civilization in the west

civilization in the west

Third Edition
Volume II: since 1555

Mark Kishlansky
Harvard University

Patrick Geary
University of California, Los Angeles

Patricia O'Brien
University of California, Irvine

LONGMAN

An Imprint of Addison Wesley Longman, Inc.

New York • Reading, Massachusetts • Menlo Park, California • Harlow, England
Don Mills, Ontario • Sydney • Mexico City • Madrid • Amsterdam

Executive Editor: Pamela Gordon
Acquisitions Editor: Bruce Borland
Development Manager: Betty Slack
Developmental Editor: Barbara Muller
Supplements Editor: Jennifer McCaffery
Marketing Manager: Sue Westmoreland
Project Editor: Dora Rizzuto
Design Supervisor and Text Designer: Rubina Yeh
Cover Designer: Christine Heibert
Cover Photo: *Flour Trade* by Giovanni Antonio Canaletto. Coll. Contessa Giustiniani, Venice, Italy.
    Camera photo/Art Resource, New York.
Art Coordinator: Rubina Yeh
Art Studio: Mapping Specialists Ltd.
Photo Researcher: Sandy Schneider
Electronic Production Manager: Su Levine
Manufacturing Manager: Willie Lane
Electronic Page Makeup: York Graphic Services, Inc.
Printer and Binder: R. R. Donnelley & Sons Company
Cover Printer: The Lehigh Press, Inc.

For permission to use copyrighted material, grateful acknowledgment is made to the copyright holders on pp. C-1 to C-8, which are hereby made part of this copyright page.

Library of Congress Cataloging-in-Publication Data

Kishlansky, Mark A.
    Civilization in the West / Mark Kishlansky, Patrick, Geary,
Patricia O'Brien. —3rd ed.
        p. cm.
    Includes bibliographical references and index.
    ISBN 0-673-98525-3 (single v.)
        1. Civilization, Western—History. I. Geary, Patrick J., 1948–
        II. O'Brien, Patricia, 1945– . III. Title.
CB245, K546   1997
909'.09812—dc21   97-13188
                                                         CIP

ISBN 0-673-98525-3 (single volume)
ISBN 0-673-98526-1 (volume I)
ISBN 0-673-98527-X (volume II)
ISBN 0-321-00283-0 (volume A)
ISBN 0-321-00285-7 (volume B)
ISBN 0-321-00287-3 (volume C)

2345678910—DOW—009998

Brief contents

detailed contents

chapter 21
industrial europe 696

special feature: industry and the
environment 722

chapter 22
social transformations
and political upheavals,
1815-1850 738

special feature: the birth of the
prison 756

chapter 23
state-building and social
change in europe,
1850-1871 778

chapter 29
postwar recovery and crisis: from the cold war to the new europe, 1945–1968   992

special feature: utopia lost 1014

chapter 30
the contemporary west, 1968 to the present   1028

special feature: television and revolutions 1038

credits c-1

index i-1

Maps

charts, tables, and figures

Documents

preface

In planning *Civilization in the West*, our aim was to write a book that students would *want* to read. Throughout our years of planning, writing, revising, rewriting, and meeting together, this was our constant overriding concern. Would students read our book? Would it be effective in conveying information while stimulating the imagination? Would it work for a variety of Western civilization courses with different levels and formats? It was not easy to keep this concern in the forefront throughout the long months of composition, but it was easy to receive the reactions of scores of reviewers to this simple question: "Would students *want* to read these chapters?" Whenever we received a resounding "No!" we began again—not just rewriting, but rethinking how to present material that might be complex in argument or detail or that might simply seem too remote to engage the contemporary student. Although all three of us were putting in long hours in front of word processors, we quickly learned that we were engaged in a teaching rather than a writing exercise. And though the work was demanding, it was not unrewarding. We hope that you will recognize and come to share with us the excitement and enthusiasm we felt in creating this text. We have enjoyed writing it, and we want students to enjoy reading it.

Judging from the reactions to our first two editions, they have. We have received literally hundreds of cards and letters from adopters and users of *Civilization in the West*. The response has been both overwhelming and gratifying. It has also been constructive. Along with praise, we have received significant suggestions for making each subsequent edition stronger. Topics such as the Crusades, the Enlightenment, and imperialism have been reorganized to present them more clearly. Subjects such as the ancient Hebrews, Napoleon, and German unification have been given more space and emphasis. New features have been added to freshen the book and keep abreast of current scholarship, and over 100 excerpts from primary sources are presented to give students a feel for the concreteness of the past. In the third edition we have added pedagogical elements to help students organize their study of each chapter. At the beginning, along with the chapter outline, we have provided study questions that highlight the most important themes in the subsequent material. At the end, we have created a section entitled "Mastering the Chapter," which isolates key terms, concepts, places, and people to aid students in reviewing what they have learned. We believe that this third edition of *Civilization in the West* not only preserves the much-praised quality of its predecessors but also enhances it.

Approach

We made a number of decisions early in the project that we believe contributed to our goal. First, we were *not* writing an encyclopedia of Western civilization. Information was not to be included in a chapter unless it related to the themes of that chapter. There was to be no information for information's sake, and each of us was called upon to defend the inclusion of names, dates, and events whenever we met to critique one another's chapters. We found, to our surprise, that by adhering to the principle that information included must contribute to or illustrate a particular point or dominating theme, we provided as much, if not more, material than books that habitually list names, places, and dates without any other context.

Second, we were committed to integrating the history of ordinary men and women into our narrative. We believe that isolated sections, placed at the end of chapters, that deal with the experiences of women or minority groups in a particular era profoundly distort historical experience. We called this technique *caboosing*, and whenever we found ourselves segregating women or families or the masses, we stepped back and asked how we might recast our treatment of historical events to account for a diversity of actors. How did ordinary men, women, and children affect the course of historical events? How did historical events affect the fabric of daily life for men and women and children from all walks of life? We tried to rethink critical historical problems of civilization as gendered phenomena. To assist us in this endeavor, we engaged two reviewers whose sole responsibility was to evaluate our chapters for the integration of these social groups into our discussion.

We took the same approach to the coverage of central and Eastern Europe that we did to women and minorities. Even before the epochal events of 1989 that returned this region to the forefront of international attention, we realized that in too many textbooks the Slavic world was treated as marginal to the history of Western civilization. Thus, with the help of a specialist reviewer, we worked to integrate more of the history of Eastern Europe into our text than is found in most others, and to do so in a way that presented these regions, their cultures and their institutions, as integral rather than peripheral to Western civilization.

To construct a book that students would *want* to read, we needed to develop fresh ideas about how to involve them with the material, how to transform them from passive recipients to active participants. We borrowed from computer science the concept of being "user-friendly." We wanted to find ways to stimulate the imagination of the student, and the more we experimented with different techniques, the more we realized that the most effective way to do this was visually. It is not true that contemporary students cannot be taught effectively by the written word; it is only true that they cannot be taught as effectively as they can by the combination of words and images. From the beginning, we realized that a text produced in full color was essential to the features we most wanted to use: the pictorial chapter openers; the large number of maps; the geographical tours of Europe at certain times in history; and the two-page special feature in every chapter, each with its own illustration.

features

It is hard to have a new idea when writing a textbook. So many authors have come before, each attempting to do something more effective, more innovative than his or her predecessor. It is probably the case that somewhere there has been a text that has used a chapter-opening feature similar to the one we use here. What we can say with certainty is that nothing else we experimented with, no other technique we attempted, has had such an immediate and positive impact on our readers or has so fulfilled our goal of involving the students in learning as our *pictorial chapter openers*. An illustration—a painting, a photograph, a picture, an artifact, an edifice—appears at the beginning of each chapter, accompanied by text through which we explore the picture, guiding students across a canvas or helping them see in an artifact or a piece of architecture details that are not immediately apparent. It is the direct combination of text and image that allows us to achieve this effect, to "unfold" both an illustration and a theme. In some chapters we highlight details, pulling out a section of the original picture to take a closer look. In others we attempt to shock the viewer into the recognition of horror or of beauty. Some chapter-opening images are designed to transport students back in time, to make them ask the question "What was it like to be there?" All of the opening images have been chosen to illustrate a dominant theme within the chapter, and the dramatic and lingering impression they make helps reinforce that theme.

We have taken a similar image-based approach to our *presentation of geography*. When teachers of Western civilization courses are surveyed, no single area of need is cited more often than that of geographical knowledge. Students simply have no mental image of Europe, no familiarity with those geophysical features that are a fundamental part of the geopolitical realities of Western history. We realized that maps, carefully planned and skillfully executed, would be an important component of our text. To complement the standard map program of the text, we have added a special geographical feature. Six times throughout the book, we pause in the narrative to take a tour of Europe. Sometimes we follow an emperor as he tours his realm; sometimes we examine the impact of a peace treaty; sometimes we follow the travels of a merchant. Whatever the thematic occasion, our intention is to guide the student around the changing contours of the geography of Western history. In order to do this effectively, we have worked with our cartographer to develop small, detailed maps to complement the overview map that appears at the beginning of each tour section. We know that only the most motivated students will turn back several pages to locate on a map a place mentioned in the text. Using small maps allows us to integrate maps directly into the relevant text, thus relieving students of the sometimes frustrating experience of attempting to locate not only a specific place on a map but perhaps even the relevant map itself. The great number of maps throughout the text, the specially designed tour-of-Europe geographical feature, and the ancillary programs of map transparencies and workbook exercises combine to provide the strongest possible program for teaching historical geography.

The third technique we have employed to engage students with historical subjects is the two-page *special feature* that appears in each chapter. These special features focus on a single event or personality chosen to enhance the student's sense that history is something that is real and alive. These features are written more dramatically and sympathetically, with a greater sense of wonder than would be appropriate in the body of the text. The prose style and the accompanying illustration are designed to captivate the reader. To help the student relate personally and directly to a historical event, we have highlighted figures such as Hypatia of Alexandria, Isabella of Castile, and nineteenth-century Zimbabwe political heroes Nehanda and Kagubi.

Finally, *Civilization in the West* contains selections from primary sources designed to stimulate students' interest in history by allowing them to hear the past speak in its own voice. We have tried to provide a mixture of "canonical" texts along with those illustrating the lives of ordinary people in order to demonstrate the variety of materials that form the building blocks of historical narrative. Each selection is accompanied by an explanatory headnote that identifies the author and work and provides the necessary historical context. Most of these extracts relate directly to discussions within the chapter, thus providing the student with a fuller understanding of a significant thinker or event.

There are many new features in our text and much that is out of the ordinary. But there are important traditional aspects of the narrative itself that also require mention. *Civilization in the West* is a mainstream text in which most of our energies have been placed in developing a solid, readable narrative of Western civilization that integrates coverage of women and minorities into the discussion. We have highlighted personalities while identifying trends. We have spotlighted social history, both in sections of chapters and in separate chapters, while maintaining a firm grip on political developments. We hope that there are many things in this book that teachers of Western civilization will find valuable. But we also hope that there are things here with which you will disagree, themes that you can develop better, arguments and ideas that will stimulate you. A textbook is only one part of a course, and it is always less important than a teacher. What we hope is that by having done our job successfully, we will have made the teacher's job easier and the student's job more enjoyable.

Mark Kishlansky
Patrick Geary
Patricia O'Brien

acknowledgments

We want to thank the many conscientious historians who gave generously of their time and knowledge to review our manuscript. Their valuable critiques and suggestions have contributed greatly to the final product. We are grateful to the following:

Sharon Bannister
University of Findlay

April Brooks
South Dakota State University

Blaine T. Browne
Broward Community College

Robert Carver
University of Missouri, Rolla

Sister Dorita Clifford, BVM
University of San Francisco

Jan M. Copes
Cleveland State University

Norman Delaney
Del Mar College

Laird Easton
California State University, Chico

Dianne E. Farrell
Moorhead State University

Frank Garosi
California State University, Sacramento

Louis Haas
Duquesne University

Margareta Handke
Mankato State University

Neil Heyman
San Diego State University

David Hudson
California State University, Fresno

Jeff Kaufmann
Muscatine Community College

Carolyn Kay
Trent University

Alexandra Korros
Xavier University

Cynthia Kosso
Northern Arizona University

Lisa M. Lane
Mira Costa College

Donna J. Maier
University of Northern Iowa

Margaret Malamud
New Mexico State University

David K. McQuilkin
Bridgewater College

Victor V. Minasian
College of Marin

John A. Nichols
Slippery Rock University

Maura O'Connor
University of Cincinnati

James H. Overfield
University of Vermont

Catherine Patterson
University of Houston

Peter O'M. Pierson
Santa Clara University

Jack B. Ridley
University of Missouri, Rolla

Constance M. Rousseau
Providence College

Timothy J. Runyan
Cleveland State University

Lixin Shao
University of Minnesota, Duluth

Ellen J. Skinner
Pace University

Patrick Smith
Broward Community College

Sherill Spaar
East Central University

Saulius Suziedelis
Millersville University

Roger Tate
Somerset Community College

Donna L. Van Raaphorst
Cuyahoga Community College

James Vanstone
John Abbott College

Faith Wallis
McGill University

We also acknowledge with gratitude the thoughtful evaluations and constructive suggestions of the historians who reviewed the first and second editions of this work.

Achilles Aavraamides
Iowa State University

Meredith L. Adams
Southwest Missouri State University

Arthur H. Auten
University of Hartford

Sharon Bannister
University of Findlay

John W. Barker
University of Wisconsin

Patrick Bass
Mount Union College

William H. Beik
Northern Illinois University

Patrice Berger
University of Nebraska

Lenard R. Berlanstein
University of Virginia

Raymond Birn
University of Oregon

Donna Bohanan
Auburn University

Werner Braatz
University of Wisconsin, Oshkosh

Thomas A. Brady, Jr.
University of Oregon

Anthony M. Brescia
Nassau Community College

Elaine G. Breslaw
Morgan State University

Ronald S. Brockway
Regis University

Daniel Patrick Brown
Moorpark College

Ronald A. Brown
Charles County Community College

Edward J. Champlin
Princeton University

Stephanie Evans Christelow
Western Washington University

Gary B. Cohen
University of Oklahoma

John J. Contreni
Purdue University

Tim Crain
University of Wisconsin, Stout

Samuel E. Dicks
Emporia State University

Frederick Dumin
Washington State University

Margot C. Finn
Emory University

Allan W. Fletcher
Boise State University

Elizabeth L. Furdell
University of North Florida

Thomas W. Gallant
University of Florida

Lorne E. Glaim
Pacific Union College

Joseph J. Godson
Hudson Valley Community College

Sue Helder Goliber
Mount St. Mary's College

Manuel G. Gonzales
Diablo Valley College

Eric Haines
Bellevue Community College

Margaretta S. Handke
Mankato State University

David A. Harnett
University of San Francisco

Paul B. Harvey, Jr.
Pennsylvania State University

Daniel W. Hollis
Jacksonville State University

Kenneth G. Holum
University of Maryland

Patricia Howe
University of St. Thomas

Charles Ingrao
Purdue University

George F. Jewsbury
Oklahoma State University

Donald G. Jones
University of Central Arkansas

William R. Jones
University of New Hampshire

Richard W. Kaeuper
University of Rochester

David Kaiser
Carnegie-Mellon University

William R. Keylor
Boston University

Joseph Kicklighter
Auburn University

Charles L. Killinger, III
Valencia Community College

Alan M. Kirshner
Ohlone College

David C. Large
Montana State University

Bryan LeBeau
Creighton University

Roberta T. Manning
Boston College

Lyle McAlister
University of Florida

Therese M. McBride
College of the Holy Cross

David B. Mock
Tallahassee Community College

Robert Moeller
University of California, Irvine

Pierce C. Mullen
Montana State University

Thomas F. X. Noble
University of Virginia

Bruce K. O'Brien
Mary Washington College

Dennis H. O'Brien
West Virginia University

Richard A. Oehling
Assumption College

Peter C. Piccillo
Rhode Island College

Theophilus Prousis
University of North Florida

Marlette Rebhorn
Austin Community College

Jack B. Ridley
University of Missouri, Rolla

John P. Ryan
Kansas City Community College

Joanne Schneider
Rhode Island College

Steven C. Seyer
Lehigh County Community College

George H. Shriver
Georgia Southern University

Steven Schroeder
Indiana University of Pennsylvania

Bonnie Smith
University of Rochester

Peter N. Stearns
Carnegie-Mellon University

Darryl B. Sycher
Columbus State Community College

Steven Vincent
North Carolina State University

Richard A. Voeltz
Cameron University

Eric Weissman
Golden West College

Each author also received invaluable assistance and en-couragement from many colleagues, friends, and family members over the years of research, reflection, writing, and revising that went into the making of this text.

Mark Kishlansky wishes to thank Ann Adams, Robert Bartlett, Ray Birn, David Buisseret, Ted Cook, Frank Conaway, Constantine Fasolt, James Hankins, Katherine Haskins, Richard Hellie, Matthew Kishlansky, Donna Marder, Mary Beth Rose, Victor Stater, Jeanne Thiel, and the staffs of the Joseph Regenstein Library, the New-berry Library, and the Widener and Lamont Libraries at Harvard.

Patrick Geary wishes to thank Mary Geary, Catherine Geary, and Anne Geary for their patience, support, and encouragement; he also thanks Anne Picard, Dale Schofield, and Hans Hummer for their able assistance throughout the project.

Patricia O'Brien thanks Elizabeth Sagias for her en-couragement and enthusiasm throughout the project and Robert Moeller for his keen eye for organization and his suggestions for writing a gendered history.

All the authors would also like to thank Paul Halliday for his contributions to the third edition. Barbara Muller, who has been with the project since its incep-tion, has again kept us on schedule and improved the new edition at every juncture. Lily Eng was a vital re-source for our many questions and maintained a steady keel during the hurricanes that accompanied the plan-ning and production of a new edition.

supplements

for qualified college adopters

Instructor's Resource Manual

Prepared by Margot C. Finn of Emory University and David B. Mock of Tallahassee Community College. This thorough instructor's manual includes an introductory essay on teaching Western civilization and a bibliographic essay on the use of primary sources for class discussion and analytical thinking. Each chapter contains a chapter summary, key terms, geographic and map items, and discussion questions.

Discovering Western Civilization Through Maps and Views

Created by Gerald Danzer, University of Illinois at Chicago—the recipient of the American History Association's James Harvey Robinson Prize for his work in the development of map transparencies—and David Buissert, this set of 140 four-color acetates is a unique instructional tool. It contains an introduction on teaching history through maps and a detailed commentary on each transparency. The collection includes cartographic and pictorial maps, views and photos, urban plans, building diagrams, and works of art. Available to qualified college adopters.

Test Bank

Developed by John Paul Bischoff of Oklahoma State University, the Test Bank contains over 1200 multiple-choice, matching, and completion questions. Multiple-choice items are referenced by topic, text page number, and type (factual or interpretive).

TestGen EQ Computerized Testing System

This flexible, easy-to-master computerized testing system includes all of the test items in the printed test bank. The friendly interface allows instructors to easily edit, print, and expand item banks. Tests can be printed in several different formats and can include figures such as graphs and tables. Available for Windows and Macintosh computers.

QuizMaster

This new program enables you to design TestGen-generated tests that your students can take on a computer rather than in printed form. QuizMaster can be obtained free through your sales representative.

Grades

This grade-keeping and classroom management software program maintains data for up to 200 students.

Transparencies

This set of transparencies contains *all* the maps from the text, bound together with reproducible map exercises in a binder.

TimeLink computer Atlas of western civilization

This atlas, compiled by William Hamblin of Brigham Young University, is an introductory software tutorial and textbook companion. This Macintosh program covers material on European developments from 400 to 1500 A.D. Students can watch animated maps display geopolitical changes and study special topics, including the Anglo-Saxon migration to Britain and the Hundred Years' War.

For students

study guide

Compiled by John Paul Bischoff of Oklahoma State University, this study guide is available in two volumes and offers for each chapter a summary; a glossary list; map and geography questions; and identification, multiple-choice, and critical-thinking questions.

supershell II computerized tutorial

Prepared by John Paul Bischoff of Oklahoma State University, this interactive program for DOS computers helps students learn major facts and concepts through drill and practice exercises and diagnostic feedback. SuperShell II provides immediate correct answers, the text page number on which the material is discussed, and a running score of the student's performance on the screen throughout the session. This free supplement is available to instructors through their sales representative.

western civilization map workbooks

Prepared by Glee Wilson of Kent State University, these two volumes include map exercises designed to test and reinforce basic geographic literacy and to build critical thinking skills. Available shrink-wrapped at no cost with any Longman survey text.

Mapping western civilization: student activities

Written by Gerald Danzer of the University of Illinois at Chicago, this free map workbook for students is designed as an accompaniment to Discovering Western Civilization through maps and views. It features exercises designed to teach students to interpret and analyze cartographic materials as historical documents. The instructor is entitled to a free copy of the workbook for each copy of the text purchased from Longman.

about the authors

mark kishlansky

Mark Kishlansky is Professor of English and European History at Harvard University. He has taught at Northwestern University, the California Institute of Technology, and the University of Chicago. A specialist in the sixteenth and seventeenth centuries, he is the author and editor of a number of studies focused on early modern English history. His latest work, A *Monarchy Transformed*, is a volume in the new Penguin History of Britain. He lives with his wife and two children in Lexington, Massachusetts, where he coaches baseball.

patrick geary

Holding a Ph.D. in Medieval Studies from Yale University, Patrick Geary is a noted scholar and teacher. He is currently Director of the Center for Medieval and Renaissance Studies at the University of California, Los Angeles. Named outstanding undergraduate history teacher for the 1986–1987 year at the University of Florida, Professor Geary has also held academic positions at the École des Hautes Études en Sciences Sociales, Paris; the Universität Wien; and Princeton University. His many publications include *Readings in Medieval History*; *Before France and Germany: The Creation and Transformation of the Merovingian World*; *Furta Sacra: Thefts of Relics in the Central Middle Ages*; and *Phantoms of Remembrance: Memory and Oblivion at the End of the First Millennium*.

patricia o'brien

As Director of the University of California Humanities Research Institute, Patricia O'Brien works to foster collaborative interdisciplinary research in the humanities. Her academic home is the Department of History at the University of California, Irvine, and she has held appointments at Yale University and at the École des Hautes Études en Sciences Sociales in Paris. Professor O'Brien is a specialist in modern French cultural and social history and has published widely on the history of crime, punishment, cultural theory, urban history, and gender issues. Representative publications include *The Promise of Punishment: Prisons in Nineteenth-Century France*; "The Kleptomania Diagnosis: Bourgeois Women and Theft in Late Nineteenth-Century France" in *Expanding the Past: A Reader in Social History*; and "Michel Foucault's History of Culture" in *The New Cultural History*, edited by Lynn Hunt.

civilization in the west

εurope at war, 1555-1648

The Massacre of the Innocents

"War is one of the scourges with which it has pleased God to afflict men," wrote Cardinal Richelieu (1585–1642), the French minister who played no small part in spreading the scourge. War was a constant of European society and penetrated to its very core. It dominated all aspects of life. It enhanced the power of the state; it defined gender roles; it consumed lives and treasure and commodities ravenously. War affected every member of society from combatants to civilians. There were no innocent bystanders. Grain in the fields was destroyed because it was food for soldiers; houses were burned because they provided shelter for soldiers. Civilians were killed for aiding the enemy or holding out against demands for their treasure and supplies. Able-bodied men were taken forcibly to serve as conscripts, leaving women to plant and harvest as best as they could.

There was nothing new about war in the middle of the sixteenth century. The early part of the century had witnessed the dynastic struggle between the Habsburgs and the House of Valois as well as the beginnings of the religious struggle between Catholics and Protestants. But the wars that dominated Europe from 1555 to 1648 brought together the worst of both of these conflicts. War was fought on a larger scale,

it was more brutal and more expensive, and it claimed more victims, civilians and combatants alike. During this century war extended throughout the Continent. Dynastic strife, rebellion, and international rivalries joined together with the ongoing struggle over religion. Ambition and faith were an explosive mixture. The French endured 40 years of civil war; the Spanish, 80 years of fighting with the Dutch. The battle for hegemony in the east led to dynastic strife for decades on end as Poles, Russians, and Swedes pressed their rival claims to each other's crowns. Finally, in 1618, these separate theaters of war came together in one of the most brutal and terrifying episodes of destruction in European history, the Thirty Years' War.

Neither the ancient temple nor the Roman costume can conceal the immediacy of the picture here. It is as painful to look at now as it was when it was created over 350 years ago. Painted by Nicolas Poussin (1594–1665) at the height of the Thirty Years' War, *The Massacre of the Innocents* remains a horrifying composition of power, terror, and despair. The cruel and senseless slaughter of the innocent baby that is about to take place is echoed throughout the canvas. Between the executioner's legs can be seen a mother clasping her own child tightly and anticipating the fall of the sword. In the background on the right, another mother turns away from the scene and carries her infant to safety. In the foreground strides a mother holding her dead child. She tears at her hair and cries in anguish. To a culture in which the image of mother and child—of Mary and Jesus—was one of sublime peacefulness and inexpressible joy, the contrast could hardly be more shocking.

The picture graphically displays the cruelty of the soldier, the helplessness of the child, and the horror of the mother. By his grip on the mother's hair and his foot on the baby's throat, the warrior shows his brute power. The mother's futile effort to stop the sword illustrates her powerlessness. She scratches uselessly at the soldier's back. Naked, the baby boy raises his hands as if to surrender to the inevitable, as if to reinforce his innocence.

To study Europe at war, we must enter into a world of politics and diplomacy, of issues and principles, of judgment and error. We must talk about armies in terms of their cost and numbers, of generals in terms of their strategy and tactics, and of battles in terms of winners and losers. There can be no doubt that the future of Europe was decisively shaped by this century of wholesale slaughter during which dynastic and religious fervor finally ran its course. The survival of Protestantism, the disintegration of the Spanish empire, the rise of Holland and Sweden, the collapse of Poland and Muscovy, the fragmentation of Germany—these were all vital transformations whose consequences would be felt for centuries. We cannot avoid telling this story, untangling its causes, narrating its course, or revealing its outcome. But neither should we avoid facing its reality. Look again at the painting by Poussin.

Focus Questions

1. How was Henry IV able to bring peace to France after decades of civil war?
2. What were the political and religious connections between the Armada launched against England by Philip II and the revolt of the Netherlands?
3. How did Sweden rise to become one of Europe's great powers in the first half of the seventeenth century?
4. How did religion help spark and spread the Thirty Years' War?
5. What were the effects of the Peace of Westphalia on political arrangements in the heart of Europe?

the crises of the western states

"*Un roi, une foi, une loi*"—one king, one faith, one law. This was a prescription that members of all European states accepted without question in the sixteenth century. Society was an integrated whole, equally dependent upon monarchical, ecclesiastical, and civil authority for its effective survival. A European state could no more tolerate the presence of two churches than it could the presence of two kings. But the Reformation had created two churches.

In Germany, where the problem first arose, the Peace of Augsburg (1555) enacted the most logical solution. The religion of the ruler was to be the religion of the subjects. Princes, town governments, and bishops would determine faith. Not surprisingly, this was a policy more convenient for rulers than for the ruled. Sudden conversions of princes, a hallmark of Protestantism, threw the state into disarray. Those closely identified with Catholicism and those who firmly believed in its doctrines had no choice but to move to a neighboring Catholic community and begin again. Given the dependence of ordinary people upon networks of kin and neighbors, enforced migration was devastating. Protestant minorities in Catholic states suffered the same fate. The enmity between the two groups came as much from bitter experience as from differences of belief.

Thus compromises that might have brought Protestants back into a reformed Catholic church were doomed from the start. Doomed too was the practical solution of toleration. To the modern mind, toleration seems so logical that it is difficult to understand why it took over a century of bloodshed before it came to be grudgingly accepted by those countries most bitterly divided. But toleration was not a practical solution in a society that admitted no principle of organization other than one king, one faith. In such a world, toleration was more threatening than warfare. Pope Clement VIII (1592–1605) described liberty of conscience as "the worst thing in the world." Those who advocated limited forms of toleration were universally despised. Those occasions during which toleration was a reluctant basis for a cease-fire were moments for catching breath before resuming the struggle for total victory. Only Poland-Lithuania, Hungary, and a few German states experimented with religious toleration during the sixteenth century.

Religious Divisions in France

The crises of the western European states that stretched from the middle of the sixteenth century to the middle of the seventeenth were as much internal and domestic as they were external and international. In France, a half century of religious warfare sapped the strength of both the monarchy and the nation. In Spain, the protracted revolt of the Netherlands drained men, money, and spirit from the most powerful nation in Europe. Decades of intermittent warfare turned the golden age of Spain to lead and hastened the decline of the Spanish empire. Each crisis had its own causes and its own history. Yet it was no coincidence that they occurred together or that they starkly posed the conflict between the authority of the state and the conscience of the individual. The century between the Peace of Augsburg (1555) and the Peace of Westphalia (1648) was the century of total war.

the french wars of religion

No wars are more terrible than civil wars. They tear at the very fabric of society, rending its institutions and destroying the delicate web of relationships that underlie all communal life. The nation is divided; communities break into factions; families are destroyed. Civil wars are wars of passion. Issues become elevated into causes and principles that form the rallying cry of heroic self-sacrifice or wanton destruction. Civil wars feed on themselves. Each act of war becomes an outrage to be revenged, each act of revenge a new outrage. Passions run deep and, however primitive, the rules for the civilized conduct of war are quickly broken. The loss of lives and property is staggering, but the loss of communal identity is greater still. Generations pass before societies recover from their civil wars. Such was the case with the French wars of religion.

Protestantism came late to France. It was not until after Calvin reformed the church in Geneva and began to export his brand of Protestantism that French society began to divide along religious lines. By 1560 there were over 2000 Protestant congregations in France, whose membership totaled nearly 10 percent of the French population. Calvin and his successors concentrated their efforts on large provincial towns and had their greatest success among the middle ranks of urban society, merchants, traders, and artisans. They also found a receptive audience among aristocratic women, who eventually converted their husbands and their sons.

The wars of religion, however, were brought on by more than the rapid spread of Calvinism. Equally important was the vacuum of power that had been created when Henry II (1547–59) died in a jousting tournament. Surviving Henry were his extraordinary widow, Catherine de Médicis, three daughters, and four sons, the oldest of whom, Francis II (1559–60), was only 15. Under the influence of his beautiful young wife, Mary, Queen of Scots, Francis II allowed the Guise family to dominate the great offices of state and to exclude their rivals from power. The Guises controlled the two most powerful institutions of the state, the army and the Church.

The Guises were staunchly Catholic, and among their enemies were the Bourbons, princes of the blood with a direct claim to the French throne but also a family with powerful Protestant members. The revelation of a Protestant plot to remove the king from Paris provided the Guises with an opportunity to eliminate their most potent rivals. The Bourbon duc de Condé, the leading Protestant peer of the realm, was sentenced to death. But five days before Condé's execution, Francis II died and Guise power evaporated. The new king, Charles IX (1560–74), was only ten years old and firmly under the grip of his mother, Catherine de Médicis, who now declared herself regent of France. (See "The Monstrous Regiment of Women," pp. 448–449.)

Condé's death sentence convinced him that the Guises would stop at nothing to gain their ambitions. Force would have to be met with force. Protestants and Catholics alike raised armies, and in 1562 civil war erupted. Because of the tangle of motives among the participants, each side in the struggles had different objectives. Catherine wanted peace and was willing to accept almost any strategy for securing it. War weakened the state and weakened loyalty to the monarch. At first she negotiated with the Bourbons, but she was ultimately forced to accept the fact that the Guises were more powerful. The Guises wanted to suppress Protestantism and eliminate Protestant influence at court. They were willing to undertake the task with or without the king's express support.

Once the wars began, the leading Protestant peers fled the court, but the position of the Guises was not altogether secure. Henry Bourbon, king of Navarre, was the next in line to succeed to the throne should Charles IX and his two brothers die without male heirs. Henry

Catherine de Médicis (1519–98), the wife of Henry II of France, was the real power behind the throne during the reigns of her sons Charles IX (1560–74) and Henry III (1574–89). Her overriding concern was to ensure her sons' succession and to preserve the power of the monarchy.

D·MEDICIS ROYNE DE FRANCE

The monstrous regiment of women

"To promote a woman to bear rule, superiority, dominion or empire above any realm, nation, or city is repugnant to nature, contumely to God, and the subversion of good order, of all equity and justice." So wrote the Scottish theologian John Knox (1513–72) in *The First Blast of the Trumpet Against the Monstrous Regiment of Women* (1558). Although he made his points more emphatically than many others, Knox was only repeating the commonplace notions of his day. He could quote Aristotle and Aquinas as well as a host of secular authorities to demonstrate female inadequacies: "Nature, I say, doth paint them forth to be weak, frail, impatient, feeble, and foolish." He could quote Saint Paul along with the ancient Fathers of the Church to demonstrate the "proper" place of women—"Man is not of the woman, but the woman of the man."

But no stacking up of authorities, no matter how numerous or revered, could erase the fact that all over Europe in the sixteenth century women could and did rule. In the Netherlands, Mary, Queen of Hungary (1531–52), and Margaret of Parma (1559–67) were successful regents. Jeanne d'Albret (1562–72) was queen of the tiny state of Navarre, territory claimed by both France and Spain but kept independent by this remarkable woman. Catherine de Médicis (1560–89), wife of one king of France and mother of three others, was the effective ruler of that nation for nearly 30 years. Mary, Queen of Scots (1542–87), was the nominal ruler of Scotland almost from her birth. England was ruled by two very different women, the Catholic Mary I (1553–58) and her Protestant half-sister Elizabeth I (1558–1603).

The problems faced by this long list of queens and regents were more than just the ordinary cares of government. The belief that women were inherently inferior in intelligence, strength, and character was so pervasive that, for men like Knox, a woman ruler was almost a contradiction in terms. Yet this was not the view taken by everyone, and female rule had its defenders as well as its detractors. One set of objections was overcome by the traditional medieval theory of the two bodies of the monarch. This argument was developed to reconcile the divine origins and functions of monarchs with their very real human frailties. In the theory of the two bodies, there was the body natural and the body politic. Both were joined together in the person of the ruler, but the attributes of each could be separated. Rule of a woman did nothing to disrupt this notion. In fact, it made it easier to argue that the frailties of the body natural of a woman were in no way related to the strengths of the body politic of a monarch.

While such ideas might help a female ruler win the acceptance of her subjects, they did little to invigorate her own sense of her role. Female rulers often strained against the straitjacket that definitions of gender placed them in. When angered, Elizabeth I would proclaim that she had more courage than her father, Henry VIII, "though I am only a woman." Mary, Queen of Scots, once revealed that her only regret was that she "was not a man to know what life it was to lie all night in the fields or to walk with a buckler and a broadsword." Some queens assumed masculine traits, riding in armor or leading forces to battle. Elizabeth's presence in armor at the threat of the landing of the Spanish Armada was viewed as one of the heroic moments of her reign. Other women rulers combined characteristics that were usually separated by gender definitions. Margaret of Parma was considered one of the most accomplished horse riders of her day. After leading her courtiers through woods and fields at breakneck speed, she would then attend council meetings and work on her needlepoint. Mary, Queen of Scots, loved hawking, a traditional kingly sport, in the Scottish wilds. After relishing the hawk's destruction of its prey, she liked to negotiate matters of state by beginning with tears and entreaties and ending with accusations and threats. The effect was more than disconcerting.

Women were no more or less successful as rulers than were men. Women's achievements, like men's, depended upon strength of character and the circumstances of the times. All the women rulers of the sixteenth century had received outstanding educations. Whether raised Catholic or Protestant, each was trained in Latin as well as modern languages, in the liberal arts, and in fine arts. Mary and Elizabeth Tudor of England wrote poetry and played musical instruments with considerable accomplishment. Mary, Queen of Scots, who was raised at the court of France, was considered particularly apt at learning, praise not often accorded a foreigner by the French. Catherine de Médicis, orphaned as an infant, was raised in convents and instructed in the new learning by Italian nuns. It was said that her political instincts were in her blood: Machiavelli had dedicated The Prince to her father. Marguerite of Navarre chose one of the leading French humanists to supervise the training of her daughter, Jeanne d'Albret.

Mary, Queen of Scots, was the only one of these female rulers born to rule. She was the sole survivor of her father, who died shortly after her birth. Mary and Elizabeth Tudor came to their thrones after the death of their younger brother Edward VI; Mary of Hungary and Margaret of Parma came to theirs as princesses of the House of Habsburg. The rule of Catherine de Médicis was the most unexpected of all. Her vigorous husband, Henry II, died during a jousting tournament, and her eldest son, Francis II, husband of Mary, Queen of Scots,

died the following year. Instead of retirement as a respected queen dowager (the widow of a previous king) Catherine de Médicis was forced into the vortex of French politics to protect the rights of her ten-year-old son, Charles IX.

For most of these queens and regents, marriage was of central importance to their position. Both Mary, Queen of Hungary, and Mary, Queen of Scots, married kings whose reigns were exceedingly brief. Lewis of Hungary died at the battle of Mohács in 1526, just four years after Mary had become his queen. Mary, Queen of Scots, was widowed even sooner, and throughout the rest of her remarkable career schemed to remarry. To strengthen her claim to the throne of England, she married the Scottish Lord Darnley. When he proved unsatisfactory to her plans, she plotted his murder and then married one of his assassins. When this husband died, she sought a match with a powerful English lord who might help her capture Elizabeth's throne. These intrigues finally led to her execution in England in 1587. Mary Tudor married Philip II of Spain in hope of reestablishing Catholicism in England through a permanent alliance with the most powerful Catholic state in Europe. Her dreams went unfulfilled when she failed to produce an heir, and the throne passed to her sister, Elizabeth, who, alone among the women rulers of the period, did not marry.

Unfortunately, the accomplishments of women rulers did little to dispel prejudices against women as a whole or to alter the definition of gender roles. Except for Mary, Queen of Scots, whose principal achievement was to provide an heir to the English throne, all the queens and regents of the sixteenth century were successful rulers. Margaret of Parma steered the careful middle course in the conflict between Spain and the Netherlands. She opposed the intervention of the Duke of Alba, and, had her advice been followed, the 80 years of war between Spain and the Netherlands might have been avoided. Catherine de Médicis held the crown of France on the heads of her sons, navigated the treacherous waters of civil war, and provided the model for religious toleration that finally was adopted in the Edict of Nantes. Elizabeth I of England became one of the most beloved rulers in that nation's history. A crafty politician who learned to balance the factions at her court and who turned the aristocracy into a service class for the crown, she brought nearly a half century of stability to England at a time when the rest of Europe was in flames.

had been raised in the Protestant faith by his mother, Jeanne d'Albret, whose own mother, Marguerite of Navarre, was among the earliest protectors of the French Protestants. The objectives of the Huguenots, as the French Calvinists came to be called, were less clear-cut. The townspeople wanted the right to practice their faith, the clergy wanted the right to preach and make converts, and the nobility wanted their rightful place in local government. Almost from the beginning, the Huguenots were on the defensive, fighting to preserve what they already had and to avoid annihilation.

The inconclusive nature of the early battles might have allowed for the pragmatic solution sought by Catherine de Médicis had it not been for the assassination of the duc de Guise in 1563 by a Protestant fanatic. This act added a personal vendetta to the religious passions of the Catholic leaders. They encouraged the slaughter of Huguenot congregations and openly planned the murder of Huguenot leaders. Protestants gave as good as they got. In open defiance of Valois dynastic interests, the Guises courted support from Spain, while the Huguenots imported Swiss and German mercenaries to fight in France. Noble factions and irreconcilable religious differences were pulling the government apart.

By 1570 Catherine was ready to attempt another reconciliation. She announced her plans for a marriage between her daughter Margaret and Henry of Navarre, a marriage that would symbolize the spirit of conciliation between the crown and the Huguenots. The marriage was to take place in Paris during August 1572. The arrival of Huguenot leaders from all over France to attend the marriage ceremony presented an opportunity of a different kind to the Guises and their supporters. If leading Huguenots could be assassinated in Paris, the Protestant cause might collapse and the truce that the wedding signified might be turned instead into a Catholic triumph.

Saint Bartholomew was the apostle that Jesus described as a man without guile. Ironically, it was on his feast day that the Huguenots who had innocently come to celebrate Henry's marriage were led like lambs to the slaughter. On 24 August 1572 the streets of Paris ran red with Huguenot blood. Although frenzied, the slaughter was inefficient. Henry of Navarre and a number of other important Huguenots escaped the carnage and returned to their urban strongholds. In the following weeks the violence spread from Paris to the countryside and thousands of Protestants paid for their beliefs with their lives. Until the French Revolution, no event in French history would evoke as much passion as the memory of the Saint Bartholomew's Day Massacre.

one κing, two faiths

The Saint Bartholomew's Day Massacre was a transforming event in many ways. In the first place, it prolonged the wars. A whole new generation of Huguenots

This scene depicts the mistreatment of French Catholics by the Protestants in the town of Angoulême. They were deprived of all nourishment, dragged over a taut rope, and then slowly roasted at the stake.

now had an emotional attachment to the continuation of warfare: their fathers and brothers had been mercilessly slaughtered. By itself the event was shocking enough. But in the atmosphere of anticipated reconciliation created by the wedding, it screamed out for revenge. And the target for retaliation was no longer limited to the Guises and their followers. By accepting the results of the massacre, the monarchy sanctioned it and spilled Huguenot blood on itself. For over a decade Catherine de Médicis had maintained a distance between the crown and the leaders of the Catholic movement. That distance no longer existed.

Nor could the Huguenots continue to maintain the fiction that they were fighting against the king's evil advisers rather than against the king. After Saint Bartholomew's Day, Huguenot theorists began to develop the idea that resistance to a monarch whose actions violated divine commandments or civil rights was lawful. For the first time, Huguenot writers provided a justification for rebellion. Perhaps most importantly, a genuine revulsion against the massacres swept the nation. A number of Catholic peers now joined with the Huguenots to protest the excesses of the crown and the Guises. These Catholics came to be called *politiques* from their desire for a practical settlement of the wars. They were led by the duc d'Anjou, next in line to the throne after Henry III (1574–89) became king.

Against them, in Paris and a number of other towns, the Catholic League was formed, a society that pledged its first allegiance to religion. The League took up where the Saint Bartholomew's Day Massacre left off, and the slaughter of ordinary people who unluckily professed the wrong religion continued. Matters grew worse in 1584, when Anjou died. With each passing year it was becoming apparent that Henry III would produce no male heir. After Anjou's death, the Huguenot Henry of Navarre was the next in line for the throne. Catholic Leaguers talked openly of altering the royal succession and began to develop theories of lawful resistance to monarchical power. By 1585, when the final civil war began—the war of the three Henrys, named for Henry III, Henry Guise, and Henry of Navarre—the crown was in the weakest possible position. Paris and the Catholic towns were controlled by the League, the Protestant strongholds by Henry of Navarre. King Henry III could not abandon his capital or his religion, but neither could he gain control of the Catholic party. The extremism of the Leaguers kept the politiques away from court, and without the politiques, there could be no settlement.

In December 1588 Henry III summoned Henry Guise and Guise's brother to a meeting in the royal bedchamber. There they were murdered by the king's order. The politiques were blamed for the murders—revenge was

Painting of the Saint Bartholomew's Day Massacre. The massacre began in Paris on 24 August 1572, and the violence soon spread throughout France.

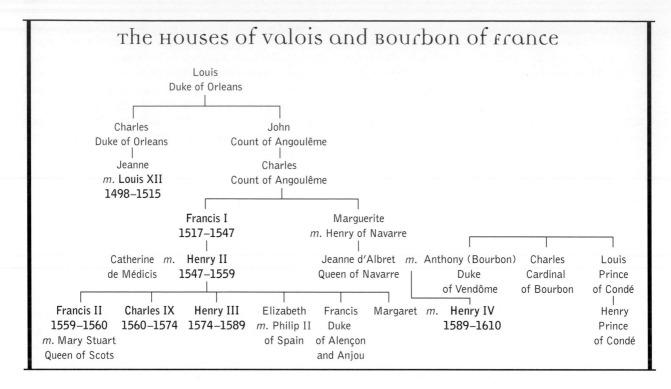

The Houses of Valois and Bourbon of France

Louis
Duke of Orleans

Charles
Duke of Orleans

Jeanne
m. **Louis XII**
1498–1515

John
Count of Angoulême

Charles
Count of Angoulême

Francis I
1517–1547

Marguerite
m. Henry of Navarre

Catherine   *m.*   **Henry II**
de Médicis   **1547–1559**

Jeanne d'Albret   *m.*   Anthony (Bourbon)
Queen of Navarre   Duke
of Vendôme

Charles
Cardinal
of Bourbon

Louis
Prince
of Condé

Francis II   **Charles IX**   **Henry III**
1559–1560   **1560–1574**   **1574–1589**
m. Mary Stuart
Queen of Scots

Elizabeth
m. Philip II
of Spain

Francis
Duke
of Alençon
and Anjou

Margaret   *m.*   **Henry IV**
1589–1610

Henry
Prince
of Condé

taken on a number of them—and Henry III was forced to flee his capital. Paris was still firmly in the hands of the League, and Henry was in danger of becoming a king without a country. He made a pact with Henry of Navarre, and together royalist and Huguenot forces besieged Paris. All supplies were cut off from the city and only the arrival of a Spanish army prevented its fall. In 1589 Catherine de Médicis died, her ambition to reestablish the authority of the monarchy in shambles, and in the same year a fanatic priest gained revenge for the murder of the Guises by assassinating Henry III.

Now Henry of Navarre came into his inheritance. After nearly 30 years of continuous civil war, it was certain that a Huguenot could never rule France. The League had already proclaimed a Catholic rival as king, and the pope excommunicated Henry of Navarre and absolved France from loyalty to him. If Henry was to become king of all France, he would have to become a Catholic king. It is not clear when Henry made the decision to accept the Catholic faith—"Paris is worth a mass," he reportedly declared—but he did not announce his decision at once. Rather he strengthened his forces, tightened his bonds with the politiques, and urged his countrymen to expel the Spanish invaders. He finally made his conversion public and in 1594 was crowned Henry IV

(1589–1610). A war-weary nation was willing to accept the sincerity of its new king rather than endure a seemingly endless struggle. Even the Leaguers were exhausted. Their claimant to the throne had died, and they were now seen as rebels rather than patriots. War had sapped both their treasuries and their spirit. Most of the leading peers on both sides were nearly bankrupt, and Henry IV was willing to pay large cash settlements to all those who would return to their estates and pledge allegiance to him.

Resistance to the reestablishment of the monarchy continued for several years, but Henry IV was a strong and capable ruler. He declared war on Spain to unite his nation against foreign aggression, and he carefully reestablished the balance of aristocratic factions at his court. The League collapsed, and moderate Catholics rallied around the king. Although Huguenots and Calvinists everywhere were shocked by Henry's conversion, they were hardly in a position to wage a successful war against their former leader. Henry's accession gave them their first real hope for an enduring settlement with the crown.

In 1598 Henry proclaimed the Edict of Nantes, which granted limited toleration to the Huguenots. It was the culmination of decades of attempts to find a solution to

Henry IV renounced Protestantism and embraced the Roman Catholic church to gain the throne of France, saying, "Paris is worth a mass."

the existence of two religions in one state. It was a compromise that satisfied no one, but it was a compromise that everyone could accept. One king, two faiths was as apt a description of Henry IV as it was of the settlement. Yet neither Henry's conversion nor the Edict of Nantes stilled the passions that had spawned and sustained the French wars of religion. Sporadic fighting between Catholics and Huguenots continued, and fanatics on both sides fanned the flames of religious hatred. Henry IV survived 18 attempts on his life before he was finally felled by an assassin's knife in 1610, but by then he had reestablished the monarchy and brought a semblance of peace to France.

the world of philip II

By the middle of the sixteenth century, Spain was the greatest power in Europe. The dominions of Philip II (1556–98) of Spain stretched from the Atlantic to the Pacific, his continental territories included the Netherlands in the north and Milan and Naples in Italy. In 1580 Philip became king of Portugal, uniting all the states of the Iberian Peninsula. With the addition of Portugal's Atlantic ports and its sizable fleet, Spanish maritime power was now unsurpassed. Spain was also a great

catholics and Huguenots

The Edict of Nantes (1598) was a milestone in the development of religious toleration in Europe. It was granted by King Henry IV to the Huguenots at the end of the French wars of religion. The Edict of Nantes established the rights of Protestants and was in effect for nearly a century.

We ordain that the Catholic, Apostolic and Roman religion shall be restored and re-established in all places and districts of this our kingdom and the countries under our rule, where its practice has been interrupted, so that it can be peacefully and freely practiced there, without any disturbance or hindrance. We forbid very expressly all persons of whatever rank, quality or condition they may be, under the aforesaid penalties, to disturb, molest or cause annoyance to clerics in the celebration of the Divine worship. . . .

And in order not to leave any cause for discords and disputes between our subjects, we have permit-ted and we permit those of the so-called Reformed religion to live and dwell in all the towns and districts of this our kingdom and the countries under our rule, without being annoyed, disturbed, molested or constrained to do anything against their conscience, or for this cause to be sought out in their houses and districts where they wish to live, provided that they conduct themselves in other respects according to the provisions of our present Edict. . . .

From the Edict of Nantes.

The French Wars of Religion

1559	Death of Henry II
1560	Protestant duc de Condé sentenced to death
1562	First battle of wars of religion
1563	Catholic duc de Guise assassinated; Edict of Amboise grants limited Protestant worship
1572	Saint Bartholomew's Day massacre
1574	Accession of Henry III
1576	Formation of Catholic League
1584	Death of duc d'Anjou makes Henry of Navarre heir to throne
1585	War of the three Henrys
1588	Duc de Guise murdered by order of Henry III
1589	Catherine de Médicis dies; Henry III assassinated
1594	Henry IV crowned
1598	Edict of Nantes

There was good reason why this slightly stooped king appeared as if he had the weight of the world on his shoulders. In the Mediterranean, Spain alone stood out against the expansion of Ottoman power. The sultan's navy continually threatened to turn the Mediterranean into a Turkish lake, while his armies attempted to capture and hold Italian soil. All Europe shuddered at the news of each Ottoman advance. Popes called for holy wars against the Turks, but only Philip heeded the cry. From nearly the moment that he inherited the Spanish crown, he took up the challenge of defending European Christianity. For over a decade Philip maintained costly coastal garrisons in North Africa and Italy and assembled large fleets and larger armies to discourage or repel Turkish invasions. This sparring could not go on indefinitely, and in 1571 both sides prepared for a decisive battle. A combined Spanish and Italian force of over 300 ships and 80,000 men met an even larger Ottoman flotilla off the coast of Greece. The Spanish naval victory at Lepanto was considered one of the great events of the sixteenth century, celebrated in story and song for the next 300 years. Although the Turks continued to menace the Mediterranean islands, Lepanto marked the end of Ottoman advances.

If Philip II saw himself as a Christian monarch fending off the advance of the infidel, he also saw himself as a Catholic monarch fending off the spread of heresy. There can be no doubt of Philip's personal devotion to Catholicism or of his oft-expressed conviction "I would prefer to lose all my dominions and a hundred lives if I had them rather than be lord over heretics." The lives

cultural and intellectual center. The fashions and tastes of its golden age dominated all the courts of Europe.

Great power meant great responsibilities, and few monarchs took their tasks more seriously than did Philip II. Trained from childhood for the cares of office, he exceeded all expectations. Philip II earned his reputation as "King of Paper" by maintaining a grueling work schedule. Up at eight and at mass soon afterwards, he met with his advisers and visitors on official business until noon. After a brief lunch, he began the real business of the day, the study of the mountains of papers that his empire generated. Although summaries were prepared of the hundreds of documents he handled each day, Philip II frequently read and annotated the longer originals. No detail was too small to escape his attention. His workday often lasted ten hours or longer. Even when he was traveling, his secretaries carried huge chests of state papers that Philip studied in his carriage and annotated on a portable desk that always accompanied him.

The Habsburg Empire Under Philip II

that were to be lost in battling heretics were numbered not in hundreds, but in hundreds of thousands. Philip II came to the throne at just the moment that Calvinism began its rapid growth in northern Europe. He supported the Catholic cause in France throughout the civil wars, sending money, advisers, and ultimately an army to relieve Paris. His ambassadors urged Catherine de Médicis and her sons to take the most repressive measures against the Huguenots, including the Saint Bartholomew's Day Massacre.

El Greco, The Adoration of the Name of Jesus (ca. 1580). The painting is an allegory of the Holy League of Spain, Venice, and the papacy. The League's victory over the Turks in the naval battle at Lepanto in 1571 halted the Ottoman advance in Europe. The figures kneeling at the bottom of the painting are Philip II of Spain, the doge of Venice, and the pope.

Philip was equally aggressive against English Protestants. For a brief time he had been king in England through his marriage to Mary I (1553–58). He encouraged Mary's efforts to restore the Catholic church in England and supported her policies of repression. When Mary died and Elizabeth I (1558–1603) rejected his marriage proposal, his limited rule in England came to an end. From then on, England and Spain entered a long period of hostility. English pirates raided Spanish treasure ships returning to Europe, and Elizabeth covertly aided both French and Dutch Protestants. Finally, in 1588, Philip decided upon invasion. A great fleet set sail from the Portuguese coast to the Netherlands, where a large Spanish army stood waiting to be conveyed to England.

The Spanish Armada comprised over 130 ships, many of them the pride of the Spanish and Portuguese navies. They were bigger and stronger than anything possessed by the English, whose forces were largely merchant vessels hastily converted for battle. But the English ships were faster and more easily maneuverable in the unpredictable winds of the English Channel. They also contained guns that could easily be reloaded for multiple firings, while the Spanish guns were designed to discharge only one broadside before hand-to-hand combat ensued. With these advantages the English were able to prevent the Armada from reaching port in the Netherlands and to destroy many individual ships as they were blown off course. The defeat of the Spanish Armada was less a military than a psychological blow to Philip II: he could more easily replace ships than restore confidence in Spanish power.

The Burgundian Inheritance

This confidence was all the more necessary when Philip II faced the gravest crisis of his reign: the revolt of the Netherlands. Although Philip's father, Charles V, had amassed a great empire, he had begun only as the duke of Burgundy. Charles's Burgundian inheritance encompassed a diverse territory in the northwestern corner of Europe. The 17 separate provinces of this territory were called the Netherlands, or the Low Countries, because of the flooding that kept large portions of them under water. The Netherlands was one of the richest and most populous regions of Europe, an international leader in manufacturing, banking, and commerce. Antwerp and Amsterdam were bustling port cities with access to the

North Sea; inland were the prosperous industrial towns of Ghent and Brussels. The preeminence of the Netherlands was all the more remarkable because the provinces themselves were divided geographically, culturally, and linguistically. Rivers, lakes, and flooded plains separated the southern provinces, where French was the background and language of the inhabitants, from the northern ones, where Germans had settled and Dutch was spoken. Charles V attempted to unify the provinces by removing them from the jurisdiction of the Holy Roman Empire and establishing a separate regency under his eldest son, Philip II. Thus the future of the Netherlands was tied to Spain and the New World when Philip II set sail for Castile in 1559 to claim the crown of Spain.

Although Philip II had every intention of returning to the Low Countries, in fact the Netherlands had seen the last of their king. Philip left his half-sister, Margaret of Parma, as regent, providing her with a talented group of Spanish administrators to carry out policies that were to be formulated in Madrid. As Philip's own grasp on the affairs of the Netherlands loosened, so did the loyalty of the native nobility to the absent monarch. The resentments that built up were traditional ones—hostility to foreigners, distrust of royal advisers, and contempt for policies that lacked understanding of local

conditions. All of these discontents came together over Philip's religious policies.

The Low Countries had accepted the Peace of Augsburg in a spirit of conciliation in which it was never intended. Here Catholics, Lutherans, Anabaptists, and Calvinists peaceably coexisted. As in France, this situation changed dramatically with the spread of Calvinism. The heavy concentration of urban populations in the Low Countries provided the natural habitat for Calvinist preachers, who made converts across the entire social spectrum. As Charles V, Holy Roman Emperor, he may have made his peace with Protestants, but as Charles I, king of Spain, he had not. Charles V had maintained the purity of the Spanish Catholic church through a sensible combination of reform and repression.

Philip II intended to pursue a similar policy in the Low Countries. With papal approval he initiated a scheme to reform the hierarchy of the Church by expanding the number of bishops, and he invited the Jesuits to establish schools for orthodox learning. Simultaneously, he strengthened the power of the Inquisition and ordered the enforcement of the decrees of the Council of Trent. The Protestants sought the protection of their local nobility who—Catholic or Protestant—had their own reasons for opposing Provincial nobility, and magistrates resented both the policies

This painting by an unknown artist depicts the clash between the Spanish and English fleets during the Armada invasion in 1588.

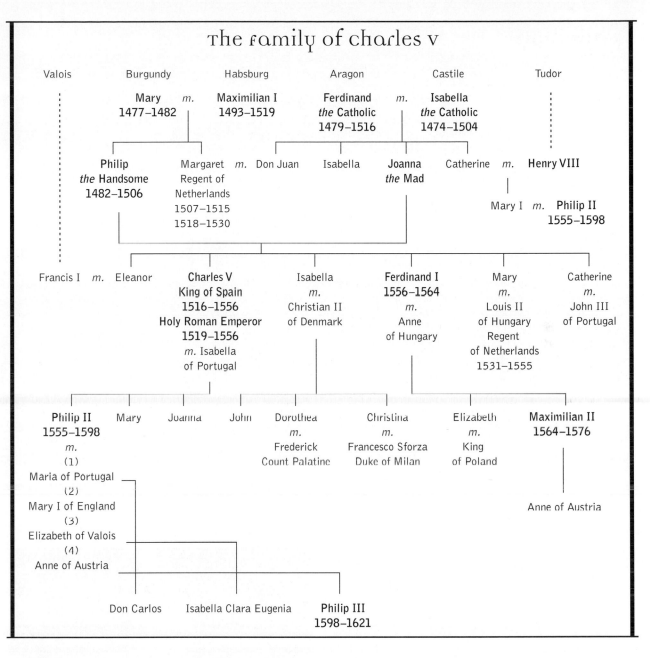

The family of charles v

Valois · Burgundy · Habsburg · Aragon · Castile · Tudor

Mary *m.* Maximilian I
1477–1482   1493–1519

Ferdinand *m.* Isabella
the Catholic   *the* Catholic
1479–1516   1474–1504

Philip · Margaret *m.* Don Juan · Isabella · Joanna · Catherine *m.* Henry VIII
the Handsome · Regent of · *the* Mad
1482–1506 · Netherlands
· 1507–1515
· 1518–1530

Mary I *m.* Philip II
1555–1598

Francis I *m.* Eleanor · Charles V · Isabella · Ferdinand I · Mary · Catherine
· King of Spain · *m.* · 1556–1564 · *m.* · *m.*
· 1516–1556 · Christian II · *m.* · Louis II · John III
· Holy Roman Emperor · of Denmark · Anne · of Hungary · of Portugal
· 1519–1556 · · of Hungary · Regent
· *m.* Isabella · · · of Netherlands
· of Portugal · · · 1531–1555

Philip II · Mary · Joanna · John · Dorothea · Christina · Elizabeth · Maximilian II
1555–1598 · · · · *m.* · *m.* · *m.* · 1564–1576
m. · · · · Frederick · Francesco Sforza · King
(1) · · · · Count Palatine · Duke of Milan · of Poland
Maria of Portugal
(2)
Mary I of England
(3)
Elizabeth of Valois
(4)
Anne of Austria

Anne of Austria

Don Carlos · Isabella Clara Eugenia · Philip III
1598–1621

---

that were being pursued and the fact that they disregarded local autonomy. Town governors and noblemen refused to cooperate in implementing the new laws. Leading Protestants like Prince William of Orange, one of the largest landholders in the Netherlands, and Count Egmont, an outstanding military leader, urged Margaret to adopt a policy of toleration along the lines of the Peace of Augsburg and made clear that they would resign from office rather than support anything else.

The revolt of the netherlands

The passive resistance of nobles and magistrates was soon matched by the active resistance of the Calvinists.

cannibals

Michel de Montaigne (1533–92) came from a wealthy family in the Bordeaux region of France and ultimately inherited the chateau from which his name derives. Before his early retirement he worked in the legal profession. His *Essays* (1572–88) combined humanist learning with the new philosophy of skepticism. The following excerpt, from "Of Cannibals," shows both his penetrating intelligence and his detached observation of the world around him.

These nations, then, seem to me barbarous in this sense, that they have been fashioned very little by the human mind, and are still very close to their original naturalness. The laws of nature still rule them, very little corrupted by ours; and they are in such a state of purity that I am sometimes vexed that they were unknown earlier, in the days when there were men able to judge them better than we. I am sorry that Lycurgus and Plato did not know of them; for it seems to me that what we actually see in these nations surpasses not only all the pictures in which poets have idealized the golden age and all their inventions in imagining a happy state of man, but also the conceptions and the very desire of philosophy. . . .

For the rest, they live in a country with a very pleasant and temperate climate, so that according to my witnesses it is rare to see a sick man there; and they have assured me that they never saw one palsied, bleary-eyed, toothless, or bent with age. They are settled along the sea and shut in on the land side by great high mountains, with a stretch about a hundred leagues wide in between. They have a great abundance of fish and flesh which bear no resemblance to ours, and they eat them with no other artifice than cooking.

They have their wars with the nations beyond the mountains, further inland, to which they go quite naked, with no other arms than bows or wooden swords ending in a sharp point, in the manner of the tongues of our boar spears. It is astonishing what firmness they show in their combats, which never end but in slaughter and bloodshed; for as to routs and terror, they know nothing of either.

Each man brings back as his trophy the head of the enemy he has killed, and sets it up at the entrance to his dwelling. After they have treated their prisoners well for a long time with all the hospitality they can think of, each man who has a prisoner calls a great assembly of his acquaintances. He ties a rope to one of the prisoner's arms by the end of which he

Portrait of Philip II by Alonso Sánchez Coello, ca. 1582. Philip tried for twelve years to suppress rebellion in the Protestant Netherlands, and he sent troops to aid Catholic forces in battle with the Huguenots in France. He fared badly in his attempts to deal with England, his Spanish Armada suffering a humiliating defeat in 1588 that marked the beginning of the decline of Spanish power.

holds him, a few steps away, for fear of being hurt, and gives his dearest friend the other arm to hold in the same way; and these two, in the presence of the whole assembly, kill him with their swords. This done, they roast him and eat him in common and send some pieces to their absent friends. This is not, as people think, for nourishment, as of old the Scythians used to do; it is to betoken an extreme revenge. And the proof of this came when they saw the Portuguese, who had joined forces with their adversaries, inflict a different kind of death on them when they took them prisoner, which was to bury them up to the waist, shoot the rest of their body full of arrows, and afterward hang them. They thought that these people from the other world, being men who had sown the knowledge of many vices among their neighbors and were much greater masters than themselves in every sort of wickedness, did not adopt this sort of vengeance without some reason, and that it must be more painful than their own; so they began to give up their old method and to follow this one.

I am not sorry that we notice the barbarous horror of such acts, but I am heartily sorry that, judging their faults rightly, we should be so blind to our own. I think there is more barbarity in eating a man alive than in eating him dead; and in tearing by tortures and the rack a body still full of feeling, in roasting a man bit by bit, in having him bitten and mangled by dogs and swine (as we have not only read but seen within fresh memory, not among ancient enemies, but among neighbors and fellow citizens, and what is worse, on the pretext of piety and religion), than in roasting and eating him after he is dead. . . .

So we may well call these people barbarians, in respect to the rules of reason, but not in respect to ourselves, who surpass them in every kind of barbarity.

Their warfare is wholly noble and generous, and as excusable and beautiful as this human disease can be; its only basis among them is their rivalry in valor. They are not fighting for the conquest of new lands, for they still enjoy that natural abundance that provides them without toil and trouble with all necessary things in such profusion that they have no wish to enlarge their boundaries. They are still in that happy state of desiring only as much as their natural needs demand; anything beyond that is superfluous to them. . . . Truly here are real savages by our standards, for either they must be thoroughly so, or we must be; there is an amazing distance between their character and ours.

From Montaigne, "Of Cannibals."

Unable to enforce Philip's policy, Margaret and her advisers agreed to a limited toleration. But in the summer of 1566, before it could be put into effect, bands of Calvinists unleashed a storm of iconoclasm in the provinces, breaking stained glass windows and statues of the Virgin and the saints, which they claimed were idolatrous. Catholic churches were stormed and turned into Calvinist meeting houses. Local authorities were helpless in the face of determined Calvinists and apathetic Catholics; they could not protect Church property. Iconoclasm gave way to open revolt. Fearing social rebellion, even the leading Protestant noblemen took part in suppressing these riots.

In Spain, the events in the Netherlands were treated for what they were: open rebellion. Despite the fact that Margaret had already restored order, Philip II was determined to punish the rebels and enforce the heresy laws.

A large military force under the command of the Duke of Alba (1507–82)—whose record of success was matched only by his record of brutality—was sent from Spain as an army of occupation. As befit a warrior who had made his reputation leading imperial troops against the Lutherans, Alba gave no quarter to the Protestants of the Netherlands. "Everyone must be made to live in constant fear of the roof breaking down over his head," he wrote.

Alba lured Count Egmont and other Protestant noblemen to Brussels, where he publicly executed them in 1568. He also established a military court to punish participants in the rebellion, a court that came to be called the Council of Blood. The Council handed down over 9000 convictions, a thousand of which carried the death penalty. As many as 60,000 Protestants fled beyond Alba's jurisdiction. Alba next made an example of sev-

The Revolt of the Netherlands

eral small towns that had been implicated in the iconoclasm. He allowed his soldiers to pillage the towns at will before slaughtering their entire populations and razing them to the ground. By the end of 1568, royal policy had gained a sullen acceptance in the Netherlands, but the hostilities did not end. For the next 80 years, with only occasional truces, Spain and the Netherlands were at war.

Alba's policies drove Protestants into rebellion. This forced the Spanish government to maintain its army by raising taxes from those provinces that had remained loyal. Soon the loyal provinces too were in revolt, not over religion, but over taxation and local autonomy. Tax resistance and fear of an invasion from France left Alba unprepared for the series of successful assaults Protestants launched in the northern provinces during 1572. Protestant generals established a permanent base in the northwestern provinces of Holland and Zeeland. By 1575 the Protestants had gained a stronghold that they would never relinquish. Prince William of Orange assumed the leadership of the two provinces that were now united against the tyranny of Philip's rule.

Spanish government was collapsing all over the Netherlands. William ruled in the north and the States-General, a parliamentary body composed of representatives from the separate provinces, ruled in the south. Margaret of Parma had resigned in disgust at Alba's tactics, and Alba had been relieved of his command when his tactics had failed. No one was in control of the Spanish army. The soldiers, who had gone years with only partial pay, now roamed the southern provinces looking for plunder. Brussels and Ghent both had been targets, and in 1576 the worst atrocities of all occurred when mutinous Spanish troops sacked Antwerp. One of the wealthiest cities in Europe, home to the most important mercantile and banking establishments in the world, Antwerp was torn apart like a roasted pig. The rampage lasted for days. When it ended, over 7000 people had been slaughtered and nearly a third of the city burned to the ground.

The "Spanish fury" in Antwerp effectively ended Philip's rule over his Burgundian inheritance. The Protestants had established a permanent home in the north. The States-General had established its ability to rule in the south, and Spanish policy had been totally discredited. To achieve a settlement, the Pacification of Ghent of 1576, the Spanish government conceded local autonomy in taxation, the central role of the States-

General in legislation, and the immediate withdrawal of all Spanish troops from the Low Countries. Five southern provinces pledged to remain Catholic and to accept the authority of the king's regent. This rift between the provinces was soon followed by a permanent split. In 1581 one group of provinces voted to depose Philip II, while a second group decided to remain loyal to him.

Philip II refused to accept the dismemberment of his inheritance and refused to recognize the independent Dutch state that now existed in Holland. Throughout the 1580s and 1590s military expeditions attempted to reunite the southern provinces and to conquer the northern ones. But Spanish military successes in the south were outweighed by the long-term failure of their objectives in the north. In 1609 Spain and the Netherlands concluded the Twelve Years' Truce, which tacitly recognized the existence of the state of Holland. By the beginning of the seventeenth century, Holland was not only an independent state, it was one of the greatest rivals of Spain and Portugal for the fruits of empire.

Revolt of the Netherlands

1559	Margaret of Parma named regent of the Netherlands
1566	Calvinist iconoclasm begins revolt
1567	Duke of Alba arrives in Netherlands and establishes Council of Blood
1568	Protestant Count Egmont executed
1572	Protestants capture Holland and Zeeland
1573	Alba relieved of his command
1576	Sack of Antwerp; pacification of Ghent
1581	Catholic and Protestant provinces split
1585	Spanish forces take Brussels and Antwerp
1609	Twelve Years' Truce

The struggles in Eastern Europe

In eastern Europe dynastic struggles outweighed the problems created by religious reform. Muscovy remained the bulwark of Eastern Orthodox Christianity, immune from the struggles over the Roman faith. Protestantism did spread into Poland-Lithuania, but unlike its reception in the west, its presence was tolerated by the Polish state. The spread of dissent was checked not by repression, but by a vigorous Catholic reformation led by the Jesuits. The domestic crises in the east were crises of state rather than of church. In Muscovy, the disputed succession that followed the death of Ivan the Terrible plunged the state into anarchy and civil war. Centuries of conflict between Poland-Lithuania and Muscovy came to a head with the Poles' desperate gamble to seize control of their massive eastern neighbor. War between Poland-Lithuania and Muscovy inevitably dominated the politics of the entire region. The Baltic states, of which Sweden was to become the most important, had their own ambitions for territory and economic gain. They soon joined the fray, making alliances in return for concessions and conquering small pieces of the mainland.

The troops of Philip II of Spain under the Duke of Alba inflicted countless cruelties on the people of the Netherlands.

kings and diets in poland

Until the end of the sixteenth century, Poland-Lithuania was the dominant power in the eastern part of Europe. It was economically healthy and militarily strong. Through its Baltic ports, especially Gdansk, Poland played a central role in international commerce and a dominant role in the northern grain trade. The vast size of the Polish state made defense difficult, and during the course of the sixteenth century it had lost lands to Muscovy in the east and to the Crimean Tartars in the south. But the permanent union with Lithuania in 1569 and the gradual absorption of the Baltic region of Livonia more than compensated for these losses. Matters of war and peace, of taxation and reform, were placed under the strict supervision of the Polish Diet, a parliamentary body that represented the Polish landed elite. The Diet also carefully controlled religious policy. Roman Catholicism was the principal religion in Poland, but the state tolerated numerous Protestant and Eastern creeds. In the Warsaw Confederation of 1573, the Polish gentry vowed, "We who differ in matters of religion will keep the peace among ourselves."

The biological failure of the Jagiellon monarchy in Poland ended that nation's most successful line of kings. Without a natural heir, the Polish nobility and gentry, who officially elected the monarch, had to peddle their throne among the princes of Europe. When Sigismund III (1587–1632) was elected to the Polish throne in 1587, he was also heir to the crown of Sweden. Sigismund accepted the prohibitions against religious repression that were outlined in the Warsaw Confederation, but he actively encouraged the establishment of Jesuit schools, the expansion of monastic orders, and the strengthening of the Roman Catholic church.

All these policies enjoyed the approval of the Polish ruling classes. But the Diet would not support Sigismund's efforts to gain control of the Swedish crown, which he inherited in 1592 but from which he was deposed three years later. If Sigismund triumphed in Sweden, all Poland would get was a part-time monarch. The Polish Diet consistently refused to give the king the funds necessary to invade Sweden successfully. Nevertheless, Sigismund mounted several unsuccessful campaigns against the Swedes that sapped Polish money and manpower.

Eastern Europe, ca. 1550

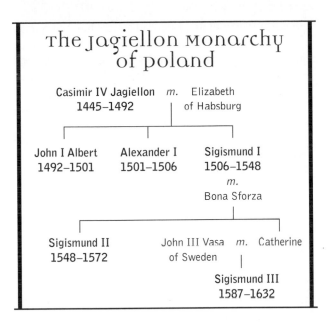

The Jagiellon Monarchy of Poland

Casimir IV Jagiellon   *m.*   Elizabeth
1445–1492   of Habsburg

John I Albert   Alexander I   Sigismund I
1492–1501   1501–1506   1506–1548
                                            m.
                                       Bona Sforza

Sigismund II   John III Vasa   *m.*   Catherine
1548–1572   of Sweden

                    Sigismund III
                    1587–1632

Muscovy's Time of Troubles

The wars of Ivan the Great and Ivan the Terrible in the fifteenth and sixteenth centuries were waged to secure agricultural territory in the west and a Baltic port in the north; both objectives came at the expense of Poland-

Lithuania. But following the death of Ivan the Terrible in 1584, the Muscovite state began to disintegrate. For years it had been held together only by conquest and fear. Ivan's conflicts with the boyars, the hereditary nobility, had created an aristocracy unwilling and unable to come to the aid of his successors. By 1601 the crown was plunged into a crisis of legitimacy known as the Time of Troubles. Ivan had murdered his heir in a fit of anger and left his half-witted son to inherit the throne. This led to a vacuum of power at the center as well as a struggle for the spoils of government. Private armies ruled great swaths of the state and pretenders to the crown—all claiming to be Dimitri, the lost brother of the last legitimate tsar—appeared everywhere. Ambitious groups of boyars backed their own claimants to the throne. So, too, did ambitious foreigners who eagerly sought to carve up Muscovite possessions.

Muscovy's Time of Troubles was Poland's moment of opportunity. While anarchy and civil war raged, Poland looked to regain the territory that it had lost to Muscovy over the previous century. Sigismund abandoned war with Sweden in order to intervene in the struggle for the Russian crown. Polish forces crossed into Muscovy and Sigismund's generals backed one of the strongest of the false Dimitris, but their plan to put him on the throne failed when he was assassinated. Sigismund used the

An assembly of the Polish Diet, the parliamentary body composed of the landed elite. On the throne is Sigismund III. Rivalry among the magnates weakened the Diet, and conflicts with the elected monarchs were frequent.

Legend:
- Russia in 1462
- Territory added by 1533
- Territory added by 1598

The Rise of Russia

partner in Baltic affairs. Denmark controlled the narrow sound that linked the Baltic with the North Sea, and its prosperity derived from the tolls it collected on imports and exports. When, in 1523, Gustav I Vasa led the uprising of the Swedish aristocracy that ended Danish domination, he won the right to rule over a poor, sparsely populated state with few towns or developed seaports. The Vasas ruled Sweden in conjunction with the aristocracy. Although the throne was hereditary, the part played by the nobility in elevating Gustav I Vasa (1523–60) gave the nobles a powerful voice in Swedish affairs. Through the council of state, known as the Rad, the Swedish nobility exerted a strong check on the monarch. Sweden's aggressive foreign policy began accidentally. When in the 1550s the Teutonic Knights found themselves no longer capable of ruling in Livonia, the Baltic seaports that had been under their dominion scrambled for new alliances. Muscovy and Poland-Lithuania were the logical choices, but the town of Reval, an important outlet for Russian trade near the mouth of the Gulf of Finland, asked Sweden for protection. After some hesitation, since the occupation of ter-

death of the last false Dimitri as a pretext to assert his own claim to the Muscovite crown. More Polish forces poured across the frontier. In 1610 they took Moscow and Sigismund proclaimed himself tsar, intending to unite the two massive states.

The Russian boyars, so long divided, now rose against the Polish enemy. The Polish garrison in Moscow was starved into submission, and a native Russian, Michael Romanov (1613–45), was chosen tsar by an assembly of landholders, the Zemsky Sobor. He made a humiliating peace with the Swedes—who had also taken advantage of the Time of Troubles to invade Muscovy's Baltic provinces—in return for Swedish assistance against the Poles. Intermittent fighting continued for another 20 years. In the end, Poland agreed to peace and a separate Muscovite state, but only in exchange for large territorial concessions.

the Rise of sweden

Sweden's rise to power during the seventeenth century was as startling as it was swift. Until the Reformation, Sweden had been part of the Scandinavian confederation ruled by the Danes. Although the Swedes had a measure of autonomy, they were very much a junior

Michael Romanov was chosen to be tsar in 1613. His father, the Patriarch Philaret of Moscow, acted as joint ruler with Michael until the patriarch's death in 1633.

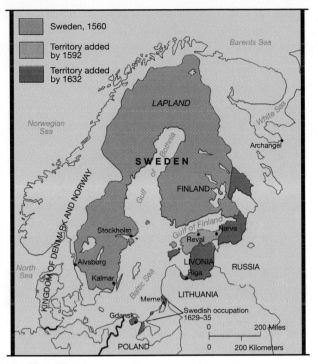

The Rise of Sweden

Legend:
- Sweden, 1560
- Territory added by 1592
- Territory added by 1632

dermine their Lutheran church. Sigismund was deposed in favor of his uncle Charles IX (1604–11). War with Poland resulted from Sigismund's efforts to regain the Swedish crown. The Swedes used the opportunity to blockade Riga and to occupy more Livonian territory. The Swedish navy was far superior to any force that the Poles could assemble, but on land Polish forces were masters. The Swedish invasion force suffered a crushing defeat and had to retreat to its coastal enclaves. The Poles now had an opportunity to retake all of Livonia but, as always, the Polish Diet was reluctant to finance Sigismund's wars. Furthermore, Sigismund had his eyes on a bigger prize. Rather than follow up its Swedish victory, Poland invaded Muscovy.

Meanwhile, the blockade of Riga and the assembly of a large Swedish fleet in the Baltic threatened Denmark. The Danes continued to claim sovereignty over Sweden and took the opportunity of the Polish-Swedish conflict to reassert it. In 1611, under the energetic leadership of

A Livonian peasant. Livonia was conquered by Ivan the Terrible in his campaign of 1563 but was soon reclaimed by the Poles. In 1660 Livonia became part of the Swedish empire. Livonia was originally inhabited by the Livs, a Finnish people.

ritory on the southern shores of the Baltic would involve great expense, Sweden fortified Reval in 1560. A decade later, Swedish forces captured Narva, farther to the east, and consolidated their hold on the Livonian coast. By occupying the most important ports on the Gulf of Finland, Sweden could control a sizable portion of the Muscovite trade.

Now only two obstacles prevented them from dominating trade with Muscovy: Archangel in the north and Riga in the south. In the 1580s, the Muscovites established a port at Archangel on the White Sea. With this new port they opened a trading route to the west, around northern Scandinavia. Sweden benefited from the White Sea trade by claiming the northern portions of the Scandinavian peninsula necessary to make the trade secure. In all of their dealings with Muscovy the Swedes sought further privileges at Archangel while laying plans for its conquest. Riga was a problem of a different sort. As the Swedes secured the northern Livonian ports, more of the Muscovy trade moved to the south and passed through Riga, which would have to be captured or blockaded if the Swedes were to control commerce in the eastern Baltic.

Sigismund's aggressive alliance with the Polish Jesuits persuaded the Swedish nobility that he would un-the Danish king Christian IV (1588–1648), Denmark invaded Sweden from both the east and the west. The Danes captured the towns of Kalmar and Alvsborg and threatened to take Stockholm. To end the Danish war, Sweden accepted humiliating terms in 1613. Sweden renounced all claims to the northern coasts and recognized Danish control of the Arctic trading route.

Paradoxically, these setbacks became the springboard for Swedish success. Fear of the Danes led both the English and the Dutch into alliances with Sweden. The countries all shared Protestant interests, and the English were heavily committed to the Muscovy trade, which was still an important part of Swedish commerce. Fear of the Poles had a similar effect upon Muscovy. In 1609 the Swedes agreed to send 5000 troops to Muscovy to help repel the Polish invasion. In return, Muscovy agreed to cede to Sweden its Baltic possessions. This was accomplished in 1617, giving Sweden complete control of the Gulf of Finland.

In 1611, during the middle of the Danish war, Charles IX died and was succeeded by his son Gustavus Adolphus (1611–32). Unlike his father and cousin before him, who had come by chance to the Swedish throne, Gustavus Adolphus was raised to be king. Gruff and affable by turns, he was one of the leading Protestant princes of his day, in every way a match for Christian IV of Denmark. Gustavus's greatest skills were military. He inherited an ample navy and an effective army. Unlike nearly every other European state, Sweden raised its

forces from its own citizens. Gustavus's predecessors had made important innovations in the training of soldiers and in their battlefield tactics. These the new king improved upon. He introduced new weapons such as the light mobile gun and reshaped his army into standard-size squadrons and regiments, which were easier to administer and deploy.

The calamitous wars inherited from his father occupied Gustavus during the early years of his reign. He was forced to conclude the humiliating peace with the Danes in 1613 and to go to war with the Russians in 1614 in order to secure the Baltic coastal estates that had been promised in 1609. Gustavus's first military initiative was to resume war with Poland in order to force Sigismund to renounce his claim to the Swedish throne. In 1621 Gustavus landed in Livonia and within two weeks had captured Riga, the capstone of Sweden's Baltic ambitions. Occupation of Riga increased Swedish control of the Muscovy trade and deprived Denmark of a significant portion of its customs duties. Gustavus now claimed Riga as a Swedish port and successfully demanded that ships sailing from there pay tolls to Sweden rather than Denmark. The capture of Riga firmly established Sweden as a coequal Baltic power.

By the mid-seventeenth century, the Sweden of Gustavus Adolphus was well on its way to international prominence. The capture of Riga gave Sweden complete control of the eastern Baltic and ended Polish pretensions to the Swedish throne. A negotiated settlement

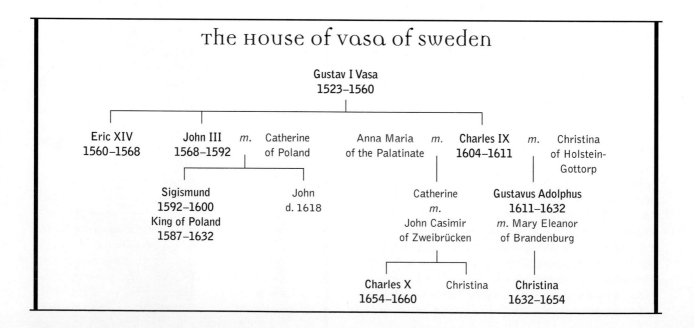

The House of Vasa of Sweden

Gustav I Vasa
1523–1560

Eric XIV
1560–1568

John III
1568–1592   *m.*   Catherine of Poland

Anna Maria of the Palatinate   *m.*   Charles IX
1604–1611   *m.*   Christina of Holstein-Gottorp

Sigismund
1592–1600
King of Poland
1587–1632

John
d. 1618

Catherine
m.
John Casimir
of Zweibrücken

Gustavus Adolphus
1611–1632
m. Mary Eleanor
of Brandenburg

Charles X
1654–1660

Christina

Christina
1632–1654

with the Danes over the collection of tolls enhanced Swedish prestige and increased Sweden's commercial prosperity. Moreover, Gustavus's marriage into the family of the Protestant rulers of Prussia gave Sweden a presence in Germany as well. For the time being Sweden faced east. But the storm clouds of religious warfare were already bursting over the Holy Roman Empire. Gustavus Adolphus now took his place among the Protestant princes of Europe, and Sweden ranked among the leading Protestant powers.

The Thirty Years' War, 1618-1648

Perhaps it was just a matter of time before the isolated conflicts that dotted the corners of Europe were joined together. In 1609 Spain and the Dutch Republic had signed a truce that was to last until 1621. In over 40 years of nearly continuous fighting, the Dutch had carved out a state in the northern Netherlands. They used the truce to consolidate their position and increase their prosperity, largely at the expense of Spain and Portugal. Thus, to the insult of rebellion was added the injury of commercial competition. Spain had reluctantly accepted Dutch independence, but Philip III (1598–1621) never abandoned the objective of recovering his Burgundian inheritance. By the opening of the seventeenth century, Philip had good reasons for hope. Beginning in the 1580s, Spanish forces had reconquered the southern provinces of the Netherlands. The prosperous towns of Brussels, Antwerp, and Ghent were again under Spanish control, and they provided a springboard for another invasion.

The Twelve Years' Truce gave Spain time to prepare for the final assault. During this time Philip III attempted to resolve all of Spain's other European conflicts so that he could then give full attention to a resumption of the Dutch war. Circumstance smiled upon his efforts. In 1603 the pacific James I (1603–25) came to the English throne. Secure in his island state, James I desired peace among all Christian princes. He quickly concluded the war with Spain that had begun with the invasion of the Spanish Armada and entered into negotiations to marry his heir to a Spanish princess. In 1610 the bellicose Henry IV of France was felled by an assassin's knife. French plans to renew war with Spain were abandoned with the accession of the eight-year-old Louis XIII (1610–43). As the sands of the Twelve Years' Truce ran

Marie de Médicis, the widow of Henry IV, with her son Louis XIII.

out, Spain and the Netherlands readied for war. But not even the greatest empire in Europe could control its own destiny. War was in the air all over the Continent, and not everyone could wait until 1621.

Bohemia Revolts

The Peace of Augsburg had served the German states well. The principle that the religion of the ruler was the religion of the state complicated the political life of the Holy Roman Empire, but it also pacified it. Although rulers had the right to enforce uniformity on their subjects, in practice many of the larger states tolerated more than one religion. By the beginning of the seventeenth century, Catholicism and Protestantism had achieved a rough equality within the German states, symbolized by the fact that of the seven electors who chose the Holy Roman Emperor, three were Catholic,

war is hell

No source has better captured the brutality of the Thirty Years' War than the novel *Simplicissimus* (1669). In a series of loosely connected episodes, the hero (whose name means "the simplest of the simple") is snatched from his village to serve in marauding armies whose confrontations with local villagers are usually more horrifying than the episode narrated here.

These troopers were even now ready to march, and had the pastor fastened by a rope to lead him away. Some cried, "Shoot him down, the rogue!" Others would have money from him. But he, lifting up his hands to heaven, begged, for the sake of the Last Judgment, for forbearance and Christian compassion, but in vain; for one of them rode down and dealt him such a blow on the head that he fell flat, and commended his soul to God. Nor did the remainder of the captured peasants fare any better. But even when it seemed these troopers, in their cruel tyranny, had clean lost their wits, came such a swarm of armed peasants out of the wood, that it seemed a wasps'-nest had been stirred. And these began to yell so frightfully and so furiously to attack with sword and musket that all my hair stood on end; and never had I been at such a merrymaking before: for the peasants of the Spessart and the Vogelsberg are as little wont as are the Hessians and men of the Sauerland and the Black Forest to let themselves be crowed over on their own dunghill. So away went the troopers, and not only left behind the cattle they had captured, but threw away bag and baggage also, and so cast all their booty to the winds lest themselves should become booty for the peasants: yet some of them fell into their hands. This sport took from me well-nigh all desire to see the world, for I thought, if 'tis all like this, then is the wilderness far more pleasant.

From Hans Von Grimmelshausen, *The Adventurous Simplicissimus*.

three Protestant, and the seventh was the emperor himself, acting as king of Bohemia. This situation was not unwelcome to the leaders of the Austrian Habsburg family who succeeded Emperor Charles V. By necessity, the eastern Habsburgs were more tolerant than their Spanish kinfolk. Protestants fought the Ottomans with as much zeal as did Catholics, and the Ottomans were the empire's more potent enemy. The unofficial policy of toleration not only helped the Austrian Habsburgs defend their state, it allowed them to expand it. The head of their house was elected king of Bohemia and king of Hungary, both states with large Protestant populations.

In 1617 Mathias, the childless Holy Roman Emperor, began making plans for his cousin, Ferdinand Habsburg, to succeed him. In order to ensure a Catholic majority among the electors, the emperor relinquished his Bohemian title and pressed for Ferdinand's election as the new king of Bohemia. Ferdinand was Catholic, very devout, and very committed. He had been educated by Jesuits and practiced what had been preached to him. On his own estates, Ferdinand abandoned the policy of toleration. Jesuit schools were founded and the precepts of the Council of Trent were enforced. Protestant preachers were barred from their offices, Protest. ooks were publicly burned, and thousands of comm. people were forced to flee, many into nearby Bohemia, where Protestants constituted the majority of the population.

Thus Ferdinand's election as king of Bohemia was no foregone conclusion. Although in the end the Protestant nobles of Bohemia could not prevent his election, they forced the new king to accept the strictest limitations upon his political and religious powers. But once elected, Ferdinand had not the slightest intention of honoring the provisions that had been thrust upon him. His opponents were equally strong willed. When Ferdinand violated Protestant religious liberties, a group of noblemen marched to the royal palace in Prague in May 1618, found two of the king's chief advisers, and hurled them out of an upper-story window. The officials' lives—if not their dignity—were preserved by the pile of manure in which they landed.

The Defenestration of Prague, as this incident came to be known, initiated a Protestant counteroffensive throughout the Habsburg lands. Fear of Ferdinand's policies led to Protestant uprisings in Hungary as well as Bohemia. Those who seized control of the government declared Ferdinand deposed and the throne vacant, but they had no candidate to accept their crown. When Emperor Mathias died in 1619, the stalemate was broken. Ferdinand succeeded to the imperial title as Ferdinand II (1619–37) and Frederick V, one of the Protestant electors, accepted the Bohemian crown.

Frederick was a sincere but weak Calvinist whose credentials were much stronger than his abilities. His mother was a daughter of Prince William of Orange and his wife, Elizabeth, a daughter of James I of England. It was widely believed that it was Elizabeth's resolution that she would "rather eat sauerkraut with a King than roast meat with an Elector" that decided the issue. No decision could have been more disastrous for the fate of Europe. Frederick ruled a geographically divided German state known as the Palatinate. One hundred miles separated the two segments of his lands, but both were strategically important. The Lower Palatinate bordered on the Catholic Spanish Netherlands and the Upper Palatinate on Catholic Bavaria.

Once Frederick accepted the Bohemian crown, he was faced with a war on three fronts. It was over almost before it began. Ferdinand II had no difficulty enlisting allies to recover the Bohemian crown, since he could pay them with the spoils of Frederick's lands. Spanish troops from the Netherlands occupied the Lower Palatinate, and Bavarian troops occupied the Upper Palatinate. Frederick, on the other hand, met rejection wherever he turned. Neither the Dutch nor the English would send more than token aid—both had advised him against breaking the imperial peace. The Lutheran princes of Germany would not enter into a war between Calvinists and Catholics, especially after Ferdinand II promised to protect the Bohemian Lutherans.

At the Battle of the White Mountain in 1620, Ferdinand's Catholic forces annihilated Frederick's army. Frederick and Elizabeth fled north, first to Denmark and then to Holland. Bohemia was left to face the wrath of Ferdinand, the victorious king and emperor. The retribution was horrible. Mercenaries who had fought for Ferdinand II were allowed to sack Prague for a week. Elective monarchy was abolished, and Bohemia became part of the hereditary Habsburg lands. Free peasants were enserfed and subjected to imperial law. Those nobles who had supported Frederick lost their lands and their privileges. Calvinism was repressed and thoroughly rooted out, consolidating forever the Catholic character of Bohemia. Frederick's estates were carved up and his rights as elector transferred to the Catholic duke of Bavaria. The Battle of the White Mountain was a turning point in the history of central Europe.

The war widens

For the Habsburgs, religious and dynastic interests were inseparable. Ferdinand II and Philip III of Spain fought for their beliefs and for their patrimony. Their victory gave them more than they could have expected: Ferdinand swallowed up Bohemia and strengthened his position in the empire, and Philip gained possession of a vital link in his supply route between Italy and the Netherlands. The Habsburgs were now more dangerous than ever. Ferdinand's aggressive Catholicism threatened the Protestant princes of Germany, who prudently began to seek allies outside the empire. Spanish expansion threatened France. The occupation of the Lower Palatinate placed a ring of Spanish armies around the French borders from the Pyrenees to the Low Countries. The French too searched for allies. But French opinion remained divided over which was the greater evil: Spain or Protestantism.

Frederick, now in Holland, refused to accept the judgment of battle. He lobbied for a grand alliance to repel the Spaniards from the Lower Palatinate and to restore the religious balance in the empire. Although his personal cause met with little sympathy, his political logic was impeccable, especially after Spain again declared war upon the Dutch in 1621. A grand Protestant alliance—secretly supported by the French—brought together England, Holland, a number of German states, and Denmark. It was the Danes who led this potentially powerful coalition. In 1626 a large Danish army under the command of King Christian IV engaged imperial forces on German soil. But Danish forces could not match the superior numbers and the superior leadership of the Catholic mercenary forces under the command of the ruthless and brilliant Count Albrecht von Wallenstein (1583–1634). In 1629 the Danes withdrew from the empire and sued for peace.

If the Catholic victory at the White Mountain in 1620 threatened the well-being of German Protestantism, the Catholic triumph over the Danes threatened its survival. More powerful than ever, Ferdinand II determined to turn the religious clock back to the state of affairs that had existed when the Peace of Augsburg was concluded in 1555. He demanded that all lands that had then been Catholic but had since become Protestant must now be returned to the fold. He also proclaimed that as the

Peace of Augsburg made no provision for the toleration of Calvinists, they would no longer be tolerated in the empire. These policies together constituted a virtual revolution in the religious affairs of the German states, and they proved impossible to impose. Ferdinand succeeded in only one thing—he united Lutherans and Calvinists against him.

In 1630 King Gustavus Adolphus of Sweden decided to enter the German conflict. To protect Swedish interests, he reasoned, he must defend the Protestant states of northern Germany. Moreover, France was willing to pay much of the cost of a war against Ferdinand. The French too felt the pressure of increasing imperial and Spanish power. Gustavus Adolphus had more success gaining the support of Catholic France than he did gaining the support of the Protestant German princes. Saxony and Brandenburg, the two largest states, feared the consequences of renewed war. Gustavus believed that he could defend the north German states from Ferdinand's aggression and by doing so protect Sweden's Baltic empire. "I seek not my own advantage in this war, nor any gain save the security of my Kingdom," he lectured the reluctant Germans. It was a farsighted strategy. In fact, the only thing he could not foresee when he landed in Germany early in 1630 was how successful his intervention would be.

While Gustavus Adolphus struggled to construct his alliance, imperial forces continued their triumphant progress. In 1631 they besieged, captured, and put to the torch the town of Magdeburg. In a war noted for cruelty between combatants and atrocities against civilians, the destruction of Magdeburg set new standards. Perhaps three-fourths of the 40,000 inhabitants of the town were slaughtered—"in the midst of a horrible din of heart-rending shrieks and cries they were tortured and put to death in so cruel a manner that no words would suffice to describe nor no tears to bewail it," was the report in one pamphlet. The sack of Magdeburg marked a turning point in Protestant fortunes. It gave the international Protestant community a unifying symbol that enhanced Gustavus's military efforts. Hundreds of pamphlets, woodcuts, and newspaper accounts brought the horror of Magdeburg home to Protestants throughout the Continent. Brandenburg and Saxony joined Gustavus Adolphus, not only enlarging his forces, but allowing him to open a second front in Bohemia. He would soon have 140,000 men under his command, only 13,000 of whom were Swedish. In the

Gustavus Adolphus of Sweden, shown at the battle of Breitenfeld in 1631. The battle was the first important Protestant victory of the Thirty Years' War. Gustavus died on the battlefield at Lützen in the following year.

autumn of 1631, this combination overwhelmed the imperial armies. Gustavus won a decisive triumph at Breitenfeld, while the Saxons occupied Prague. For the first time since 1618, Protestant forces were ascendant, and they brought the war into the Catholic heartland of the empire.

Gustavus Adolphus lost no time in pressing his advantage. The Swedes marched west to the Rhine, easily conquering the richest of the Catholic cities and retaking the Lower Palatinate. In early 1632 Protestant forces plundered Bavaria. It was the Bavarian ruler Maximilian who had gained most from the years of war. His troops had occupied the Upper Palatinate, and he had received Frederick's rights as imperial elector in return for support of Ferdinand. Moreover, Maximilian had played a double game of negotiating with the French for neutrality and with the emperor for the spoils of victory. So there was poetic justice when Maximilian's state was invaded, his castles looted, and his lands plundered. But there was no justice at all for the wretched inhabitants of this stronghold of German Catholicism. Town and countryside were laid waste. Not until the winter of 1632 did the armies of Gustavus and Wallenstein finally meet. At the battle of Lützen the Swedes won the field but lost their beloved king. Wounded in the leg, the back, and the head, Gustavus Adolphus died. In less than two years he had decisively transformed the course of the war and the course of Europe's future.

Population Loss in Germany During the Thirty Years' War

Protestant forces now occupied most of central and northern Germany. Ferdinand's ability to redraw the religious map of the empire was at an end.

The siege of Magdeburg, 1631. The sack of the city by the Imperial troops of Tilly's army was one of the most barbarous incidents of the brutal Thirty Years' War.

fire and sword

No event of the Thirty Years' War had a greater effect on public opinion than the annihilation of the Protestant city of Magdeburg, in 1631. Dozens of pamphlets and woodcuts, including this anonymous account, detailed the slaughter of civilians and the devastation of property. It was commonly believed that neither a human nor an animal escaped the destruction.

Thus it came about that the city and all its inhabitants fell into the hands of the enemy, whose violence and cruelty were due in part to their common hatred of the adherents of the Augsburg Confession, and in part to their being imbittered by the chain shot which had been fired at them and by the derision and insults that the Magdeburgers had heaped upon them from the ramparts.

Then was there naught but beating and burning, plundering, torture, and murder. Most especially was every one of the enemy bent on securing much booty. When a marauding party entered a house, if its master had anything to give he might thereby purchase respite and protection for himself and his family till the next man, who also wanted something, should come along. . . .

Thus in a single day this noble and famous city, the pride of the whole country, went up in fire and smoke; and the remnant of its citizens, with their wives and children, were taken prisoners and driven away by the enemy with a noise of weeping and wailing that could be heard from afar, while the cinders and ashes from the town were carried by the wind to Wanzleben, Egeln, and still more distant places . . . .

The Long Quest for Peace

The Thirty Years' War was barely half over when Gustavus Adolphus fell at Lützen. But from that time forward, its central European phase receded in importance. The final stages of the war involved the resumption of the century-old struggle between France and Spain. When the Twelve Years' Truce expired in 1621, Spain again declared war upon the Dutch. Philip III's hopes of concentrating all his resources against Holland had been disappointed by the outbreak of war in central Europe. Not until after the Bohemian revolt had been repressed did the Spanish army begin the long, laborious process of besieging the well-fortified and well-defended towns of the Netherlands. The resumption of war in the Netherlands, combined with the continued successes of Habsburg forces in central Europe, convinced Louis XIII and his chief minister, Cardinal Richelieu, that the time for active French involvement in European affairs was now at hand. Throughout the early stages of the war, France had secretly aided anti-Habsburg forces. Now the time had come to take an open stand. In 1635 France declared war on Spain.

Neither country was prepared for large-scale military action, and neither could afford it. The war resembled nothing so much as two punch-drunk fighters pounding each other, both receiving as much punishment as they

The Thirty Years' War

1618	Defenestration of Prague
1619	Ferdinand Habsburg elected Holy Roman Emperor; Frederick of the Palatinate accepts the crown of Bohemia
1620	Catholic victory at battle of White Mountain
1621	End of Twelve Years' Truce; war between Spain and Netherlands
1626	Danes form Protestant alliance under Christian IV
1627	Spain declares bankruptcy
1630	Gustavus Adolphus leads Swedish forces into Germany
1631	Sack of Magdeburg; Protestant victory at Breitenfeld
1632	Protestant victory at Lützen; death of Gustavus Adolphus
1635	France declares war on Spain
1640	Portugal secedes from Spain
1643	Battle of Rocroi; French forces repel Spaniards
1648	Peace of Westphalia

Legend:
- Spanish dominions
- Austrian dominions
- Brandenburg-Prussia
- Swedish dominions
- Boundary of Holy Roman Empire

The Peace of Westphalia, Europe, 1648

inflicted. France took the offensive first, invading the Spanish Netherlands. In 1636 a Spanish army struck back, pushing to within 25 miles of Paris before it was repelled. Both sides soon began to search for a settlement, but pride prevented them from laying down their gloves. Spain toppled first. Its economy in shambles and its citizens in revolt over high prices and higher taxes, it could no longer maintain its many-fronted war. The Swedes again defeated imperial forces in Germany, the Dutch destroyed much of Spain's Atlantic fleet in 1639, and the Portuguese rose up against the union of crowns that had brought them nothing but expense and the loss of crucial portions of their empire. In 1640 the Portuguese regained their independence. In 1643 Spain gambled once more on a knockout blow against the French. But at the battle of Rocroi, exhausted French troops held out and the Spanish invasion failed.

By now the desire for peace was universal. Most of the main combatants had long since perished: Philip III, ever optimistic, in 1621; Frederick V, an exile to the end, in 1632; Gustavus Adolphus, killed at Lützen in the same year; Wallenstein, murdered by order of Ferdinand II in 1634; Ferdinand himself in 1637; and Louis XIII in 1643, five days before the French triumph at Rocroi. Those who succeeded them had not the same passions, and after so many decades the longing for peace was the strongest emotion on the Continent. But the tangle of wars and alliances was not easily unsnarled, and those who saw themselves as victors at one stage or another still sought desperately for their spoils. Some wanted to reconstruct the political world as it had existed in 1618, others to reestablish it as it was after the first round of Catholic victories in 1627. The Swedes, who had gained most from the struggle—they now occupied much of northern Germany and, after a brief war with Denmark, much territory in the western Baltic as well—wished to settle things largely as they stood. Fighting persisted as each effort to reach a universal peace failed. Finally, at the beginning of 1648, Spain and the Netherlands concluded their 80 years of fighting. This bilateral agreement broke the logjam. One by one the combatants agreed to end their hostilities with one another, and soon the stage was set for a Continent-wide settlement.

A series of agreements, collectively known as the Peace of Westphalia, established the outlines of the political geography of Europe for the next century. Its focus was on the Holy Roman Empire, and it reflected Protestant successes in the final two decades of war. Sweden gained further territories on the Baltic, making it master of the north German ports. France, too, gained in territory and prestige. It kept the vital towns in the Lower Palatinate through which Spanish men and material had moved, and though it did not agree to come to terms with Spain immediately, France's fear of encirclement was at an end. The Dutch gained statehood through official recognition by Spain and through the power they had displayed in building and maintaining an overseas empire.

Territorial boundaries were reestablished as they had existed in 1624, giving the Habsburgs control of both Bohemia and Hungary. The independence of the Swiss cantons was now officially recognized, as were the rights of Calvinists to the protection of the Peace of Augsburg, which again was to govern the religious affairs of the empire. Two of the larger German states were strengthened to balance the emperor's power. Bavaria was allowed to retain the Upper Palatinate, and Brandenburg, which ceded some of its coastal territory to Sweden, gained extensive territories in the east.

The emperor's political control over the German states was also weakened. German rulers were given independent authority over their states, and the imperial diet, rather than the emperor, was empowered to settle disputes. Thus weakened, future emperors ruled in the Habsburg territorial lands with little ability to control, influence, or even arbitrate German affairs. The judgment that the Holy Roman Empire was neither holy, nor Roman, nor an empire was now irrevocably true.

The Peace of Westphalia put the pieces of the map of European states back together. Protestantism and Catholicism now coexisted and there was to be little further change in the geography of religion. The northwest of Europe—England, Holland, Scandinavia, and the north German states—was Protestant, while the south was Catholic. The empire of the German peoples was now at an end, the Austro-Hungarian empire at a beginning. Holland and Sweden had become international powers; Spain and Denmark faded from prominence. Muscovy began a long period of isolation from the west, attempting to restore a semblance of government to its people. But if the negotiators at Westphalia could resolve the political and religious ambitions that gave rise to a century of nearly continuous warfare, they could do nothing to eradicate the effects of war itself. The devastation of humanity in the name of God with which the reform of religion had begun was now exhausted. The costs were horrific. The population of Germany fell from 15 million in 1600 to 11 million in 1650. The armies brought destruction of all kinds in their wake. Plague again raged in Europe—the town of Augsburg lost 18,000 inhabitants in the early 1630s. Famine, too, returned to a continent that 50 years earlier had been self-sufficient in grain. The war played havoc with all of the economies that it touched. Inflation, devaluation of coinage, and huge public and private debts were all directly attributable to the years of fighting. And the toll taken on the spirit of those generations that never knew peace is incalculable.

mastering the chapter

To review the main points of the chapter, be sure you can explain the significance of each of the following.

Terms/Concepts/Events	People	Places
Saint Bartholomew's Day Massacre	Catherine de Médicis	Netherlands
politiques	Guises	Brussels
Catholic League	Bourbons	Ghent
Edict of Nantes	Huguenots	Antwerp
Spanish Armada	Henry of Navarre	Warsaw
Pacification of Ghent	Philip II	Muscovy
Polish Diet	Prince William of Orange	Gulf of Finland
Time of Troubles	James I	Bohemia
Defenestration of Prague	Gustavus Adolphus	Palatinate
Peace of Westphalia	Cardinal Richelieu	Bavaria

suggestions for further reading

general reading

* J. H. Elliott, *Europe Divided, 1559–1598* (New York: Harper & Row, 1968). An outstanding synthesis of European politics in the second half of the sixteenth century.

* Geoffrey Parker, *Europe in Crisis, 1598–1648* (London: William Collins and Sons, 1979). An up-to-date study of European states in the early seventeenth century.

* Richard Bonney, *The European Dynastic States, 1494–1660* (Oxford: Oxford University Press, 1991.) The most up-to-date introduction to the period, by a noted historian of France.

* Jan de Vries, *The European Economy in an Age of Crisis* (Cambridge: Cambridge University Press, 1976). A comprehensive study of economic development, including long-distance trade and commercial change.

* Richard Dunn, *The Age of Religious Wars, 1559–1715* (New York: Norton, 1979). A well-written survey of early modern society.

* H. G. Koenigsberger, *Early Modern Europe* (London: Longman, 1987). A general overview designed for beginning students.

The crises of the western states

J. H. M. Salmon, *Society in Crisis* (New York: St. Martin's Press, 1975). The best single-volume account of the French civil wars; difficult but rewarding.

N. M. Sutherland, *The Massacre of St. Bartholomew and the European Conflict* (London: Macmillan, 1973). Argues the case for the importance of Spanish influence on the massacre and the course of the wars of religion.

Robert Kingdon, *Myths about the St. Bartholomew's Day Massacres, 1572–76* (Cambridge, MA: Harvard University Press, 1988). A study of the impact of a central event in the history of France.

David Buisseret, *Henry IV* (London: Allen & Unwin, 1984). A stylish biography of a problematic personality.

* Mark Greengrass, *France in the Age of Henri IV* (London: Longman, 1984). An important synthesis of French history in the early seventeenth century.

Geoffrey Parker, *Philip II* (Boston: Little, Brown, 1978). The best introduction.

* Garrett Mattingly, *The Armada* (Boston: Houghton Mifflin, 1959). Still the classic account, despite recent reinterpretations.

Colin Martin and N. G. Parker, *The Spanish Armada* (London: Hamilton Press, 1988). A recent study based on archaeological finds and a fresh look at the evidence.

* John Lynch, *Spain, 1516–1598: From Nation State to World Empire* (Cambridge, MA: Blackwell, 1994). The most up-to-date survey.

* Henry Kamen, *Spain, 1469–1714* (London: Longman, 1983). A recent survey with up-to-date interpretations.

* A. W. Lovett, *Early Habsburg Spain* (Oxford: Oxford University Press, 1986). An accessible survey of the recent work on sixteenth century Spain.

* Geoffrey Parker, *The Dutch Revolt* (London: Penguin Books, 1977). An outstanding account of the tangle of events that comprised the revolts of the Netherlands.

* Pieter Geyl, *The Revolt of the Netherlands* (London: Ernest Benn, 1962). Still worth reading for its passion and enthusiasm.

* Jonathan Israel, *The Dutch Republic and the Hispanic World 1606–1661* (Oxford : Clarendon, 1986). A panoramic survey of the stormy relations between Empire and Republic.

* C. V. Wedgwood, *William the Silent, William of Nassau, Prince of Orange, 1533–1584* (New York: Norton, 1968). A stylish biography.

* Peter Limm, *The Dutch Revolt, 1559–1648* (London: Longman, 1989). A brief introduction with source excerpts.

James D. Tracy, *Holland Under Habsburg Rule, 1506–1566* (Berkeley: University of California Press, 1990). A history of the political formation of the Dutch state.

* Penry Williams, *The Later Tudors* (Oxford: Oxford University Press, 1995). The newest survey in the Oxford history of England.

* J. A. Guy, *Tudor England* (Oxford: Oxford University Press, 1988). A magisterial survey by the leading scholar of Tudor England.

* Wallace Maccaffrey, *Elizabeth I* (New York: Edward Arnold, 1993). The latest scholarly biography.

W. E. F. Reddawaay, et al., eds., *The Cambridge History of Poland to 1696* (Cambridge: Cambridge University Press, 1950). A difficult but thorough narrative of Polish history.

Michael Roberts, *Gustavus Adolphus and the Rise of Sweden* (London: English Universities Press, 1973). A highly readable account of Sweden's rise to power.

the struggles in eastern europe

* S. F. Platonov, *The Time of Troubles* (Lawrence: University Press of Kansas, 1970). A good narrative of the disintegration of the Muscovite state.

Maureen Perrie, *Pretenders and Popular Monarchisms in Early Modern Russia* (Cambridge: Cambridge University Press, 1995). Recent scholarship on the Time of Troubles, focusing on the royal impostors.

Stewart Oakley, *War and Peace in the Baltic, 1560–1790* (New York: Routledge, 1992). A solid account of military history during the period of Sweden's rise.

David Kirby, *Northern Europe in the Early Modern Period: The Baltic World, 1492–1772* (London: Longman, 1990). The best single volume on Baltic politics.

Michael Roberts, *The Swedish Imperial Experience* (Cambridge: Cambridge University Press, 1979). Reflections on Swedish history by the preeminent historian of early modern Sweden.

the thirty years' war

* C. V. Wedgwood, *The Thirty Years' War* (New York: Doubleday, 1961). An heroic account; the best narrative history.

* Geoffrey Parker, ed., *The Thirty Years' War* (London: Routledge & Kegan Paul, 1984). A multiauthor account that views the war from a variety of vantage points.

* Peter Limm, *The Thirty Years' War* (London: Longman, 1984). An excellent brief survey with documents.

* Josef Polisensky, *Tragic Triangle* (Prague: Charles University Press, 1991). The origins of the Thirty Years' War from the Bohemian point of view.

* J. H. Elliott, *Richelieu and Olivares* (Cambridge: Cambridge University Press, 1984). A comparison of statesmen and statesmanship in the early seventeenth century.

*Paperback edition available.

The Experiences of Life in Early Modern Europe, 1500-1650

Haymaking

It is summer in the Low Countries. The trees are full, the meadows green; flowers rise in clumps and bushes hang heavy with fruit. The day has dawned brightly for haymaking. Yesterday the long meadow was mowed, and today the hay will be gathered and the first fruits and vegetables of the season harvested. From throughout the village families come together to labor. Twice each summer the grass is cut, dried, and stacked. Some of it will be left in the fields for the animals until autumn; some will be carried into large lofts and stored for the winter.

This scene of communal farming is repeated with little variation throughout Europe in the early modern era. The village we are viewing is fairly prosperous. We can see at least three horses and a large wheeled cart. Horses are still a luxury for farmers; they can be used for transportation as well as labor, but they are weaker than oxen and must be fed on grain rather than grass. The houses of the village also suggest comfort. The one at the far right is typical. It contains one floor for living and a loft for storage. The chimney separates a kitchen in the back from the long hall where the family works, sleeps, and entertains itself. The bed—it is not uncommon for there to be only one for the whole family—would be near the fireplace. It will be restuffed with straw after the harvest. The spinning wheel and whatever other machines the family possesses would be situated nearest the single window, which lets in light and air on good days and cold and rain on bad ones. The window is covered by oiled animal skin, since glass is still too expensive for use in rural housing. The long end of the hall, farthest from heat and light, will be home to the family's animals once winter sets in. But now, in summer, it is luxurious space where children can play or parents claim a little privacy.

The church is easily distinguished by its steeple and arched doorway and is made of brick. The steeple has 16 windows, probably all set with expensive glass and some even stained. The church would have been built over several generations at considerable cost to the villagers. Even the most prosperous houses in the far meadow are made of timber and thatch. The layout of the buildings shows us how the village must have grown. The original settlement was all on the rise above the church. The houses nearer the center of the picture were undoubtedly added later, perhaps to allow the sons of the more prosperous village farmers to begin their own families before their parents' death.

In the center of the scene are a large number of laborers. Four men with pitchforks load the cart while two women sweep the hay that falls back into new piles. Throughout the field, men and women, distinguished only by their clothing, rake hay into large stacks for successive loadings of the cart. At least 25 individuals work at these tasks. Men perform the heaviest work of loading the haycart and hammering the scythes while men and women share all the other work. Although no children appear in the scene, some are undoubtedly at work picking berries and beans.

Perhaps the three women returning to work are of the same family, a young girl flanked by her grandmother and mother. The expression of the eldest woman tells a tale of lifelong exertion as she holds her rake loosely and balances it carefully on her shoulder to lessen its weight. The woman on the other end has a look of determination. She is holding her hat rather than wearing it, and her thick, muscular shoulders suggest a regimen of heavy labor. She has made this journey many times before. The young girl seems almost serene, still invigorated rather than ground down by the day's exercise.

As a trio they remind us that the life of ordinary people in the early modern period was neither romantic nor despondent, neither quaint nor primitive. It had its own joys and sorrows, its own triumphs and failures, its own measures of progress and decay. Inevitably, we

FOCUS QUESTIONS

1. What physical forces and social customs shaped the everyday life of Europe's rural population?
2. What was the nature of demographic change in the sixteenth century, and what was its impact on the European economy?
3. How are the terms "stratification," "hierarchy," and "status" useful for understanding social relations in early modern Europe?
4. How were the different roles of men and women within the family reflected in the different lives of men and women in the wider community?

compare it to our experiences and contrast it to our comforts. By our standards, a sixteenth-century prince endured greater material hardships than a twentieth-century welfare recipient. There was no running water, no central heating, no lavatories, no electricity. There was no relief for toothache, headache, or numbing pain. Travel was dangerous and exhausting. There was no protection from the open air, and many nights were spent on the bare ground. Waiting for winds to sail was more tedious than waiting to board a plane. Entertainment was sparse, and the court jester was little match for stereo and video. But though we cannot help but be struck by these differences, we will not understand very much about the experiences of life in sixteenth-century Europe if we judge it by our own standard of living. We must exercise our historical imagination if we are to appreciate the conditions of early modern European society.

Economic Life

There was no typical sixteenth-century European. Travelers' accounts and ambassadors' reports indicate that contemporaries were constantly surprised by the habits and possessions of other Europeans. Language, custom, geography, and material conditions separated peoples in one place from those in another. Contrasts between social groups were more striking still. A Muscovite boyar had more in common with an English nobleman than either had with his country's peasants. A Spanish goldsmith and a German brass maker lived remarkably similar lives when compared to that of a shepherd anywhere in Europe. No matter how carefully historians attempt to distinguish between country and town life, between social or occupational groups, or between men and women, they are still smoothing out edges that are very rough, still turning individuals into aggregates, still sacrificing the particular for the general. No French peasant family ever had 3.5 children even if, on average, they all did. There was no typical sixteenth-century European.

But there were experiences that most Europeans shared and common structures through which their activities were channeled that separated them from their predecessors and their successors. There was a distinctive sixteenth-century experience that we can easily discern and that they could dimly perceive. Much of it was a natural progression in which one generation improved upon the situation of another. Agriculture increased: more land was cleared, more crops were grown, and better tools were crafted. Some of the experience was natural regression. Irreplaceable resources were lost: more trees were felled, more soil was eroded, and more fresh water was polluted. But some of what was distinctive about sixteenth-century life resulted from dynamic changes in economic and social conditions. The century-long population explosion and increase in commodity prices fundamentally altered people's lives. Not since the Black Death had Europe experienced so thorough a transformation in its economic development and its social organization. Change and reactions to change became dominant themes of everyday life.

Rural Life

In the early modern era, as much as 90 percent of the European population lived on farms or in small towns in which farming was the principal occupation. Villages were small and relatively isolated, even in densely populated regions like Italy and the Low Countries. They might range in size from 100 families, as was common in France and Spain, to fewer than 20 families, which was the average size of Hungarian villages. These villages, large or small, prosperous or poor, were the bedrock of the sixteenth-century state. A surplus peasant population fed the insatiable appetite of towns for laborers and of crowns for soldiers. The manor, the parish, and the rural administrative district were the institutional infrastructures of Europe. Each organized the peasantry for its own purposes. Manorial rents supported the lifestyle of the nobility; parish tithes supported the works of the Church; local taxes supported the power of the state. Rents, tithes, and taxes easily absorbed more than half of the wealth produced by the land. From the remaining half, the peasant had to make provision for the present and the future.

This picture, painted in 1530, shows farmworkers threshing grain. The figure at the door seems to be an overseer. He has just sold a sack of grain, indicating the transition from a system of self-sufficient manors to a market economy.

To survive, the village community had to be self-sufficient. In good times there was enough to eat and some to save for the future. Hard times meant hunger and starvation. Both conditions were accepted as part of the natural order, and both occurred regularly. One in every three harvests was bad; one in every five was disastrous. Bad harvests came in succession. Depending upon the soil and crop, between one-fifth and one-half of the grain harvested had to be saved as seed for the next planting season. When hunger was worst, people faced the agonizing choice of eating or saving their seed corn.

Hunger and cold were the constant companions of the average European. In Scandinavia and Muscovy, winter posed as great a threat to survival as did starvation. There the stove and garments made from animal fur were essential requirements, as were the hearth and the woolen tunic in the south. Everywhere in Europe homes were inadequate shelter against the cold and damp. Most were built of wood and roofed in thatch. Inside walls were patched with dried mud and sometimes covered with bark or animal skins. Windows were few and narrow. Piled leaves or straw, which could easily be replaced, covered the ground and acted as insulation. The typical house was one long room with a stone hearth at the end. The hearth provided both heat and light and belched forth soot and smoke through a brick chimney.

People had relatively few household possessions. The essential piece of furniture was the wooden chest, which was used for storage. A typical family could keep all of its belongings in the chest, which could then be buried or carried away in times of danger. The chest had other uses as well. Its flat top served as a table or bench or as a sideboard on which food could be placed. Tables and stools were becoming more common during the sixteenth century, though chairs were still a great luxury. Most domestic activities, of which cooking, eating, and sleeping were dominant, took place close to the ground, and squatting, kneeling, and sitting were the usual postures of family members. In areas in which

Living by one's wits

The Life of Lazarillo des Tormes (1554) is among the first modern novels, one of a variety of sixteenth-century Spanish stories that are called picaresque after the wandering beggars that are their heroes. Although the picaresque novel was a fictional account, much of the descriptive detail accurately portrays the social conditions for the vast majority of the Spanish population in the so-called Golden Age.

We began our journey, and in a few days he taught me thieves' jargon, and when he saw me to be of a good wit, was well pleased, and used to say: "Gold or silver I cannot give thee, but I will show thee many pointers about life." And it was so; for after God this man gave me my life, and although blind lighted and guided me in the career of living.

He used to carry bread and everything else in a linen sack which closed at the mouth with an iron ring and a padlock and key, and when he put things in and took them out, it was with so much attention, so well counted, that the whole world wouldn't have been equal to making it a crumb less. But I would take what stingy bit he gave me, and finish it in less than two mouthfuls. After he had fastened the lock and stopped worrying about it, thinking me to be engaged in other things, by a little seam, which I unsewed and sewed up again many times in the side of the sack, I used to bleed the miserly sack, taking out bread—not measured quantities but good pieces—and slices of bacon and sausage; and thus would seek a convenient time to make good the devilish state of want which the wicked blind man left me in.

When we ate he used to put a little jug of wine near him. I would quickly seize it and give it a couple of silent kisses and return it to its place; but this plan didn't work long, for he noticed the deficiency in his draughts, and in order to keep his wine safe, he never after let go the jug, but kept hold of the handle. But there is no lode-stone that draws things to it so strongly as I with a long rye straw, which I had prepared for that purpose, and placing which in the mouth of the jug, I would suck up the wine to a fare-ye-well. But the villain was so clever that I think he

heard me; and from then on he changed procedure and set his jug between his legs and covered it with his hand, and thus drank secure.

We were at Escalona, town of the Duke of that ilk, in an inn, and he gave me a piece of sausage to roast. When he had basted the sausage and eaten the basting, he took a maravedi from his purse and bade me fetch wine from the tavern. The devil put the occasion before my eyes, which, as the saying is, makes the thief; and it was this: there lay by the fire a small turnip, rather long and bad, and which must have been thrown there because it was not fit for the stew. And as nobody was there at the time but him and me alone, as I had an appetite whetted by having got the toothsome odour of the sausage inside me (the only part, as I knew, that I had to enjoy myself with), not considering what might follow, all fear set aside in order to comply with desire—while the blind man was taking the money out of his purse, I took the sausage, and quickly put the above-mentioned turnip on the spit, which my master grasped, when he had given me the money for the wine, and began to turn before the fire, trying to roast what through its demerit had escaped being boiled. I went for the wine, and on the way did not delay in despatching the sausage, and when I came back I found the sinner of a blind man holding the turnip ready between two slices of bread, for he had not yet recognized it, because he had not tried it with his hand. When he took the slices of bread and bit into them, thinking to get part of the sausage too, he found himself chilled by the chilly turnip.

From *Lazarillo des Tormes*.

spinning, weaving, and other domestic skills were an important part of the family's economy, a long bench was propped against the wall, usually beneath a window. Bedsteads were also becoming more common as the century wore on. They raised the straw mattresses off the ground, keeping them warmer and drier. All other family possessions related to food production. Iron spits and pots, or at least metal rings and clamps for wooden ones, were treasured goods that were passed from generation to generation. Most other implements were wooden. Long-handled spoons; boards known as trenchers, which were used for cutting and eating; and one large cup and bowl were the basic stock of the kitchen. The family ate from the long trencher and passed the bowl and cup. Knives were essential farm tools that doubled for kitchen and mealtime duty, but forks were still a curiosity.

The scale of life was small, and its pace was controlled by the limits that nature imposed. It was a civilization of daylight—up at dawn, asleep at dusk; long working hours in summer, short ones in winter. For most people, the world was bounded by the distance that could be traveled on foot. Those who stayed all their lives in their rural villages may never have seen more than a hundred other people at once or have heard any noise louder than a human voice and terrifying thunder. Their wisdom—hard won and carefully preserved—was of the practical experience necessary to survive the struggle with nature. This was the most important legacy that parents left their children.

Peasant life centered on agriculture. Technology and technique varied little across the continent, but there were significant differences depending upon climate and soil. The lives of those who grew crops contrasted with the experiences of those who raised animals. Across the great plain, the breadbasket that stretched from the Low Countries to Poland-Lithuania, the most common form of crop growing was still the three-field rotation system. In this method winter crops like wheat or rye were planted in one field; spring crops like barley, peas, or beans were planted in another; and the third field was left fallow. Over 80 percent of what was grown on the farm was consumed on the farm. In most parts of Europe, wheat was a luxury crop, sold at market rather than eaten at home. Wheat bread was prized for its taste, texture, and white color. Rye and barley were the staples for peasants. These grains were cheaper to grow, had higher yields, and could be brewed as well as baked. Most of this grain was baked into the coarse

An illustration for the month of December from a sixteenth-century Book of Hours shows pig-killing and baking. The loaves were prepared in individual homes and baked in communal ovens.

black bread that was the monotonous fare of the peasant diet. Two to three pounds a day for an adult male was an average allotment when grain was readily available. Beer and gruels of grain and skimmed milk or water flavored with fruit juice supplemented peasant fare. In one form or another, grain provided over 75 percent of the calories in a typical diet.

The warm climate and dry weather of Mediterranean Europe favored a two-crop rotation system. With less water and stronger sunlight, half the land had to be left fallow each year to restore its nutrients. Here fruit, especially grapes and olives, was an essential supplement to diet. With smaller cereal crops, wine replaced beer as a nutritious beverage. The fermentation of grapes and grain into wine and beer also provided convenient ways of storing foodstuffs, a constant problem during the winter and early spring. Wine and olive oil were also luxury products and were most commonly exchanged for meat, which was less plentiful on southern European farms.

Animal husbandry was the main occupation in the third agricultural area of Europe, the mountainous and hilly regions. Sheep were the most common animal that Europeans raised. Sheep provided the raw material for almost all clothing, their skins were used for parchment and as window coverings, and they were a ready source of inexpensive meat. They were bred in hundreds of thousands, migrating across large areas of grazing land, especially in western Europe, where their wool was the main export of both England and Spain. Pigs were domestic animals prevalent in woodland settlements. They foraged for food and were kept, like poultry, for slaughter. Cattle, on the other hand, were essential farm animals. "The fundamentals of the home," wrote the Spanish poet Luis de Leon (1527–91), "are the woman and the ox, the ox to plow and the woman to manage things." In the dairying areas of Europe, cattle produced milk, cheese, and butter; in Hungary and Bohemia, the great breeding center of the continent, they were raised for export; and most everywhere else they were used as beasts of burden.

Because agriculture was the principal occupation of Europeans, land was the principal resource. Most land was owned, not by those who worked it, but by lords who let it out in various ways. The land was still divided into manors, and the manor lord, or seigneur, was still responsible for maintaining order, administering justice, and arbitrating disputes. Although the personal bonds between lords and tenants were gradually loosening, political and economic ties were as strong as ever. Lords were not necessarily individual members of the nobility; in fact, they were more commonly the Church or the State. In western Europe, peasants generally owned between a third and a half of the land they worked, while eastern European peasants owned little if any land. But by the sixteenth century, almost all peasants enjoyed security of tenure on the land they worked. In return for various forms of rents, they used the land as they saw fit and could hand it down to their children. Rents were only occasionally paid in coin, though money rents became more common as the century progressed. More frequently, the lord received a fixed proportion of the yield of the land or received labor from the peasant. Labor service was being replaced by monetary payments in northern and western Europe, but it continued in the east, where it was known as the *robot*. German and Hungarian peasants normally owed two or three days' labor on the lord's estate each week, while Polish peasants might owe as much as four days. Labor service tied the peasants to the land they worked. Eastern European peasants were less mobile than peasants in the west, and as a result towns were fewer and smaller in the east.

Although the land in each village was set out in large fields so that crops could be rotated, families owned their own pieces within the field, usually in scattered strips that they plowed, manured, and planted individually. There were also large common fields used as pasture, as well as common woodlands where animals foraged, fuel was gathered, and game hunted. Even the common fields and woodlands were not shared equally. Those who held the most land in the fields possessed greater shares of the commons. Villagers disputed frequently over rights to sticks and branches of trees and over the number of sheep or cows that could be grazed in the meadows, especially when resources were scarce.

Farm work was ceaseless toil. Six or seven times a year farmers tilled the fields to spread animal manure below the surface of the soil. While most villages possessed metal plows, the team of draught animals was the single essential component for farming. The births of foals and calves were more-celebrated events than the births of children; the death of an ox or horse was a catastrophe that could drive a family into debt or from the land entirely. Calamities lurked everywhere, from rain and drought to locusts and crows. Most farms could support only one family at subsistence level, and excess sons and daughters had to fend for themselves, either through marriage in the village or by migration to a town.

Town Life

In the country men and women worked to the natural rhythm of the day: up at the cock's crow, at work in the cooler hours, at rest in the hotter ones. Rain and cold kept them idle; sunlight kept them busy. Each season brought its own activity. In the town the bell tolled every hour. In the summer the laborers gathered at the town gates at four in the morning, in the winter at seven. The bell signaled the time for morning and afternoon meals as well as the hour to lay down tools and return home. Wages were paid for hours worked: 7 in winter, as many as 16 in June and July.

In all towns there was an official guild structure that organized and regulated labor. Rules laid down the re-

Grain Supply and Trade in Sixteenth-Century Europe

While the life of the peasant community turned on self-sufficiency, that of the town turned on interdependence. Exchange was the medium that transformed labor and skill into food and shelter. The town was one large marketplace in which the circulation of goods dictated the survival of the residents. Men and women in towns worked as hard as did those on farms, but town dwellers received a more varied and more comfortable life in return. This is not to suggest that hunger and hardship were unknown in towns. Urban poverty was endemic and grew worse as the century wore on. In most towns, as much as a quarter of the entire population might be destitute, living from casual day labor, charity, or crime. But even for these people, food was more readily available in greater varieties than in the countryside, and the institutional network of support for the poor and homeless was stronger. In Lyon the overseers of the poor distributed a daily ration of a pound and a half of bread, more than half of what a farm laborer would consume. The urban poor fell victim more often to disease than to starvation.

Towns were distinguished by the variety of occupations that existed within them. The preparation and exchange of food dominated small market towns. Peasants would bring in their finest produce for sale and exchange it for vital manufactured goods like iron spits and pots for cooking or metal and leather tools for farm work. In smaller towns there was as much barter as sale; in larger places, money was exchanged for commodities. Women dominated the food trades in most market towns, trading, buying, and selling in the shop fronts that occupied the bottom story of their houses. Because

quirements for training, the standards for quality, and the conditions for exchange. Only those officially sanctioned could work in trades, and each trade could perform only specified tasks. In the German town of Nuremberg a sword maker could not make knives, nor could a pin maker make thimbles. Specialization went even further in London, Paris, and other large cities.

In the early sixteenth century, the port city of Antwerp became Europe's leading commercial center. The city's rulers adopted tolerant policies that encouraged economic activity, including international trade with Spanish and Portuguese territories in the Americas. The bustling crowd in the marketplace reflects the city's status as a center of commerce.

of their skills in food preparation, they were better able to obtain the best prices and advantageously display the best goods. In these small towns, men divided their time between traditional agricultural pursuits—there were always garden plots and even substantial fields attached to towns—and manufacturing. Half of the households in the Spanish town of Ciudad Real derived their income entirely from farming. Almost every town made and distributed to the surrounding area some special product that drew to the town the wealth of the countryside.

In larger towns the specialization of labor was more intense and wage earning more essential. Large traders dominated the major occupations like baking, brewing, and cloth manufacture, leaving distribution in the hands of the family economy, where there might still be a significant element of bartering. Piecework handicrafts became the staple for less prosperous town families, who prepared raw materials for the large manufacturers or finished products before their sale. Occupations were normally organized geographically, with metal- or glassworking taking place in one quarter of the town, brewing or baking in another. There was a strong family and kin network to these occupations, as each craft required long years of technical training, which was handed down from parents to children.

In large towns there were also specialized trades performed by women. There were 55 midwives in Nuremberg in the middle of the sixteenth century, and a board of women chosen from among the leading families of the town supervised their work. Nursing the sick was a logical extension of these services and also appears to have been an exclusively female occupation. So, too, was prostitution, which was an officially sanctioned occupation in most large towns in the early modern era. There were town brothels, situated in specified districts, subject to taxation and government control. Public bathhouses, which employed skilled women workers, served as unofficial brothels for the upper ranks of urban society. They too were regulated, especially after the first great epidemic of venereal disease in the early sixteenth century.

Most town dwellers, however, lived by unskilled labor. The most lucrative occupations were strictly controlled, so those who flocked to towns in search of employment usually hired themselves out as day laborers, hauling and lifting goods onto carts or boats, stacking materials at building sites, or delivering water and food. After the first decades of the century, the supply of laborers exceeded the amount of work to occupy them

A *woodcut from* De conceptu et generatione hominis (1554), *a famous handbook for midwives. During the birth, astrologers cast the infant's horoscope in the background.*

and town authorities were constantly attempting to expel them. The most fortunate might succeed in becoming servants.

Domestic service was a critical source of household labor. Even families on the margins of subsistence employed servants to undertake the innumerable household tasks, which allowed parents to pursue their primary occupations. Everything was done by hand and on foot, and extra pairs of each were essential. In Münster at midcentury there were 400 servants for 1000 households. Domestics were not apprentices, though they might aspire to become apprentices to the trade followed in the family with whom they lived. If they had kinship bonds in the town, apprenticeship was a likely outcome. But more commonly, domestics remained household servants, frequently changing employers in hope of more comfortable housing and better food. Their lives were always precarious. Any number of circumstances, from the death of their employer to allegations of misconduct, could cost them their places. Male servants were scapegoats for missing household items; female servants were vulnerable to sexual assaults.

Just as towns grew by the influx of surplus rural population, they sustained themselves by the import of surplus agricultural production. Most towns owned tracts of land, which they leased to peasants or farmed by hired labor. The town of Nuremberg controlled 25 square miles of forest and farmlands, while the region around Toledo was inhabited by thousands of peasants who paid taxes and rents to city landlords. Agriculture was the fourth largest occupation in the Spanish city of Barcelona, which had a population of over 35,000 in the early sixteenth century. All towns had municipal storehouses of grain to preserve their inhabitants from famine during harvest failures. Grain prices were strictly regulated and frequently subsidized to ensure that laborers were adequately fed. The diet of even a casual laborer would have been envied by an average peasant. Male grape pickers in Stuttgart received meat, soup, vegetables, wine, and beer; females got soup, vegetables, milk, and bread. In addition they received their wages. It is hardly surprising that towns were enclosed by thick walls and defended by armed guards.

Economic Change

Over the course of the sixteenth century, the European population increased by about a third, with much of the growth taking place in the first 50 years. Rough estimates suggest the rise to have been from about 80 to 105 million. Patterns of growth varied by region. The population of the eastern part of Europe seems to have increased more steadily across the century, while western Europe experienced a population explosion in the early decades. The population of France may have doubled between 1450 and 1550, from 10 to 20 million. The population of England nearly doubled between 1500 and 1600, from over 2 million to over 4 million. Castile, the largest region in Spain, grew 50 percent in 50 years. Europe had finally recovered from the devastation of the Black Death, and by 1600 its population was greater than it had ever been. Demographic growth was even more dramatic in the cities. In 1500, only four cities had populations greater than 100,000; in 1600, there were eight. Naples grew from 150,000 to 280,000, and both Paris and London to more than 200,000 inhabitants. Fifteen large cities more than doubled their populations, with London experiencing a phenomenal 400 percent increase.

The rise in population dramatically affected the lives of ordinary Europeans. In the early part of the century, the first phase of growth brought prosperity. The land was still not farmed to capacity, and extra hands meant increased productivity. As there was uncultivated land that could be plowed, convenient room for new housing, and enough commons and woodlands to be shared, the population increase was a welcome development. Even when rural communities began to reach their natural limits as people's needs pressed against nature's resources, opportunity still existed in the burgeoning towns and cities. At first the cycle was beneficial. Surplus on the farms led to economic growth in the towns. Growth in the towns meant more opportunities for those on the farms. More food supported more workers, and more workers produced more goods and services, which were exchanged for more food.

The first waves of migrants to the towns found opportunity everywhere. Even the most lucrative textile and provisioning trades were recruiting new members, and apprenticeships were easy to find. A shortage of casual labor kept wages at a decent rate. Successful migrants encouraged kin from their villages to move to the towns and sponsored their start in trade or service. For a while, rural families did not have to make elaborate preparations to provide for their younger sons and daughters: they could be sent to the towns. Instead of saving every extra penny to give their children a start in life, farmers could purchase some luxury goods or expand their landholdings.

Such an opportunity could not last. With more mouths to feed, more crops had to be planted. Since the most productive land was already under the plow, new fields were carved from less fertile areas. In some villages land was taken from the common waste, the woodlands or scrublands that were used for animal forage and domestic fuel. This land was less suitable for crops, and it became unavailable for other important uses. In Spain, for example, the land that was reclaimed came at the expense of sheep grazing. This reduced the size of the flocks of sheep and damaged both the domestic and the foreign wool trade. It also reduced the amount of fertilizer available for enriching the soil. In England and the Low Countries, large drainage projects were undertaken to reclaim land for crops. In the east, so-called forest colonies sprang up, clearing space in the midst of woodlands for new farms. Colonization of areas in Poland-Lithuania, Muscovy, and the Ukraine can be compared to the overseas ventures of Spain and Portugal.

By midcentury there was a natural limit to the number of workers who could profitably engage in any given trade, and those safely in were pulling the ladder up behind them. Town governments came under pressure from the guilds to enforce apprenticeship requirements

Population Density in Europe, ca. 1600

that had been relaxed during the period of growth. Guilds raised fees for new entrants and designated only a small number of places where their goods could be purchased. Most apprenticeships were limited to patrimony: one son for each full member. Such restrictions meant that newly arrived immigrants could enter only into the less profitable small crafts.

As workers continued to flood into the towns, real wages began to fall, not only among the unskilled but throughout the work force. A black market in labor developed to take advantage of the surplus population. In terms of purchasing power, the wages of a craftsman in the building trade in England fell by one-half during the sixteenth century. A French stonemason, a highly paid skilled laborer, could buy 33 pounds of bread with his daily wage in 1480; by 1550 he could buy fewer than 10.

Peasants in the French region of Languedoc who hired out for farm labor lost 56 percent of their purchasing power during the century. Only reapers, who were the physically strongest agricultural laborers, appear to have kept pace with inflation; grape pickers, among the least skilled, endured declines of up to 300 or 400 percent.

The fall in real wages took place against a backdrop of inflation that has come to be called the Price Revolution. Between 1500 and 1650, cereal prices increased between five- and sixfold, manufactured goods between two- and threefold. Most of the rapid increase came in the second half of the sixteenth century, a result of both population growth and the import of precious metals from the New World. Sixteenth-century governments understood little about the relationship between money supply and prices. Gold and silver from America flooded the international economy, raising commodity prices. As prices rose so did the deficits of the state, which was the largest purchaser of both agricultural and manufactured goods. With huge deficits, states began to devalue their coins in the mistaken belief that this would lower their debt. But debased coinage resulted in still higher prices, and higher prices resulted in greater debt. The Price Revolution was felt throughout the Continent and played havoc with government finances, international trade, and the lives of ordinary people.

A 500 percent inflation in agricultural products over a century is not much by modern standards. Compounded, the rate averages less than 2 percent a year. But the Price Revolution did not take place in a modern society or within a modern market economy. In the sixteenth century, this level of rising prices disrupted everything. In the Spanish town of Seville, almost all buildings were rented on 99-year leases to the families who lived and worked in them. This was a fairly common practice throughout Europe. It meant that a landlord who rented a butcher shop and living quarters in 1501 could not raise the rent until 1600! Similarly, lords frequently held the right to purchase agricultural produce at specified prices. This system, similar to today's commodity market, helped both lords and peasants plan ahead. It assured the lord a steady supply and the peasant a steady market. But it assumed steady prices. Until the middle of the seventeenth century, the king of England had the right to purchase wheat at prices set 300 years earlier.

Thus an enduring increase in prices created profound social dislocation. Some people became destitute; others became rich beyond their dreams. The towns were particularly hard hit, for they exchanged manufactured goods for food and thus suffered when grain prices rose faster than those of other commodities. Landholders who derived their income from rents were squeezed; those who received payment in kind reaped a windfall of more valuable agricultural goods. Peasants were largely protected from the rise in food prices, but they were not insulated from its consequences. As long as they consumed what they raised, the nominal value of commodities was of no great matter. But if some part of their subsistence had to be obtained by labor, they were in grave peril.

There was now an enormous incentive to produce a surplus for market and to begin to specialize in particular grains that were in high demand. Every small scrap of land that individual peasant families could bring under cultivation would now yield foodstuffs that could be exchanged for manufactured luxury goods. The tendency for all peasants to hold roughly equivalent amounts of land abruptly ceased. The fortunate could become prosperous by selling their surplus. The unfortunate found ready purchasers for their strips and common rights. Villagers began to be divided into those who held large

Joris Hoefnagel, Wedding Feast at Bermondsey (ca. 1590). In this painting of an Elizabethan wedding feast, as depicted by the Flemish painter Joris Hoefnagel, bakers and violinists usher in the wedding party to the feast. In the background in the left of the picture is the imposing Tower of London.

The new money economy inspired this satirical portrait by Quentin Massys. It shows a moneylender counting his receipts while his wife is distracted from her Bible by the pile of coins. Many such merchants won fame and power and even titles.

amounts of land and sold their surplus at a profit and those who held small amounts of land and hired out as laborers to their more fortunate neighbors.

The beneficial cycle now turned vicious. Those who had sold out and left the land looking for prosperity in the towns were forced to return to the land as agrarian laborers. In western Europe they became the landless poor, seasonal migrants without the safety net of rooted communal life. In eastern Europe labor service enriched the landed nobility, who were able to sell stores of grain in the export market. They used the law to tie the peasants to the land in order to ensure that grain would be cultivated for the market. Poland-Lithuania became a major supplier of cereals to northern Europe, and Gdansk became the most important agricultural seaport in the world. But agricultural surplus from the east could not make up for the great shortfall in the west. By the beginning of the seventeenth century, the western European states faced a crisis of subsistence. Everyone was hungry; many were starving.

social Life

Social organization combines elements of tradition, belief, and function, but these elements are so fused together that it is impossible to determine where one ends and the other begins. Society is a human construct, subject to the strengths and frailties of its creators. The basic assumption of sixteenth-century European society was inequality, and its basic form of social organization was stratification. The group, rather than the individual, was the predominant unit in society. The first level of the social order was the family and the household; then came the village or town community; and finally the gradations of ranks and orders of society at large. Elaborate rituals helped define membership in each of these groups, from the marriage ceremony to the initiation rites of citizens and to the processions and ceremonial displays of the nobility. All stressed the significance of the rights and obligations of different levels of society. Each group had its own place in the social order and each performed its own essential function. Society was the sum of its parts.

This traditional social organization was severely tested over the course of the early modern period. Economic change reshaped ideas of mobility and drew sharper distinctions between rural and urban life. The growth of towns and their domination of the countryside around them challenged beliefs about the primacy of agricultural production and the subordinate nature of trade and commerce. The rise to new wealth and prominence of some social groups challenged traditional elites' hold on power and prestige. The transformation of landholding patterns in the villages challenged the stability of rural communities. The rising numbers of both urban and rural poor challenged the institutions of charitable relief and posed the threat of crime and disorder. Eventually these developments led to bloody confrontations between social groups.

social constructs

Hierarchy was the dominant principle of social organization in the early modern era. Hierarchy existed at every level, from the basic distinction between lords and commoners to the fastidious complexity of the ranks of the nobility. The hierarchy of masters, journeymen, and apprentices dominated trades; trades themselves existed in a hierarchy. In the hierarchy of civic government, each official held a place in an ascending

An illumination from a sixteenth-century manuscript shows a prosperous Venetian merchant entertaining visitors at his mainland country estate.

order, up to the elite of councillors and mayors. On the land was the hierarchy of freeholder, laborer, and lease-holder among the peasants. The family itself was hierarchically organized, with the wife subordinate to her husband, the children to their parents, and the apprentices and servants to their master and mistress. "All things observe degree, priority and place," Shakespeare wrote of both natural and human order in *Troilus and Cressida* (1601–02). "Take but degree away, untune that string, and hark what discord follows."

Hierarchy was a principle of orderliness that helped govern social relations. It is tempting to approach hierarchy through wealth, to divide groups and individuals into rich and poor. Many gradations in the sixteenth-century social hierarchy corresponded to levels of wealth, but they were threshold levels rather than absolute levels. Lords, by definition, did not engage in manual labor. They were wealthier than peasants. The governing elites of towns needed sufficient wealth to neglect their own affairs while occupied in public service. They were wealthier than wage earners. But the ranks of the nobility cannot be explained by gradations of wealth among nobles, and there were many rich town dwellers who were not members of the governing elite.

Status, rather than wealth, determined the social hierarchy. It conferred privileges and exacted responsibilities according to rank. Status was everywhere apparent. It was confirmed in social conventions like bowing and hat doffing. In towns and cities the clothing that people were allowed to wear—even the foods that they were allowed to eat—reflected status. Status was signified in titles: not just in the ranks of the nobility or between nobles and commoners, but even in ordinary communities masters and mistresses, goodmen and goodwives, squires and ladies, adopted the English equivalents of European titles. The acceptance of status was an everyday, uncomplicated, unreflective act, like stopping at a red light. Inequality was a fact of European social life that was as unquestioned as it was unquestionable.

Images that people used to describe both the natural world and their social world reinforced the functional nature of hierarchy. The first, and most elaborate image, was that of the Great Chain of Being. The Great Chain was a description of the universe in which everything had a place, from God at the top of the chain to inanimate objects like rocks at the bottom. Complex accounts of the chain listed the seven orders of angels, the multiple ranks of humans, even the degrees of animals and plants, from which lions emerged as kings of the jungle. Spanish botanists were dispatched to the New World to help identify the unknown flora and fauna in terms of their places in the chain. Native Americans were first thought to be the lost tribes of Israel, as these were the only humans missing from traditional accounts of the chain. For ordinary people, the Great Chain of Being expressed the belief that all life was interconnected, that every link was a part of a divinely ordered universe and was as necessary as every other.

The second metaphor used to describe society stressed this notion of interdependency even more strongly. This was the image of the Body Politic. In the Body Politic, the head ruled, the arms protected, the stomach nourished, and the feet labored. The image described a small community as well as a large state. In the state the king was the head, the Church the soul, the nobles the arms, the artisans the hands, and the peasants the feet. Each performed its own function, and each function was essential to the health of the body. The Body Politic was an organic unity of separate parts working harmoniously for a common goal. Like the Great Chain of Being, it was a profoundly conservative concept of social organization. Taken literally, it precluded the idea of social mobility, of people rising or falling from one group to another.

social structure

The Great Chain of Being and the Body Politic were static concepts of social organization. But in the early modern era, European society was in a state of dynamic change. Fundamentally, all European societies were divided into nobles and commoners. This was a basic distinction that existed throughout the Continent, though relationships between the two orders differed from place to place. Nobility was a legal status that conferred certain privileges upon its holders. The first was rank and title, a well-defined place at the top of the social order that was passed from one generation to the next. Each rank had its own privileges and each was clearly demarcated from the next by behavior, dress, and title. The escutcheon—the coat of arms—was a universally recognized symbol of rank and family connection. The coat of arms was woven in garments; emblazoned on windows, carriages, and household goods; and displayed on banners during formal processions. Although there were various systems of title in use across the Continent and the nobility of one state could not claim noble privileges in another state, the hierarchy of prince, duke, earl, count, and baron was roughly standard.

Because rulers conferred these titles on individuals, elevating some to higher ranks and others from commoner to noble, the nobility was a political order as well as a social one. Political privileges were among the nobility's most important attributes. In many countries, the highest offices of the state and the military were reserved for members of the nobility. In Poland, for example, all offices were held by noblemen. This was a privilege that could work both ways, either restricting officeholders to those already ennobled or, as in town councils in France and Spain, ennobling those who achieved certain offices. The nobility was also granted rights of political participation in the deliberative bodies of the state. In England the peerage was defined as all those who were summoned to the House of Lords. In most parts of central Europe, the nobility alone composed the diets that advised the monarch. In the empire, the rank of imperial free knights allowed the nobility to separate itself entirely from the jurisdiction of towns or individual principalities.

Finally, members of the nobility held economic privileges, a result both of their rank and of their role as lords on the lands they owned. In almost every state, the nobility was exempt from most taxation. This was an area in which the interests of the nobles conflicted directly with those of the ruler. The larger the number of tax exemptions for the nobility, the stronger was its power in relation to the monarch. Tax exemptions of the nobility were most extensive in eastern and central Europe. There the crowns were elective rather than hereditary, allowing the nobles to bargain their support. The Polish nobility was exempt from the salt tax, the alcohol tax, and all internal tolls and customs. As Polish agriculture developed into an export industry, exemption from tolls gave the nobility a competitive advantage over merchants in the marketing of goods. The Hungarian nobility was exempt from all direct taxes, including the land tax. The nobility in western Europe enjoyed fewer immunities but not necessarily less valuable ones. French nobles were exempt from the taille, Spanish nobles from the hearth tax. As French nobles had vast incomes and Spanish nobles' houses had many hearths, both were important exclusions. The English nobility enjoyed no exemptions from direct taxation, but then there was little direct taxation from which to be exempted. The most important English taxes were on exports of wool and cloth, and thus fell on merchants rather than landholders.

Privileges implied obligations. Initially the nobility was the warrior caste of the state and its primary obligations were to raise, equip, and lead troops into battle. Much of the great wealth that nobles possessed was

Georges de La Tour, The Fortune Teller. In the painting, which serves as a warning to the naive about the wicked ways of the world, a fashionably dressed young innocent is drawn into the snare of the wily fortune teller.

at the service of the ruler during times of war, and war was a perpetual activity. By the sixteenth century, the military needs of the state had far surpassed the military power of its nobility. Warfare had become a national enterprise that required central coordination. Nobles became administrators as much as warriors, though it is fair to say that many did both. The French nobility came to be divided into the nobility of the sword and the nobility of the robe—that is, warriors and officeholders. The old military nobility could hardly understand the new service nobility. "I have continually been astounded," one of them remarked, "that so many young men could thus amuse themselves in a law court, since ordinarily youthful blood is boiling." A glorious battlefield death was still an ideal for most of Europe's noblemen.

Nobles also had the obligation of governing at both the national and the local level. At the discretion of the ruler, they could be called to engage in any necessary occupation, no matter how disruptive to their economic or family affairs. On their land, they administered their estates and settled the disputes of their tenants. In times of want they were expected to provide for the needy, in times of dearth for the hungry. There was an

obligation of good lordship that was implicitly understood, if not always explicitly carried out, between lord and peasant.

The principal distinction in sixteenth-century society was between lord and commoners, but it was not the only one. In both town and countryside a new social group was emerging. It had neither the legal nor the social privileges of nobility, but it performed many of the same functions. Over the course of the century this group carved out a place that was clearly distinct from that of the commoners, even if it was not clearly identical to the lords. It is easiest to describe in the towns, for the towns remained a separate unit of social organization in most states. Towns enjoyed many of the same political and economic privileges as the nobility. In many states, the towns sent representatives to meet with the nobles and the king and were the most important part of national deliberative assemblies such as the English Parliament, the French Estates, or the Spanish Cortes. Towns were granted legal rights to govern their own citizens, to engage in trade, and to defend themselves by raising and storing arms. Although they paid a large share of most taxes, towns also received large tax concessions.

Yet, as individuals, members of the town elite held no special status in society at large. Some were among the richest people in the state—great bankers and merchants wealthier than dukes—but they had to devise their own systems of honor and prestige. In Venice, the *Book of Gold* distinguished the local elite from the ranks of ordinary citizens. Members of the "Old Families," who monopolized the highest civic offices, ruled Nuremberg. In France and Spain, some of the highest officers of leading towns were granted noble status, like the "honored citizens" of Barcelona who were ennobled by King Ferdinand of Aragon. German burghers, as prosperous townsmen were called, remained caught in a state between noble and common, despised from above because they worked with their hands, envied from below for their wealth and comfort. In Münster, many withdrew from urban affairs and sought the privileges of the lower nobility.

In rural society the transformation of agricultural holdings in many places also created a group that fit uncomfortably between lords and commoners. The accumulation of larger and larger estates through purchase from the nobility, the state, or the Church made lords—in the sense of landowners with tenants—out of many who were not lords in rank. They received rents and dues from their tenants, administered their estates, and preserved the so-called moral economy that sustained the peasants during hard times. In England this group came to be known as the gentry, and there were parallel groups in Spain, France, and the empire. The gentry aspired to the privileges of the nobility. In England members of the gentry had the right to have a coat of arms and could be knighted. But knighthoods were not hereditary and did not confer membership in the House of Lords. In Spain, the caballeros and hidalgos gained noble privileges but were still of lower status than the grandees. The gentry aped the habits of the nobility, often outdoing nobles in lavish displays of wealth and spending.

Social stratification did not only apply to the wealthy groups within European societies. Although it is more difficult to reconstruct the principles upon which rural communities based their complicated systems of status and order, there can be no doubt that systems existed and that they helped create the bonds that tied communities together. In many German villages, a principal distinction was between those who held land in the ancient part of the settlement—the *Esch*—and those who held land in those areas into which the village had expanded. The *Esch* was normally the best land, and thus the distinction was likely to correlate with the relative

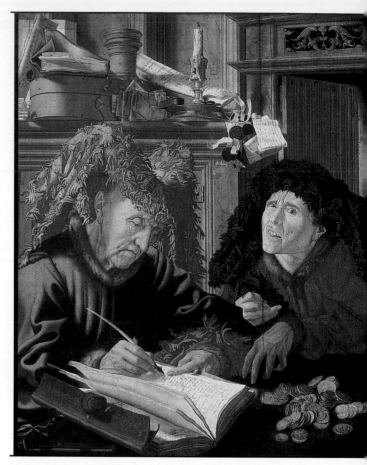

Marinus van Reymerswaele, The Two Tax Gatherers. *The figure on the left is a city treasurer who is posting in the book an account of the city's revenues from taxes on wine, beer, fish, and other commodities. The painting is probably a satirical composition intended to expose the iniquity of covetousness, usury, or extortion.*

wealth of the two groups. But interestingly, the holders of the *Esch* were tied to the lord of the estate, while holders of the less desirable lands were free peasants. Here freedom to move from place to place was less valued than the right to live in the heart of the village.

Just the opposite set of values prevailed in English villages, where freeholders were in the most enviable position. They led the movements to break up the common fields for planting and were able to initiate legal actions against their lord. They might not have the best lands in the village, but whenever village land was converted to freehold, unfree tenants would go into debt to buy it. Increasingly, French peasants came to own the land that they farmed. They protested against the very title of *villein*, claiming that its older association with serfdom discouraged others from trading with those so labeled. The relationship of free and unfree went even further in Muscovy, where thousands of starving laborers sold themselves into slavery. Perhaps as much as 10 percent of the population of Muscovy accepted their loss of freedom and became domestic slaves of the military and noble orders.

In towns, the order of rank below the elite pertained as much to the kind of work that one performed as it did to the level at which it was undertaken. The critical division in town life was between those who had the freedom of the city—citizens—and those who did not. Citizenship was restricted to membership in certain occupations and was closely regulated. It could be purchased, especially by members of learned professions whose services were becoming vital in the early modern era, but most citizenship was earned by becoming a master in one of the guilds after a long period of apprenticeship and training. Only males could be citizens. In Germany, the feminine equivalent for the word used to denote a male citizen in good standing meant "prostitute"! But women who were married to citizens enjoyed their husbands' privileges, and widows of citizens could pass the privileges to their new husbands when they remarried. In both town and countryside, the privileges and obligations of each social group were the glue that held communities together.

social change

In the sixteenth century, social commentators believed that change was transforming the world in which they lived. In 1600 a Spanish observer blamed the rise of the rich commoners for the ills of the world: "They have obtained a particular status, that of a self-made group; and since they belong neither to the rich nor to the poor nor to the middle, they have thrown the state into the confusion we now see it in." An Englishman commenting on the rise of the gentry could give no better definition of its status than to say that a gentleman was one who lived like a gentleman. The challenge that the new nobility of the robe posed to the old nobility of the sword poisoned relations between these two segments of the French ruling elite. The military service class in Muscovy, who were of more use to the Muscovite princes than were the traditional landed nobility, posed an even greater threat to the privileges of the boyars.

Pressures on the ruling elites of European society came from above as well as below. The expansion of the state and the power of the prince frequently came as a result of direct conflict with the nobility. Only in east-central Europe—in Hungary, Bohemia, and Poland-

Lithuania—did the consolidation of the state actually enhance the privileges of the traditional noble orders, and these were areas in which towns were small and urban elites weak.

There were many reasons why the traditional European social hierarchy was transformed during the course of the early modern era. In the first place, population increase necessitated an expansion of the ruling orders. With more people to govern, there had to be more governors who could perform the military, political, and social functions of the state. The traditional nobility grew slowly, as titles could be passed to only one son and intermarriage within the group was very high. Second, opportunities to accumulate wealth expanded dramatically with the Price Revolution. Traditionally wealth was calculated in land and tenants rather than in the possession of liquid assets like gold and silver. But with the increase in commodity prices, surplus producers could rapidly improve their economic position. What previously might have taken a generation or two of good fortune to amass could now be gathered seemingly overnight. Moreover, state service became a source of unlimited riches. The profits to be made from tax collecting, officeholding, or administering the law could easily surpass those to be made from landholding, especially after the economic downturn at the end of the century. The newly rich clamored for privileges, and many were in a position to lobby rulers effectively for them. Across European society the nobility grew, fed from fortunes made on the land, in trade, and in office.

Social change was equally apparent at the bottom of the social scale, but here it could not be so easily absorbed. The continuous population growth created a group of landless poor who squatted in villages and clogged the streets of towns and cities. Although poverty was not a new development of the early modern era, its growth created new problems. Rough estimates suggest that as many as a quarter of all Europeans were destitute. This was a staggering figure in great cities. There were tens of thousands of destitute people in London or Paris, where, it was observed, "the crowds of poor were so great that one could not pass through the streets."

Traditionally, local communities cared for their poor. Widows, orphans, and the handicapped, who would normally constitute over half of the poor in a village or town, were viewed as the "deserving poor," worthy of the care of the community through the Church or through private almsgiving. Catholic communities like Venice created a system of private charity that paralleled the institutions of the Church. Although Protestant communities took charity out of the control of the church, they were no less concerned about the plight of the deserving poor. In England a special tax, the poor rate, supported the poor and provided them with subsistence until they remarried or found employment. Perhaps the most elaborate system of all existed in the French town of Lyon. There all the poor were registered and given identity cards. Each Sunday they would receive a week's worth of food and money. Young girls were provided with dowries, and young boys were taught crafts. Vagrants from the surrounding countryside were given one week's allotment to enable them to travel on. But this enlightened system was only for the deserving poor, and as the century progressed it was overwhelmed.

Charity began at home—it was an obligation of the community. But as the sixteenth century progressed, the number of people who lived on the margins of sub-

Feeding the Hungry *by Cornelius Buys, 1504. A maidservant is doling out small loaves to the poor and the lame at the door of a wealthy person's home. The poor who flocked to the towns were often forced to rely on charity to survive.*

sistence grew beyond the ability of the local community to care for them. Perhaps more importantly, many of those who now begged for alms fell outside the traditional categories of the deserving poor. In England they were called the sturdy beggars, men and women capable of working but incapable of finding more than occasional labor. To support themselves and their families, they left their native communities in search of employment and thus forfeited their claims on local charity. Most wound up in the towns and cities, where they slept and begged in the streets. Some disfigured themselves to enhance their abilities as beggars. As strangers they had no claim on local charity; as able-bodied workers they had no claim on local sympathy. Poor mothers abandoned their newborn infants on the steps of foundling hospitals or the houses of the rich. It is estimated that 10 percent of all newborn babies in the Spanish city of Valladolid were abandoned.

The problem of crime complicated the problems of poverty and vagrancy. Increasing population and increasing wealth equaled increasing crime; the addition of the poor to the equation aggravated the situation. The poor, destitute outsiders to the community, without visible means of support, were the easiest targets of official retribution. Throughout the century, numerous European states passed vagrancy laws in an effort to alleviate the problem of the wandering poor. In England the poor were whipped from village to village until they were returned home. The sturdy beggars were branded with the letter V on their chests to identify them as vagrants, and therefore as potential criminals. Both Venetian and Dutch vagrants were regularly rounded up for galley service, while vagrants in Hungary were sold into slavery. Physical mutilation was used in an ineffective method of deterrence; thieves had fingers chopped off—which, of course, made it impossible for them to perform manual labor, and thus likely to steal again. Sexual offenses were criminalized—especially bastardy, since the birth of illegitimate children placed an immediate burden on the community. Prostitutes, who had long been tolerated and regulated in towns, were now persecuted. Rape increased. Capital punishment was reserved for the worst crimes—murder, incest, and grand larceny being most common—but, not surprisingly, executions were carried out mostly on outsiders to the community, single women, the poor, and the vagrant being the most frequent victims.

Peasant Revolts

The economic and social changes of the sixteenth century bore serious consequences. Most telling was the upswing of violent confrontations between peasants and their lords. There was more than one difference between rich and poor in sixteenth-century society, but when conflict arose between them the important difference was that the wealthy controlled the means of coercion: the military and the law. Across Europe, and with alarming regularity, peasants took up arms to defend themselves from what they saw as violations of traditional rights and obligations. Peasant revolts were not hunger riots. Although they frequently occurred in periods of want, after bad harvests or marauding armies had impoverished villages, peasant revolts were not desperate attacks against warehouses or grain silos. Nor did those who took part in them form an undisciplined mob. Most revolts chose leaders, drew up petitions of grievances, and organized the rank and file into a semblance of military order. Leaders were literate—usually drawn from the lower clergy or minor gentry rather than from the peasantry—political demands were moderate, and tactics were sophisticated. But peasant revolts so profoundly threatened the social order that they were met with the severest repression. Confronted with the execution of their estate agents, rent strikes, and confiscation of their property, lords responded as if they were at war. Veteran soldiers and trained mercenaries were called out to fight peasant armies composed mostly of raw recruits. The results were horrifying.

It is essential to realize that while peasants revolted against their lords, fundamentally their anger and frustration were products of agrarian changes that could be neither controlled nor understood. As population increased and market production expanded, many of the traditional rights and obligations of lords and peasants became oppressive. One example is that of forest rights. On most estates, the forests surrounding a village belonged to the lord. Commonly the village had its own woodlands in which animals foraged and fuel and building material were available. As the population increased, more farms came into existence. New land was put under the plow, and grain fields pressed up against the forest. There were more animals in the village, and some of them were let loose to consume the young sprouts and saplings. Soon there was not enough food for the wild game that was among the lord's most valuable property. So the game began to feed on the peasants' crops, which were now placed so appetizingly close to the forests. It was a capital crime for a peasant to kill wild game, but peasants couldn't allow the game to consume their crops.

A similar conflict arose over enclosing crop fields. An enclosure was a device—normally a fence or hedge that surrounded an area—to keep a parcel of land separate from the planted strips of land owned by the villagers. The parcel could be used for grazing animals or raising a specialty crop for the market. But an enclosure de-

Rebellious peasants carrying a standard called the Banner of the Shoe surround a knight.

stroyed the traditional form of village agriculture, whereby decisions on which crops to plant were made communally. It became one of the chief grievances of the English peasants. But while enclosures broke up the old field system in many villages, they were a logical response to the transformation of land ownership that had already taken place. As more land was accumulated by fewer families, it made less sense for them to work widely scattered strips all over the village. If a family could consolidate its holdings by swaps and sales, it could gain an estate large enough to be used for both crops and grazing. An enclosed estate allowed wealthy farmers to grow more luxury crops for market or to raise only sheep on a field that had once been used for grain.

Enclosure was a process that both lord and rich peasant undertook, but it drove the smallholders from the land and was thus a source of bitter resentment for the poorer peasants. It was easy to protest the greed of the lords who, owning the most land, were the most successful enclosers. But enclosures were more a result of the process in which villages came to be characterized by a very small elite of large landholders and a very large mass of smallholders and landless poor. It was an effect rather than a cause.

From Hungary to England, peasant revolts brought social and economic change into sharp relief. A call for a crusade against Ottoman advances in 1514 provided the opportunity for Hungarian peasants to revolt against their noble landlords. Thousands dropped their plowshares and grasped the sword of a holy war. However, in fact, war against the Ottomans did not materialize. Instead, the mobilized peasants, under the leadership of disaffected army officers and clergymen, issued grievances against the labor service that they owed to their lords as well as numerous violations of customary agricultural practices. Their revolt turned into a civil war that was crushed with great brutality. In England, severe economic conditions led to a series of revolts in 1549. Participants in the Western Rising, who succeeded in storming the town of Exeter, also combined religious and economic grievances. Cornish rebels added a social dimension with their slogan "Kill the gentlemen." In eastern England, Ket's Rebellion arose from peasant opposition to enclosure. The rebels occupied Norwich, the second largest city in the realm, but their aspirations were for reform rather than revolution. They, like the Hungarian peasants, were crushed by well-trained forces.

The complexity of the peasants' problems is perhaps best revealed in the series of uprisings that are known collectively as the German Peasants' War. It was by far the most widespread peasant revolt of the sixteenth century, involving tens of thousands of peasants, and it combined a whole series of agrarian grievances with an awareness of the new religious spirit preached by Martin Luther. Luther condemned both lords and peasants: the lords for their rapaciousness, the peasants for their rebelliousness. Although he had a large following among the peasants, his advice that earthly oppression be passively accepted was not followed. The Peasants' War was directed against secular and ecclesiastical lords, and the rebels attacked both economic and religious abuses. Their combination of demands, such as the community's right to select its own minister and the community's right to cut wood freely, attracted a wide following in the villages and small towns of southern and central Germany. The printed demands of the peasantry, the most famous of which was the Twelve Articles of the Peasants of Swabia (1525), helped spread the movement far beyond its original bounds. The peasants organized themselves into large armies led by experienced soldiers. Initially they were able to besiege castles and abbeys and plunder lords' estates. Ultimately, those movements that refused compromise were ruthlessly crushed. By conservative estimates, over 100,000 peasants were slaughtered during and after the war, many to serve as warning against future uprisings.

At base the demands of the peasantry addressed the agrarian changes that were transforming German villages. Population growth was creating more poor villagers who could only hire out as laborers but who demanded a share of common grazing and woodlands. Because the presence of these poor increased the taxable wealth of the village, they were advantageous to the lord. But the strain they placed on resources was felt by both the subsistence and the surplus farmers. Tensions within the village were all the greater because the landless members were the kin of the landed—sons and daughters, brothers and sisters. If they were to be settled properly on the land, then the lord would have to let the village expand. If they were to be kept on the margins of subsistence, then the more prosperous villagers would have to be able to control their numbers and their conduct. In either case, the peasants needed more direct responsibility for governing the village than existed in their traditional relationship with their lord. Thus the grievances of the peasants of Swabia demanded release of the village peasantry from the status of serfs. They wanted to be allowed to move off the land, to marry out of the village without penalty, and to

the peasants' Revolt

In 1524 and 1525 a series of local protests over economic conditions coalesced into one of the largest concerted peasant uprisings in German history. The Peasants' Revolt was not a disorganized uprising of the hungry and dispossessed, but rather a carefully coordinated movement that attempted to win widespread social reforms. The Twelve Articles of the Peasants of Swabia show both the nature of the peasants' grievances and their ability to articulate them.

The First Article. First, it is our humble petition and desire, as also our will and resolution, that in the future we should have power and authority so that each community should choose and appoint a pastor, and that we should have the right to depose him should he conduct himself improperly. The pastor thus chosen should teach us the gospel pure and simple, without any addition, doctrine, or ordinance of man.

The Second Article. According as the just tithe is established by the Old Testament and fulfilled in the New, we are ready and willing to pay the fair tithe of grain. . . . We will that for the future our church provost, whomsoever the community may appoint, shall gather and receive this tithe. . . .

The Tenth Article. In the tenth place, we are aggrieved by the appropriation by individuals of meadows and fields which at one time belonged to a community. These we will take again into our own hands. . . .

Conclusion. In the twelfth place, it is our conclusion and final resolution that if any one or more of the articles here set forth should not be in agreement with the word of God, as we think they are, such article we will willingly retract if it is proved really to be against the word of God by a clear explanation of the Scripture.

From the Twelve Articles of the Peasants of Swabia.

be free of the death taxes that further impoverished their children. These concessions would make it easier for the excess population to adjust to new conditions. They also wanted stable rents fixed at fair rates, a limit placed on labor service, and a return to the ancient customs that governed relations between lords and peasants. All these proposals were backed by an appeal to Christian principles of love and charity. They were profoundly conservative.

The demands of the German peasants reflected a traditional order that no longer existed. In many places, the rents and tithes that the peasants wanted to control no longer belonged to the lords of the estates. They had been sold to town corporations or wealthy individuals who purchased them as an investment and expected to realize a fair return. Most tenants did enjoy stable and fixed rents, but only on their traditional lands. As they increased their holdings, perhaps to keep another son in the village or to expand production for the market, they were faced with the fact that rents were higher and land more expensive than it had been before. Marriage fines, death duties, and labor service were oppressive, but they balanced the fact that traditional rents were very low. In many east German villages, peasants willingly increased their labor service for a reduction in their money rents. It was hardly likely that they could have both. If the peasants were being squeezed, and there can be little doubt that they were, it was not only the lords who were doing the squeezing. The Church took its tenth, the state increased its exactions, and the competition for survival and prosperity among the peasants themselves was ferocious. Peasants were caught between the jaws of an expanding state and a changing economy. When they rebelled, the jaws snapped shut.

private Life

The great events of the sixteenth century—the discovery of the New World, the consolidation of states, the increasing incidence and ferocity of war, the reform of religion—all had profound impact on the lives of ordinary people. There could be no private life separate from these developments. However slowly they penetrated to isolated village communities, however intermittent their effect, they were inextricably bound up with the experiences and the worldview of all Europeans. The states offered more protection and demanded more resources. Taxes increased, and tax collecting became more efficient. Wars took village boys and made them soldiers. Armies brought devastation to thousands of communities. The New World offered new opportunities, brought new products, and increased the wealth of the Continent. Religious reform, both Protestant and Catholic, penetrated into popular beliefs and personal piety. All these sweeping changes blurred the distinction between public and private life.

Still, the transformations wrought by political and intellectual developments were not necessarily the most important ones in people's lives. The lives of most Europeans centered on births and deaths, on the harvest, and on the social relations in their communities. For them, great events were the successful crop, the marriage of an heir, or the festivals that marked the progress of the year. Their beliefs were based as much on the customs they learned as children as on the religion they learned at church. Their strongest loyalties were to family and community rather than to church or state.

The Family

Sixteenth-century life centered on the family. The family was a crucial organizing principle for Europeans of all social ranks, and it served a variety of functions. In the most obvious sense, the family was the primary kin group. European families were predominantly nuclear, composed of a married couple and their children. In western Europe, a small number of families contained the adult siblings of the family head, uncles and aunts who had not yet established their own families. This pattern was more common in the east, especially in Hungary and Muscovy, where taxation was based on households and thus encouraged extended families. There several nuclear families might live under the same roof. Yet however families were composed, kinship had a wider orbit than just parents and children. In-laws, step-relations, and cousins were considered part of the kin group and could be called upon for support in a variety of contexts, from charity to employment and business partnerships. In towns such family connections created large and powerful clans.

In a different sense, family was lineage, the connections between preceding and succeeding generations. This was an important concept among the upper ranks of society, where ancient lineage, genuine or fabricated,

was a valued component of nobility. This concept of family imparted a sense of stability and longevity in a world in which individual life was short. Even in peasant communities, however, lineage existed in the form of the family farm, that is, the strips in the field that were passed from generation to generation and named for the family that owned them. The village's fields and landmarks also bore the names of individual families, and membership in one of the ancient families of the village was a mark of social distinction.

The family was also an economic unit. Here family overlapped with the household—all those who lived under the same roof, including servants and apprentices. In its economic functions, the family was the basic unit for the production, accumulation, and transmission of wealth. Occupation determined the organization of the economic family. Every member of the household had his or her own functions that were essential to the survival of the unit. Tasks were divided by gender and by age, but there was far more intermixture than is traditionally assumed. On farms women worked at nearly every occupation with the exception of mowing and plowing. In towns they were vital to the success of shops and trades, though they were denied training in the skilled crafts. As laborers, they worked in the town fields—for little more than half the wages of men performing the same tasks—and in carrying and delivering goods and materials. Children contributed to the economic vitality of the household from an early age.

Finally, the family was the primary unit of social organization. In the family children were educated and the social values of hierarchy and discipline were taught. Authority in the family was strictly organized in a set of three overlapping categories. At the top was the husband, head of the household, who ruled over his wife, children, and servants. All members of the family owed obedience to the head. The family was like "a little commonwealth," as English writers put it, in which the adult male was the governor and all others the governed. But two other categories of relationships in the family dispersed this authority. Children owed obedience to their parents, male or female. In this role the wife and mother was governor as well as governed. Similarly, servants owed obedience to both master and mistress. Male apprentices were under the authority of the wife, mother, and mistress of the household. The importance of the family as a social unit was underscored by the fact that people unattached to families attracted suspicion in sixteenth-century society. Single men were often viewed as potential criminals; single women as poten-

Peasant Family (*ca.* 1640), *a realistic scene of peasant life in France by the genre painter Louis Le Nain.*

tial prostitutes. Both lived outside the discipline and social control of families.

Although the population of Europe was increasing in the early modern era, families were not large. Throughout northern and western Europe, the size of the typical family was two adults and three or four children. Late marriages and breast-feeding helped control family size: the former restricted the number of childbearing years while the latter increased the space between pregnancies. Women married around age 25, men slightly later. A woman could expect about 15 fertile years and seven or eight pregnancies if neither she nor her husband died in the interim. Only three or four children were likely to survive beyond the age of ten. In her fertile years, a woman was constantly occupied with infants. She was either about to give birth or about to become pregnant. If she used a wet nurse rather than feed her own babies, as many women in the upper ranks of society did, then she was likely to have 10 or 12 pregnancies during her fertile years and correspondingly more surviving children.

Constant pregnancy and child care may help explain some of the gender roles that men and women assumed in the early modern era. Biblical injunctions and traditional stereotypes help explain others. Pregnant or not, women's labor was a vital part of the domestic economy, especially until the first surviving children were strong enough to assume their share. The woman's sphere was the household. On the farm she was in charge of the preparation of food, the care of domestic animals, the care and education of children, and the manufacture and cleaning of the family's clothing. In towns women supervised the shop that was part of the household. They sold goods, kept accounts, and directed the work of domestics or apprentices. Mothers trained their daughters to perform these tasks in the same way that fathers trained their sons to work the fields or ply their craft.

The man's sphere was public—the fields in rural areas, the streets in towns. Men plowed, planted, and did the heavy reaping work of farming. They made and maintained essential farm equipment and had charge of the large farm animals. They marketed surplus produce and made the few purchases of equipment or luxury goods. Men performed the labor service that was normally due the lord of the estate, attended the local courts in various capacities, and organized the affairs of the village. In towns men engaged in heavy labor, procured materials

In an age of high infant mortality and short life expectancy, women were expected to bear many children to ensure family continuity. This embroidery depicts a mother with her thirteen daughters.

for craft work, and marketed their product if it was not sold in the household shop. Only men could be citizens of the towns or full members of most craft guilds, and only men were involved in civic government.

This separation of men and women into the public and the domestic spheres meant that marriage was a blending of complementary skills. Each partner brought to the marriage essential knowledge and abilities that were fundamental to the economic success of the union. Except in the largest towns, nearly everyone was married for at least a part of his or her life. Remarriage was more common for men than women, however, because a man continued to control the family's property after the death of his wife, whereas a widow might have only a share of it after bequests to children and provisions for apprentices. In the French town of Nantes, a quarter of the annual weddings were remarriages.

While male roles were constant throughout the life cycle, as men trained for and performed the same occupations from childhood to death, female roles varied greatly depending upon the situation. While under the care of fathers, masters, or husbands, women worked in the domestic sphere; once widowed, they assumed the public functions of head of household. Many women inherited shops or farmland; most became responsible for the placement and training of their children. But because of the division of labor upon which the family depended and because of the inherent social and economic prejudices that segregated public and domestic roles, widows were particularly disadvantaged. The most fortunate among them remarried—"The widow weeps with one eye and casts glances with the other," an English proverb held. Their financial and personal independence from men, prized today, was a millstone in the early modern world.

communities

Despite its central place in all aspects of sixteenth-century life, the family was a fragile and impermanent institution. Even without divorce—permitted in Protestant communities, though never very common—marriages were short. The early death of one of the partners abbreviated the life of the natural family. New marriage partners or social welfare to aid the indigent was sought from within the wider community. On the farm, this community was the rural village; in the town, it was the ward, quarter, or parish in which the family lived. Community life must not be romanticized. Interpersonal violence, lawsuits, and feuds were extraordinarily common

A feminine perspective

Arcangela Tarabotti was born in Venice in the early seventeenth century. Her family did not have the means to provide her with a sufficient dowry, so she was sent to live in a Catholic convent, where she unhappily remained for the rest of her life. She wrote two major works. The first, *Monastic Hell,* gives the flavor of her attitude toward her fate. The second was *Innocence Undone,* from which the following excerpt is taken.

Since woman is the epitome of all perfections, she is the last of the works of God, as far as material creation is concerned, but otherwise she dates from the beginning, and is the first-generated of all creatures, generated by the breath of God himself, as the Holy Spirit inferred, through the mouth of Solomon in the Ecclesiastes where he introduces the Most Holy Virgin to sing of herself: *The Lord possessed me in the beginning of his ways, before he made any thing from the beginning.*

This creature, although a woman, did not need to be made with a rib taken from man, because, so to speak, she was born before the beginning of time as well as before men, who, blinded by their ambition to dominate the world alone, astutely fail to mention this infallible truth, that the woman has existed in the Divine mind from the beginning. *I was set up from eternity, and of old before the earth was made. The depths were not as yet, and I was already conceived.*

They cannot deny the fact, although their malice prevents them from speaking it openly; but let us try to make them admit, in accordance with the Holy Scriptures rather than with some ill-informed preachers, that the woman made the man perfect and not vice versa.

After the Supreme Being created the world and all the animals (as I have said before), the text says *And God saw all the things that he had made; and they were very good.* Foreseeing that the man without woman would be the compendium of all imperfections, God said: *It is not good for man to be alone: let us make him a help like unto himself.* And therefore he created a companion for him that would be the universal glory of humanity and make him rich with merits.

Almighty God, having kept the creation of the woman as the last act of his wonderful work, desired to bestow privileges upon her, reinforce her graces and gladden the whole world with her splendour. If the supreme Architect's greatness, wisdom and love towards us shone brightly in his other works, he planned to make the woman, this excellent last addition to his splendid construction, capable of filling with wonder whoever looked at her. He therefore gave her the strength to subdue and dominate the proudest and wildest hearts and hold them in sweet captivity by a mere glance or else by the power of her pure modesty. God formed Man, who is so proud, in the field of Damascus; and from one of his ribs he formed woman in the garden of Eden.

If I were not a female, I would deduce from this that the woman, both because of her composition and because of the place in which she was created, is nobler, gentler, stronger and worthier than the man.

What is true strength anyway, if not domination over one's feelings and mastery over one's passions? And who is better at this than the female sex, always virtuous and capable of resisting every temptation to commit or even think evil things? Is there anything more fragile than your head? Compare it to the strength of a rib, the hard bone that is the material from which we were created, and you will be disappointed. Anyone knows that women show more strength than men when they conceive and give birth, by tirelessly carrying all that weight around for nine months.

But you cruel men, who always go around preaching evil for good and good for evil, you pride yourselves in your strength because, like the inhuman creatures you are, you fight and kill each other like wild beasts. . . . Thus, if strength is the ability to bear misfortunes and insults, how can you call yourselves strong when you shed other people's blood sometimes for no reason at all and take the life of innocent creatures at the slightest provocation of a word or a suspicion?

Strength is not mere violence; it requires an indomitable soul, steadfast and constant in Christian fortitude. How can you, o most inconstant ones, ever boast of such virtù? Improperly and deceitfully you have called yourselves virtuous, because only those who fill the world with people and virtù can be called strong.

And those are women. Listen to Solomon, whose words about women reinforce my argument: *Strength and dignity are her clothing.*

From Tarabotti, *Innocence Undone.*

in both rural and urban communities. The community was not an idyllic haven of charity and love, where everyone knew and respected neighbors and worked toward a common goal. Like every other aspect of society, the community was socially and economically stratified, gender roles were segregated, and resources were inequitably divided. But the community was the place where people found their social identity. It provided marriage partners for its families, charity for its poor, and a local culture for all of its inhabitants.

The two basic forces that tied the rural community together were the lord and the priest. The lord set conditions for work and property ownership that necessitated common decision-making on the part of the village farmers. The lord's presence, commonly in the form of an agent, could be both a positive and a negative force for community solidarity. Use of the common lands, the rotation of labor service, and the form in which rents in kind were paid were all decisions that had to be made collectively. Village leadership remained informal, though in some villages headmen or elders bargained with the lord's agent or resolved petty disputes among the villagers. Communal agreement was also expressed in communal resistance to violations of custom or threats to the moral economy. All these forms of negotiation fused individual families into a community. So, too, in a different way did the presence of the parish priest or minister, who attended all the pivotal events of life—birth, marriage, and death. The church was the only common building of the community; it was the only space that was not owned outright by the lord or an individual family. The scene of village meetings and ceremonies, it was the center of both spiritual and social life. The parish priest served as a conduit for all the news of the community and the focal point for the village's festive life. In rural communities, the church was the only organization to which people belonged.

Communities were bound together by the authorities who ruled them and by their common activities. But they were also bound together by their own social customs. Early modern communities used a number of ceremonial occasions as opportunities for expressing solidarity and confirming, in one way or another, the values to which they adhered. In rural parishes there was the annual perambulation, a walk around the village fields that usually occurred before planting began. It was led by the priest, who carried with him any particularly sacred objects that the parish possessed. Behind

him followed the village farmers, in some places all members of the village who were capable of walking the distance. The perambulation had many purposes. The priest blessed the fields and prayed for a bountiful crop; the farmers surveyed their own strips and any damage that had been done to the fields during the winter; the community defined its geographical space in distinc-

Jan van Eyck, The Marriage of Giovanni Arnolfini and Giovanna Cenami. *This outstanding fifteenth-century painting of a nuptial scene teems with symbols, including the religious symbols of the rosary, the roundels on the mirror frame, and the post of the chair. The little dog in the foreground may represent fidelity, and the candles in the chandelier may be a symbol of marriage. The mirror reflects the image of two witnesses, who would have been standing where spectators viewing the picture would stand. The inscription on the wall, "Jan van Eyck was here, 1434," suggests that one of the figures is a self-portrait of the artist.*

tion to the space of others; and all the individuals who took part reaffirmed their shared identity with others in the village.

In towns ceremonial processions were far more elaborate. Processions might take place on saints' days in Catholic communities or on anniversaries of town liberties. The order of the march, the clothing worn by the participants, and the objects displayed reflected the strict hierarchies of the town's local organizations. In Catholic towns the religious orders led the town governors in their robes of office. Following the governors were the members of guilds, each guild placed according to its rank of importance and each organized by masters, journeymen, and apprentices. In some towns the wives of citizens marched in procession; in others they were accorded special places from which to view the ceremony. Village and civic ceremonies normally ended with communal feasting and dancing, which were the most popular forms of recreation.

Not all ceremonial occasions were so formal. The most common ceremony was the wedding, a rite of passage that was simultaneously significant to the individual, the family, and the community. The wedding was a public event that combined a religious ceremony and a community procession with feasting and festivity. It took different forms in different parts of Europe and in different social groups. But whether eastern or western, noble or common, the wedding was celebrated as the moment when the couple entered fully into the community. Marriage involved more than just the union of bride and groom. Parents were a central feature in the event, both in arranging the economic aspects of the union—dowry and inheritance—and in approving the occasion. Many couples were engaged long before they were married, and in many places it was the engagement that was most important to the individuals and the wedding that was most important to the community. One German townsman described how he "had taken a wife but they have not held the wedding yet."

Traditional weddings involved the formal transfer of property, an important event in rural communities, where the ownership of strips of land or common rights concerned everyone. The bridal dowry and the groom's inheritance were formally exchanged during the wedding, even if both were small. The public procession—"the marriage in the streets" as it was sometimes called in towns—proclaimed the union throughout the community and was considered to be as important as the

Carnivals were occasions for games and feasting. A Carnival on the Feast Day of Saint George in a Village Near Antwerp, *painted around 1605 by Abel Grimmer, shows the revels of the villagers presided over by the religious figure on the banner at the right.*

religious ceremony. It was followed by a feast as abundant as the families of bride and groom could afford. In peasant communities, gifts of food for the feast were as common as were gifts to the couple. There were always provisions made that excess food should be sent to the poor or unfortunate after the wedding.

Weddings also legitimated sexual relations. Many of the dances and ceremonies that followed the feast symbolized the sexual congress. Among German burghers it was traditional for the bride to bring the bed to her new home, and bridal beds were passed from mothers to daughters. Among the nobility, the consummation of the marriage was a vital part of the wedding, for without it the union could be annulled. Finally, the marriage inaugurated both bride and groom into new roles in the community. Their place at the wedding table next to their parents elevated them to the status of adults.

Other ceremonies were equally important in creating a shared sense of identity within the community. In both town and countryside, the year was divided by a number of festivals that defined the rhythm of toil and rest. They coincided with both the seasonal divisions of agricultural life and the central events of the Christian calendar. There was no essential difference between the popular and Christian elements in festivals, however strongly the official church insisted upon one. Christmas and Easter were probably the most widely observed Christian holidays, but Carnival, which preceded Lent, was a frenzied round of feasts and parties that resulted in a disproportionate number of births nine months later. The Twelve Days of Christmas, which inaugurated the slow, short days of winter, were only loosely attached to the birth of Jesus and were even abolished by some Protestant churches. The rites of May, which celebrated the rebirth of spring, were filled with sexual play among the young adults of the community. Youth groups went "a-Maying" by placing flowers at the homes of marriageable girls, electing a Queen of the May, and dancing and reveling before the hard work of planting. All Hallows' Eve was a celebration for the community's dead. Their spirits wandered the village on that night, visiting kin and neighbors.

Festivals helped maintain the sense of community that might be weakened during the long months of increased work or enforced indoor activity. They were first and foremost celebrations in which feasting, dancing, and play were central. But they also served as safety valves for the pressures and conflicts that built up over the year. There were frequently group and individual sports, like soccer or wrestling, which served to channel

aggressions. Village elders would arbitrate disputes, and marriage alliances or property transactions would be arranged.

Festivals further cemented the political cohesion of the community. Seating arrangements reflected the hierarchy of the community, and public punishment of offenders reinforced deference and social and sexual mores. Youth groups, or even the village women, might band together to shame a promiscuous woman or to place horns on the head of a cuckolded husband. Sometimes a man who had been beaten or abused by his wife, or who had simply failed to enforce obedience from her, was forced to ride backward on a horse or donkey to symbolize the misrule in his family. At such processions, which the French called *charivaris* and the English *skimmingtons*, rough music was played and the offense of the individual or couple was elaborately recreated. (See "Sex and the Married Man," pp. 508–509.) These forms of community ritual worked not only to punish offenders but also to reinforce the social and sexual values of the village as a whole.

popular Beliefs

Ceremony and festival are reminders that sixteenth-century Europe was still a preliterate society. Despite the introduction of printing and the millions of books that were produced during the period, the vast majority of Europeans conducted their affairs without the benefit of literacy. Their culture was oral and visual. They had need of an exact memory, and they developed a shorthand of adages, charms, and spells that helped them organize their activities and pass down their knowledge. It is difficult for us to re-create this mental world, in which almost all natural events were unpredictable and in which there was little certainty. Outside a small circle of intellectuals, there was little effective knowledge about either human or celestial bodies. The mysteries of the sun, moon, and stars were as deep as those of health and sickness. But this does not mean that ordinary people lived in a constant state of terror and anxiety. They used the knowledge they did have to form a view of the universe that conformed to their experiences and that responded to their hopes. Although many of their beliefs seem mere superstitions, they allowed people to form a coherent explanation of the natural world and of their relationship to it.

These beliefs blended Christian teaching and folk wisdom with a strong strain of magic. Popular belief in

THE DEVIL'S DUE

Evidence of the supernatural world abounded for the people of premodern Europe. Natural disasters such as plague and human disasters such as war promoted fear of witchcraft. When the world seemed out of balance and the forces of good retreated before the forces of evil, people sought someone to blame for their troubles. Witches were an obvious choice. Accused witches were most commonly women on the margins of society. Once brought before the authorities, many admitted their traffic with Satan, especially under torture. *The Witch Hammer* is a set of detailed instructions for the rooting out of witches, including procedures to induce their confessions.

The method of beginning an examination by torture is as follows: First, the jailers prepare the implements of torture, then they strip the prisoner (if it be a woman, she has already been stripped by other women, upright and of good report). This stripping is lest some means of witchcraft may have been sewed into the clothing—such as often, taught by the Devil, they prepare from the bodies of unbaptized infants, [murdered] that they may forfeit salvation. And when the implements of torture have been prepared, the judge, both in person and through other good men zealous in the faith, tries to persuade the prisoner to confess the truth freely; but, if he will not confess, he bids attendants make the prisoner fast to the strappado or some other implement of torture. The attendants obey forthwith, yet with feigned agitation. Then, at the prayer of some of those present, the prisoner is loosed again and is taken aside and once more persuaded to confess, being led to believe that he will in that case not be put to death.

But if, neither by threats nor by promises such as these, the witch cannot be induced to speak the truth, then the jailers must carry out the sentence, and torture the prisoner according to the accepted methods, with more or less of severity as the delinquent's crime may demand. And, while he is being tortured, he must be questioned on the articles of accusation, and this frequently and persistently, beginning with the lighter charges—for he will more readily confess the lighter than the heavier. And,

while this is being done, the notary must write down everything in his record of the trial—how the prisoner is tortured, on what points he is questioned, and how he answers.

And note that, if he confesses under the torture, he must afterward be conducted to another place, that he may confirm it and certify that it was not due alone to the force of the torture.

But, if the prisoner will not confess the truth satisfactorily, other sorts of tortures must be placed before him, with the statement that, unless he will confess the truth, he must endure these also. But, if not even thus he can be brought into terror and to the truth, then the next day or the next but one is to be set for a *continuation* of the tortures—not a *repetition*, for they must not be repeated unless new evidence be produced. . . .

And during the interval, before the day assigned, the judge, in person or through approved men, must in the manner above described try to persuade the prisoner to confess, promising her (if there is aught to be gained by this promise) that her life shall be spared.

The judge shall see to it, moreover, that throughout this interval guards are constantly with the prisoner, so that she may not be left alone; because she will be visited by the Devil and tempted into suicide.

From *The Witch Hammer.*

magic could be found everywhere in Europe, and it operated in much the same way as science does today. Only skilled practitioners could perform magic. It was a technical subject that combined expertise in the properties of plants and animals with theories about the composition of human and heavenly bodies. It had its own language, a mixture of ancient words and sounds with significant numbers and catchphrases. Magicians specialized: some concentrated on herbs and plants, others on the diseases of the body. Alchemists worked with rocks and minerals, astrologers with the movement of the stars. Witches were thought to understand the

sex and the married man

On 27 May 1618 the peace of the small hamlet of Quemerford, in the west of England, was shattered by the appearance of a large crowd from the neighboring market town of Calne. Men marched with fowling pieces and muskets to a cacophony of drums, clanging pots, whistles, and shouts. Among them, on a red horse, rode an outlandishly costumed man—a smock covering his body; on his head a nightcap with two long shoehorns tied to his ears; and on his face a false beard made from a deer's tail. The crowd escorted the rider to the home of Thomas Mills, who worked in Calne as a cutler. There they stopped. Guns were discharged into the air; an even greater clamor of rough music arose from drums, pipes, and metal objects; and when Mills opened his door, members of the crowd waved aloft the horns of goats or rams mounted on sticks. Then a few strong men entered the house; seized hold of his wife, Agnes; and dragged her to a village mud hole where she was ducked and covered in filth. She was rescued from being set on the horse and ridden to Calne.

This event, known as a skimmington in the west of England, and a charivari in France, was a shaming ritual. It was an element of popular culture that took place against the wishes of local authorities and without their connivance. Its purpose was twofold: to identify and punish sexual misconduct and to maintain the male-dominated gender system. These shaming rituals resulted from conduct that the male members of the community believed threatened local order (few women are known to have taken part in these events). In France most charivaris were conducted against husbands who were beaten by their wives; in England many skimmingtons were directed against husbands whose wives had been unfaithful. In both they were designed to shame men into disciplining women and to warn women to remain obedient.

Although skimmingtons and charivaris differed from place to place, they all contained similar elements. These were designed to invert normal behavior in one way or another. The rough music symbolized the disharmony of a household in which the woman dominated, either by her physical conduct—adultery or husband beating—or her verbal conduct—cursing or abusing her husband or other men. The music was made with everyday objects rather than instruments, and pots and pans were universally present. The "riding" of the husband was another common feature. In many rituals the "husband," played by a neighbor, was placed facing the tail of the horse or donkey to symbolize the backwardness of his behavior. In some, a "wife," also acted by a neighbor, rode behind the man and beat him with a stick or, in England, with the long-handled ladle used to skim cream that was known as a skimmington. In the end, the real husband or wife was captured, the man to ride in shame throughout the town, the woman to be sat on a cucking stool and dunked in water.

The presence of horns on the male riding the horse and on sticks carried by members of the crowd or worn atop their heads was the universal symbol of adultery. The cuckold—a word derived from the name of a promiscuous female bird—was an object of derision throughout European society. Codes of conduct from noble to peasant stressed the importance of female sexual fidelity in maintaining the purity of bloodlines and the order of the household. The cuckold was shorn of his masculinity; he had lost his "horns," in common parlance. His personal indignity was a cause for jest and insult, but the disorderliness implicit in the conduct of his wife was a cause for community concern. In local society, reputation was equated with personal worth, and no one had less reputation than the cuckold. Among the nobility, duels were fought over the slightest suggestion of a wife's unfaithfulness, while among ordinary folks the raising of the forefinger and pinkie—the sign of horns—initiated brawls.

The skimmington or charivari combined festive play with the enforcement of social norms. It was rough justice, as the objects of shame were allowed neither explanation nor defense. They were guilty by common fame, that is, by the report of their neighbors and the gossip of the local alehouse rather than by any examination of evidence. Women who yelled at their husbands were sometimes assumed to have beaten them; women who had beaten their husbands were assumed to have cuckolded them. The crimes were all interrelated, and protestations of innocence were useless. The crowds that gathered to perform the ceremony usually had bolstered their courage at the local tavern, and among them were village toughs and those who held grudges against the targeted family. Assault, property damage, and theft occasionally accompanied a skimmington. But most of the crowd was there to have a bit of sport and revel in the discomfort of the victims. Their conduct was the inverse of a legal procedure, as disorderly as the conduct of those to be punished. However, their purpose was not to turn the world upside down, but to set it right side up again by restoring the dominance of husbands over wives.

While shaming rituals like the charivari and the skimmington had a long history in Europe, they seem to have exploded into prominence in the late sixteenth and early seventeenth centuries. Population pressures and economic hardship are two conventional explanations for why there were greater local tensions during this period. Skimmingtons and charivaris frequently had rough edges, with some participants motivated by hatred or revenge. But it is also likely that there were more inversion rituals because there was more inversion. Women were taking a larger role in economic affairs and were becoming increasingly literate and active in religion, especially in Protestant countries. Assertive, independent women threatened the male-dominated social order as much as demographic and social change. That these threats were most identified with sexual misconduct and with the stripping of a husband's masculinity was hardly surprising. The image of the obedient female was conventionally the image of chastity. Thus the image of the independent female had to become one of promiscuity. Through the use of skimmingtons and charivaris, men attempted to restore norms of sexual conduct and gender relations that were increasingly under attack. As one English poet put it:

Ill fares the hapless family that shows
A cock that's silent, and a Hen that crows.
I know not which live more unnatural lives,
Obedient husbands, or commanding wives.

A German manuscript of 1464 shows an astrologer "diagnosing and prognosticating." The interest of astrologers in the heavens foreshadowed the rise of the science of astronomy in the sixteenth and seventeenth centuries.

properties of animals especially well. The witches of Shakespeare's *Macbeth* chanted their exotic recipe for witch's gruel:

> Eye of newt and toe of frog,
> Wool of bat and tongue of dog,
> Adder's fork and blindworm's sting,
> Lizard's leg and owlet's wing,
> For a charm of powerful trouble,
> Like a hell-broth boil and bubble.

Magical practices appealed to people at all levels of society. The wealthy favored astrology and paid handsomely to discover which days and months were the most auspicious for marriages and investments. So-called cunning men predicted the future for those of the lower orders who would not be able to give an astrologer such vital information as the date of their birth or to pay such exorbitant fees. The poorest villagers sought the aid of herbalists to help control the constant aches and pains of daily life. Sorcerers and wizards were called upon in more extreme circumstances, such as a threatened harvest or matters of life and death. These magicians competed with the remedies offered by the Church. Special prayers and visits to the shrines of particular saints were believed to have similar curative value. Magical and Christian beliefs did not oppose each other; they existed on a continuum and were practiced simultaneously. In some French villages, for example, four-leaf clovers were considered especially powerful if they were found on a particular saint's day. It was not until the end of the century, when Protestant and Catholic leaders condemned magical practices and began a campaign to root them out, that magic and religion came into conflict.

Magical practices served a variety of purposes. Healing was the most common, and many "magical" brews were effective remedies of the minor ailments for which they were prescribed. Most village magicians were women because it was believed that women had unique knowledge and understanding of the body. Women were also familiar with the properties of the herbs from which most remedies were derived. Magic was also used for predictive purposes. Certain charms and rituals were believed to have the power to affect the weather, the crops, and even human events. As always, affairs of the heart were as important as those of the stomach. Magicians advised the lovesick on potions and spells that would gain them the object of their desires. Cats were particularly associated with love spells, as were the petals of certain flowers. "He loves me, he loves me not" was more than a child's game. Magic was believed to have the power to alter the course of nature, and it could be used for both good and evil purposes.

Magic for evil was black magic, or witchcraft, which utilized beliefs in the presence of spiritual forces in nature. Witches were believed to possess special powers that put them into contact with the devil and the forces of evil, which they could then use for their own purposes. Belief in the prevalence of good and evil spirits was Christian as well as magical. But the Church had gradually consigned the operation of the devil to the afterlife and removed his direct agency from earthly affairs. Beginning in the late fifteenth century, Church authorities began to prosecute large numbers of suspected witches. By the end of the sixteenth century, there was a continent-wide witch craze. Unexplained misfortune or simple malice could set off accusations that might include dozens or even hundreds of suspected witches. Confessions were obtained under torture, as were further accusations. In the period from 1550 to 1650 there were more than 30,000 prosecutions in Germany alone.

Witches were usually women, most often those unmarried or widowed. Although male sorcerers and wizards were thought to have powers over evil spirits, by the sixteenth century it was females who served as the mediators between humans and the diabolical. In a sample of more than 7000 cases of witchcraft prosecuted in early modern Europe, over 80 percent of the defendants were women. There is no clear explanation why women fulfilled this important and powerful role. Belief in women's special powers over the body through their singular ability to give birth is certainly one part of the explanation, for many stories about the origins of witches suggest that they were children fathered by the devil and left to be raised by women. The sexual element of union with the devil and the common belief that older women were sexually aggressive combined to threaten male sexual dominance. Witches were also believed to have peculiar physical characteristics. A group of Italian witches, male and female, were distinguished by having been born with a caul (a membrane around their heads that was removed after birth). Accused witches were strip-searched to find the devil's mark, which might be any bodily blemish. Another strand of explanation lies in the fact that single women existed on the fringes of society, isolated and exploited by the community at large. Their occult abilities thus became a protective mechanism that gave them a function within the community while they remained outside it.

It is difficult to know how important black magical beliefs were in ordinary communities. Most of the daily magic that was practiced was the mixture of charms, potions, and prayers that mingled magical, medical, and Christian beliefs. But as the century progressed, more and more notice was taken of black magic. Misfortunes that befell particular families or social groups were

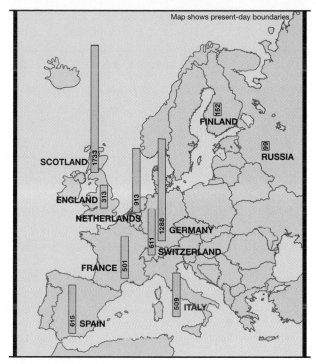

Witchcraft Persecutions

blamed upon the activities of witches. The campaign of the established churches to root out magic was largely directed against witches. The churches transposed witches' supposed abilities to communicate with the devil into the charge that they worshipped the devil. Because there was such widespread belief in the presence of diabolical spirits and in the capabilities of witches to

A reluctant witch rides off to hell with the devil while indifferent peasants go about their business. This woodcut is from Historia de gentibus septentrionalibus (History of the Northern Folk) *by Olaus Magnus, published at Rome in 1555.*

control them, Protestant and Catholic church courts could easily find witnesses to testify in support of the charges against individual witches. Yet wherever sufficient evidence exists to understand the circumstances of witchcraft prosecutions, it is clear that the community itself was under some form of social or economic stress. Sacrificing a marginal member of the community might be the means to restore village solidarity.

Population growth, economic diversification, and social change characterized life in early modern Europe. It was a century of extremes. The poor were getting poorer and the rich were getting richer. The early part of the century has been called the golden age of the peasantry; the later part has been called the crisis of subsistence. At all levels of the social scale, the lives of grandparents and grandchildren were dramatically different. For surplus producers, the quality of life improved throughout the century. The market economy expanded. Agricultural surplus was exchanged for more land and a wider variety of consumer goods. Children could be provided with an education, and domestic and agricultural labor was cheap and plentiful. For subsistence producers, the quality of life eroded. In the first half of the century, their diet contained more meat than it would for the next 300 years. Their children could be absorbed on new farms or sent to towns where there was a shortage of both skilled and unskilled labor. But gradually the outlook turned bleak. The land could support no more new families, and the towns needed no more labor. As wages fell and prices rose, peasants in western Europe were caught between the crushing burdens of taxation from lord, state, and church and the all-too-frequent catastrophes of poor harvests, epidemic disease, and warfare. In eastern Europe the peasantry was tied to the land in a new serfdom that provided minimum subsistence in return for the loss of freedom and opportunity. When peasants anywhere rose up against these conditions, they were cut down and swept away like new-mown hay.

Mastering the Chapter

To review the main points of the chapter, be sure you can explain the significance of each of the following.

Terms/Concepts/Events

tithes
three-field rotation
Price Revolution
Great Chain of Being
Body Politic
deserving poor
sturdy beggars
enclosure
nuclear families
charivaris

suggestions for further Reading

general Reading

Henry Kamen, *European Society, 1500–1700* (London: Hutchinson, 1984). A general survey of European social history.

* Robert Mandrou, *Introduction to Modern France* (New York: Harper & Row, 1977). Explores a variety of subjects in French social history from the mental to the material world.

* Peter Laslett, *The World We Have Lost: Further Explored* (New York: Scribners, 1984). One of the pioneering works in the family and population history of England.

* George Huppert, *After the Black Death* (Bloomington: Indiana University Press, 1986). An up-to-date and detailed study of social history in all parts of the Continent.

economic Life

* Fernand Braudel, *Civilization and Capitalism: The Structures of Everyday Life* (New York: Harper & Row, 1981). Part of a larger work filled with fascinating detail about the social behavior of humankind during the early modern period.

Emmanuel Le Roy Ladurie, *The French Peasantry 1450–1660* (London: Scholar Press, 1987). A complex study of the lives of the French peasantry.

* Gerald Strauss, *Nuremberg in the Sixteenth Century* (New York: John Wiley & Sons, 1966). A political and social history of a typical German town.

David Palliser, *Tudor York* (Oxford: Oxford University Press, 1979). A study of the second largest English urban area and its decline in the sixteenth century.

* Natalie Z. Davis, *Society and Culture in Early Modern France* (Stanford, CA: Stanford University Press, 1975). A collection of compelling essays drawn from the author's research on the French town of Lyon.

* Carlo Cipolla, ed., *Fontana Economic History of Europe*. Vol. 2, *The Sixteenth and Seventeenth Centuries* (London: Harvester Press, 1977). A multiauthored compendium of information and analysis on all aspects of European economic life.

* Peter Kriedte, *Peasants, Landlords and Merchant Capitalists* (Cambridge: Cambridge University Press, 1983). A Marxist interpretation of the transformations of the European economy

Hermann Kellenbenz, *The Rise of the European Economy* (London: Weidenfeld and Nicolson, 1976). A general survey of economic life with good material from Scandinavian and German sources.

social Life

* E. M. W. Tillyard, *The Elizabethan World Picture* (New York: Harper & Row, 1960). The classic account of the social constructs of English society.

* Arthur Lovejoy, *The Great Chain of Being* (New York: Random House, 1959). An intellectual history of an idea through its centuries of development.

Michael Bush, *Noble Privilege* (New York: Holmes & Meier, 1983). An analytic account of the types of privileges enjoyed by the European nobility, based on wide reading.

Antoni Maczak, Henryk Samsonowicz, and Peter Burke, eds., *East-Central Europe in Transition* (Cambridge: Cambridge University Press, 1985). Essays by leading historians of eastern Europe, most of which focus upon economic development.

Michael Weisser, *The Peasants of the Montes* (Chicago: University of Chicago Press, 1972). A study of the lives of the Spanish peasants who lived in the shadow of Toledo.

* Margaret Spufford, *Contrasting Communities* (Cambridge: Cambridge University Press, 1974). A detailed reconstruction of three English villages that explores social, economic, and religious life in the late sixteenth and early seventeenth centuries.

* R. Scribner and G. Benecke, *The German Peasant War*, 1525 (London: Allen & Unwin, 1979). Essays by leading scholars on different aspects of the most important of all peasant revolts.

* Peter Blickle, *The Revolution of* 1525 (Baltimore, MD: Johns Hopkins University Press, 1981). A provocative interpretation of the causes and meaning of the German Peasants' War.

* Yves-Marie Bercé, *Revolt and Revolution in Early Modern Europe* (New York: St. Martin's Press, 1987). A study of the structure of uprisings throughout Europe by a leading French historian.

private Life

* Roger Chartier, ed., A *History of Private Life*. Vol. 3, *Passions of the Renaissance* (Cambridge, MA: Harvard University Press, 1989). A lavishly illustrated study of the habits, mores, and structures of private life from the fifteenth to the eighteenth centuries.

* Michael Mitterauer and Reinhard Sieder, *The European Family* (Chicago: University of Chicago Press, 1982). A sociological survey that presents the varying ways in which European families were structured.

* Ralph Houlbrooke, *The English Family*, 1450–1700 (London: Longman, 1984). A thorough survey of family history for the society that has been most carefully studied.

* Jean-Louis Flandrin, *Families in Former Times* (Cambridge: Cambridge University Press, 1976). Studies of kinship, household, and sexuality by one of the leading French family historians.

* Beatrice Gottlieb, *The Family in the Western World From the Black Death to the Industrial Age* (Oxford: Oxford University Press, 1994). An outstanding introduction to the transformations in the lives of families.

* Paul Zumthor, *Daily Life in Rembrandt's Holland* (Stanford, CA: Stanford University Press, 1994). A fascinating recovery of the lives of ordinary people.

* A. T. Van Deursen, *Plain Lives in a Golden Age* (Cambridge: Cambridge University Press, 1991). A study of Dutch popular culture and religious belief that makes excellent use of the visual arts.

Merry Wiesner, *Working Women in Renaissance Germany* (New Brunswick, NJ: Rutgers University Press, 1986). A survey of women's work in Germany and the ways in which it changed during the sixteenth century.

* Margaret Sommerville, *Sex and Subjection* (London: Macmillan, 1995). The origins of modern views on women.

Anthony Fletcher, *Gender, Sex & Subordination in England 1500–1800* (New Haven, CT: Yale University Press, 1995). A sensitive reading of relations between men and women in the early modern world.

* Merry E. Wiesner, *Women and Gender in Early Modern Europe* (Cambridge: Cambridge University Press, 1993). The best introduction to European women's history.

Brian Pullan, *Rich and Poor in Renaissance Venice* (Cambridge, MA: Harvard University Press, 1971). A massive history of social classes in Venice with a detailed account of poverty and vagrancy.

* Robert Jutte, *Poverty and Deviance in Early Modern Europe* (Cambridge: Cambridge University Press, 1994). The poor, crime and criminality.

* Peter Burke, *Popular Culture in Early Modern Europe* (New York: Harper & Row, 1978). A lively survey of cultural activities among the European populace.

* R. Muchembled, *Popular Culture and Elite Culture in France*, 1400–1750 (Baton Rouge: Louisiana State University Press, 1985). A detailed treatment of the practices of two conflicting cultures.

* R. A. Houston, *Literacy in Early Modern Europe* (London: Longman, 1988). How literacy and education became part of popular culture from 1500 to 1800.

* D. Underdown, *Revel, Riot and Rebellion* (Oxford: Oxford University Press, 1985). An engaging study of popular culture and its relationship to social and economic structures in England.

* Keith Thomas, *Religion and the Decline of Magic* (New York: Scribners, 1971). A gargantuan descriptive and anecdotal account of the forms of religious and magical practice in England.

* Jean Delumeau, *Sin and Fear* (New York: St. Martin's Press, 1990). A cultural history of emotion based on a dazzling study of mainly Catholic writers.

* Brian Levack, *The Witch-Hunt in Early Modern Europe* (London: Longman, 1987). A study of the causes and meaning of the persecution of European witches in the sixteenth and seventeenth centuries.

*Paperback edition available.

The Royal State in the seventeenth century

Fit for a King

Behold Versailles: the greatest palace of the greatest king of the greatest state in seventeenth-century Europe. Everything about it was stupendous, a reflection of the grandeur of Louis XIV and of France. Sculptured gardens in dazzling geometric forms stretched for acres, scenting the air with exotic perfumes. Nearly as beautiful as the grounds were the 1400 fountains, especially the circular basins of Apollo and Latona, the sun god and his mother. The hundreds of water jets that sprayed at Versailles defied nature as well as the senses, for the locale was not well irrigated and water had to be pumped through elaborate mechanical works all the way from the Seine. Gardens and fountains provided the setting for the enormous palace with its hundreds of rooms for both use and show. Five thousand people, a tenth of whom served the king alone, inhabited the palace. Thousands of others flocked there daily. Most lived in the adjacent town, which had grown from a few hundred people to over 40,000 in a single generation. The royal stables quartered 12,000 horses and hundreds of carriages. The cost of all of this magnificence was equally astounding. Fragmentary accounts indicate that construction costs were over 100 million French pounds. Louis XIV ordered the official receipts burned.

Like the marble of the palace, nature itself was chiseled to the requirements of the king. Forests were pared to make leafy avenues or trimmed to conform to the geometric patterns of the gardens. In spring and summer, groves of orange trees grown in tubs were everywhere; in winter and fall they were housed indoors at great expense. Life-size statues and giant carved urns lined the carefully planned walkways that led to breathtaking views or sheltered grottoes. A cross-shaped artificial canal, over a mile long, dominated the western end of the park. Italian gondolas skimmed along its surface, carrying visitors to the zoo and aviary on one side or to the king's private chateau on the other.

But this great pile of bricks and stone, of marble and precious metals, expressed the contradictions of its age as well as its grandeur. The seventeenth century was an era when the rich got richer and the poor got poorer. It was a time when the monarchical state expanded its power and prestige even as it faced grave challenges to its very existence. It was an epoch of unrelenting war amid a nearly universal desire for lasting peace. Thus it was fitting that this prodigious monument was uncomfortable to live in, so unpleasant that Louis had a separate chateau built on the grounds as a quiet retreat. His wife and his mistresses complained constantly of accommodations in which all interior comforts had been subordinated to the external facade of the building. Versailles was a seat of state as well as the home of the monarch, and it is revealing that the private was sacrificed to the public.

The duc de Saint-Simon, who passed much of his time at Versailles, was well aware of the contradictions: "The beautiful and the ugly were sown together, the vast and the constricted." Soldiers, artisans, and the merely curious clogged the three great avenues that led from Paris to the palace. When the king dined in public, hordes of Parisians drove out for the spectacle, filing past the monarch as if he were an exhibit at a museum. The site itself was poorly drained. "Its mud is black and stinking with a stench so penetrating that you can smell it for several leagues around." The orange groves and the stone urns filled with flower petals were more practical than beautiful: they masked the stench of sewage that was particularly noxious in the heat and the rain. Even the gardens were too vast to be enjoyed. In the planted areas, the smell of flowers was overpowering while the acres of mown lawn proved unattractive to an aristocracy little given to physical exercise. "The gardens were admired and avoided," Saint-Simon observed acidly. In these contrasts of failure amid achievement, Versailles stands as an apt symbol of its age: a gaudy mask to hide the wrinkles of the royal state.

Focus Questions

1. How did war in the seventeenth century contribute to the creation of more powerful monarchical states?
2. What religious and political ideas were developed to justify resistance to monarchical authority?
3. What political and religious problems combined to bring England to civil war, and what results did the conflict produce in English government?
4. How did rulers like Frederick William of Brandenburg, Peter the Great, or Louis XIV, and theorists like Hobbes and Bossuet, justify absolute monarchical power?

The Rise of the Royal state

The religious and dynastic wars that dominated the early part of the seventeenth century had a profound impact upon the western European states. Not only did they cause terrible suffering and deprivation, but they also demanded efficient and better-centralized states to conduct them. War was both a product of the European state system and a cause of its continued development. As armies grew in size, the resources necessary to maintain them grew in volume. As the battlefield spread from state to state, defense became government's most important function. More and more power was absorbed by the monarch and his chief advisers; more and more of the traditional privileges of aristocracy and towns were eroded. At the center of these rising states, particularly in western Europe, were the king and his court. In the provinces were tax collectors and military recruiters.

Divine Kings

"There is a divinity that doth hedge a king," wrote Shakespeare. Never was that hedge more luxuriant than in the seventeenth century. In the early sixteenth century, monarchs treated their states and their subjects as personal property. Correspondingly, rulers were praised in personal terms: for their virtue, wisdom, or strength. By the early seventeenth century, the monarchy had been transformed into an office of state. Now rulers embodied their nation and, no matter what their personal characteristics, they were held in awe because they were monarchs.

Thus, as rulers lost direct personal control over their patrimony, they gained indirect symbolic control over their nation. This symbolic power was to be seen everywhere. By the beginning of the seventeenth century, monarchs had set permanent seats of government attended by vast courts of officials, place seekers, and servants. The idea of the capital city emerged, with Madrid, London, Paris, and Vienna as the models. Here the grandiose style of the ruler stood proxy for the wealth and glory of the nation. Great display bespoke great pride, and great pride was translated into great strength.

Portraits of rulers in action and repose conveyed the central message. Elizabeth I was depicted bestriding a map of England or clutching a rainbow and wearing a gown woven of eyes and ears to signify her power to see and hear her subjects. The Flemish painter Sir Anthony Van Dyck (1599–1641) created powerful images of three generations of Stuart kings of England. He was court painter to Charles I, whose qualities he portrayed with great sympathy and not a little exaggeration. Diego Velázquez (1599–1660) was court painter to Philip IV of Spain. His series of equestrian portraits of the Habsburgs—kings, queens, princes, and princesses—exude the spirit of the seventeenth-century monarchy, the grandeur and pomp, the power and self-assurance. Peter Paul Rubens (1577–1640) represented 21 separate episodes in the life of Marie de Médicis, queen regent of France.

The themes of writers were no different than those of artists. Monarchy was glorified in a variety of forms of literary representation. National history, particularly of recent events, enjoyed wide popularity. Its avowed purpose was to draw the connection between the past and the present glories of the state. One of the most popular French histories of the period was entitled *On the Excellence of the Kings and the Kingdom of France*. Francis Bacon (1561–1626), who is remembered more as a philosopher and scientist, wrote a laudatory history of Henry VII, founder of the Tudor dynasty.

In England it was a period of renaissance. Poets, playwrights, historians, and philosophers by the dozens gravitated to the English court. One of the most remarkable of them was Ben Jonson (1572–1637). He began life as a bricklayer, fought against the Spanish in Flanders, and then turned to acting and writing. His wit and talent brought him to court, where he made his mark by writing and staging masques, light entertainment that included music, dance, pantomime, and acting. Jonson's masques were distinguished by their lavish productions and exotic costumes and the inventive set designs of the great architect Inigo Jones (1573–1652). They were frequently staged at Christmastime and starred members of the court as players. The masques took the grandeur of England and its rulers for their themes.

The role of William Shakespeare (1564–1616) in the celebration of monarchy was more ambiguous. Like Jonson, Shakespeare came from an ordinary family, had little formal education, and began his astonishing career as an actor and producer of theater. He soon began to write as well as direct his plays and his company, the King's Players, received royal patronage. He set many of his plays at the courts of princes, and even comedies like *The Tempest* (1611) and *Measure for Measure* (1604) centered on the power of the ruler to dispense justice and to bring peace to his subjects. Both plays were staged at court. Shakespeare's history plays focused entirely on the character of kings. In *Richard II* (1597) and *Henry VI* (three parts, 1591–94) Shakespeare exposed the harm that weak rulers inflicted on their states, while in *Henry IV* (two parts, 1598–1600) and *Henry V* (1599) he highlighted the benefits to be derived from strong rulers.

Shakespeare's tragedies made this point in a different way. The tragic flaw in the personality of rulers exposed the world around them to ruin. In *Macbeth* (1606) this flaw was ambition. Macbeth killed to become a king and had to keep on killing to remain one. In *Hamlet* (1602) the tragic flaw was irresolution. The inability of the Prince of Denmark to act decisively and reclaim the crown that was his by right brought his state to the brink of collapse. Shakespeare's plays were viewed in London theaters by members of all social classes, and

Queen Elizabeth I of England. This portrait was commissioned by Sir Henry Lee to commemorate the queen's visit to his estate at Ditchley. Here the queen is the very image of Gloriana—ageless and indomitable.

his concentration on the affairs of rulers helped reinforce their dominating importance in the lives of all of their subjects.

The political theory of the divine right of kings further enhanced the importance of monarchs. This theory held that the institution of monarchy had been created by God and that the monarch functioned as God's representative on earth. One clear statement of divine-right theory was actually written by a king, James VI of Scotland, who later became James I of England (1603–25). In *The True Law of Free Monarchies* (1598), James reasoned that God had placed kings on earth to rule and that he would judge them in heaven for their transgressions.

The idea of the divine origin of monarchy was uncontroversial, and it was espoused not only by kings. One of the few things that the French Estates-General actually agreed upon during its meeting in 1614—the last for over 175 years—was the statement: "The king is sovereign in France and holds his crown from God only." This sentiment echoed the commonplace view of French political theorists. The greatest writer on the subject, Jean Bodin (1530–96), called the king "God's image on earth." In *The Six Books of the Commonwealth* (1576), Bodin defined the essence of the monarch's power: "The principal mark of sovereign majesty is essentially the right to impose laws on subjects generally without their consent."

Although at first glance the theory of the divine right of kings appears to be a blueprint for arbitrary rule, in fact it was yoked together with a number of principles that restrained the conduct of the monarch. As James I pointed out, God had charged kings with obligations: "to minister justice; to establish good laws; and to procure peace."

Kings were bound by the law of nature and the law of nations. They could not deprive their subjects of their lives, their liberties, or their property without due cause established by law. As one French theorist held, "While the kingdom belongs to the king, the king also belongs to the kingdom." Wherever they turned, kings were instructed in the duties of kingship. In tracts, letters, and literature they were lectured on the obligations of their office. "A true king should be first in government, first in council, and first in all the offices of state."

The court and the courtiers

For all of the bravura of divine-right theory, far more was expected of kings than they could possibly deliver. The day-to-day affairs of government had grown beyond the capacity of any monarch to handle them. The expansion in the powers of the western states absorbed more officials than ever. At the beginning of the sixteenth century, the French court of Francis I employed 622 officers; at the beginning of the seventeenth century, the court of Henry IV employed over 1500. Yet the difference was not only in size. Members of the seventeenth-century court were becoming servants of the state as well as of the monarch.

Expanding the court was one of the ways in which monarchs co-opted potential rivals within the aristocracy. In return, those who were favored enhanced their power by royal grants of titles, lands, and income. As the court expanded, so did the political power of courtiers. Royal councils—a small group of leading officeholders who advised the monarch on state business—grew in significance. Not only did the council assume the management of government, it also began to advocate policies for the monarch to adopt.

Yet, like everything else in seventeenth-century government, the court revolved around the monarch. The monarch appointed, promoted, and dismissed office-holders at will. As befit this type of personal govern-

ment, most monarchs chose a single individual to act as a funnel for private and public business. This was the "favorite," whose role combined varying proportions of best friend, right-hand man, and hired gun. Some favorites, like Cardinal Richelieu of France and Spain's Count-Duke Olivares, were able to transform themselves into chief ministers with a political philosophy and a vision of government. Others, like the English duke of Buckingham, simply remained royal companions. Favorites walked a not very tight rope. They could retain their balance only as long as they retained their influence with the monarch. Richelieu claimed that it was "more difficult to dominate the four square feet of the king's study than the affairs of Europe." The parallel careers of Richelieu, Olivares, and Buckingham neatly illustrate the dangers and opportunities of the office.

Cardinal Richelieu (1585–1642) was born into a French noble family of minor importance. A younger son, he trained for the law and then for a position that his family owned in the Church; he was made a cardinal in 1622. After skillful participation in the meeting of the Estates-General of 1614, Richelieu was given a court

A glimpse of a king

Louis de Rouvroy, duc de Saint-Simon, spent much of his career at the court of Louis XIV. His *Memoires* provide a fascinating study of life at Versailles, as well as poison pen portraits of the king and his courtiers. Here he describes some habits of the king.

He always took great pains to find out what was going on in public places, in society, in private houses, even family secrets, and maintained an immense number of spies and tale-bearers. These were of all sorts; some did not know that their reports were carried to him; others did know it; there were others, again, who used to write to him directly, through channels which he prescribed; others who were admitted by the backstairs and saw him in his private room. Many a man in all ranks of life was ruined by these methods, often very unjustly, without ever being able to discover the reason; and when the King had once taken a prejudice against a man, he hardly ever got over it. . . .

No one understood better than Louis XIV the art of enhancing the value of a favour by his manner of bestowing it; he knew how to make the most of a word, a smile, even of a glance. If he addressed any

one, were it but to ask a trifling question or make some commonplace remark, all eyes were turned on the person so honored; it was a mark of favour which always gave rise to comment. . . .

He loved splendour, magnificence, and profusion in all things, and encouraged similar tastes in his Court; to spend money freely on equipages and buildings, on feasting and at cards, was a sure way to gain his favour, perhaps to obtain the honour of a word from him. Motives of policy and something to do with this; by making expensive habits the fashion, and, for people in a certain position, a necessity, he compelled his courtiers to live beyond their income, and gradually reduced them to depend on his bounty for the means of subsistence.

From duc de Saint-Simon, *Memoires.*

This portrait of Richelieu by Philippe de Champaigne shows the cardinal's intellectual power and controlled determination.

The Spanish master Diego Velázquez painted this portrait of the Count-Duke Olivares.

post through the patronage of Queen Marie de Médicis, mother of Louis XIII. The two men made a good match. Louis XIII hated the work of ruling and Richelieu loved little else.

Although Richelieu received great favor from the king—he became a duke and amassed the largest private fortune in France—his position rested on his managerial abilities. Richelieu never enjoyed a close personal relationship with his monarch, and he never felt that his position was secure. In 1630 Marie de Médicis turned against him and he very nearly was ousted from office. His last years were filled with suppressing plots to undermine his power or to take his life.

Count-Duke Olivares (1587–1645) was a younger son of a lesser branch of a great Spanish noble family. By

the time he was 20 he had become a courtier with a title, a large fortune, and, most unusually, a university education. Olivares became the favorite of King Philip IV (1621–65). He was elevated to the highest rank of the nobility and lost no time consolidating his position.

Olivares used his closeness to the monarch to gain court appointments for his relatives and political supporters, but he was more interested in establishing political policy than in building a court faction. His objective was to maintain the greatness of Spain, whose fortunes, like his moods, waxed and waned. Like Richelieu, Olivares attempted to further the process of centralizing royal power, which was not very advanced in Spain. Olivares's plans for a nationally recruited and financed army ended in disaster. His efforts at tax reform went unrewarded. He advocated the aggressive foreign policy that mired Spain in the Thirty Years' War and 80 years of war in the Netherlands. As domestic and foreign crises mounted, Philip IV could not resist the pressure to dismiss his chief minister. In 1643 Olivares was removed from office and two years later, physically exhausted and mentally deranged, he died.

The duke of Buckingham (1592–1628) was also a younger son, but not of the English nobility. He received the aimless education of a country gentleman, spending several years in France learning the graces of fashion and dancing. Reputedly one of the most handsome men in Europe, Buckingham hung about the fringes of the English court until his looks and charm brought him to the attention of Queen Anne, James I's wife. She recommended him for a minor office that gave him frequent access to the king. Buckingham quickly caught the eye of James I, and his rise was meteoric. In less than seven years he went from commoner to duke, the highest rank of the English nobility.

Along with his titles, Buckingham acquired political power. He assumed a large number of royal offices, among them Admiral of the Navy, and placed his relatives and dependents in many others. Buckingham took his obligations seriously. He began a reform of naval administration, for example, but his rise to power had been so sudden that he found enemies at every turn. These increased dramatically when James I died in 1625. But Buckingham succeeded where so many others had failed by becoming the favorite and chief minister of the new king, Charles I (1625–49). His accumulation of power and patronage proceeded unabated, as did the enmity he aroused. But Charles I stood firmly behind him. In 1628 a discontented naval officer finally accomplished what the most powerful men in England could not: Buckingham was assassinated. While Charles I wept inconsolably at the news, ordinary Londoners drank to the health of his killer.

The Drive to Centralize Government

Richelieu, Olivares, and Buckingham met very different ends. Yet in their own ways they shared a common goal: to extend the authority of the monarch over his state and to centralize his control over the machinery of governance.

One of the chief means by which kings and councillors attempted to expand the authority of the state was through the legal system. Administering justice was one of the sacred duties of the monarchy. The complexities

George Villiers, duke of Buckingham. The royal favorite virtually ruled the country between 1618 and 1628. The general rejoicing at his death embittered the king and helped bring about the 11 years' rule without Parliament.

of ecclesiastical, civil, and customary law gave trained lawyers an essential role in government. As legal experts and the demands for legal services increased, royal law courts multiplied and expanded. In France, the Parlement of Paris, the main law court of the state, became a powerful institution that contested with courtiers for the right to advise the monarch. The number of regional parlements increased, bringing royal justice to the farthest reaches of the realm. Members of the Parlement of Paris and of the expanding provincial parlements were known as nobility of the robe, because of the long gowns lawyers and judges wore.

In Spain the *letrados*—university-trained lawyers who were normally members of the nobility—were the backbone of royal government. Formal legal training was a requirement for many of the administrative posts in the state. In Castile members of all social classes frequently used the royal courts to settle personal disputes. The expansion of a centralized system of justice thus joined the interests of subjects and the monarchy.

In England the legal system expanded differently. Central courts, situated in the royal palace of Westminster, grew and the lawyers and judges who practiced in them became a powerful profession. They were especially active in the House of Commons of the English Parliament, which, along with the House of Lords, had extensive advisory and legislative powers. More important than the rise of the central courts, however, was the rise of the local ones. The English Crown extended royal justice to the counties by granting legal authority to members of the local social elite. These justices of the peace, as they were known, became agents of the Crown in their own localities. Justices were given power to hear and settle minor cases and to imprison those who had committed serious offenses until the assizes, the semi-annual sessions of the county court.

Assizes combined the ceremony of rule with its process. Royal authority was displayed in a great procession to the courthouse that was led by the judge and the county justices, followed by the grand and petty juries of local citizens who would hear the cases, and finally by the carts carrying the prisoners to trial. Along with the legal business that was performed, assizes were occasions for edifying sermons, typically on the theme of obedience. Their solemnity—marked by the black robes of the judge, the Latin of the legal proceedings, and the public executions with which assizes invariably ended—all served to instill a sense of the power of the state in the throngs of ordinary people who witnessed them.

Efforts to integrate center and locality extended to more than the exercise of justice. The monarch also needed officials who could enforce royal policy in those localities where the special privileges of groups and individuals remained strong. The best strategy was to appoint local leaders to royal office. But with so much of the aristocracy resident at court, this was not always an effective course. In France, the provincial governors were traditionally members of the ancient nobility who enjoyed wide powers in matters of military recruitment, revenue collection, and judicial administration. But many governors spent far more time in Paris than in the locality that they were to administer and often opposed the exactions demanded by the monarch. By the beginning of the seventeenth century, the French monarchy began to rely on new central officials known as intendants to perform many of the tasks of the provincial governors. Cardinal Richelieu expanded the use of the intendants, and by the middle of the century they had become a vital part of royal government.

The Lords Lieutenant were a parallel institution created in England. Unlike every other European state, England had no national army. Every English county was required to raise, equip, and train its own militia. Lords Lieutenant were in charge of these trained bands. Since the aristocracy was the ancient military class in the state, the lieutenants were chosen from the greatest nobles of the realm. But they delegated their work to members of the gentry, large local landholders who took on their tasks as a matter of prestige rather than profit. Perhaps not surprisingly, the English military was among the weakest in Europe and nearly all its foreign adventures ended in disaster.

Efforts to centralize the affairs of the Spanish monarchy could not proceed so easily. The separate regions over which the king ruled maintained their own laws and privileges. Attempts to apply Castilian rules or implant Castilian officials always drew opposition from other regions. Olivares frequently complained that Philip IV was the king of Castile only and nothing but a thorough plan of unification would make him the king of Spain. He proposed such a plan in 1625 to attempt to solve the dual problems of military manpower and military finance. After 1621, Spain was again deeply involved in European warfare. Fighting in the Netherlands and in Germany demanded large armies and larger sums of money. Olivares launched a plan for a Union of Arms to which all the separate regions of the empire—including Mexico and Peru in the west, Italy in the east, and the separate regions in Iberia—would contribute. He envisioned an army of 140,000 but soon lowered his sights. Not all of the Iberian provinces were persuaded to contribute. Catalonia stood upon its ancient privileges and refused to grant either troops or funds. But Olivares was able to establish at least the principle of unified cooperation.

The Taxing Demands of War

More than anything else, war propelled the consolidation of the state. Whether offensive or defensive, continuous or intermittent, successful or calamitous, war was the irresistible force of the seventeenth-century monarchy. War taxation was its immovable object. Perhaps half of all revenue of the western states went to finance war. To maintain its armies and navies, its fortresses and outposts, the state had to squeeze every penny from its subjects. Old taxes had to be collected more efficiently; new taxes had to be introduced and enforced. As one Spanish jurist observed, in a familiar refrain, "There can be no peace without arms, no arms without money, and no money without taxation." However, the unprecedented demands for money by the state were always resisted. The privileged challenged the legality of levying taxes; the unprivileged did whatever they could to avoid paying them.

The claims and counterclaims of subjects and sovereigns were very strong. In the first place, armies had grown bigger and more expensive. In 1625 Philip IV had nearly 300,000 men in arms throughout his empire. The expense of maintaining Spanish fortresses alone had quintupled since the time of Philip II. Not only were there more men to pay, equip, and supply, but the cost of war materials continued to rise with inflation. Similarly, the cost of food and fodder rose. Marauding armies might be able to plunder sufficient grain during the spring and autumn, but they still consumed massive amounts of meat and drink that could not be supplied locally.

The economic hardships caused by the ceaseless military activity touched everyone. Those in the direct path of battle had little left to feed themselves, let alone to provide to the state. The disruption of the delicate cycle of planting and harvesting devastated local communities. Armies plundered ripened grain and trampled seedlings as they moved through fields. The conscription of village men and boys removed vital skills from the community and upset the gender-based division of labor. Peasants were squeezed by the armies for crops, by the lords for rents, and by the state for taxes.

In fact, the inability of the lower orders of European society to finance a century of warfare was clear from the beginning. In Spain and France, the principal problem was that so much of the wealth of the nation was beyond the reach of traditional royal taxation. The nobility and many of the most important towns had long achieved exemption from basic taxes on consumption and wealth. European taxation was regressive, falling most heavily on those least able to pay. Rulers and subjects alike recognized the inequities of the system. Regime after regime began with plans to overhaul the

Diego de Velázquez, Surrender of Breda (1634–35). Although the incident represented in the painting is fictitious—the leader of the forces of the United Provinces never handed over to the victorious Spanish general the keys to the fortress at Breda—the emotional quality the artist has evoked makes it seem real. Both the victor and the vanquished have been bowed by war, yet meet each other on an almost equal footing in the center of the picture. On either side the faces of the Dutch and Spanish soldiers clearly reflect the fortunes of war.

national system of taxation before settling for propping up new emergency levies against the rotting foundations of the old structure. Nevertheless, the fiscal crisis that the European wars provoked did result in an expansion of state taxation.

In France, for example, royal expenditures rose 60 percent during the first two decades of the seventeenth century, while the yield from the *taille*, the crown's basic commodity tax, remained constant. Thus the crown was forced to search for new revenues, the most important of which was the *paulette*, a tax on officeholding. To raise money, especially in emergencies, the crown had been forced to sell government offices, until by the seventeenth century a majority of offices had been obtained by direct purchase. The sale of an office provided a one-time windfall for the crown, but after that the cost of salaries and benefits was a perpetual drain. So, too, were the administrative costs of potentially inefficient officeholders. Many purchased their posts as an investment and treated them as personal property. For an annual payment of one-sixtieth of the value of the office, the paulette allowed the current holder to sell or bequeath it as desired. Henry IV instituted the paulette in 1604 and it became a vital source of royal revenue as well as an acute source of aristocratic and legal complaint. In the early 1620s, revenue from the sale of offices amounted to one-third of the crown's income.

The purchase of office was inherently corrupt, but it was not necessarily inefficient. Sons who were to inherit offices could be trained for their posts, if for no other reason than to operate them profitably. The crown received money from classes in society that were generally beyond the reach of taxation, while members of these classes received power, prestige, and experience in public service. As long as profit and efficiency went hand in hand, both officeholder and monarch might be well served. Unfortunately, it was the king rather than his officers who had the greatest incentive to manipulate the system. The more offices that could be created, the larger the income from the paulette. During fiscal emergencies this was a temptation to which all French monarchs succumbed.

"Fiscal emergency" was just another name for the routine problems of the Spanish monarchy. As the greatest military power in Europe, Spain necessarily had the greatest military budget, and thus the most extensive system of taxation. The crown taxed both domestic and imperial trade and took a healthy share of the gold and silver that continued to be mined in America. But all these revenues fell short of the state's needs.

In the 1590s Philip II established an important new source of internal taxation. In an agreement with the Cortes of Castile, he introduced the *milliones*, a tax on consumption that was to yield millions of ducats a year for war costs. An extremely regressive measure, the milliones taxed the sale of meat, wine, and oil—the basic elements of diet. This tax, which hit urban areas particularly hard, was originally designed to last only six years. But the crises that the crown pleaded in the 1590s were even deeper at the turn of the century. The milliones became a permanent tax and a permanent grievance throughout Castile.

By contrast, the English crown was never able to persuade Parliament to grant permanent additional revenues. Although uninvolved in European conflicts, England was not immune from military spending. War with Ireland in the 1590s and with Spain between 1588 and 1604 depleted the reserves that the crown had obtained

The oppression of the peasantry is the theme of this engraving published in the mid-seventeenth century: "This noble is the spider and the peasant the fly." The poor man is handing over goods and money to the fat milord, who says, "You must pay or serve." The peasant replies, "To all masters, all honors."

when Henry VIII dissolved the monasteries. Disastrous wars against France and Spain in the 1620s provoked fiscal crisis for a monarchy that had few direct sources of revenue. While the great wealth of the kingdom was in land, the chief sources of revenue for the crown were in trade. In the early seventeenth century, customs duties, or impositions, became a lucrative source of income when the judges ruled that the king could determine which commodities could be taxed and at what rate. Impositions fell heavily upon the merchant classes and urban consumers, but unlike the milliones, impositions were placed on luxury import goods rather than on basic commodities.

Because so much of the crown's revenues derived from commerce and because foreign invasion could only come from the sea, the most pressing military need of the English monarchy was for naval defense. Even during the Armada crisis, the largest part of the English fleet had been made up of private merchant ships pressed into service through the emergency tax of Ship Money. This was a tax on each port town to hire a merchant ship and fit it out for war. In the 1630s Charles I revived Ship Money and extended it to all English localities. His innovation aroused much opposition from the gentry, especially after his refusal to call Parliament into session to have the tax confirmed.

War finance was like an all-consuming monster. No matter how much new revenue was fed into it, its appetite grew for more. New taxes and increased rates of traditional taxation created suffering and a sense of grievance throughout the western European states. Opposition to taxation was not based on greed: the state's right to tax was not yet an established principle. Monarchs received certain forms of revenue in return for grants of immunities and privileges to powerful groups in their state. The state's efforts to go beyond these restricted grants were viewed as theft of private property. In the case of Ship Money, challengers argued that the king had no right to what belonged to his subjects except in a case of national emergency. This was a claim that the king accepted, arguing that such an emergency existed in the presence of pirates who were attacking English shipping. But if Charles I did not make a convincing claim for national emergency, the monarchs of France and Spain, the princes of Germany, and the rulers of the states of eastern Europe all did.

Throughout the seventeenth century, monarchy solidified itself as a form of government. The king's authority came from God, but his power came from his people. By administering justice, assembling armies, and extracting resources through taxation, the monarch ruled as well as governed. The richer the king and the more powerful his might, the more potent was his state. Europeans began to identify themselves as citizens of a nation and to see themselves in distinction to other nations.

The crises of the Royal state

The expansion of the functions, duties, and powers of the state in the early seventeenth century was not universally welcomed in European societies. The growth of central government came at the expense of local rights and privileges held by corporate bodies like the Church and the towns or by individuals like provincial officials and aristocrats. The state proved a powerful competitor, especially in the contest for the meager surplus produced on the land. As rents and prices stabilized in the early seventeenth century after a long period of inflation, taxation increased, slowly at first and then at a pace with the gathering momentum of the Thirty Years' War. State exactions burdened all segments of society. Peasants lost the small benefit that rising prices had conferred on producers. The surplus that parents had once passed on to children was now taken by the state. Local officials, never altogether popular, came to be seen as parasites and were easy targets for peasant rebellions. Larger landholders, whose prosperity depended on rents and services from an increasingly impoverished peasantry, suffered along with their tenants. Even the great magnates were appalled by the state's insatiable appetite.

Taxation was not the only thing that aroused opposition. Social and economic regulation meant more laws. More laws meant more lawyers and agents of enforcement. State regulation may have been more efficient (though many believed it was more efficient only for the state) but it was certainly disruptive. It was also expensive at a time when the fragile European economy was in a phase of decline. The early seventeenth century was a time of hunger in most of western Europe. Subtle changes in climate reduced the length of growing seasons and the size of crops. Bad harvests in the 1620s and 1640s left disease and starvation in their wake. And the wars ground on. Armies brought misery to those who were forcibly recruited to fight, those who were taxed into destitution, and those who simply had the misfortune to live in the path of destruction.

By the middle of the seventeenth century, a European crisis was taking shape, though its timing and forms differed from place to place. Rural protests, like grain riots and mob assaults on local institutions, had a long history in all of the European states. Popular revolt was not the product of mindless despair, but rather the natural form of political action for those who fell outside the institutionalized political process. Bread riots and tax revolts became increasingly common in the early seventeenth century. More significantly, as the focus of discontent moved from local institutions to the state, the forms of revolt changed. So, too, did the participants. Members of the political elite began to formulate their own grievances against the expansion of state power. A theory of resistance, first developed in the French wars of religion, came to be applied to political tyranny and posed a direct challenge to the idea of the divine right of kings. By the 1640s, all of these forces had converged, and rebellion exploded across the Continent. In Spain, the ancient kingdoms of Catalonia and Portugal asserted their independence from Castilian rule; in France, members of the aristocracy rose against a child monarch and his regent. In Italy, revolts rocked Naples and Sicily. In England, a constitutional crisis gave way to civil war, and then to the first political revolution in European history.

The Need to Resist

Europeans lived more precariously in the seventeenth century than in any period since the Black Death. One benchmark of crisis was population decline. In the Mediterranean, Spain's population fell from 8.5 to 7 million and Italy's population from 13 to 11 million. The ravages of the Thirty Years' War were most clearly felt in central Europe: Germany lost nearly a third of its people, Bohemia nearly half. Northwestern Europe—England, the Netherlands, and France—was hardest hit in the first half of the century and only gradually recovered by 1700. Population decline had many causes and, rather remarkably, direct casualties from warfare were a very small component. The indirect effects of war, the disruption of agriculture, and the spread of disease were far more devastating. Spain alone lost a half million people at the turn of the century and another half million between 1647 and 1652. Severe outbreaks of plague in 1625 and in 1665 hit England, while France endured three consecutive years of epidemics, from 1629 to 1631.

All sectors of the European economy, from agriculture to trade, stagnated or declined in the early seventeenth century. Not surprisingly, peasants were hardest hit. The surplus from good harvests did not remain in rural communities to act as a buffer for bad ones. Tens of thousands died during the two great subsistence crises in the late 1620s and the late 1640s. Predictably, acute economic crisis led to rural revolt. As the French peasants reeled from visitations of plague, frost, and floods, the French state was raising the taille, the tax that fell most heavily on the lower orders. A series of French rural revolts in the late 1630s focused on opposition to tax increases. The Nu-Pieds—"the barefooted"—rose against changes in the salt tax; others rose against new levies on wine. These revolts began in the same way: with the murder of a local tax official, the organization of a peasant militia, and the recruitment of local clergy and notables. The rebels forced temporary concessions from local authorities, but they never achieved lasting reforms. Each revolt ended with the reimposition of order by the state. In England the largest rural protests, like the Midland Revolt of 1607, centered on opposition to the enclosure of grain fields and their conversion to pasture.

The most spectacular popular uprisings occurred in Spanish-occupied Italy. In the spring of 1647 the Sicilian city of Palermo exploded under the pressure of a disastrous harvest, rising food prices, and relentless taxation. A city of 130,000 inhabitants, Palermo imported nearly all of its foodstuffs. As grain prices rose, the city government subsidized the price of bread, running up huge debts in the process. When the town governors could no longer afford the subsidies, they decided to reduce the size of the loaf rather than increase its price. This did not fool the women of the city, who rioted when the first undersized loaves were placed on sale. Soon the entire city was in revolt. "Long live the king and down with taxes!" became the rebel slogan. Commoners who were not part of the urban power structure led the revolt in Palermo. For a time they achieved the abolition of Spanish taxes on basic foodstuffs. Their success provided the model for a similar uprising in Naples, the largest city in Europe. The Neapolitan revolt began in 1647 after the Spanish placed a tax on fruit. A crowd gathered to protest the new imposition, burned the customs house, and murdered several local officials. The protesters were led first by a fisherman and then by a blacksmith, and again the rebels achieved the temporary suspension of Spanish taxation. But neither of the Italian urban revolts could attract support

The Plague in Milan, *a painting by Caspar Crayer of the seventeenth-century Flemish school. The victims of the epidemic are being consoled by a priest.*

from the local governors or the nobility. Both uprisings were eventually crushed.

The Right to Resist

Rural and urban revolts by members of the lower orders of European society were doomed to failure. Not only did the state control vast military resources, but it could count on the loyalty of the governing classes to suppress local disorder. It was only when local elites rebelled and joined their social and political discontent to the economic grievances of the peasants that the state faced a genuine crisis. Traditionally, aristocratic rebellion focused on the legitimacy rather than the power of the state. Claimants to the throne initiated civil wars for the prize of the crown. By the early seventeenth century, however, hereditary monarchy was too firmly entrenched to be threatened by aristocratic rebellions. When Elizabeth I of England died without an heir, the throne passed to her cousin, James I, without even a murmur of discontent. The assassination of Henry IV in 1610 left a child on the French throne, yet it provoked little more than intrigue over which aristocratic faction would advise him. The principles of hereditary monarchy and the divine right of kings laid an unshakable foundation for royal legitimacy. But if the monarch's right to rule could no longer be challenged, was the method of rule equally unassailable? Were subjects bound to their sovereign in all cases whatsoever?

Luther and Calvin had preached a doctrine of passive obedience. Magistrates ruled by divine will and must be obeyed in all things, they argued. Both left a tiny crack in the door of absolute submission, however, by recognizing the right of lesser magistrates to resist their superiors if divine law was violated. It was during the French civil wars that a broader theory of resistance began to develop. In attempting to defend themselves from accusations that they were rebels, a number of Huguenot writers responded with an argument that accepted the divine right of kings but limited royal power. They claimed that kings were placed on earth by God to uphold piety and justice. When they failed to do so, lesser magistrates were obliged to resist them. As God would not institute tyranny, oppressive monarchs could not be acting by divine right. Therefore, the king who violated divine law could be punished. In the most influential of these writings, A *Defense of Liberty Against Tyrants* (1579), Philippe Duplessis-Mornay (1549–1623) took the critical next step and argued that the king who violated the law of the land could also be resisted.

In the writings of both Huguenot and Dutch Protestants there remained strict limits to this right to resist. These authors accepted all the premises of divine-right theory and restricted resistance to other divinely ordained magistrates. Obedience tied society together at all levels, and loosening any of the knots might unravel everything. In fact, one crucial binding had already come loose when the arguments used to justify resistance in matters of religion came to be applied to matters of state. Logic soon drove the argument further. If it was the duty of lesser magistrates to resist monarchical tyranny, why was it not the duty of all citizens to do so?

European Population Data (in millions)

Year	1550	1575	1600	1625	1650	1675	1700
England	3		4	4.5		5.8	5.8
France		20					19.3
Italy	11	13	13	13	12	11.5	12.5
Russia	9		11	8	9.5	13	16
Spain	6.3		7.6		5.2		7
All Europe	85	95	100	100	80	90	100

This was a question posed not by a Protestant rebel, but by a Jesuit professor, Juan de Mariana (1536–1624). In *The King and the Education of the King* (1598), Mariana described how human government developed from the need of individuals to have leaders to act for their convenience and well-being. These magistrates were established by the people and then legitimated by God. Magistrates were nothing other than the people's representatives, and if it was the duty of magistrates to resist the tyranny of monarchs, then it must also be the duty of every individual citizen. "If the sacred fatherland is falling into ruins, he who tries to kill the tyrant will be acting in no ways unjustly."

Mariana was careful to specify that only the most willful and deliberate lawbreakers were actually tyrants. He also advocated the use of national assemblies rather than individual assassins to make the decision to punish them. But there was no escaping the implications of his argument. If anyone could judge the conduct of kings, then there would be no standards of judgment. As Cardinal Richelieu observed succinctly: "Tyranny is monarchy misliked." In 1605 a Catholic conspiracy to murder James I of England was foiled by government agents at the last moment. In 1610 a religious fanatic assassinated Henry IV of France. The right of individuals to resist tyrants was rapidly developing into the right of subjects to overthrow their monarchs.

In fact, there remained one more vital link in the chain. This was supplied by the great English poet John Milton (1608–74) in his defense of the English Revolution. Milton built upon traditional resistance theory as it had developed over the previous 50 years. Kings were instituted by the people to uphold piety and justice. Lesser magistrates had the right to resist monarchs. An unjust king forfeited his divine right and was to be punished as any ordinary citizen. In *The Tenure of Kings and Magistrates* (1649), Milton expanded upon the conventional idea that society was formed by a covenant, or contract, between ruler and ruled. The king in his coronation oath promised to uphold the laws of the land and rule for the benefit of his subjects. The subjects promised to obey. Failure by either side to meet obligations broke the contract.

By the middle of the seventeenth century, resistance theory provided the intellectual justification for a number of different attacks on monarchical authority. In 1640 simultaneous rebellions in the ancient kingdoms of Portugal and Catalonia threatened the Spanish monarchy. The Portuguese successfully dissolved the rather artificial bonds that had been created by Philip II and resumed their separate national identity. Catalonia, the easternmost province of Spain, which Ferdinand of Aragon had brought to the union of crowns in the fifteenth century, presented a more serious challenge. Throughout the 1620s Catalonia, with its rich Mediterranean city of Barcelona, had consistently rebuffed Olivares's attempts to consolidate the Spanish provinces. The Catalonian Cortes—the representative institution of the towns—refused to make even small contributions to the Union of Arms or to successive appeals for emergency tax increases. Catalonian leaders feared that these demands were only the thin edge of the wedge. They did not want their province to go the way of Castile, where taxation was as much an epidemic as plague.

Catalonia relied on its ancient laws to fend off demands for contributions to the Spanish military effort. But soon the province was embroiled in the French war, and Olivares was forced to bring troops into Catalonia. The presence of the soldiers and their conduct inflamed the local population. In the spring of 1640 an unconnected series of peasant uprisings took place. Soldiers and royal officials were slain, and the Spanish viceroy of the province was murdered. But the violence was not directed only against outsiders. Attacks on wealthy citizens raised the specter of social revolt.

At this point a peasant uprising broadened into a provincial rebellion. The political leaders of Barcelona

The execution of François Ravaillac, the assassin of Henry IV of France.

not only decided to approve the rebellion but decided to lead it. They declared that Philip IV had violated the fundamental laws of Catalonia and that as a consequence their allegiance to the crown of Spain was dissolved. Instead they turned to Louis XIII of France, offering him sovereignty if he would preserve their liberties. In fact, the Catalonians simply exchanged a devil they knew for one they did not. The French happily sent troops into Barcelona to repel a Spanish attempt to crush the rebellion, and now two armies occupied Catalonia. The Catalonian rebellion lasted for 12 years. When the Spanish finally took Barcelona in 1652, both rebels and ruler were exhausted from the struggle.

The revolt of the Catalonians posed a greater external threat to the Spanish monarchy than it did an internal one. In contrast, the French Fronde, an aristocratic rebellion that began in 1648, was more directly a challenge to the underlying authority of the state. It too began in response to fiscal crises brought on by war. Throughout the 1640s the French state had tottered on the edge of bankruptcy. It had used every means of creative financing that its ministers could devise, mortgaging as much of the future as anyone would buy. Still, it was necessary to raise traditional taxes and institute new ones. The first tactic revived peasant revolts, especially in the early years of the decade; the second led to the Fronde.

The Fronde was a rebellion against the regency government of Louis XIV (1643–1715), who was only four years old when he inherited the French throne. His mother, Anne of Austria (1601–66), ruled as regent with the help of her Italian adviser, Cardinal Mazarin (1602–61). In the circumstances of war, agricultural crisis, and financial stringency, no regency government was going to be popular, but Anne and Mazarin made the worst of a bad situation. They initiated new taxes on officeholders, Parisian landowners, and the nobility. Soon all three united against them, led by the Parlement of Paris, the highest court in the land, in which new decrees of taxation had to be registered. When the Parlement refused to register a number of the new taxes proposed by the government and soon insisted on the right to control the crown's financial policy, Anne and Mazarin struck back by arresting a number of leading members of the Parlement. But in 1648 barricades went up in Paris, and the court, along with the nine-year-old king, fled the capital. Quickly the Fronde—which took its name from the slingshots that children used to hurl stones at carriages—became an aristocratic revolt aimed not at the king, but at his advisers. Demands for Mazarin's resignation, the removal of the new taxes, and greater participation in government by nobles and Parlement were coupled with profuse statements of loyalty to the king.

The duc de Condé, leader of the Parisian insurgents, courted Spanish aid against Mazarin's forces, and the cardinal was forced to make concessions in order to prevent a Spanish invasion of France. The leaders of the Fronde agreed that the crown must overhaul its finances and recognize the rights of the administrative nobility to participate in formulating royal policy, but they had no concrete proposals to accomplish either aim. Nor could they control the deteriorating political situation in Paris and a number of provincial capitals where urban and rural riots followed the upper-class attack upon the state. The catastrophic winter of 1652, with its combination of harvest failure, intense cold, and epidemic disease, brought the crisis to a head. Louis XIV was declared old enough to rule and his forces recaptured Paris, where he was welcomed as a savior. Born of frustration, fear, and greed, the Fronde accomplished little. It demonstrated only that the French aristocracy remained an independent force in politics. Like the Catalonian revolt, it revealed the fragility of the absolute state on the one hand, yet its underlying stability on the other.

The English Civil War

On the surface, it is difficult to understand why the most profound challenge to monarchical authority took place in England. Among the nations of Europe, England alone enjoyed peace in the early seventeenth century. Except for a brief period around 1620, the English economy sputtered along. The monarchy itself was stable. James I had succeeded his cousin Elizabeth I without challenge and already had as many children as the Tudors had produced in nearly a century.

James I was not a lovable monarch, but he was capable, astute, and generous. In the eyes of his critics he had two great faults: he succeeded a legend and he was Scottish. There was little he could do about either. Elizabeth I had ruled England successfully for over 40 years. As the economy soured and the state tilted toward bankruptcy in the 1590s, the queen remained above criticism. She sold off royal lands worth thousands of pounds and ran up huge debts at the turn of the century, yet the gleaming myth of the glorious virgin queen tarnished not the least bit. When she died, the general population wept openly and the governing elite

An episode from the second Fronde, one of two French civil wars that occurred during the minority of Louis XIV.

breathed a collective sigh of relief. There was so much to be done to set things right.

At first James I endeared himself to the English gentry and aristocracy by showering them with the gift of social elevation. On his way to London from Scotland, the first of the Stuart kings knighted thousands of gentlemen who had waited in vain for favor from the queen. He promoted peers and created new titles to meet the pent-up demands of decades of stinginess. But he showered favor equally on his own countrymen, members of his royal Scottish court who accompanied him to England. A strong strain of ethnic prejudice combined with the disappointed hopes of English courtiers to generate immediate hostility to the new regime. If Elizabeth could do no wrong, James could do little right. Although he relied upon Elizabeth's most trusted ministers to guide state business, James was soon plunged into financial and political difficulties. He never escaped from either.

His financial problems resulted directly from the fact that the tax base of the English monarchy was undervalued. For decades the monarchy had staved off a crisis by selling lands that had been confiscated from the Church in the mid-sixteenth century. But this solution reduced the crown's long-term revenues and made it dependent on extraordinary grants of taxation from Parliament. Royal demands for money were met by parliamentary demands for political reform, and these differing objectives provoked unintentional political controversies in the 1620s. The most significant, in 1628, during the reign of Charles I, led to the formulation of the Petition of Right, which restated the traditional English freedoms from arbitrary arrest and imprisonment (habeas corpus), nonparliamentary taxation, and the confiscation of property by martial law.

Religious problems mounted on top of economic and political difficulties. Demands were made for thoroughgoing church reforms by groups and individuals who had little in common apart from the name given to them by their detractors: Puritans. One of the most contentious issues raised by Puritans was the survival in the Anglican church of the Catholic hierarchy of archbishops and bishops. They demanded the abolition of this episcopal form of government and its replacement with a presbyterial system similar to that in Scotland, in which congregations nominated their own representatives to a national assembly. As the king was the supreme head of the English church, an attack upon church structure was an attack upon the monarchy. "No bishop, no king," James I declared as he rejected the first formal attempts at reform. But neither James I nor his son, Charles I, opposed religious reform. They too wanted a better educated clergy, a plain and decorous worship service, and godly citizens. But to achieve their reforms they strengthened episcopal power. In the 1620s Archbishop William Laud (1573–1645) rose to power in the English church by espousing a Calvinism so moderate that many denied it was Calvinism at all. Laud preached the beauty of holiness and strove to reintroduce decoration in the church and a formal decorum in the service. One of Laud's first projects after he was appointed archbishop of Canterbury was to establish a consistent divine service in England and Scotland by creating new prayer books.

It fell to the unfortunate dean of St. Giles Cathedral in Edinburgh to introduce the new Scottish prayer book in 1637. The reaction was immediate: someone threw a stool at his head and dozens of women screamed that "popery" was being brought to Scotland. There were riots by citizens and resistance to the use of the new prayer book by clergy and the nobility. To Charles I the opposition was rebellion, and he began to raise forces to suppress it. But Scottish soldiers were far more determined to preserve their religious practice than were English soldiers to impose the king's. By the end of 1640, a Scottish army had successfully invaded England.

Now the fiscal and political problems of the Stuart monarchs came into play. For 11 years Charles I had managed to do what he was in theory supposed to do: live from his own revenues. He had accomplished this by a combination of economy and the revival of ancient feudal rights that struck hard at the governing classes. He levied fines for unheard-of offenses, expanded traditional taxes, and added a brutal efficiency to the collection of revenue. While these expedients sufficed during peacetime, now that an army had to be raised and a war fought, Charles I was again dependent upon grants from Parliament, which he reluctantly summoned in 1640.

The Long Parliament, which met in November 1640 and sat for 13 years, saw little urgency in levying taxes to repel the Scots. After all, the Scots were resisting Laud's religious innovations, and there were many Englishmen who believed that they should be resisted. More to the point, members of Parliament had a host of political grievances to be redressed before they granted the king his money. Parliament proposed a number of constitutional reforms that Charles I reluctantly accepted. The Long Parliament would not be dismissed without its own consent. In the future, Parliaments would be summoned once every three years. Due process in common law would be observed, and the ancient taxes that the crown had revived would be abolished. To show its seriousness of purpose, Parliament, as the highest court in the land, tried and executed Charles's leading political adviser, the Earl of Strafford, and imprisoned Archbishop Laud.

At first Charles I could do nothing but bide his time and accept these assaults on his power and authority. Once he had crushed the Scots he would be able to bargain from a position of strength. But as the months passed, it became clear that Parliament had no intention of providing him with money or forces. Rather, the members sought to negotiate with the Scots themselves and to continue to demand concessions from the king as long as the Scottish threat remained. By the end of 1641, Charles's patience had worn thin. He bungled an attempt to arrest the leaders of the House of Commons, but he successfully spirited his wife and children out of London. Then he too left the capital and headed north where, in the summer of 1642, he raised the royal standard and declared the leaders of Parliament rebels and traitors. England was plunged into civil war.

Parliament had finally pushed too hard, and its members now found themselves in the unprecedented situation of having to fight a war against their sovereign, a war that few of them wanted and that hardly anyone believed they could win. One of the Parliament's generals summed up the futility of the situation: "If we defeat the king ninety-nine times, yet still he is king. But if he defeat us once we will all be hanged as traitors." Nevertheless, there were strong passions on both sides. Parliamentarians believed that they were fighting to defend their religion, their liberties, and the rule of law. Royalists believed they were fighting to defend their monarch, their church, and social stability. After nearly three years of inconclusive fighting, in June 1645 Parliament won a decisive victory at Naseby and brought the war to an end the following summer. The king was in captivity, bishops had been abolished, a Presbyterian church had been established, and limitations were placed on royal power. All that remained necessary to end three years of civil war was the king's agreement to abide by the judgment of battle.

But Charles I had no intention of surrendering either his religion or his authority. Despite the rebels' successes, they could not rule without him, and he would concede nothing as long as opportunities to maneuver remained. In 1647 there were opportunities galore. The war had proved ruinously expensive to Parliament. It owed enormous sums to the Scots, to its own soldiers, and to the governors of London. Each of these elements had its own objectives in a final settlement of the war, and they were not altogether compatible. London feared the parliamentary army, unpaid and camped dangerously close to the capital. The Scots and the English Presbyterians in Parliament feared that the religious settlement already made would be sacrificed by those known as Independents, who desired a more decentralized church. The Independents feared that they would be persecuted just as harshly by the Presbyterians as they had been by the king. In fact, the war had settled nothing.

The English Revolutions

Charles I happily played both ends against the middle until the army decisively ended the game. In June 1647 soldiers kidnapped the king and demanded that Parliament pay their arrears, protect them from legal retribution, and recognize their service to the nation. Those in

The English Civil War

Charles I turning from his panic-stricken troops at the battle of Naseby. Cromwell's victory in the battle ended the civil war and sealed Charles's fate.

Parliament who opposed the army's intervention were impeached, and when London Presbyterians rose up against the army's show of force, troops moved in to occupy the city. The civil war, which had come so close to resolution in 1647, had now become a military revolution. Religious and political radicals flocked to the army and encouraged the soldiers to support their programs and resist disbandment. New fighting broke out in 1648 as Charles encouraged his supporters to resume the war. But forces under the command of Sir Thomas Fairfax (1612–71) and Oliver Cromwell (1599–1658) easily crushed the royalist uprisings in England and Scotland. The army now demanded that Charles I be brought to justice for his treacherous conduct both before and during the war. When the majority in Parliament refused, still hoping against hope to reach an accommodation with the king, the soldiers again acted decisively. In December 1648 army regiments were sent to London to purge the two houses of Parliament of those who opposed the army's demands. The remaining members, contemptuously called the Rump Parliament, voted to bring the king to trial for his crimes against the liberties of his subjects. On 30 January 1649, Charles I was executed and England was declared to be a commonwealth. (See "'King Charles's Head,'" pp. 536–537.) The monarchy and the House of Lords were abolished, and the nation was to be governed by what was left of the membership of the House of Commons.

For four years the members of the Rump Parliament struggled with proposals for a new constitution while balancing the demands of moderate and radical reformers and an increasingly hostile army. It achieved little other than to raise the level of frustration. In 1653 Oliver Cromwell, with the support of the army's senior officers, forcibly dissolved the Rump and became the leader of the revolutionary government. At first he ruled along with a Parliament hand-picked from among the supporters of the commonwealth. When Cromwell's Parliament proved no more capable of governing than had the Rump, a written constitution, The Instrument of Government (1653), established a new polity. Cromwell was given the title Lord Protector, and he was to rule along with a freely elected Parliament and an administrative body known as the Council of State.

Cromwell was able to hold the revolutionary cause together through the force of his own personality. A member of the lesser landed elite who had opposed the arbitrary policies of Charles I, he was a devout Puritan who believed in a large measure of religious toleration for Christians. As both a member of Parliament and a senior officer in the army, he had been able to temper the claims of each when they conflicted. Cromwell saw God's hand directing England toward a more glorious future, and he believed that his own actions were divinely ordained: "No man climbs higher than he that knows not whither he goes." Although many urged him to accept the crown of England and begin a new monarchy, Cromwell steadfastly held out for a government in which fundamental authority resided in Parliament. Until his death he defended the achievements of the revolution and held its conflicting constituents together.

But a sense that only a single person could effectively rule a state remained too strong for the reforms of the revolutionary regimes to have much chance of success. When Cromwell died in 1658 it was only natural that his eldest son, Richard, should be proposed as the new Lord Protector despite the fact that Richard had very little experience in either military or civil affairs. Nor did he have the sense of purpose that was his father's greatest source of strength. Without an individual to hold the movement together, the revolution fell apart. In 1659 the army again intervened in civil affairs, dismissing the recently elected Parliament and calling for the restoration of the monarchy

A short, sharp shock

Charles I was executed at Westminster on a bitter January afternoon in 1649. This excerpt comes from an eyewitness account of his last moments. Charles, who was accompanied on the scaffold by the bishop of London, discovered that the chopping block was very short so that he could be held down if he resisted.

And to the executioner he said, "I shall say but very short prayers, and when I thrust out my hands—"

Then he called to the bishop for his cap, and having put it on, asked the executioner, "Does my hair trouble you?" who desired him to put it all under his cap; which, as he was doing by the help of the bishop and the executioner, he turned to the bishop, and said, "I have a good cause, and a gracious God on my side."

The bishop said, "There is but one stage more, which, though turbulent and troublesome, yet is a very short one. You may consider it will soon carry you a very great way; it will carry you from earth to heaven; and there you shall find to your great joy the prize you hasten to, a crown of glory."

The king adjoins, "I go from a corruptible to an incorruptible crown; where no disturbance can be, no disturbance in the world."

The bishop. "You are exchanged from a temporal to an eternal crown—a good exchange."

Then the king asked the executioner, "Is my hair well?" . . . and looking upon the block, said . . . "You must set it fast."

The executioner. "It is fast, sir."

King. "It might have been a little higher."

Executioner. "It can be no higher, sir."

King. "When I put out my hands this way, then—"

Then having said a few words to himself, as he stood, with hands and eyes lifted up, immediately stooping down he laid his neck upon the block; and the executioner, again putting his hair under his cap, his Majesty, thinking he had been going to strike, bade him, "Stay for the sign."

Executioner. "Yes, I will, an it please your Majesty."

After a very short pause, his Majesty stretching forth his hands, the executioner at one blow severed his head from his body; which, being held up and showed to the people, was with his body put into a coffin covered with black velvet and carried into his lodging.

His blood was taken up by divers persons for different ends: by some as trophies of their villainy; by others as relics of a martyr; and in some hath had the same effect, by the blessing of God, which was often found in his sacred touch when living.

"king charles's head"

They could have killed him quietly: the executioners slipping away silently in the night, unauthorized, unknown. It was the quickest way, and it would end all doubts. Since June 1647, Charles I had been prisoner of the parliamentary army, and there had been more than one moment in which his elimination would have settled so many vexing problems. They could have let him escape: a small boat, an unlocked door, a guard conveniently asleep. Let him take his chances on the open sea. Let him live out his life in exile. Dangerous, perhaps, but still he would be gone and a new government in the name of the people could get on with creating a new order. They could have done it quietly.

Instead, the leaders of Parliament and the army decided on a trial, a public presentation of charges against the king. A high court of justice, enforcing the laws of England, would try its king for treason against the state. The logic was simple: If Parliament had fought for the preservation of the liberties of all Englishmen, then they could only proceed against the king by law. If they followed any other course, then they were usurpers, ruling by might rather than law. But if the logic was simple, everything else was hopelessly complex. English law was a system of precedents, one case stacked upon another to produce the weighty judgments of what was lawful. Never had there been a treason case like this one. Indeed, how could the king commit treason? How could he violate his own allegiance?

Nor was it clear what court had jurisdiction over this unprecedented case. The royal judges would have no part of it; neither would the House of Lords. The House of Commons was forced to create its own high court of justice, 135 supporters of the parliamentary cause drawn from its own members, from the army, and from among the leading citizens of London. Barely half attended any of the sessions. Judge John Bradshaw, who presided over two provincial royal courts, was chosen to preside at the king's trial after several of his more distinguished colleagues tactfully declined the post. Bradshaw took the precaution of lining his hat with lead against the chance that he would be shot at from the galleries rather than the floor.

These shortcomings did not deter the leaders of the parliamentary cause. These were unprecedented times, and the ossified procedures of lawyers and law courts could not be allowed to detract from the undeniable justice of their cause. Charles I had committed treason against his nation. He had declared war on his people. He had brought Irish and Scottish armies into England to repress Parliament, and when that had failed he had negotiated with French, Danish, and Dutch troops for the same purpose. Even when he had been defeated in battle, when the judgment of God was clear for all to see: even then he plotted and he tricked. His lies were revealed by his own hand, his captured correspondence detailing how he intended to double-cross those to whom he swore he would be faithful. Cromwell called him "a man against whom the Lord had witnessed," and the prosecution needed no better testimony than that. If there were no precedents, then this trial would set one.

Nevertheless, the makeshift nature of the court provided the king with his line of attack. If there was to be a public display, then Charles I was determined to turn it to his advantage. Even as his royal palace was being converted into a courtroom and an execution platform was being hastily erected on one of its balconies, even now the king could not conceive that the nation could be governed without him. Royal government had guided England for a millennium, and for all he could see would do so for another.

About the trial itself, he worried not at all. There could be no court in the land that could try its king, no authority but his own that could determine a charge of treason. When it was read out that he was a tyrant and traitor, he burst out laughing: "Remember, I am your king, your lawful king and what sins you bring upon your heads and the judgment of God upon this land, think well upon it," he told his accusers.

The trial began on Saturday, 20 January 1649. Armed soldiers in battle dress cleared the floor of the large chamber. Curious onlookers packed the galleries. Despite the fact that all former royalists had been ordered out of the city before the trial began, the king had more than one supporter well placed to heckle the commissioners. The king wore the enormous golden star of the Order of the Garter on his cloak but was allowed no other symbol of royalty to overawe his accusers.

The charge of "treason and high misdemeanors" had carefully been prepared. The king was accused of making war on his people "whereby much innocent blood of the free people of this nation hath been spilt." When the resounding indictment concluded, all eyes turned toward Charles I. Now he would have to answer the charge, guilty or not guilty, and in answering show the line of his defense. But the king chose a different strategy. Rather than answer the charge, he questioned the authority of the court. "I would know by what power I am called hither, a king cannot be tried by any superior jurisdiction here on earth." This was the weakest point of the parliamentary strategy. Judge Bradshaw could only assert that the court represented the free people of England. But Charles was relentless. He demanded precedents and refused to be silenced by the assertion that his objections were overruled.

The prosecutors had prepared a case against the king and were ready to call their witnesses. They hoped to place the king's evil conduct before the eyes of the nation. But in English law, a defendant who refused to plead was presumed to have pleaded guilty. Thus the king's trial ended as soon as it had begun. After three fruitless sessions and much behind-the-scenes maneuvering, it was decided that the king should be condemned and sentenced to die. On 27 January, Judge Bradshaw appeared in the scarlet robes of justice and issued the sentence. Charles had prepared a statement for maximum effect and waited patiently to deliver it. Now it was the king's turn to be surprised. After pronouncing sentence, Bradshaw and the commissioners rose from the bench. "Will you not hear me a word, Sir," called a flustered Charles I. "No," replied the judge. "Guards, withdraw your prisoner."

Tuesday, 30 January, dawned cold and clear. It had been a bitter winter. Charles put on two shirts so that if he trembled from the cold it would not be interpreted as fear. In fact, he made a very good end. He spoke briefly and to the point, denying that he had acted against the true interests and rights of his subjects. Then he lay down on the platform, placed his head upon the block, and prayed. As the axe fell, one witness recorded, "such a groan as I never heard before and hope never to hear again" broke forth from the crowd. The English Revolution had begun.

Allegorical view of Cromwell as savior of England. Babylon and Error are trampled under his feet. On the pillar at the right, England, Scotland, and Ireland pay him homage, and the left pillar enumerates the legal bases of his power.

stituted reform. Absolute monarchy had become constitutional monarchy, with the threat of revolution behind the power of Parliament and the threat of anarchy behind the power of the crown.

Both threats proved potent in 1685 when James II (1685–88) came to the throne. A declared Catholic, James attempted to use his power of appointment to foil the constraints that Parliament imposed on him. He elevated Catholics to leading posts in the military and in the central government and began a campaign to pack a new Parliament with his supporters. This proved too much for the governing classes, who entered into negotiations with William, Prince of Orange, husband of Mary Stuart, James's eldest daughter. In 1688 William landed in England with a small force. Without support, James II fled to France, the English throne was declared vacant, and William and Mary were proclaimed king and queen of England. There was little bloodshed in England and little threat of social disorder, and the event soon came to be called the Glorious Revolution. Its achievements were set down in the Declaration of Rights (1689), which was presented to William and Mary before they took the throne. The Declaration reasserted the fundamental principles of constitutional monarchy as they had developed over the previous half century. Security of property and the regularity of Parliaments were guaranteed. The Toleration Act (1689) granted religious freedom to nearly all groups of Protestants. The liberties of the subject and the rights of the sovereign were to be in balance.

The events of 1688 in England reversed a trend toward increasing power on the part of the Stuarts. This second episode of resistance resulted in the development of a unique form of government that a century later would spawn dozens of imitators. John Locke (1632–1704) was the theorist of the Revolution of 1689. He was heir to the century-old debate on resistance, and he carried the doctrine to a new plateau. In *Two Treatises on Civil Government* (1690), Locke developed the contract theory of government. Political society was a compact that individuals entered into freely for their own well-being. It was designed to maintain each person's natural rights—life, liberty, and property. Natural rights were inherent in individuals; they could not be given away. The contract between rulers and subjects was an agreement for the protection of natural rights. "Arbitrary power cannot consist with the ends of society and government. Men would not

to provide stability to the state. After a period of negotiation in which the king agreed to a general amnesty with only a few exceptions, the Stuarts were restored when Charles II (1649–85) took the throne in 1660.

Twenty years of civil war and revolution had had their effect. Parliament became a permanent part of civil government and now had to be managed rather than ignored. Royal power over taxation and religion was curtailed, though in fact Parliament proved more vigorous in suppressing religious dissent than the monarchy ever had. England was to be a reformed Protestant state, although there remained much dispute about what conquit the freedom of the state of nature were it not to preserve their lives, liberties, and fortunes and by stated rules to secure their peace and happiness." When rulers acted arbitrarily, they were to be deposed by their subjects, preferably in the relatively peaceful manner in which James II had been replaced by William III.

The efforts of European monarchies to centralize their power came at the expense of the Church, the aristocracy, and the localities. It was a struggle that took place over decades and was not accomplished easily. In France, the Fronde was an aristocratic backlash; in Spain, the revolt of the Catalonians pitted the Castilian crown against a proud ethnic province. In England, a civil war fought to prevent the encroachments of the crown against the rights of the community gave way to a bloody revolution that combined religious and constitutional grievances—the excesses of monarchy were succeeded by the excesses of parliamentary rule. But the lesson learned by the English ruling elites was that for a nation to enjoy the benefits of a powerful central authority, it was necessary to restrain that authority. The Glorious Revolution of 1689 helped create a constitutional balance between ruler and ruled.

The zenith of the Royal state

The crises of midcentury tested the mettle of the royal states. Over the long term, these crises had two different consequences. First, they provided a check to the exercise of royal power. Fear of recurring rebellions had a chilling effect upon policy, especially taxation. Reforms of financial administration, long overdue, were one of the themes of the later seventeenth century. Even as royal government strengthened itself, it remained concerned about the impact of its policies. Second, the memory of rebellion served to control the ambitions of factious noblemen and town oligarchs.

If nothing else, these episodes of opposition to the rising royal states made clear the universal desire for

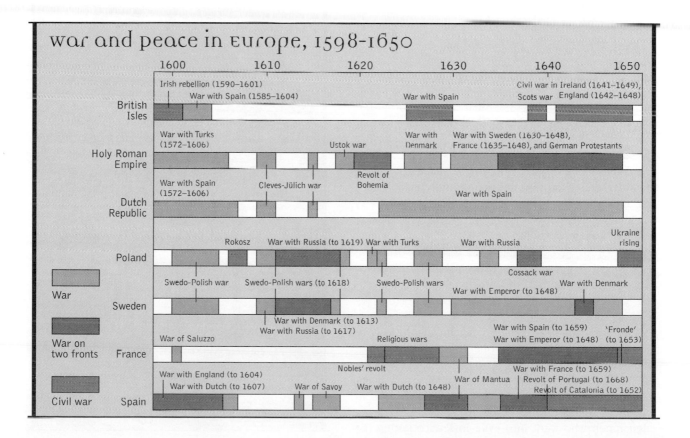

stable government, which was seen as the responsibility of both subjects and rulers. By the second half of the seventeenth century, effective government was the byword of the royal state. As Louis XIV proclaimed, rule was a trade that had to be constantly studied and practiced. The natural advantages of monarchy had to be merged with the interests of the state's citizens and their desires for wealth, safety, and honor. After so much chaos and instability, the monarchy had to be elevated above the fray of day-to-day politics; it had to become a symbol of the power and glory of the nation. Control no longer meant the greedy grasp of royal officials but rather their practiced guidance of affairs.

In England, Holland, and Sweden, a form of constitutional monarchy developed in which rulers shared power, in varying degrees, with other institutions of state. In England it was Parliament, in Holland the town oligarchies, and in Sweden the nobility. But in most other states in Europe there developed a pure form of royal government known as absolutism. Absolute monarchy revived the divine-right theories of kingship and added to them a cult of the personality of the ruler. Absolutism was practiced in states as dissimilar as Denmark, Brandenburg-Prussia, and Russia. It reached its zenith in France under Louis XIV, the most powerful of the seventeenth-century monarchs.

The Nature of Absolute Monarchy

Locke's theory of contract provided one solution to the central problem of seventeenth-century government: how to balance the monarch's right to command and the subjects' duty to obey. By establishing a constitutional monarchy in which power was shared between the ruler and a representative assembly of subjects, England found one path out of this thicket. But it was not a path that many others could follow. The English solution was most suited to a state that was largely immune from invasion and land war. Constitutional government required a higher level of political participation of citizens than did an absolute monarchical one. Greater participation in turn meant greater freedom of expression, greater toleration of religious minorities, and greater openness in the institutions of government. All were dangerous. The price that England paid was a half century of governmental instability.

The alternative to constitutional monarchy was absolute monarchy. It too found its greatest theorist in England. Thomas Hobbes (1588–1679) was one of many Englishmen who went into exile in France during the

course of the English civil wars. In his greatest work, *Leviathan* (1651), Hobbes argued that before civil society had been formed, humans lived in a savage state of nature, "in a war of every man against every man." This was a ghastly condition without morality or law—"the notions of right and wrong, of justice and injustice have there no place." People came together to form a government for the most basic of all purposes: self-preservation. Without government they were condemned to a life that was "solitary, poor, nasty, brutish, and short." To escape the state of nature, individuals pooled their power and granted it to a ruler. The terms of the Hobbesian contract were simple. Rulers agreed to rule; subjects agreed to obey. When the contract was intact, people ceased to live in a state of nature. When it was broken, they returned to it. With revolts, rebellions, and revolutions erupting in all parts of Europe, Hobbes's state of nature never seemed very far away.

The title page of the first edition of Thomas Hobbes's Leviathan, *published in 1651. The huge figure, composed of many tiny human beings, symbolizes the surrender of individual human rights to those of the state.*

For most states of Europe in the later seventeenth century, absolute monarchy became not only a necessity but an ideal. The consolidation of power in the hands of the divinely ordained monarch who nevertheless ruled according to principles of law and justice was seen as the perfect form of government. Absolutism was an expression of control rather than of power. If the state was sometimes pictured as a horse, the absolute monarch gripped the reins more tightly than the whip. "Many writers have tried to confound absolute government with arbitrary government. But no two things could be more unlike," wrote Bishop Jacques Bossuet (1627–1704), who extolled absolutism in France. The absolute ruler ruled in the interests of his people: "The prince is the public person, the whole state is included in him, the will of all the people is enclosed within his own."

The main features of absolute monarchy were all designed to extend royal control. As in the early seventeenth century, the person of the monarch was revered. Courts grew larger and more lavish in an effort to enhance the glory of the monarchy, and thereby of the state. "L'état, c'est moi"—"I am the state"—Louis XIV was supposed to have said. No idea better expresses absolutism's connection between governor and governed. As the king grew in stature, his competitors for power all shrank. Large numbers of nobles were herded together at court under the watchful eye of monarchs who now ruled rather than reigned. The king shed the cloak of his favorites and rolled up his own sleeves to manage state affairs. Representative institutions, especially those that laid claim to control over taxation, were weakened or cast aside for obstructing efficient government and endangering the welfare of the state. Monarchs needed standing armies, permanent forces that could be drilled and trained in the increasingly sophisticated arts of war. Thus the military was expanded and made an integral part of the machinery of government. The military profession developed within nations, gradually replacing mercenary adventurers who had fought for booty rather than for duty.

Yet the absolute state was never as powerful in practice as it was in theory, nor did it ever exist in its ideal shape. Absolutism was always in the making, never quite made. Its success depended upon a strong monarch who knew his own will and could enforce it. It

Fathers Know Best

Sir Robert Filmer's *Patriarcha* (1680) is one of the clearest statements of the divine origins of monarchy in human society. Filmer believed that Adam, the first father, was monarch of the universe and that his children owed him absolute obedience. *Patriarcha* was written a half century before it was published in 1680.

In all kingdoms or commonwealths in the world, whether the prince be the supreme father of the people or but the true heir of such a father . . . there is, and always shall be continued to the end of the world, a natural right of a supreme father over every multitude, although, by the secret will of God, many at first do most unjustly obtain the exercise of it.

To confirm this natural right of regal power, we find in the decalogue that the law which enjoins obedience to kings is delivered in the terms of 'honour thy father' [Exodus, xx, 12] as if all power were originally in the father. If obedience to parents be immediately due by a natural law, and subjection to princes but by the mediation of an human ordinance, what reason is there that the law of nature should give place to the laws of men? . . .

If we compare the natural duties of a father with those of a king, we find them to be all one, without any difference at all but only in the latitude or extent of them. As the father over one family, so the king, as father over many families, extends his care to preserve, feed, clothe, instruct and defend the whole commonwealth. His wars, his peace, his courts of justice and all his acts of sovereignty tend only to preserve and distribute to every subordinate and inferior father, and to their children, their rights and privileges, so that all the duties of a king are summed up in an universal fatherly care of his people.

From Sir Robert Filmer, *Patriarcha*.

depended upon unity within the state and the absence or ruthless suppression of religious or political minorities. The absolute ruler needed to control information and ideas, to limit criticism of state policy. Ultimately, the absolute state rested upon the will of its citizens to support it. The seventeenth-century state remained a loose confederation of regions, many acquired by conquest, whose loyalty was practical rather than instinctive. There was no state police force to control behavior or attitudes, no newspapers or mass communication to spread propaganda. Censorship might restrict the flow of forbidden books, but it could do little to dam up the current of ideas.

Absolutism in the East

Frederick William, the Great Elector of Brandenburg-Prussia (1640–88), was one of the European princes who made the most effective use of the techniques of absolutism. In 1640 he inherited a scattered and ungovernable collection of territories that had been devastated by the Thirty Years' War. Brandenburg, the richest of his possessions, had lost nearly half of its population. The war had a lasting impact on Frederick William's character. As a child he had hidden in the woods to escape bands of marauding soldiers; as a teenager he had followed to its burial the corpse of Gustavus Adolphus, the man he most admired and wished to emulate. A long stay in Holland during the final stages of the Dutch Revolt impressed on him the importance of a strong army and a strong base of revenue to support it.

Frederick William had neither. In 1640 his forces totaled no more than 2500 men, most of them, including the officers, the dregs of German society. Despite the fact that he was surrounded by powerful neighbors—Sweden and Poland both claimed sovereignty over parts of his inheritance—the territories under his control had no tradition of military taxation. The nobility, known as the Junker, enjoyed immunity from almost all forms of direct taxation, and the towns had no obligation to furnish either men or supplies for military operations beyond their walls. When Frederick William attempted to introduce an excise—the kind of commodity tax on consumption that had so successfully financed the Dutch Revolt and the English Revolution—he was initially rebuffed. But military emergency

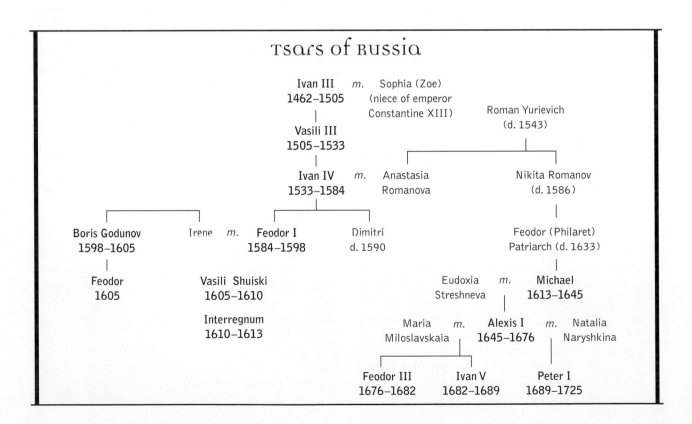

Tsars of Russia

Ivan III *m.* Sophia (Zoe) (niece of emperor Constantine XIII)

Vasili III 1505–1533

Ivan IV 1533–1584 *m.* Anastasia Romanova

Roman Yurievich (d. 1543)

Nikita Romanov (d. 1586)

Boris Godunov 1598–1605

Irene *m.* Feodor I 1584–1598

Dimitri d. 1590

Feodor (Philaret) Patriarch (d. 1633)

Feodor 1605

Vasili Shuiski 1605–1610

Interregnum 1610–1613

Eudoxia Streshneva *m.* Michael 1613–1645

Maria Miloslavskaia *m.* Alexis I 1645–1676 *m.* Natalia Naryshkina

Feodor III 1676–1682

Ivan V 1682–1689

Peter I 1689–1725

overcame legal precedents. By the 1650s Frederick William had established the excise in the towns, though not on the land.

With the excise as a steady source of revenue, the Great Elector could now create one of the most capable standing armies of the age. The strictest discipline was maintained in the new army, and the Prussian army developed into a feared and efficient fighting machine. Frederick William organized one of the first departments of war to oversee all of the details of the creation of his army, from housing and supplies to the training of young officer candidates. This department was also responsible for the collection of taxes. By integrating military and civilian government, Frederick William was able to create an efficient state bureaucracy that was particularly responsive in times of crisis. The creation of the Prussian army was the force that led to the creation of the Prussian state.

The same materials that forged the Prussian state led to the transformation of Russia. Soon after the young tsar Peter I (1682–1725) came to the throne, he realized that he could compete with the western states only by learning to play their game. In 1697 Peter visited the West, ostensibly to build an alliance against the Turks but actually to learn as much as he could about Western military technology. He loved novelty and introduced new agricultural products like wine and potatoes to his subjects. When he determined that Russians should no longer wear beards, he took a hand in cutting them off. When he was persuaded of the benefits of dentistry, he practiced it himself on his terrified subjects. His campaign to westernize Russia frequently confused the momentous with the inconsequential, but it had an extraordinary impact at all levels of government and society.

Like those of Frederick William, Peter's greatest reforms were military. Peter realized that if Russia were to flourish in a world dominated by war and commerce, it would have to reestablish its hold on the Baltic ports. This meant dislodging the Swedes from the Russian mainland and creating a fleet to protect Russian trade. Neither goal seemed likely. The Swedes were one of the great powers of the age, constant innovators in battlefield tactics and military organization. Peter studied their every campaign. His first wars against the Swedes ended in humiliating defeats, but with each failure came a sharper sense of what was needed to succeed.

First Peter introduced a system of conscription that resulted in the creation of a standing army. Conscripts were branded to inhibit desertion, and a strict disci-

In his campaign to modernize Russia, Peter the Great declared that the nobles should shear off their beards, which were a symbol of their status. In this illustration, a clean-shaven Peter wields the scissors himself.

pline was introduced to prepare the soldiers for battle. Peter unified the military command at the top and stratified it in the field. He established promotion based on merit. For the first time, Russian officers were given particular responsibilities to fulfill during both training and battle. Peter created military schools to train cadets for the next generation of officers.

Finally, in 1709, Peter realized his ambitions. At the battle of Poltava, the Russian army routed the Swedes, wounding King Charles XII, annihilating his infantry, and capturing dozens of his leading officers. That night Peter toasted the captured Swedish generals. He claimed that everything he knew about warfare he had learned from them, and he congratulated them on their success as teachers. After the battle of Poltava, Russia gradually replaced Sweden as the dominant power in the Baltic.

A close shave

Peter the Great made many efforts to westernize Russia after his travels in Holland and England. He reformed the navy, built a great seaport at St. Petersburg, and instituted an array of governmental reforms. But nothing was so prominent as or affected ordinary people more than his edicts on beards and clothing.

The tsar labored at the reform of fashions, or, more properly speaking, of dress. Until that time the Russians had always worn long beards, which they cherished and preserved with much care, allowing them to hang down on their bosoms, without even cutting the moustache. With these long beards they wore the hair very short, except the ecclesiastics, who, to distinguish themselves, wore it very long. The tsar, in order to reform that custom, ordered that gentlemen, merchants, and other subjects, except priests and peasants, should each pay a tax of one hundred rubles a year if they wished to keep their beard; the commoners had to pay one kopeck each. Officials were stationed at the gates of the towns to collect that tax, which the Russians regarded as an enormous sin on the part of the tsar and as a thing which tended to the abolition of their religion.

These insinuations, which came from the priests, occasioned the publication of many pamphlets in Moscow, where for that reason alone the tsar was regarded as a tyrant and a pagan; and there were many old Russians who, after having their beards shaved off, saved them preciously, in order to have them placed in their coffins, fearing that they would not be allowed to enter heaven without their beards. As for the young men, they followed the new customs with the more readiness as it made them appear more agreeable to the fair sex.

From the reform in beards we may pass to that of clothes. Their garments, like those of the Orientals, were very long, reaching to the heel. The tsar issued an ordinance abolishing that costume, commanding all the boyars (nobles) and all those who had positions at the court to dress after the French fashion, and likewise to adorn their clothes with gold or silver according to their means. . . .

The same ordinance also provided that in the future women, as well as men, should be invited to entertainments, such as weddings, banquets, and the like, where both sexes should mingle in the same hall, as in Holland and England. It was likewise added that these entertainments should conclude with concerts and dances, but that only those should be admitted who were dressed in English costumes. His Majesty set the example in all these changes.

From "De Missy's Life of Peter."

Like everything else about him, Peter the Great's absolutism was uniquely his own. But though Peter's power was unlimited, it was not uncontested. He secularized the Russian Orthodox church, subjecting it to the control of state power and confiscating much of its wealth in the process. He broke the old military service class, which attempted a coup d'état when Peter was abroad in the 1690s. By the end of his reign, the Russian monarchy was among the strongest in Europe.

The origins of french Absolutism

Nowhere was absolutism as successfully implanted as in France. Louis XIII (1610–43) was only eight years old when he came to the throne, and he grew slowly into his role under the tutelage of Cardinal Richelieu. It was Richelieu's vision that stabilized French government. As chief minister, Richelieu saw clearly that the prosperity and even the survival of France depended upon strengthening royal power. He preached a doctrine of *raison d'état*—reason of state—in which he placed the needs of the nation above the privileges of its most important groups. Richelieu saw three threats to stable royal government: "The Huguenots shared the state, the nobles conducted themselves as if they were not subjects, and the most powerful governors in the provinces acted as if they were sovereign in their office."

Richelieu took measures to control all three. The power of the nobles was the most difficult to attack. The nobles' long tradition of independence from the crown

Russia Under Peter the Great

The Battle of Poltava (1709). The defeat of King Charles XII led to the decline of Swedish power in the Baltic.

had been enhanced by the wars of religion. Perhaps more importantly, the ancient aristocracy, the nobility of the sword, felt themselves in a particularly vulnerable position. Their world was changing and their traditional roles were becoming obsolete. Professional soldiers replaced them at war, professional administrators at government. Mercantile wealth threatened their economic superiority; the growth of the nobility of the robe—lawyers and state officials—threatened their social standing. They were hardly likely to take orders from a royal minister like Richelieu, especially when he attacked one of the great symbols of their power, the duel.

To limit the power of local officials, Richelieu used intendants to examine their conduct and to reform their administration. He made careful appointments of local governors and brought more regions under direct royal control. Against the Huguenots, Richelieu's policy was more subtle. He was less interested in challenging their religion than their autonomy. In 1627, when the English sent a force to aid the Huguenots against the government, Richelieu and Louis XIII abolished the Huguenots' privileges altogether. They were allowed to maintain their religion, but not their special status. They would have no privileges other than to be subjects of the king of France.

Richelieu's program was a vital prelude to the development of absolute monarchy in France. But the cardinal was not a king. While it is clear that Richelieu did not act without the full support of Louis XIII and clear that the king initiated many reforms for which the cardinal received credit, there can be no doubt that Richelieu was the power behind the throne. Louis XIII hated the business of government and even neglected his principal responsibility of providing the state with an heir. For years he and his wife slept in separate palaces, and only a freak rainstorm in Paris forced him to spend a night with the queen, Anne of Austria, in 1637. It was the night Louis XIV was conceived. Louis XIII and Richelieu died within six months of each other in 1642 and 1643, and the nation again endured the turmoil of a child king. Richelieu's aggressive policy to curb the nobility and his stringent financial program in the 1630s helped precipitate the Fronde. Louis XIV (1643–1715) was never to forget the terror of the aristocratic rebellion in Paris: how he was forced to flee the capital in the dead of night, how he endured the penury of exile, how he suffered the humiliation of being bossed about by the rebels. He would never forget, and he would have a long time to remember.

Louis le Grand

Not quite five years old when he came to the throne, Louis XIV was tutored by Cardinal Jules Mazarin (1602–61), Richelieu's successor as chief minister. If anything, Mazarin was more ruthless and less popular than his predecessor. An Italian from a modest background, Mazarin won the money to launch his career at the gaming table. Good fortune seemed to follow him everywhere. He gambled with his life and his career, and each time he raked in the stakes. He died with the largest private fortune that had ever been accumulated by a French citizen, easily surpassing the fortune of Richelieu. Like Richelieu, whom he emulated, Mazarin was an excellent administrator who had learned well the lessons of raison d'état. At the conclusion of the Thirty Years' War, for example, Mazarin refused to make peace with Spain, believing that the time was ripe to deliver a knockout blow to the Spanish Habsburgs.

In order to pacify the rebellious nobility of the Fronde, who opposed Mazarin's power, Louis XIV was declared to have reached his majority at the age of 13. But it was not until Mazarin died ten years later in 1661 that the king began to rule. Louis was blessed with able and energetic ministers. The two central props of his state—money and might—were in the hands of dynamic men, Jean-Baptiste Colbert (1619–83) and the Marquis de Louvois (1639–91). Colbert—to whom credit belongs for the building of the French navy, the reform of French legal codes, and the establishment of national academies of culture—was Louis's chief minister for finance. Colbert's fiscal reforms were so successful that in less than six years a debt of 22 million French pounds had become a surplus of 29 million. Colbert achieved this astonishing feat not by raising taxes but by increasing the efficiency of their collection. Until Louis embarked on his wars, the French state was solvent.

To Louvois, Louis's minister of war, fell the task of reforming the French army. During the Fronde, royal troops were barely capable of defeating the makeshift forces of the nobility. By the end of the reign, the army had grown to 400,000 and its organization had thoroughly been reformed. Louvois introduced new ranks for the field officers who actually led their men into battle, and promotions were distributed by merit rather than purchase. He also solved one of the most serious logistical problems of the age by establishing storehouses of arms and ammunition throughout the realm. The greatest achievements of the reign were built on

This Hyacinthe Rigaud portrait of Louis XIV in his coronation robes shows the splendor of Le Roi Soleil *(the Sun King), who believed himself to be the center of France as the sun is the center of the solar system.*

the backs of fiscal and military reforms, which were themselves a product of the continuing sophistication of French administration.

Louis XIV furthered the practice of relying on professional administrators to supervise the main departments of state and offer advice on matters of policy. He created a separation between courtiers and officeholders and largely excluded the nobility of the sword from the inner circles of government, which were composed of ministers of departments and small councils that handled routine affairs. These councils were connected to the central advisory body of government, the secret council of the king. Within each department, ministers furthered the process of professionalization that led to the advancement of talented clerks, secretaries, and administrators. Although there still remained a large gulf between the promulgation of policy at Versailles and its enforcement in the provinces, it was now a gulf that could be measured and ultimately bridged. Louis XIV built on the institution of the intendant that Richelieu had developed with so much success. Intendants were now a permanent part of government, and their duties expanded from their early responsibilities as coordinators and mediators into areas of policing and tax collection. It was through the intendants that the wishes of central government were made known in the provinces.

Although Louis XIV was well served, it was the king himself who set the tone for French absolutism. "If he was not the greatest king, he was the best actor of majesty that ever filled the throne," wrote an English observer. The acting of majesty was central to Louis's rule. His residence at Versailles was the most glittering court of Europe, renowned for its beauty and splendor. It was built on a scale never before seen, and Louis took a personal interest in making sure it was fit for a king. When the court and king moved there permanently in 1682, Versailles became the envy of the Continent. But behind the imposing facade of Versailles stood a well-thought-out plan for domestic and international rule.

Louis XIV attempted to tame the French nobles by requiring their attendance at his court. Louis established a system of court etiquette so complex that constant study was necessary to prevent humiliation. While the nobility studied decorum they could not plot rebellion. At Versailles one never knocked on a door; one scratched with a fingernail. This insignificant custom had to be learned and remembered—it was useless anywhere else—and practiced if one hoped for the favor of the king. Leading noblemen of France rose at dawn so that they could watch Louis be awakened and hear him speak his first words. Dozens followed him from hall to gallery and from gallery to chamber as he washed, dressed, prayed, and ate.

This aura of court culture was equally successful in the royal art of diplomacy. During Louis's reign, France replaced Spain as the greatest nation in Europe. Massive royal patronage of art, science, and thought brought French culture to new heights. The French language replaced Latin as the universal European tongue.

France was the richest and most populous European state, and Louis's absolute rule finally harnessed these resources to a single purpose. France became a commercial power rivaling the Netherlands, a naval power rivaling England, and a military power without peer. It was not only for effect that Louis took the image of the sun as his own. In court, in the nation, and throughout Europe everything revolved around him.

France's rise to preeminence in Europe was undoubtedly the greatest accomplishment of the absolute monarchy of Louis XIV. But it did not come without costs. Louis XIV made his share of mistakes, which were magnified by the awe in which his opinions were held. His aggressive foreign policy ultimately bankrupted the crown. But without doubt his greatest error was to persecute the Huguenots. As an absolute ruler, Louis believed that it was necessary to have absolute conformity and obedience. The existence of the Huguenots, with their separate communities and distinct forms of wor-

Gian Lorenzo Bernini, The Ecstasy of St. Theresa. In this work, depicting the ecstatic vision of St. Theresa, the sixteenth-century Spanish Carmelite reformer, the saint floats toward heaven on seemingly weightless marble as an angel is about to pierce her breast with a burning arrow. The artist's creation depicts a mystic vision St. Theresa experienced and described in her writings.

A symbolic drawing shows how heretics will be driven from France by the Sun King. Such a policy proved shortsighted, however, as thousands of Huguenot émigrés enriched Louis's potential enemies with their valuable skills.

ship, seemed an affront to his authority. Almost from the beginning, Louis allowed the persecution of Protestants, despite the protection provided by the Edict of Nantes. Protestant churches were pulled down, conversions to Catholicism were bought with the lure of immunities from taxation, and children were separated from their families to be brought up in Catholic schools. Finally, in 1685 Louis XIV revoked the Edict of Nantes. All forms of Protestant worship were outlawed, and the ministers who were not hunted down and killed were forced into exile. Despite a ban on Protestant emigration, over 200,000 Huguenots fled the country, many of them carrying irreplaceable skills with them to Holland and England in the west and Brandenburg in the east.

Supporters of the monarchy celebrated the revocation of the Edict of Nantes as an act of piety. Religious toleration in seventeenth-century Europe was still a policy of expediency rather than of principle. Even the English, who prided themselves on developing the concept of toleration, and the Dutch, who welcomed Jews to Amsterdam, would not officially tolerate Catholics. But the persecution of the Huguenots was a social and political disaster for France. Those who fled to other Protestant states spread the stories of atrocities that stiffened European resolve against Louis. Those who remained became an embittered minority who pulled at the fabric of the state at every chance. Nor did the official abolition of Protestantism have much effect upon its existence. Against these policies, the Huguenots held firm to their beliefs. There were well over a million French Protestants, undoubtedly the largest religious minority in any state. Huguenots simply went underground, practicing their religion secretly and gradually replacing their numbers. No absolutism, however powerful, could succeed in eradicating religious beliefs.

Louis XIV gave his name to the age that he and his nation dominated, but he was not its only towering figure. The Great Elector, Peter the Great, Louis the Great—so they were judged by posterity, kings who had forged nations for a new age. Their style of rule showed the royal state at its height, still revolving around the king but more and more dependent upon permanent institutions of government that followed their own imperatives. The absolute state harnessed the economic and intellectual resources of the nation to the political will of the monarch. It did so to ensure survival in a dangerous world. But while monarchs ruled as well as reigned, they did so by incorporating vital elements of the state into the process of government. In England the importance of the landholding classes was recognized in the constitutional powers of Parliament. In Prussia the military power of the Junker was asserted through command in the army, the most important institution of the state. In France Louis XIV co-opted many nobles at his court while making use of a talented pool of lawyers, clergymen, and administrators in his government. A delicate balance existed between the will of the king and the will of the state, a balance that would soon lead these continental powers into economic competition and military confrontation.

Mastering the chapter

To review the main points of the chapter, be sure you can explain the significance of each of the following.

Terms/Concepts/Events	People	Places
divine right of kings	Elizabeth I	Catalonia
intendants	James VI and I	Barcelona
resistance theory	Cardinal Richelieu	Naseby
Fronde	Louis XIV	Brandenburg-Prussia
Petition of Right	Cardinal Mazarin	Poltava
Puritans	Oliver Cromwell	Versailles
Long Parliament	John Locke	
Glorious Revolution	Thomas Hobbes	
Toleration Act	Peter the Great	
revocation of the Edict of Nantes	Jean-Baptiste Colbert	

suggestions for further Reading

General Reading

* Thomas Munck, *Seventeenth Century Europe, 1598–1700* (New York: St. Martin's Press, 1990). The most up-to-date survey.

* William Doyle, *The Old European Order* (Oxford: Oxford University Press, 1978). An important synthetic essay, bristling with ideas.

* Geoffrey Parker, *Europe in Crisis, 1598–1648* (London: William Collins and Sons, 1979). The best introduction to the period.

  Perry Anderson, *Lineages of the Absolutist State* (London: NLB Books, 1974). A sociological study of the role of absolutism in the development of the Western world.

* Eric Cochrane, C. M. Gray, and Mark Kishlansky, eds., *Early Modern Europe: Crisis of Authority* (Chicago: University of Chicago Press, 1987). A collection of source materials from the University of Chicago readings in Western Civilization.

The Rise of the Royal State

* Graham Parry, *The Golden Age Restor'd* (New York: St. Martin's Press, 1981). A study of English court culture in the reigns of James I and Charles I.

  J. H. Elliott and Jonathan Brown, *A Palace for a King* (New Haven, CT: Yale University Press, 1980). An outstanding work on the building and decorating of a Spanish palace.

* J. N. Figgis, *The Divine Right of Kings* (Cambridge: Cambridge University Press, 1914). Still the classic study of this central doctrine of political thought.

* Yves-Marie Bercé, *The Birth of Absolutism* (London: Macmillan, 1996). A history of France from the reign of Louis XIV to the eve of the Revolution by a leading historian of France.

  Glenn Burgess, *Absolute Monarchy and the Stuart Constitution* (New Haven, CT: Yale University Press, 1996). The interrelationship of theories of monarchy and absolutism in England.

* J. H. Elliott, *Richelieu and Olivares* (Cambridge: Cambridge University Press, 1984). A brilliant dual portrait.

* Roger Lockyer, *Buckingham* (London: Longman, 1984). A stylish biography of the favorite of two monarchs.

The Crises of the Royal State

* Quentin Skinner, *The Foundations of Modern Political Thought*. 2 vols. (Cambridge: Cambridge University Press, 1978). A seminal work on the history of ideas from Machiavelli to Calvin.

* Perez Zagoin, *Rebels and Rulers*. 2 vols. (Cambridge: Cambridge University Press, 1982). A good survey of revolutions, civil war, and popular protests throughout Europe.

* Trevor Aston, ed., *Crisis in Europe, 1600–1660* (Garden City, NY: Doubleday, 1967). Essays on the theme of a general crisis in Europe by distinguished historians.

  G. Parker and L. Smith, eds., *The General Crisis of the Seventeenth Century* (London: Routledge & Kegan Paul, 1978). A collection of essays on the problem of the general crisis.

  M. A. Kishlansky, *A Monarchy Transformed* (London: Penguin Books, 1996). The most recent survey of a remarkable era.

* Lawrence Stone, *The Causes of the English Revolution* (New York: Harper & Row, 1972). A vigorously argued explanation of why England experienced a revolution in the mid-seventeenth century.

* Ann Hughes, *The Causes of the English Civil War* (New York: St. Martin's Press, 1991). A lucid introduction to the scholarship of a vast subject.

* D. E. Underdown, *Pride's Purge* (London: Allen & Unwin, 1985). The most important work on the politics of the English Revolution.

Jonathan Israel, ed., *The Anglo-Dutch Moment* (Cambridge: Cambridge University Press, 1991). Essays by an international team of scholars on the European dimensions of the Revolution of 1688.

* W. A. Speck, *The Revolution of 1688* (Oxford: Oxford University Press, 1988). The best single volume on the event that transformed England into a global power.

The zenith of the Royal State

* Geoffrey Parker, *The Military Revolution* (Cambridge: Cambridge University Press, 1988). A lucid discussion of how power was organized and deployed in the early modern state.

* H. W. Koch, *A History of Prussia* (London: Longman, 1978). A comprehensive study of Prussian history, with an excellent chapter on the Great Elector.

* Paul Dukes, *The Making of Russian Absolutism* (London: Longman, 1982). A thorough survey of Russian history in the seventeenth and eighteenth centuries.

* Vasili Klyuchevsky, *Peter the Great* (London: Random House, 1958). A classic work, still the best study of Peter.

* W. E. Brown, *The First Bourbon Century in France* (London: University of London Press, 1971). A good introduction to French political history.

* William Beik, *Absolutism and Society in Seventeenth Century France* (Cambridge: Cambridge University Press, 1985). The single best study of the government of a French province in the seventeenth century.

Joseph Bergin, *The Rise of Richelieu* (New Haven, CT: Yale University Press, 1991). A fascinating portrait of a consummate politician.

Richard Bonney, *Society and Government in France Under Richelieu and Mazarin, 1624–61* (Basingstoke: Macmillan, 1988). An excellent introduction by a master of the period.

Peter Burke, *The Fabrication of Louis XIV* (New Haven, CT: Yale University Press, 1992). A compelling account of a man and a myth.

* Peter R. Campbell, *Louis XIV, 1661–1715* (London: Longman, 1993). A brief account accompanied by source material and an up-to-date bibliography.

* John Wolf, *Louis XIV* (New York: Norton, 1968). An outstanding biography of the Sun King.

*Paperback edition available.

science and commerce in early modern europe

Rembrandt's Lessons

By the early seventeenth century, interest in scientific investigation had spread out from narrow circles of specialists to embrace educated men and women. One of the more spectacular demonstrations of new knowledge was public dissection, by law performed only on the corpses of criminals. Here the secrets of the human body were revealed both for those who were training to be physicians and those who had the requisite fee and strong stomach. Curiosity about the human body was becoming a mark of education. New publications, both scientific and popular, spread ancient wisdom as well as the controversial findings of the moderns. Pictures drawn on the basis of dissections filled the new medical texts, like the one on the stand at the feet of the corpse in *The Anatomy Lesson of Dr. Nicolaes Tulp* (1632) by Rembrandt van Rijn (1606–69).

Dr. Tulp's anatomy lesson was not meant for the public. In fact, those gathered around him in various poses of concentration were not students at all. They were members of the Amsterdam company of surgeons, the physicians' guild of the early seventeenth century. The sitters had commissioned the picture, which was a celebration of themselves as well as of the noted Professor Tulp. They hired the young Rembrandt to compose the picture with the assurance that each of the sitters (whose names are written on the paper one of them holds in his hand) would appear as if he alone were the subject of a portrait. Rembrandt succeeded beyond expectation. Each individual was given his due. The expressions on their faces as much as their physical characteristics mark each one out from the group. Yet the portraits were only one part of the painting. The scene that Rembrandt depicted unified them. They became a group by their participation in the anatomy lesson. Rembrandt has chosen a moment of drama to stop the action. Dr. Tulp is demonstrating how the gesture he is making with his left hand would be made by the tendons in the arm of the gruesome cadaver. The central figures of the group are rapt in attention, though only one of them is actually observing the procedure of the dissection. Each listens to Tulp, comparing his own experience and knowledge to that of the professor and the text that stands open.

The *Anatomy Lesson* established the 25-year-old Rembrandt as one of the most gifted and fashionable painters in Amsterdam. If any people could be said to be consumers of art in seventeenth-century Europe, it was the Dutch. Artists flourished and pictures abounded. Travelers were struck by the presence of artwork in both public and private places and in the homes of even moderately prosperous people. The group portrait, which Rembrandt brought to new levels of expression, was becoming a favorite genre. It was used to celebrate the leaders of Dutch society, who— unlike the leaders of most other European states—were not princes and aristocrats, but rather merchants, guild officials, and professionals. Rembrandt captured a spirit of civic pride in his group portraits. Here it was the surgeons' guild; later it would be the leaders of the cloth merchants' guild, another time a militia company.

Like the leaders of the surgeons' guild, who hung their commissioned portraits in their company's hall, the Dutch Republic swelled with pride in the seventeenth century. Its long war with Spain was finally drawing to a close, and it was time to celebrate the birth of a new state. The Dutch were a trading people, and their trade flourished as much in times of war as in times of peace. Their ships traveled to all parts of the globe, and they dominated the great luxury trades of the age. Bankers and merchants were the backbone of the Dutch Republic. Yet this republic of merchants was also one of the great cultural centers of the Continent. Intellectual creativity was cultivated in the same manner as was a trading partner. In the burgeoning port of Amsterdam, the fastest-growing city in Europe, artists, philosophers, and mathematicians lived cheek by jowl. The free exchange of ideas made Amsterdam home to those exiled for their beliefs. The Dutch practiced religious toleration as did no one else. Catholics, Protestants, and Jews all were welcomed to the Dutch Republic and found that they could pursue their own paths without persecution. Freedom of thought and freedom of expression helped develop a new spirit of scientific inquiry, like that portrayed in *The Anatomy Lesson of Dr. Nicolaes Tulp*.

Focus Questions

1. What was new about the methods and ideas of Copernicus, Brahe, Kepler, and Galileo, and why were they threatening to Catholic doctrine?
2. In what ways did the new science build upon traditional ideas associated with alchemy, astrology, and Hermetic thinking; in what ways was it a departure?
3. What new technologies, trading practices, and financial devices assisted the expansion of long-distance trading?
4. Why were the Dutch especially well suited to participate in the worldwide expansion of European commerce?
5. How did the governments of the various European nations promote their own commercial interests?

The New Science

And new Philosophy calls all in doubt,
The element of fire is quite put out;
The sun is lost and the earth, and no man's wit
Can well direct him where to look for it.

So wrote the English poet John Donne (1572–1631) about one of the most astonishing yet perplexing moments in the history of Western thought: the emergence of the new science. It was astonishing because it seemed truly new. The discoveries of the stargazers, like those of the sea explorers, challenged people's most basic assumptions and beliefs. Men dropping balls from towers or peering at the skies through a glass claimed that they had disproved thousands of years of certainty about the nature of the universe: "And new Philosophy calls all in doubt." But the new science was perplexing because it seemed to loosen the moorings of everything that educated people thought they knew about their world. Nothing could be more disorienting than to challenge common sense. One needed to do little more than wake up in the morning to know that the sun moved from east to west while the earth stood still. But mathematics, experimentation, and deduction were needed to understand that the earth was in constant motion and that it revolved around the sun—"And no man's wit/ Can well direct him where to look for it."

The scientific revolution was the opening of a new era in European history. After two centuries of classical revival, European thinkers had finally come against the limits of ancient knowledge. Ancient wisdom had served Europeans well, and it was not to be discarded lightly. But one by one, the certainties of the past were being called into question. The explanations of the universe and the natural world that had been advanced by Aristotle and codified by his followers no longer seemed adequate. There were too many contradictions between theory and observation, too many things that did not fit. Yet breaking the hold of Aristotelianism was no easy task. A full century was to pass before even learned people would accept the proofs that the earth revolved around the sun. Even then, the most famous of them—Galileo—had to recant these views or be condemned as a heretic.

The two essential characteristics of the new science were that it was materialistic and mathematical. Its materialism was contained in the realization that the universe is composed of matter in motion. This meant that the stars and planets were not made of some perfect ethereal substance but of the same matter that was found on earth. They were thus subject to the same rules of motion as were earthly objects. The mathematics of the new science was contained in the realization that calculation had to replace common sense as the basis for understanding the universe. Mathematics itself was transformed with the invention of logarithms, analytic geometry, and calculus. More importantly, scientific experimentation took the form of measuring repeatable phenomena. When Galileo attempted to develop a theory of acceleration, he rolled a brass ball down an inclined plane and recorded the time and distance of its descent 100 times before he was satisfied with his results.

The new science was also a Europe-wide movement. The spirit of scientific inquiry flourished everywhere. The main contributors to astronomy were a Pole, a Dane, a German, and an Italian. The founder of medical chemistry was Swiss; the best anatomist was Belgian. England contributed most of all—the founders of modern chemistry, biology, and physics. By and large, these scientists operated outside the traditional seats of learning at the universities. Although most were university trained and not a few taught the traditional Aristotelian subjects, theirs was not an academic movement. Rather, it was a public one made possible by the printing press. Once published, findings became building blocks for scientists throughout the Continent and from one generation to the next. Many discoveries were made in the search for practical solutions to ordinary problems, and what was learned fueled advances in technology and the natural sciences. The new science gave seventeenth-century Europeans a sense that they might finally master the forces of nature.

Heavenly Revolutions

There was much to be said for Aristotle's understanding of the world, for his cosmology. For one thing, it was harmonious. It incorporated a view of the physical world that coincided with a view of the spiritual and moral one. The heavens were unchangeable, and therefore they were better than the earth. The sun, moon, and planets were all faultless spheres, unblemished and immune from decay. Their motion was circular because the circle was the perfect form of motion. The earth was at the center of the universe because it was the heaviest planet and because it was at the center of

This chart of the heavens was engraved by Andreas Cellarius in 1660. It portrays the heliocentric universe described by Nicolaus Copernicus and accepted by Galileo. Earth and Jupiter are shown with moons orbiting them.

the Great Chain of Being, between the underworld of spirits and the upper world of gods. The second advantage to the Aristotelian world view was that it was easily incorporated into Christianity. Aristotle's description of the heavens as being composed of a closed system of crystalline rings that held the sun, moon, and planets in their circular orbits around the earth left room for God and the angels to reside just beyond the last ring.

There were, of course, problems with Aristotle's explanation of the universe as it was preserved in the work of Ptolemy, the greatest of the Greek astronomers. For one thing, if the sun revolved in a perfect circle around the earth, then why were the seasons not perfectly equal? If the planets all revolved around the earth in circles, then why did they look nearer or farther, brighter or darker at different times of year? To solve these problems, a host of ingenious hypotheses were advanced. Perhaps the sun revolved around the earth in an eccentric circle, that is, a circle not centered on the earth. This would account for the differing lengths of seasons. Perhaps the planets revolved in circles that rested on a circle around the earth. Then, when the planet revolved

within the larger circle, it would seem nearer and brighter, and when it revolved outside it, it would seem farther away and darker. This was the theory of epicycles. Yet to account for the observable movement of all the known planets, there had to be 55 of these epicycles, these circles within circles. As ingeniously complex as they were, the modifications of Aristotle's views made by the theories of eccentric circles and epicycles had one great virtue. they accurately predicted the movements of the planets. Although they were completely hypothetical, they answered the most troubling questions about the Aristotelian system.

In the 1490s, Nicolaus Copernicus (1473–1543) came to the Polish University of Krakow, which had one of the leading mathematical faculties in Europe. There they taught the latest astronomical theories and vigorously debated the existence of eccentric circles and epicycles. Copernicus came to Krakow for a liberal arts education before pursuing a degree in Church law. He became fascinated by astronomy and puzzled by the debate over planetary motion. Copernicus believed, like Aristotle, that the simplest explanations were the best. If the sun

Epicycle and Eccentric circles

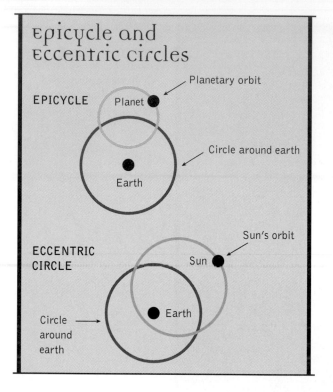

EPICYCLE

Planet

Planetary orbit

Circle around earth

Earth

ECCENTRIC CIRCLE

Sun's orbit

Sun

Earth

Circle around earth

was at the center of the universe and the earth simply another planet in orbit, then many of the most elaborate explanations of planetary motion were unnecessary. "At rest, in the middle of everything is the sun," Copernicus wrote in *On the Revolutions of the Heavenly Spheres* (1543). "For in this most beautiful temple who would place this lamp in another or better position than that from which it can light up the whole thing at the same time?" Because Copernicus accepted most of the rest of the traditional Aristotelian explanation, especially the belief that the planets moved in circles, his sun-centered universe was only slightly better at predicting the position of the planets than the traditional earth-centered one, but Copernicus's idea stimulated other astronomers to make new calculations.

Under the patronage of the king of Denmark, Tycho Brahe (1546–1601) built a large observatory to study planetary motion. In 1572 Brahe discovered a nova, a brightly burning star that was previously unknown. This discovery challenged the idea of an immutable universe composed of crystalline rings. In 1577 the appearance of a comet cutting through the supposedly

stargazing

Nicolaus Copernicus was born in Poland and educated at the University of Krakow, which had one of the greatest mathematics faculties of the age. He prepared for a career in the church, but his abiding interest was the study of astronomy. Through observation and calculation, Copernicus worked out a heliocentric view of the universe in which the earth revolved on an axis and orbited the sun. His pathbreaking work was not published until the year of his death, and he was fully aware of the implications of his discovery.

For, first, the mathematicians are so unsure of the movements of the Sun and Moon that they cannot even explain or observe the constant length of the seasonal year. Secondly, in determining the motions of these and of the other five planets, they use neither the same principles and hypotheses nor the same demonstrations of the apparent motions and revolutions. . . . Nor have they been able thereby to discern or deduce the principal thing—namely the shape of the Universe and the unchangeable symmetry of its parts. . . .

Thus assuming motions, which in my work I ascribe to the Earth, by long and frequent observations

I have at last discovered that, if the motions of the rest of the planets be brought into relation with the circulation of the Earth and be reckoned in proportion to the circles of each planet, not only do their phenomena presently ensue, but the orders and magnitudes of all stars and spheres, nay the heavens themselves, become so bound together that nothing in any part thereof could be moved from its place without producing confusion of all the other parts of the Universe as a whole.

From Copernicus, *On the Revolutions of Heavenly Spheres* (1543).

STELLÆBURGUM sive OBSERVATORIUM SUBTERRANEVM, A TYCHONE BRAHE Nobili Dano
IN INSULA HVÆNA, EXTRA ARCEM URANIAM. EXTRVCTVM CIRCA ANNVM M D LXXXIIII.

Tycho Brahe designed and built this observatory, much of which was constructed underground. In each of the large cupolas were instruments through which Brahe and his collaborators could make their celestial observations. Astronomers could also view the heavens through apertures in the flat roofs of the underground chambers.

impenetrable rings punched another hole into the old cosmology. Brahe's own views were a hybrid of old and new. He believed that all planets but the earth revolved around the sun and that the sun and the planets revolved around a fixed earth. To demonstrate this theory, Brahe and his students compiled the largest and most accurate mathematical tables of planetary motion yet known. From this research, Brahe's pupil Johannes Kepler (1571–1630), one of the great mathematicians of the age, formulated laws of planetary motion. Kepler discovered that planets orbited the sun in an elliptical rather than a circular path. This accounted for their movements nearer and farther from the earth. More importantly, he demonstrated that there was a precise mathematical relationship between the speed with which a planet revolved and its distance from the sun. Kepler's findings supported the view that the galaxy was heliocentric and that the heavens, like the earth, were made of matter that was subject to physical laws.

What Kepler demonstrated mathematically, the Italian astronomer Galileo Galilei (1564–1642) confirmed by observation. Creating a telescope by using magnifying lenses and a long tube, Galileo saw parts of the heavens that had never been dreamed of before. In 1610 he discovered four moons of Jupiter, proving conclusively that all heavenly bodies did not revolve around the earth. He observed the landscape of the earth's moon and described it as full of mountains, valleys, and rivers. It was of the same imperfect form as the earth itself. He even found spots on the sun, which suggested that it, too, was composed of ordinary matter. Through the telescope, Galileo gazed upon an unimaginable universe. "The Galaxy is nothing else but a mass of innumerable stars," he wrote. Galileo's greatest scientific discoveries had to do with motion—he was the first to posit a law of inertia—but his greatest contribution to the new science was his popularization of the Copernican theory. He took the debate over the structure of the universe to the public, popularizing the discoveries of scientists in his vigorous Italian tracts.

As news of his experiments and discoveries spread, Galileo became famous throughout the Continent, and his support for heliocentrism became a celebrated cause. In 1616 the Roman Catholic church cautioned him against promoting his views. In 1633, a year after publishing his A *Dialogue Between the Two Great Systems of the World*, Galileo was tried by the Inquisition and forced

The Telescope

No single individual is as much associated with the Scientific Revolution as Galileo Galilei. He made formative contributions to mathematics, physics, and astronomy, but he also served as a lightning rod for the dissemination of the newest ideas. He popularized the work of Copernicus and was condemned by the Catholic church for his views and publications. He ended his life under house arrest. Among his other accomplishments, Galileo was the first to use a telescope to make scientific observations.

About ten months ago a report reached my ears that a certain Fleming had constructed a spyglass by means of which visible objects, though very distant from the eye of the observer, were distinctly seen as if nearby. Of this truly remarkable effect several experiences were related, to which some persons gave credence while others denied them. A few days later the report was confirmed to me in a letter from a noble Frenchman at Paris, Jacques Badovere, which caused me to apply myself wholeheartedly to inquire into the means by which I might arrive at the invention of a similar instrument. This I did shortly afterwards, my basis being the theory of refraction. First I prepared a tube of lead, at the ends of which I fitted two glass lenses, both plane on one side while on the other side one was spherically convex and the other concave. Then placing my eye near the concave lens I perceived objects satisfactorily large and near, for they appeared three times closer and nine times larger than when seen with the naked eye alone. Next I constructed another one, more accurate, which represented objects as enlarged more than sixty times. Finally, sparing neither labor nor expense, I succeeded in constructing for myself so excellent an instrument that objects seen by means of it appeared nearly one thousand times larger and over thirty times closer than when regarded with our natural vision.

It would be superfluous to enumerate the number and importance of the advantages of such an instrument at sea as well as on land. But forsaking terrestrial observations, I turned to celestial ones, and first I saw the moon from as near at hand as if it were scarcely two terrestrial radii. . . .

. . . Let us speak first of that surface of the moon which faces us. For greater clarity I distinguish two parts of this surface, a lighter and a darker; the lighter part seems to surround and to pervade the whole hemisphere, while the darker part discolors the moon's surface like a kind of cloud, and makes it appear covered with spots. . . . From observation of these spots repeated many times I have been led to the opinion and conviction that the surface of the moon is not smooth, uniform, and precisely spherical as a great number of philosophers believe it (and the other heavenly bodies) to be, but is uneven, rough, and full of cavities and prominences, being not unlike the face of the earth, relieved by chains of mountains and deep valleys.

From Galileo, *The Starry Messenger* (1610).

specifically to recant the idea that the earth moves. He spent the rest of his life under house arrest. Galileo insisted that there was nothing in the new science that was anti-Christian. He rejected the view that his discoveries refuted the Bible, arguing that the words of the Bible were often difficult to interpret and that nature was another way in which God revealed himself. In fact, Galileo feared that the Church's opposition to what he deemed as scientific truth could only bring the Church into disrepute. (See "The Trials of Galileo," pp. 560–561.)

The Natural World

The new science originated from a number of traditions that were anything but scientific. Inquiry into nature and the environment grew out of the discipline of natural philosophy and was nurtured by spiritual and mystical traditions. Much of the most useful medical knowledge had come from the studies of herbalists; the most reliable calculations of planetary motion had come from astrologers. Although the first laboratories and observatories were developed in aid of the new science, practice in them was as much magical as experimental. For those attempting to unlock the mysteries of the universe, there was no separation between magic and science. Some of the most characteristic features of modern science, such as the stress on experimentation and empirical observation, developed only gradually. What was new about the new science was the determination to develop systems of thought that could help humans understand and control their environment. Thus there was a greater openness and spirit of cooperation about discoveries than in the past, when experiments were conducted secretly and results were kept hidden away.

Aristotelianism was not the only philosophical system to explain the nature and composition of the universe. During the Renaissance the writings of Plato had attracted a number of Italian humanists, most notably Marsilio Ficino (1433–99) and Pico della Mirandola (1463–94). These Neoplatonic humanists taught Plato's theory that the world was composed of ideas and forms that were hidden by the physical properties of objects. They believed that the architect of the universe possessed the spirit of a geometrician and that the perfect disciplines were music and mathematics. These elements of Neoplatonism created an impetus for the mathematically based studies of the new scientists. They were especially important among the astronomers, who used both calculation and geometry in exploring the heavens. But they also served to bolster the sciences of alchemy and astrology. Alchemy was the use of fire in the study of metals, an effort to find the essence of things through their purification. While medieval alchemists mostly attempted to find gold and silver as the essence of lead and iron, the new experimentation focused on the properties of metals in general. Astrology was the study of the influence of the stars on human behavior, calculated by planetary motion and the harmony of the heavenly spheres. Astrologers made careful calculations based on the movement of the planets and were deeply involved in the new astronomy. The Neoplatonic emphasis on mathematics also accorded support for a variety of mystical sciences based on numerology. These were efforts to predict events from the combination of particular numbers.

The most influential of these mystical traditions was that associated with Hermes Trismegistus ("Thrice Greatest"), an Egyptian who was reputed to have lived in the second century A.D. and to have known the secrets of the universe. A body of writings mistakenly attributed to Hermes was discovered during the Renaissance and formed the basis of a Hermetic tradition. The core of Hermetic thinking was belief in a universal spirit that was present in all objects and that spontaneously revealed itself. Kepler was one of many of the new scientists influenced by Hermeticism. His efforts to understand planetary motion derived from his search for a unifying spirit.

A combination of Neoplatonic and Hermetic traditions was central to the work of one of the most curious of the new scientists, the Swiss alchemist Paracelsus (1493–1541). Paracelsus studied with a leading German alchemist before following in his father's footsteps by becoming a physician. Although he worked as a doctor, his true vocation was alchemy, and he conducted innumerable experiments designed to extract the essence of particular metals. Paracelsus taught that all matter was composed of combinations of three principles: salt, sulfur, and mercury. This view replaced the traditional belief in the four elements of earth, water, fire, and air.

Although the Paracelsian system was peculiar, it transformed ideas about chemistry and medicine. Paracelsus rejected the theory that disease was caused by an imbalance in the humors of the body—the standard view of Galen, the great Greek physician of the second century A.D. Instead, Paracelsus argued that each disease had its own cause, which could be diagnosed and remedied. Where traditional doctors treated disease by bloodletting or sweating to correct the patient's imbalance of humors, Paracelsus prescribed the ingestion of particular chemicals—especially distilled metals like mercury, arsenic, and antimony—and he favored administering them at propitious astrological moments.

Paracelsus's experimentation with metals and his practice of diagnostic medicine gave a practical turn to the study of alchemy. Efforts to cure new diseases like syphilis led to the continued study of the chemical properties of substances and to a new confidence about medical science. Although established physicians and medical faculties rejected Paracelsian cures and methods, his influence spread among ordinary practitioners. It ultimately had a profound impact on the studies of Robert Boyle (1627–91), an Englishman who helped es-

The Trials of Galileo

For eight years he had held his peace. Since 1616 he had bided his time, waiting for a change in the attitudes of the Catholic authorities—or, as he believed, waiting for reason to prevail. For a time he had even abandoned his astronomical investigations for the supposedly safer fields of motion and physics. Even there, Aristotle had been wrong. No matter what he touched, his reason showed him that the conclusions of Aristotle, the conclusions adopted and supported by the Roman Catholic church, were wrong. Now finally, with the accession of Pope Urban VIII, old Cardinal Barbarini, who was himself a mathematician, Galileo felt confident that he could resume his writing and publishing.

Galileo's rebellion began early, when he decided to study mathematics rather than medicine. Galileo was fascinated with the manipulation of numbers, and by the age of 25 was teaching at the University of Pisa. There he began to conduct experiments to measure rates of motion. Galileo was soon in trouble with his colleagues and was forced to leave Pisa for Padua.

It was in Padua that his real difficulties began. After seeing a small prototype made in Holland, Galileo developed a telescope that could magnify objects to 30 times their size, which made it possible to see clearly the stars and planets that had been only dimly perceptible before. In 1610 Galileo had looked at the moon and discovered that its properties were similar to those of the earth. He had seen four moons of Jupiter, the first conclusive proof that there were heavenly bodies that did not revolve around the earth. Even before he had gazed at the stars, Galileo was persuaded that Copernicus must be right in arguing that the earth revolved around the sun. Now he believed he had irrefutable proof: the proof of his own eyes.

From the publication of *The Starry Messenger* in 1610, Galileo became the most active and best known advocate of the Copernican universe. In 1616 he was called to Rome and warned about his opinions. Belief in the theories of Copernicus was heresy, he was told. If Galileo held or maintained them, he would incur a heavy penalty. The Church accepted unequivocally the Ptolemaic explanations of the structure of the universe and could cite innumerable passages in the Bible to support them. It was willful and stubborn to oppose official doctrine, doctrine that had been frequently and fully examined. At first it seemed that Galileo would be silenced, but the erudite Cardinal Bellarmine, to whom the case had been assigned, wished only to caution him. Galileo might still examine the Copernican hypotheses; he might still discuss them with his learned colleagues, as long as he did not hold or maintain them to be true.

For eight years Galileo kept his peace. When he decided to write again, it was in the belief that things were changing. He created a dialogue between a Ptolemaist and a Copernican. Let the one challenge the other on the most basic points, just as if they were in formal academic dispute. How did each explain the most difficult things that there were to explain, the existence of spots on the sun or the movement of the tides? Especially the tides. . . . If the earth stood still and the sun moved, why were there tides in the seas that moved with such regularity that they could be predicted?

Galileo was no heretic. He had no desire to challenge the Church. He would not print his tract anonymously in a Protestant country. Rather, he would create a true dialogue, one with which not even the most narrow-minded censor of the Roman church could find fault. He submitted his book to the official censor in Rome for approval, then to the official censor in Florence. The censors struck out passages, changed some words and deleted others. They demanded a new preface, even a new title: *A Dialogue Between the Two Great Systems of the World.* Finally, in 1632, the book went to press and was an immediate success.

Indeed, it was a success that could not be ignored. The Jesuits, who regarded learning and education as their special mission, demanded that action be taken against Galileo. Their teachings had been held up to ridicule; their official astronomers had been challenged; their doctrines had been repudiated. There was much at stake. Galileo's book had not been the vigorous academic dispute that he promised, and it had not concluded with the triumph of Church doctrine over the speculations of Copernicus. No, it had been advocacy. Anyone could see where the author's true sympathies lay. The character chosen to speak the part of Aristotle was not named Simplicio for nothing. Although this was the name of an ancient Aristotelian, it was also a perfect description of the arguments that the speaker advanced. Especially in the matter of the tides, Galileo had reduced the Aristotelian position to nonsense. The Jesuits brought their case directly to the pope and won an investigation, an investigation that they knew would end with Galileo's condemnation.

Although initially Pope Urban VIII was reluctant to prosecute the 70-year-old astronomer, "the light of Italy," ultimately he had no choice. The great war to stamp out heresy was going badly for the Church. The pope needed the support of the Jesuits in Vienna and in Madrid much more than he needed the support of a scientist who had seen the moons of Jupiter. Nevertheless, when the case was turned over to the Inquisition, it proved weak in law. Galileo had only to present the book itself to show that he had received the official sanction of not one, but two censors of the Roman Catholic church. If there was still anything in his book that offended, could the fault be his alone?

The argument stymied the prosecutors, who were forced to find evidence where none existed. Resurrecting the agreement between Galileo and Bellarmine, they attempted to make it say that Galileo was under an ab-

These drawings of Galileo's moon observations accompanied the first draft of The Starry Messenger. Galileo correctly interpreted the bright spots that appear on the dark part of the moon as mountain peaks.

solute ban from even discussing the Copernican theories. Either Galileo would agree to recant his views, admit his errors, and beg the forgiveness of the Church or he would be tried and burned as a heretic. But though he could be forced to recant his view that the earth orbits the sun, Galileo could not be forced to change his mind.

After his recantation, Galileo was sentenced to live out his days under house arrest. Five years after his death in 1642, his greatest scientific work, *The Two New Sciences*, was smuggled out of Italy and printed anonymously in Holland.

The alchemist Heinrich Khunrath included this picture of himself in his book on alchemy (1609). The chapel and laboratory combined symbolizes the union of the physical processes with divine principles.

tablish the basis of the science of chemistry. Boyle devoted his energies to raising the study of medical chemistry above that of merely providing recipes for the cure of disease. He worked carefully and recorded each step in his experiments. Boyle's first important work, *The Sceptical Chymist* (1661), attacked both Aristotelian and Paracelsian views of the basic components of the natural world. Boyle rejected both the four humors and the three principles. Instead he favored an atomic explanation in which matter "consisted of little particles of all sizes and shapes." Changes in these particles, which would later be identified as the chemical elements, resulted in changes in matter. Boyle's most important experiments were with gases—a word invented by Paracelsus. He formulated the relationship between the volume and pressure of a gas (Boyle's law) and invented the air pump.

The new spirit of scientific inquiry also affected medical studies. The study of anatomy through dissection had helped the new scientists reject many of the descriptive errors in Galen's texts. The Belgian doctor Andreas Vesalius (1514–64), who was physician to the emperor Charles V, published the first modern set of anatomical drawings in 1543, the same year that Copernicus published his work. But accurate knowledge of the composition of the body did not also mean better understanding of its operation. Dead bodies didn't easily yield the secrets of life. Much of what was known about matters as common as reproduction was a combination of ancient wisdom and the practical experiences of midwives and doctors. Both were woefully inadequate.

One of the greatest mysteries was the method by which blood moved through the vital organs. It was generally believed that the blood originated in the liver, traveled to the right side of the heart, and then passed to the left side through invisible pores. Anatomical investigation proved beyond doubt that there was blood in both sides of the heart, but no one could discover the pores through which it passed. William Harvey (1578–1657), an Englishman who had received his medical education in Italy, offered an entirely different explanation. Harvey was employed as royal physician to both James I and Charles I and had one of the most lucrative medical practices in Europe. His real interest, however, was in studying the anatomy of the heart. Harvey examined hearts in more than 40 species before concluding that the heart worked like a pump or, as he

put it, a water bellows. Harvey observed that the valves of the heart's chambers allowed the blood to flow in only one direction. He thus concluded that the blood was pumped by the heart and circulated throughout the entire body.

The greatest of all English scientists was the mathematician and physicist Sir Isaac Newton (1642–1727). It was Newton who brought together the various strands of the new science. He merged the materialists and Hermeticists, the astronomers and astrologers, the chemists and alchemists. He made stunning contributions to the sciences of optics, physics, astronomy, and mathematics, and his magnum opus, *Mathematical Principles of Natural Philosophy* (1687), is one of a handful of the most important scientific works ever composed. Most important, Newton solved the single most perplexing problem: if the world was composed of matter in motion, what was motion?

Newton came from a moderately prosperous background and was trained at a local grammar school before entering Cambridge University. There was little in his background or education to suggest his unique talents, and in fact his most important discoveries were not appreciated until years after he had made them. Newton was the first to understand the composition of light, the first to develop a calculus, and the first to build a reflecting telescope. Newton became a professor at Cambridge, but he spent much of his time alone. He made a great study of Hermetic writings and from them revived the mystical notions of attraction and repulsion.

Although Galileo had developed a *theory of inertia*, the idea that a body at rest stays at rest, most materialists believed that motion was inherent in objects. In contrast, Newton believed that motion was the result of the interaction of objects and that it could be calculated mathematically. From his experiments he formulated the concept of force and his famous laws of motion: (1) that objects at rest or of uniform linear motion remain in such a state unless acted upon by an external force; (2) that changes in motion are proportional to force; and (3) that for every action there is an equal and opposite reaction. From these laws of motion, Newton advanced one step further. If the world was no more than matter in motion and if all motion was subject to the same laws, then the movement of the planets could be explained in the same way as the movement of an apple falling from a tree. There was a mathematical relationship between attraction and repulsion—a universal gravitation, as Newton called it—that governed the

Tenth "Muscle Plate" from Andreas Vesalius's De Humani Corporis Fabrica (Concerning the Fabric of the Human Body), *published in 1543. The muscles of the back of the body are laid bare.*

movement of all objects. Newton's theory of gravity joined together Kepler's astronomy and Galileo's physics. The mathematical, materialistic world of the new science was now complete.

science enthroned

By the middle of the seventeenth century, the new science was firmly established throughout Europe. Royal and noble patrons supported the enterprise by paying some of the costs of equipment and experimentation. Royal observatories were created for astronomers, colleges of physicians for doctors, and laboratories for chemists. Both England and France established royal societies of learned scientists to meet together and discuss their discoveries. The French Académie des Sciences (1666) was composed of 20 salaried scientists and an equal number of students, representing the different branches of scientific learning. They met twice weekly throughout the year, and each member worked on a project of his own devising. The English Royal Society (1662) boasted some of the greatest minds of the age. It was there that Newton first made public his most important discoveries. Scientific bodies were also formed outside the traditional universities. These were the so-called mechanics colleges, like Gresham College in London, where the practical applications of mathematics and physics were studied and taught. Navigation was a particular concern of the college, and the faculty established close ties with the Royal Navy and with London merchants.

The establishment of learned scientific societies and practical colleges fulfilled part of the program advocated by Sir Francis Bacon (1561–1626), one of the leading supporters of scientific research in England. In *The Advancement of Learning* (1605), Bacon had proposed a scientific method through inductive empirical experimentation. Bacon believed that experiments should be carefully recorded so that results were both reliable and repeatable. He advocated the open world of the scientist over the secret world of the magician. In his numerous writings, he stressed the practical impact of scientific discovery and even wrote a utopian work in which science appeared as the savior of humanity. Although he was not himself a scientific investigator, Bacon used his considerable influence to support scientific projects in England.

Bacon's support for the new science contrasts markedly with the stance taken by the Roman Catholic church. Embattled by the Reformation and the wars of religion, the Church had taken the offensive in preserving the core of its heritage. By the early seventeenth century, the missionary work of the Jesuits had won many reconversions and had halted the advance of

Joseph Wright of Derby, An Experiment on a Bird in the Air Pump (1768). Traveling lecturers fed the growing popular interest in science and often enlivened their talks with demonstrations of the air pump. The demonstration usually involved placing a live animal in a glass receiver attached to a pumping apparatus. Air was pumped out to demonstrate the animal's reaction to the loss of air. If air was readmitted in time, the animal would revive. Normally the bird used in the experiment would have been a sparrow or some other common species. The artist has taken some liberty—and created a decidedly more dramatic picture— by depicting a white cockatoo as the subject of the demonstration.

Protestantism. Now the new science appeared to be another heresy. Not only did it confound ancient wisdom and contradict Church teachings, but it was also a lay movement that was neither directed nor controlled from Rome. The trial of Galileo slowed the momentum of scientific investigation in Catholic countries and starkly posed the conflict between authority and knowledge. But the stand taken by the Church was based on more than narrow self-interest. Ever since Copernicus had published his views, a new skepticism had emerged among European intellectuals. Every year new theories competed with old ones, and dozens of contradictory explanations for the most common phenomena were advanced and debated. The skeptics concluded that nothing was known and nothing was knowable. Their position led inevitably to the most shocking of all possible views: atheism.

There was no necessary link between the new science and an attack upon established religion: so Galileo had argued all along. Few of the leading scientists ever saw a contradiction between their studies and their faith. Sir Robert Boyle endowed a lectureship for the advancement of Christian doctrine and contributed money for the translation of the New Testament into Turkish. Still, by the middle of the century attacks on the Church were increasing, and some blamed the new science for them. Thus it was altogether fitting that one of the leading mathematicians of the day should also provide the method for harmonizing faith and reason.

René Descartes (1596–1650) was the son of a provincial lawyer and judge. He was trained in one of the best Jesuit schools in France before taking a law degree in 1616. While it was his father's intention that his son practice law, it was René's intention that he become educated in "the school of life." He entered military service in the Dutch Republic, and after the outbreak of the Thirty Years' War served in the Duke of Bavaria's army. Descartes was keenly interested in mathematics, and during his military travels he met and was tutored by a leading Dutch mathematician. For the first time he learned of the new scientific discoveries and of the advances made in mathematics. In 1619 he dreamed that he had discovered the scientific principles of universal knowledge. After this dream, Descartes returned to Holland and began to develop his system. He was on the verge of publishing his views when he learned of the Church's condemnation of Galileo. Reading Galileo's *Dialogue Between the Two Great Systems of the World*, Descartes discovered that he shared many of the same opinions

and had worked out mathematical proofs for them. He refrained from publishing until 1637 when he brought out his *Discourse on Method*.

In the *Discourse on Method*, Descartes demonstrated how skepticism could be used to produce certainty. He began by declaring that he would reject everything that could not be clearly proved beyond doubt. Thus he rejected his perception of the material world, the testimony of his senses—all known or imagined opinions. He was left only with doubt. But what was doubt, if not thought, and what was thought, if not the workings of his mind? The only thing of which he could be certain, then, was that he had a mind. Thus his famous formulation: "I think, therefore I am." From this first certainty came another: the knowledge of perfectibility. He knew that he was imperfect and that a perfect being had to

René Descartes, the seventeenth-century French mathematician, philosopher, and scientist. He remained a faithful Catholic all his life while questioning the very foundations of Catholic philosophy.

have placed that knowledge within him. Therefore, a perfect being—God—existed.

Descartes's philosophy, known as Cartesianism, rested on the dual existence of matter and mind. Matter was the material world, subject to the incontrovertible laws of mathematics. Mind was the spirit of the creator. Descartes was one of the leading mechanistic philosophers, believing that all objects operated in accord with natural laws. He invented analytic geometry and made important contributions to the sciences of optics and physics on which Newton would later build. Yet it was in his proof that the new science could be harmonized with the old religion that Descartes made his greatest contribution to the advancement of learning. Despite the fact that his later work was condemned by the Catholic church and that he preferred the safety of Protestant Holland to the uncertainty of his Catholic homeland, Cartesianism became the basis for the unification of science and religion.

"I shall attempt to make myself intelligible to everyone," Descartes wrote. Like many of the new scientists, he preferred the use of vernacular languages to elite Latin, hoping that his work would reach beyond the narrow bounds of high culture. Descartes was one of many new scientists who saw the practical import of what they had learned and who hoped to bring that knowledge to the aid of the material well-being of their contemporaries. John Dee (1527–1608) translated the Greek geometrician Euclid into English so that ordinary people might "find out and devise new works, strange engines and instruments for sundry purposes in the commonwealth." Although many of the breakthrough discoveries of the new scientists would not find practical use for centuries, the spirit of discovery was to have great impact in an age of commerce and capital. The quest for mathematical certainty and prime movers led directly to improvements in agriculture, mining, navigation, and industrial activity. It also brought with it a sense of control over the material world that provided a new optimism for generations of Europeans.

empires of goods

Under the watchful eye of the European states, a worldwide marketplace for the exchange of commodities had been created. First the Dutch and then the

The Geographer *by Jan Vermeer van Delft, 1669. A Dutch cartographer, holding dividers, is shown surrounded by charts, a globe, and other paraphernalia of his craft. Such cartographers combined the skills of artist and mathematician.*

English had established monopoly companies to engage in exotic trades in the East. First the Spanish and Portuguese, then the English and French had established colonial dependencies in the Atlantic that they carefully nurtured in hope of economic gain. Protected trade had flourished beyond the wildest dreams of its promoters. Luxury commodities became staples; new commodities became luxuries. Trade enhanced the material life of all Europeans, though it came at great cost to the Asians, Africans, and Latin Americans whose labor and raw materials were converted into the new crazes of consumption.

While long-distance trade was never as important to the European economy as inland and intracontinental trade, its development in the seventeenth and eighteenth centuries had a profound impact on lifestyles, economic policy, and, ultimately, warfare. The Dutch became the first great commercial power. Their achievements were based on innovative techniques, rational management, and a social and cultural environment that supported mercantile activities. Dutch society was freer than any other; it was open to new capital, new ventures, and new ideas. The Dutch improved the organization of trade by developing the concept of the entrepôt, a place where goods were brought for storage before being exchanged. They pioneered in finance by establishing the Bank of Amsterdam. They led in shipbuilding by developing the flyboat, a long, flat-hulled vessel designed specifically to carry bulky cargoes like grain. They traded around the globe with the largest mercantile fleet yet known. It was not until the end of the seventeenth century that England and France surpassed the Dutch. This reversal owed less to new innovations than it did to restrictions on trade. Because the Dutch dominated the European economy, the French and English began to pass laws to eliminate Dutch competition. The English banned imports carried in Dutch ships; the French

banned Dutch products. Both policies cut heavily into the Dutch superiority, and both ultimately resulted in commercial warfare.

The Marketplace of the World

By the sixteenth century, all the major trading routes had already been opened. The Spanish moved back and forth across the Atlantic; the Dutch and Portuguese sailed around the tip of Africa to the Indian Ocean. The Baltic trade connected the eastern and western parts of Europe as Danes, Swedes, and Dutch exchanged Polish and Russian raw materials for English and French manufactured goods. The Mediterranean, which had dominated world trade for centuries, was still a vital artery of intercontinental trade, but its role was diminishing. In 1600 almost three-quarters of the Asian trade was still land based, much of it carried through the Middle East to the Mediterranean. A century later, nearly all Asian trade was carried directly to western Europe by Dutch and English vessels. Commercial power was shifting to the northern European states just as dramatically as military and political power.

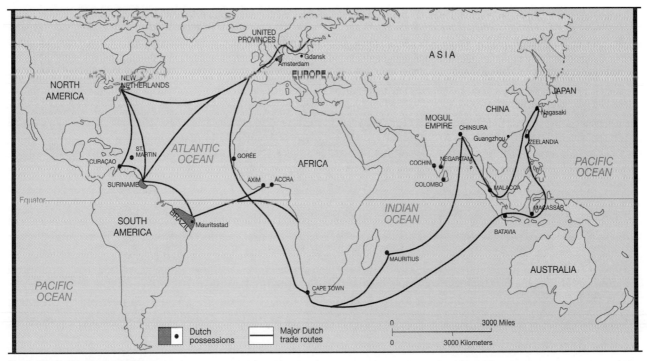

Dutch Trade Routes, ca. 1650

The technology associated with commerce achieved no breakthroughs to compare with the great transformations of the fifteenth century, when new techniques of navigation made transatlantic travel possible. It is certainly true that there continued to be improvements. The astronomical findings of the new science were a direct aid to navigation, as were the recorded experiences of so many practiced sea travelers. The materials used to make and maintain ships improved with the importation of pitch and tar from the east and with the greater availability of iron and copper from Scandinavia. It was the Dutch who made the single most important innovation in shipbuilding. To gain maximum profit from their journeys to the Baltic, the Dutch designed the so-called flyboats. Flyboats sacrificed speed and maneuverability, but they were cheap to build and could be manned by small crews. They carried no heavy armaments and were thus well adapted to the serene Baltic trade.

It was unspectacular developments like the flyboat that had such an impact on seventeenth- and eighteenth-century transcontinental trade. Innovation, organization, and efficient management were the principal elements of what historians have called the commercial revolution. Concerted efforts to maximize opportunities and advantages accounted for the phenomenal growth in the volume and value of commercial exchange. One of the least spectacular and most effective breakthroughs was the replacement of bilateral with triangular trade. In bilateral trade, the surplus commodities of one community were exchanged for those of another. This method, of course, restricted the range of trading partners to those with mutually desirable surplus production: England and Italy were unlikely to swap woolens or Sicily and Poland to trade grain. For those with few desirable commodities, bilateral trade meant the exchange of precious metals for goods, and throughout much of the sixteenth and early seventeenth centuries, bullion was by far the most often traded commodity. Triangular trade created a larger pool of desirable goods. British manufactured goods could be traded to Africa for slaves, the slaves could be traded in the West Indies for sugar, and the sugar could be consumed in Britain. Moreover, the merchants involved in shifting these goods from place to place could achieve profits on each exchange. Indeed, their motive in trading could now change from dumping surplus commodities to matching supply and demand.

Equally important were the changes made in the way trade was financed. As states, cities, and even individuals could stamp their own precious metal, there were hundreds of different European coins with different nominal and metallic values. The influx of American silver further destabilized an already unstable system of exchange. The Bank of Amsterdam was created in 1609 to establish a uniform rate of exchange for the various currencies traded in that city. From this useful function a second developed—transfer, or giro, banking, a system that had been invented in Italy. In giro banking, various merchant firms held money on account and issued bills of transfer from one to another. This transfer system meant that merchants in different cities did not have to transport their precious metals or endure long delays in having their accounts settled.

Giro banking also aided the development of bills of exchange, an early form of checking. Merchants could conclude trades by depositing money in a given bank or merchant house and then having a bill drawn for the sum they owed. Bills of exchange were especially important in international trade, as they made large-scale shipments of precious metals to settle trade deficits unnecessary. By the end of the seventeenth century bills of exchange had become negotiable; that is, they could pass from one merchant to another without being redeemed. Thus a Dutch merchant could buy French wines in Bordeaux with a bill of exchange drawn on an account in the Bank of Amsterdam. The Bordeaux merchant could then purchase Spanish oranges and use the same bill of exchange as payment. There were two disadvantages to this system: ultimately the bill had to return to Amsterdam for redemption; and when it did, the account on which it was drawn might be empty. The establishment of the Bank of England in 1694 overcame these difficulties. The Bank of England was licensed to issue its own bills of exchange, or bank notes, which were backed by the revenue from specific English taxes. This security of payment was widely sought after, and the Bank of England soon became a clearinghouse for all kinds of bills of exchange. The Bank would buy in bills at a discount, paying less than their face value, and pay out precious metal or their own notes in exchange.

The effects of these and many other small-scale changes in business practice helped fuel prolonged growth in European commerce. It was the European merchant who made this growth possible by accepting the risks of each individual transaction and building up small pools of capital from which successive transactions could take place. Most mercantile ventures were conducted by individuals or families and were based on the specialized trade of a single commodity. Trade offered high returns because it entailed high risks. The long delays in moving goods and their uncertain arrival; the unreliability of agents and the unscrupulousness of other traders; and the inefficiencies in transport and communication all weighed heavily against success. Those who succeeded did so less by luck than by hard work. They used family members to receive shipments. They lowered shipping costs by careful packaging. They lowered protection costs by securing their trade routes. Financial publications lowered the costs of information. Ultimately, lower costs meant lower prices. For centuries luxury goods had dominated intercontinental trade. But by the eighteenth century, European merchants had created a world marketplace in which the luxuries of the past were the common fare of the present.

consumption choices

As long-distance trade became more sophisticated, merchants became more sensitive to consumer tastes. Low-volume, high-quality goods like spices and silks could not support the growing merchant communities in the European states. These goods were the preserve of the largest trading companies and, more importantly, they had reached saturation levels by the early seventeenth century. The price of pepper, the most used of all spices, fell nearly continuously after 1650. Moreover, triangular trade allowed merchants to provide a better match of supplies and demands. The result was the rise to prominence of a vast array of new commodities, which not only continued the expansion of trade but also reshaped diet, lifestyles, and patterns of consumption. New products came from both East and West. Dutch and English incursions into the Asian trade provoked competition with the Portuguese and expanded the range of commodities that were shipped back to Europe. An aggressive Asian triangle was created in which European bullion bought Indonesian spices that were exchanged for Persian silk and Chinese and Japanese finished goods. In the Atlantic, the English were quick to develop both home and export markets for a variety of new or newly available products.

European trade with Asia had always been designed to satisfy consumer demand rather than to exchange surplus goods. Europeans manufactured little that was desired in Asia, and neither merchants nor governments saw fit to attempt to influence Asian tastes in the way they did those of Europeans. The chief commodity imported to the East was bullion: tons of South American silver, perhaps a third of all that was produced. In return came spices, silk, coffee, jewels, jade, porcelain,

dyes, and a wide variety of other exotic goods. By the middle of the seventeenth century, the Dutch dominated the spice trade, obtaining a virtual monopoly over cinnamon, cloves, nutmeg, and mace and carrying the largest share of pepper. Each year Europeans consumed perhaps a million pounds of the four great spices and seven million pounds of pepper. Both Dutch and English competed for preeminence in the silk trade. The Dutch concentrated on Chinese silk, which they used mostly in trade with Japan. The English established an interest in lower-quality Indian silk spun in Bengal and even hired Italian silk masters to try to teach European techniques to the Indian spinners.

The most important manufactured articles imported from the East to Europe were the lightweight, brightly colored Indian cottons known as calicoes. The Dutch first realized the potential of the cotton market. Until the middle of the seventeenth century, cotton and cotton blended with silk were used in Europe only for wall hangings and table coverings. Colorful Asian chintz contained floral patterns that Europeans still considered exotic. But the material was also soft and smooth to the touch, and it soon replaced linen for use as underwear and close-fitting garments among the well-to-do. The fashion quickly caught on, and the Dutch began exporting calicoes throughout the Continent. The English and French followed suit, establishing their own trading houses in India and bringing European patterns

Detail of an Indian textile from the Madras region, ca. 1650. Calicut gave its name to the cotton cloth called calico. This is an example of a "painted Calicut," a wall hanging that shows richly dressed Indian women.

Photograph © 1980 The Metropolitan Museum of Art

and designs with them for the Asians to copy. The calico trade was especially lucrative because the piece goods were easy to pack and ship and, unlike consumables, could be stored indefinitely. When the English finally came to dominate the trade in the middle of the eighteenth century, they were shipping over a million cloths a year into London. The craze for calicoes was so great that both the English and French governments attempted to ban their import to protect their own clothing industries.

Along with the new apparel from the East came new beverages. Coffee, which was first drunk in northern Europe in the early seventeenth century, had become a fashionable drink by the end of the century. Coffeehouses sprang up in the major urban areas of northern Europe. There political and intellectual conversation was as heady as the strong Middle Eastern brew that was served. The Dutch and English both established themselves in the coffee trade, which was centered in the Middle Eastern seaport of Mocha. By the beginning of the eighteenth century, the Dutch had begun to grow their own coffee for export from their island colony of Java, and the two different types of coffee competed for favor.

As popular as coffee became among the European elites, it paled in comparison to the importance of tea as both an import commodity and a basic beverage. While coffee drinking remained the preserve of the wealthy, tea consumption spread throughout European society. It was probably most prevalent in England, where the combination of China tea and West Indian sugar created a virtual revolution in nutrition. The growth in tea consumption was phenomenal. In 1706 England imported 100,000 pounds of tea. By the end of the century the number had risen to over 15 million pounds. The English imported most of this tea directly from China, where an open port had been established at Canton. Originally just one of a number of commodities that were carried on an Asian voyage, tea soon became the dominant cargo of the large English merchant ships. Some manufactured goods would be brought to India on the outward voyage in order to fill as much cargo space as possible, but once the ships had loaded the green and black teas, they sailed directly home. Almost all tea was purchased with bullion, as the Chinese had even less use for European goods than did other Asians. It was not until the discovery that the Chinese consumed large quantities of opium, which was grown in India and Southeast Asia, that a triangular trade developed.

The success of tea was linked to the explosive growth in the development of sugar in Europe's Atlantic colonies. The Portuguese had attempted to cultivate sugar in the Azores at the end of the fifteenth century, but it was not until the settlement of Brazil, whose hot, humid climate was a natural habitat for the cane plants, that widespread cultivation began. The island of Barbados became the first English sugar colony. Barbados turned to sugar production accidentally, when its first attempts to market tobacco failed. The planters modeled their methods on those of Brazil, where African slaves were used to plant, tend, and cut the giant canes from which the sugar was extracted. For reasons that will never be fully understood, the English had an insatiable appetite for sugar's sweetness. It was taken plain, like candy; used in small quantities in almost all types of recipes; and diluted in ever-increasing quantities of tea. Hot, sweet tea became a meal for the lower orders of English society, a meal which—unlike beer—provided a quick burst of energy. By 1700 the English were sending home over 50 million pounds of sugar besides what they were shipping directly to the North American colonies. This quantity doubled by 1730, and still there was no slackening of demand. What might have become a valuable raw material in English trade instead became a staple of consumption.

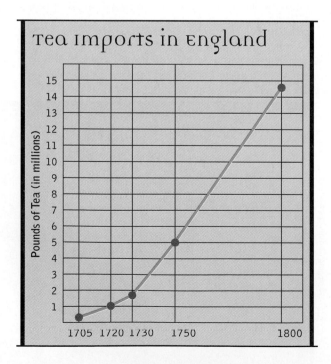

Tea Imports in England

Pounds of Tea (in millions)

1705 1720 1730   1750   1800

The triangular trade of manufactures—largely reexported calicoes—to Africa for slaves, who were exchanged in the West Indies for sugar, became the dominant form of English overseas trade. Colonial production depended upon the enforced labor of hundreds of thousands of Africans. Gold and silver, tobacco, sugar, rice, and indigo were all slave crops. Africans were enslaved by other Africans and then sold to Europeans to be used in the colonies. Over 6 million black slaves were imported into the Americas during the course of the eighteenth century. While rum and calicoes were the main commodities exchanged for slaves, the African tribes that dominated the slave trade organized a highly competitive market. Every colonial power participated in this lucrative trade. Over 3 million slaves were imported into the Portuguese colony of Brazil; by the end of the eighteenth century, there were 500,000 slaves and only 35,000 French inhabitants on the sugar island of Saint Domingue. But it was the English, with their sugar colonies of Barbados and Jamaica and their tobacco colonies of Virginia and Maryland, who ultimately came to control the slave trade. The prosperity of Newport, Rhode Island, in North America and the port of Liverpool in Lancashire were built entirely on the slave trade, as were hundreds of plantation fortunes. The sweet tooth of Europe was fed by the sweat of black Africans.

Sugar was by far the dominant commodity of the colonial trade, but it was not the only one. Furs and fish had first driven Europeans toward North America, and both remained important commodities. Beaver and rabbit skins were the most common materials for making headgear in an age in which everyone wore a hat. The schools of cod in Canadian waters were among the richest in the world, and the catch was shipped back either salted or dried. The English established what amounted to a manufacturing industry on the Newfoundland coast, where they dried the tons of fish that they caught. In the eighteenth century, rice was grown for export in the southern American colonies, particularly South Carolina. Rice never achieved great popularity in England, though it was in constant demand in the German states. Tobacco was the first new American product to come into widespread use in Europe, and its popularity—despite various official efforts to ban its use as dirty and unhealthy—grew steadily. American tobacco was grown principally in the colonies of Virginia and Maryland and shipped across the ocean, where it was frequently

Scale of Feet

PLAN OF A SLAVE VESSEL.

This diagram shows how slaves were packed into cargo holds for the notorious Middle Passage to the Americas. The plan was a model of efficiency, for slave traders sought to maximize profits.

THE SLAVE TRADE.

The motion in the House of Lords made by Lord Denman, on Tuesday night, has naturally revived the interest of the measures for the extinction of this vile traffic of "man-selling and man-stealing." The close of the session is marked by these humane exertions, as was its commencement, in the comprehensive speech of Lord George Bentinck, in the House of Commons, on February 3. His Lordship then held in his hand a communication from Captain Pilkington, of the Royal Navy, on the subject of the slave-trade, accompanied with a plan of one of the slave vessels (which we now Engrave). They were sit-

Water Line

entertainment enlivened by some most exquisite performances on the national instrument, the harp, much to the delight of all assembled. From the dinner-table the company retired at an early hour to the School-rooms, where the *conversazioni* were held.

WEDNESDAY.

On Wednesday, as the Geological and Natural History Sections were unable to finish the business before them, they each held meetings; but as a great number of members had left Swansea that morning by the *Lord Beresford* steamer, and others were examining the works in the neighbourhood, the Sections were very slightly attended, and the papers communicated were of small general interest.

A dinner, given by Lewis W. Dillwyn, Esq., who is himself one of the oldest members of the Royal Society, may be regarded as the close of the proceedings.

The last General Meeting was held in the afternoon, when it appeared, that, notwithstanding the inferiority of Swansea as respects population, this meeting has added considerably to the funds of the Association.

In concluding our notice of an Association which numbers among its members all the most eminent men in every department of physical and natural science, we cannot but express our satisfaction at the business-like character of this meeting. It is true that it has not startled the word by the announcement of any great discovery; but it will be found, upon examination, to present a fair average rate of progress. The vulnerable points have been less apparent than hitherto; and by the exclusion from the sections of all subjects which were not purely scientific, and by particularly avoiding those communications which have frequently been introduced as mere trading advertisements, of which we witnessed but one, that on gutta percha, which in our opinion should not have been received, the Association has placed itself upon exalted ground, and en-blended with European varieties. Although the English were the principal importers, it was the Dutch who dominated the European tobacco trade, making the most popular blends.

The new commodities flooded into Europe from all parts of the globe. By the middle of the eighteenth century, tea, coffee, cocoa, gin, and rum were among the most popular beverages. These were all products that had largely been unknown a century earlier. Among the wealthy, tea was served from porcelain pots imported from China; among all classes it was drunk with sugar imported from America. Beaver hats and Persian silks were fashionable in the upper reaches of society, rabbit caps and calico prints in the lower. New habits were created as new demands were satisfied. Tea and sugar passed from luxury to staple in little more than a generation, and the demand for both products continued to increase. To meet it, the European trading powers needed to create and maintain a powerful and efficient mercantile system.

This illustration of a Caribbean tobacco plantation shows an overseer directing the planting of the tobacco shoots while slaves in the drying sheds roll the leaves for export.

Dutch Masters

For the nearly 80 years between 1565 and 1648 that the Dutch were at war, they grew ever more prosperous. While the economies of most other European nations were sapped by warfare, the Dutch seemed to draw strength from their interminable conflict with the Spanish empire. They did have the advantage of fighting defensively on land and offensively on sea. Land war was terribly costly to the aggressor, who had to raise large armies, transport them to the site of battles or sieges, and feed them while they were there. The defender simply had to fortify strong places, keep its water routes open to secure supplies, and wait for the weather to change. Sea war—or piracy, depending on one's viewpoint—required much smaller outlays for men and material and promised the rewards of captured prizes. The Dutch became expert at attacking the Spanish silver fleets, hunting like a lion against a herd by singling out the slower and smaller vessels for capture. The Dutch also benefited from the massive immigration into their provinces of Protestants who had lived and worked in the southern provinces. These immigrants brought with them vital skills in manufacturing and large reserves of capital for investment in Dutch commerce.

The Dutch grounded their prosperity on commerce. Excellent craftsmen, they took the lead in the skilled occupations necessary for finishing cloth, refining raw materials, and decorating consumer goods. They were also successful farmers, especially given the small amounts of land with which they had to work and the difficult ecological conditions in which they worked it. But their greatest abilities were in trade.

Although the Dutch Republic comprised seven separate political entities, with a total population of about two million, the province of Holland was preeminent among them. Holland contained more than a quarter of this population, and its trading port of Amsterdam was one of the great cities of Europe. The city had risen dramatically in the seventeenth century, growing from a midsized urban community of 65,000 in 1600 to a metropolis of 170,000 fifty years later. The port was one of the busiest in the world, for it was built to be an entrepôt. Vast warehouses and docks lined its canals. Visitors were impressed by the bustle, the cleanliness, and the businesslike appearance of Amsterdam. There were no great public squares and few recognizable monuments. The central buildings were the Bank and the Exchange, testimony to the dominant activities of the residents.

The Dutch dominated all types of European trade. They carried more English coal than England, more French wine than France, more Swedish iron than Sweden. Dutch ships outnumbered all others in every important port of Europe. Goods were brought to Amsterdam to be redistributed throughout the world. Dutch prosperity rested first upon the Baltic trade. Even after it ceased to expand in the middle of the seventeenth century, the Baltic trade composed over one-quarter of all of Holland's commercial enterprise. The Dutch also were the leaders in the East Indian trade throughout the seventeenth century. They held a virtual monopoly on the sale of exotic spices and the largest share of the pepper trade. Their imports of cottons, and especially of porcelain, began new consumer fads that soon resulted in the development of European industries. Dutch potteries began to produce china, as lower-quality ceramic goods came to be known. Dutch trade in the Atlantic was of less importance, but the Dutch did have a colonial presence in the New World, controlling a number of small islands and the rapidly growing mainland settlement of New Netherland. Yet the Dutch still dominated the secondary market in tobacco and sugar, becoming the largest processor and refiner of these important commodities.

In all of these activities the Dutch acted as merchants rather than as consumers. Unlike most other Europeans, they regarded precious metal as a commodity like any other and took no interest in accumulating it for its own sake. This attitude enabled them to pioneer triangular trading and develop the crucial financial institutions necessary to expand their overseas commerce. The Dutch were not so much inventors as improvers. They saw the practical value in Italian accounting and banking methods and raised them to new levels of efficiency. They made use of marine insurance to help diminish the risks of mercantile activity. Their legal system favored the creation of small trading companies by protecting individual investments. The European stock and commodity markets were centered in Amsterdam. By the 1670s, over 500 commodities were traded on the Amsterdam exchange, and even a primitive futures market had evolved for those who wished to speculate.

There were many explanations for the unparalleled growth of this small maritime state into one of the greatest of European trading empires. Geography and climate provided one impetus, the lack of sufficient

A *prosperous Dutch trader in the East Indies poses with his wife on a hill near the port of Batavia (now Jakarta, Indonesia).*

foodstuffs another. Yet there were cultural characteristics as well. One was the openness of Dutch society. Even before the struggle with Spain, the northern provinces had shown a greater inclination toward religious toleration than had most parts of Europe. Amsterdam became a unique center for religious and intellectual exchange. European Jews flocked there, as did Catholic dissidents like Descartes. These people brought with them a wide range of skills and knowledge, along with capital that could be invested in trade. There was no real nobility among the Dutch, and certainly no set of values that prized investment in land over investment in trade. The French and Spanish nobility looked with scorn upon their mercantile classes and shunned any form of commercial investment; and the English, though more open to industry and trade, sank as much of their capital as possible into landed estates and country houses. The Dutch economic elite invested in trade. By the middle of the seventeenth century, the Dutch Republic enjoyed a reputation for cultural creativity that was the envy of the Continent. A truly extraordinary school of Dutch artists led by Rembrandt celebrated this new state born of commerce with vivid portrayals of its people and its prosperity.

mercantile organization

Elsewhere in Europe, trade was the king's business. The wealth of the nation was part of the prestige of the monarch, and its rise or fall part of the crown's power. Power and prestige were far more important to absolute rulers than was the profit of merchants. Indeed, in all European states except the Dutch Republic, the activities of merchants were scorned by both the landed elite and the salaried bureaucrats. Leisure was valued by the one and royal service by the other. The pursuit of wealth by buying and selling somehow lacked dignity, yet the activities of the mercantile classes took on increasing importance for the state for two reasons. First, imported goods, especially luxuries, were a noncontroversial target for taxation. Customs duties and excise taxes proliferated all over Europe. Representative assemblies composed of landed elites were usually happy to grant

The Fishmarket at Leiden *by Jan Steen (ca. 1626–79) illustrates the importance of the fishing industry to the Dutch economy.*

them to the monarch, and merchants could pass them on to consumers in higher prices. Second, the competition for trade was seen as a competition between states rather than individual merchants. Trading privileges involved special arrangements with foreign powers, arrangements that recognized the sovereign power of European monarchs. In this way, trade could bring glory to the state.

The competition for power and glory derived from the theory of mercantilism, a set of assumptions about economic activity that were commonly held throughout Europe and that guided the policies of almost every government. There were two interrelated ideas. One was that the wealth of a nation resided in its stock of precious metal, and the other was that economic activity was a zero-sum game. There was thought to be a fixed amount of money, a fixed number of commodities, and a fixed amount of consumption. Thus, what one country gained, another lost. If England bought wine from France and paid £100,000 in precious metal for it, then England was £100,000 poorer and France £100,000 richer. If one was to trade profitably, it was absolutely necessary to wind up with a surplus of precious metal. Therefore, it was imperative that governments regulate trade so that the stocks of precious metal were protected from the greed of the merchants. The first and most obvious measure of protection, then, was to prohibit the export of coin except by license, a prohibition that was absolutely unenforceable and was violated more often by government officials than by merchants.

These ideas about economic activity led to a variety of forms of economic regulation. The most common was the monopoly, a grant of special privileges in return for both financial considerations and an agreement to abide by the rules set out by the state. In the context of the seventeenth-century economy, there were a number of advantages to monopolies. First, of course, were those that accrued to the crown. There were direct and indirect revenues: monopolists usually paid considerable fees for their rights, and their activities were easy to monitor for purposes of taxation. The crown could use the grant of monopoly to reward past favors or to purchase future support from powerful individuals. There were also advantages for the monopolists. They could make capital investments with the expectation of long-term gains. This advantage was especially important in attracting investors for risky and expensive ventures like long-distance trade. Indeed, there were even benefits for the economy as a whole, as monopolies increased productive investment at a time when most

capital was being used to purchase land, luxury goods, or offices.

Two monopoly companies, the English and the Dutch East India companies, dominated the Asian trade. The English East India Company, founded in 1600 with a capital of £30,000, was given the exclusive right to the Asian trade and immediately established itself throughout the Indian Ocean. The Dutch East India Company was formed two years later with ten times the capital of its English counterpart. By the end of the century, the Dutch company employed over 12,000 people. Both companies were known as joint-stock companies, an innovation in the way in which businesses were organized. Subscribers owned a percentage of the total value of the company, based on the number of shares they bought, and were entitled to a distribution of profits on the same basis. Initially, the English company determined profits on single voyages and was supposed to distribute all of its assets to its shareholders after a given period. But changes in legal practice gave the company an identity separate from the individuals that held the shares. Now shares could be exchanged without the breakup of the company as a whole. Both Amsterdam and London soon developed stock markets to trade the shares of monopoly companies.

Both East India companies were remarkably good investments. The Dutch East India Company paid an average dividend of 18 percent for over 200 years. The value of English East India Company shares rose fivefold in the second half of the seventeenth century alone. Few other monopoly companies achieved a record comparable to that of the East India companies. The English Royal African Company, founded in 1672 to provide slaves for the Spanish colonies, barely recouped costs and was soon superseded by private trade. Even the French East Indian and African companies, which were modeled on the Dutch and English, were forced to abandon their monopolies. The Dutch and English companies were successful not because of their special privileges but because they were able to lower the costs of protecting their ships and cargoes.

Monopolies were not the only form of regulation in which seventeenth-century government engaged. For those states with Atlantic colonies, regulation took the form of restricting markets rather than traders. In the 1660s the English government, alarmed at the growth of Dutch mercantile activity in the New World, passed a series of Navigation Acts designed to protect English shipping. Colonial goods—primarily tobacco and sugar—could be shipped to and from England only in

Rembrandt, The Syndics of the Cloth Guild (1662). *This work was painted for the Drapers' or Cloth Guild and installed at the Guild's headquarters in Amsterdam. The five hatted Syndics look as though they have been caught in a momentary interruption of business. The bareheaded figure in the background is the valet, who unlike the Syndics, was not required to pay for his portrait.*

English boats. If the French wanted to purchase West Indian sugar, they could not simply send a ship to the English colony of Barbados loaded with French goods and exchange them for sugar. Rather, they had to make their purchases from an English import-export merchant and the goods had to be unloaded in an English port before they could be reloaded to be shipped to France. As a result, the English reexport trade skyrocketed. In the year 1700, reexports amounted to nearly 40 percent of all English commerce. With such a dramatic increase in trading, all moved in English ships, shipbuilding boomed. English coastal towns enjoyed heightened prosperity, as did the great colonial ports of Bristol and Liverpool. For a time, colonial protection proved effective.

French protectionism was as much internal as colonial. The French entered the intercontinental trade later than their North Atlantic rivals, and they were less dependent on trade for their subsistence. Of all the states of Europe, only France could satisfy its needs from its own resources. But to achieve such self-sufficiency required coordination and leadership. In the 1670s, Louis XIV's finance minister, Jean-Baptiste Colbert (1619–83),

developed a plan to bolster the French economy by protecting it against European imports. First Colbert followed the English example of restricting the reexport trade by requiring that imports come to France either in French ships or in the ships of the country from which the goods originated. In addition, he used tariffs to make imported goods unattractive in France. He sponsored a drive to increase French manufacturing, especially of textiles, tapestries, linens, glass, and furniture. To protect the investments in French manufacturing, enormous duties were placed on the import of similar goods manufactured elsewhere. The Venetian glass industry, for example, suffered a serious blow from Colbert's tariffs. English woolen manufacturers were also damaged, and the English sought retaliatory measures. But in fact, the English had already begun to imitate this form of protection. In the early eighteenth century, England attempted to limit the importation of cotton goods from India to prevent the collapse of the domestic clothing industry.

The Navigation Acts and Colbert's program of protective tariffs were directed specifically against Dutch reexporters. The Dutch were the acknowledged leaders in all branches of commerce in the seventeenth century. There were many summers when there were more Dutch vessels in London Harbor than there were English ships. In the 1670s the Dutch merchant fleet was probably larger than the English, French, Spanish, Portuguese, and German fleets combined! Restrictive navigation practices were one way to combat an advantage that the Dutch had built through heavy capital investment and by breaking away from the prevailing theories about the relationship between wealth and precious metals. The English and French Navigation Acts cut heavily into the Dutch trade, and ultimately both the English and French overtook them. But protectionism had its price. Just as the dynastic wars were succeeded by the wars of religion, so the wars of religion were succeeded by the wars of commerce.

"The discovery of America and that of a passage to the East Indies by the Cape of Good Hope are the two

Eastern Traders

The Dutch East India Company was the most important of the monopoly trading companies that were founded in the early seventeenth century. It was organized as a stock company and its shares traded on the Amsterdam bourse. Merchants could purchase portions of its ships for both imports and exports, and the company was given total control over the eastern spice trade. It was also given political and diplomatic powers in the areas in which it traded, and its overseas members behaved as much as foreign ambassadors as merchants. This excerpt, from an early history of the company, provides details of its original charter.

After various private merchants joined with others in the 1590s and after the turn of the century to form companies, first in Amsterdam and then in other cities of Holland and Zeeland, to open up and undertake travel and trade with the East Indies, and from time to time equipped and sent out many ships, which returned, on the average, with no small success, the States General came to the conclusion that it would be more useful and profitable not only for the country as a whole but also for its inhabitants individually, especially all those who had undertaken and shared in navigation and trade, that these companies should be combined and this navigation and trade be placed and maintained on a firm footing, with order and political guidance. After much argument and persuasion, this union was worked out by Their High Mightinesses [the government of the United Provinces], in their own words, to advance the prosperity of the United Netherlands, to conserve and increase its industry and to bring profit to the Company and to the people of the country.

. . . The Company's charter authorized it to make alliances with princes and potentates east of the Cape of Good Hope and beyond the Straits of Magellan, to make contracts, build fortresses and strongholds, name governors, raise troops, appoint officers of justice, and perform other necessary services for the advancement of trade; to dismiss the said governors and officers of justice if their conduct was found to be harmful and disloyal, provided that these governors or officers could not be prevented from returning here to present such grievances or complaints as they think they might have. . . .

The inhabitants of this country were permitted to invest as much or as little as they pleased in shares of the Company.

The subscription had to be made before September 1, 1602. . . .

. . . When the time for this investment or subscription had expired, various competent persons in different places presented requests in person or by sealed letter to the assembly of the XVII, asking that they be permitted to join the Company with the investment of certain sums of money; it was decided that no one else should be permitted to join in violation of the charter and to the detriment of the shareholders who had paid in their subscriptions before the expiration of the date fixed, and that the subscribed capital should be neither increased nor reduced.

defining commerce

Adam Smith was a Scottish political theorist whose work *The Wealth of Nations* (1776) was the first great work of economic analysis in European history. Smith had wide-ranging interests and wrote with equal authority about manufacturing, population, and trade. He was the first to develop the doctrine of free trade, which he called laissez-faire. Smith argued that the government that governed least governed best, and he was an early critic of protective tariffs and monopolies.

Every individual necessarily labours to render the annual revenue of the society as great as he can. He generally, indeed, neither intends to promote the public interest, nor knows how much he is promoting it. By preferring the support of domestic to that of foreign industry, he intends only his own security; and by directing that industry in such a manner as its produce may be of the greatest value, he intends only his own gain, and he is in this, as in many other cases, led by an invisible hand to promote an end which was no part of his intention. Nor is it always the worse for the society that it was no part of it. By pursuing his own interest he frequently promotes that of the society more effectually than when he really intends to promote it. I have never known much good done by those who affected to trade for the public good. . . .

. . . Each nation has been made to look with an invidious eye upon the prosperity of all the nations with which it trades, and to consider their gain as its own loss. Commerce, which ought naturally to be, among nations as among individuals, a bond of union and friendship, has become the most fertile source of discord and animosity. The capricious ambition of kings and ministers has not, during the present and the preceding century, been more fatal to the repose of Europe, than the impertinent jealousy of merchants and manufacturers. The violence and injustice of the rulers of mankind is an ancient evil, for which, I am afraid, the nature of human affairs can scarce admit of a remedy. But the mean rapacity, the monopolizing spirit of merchants and manufacturers, who neither are, nor ought to be, the rulers of mankind, though it cannot perhaps be corrected, may very easily be prevented from disturbing the tranquillity of anybody but themselves. . . .

The natural advantages which one country has over another in producing particular commodities are sometimes so great, that it is acknowledged by all the world to be in vain to struggle with them. . . . Very good grapes can be raised in Scotland, and very good wine too can be made of them at about thirty times the expense for which at least equally good can be brought from foreign countries. Would it be a reasonable law to prohibit the importation of all foreign wines merely to encourage the making of claret and burgundy in Scotland?

From Adam Smith, *The Wealth of Nations* (1776).

greatest and most important events in the history of mankind." So wrote the great Scottish economist Adam Smith (1723–90) in *The Wealth of Nations* (1776). For Smith and his generation, the first great age of commerce was coming to an end. The innovations of the Dutch had given way to a settled pattern of international long-distance trade. States now viewed commerce as a part of their national self-interest. They developed overseas empires, which they protected as markets for their goods and sources for their raw materials. These were justified by the theory of mercantilism and the demands of a generation of consumers who saw the luxuries of the past as the necessities of the present.

The wars of commerce

The belief that there was a fixed amount of trade in the world was still strong in the late seventeenth century. One country's gains in trade were another's losses. There was not more than enough to go around, and it could not be easily understood how the expansion of one country's trade could benefit all countries. Competition for trade was the same as competition for territory or subjects, part of the struggle by which the state grew powerful. It was not inevitable that economic competition would lead to warfare, only that restrictive competition would.

Thus the scramble for colonies in the seventeenth century led to commercial warfare in the eighteenth. As the English gradually replaced the Dutch as the leading commercial nation, so the French replaced the English as the leading competitor. Hostility between the English and the French had existed for centuries, and it was not without cause that the commercial wars of the eighteenth century should be likened to the territorial wars of the Middle Ages. The greed of merchants and the glory of princes fueled a struggle for the dominance of world markets that brought European warfare to every corner of the globe.

The mercantile wars

Commercial warfare in Europe began between the English and the Dutch in the middle of the seventeenth century. Both had established aggressive overseas trading companies in the Atlantic and in Asia. In the early seventeenth century, the Dutch were the undisputed leaders, their carrying capacity and trade monopolies the greatest in the world. But the English were rising quickly. Their Atlantic colonies began to produce valuable new commodities like tobacco and sugar, and their Asian trade was expanding decade after decade. Conflict was inevitable, and the result was a series of three naval wars fought between 1652 and 1674.

The Dutch had little choice but to strike out against English policy, but they also had little chance of overall success. Their spectacular naval victory in 1667, when the Dutch fleet surprised many English warships at port and burned both ships and docks at Chatham, obscured the fact that Dutch commercial superiority was slipping. In 1664 the English conquered New Netherland on the North American mainland and renamed it New York. With this defeat, the Dutch lost their largest colonial possession. The wars were costly to both states, nearly bankrupting the English Crown in 1672. Anglo-Dutch rivalry was finally laid to rest after 1688, when William of Orange, stadtholder of Holland, became William III (1689–1702), king of England.

Painter Jan Peter depicts an incident in the naval warfare caused by trade rivalry between the Dutch and the English. The Dutch fleet sailed up the Medway River and destroyed many English vessels, towing away a battleship.

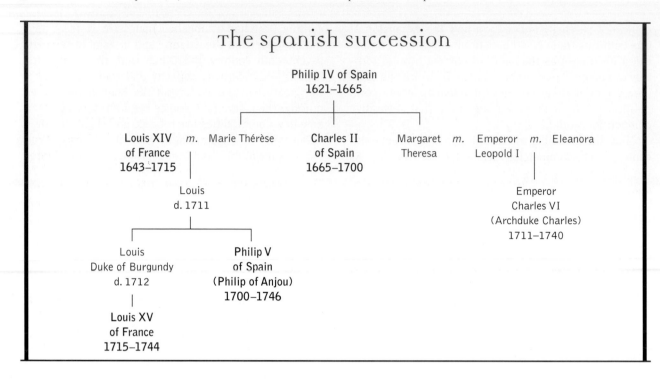

The spanish succession

Philip IV of Spain
1621–1665

Louis XIV *m.* Marie Thérèse   Charles II   Margaret *m.* Emperor *m.* Eleanora
of France   of Spain   Theresa   Leopold I
1643–1715   1665–1700

Louis
d. 1711

Emperor
Charles VI
(Archduke Charles)
1711–1740

Louis   Philip V
Duke of Burgundy   of Spain
d. 1712   (Philip of Anjou)
                      1700–1746

Louis XV
of France
1715–1744

The Anglo-Dutch commercial wars were just one part of a larger European conflict. Dutch commerce was as threatening to France as it was to England, though in a different way. Under Colbert, France pursued a policy of economic independence. The state supported internal industrial activity through the financing of large workshops and the encouragement of new manufacturing techniques. To protect French products, Colbert levied a series of punitive tariffs on Dutch imports, which severely depressed both trade and manufacture in Holland. Although the Dutch retaliated with restrictive tariffs of their own—in 1672 they banned the import of all French goods for an entire year—the Dutch economy depended on free trade. The Dutch had much more to lose than did France in a battle of protective tariffs.

But the battle that Louis XIV had in mind was to be more deadly than one of tariffs. Greedily he eyed the Spanish Netherlands—to which he had a weak claim through his Habsburg wife—believing that the Dutch stood in the way of his plans. The Dutch had entered into an alliance with the English and Swedes in 1668 to counter French policy, and Louis was determined to crush them in retaliation. He successfully bought off both of Holland's supposed allies, providing cash pensions to the kings of England and Sweden in return for

England's active participation and Sweden's passive neutrality in the impending war. In 1672 Louis's army, over 100,000 strong, invaded the Low Countries and swept all before them. Only the opening of the dikes prevented the French from entering the province of Holland itself.

The French invasion coincided with the third Anglo-Dutch war, and the United Provinces found themselves besieged on land and sea. Their international trade was disrupted, their manufacturing industries were in ruins, and their military budget skyrocketed. Only able diplomacy and skillful military leadership prevented total Dutch demise. A separate peace was made with England, and Spain, whose sovereign territory had been invaded, entered the war on the side of the Dutch, as did a number of German states. Louis's hope for a lightning victory faded, and the war settled into a series of interminable sieges and reliefs of fortified towns. The Dutch finally persuaded France to come to terms in the Treaty of Nijmegen (1678–79). While Louis XIV retained a number of the territories he had taken from Spain, his armies withdrew from the United Provinces and he agreed to lift most of the commercial sanctions against Dutch goods. The first phase of mercantile warfare was over.

the wars of Louis XIV

It was Louis XIV's ambition to restore the ancient Burgundian territories to the French crown and to provide secure northern and eastern borders for his state. Pursuit of these aims involved him in conflicts with nearly every other European state. Spain had fought for 80 years to preserve the Burgundian inheritance in the Low Countries. By the Peace of Westphalia (1648), the northern portion of this territory became the United Provinces, while the southern portion remained loyal to the crown and became the Spanish Netherlands. This territory provided a barrier between Holland and France that both states attempted to strengthen by establishing fortresses and bridgeheads at strategic places. In the east, Louis eyed the duchies of Lorraine and Alsace and the large swath of territory farther south known as Franche-Comté. The Peace of Westphalia had granted France control of a number of Imperial cities in these duchies, and Louis aimed to link them together. All these territories were ruled by Habsburgs: Alsace and Lorraine by the Austrian Holy Roman Emperor, Franche-Comté by the Spanish king.

In the late seventeenth century, ambassadors and ministers of state began to develop the theory of a bal-ance of power in Europe. This was a belief that no state or combination of states should be allowed to become so powerful that its existence threatened the peace of the others. Behind this purely political idea of the balance of power lay a theory of collective security that knit together the European state system. French expansion in either direction not only threatened the other states directly involved but also posed a threat to European security in general.

Louis showed his hand clearly enough in the Franco-Dutch war that had ended in 1679. Although he withdrew his forces from the United Provinces and evacuated most of the territories he had conquered, France absorbed Franche-Comté by the Treaty of Nijmegen, as well as portions of the Spanish Netherlands. Louis began plotting his next adventure almost as soon as the treaty was signed. Over the next several years, French troops advanced steadily into Alsace, ultimately forcing the city of Strasbourg, a vital bridgehead on the Rhine, to recognize French sovereignty. Expansion into northern Italy was similarly calculated. Everywhere Louis looked, French engineers rushed to construct fortresses and magazines in preparation for another war.

It finally came in 1688 when French troops poured across the Rhine to seize Cologne. A united German empire led by Leopold I, archduke of Austria, combined with the maritime powers of England and Holland, led by William III, to form the Grand Alliance, the first of the great balance-of-power coalitions. In fact, the two sides proved so evenly matched that the Nine Years' War (1688–97) settled very little, but it demonstrated that a successful European coalition could be formed against France. It also signified the permanent shift in alliances that resulted from the Revolution of 1688 in England. Although the English had allied with France against the Dutch in 1672, after William became king he persuaded the English Parliament that the real enemy was France. Louis's greatest objective, to secure the borders of his state, had withstood its greatest test. He might have rested satisfied but for the vagaries of births, marriages, and deaths.

Like his father, Louis XIV had married a daughter of the king of Spain. Philip IV had married his eldest daughter to Louis XIV and a younger one to Leopold I of Austria, who subsequently became the Holy Roman Emperor (1658–1705). Before he died, Philip finally fathered a son, Charles II (1665–1700), who attained the Spanish crown at the age of four but was mentally and physically incapable of ruling his vast empire. For decades it was apparent that there would be no direct

France Under Louis XIV

Habsburg successor to an empire that, despite its recent losses, still contained Spain, South America, the Spanish Netherlands, and most of Italy. Louis XIV and Leopold I both had legitimate claims to an inheritance that would have irreversibly tipped the European balance of power.

As Charles II grew increasingly feeble, efforts to find a suitable compromise to the problem of the Spanish succession were led by William III, who, as stadtholder of Holland, was vitally interested in the fate of the Spanish Netherlands and, as king of England, in the fate of the Spanish American colonies. In the 1690s two treaties of partition were drawn up. The first achieved near universal agreement but was nullified by the death of the German prince who was to inherit the Spanish crown. The second, which would have given Italy to Louis's son and everything else to Leopold's son, was opposed by Leopold, who had neither naval nor commercial interests and who claimed most of the Italian territories as imperial fiefs.

All these plans had been made without consulting the Spanish. If it was the aim of the European powers to partition the Spanish empire in order to prevent any one state from inheriting too much of it, it was the aim of the Spanish to maintain their empire intact. To this end, they devised a brilliant plan. Charles II bequeathed his entire empire to Philip of Anjou, the younger grandson of Louis XIV, with two stipulations: first, that Philip renounce his claim to the French throne; and second, that he accept the empire intact, without partition. If he—or more to the point, if his grandfather Louis XIV—did not accept these conditions, then the empire would pass to Archduke Charles, the younger son of Leopold I. Such provisions virtually assured war between France and the empire unless compromise between the two powers could be reached. But before terms could even be suggested, Charles II died and Philip V (1700–46) was proclaimed king of Spain and its empire.

Thus the eighteenth century opened with the War of the Spanish Succession (1702–14). Emperor Leopold rejected the provisions of Charles's will and sent his troops to occupy Italy. Louis XIV confirmed the worst fears of William III when he provided his grandson with French troops to "defend" the Spanish Netherlands. William III revived the Grand Alliance and initiated a massive land war against the combined might of France and Spain. The allied objectives were twofold: to prevent the unification of the French and Spanish thrones and to partition the Spanish empire so that both Italy and the Netherlands were ceded to Austria. The objective of Louis XIV was simply to preserve as much as possible of the Spanish inheritance for the house of Bourbon.

The ratification of the Treaty of Münster (1648). Under the treaty, Spain finally recognized Dutch independence.

War of the Spanish Succession

Leopold's younger son, Archduke Charles, inherited the empire as Charles VI (1711–40) and raised the prospect of an equally dangerous combined Austrian-Spanish state.

Between 1713 and 1714, a series of treaties at Utrecht settled the War of the Spanish Succession. Spanish possessions in Italy and the Netherlands were ceded to Austria; France abandoned all its territorial gains east of the Rhine and ceded its North American territories of Nova Scotia and Newfoundland to England. England also acquired from Spain Gibraltar, on the southern coast of Spain, and the island of Minorca in the Mediterranean. Both were strategically important to English commercial interests. English intervention in the Nine Years' War and the War of the Spanish Succession did not result in large territorial gains, but it did result in an enormous increase in English power and

William III died in 1702 and was succeeded by Anne (1702–14). John Churchill (1650–1722), duke of Marlborough and commander in chief of the army, continued William's policy. England and Holland again provided most of the finance and sea power, but, in addition, the English also provided a land army nearly 70,000 strong. Prussia joined the Grand Alliance, and disciplined Prussian troops helped offset the addition of the Spanish army to Louis's forces. In 1704 Churchill defeated French forces at Blenheim in Germany, and in 1706 at Ramillies in the Spanish Netherlands. France's military ascendancy was over.

Efforts to negotiate a peace settlement took longer than the war itself. The Austrians had taken control of Italy, the English and Dutch had secured the Spanish Netherlands, and the French had been driven back beyond the Rhine. The Allies believed that they could now enforce any treaty they pleased on Louis XIV and, along with concessions from France, attempted to oust his grandson, Philip V, from the Spanish throne. This proved impossible to achieve, though it took more than five years to learn the lesson. By then the European situation had taken another strange twist. Both Emperor Leopold and his eldest son had died. Now

An eighteenth-century English playing card showing Philip of Anjou, the grandson of Louis XIV, stealing the Spanish crown.

English artist Sir James Thornhill paid tribute to the new English rulers William and Mary in this extravagant depiction, which adorns the ceiling of the Painted Hall in the naval hospital at Greenwich.

of Great Britain (as England was known after its union with Scotland in 1707). In addition to receiving Gibraltar and Minorca from Spain, Britain was also granted the monopoly to provide slaves to the Spanish American colonies and the right to send one trading ship a year to them. In east and west, Britain was becoming the dominant commercial power in the world.

At least some of the reason for Britain's preeminence was the remarkable growth of the Atlantic colonies. The colonial economy was booming, and consumer goods that were in demand in London, Paris, and Amsterdam were also in demand in Boston, Philadelphia, and New York. Like every other colonial power, the British held a monopoly on their colonial trade. They were far less successful than the Spanish and French in enforcing the notion that colonies existed only for the benefit of the parent country, but the English Parliament continued to pass legislation aimed at restricting colonial trade with other nations and other nations' colonies. Like almost all other mercantile restrictions, these efforts were stronger in theory than in practice. Tariffs on imports and customs duties on British goods provided a double incentive for smuggling.

France emerged as Britain's true colonial rival. In the Caribbean, the French had the largest and most profitable of the West Indian sugar islands, Saint Domingue

prestige. Over the next 30 years England would assert its own imperial claims.

The colonial wars

The Treaty of Utrecht (1713–14) ushered in almost a quarter century of peace in western Europe. Austrian rule in the Netherlands and Italy remained a major irritant to the Spanish, but Spain was too weak to do more than sulk and snarl. The death of Louis XIV in 1715 quelled French ambitions for a time and even led to an Anglo-French accord that guaranteed the preservation of the settlement reached at Utrecht. Peace allowed Europe to rebuild its shattered economy and resume the international trade that had been so severely disrupted over the last 40 years. The Treaty of Utrecht had resolved a number of important trading issues, all in favor

The Treaty of Utrecht, Europe 1714

The Seven Years' War

Portrait of John Churchill, Duke of Marlborough, by Sir Godfrey Kneller, ca. 1706. Justice smiles down from the clouds at the triumphant duke as Victory reaches down to crown him with laurel. Trampled under the horse's hooves is the disheveled figure of Discord.

(modern-day Haiti). In North America, France not only held Canada but laid claim to the entire continent west of the Ohio River. The French did not so much settle their colonial territory as occupy it. They surveyed the land, established trading relations with the Native Americans, and built forts at strategic locations. The English, in contrast, had developed fixed communities, which grew larger and more prosperous by the decade. France determined to defend its colonies by establishing an overseas military presence. Regular French troops were shipped to Canada and installed in Louisbourg, Montreal, and Quebec. The British responded with troops of their own and sent an expeditionary force to clear the French from the Ohio River Valley. This action was the immediate cause of the Seven Years' War (1756–63).

Although the Seven Years' War had a bitter Continental phase, it was essentially a war for empire between the English and the French. There were three main theaters: the North American mainland, the West Indian sugar plantations, and the eastern coast of India. All over the globe, the British won smashing victories. The British navy blockaded the water route to Canada, inflicting severe hardship on French settlers in Montreal and Quebec. British forces ultimately captured both towns. After some initial successes, the French were driven back west across the Mississippi River, and their line of fortresses in the Ohio Valley fell into English hands. The English also succeeded in taking all the French sugar islands except Saint Domingue. British success in India was equally complete. The French were chased from their major trading zone and English dominance was secured.

By the end of the Seven Years' War, Britain had become a global imperial power. In the Peace of Paris (1763), France ceded all of Canada in exchange for the return of its West Indian islands. British dominion in the East Indian trade was recognized and led ultimately to British dominion of India itself. In less than a century, the ascendancy of France was broken and Europe's first modern imperial power had been created.

European commercial expansion was the first step in a long process that would ultimately transform the material life of all human beings. The quest for new commodities led to increased sophistication in transportation, marketing, and distribution—all vital developments for agricultural changes in the future. The ability to move large quantities of goods from place to place and to exchange them between different parts of the globe laid the foundation for organized manufacturing. The practical impact of scientific discovery, as yet only dimly glimpsed, would soon spur the transformation of handicrafts into industries. In the eighteenth century the material world was still being conquered, and the most unattractive features of this conquest were all too plainly visible. Luxuries for the rich were won by the labors of the poor. The pleasures of sugar and tobacco were purchased at the price of slavery for millions of Africans. The greed of merchants and the glory of princes was an unholy alliance that resulted in warfare around the globe. But it was a shrinking globe, one whose peoples were becoming increasingly interdependent, tied together by the goods and services that they could provide to each other.

mastering the chapter

To review the main points of the chapter, be sure you can explain the significance of each of the following.

Terms/Concepts/Events	People	Places
Aristotelianism	Nicolaus Copernicus	Mocha
Royal Society	Johannes Kepler	Azores
triangular trade	Galileo Galilei	Barbados
Bank of England	Paracelsus	Liverpool
mercantilism	Robert Boyle	Amsterdam
joint-stock companies	Andreas Vesalius	Bristol
Navigation Acts	William Harvey	Spanish Netherlands
War of the Spanish Succession	Sir Isaac Newton	Lorraine
Treaty of Utrecht	Sir Francis Bacon	Alsace
Seven Years' War	René Descartes	Franche-Comté

suggestions for further reading

general reading

* A. Rupert Hall, *The Revolution in Science, 1500–1750* (London: Longman, 1983). The best introduction to the varieties of scientific thought in the early modern period. Detailed and complex.

* Jan de Vries, *The European Economy in an Age of Crisis* (Cambridge: Cambridge University Press, 1976). A comprehensive study of economic development, including long-distance trade and commercial change.

* K. H. D. Haley, *The Dutch in the Seventeenth Century* (London: Thames and Hudson, 1972). A well-written and well-illustrated history of the golden age of Holland.

* Derek McKay and H. M. Scott, *The Rise of the Great Powers, 1648–1815* (London: Longman, 1983). An outstanding survey of diplomacy and warfare.

* Jeremy Black, *The Rise of the European Powers, 1679–1793* (New York: Edward Arnold, 1990). A new look at diplomatic history from an English point of view.

The New science

* Margaret C. Jacob, *The Cultural Meaning of the Scientific Revolution* (New York: Alfred A. Knopf, 1988). Scientific thought portrayed in its social context.

* H. F. Cohen, *The Scientific Revolution* (Chicago: University of Chicago Press, 1994). The history of the idea of the scientific revolution and of the events that comprised it.

* Stillman Drake, *Galileo* (New York: Hill and Wang, 1980). A short but engaging study of the great Italian scientist.

* Mario Biagioli, *Galileo, Courtier* (Chicago: University of Chicago Press, 1993). A remarkable study of Galileo that sets his science within the context of the culture of absolutism.

* Londa Schiebinger, *The Mind Has No Sex?: Women in the Origins of Modern Science* (Cambridge, MA: Harvard University Press, 1990). The role of women in the scientific revolution.

* Allen Debus, *Man and Nature in the Renaissance* (Cambridge: Cambridge University Press, 1978). An especially good account of the intellectual roots of scientific thought.

* Richard Westfall, *The Construction of Modern Science. Mechanisms and Mechanics* (Cambridge: Cambridge University Press, 1977). A survey of scientific developments from Kepler to Newton. A good introduction to both mechanics and mathematics.

  Charles Webster, *The Great Instauration: Science, Medicine, and Reform* (London: Duckworth, 1975). A complicated but rewarding analysis of experimental science and the origins of scientific medicine.

* David Lindberg and Robert Westman, eds., *Reappraisals of the Scientific Revolution* (Cambridge: Cambridge University Press, 1990). A collection of essays that survey recent scholarship on the scientific revolution.

* Frank E. Manuel, *Sir Isaac Newton: A Portrait* (Cambridge, MA: Harvard University Press, 1968). A readable account of one of the most complex intellects in European history, from a psychoanalytic point of view.

* Richard Westfall, *The Life of Isaac Newton* (Cambridge: Cambridge University Press, 1993). The best short biography.

empires of goods

* Ralph Davis, *The Rise of the Atlantic Economies* (Ithaca, NY: Cornell University Press, 1973). A nation-by-nation survey of the colonial powers.

  J. N. Ball, *Merchants and Merchandise: The Expansion of Trade in Europe* (London: Croom Helm, 1977). A good overview of European overseas economies.

* James D. Tracy, *The Rise of Merchant Empires: Long-Distance Trade in the Early Modern World, 1350–1750* (Cambridge: Cambridge University Press, 1993). An outstanding collection of essays by internationally recognized scholars.

  K. N. Chaudhuri, *The Trading World of Asia and the English East India Company* (Cambridge: Cambridge University Press, 1978). A brilliant account of the impact of the Indian trade on both Europeans and Asians.

* Sidney Mintz, *Sweetness and Power* (New York: Viking Press, 1985). An anthropologist explores the lure of sugar and its impact on Western society.

* Philip Curtin, *The Atlantic Slave Trade* (Madison: University of Wisconsin Press, 1969). A study of the importation of African slaves into the New World, with the best estimates of the numbers of slaves and their destinations.

* Joseph Miller, *Way of Death: Merchant Capitalism and the Angolan Slave Trade, 1730–1830* (Madison: University of Wisconsin Press, 1988). An illuminating portrait of the eighteenth-century slave trade, with an unforgettable account of the slave voyages.

* Jonathan Israel, *Dutch Primacy in World Trade, 1585–1740* (Oxford: Oxford University Press, 1989). The triumph of Dutch traders and techniques written by the leading authority.

* Simon Schama, *The Embarrassment of Riches* (New York: Alfred A. Knopf, 1987). A social history of the Dutch Republic that explores the meaning of commerce in Dutch society.

Jonathan Israel, *The Dutch Republic* (Oxford: Oxford University Press, 1995). A comprehensive history of the Dutch rise to world prominence and its subsequent decline.

* Holden Furber, *Rival Empires of Trade in the Orient, 1600–1800* (Minneapolis: University of Minnesota Press, 1976). A comprehensive survey of the battle for control of the Asian trade in the seventeenth and eighteenth centuries.

The wars of commerce

A. C. Carter, *Neutrality or Commitment: The Evolution of Dutch Foreign Policy, 1667–1795* (London: Edward Arnold, 1975). A tightly written study of the objectives and course of Dutch diplomacy.

Charles Wilson, *Profit and Power* (London: Longman, 1957). Still the best study of the Anglo-Dutch wars of the mid-seventeenth century.

* Jeremy Black, *A System of Ambition?: British Foreign Policy, 1660–1793* (London: Longman, 1991). The best survey of Britain's international relations during the long eighteenth century.

Herbert Rowan, *The Princes of Orange* (Cambridge: Cambridge University Press, 1988). An engrossing history of the family that ruled the Dutch Republic.

Paul Langford, *The Eighteenth Century, 1688–1815* (New York: St. Martin's Press, 1976). A reliable guide to the growth of British power.

Ragnhild Hatton, ed., *Louis XIV and Europe* (London: Macmillan, 1976). An important collection of essays on French foreign policy in its most aggressive posture.

Richard Pares, *War and Trade in the West Indies, 1739–63* (Oxford: Oxford University Press, 1936). A blow-by-blow account of the struggle for colonial supremacy in the sugar islands.

*Paperback edition available.

SWEDEN

Oostvinlandt

RUSSIA

LYTLANDT

COURLANT

EUROPA

PRUSSEN

Province

Hongarn

Wallaen

SLAVONIA

GRACIA

NATOLIA

The Balance of Power in Eighteenth-Century Europe

CHAPTER 18

Calling the Tune

Frederick the Great loved music. During his youth it was one of his private passions that so infuriated his father. Mathematics, political economy, modern languages—even the dreaded French—these were the subjects that a future king of Prussia should learn. But music, never. Rather, the boy should be at the hunt watching the dogs tear apart a stag, or on maneuvers with the Potsdam guards, a troop of soldiers all nearly 7 feet tall. This was the regimen King Frederick William I prescribed for his son. It was no longer enough to reign over one's subjects; to be a successful monarch in the power politics of the eighteenth century, a king had to be a soldier.

But Frederick the Great loved music. He secretly collected all the books and manuscripts he could find on the subject, outspending his tiny allowance in the process. He had Johann Quantz (1697–1773), the greatest flutist of the day, placed on his staff to teach him and to conspire with him against his father. At night, while the old king drank himself into a stupor—an activity he warmly recommended to his son—Frederick powdered his hair, put on a jacket of the latest French style, and regaled his friends with his newest compositions. A lookout guarded the door in case the king wandered by unexpectedly. Once the musicians were almost discovered and Frederick's fine new jacket was tossed on the fire, but the flutes and musical scores remained safely hidden.

After he became king, Frederick the Great could indulge his passion more openly. Yet he preferred to hold his concerts, usually small gatherings, at the Palace of San Souci, which he built in Potsdam. A special music room was designed for the king's use, and he lavished attention on it. The great chandelier, lit by a circle of candles, illuminated the center of the room and highlighted the soloist. The entire palace reflected Frederick's personal taste. Unlike most great palaces of state, it was small, functional, and beautiful. Here Frederick could escape the mounting cares of governing one of the most powerful states in Europe by reading, corresponding with eminent French intellectuals, and playing the flute. In this picture, *Das Flötenkonzert* (The Flute Concert), Frederick is portrayed performing in his great music room. Before a small audience of courtiers and intimates, he plays to the accompaniment of cello, violins, and piano.

Frederick's talent was real enough. A British visitor to Sans Souci, who had little reason to flatter the king, reported: "I was much pleased and surprised with the neatness of his execution. His performance surpassed anything I had ever heard among the dilettanti or even professors." This judgment is reinforced when one studies the expressions of the three men in the left corner of the painting. They are taking genuine pleasure in the music they are hearing (all the more genuine in that the king's back is to them). So, too, are the musicians who are accompanying the king. There is as much joy as concentration upon their faces.

Frederick's musical accomplishment was not unique among eighteenth-century monarchs: Joseph II of Austria was also a skilled flutist. But it was not so much music as accomplishment that was coming to be valued among the monarchs of the new European powers. Catherine the Great of Russia corresponded with philosophers; Frederick the Great brought the great French intellectual Voltaire (1698–1778) to his court—though they quickly took a dislike to each other. The acquisition of culture seemed to matter more and more as the century wore on. Museums, opera houses, and great art collections were established all over the Continent. The Hermitage in Saint Petersburg was

Focus Questions

1. What were the great powers of Europe in the eighteenth century and in what ways was there a "balance of power" among them?
2. What did Peter I and Catherine II of Russia accomplish during their reigns that justifies the title "the great"?
3. How was the tiny state of Brandenburg-Prussia able to make itself into one of Europe's major powers and what did this mean for the Austrian empire?
4. How did Britain's theory of mixed government and its parliamentary party system assist its rise to become Europe's great imperial power?
5. How and why did the "balance of power" shift during the eighteenth century?

stocked with the works of Dutch and English masters. The British Museum was founded in London with the support of King George II, who deposited his great library there. Whether this veneer of culture did anything to lessen the brutality of warfare and power politics is a matter of opinion. But as a veneer it was as highly polished as the flute that Frederick the Great is so delicately pressing to his mouth.

Europe in 1714

Within a relatively short span of time at the beginning of the eighteenth century, two treaties brought about a considerable reorganization of the political geography of Europe. The Treaty of Utrecht (1713–14) created a new Europe in the west. The Treaty of Nystad (1721) cre-

ated a new Europe in the east. Both agreements reflected the dynamics of change that had taken place over the previous century. The rise of France on the Continent and Britain's colonial empire around the globe were facts that could no longer be ignored. The decline of Sweden and Poland and the emergence of Russia as a great power were the beginning of a long-

Europe in 1714

term process that would continue to dominate European history.

All of this could be seen on a map of Europe in the early eighteenth century. France's absorption of Alsace and encroachments into Lorraine would be bones of contention between the French and the Germans for two centuries and would ultimately contribute to the outbreak of World Wars I and II. The political footballs of the Spanish Netherlands and Spanish Italy, now temporarily Austrian, continued to be kicked about until the nationalist movements of the nineteenth century gave birth to Belgium, Luxembourg, and a united Italy. The emergence of Brandenburg-Prussia on the north German coast and the gradual decline of the Holy Roman Emperor's power were both vital to the process that created a unified Germany and a separate Austria. In the southeast, the slow but steady reconquest of the Balkans from Ottoman dominion restored the historic southern border of the Continent. The inexorable expansion of Russia was also already apparent.

expansion in the west

Perhaps the most obvious transformation in the political geography of western Europe was the expansion of European power around the globe. In the Atlantic, Spain remained the largest colonial power. Through its viceroyalty system it controlled all of Mexico and Central America; the largest and most numerous of the Caribbean islands; North America from Colorado to California (as well as Florida); and most of South America. The other major colonial power in the region was Portugal, which shared dominion over the South American continent. In the Portuguese colony of Brazil, production of sugar, dyestuffs, timbers, and exotic commodities amply repaid the meager investment the Portuguese had made.

In North America, the French and British shared the eastern half of the continent. The French controlled most of it. They had landed first in Canada and then slowly made their way down the Saint Lawrence River. New France, as their colonial empire was called, was a trading territory, and it expanded along the greatest of the waterways: the Great Lakes and the Ohio, Missouri, and Mississippi rivers. French settlements had sprung up as far south as the Gulf of Mexico. France also claimed the territory of Louisiana, named for Louis XIV, which stretched from New Orleans to Montana. The British settlements were all coastal, stretching from

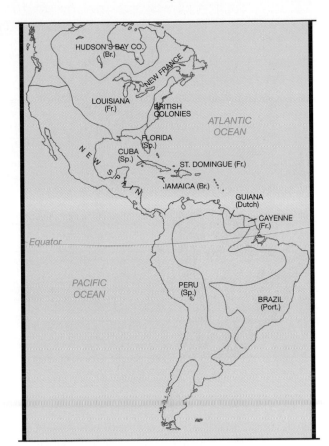

The Americas

Maine to Georgia on the Atlantic seaboard. Unlike the French, the British settled their territory and were only interested in expansion when their population, which was doubling every 25 years, outgrew its resources. By the early eighteenth century, the ports of Boston, New York, Philadelphia, and Charleston were thriving commercial centers.

Europeans managed their eastern colonial territories differently than they did those in the Atlantic. Initially the Portuguese and the Dutch had been satisfied with establishing trading factories—coastal fortresses in Africa and Asia that could be used as warehouses and defended against attack. But in the seventeenth century, the European states began to take control of vital ports and lucrative islands. Here the Dutch were the acknowledged leaders, replacing the Portuguese, who had begun the process at the end of the sixteenth century. Holland held by force or in conjunction with local leaders all the Spice Islands in the Pacific. The Dutch also occupied both sides of the Malay Peninsula and nearly

The Dutch East India Company's trading station on the Hooghly River in Bengal, 1665. The station was one of a network of bases the company established throughout its eastern trading empire.

all the coastal areas of the islands in the Java Sea. Dutch control of Ceylon was strategically important for its Indian trade. Compared to the Dutch Republic, all other European states had only a minor territorial presence in the East, with the exception of Spain, which still controlled the Philippines. The British had limited their eastern outposts to trading establishments, and through these they maintained a significant presence in India. During the eighteenth century, the British began to colonize the Indian subcontinent directly.

Imperial expansion was the most obvious change in the geopolitical boundaries of Europe, but it was not the only one. A brief tour of the western states after the Treaty of Utrecht reveals some others. In 1707 England and Scotland formally joined together to form Great Britain. In addition to its eastern and western colonies, Britain had also gained control of Gibraltar at the foot of Spain and the island of Minorca in the Mediterranean. Both territories were strategically important to British commerce.

Across the English Channel were the Low Countries, now permanently divided between the United Provinces in the north, led by Holland, and those provinces in the south that had remained loyal to the Spanish crown in the sixteenth century. By 1714 the golden age of the Dutch was over. Although the Dutch continued as a colonial and maritime power, their small numbers and meager natural resources eventually outweighed their abilities as innovators and managers. They lost their eastern empire to Britain and their predominance in European trade to France. What the Dutch gained at Utrecht was the right to maintain their forces in the towns along the border between France and the old

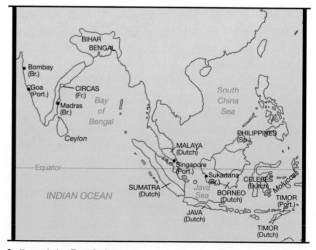

India and the East Indies

Great Britain and the Low Countries

France and Spain

Spanish Netherlands. The Spanish Netherlands, the original Burgundian inheritance, were now being slowly dismembered. Since the accession of Louis XIV, France had plucked small pieces from the territories that had been contested between France and Spain since the fifteenth century. Between French aggression and the Dutch occupation of such important places as Ghent and Ypres, the ability of the southern provinces to maintain a separate identity suffered a grave blow. But not as grave as that formalized at Utrecht, when sovereignty over this territory was assigned to Austria, ostensibly because the emperor was a Habsburg, but really because the balance of power in western Europe demanded it.

To the south lay France, still the most powerful nation in Europe despite its losses in the War of the Spanish Succession. By 1714 Louis XIV had broken forever the danger of Spanish encirclement that had been the worry of every French king since Francis I in the early sixteenth century. Louis had methodically set out to occupy those territories that were strategically necessary to defend his state from invasion by the Dutch, the Spanish, the British, or the emperor. In the northeast he absorbed the Duchy of Bar. In the north he absorbed a healthy portion of Flanders, including Dunkirk on the English Channel and the prosperous clothing town of

Lille. He pushed the eastern boundary of his state to the Rhine by overrunning Alsace and parts of Lorraine. Strasbourg remained French under the settlement of 1714, testimony to the fact that it was possible to hold France only at the western banks of the Rhine. Finally, farther to the south, Louis had won and held Franche-Comté, once the center of Burgundy. In 1714 France was larger, stronger, and better able to defend its borders than ever before. It was also exhausted.

As France expanded, so Spain contracted. Less than two centuries earlier, a Spanish king had dreamed of being monarch over all of Europe. Now a French Bourbon sat on the great Habsburg throne and Spain was slowly being sliced to pieces. By 1714 the European territories of the Spanish empire had been reduced to Iberia itself. But the loss of its European empire was to prove a blessing in disguise for Spain, which now entered upon a new and unexpected phase of growth and influence.

The center of Europe remained occupied by the agglomeration of cities, bishoprics, principalities, and small states known collectively as the Holy Roman Empire, but now more accurately called the German empire. There were still over 300 separate jurisdictions, most of them vulnerable to preying neighbors such as Louis XIV. Bavaria in the south and Saxony, Brandenburg, and Hanover in the north were among the most important of the large states, with the added twist that Hanover was now ruled by the king of Great Britain. The emperor, now officially prohibited from interference in the internal administration of the large states, was less dominant in German affairs than he had been before the Thirty Years' War.

Increasingly, Habsburg power centered on Austria, Bohemia, and Hungary. This was especially true during the reign of Leopold I (1655–1705). Withstanding threats on all sides, Leopold was able to expand his state both to the west and to the south and to bring Austria into the ranks of the great European powers. Such an outcome could hardly have been foreseen in the middle of the seventeenth century, when the Ottomans made their last great thrust into the interior of Europe. In 1683 the Ottomans besieged Vienna itself, and only the arrival of 70,000 Polish-led troops saved it from falling. But from that time forward, Austrian forces scored stunning victories. By 1699 almost all of Hungary had been retaken by Austria; with the Treaty of Passarowitz in 1718 Austria gained the rest of Hungary and Serbia. When the Treaty of Utrecht granted Austria control of the Netherlands, Lombardy, and Naples, the Austrian Habsburgs became rulers of a European empire.

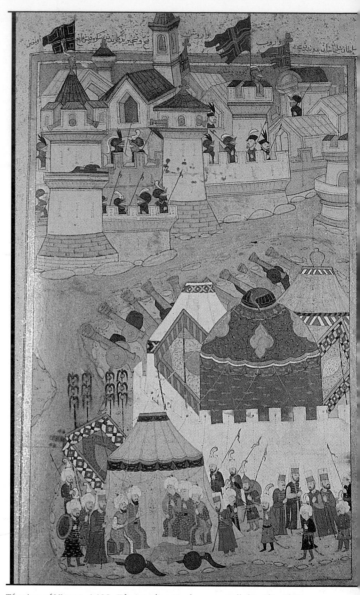

The siege of Vienna, 1683. The invading Turks were repelled in this, their last great advance in Europe.

The Holy Roman Empire

Austria's Italian possessions included the vast southern territories of Naples (including Sicily after 1720) and the rich industrial area surrounding Milan in the north. Alongside the Austrian territories, a number of independent city-states continued to flourish on the Italian peninsula. Both Venice and Genoa remained prosperous and independent. The Grand Duchy of Tuscany, with its great city of Florence, and the Papal States had both expanded over the course of the seventeenth century, absorbing their smaller neighbors until both were large consolidated territories. To the west of the Italian states was the Duchy of Savoy. Savoy had pursued a flexible foreign policy, pleasing whichever of its powerful neighbors was most dangerous and accepting the patronage of whichever seemed most friendly. As a client of the Spanish, French, and Austrians, Savoy grew and prospered. After the War of the Spanish Succession, Savoy was counted among the victors, though it had fought on both sides. Duke Victor Amadeus II became a king when he received the island of Sicily, which he exchanged with Austria for Sardinia in 1720.

Thus the Treaty of Utrecht signaled a new configuration of political power. England, France, Prussia, and Austria were the ascending powers, Holland and Spain the declining ones. Italy and the southern Netherlands were the bones over which the biggest dogs fought, sometimes playfully, sometimes in deadly earnest.

Realignment in the East

This was western Europe in 1714. In the east, it was the Treaty of Nystad (1721), ending the Great Northern War (1700–21), that fixed the political geography. Here the emerging powers were Russia and Prussia, while those in decline were Sweden and Poland. The critical factor in eastern European politics remained access to the sea. Outlets to the Baltic Sea in the north and the Black Sea in the south were the vital lifeline for this part of the Continent, and control of these outlets was the central motivation for the long years of war fought among the eastern states.

The expansion of Russia is one of the central events in European history, and the early eighteenth century is its pivotal period. During the long years of social and economic recovery after the death of Ivan the Terrible in 1584, Russia had been easy prey for its powerful neighbors Sweden and Poland. Through a series of wars and political pacts, Russia had ceded most of its Baltic territories to Sweden, while it had relinquished land and population in the west to Poland. Peter the Great (1682–1725) set out to reclaim what had been lost. As a result of the Great Northern War, Russia regained the eastern Baltic coastline from the southeastern end of Finland to Riga in the west. Russia now controlled all of the vital Baltic ports in the east. Peter built a new capital on the Gulf of Finland. In this new city, named Saint Petersburg, he laid the foundation for the Russian navy.

What Russia gained, Sweden lost. At the height of its power in the middle of the seventeenth century, Sweden

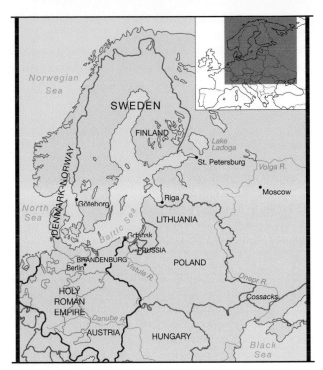

Russia and Sweden

had dominated the Baltic. It occupied all of Finland, controlled the important eastern coast of Norway, and had gained a foothold in Germany. Most importantly, Sweden had captured the southern tip of its own peninsula from the Danes, making the mainland portion of its state whole. But Sweden's century-long rise to power was followed by a rapid period of decline. The small and relatively poor population could not long succeed in governing an empire. The Great Northern War ended whatever pretensions Sweden still had. It lost all of its German territories: those on the North Sea went to Hanover, those on the Baltic to Prussia. Livonia, Estonia, and the eastern provinces were returned to Russia, but Sweden was able to hold on to its vital gains from the Danes. Sweden had built its own window to the west at Göteborg on the North Sea, and from there it could carry on a direct trade with Britain and the Netherlands.

Since the end of the Thirty Years' War, Brandenburg-Prussia had been growing steadily. A strange configuration of a state, with its geographical heart in Brandenburg, it was one of the domains of the Holy Roman Empire. From the capital at Berlin the princes of Brandenburg directed the accumulation of small neighboring German lands: Magdeburg and Halle to the southwest, a piece of Pomerania to the northeast. But while Brandenburg expanded in every direction, it could do little to join itself to the kingdom of Prussia. A huge swath of Poland, cutting between the two, stood in the way. This division of Brandenburg-Prussia was its most important geopolitical feature. In the eighteenth century, the determination to join together dominated Prussian history.

This aim, of course, meant eventual conflict with Poland. Despite its political weakness, Poland was one of the largest landmasses in Europe. On its southern border it held back Ottoman expansion; on its eastern border it held back the Russians. Its great port of Gdansk on the Baltic dominated the grain and timber trade with northern Europe as well as local Baltic commerce between Scandinavia and the mainland. Sweden and Russia, the eastern powers, controlled Poland politically, helping nominate its elected kings and ensuring that its decentralized form of aristocratic government kept Poland weak. Poland served as a useful counterweight in the balance of power in eastern Europe. Except for its Baltic territories, Poland was not yet seen as a great prize to be fought over. But by the beginning of the eighteenth century it was a helpless giant ready to be toppled.

Thus a potent Prussia and Russia and a prostrate Poland characterized the realignment of the eastern portion of Europe. Most importantly, the separation between east and west was narrowing. Prussia's German orientation and the westernization of Russia led to closer ties with the west.

This portrait of Peter the Great by his court painter Louis Caravaque pays homage to Peter's intense interest in naval matters. Ships flying English, Dutch, Danish, and Russian flags prepare for maneuvers under his command.

The Rise of Russia

At the beginning of the eighteenth century, Russia was scarcely known about or cared about in the rest of Europe. Peter the Great changed all that. The Treaty of Nystad had confirmed the magnitude of his victory over the Swedes in the Great Northern War, both in territory and prestige. The change created consternation in the courts of Europe. Just a quarter century before, no one had cared very much what the king of Russia called himself. In fact, little was known for sure about the Russian ruler or his state. What little mercantile contact there was between Russia and the West was conducted entirely by westerners. Foreign merchants were allowed to live in Moscow in a separate ghetto called "German-

town." Their letters were the main source of western knowledge about the vast Muscovite empire.

Peter the Great brought Europe to Russia and Russia to Europe. Twice he visited Europe to discover the secrets of western prosperity and might. He arranged marriages between the closest heirs to his throne, including his son Alexis, and the sons and daughters of German princes and dukes. By 1721 he had established 21 separate foreign embassies. The sons of the Russian gentry and nobility were sent west—sometimes forcibly—to further their education and to learn to adapt to western outlooks. Peter recruited Europeans to fill the most important skilled positions in the state: foreign engineers and gunners to serve in the army; foreign architects to build the new capital at Saint Petersburg; foreign scholars to head the new state schools; foreign administrators to oversee the new departments of state. Peter borrowed freely and adapted sensibly. If necessary, he would drag his countrymen kicking and screaming into the modern world.

By 1721 Russia was recognized all over Europe as an emerging power. The military defeat of the seemingly invincible Swedes had made monarchs from Louis XIV to William III sit up and take notice. And the great Russian victory over Sweden at Poltava in 1709 was no fluke. Peter's forces followed it up with several strong campaigns, which proved that Russia could organize, equip, finance, and train an up-to-date military force. Moreover, Peter's absorption of Sweden's Baltic territories made Russia a power in the north. The Russian navy, built mostly by foreigners, was now capable of protecting Russian interests and defending important ports such as Riga and Saint Petersburg. Even the Dutch, who had long plotted the decline of Swedish might, now became nervous. Thus it was unsettling that Peter wished to be recognized as emperor.

The Reforms of Peter the Great

Peter the Great was not the first Russian tsar to attempt to borrow from western developments. The process had been under way for decades. The opening of the northern port of Archangel in 1584 led to direct contact with British and Dutch traders, who brought with them new ideas and useful products, which were then adapted to Russian needs and conditions. Russia was a vast state, and Europe was only one of its neighbors. Its religion had come from Byzantium rather than Rome, thus giving Russian Christianity an eastern flavor. Its Asian territories mixed the influence of Mongols and Ottomans; its southern borders met Tartars and Cossacks. While most European states were racially and ethnically homogeneous, Russia was a loose confederation of diverse peoples. Yet it was the western states that posed the greatest threat to Russia in the seventeenth century, and it was to the west that Peter, like his father before him, turned his attention.

It would be wrong to see Peter's westernizing innovation as a systematic program. More to the point, nearly all of his reforms—economic, educational, administrative, social, military—were done to enhance military efficiency rather than civil progress. In his 30 years of active rule there was only one year—1724—during which he was not at war. Vital reforms like the poll tax

Peter the Great was a precocious child. He began his education at the age of two, using a book similar to the illustrated Russian speller whose "Z" page is shown here.

(1724), which changed the basis of taxation from the household to the individual adult male, had enormous social consequences. The new policy of taxing individuals officially erased whole social classes. A strict census taken (and retaken) to inhibit tax evasion became the basis for further governmental encroachments on the tsar's subjects. Yet the poll tax was not designed for any of these purposes. It was instituted to increase tax revenue for war. Similarly, compulsory lifetime military service required of the landowning classes (the nobility and gentry) was established to provide officers and state servants for an expanding military machine.

Yet if Peter's reforms were not systematic and developed from little other than military necessity, nevertheless they constituted a fundamental transformation in the life of all Russian people. The creation of a gigantic standing army and an entirely new navy meant conscription of the Russian peasantry on a grand scale. In a ten-year period of the Great Northern War, the army absorbed 330,000 conscripts, most of whom never returned to their homes. Military service was not confined to the peasantry. Traditionally, the rural gentry raised and equipped the local conscript forces and gave them what training they could. Most gentry lived on estates that had been granted to them, along with the resident peasants, as a reward for their military contributions. Peter the Great intensified the obligations of the gentry. Not only were they to serve the state for life, but they were to accompany their regiments to the field and lead them in battle. When too old for active military service, they were to perform administrative service in the new departments of state.

The expansion of military forces necessitated an expansion of military administration as well. Peter's first innovation was the creation of the Senate, a group of nine senior administrators who were to oversee all aspects of military and civil government. The Senate became a permanent institution of government led by an entirely new official, the Procurator-General, who presided over its sessions and could propose legislation as well as oversee administration. From the Senate emanated 500 officials known as the fiscals, who traveled throughout the state looking for irregularities in tax assessment and collection. They quickly developed into a hated and feared internal police force.

Peter's efforts to reorganize his government went a step further in 1722, when he issued the Table of Ranks. This was an official hierarchy of the state that established the social position or rank of individuals. It was divided into three categories—military service, civil service, and owners of landed estates. Each category contained 14 ranks, and it was decreed that every person who entered the hierarchy did so at the bottom and worked his way up. The creation of the Table of Ranks was significant in a number of ways. It demonstrated Peter's continued commitment to merit as a criterion for advancement. This standard had been shown in the military, where officers were promoted on the basis of service and experience rather than birth or background. Equally important was Peter's decision to make the military service the highest of the three categories. This reversed the centuries-old position of the landed aristocracy and the military service class. Although the old nobility also served in the military and continued to dominate state service, the Table of Ranks opened the way for the infusion of new elements into the Russian elite.

Many of those who were able to advance in the Table of Ranks did so through attendance at the new institutions of higher learning that Peter founded. His initial educational establishments were created to further the military might of the state. The Colleges of Mathematics, Engineering, and Artillery, which became the training grounds for his army officers, were all founded during the Great Northern War. But Peter was interested in liberal education as well. He had scores of western books translated into Russian. He had a press established in Moscow to print original works, including the first Russian newspaper. He decreed that a new, more westernized alphabet replace the one used by the Russian Orthodox church and that books be written in the language that the people spoke rather than in the formal literary language of religious writers. He also introduced Arabic numerals into official accounting records.

Peter's reforms of government and society were matched by his efforts to energize the economy. No state in Europe had as many natural resources as did Russia, yet manufacturing barely existed there. As with everything else he did, Peter took a direct hand in establishing factories for the production of textiles, glass, leather, and, most importantly, iron and copper. The state directly owned about half of these establishments, most of them on a larger scale than any known in the west. By 1726, more than half of all Russian exports were manufactured goods and Russia had become the largest producer of iron and copper in the world.

In all these ways and more, Peter the Great transformed Russia. But the changes Peter wrought did not come without cost. The traditions of centuries were not easily broken. Intrigue against Peter led first to confrontation with the old military elite, and later to conflict with his only son, Alexis. It remains unclear whether the plot with which Alexis was connected actually existed or whether it was a figment of Peter's imagination, but it is abundantly clear that Alexis's death from torture plunged the state into a succession crisis in 1725. Finally, the great costs of westernization were paid by the masses of people, who benefited little from the improvement in Russia's international standing or from the social and economic changes that affected the elites.

Life in Rural Russia

At the beginning of the eighteenth century, nearly 97 percent of the Russian people lived on the land and practiced agriculture. Farming techniques and agrarian lifestyles had changed little for centuries. Most of the country's soil was poor. Harsh climate and low yields characterized Russian agriculture. Thirty-four of the 100 Russian harvests during the eighteenth century can be termed poor or disastrous, yet throughout the century state taxation was making larger and larger demands upon the peasantry. During Peter's reign alone, direct taxation increased by 500 percent.

The theory of the Russian state was one of service, and the role of Russian peasants was to serve their master. Beginning in the mid-seventeenth century, the peasantry had undergone a change in status. The law code of 1649 formalized a process that had been under way for over a century whereby peasants were turned into the property of their landlords. During the next century, laws curtailed the ability of peasants to move freely from one place to another, eliminated their right to hold private property, and abolished their freedom to petition the tsar against their masters. At the same time that landlords increased their hold over peasants, the state increased its hold over landlords. They were made responsible for the payment of taxes owed by their peasants and for the military service due from them. By the middle of the eighteenth century, over half of all peasants—6.7 million adult males by 1782—had thus become serfs, the property of their masters, without any significant rights or legal protection.

Private landlords reckoned their wealth in the number of serfs they owned, but in fact most owned only a small number—fewer than 50—in the middle of the eighteenth century. This resulted from the common practice whereby a father divided his estate among all of his surviving sons. Most gentry were small landholders, constantly in debt and rarely able to meet their financial and service obligations to the state. This life of poverty at the top was, of course, magnified at the bottom. The vast majority of serfs lived in small villages where they divided up their meager surplus to pay their taxes and drew lots to see who would be sent for military service. When the debts of their lords became too heavy, it was the serfs who were foreclosed.

If serfs made up the bottom half of the Russian peasantry, there were few advantages to being in the top half, among the state peasants. State peasants lived on lands owned by the monarchy itself. Like the serfs, they were subject to the needs of the state for soldiers and workers. The use of forced labor was a feature of each of Peter's grandiose projects. Saint Petersburg was built by the backbreaking labor of peasant conscripts. From 1709, when the project began, perhaps as many as 40,000 laborers a year were forced to work on the various sites. The unhealthy conditions of the swampy environment from which the new capital rose claimed the lives of thousands of these workers, as did the appalling conditions of overwork and undernourishment in which they lived.

Many Russian peasants developed a philosophy of submission and a rich folk culture that valued a stubborn determination to endure. For those who would no longer bend to the knout—the heavy leather whip that was the omnipresent enforcer of obedience—there was only flight or rebellion. Hundreds of thousands of serfs fled to state-owned lands in hope of escaping the cruelties of individual landlords. Although severe penalties were imposed for aiding runaway serfs, in fact most state overseers and many private landlords encouraged runaways to settle on their lands. In their social and economic conditions, eighteenth-century Russian peasants were hardly distinguishable from medieval European serfs.

The Enlightened Empress Catherine

Of all the legacies of Peter the Great, perhaps the one of most immediate consequence was that government could go on without him. During the next 37 years, six tsars ruled Russia, "three women, a boy of twelve, an infant, and a mental weakling," as one commentator acidly observed. More to the point, each succession was contested, as there were no direct male heirs to the throne in this period. Nevertheless, despite turmoil at the top, government continued to function smoothly and Peter's territorial conquests were largely maintained. Russia also experienced a remarkable increase in numbers during this period. Between 1725 and 1762 the population increased from 13 to 19 million, a jump of nearly one-half in a single generation. This explosion of people dramatically increased the wealth of the landholding class, who reckoned their status by the number of serfs they owned.

The expansion of the economic resources of the nobility was matched by a rise in legal status and political power. This was the period sarcastically dubbed "the emancipation of the nobility," a phrase that captures not only the irony of the growing gap between rich and poor but also the contrast between the social structures of Russia and those of western Europe. In return for their privileges and status, Peter the Great extended the duties the landowning classes owed to the state. By granting unique rights, like the ownership of serfs, to the descendants of the old military service class, Peter had forged a Russian nobility. Lifetime service, however, was the price of nobility.

In order to gain and hold the throne, each succeeding tsar had to make concessions to the nobility to gain their loyalty. At first it was a few simple adjustments. The sons of wealthy landowners who completed a course of education at one of the state academies were allowed to enter the Table of Ranks in the middle of the hierarchy rather than at the bottom. Then life service was commuted to a term of 25 years, still a long time in a world of short lives and sudden deaths. But these concessions were not enough.

Twenty-five years of service did not solve the problem of estate management, especially as the tasks of management grew along with the population of serfs. Thus the next capitulation was that a single son could remain on the estate and escape service altogether. The births of younger sons were concealed; owners of multiple estates claimed the exemption of one son for each. Most decisively, the talented remained at home to serve the family while the wastrels were sent to serve the state. Finally, in 1762, the obligation for state service by the nobility was abolished entirely.

The abolition of compulsory service was not the same as the abolition of service itself. In fact the end of compulsory service enabled Catherine II, "the Great" (1762–96), to enact some of the most important reforms of her reign. (See "Catherine Before She Was Great," pp. 604–605.) At first, Catherine's accession seemed nothing more than a continuation of monarchical instability—her first two acts were to have her husband, Peter III, murdered and to lower the salt tax. Each brought her a measure of security.

Catherine was a dynamic personality who alternately captivated and terrified those with whom she came into contact. Her policies were as complex as her personality, influenced on the one hand by the new French ideas of social justice and the nobility of the human race, and on the other hand by the traditional Russian ideas of absolute rule over an enserfed and subhuman population. Catherine handled these contrasting dimensions of her rule masterfully, gaining abroad the reputation as the most enlightened of European monarchs and at home the sincere devotion of her people.

The most important event in the early years of Catherine's reign was the establishment of a legislative commission to review the laws of Russia. Catherine herself wrote the *Instruction* (1767), by which the elected commissioners were to operate. She borrowed her theory of law from the French jurist Baron de Montesquieu (1689–1755) and her theory of punishment from the Italian reformer Cesare Beccaria (1738–94). Among other things, Catherine advocated the abolition of capital punishment, torture, serf auctions, and the breakup of serf families by sale. Few of these radical reforms were ever put into practice.

But in 1775 Catherine did restructure local government. Russia was divided into 50 provincial districts, each with a population of between 300,000 and 400,000 inhabitants. Each district was to be governed by both a

childhood Traumas

Catherine the Great left a fascinating account of her early years, which is in sharp contrast to her reputation for ruthlessness as a ruler.

My father, whom I saw very seldom, considered me to be an angel, my mother did not bother much about me. She had had, eighteen months after my birth, a son whom she passionately loved, whereas I was merely tolerated and often repulsed with violence and temper, not always with justice. I was aware of all this, but not always able to understand what I really felt about it.

At the age of seven I was suddenly seized with a violent cough. It was the custom that we should kneel every night and every morning to say our prayers. One night as I knelt and prayed I began to cough so violently that the strain caused me to fall on my left side, and I had such sharp pains in my chest that they almost took my breath away.

Finally, after much suffering, I was well enough to get up and it was discovered, as they started to put on my clothes, that I had in the meantime assumed the shape of the letter Z: my right shoulder was much higher than the left, the backbone running in a zigzag and the left side falling in.

From Catherine the Great, *Memoirs* (1755).

central official and elected local noblemen. This reform was modeled upon the English system of justices of the peace. Previous local reforms had failed because of the absence of a resident local nobility. The abolition of compulsory service finally made possible the establishment of local institutions. In 1785 Catherine issued the Charter of the Nobility, a formal statement of the rights and privileges of the noble class. The Charter incorporated all the gains the nobility had made since the death of Peter the Great, but it also instituted the requirements for local service that had been the basis of Catherine's reforms. District councils with the right to petition directly to the tsar became the centerpiece of Russian provincial government.

In order to train the local nobility for government service, Catherine introduced educational reforms. Peter had established military schools for the nobility and had staffed them with foreigners. The University of Moscow had been founded in 1755, and its faculty too was dominated by European emigrants. Catherine saw the need to broaden the educational system. Borrowing from the Austrian system, she established provincial elementary schools to train the sons and daughters of the local nobility. To staff these, Catherine created teachers' colleges so that the state would have its own educators. Although the program called for the equal education of women, except in Saint Petersburg and Moscow few women attended either elementary or high schools.

Catherine's reforms did little to enhance the lives of the vast majority of her people. Although she often spoke in the terms of the French philosophers who saw the enserfment of fellow humans as a blot on civilization, Catherine took no effective action either to end serfdom or to soften its rigors. In fact, by grants of state land Catherine gave away 800,000 state peasants, who became serfs. So, too, did millions of Poles who became her subjects after the partition of Poland in 1793 and 1795.

The most significant uprising of the century, Pugachev's revolt (1773–75), took place during Catherine's reign. Emelyan Pugachev (1726–75) was a Cossack who in his youth had been a military adventurer. Disappointed in his career, he made his way to the Ural mountains, where he recruited Asian tribesmen and laborers forced to work in the mines. By promising freedom and land ownership, he drew peasants to his cause. In 1773 Pugachev declared himself to be Tsar Peter III, the murdered husband of Catherine II. He began with small raiding parties against local landlords and military outposts and soon had gained the allegiance of

Chained but undaunted, Emelyan Pugachev awaits punishment for leading a peasant rebellion in the southern Urals.

tens of thousands of peasants. In 1774, with an army of nearly 20,000, Pugachev took the city of Kazan and threatened to advance on Moscow. It was another year before state forces could effectively control the rebellion. Finally, Pugachev was betrayed by his own followers and sent to Moscow, where he was executed.

During the reigns of Peter and Catherine the Great, Russia was transformed into an international power. Saint Petersburg, a window to the west, was a capital worthy of a potent monarch, and during the course of the eighteenth century it attracted many of Europe's leading luminaries. At court French was spoken, the latest fashions were worn, and the newest ideas for economic and educational reform were aired. The Russian nobility mingled comfortably with its European counterparts, while the military service class developed into bureaucrats and administrators. But if life glittered at court, it remained the same dull regimen in the country. Millions of peasants were owned either by the state or by private landlords, and their quality of life was no dif-

catherine Before she was Great

Catherine the Great wasn't always called the Empress of All the Russias. In fact, she wasn't always called Catherine. Sophie of Anhalt-Zerbst was the daughter of a petty German prince whose estates were too poor to provide for his family. He hired out as a military officer to the kings of Prussia and became governor of the dreary Baltic port of Stettin. Here Sophie passed her childhood. The family lived comfortably, and Sophie was provided with a French governess, Babette Cardel. From Babette she learned not only the language of the French but their ways. Sophie was no easy child to handle. Her natural curiosity led to some narrow escapes, and she was nearly killed at the age of three when she pulled a cupboard down. To curiosity was added spirit, and the shouting matches in which she and Babette engaged were long remembered. Indeed, Babette took to bribing young Sophie with sweets, which in the long run did less to soften her temper than to ruin her teeth.

By far the most significant event of Sophie's childhood was the sudden sickness that overtook her at the age of seven. She was seized by coughing, fevers, and fits that incapacitated her for weeks. For a time her life was in danger. It was not unusual in those days for unexplained illness to appear and disappear with bewildering suddenness, and this is what happened to Sophie. One morning she awoke without fever and without the racking cough that had seared her body. But in its place had come a physical change. Weeks of lying on her side had deformed her physique: "I had assumed the shape of a letter Z. My right shoulder was much higher than the left, the backbone running in a zigzag and the left side falling in," she later recalled. Such a result was as mysterious as the illness that occasioned it. Doctors were sought for advice. None could help until at last a veterinarian who practiced on the limbs of horses and cows was found. He prescribed a useless concoction of medicines but also built a body frame for Sophie that was designed to reshape her deformity. She wore this for four years until she regained her former posture.

Sophie's father was a strict Lutheran who prescribed a regimen for the education of his children that was to be followed precisely. Just after her recovery, Sophie was told that she could no longer play with her toys but must behave as an adult. Tutors were brought to teach her history and geography, and a Lutheran minister was deputed to train her in religion. Sophie took delight in confounding her religion instructor and in general showed the same high spirits as she had in childhood.

Although Sophie did not have a close relationship with her mother—in later years they quarreled incessantly—it was her mother who showed her the world outside Stettin. Joanna of Holstein-Gottorp had grown up surrounded by courtly pomp While her family, too, came from the ranks of the minor princes of the Holy Roman Empire, marriages and inclination had brought them into the circle of German aristocratic life. This was a world for which Joanna longed, and every year she visited her relations in Brunswick. Sophie began to accompany her mother on these trips, and they became for her the means to escape the boredom of Stettin. On one visit to Berlin she was introduced to Frederick William I, king of Prussia. Her relatives included a future king of Sweden and a future queen of Britain. These trips to Brunswick and Berlin opened Sophie's eyes to the possibility of a different life, the possibility of life with one of the crown princes of Europe.

As it happened, Sophie had little need to wish. By a twist of fate, another of her mother's innumerable cousins had recently been declared heir to the throne of Russia.

This was Peter, soon to be duke of Holstein-Gottorp and ultimately Peter III of Russia. Empress Elizabeth of Russia was childless, and Peter was her nearest relative. She determined to have him married to an eligible German princess, and after much casting about, the choice fell on Sophie. In 1744 Sophie was summoned to Russia. Joanna was thrilled with the prospect, not only because of the possibility of a successful marriage for her daughter, but also because she was to have a role in the affair. No one asked Sophie what she thought, since her opinion hardly mattered.

The journey to Russia was a trip that Sophie would never forget. Stettin was no tropical paradise, but the climate there had little prepared Sophie and her mother for the rigors of the east. Carriages gave way to sleighs, and her heavy cloth clothing to sable. Sophie and Joanna huddled together for warmth, covering their faces and hands from the bitter arctic winds. It took nearly four weeks to reach Saint Petersburg, and when they arrived they were informed that they must hurry to join the royal court at Moscow. There they were received with unusual warmth, as it was the sixteenth birthday of the new heir to the throne and all of Russian society was eager to see his bride-to-be.

Sophie's earliest meetings with her fiancé were not entirely satisfactory. In a strange land she might have expected strange customs, but Peter was a German like herself. Thus she was unprepared for their first interview, in which Peter professed his passionate love for one of the ladies of the court. Sophie was only 15 and, by her own account at least, innocent in sexual matters. Peter's frank confession, which was accompanied by assurances that he would marry Sophie anyhow, caused her as much confusion as it did anger and resentment. She resolved to keep her own counsel and to attempt to please the empress, if not the heir. Sophie spent the days before her marriage learning both the Russian language and the Eastern Orthodox religion. She would have to convert to the old faith before she could be betrothed. As part of her conversion, she had to take a Russian name, and thus she came to be called Catherine. Whether her change of religion was sincere or not, it was required. Sophie was shrewd enough to realize the importance of the Church, and she won many admirers at court when, after being taken suddenly ill, she asked for an Orthodox priest rather than a Lutheran minister or a doctor.

Sophie's marriage took place in 1745 in one of the most magnificent ceremonies anyone could recall. By then she knew that she was alone in the world. She had fought bitterly with her mother. Sophie shared nothing with her new husband—including the marriage bed. The household set up for her was composed entirely of spies for the empress, and even her correspondence was monitored. She spent the next 15 years supplementing the education that she had received as a child. She read everything she could get hold of. Her Russian improved dramatically as she read Russian and French or German versions of the same works. She devoured the classics, especially history and philosophy, and for the first time became acquainted with the works of the new European writers whose reputations had reached as far as Russia. Sophie indulged her enthusiasm for riding, an exercise not usually taken by women. She also developed a passion for the handsome guardsmen who inhabited the palace. Perhaps in revenge for her husband's conduct, perhaps in return for his neglect, she took the first of more than 20 lovers. When she became pregnant in 1754, it was almost certainly not with Peter's child. Eight years later, Empress Elizabeth died and the private life of Sophie of Anhalt-Zerbst ended. The half-mad Peter III acceded to the throne, and Sophie, now known to the world as Catherine, began her remarkable public career.

ferent at the end of the campaign of westernization than it had been at the beginning.

The Two Germanies

The Thirty Years' War, which ended in 1648, initiated a profound transformation of the Holy Roman Empire. Warfare had devastated imperial territory. It was decades before the rich imperial lands recovered, and then the political consequences of the war had taken effect. There were now two empires, a German and an Austrian, though both were ruled by the same person. In the German territories, whether Catholic or Protestant, the Holy Roman Emperor was more a constitutional monarch than the absolute ruler he was in Austria. The larger states like Saxony, Bavaria, and Hanover made their own political alliances despite the jurisdictional control that the emperor claimed to exercise. Most decisively, so did Brandenburg-Prussia. By the beginning of the eighteenth century, the electors of Brandenburg had become the kings of Prussia, and Prussia's military power and efficient administrative structure became the envy of its German neighbors.

The Austrian empire was composed of Austria and Bohemia, the Habsburg hereditary lands, and as much of Hungary as could be controlled. In Austria, the Habsburgs clung tightly to their power. For decades Austria was the center of the still-flourishing Counter-Reformation, and the power and influence of the Jesuits was as strong here as it was in Spain. The War of the Spanish Succession, which gave the Habsburgs control of the southern Netherlands and parts of Italy, brought Austria an enhanced role in European affairs. Austria remained one of the great powers of Europe and the leading power in the Holy Roman Empire despite the rise of Prussia. Indeed, from the middle of the eighteenth century, the conflict between Prussia and Austria was the defining characteristic of central European politics.

The Rise of prussia

The transformation of Brandenburg-Prussia from a petty German principality to a great European power was one of the most significant and least expected developments of the eighteenth century. Frederick William, the Great Elector (1640–88), had begun the process of forging Brandenburg-Prussia into a power in its own right by building a large and efficient military

The Expansion of Prussia

A King's-eye View

Frederick the Great wrote philosophical and military tracts as well as composing dozens of compositions for the flute. Here is his definition of the enlightened despot.

The sovereign is attached by indissoluble ties to the body of the state; hence it follows that he, by repercussion, is sensible to all the ills which afflict his subjects; and the people, in like manner, suffer from the misfortunes which affect their sovereign. There is but one general good, which is that of the state. . . . The sovereign represents the state; he and his people form but one body, which can only be happy as far as united by concord. The prince is to the nation he governs what the head is to the man; it is his duty to see, to think, and act for the whole community, so that he may procure it every advantage of which it is capable. . . . Such are in general the duties imposed upon a prince, from which, in order that he may never depart, he ought often to recollect that he himself is but a man, like the least of his subjects. If he be the first general, the first minister of the realm, it is not so that he should shelter in the shadow of authority, but that he should fulfill the duties of such titles. He is only the first servant of the state, who is obliged to act with probity and prudence; and to remain as totally disinterested as if he were each moment liable to render an account of his administration to his fellow citizens.

From Frederick the Great, *An Essay on Forms of Government.*

machine. At the beginning of the eighteenth century, Prussia was on the winning side in both the War of the Spanish Succession and the Great Northern War. When the battlefield dust had settled, Prussia found itself in possession of Pomerania and the Baltic port of Stettin. It was now a recognized power in eastern Europe.

Frederick William I (1713–40) and his son Frederick II, "the Great" (1740–86), turned this promising beginning into an astounding success. A devout Calvinist, Frederick William I deplored waste and display as much on moral as on fiscal grounds. The reforms he initiated were intended to subordinate both aristocracy and peasantry to the needs of the state and to subordinate the needs of the state to the demands of the military.

Because of its geographical position, Prussia's major problem was to maintain an efficient and well-trained army during peacetime. Defense of its exposed territories required a constant state of military preparedness, yet the relaxation of military discipline and the desertion of troops to their homes inevitably followed the cessation of hostilities. Frederick William I solved this problem by integrating the economic and military structures of his state. First he appointed only German officers to command his troops, eliminating the mercenaries who sold their services to the highest bidders. Then he placed these noblemen at the head of locally recruited regiments. Each adult male in every district was required to register for military service in the regiment of the local landlord. These reforms dramatically increased the effectiveness of the army by shifting the burden of recruitment and training to the localities.

Yet despite all the attention that Frederick William I lavished on the military—by the end of his reign nearly 70 percent of state expenditures went to the army—his foreign policy was largely pacific. In fact, his greatest achievements were in civil affairs, reforming the bureaucracy, establishing a sound economy, and raising state revenues. Through generous settlement schemes and by welcoming Protestant and Jewish refugees, Frederick William was able to expand the economic potential of these eastern territories. Frederick William I pursued an aggressive policy of land purchase to expand the royal domain, and the addition of so many new inhabitants in Prussia further increased his wealth. While the major western European powers were discovering deficit financing and the national debt, Prussia was running a surplus.

Financial security was vital to the success of Frederick the Great. Father and son had quarreled bitterly throughout Frederick's youth—not only about music—and most observers expected that out of spite Frederick would tear down all that his father had built up. In fact father and son were cast in the same mold, with the unexpected difference that the son was more ruthless and ambitious. With his throne, Frederick II inherited the fourth largest army in Europe and the richest treasury.

He wasted no time in putting both to use. His two objectives were to acquire the Polish corridor of West Prussia that separated his German and Prussian territories and to acquire the agriculturally and industrially rich Austrian province of Silesia to the southeast of Berlin. Just months after his coronation, Frederick conquered Silesia, increasing the size of Prussia by nearly a quarter. Within a decade the province dominated the Prussian economy, outproducing and outconsuming all other areas of Frederick's state.

It was Frederick's military prowess that earned him the title "the Great." But this was only a part of his achievement. More than his father, Frederick II forged an alliance with the Prussian nobility, integrating them into a unified state. A tightly organized central administration, which depended upon the cooperation of the local nobility, directed both military and bureaucratic affairs. At the center, Frederick worked tirelessly to oversee his government. Where Louis XIV had proclaimed, "I am the state," Frederick the Great announced, "I am the first servant of the state." He codified the laws of Prussia, abolished torture and capital punishment, and instituted agricultural techniques imported from the states of western Europe. By the end of Frederick's reign, Prussia had become a model for bureaucratic organization, military reform, and enlightened rule.

Austria survives

Austria was the great territorial victor in the War of the Spanish Succession, acquiring both the Netherlands and parts of Italy. Austrian forces recaptured a large part of Hungary from the Turks, thereby expanding their territory to the south and the east. As hereditary ruler of Austria and Bohemia, king of Hungary, and Holy Roman Emperor of the German nation, Charles VI (1711–40) was recognized as one of Europe's most potent rulers. But appearances were deceptive. The apex of Austrian power and prestige had already passed. Austria had benefited from balance-of-power politics, not so much from its own strength as from the leverage it could give to others. With the rise of Russia and Prussia, there was now more than one fulcrum to power in eastern Europe.

The difficulties facing Austria ran deep. The Thirty Years' War had made the emperor more an Austrian monarch than an imperial German ruler. On the

Prussian infantry officers display their uniforms in this painting from the late eighteenth century. Distinctive, colorful, and elaborate uniforms, different for each regiment, were common in European armies before the field-gray and khaki era of the twentieth century.

military Discipline

Herman Maurice de Saxe was the illegitimate son of the king of Poland. He had extensive military experience in both eastern and western Europe. He ultimately achieved the office of Marshal of France, where he was celebrated as a military reformer. He modeled many of his reforms on the Prussian army.

Would it not be much better to establish a law obliging men of all conditions of life to serve their king and country for the space of five years? A law, which could not reasonably be objected against, as it is both natural and just for people to be engaged in the defense of that state of which they constitute a part, and in choosing them between the years of twenty and thirty, no manner of inconvenience can possibly be the result; for those are years devoted, as it were, to libertinism; which are spent in adventures and travels, and, in general, productive of but small comfort to parents. An expedient of this kind could not come under the denomination of a public calamity, because every man, at the expiration of his five years service, would be discharged. It would also create an inexhaustible fund of good recruits, and such as would not be subject to desertion. In course of time,

everyone would regard it as an honor rather than a duty to perform his task; but to produce this effect upon a people, it is necessary that no sort of distinction should be admitted, no rank or degree whatsoever excluded, and the nobles and rich rendered, in a principal manner, subservient to it. This would effectually prevent all murmur and repining, for those who had served their time, would look upon such, as betrayed any reluctance, or dissatisfaction at it, with contempt; by which means, the grievance would vanish insensibly, and every man at length esteem it an honor to serve his term. The poor would be comforted by the example of the rich; and the rich could not with decency complain, seeing themselves on a footing with the nobles.

From Marshal de Saxe, *Memoirs on the Art of War* (1757)

Austrian hereditary estates, the Catholic Counter-Reformation continued unabated, bringing with it the benefits of Jesuit education, cultural revival, and the religious unity necessary to motivate warfare against the Ottomans. But these benefits came at a price. Perhaps as many as 200,000 Protestants fled Austria and Bohemia, taking with them their skills and capital. For centuries the vision of empire had dominated Habsburg rule. This meant that the Austrian monarchy was a multiethnic confederation of lands loosely tied together by loyalty to a single head. The components preserved a high degree of autonomy: Hungary elected the Habsburg emperor its king in a separate ceremony. Local autonomy continually restricted the imposition of central policy, and never were the localities more autonomous than in the matter of taxation. Thus it was hard for Austria to centralize in the same way as had Prussia.

Austria was predominantly rural and agricultural. Less than 5 percent of the population lived in towns of 10,000 or more; less than 15 percent lived in towns at all. On the land, the local aristocracy, whether nobility or gentry, exploited serfs to the maximum. Not only

were serfs required to give labor service three days a week (and up to six during planting and harvest times), but the nobility maintained a full array of feudal privileges, including the right to mill all grain and brew all beer. When serfs married, when they transferred property, even when they died, they paid taxes to their lord. As a result they had little left to give the state. In consequence, the Austrian army was among the smallest and the poorest of the major powers despite the fact that it had the most active enemies along its borders.

Lack of finance, human resources, and governmental control were the underlying problems of Austria, but they were not the most immediate difficulties facing Charles VI. With no sons to succeed him, Charles feared that his hereditary and elective states would go their separate ways after his death and that the great Habsburg monarchy would end. For 20 years his abiding ambition was to gain recognition for the principle that his empire would pass intact to his daughter, Maria Theresa. He expressed the principle in a document known as the Pragmatic Sanction, which stated that all Habsburg lands would pass intact to the eldest heir, male or female. Charles VI made concession after concession to gain acceptance of the Pragmatic Sanction. But the leaders of Europe licked their lips at the prospect of a dismembered Austrian empire.

Maria Theresa (1740–80) inherited the imperial throne in 1740 and quickly discovered what it was like to be a woman in a man's world. In 1740 Frederick of Prussia invaded the rich Austrian province of Silesia and attracted allies for an assault upon Vienna. Faced with Bavarian, Saxon, and Prussian armies, Maria Theresa might well have lost her inheritance had she not shown her remarkable capacities so early in her reign. She appeared before the Hungarian estates, accepted their crown, and persuaded them to provide her with an army capable of halting the allied advance. Although she was unable to reconquer Silesia, Hungarian aid helped her hold the line against her enemies.

The loss of Silesia, the most prosperous part of the Austrian domains, signaled the need for fundamental

Maria Theresa and her family. Eleven of Maria Theresa's 16 children are posed with the empress and her husband, Francis of Lorraine. Standing next to his mother is the future emperor Joseph II.

reform. The new eighteenth-century idea of building a state replaced the traditional Habsburg concern with maintaining an empire. Maria Theresa and her son Joseph II (1780–90) began the process of transformation. For Austria, state building meant first the reorganization of the military and civil bureaucracy to clear the way for fiscal reform. As in Prussia, a central directory was created to oversee the collection of taxes and the disbursement of funds. Maria Theresa personally persuaded her provincial estates both to increase taxation and to extend it to the nobles and the clergy. While her success was limited, she finally established royal control over the raising and collection of taxes.

The second element in Maria Theresa's reform program involved the condition of the Austrian peasantry. Maria Theresa established the doctrine that "the peasant must be able to support himself and his family and pay his taxes in time of peace and war." She limited labor service to two days per week and abolished the most burdensome feudal dues. Joseph II ended serfdom altogether. The new Austrian law codes guaranteed peasants' legal rights and established their ability to seek redress through the law. Joseph II hoped to extend reform even further. In the last years of his life, he abolished obligatory labor service and ensured that all peasants kept one-half of their income before paying local and state taxes. Such a radical reform met a storm of opposition and was ultimately abandoned at the end of the reign.

The reorganization of the bureaucracy, the increase in taxation, and the social reforms that created a more productive peasantry revitalized the Austrian state. The efforts of Maria Theresa and Joseph II to overcome provincial autonomy worked better in Austria and Bohemia than in Hungary. The Hungarians declined to contribute at all to state revenues, and Joseph II took the unusual step of refusing to be crowned king of Hungary so that he would not have to make any concessions to Hungarian autonomy. He even imposed a tariff on Hungarian goods sold in Austria. More seriously, parts of the empire already had been lost before the process of reform could begin. Prussia's seizure of Silesia was the hardest blow of all. Yet in 1740, when Frederick the Great and his allies swept down from the north, few would have predicted that Austria would survive.

The politics of power

Frederick the Great's invasion of Silesia in 1740 was callous and cynical. Since the Pragmatic Sanction bound him to recognize Maria Theresa's succession, Frederick cynically offered her a defensive alliance in return for which she would simply hand over Silesia. It was an offer she should not have refused. Although Frederick's action initiated the War of the Austrian Succession, he was not alone in his desire to shake loose parts of Austria's territory. Soon nearly the entire Continent became embroiled in the conflict.

The War of the Austrian Succession (1740–48) resembled a pack of wolves stalking its injured prey. It quickly became a major international conflict, involving Prussia, France, and Spain on one side and Austria, Britain, and Holland on the other. Spain joined the fighting to recover its Italian possessions, Saxony claimed Moravia, France entered Bohemia, and the Bavarians moved into Austria from the south. With France and Prussia allied, it was vital that Britain join with Austria to maintain the balance of power. Initially the British did little more than subsidize Maria Theresa's forces, but once France renewed its efforts to conquer the Netherlands, both Britain and the Dutch Republic joined in the fray.

That the British cared little about the fate of the Habsburg empire was clear from the terms of the treaty that they dictated at Aix-la-Chapelle (Aachen) in 1748. Austria recognized Frederick's conquest of Silesia, as well as the loss of parts of its Italian territories to Spain. France, which the British had always regarded as the real enemy, withdrew from the Netherlands in return for the restoration of a number of colonial possessions. The War of the Austrian Succession made Austria and Prussia permanent enemies and gave Maria Theresa a crash course in international diplomacy. She learned firsthand that self-interest rather than loyalty underlay power politics.

This lesson was reinforced in 1756 when Britain and Prussia entered into a military accord at the beginning of the Seven Years' War (1756–63). Prussian expansion and duplicity had already alarmed both Russia and France, and Frederick II feared that he would be squeezed from east and west. He could hardly expect help from Maria Theresa, so he extended overtures to the British, whose interests in protecting Hanover, the hereditary estates of their German-born king, outweighed their prior commitments to Austria. Frederick's actions drove France into the arms of both the Austrians and the Russians, and an alliance that included the German state of Saxony was formed in defense. Thus was initiated a diplomatic revolution in which France and Austria became allies after 300 years as enemies.

Once again Frederick the Great took the offensive, and once again he won his risk against the odds. His attack on Saxony and Austria in 1756 brought a vigorous response from the Russians, who interceded on Austria's behalf with a massive army. Three years later, at the battle of Kunersdorf, Frederick suffered the worst military defeat of his career when the Russians shattered his armies. In 1760 his forces were barely a third of the size of those massed by his opponents, and it was only a matter of time before he was fighting defensively from within Prussia.

In 1762 Empress Elizabeth died. She was succeeded by her nephew, the childlike Peter III, a German by birth who worshipped Frederick the Great. When Peter came

A satire on the Treaty of Paris, which ended the Seven Years' War.

to the throne, he immediately negotiated peace with Frederick, abandoning not only his allies but also the substantial territorial gains that the Russian forces had made within Prussia. It was small wonder that the Russian military leadership joined in the coup d'état that brought Peter's wife, Catherine, to the throne in 1762. With Russia out of the war, Frederick was able to fend off further Austrian offensives and to emerge with his state, including Silesia, intact.

The Seven Years' War did little to change the boundaries of the German states, but it had two important political results. The first was to establish beyond doubt the status of Prussia as a major power and a counterbalance to Austria in central Europe. The existence of the dual Germanies, one led by Prussia and the other by Austria, was to have serious consequences for German unification in the nineteenth century and for the two world wars in the twentieth. The second result of the Seven Years' War was to initiate a long period of peace in eastern Europe. Both Prussia and Austria were financially exhausted from two decades of fighting. Both states needed a breathing spell to initiate administrative and economic improvements, and the period following the Seven Years' War witnessed the sustained programs of internal reforms for which Frederick the Great, Maria Theresa, and Joseph II were famous in the decades following 1763.

Peace among the eastern European powers did not mean that they abandoned their territorial ambitions. All over Europe, absolute rulers reformed their bureaucracies, streamlined their administrations, increased their sources of revenue, and built enormous standing armies. All over Europe except in Poland. There the autonomous power of the nobility remained as strong as ever. No monarchical dynasty was ever established, and each elected ruler not only confirmed the privileges of the nobility but usually was forced to extend them. In the Diet, the Polish representative assembly, small special-interest groups could bring legislative business to a halt by exercising their veto power. Given the size of Poland's borders, its army was pathetically inadequate for the task it had to face. The Polish monarchy was helpless to defend its subjects from the destruction on all sides.

In 1764 Catherine the Great and Frederick the Great joined to place one of Catherine's former lovers on the Polish throne and to turn Poland into a weak dependent. Russia and Prussia had different interests in Poland's fate. For Russia, Poland represented a vast

buffer state that kept the German powers at a distance from Russia's borders. It was more in Russia's interest to dominate Polish foreign policy than to conquer its territory. For Prussia, Poland looked like another helpless flower, "to be picked off leaf by leaf," as Frederick observed. Poland seemed especially appealing because Polish territory, including the Baltic port of Gdansk, separated the Prussian and Brandenburg portions of Frederick's state.

By the 1770s the idea of carving up Poland was being actively discussed in Berlin, Saint Petersburg, and Vienna. Austria, too, had an interest in a Polish partition,

This engraving by Le Mire is called "The Cake of the Kings: First Partition of Poland, 1773." The monarchs of Russia, Austria, and Prussia join in carving up Poland. The Polish king is clutching his tottering crown.

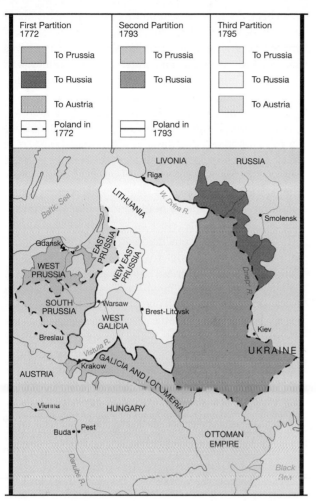

First Partition 1772	Second Partition 1793	Third Partition 1795
To Prussia	To Prussia	To Prussia
To Russia	To Russia	To Russia
To Austria		To Austria
Poland in 1772	Poland in 1793	

The Partition of Poland

Austria, despite its lost territory, proved capable of surviving the accession of a female ruler and of fighting off an attempt to dismember its empire. Its participation in the partition of Poland strengthened its role in the politics of the eastern powers, while its alliance with France fortified its role in the west. From one empire there were now two states, and the relationship between Prussia and Austria would dominate central Europe for the next century.

The Greatness of Great Britain

By the middle of the eighteenth century, Great Britain had become the leading power of Europe. It had won its spurs in Continental and colonial wars. Britain was unsurpassed as a naval power, able to protect its far-flung trading empire and to make a show of force in almost any part of the world. Perhaps more impressively for a nation that did not support a large standing army, British soldiers had won decisive victories in the European land wars. Until the American Revolution, Britain came up a winner in every military venture it undertook. But might was only one part of British success. Economic preeminence was every bit as important. British colonial possessions in the Atlantic and Indian oceans poured consumer products into Britain for export to the European marketplaces. Growth in overseas trade was matched by growth in home production. British advances in agricultural technique had transformed Britain from an importer to an exporter of grain. The manufacturing industries that other European states attempted to create with huge government subsidies flourished in Britain through private enterprise.

British military and economic power was supported by a unique system of government. In Britain the nobility served the state through government. The British constitutional system, devised in the seventeenth century and refined in the eighteenth, shared power between the monarchy and the ruling elite through the institution of Parliament. Central government integrated monarch and ministers with chosen representatives from the localities. Such integration not only provided the Crown with the vital information necessary to formulate national policy, but it eased acceptance and enforcement of government decisions. Government

especially to maintain its power and status with the other two states, and perhaps to use Polish territory as a potential bargaining chip for the return of Silesia. Finally, in 1772, the three great eastern powers struck a deal. Russia would take a large swath of the grain fields of northeast Poland, which included over one million people, while Frederick would unite his lands by seizing West Prussia. Austria gained both the largest territories, including Galicia, and the greatest number of people, nearly two million Polish subjects.

In a half century the balance of power in central Europe had shifted decisively. Prussia's absorption of Silesia and parts of Poland made it a single geographical entity, as well as a great economic and military power.

was seen as the rule of law that, however imperfect, was believed to operate for the benefit of all.

The parliamentary system gave Britain some of its particular strengths, but they came at a cost. Politics was a national pastime rather than the business of an elite of administrators and state servants. Decentralization of decision-making led to half-measures designed to placate competing interests. Appeals to public opinion, especially by candidates for Parliament, often played upon fears and prejudices that divided rather than united the nation. Moreover, the relative openness of the British system hindered diplomatic and colonial affairs, in which secrecy and rapid changes of direction were often the monarch's most potent weapons. These weaknesses came to light most dramatically during the struggle for independence waged by Britain's North American colonists. There the clash of principle and power was most extreme and the strengths and weaknesses of parliamentary rule were ruthlessly exposed.

The British constitution

The British Constitution was a patchwork of laws and customs that was gradually sewn together to form a workable system of government. Many of its greatest innovations came about through circumstance rather than design, and circumstance continued to play an essential role in its development in the eighteenth century. At the apex of the government stood the king, not an absolute monarch like his European counterparts, but not necessarily less powerful for having less arbitrary power. The British people revered monarchy and the monarch. The theory of mixed government depended upon the balance of interests represented by the monarchy in the Crown, the aristocracy in the House of Lords, and the people in the House of Commons. Less abstractly, the monarch was still regarded as divinely ordained and a special gift to the nation. The monarch was the actual and symbolic leader of the nation as well as the Supreme Head of the Church of England. Allegiance to the Anglican church, whether as a political creed among the elite or as a simple matter of devotion among the populace, intensified allegiance to the king.

The partnership between Crown and representative body was best expressed in the idea that the British government was composed of King-in-Parliament. Parliament consisted of three separate organs: monarch, lords, and commons. Although each existed separately

as a check upon the potential excesses of the others, it was only when the three functioned together that parliamentary government could operate. The king was charged with selecting ministers, initiating policy, and supervising administration. The two houses of Parliament were charged with raising revenue, making laws, and presenting the grievances of subjects to the Crown.

There were 558 members of the House of Commons after the union with Scotland in 1707. Most members of the lower house were nominated to their seats. The largest number of seats were located in small towns where a local oligarchy, or neighboring patron, had a customary right to make nominations that were invariably accepted by the electorate. Even in the largest cities, influential citizens made arrangements for nominating members in order to avoid the cost and confusion of an actual election. Campaigns were ruinously expensive for the candidates—an election in 1754 cost the losing candidates £40,000—and potentially dangerous to the local community, where bitter social and political divisions boiled just below the surface.

The British gentry dominated the Commons, occupying over 80 percent of the seats in any session. Most of these members also served as unpaid local officials in the counties, as justices of the peace, captains of the local militias, or collectors of local taxes. They came to Parliament not only as representatives of the interests of their class, but as experienced local governors who understood the needs of both Crown and subject.

Nevertheless, the Crown had to develop methods to coordinate the work of the two houses of Parliament and facilitate the passage of governmental programs. The king and his ministers began to use the deep royal pockets of offices and favors to bolster their friends in Parliament. Not only were those employed by the Crown encouraged to find a place in the House of Commons, but those who had a place in Parliament were encouraged to take employment from the Crown. Despite its potential for abuse, this was a political process that integrated center and locality, and at first it worked rather well. Those with local standing were brought into central offices. There they could influence central policy-making while protecting their local constituents. These officeholders, who came to be called placemen, never constituted a majority of the members of Parliament. They formed the core around which eighteenth-century governments operated, but it was a core that needed direction and cohesion. It was such leadership and organization that was the essential contribution of eighteenth-century politics to the British Constitution.

Thomas Gainsborough, Robert Andrews and His Wife, *ca. 1748–50. Gainsborough began as a landscape painter but eventually became the favorite portraitist of British high society. This is one of his early portraits and shows the country squire and his wife with casual grace in their home setting.*

parties and ministers

Although parliamentary management was vital to the Crown, it was not the Crown that developed the basic tools of management. Rather, these techniques originated within the political community itself, and their usefulness was only slowly grasped by the monarchy. The first and, in the long term, most important tool was the party system.

Political parties initially developed in the late seventeenth century around the issue of the Protestant succession. Those who opposed James II because he was a Catholic attempted to exclude him from inheriting the crown. They came to be called by their opponents *Whigs*, which had come to mean "horse thieves" (the term originally derived from *Wiggamore*, a name for Western Isle Scots who cried "Whig, whig!" to spur their horses on). Those who supported James's hereditary rights but who also supported the Anglican church came to be called by their opponents *Tories*, which in Gaelic meant "cattle rustlers."

The Tories cooperated in the Revolution of 1688 that placed William and Mary on the throne because James had threatened the Anglican church by tolerating Catholics and because Mary had a legitimate hereditary right to be queen. After the death of Queen Anne in 1714, the Tories supported the succession of James III, James II's Catholic son, who had been raised in France, rather than of George I (1714–27), prince of Hanover and Protestant great-grandson of James I. An unsuccessful rebellion to place James III on the throne in 1715 discredited the leadership of the Tory party but did not weaken its importance in both local and parliamentary politics.

The Whigs supported the Protestant succession and a broad-based Protestantism. They attracted the allegiance of large numbers of dissenters, heirs to the Puritans of the seventeenth century who practiced forms of Protestantism different from that of the Anglican church. The struggle between Whigs and Tories was less a struggle for power than it was for loyalty to their opposing viewpoints. As the Tories opposed the Hanoverian succession and the Whigs supported it, it was no mystery which party would find favor with George I. Moreover, as long as there was a pretender to the British throne—another rebellion took place in Scotland in 1745 led by the grandson of James II—the Tories continued to be tarred with the brush of disloyalty.

The division of political sympathies between Whigs and Tories helped create a set of groupings to which parliamentary leadership could be applied. A national rather than a local or regional outlook could be used to organize support for royal policy as long as royal policy conformed to that national outlook. The ascendancy of the Whigs enabled George I and his son George II (1727–60) to govern effectively through Parliament, but at the price of dependence upon the Whig leaders. Although the monarch had the constitutional freedom to choose his ministers, realistically he could choose only Whigs, and practically none but the Whig leaders of the House of Commons. Happily for the first two Georges, they found a man who was able to manage Parliament but desired only to serve the Crown.

Sir Robert Walpole (1676–1745) came from a long-established gentry family in Norfolk. Walpole was an early supporter of the Hanoverian succession and an early victim of party warfare. But once George I was securely on the throne, Walpole became an indispensable leader of the House of Commons. His success rested upon his extraordinary abilities: he was an excellent public speaker; he relished long working days and the details of government; and he understood better than anyone else the intricacies of state finance. Walpole became First Lord of the Treasury, a post that he transformed into first minister of state. From his treasury post, Walpole assiduously built a Whig parliamentary party. He carefully dispensed jobs and offices, using them as bait to lure parliamentary supporters. Walpole's organization paid off both in the passage of legislation desired by the Crown and at the polls, where Whigs were returned to Parliament time and again.

From 1721 to 1742 Walpole was the most powerful man in the British government. He refused an offer of a peerage so that he could continue to lead the House of Commons. Walpole's long tenure in office was as much a result of his policies as of his methods of governing. He brought a measure of fiscal responsibility to government by establishing a fund to pay off the national debt. In foreign policy he pursued peace with the same fervor that both his predecessors and successors pursued war. The long years of peace brought prosperity to both the landed and merchant classes, but they also brought

criticism of Walpole's methods. The way in which he used government patronage to build his parliamentary party was attacked as corruption. So, too, were the ways in which the pockets of Whig officeholders were lined. During his last decade in office, Walpole struggled to survive. His attempt to extend the excise tax on colonial goods nearly led to his loss of office in 1733. His refusal to respond to the clamor for continued war with Spain in 1741 finally led to his downfall.

Walpole's 20-year rule established the pattern of parliamentary government. The Crown needed a "prime" minister who was able to steer legislation through the House of Commons. It also needed a patronage broker who could take control of the treasury and dispense its largess in return for parliamentary backing. Walpole's personality and talents had combined these two roles. Hereafter they were divided. Those who had grown up under Walpole had learned their lessons well. The Whig monopoly of power continued unchallenged for nearly another 20 years. The patronage network Walpole had created was vastly extended by his Whig successors. Even minor posts in the customs or the excise offices were now exchanged for political favor, and only those approved by the Whig leadership could claim them. The cries of corruption grew louder not only in the country houses of the long-disenfranchised Tories, but in the streets of London, where a popular radicalism developed in opposition to the Whig oligarchy. They were taken up as well in the North American colonies, where two million British subjects champed at the bit of imperial rule.

America Revolts

Britain's triumph in the Seven Years' War (1756–63) had come at great financial cost to the nation. At the beginning of the eighteenth century, the national debt stood at £14 million; by 1763 it had risen to £130 million, despite the fact that Walpole's government had been paying off some of it. Then, as now, the cost of world domination was staggering. George III (1760–1820) came to the throne with a taste for reform and a desire to break the Whig stranglehold on government. He was to have limited success on both counts, though not for want of trying. In 1763 the king and his ministers agreed that reform of colonial administration was long overdue. Such reform would have the twin benefit of shifting part of the burden of taxation from Britain to North America and of making the commercial side of colonization pay.

This was sound thinking all around, and in due course Parliament passed a series of duties on goods

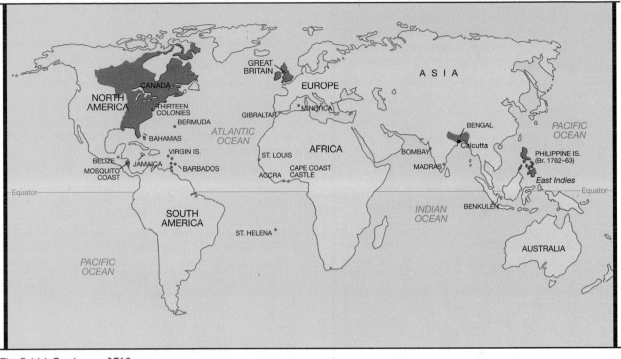

The British Empire, ca. 1763

imported into the colonies, including glass, wine, coffee, tea, and, most notably, sugar. The so-called Sugar Act (1764) was followed by the Stamp Act (1765), a tax on printed papers such as newspapers, deeds, and court documents. Both acts imposed taxes in the colonies similar to those that already existed in Britain. Accompanying the acts were administrative orders designed to cut into the lucrative black market trade. The government instituted new rules for searching ships and transferred authority over smuggling from the local colonial courts to Britain's Admiralty courts. Although British officials could only guess at the value of the new duties imposed, it was believed that with effective enforcement £150,000 would be raised. All this would go to pay the vastly greater costs of colonial administration and security.

British officials were more than perplexed when these mild measures met with a ferocious response. Assemblies of nearly every colony officially protested the Sugar Act. They sent petitions to Parliament begging for repeal and warning of dire economic and political consequences. Riots followed passage of the Stamp Act. Tax collectors were hounded out of office, their resignations precipitated by threats and acts of physical violence. In Massachusetts, mobs that included political leaders in the colony razed the homes of the collector

and the lieutenant-governor. However much the colonists might have regretted the violence that was done, they believed that an essential political principle was at stake. It was a principle of the freedom of an Englishman.

At their core, the protests of the American colonists underscored the vitality of the British political system. The Americans argued that they could not be taxed without their consent and that their consent could come only through representation in Parliament. Since there were no colonists in Parliament, Parliament had no jurisdiction over the property of the colonists. Taxation without representation was tyranny. There were a number of subtleties to this argument that were quickly lost as political rhetoric and political action heated up. In the first place, the colonists did tax themselves through their own legislatures and much of that money paid the costs of administration and defense. Second, as a number of pamphleteers pointed out, no one in the colonies had asked the British government to send regiments of the army into North America. The colonists had little reason to put their faith in British protection. Hard-fought colonial victories were tossed away at European negotiating tables, while the British policy of defending Indian rights in the Ohio Valley ran counter to the interests of the settlers. When defense was nec-

The Bostonian's Paying the Excise-Man, or Tarring & Feathering

In Britain's North American colonies, public sentiment against the importation of tea and other British goods often found expression in a coat of tar and feathers applied to the bare skin of the offending importer. Note the symbols in The Bostonians Paying the Excise-Man: *the Liberty Tree from which dangles a hangman's noose and the overturned copy of the Stamp Act. In the background, Bostonians dump chests of tea into the harbor.*

essary, the colonists had proved themselves both able and cooperative in providing it. A permanent tax meant a permanent army, and a standing army was as loathed in Britain as it was in the colonies.

In opposing the Stamp Act, colonists also tried to draw a distinction between internal and external taxation. They deemed regulation of overseas commerce a legitimate power of Parliament but argued that the regulation of internal exchange was not. But this distinction was lost once the issue of parliamentary repre-

sentation was raised. If the colonists had not consented to British taxation, then it made no difference whether taxation was internal or external. The passion generated in the colonies was probably no greater than that generated in Britain. The British government also saw the confrontation as a matter of principle, but for Britain the principle was parliamentary sovereignty. This, above all, was the rock upon which the British constitution had been built over the last century. Parliament had entered into a partnership with the Crown. The Crown had surrendered—willingly or not—many of its prerogatives. In return, Parliament had bound the people to obedience. There were well-established means by which British subjects could petition Parliament for redress of grievances against the monarch, but there were no channels by which they could question the sovereignty of Parliament.

Once the terms of debate had been so defined, it was difficult for either side to find a middle ground. Parlia-

The New European Powers

1707	England and Scotland unite to form Great Britain
1713–1714	Peace of Utrecht ends War of the Spanish Succession (1702–1714)
1714	British crown passes to House of Hanover
1721	Treaty of Nystad ends Great Northern War (1700–1721)
1721–1742	Sir Robert Walpole leads British House of Commons
1722	Peter the Great of Russia creates Table of Ranks
1740	Frederick the Great of Prussia invades Austrian province of Silesia
1748	Treaty of Aix-la-Chapelle ends War of the Austrian Succession (1740–1748)
1756–1763	Seven Years' War pits Prussia and Britain against Austria, France, and Russia
1773–1775	Pugachev's revolt in Russia
1774	Boston Tea Party
1775	American Revolution begins
1785	Catherine the Great of Russia issues Charter of the Nobility

unalienable rights

The Declaration of Independence, written by Thomas Jefferson (1776), succinctly summarized the principles on which the American Colonists were to build a new form of democratic government.

We hold these truths to be self-evident, that all men are created equal, that they are endowed by their Creator with certain unalienable Rights, that among these are Life, Liberty and the pursuit of Happiness. That to secure these rights, Governments are instituted among Men, deriving their just powers from the consent of the governed. That whenever any Form of Government becomes destructive of these ends, it is the Right of the People to alter or to abolish it, and to institute new Government, laying its foundation on such principles and organizing its powers in such form, as to them shall seem most likely to effect their Safety and Happiness. Prudence, indeed, will dictate that Governments long established should not be changed for light and transient causes; and accordingly all experience hath shown, that mankind are more disposed to suffer, while evils are sufferable, than to right themselves by abolishing the forms to which they are accustomed. But when a long train of abuses and usurpations, pursuing invariably the same Object, evinces a design to reduce them under absolute Despotism, it is their right, it is their duty, to throw off such Government, and to provide new Guards for their future security.

From the Declaration of Independence.

mentary moderates managed repeal of the Stamp Act and most of the clauses of the Sugar Act, but they also joined in passing the Declaratory Act (1766), which stated unequivocally that Parliament held sovereign jurisdiction over the colonies "in all cases whatsoever." This was a claim that became more and more difficult to sustain as colonial leaders began to cite the elements of resistance theory that had justified the Revolution of 1688. Then the protest had been against the tyranny of the king; now it was against the tyranny of Parliament. American propagandists claimed that a conspiracy existed to deprive the colonists of their property and rights and to enslave them for the benefit of special interests and corrupt politicians.

The techniques of London radicals who opposed parliamentary policy were imported into the colonies. Newspapers were used to whip up public support, boycotts brought ordinary people into the political arena; public demonstrations like the Boston Tea Party (1774) were carefully designed to intimidate; mobs were occasionally given free rein. Although the government had faced down these tactics when they were used in London to support John Wilkes (1725–97), an ardent critic of royal policy, they were less successful when the crisis lay an ocean away. When, in 1770, British troops fired on a Boston mob, American propagandists were provided with empirical evidence that Britain intended to enslave the colonies. Violence was met by violence, passion by passion. In 1775 full-scale fighting was under way. Eight years later Britain withdrew from a war it could not win, and the American colonies were left to govern themselves.

By the end of the third quarter of the eighteenth century, Europe had a new political configuration. A continent once dominated by a single power—Spain in the sixteenth century and France in the seventeenth—was now dominated by a state system in which alliances among several great powers held the balance. Despite the loss of its American colonies, Great Britain had proved the most potent of the states. Its victories over the French in the Seven Years' War and over France and Prussia in the War of the Austrian Succession secured its position. But it was a position that could be maintained only through alliances with the German states, with either Prussia or Austria. The rise of

Prussia provided a counterweight to French domination of the Continent. Although these two states became allies in the middle of the century, the ambitions of their rulers made them natural enemies, and it would not be long before French and Prussian armies were again pitted against each other. France, still the wealthiest and most populous of European states, had slumbered through the eighteenth-century reorganization. The legacies of Louis XIV took a long time to reach fruition. He had claimed glory for his state, giving the French people a sense of national identity and national destiny, but making them pay an enormous price in social and economic dislocation. Thus the mid-eighteenth century was to be an age of the greatest literary and philosophical achievement for France, but the late eighteenth century was to be an age of the greatest social upheaval that Europe had ever known.

Mastering the chapter

To review the main points of the chapter, be sure you can explain the significance of each of the following.

Terms/Concepts/Events	People	Places
Great Northern War	Peter the Great	Gibraltar
Pragmatic Sanction	Catherine the Great	Minorca
War of the Austrian Succession	Emelyan Pugachev	United Provinces
Seven Years' War	Frederick William	Austrian Netherlands
Polish Diet	Frederick the Great	Hanover
Partition of Poland	Charles VI	Austrian Empire
British Constitution	Maria Theresa	Tuscany
Whigs	Joseph II	Duchy of Savoy
Tories	George I	Saint Petersburg
Hanoverian succession	Sir Robert Walpole	Berlin

Suggestions for further Reading

General Reading

* Olwen Hufton, *Europe: Privilege and Protest, 1730–1789* (Ithaca, NY: Cornell University Press, 1980). An excellent survey of the political and social history of the mid-eighteenth century.

* Leonard Krieger, *Kings and Philosophers, 1689–1789* (New York: Norton, 1970). A brilliant depiction of the personalities and ideas of eighteenth-century Europe.

* Jeremy Black, *Eighteenth Century Europe* (London: Macmillan, 1990). The eighteenth century arranged thematically by society, culture, and economy.

* M. S. Anderson, *Europe in the Eighteenth Century, 1713–1783*, 3d ed. (London: Longman, 1987). A country-by-country survey of political developments.

Nicholas Riasanovsky, *A History of Russia* (New York: Oxford University Press, 1993). The best one-volume history of Russia.

* David Kirby, *Northern Europe in the Early Modern Period* (London: Longman, 1991). Political history from a Baltic perspective, with excellent chapters on Sweden and Russia.

europe in 1714

* Derek McKay and H. M. Scott, *The Rise of the Great Powers* (London: Longman, 1983). An outstanding survey of diplomacy and warfare.

the rise of russia

* Paul Dukes, *The Making of Russian Absolutism*, 1613–1801 (London: Longman, 1982). An extensive survey of the Russian monarchy in its greatest period.

* B. H. Sumner, *Peter the Great and the Emergence of Russia* (New York: Collier Books, 1962). A short and readable study; the best introduction.

* M. S. Anderson, *Peter the Great* (London: Thames and Hudson, 1978). A well-constructed, comprehensive biography.

  John P. LeDonne, *Absolutism and Ruling Class: The Formation of the Russian Political Order, 1700–1825* (New York: Oxford University Press, 1991).

* Jerome Blum, *Lord and Peasant in Russia* (New York: Columbia University Press, 1961). The best work on the social life of Russians.

* Isabel de Madariaga, *Catherine the Great, a Short History* (New Haven, CT: Yale University Press, 1990). The best brief life.

the two germanies

* H. W. Koch, *A History of Prussia* (London: Longman, 1978). The most recent study of the factors that led to Prussian dominance of Germany.

* Rudolf Vierhaus, *Germany in the Age of Absolutism* (Cambridge: Cambridge University Press, 1989). A synoptic survey of society, culture, and politics.

* Charles Ingrao, *The Habsburg Monarchy 1618–1815* (Cambridge: Cambridge University Press, 1994). Divided evenly between foreign and domestic affairs; rewarding for readers of all levels.

* J. Gagliardo, *Germany Under the Old Regime* (London: Longman, 1991). The best single-volume history.

* Gerhard Ritter, *Frederick the Great* (Berkeley: University of California Press, 1974). A classic biography, short and readable.

* Walther Hubatsch, *Frederick the Great of Prussia* (London: Thames and Hudson, 1975). A full account of the reign of Prussia's greatest leader.

* Ernst Wangermann, *The Austrian Achievement* (New York: Harcourt Brace Jovanovich, 1973). The most readable study of Austrian politics, culture, and society in the eighteenth century.

* T. C. W. Blanning, *Joseph II and Enlightened Despotism* (London: Longman, 1970). Displays the relationship between new ideas, reform policies, and the practical necessities of government.

  C. A. Macartney, *Maria Theresa and the House of Austria* (Mystic, CT: Verry Inc., 1969). Still the best introductory study.

* Reed S. Browning, *The War of Austrian Succession* (London: Macmillan, 1995). A comprehensive history of a complicated event.

  John Stoye, *Marsigli's Europe* (New Haven, CT: Yale University Press, 1994). European civilization seen through the eyes of a virtuoso statesman and soldier.

the greatness of great britain

* J. C. D. Clark, *English Society*, 1688–1832 (Cambridge: Cambridge University Press, 1985). A bold reinterpretation of the most important features of English society.

* J. H. Plumb, *The Origins of Political Stability, England 1675–1725* (Boston: Houghton Mifflin, 1967). The fullest of the contributions of Walpole to the establishment of the British constitution.

* Linda Colley, *Britons* (New Haven, CT: Yale University Press, 1992). A lively account of how a nation was forged from Welsh, Scots, and English and how unity and diversity intermixed.

Ragnhild Hatton, *George I Elector and King* (Cambridge, MA: Harvard University Press, 1978). An outstanding biography that shows the German side of a British monarch.

* John Brewer, *Party Ideology and Popular Politics at the Accession of George III* (Cambridge: Cambridge University Press, 1976). An important book about the pressures on the political system in the late eighteenth century.

* Paul Langford, A *Polite and Commercial People: England 1727–1783* (Oxford: Oxford University Press, 1989). The standard survey in the Oxford history series.

* Gordon Wood, *The Radicalism of the American Revolution* (New York: Alfred A. Knopf, 1992). How the ideals of the American Revolution shaped an emerging nation.

* Ian Christie and Benjamin W. Labaree, *Empire or Independence, 1760–1777* (New York: Norton, 1977). The American troubles from the British point of view.

* Bernard Bailyn, *The Ideological Origins of the American Revolution* (Cambridge, MA: Harvard University Press, 1967). A brilliant interpretation of the underlying causes of the break between Britain and the North American colonies.

* Robert Middlekauff, *The Glorious Cause. The American Revolution, 1763–1789* (New York: Oxford University Press, 1982). A lively narrative account from the American perspective.

*Paperback edition available.

culture and society in eighteenth-century europe

happy families

"Happy families are all alike," wrote Lev Tolstoy in the nineteenth century when the idea of a happy family was already a cliché. Such an idea would never have occurred to his eighteenth-century forebears. For them the happy family was new. Personal happiness was an invention of the Enlightenment, the result of novel attitudes about human aspirations and human capabilities. "Happiness is a new idea in Europe," wrote Louis de Saint-Just (1767–94). It emerged in response to the belief that what was good brought pleasure and what was evil brought pain. Happiness, both individual and collective, became the yardstick by which life was measured. This meant a reorientation in personal conduct and, most of all, a reorientation of family life. Especially for those with an economic cushion, a pleasurable family life became essential. Husbands and wives were to be companions, filled with romantic love for each other and devoted to domestic bliss. Children, the product of their affection, were to be doted on, treated not as miniature adults to be lectured and beaten, but as unfilled vessels into which was poured all that was good.

Were ever a couple more in love than the husband and wife depicted in A Visit to the Wet Nurse by Jean-Honoré Fragonard (1732–1806)? The man clasps his wife's arm to his cheek, she lays her hand on his shoulder. Their sighs are almost audible! Together they admire the fruit of their love, the baby asleep in the cradle. It is hard to guess which parent dotes more, the mother with her rapturous expression or the father with his intensity. He kneels on a cushion in almost religious devotion, his hands folded as if in prayer. Who can doubt their companionship or their love for their babe? They have come together to see how the wet nurse is caring for their child.

At the beginning of the eighteenth century, the use of a wet nurse was still common among the families of the French bourgeoisie, the class to which this couple belongs. As time passed, however, more and more families began to keep their children at home and more mothers began to nurse their babies themselves. In part this change was a response to the higher mortality rate among infants sent out to wet nurses. But a wet nurse who could be supervised, that is, one who lived near enough to be visited, but far enough away from the town to enjoy wholesome air, might be the best of both worlds. This is just what the couple here has found, and today they come, with their other child (the boy in the hat), to see their baby sleeping peacefully, the wet nurse sitting attentively at the infant's side.

But there are two families in this picture, and they are hardly alike. At first glance, the wet nurse looks like an old woman, perhaps even an aging nanny. She sits with her distaff in her hand, for the arrival of her clients has interrupted her spinning. It is shocking to realize that she cannot be much older than 30, an age beyond which wealthy families would not hire her for fear either that she would not have much milk or that it would be sour. The two younger children are undoubtedly hers, the youngest probably just weaned so that all of the milk would go to the baby. No adoring husband sits beside the wet nurse. Her husband, if he is still alive, is hard at work with no leisure time for visits to the country. Not only does the wet nurse have to sell her milk, but she also spins, to keep her family clothed and to earn a little extra to put away for hard times.

The newest fads of the age have passed her family by. While the child in the cradle will be spoiled by toys manufactured especially for children—puzzles, games, rocking horses, and balls—the children of the wet nurse must make do with household objects and their own imagination. A ball of yarn thrown to the cat helps the elder child while away the hours. Like much else in the eighteenth century, the world of the family was divided between high and low.

focus questions

1. What were the main elements of Enlightenment thought?
2. What social, moral, and religious traditions were challenged by the ideas of thinkers such as Voltaire, Hume, Montesquieu, and Rousseau?
3. How did the European nobility maintain its social eminence in the face of a new bourgeois culture created by an expanding middle class?
4. Why did Europe's population begin to grow so dramatically in the eighteenth century and how did society respond to the challenges this posed?

The seven-year-old musical prodigy Wolfgang Amadeus Mozart plays the harpsichord while his father Leopold plays the violin and his sister Nannerl sings. The boy won great ovations on concert tours throughout Europe.

Eighteenth-century culture

The eighteenth century spawned a rich and costly culture. Decorative architecture, especially interior design, reflected the increasing sociability of the aristocracy. Entertainment became a central part of aristocratic life, losing its previous formality. In this atmosphere music became a cultural passion. The string quartet made its first appearance in the eighteenth century, and chamber music enjoyed unparalleled popularity. Only the wealthiest could afford to stage private operas, the other musical passion of the age. The Esterhazys of Hungary employed 22 musicians and a conductor, who for most of the late eighteenth century was Joseph Haydn (1732–1809), the father of the modern symphony. Haydn's post was not an honorary one. In addition to hiring and managing the orchestra, he was expected to direct two operas and two concerts a week, as well as the music for Sunday services. An aristocratic patron was essential for the aspiring composer. If he could not find one or if, like Wolfgang Amadeus Mozart (1756–91), he could not bend his will to one, he could not flourish. While Haydn lived comfortably in a palace, Mozart, probably the greatest musical genius in Western history, lived impoverished in a garret and died at age 35 from lack of medical attention.

Musical entertainments in European country houses were matched by the literary and philosophical entertainments of the urban salons. Papers on scientific and literary subjects were read at gala dinner parties and discussed with great seriousness in drawing rooms. In the salons, most of which were organized by the wives and daughters of the nobility, were to be found the most influential thinkers of the day presenting the ideas of the Enlightenment, a new European outlook on religion, society, and politics.

The Enlightenment

The Enlightenment was less a set of ideas than it was a set of attitudes. At its core was criticism, a questioning of traditional institutions, customs, and morals. In 1762 the French philosopher Jean-Jacques Rousseau (1712–78) published one of the most important works on social theory, *The Social Contract*, which opened with the gripping maxim "Man is born free and everywhere he is in chains." But most of the great thinkers of the Enlightenment were not so much philosophers as savants, knowledgeable popularizers whose skills were in simplifying and publicizing a hodgepodge of new views.

In France, Enlightenment intellectuals were called *philosophes* and claimed all the arts and sciences as their purview. The *Encyclopedia* (35 volumes, 1751–80), edited by Denis Diderot (1713–84), was one of the greatest achievements of the age. Titled *Systematic Dictionary of the Sciences, Arts, and Crafts*, it attempted to summarize all acquired knowledge and to dispel all imposed superstitions. There was no better definition of a philosophe than that given them by one of their enemies: "Just what is a philosophe? A kind of monster in society who feels under no obligation towards its manners and morals, its proprieties, its politics, or its religion. One may expect anything from men of their ilk."

The influence of French counterculture on enlightened thought was great, but the Enlightenment was by no

Painting of a lively dinner conversation among philosophes. Voltaire, with raised arm, is shown seated to the left of Diderot.

means a strictly French phenomenon. Its greatest figures included the Scottish economist Adam Smith (1723–90), the Italian legal reformer Cesare Beccaria (1738–94), and the German philosopher Immanuel Kant (1724–1804). In France it began among anti-establishment critics; in Scotland and the German states it flourished in the universities, and in Prussia, Austria, and Russia it was propagated by the monarchy. The Enlightenment began in the 1730s and was still going strong a half century later when its attitudes had been absorbed into the mainstream of European thought.

No brief summary can do justice to the diversity of enlightened thought in eighteenth-century Europe. Because it was an attitude of mind rather than a set of shared beliefs, there are many contradictory strains to follow. In his famous essay *What Is Enlightenment?* (1784), Immanuel Kant described it simply as freedom to use one's own intelligence. "I hear people clamor on all sides: Don't argue! The officer says: Don't argue, drill! The tax collector says: Don't argue, pay. The pastor says: Don't argue, believe." To all of them Kant replied: "Dare to know! Have the courage to use your own intelligence."

The Spirit of the Enlightenment. In 1734 there appeared in France a small book titled *Philosophical Letters Concerning the English Nation.* Its author, Voltaire (1694–1778), had spent two years in Britain, and while there he had made it his business to study the differences between the peoples of the two nations. In a simple but forceful style, Voltaire demonstrated time and again the superiority of the British. They practiced religious toleration and were not held under the sway of a venal clergy. They valued people for their merits rather than their birth. Their political constitution was a marvel—"The English nation is the only one on earth that has succeeded in controlling the power of kings by resisting them." They made national heroes of their scientists, poets, and philosophers. In all of this Voltaire contrasted British virtue with French vice. He attacked the French clergy and nobility directly, the French monarchy implicitly. Not only did he praise the genius and accomplishments of Sir Isaac Newton above those

The All-knowing

The *Encyclopedia* was one of the great collaborative ventures of the new spirit of reason that so characterized the Enlightenment. Following is the *Encyclopedia*'s entry on itself, the purpose of compiling human knowledge in book form.

Encyclopedia . . . In truth, the aim of an *encyclopedia* is to collect all the knowledge scattered over the face of the earth, to present its general outlines and structure to the men with whom we live, and to transmit this to those who will come after us, so that the work of past centuries may be useful to the following centuries, that our children, by becoming more educated, may at the same time become more virtuous and happier, and that we may not die without having deserved well of the human race. . . .

I have said that it could only belong to a philosophical age to attempt an *encyclopedia*; and I have said this because such a work constantly demands more intellectual daring than is commonly found in [less courageous periods]. All things must be examined, debated, investigated without exception and without regard for anyone's feelings. . . . We must ride roughshod over all these ancient puerilities, overturn the barriers that reason never erected, give back to the arts and sciences the liberty that is so precious to them. . . . We have for quite some time needed a reasoning age when men would no longer seek the rules in classical authors but in nature. . . .

From Denis Diderot, *Encyclopedia* (1751–72).

---

of René Descartes, but he also graphically contrasted the Catholic church's persecution of Descartes with the British state's celebration of Newton. "England, where men think free and noble thoughts," Voltaire enthused.

It is difficult now to recapture the psychological impact that the *Philosophical Letters* had on the generation of educated Frenchmen who first read them. The book was officially banned and publicly burned, and a warrant was issued for Voltaire's arrest. The *Letters* dropped like a bombshell upon the moribund intellectual culture of the Church and the universities and burst open the complacent, self-satisfied Cartesian worldview. The book ignited in France a movement that would soon be found in nearly every corner of Europe.

Born in Paris in 1694 into a bourgeois family with court office, François-Marie Arouet, who later took the pen name Voltaire, was educated by the Jesuits, who encouraged his poetic talents and instilled in him an enduring love of literature. He was a difficult student, especially as he had already rejected the core of the Jesuits' religious doctrine. He was no less difficult as he grew and began a career as a poet and playwright. It was not long before he was imprisoned in the Bastille for penning verses that maligned the honor of the regent of France. Released from prison, he insulted a nobleman, who retaliated by having his servants publicly beat Voltaire. Voltaire issued a challenge for a duel, a greater insult than the first, given his low birth. Again he was sent to the Bastille and was only released on the promise that he would leave the country immediately.

Thus Voltaire found himself in Britain, where he spent two years learning English, writing plays, and enjoying his celebrity free from the dangers that celebrity entailed in France. When he returned to Paris in 1728, it was with the intention of popularizing Britain to Frenchmen. He wrote and produced a number of plays and began writing the *Philosophical Letters*, a work that not only secured his reputation but also forced him into exile at the village of Cirey, where he moved in with the Marquise du Châtelet (1706–49).

The Marquise du Châtelet, though only 27 at the time of her liaison with Voltaire, was one of the leading advocates of Newtonian science in France. She built a laboratory in her home and introduced Voltaire to experimental science. While she undertook the immense challenge of translating Newton into French, Voltaire worked on innumerable projects: poems, plays, philosophical and antireligious tracts (which she wisely kept him from publishing), and histories. It was one of the most productive periods of his life, and when the Marquise du Châtelet died in 1749, Voltaire was crushed.

Now past 50 years old, Voltaire began his travels. He was invited to Berlin by Frederick the Great, who admired him most of all the intellectuals of the age. The relationship between these two great egotists was predictably stormy and resulted in Voltaire's arrest in Frankfurt. Finally allowed to leave Prussia, Voltaire eventually settled in Geneva, where he quickly became embroiled in local politics and was none too politely asked to leave. He was tired of wandering and tired of being chased. His youthful gaiety and high spirits, which remained in Voltaire long past youth, were dealt a serious blow by the tragic earthquake in Lisbon in 1755, when thousands of people attending church services were killed.

Optimism in the face of such a senseless tragedy was no longer possible. His black mood was revealed in *Candide* (1759), which was to become his enduring legacy. *Candide* introduced the ivory-tower intellectual Dr. Pangloss, the overly optimistic Candide, and the very practical philosophy "We must cultivate our own garden." It was Voltaire's capacity to challenge all authority that was probably his greatest contribution to Enlightenment attitudes. He held nothing sacred. He questioned his own paternity and the morals of his mother; he lived openly with the Marquise du Châtelet and her husband; and he spoke as slightingly of kings and aristocrats as he did of his numerous critics. At the height of the French Revolution, Voltaire's body was removed from its resting place in Champagne and taken in great pomp to Paris, where it was interred in the Panthéon, where the heroes of the nation were put to rest. "Voltaire taught us to be free" was the slogan that the Parisian masses chanted during the funeral procession. It was an ending perhaps too solemn and conventional for one as irreverent as Voltaire. When the monarchy was restored after 1815, his bones were unceremoniously dumped in a lime pit.

Some enlightened thinkers based their critical outlook on skepticism, the belief that nothing could be known for certain. When the Scottish philosopher David Hume (1711–76) was accused of being an atheist, he countered the charge by saying he was too skeptical to be certain that God did not exist. Hume's first major philosophical work, A *Treatise of Human Nature* (1739), made absolutely no impression upon his contemporaries. For a time he took a post as a merchant's clerk; then he served as a tutor; and finally he found a position as a private secretary. During the course of these various employments he continued to write, publishing a series of essays on the subject of morality and rewriting his treatise into An *Enquiry Concerning Human Understanding* (1748), his greatest philosophical work.

Hume made two seminal contributions to Enlightenment thought. He exploded the synthesis of Descartes by arguing that neither matter nor mind could be proved to exist with any certainty. Only perceptions existed, either as impressions of material objects or as

The Human condition

More than anyone else, Voltaire symbolized the new thinking of the Enlightenment. Witty, ironic, irreverent, and penetrating, his writings provoked howls of protest and squeals of delight. Among the most widely read was his philosophical dictionary, from which this definition of evil is drawn.

People clamor that human nature is essentially perverse, that man is born the child of the devil, and of evil. Nothing is more ill-advised; for, my friend, in preaching at me that everybody is born perverse, you warn me that you were born that way, that I must distrust you as I would a fox or a crocodile. . . . It would be much more reasonable, much nobler, to say to me: "You were all born good; see how frightful it would be to corrupt the purity of your being." We should treat mankind as we should treat all men individually. . . .

Man is not born evil; he becomes evil, as he becomes sick. . . . Gather together all the children of the universe; you will see in them nothing but innocence, gentleness, and fear. . . .

If men were essentially evil, if they were all born the subjects of a being as malevolent as it is unhappy, who inspired them with all this frenzy to avenge his own torment, we would see husbands murdered by their wives, and fathers by their children every morning. . . .

From Voltaire, *The Philosophical Dictionary* (1764).

David Hume.

society, and European religion all bound together by the story of a Persian despot who leaves his harem to learn about the ways of the world. The use of the Persian outsider allowed Montesquieu to comment on the absurdity of European customs in general and French practices in particular. The device of the harem allowed him to titillate his audience with exotic sexuality.

After this success, Montesquieu decided to sell his office and make the grand tour. He spent nearly two years in England, for which, like Voltaire, he came to have the greatest admiration. Back in Bordeaux, Montesquieu began to assemble his thoughts for what he believed would be a great work of political theory. The two societies that he most admired were ancient Rome and present-day Britain, and he studied the forms of their government and the principles that animated them. *The Spirit of the Laws* was published in 1748, and despite its gargantuan size and densely packed examples, it was immediately recognized as a masterpiece. Catherine the Great of Russia kept it at her bedside, and it was the single most influential work for the framers of the United States Constitution.

In both *Persian Letters* and *The Spirit of the Laws* Montesquieu explored how liberty could be achieved and despotism avoided. He divided all forms of government into republics, monarchies, and despotisms. Each form had its own peculiar spirit: virtue and moderation in republics, honor in monarchies, and fear in despotisms. Like each form, each spirit was prone to abuse and had to be restrained if republics were not to give way to vice and excess, monarchies to corruption, and despotisms to repression. Montesquieu classified regimes as either moderate or immoderate, and through the use of extensive historical examples attempted to demonstrate how moderation could be maintained through rules and restraints, through the spirit of the law.

For Montesquieu, a successful government was one in which powers were separated and checks and balances existed within the institutions of the state. As befit a provincial magistrate, he insisted on the absolute separation of the judiciary from all other branches of government. The law needed to be independent and impartial, and it needed to be just. Montesquieu advocated that law codes be reformed and reduced mainly to regulate crimes against persons and property. Punishment should fit the crime but should be humane. Montesquieu was one of the first to advocate the abolition of torture. Like most Europeans of his age, he saw monarchy as the only realistic form of government, but he argued that for a monarchy to be successful, it needed a strong and independent aristocracy to re-

ideas. If human understanding was based on sensory perception rather than on reason, then there could be no certainty in the universe. Hume's second point launched a frontal attack upon established religion. If there could be no certainty, then the revealed truths of Christian religion could have no basis. In his historical analysis of the origins of religion, Hume argued that "religion grows out of hope or fear." He attacked the core of Christian explanations based on either Providence or miracles by arguing that to anyone who understood the basis of human perception it would take a miracle to believe in miracles.

In 1749 Hume received in the mail a work from an admiring Frenchman, titled *The Spirit of the Laws*. The sender was Charles-Louis de Secondat, Baron Montesquieu (1689–1755). Born in Bordeaux, he ultimately inherited both a large landed estate and the office of president of the Parlement of Bordeaux. His novel *Persian Letters* (1721) was a brilliant satire of Parisian morals, French

of the people

Baron de Montesquieu's *The Spirit of the Laws* (1750) was one of the most important political works of the Enlightenment. It analyzed the various forms of government and estimated their strengths and weaknesses. Montesquieu provided inspiration for the American Declaration of Independence and the Constitution.

In a democracy the people are in some respects the sovereign, and in others the subject. There can be no exercise of sovereignty but by their suffrages, which are . . . fundamental to this government. And indeed it is as important to regulate in a republic, in what manner, by whom, to whom, and concerning what suffrages are to be given, as it is in a monarchy to know who is the prince, and after what manner he ought to govern. . . .

The people are extremely well qualified for choosing those whom they are to intrust with part of their authority. . . . They can tell when a person has fought many battles, and been crowned with success; . . . They can tell when a judge is assiduous in his office, gives general satisfaction, and has never been charged with bribery. . . . But are they capable of conducting an intricate affair, of seizing and improving the opportunity and critical moment of action? No; this surpasses their abilities. . . .

As most citizens have sufficient ability to choose, though unqualified to be chosen, so the people, though capable of calling others to an account for their administration, are incapable of conducting the administration themselves. . . .

Again, there is no liberty if the judiciary power be not separated from the legislative and executive. Were it joined with the legislative, the life and liberty of the subject would be exposed to arbitrary control; for the judge would be then the legislator. Were it joined to the executive power the judge might behave with violence and oppression.

From Montesquieu, *The Spirit of the Laws.*

strain its tendency toward corruption and despotism. He based his arguments on what he believed was the case in Britain, which he praised as the only state in Europe in which liberty resided.

Enlightened thinkers attacked established institutions, above all the Church. Most were deists who believed in the existence of God on rational grounds only. Following the materialistic ideas of the new science, deists believed that nature conformed to its own material laws and operated without divine intervention. God, in a popular Enlightenment image, was like a clockmaker who constructed the elaborate mechanism, wound it, and gave the pendulum its first swing. After that the clock worked by itself. Deists were accused of being anti-Christian, and they certainly opposed the ritual forms of both Catholic and Protestant worship. They also opposed the role of the Church in education, for education was the key to an enlightened view of the future. This meant, above all, conflict with the Jesuits. "Let's eat a Jesuit" was Voltaire's half-facetious comment.

Jean-Jacques Rousseau attacked the educational system. His tract on education, disguised as the romantic novel *Émile* (1762), argued that children should be taught by appealing to their interests rather than with strict discipline. Education was crucial because the Enlightenment was dominated by the idea of the British philosopher John Locke (1632–1704) that the mind was blank at birth, a *tabula rasa*—"white paper void of all characters"—and that it was filled up by experience. Contrary to the arguments of Descartes, Locke wrote in *An Essay Concerning Human Understanding* (1690) that there were no innate ideas and no good or evil that was not conditioned by experience. For Locke, as for a host of thinkers after him, good and evil were defined as pleasure and pain. We do good because it is pleasurable and we avoid evil because it is painful. Morality was a sense experience rather than a theological one. It was also relative rather than absolute. This was an observation that derived from increased interest in non-European cultures. The *Persian Letters* of Baron Montesquieu was the most popular of a genre describing non-European societies that knew nothing of Christian morality.

By the middle of the eighteenth century, the pleasure/pain principle enunciated by Locke had come to be applied to the foundations of social organization. If per-

The frontispiece from Montesquieu's The Spirit of the Laws *has a medallion of the author surrounded by allegorical figures, including the blind Justice. In the lower left corner are copies of the author's works.*

sonal good was pleasure, then social good was happiness. The object of government, in the words of the Scottish moral philosopher Francis Hutcheson (1694–1746), was "the greatest happiness of the greatest number." This principle was at the core of *Crimes and Punishments* (1764), Cesare Beccaria's pioneering work of legal reform. Laws were instituted to promote happiness within society. They had to be formulated equitably for both criminal and victim. Punishment was to act as a deterrent to crime rather than as retribution. Therefore, Beccaria advocated the abolition of torture to gain confessions, the end of capital punishment, and the rehabilitation of criminals through the improvement of penal institutions. By 1776 happiness was established as one of the basic rights of man, enshrined in the American Declaration of Independence as "life, liberty, and the pursuit of happiness."

It was in refashioning the world through education and social reform that the Enlightenment revealed its orientation toward the future. *Optimism* was a word invented in the eighteenth century to express this feeling of liberation from the weight of centuries of traditions. "This is the best of all possible worlds and all things turn out for the best," was the satirical slogan of Voltaire's *Candide*. But if Voltaire believed that enlightened thinkers had taken optimism too far, others believed that it had to be taken further still.

Progress, an idea that not all enlightened thinkers shared, was another invention of the age. It was expressed most cogently by the French philosopher the Marquis de Condorcet (1743–94) in *The Progress of the Hu-*

The good of all

The Social Contract (1762) was one of the greatest visionary tracts of the eighteenth century. In it Jean-Jacques Rousseau envisioned a harmonious society capable of eliminating want and controlling evil. Here he discusses his famous idea of the general will.

As long as men united together look upon themselves as a single body, they have but one will relating to the common preservation and general welfare. Then all the energies of the state are vigorous and simple: its maxims are clear and luminous; there are no mixed contradictory interests; the common prosperity shows itself everywhere, and requires only good sense to be appreciated. Peace, union, and equality are enemies of political subtleties. Upright, honest men are difficult to deceive, because of their simplicity: decoys and pretexts do not impose upon them, they are not cunning enough to be dupes. When we see among the happiest people in the world troops of peasants regulating the affairs of state under an oak, and conducting themselves wisely, can we help despising the refinements of other nations, who make themselves illustrious and miserable with so much art and mystery?

From Jean-Jacques Rousseau, *The Social Contract.*

Jean-Jacques Rousseau.

man Mind (1795), in which he developed an almost evolutionary view of human development from a savage state of nature to a future of harmony and international peace.

The Impact of the Enlightenment. As there was no single set of Enlightenment beliefs, so there was no single impact of the Enlightenment. Its general influence was felt everywhere, even seeping to the lowest strata of society. Its specific influence is harder to gauge. Paradoxically, enlightened political reform took firmer root in eastern Europe, where the ideas were imported, than in western Europe, where they originated. It was absolute rulers who were most successful in borrowing Enlightenment reforms.

It is impossible to determine what part enlightened ideas and what part practical necessities played in the eastern European reform movement that began around midcentury. In at least three areas the coincidence between ideas and actions was especially strong: law, education, and the extension of religious toleration. Law was the basis of Enlightenment views of social interaction, and the influence of Montesquieu and Beccaria spread quickly. In Prussia and Russia the movement to codify and simplify the legal system did not reach fruition in the eighteenth century, but in both places it was well under way. The Prussian jurist Samuel von

Cocceji (1679–1755) initiated the reform of Prussian law and legal administration. Cocceji's project was to make the enforcement of law uniform throughout the realm, to prevent judicial corruption, and to produce a single code of Prussian law. The code, finally completed in the 1790s, reflected the principles of criminal justice articulated by Beccaria. In Russia, the Law Commission summoned by Catherine the Great in 1767 never did complete its work. Nevertheless, profoundly influenced by Montesquieu, Catherine attempted to abolish torture and to introduce the Beccarian principle that the accused was innocent until proved guilty. In Austria, Joseph II presided over a wholesale reorganization of the legal system. Courts were centralized, laws codified, and torture and capital punishment abolished.

Enlightenment ideas also underlay the efforts to improve education in eastern Europe. The religious orders, especially the Jesuits, were the most influential educators of the age, and the Enlightenment attack upon them created a void that had to be filled by the state. Efforts at compulsory education were first undertaken in Russia under Peter the Great, but these were aimed at the compulsory education of the nobility. It was Catherine who extended the effort to the provinces, attempting to educate a generation of Russian teachers. She was especially eager that women receive primary schooling, although the prejudice against educating women was too strong to overcome. Austrian and Prussian reforms were more successful in extending the reach of primary education, even if its content remained weak.

Religious toleration was the area in which the Enlightenment had its greatest impact in Europe, though again it was in the eastern countries that this was most visible. Freedom of worship for Catholics was barely whispered about in Britain, while neither France nor Spain were moved to tolerate Protestants. Nevertheless, within these parameters there were some important changes in the religious makeup of the western European states. In Britain, Protestant dissenters were no longer persecuted for their beliefs. By the end of the eighteenth century, the number of Protestants outside the Church of England was growing; and by the early nineteenth century discrimination against Protestants was all but eliminated. In France and Spain, relations between the national church and the papacy were undergoing a reorientation. Both states were asserting more independence—both theologically and financially—from Rome. The shift was symbolized by disputes over the role of the Jesuits, who were finally expelled from France in 1764 and from Spain in 1767.

In eastern Europe, enlightened ideas about religious toleration did take effect. Catherine the Great abandoned persecution of a Russian Orthodox sect known as the Old Believers. Prussia had always tolerated various Protestant groups, and with the conquest of Silesia it acquired a large Catholic population. Catholics were guaranteed freedom of worship, and Frederick the Great even built a Catholic church in Berlin to symbolize this policy. Austria extended enlightened ideas about toleration the furthest. Maria Theresa was a devout Catholic and had actually increased religious persecution in her realm, but Joseph II rejected his mother's dogmatic position. In 1781 he issued the Patent of Toleration, which granted freedom of worship to Protestants and members of the Eastern Orthodox church. The following year he extended this toleration to Jews. Joseph's attitude toward toleration was as practical as it was enlightened. He believed that the revocation of the Edict of Nantes—which had granted limited toleration to Protestants—at the end of the seventeenth century had been an economic disaster for France, and he encouraged religious toleration as a means to economic progress.

A science of economics was first articulated during the Enlightenment. A group of French thinkers known as the Physiocrats subscribed to the view that land was wealth and thus argued that agricultural activity, especially improved means of farming and livestock breeding, should take first priority in state reforms. As wealth came from land, taxation should be based only on land ownership, a principle that was coming into increased prominence despite the opposition of the landowning class. Physiocratic ideas combined a belief in the sanctity of private property with the need for the state to increase agricultural output. Ultimately the Physiocrats, like the great Scottish economic theorist Adam Smith, came to believe that government should cease to interfere with private economic activity. They articulated the doctrine *Laissez faire, laissez passer*—"Let it be, let it go." The ideas of Adam Smith and the Physiocrats ultimately formed the basis for nineteenth-century economic reform.

If the Enlightenment did not initiate a new era, it did offer a new vision, whether in Hume's psychology, Montesquieu's political science, Rousseau's sociology, or Smith's economic theory. All of these subjects, which have such a powerful impact on contemporary life, had their modern origins in the Enlightenment. As the British poet Alexander Pope (1688–1744) put it: "Know then thyself, presume not God to scan/ The proper

major works of the enlightenment

1690	*An Essay Concerning Human Understanding* (Locke)
1721	*Persian Letters* (Baron Montesquieu)
1734	*Philosophical Letters Concerning the English Nation* (Voltaire)
1739	*A Treatise of Human Nature* (Hume)
1740	*Pamela* (Richardson)
1748	*An Enquiry Concerning Human Understanding* (Hume); *The Spirit of the Laws* (Baron Montesquieu)
1751–1780	*Encyclopedia* (Diderot)
1759	*Candide* (Voltaire)
1762	*Émile; The Social Contract* (Rousseau)
1764	*Crimes and Punishments* (Beccaria)
1784	*What Is Enlightenment?* (Kant)
1795	*The Progress of the Human Mind* (Marquis de Condorcet)
1798	*An Essay on the Principles of Population* (Malthus)

study of mankind is man." Enlightened thinkers challenged existing ideas and existing institutions. A new emphasis on self and on pleasure led to a new emphasis on happiness. All three fed into the distinctively Enlightenment idea of self-interest. Happiness and self-interest were values that would inevitably corrode the old social order, which was based upon principles of self-sacrifice and corporate identity. It was only a matter of time.

eighteenth-century society

Eighteenth-century society was a hybrid of old and new. It remained highly stratified socially, politically, and economically. Birth and occupation determined wealth, privilege, and quality of life as much as they had in the past. But in the eighteenth century the gulf between top and bottom was being filled by a thriving middle class, a *bourgeoisie*, as they were called in France. There were now more paths toward the middle and upper classes, more wealth to be distributed among those above the level of subsistence. It was bourgeois culture and bourgeois values that were new in the eighteenth century. At the bottom of society, poverty still gripped the mass of European people. Changes in agriculture allowed more to survive than ever before, but their survival was still perilous, dependent upon chance rather than effort.

The Nobility

Nobles were defined by their legal rights. They had the right to bear arms, the right to special judicial treatment, the right to tax exemptions. In Russia only nobles could own serfs; in Poland only nobles could hold government office. In France and Britain the highest court positions were always reserved for noblemen. Nobles dominated the Prussian army. In 1786, out of nearly 700 senior officers only 22 were not noblemen. The Spanish nobility claimed the right to live idly. Rich or poor, they shunned all labor as a right of their heritage. Swedish and Hungarian noblemen had their own legislative chambers, just as the British had the House of Lords. Noble privilege was as vibrant as ever.

Although all who enjoyed these special rights were noble, not all nobles were equal. In many states the noble order was subdivided into easily identifiable groups. The Spanish grandees, the upper nobility, were numbered in the thousands; the Spanish hidalgos, the lower nobility, in the hundreds of thousands. In Hungary, out of 400,000 noblemen only about 15,000 belonged to the landed nobility, who held titles and were exempt from taxes. The landed nobility were personally members of the upper chamber of the Hungarian Diet, while the lesser nobility sent representatives to the lower chamber. This was not unlike the situation in England, where the elite class was divided between the peerage and the gentry. The peerage held titles, were members of the House of Lords, and had a limited range of judicial and fiscal privileges. In the mid-eighteenth century, there were only 190 British peers. The gentry, which numbered over 20,000, dominated the House of Commons and local legal offices but were not strictly members of the nobility. The French nobility was informally distinguished among the small group of peers known as the Grandes, whose ancient lineage, wealth, and power set them apart from all others; a rather larger service nobility whose privileges derived in one way or another from municipal or judicial service; and what might be called the country nobility, whose small estates and local outlook made their fiscal immunities vital to their survival.

These distinctions among the nobilities of the European states masked a more important one: wealth. As the saying went, "All who were truly noble were not wealthy, but all who were truly wealthy were noble." In the eighteenth century, despite the phenomenal increase in mercantile activity, wealth was still calculated

European artists often created allegorical paintings contrasting "civilized" Europe with "savage" America. In this work, by Italian artist Giovanni Battista Tiepolo, the figure of America is adorned with gold and feathers and riding on the back of an alligator. She receives tributes of stags, bundles of brazil wood, and ripe fruit. In the right foreground, a pile of severed heads pierced with arrows recalls America's savage heritage.

in profits from the ownership of land, and it was the wealthy landed nobility who set the tone of elite life in Europe.

All That Glitters. Eighteenth-century Europe was a society of orders gradually transforming itself into a society of classes. At the top, as vigorous as ever, was the nobility, the privileged order in every European state. In different parts of Europe the nobility used different methods to maintain their land-based wealth. In places like Britain, Spain, Austria, and Hungary, forms of entail were the rule. In simple terms, an entail was a restriction prohibiting the breakup of a landed estate either through sale or inheritance. The owner of the estate was merely a caretaker for his heir, and while he could add land, he could not easily subtract any. Entailed estates grew larger and larger and, like magnets, attracted other entailed estates through marriage. In Britain, where primogeniture—inheritance by the eldest son—accompanied entail, 400 families owned one-quarter of the entire country. Yet this concentration of landed wealth paled into insignificance when compared to the situation in Spain, where just four families owned one-third of all the cultivable land. In the east, where land was plentiful, the Esterhazys of Hungary and the Radziwills of Poland owned millions of acres.

The second method by which the European nobility ensured that the wealthy would be noble was by absorption. There were several avenues to upward mobility, but by the eighteenth century the holding of state offices was the most common. In France, for example, a large number of offices were reserved for the nobility. Many of these were owned by their holders and passed on to their children, but occasionally an office was sold on the market and the new holder was automatically ennobled. The office of royal secretary was one of the most common routes to noble status. The number of secretaries increased from 300 to 900 during the course of the eighteenth century, yet despite this dilution the value of the offices continued to skyrocket. An office that was worth 70,000 French pounds at the beginning of the century was worth 300,000 by the 1780s. In fact, in most European societies there was more room for new nobles than there were aspiring candidates. This was because of the costs that maintaining the new status imposed. In Britain, anyone who could live like a gentleman was accounted one. But the practice of entail made it very difficult for a newcomer to purchase the requisite amount of land. Philip V increased the number of Spanish grandees in an effort to dilute their power, yet when he placed a tax on entrance into the lower nobility, the number of hidalgos dropped precipitously.

For the wealthy, aristocracy was becoming an international status. The influence of Louis XIV and the court of Versailles lasted for well over a century and spread to town and country life. Most nobles maintained multiple residences. The new style of aristocratic entertainment required more public space on the first floor, while the increasing demand for personal and familial privacy necessitated more space in the upper stories. The result was larger and more opulent homes. Here the British elite led all others. Over 150 country houses were built in the early eighteenth century alone, including Blenheim Palace, which was built for John Churchill, duke of Marlborough, at a cost of £300,000. To the expense of architecture was added the expense of decoration. New materials such as West Indian mahogany occasioned new styles, and both drove up costs. The high-quality woodwork and plastering made fashionable by the English Adam brothers was quickly imitated on the Continent. Only the Spanish nobility shunned country estates, preferring to reside permanently in towns.

The building of country houses was only one part of the conspicuous consumption of the privileged orders. Improvements in travel, both in transport and roads, permitted increased contact between members of the national elites. The stagecoach linked towns, and canals linked waterways. Both made travel quicker and more enjoyable. The grand tour of historical sites continued to be used as a substitute for formal education. Young men would pass from country house to country house buying up antiquities, paintings, and books along the way. The grand tour was a means of introducing the European aristocracies to each other, and also a means of communicating taste and fashion among them. Whether it was a Russian noble in Germany, a Swede in Italy, or a Briton in Prussia, all spoke French and shared a cultural outlook.

Much of this was cultivated in the salons, a social institution begun in the seventeenth century by French women that gradually spread throughout the Continent. In the salons, especially those in Paris, the aristocracy and bourgeoisie mingled with the leading intellectuals of the age. Here wit and insight replaced polite conversation. At formal meetings, papers on scientific or philosophical topics were read and discussed. At informal gatherings new ideas were examined and exchanged. The British ambassador to Spain was appalled to discover that men and women were still kept separate in the salons of Madrid and that there was no seri-

Blenheim Palace, Oxfordshire, was built for the duke of Marlborough by a grateful nation and named after his famous victory.

ous conversation during evenings out. It was in the salons that the impact of the Enlightenment, the great European intellectual movement of the eighteenth century, first made itself felt.

The Bourgeoisie

Bourgeois is a French word, and it carried the same tone of derision in the eighteenth century that it does today. The bourgeois was a man on the make, scrambling after money or office or title. He was neither well-born nor well-bred, or so said the nobility. Yet the bourgeoisie served vital functions in all European societies. They dominated trade, both nationally and internationally. They made their homes in cities and did much to improve the quality of urban life. They were the civilizing influence in urban culture, for unlike the nobility, they were the city's permanent denizens. Perhaps most importantly, the bourgeoisie provided the safety valve between the nobility and those who were acquiring wealth and power but lacked the advantages of birth and position. By developing their own culture and class identity, the bourgeoisie provided successful individuals with their own sense of pride and achievement and eased the explosive buildup of social resentments.

During the eighteenth century, the bourgeoisie grew in both numbers and importance. An active commercial and urban life gave many members of this group new social and political opportunities, and many of them passed into the nobility through the purchase of land or office. But for those whose aspirations or abilities were different, this social group began to define its own values, which centered on the family and the home. A new interest in domestic affairs touched both men and women of the European bourgeoisie. Their homes became social centers for kin and neighbors, and their outlook on family life reflected new personal relationships. Marriages were made for companionship as much as for economic advantage. Romantic love between husbands and wives was newly valued. So were children, whose futures came to dominate familial concern. Childhood was recognized as a separate stage of life and the education of children as one of the most important of all parental responsibilities. The image of the affectionate father replaced that of the hard-bitten businessman; the image of the doting mother replaced that of the domestic drudge.

Urban Elites. In the society of orders, nobility was the acid test. The world was divided into the small number

This dining room from Landsdowne House in London is one of the finest examples of Robert Adam's style. Characteristic of Adam's style are the vases, trophies of arms, leaf garlands, sprays, rosettes, scrolls, and fan-shaped motifs cast in plaster adorning the room.

of those who had it and the large number of those who did not. At the apex of the non-noble pyramid was the bourgeoisie, the elites of urban Europe whose place in the society of orders was ambiguous. *Bourgeois*, or *burgher*, simply meant "town dweller," but as a social group it had come to mean wealthy town dweller. The bourgeoisie was strongest where towns were strongest: in western rather than in eastern Europe and in northern rather than southern Europe, with the notable exception of Italy. Holland was the exemplar of a bourgeois republic. More than half of the Dutch population lived in towns, and there was no significant aristocratic class to compete for power. The Regents of Amsterdam were the equivalent of a European court nobility in wealth, power, and prestige, though not in the way in which they had accumulated their fortunes. The size of the bourgeoisie in various European states cannot be determined absolutely. At the end of the eighteenth century, the British middle classes probably constituted around 15 percent of the population, the French bourgeoisie less than 10 percent. By contrast, the Russian or Hungarian urban elites were less than 2 percent of the population in those states.

Like the nobility, the bourgeoisie constituted a diverse group. At the top were great commercial families engaged in the expanding international marketplace and reaping the profits of trade. In wealth and power they were barely distinguishable from the nobility. At the bottom were the so-called petite bourgeoisie; shopkeepers, artisans, and small manufacturers. The solid core of the bourgeoisie was employed in trade, exchange, and service. Most were engaged in local or national commerce. Trade was the lifeblood of the city, for by itself the city could neither feed nor clothe its inhabitants. Most bourgeois fortunes were first acquired in trade. Finance was the natural outgrowth of commerce, and another segment of the bourgeoisie accumulated or preserved their capital through the sophisticated financial instruments of the eighteenth century. While the very wealthy loaned directly to the central government or bought shares in overseas trading companies, most bourgeois participated in government credit markets. They purchased state bonds or lifetime annuities and lived on the interest. The costs of war flooded the urban credit markets with high-yielding and generally stable financial instruments. Finally, the bourgeoisie were members of the burgeoning professions that provided services for the rich. Medicine, law, education, and the bureaucracy were all bourgeois professions, for the cost of acquiring the necessary skills could be borne only by those already wealthy.

During the course of the eighteenth century, this combination of occupational groups was expanding, both in numbers and in importance, all over Europe. So was the bourgeois habitat. The urbanization of Europe continued steadily throughout the eighteenth century. A greater percentage of the European population were living in towns, and a greater percentage were living in large towns of over 10,000 inhabitants, which, of necessity, were developing complex socioeconomic structures. In France alone there were probably over a hundred such towns, each requiring the services of the bourgeoisie and providing opportunities for their expansion. And the larger the metropolis, the greater the need. In 1600, only 20 European cities contained as many as 50,000 people; in 1700 that number had risen to 32; and by 1800 to 48. During the course of the eighteenth century, the number of cities with 75,000 inhabitants doubled. London, the largest city, had grown to 865,000, a remarkable feat considering that in 1665 over one-quarter of the London population had died in the Great Plague. In such cities the demand for lawyers, doctors, merchants, and shopkeepers was almost insatiable.

Besides wealth, the urban bourgeoisie shared another characteristic: mobility. The aspiration of the bourgeoisie was to become noble, either through office or by acquiring rural estates. In Britain, a gentleman was still defined by lifestyle: "All are accounted gentlemen in England who maintain themselves without manual labor." Many trading families left their wharves and countinghouses to acquire rural estates, live off rents, and practice the openhanded hospitality of gentlemen. In France and Spain, nobility could still be purchased, though the price was constantly going up. For the greater bourgeoisie, the transition was easy; for the lesser, the failure to move up was all the more frustrating for being just beyond their grasp. The bourgeoisie did not only imagine their discomfort, they were made to feel it at every turn. They were the butt of jokes, theater, and popular songs. They were the first victims in the shady financial dealings of

The Dutton Family by John Zoffany. This eighteenth-century painting shows the comforts enjoyed by the British upper middle class.

crown and court, the first casualties in urban riots. Despised from above and envied from below, the bourgeoisie were uncomfortable with the present yet profoundly conservative about the future. The one consolation to their perpetual misery was that as a group they got richer and richer. And as a group they began to develop a distinctive culture that reflected their qualities and aspirations.

Bourgeois Values. Many bourgeoisie viewed their condition as temporary and accepted the pejorative connotations of the word *bourgeois*. They had little desire to defend a social group out of which they fervently longed to pass. Others, whose aspirations were lower, were nevertheless uncomfortable with the status that they had already achieved. They had no ambition to wear the silks and furs reserved for the nobility or to attend the opening night at the opera decked in jewels and finery. In fact, such ostentation was alien to their existence and to the success that they had achieved. There was a real tension between the values of noble and bour-

geois. The ideal noble was idle, wasteful, and ostentatious; the ideal bourgeois was industrious, frugal, and sober. Voltaire, who made his fortune as a financial speculator rather than as a man of letters, aped the lifestyle of the nobility. But he could never allow himself to be cheated by a tradesman, a mark of his origins. When Louis XVI tried to make household economies in the wake of a financial crisis, critics said that he acted "like a bourgeois."

Even if the bourgeoisie did not constitute a class, they did share certain attitudes that constituted a culture. The wealthy among them participated in the new world of consumption, whether they did so lavishly or frugally. For those who aspired to more than their birth allowed, there was a loosening of the strict codes of dress that reserved certain fabrics, decorative materials, and styles to the nobility. Merchants and bankers could now be seen in colored suits or with piping made of cloth of gold; their wives could be seen in furs and silks. They might acquire silverware, even if they did not go so far as the nobility and have a coat of arms engraved

L'Amour au Théâtre Français (*Love in the French Theater*) (*ca.* 1716), *by Antoine Watteau. The painting is thought to portray a scene from* Les Fêtes de l'Amour et de Bacchus, *a comic opera composed in* 1672.

upon it. Coaches and carriages were also becoming common among the bourgeoisie, to take them on the Sunday rides through the town gardens or to their weekend retreats in the suburbs. Parisian merchants, even master craftsmen like clockmakers, were now acquiring suburban homes, although they could not afford to retire to them for the summer months.

But more and more, the bourgeoisie was beginning to travel. In Britain whole towns were established to cater to leisure travelers. The southwestern town of Bath, which was rebuilt in the eighteenth century, was the most popular of all European resort towns, famous since Roman times for the soothing qualities of its waters. Bath was soon a social center as notable for its marriage market as for its recreations. Brighton, a seaside resort on the south coast, quadrupled in size in the second half of the eighteenth century. Bathing—what we would call swimming—either for health or recreation, became a middle-class fad, displacing traditional fear of the sea.

The leisure that wealth bestowed on the bourgeoisie, in good bourgeois fashion, quickly became commercialized. Theater and music halls for both light and serious productions proliferated. By the 1760s an actual theater district had arisen in London and was attracting audiences of over 20,000 a week. London was unusual, both for its size and for the number of well-to-do visitors who patronized its cultural events. The size of the London audiences enabled the German-born composer Georg Friedrich Handel (1685–1759) to earn a handsome living by performing and directing concerts. He was one of the few musicians in the eighteenth century to live without noble patronage. But it was not only in Britain that theater and music flourished. Voltaire's plays were performed before packed houses in Paris, with the author himself frequently in attendance to bask in the adulation of the largely bourgeois audiences who attended them. In Venice it was estimated that over 1200 operas were produced in the eighteenth century. Rome and Milan were even better known, and Naples was the center for Italian opera. Public concerts were a mark of bourgeois culture, for the court nobility was entertained at the royal palaces or great country houses. Public concerts began in Hamburg in the 1720s, and Frederick the Great helped establish the Berlin Opera House some decades later.

Theater and concert going were part of the new attitude toward socializing that was one of the greatest contributions of the Enlightenment. Enlightened thinkers spread their views in the salons, and the salons soon spawned the academies, local scientific societies that, though led and patronized by provincial nobles, included large numbers of bourgeois members. The academies sponsored essay competitions, built up libraries, and became the local centers for intellectual interchange. A less structured form of sociability took place in the coffeehouses and tearooms that came to be a feature of even small provincial towns. In the early eighteenth century, there were over 2000 London coffee shops where men—for the coffeehouse was largely a male preserve—could talk politics, read the latest newspapers and magazines, and indulge their taste for this still-exotic beverage. More exclusive clubs were also a form of middle-class sociability, some centering on political issues, some (like the chambers of commerce) centering on professional interests. Parisian clubs, called *sociétés*, covered a multitude of diverse interests. Literary sociétés were the most popular, maintaining their purpose by forbidding drinking, eating, and gambling on their premises.

Above all, bourgeois culture was literate culture. Wealth and leisure led to mental pursuits—if not always to intellectual ones. The proliferation of relatively cheap printed material had an enormous impact on the lives of those who were able to afford it. Holland and Britain were the most literate European societies and also, because of the absence of censorship, the centers of European printing.

This was the first great period of the newspaper and the magazine. The first daily newspaper appeared in London in 1702; eighty years later, 37 provincial towns had their own newspapers, while the London papers were read all over Britain. Then as now, the newspaper was as much a vehicle for advertisement as for news. News reports tended to be bland, avoiding controversy and concentrating on general national and international events. Advertising, on the other hand, tended to be lurid, promising cures for incurable ills and the most exquisite commodities at the most reasonable prices.

For entertainment and serious political commentary, the British reading public turned to magazines, of which there were over 150 separate titles by the 1780s. The most famous were *The Spectator*, which ran in the early part of the century and did much to set the tone for a cultured middle-class life, and *The Gentleman's Magazine*, which ran in midcentury and was said to have had a circulation of nearly 15,000. The longest-lived of all British magazines was *The Ladies' Diary*, which continued in existence from 1704 to 1871 and doled out self-improvement, practical advice, and fictional romances in equal proportion.

The Ladies' Diary was not the only literature aimed at the growing number of leisured and lettered bourgeois women. Although enlightened thinkers could be ambivalent about the place of women in the new social order, they generally stressed the importance of female education and welcomed women's participation in intellectual pursuits. Whether it was new ideas about women or simply the fact that more women had leisure, a growing body of both domestic literature and light entertainment was available to them. This included a vast number of teach-yourself books aimed at instructing women how best to organize domestic life and how to navigate the perils of polite society. Moral instruction, particularly on the themes of obedience and sexual fidelity, was also popular. But the greatest output directed toward women was in the form of fanciful romances, from which a new genre emerged. The novel first appeared in its modern form in the 1740s. Samuel Richardson (1689–1761) wrote *Pamela* (1740), the story of a servant girl who successfully resisted the advances

of her master until he finally married her. It was composed in long episodes, or chapters, that developed Pamela's character and told her story at the expense of the overt moral message that was Richardson's original intention. Richardson's novels were printed in installments and helped to drive up the circulation of national magazines.

Family Life. While the public life of the bourgeoisie can be measured in the sociability of the coffeehouse and the academy, private life must be measured in the home. There a remarkable transformation was under way, one that the bourgeoisie shared with the nobility. In the pursuit of happiness encouraged by the Enlightenment, one of the newest joys was domesticity. The image—and sometimes the reality—of the happy home, where love was the bond between husband and wife and care the bond between parents and children, came to dominate both the literary and visual arts. Only those wealthy enough to afford to dispense with women's work could partake of the new domesticity; only those touched by Enlightenment ideas could attempt to make the change. But where it occurred, the transformation in the nature of family life was one of

This writing desk, designed by Jean-Francois Oeben, who was appointed cabinetmaker to Louis XV of France in 1754, features the intricate pictorial marquetry and elaborate ormolu (a brass imitation of gold) that are characteristic of French Rococo style.

the most profound alterations in eighteenth-century culture.

The first step toward the transformation of family relationships was in centering the conjugal family in the home. In the past, the family was a less important structure for most people than the social groups to which they belonged or the neighborhood in which they lived. Marriage was an economic partnership and a means to carry on lineage. Individual fulfillment was not an object of marriage, and this attitude could be seen among the elites in the great number of arranged marriages, the speed with which surviving spouses remarried, and the formal and often brutal personal relationships between husbands and wives.

Patriarchy was the dominant value within the family. Husbands ruled over wives and children, making all of the crucial decisions that affected both the quality of their lives and their futures. As late as the middle of the eighteenth century, a British judge established the "rule of thumb," which asserted that a husband had a legal right to beat his wife with a stick, but the stick should be no thicker than a man's thumb. It was believed that children were stained with the sin of Adam at birth and that only the correct upbringing could clean some of it away. In nearly 200 child-rearing advice books published in England before the middle of the eighteenth century, only three did not advise the beating of children. John Wesley (1703–91), the founder of Methodism, remembered his own mother's dictum that "children should learn to fear the rod and cry softly." Children were sent out first for wet-nursing; then at around the age of seven for boarding, either at school or in a trade; and finally into their own marriages.

There can be no doubt that this profile of family life began to change, especially in western Europe, during the second half of the eighteenth century. Although the economic elements of marriage remained strong—newspapers actually advertised the availability of partners and the dowries or annual income that they would bring to the marriage—other elements now appeared. Fed by an unending stream of stories and novels and a new desire for individual happiness, romantic and sexual attraction developed into a factor in marriage. Potential marriage partners were no longer kept away from each other or smothered by chaperons. The social season of polite society, in which prospective partners could dance, dine, and converse with each other to determine compatibility, gave greater latitude to courtship. Perhaps more importantly, the role of potential spouses in choosing a partner appears to have in-

creased. This was a subtle matter, for even in earlier centuries parents did not simply assign a spouse to their children. But by the eighteenth century, adolescents themselves searched for their own marriage partners and exercised a strong negative voice in identifying unsuitable ones.

The quest for compatibility, no less than the quest for romantic love, led to a change in personal relationships between spouses. The extreme formality of the past was gradually breaking down. Husbands and wives began spending more time with each other, developing common interests and pastimes. Their personal life began to change. For the first time, houses were built to afford a couple privacy from their children, servants, and guests. Rooms were designed for specific functions and were set off by hallways. Corridors were an important innovation in creating privacy. In earlier architecture, one walked through a room to the next one behind it. Now rooms were separated and doors could be closed. This new design allowed for an intimate life that earlier generations did not find necessary and that they could not, in any case, put into practice.

Couples had more time for each other because they were beginning to limit the size of their families. There were a number of reasons for this development, which again pertained only to the upper classes. For one thing, child mortality rates were declining among wealthy social groups. Virulent epidemic diseases like the plague, which knew no class lines, were gradually disappearing. Moreover, though there were few medical breakthroughs in this period, sanitation was improving. Bearing fewer children had an enormous impact on the lives of women, reducing the danger of death and disablement in childbirth and giving them leisure time to pursue domestic tasks. This is not to say that the early part of a woman's marriage was not dominated by children; in fact, because of new attitudes toward child-rearing it may have been dominated more than ever. Many couples appear to have made a conscious decision to space births, though success was limited by the fact that the most common technique of birth control was coitus interruptus, or withdrawal.

The transformation in the quality of relationships between spouses was mirrored by an even greater transformation in attitudes toward children. There were many reasons why childhood now took on a new importance. Decline in mortality rates had a profound psychological impact. Parents could feel that their emotional investment in their children had a greater chance of fulfillment. But equally important were the new ideas about education, especially Locke's belief that the child enters the world a blank slate whose personality is created through early education. This view not only placed a new responsibility on parents but also gave them the concept of childhood as a stage through which individuals passed. This idea could be seen in the commercial sphere as well as in any other. In 1700 there was not a single shop in London that sold children's toys exclusively; by the 1780s there were toy shops everywhere, three of which sold nothing but rocking horses. Children's toys abounded: soldiers and forts, dolls and dollhouses. The jigsaw puzzle was invented in the 1760s as a way to teach children geography. There were also shops that sold nothing but clothes specifically designed for children, no longer simply adult clothes in miniature.

Most important of all was the development of materials for the education of children. This took place in two stages. At first so-called children's books were books whose purpose was to help adults teach children. Later came books directed at children themselves, with large print, entertaining illustrations, and nonsensical characters, usually animals who taught moral lessons. In Britain the Little Pretty Pocket Book series, created by John Newbery (1713–67), not only encompassed educational primers but also included books for the enter-tainment of the child. Newbery published a Mother Goose book of nursery rhymes and created the immortal character of Miss Goody Two-Shoes. Instruction and entertainment also lay behind the development of children's playing cards, in which the French specialized. Dice games, like one in which a child made a journey across Europe, combined geographical instruction with the amusement of competition.

The commercialization of childhood was, of course, directed at adults. The new books and games that were designed to enhance a child's education not only had to be purchased by parents but had to be used by them as well. More and more mothers were devoting their time to their children. Among the upper classes, the practice of wet-nursing began to decline. Mothers wanted to nurture their infants—both literally, by breast-feeding, and figuratively, by teaching them. Children became companions to be taken on outings to the increasing number of museums or shows of curiosities, which began to discount children's tickets by the middle of the century.

The preconditions of this transformation of family life could not be shared by the population at large. Working women could afford neither the cost of instructional materials for their children nor the time to use them. Ironically, they now began using wet nurses, once

The Snatched Kiss, *or* The Stolen Kiss (1750s), *by Jean-Honoré Fragonard, was one of the* "series paintings" *popular in the late eighteenth century. A later canvas entitled* The Marriage Contract *shows the next step in the lives of the lovers.*

the privilege of the wealthy, for increasingly a working woman's labor was the margin of survival for her family. Working women enjoyed no privacy in the hovels in which they lived, with large families in single rooms. Wives and children were still beaten by husbands and fathers and were unacquainted with enlightened ideas of the worth of the individual and the innocence of the child. By the end of the eighteenth century, two distinct family cultures coexisted in Europe: one based on companionate marriage and the affective bonds of parents and children; the other based on patriarchal dominance and the family as an economic unit.

The Masses

The paradox of the eighteenth century was that for the masses, life was getting better by getting worse. More Europeans were surviving than ever before, and more food was available to feed them; there was more housing, better sanitation, and even better charities. Yet for all of this, there was more misery. Those who would have succumbed to disease or starvation a century before now survived from day to day, beneficiaries—or victims—of increased farm production and improved agricultural marketing. The market economy organized a more effective use of land, but it created a widespread social problem. The landless agrarian laborer of the eighteenth century was the counterpart of the sturdy sixteenth-century beggar, capable of working but incapable of finding work. In the cities, the plight of the poor was as desperate as ever. Men and women sold their labor or their bodies for a pittance, while beggars slept at every doorway. Even the most openhearted charitable institutions were unable to cope with the massive increase in the poor. By the thousands, mothers abandoned their children to the foundling hospitals, where it was believed they would have a better chance of survival, even though hospital death rates were nearly 80 percent.

Not all members of the lower orders succumbed to poverty or despair. In fact, many were able to benefit from existing conditions and lead a more fulfilling life than ever before. The richness of popular culture, signified by a spread of literacy into the lower reaches of European society, was one indication of this change. So, too, were the reforms urged by enlightened thinkers to improve basic education and the quality of life in the cities. For the segment of the lower orders that could keep its head above water, the eighteenth century offered new opportunities and new challenges.

Jean Baptiste Greuze (1725–1805), Broken Eggs. French artist Greuze studied in Lyon and Paris but was deeply influenced by Dutch genre painting. Greuze's depictions of village life are in marked contrast to the extravagant Rococo style of his contemporaries.

Breaking the Cycle. Of all the legacies of the eighteenth century, none was more fundamental than the steady increase in European population that began around 1740. This was not the first time that Europe had experienced sustained population growth, but it was the first time that such growth was not checked by a demographic crisis. Breaking the cycle of population growth and crisis was a momentous event in European history, despite the fact that it went unrecorded at the time and unappreciated for centuries after.

The figures tell one part of the story. In 1700 European population is estimated to have been 120 million. By 1800 it had grown 50 percent, to over 180 million. And the aggregate hides significant regional variations. While France, Spain, and Italy expanded between 30 and 40 percent, Prussia doubled and Russia and Hungary may have tripled in number. Britain increased by 80 percent, from about 5 to 9 million, but the rate of growth was accelerating. In 1695 the English population stood at 5 million. It took 62 years to add the next million and 24 years to add the million after that. In 1781 the population was 7 million, but it took only 13 years to reach 8 million and only 10 more years to reach 9 million. Steady population growth had continued without significant checks for well over a half century.

Ironically, the traditional pattern of European population found its theorist at the very moment that it was about to disappear. In 1798 Thomas Malthus (1766–1834) published *An Essay on the Principles of Population*. Reflecting on the history of European population, Malthus observed the cyclical pattern by which growth over one or two generations was checked by a crisis that significantly reduced population. From these lower levels new growth began until it was checked and the cycle repeated itself. Because people increased more quickly than did food supplies, the land could only sustain a certain level of population. When that level was near, population became prone to a demographic check. Malthus divided population checks into two categories: positive and preventive. Positive checks were war, disease, and famine, all of which Malthus believed were natural, although brutal, means of population control. Famine was the obvious result of the failure of food supplies to keep pace with demand; war was the competition for scarce resources; and disease often accompanied both. It was preventive checks that most interested Malthus. These were the means by which societies could limit their growth to avoid the devastating consequences of positive checks. Celibacy, late marriages, and sexual abstinence were among the choices that Malthus approved, though abortion, infanticide, and contraception were also commonly practiced.

In the sixteenth and seventeenth centuries, the dominant pattern of the life cycle was high infant and child mortality, late marriages, and early death. All controlled population growth. Infant and child mortality rates were staggering: only half of all those born reached the age of ten. Late marriage was the only effective form of birth control—given the strong social taboos against sexual relations outside marriage—for a late marriage reduced a woman's childbearing years. Women in western Europe generally married between the ages of 24 and 26; they normally ceased bearing children at the age of 40. But not all marriages lasted this 14- or 16-year span, as one or the other partner died. On average, the childbearing period for most women was between 10 and 12 years, long enough to endure six pregnancies, which would result in three surviving children. (See "Giving Birth in the Eighteenth Century," pp. 648–649.)

Three surviving children for every two adults would, of course, have resulted in a 50 percent rise in population in every generation. Celibacy was one limiting factor; cities were another. Perhaps as much as 15 percent of the population in western Europe remained celibate, either by entering religious orders that imposed celibacy or by lacking the personal or financial attributes necessary to make a match. Religious orders that enforced celibacy were still central features of Catholic societies, and spinsters, as unmarried women were labeled, were increasing everywhere. Cities were like sticky webs, trapping the surplus rural population for the spiders of disease, famine, and exposure to devour. Throughout the early modern period, urban areas grew through migration. Settled town dwellers might have been able to sustain their own numbers despite the unsanitary conditions of cities, but it was migrants who brought about the cities' explosive growth. Rural migrants accounted for the appallingly high urban death rates. When we remember that the largest European cities were continuously growing—London from 200,000 in 1600 to 675,000 in 1750; Paris from 220,000 to 576,000; Rome from 105,000 to 156,000; Madrid from 49,000 to 109,000; Vienna from 50,000 to 175,000—then we can appreciate how many countless thousands of immigrants perished before marriage. If urban perils were not enough, there were still the positive checks. Plagues carried away hundreds of thousands, wars halved populations of places in their path, and famine overwhelmed the weak and the poor. The worst famine in European history came as late as

1697, when one-third of the population of Finland starved to death.

The late seventeenth and early eighteenth centuries was a period of population stagnation, if not actual decline. It was not until the third or fourth decade of the eighteenth century that another growth cycle began. It rapidly gained momentum throughout the Continent and showed no signs of abating after two full generations. More important, this upward cycle revealed unusual characteristics. In the first place, fertility was increasing. This had several causes. In a few areas, most notably in Britain, women were marrying younger, thereby increasing their childbearing years. This pattern was also true in eastern Europe, where women traditionally married younger. In the late eighteenth century, the average age at marriage for Hungarian women had dropped to 18.6 years. Elsewhere, most notably in France, the practice of wet-nursing was becoming more common among the masses. As working women increasingly took jobs outside the house, they were less able to nurse their own children. Finally, sexual activity outside marriage was rising. Illegitimacy rates, especially in the last decades of the century, were spurting everywhere. Over the course of the century, they rose by 60 percent in France, more than doubled in England, and nearly quadrupled in Germany. So, too, were the rates of premarital pregnancy on the rise. The number of couples rushed to the altar in 1800 was nearly double that before 1750 in most of western Europe.

But increasing fertility was only part of the picture. More significant was decreasing mortality. The positive checks of the past were no longer as potent. European warfare not only diminished in scale after the middle of the century, it changed location as well. Rivalry for colonial empires removed the theater of conflict from European communities. So did the increase in naval warfare. The damage caused by war had always been more by aftershock than by actual fighting. The destruction and pillage of crops and the wholesale slaughter of livestock created food shortages that weakened local populations for the diseases that came in train with the armies. As the virulence of warfare abated, so did that of epidemic disease. The plague had all but disappeared from western Europe by the middle of the eighteenth century. The widespread practice of quarantine—especially in Hungary, which had been the crucial bridge between eastern and western epidemics—went far to eradicate the scourge of centuries.

Without severe demographic crises to maintain the cyclical pattern, the European population began a gentle but continuous rise. Urban sanitation, at least for permanent city dwellers, was becoming more effective. Clean water supplies, organized waste and sewage disposal, and strict quarantines were increasingly part of urban regulations. The use of doctors and trained midwives helped lower the incidence of stillbirth and decreased the number of women who died in childbirth. Almost everywhere levels of infant and child mortality were decreasing. More people were being born, more were surviving the first ten dangerous years, and thus more were marrying and reproducing. Increased fertility and decreased mortality could have only one result: renewed population growth. No wonder Malthus was worried.

Daily Bread. In the past, if warfare or epidemic diseases failed to check population growth, famine would have done the job. How the European economy conquered famine in the eighteenth century is a complicated story. There was no single breakthrough that accounts for the ability to feed the tens of millions of additional people who now inhabited the continent. Holland and Britain, at the cutting edge of agricultural

The poverty of eighteenth-century London slums was a favorite subject of the English artist William Hogarth. Gin Lane *depicts the London poor in alcoholic delirium, their only escape from the misery of their daily lives.*

giving birth in the eighteenth century

"In sorrow thou shalt bring forth children." Such was Eve's punishment for eating of the forbidden tree, and that sorrow continued for numberless generations. Childbirth was painful, dangerous, and all too often deadly. Although successful childbirth needed no outside intervention, without the accumulated wisdom of the ages, babies and mothers routinely perished. That wisdom was passed from mother to daughter and finally was collected by skilled women who practiced the craft of midwifery. Every village, no matter how small, had women who were capable of assisting others in childbirth. Midwives' skills ranged widely, from the use of herbal potions and strong drink to ease the pain of labor to a rudimentary understanding of how to assist a complicated delivery when the fetus was not in the proper position.

Midwives, who until the late seventeenth century were always women, were part of the support group that attended a woman during her labor. Typically, childbirth was a social occasion. Along with the midwife would be a wet nurse and female kin and neighbors, who would offer encouragement, bring refreshments, and tend to the chores that the pregnant woman would have performed herself. Without chemicals to induce contractions and without the ability to intervene in the delivery, labor was usually long. Ordinarily, it did not take place in bed, but rather in a room or a part of a room that had been set aside for the occasion. By the eighteenth century, at least in larger urban areas, poor women who had no separate space for labor could give birth in lying-in hospitals. Within the birthing room, the conclave of women was much like a social gathering. The pregnant woman was advised to adopt any position that made her feel comfortable; standing and walking were favored in the belief that the effects of gravity helped the baby move downward. The woman might sit on a neighbor's lap or on a birthing stool, a chair open at the bottom, during contractions and delivery.

Most midwives subscribed to the philosophy of letting nature take its course. Because the difficulties and length of labor differed markedly from woman to woman, the midwife's most important contribution was to offer comfort and reassurance based on her long experience. By the seventeenth century, manuals for midwives were being published, some of them written by women, but most by male doctors with surgical experience. Midwives and doctors were always at daggers drawn. Trained physicians increasingly saw childbirth as a process that could be improved by the application of new medical knowledge, but as childbirth was a female experience, midwives jealously guarded their role in it. No matter how skilled they were, they were denied access to medical training that might have enabled them to develop lucrative practices on their own. Thus they had no intention of letting male doctors into their trade. For a time the compromise was the handbooks, which contained guides to anatomy, descriptions of the most common complications, and the direst warnings to call trained physicians when serious problems arose.

By the beginning of the eighteenth century, the "man-midwife" had made his appearance in western Europe. Medically trained and usually experienced in other forms of surgery, the emergence of the man-midwife led to a number of breakthroughs in increasing the safety of childbirth. There can be no question that more mothers and children survived as a result of the man-midwives' knowledge and skills. But at the same time, the social experience of childbirth changed dramatically. What had been a female rite of passage, experienced by and with other women, now became a private event experienced by an individual woman and her male doctor. As female midwives were still excluded from medical training and licensing, their ability to practice their trade eroded in the face of new techniques and information to which they were denied access.

Although most man-midwives trained in hospitals where the poor came to give birth, they practiced among the rich. New attitudes toward marriage and children made the pain and danger of childbirth less acceptable to husbands, who sought every remedy they could afford. British and French man-midwives made fortunes practicing their trade. Their first task was to ascertain that the fetus was in the proper position to descend. In order to do this, however, they had to make an examination that was socially objectionable. Although advanced thinkers could face their man-midwife with the attitude that shame was better than death—"I considered that through modesty I was not to give up my life," as one English noblewoman reasoned—many women and more husbands were unprepared for the actual practice of a man. Thus students were taught as much about bedside manner as about medicine. They were not to examine the patient unless there was another person present in the room, they were not to ask direct questions, and they were not to face the patient during any of their procedures. They were taught to keep a linen cloth on top of the woman's abdomen and to make the examination only by touch—incredulous students were reminded that the most famous French man-midwife was blind! If the fetus was in the correct position, nothing further would be done until the delivery itself. It was only when the fetus was in what was labeled an "unnatural" position that the skill of the physician came into play.

For the most part, a child that could not be delivered head first, face down was in serious risk of being stillborn and the mother in serious risk of dying in labor. This was the problem to which the physicians addressed themselves in the eighteenth century and for which they found remarkable solutions. Most answers came from better understanding of female anatomy and a better visualization of the way in which the fetus moved during labor. The first advance was the realization that the fetus could be turned while still in the womb. Pressure applied on the outside of the stomach, especially in early stages of labor, could help the fetus drop down correctly. A baby who emerged feet first had to be turned face down before it was pulled through the birth canal.

For babies who could not be manually manipulated, the greatest advance of the eighteenth century was the invention of the forceps, or the *tire-tête*, as the French called them. With forceps, the physician could pull the baby by force when the mother was incapable of delivery. Forceps were used mostly in breech births but were also a vital tool when the baby was too large to pass through the cervix by contraction. The forceps were invented in Britain in the middle of the seventeenth century but were kept secret for more than 50 years. During that time they were used by three generations of a single family of man-midwives. In the eighteenth century, they came into general use when the Scotsman William Smellie (1697–1765) developed a short, leather-covered instrument that enabled the physician to do as little damage as possible to either mother or child. Obstetrics now emerged as a specialized branch of medical practice. If neither the pain nor the sorrow of childbirth could be eliminated, its dangers could be lessened.

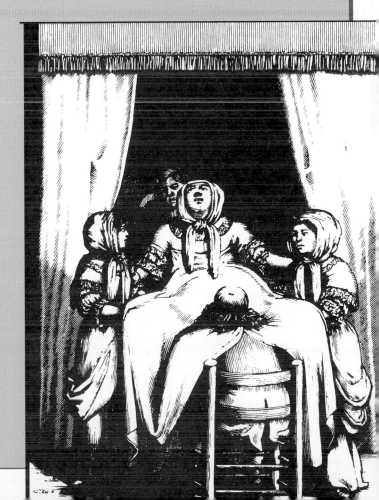

improvement, employed dynamic new techniques that would ultimately provide the means to support continued growth, but most European agriculture was still mired in the time-honored practices that had endured for centuries. Still, not everyone could be fed or fed adequately. Widespread famine might have disappeared, but slow starvation and chronic undernourishment had not. It is certainly the case that hunger was more common at the end of the eighteenth century than at the beginning and that the nutritional content of a typical diet may have reached its lowest point in European history.

Nevertheless, the capacity to sustain rising levels of population can only be explained in terms of agricultural improvement. Quite simply, European farmers were now producing more food and marketing it better. In the most advanced societies, this was a result of conscious efforts to make agriculture more efficient. In traditional open-field agriculture, communities quickly ran up against insurmountable obstacles to growth. The three-field crop rotation system left a significant proportion of land fallow each year, while the concentration on subsistence cereal crops progressively eroded the land that was in production. Common farming was only as strong as the weakest member of the community. There was little incentive for successful individuals to plow profits back into the land, either through the purchase of equipment or the increase of livestock. Livestock was a crucial variable in agricultural improvement. As long as there was only enough food for humans to eat, only essential livestock could be kept alive over the winter. Oxen, which were still the ordinary beasts of burden, and pigs and poultry, which required only minimal feed, were the most common. But few animals meant little manure, and without manure the soil could not easily be regenerated.

It was not until the middle of the seventeenth century that solutions to these problems began to appear. The first change was consolidation of landholdings so that traditional crop rotations could be abandoned. A second innovation was the introduction of fodder crops, some of which—like clover—added nutrients to the soil, while others—like turnips—were used to feed livestock. Better grazing and better winter feed increased the size of herds, while new techniques of animal husbandry, particularly crossbreeding, produced hardier strains. It was quite clear that the key to increased production lay in better fertilization, and by the eighteenth century some European farmers had broken through the "manure barrier." Larger herds, the introduction of clover crops, the use of human waste from towns, and even the first experiments with lime as an artificial fertilizer were all part of the new agricultural methods. The impact of new farming techniques was readily apparent. In Britain and Holland, where they were used most extensively, grain yields exceeded ten kernels harvested for each one planted, while in eastern Europe, where they were hardly known, yields were less than five to one.

Along with the new crops that helped nourish both soil and animals came new crops that helped nourish people. Indian corn, or maize, was a staple crop for Native Americans and gradually came to be grown in most parts of western Europe. Maize not only had higher nutritional value than most other cereals, it also yielded more food per acre than traditional grains, reaching levels as high as 40 to 1. So, too, did the potato, which also entered the European diet from the New World. The potato grew in poor soil, required less labor, and yielded an abundant and nutritious harvest. It rapidly took hold in Ireland and parts of Prussia, from which it spread into eastern Europe. French and Spanish peasants reluctantly introduced it into their diet. Wherever it took root, the potato quickly established itself as survival food. It allowed families to subsist on smaller

Cereal Crops

amounts of land and with less capital outlay. As a result, potato cultivation enabled people in some parts of Europe to marry younger, and thus to produce more children.

It must be stressed, however, that these new developments involved only a very narrow range of producers. The new techniques were expensive, and knowledge of the new crops spread slowly. Change had to overcome both inertia and intransigence. With more mouths to feed, profits from agriculture soared without landowners having to lift a finger. Only the most ambitious were interested in improvement. At the other end, peasant farmers were more concerned with failure than success. An experiment that did not work could devastate a community; one that did only meant higher taxes. Thus the most important improvements in agricultural production were more traditional ones. Basically, there was an increase in the amount of land that was utilized for growing. In most of western Europe there was little room for agricultural expansion, but in the east there remained great tracts of uncultivated land. In Russia, Prussia, and Hungary, hundreds of thousands of new acres came under the plow, though it must be admitted that some of it simply went to replace land that had been wastefully exhausted in previous generations. In one German province, nearly 75 percent more land was in cultivation at the end of the eighteenth century than had been at the beginning. Even in the west, drainage schemes and forest clearance expanded productive capacity.

There was also an upswing in the efficiency with which agricultural products were marketed. From the seventeenth century onward, market agriculture was gradually replacing subsistence agriculture in most parts of Europe. Market agriculture had the advantage of allowing specialization on farms. Single-crop farming enabled farmers to benefit from the peculiarities of their own soil and climate. They could then exchange their surplus for the range of crops they needed to subsist. Market exchange was facilitated by improved transportation and communication, and above all by the increase in the population of towns, which provided demand. On a larger scale, market agriculture was able to respond to regional harvest failures in a way that subsistence agriculture could not. The most hated figure in the eighteenth century was the grain engrosser, a middleman who bought up local surplus and shipped it away. Engrossers were accused of driving up prices—which they did—and of creating famines—which they did not. In fact, the national and international trade in

Agricultural techniques are illustrated in this plate from Diderot's Encyclopedia. In the foreground, a man steers a high-wheeled horse-drawn plow while a woman operates a hopper device to sow seeds.

large quantities of grain evened out regional variations in harvests and went a long way toward reducing local grain shortages. The upkeep of roads, the building of canals, and the clearing of waterways created a national lifeline for the movement of grain.

Finally, it is believed that the increase in agricultural productivity owed something to a change in climate that took place in the late eighteenth century. This is very difficult to substantiate and impossible to explain. It is thought that the annual ring of growth inside tree trunks is an indicator of changes in climate. Hot years produce markedly different rings than cold ones; wet years are etched differently than dry ones. Examination of trees that are centuries old seems to indicate that the European climate was unusually cold and wet during the seventeenth century—some have even called it a little ice age—and that it gradually warmed during the eighteenth century. Even moderate climatic change, when combined with new techniques, new crops, expanded cultivation, and improved marketing, would go a long way toward explaining how so many more people were being fed at the end of the eighteenth century.

The Plight of the Poor. "Of every ten men one is a beggar, five are too poor to give him alms, three more are ill at ease, embarrassed by debts and lawsuits, and the tenth does not represent a hundred thousand families." So observed an eighteenth-century Frenchman about the distribution of wealth in his country. There can be no doubt that the most serious social problem of the eighteenth century was the explosion of poor people throughout Europe. There was grim irony in the fact that advances in the production and distribution of food and the retreat of war and plague allowed more people to survive hand-to-mouth than ever before. Where their ancestors had succumbed to quick death from disease or starvation, they eked out a miserable existence of constant hunger and chronic pain, with death at the end of a seemingly endless corridor.

It is impossible to gauge the number of European poor or to separate them into categories of greater and greatest misery. The truly indigent, the starving poor, probably composed 10 to 15 percent of most societies, perhaps as many as 20 million people throughout the Continent. They were most prevalent in towns but were an increasing burden on the countryside, where they wandered in search of agricultural employment. The wandering poor had no counterpart in the east, where serfdom kept everyone tied to the land, but the hungry and unsheltered certainly did. Yet the problem of poverty was not only to be seen among the destitute. In fact, the uniqueness of the poor in the eighteenth century is that they were drawn from social groups that even in the hungry times of the early seventeenth century had been successful subsistence producers. Perhaps another 40 percent of the population in western Europe was described by contemporaries as those without a fixed interest: in the country, those without land; in the towns, those without steady jobs.

It was easy to see why poverty was increasing. The relentless advance of population drove up the price of food and drove down the price of wages. In the second half of the eighteenth century, the cost of living in France rose by over 60 percent while wages rose only by

Der Pesthof (The Plague Ward), 1746, *illustrates the conditions in eighteenth-century medical facilities. The centerpiece is a gruesome amputation.*

25 percent. In Spain the cost of living increased by 100 percent while wages rose only 20 percent. Only in Britain did wages nearly keep pace with prices. Rising prices made land more valuable. At the beginning of the eighteenth century, as the first wave of population expansion hit western Europe, small holdings began to decrease in size. The custom of partible inheritance, by which each son received a share of land, shrank the average size of a peasant holding below that necessary to sustain an average-size family, let alone one that was growing larger. In one part of France it was estimated that 30 acres was a survival plot of land in good times. At the end of the seventeenth century 80 percent of the peasants there owned less than 25 acres.

As holdings contracted, the portion of the family income derived from wage labor expanded. In such circumstances, males were more valuable than females, both as farmers and laborers, and there is incontrovertible evidence that European rural communities practiced female infanticide. In the end, however, it became increasingly difficult for the peasant family to remain on the land. Mediterranean sharecroppers fell further and further into debt until they finally lost their land entirely. Small freeholders were forced to borrow against future crops until a bad harvest led to foreclosure. Many were allowed to lease back their own lands, on short terms and at high rents, but most swelled the ranks of agricultural laborers, migrating during the planting and harvest seasons and suffering cruelly during winter and summer. In Britain the rural landless outnumbered the landed by two to one. In France there were as many as 8 million peasants who no longer owned their own land.

Emigration was the first logical consequence of poverty. In places where rural misery was greatest, like Ireland, whole communities pulled up stakes and moved to America. Frederick the Great attracted hundreds of thousands of emigrants to Prussia by offering them land. But most rural migrants did not move to new rural environments. Rather, they followed the well-trodden paths to the cities. Many traditional domestic crafts were evolving into industrial activities. In the past, peasants had supplemented their family income by processing raw materials in the home. Spinning, weaving, and sewing were common cottage industries in which the workers took in the work, supplied their own equipment, and were paid by the piece. Now, especially in the cloth trades, a new form of industrial activity was being organized. Factories, usually located in towns or larger villages, assembled workers together, set them at larger and more efficient machines, and paid them for their time rather than for their output.

Families unable to support themselves from the land had no choice but to follow the movement of jobs.

Urban poverty seemed more extreme to observers because there were more poor to observe. They crowded into towns in search of work or charity, though they were unlikely to find much of either. It was certainly true that urban areas were better equipped to assist the poor than were the rural communities from which they came. But the likelihood of finding aid only attracted more and more poor, straining and finally breaking the capacities of urban institutions. The death rate of these migrants and their children was staggering. It is perhaps best typified by the dramatic increase in the numbers of abandoned babies throughout western European cities. The existence of foundling hospitals in cities meant that unwed or poor mothers could leave their children in the hope that they would receive better care than the mother herself could provide. In fact, this was rarely the case. In the largest foundling hospital in Paris, only 15 percent of the children survived their first year of "care." But this did little to deter abandonment. In 1772 over 7500 babies were left in this charnel house, representing 40 percent of all the children born in Paris that year. The normal rates of abandonment of between 10 and 15 percent of all children born in such diverse cities as Madrid and Brussels were little better.

Neither state nor private charities could cope with the flood of poor immigrants. Although the English pundit Samuel Johnson (1709–84) opined that "a decent provision for the poor is the true test of civilization," what he meant was provision for the deserving poor, those unfortunates who were physically or mentally unable to support themselves. The distinction between the worthy and unworthy poor was one involved with changing definitions of charity itself. In earlier times, charity was believed to benefit the soul of the giver as much as the body of the recipient. Thus the poor were socially useful, providing the rich with the opportunity to do good works. But now the poor were coming to be viewed as a problem of social administration. Hospitals, workhouses, and, more ominously, prisons were established or expanded to deal with them.

Hospitals were residential asylums rather than places for health care. They took in the old, the incapacitated, and, increasingly, the orphaned young. Those in France were aptly named "Hotels of God," considering their staggering death rates. "There children dwell who know no parents' care/Parents who know no children's care dwell there," one poet lamented. Workhouses existed for those who were capable of work but incapable of finding it. They were supposed to improve the values of the idle by keeping them busy, though in most places they served only to improve the profits of the industrialists, who rented out workhouse inmates at below-market wages. Prisons grew with crime. There were spectacular increases in crimes against property in all eighteenth-century cities, and despite severe penalties that could include hanging for petty theft, more criminals were incarcerated than executed. Enlightened arguments for the reform of prisons and punishment tacitly acknowledged the social basis of most crime. As always, the victims of crime were mostly drawn from the same social backgrounds as the perpetrators. Along with all of their other troubles, it was the poor who were most commonly robbed, beaten, and abused.

Popular Culture. However depressing this story of the unrelieved misery of the poor is, we should not think of the masses of eighteenth-century society only as the downtrodden victims of social and economic forces beyond their control. For the peasant farmer about to lose his land or the urban artisan without a job, security was an overwhelming concern. While many were to endure such fates, many others lived comfortably by the standards of the age, and almost everyone believed that things were better now than they had ever been before. Popular culture was a rich mixture of family and community activities that provided outlets from the pressures of work and the vagaries of fortune. It was no less sustaining to the population at large than was the purely literate culture of the elite, no less vital as a means of explanation for everyday events than the theories of the philosophers or the programs of the philosophes.

In fact, the line between elite and popular culture in the eighteenth century is a thin one. For one thing, there was still much mixing of social classes in both rural and urban environments. Occasions of display such as festivals, village fairs, and religious holidays brought entire communities together and reinforced their collective identities. Moreover, there were many shared elements between the two cultures. All over Europe, literacy was increasing, the result of primary education, of new business techniques, and of the millions of books that were available in editions tailored to even the most modest purse. Nearly half of the inhabitants of France were literate by the end of the eighteenth century, perhaps 60 percent of those in Britain. Men were more likely to have learned to read than women, as were those who lived in urban areas. More than a quar-

A 1781 *colored mezzotint by J. R. Smith shows a lady leaving a lending library with a book.*

ter of French women could read, a number that had doubled over the century. As the rates of female literacy rose, so did overall rates, for women took the lead in teaching children.

Popular literacy spawned popular literature in remarkable variety. Religious works remained the most important, but they were followed by almanacs, romances, and (perhaps surprisingly) chivalric fiction. Religious tracts aimed at the populace were found throughout Europe. They contained stories of the saints in Catholic countries and of the martyrs in Protestant ones, proverbs intended to increase spirituality, and prayers to be offered for all occasions. Almanacs combined prophecies, home remedies, astrological tables, predictions about the weather, and advice on all varieties of agricultural and industrial activities. In the middle of the century, just one of the dozens of British almanacs was selling over 80,000 copies a year. Romances were the staple of lending libraries, which were also becoming a common feature of even small towns. These books were usually published in inexpensive installments spaced according to the time working families needed to save the pennies to purchase them. Written by middle-class authors, popular romances had a strong moral streak, promoting chastity for women and sobriety for men. Yet the best-selling popular fiction, at least in western Europe, was melodramatic tales of knights and ladies from the age of chivalry. These themes had seeped into popular consciousness after having fallen out of favor among the elites. But cultural tastes did not only trickle down. The masses kept the chivalric tradition alive during the eighteenth century; it would percolate up into elite culture in the nineteenth.

Nevertheless, literate culture was not the dominant form of popular culture. Traditional social activities continued to reflect the violent and even brutal nature of day-to-day existence. Village festivals were still the safety valve of youth gangs who enforced sexual morals by shaming husbands whose wives were unfaithful or women whose reputations were sullied. Many holidays were celebrated by sporting events that pitted the inhabitants of one village against those of another. These almost always turned into free-for-alls in which broken bones were common and deaths not unknown. In fact, the frequent breakdown of sporting activities into gang wars was the principal cause for the development of rules for soccer, as well as more esoteric games like cricket in Britain. Well-organized matches soon became forms of popular entertainment. Over 20,000 spectators attended one eighteenth-century cricket match, and soccer and cricket soon became as popular for gambling as was horse racing among the wealthy.

Even more popular were the so-called blood sports, which continued to be the most common form of popular recreation. These were brutal competitions in which, in one way or another, animals were maimed or slaughtered. Dog- and cockfighting were among those that still survive today. Less attractive to the modern mind were blood sports like bearbaiting or bull running, in which the object was the slaughter of a large beast over a prolonged period of time. Blood sports were certainly not confined to the masses—foxhunting and bullfighting were pastimes for the very rich—but they formed a significant part of local social activity.

So, too, did the tavern or alehouse, which in town or country was the site for local communication and recreation. There women and men gossiped and gambled to while away the hours between sundown and bedtime. Discussions and games became animated as the

William Hogarth, The Cockpit (ca. 1759) *The central figure is a blind nobleman who was said never to have missed an important cockfight. The steel spurs on the birds' legs enabled them to inflict serious damage in the heat of battle.*

evening wore on, for staggering amounts of alcohol were consumed. "Drunk for a penny, dead drunk for two pennies, straw for nothing," advertised one of the thousands of British gin mills that dominated the poorer quarters of towns. The increased use of spirits—gin, brandy, rum, and vodka—changed the nature of alcohol consumption in Europe. Wine and beer had always been drunk in quantities that we would find astounding, but these beverages were also an important part of diet. The nutritional content of spirits was negligible. People drank spirits to get drunk. The British reformer Francis Place (1771–1854), who grew up in a working-class family, commented that the British masses had only two pleasures, "sex and drinking. And drunkenness is by far the most desired." The level to which it rose in the eighteenth century speaks volumes about the changes in social and economic life that the masses of European society were now experiencing.

Eighteenth-century society was a hybrid of old and new. It remained highly stratified. Birth and occupation determined wealth, privilege, and quality of life as much as they had in the past, but there were now more paths toward the middle and upper classes, more wealth to be distributed among those above the level of subsistence. Opulence and poverty increased in step as the fruits of commerce and land enriched the upper orders while rising population impoverished the lower ones. Enlightenment ideas highlighted the contradictions. The attack on traditional authority, especially the Roman Catholic church, was an attack on a conservative, static world view. Enlightenment thinkers looked to the future, to a new world shaped by reason and knowledge, a world ruled benevolently for the benefit of all human beings. Government, society, the individual—all could be improved if only the rubble of the past was cleared away. These thinkers could hardly imagine how potent their vision would become.

mastering the chapter

To review the main points of the chapter, be sure you can explain the significance of each of the following.

Terms/Concepts/Events	People	Places
philosophes	Joseph Haydn	Bath
Encyclopedia	Wolfgang Amadeus Mozart	
Physiocrats	Jean-Jacques Rousseau	
bourgeoisie	Denis Diderot	
entail	Adam Smith	
salons	Voltaire	
coffeehouse	Marquise du Châtelet	
The Spectator	David Hume	
foundling hospitals	Baron Montesquieu	
workhouses	Thomas Malthus	

suggestions for further reading

general reading

* Olwen Hufton, *Europe: Privilege and Protest*, 1730–1789 (Ithaca, NY: Cornell University Press, 1980). An excellent survey of the political and social history of the mid-eighteenth century.

* Leonard Krieger, *Kings and Philosophers*, 1689–1789 (New York: Norton, 1970). A brilliant depiction of the personalities and ideas of eighteenth-century Europe.

* Isser Woloch, *Eighteenth Century Europe, Tradition and Progress*, 1715–89 (New York: Norton, 1982). Especially strong on social movements and popular culture.

* William Doyle, *The Old European Order*, 1660–1800 (Oxford: Oxford University Press, 1978). An important essay on the structure of European societies and the ways in which they held together.

Raymond Birn, *Crisis, Absolutism, Revolution: Europe*, 1648–91 (New York: Holt, Rinehart and Winston, 1977). A reliable survey with especially good chapters on the Enlightenment.

eighteenth-century culture

* Norman Hampson, *The Enlightenment* (London: Penguin Books, 1982). The best one-volume survey.

* Peter Gay, *The Enlightenment: An Interpretation*. 2 vols. (New York: Alfred A. Knopf, 1966–1969). A difficult but rewarding study by one of the leading historians of the subject.

Ulrich Im Hof, *The Enlightenment* (Oxford: Blackwell, 1994). A wide-ranging survey from a German perspective.

Carolyn Lougee, *Le Paradis des Femmes: Women, Salons, and Social Stratification* (Princeton, NJ: Princeton University Press, 1976). A study of the foundation of the French salons and the role of women in it.

* Judith Sklar, *Montesquieu* (Oxford: Oxford University Press, 1987). A concise, readable study of the man and his work.

Theodore Besterman, *Voltaire* (Chicago: University of Chicago Press, 1976). The best of many biographies of an all-too-full life.

A. J. Ayer, *Voltaire* (New York: Random House, 1986). A brief and vibrant study.

* Dorinda Outram, *The Enlightenment* (Cambridge: Cambridge University Press, 1995). A survey of the different theories on the Enlightenment.

* Peter Gay, *The Enlightenment. A Comprehensive Anthology* (New York: Simon & Schuster, 1985). The best single volume for selections of the major works of the Enlightenment.

* John G. Gagliardo, *Enlightened Despotism* (New York: Thomas Y. Crowell, 1967). A sound exploration of the impact of Enlightenment ideas on the rulers of Europe, with emphasis on the east.

* John W. Yolton, ed., *The Blackwell Companion to the Enlightenment* (Cambridge, MA: Blackwell, 1995). A comprehensive dictionary that identifies major people, works, and events.

eighteenth-century society: the nobility

Michael Bush, *Noble Privilege* (New York: Holmes & Meier, 1983). A good analytic survey of the rights of European nobles.

J. V. Beckett, *The Aristocracy in England* (London: Basil Blackwell, 1986). A comprehensive study of a tightly knit national aristocracy.

* Jonathan Dewald, *The European Nobility 1400–1800* (Cambridge: Cambridge University Press, 1996). An insightful survey.

* H. M. Scott, *The European Nobilities in the Seventeenth and Eighteenth Centuries* (London: Longman, 1995). An exploration of the wealth and power of Europe's dominant social class.

* Albert Goodwin, ed., *The European Nobility in the Eighteenth Century* (New York: Harper & Row, 1967). Separate essays on national nobilities, including those of Sweden, Poland, and Spain.

eighteenth-century society: the bourgeoisie

Jan de Vries, *European Urbanization*, 1500–1800 (Cambridge, MA: Harvard University Press, 1984). An important, though difficult, study of the transformation of towns into cities, with the most reliable estimates of size and rates of growth.

* P. J. Corfield, *The Impact of English Towns* 1700–1800 (Oxford: Oxford University Press, 1982). A thorough survey of the role of towns in English social and economic life.

Peter Earle, *The Making of the English Middle Class* (London: Methuen, 1989). The manners, mores, and mindset of the group that would come to dominate nineteenth-century Britain.

* Elinor Barber, *The Bourgeoisie in Eighteenth-Century France* (Princeton, NJ: Princeton University Press, 1955). Still the best study of the French bourgeoisie.

* Simon Shama, *The Embarrassment of Riches* (Berkeley: University of California Press, 1987). The social life of Dutch burghers, richly portrayed.

* Ian Watt, *The Rise of the Novel* (Berkeley: University of California Press, 1957). An important essay on the relationship between literature and society in the eighteenth century.

David Garrioch, *Neighborhood and Community in Paris*, 1740–90 (Cambridge: Cambridge University Press, 1986). A good microstudy of Parisian neighborhoods and the people who inhabited them.

George Sussman, *Selling Mothers' Milk: The Wet-Nursing Business* (Bloomington: Indiana University Press, 1982). A study of buyers and sellers in this important social marketplace.

* Samia Spencer, *French Women and the Age of Enlightenment* (Bloomington: Indiana University Press, 1992). A survey of the role of women in French high culture.

* Lawrence Stone, *The Family, Sex and Marriage in England* 1500–1800 (New York: Harper & Row, 1979). A controversial but extremely important argument about the changing nature of family life.

* Jean-Louis Flandrin, *Families in Former Times* (Cambridge: Cambridge University Press, 1979). Strong on family and household organization.

eighteenth-century society: the masses

* Michael W. Flinn, *The European Demographic System* (Baltimore, MD: Johns Hopkins University Press, 1981). The best single-volume study especially for the nonspecialist.

E. A. Wrigley and R. S. Schofield, *The Population History of England* (Cambridge, MA: Harvard University Press, 1981). The most important reconstruction of a national population, by a team of researchers.

Olwen Hufton, *The Poor in Eighteenth-Century France* (Oxford: Oxford University Press, 1974). A compelling study of the life of the poor.

* Roy Porter, *English Society in the Eighteenth Century* (London: Penguin Books, 1982). A breezy, entertaining survey of English social life.

* J. M. Beattie, *Crime and the Courts in England* (Princeton, NJ: Princeton University Press, 1986). A difficult but sensitive analysis of crime and criminal justice.

* Peter Linebaugh, *The London Hanged: Crime and Civil Society in the Eighteenth Century* (Cambridge: Cambridge University Press, 1993). A controversial study of capital punishment and its uses in the war between the classes.

* Peter Burke, *Popular Culture in Early Modern Europe* (New York: Harper & Row, 1978). A wide survey of practices throughout the continent.

* Robert Muchembled, *Popular Culture and Elite Culture in France*, 1400–1750 (Baton Rouge: Louisiana State University Press, 1985). A complex but richly textured argument about the relationship between two cultures.

* Robert Malcolmson, *Popular Recreation in English Society*, 1700–1850 (Cambridge: Cambridge University Press, 1973). Sport and its role in society.

*Paperback edition available.

The French Revolution and the Napoleonic Era, 1789–1815

"Let Them Eat Cake"

The Queen of France was bored. Try as she might, Marie Antoinette (1755–93) found insufficient diversion in her life at the great court of Versailles. When she was 14, she had married the heir to the French throne, the future Louis XVI. By the age of 19, she was queen of the most prosperous state in continental Europe. Still, she was bored. Her life, she complained to her mother, Empress Maria Theresa of Austria, was futile and meaningless. Maria Theresa advised the unhappy queen to suffer in silence or risk unpleasant consequences.

Sometimes mothers know best.

Unpopular as a foreigner from the time she arrived in France, Marie Antoinette suffered a further decline in her reputation as gossip spread about her gambling and affairs at court. The public heard exaggerated accounts of the fortunes she spent on clothing and jewelry. In 1785 she was linked to a cardinal in a nasty scandal over a gift of a diamond necklace. In spite of her innocence, rumors of corruption and infidelity surrounded her name. Dubbed "Madame Deficit," she came to represent all that was considered decadent in royal rule.

She continued to insist, "I am afraid of being bored." To amuse herself, she ordered a life-size play village built on the grounds of Versailles, complete with cottages, a chapel, a mill, and a running stream. Then, dressed in silks and muslins intended as the royal approximation of a milkmaid's garb, she whiled away whole days with her friends and children, all pretending they were inhabitants of this picturesque "hamlet." Her romantic view of country life helped pass the time, but it did little to bring her closer to the struggling peasants who made up the majority of French subjects.

Marie Antoinette's problems need not have mattered much. Monarchs before her had been considered weak and extravagant. The difference was that her foibles became public in an age when the opinion of the people affected political life. Rulers, even those believed to be divinely appointed, were subjected to a public scrutiny all the more powerful because of the growth of the popular press. Kings, their ministers, and their spouses were held accountable—a dangerous phenomenon for an absolute monarchy.

This Austrian-born queen may not have been more shallow or wastefully extravagant than other queens, but it mattered that people came to see her that way. The queen's reputation sank to its nadir when it was reported that she dismissed the suffering of her starving subjects with the haughty retort "Let them eat cake."

Marie Antoinette never said "Let them eat cake," but everyone thought she did. This was the kind of callousness that people expected from the monarchy in 1789. Marie Antoinette understood the plight of her starving subjects, as her correspondence indicates. Probably a courtier at Versailles was the real source of the brutal retort, but the truth did not matter. Marie Antoinette and her husband were being indicted by the public for all the political, social, and fiscal crises that plagued France.

In October 1793, Marie Antoinette was put on trial by the Revolutionary Tribunal and found guilty of treason. She was stripped of all the trappings of monarchy and forced to don another costume. Dressed as a poor working woman, her hair shorn, the former queen mounted the guillotine, following in the footsteps of her husband, who had been executed earlier that year.

The monarchy did not fall because of a spendthrift queen or an inept king. The monarchy had ceased to be responsive to the profound changes that shook France. It fell because of a new concern among the people for royal accountability in words and deeds. A rising democratic tide carried with it ideas about political representation, participation, and equality. If a queen could change places with a milkmaid, why should not a milkmaid be able to change places with a queen?

Focus Questions

1. To what extent was the French nobility responsible for the crisis that destroyed the *ancien régime*?
2. How did commoners, men and women, transform a crisis of government into a revolution?
3. Why did the leaders of the Revolution resort to a "reign of terror" and what effect did this have on the Revolution?
4. What problems in France and beyond contributed to the rise of Napoleon?
5. What did Napoleon accomplish in France, and what brought about his fall?

The crisis of the old Regime in France, 1715-1788

France in the eighteenth century, the age of the Enlightenment, was a state invigorated by new ideas, but it was also dominated by tradition. The traditional institutions of monarchy, Church, and aristocracy defined power and status. Talk of reform, progress, and perfectibility coexisted with the social realities of privileges and obligations determined by birth. The eighteenth century was a time when old ways prevailed even as a new view of the world was taking shape.

At the end of the eighteenth century, a number of foreign visitors to France commented on the disparities that characterized French social and political life. One English visitor in particular—Arthur Young (1741–1820), an agronomist writing on his travels in France in the 1780s—observed that though a prosperous land, France was pocked with extreme poverty; though a land of high culture and great art, it was riddled with ignorance, illiteracy, and superstition; though a land with a centralized bureaucracy, it was also saddled with local pettiness and obsolete practices.

The tensions generated by the clash of continuity and change made this an exciting and complex period in France. Reformers talked of progress while peasants still used wooden plows. The philosophes glorified reason in a world of violence, superstition, and fear. The great crisis of eighteenth-century France, the French Revolution, destroyed the *ancien régime* (old regime). But the revolution was as much a product of continuities and traditions as it was a product of change and the challenge of new ideas.

Louis XV's France

When Louis XV (1715–74) died, he was a hated man. In his 59-year reign, he managed to turn the public against him. He was denounced as a tyrant who was trying to starve his people, a slave to the mistresses who ruled his court, and an indecisive sybarite dominated by evil ministers. Louis XV's apathy and ineptitude contributed to his poor image. The declining fortunes and the damaged prestige of the monarchy, however, reflected more than the personality traits of an ineffectual king: they reflected structural challenges to fiscal solvency and absolutist rule that the monarchy was unable to meet.

Louis XV, like his great-grandfather Louis XIV, laid claim to rule as an absolute monarch. He insisted that

"the rights and interests of the nation . . . are of necessity one with my own, and lie in my hands only." Such claims failed to mask the weaknesses of royal rule. Louis XV lacked a sufficiently developed bureaucracy to administer and tax the nation in an evenhanded fashion. By the beginning of the eighteenth century, the absolute monarchy had extended royal influence into the new areas of policing, administration, lawmaking, and taxation. But none of these changes proved sufficient to meet the growing needs of the state.

The heightened tensions between the monarch and the aristocracy found expression in various institutions, especially the parlements, the 13 sovereign courts in the French judicial system, with their seats in Paris and a dozen provincial centers. The magistrates of each parlement were members of the aristocracy, some of them nobles of recent origin and others of long standing, depending on the locale. The king needed the parlements to record royal decrees before they could become law. This recording process conferred real political power on the parlements, which could withhold approval for the king's policies by refusing to register his decrees. When decrees involved taxation, the magistrates often refused to endorse them. By successfully challenging the king, the parlements became a battleground between the elite, who claimed that they represented the nation, and the king, who said the nation was himself.

The king repeatedly attempted to neutralize the power of the parlements by relying instead on his own state bureaucracy. His agents in the provinces, called intendants, were accountable directly to the central government. The intendants, as the king's men, and the magistrates who presided in the parlements represented contradictory claims to power. As the king's needs increased in the second half of the eighteenth century, the situation was becoming intolerable for those exercising power and those aspiring to rule in the name and for the good of the nation.

The nadir of Louis XV's reign came in 1763, with the French defeat in the Seven Years' War both on the Continent and in the colonies. In the Treaty of Paris, France ceded territory, including its Canadian holdings, to Great Britain. France lost more than lands: it lost its footing in the competition with its chief rival, Great Britain, which had been pulling ahead of France in international affairs since the mid-eighteenth century. The war was also a financial debacle, paid for by loans secured against the guarantee of victory. The defeat not only left France barren of funds, it also promoted further expenditures for strengthening the French navy

This cartoon from 1789 depicts Necker (at left) showing the king how to conceal the size of the deficit from the Estates. On the wall, a list of royal loans is headed "New ways to revive France"—but the total is "Deficit."

be curbed. In 1770, in an attempt to coerce the magistrates into compliance with the king's wishes, he engineered the overthrow of the Parlement of Paris, the most important of the high courts. Those magistrates who remained obdurate were sent into exile. New courts, whose membership was based on appointment instead of the sale of offices, took their place amid much public criticism. Ultimately, Maupeou's attempt failed. His action did nothing to improve the monarch's image, and it did even less to solve the fiscal problems of the regime. The conflict between Louis XV and the parlements revealed the dependent nature of the monarchy that claimed to be absolute and accountable only to God.

The dignity and prestige of the monarchy were seriously damaged in the course of Louis XV's long reign. His legacy was well captured in the expression erroneously attributed to him, *Après moi le deluge*—"After me, the flood." Continuing to live the good life at the court, he failed dismally to offset rising state expenditures—caused primarily by military needs—with new sources of revenue. In 1774 Louis XV died suddenly of smallpox. His unprepared 20-year-old grandson, Louis XVI (1774–92), a young man who amused himself by hunting and pursuing his hobby as an amateur locksmith, was left to try to stanch the flood.

Louis XVI and the National Debt

Louis XV left to his heir Louis XVI the legacy of a disastrous deficit. From the beginning of his reign, Louis XVI was caught in the vicious circle of excessive state spending—above all, military spending—followed by bouts of heavy borrowing. Borrowing at high rates required the government to pay out huge sums in interest and service fees on the loans that were keeping it afloat. These outlays in turn piled the state's indebtedness ever higher, requiring more loans, and threatening to topple the whole financial structure of the state and the regime itself.

In inheriting this trouble-ridden fiscal structure, Louis XVI made his own contribution to it. Following in the footsteps of his grandfather, he involved France in a costly war, the War of American Independence (1775–83), by supporting the 13 colonies in their revolt against Great Britain. This involvement brought the French monarchy to the brink of bankruptcy. Contrary to public opinion, most of the state's expenditures did not go toward lavishing luxuries on the royal court and the royal family at Versailles. They went to pay off loans.

against the superior British fleet. New taxation was the way out of the financial trap in which the king now found himself.

Louis XV's revenue problem was not easily solved. In order to raise taxes, the king had to turn to the recording function of the parlements. Following the costly Seven Years' War, the parlements chose to exercise the power of refusal by blocking a proportional tax to be imposed on nobles and commoners alike. The magistrates resisted taxation, arguing that the king was attacking the liberty of his subjects by attempting to tax those who were exempt by virtue of their privileged status.

René Nicolas Charles Augustin de Maupeou (1714–92), Louis XV's chancellor from 1768 to 1774, decided that the political power of the parlements had to

More than half of the state budget in the 1780s represented interest on loans taken to pay for foreign military ventures.

The king needed money, and he needed it fast. To those who could afford to purchase them, the king continued to sell offices that carried with them titles, revenues, and privileges. He also relied on the sale of annuities that paid high interest rates and that attracted speculators, large and small. The crown had leased out its rights to collect the salt tax in return for large lump-sum advances from the Royal General Farms, a syndicate of about 100 wealthy financier families. The Royal General Farms reaped healthy profits on their annual transactions at the state's expense. The combined revenues collected by the king through these various stratagems were little more than a drop in the vast ocean of debt that threatened to engulf the state.

The existing tax structure proved hopelessly inadequate to meet the state's needs. The *taille*, a direct tax, was levied, either on persons or on land, according to region. Except for those locales where the taille was attached to land, the nobility was always exempt from direct taxation. Members of the bourgeoisie could also avoid the direct tax as citizens of towns enjoying exemption. That meant that the wealthy, those best able to pay, were often exempt. Indirect taxes, like those on salt (the *gabelle*) and on food and drink (the *aide*), and internal and external customs taxes were regressive taxes that weighed heavily on those least able to pay. The peasantry bore the brunt of the nation's tax burden, and Louis XVI knew all too well that he could not squeeze blood from a stone by increasing indirect taxes. A peasantry too weighted down would collapse—or rebel.

The privileged elite persisted in rejecting the crown's attempts to tax them. As one of the first acts of his reign, in 1775 Louis XVI had restored the magistrates to their posts in the parlements, treating their offices as a form of property of which they had been deprived. In his conciliatory act, Louis XVI nevertheless stressed that the self-interest of the aristocracy was at odds with the common good of the nation and urged the approval of his programs. Nevertheless, by 1776 the Parlement of Paris was again obstructing royal decrees.

Louis XVI appointed Anne Robert Jacques Turgot (1727–81) as his first controller-general. Turgot's reformist economic ideas were influenced by Enlightenment philosophes. In order to generate revenues, Turgot reasoned, France needed to prosper economically. The government was in a position to stimulate economic growth by eliminating regulations, economiz-

ing at court, and improving the network of roads through a tax on landowners. Each of Turgot's reforms offended established interests, thereby ensuring his early defeat. Emphasis on a laissez-faire economy outraged the guilds; doing away with the forced labor of peasants on the roads (the *corvée*) threatened privileged groups who had never before been taxed.

As he floundered about for a solution to his economic difficulties, the king turned to a new adviser, Jacques Necker (1732–1804), a Swiss-born Protestant banker. The king and the public expected great things from Necker, whose international business experience was counted on to save the day. Necker, a prudent man, applied his accounting skills to measuring—for the first time—the total income and expenditures of the French state. The budget he produced and widely circulated allayed everyone's fears of certain doom and assured the nation that no new taxes were necessary—an assurance based on disastrous miscalculations. Instead of raising taxes, Necker committed his ministry to eliminating costly inefficiencies. He set his sights on contracts of the farmers-general, collectors of the indirect salt taxes, whom he likened to weeds sprouting in a swamp. Necker's aim was to reduce ordinary expenses of the realm in order to be ready for the extraordinary ones associated with waging a war. Such policies made him enemies in high places and numbered his days in office.

Necker and those who preceded him in controlling and directing the finances of the state under Louis XV and Louis XVI were committed to reforming the system. All the advisers recognized that the state's fiscal problems were structural and required enlightened solutions, but no two of them agreed on the same program of reforms. Necker had somehow captivated popular opinion, and there was widespread regret expressed over his forced resignation.

Charles Alexandre de Calonne (1734–1802), appointed controller-general in 1783, had his own ideas of how to bail out the ship of state. He authored a program of reforms that would have shifted the tax burden off those least able to pay and onto those best able to support the state. Specifically, he proposed a tax on land proportional to land values, a measure that would have most seriously affected the land-rich nobility. In addition, taxes that affected the peasantry were to be lightened or eliminated. Finally, Calonne proposed the sale of Church lands for revenues. In an attempt to bypass the recalcitrant parlements, Calonne advised the crown in 1787 to convene an Assembly of Notables made up of 150 individuals from the magistracy, the

Church hierarchy, the titled nobility, and municipal bodies, for the purpose of enlisting their support for reforms. Louis listened to Calonne, who was denounced by the Assembly of Notables for attacking the rights of the privileged. He too was forced to resign. All of Louis XVI's attempts to persuade the nobility to agree to tax reforms had failed.

A new controller-general, Archbishop Loménie de Brienne (1727–94), recommended emergency loans. The crown once again disbanded the Paris Parlement, which was now threatening to block loans as well as taxes. Aristocratic magistrates now insisted on a constitution, in which their own right to govern would be safeguarded and the accountability of the king would be defined. In opposing the royal reforms, nobles spoke of the "rights of man" and used the term *citizen*. They had no sympathy for tax programs that threatened their privileges.

The Three Estates

Louis XVI was a desperate man in 1788, so desperate that he yielded to the condition placed on him by the Paris Parlement. he agreed to convene the Estates-General, a medieval body that had not met since 1614 and that had been considered obsolete with the rise of a centralized bureaucratic government. However, eighteenth-century French society continued to be divided by law and custom into a pyramid of three tiers called orders or estates. At the top were those who prayed (the clergy), followed by those who fought (the nobility). The base of the pyramid was formed by the largest of the three estates, those who worked—the bourgeoisie, the peasantry, and urban and rural workers. The Estates-General included equal representation from these three estates of the clergy, nobility, and commoners. Yet only about 200,000 subjects belonged to the first two estates. The Third Estate was composed of all those members of the realm who enjoyed a common identity only in their lack of privilege—over 23 million French people. Traditionally each of the three orders was equally weighted. This arrangement favored the nobility, who controlled the first two estates. The nobility, therefore, was understandably not worried about the prospect of having the Estates-General decide the tax-reform program.

In the second half of the eighteenth century, these traditional groups no longer reflected social realities—a situation that proved to be a source of serious problems for the Estates-General. The piety of the first order

had been called into doubt as religious leaders were criticized for using the vast wealth of the Church for personal benefit instead of public worship. The protective military function of the second order had ceased to exist with the rise of the state and the changing nature of war. Some members of the bourgeoisie—those who worked with their heads, not their hands—shared privileges with the nobility and aspired to a noble lifestyle, in spite of their legal and customary presence in the ranks of the Third Estate alongside peasants and urban workers.

The vast majority of French subjects who constituted the Third Estate certainly were identified by work, but the array of mental and physical labor—and lack of work—splintered the estate into a myriad of occupations, aspirations, and identities. All power flowed upward in this arrangement, with the First and Second Estates dominating the social and political universe. Women and men accepted this hierarchy as the natural organization of society in eighteenth-century France.

This cartoon depicts the plight of the French peasants. An old farmer is bowed down under the weight of the privileged aristocracy and clergy while birds and rabbits, protected by unfair game laws, eat his crops.

The king continued to stand at the pinnacle of the eighteenth-century social pyramid. Traditionally revered as the "father" of his subjects, he claimed to be divinely appointed by God. Kingship in this era had a dual nature. The king was both supreme overlord (a legacy from feudal times) and absolute monarch. As supreme overlord he stood dominant over the aristocracy and the court. As absolute monarch he stood at the head of the state and society. When the king equated himself with the state—"L'état, c'est moi," as Louis XIV boasted—all problems—economic, social, and political—also came to be identified with the king. Absolutism required a weakened nobility and a bureaucracy strong enough to help the monarchy to adjust to changes. After the death of Louis XIV in 1715, Louis XV and Louis XVI faced a resurgent aristocracy without the support of a state bureaucracy capable of successfully challenging aristocratic privilege or of solving fiscal problems.

"To live nobly," that is, to live as a noble, was the social ideal to which one could aspire in the eighteenth century. While the system of orders set clear boundaries of social status, distinctions within estates created new hierarchies. The clergy, a privileged order, contained both commoners and nobles, but leadership in the Church depended on social rank. The aristocracy retained control of the bishoprics even as an activist element among the lower clergy agitated for reforms and better salaries. In a state in which the king claimed to rule by God's will, Catholicism, virtually the state religion, was important in legitimizing the divine claims of the monarchy.

There were two kinds of nobility: the older nobility of the sword, who claimed descent from medieval times, and the more recent nobility of the robe, who had acquired their position through the purchase of offices that conferred noble status. By increasing the numbers of the nobility of the robe, Louis XIV had hoped to undermine the power of the aristocracy as a whole and to decrease its political influence. But aristocrats rallied and closed ranks against the dilution of their power. As a result, both Louis XV and Louis XVI faced a reviving rather than a declining aristocracy. One in four nobles had moved from the bourgeoisie to the aristocratic ranks in the eighteenth century; two out of every three had been ennobled during the seventeenth or eighteenth centuries. Nobles had succeeded in restoring their economic and social power. Furthermore, a growing segment of the aristocracy, influenced by Enlightenment ideas and the example of English institutions,

was intent on increasing the political dominance of the aristocracy.

Nobles strengthened their powers in two ways. First, they monopolized high offices and closed access to non-nobles, thereby controlling posts in ministries, the Church, and the army. Second, the nobility benefited greatly from the doubling in land values brought on by the increase in the value of crops. Nobles enjoyed privileges, the greatest being, in most cases, exemption from taxes. Seeking ever higher returns from the land, some members of the aristocracy adopted new agricultural techniques to achieve greater crop yields. There were certainly poor aristocrats who lacked the lands to benefit from this trend, but those who did control sizable holdings profited greatly from higher dues paid to them and reaped increased incomes from crops. In addition, many aristocrats revived their feudal claims to ancient seigneurial, or lordly, privileges. They hired lawyers to unearth old claims and hired agents to collect dues.

A spirit of innovation characterized the values of certain members of the nobility. Although technically prevented from participating in trade by virtue of their titles and privileges, an active group among the nobility succeeded in making fortunes in metallurgy, glassmaking, and mining. Others participated in trade. These nobles were an economically dynamic and innovative segment of the aristocracy. In spite of the obsolete aspect of their privileges, aristocrats were often responsible for the introduction of modern ideas and techniques in the management of estates and in the bookkeeping involved with collection of rents. Capitalist techniques were not unknown to nobles adapting to the marketplace. These nobles formed an elite partnership with forward-looking members of the bourgeoisie.

Commoners—that is, those who did not enjoy the privileges of the nobility—constituted a broad range of the French populace. The peasantry was by far the largest group of commoners. Most French peasants were free, no longer attached to the soil as serfs were in a feudal system. Yet all peasants endured common obligations placed on them by the crown and the privileged classes. A bewildering array of taxes afflicted peasants: they owed the tithe to the Church, land taxes to the state, and seigneurial dues and rents to the landlord. In some areas, peasants repaired roads and drew lots for military service. Dues affected almost every aspect of rural life, including harvests and the sale of property. In addition, indirect taxes like that on salt

"Brooms, Brooms," a plate from a volume on the cries of Paris, shows a woman hawking brooms. Most poor women were forced to do exhausting manual labor.

was essential to the survival of the rural family. Peasant women sought employment in towns and cities as seamstresses and servants in order to send money back home to struggling relatives. Children, too, added their earnings to the family pot. In spite of various strategies for survival, more and more peasant families were disrupted by the end of the eighteenth century.

Another group of commoners in the Third Estate, the bourgeoisie, embraced within it a variety of professions, from bankers and financiers to businessmen, merchants, entrepreneurs, lawyers, shopkeepers, and artisans. Along with the nobility, wealthy bourgeois formed the urban elites that administered cities and towns. Prestigious service to the state or the purchase of offices that carried with them noble status enabled the wealthiest members of the bourgeoisie to move into the ranks of the nobility. Many bourgeois served as middlemen for the nobility by running estates and collecting dues.

Like the rest of the social universe, the world of artisans and workers was shaded with various gradations of wealth and status. Those who owned their own shops and perhaps employed other workers stood as an elite among the working class. In spite of their physical proximity, there was a vast difference between those who owned their own shops and those who earned wages or were paid by the piece. Wage earners represented about 30 percent of the population of cities and towns, and their numbers were swelling as artisans were pushed out of their guilds and peasants were pushed off their land.

Those who worked in crafts were a labor elite, and guilds were intended to protect the corporations of masters, journeymen, and apprentices through monopolistic measures. But the emphasis on free trade and the expansion of markets in the eighteenth century weakened the hold of the guilds. Merchants often took guilds over and paid workers by the piece. The effect was a reduction in the wages of skilled workers. By the 1780s, most journeymen who hoped to be masters knew that their dream would never be realized.

So, when Louis XVI announced in August 1788 that the Estates-General would meet at Versailles in May 1789, people from all walks of life hoped for some redress of the miseries. The king hoped that the clergy, nobility, and commoners would somehow solve his fiscal problems. Yet every social group, from the nobles to the poorest laborers, had its own agenda and its own ideas about justice, social status, and economic well-being.

were a serious burden for the peasantry. As if all this were not enough, peasants who were forced to take loans to survive from one harvest to another paid exorbitant interest rates. No matter how bad conditions were, peasants had to be sure to save the seed for next year's crop.

The peasants who staggered and collapsed under all these obligations were forced to work as itinerants or leave the land. The precariousness of rural life and the increase in population in the countryside contributed to the permanent displacement and destitution of a growing sector of rural society. Without savings and destroyed by poor harvests, impoverished rural inhabitants wandered the countryside looking for odd jobs and eventually begging to survive. The labor of women

The First Stage of the French Revolution, 1789-1792

Those who lived through it were sure that there had never been a time like it before. The French Revolution, or the Great Revolution, as it was known to contemporaries, was a time of creation and discovery. The ten years from 1789 to 1799 were punctuated by genuine euphoria and democratic transformations. From the privileged elites who initiated the overthrow of the existing order to the peasants and workers, men and women, who railed against tyranny, the revolution touched every segment of society.

The revolution achieved most in the area of politics. The overthrow of absolutist monarchy brought with it new social theories, new symbols, and new behavior. The excitement of anarchy was matched by the terror of repression. Revolutionary France had to contend with war throughout Europe. The revolution had its dark side of violence and instability: in its wake came internal discord, civil war, and violent repression. In the search for a new order, political forms followed one after the other in rapid succession: constitutional monarchy, republic, oligarchy. The creation of Napoleon's dictatorship at the end of the century signified that the revolution had come to an end.

Revolutionary incidents flared up throughout Europe in the second half of the eighteenth century in the Netherlands, Belgium, and Ireland. Absolute authority was challenged and sometimes modified. Across the Atlantic, American colonists concerned with the principle of self-rule had thrown off the yoke of the British in the War of Independence. But none of these events, including the American Revolution, was so violent in breaking with the old order, so extensive in involving millions of men and women in political action, and so consequential for the political futures of other European states as was the French Revolution. The triumphs and contradictions of the revolutionary experiment in democracy mark the end of the old order and the beginning of modern history. Politics would never be the same again.

Taking Politics to the People

Choosing representatives for the Estates-General in March and April 1789 stirred up hope and excitement in every corner of France. From the very beginning, there were warning signs that a more astute monarch might have noticed. The call for national elections set in motion a politicizing process the king could not control. Members of the Third Estate, traditionally excluded from political and social power, were presented with the opportunity of expressing their opinions on the state of government and society. In an increasingly literate age, pamphlets, broadsides, and political tracts representing every political persuasion blanketed France. Those who could not read stood in marketplaces and city squares or sat around evening fires and had the political literature read to them. Farmhands and urban laborers realized that they were participating in the same process as their social betters, and they believed they had a right to speak and be heard.

This was a time of great hope, especially for people who had been buffeted by the rise in prices, decline in real wages, and the hunger that followed crop failures and poor harvests. Now there was the promise of a respite and a solution. Taxes could be discussed and changed, the state bureaucracy could be reformed—or better, abolished. Intellectuals discussed political alternatives in the salons of the wealthy. Nobles and bourgeois met in philosophical societies dedicated to enlightened thought. Commoners gathered in cafes to drink and debate. Although the poor often fell outside of this network of communication, they were not immune to the ideas that emerged. In the end, people of all classes had opinions and were more certain than ever of their right to express their ideas. Absolutism was in trouble, though Louis XVI did not know it, as people began to forge a collectively shared idea of politics. People now had a forum—the Estates-General—and a focus—the politics of taxation. But most important, they had the elections.

In competing for power, some members of the Third Estate were well aware of their vast numerical superiority over the nobility. Because of it, they demanded greater representation than the 300 members per estate defined according to the practices of 1614. At the very least, they argued, the number of representatives of the Third Estate should be doubled to 600 members, giving commoners equality in numbers with nobles and priests together. Necker, recalled as director-general of finance in August 1788, agreed to the doubling in the size of the Third Estate as a compromise but left unresolved the additional demand of vote by head rather than by order. If voting was to be left as it was, in accordance with the procedures of 1614, the nobility who controlled the First and Second Estates would determine all outcomes. With a voting procedure by head instead of by order, however, the deputies of the Third

Estate could easily dominate the Estates-General, confident that they could count on parish priests and liberal nobles like the Marquis de Lafayette to defect from voting with the First and Second Estates and join their cause.

In conjunction with this political activity and in scheduled meetings, members of all three estates drew up statements of their problems. This took place in a variety of forums, including guilds and village and town meetings. The people of France set down their grievances in notebooks—known as *cahiers de doléances*—that were then carried to Versailles by the deputies elected to the Estates-General. The cahiers expressed the particular grievances of each estate. These notebooks contained a collective outpouring of problems and are important for two major reasons. First, they made clear the similarity of grievances shared throughout France. Second, they indicated the extent to which a common political culture, based on a concern with political reform, had permeated different levels of French society. Both the privileged and the nonprivileged identified a common enemy in the system of state bureaucracy to which the monarch was so strongly tied. Although the king was still addressed with respect, new concerns with liberty, equality, property, and the rule of law were voiced.

"If only the king knew!" In this phrase, French men and women had for generations expressed their belief in the inevitability of their fate and the benevolence of their king. They saw the king as a loving and wise father who would not tolerate the injustices visited on his subjects if only he knew what was really happening. In 1789 peasants and workers were questioning why their lives could not be better, but they continued to express their trust in the king. Combined with their old faith was a new hope. The peasants in the little town of Saintes recorded their newly formed expectations in their cahier:

> Our king, the best of kings and father of a great and wise family, will soon know everything. All vices will be destroyed. All the great virtues of industriousness, honesty, modesty, honor, patriotism, meekness, friendliness, equality, concord, pity, and thrift will prevail and wisdom will rule supreme.

Those who opposed the revolution later alleged that these notebooks proved the existence of a highly coordinated plot on the part of secret societies out to destroy the regime. They were wrong. Similarities in complaints, demands, and language proved the forging of a new political consciousness, not a conspiracy. Societies and clubs circulated "model" cahiers among themselves, resulting in the use of similar forms and vocabulary. People were questioning their traditional roles and now had elected deputies who would represent them before the king. In the spring of 1789, a severe economic crisis that heightened political uncertainty swept through France. For a king expected to save the situation, time was running out.

Convening the Estates-General

The elected deputies arrived at Versailles at the beginning of May 1789 carrying in their valises and trunks the grievances of their estates. The opening session of the Estates-General took place in a great hall especially constructed for the event. The 1248 deputies presented a grand spectacle as they filed to their assigned places to hear speeches by the king and his ministers.

Revolutionary France

Contrasts among the participants were immediately apparent. Seated on a raised throne under a canopy at one end of the hall, Louis XVI was vested in full kingly regalia. On his right sat the archbishops and cardinals of the First Estate, strikingly clad in the pinks and purples of their offices. On his left were the richly and decorously attired nobility. Facing the stage sat the 648 deputies of the Third Estate, dressed in plain black suits, stark against the colorful and costly costumes of the privileged. It was clear, in the most visual terms, that "clothes make the man." Members of the Third Estate had announced beforehand that they would not follow the ancient custom for commoners of kneeling at the king's entrance. Fired by the hope of equal treatment and an equal share of power, they had come to Versailles to make a constitution. The opening ceremony degenerated into a moment of confusion over whether members of the Third Estate should be able to wear their hats in the presence of the king. Many saw in the politics of clothing a tense beginning to their task.

The tension between commoners and privileged was further aggravated by the unresolved issue of how the voting was to proceed. The Third Estate was adamant in its demand for vote by head. The privileged orders were equally firm in insisting on vote by order. Paralysis set in, as days dragged into weeks and the Estates were unable to act. The body that was to save France from fiscal collapse was hopelessly deadlocked.

Two men whose backgrounds made them unlikely heroes emerged as leaders of the Third Estate. One, Abbé Emmanuel Joseph Sieyès (1748–1836), was a member of the clergy who frequented Parisian salons. The other, the comte Honoré Gabriel Victor de Mirabeau (1749–91), a black sheep among the nobility, had spent time in prison because of his father's charges that he was a defiant son who led a misspent, debauched, and profligate youth. In spite of his nobility, Mirabeau appeared at Versailles as a deputy for Aix and Marseilles to the Third Estate. His oratory and presence commanded attention from the start. As a consummate politician, Mirabeau combined forces with Sieyès, who had already established his reputation as a firebrand reformer with his eloquent pamphlet "What Is the Third Estate?" published in January 1789.

Sieyès and Mirabeau reminded members of the Third Estate of the reformist consensus that characterized their ranks. Under their influence, the Third Estate decided to proceed with its own meetings. On 17 June 1789, the Third Estate, joined by some sympathetic clergy, changed its name to the National Assembly as an assertion of its true representation of the French nation. Three days later, members of the new National Assembly found themselves locked out of their regular meeting room by the king's guard. Outraged by this insult, they moved to a nearby indoor tennis court, where they vowed to stay together for the purpose of writing a constitution. This event, known as the Oath of the Tennis Court, marked the end of the absolutist monarchy and the beginning of a new concept of the state that power resided in the people. The revolution had begun.

The drama of Versailles, a staged play of gestures, manners, oaths, and attire, also marked the beginning of a far-reaching political revolution. Although it was a drama that took place behind closed doors, it was not one unknown to the general public. Throughout May and June 1789, Parisians trekked to Versailles to watch the deliberations. Then they brought news back to the capital. Deputies wrote home to their constituents to keep them abreast of events. Newspapers that reported daily on these wranglings and pamphleteers who analyzed them spread the news throughout the nation. Information, often conflicting, stirred up anxiety; news of conflict encouraged action.

The frustration and stalemate of the Estates-General threatened to put the spark to the kindling of urban unrest. The people of Paris had suffered through a harsh winter and spring under the burdens of high prices (especially of bread), limited supplies, and relentless tax demands. The rioting of the spring had for the moment ceased as people waited for their problems to be solved by the deputies of the Estates-General. The suffering of the urban poor was not new, but their ability to connect economic hardships with the politics at Versailles and to blame the government was. As hopes began to dim with the news of political stalemate, news broke of the creation of the National Assembly. It was greeted with new anticipation.

The Storming of the Bastille

The king, who had temporarily withdrawn from sight following the death of his son at the beginning of June, reemerged to meet with the representatives of each of the three estates and propose reforms, including a constitutional monarchy. But Louis XVI refused to accept the now popularly supported National Assembly as a legitimate body, insisting instead that he must rely on the three estates for advice. He simply did not understand that the choice was no longer his to make. He summoned troops to Versailles and began concentrat-

"what is the third estate?"

As an ambitious clergyman from Chartres, Abbé Emmanuel Joseph Sieyès was a member of the First Estate. Yet Sieyès was elected deputy to the Estates-General for the Third Estate on the basis of his attacks on aristocratic privilege. He participated in the writing and editing of the great documents of the early revolution: the Oath of the Tennis Court and the Declaration of the Rights of Man and Citizen. The pamphlet for which he is immortalized in revolutionary lore was his daring "What Is the Third Estate?" Written in January 1789, it boldly confronted the bankruptcy of the system of privilege of the Old Regime and threw down the gauntlet to those who ruled France. In this document the revolution found its rallying point.

1st. What is the third estate? Everything.

2nd. What has it been heretofore in the political order? Nothing.

3rd. What does it demand? To become something therein. . . .

Who, then, would dare to say that the third estate has not within itself all that is necessary to constitute a complete nation? It is the strong and robust man whose one arm remains enchained. If the privileged order were abolished, the nation would not be something less but something more. Thus, what is the third estate? Everything; but an everything shackled and oppressed. What would it be without the privileged order? Everything; but an everything free and flourishing. Nothing can progress without it; everything would proceed infinitely better without the others. It is not sufficient to have demonstrated that the privileged classes, far from being useful to the nation, can only enfeeble and injure it; it is necessary, moreover, to prove that the nobility does not belong to the social organization at all; that, indeed, it may be a *burden* upon the nation, but that it would not know how to constitute a part thereof.

The third estate, then, comprises everything appertaining to the nation; and whatever is not the third estate may not be regarded as being of the nation. What is the third estate? Everything!

---

ing soldiers in Paris. Civilians continually clashed with members of the military, whom they jostled and jeered. The urban crowds recognized the threat of repression that the troops represented. People decided to meet force with force. To do so, they needed arms themselves—and they knew where to get them.

On 14 July 1789, the irate citizens of Paris stormed the Bastille, a royal armory that also served as a prison for a handful of debtors. The storming of the Bastille has become the great symbol in the revolutionary legend of the overthrow of the tyranny and oppression of the old regime. But it is significant for another reason. It was an expression of the power of the people to take politics into their own hands. Parisians were following the lead of their deputies in Versailles. They had formed a citizen militia known as the National Guard, and they were prepared to defend their concept of justice and law.

The people who stormed the Bastille were not the poor, the unemployed, the criminals, or the urban rabble, as their detractors portrayed them. They were bourgeois and petit-bourgeois, shopkeepers, guild members, family men and women who considered it their right to seize arms in order to protect their interests. The Marquis de Lafayette (1757–1834), a noble beloved of the people because of his participation in the American Revolution, helped organize the National Guard. Under his direction, the militia adopted the tricolor flag as its standard. The tricolor combined the red and blue colors of the city of Paris with the white of the Bourbon royal family. It became the flag of the revolution, replacing the fleur-de-lis of the Bourbons. It is the national flag of France today.

The king could no longer dictate the terms of the constitution. By their actions, the people in arms had ratified the National Assembly. Louis XVI was forced to yield. The events in Paris set off similar uprisings in cities and towns throughout France. National guards in provincial cities modeled themselves after the Parisian militia. Government officials fled their posts and abandoned their responsibilities. Commoners stood ready to fill the power vacuum that now existed. But the revolution was not just an urban phenomenon: the peasantry had their own grievances and their own way of making a revolution.

This lively amateur painting of the fall of the Bastille is by Claude Cholat, one of the attackers. Tradition has it that Cholat is manning the cannon in the background. The inscription proclaims that the painting is by one of the "conquerors of the Bastille."

The Revolution of the peasantry

In the spring and early summer of 1789, food shortages drove bands of armed peasants to attack manor houses throughout France. In the areas surrounding Paris and Versailles, peasants destroyed game and devastated the forests where the king and his nobles hunted. The anger reflected in these seemingly isolated events was suspended as the hope grew that the proceedings at Versailles would produce results. Remote as peasant involvement in the drawing up of the cahiers might have been, peasants everywhere expected that aid was at hand.

News of the events of Versailles and then of the revolutionary action in Paris did not reassure rural inhabitants. By the end of June the hope of deliverance from crippling taxes and dues was rapidly fading. The news of the Oath of the Tennis Court and the storming of the Bastille terrified country folk, who saw the actions as evidence of an aristocratic plot that threatened sorely needed reforms. As information moved along postal routes in letters from delegates to their supporters, or news was repeated in the Sunday market gatherings, distortions and exaggerations crept in. It seemed to rural inhabitants that their world was falling apart. Some peasants believed that Paris was in the hands of brigands and that the king and the Estates-General were victims of an aristocratic plot. Rural vision, fueled by empty stomachs, was apocalyptic.

This state of affairs was aggravated as increasing numbers of peasants were pushed off the land to seek employment as transient farm laborers, moving from one area to another with the cycles of sowing and harvesting. Throughout the 1780s the number of peasants without land was increasing steadily. Starving men, women, and children, filthy and poorly dressed, were frightening figures to villagers who feared that the same fate would befall them with the next bad harvest. As one landowner lamented, "We cannot lie down without fear, the nighttime paupers have tormented us greatly, to say nothing of the daytime ones, whose numbers are considerable."

Most peasants had lived in the same place for generations and knew only the confines of their own villages. They were uneasy about what existed beyond the horizon. Transients, often speaking strange dialects, disrupted and threatened the social universe of the village. In order to survive, wanderers often resorted to petty theft, stealing fruit from trees or food from unwatched hearths. Often traveling in groups, hordes of vagabonds struck fear into the hearts of farmworkers, trampling crops and sleeping in open fields. Peasants were sure that these unfortunate souls were brigands paid by the local aristocracy to persecute a peasantry already stretched to the breaking point.

Hope gave way to fear. Beginning on 20 July 1789, peasants in different areas of France reacted collectively throughout France, spreading false rumors of a great conspiracy. Fear gripped whole villages and in some areas spawned revolt. Just as urban workers had connected their economic hardships to politics, so too did desperate peasants see their plight in political terms. They banded together and marched to the residences of the local nobility, breaking into châteaus with a single mission in mind: to destroy all legal documents by which nobles claimed payments, dues, and services from local peasants. They drove out the lords and in

This engraving from the late eighteenth century shows French country houses ablaze while speeding carriages carry their frightened owners to safety. The peasants attacked and looted the houses of the gentry and burned the rolls of feudal duties.

N.° 30.

some cases burned their châteaus, putting an end to the tyranny of the privileged over the countryside. The peasants had taken matters into their own hands. They intended to consign the last vestiges of aristocratic privilege to the bonfires of aristocratic documents.

The overthrow of privileges rooted in a feudal past was not as easy as that. Members of the National Assembly were aghast at the eruption of rural violence. They knew that to stay in power they had to maintain peace. They also knew that to be credible they had to protect property. Peasant destruction of seigneurial claims posed a real dilemma for the bourgeois deputies directing the revolution. If they gave in to peasant demands, they risked losing aristocratic support and undermining their own ability to control events. If they gave in to the aristocracy, they risked a social revolution in the countryside, which they could not police or repress. Liberal members of the aristocracy cooperated with the bourgeois leaders in finding a solution.

In a dramatic meeting that lasted through the night of 4 August 1789, the National Assembly agreed to abolish the principle of privilege. The peasants had won—or thought they had. In the weeks and months ahead, rural people learned that they had lost their own prerogatives—the rights to common grazing and gathering—and were expected to buy their way out of their feudal services. In the meantime, parliamentary action had saved the day: the deputies stabilized the situation through legislating compromise.

women on the march

Women participated with men in both urban and rural revolutionary actions. Acting on their own, women were responsible for the most dramatic event of the early years of the revolution: in October 1789 they forced the king and the royal family to leave Versailles for Paris to deal in person with the problems of bread supply, high prices, and starvation. Women milling about in the marketplaces of Paris on the morning of 5 October were complaining bitterly about the high cost and shortages of bread. The National Assembly was in session, and the National Guards were patrolling the streets of Paris. But these trappings of political change had no impact on the brutal realities of the marketplace.

Women were in charge of buying the food for their families. Every morning they stood in lines with their neighbors reenacting the familiar ritual. Some mornings they were turned away, told by the baker or his assistants that there was no bread. On other days they did not have enough coins in their purses to buy this staple of their diet. Women responsible for managing the consumption of the household were most directly in touch with the state of provisioning the capital. When they were unable to feed their families, the situation became intolerable.

So it was, on the morning of 5 October 1789, that 6000 Parisian women marched out of the city and toward Versailles. They were taking their problem to the king with the demand that he solve it. Later in the day, Lafayette, sympathetic to the women's cause, led the Parisian National Guard to Versailles to mediate events. The women were armed with pikes, the simple weapon available to the poorest defender of the revolution, and they were prepared to use them. The battle came early the next morning, when the women, tired and cold from waiting all night at the gates of the palace, invaded the royal apartments and chased Marie Antoinette from her bedroom. Several members of the royal guards, hated by the people of Paris for alleged insults against the tricolor cockade, were killed by the angry women, who decapitated them and mounted their heads on pikes. A shocked Louis XVI agreed to return with the crowd to Paris. The crowd cheered Louis's decision, which briefly reestablished his personal popularity. But as monarch, he had been humiliated at the hands of women of the capital. Reduced to the roles of "the baker, the baker's wife, and the baker's son" by jeer-

ing crowds, the royal family was forced to return to Paris that very day. Louis XVI was now captive to the revolution, whose efforts to form a constitutional monarchy he purported to support.

The Revolution Threatened

The disciplined deliberations of committees intent on fashioning a constitutional monarchy replaced the passion and fervor of revolutionary oratory. The National, or Constituent, Assembly divided France into new administrative units—*départements*—for the purpose of establishing better control over municipal governments. Along with new administrative trappings, the government promoted its own rituals. On 14 July 1790, militias from each of the newly created 83 départements of France came together in Paris to celebrate the first anniversary of the storming of the Bastille. A new national holiday was born and with it a sense of devotion and patriotism for the new France liberated by the revolution. In spite of these unifying elements, however, the newly achieved revolutionary consensus began to show signs of breaking down.

In February 1790 legislation dissolved all monasteries and convents, except for those that provided aid to the poor or that served as educational institutions. As the French church was stripped of its lands, Pope Pius VI (1775–99) denounced the principles of the revolu-

A contemporary print of the women of Paris advancing on Versailles. The determined marchers are shown waving pikes and dragging an artillery piece. The women were hailed as heroines of the revolution.

Depart des Heroines de Paris pour Versailles le 5 Octobre 1789.

The fleeing Louis XVI and his family were apprehended at Varennes in June 1791.

tion. In July 1790 the government approved the Civil Constitution of the Clergy: priests now became the equivalent of paid agents of the state. By requiring an oath of loyalty to the state from all practicing priests, the National Assembly created a new arena for dissent. Catholics were forced to choose to embrace or reject the revolution. Many "nonjuring" priests who refused to take the oath went into hiding. The wedge driven between the Catholic church and revolutionary France allowed a mass-based counterrevolution to emerge. Aristocratic émigrés who had fled the country because of their opposition to the revolution were languishing for lack of a popular base. From his headquarters in Turin, the king's younger brother, the comte d'Artois, was attempting to incite a civil war in France. When the revolutionaries decided to attack the Church not just as a landed and privileged institution but also as a religious one, the counterrevolution rapidly expanded.

The Constitution of 1791, completed after over two years of deliberations, established a constitutional monarchy with a ministerial executive power answerable to a legislative assembly. Louis XVI, formerly the divinely anointed ruler of France, was now "Louis, by the grace of God and the constitutional law of the state, King of the French." In proclaiming his acceptance of the constitution, Louis expressed the sentiments of many when he said, "The end of the revolution is come. It is time that order be reestablished so that the constitution may receive the support now most necessary to it; it is time to settle the opinion of Europe concerning the destiny of France, and to show that French men are worthy of being free." Louis, who had been wrong often enough in the past, could not have been more mistaken

when he declared that the end of the revolution was at hand.

The Constitution of 1791 marked the triumph of the principles of the revolution. But it was at best a precarious political compromise. Months before the ink was dry on the final document, the actions of the king doomed the new constitution to failure. To be successful, constitutional monarchy required a king worthy of honor and respect. Louis XVI seemed to be giving the revolutionaries what they wanted by cooperating with the framers of the constitution. Yet late one night in June 1791, Louis XVI, Marie Antoinette, and their children disguised themselves as commoners, crept out of the royal apartments in the Tuileries Palace, and fled Paris. Louis intended to leave France to join foreign forces opposing the revolution at Metz. He got as far as Varennes, where he was captured by soldiers of the National Guards and brought back to a shocked Paris. The king had abandoned the revolution. Although he was not put to death for another year and a half, he was more than ever a prisoner of the revolution. The monarchy was effectively finished as part of a political solution; with its demise went liberal hopes for a constitutional settlement.

The defection of the king was certainly serious, but it was not the only problem facing the revolutionaries. Other problems plagued the revolutionary government, notably foreign war and the fiscal crisis, coupled with inflation. In order to establish its seriousness and legitimacy, the National Assembly had been willing in 1789 to absorb the debts of the old regime. The new government could not sell titles and offices, as the king had done to deal with financial problems, but it did confiscate Church property. In addition, it issued treasury bonds in the form of assignats in order to raise money. The assignats soon assumed the status of bank notes, and by the spring of 1790 they had become compulsory legal tender. Initially they were to be backed by land confiscated from the Church and now being sold by the state. But the need for money soon outran the value of the land available, and the government continued to print assignats according to its needs. Depreciation of French currency in international markets and inflation at home resulted. The revolutionary government found itself in a situation which in certain respects was worse than that experienced by Louis XVI before the calling of the Estates-General. Assignat-induced inflation produced a sharp decline in fortunes of bourgeois investors living on fixed incomes. Rising prices meant increased misery for workers and peasants.

New counterrevolutionary groups were becoming frustrated with revolutionary policies. Throughout the winter and spring of 1791–92, people rioted and demanded that prices be fixed, while the assignat dropped to less than half its face value. Peasants refused to sell crops for the worthless paper. Hoarding further drove up prices. Angry crowds turned to pillaging, rioting, and murder, which became more frequent as the value of the currency declined and prices rose.

Foreign war beginning in the fall of 1791 also challenged stability. Some moderate political leaders welcomed war as a blessing in disguise, since it could divert the attention of the masses away from problems at home and promote loyalty to the revolution. Others envisioned war as a great crusade to bring revolutionary principles to oppressed peoples throughout Europe. The king and queen, trapped by the revolution, saw war as their only hope of liberation. Louis XVI could be rightfully restored as the leader of a France defeated by the sovereigns of Europe. Some who opposed the war believed it would destabilize the revolution. France must solve its problems at home, they argued, before fighting a foreign enemy. Louis, however, encouraged those ministers and advisers eager for battle. In April 1792, France declared war against Austria.

Individuals, events, economic realities, and the nature of politics conspired against the success of the first constitutional experiment. The king's attempt to flee France in the summer of 1791 seriously wounded the attempt at compromise. Many feared that the goals of the revolution could not be preserved in a country at war and with a king of dubious loyalties.

Experimenting with Democracy: The Revolution's Second Stage, 1792-1799

The Revolution was a school for the French nation. A political universe populated by individual citizens replaced the eighteenth-century world of subjects loyal to their king. This new construction of politics, in which all individuals were equal, ran counter to prevailing ideas about collective identities defined in guilds and orders. People on all levels of society learned politics by doing it. In the beginning, experience helped. The elites, both noble and bourgeois, had served in government and administration. But the rules of the game under the old regime had been very different, with birth determining power.

After 1789, all men were declared free and equal, in opportunity if not in rights. Men of ability and talent, who had served as middlemen for the privileged elite under the old regime, now claimed power as their due. Many of them were lawyers, educated in the rules and regulations of the society of orders. They experienced firsthand the problems of the exercise of power in the old regime, and they had their own ideas about reform. But the school of the revolution did not remain the domain of a special class. Women demanded their places but continued to be excluded from the political arena, though the importance of their participation in the revolution was indisputable. Workers talked of seizing their rights, but because of the inherent contradictions of representation and participation, experimenting with democracy led to outcomes that did not look very democratic at all.

Declaring Political Rights

"Liberty consists in the ability to do whatever does not harm another." So wrote the revolutionary deputies of 1789. Sounding a refrain similar to that of the American Declaration of Independence, the Declaration of the Rights of Man and Citizen appeared on 26 August 1789. The document amalgamated a variety of Enlightenment ideas drawn from the works of political philosophy, including those of Locke and Montesquieu. "Men are born and remain free and equal in rights. Social distinctions may be based only on common utility." Perhaps most significant of all was the attention given to property,

Declaration of the Rights of Man and Citizen

Sounding a refrain similar to that of the American Declaration of Independence (1776), the Declaration of the Rights of Man and Citizen was adopted by the National Assembly on 26 August 1789. The document amalgamated a variety of Enlightenment ideas, including those of Locke and Montesquieu. The attention to property, which was defined as "sacred and inviolable," rivaled that given to liberty as a "natural" and "imprescriptible" right of man.

1. Men are born and remain free and equal in rights. Social distinctions may be founded only upon the general good.
2. The aim of all political association is the preservation of the natural and imprescriptible rights of man. These rights are liberty, property, security, and resistance to oppression.
3. The principle of all sovereignty resides essentially in the nation. No body nor individual may exercise any authority which does not proceed directly from the nation.
4. Liberty consists in the freedom to do everything which injures no one else; hence the exercise of the natural rights of each man has no limits except those which assure to the other members of the society the enjoyment of the same rights. These limits can only be determined by law.
5. Law can only prohibit such actions as are hurtful to society. Nothing may be prevented which is not forbidden by law, and no one may be forced to do anything not provided for by law.
6. Law is the expression of the general will. Every citizen has a right to participate personally, or through his representative, in its formation. It must be the same for all, whether it protects or punishes. All citizens, being equal in the eyes of the law, are equally eligible to all dignities and to all public positions and occupations, according to their abilities, and without distinction except that of their virtues and talents.
7. No person shall be accused, arrested, or imprisoned except in the cases and according to the forms prescribed by law. Any one soliciting, transmitting, executing, or causing to be executed, any arbitrary order, shall be punished. But any citizen summoned or arrested in virtue of the law shall submit without delay, as resistance constitutes an offense.
8. The law shall provide for such punishments only as are strictly and obviously necessary . . . .
9. As all persons are held innocent until they shall have been declared guilty, if arrest shall be deemed indispensable, all harshness not essential to the securing of the prisoner's person shall be severely repressed by law.
10. No one shall be disquieted on account of his opinions, including his religious views, provided their manifestation does not disturb the public order established by law.
11. The free communication of ideas and opinions is one of the most precious of the rights of man. Every citizen may, accordingly, speak, write, and print with freedom, but shall be responsible for such abuses of this freedom as shall be defined by law.
12. The security of the rights of man and of the citizen requires public military forces. These forces are, therefore, established for the good of all and not for the personal advantage of those to whom they shall be entrusted.
13. A common contribution is essential for the maintenance of the public forces and for the cost of administration. This should be equitably distributed among all the citizens in proportion to their means.
14. All the citizens have a right to decide, either personally or by their representatives, as to the necessity of the public contribution; to grant this freely; to know to what uses it is put; and to fix the proportion, the mode of assessment and of collection and the duration of the taxes.
15. Society has the right to require of every public agent an account of his administration.
16. A society in which the observance of the law is not assured, nor the separation of powers defined, has no constitution at all.
17. Since property is an inviolable and sacred right, no one shall be deprived thereof except where public necessity, legally determined, shall clearly demand it, and then only on condition that the owner shall have been previously and equitably indemnified.

which was declared a "sacred and inviolable," "natural," and "imprescriptible" right of man.

In the year of tranquillity that followed the violent summer of 1789, the new politicians set themselves the task of creating institutions based on the principle of liberty and others embodied in the Declaration of the Rights of Man and Citizen. The result was the Constitution of 1791, a statement of faith in a progressive constitutional monarchy. A king accountable to an elected parliamentary body would lead France into a prosperous and just age. The constitution acknowledged the people's sovereignty as the source of political power. It also enshrined the principle of property by making voting rights dependent on property ownership. All men might be equal before the law, but by the Constitution of 1791 only wealthy men had the right to vote for representatives and hold office.

All titles of nobility were abolished. In the early period of the revolution, civil liberties were extended to Protestants and Jews, who had been persecuted under the old regime. Previously excluded groups were granted freedom of thought, worship, and full civil liberties. More reluctantly, deputies outlawed slavery in the colonies in 1794. Slave unrest in Saint Domingue (modern-day Haiti) had coincided with the political conflicts of the revolution and exploded in rebellion in 1791, driving the revolutionaries in Paris to support black independence although it was at odds with French colonial interests. Led by Toussaint L'Ouverture (1743–1803), black rebels worked to found an independent Haitian state, which was declared in 1804. But the concept of equality with regard to race remained incompletely integrated with revolutionary principles, and slavery was reestablished in the French colonies in 1802.

Men were the subject of these newly defined rights. No references to women or their rights appear in the constitutions or the official Declarations of Rights. Women's organizations agitated for an equitable divorce law, and divorce was legalized in September 1792. Women were critical actors in the revolution from its very inception, and their presence shaped and directed the outcome of events, as the women's march to Versailles in 1789 made clear. The marquis de Condorcet (1743–94), elected to the Legislative Assembly in 1791, was one of the first to chastise the revolutionaries for overlooking the political rights of women who, he point-

Slaves revolting against the French in Saint Domingue in 1791. Napoleon sent an army to restore colonial rule in 1799, but yellow fever decimated the French soldiers, and the rebels defeated the weakened French army in 1803.

edly observed, were half of the human race. "Either no individual of the human race has genuine rights, or else all have the same; and he who votes against the right of another, whatever the religion, color, or sex of that other, has henceforth abjured his own." Condorcet argued forcefully but unsuccessfully for the right of women to be educated.

The revolutionaries had declared that liberty was a natural and inalienable right, a universal right that was extended to all with the overthrow of a despotic monarch and a privileged elite. The principle triumphed in religious toleration. Yet the revolutionary concept of liberty foundered on the divergent claims of excluded groups—workers, women, and slaves—who demanded full participation in the world of politics. In 1792 revolutionaries confronted the contradictions inherent in their political beliefs of liberty and equality now being challenged in the midst of social upheaval and foreign war. In response, the revolution turned to more radical measures to survive.

The second Revolution: The Revolution of the people

The first revolution, from 1789 through the beginning of 1792, was based on liberty—the liberty to compete, to own, and to succeed. The second revolution, which began in 1792, took equality as its rallying cry. This was the revolution of the working people of French cities. The popular movement that spearheaded political action in 1792 was committed to equality of rights in a way not characteristic of the leaders of the revolution of 1789. Urban workers were not benefiting from the revolution, but they had come to believe in their own power as political beings. Organized on the local level into sections, artisans in cities identified themselves as *sans-culottes*—literally, those trousered citizens who did not wear knee breeches (*culottes*)—to distinguish themselves from the privileged elite.

On 10 August 1792, the people of Paris stormed the Tuileries, chanting their demands for "Equality!" and "Nation!" The people tramped across the silk sheets of the king's bed and broke his fine furniture, reveling in the private chambers of the royal family. Love and respect for the king had vanished. What the people of Paris demanded now was universal manhood suffrage and participation in a popular democracy. Working people were acting independently of other factions, and the bourgeois political leadership became quickly aware of the need to scramble to maintain order.

Who constituted the popular movement? The self-designated sans-culottes were the working men and women of Paris. Some were wealthier than others, some were wage earners, but all shared a common identity as consumers in the marketplace. They hated the privileged (*les gros*), who appeared to be profiting at the expense of the people. The sans-culottes wanted government power to be decentralized, with neighborhoods ruling themselves through sectional organizations. As the have-nots, they were increasingly intent on pulling down the haves, and they translated this sense of vengeance into a new revolutionary justice. When they invaded the Tuileries Palace on the morning of 10 August, the sans-culottes did so in the name of the people. They saw themselves as patriots whose duty it was to brush the monarchy aside. The people were now a force to be reckoned with and feared.

"Terror is the order of the Day"

Political factions characterized revolutionary politics from the start. The terms *Left* and *Right*, which came to represent opposite ends of the political spectrum, originated in a description of where people sat in the Assembly in relation to the podium. Political designations were refined in successive parliamentary bodies. The Convention was the legislative body elected in September 1792 that succeeded the Legislative Assembly and had as its charge determining the best form of government after the collapse of the monarchy. On 21 September 1792, the monarchy was abolished in France; on the following day the Republic, France's first, came into being. Members of the Convention conducted the trial of Louis XVI for treason and pronounced his sentence: execution by the guillotine in January 1793.

The various political factions of the Convention were described in terms borrowed from geography. The Mountain, sitting on the upper benches on the left, was made up of members of the Jacobin Club (named for its meeting place in an abandoned monastery). The Jacobins were the most radical element in the National Convention, supporting democratic solutions and speaking in favor of the cause of people in the streets. The Plain held the moderates, who were concerned with maintaining public order against popular unrest. Many members of the Plain came to be called Girondins in the mistaken belief that they originated in the département of the Gironde.

Both Girondins and Jacobins were from the middle ranks of the bourgeoisie, and both groups were dedi-

French towns and villages set up "Liberty Trees" to show their revolutionary fervor. The trees were hung with cockades and topped with red caps. This drawing shows a tree near the captured Bastille. In the background sans-culottes rout an Austrian army.

These women are Jacobin tricoteuses, the lowest class of women radicals, who met to applaud radical motions in the Jacobin Club. Militant women of the Revolution failed to achieve their major goal—political equality with men.

cated to the principles of the revolution. Although they controlled the ministries, the Girondins began to lose their hold on the revolution and the war. The renewed European war fragmented the democratic movement, and the Girondins, unable to control violence at home, saw political control slipping away. They became prisoners of the revolution when 80,000 armed Parisians surrounded the National Convention in June 1793.

Girondin power had been eroding in the critical months between August 1792 and June 1793. A new leader was working quietly and effectively behind the scenes to weld a partnership between the popular movement of sans-culottes and the Jacobins. He was Maximilien Robespierre (1758–94), leader of the Mountain and the Jacobin Club. Robespierre was typical of the new breed of revolutionary politician. Only 31 years old in 1789, he wrote mediocre poems and attended the local provincial academy to discuss the new ideas when he was not practicing law in his hometown of Arras. Elected to the Estates-General, he joined the Jacobin Club and quickly rose to become its leader. He was willing to take controversial stands on issues: unlike most of his fellow members of the Mountain—including his rival, the popular orator Georges-Jacques Danton (1759–94)—he opposed the war in 1792. Although neither an original thinker nor a compelling orator, Robespierre discovered with the revolution that he was an adroit political tactician. He gained a following and learned how to manipulate it. It was he who engineered the Jacobins' replacement of the Girondins as leaders of the government.

Robespierre's chance for real power came when he assumed leadership of the Committee of Public Safety in July 1793. Faced with the threat of internal anarchy and external war, the elected body, the National Convention, yielded political control to the 12-man Committee of Public Safety that ruled dictatorially under Robespierre's direction. The Great Committee, as it was known at the time, orchestrated the Reign of Terror (1793–94), a period of systematic state repression that meted out justice in the people's name. Summary trials by specially created revolutionary tribunals were followed by the swift execution of the guilty under the blade of the guillotine.

Influenced by *The Social Contract* (1762) and other writings of Jean-Jacques Rousseau, Robespierre believed that sovereignty resided with the people. For him, individual wills and even individual rights did not matter when weighed against the will of the nation. The king was dead; the people were the new source of political power. Robespierre saw himself in the all-important role of interpreting and shaping the people's will. His own task was to guide the people "to the summit of its destinies." As he explained to his critics, "I am defending not my own cause but the public cause." As head of the Great Committee, Robespierre oversaw a revolutionary machinery dedicated to economic regulation, massive military mobilization, and a punitive system of revolutionary justice characterized by the slogan "Terror Is the Order of the Day." Militant revolutionary committees and revolutionary tribunals were established throughout France to identify traitors and to mete out the harsh justice that struck hardest against those members of the bourgeoisie perceived as opponents of the government.

The guillotine became the symbol of revolutionary justice, but it was not the only means of execution. In Lyon, officials of the Reign of Terror had prisoners tied to stakes in open fields and fired on with cannon. In Nantes, a Parisian administrator of the new justice had

enemies of the revolution chained to barges and drowned in the estuary of the Loire. The civil war, which raged most violently in the Vendée in the west of France, consisted often of primitive massacres that sent an estimated quarter of a million people to their deaths. The bureaucratized Reign of Terror was responsible for about 40,000 executions in a nine-month period, resulting in the image of the republicans as "drinkers of blood." (See "The Guillotine and Revolutionary Justice," pp. 682–683.)

The Cult of the Supreme Being, a civic religion without priests or churches and influenced by Rousseau's ideas about nature, followed de-Christianization. The cathedral of Notre Dame de Paris was turned into the Temple of Reason, and the new religion established its own festivals to undermine the persistence of Catholicism. The cult was one indication of the Reign of Terror's attempt to create a new moral universe of revolutionary values.

Women remained conspicuously absent from the summit of political power. After 1793, Jacobin revolutionaries, who had been willing to empower the popular movement of workers, turned against women's participation and denounced it. Women's associations were outlawed and the Society of Revolutionary Republican Women was disbanded. Olympe de Gouges, revolutionary author of the Declaration of the Rights of Woman and Citizen, was guillotined. Women were declared unfit for political participation, according to the Jacobins, because of their biological functions of reproduction and child-rearing. Rousseau's ideas about family policy were probably more influential than his political doctrines. His best-selling books *La Nouvelle Héloïse* (1761) and *Émile* (1762), which combined went into 72 editions before 1789, were moral works that transformed people's ideas about family life. Under his influence, the reading public came to value a separate and private sphere of domestic and conjugal values. Following Rousseau's lead, Robespierre and the Jacobins insisted that the role of women as mothers was incompatible with women's participation in the political realm.

By attacking his critics on both the Left and the Right, Robespierre undermined the support he needed to stay in power. He abandoned the alliance with the popular movement that had been so important in bringing him to power. Robespierre's enemies—and he had many—were able to break the identification be-

The Guillotine and Revolutionary Justice

In the sultry summer days of 1792, Parisians found a new way to entertain themselves. They attended executions. French men, women, and children were long accustomed to watching criminals being tortured and put to death in public view. During the old regime, spectators could enjoy the variety of a number of methods: drawing and quartering, strangling, or hanging. Decapitation, reputedly a less painful death, was a privilege reserved for nobles sentenced for capital crimes. The French Revolution extended this formerly aristocratic privilege to all criminals condemned to death. What especially attracted people to public squares in the third year of the revolution was the introduction of a novel method of decapitation. In 1792 the new instrument of death, the guillotine, became the center of the spectacle of revolutionary justice.

The guillotine promised to eliminate the suffering of its victims. Axes, swords, and sabers—the traditional tools of decapitation and dismemberment—were messy and undependable, producing slow and bloody ordeals when inept or drunken executioners missed their mark or victims flinched at the fatal moment. The design of the guillotine took all of this into account. On its easel-like wooden structure, victims, lying on their stomachs, were held in place with straps and a pillory. Heavy pulleys guaranteed that the sharp blade would fall efficiently from its great height. A basket was placed at the base of the blade to catch the severed head; another was used to slide the headless body through the base of the scaffolding for removal. In place of unintended torture and gore, the guillotine was devised as a humanitarian instrument to guarantee swift and painless death.

It should have been called the Louisette, after its inventor, Dr. Antoine Louis. In what now seems a dubious honor, the new machine was named instead after its greatest supporter, Dr. Joseph Ignace Guillotin, a delegate to the National Assembly. Both Guillotin and Louis were medical doctors, men of science influenced by Enlightenment ideas and committed to the revolution's elimination of the cruelty of older forms of punishment. In the spirit of scientific experimentation, Louis's invention was tested on sheep, cadavers, and then convicted thieves. In 1792 it was used for the first time against another class of offenders: political prisoners.

Early in the revolution, the Marquis de Condorcet, philosophe and mathematician, had opposed capital punishment with the argument that the state did not have the right to take life. Ironically, Maximilien Robespierre, future architect of the Reign of Terror, was one of the few revolutionaries who agreed with Condorcet. Those who favored justice by execution of the state's enemies prevailed. The revolutionary hero and associate of the radical Jacobins Jean-Paul Marat (1743–93), who was himself stabbed to death in his bathtub, advocated the state's use of violence against its enemies: "In order to ensure public tranquillity, 200,000 heads must be cut off." By the end of 1792, as revolution and civil war swept over France, 83 identical guillotines were constructed and installed in each of the départements of France. For the next two years, the guillotine's great blade was rhythmically raised and lowered daily in public squares all over France. In the name of the revolution, the "axe of the people" dispatched over 50,000 victims.

Although intended as a humanitarian instrument, the guillotine became the symbol of all that was arbitrary and repressive about a revolution run amok. Day and night, the Revolutionary Tribunal in Paris delivered the death sentence to the "enemies of the people." Most of those executed were members of what had been the Third Estate: members of the bourgeoisie, workers, peasants. Only 15 percent of the condemned were nobles and priests. During the Terror, the guillotine could be used to settle old scores. Sans-culottes turned in their neighbors, sometimes over long-standing grievances that owed more to spite than politics. The most fanatical revolutionaries had fantasies that guillotines were about to be erected on every street corner to dispense with hoarders and traitors. Others suggested that guillotines be made portable so that by putting justice on wheels, it could be taken directly to the people.

As usual, Paris set the style. The most famous of the guillotines stood on the Place du Carrousel, deliberately placed in front of the royal palace of the Tuileries. It was eventually moved to the larger Place de la Révolution in order to accommodate the growing numbers of spectators. Famous victims drew especially large crowds. The revolutionary drama took on the trappings of a spectacle as hawkers sold toy guillotines, miniature pikes, and liberty caps as souvenirs, along with the usual food and drink. Troops attended these events, but not to control the crowd. Members of the National Guard in formation, their backs to the people, faced the stage of the scaffold. They, like the citizenry, were there to witness the birth of a new nation and, by their presence, to give legitimacy to the event. The crowd entered into the ritual, cheering the victim's last words and demanding that the executioner hold high the severed head. In the new political culture, death was a festival.

For two centuries Western societies have debated the legitimacy of the death sentence and have periodically considered the relative merits of the guillotine, the gas chamber, and the electric chair. For the French, the controversy temporarily ceased in 1794, when people were convinced that justice had gotten out of hand and that they had had enough. For the time being, the government put an end to capital punishment. The guillotine would return. But at the height of its use, between 1792 and 1794, it had played a unique role in forging a new system of justice: the guillotine had been the great leveler. In the ideology of democracy, people were equal—in death as well as in life. The guillotine came to be popularly known as the "scythe of equality." It killed king and commoner alike.

Declaration of the Rights of Woman and Citizen

"Woman, wake up!" Thus did Olympe de Gouges (d. 1793), a self-educated playwright, address French women in 1791. Aware that women were being denied the new rights of liberty and property extended to all men by the Declaration of the Rights of Man and Citizen, Gouges composed her own Declaration of the Rights of Woman and Citizen, modeled on the 1789 document. Persecuted for her political beliefs, she foreshadowed her own demise at the hands of revolutionary justice in article 10 of her declaration. The Declaration of the Rights of Woman and Citizen became an important document in women's demands for political rights in the nineteenth century, and Gouges herself became a feminist hero.

Article I

Woman is born free and lives equal to man in her rights. Social distinctions can be based only on the common utility.

Article II

The purpose of any political association is the conservation of the natural and imprescriptible rights of woman and man; these rights are liberty, property, security, and especially resistance to oppression.

Article III

The principle of all sovereignty rests essentially with the nation, which is nothing but the union of woman and man; no body and no individual can exercise any authority which does not come expressly from it [the nation].

Article IV

Liberty and justice consist of restoring all that belongs to others; thus, the only limits on the exercise of the natural rights of woman are perpetual male tyranny; these limits are to be reformed by the laws of nature and reason.

Article V

Laws of nature and reason proscribe all acts harmful to society; everything which is not prohibited by these wise and divine laws cannot be prevented, and no one can be constrained to do what they do not command.

Article VI

The law must be the expression of the general will; all female and male citizens must contribute either personally or through their representatives to its formation; it must be the same for all: male and female citizens, being equal in the eyes of the law, must be equally admitted to all honors, positions, and public employment according to their capacity and without other distinctions besides those of their virtues and talents.

Article VII

No woman is an exception; she is accused, arrested, and detained in cases determined by law. Women, like men, obey this rigorous law.

---

tween political power and the will of the people that Robespierre had established. As a result, he was branded a traitor by the same process that he had used against many of his own enemies. He saved France from foreign occupation and internal collapse, but he could not save democracy through terror. In the summer of 1794, Robespierre was guillotined. The Reign of Terror ceased with his death in the revolutionary month of Thermidor 1794.

The revolution did not end with the Thermidorian Reaction, as the fall of Robespierre came to be known, but his execution initiated a new phase. For some,

democracy lost its legitimacy. The popular movement was reviled, and sans-culotte became a term of derision. Jacobins were forced underground. Price controls were abolished, resulting in extreme hardship for most urban residents. Out of desperation, in April 1795 the Jacobins and the sans-culottes renewed their alliance and united to demand "bread and the Constitution of 1793." The politics of bread had never been more accurately captured in slogan. Those who took to the streets in 1795 saw the universal manhood suffrage of the unimplemented 1793 constitution as the way to solve their economic problems. But their de-

Article VIII

The law must establish only those penalties that are strictly and obviously necessary. . . .

Article IX

Once any woman is declared guilty, complete rigor is [to be] exercised by the law.

Article X

No one is to be disquieted for his very basic opinions; woman has the right to mount the scaffold; she must equally have the right to mount the rostrum, provided that her demonstrations do not disturb the legally established public order.

Article XI

The free communication of thoughts and opinions is one of the most precious rights of woman, since that liberty assures the recognition of children by their fathers. Any female citizen thus may say freely, I am the mother of a child which belongs to you, without being forced by a barbarous prejudice to hide the truth; [an exception may be made] to respond to the abuse of this liberty in cases determined by the law.

Article XII

The guarantee of the rights of woman and the female citizen implies a major benefit; this guarantee must be instituted for the advantage of all, and not for the particular benefit of those to whom it is entrusted.

Article XIII

For the support of the public force and the expenses of administration, the contributions of woman and man are equal; she shares all the duties [corvées] and all the painful tasks; therefore, she must have the same share in the distribution of positions, employment, offices, honors and jobs [industrie].

Article XIV

Female and male citizens have the right to verify, either by themselves or through their representatives, the necessity of the public contribution. This can only apply to women if they are granted an equal share, not only of wealth, but also of public administration, and in the determination of the proportion, the base, the collection, and the duration of the tax.

Article XV

The collectivity of women, joined for tax purposes to the aggregate of men, has the right to demand an accounting of his administration from any public agent.

Article XVI

No society has a constitution without the guarantee of rights and the separation of powers: the constitution is null if the majority of individuals comprising the nation have not cooperated in drafting it.

Article XVII

Property belongs to both sexes whether united or separate; for each it is an inviolable and sacred right; no one can be deprived of it, since it is the true patrimony of nature, unless the legally determined public need obviously dictates it, and then only with a just and prior indemnity.

mands went unheeded; the popular revolution had failed.

The End of the Revolution

In the four years after Robespierre's fall, a new government by committee, called the Directory, appeared to offer mediocrity, caution, and opportunism in place of the idealism and action of the early years of the revolution. No successor to Robespierre stepped forward to command center stage. There were no heroes like Lafayette or the great Jacobin orator Georges-Jacques Danton to inspire patriotic fervor. Nor were there women like Olympe de Gouges to demand in the public arena equal rights for women. Most people, numbed after years of change, barely noticed that the revolution was over. Ordinary men in parliamentary institutions effectively did the day-to-day job of running the government. They tried to steer a middle path between royalist resurgence and popular insurrection. This nearly forgotten period in the history of the French Revolution was

The French Revolution

August 1788	Louis XVI announces meeting of Estates-General to be held May 1789
5 May 1789	Estates-General convenes
17 June 1789	Third Estate declares itself the National Assembly
20 June 1789	Oath of the Tennis Court
14 July 1789	Storming of the Bastille
20 July 1789	Revolution of peasantry begins
26 August 1789	Declaration of the Rights of Man and Citizen
5 October 1789	Parisian women march to Versailles; force Louis XVI to return to Paris
February 1790	Monasteries, convents dissolved
July 1790	Civil Constitution of the Clergy
June 1791	Louis XVI and family attempt to flee Paris; are captured and returned
April 1792	France declares war on Austria
10 August 1792	Storming of the Tuileries
22 September 1792	Revolutionary calendar implemented
January 1793	Louis XVI executed
July 1793	Robespierre assumes leadership of Committee of Public Safety
1793–1794	Reign of Terror
1794	Robespierre guillotined
1799	Napoleon overthrows the Directory and seizes power

conscription in 1798 met with widespread protest and resistance. No matter what their political leanings, people were weary. They turned to those who promised stability and peace.

In the democratic experiment at the heart of the second stage of the French Revolution, the sovereign will of the people permanently replaced the monarch's claim to divine right to rule. Yet with democracy came tyranny. The severe repression of the terror revealed the pressures that external war and civil unrest created for the new Republic. The Thermidorian Reaction and the elimination of Robespierre as the legitimate interpreter of the people's will ushered in a period of conciliation, opportunism, and a search for stability. Ironically, the savior that France found to answer its needs for peace and a just government was a man of war and a dictator.

The Reign of Napoleon, 1799-1815

The great debate that rages to this day about Napoleon revolves around the question of whether he fulfilled the aims of the revolution or perverted them. In his return to a monarchical model, Napoleon resembled the enlightened despots of eighteenth-century Europe. In a modern sense, he was also a dictator, manipulating the French population through a highly centralized administrative apparatus. He locked French society into a program of military expansion that depleted its human and material resources. Yet, in spite of destruction and war, he dedicated his reign to building a French state according to the principles of the Revolution. Napoleon is one of those individuals about whom one can say that if he had not lived, history would have been different. He left his mark on an age and a continent.

Bonaparte Seizes Power

In Paris in 1795 a young, penniless, and unknown military officer moved among the wealthy and the beautiful of Parisian society and longed for fame. Already nicknamed at school "the Little Corporal" on account of his short stature, he was snubbed because of his background and ridiculed for his foreign accent. His story is typical of all stories of thwarted ambition. Yet the outcome of this story is unique: within four years this young man would become ruler of France. The story of

the fulfillment of the liberal hopes of 1789 for a stable constitutional rule.

The Directory, however, continued to be dogged by European war. A mass army of conscripts and volunteers had successfully extended France's power and frontiers. France expelled foreign invaders and annexed territories, including Belgium, while increasing its control in Holland, Switzerland, and Italy. But the expansion of revolutionary France was expensive and increasingly unpopular. Military defeats and the corruption of the Directory undermined government control. The Directory might have succeeded in the slow accretion of a parliamentary tradition, but reinstatement of his ascent to power is also a story of the demise of the revolution.

Napoleon Bonaparte (1769–1821) was a true child of the eighteenth century. He shared the philosophes' belief in a rational and progressive world. Born in Corsica, which until a few months before his birth was part of the Republic of Genoa, he received his training in French military schools. As a youth, he was arrogant and ambitious. But he could have never aspired to a position of leadership in the army during the old regime because he lacked the noble birth necessary for advancement. The highest rank Napoleon could hope to achieve was that of captain or major.

The revolution changed everything for him. First, it opened up careers previously restricted by birth, including those in the military, to talent. Second, the revolution made new posts available when aristocratic generals defected and crossed over to the enemy side, both before and after the execution of the king. Finally, the revolution created great opportunities for military men to test their mettle.

Foreign war and civil war required military leaders devoted to the revolution. Forced to flee Corsica because he had sided with the Jacobins, Napoleon and his troops were given the task of crushing Parisian protesters who rioted against the Directory in 1795. His victories in the Italian campaign in 1796–97 launched his political career. As he extended French rule into central Italy, he became the embodiment of revolutionary values and energy.

The revolutionary wars had begun as wars to liberate humanity in the name of liberty, equality, and fraternity. Yet concerns for power, territory, and riches soon replaced earlier concerns with defense of the nation and of the revolution. This aggrandizement was nowhere more evident than in the Egyptian campaign of 1798, in which Napoleon Bonaparte headed an expedition whose goal was to enrich France by hastening the collapse of the Turkish empire, crippling British trade routes, and handicapping Russian interests in the region. With Napoleon's highly publicized campaigns in Egypt and Syria, the war left the European theater and moved to the East, leaving behind its original revolutionary ideals. The Egyptian campaign, which was in reality a disaster, made Napoleon a hero at home. Yet in 1799 he readily joined a conspiracy that pulled down the Directory, the government he had earlier preserved, and became the First Consul of a triumvirate of consuls.

Napoleon set out to secure his position of power by eliminating his enemies on the Left and weakening those on the Right. He guaranteed the security of property acquired in the revolution, a move that undercut royalists who wanted to return property to its original owners. Through policing forces and special criminal courts, law and order prevailed and civil war subsided. The First Consul promised a balanced budget and appeared to deliver it. Bonaparte spoke of healing the nation's wounds, especially those opened by de-Christianization during the revolution. Realizing the importance of religion in maintaining domestic peace, Napoleon reestablished relations with the pope in 1801 by the Concordat, which recognized Catholicism as the religion of the French and restored the Roman Catholic hierarchy.

Napoleon's popularity as First Consul flowed from his military and political successes and his religious reconciliation. He had come to power in 1799 by appealing for the support of the army. In 1802 Napoleon decided to extend his power by calling for a plebiscite in which he asked the electorate to vote him First Consul for life. Public support was overwhelming. An electoral landslide gave Napoleon greater political power than any of his Bourbon predecessors. Using revolutionary mechanisms, Napoleon laid the foundation for a new dynasty.

Napoleon's Empire

War and More War

Napoleon was either at war or preparing for war during his entire reign. He certainly seemed up to the task of defeating the European powers. His military successes before 1799, real and apparent, had been crucial in his bid for political power. By 1802 he had signed favorable treaties with both Austria and Great Britain. He appeared to deliver a lasting peace and to establish France as the dominant power in Europe. But the peace was short-lived. In 1803 France embarked on an 11-year period of continuous war. Under Napoleon's command, the French army delivered defeat after defeat to the European powers. Austria fell in 1805, Prussia in 1806, and the Russian armies of Alexander I were defeated at Friedland in 1807. In 1808 Napoleon invaded Spain to drive out British expeditionary forces intent on invading France. The great painter of the Spanish court, Francisco Goya (1746–1828), produced a series of etchings, *The Disasters of War*, that depicted the atrocities accompanying the Napoleonic invasion. Spain became a satellite kingdom of France, though the conflict continued.

Britain was the one exception to the string of Napoleonic victories. Napoleon initially considered sending a French fleet to invade the island nation. Lacking the strength necessary to achieve this, he turned to economic warfare, blockading European ports against British trade. Beginning in 1806, the Continental System, as the blockade was known, erected a structure of protection for French manufactures in all continental European markets. The British responded to the tariff walls and boycotts with a naval blockade that succeeded in cutting French commerce off from its Atlantic markets. The Continental System did not prove to be the decisive policy that Napoleon had planned: the British economy was not broken and the French economy did not flourish when faced with restricted resources and the persistence of a black market in smuggled goods.

Still, by 1810 the French leader was master of the Continent. French armies had extended revolutionary reforms and legal codes outside France and brought with them civil equality and religious toleration. They had also drained defeated countries of their resources and had inflicted the horrors of war with armies of occupation, forced billeting, and pillage. Napoleon's empire extended across Europe, with only a diminished Austria, Prussia, and Russia remaining independent. He placed his relatives and friends on the thrones of the new satellite kingdoms of Italy, Naples, Westphalia, Holland, and Spain. It was a fine empire, Napoleon later recalled in the loneliness of exile. Napoleon's empire did not endure, but at its acme, it seemed as though it would never fall.

Peace at Home

Napoleon measured domestic prosperity in terms of the stability of his reign. Through the 1802 plebiscite that voted him First Consul for life, he maintained the

This engraving, from the series Disasters of War by Francisco Goya, depicts the horrors of war. The series was inspired by Napoleon's invasion and occupation of Spain from 1808 to 1813.

German caricature of Napoleon (1814). The anonymous artist who created this caricature has depicted on the French general's face the victims of Napoleon's doomed Russian campaign.

impediment to the development of a national market by creating a uniform system of weights and measures. The metric system was established by 1799. But Napoleon felt the need to go further: France must be first in scientific research and application. To assure French predominance, Napoleon became a patron of science, supporting important work in the areas of physics and chemistry. Building for the future, Napoleon made science a pillar in the new structure of higher education.

The Directory had restored French prosperity through stabilization of the currency, fiscal reform, and support of industry. Napoleon's contribution to the French economy was the much needed reform of the tax system. He authorized the creation of a central banking system. French industries flourished under the protection of the state. The blockade forced the development of new domestic crops such as sugar beets and indigo, which became substitutes for colonial products. Napoleon extended the infrastructure of roads so necessary for the expansion of national and European markets.

Perhaps his greatest achievement was the codification of law, a task begun under the revolution. Many of the new articles of the Napoleonic Code were hammered out in Napoleon's presence, as he presided regularly over meetings with legal reformers. Combined with economic reforms, the Napoleonic Code facilitated trade and the development of commerce by regularizing contractual relations and protecting property rights and equality before the law.

The civil laws of the new code carved out a family policy characterized by hierarchy and subordination. Married women were neither independent nor equal to men in ownership of property, custody of children, and access to divorce. Women also lacked political rights. In the Napoleonic Code, women, like children, were subjected to paternal authority. The Napoleonic philosophy of woman's place is well captured in an anecdote told by Madame Germaine de Staël (1766–1817), a leading intellectual of her day. As the daughter of Jacques Necker, the Swiss financier and adviser to Louis XVI at the time of the revolution, she had been taught Enlightenment ideas from an early age. On finding herself seated next to Napoleon at a dinner party, she asked him what was very likely a self-interested question: whom did he consider the greatest woman, alive or dead? Napoleon had no name to give her but responded, without pausing: "The one who has had the most children."

Napoleon turned his prodigious energies to every aspect of French life. He encouraged the arts while cre-

charade of constitutional rule while he ruled as virtual dictator. In 1804 he abandoned all pretense and had himself proclaimed emperor of the French. Mimicking the rituals of kingship, he staged his own coronation and that of his wife Josephine at the cathedral of Notre Dame de Paris. Breaking the tradition set by Charlemagne, Napoleon took the crown from the hands of Pope Pius VII (1800–23) and placed it on his own head.

Secure in his regime, surrounded by a new nobility that he created based on military achievement and talent and that he rewarded with honors, Napoleon set about implementing sweeping reforms in every area of government. Like many of the men of the revolutionary assemblies who had received scientific educations in their youth, he recognized the importance of science for both industry and war. The revolution had removed an ating a police force. He had monuments built but did not forget about sewers. He organized French administrative life in a fashion that has endured. In place of the popular democratic movement, he offered his own singular authority. In place of elections, clubs, and free associations, he gave France plebiscites and army service. To be sure, Napoleon believed in constitutions, but he thought they should be "short and obscure." For Napoleon the great problem of democracy was its unpredictability. His regime solved that problem by eliminating choices.

Decline and Fall

Militarily, Napoleon went too far. The first cracks in the French façade began to show in the Peninsular War (1808–14) with Spain, in which Spanish guerrilla tactics proved costly for French troops. Napoleon's biggest mistake, the one that shattered the myth of his invincibility, occurred when he decided to invade Russia in June 1812. Having decisively defeated Russian forces in

1807, Napoleon had entered into a peace treaty with Tsar Alexander I that guaranteed Russian allegiance to French policies. Alexander repudiated the Continental System in 1810 and appeared to be preparing for his own war against France. Napoleon seized the initiative, sure that he could defeat Russian forces once again. With an army of 500,000 men, Napoleon moved deep into Russia in the summer of 1812. The tsar's troops fell back in retreat. It was a strange war, one that pulled the French army to Moscow like a bird following bread crumbs. When Napoleon and his men entered Moscow in September, they found a city in flames. The people of Moscow had destroyed their own city to deprive the French troops of winter quarters.

Winter comes early in Moscow, Napoleon's men discovered. They had left France basking in the warmth of summer and sure of certain and early victory. They now found themselves facing a severe Russian winter without overcoats, supplies, or food. Russia's strategy has become legendary. The Russians destroyed grain and shelter that might be of use to the French. Napoleon and his starving and frostbitten troops were forced into retreat. The horses of the French cavalry died because they were not properly shod for cold weather. The French army was decimated. Fewer than 100,000 men made it back to France.

Britain, unbowed by the Continental System, remained Napoleon's sworn enemy. Prussia joined Great Britain, Sweden, Russia, and Austria in opposing France anew. In the Battle of Nations at Leipzig in October 1813, France was forced to retreat. Napoleon refused a negotiated peace and fought on until the following March, when the victorious allies marched down the streets of Paris and occupied the French capital. Only then did Napoleon abdicate in favor of his young son, François, the titular king of Rome (1811–32). Napoleon was exiled to the Mediterranean island of Elba.

The allies refused to accept the young "Napoleon II" and supported instead the Bourbon claimant to the throne, the brother of the guillotined Louis XVI. Naming himself Louis XVIII (skipping "XVII" in deference to his nephew dead at the hands of the Revolution), the new king claimed to rule over a "restored" France.

Still it was not quite the end for Napoleon. While the European heads of state sat in Vienna trying to determine the future of Europe and France's place in it, Napoleon returned from his exile on the Mediterranean island of Elba to reclaim leadership of France. On 15 June 1815, Napoleon once again, and for the final time, confronted the European powers in one of the most fa-

The Reign of Napoleon

1799	Napoleon establishes consulate, becomes First Consul
1801	Napoleon reestablishes relations with pope, restores Roman Catholic hierarchy
1802	Plebiscite declares Napoleon First Consul for life
1804	Napoleon proclaims himself Emperor of the French
1806	Continental System implemented
1808–1814	France engaged in Peninsular War with Spain
June 1812	Napoleon invades Russia
September 1812	French army reaches Moscow, is trapped by Russian winter
1813	Napoleon defeated at Battle of Nations at Leipzig
March 1814	Napoleon abdicates and goes into exile on island of Elba
March 1815	Napoleon escapes Elba and attempts to reclaim power
15 June 1815	Napoleon is defeated at Waterloo and exiled to island of Saint Helena

This 1835 painting by De Boisdenier depicts the suffering of Napoleon's Grand Army on the retreat from Moscow. The Germans were to meet a similar fate over 100 years later when they invaded Russia without adequate supplies for the harsh winter.

mous military campaigns in history. With 125,000 loyal French forces, Napoleon seemed within hours of reestablishing the French empire in Europe.

But he had underestimated his opponents. The defeat of Napoleon's forces at Waterloo was decisive. Napoleon later explained, "Everything failed me just when everything had succeeded!" He had met his Waterloo, and with his defeat a new expression entered the language to describe devastating, permanent, irreversible downfall. Napoleon's return proved brief—it lasted only 100 days. An era had come to an end. Napoleon was exiled to the inhospitable island of Saint Helena in the South Atlantic. For the next six years, Napoleon wrote his memoirs under the watchful eyes of his British jailers. He died a painful death from cancer on 5 May 1821.

The period of revolution and empire from 1789 to 1815 radically changed the face of France. A new, more cohesive elite of bourgeois and nobles emerged, sharing power based on wealth and status. Ownership of land remained a defining characteristic of both old and new elites. A new state bureaucracy, built on the foundations of the old, expanded and centralized state power.

The people as sovereign now legitimated political power. Napoleon at his most imperial never doubted that he owed his existence to the people. In this sense, Napoleon was the king of the revolution—an apparently contradictory fusion of old forms and new ideology. Napoleon channeled democratic forces into enthusiasm for empire. He learned his lessons from the failure of the Bourbon monarchy and the politicians of the revolution. For 16 years Napoleon successfully reconciled the old regime with the new France. Yet he could not resolve the essential problem of democracy: the relationship between the will of the people and the exercise of political power. The picture in 1815 was not dramatically different from the situation in 1789. The revolution might be over, but changes fueled by the revolutionary tradition were just beginning. The struggle for a workable democratic government continued in France for another century, and elsewhere in Europe throughout the twentieth century.

Mastering the Chapter

To review the main points of the chapter, be sure you can explain the significance of each of the following.

Terms/Concepts/Events	People	Places
Estates-General	Louis XV	Versailles
cahiers de doléances	Jacques Necker	Bastille
Oath of the Tennis Court	Charles Alexandre de Calonne	Tuileries Palace
Constitution of 1791	Abbé Sieyès	Metz
Declaration of the Rights of Man	Mirabeau	Varennes
Jacobins	Toussaint L'Ouverture	the Vendée
Committee of Public Safety	Maximilien Robespierre	Corsica
Thermidorian Reaction	Georges-Jacques Danton	Elba
Directory	Olympe de Gouges	Waterloo
Napoleonic Code	Napoleon Bonaparte	Saint Helena

Suggestions for Further Reading

The Crisis of the Old Regime in France

C. B. A. Behrens, *Society, Government, and the Enlightenment* (New York: Harper & Row, 1985). A comparative study of eighteenth-century France and Prussia, focusing on the relationship between government and the ruling classes, that explains how pressures for change in both countries led to different outcomes: revolution in France and reform in Prussia.

* Roger Chartier, *The Cultural Origins of the French Revolution*, tr. Lydia G. Cochrane (Durham, NC: Duke University Press, 1991). Argues for the importance of the rise of critical modes of thinking in the public sphere in the eighteenth century and of long-term de-Christianization in shaping the desire for change in French society and politics.

Olwen Hufton, *The Poor in Eighteenth-Century France, 1750–1789* (Oxford: Clarendon, 1974). Examines the lives of the poor before the revolution and the institutions that attempted to deal with the problem of poverty.

Olwen Hufton, *Europe: Privilege and Protest, 1730–1789* (Sussex, England: Harvester Press, 1980). An overview of the impact of rapid social, ideological, and economic changes on the concept and exercise of privilege.

* Daniel Roche, *The People of Paris* (Berkeley: University of California Press, 1987). An essay on popular culture in the eighteenth century in which the author surveys the lives of the Parisian popular classes—servants, laborers, and artisans—and examines their housing, furnishing, dress, and leisure activities.

Isser Woloch, *Eighteenth-Century Europe: Tradition and Progress, 1715–1789* (New York: Norton, 1982). A discussion of eighteenth-century Europe comparing social, economic, political, and intellectual developments elsewhere on the Continent to the French experience, with special attention to cultural aspects such as popular beliefs and religion.

The first stage of the French Revolution

François Furet and Denis Richet, *The French Revolution* (New York: Macmillan, 1970). Two experts on the French Revolution present a detailed overview of the period from 1789 to 1798, when Bonaparte returned to Paris.

* Georges Lefebvre, *The Great Fear of 1789* (New York: Pantheon Books, 1973). This classic study analyzes the rural panic that swept through parts of France in the summer of 1789. The Great Fear is presented as a distinct episode in the opening months of the revolution, with its own internal logic.

Colin Lucas, ed., *Rewriting the French Revolution* (Oxford: Clarendon Press, 1991). Responding to the historiographic challenge of the bicentenary of the French Revolution, eight scholars present new interpretations in the areas of social development, ideas, politics, and religion.

* D. M. G. Sutherland, *France, 1789–1815: Revolution and Counter-Revolution* (New York: Oxford University Press, 1986). An interpretation of the revolutionary period that stresses the struggle against counterrevolution and presents the revolution as a complex and contradictory process of social and political conflict over incompatible rights and privileges enjoyed by significant portions of the population.

* Michel Vovelle, *The Fall of the French Monarchy* (Cambridge: Cambridge University Press, 1984). A social history of the origins and early years of the revolution, beginning with a brief examination of the old regime and paying special attention to social and economic changes initiated by the revolution, the role of the popular classes, and the creation of revolutionary culture.

Experimenting with Democracy: The Revolution's second stage, 1792–1799

* François Furet, *Interpreting the French Revolution* (Cambridge: Cambridge University Press, 1981). A series of essays challenging many of the assumptions about the causes and outcome of the revolution and reviewing its historiography. The author argues that political crisis, not class conflict, was the revolution's primary cause and that revolutionary ideas concerning democracy are central to an understanding of the Reign of Terror.

Carla Hesse, *Publishing and Cultural Politics in Revolutionary Paris, 1789–1810* (Berkeley: University of California Press, 1991). Reconstructs the publishing world that emerged from the revolutionary struggles of publishers and printers of Paris and examines the political, legal, and socioeconomic forces shaping the new cultural politics between 1789 and 1810.

* Lynn Hunt, *Politics, Culture, and Class in the French Revolution* (Berkeley: University of California Press, 1984). A study of the revolution as the locus of the creation of modern political culture. The second half of the book examines the social composition and cultural experiences of the new political class that emerged during the revolution.

Lynn Hunt, *The Family Romance of the French Revolution* (Berkeley: University of California Press, 1992). Studies recurrent images of the family in French revolutionary politics in order to understand the gendered nature of the revolution and republicanism.

* Joan B. Landes, *Women and the Public Sphere in the Age of the French Revolution* (Ithaca, NY: Cornell University Press, 1988). Landes examines the genesis of the modern notion of the public sphere from a feminist perspective and argues that within the revolutionary process women were relegated to the private sphere of the domestic world.

* Sara E. Melzer and Leslie Rabine, eds., *Rebel Daughters: Women and the French Revolution* (New York: Oxford University Press, 1992). Contributors from a variety of disciplines examine the importance of women in the French Revolution, with special attention to the exclusion of women from the new politics.

Dorinda Outram, *The Body of the French Revolution: Sex, Class and Political Culture* (New Haven, CT: Yale University Press, 1989). Examines how images of the body in the late eighteenth century differed from class to class and how bourgeois attitudes toward physicality resulted in a gendered political discourse in which the hero replaced the king.

* Albert Soboul, *The Sans-Culottes* (New York: Anchor, 1972). An exhaustive study of the artisans who composed the core of popular political activism in revolutionary Paris. Soboul examines

the political demands and ideology of the sans-culottes, as well as the composition, culture, and actions of the popular movement during the revolution.

The Reign of Napoleon

* Louis Bergeron, *France Under Napoleon* (Princeton, NJ: Princeton University Press, 1981). An analysis of the structure of Napoleon's regime, its social bases of support, and its opponents.

* Felix Markham, *Napoleon* (New York: New American Library, 1963). This classic study treats both Napoleon's life and legend while giving a balanced account of the social and intellectual life of the period and the impact of the Napoleonic Empire on Europe.

Jean Tulard, *Napoleon: The Myth of the Saviour* (London: Weidenfeld and Nicolson, 1984). This biography of Napoleon situates his rise to power within the crisis of legitimacy created by the destruction of the monarchy during the revolution. The Napoleonic Empire is presented as a creation of the bourgeoisie, who desired to end the revolution and consolidate their gains and control over the lower classes.

Isser Woloch, *The New Regime: Transformations of the French Civic Order* (New York: Norton, 1994). Woloch's study emphasizes the break of the new regime from the old, placing the institutions created or revamped after 1789 in the context of a new civic order and citizenship.

*Paperback edition available.

SWEDEN

Oostvrinlandt

RUSSIA

Lytlandt

COURLANT

EUROPA

PRUSSIA

Hongaria

Moldavia

SCLAVONIA

Bulgaria

GRÆCIA

NATOLIA

industrial europe

portrait of an age

The Normandy train has reached Paris. The coast and the capital are once again connected. Passengers in their city finery disembark and are greeted by others who have awaited their scheduled arrival. Workmen stand ready to unload freight, porters to carry luggage. Steam billows forth from the resting engine, which is the object of all human activity. The engine stares at us as enigmatically as any character in a Renaissance portrait. We hardly think to ask what lies behind the round black face with its headlight for an eye and its chimney for a snout. Yet the train that has arrived in *La Gare Saint-Lazarre* by Claude Monet (1840–1926) is as much the central character in this portrait of the industrial age as was any individual in portraits of ages past.

The train's iron bulk dwarfs the people around it. Indeed, iron dominates our attention. Tons of it are in view. The rails, the lampposts, the massive frame of the station, no less than the train itself, are all formed from iron—pliable, durable, inexpensive iron—the miracle product of industrialization. The iron station with its glass panels became as central a feature of nineteenth-century cities as stone cathedrals were in the Middle Ages. Railway stations changed the shape of urban settings, just as railway travel changed the lives of millions of people.

There had never been anything like it before. Ancient Romans had hitched four horses to their chariots; nineteenth-century Europeans hitched four horses to their stagecoaches. The technology of overland transportation had hardly changed in 2000 years. Coach journeys were long, uncomfortable, and expensive. They were governed by the elements and the muddy, rutted roads, which caused injuries to humans and horses with alarming regularity. First-class passengers rode inside, where they were jostled against one another and breathed the dust that the horses kicked up in front of them. Second-class passengers rode on top, braving the elements and risking life and limb in an accident.

Railway travel was a quantum leap forward. It was faster, cheaper, and safer. Overnight it changed conceptions of time, space, and, above all, speed. People could journey to what once were distant places in a single day. Voyages became trips, and the travel holiday was born. Commerce was transformed, as was the way in which it was conducted. Large quantities of goods could be shipped quickly from place to place; orders could instantly be filled. The whole notion of locality changed, as salesmen could board a morning train for what only recently had been an unreachable market. Branch offices could be overseen by regional directors, services and products could be standardized, and the gap between great and small cities and between town and countryside could be narrowed.

Wherever they went, the railroads created links that had never been forged before. In Britain the railroad schedule became the source of the creation of official time. Trains that left London were scheduled to arrive at their destinations according to London time, which came to be kept at the royal observatory in Greenwich. Trains carried fresh fish inland from the coasts and fresh vegetables from rural farms to city tables. Mail moved farther and more quickly; news spread more evenly. Fashionable ideas from the capital cities of Europe circulated everywhere, as did new knowledge and discoveries. The railroads brought both diversity and uniformity.

They also brought wonderment. The engine seemed to propel itself with unimaginable power and at breathtaking speed. The English actress Fanny Kemble (1809–93) captured the sensation memorably: "You can't imagine how strange it seemed to be journeying on thus, without any visible cause of progress other than the magical machine, with its flying white breath and rhythmical, unvarying pace. I felt no fairy tale was ever half so wonderful as what I saw." For many the railroad symbolized the genius of the age in which they were living, an age in which invention, novelty, and progress were everywhere to be seen. It combined the great innovations of steam, coal, and iron that were transforming nearly every aspect of ordinary life. But for others, the railway was just as centrally a symbol of disquiet, of the passing of a way of life that was easier to understand and to control. "Seated in the old mail-coach we needed no evidence out of ourselves to indicate the velocity," wrote the English author Thomas De Quincey (1785–1859) in his obituary for the passing of horse travel. "We heard our speed, we saw it, we felt it. This speed was not the product of blind, insensate agencies, that had no sympathy to give, but was incarnated in the fiery eyeballs of the noblest among brutes."

Focus Questions

1. Why did early manufacturing develop in the countryside, and what effect did this have on manufacturing practices and social relations?
2. In what ways were the ideas about organization of manufacturers like Josiah Wedgwood and Robert Owen as significant as new technology in the development of industry in Britain?
3. How did British society address some of the changes in peoples' lives that were brought about by industrialization?
4. How did industrialization on the Continent differ from industrialization in England?
5. Why did some nations develop little industry at all?

The fruits of the railways, like the fruits of industrialization, were not all sweet. As the nineteenth century progressed, there could be no doubt that, year by year, one way of life was being replaced by another. More and more laborers were leaving the farms for the factories; more and more products were being made by machines. Everywhere there was change, but it was not always or everywhere for the better. Millions of people poured into cities that mushroomed up without plan or intention. Population growth, factory labor, and ultimately the grinding poverty that they produced overwhelmed traditional means of social control. Families and communities split apart; the expectations of ordinary people were no longer predictable. Life was spinning out of control for individuals, groups, and even whole societies. It was an engine racing down a track that only occasionally ended as placidly as did the Normandy train at the Gare Saint-Lazarre.

The Traditional Economy

The curse of Adam and Eve was that they would earn their daily bread by the sweat of their brows. For generation after generation, age after age, economic life was dominated by toil. Man, woman, and child labored to secure their supply of food against the caprice of nature. There was nothing even vaguely romantic about the backbreaking exertion needed to crack open the hard ground, plant seeds in it, and protect the crops from the ravages of insects, birds, and animals long enough to be harvested. Every activity was labor-intensive. Wood for shelter or fuel was chopped with thick, blunt axes. Water was drawn from deep wells by the long, slow turn of a crank or dragged in buckets from the nearest stream. Everything that was consumed was pulled or pushed or lifted. French women carried soil and water up steep terraces in journeys that could take as long as seven hours. "The women seemed from their persons and features to be harder worked than horses," Arthur Young (1741–1820), the English agricultural expert, observed with a combination of admiration and disgust. The capital that was invested in the traditional economy was human capital, and by the middle of the eighteenth century nearly eight out of every ten Europeans still tilled the soil, earning their bread by the sweat of their brow.

Although the traditional economy was dominated by agriculture, an increasing amount of labor was devoted to manufacture. The development of a secure and expanding overseas trade created a worldwide demand for consumer goods. In the countryside, small domestic textile industries grew up. Families would take in wool for spinning and weaving to supplement their income from agriculture. When times were good, they would expend proportionately less effort in manufacturing; when times were bad, they would expend more. Their tasks were set by an entrepreneur who provided raw materials and paid the workers by the piece. Wages paid to rural workers were lower than those paid to urban laborers because they were not subject to guild restrictions and because they supplemented farm income. Thus entrepreneurs could profit from lower costs, although they had to bear the risk that the goods produced in this fashion would be of lesser quality or that markets would dry up in the interval. Although domestic industry increased the supply of manufactured commodities, it demanded even more labor from an already overworked sector of the traditional economy.

Throughout the traditional economy, the limits on progress were set by nature. Good harvests brought prosperity, bad harvests despair. Over the long run, the traditional economy ran in all-too-predictable cycles. Sadly, the adage "Eat, drink, and be merry, for tomorrow we may die," was good advice. Prosperity was sure to bring misery in its train. The good fortune of one generation was the hard luck of the next, as more people competed for a relatively fixed quantity of food. No amount of sweat and muscle and, as yet, ingenuity could rescue the traditional economy from its pendulum swings of boom and bust.

By the eighteenth century, the process that would ultimately transform the traditional economy was already under way. It began with the agricultural revolution, one of the great turning points in human history. Before it occurred, the life of every community and of every citizen was always held hostage to nature. The struggle to secure an adequate food supply was the dominant fact of life to which nearly all productive labor was dedicated. After the agricultural revolution, an inadequate food supply was a political rather than an economic fact of life. Fewer and fewer farmers were required to feed more and more people. In Britain, where nearly 70 percent of the population was engaged in agriculture at the end of the seventeenth century, fewer than 2 percent now work on farms. By the middle of the nineteenth century, the most advanced economies were capable of producing vast surpluses of basic commodities. The agricultural revolution was not an event, and it did not happen suddenly. It would not deserve the label "revolution" at all were it not for its momentous consequences: Europe's escape from the shackles of the traditional economy.

Farming Families

Over most of Europe, agricultural activity in the eighteenth century followed methods of crop rotation that had been in place for over a thousand years. Fields were divided into strips of land, and each family "owned" a certain number of strips, which they cultivated for their livelihood. Between one-half and one-third of village land lay fallow each year so that its nutrients could be restored. Open-field farming, as this system was called, was communal rather than individual. Decisions about which crops to grow in the productive fields, where animals would be pastured, or how much wood could be cut from the common wastes affected everyone. Moreover, many activities, such as plowing, gleaning, and manuring, could not conveniently observe the distinctions of ownership of separate strips. Nor, given the realities of nature, could individual families be self-sustaining without the services of a village tanner or milkmaid or hog minder drawn from the closely intertwined group of kin and neighbors that constituted the community. Communal agriculture was effective, but it also limited the number of people that could survive on the produce from a given amount of land.

There were a number of reasons why this pattern of agricultural production remained unchanged century after century. In the first place, there was little incentive for the peasantry to change it. Although they worked hard to ensure their subsistence, they had little desire to create a surplus. For one thing, almost every commodity produced in the village was perishable, and unless it could be consumed or converted at market into durable goods or cash it was largely worthless. For another thing, peasants owed much of their productivity—in one form or another—to their lords. In eastern Europe, serfdom tied the peasantry to the land, where they were used as laborers for the production of foodstuffs for export. Peasants in central Europe were still obligated to perform labor service for their lords, though in parts of Germany in the eighteenth century this obligation was being commuted to money rents. In France and Scandinavia peasants "owned" much of their land in the sense that within the constraints imposed by the village, they could cultivate it as they saw fit and bequeath it to their heirs. But they paid dearly for these rights. Manorial taxes, in both money and kind, could take as much as half of each year's output, while demands from the state and the Church might absorb another quarter. The surplus wealth produced by the European peasantry, whether free or unfree, was extracted by their lords.

This is not to say that European peasants were uninterested in bettering their immediate economic circumstances or that they obstructed agricultural change. Agriculture was a profoundly conservative occupation, for the risk of experimentation was nothing less than survival. Lords and peasants both practiced defensive innovation, introducing change only after its practical benefits were easily demonstrable. For example, in the mid-seventeenth century two French provincial parlements banned the cultivation of potatoes in the mistaken belief that they caused leprosy. Yet both potatoes and corn became peasant crops and spread rapidly throughout southern Europe, not least because as new commodities they were untaxed. Peasants bartered their surplus, hoarded their profits, and took what few advantages they could out of a system in which the deck was stacked against them.

As the European population entered a new cycle of growth in the second quarter of the eighteenth century, the traditional economy began to increase agricultural productivity in traditional ways. In the east, new lands were colonized and slowly brought under cultivation. Frederick the Great welcomed immigrants to Prussia, where land was plentiful, if not very fertile. In settled communities, less productive land, which had provided fodder for animals at the end of the seventeenth century, now had to provide food for humans. Scrubland was cleared and hillsides terraced. Dry ground was irrigated manually by women and children working in bucket brigades. As always, an increase in population initially meant an increase in productivity. For a time, more able-bodied workers produced more food. In the half century that ended in the 1770s, French peasants

Population Growth in Europe, 1800–1850

increased agricultural production by nearly 60 percent. The intensification of traditional methods rather than innovation accounted for the increase. The number of strips held by each family declined, but each strip was more carefully cultivated.

By the end of the eighteenth century, the European population was reaching the point at which another check on its growth might be expected. Between 1700 and 1800, total European population had increased by nearly 50 percent, and the rate of growth was continuing to accelerate. This vast expansion of rural population placed a grave strain on agricultural production. Decade by decade, more families attempted to eke out an existence from the same amount of land. The gains made by intensive cultivation were now lost to overpopulation. In areas that practiced partible inheritance, farms were subdivided into units too small to provide subsistence. Competition for these "morsels" of land, as the French called them, was intense. Older sons bought out younger brothers; better-off families purchased whatever came on the market to prevent their children from slipping into poverty. Even in areas in which primogeniture was the rule, portions for younger sons and daughters ate into the meager inheritance of the eldest son.

Over much of Europe, it was becoming increasingly difficult to live by bread alone.

Rural Manufacture

The crisis of overpopulation meant that not only were there more mouths to feed, there were more bodies to clothe. This increased the need for spun and woven cloth, and thus for spinners and weavers. Traditionally, commercial cloth production was the work of urban artisans, but the expansion of the marketplace and the introduction of new fabrics, especially cotton and silk, had eroded the monopoly of most of the clothing guilds. Merchants could sell as much finished product as they could find, and the teeming rural population provided a tempting pool of inexpensive labor for anyone willing to risk the capital to purchase raw materials. Initially, farming families took manufacturing work into their homes to supplement their income. Spinning and weaving were the most common occupations, and they were treated as occasional work, reserved for the slow times in the agricultural cycle. This was known as cottage industry. It was supplementary employment, less important and less valuable than the vital agricultural labor that all members of the family undertook.

But by the middle of the eighteenth century, cottage industry was developing in a new direction. As landholdings grew smaller, even good harvests did not promise subsistence to many families. This oversupply of labor was soon organized into the putting-out system, which mobilized the resources of the rural labor force for commercial production of large quantities of manufactured goods. The characteristics of the putting-out system were similar throughout Europe, whether it was undertaken by individual entrepreneurs or lords of the manor, or even sponsored by the state. The process began with the capital of the entrepreneur, which was used to purchase raw materials. These materials were "put out" to the homes of workers where the manufacture, most commonly spinning or weaving, took place. The finished goods were returned to the entrepreneur, who sold them at a profit, with which he bought raw materials to begin the process anew.

The simplicity of the putting-out system was one of its most valuable features. All of its essential elements were already present in rural communities. The small nest egg of a prosperous farmer or small trader was all the money needed to make the first purchase of raw materials. These raw materials could be put out to his kin or closest neighbors and the finished goods then delivered to market along with surplus crops. Not only could a small amount of cash begin the cycle of putting-out, but that capital continued to circulate to keep the process in motion.

The small scale of the initial enterprise can be seen in the fact that many entrepreneurs had themselves begun as workers. In Bohemia, for example, some of the largest putting-out operations were run by serfs who paid their lords fees for the right to engage in trade. At the end of the eighteenth century, there were over one-quarter million spinners in the Bohemian linen industry alone, most of them organized into small groups around a single entrepreneur, though one monastery employed over 650 women spinners. Putting-out also required only a low level of skill and common, inexpensive tools. Rural families did their own spinning and rural villages their own weaving. Thus, putting-out demanded little investment, either in plant, equipment, or education. Nor did it inevitably disrupt traditional gender-based tasks in the family economy. In most places spinning was women's work, weaving was done by men, and children helped at whichever task was under way. In fact, certain occupations, like lacemaking in France, were so gender-based that men would not even act as entrepreneurs. In Austria, lacemaking was considered less honorable than other forms of clothmaking because of its association with women and household-based production. Performed at home, rural manufacture remained a traditional family-oriented occupation.

Because this form of manufacturing began as supplementary work, rural laborers were willing to accept low wages. In urban areas, guild restrictions regulated the number of laborers and ensured that they were paid a living wage. Lower labor costs were probably a necessary condition for the success of domestic-based manufacturing. It was vital that the finished goods could readily be sold at market, for it was that sale that allowed the purchase of more raw material. If the entrepreneur could not dispose of his product, his network of workers collapsed. On the other hand, piecework provided farmers with the cushion they needed to survive too-small harvests or too-small plots of land. In the Swiss highlands during the late eighteenth century, farmers prospered on farms one-eighth the size of those tilled by their grandfathers. But more of their time was now occupied in cloth production than in agriculture. As long as rural manufacture supplemented agricultural income, it was seen as a benefit for everyone involved—the entrepreneur, the individual worker, and the village community.

Gradually, the putting-out system came to dominate the lives of many rural families. From small networks of isolated villages, domestic manufacture grew to cover entire regions. Perhaps as many as one-quarter of the inhabitants of the Irish province of Ulster were engaged in manufacturing linen by the end of the eighteenth century. Spinning and weaving became full-time occupations for families that kept no more than a small gar-

Linen production is the subject of an engraving from Nuremberg by Franz Philipp Florin, 1705. The flax stems were soaked to soften the tough outer fibers, which were then removed by beating. The inner fibers were spun into linen on hand looms.

This 1791 engraving by William Hincks shows women engaged in typical tasks of eighteenth-century cottage industry: spinning, reeling with the clock reel, and boiling the yarn.

den. But without agricultural earnings, piecework rates became starvation wages, and families unable to purchase their subsistence were forced to rely upon loans from the entrepreneurs who set them at work. Long hours in dank cottages performing endlessly repetitive tasks became the lot of millions of rural inhabitants, and their numbers increased annually. While the sons of farmers waited to inherit land before they formed their families, the sons of cottage weavers needed only a loom to begin theirs. They could afford to marry younger and to have more children, for children could contribute to manufacturing from an early age.

Consequently, the expansion of the putting-out system, like the expansion of traditional agriculture, fueled the continued growth of population. Like traditional agriculture, putting-out contained a number of structural inefficiencies. Both entrepreneur and worker were potential victims of unscrupulousness. Embezzlement of raw materials was a problem for the entrepreneur, arbitrary wage cuts for the laborers. Because the tasks were performed at home, the entrepreneur could not supervise the work. Most disputes in domestic manufacturing arose over specifications of quality. Workers would not receive full pay for poorly produced goods that could not be sold for full value. Inexperienced,

aged, or infirm workers could easily spoil costly raw materials. One Bohemian nobleman created village spinning rooms on his estates so that young girls could be given four weeks of training before they set up on their own. Finally, the putting-out system was labor- rather than capital-intensive. As long as there were ready hands to employ, there was little incentive to seek better methods or more efficient techniques.

The Agricultural Revolution

The continued growth of Europe's population necessitated an expansion of agricultural output. In most places this was achieved by intensifying traditional practices, bringing more land into production and more labor to work the land. But in the most advanced European economies, first in Holland and then in England, traditional agriculture underwent a long but dynamic transformation, an agricultural revolution. It was a revolution of technique rather than technology. Humans were not replaced by machines nor were new forms of energy substituted for human and animal muscle. Indeed, many of the methods that were to increase crop yields had been known for centuries and practiced during periods of population pressure. But they had never been practiced as systematically as they came to be from the seventeenth century onward, and they were never combined with a commercial attitude toward farming. It was the willingness and ability of owners to invest capital in their land that transformed subsistence farming into commercial agriculture.

As long as farming was practiced in open fields, there was little incentive for individual landowners to invest in improvements to their scattered strips. While the community as a whole could enclose a small field or plant some fodder crops for the animals, its ability to change traditional practice was limited. In farming villages, even the smallest landholder had rights in common lands, which were jealously guarded. Rights in commons meant a place in the community itself. Commercial agriculture was more suited to large rather than small estates and was more successful when the land could be utilized in response to market conditions rather than the necessities of subsistence.

The consolidation of estates along with the enclosure of fields was thus the initial step toward change. This was a long-term process that took many forms. In England, where it was to become most advanced, enclosure was already under way in the sixteenth century. Prosperous families had long been consolidating their strips in the open fields, and at some point the lord of the manor and the members of the community agreed to carve up the common fields and make the necessary exchanges to consolidate everyone's lands. Perhaps as much as three-quarters of the arable land in England was enclosed by agreement before 1760. Enclosure by agreement did not mean that the breakup of the open-field community was necessarily a harmonious process. Riots preceding or following agreed enclosures were not uncommon.

Paradoxically, it was the middling rather than the poorest villagers who had the most to lose. The breakup of the commons initially gave the poor more arable land from which to eke out their subsistence, and few of them could afford to sacrifice present gain for future loss. These smallholders were quickly bought out. It was the middle-size holders who were squeezed hardest. Although prosperous in communal farming, these families did not have access to the capital necessary to make agricultural improvements such as converting grass to grain land or purchasing large amounts of fertilizer. They could not compete in producing for the market, and gradually they, too, disappeared from the enclosed village. Their opposition to enclosure by agreement led, in the eighteenth century, to enclosure by act of Parliament. Parliamentary enclosure was legislated by government, a government composed for the most part of large landowners. A commission would view the community's lands and divide them, usually by a prescribed formula. Between 1760 and 1815, over 1.5 million acres of farmland were enclosed by act of Parliament. During the late eighteenth century, the Prussian and French governments emulated this practice by ordering large tracts of land enclosed.

The enclosure of millions of acres of land was one of the largest expenses of the new commercial agriculture. Hedging or fencing off the land and plowing up the commons required extra labor beyond that necessary for basic agrarian activities. Thus many who sold the small estates that they received on the breakup of the commons remained in villages as agricultural laborers or leaseholders. But now they practiced a different form of farming. More and more agricultural activity became market-oriented. Single crops were sown in large enclosed fields and exchanged at market for the mixture of goods that previously had been grown in the village. Market production turned attention from producing a

Commercial linen centers

- ■ Major
- ▲ Minor

Rural industry

- Intensive
- Less intensive

The European Linen Industry

balance of commodities to increasing the yield of a single one.

The first innovation was the widespread cultivation of fodder crops such as clover and turnips. Crops like clover restore nutrients to the soil as they grow, shortening the period in which land has to lie fallow. Moreover, farm animals grazing on clover or feeding on turnips return more manure to the land, further increasing its productivity. Turnip cultivation had begun in Holland and was brought to England in the sixteenth century. But it was not until the late seventeenth century that Viscount Charles "Turnip" Townsend (1675–1738) made turnip cultivation popular. Townsend and other large Norfolk landowners developed a new system of planting known as the four-crop rotation, in which wheat, turnips, barley, and clover succeeded one another. This method kept the land in productive use, and both the turnip and clover crops were used to feed larger herds of animals.

The ability of farmers to increase their livestock was as important as their ability to grow more grain. Not only were horses and oxen more productive than humans—a horse could perform seven times the labor of a man while consuming only five times the food—but the animals also refertilized the land as they worked. Light fertilization of a single acre of arable land required an average of 25,000 pounds of manure. But animals competed with humans for food, especially during the winter months when little grazing was possible. To conserve grain for human consumption, lambs were led to the slaughter and the fatted calf was killed in the autumn. Thus the development of the technique of meadow floating was a remarkable breakthrough. By flooding low-lying land near streams in the winter, English and Dutch farmers could prevent the ground from freezing during their generally mild winters. When the water was drained, the land beneath it would produce an early grass crop on which the beasts could graze. This meant that more animals could be kept alive during the winter.

The relationship between animal husbandry and grain growing became another feature of commercial agriculture. In many areas farmers could choose between growing grain and pasturing animals. When prices for wool or meat were relatively higher than those for grain, fields could be left in grass for grazing. When grain prices rose, the same fields could be plowed. Consolidated enclosed estates made this convertible husbandry possible. The decision to hire fieldworkers or shepherds could be taken only by large agricultural employers. Whatever the relative price of grain, the open-field village continued to produce grain as its primary crop. Farmers who could convert their production in tune to the market could not only maximize their profits but could also prevent shortages of raw materials for domestic manufacturers or of foodstuffs for urban and rural workers.

Convertible husbandry was but the first step in the development of a true system of regional specialization in agriculture. Different soils and climates favored different use of the land. In southern and eastern England the soil was thin and easily depleted by grain growing.

Surveyors measure a field for land enclosure. The enclosure movement eliminated large areas of what had formerly been communal land.

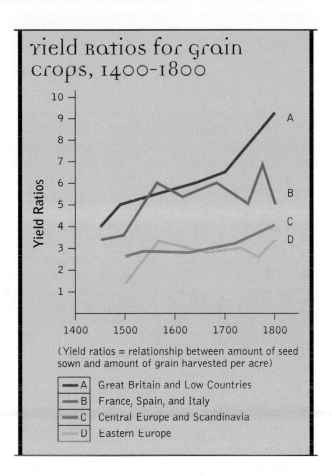

Yield Ratios for Grain Crops, 1400–1800

Yield Ratios

(Yield ratios = relationship between amount of seed sown and amount of grain harvested per acre)

—— A	Great Britain and Low Countries
—— B	France, Spain, and Italy
—— C	Central Europe and Scandinavia
—— D	Eastern Europe

farming in England produced enough food for 1.7 people; in 1800 each produced enough for 2.5. Cheaper food allowed more discretionary spending, which fueled the demand for consumer goods, which in turn employed more rural manufacturers. But there are no benefits without costs. The transformation of agriculture was also a transformation in a way of life. The open-field village was a community; the enclosed estate was a business. The plight of the rural poor was tragic enough in villages of kin and neighbors, where face-to-face charity might be returned from one generation to the next. With their scrap of land and their common rights, even the poorest villagers laid claim to a place of their own. But as landless laborers, either on farms or in rural manufacturing, they could no longer make that claim. They would soon be fodder for the factories, the "dark satanic mills" that came to disfigure the land once tilled in open-field villages. For the destitute, charity was now visited upon them in anonymous parish workhouses or in the good works of the comfortable middle class. In all of these ways the agricultural revolution changed the face of Europe.

The Industrial Revolution in Britain

Like the changes in agriculture, the changes in manufacturing that began in Britain during the eighteenth century were more revolutionary in consequence than in development. But their consequences were revolutionary indeed. A work force that was predominantly agricultural in 1750 had become predominantly industrial a century later. A population that for centuries had centered on the south and east was now concentrated in the north and west. Liverpool, Manchester, Glasgow, and Birmingham mushroomed into giant cities. While the population of England grew by 100 percent between 1801 and 1851, from about 8.5 million people to over 17 million, the populations of Liverpool and Manchester grew by over 1000 percent.

It was the replacement of animal muscle by hydraulic and mineral energy that made this continued population growth possible. Water and coal drove machinery that dramatically increased human productivity. In 1812, one woman could spin as much thread as 200 women had in 1770. What was most revolutionary about the Industrial Revolution was the wave after wave of technological innovation, a constant tinkering and improving of the ways in which things were made, which

Traditionally, these light soil areas had been used almost exclusively for sheep rearing. On the other hand, the clay soils of central England, though poorly drained and hard to work, were more suited to grain growing. The new agricultural techniques reversed the pattern. The introduction of fodder crops and increased fertilization rejuvenated thin soils, and southeastern England became the nation's breadbasket. Large enclosed estates provided a surplus of grain throughout the eighteenth century. By the 1760s, England was exporting enough grain to feed over a half million people. Similarly, the midland clays became the location of great sheep runs and cattle herds. Experiments in herd management, crossbreeding, and fattening all resulted in increased production of wool, milk, meat, leather, soap, and tallow for candles.

There can be no doubt about the benefits of the transformation of agricultural practices that began in Holland and England in the seventeenth century and spread slowly to all corners of the Continent over the next 200 years. Millions more mouths were fed at lower cost than ever before. In 1700 each person engaged in could have the simultaneous effects of cutting costs and improving quality. It was not just the great breakthrough inventions like the steam engine, the smelting of iron with coke, and the spinning jenny that were important, but also the hundreds of adjustments in technique that applied new ideas in one industry to another, opened bottlenecks, and solved problems. Ingenuity rather than genius was at the root of the Industrial Revolution in Britain.

The Industrial Revolution was a sustained period of economic growth and change brought about by the application of mineral energy and technological innovations to the process of manufacturing. It took place during the century between 1750 and 1850, though different industries moved at different paces and sustained economic growth continued in Britain until the First World War. It is difficult to define the timing of the Industrial Revolution with any great precision because, unlike a political event, an economic transformation does not happen all at once. Nor are new systems and inventions ever really new. Coal miners had been using rails and wheeled carriages to move ore since the seventeenth century. In the sixteenth century, "Jack of Newbury" had housed his cloth workers in a large shed. The one was the precursor of the railroad and the other the precursor of the factory, but each preceded the Industrial Revolution by more than a century. Before 1750, innovations made their way slowly into general use, and after 1850 the pace of growth slowed appreciably. By then, Britain had a manufacturing economy: fewer than one-quarter of its labor force engaged in agriculture and nearly 60 percent were involved in industry, trade, and transport.

Britain First

The Industrial Revolution occurred first in Britain, but even in Britain industrialization was a regional rather than a national phenomenon. There were many areas of Britain that remained untouched by innovations in manufacturing methods and agricultural techniques, though no one remained unaffected by the prosperity that industrialization brought. This was the result of both national conditions and historical developments. When industrialization spread to the Continent, it took hold—as it had in Britain—in regions where mineral resources were abundant or where domestic manufacturing was a traditional activity. There was no single model for European industrialization, however often contemporaries looked toward Britain for the key to unlock the power of economic growth. There was as much technological innovation in France, as much capital for investment in Holland. Belgium was rich in coal, while eastern Europe enjoyed an agricultural surplus that sustained an increase in population. The finest cotton in the world was made in India; the best iron was made in Sweden. Each of these factors was in some way a precondition for industrialization, but none by itself proved sufficient. Only in Britain did these circumstances meld together.

Among Britain's blessings, water was foremost. Water was its best defense, protecting the island from foreign invasion and making it unnecessary to invest in a costly standing army. Rather, Britain invested heavily in its navy to maintain its commercial preeminence around the globe. The navy protected British interests in times of war and transported British wares in times of peace. Britain's position in the Asian trade made it the leading importer of cottons, ceramics, and teas. Its colonies, especially in North America, not only provided sugar and tobacco but also formed a rich market for British manufacturing.

But the commercial advantages that water brought were not confined to oceanic trade. Britain was favored

Great Britain—Canals and Navigable Rivers

by an internal water system that tied inland communities together. In the eighteenth century, no place in Britain was more than 70 miles from the sea or more than 30 miles from a navigable river. Water transport was far cheaper than hauling goods overland; a packhorse could carry 250 pounds of goods on its back but could move 100,000 pounds by walking alongside a river and pulling a barge. Small wonder that river transport was one of the principal interests of merchants and traders. Beginning in the 1760s, private concerns began to invest in the construction of canals, first to move coal from inland locations to major arteries and then to connect the great rivers themselves. Over the next 50 years several hundred miles of canals were built by authority of Navigation Acts, which allowed for the sale of shares to raise capital. In 1760 the Duke of Bridgewater (1736–1803) lived up to his name by completing the first great canal. It brought coal to Manchester and ultimately to Liverpool. It cost more than £250,000 and took 14 years of labor to build, but it repaid the duke and his investors many times over by bringing an uneconomical coal field into production. Not the least of the beneficiaries were the people of Manchester, where the price of coal was halved.

Coal was the second of Britain's natural blessings on which it improved. Britain's reserves of wood were nearly depleted by the eighteenth century, especially

Great Britain—Coal and Iron Ore Deposits

The Worsley-Manchester Canal, as shown in Arthur Young's Six Months' Tour Through the North of England, 1770. *This view shows the mouth of the subterranean tunnel at Worsley, where the canal was driven underground to a coal mine. The crane was used to hoist blocks of stone onto canal boats.*

those near centers of population. Coal had been in use as a fuel for several centuries, and the coal trade between London and the northern coal pits had been essential to the growth of the capital. Coal was abundant, much of it almost at surface level along the northeastern coast and easily transported on water. The location of large coalfields along waterways was a vital condition of its early use. As canals and roadways improved, more inland coal was brought into production for domestic use. Yet it was in industry rather than in the home that coal was put to its greatest use. Here again Britain was favored, for large seams of coal were also located near large seams of iron. At first this coincidence was of little consequence, since iron was smelted by charcoal made from wood and iron foundries were located deep in forests. But ultimately ironmakers learned to use coal for fuel, and then the natural economies of having mineral, fuel, and transport in the same vicinity were given full play.

The factors that contributed to Britain's early industrialization were not only those of natural advantage. Over the course of years, Britain had developed an infrastructure for economic advancement. The transformation of domestic handicrafts to industrial production depended as much on the abilities of merchants as on those of manufacturers. The markets for domestic manufacturing had largely been overseas, where British merchants built up relationships over generations. Export markets were vital to the success of industrialization as production grew dynamically and most ventures needed a quick turnaround of sales to reinvest their profits in continued growth. The flexibility of English trading houses would be seen in their ability to shift from reexporting Eastern and North American goods to exporting British manufactures. Equally important, increased production meant increased demand for raw materials: Swedish bar iron for casting, Egyptian and American cotton for textiles, and Oriental silk for luxuries. The expansion of shipping mirrored the expansion of the economy, tripling during the eighteenth century to over 1 million tons of cargo capacity.

The expansion of shipping, agriculture, and investment in machines, plant, and raw material all required capital. Not only did capital have to exist, but it had to be made productive. Profits in agriculture, especially in the south and east, somehow had to be shifted to investment in industry in the north and west. The wealth of merchants, which flowed into London, had to be redistributed throughout the economy. More importantly, short-term investments had to give way to long-term financing. At the end of the seventeenth century, the creation of the Bank of England had begun the process of constructing a reliable banking system. The Bank of England dealt almost entirely with government securities, but it also served as a bill broker. It bought the debts of reputable merchants at a discount in exchange for Bank of England notes. Bank of England notes could then be exchanged between merchants, and this increased the liquidity of the English economy, especially in London. It also became the model for provincial banking by the middle of the eighteenth century.

Private family banks also grew in importance in London, handling the accounts of merchants and buying shares in profitable enterprises, of which the canals were a favorite. Regional banks, smaller and less capitalized, began to use these private London banks as correspondents, that is, as extensions of their own banks in the city. This allowed local manufacturers and city merchants to do business with one another. The connections between the regional banks and London facilitated the flow of capital from one section of the nation to the other. In 1700 there were just 12 provincial banks; by 1790 there were nearly 300. Banks remained reluctant to invest for the long term, preferring to discount bills for a few months, but after they developed a relationship with a particular firm, they were usually willing to continue to roll the debt over. Although the banking system was vital to large enterprises, in fact the capital for most industry was raised locally, from kin and neighbors, and grew by plowing back profits into the business. At least at the beginning, manufacturers were willing to take risks and to work for small returns to ensure the survival and growth of their business.

Minerals and Metals

There could have been no Industrial Revolution without coal. It was the black gold of the eighteenth century, the fuel that fed the furnaces and turned the engines of industrial expansion. The coal produced by one miner generated as much energy as 20 horses. Coal was the first capital-intensive industry in Britain, already well developed by the seventeenth century. Owners paid the costs of sinking shafts, building roads, and erecting winding machines. Miners were brought to a pit and paid piecework for their labor. Only the very wealthy could afford to invest in coal mining, and it was by chance that British law vested mineral rights in owners rather than users of the land, as was the case on the Continent. This meant that the largest English coalfields were owned by landed families of means who were able to invest agricultural profits in mining. Britain's traditional elites thus played a crucial role in the industrial transformation of the agrarian economy from which their wealth and social standing had derived.

The technical problems of coal mining grew with demand. As surface seams were exhausted it became necessary to dig deeper shafts, to lower miners farther underground, and to raise the coal greater heights to the surface. Men loosened the coal from the seam; women and children hauled it to the shaft. They also cleared the tons of debris that came loose with the coal. Underground mining was extremely dangerous. In addition to all-too-frequent cave-ins, miners struggled against inadequate ventilation and light. Better ventilation was achieved by the expensive method of sinking

Joseph Wright of Derby, A Blacksmith's Shop (1771). Many of Wright's paintings are associated with the industrial revolution of the eighteenth century, but his principal artistic interest was in the dramatic rendering of light and shade. Nevertheless the three men at the anvil shown here wear typical working clothes and strike realistic poses. The two boys on the right react differently to the scene. The boy in front turns away from the noise and the heat, while behind him the other, whose attire suggests that he is an apprentice, looks on steadily.

second and third shafts into the same seam, allowing for cross breezes. Candles and sparks created by flint wheels addressed the problem of light, though both methods suffered from the disadvantage that most pits contained combustible gases. Even after a fireman walked through the mine exploding gas with a long lighted stick, many miners preferred to work in total darkness, feeling the edges of the seam.

But by far the most difficult mining problem was water. As pits were sunk deeper they reached pools of groundwater, which enlarged as the coal was stripped away from the earth. Dripping water increased the difficulty of hewing, standing water the difficulty of hauling. The pit acted like a riverbed and filled quickly. Water drainage presented the greatest obstacle to deep-shaft mining. Women and children could carry the water out in large skin-lined baskets, which were attached to a winding wheel and pulled up by horses. Primitive pumps, also horse-powered, had been devised for the same purpose. Neither method was efficient or effective when shafts sank deeper. In 1709 Thomas Newcomen (1663–1729) introduced a steam-driven pump that enabled water to be sucked through a pipe directly from the pit bottom to the surface. Although the engine was expensive to build and needed tons of coal to create the steam, it could raise the same amount of water in a day as 2500 humans. Such economies of labor were enormous, and within 20 years of its introduction there were 78 engines draining coal and metal mines in England.

Innovations like Newcomen's engine helped increase output of coal at just the time that it became needed as an industrial fuel. Between 1700 and 1830, coal production increased tenfold despite the fact that deeper and more difficult seams were being worked. Eventually, the largest demand for coal came from the iron industry. In 1793 just two ironworks consumed as much coal as the entire population of Edinburgh. Like mining coal, making iron was both capital- and labor-intensive, requiring expensive furnaces, water-powered bellows, and mills in which forged iron could be slit into rods or rolled into sheets. Ironmaking depended upon an abundance of wood, for it took the charcoal derived from 10 acres of trees to refine 1 ton of iron ore. After the ore was mined, it was smelted into pig iron, a low-grade, brittle metal. Pig iron was converted to higher-quality bar iron in charcoal-powered forges that burned off some of its impurities. From bar iron came the rods and sheets used in casting household items like pots and nails or in making finer wrought-iron products like plows and armaments. Because each process in the making of iron was separate, furnaces, forges, and mills were located near their own supplies of wood. The shipping of the bulky ore, pig iron, and bar iron added substantially to its cost, and it was cheaper to import bars from Sweden than to carry them 20 miles overland.

The great innovations in the production of iron came with the development of techniques that allowed for the use of coal rather than wood charcoal in smelting and forging. As early as 1709, Abraham Darby (1678?–1717), a Quaker nail maker, experimented with smelting iron ore with coke, coal from which most of the gas has been burned off. Iron coking greatly reduced the cost of fuel in the first stages of production, but because most ironworks were located in woodlands rather than near coal pits, the method was not widely adopted. Moreover, although coke made from coal was cheaper than charcoal made from wood, coke added its own impurities to the iron ore. Nor could it provide the intense heat needed for smelting without a large bellows. The cost of the bellows offset the savings from the coke until James Watt (1736–1819) invented a new form of steam engine in 1775.

Like most innovations of the Industrial Revolution, Watt's steam engine was an adaptation of existing technology made possible by the sophistication of techniques in a variety of fields. Although James Watt is credited with the invention of the condensing steam engine, one of the seminal creations in human history, the success of his work depended upon the achievements of numerous others. Watt's introduction to the steam engine was accidental. An instrument maker in Glasgow, he was asked to repair a model of a Newcomen engine and immediately realized that it would work more efficiently if there were a separate chamber for the condensation of the steam. Although his idea was sound, Watt spent years attempting to implement it. He was continually frustrated that poor-quality valves and cylinders never fit well enough together to prevent steam from escaping from the engine.

Watt was unable to translate his idea into a practical invention until he became partners with the Birmingham ironmaker and manufacturer Matthew Boulton (1728–1809). At Boulton's works, Watt found craftsmen who could make precision engine valves, and at the foundries of John Wilkinson (1728–1808) he found workers who could bore the cylinders of his engine to exact specifications. Watt's partnership with Boulton and Wilkinson was vital to the success of the steam engine. But Watt himself possessed the qualities necessary to ensure that his ideas were transformed into reality. He

Women and children were the cheapest labor force in England during the Industrial Revolution. They were sometimes employed in heavy work such as mining. Here two children are being raised to ground level from the mine pit.

persevered through years of unsuccessful experimentation and searched out partners to provide capital and expertise. He saw beyond bare mechanics, realizing the practical utility of his invention long before it was perfected. Watt designed the mechanism to convert the traditional up-and-down motion of the pumping engine into rotary motion, which could be used for machines and ultimately for locomotion.

Watt's engine received its first practical application in the iron industry. Wilkinson became one of the largest customers for steam engines, using them for pumping, moving wheels, and ultimately increasing the power of the blast of air in the forge. Increasing the heat provided by coke in the smelting and forging of iron led to the transformation of the industry. In the 1780s, Henry Cort (1740–1800), a naval contractor, experimented with a technique for using coke as fuel in removing the impurities from pig iron. The iron was melted into puddles and stirred with rods. The gaseous carbon that was brought to the surface burned off, leaving a purer and more malleable iron than even charcoal could produce. Because the iron had been purified in a molten state, Cort reasoned that it could be rolled directly into sheets rather than first made into bars. He erected a rolling mill adjacent to his forge and combined two separate processes into one.

Puddling and rolling had an immediate impact upon iron production. There was no longer any need to use charcoal in the stages of forging and rolling. From mineral to workable sheets, iron could be made entirely with coke. Ironworks moved to the coalfields, where the economies of transporting fuel and finished product were great. Moreover, the distinct stages of production were eliminated. Rather than separate smelting, forging, and finishing industries, one consolidated manufacturing process had been created. Forges, furnaces, and rolling machines were brought together and powered by steam engines. Cort's rolling technique alone increased output 15 times. By 1808, output of pig iron had grown from 68,000 to 250,000 tons and of bar iron from 32,000 to 100,000 tons.

cotton is king

Traditionally, British commerce had been dominated by the woolen cloth trade, in which techniques of production had not changed for hundreds of years. Running water was used for cleaning and separating fleece; crude wooden wheels spun the thread; simple handlooms wove together the long warp threads and the short weft ones. It took nearly four female spinners to provide the materials for one male weaver, the tasks having long been gender-specific. During the course of the seventeenth century, new fabrics appeared on the domestic market, particularly linen, silk, and cotton. It was cotton that captured the imagination of the eigh-

An engraving of the Soho Engineering Works at Birmingham, England. Here James Watt and his partner Matthew Boulton manufactured steam engines from 1775 to 1810.

Great Britain—Textile Centers

teenth-century consumer, especially brightly colored, finely spun Indian cotton.

Spinning and weaving were organized as domestic industries. Work was done in the home on small, inexpensive machines to supplement the income from farming. Putters-out were especially frustrated by the difficulty in obtaining yarn for weaving in the autumn, when female laborers were needed for the harvest. Even the widespread development of full-time domestic manufacturers did not satisfy the increased demand for cloth. Limited output and variable quality characterized British textile production throughout the early part of the eighteenth century. The breakthrough came with technological innovation. Beginning in the mid-eighteenth century, a series of new machines dramatically increased output and, for the first time, allowed English textiles to compete with Indian imports.

The first innovation was the flying shuttle, invented by John Kay (1704–64) in the 1730s. A series of hammers drove the shuttle, which held the weft, through the stretched warp on the loom. The flying shuttle allowed weavers to work alone rather than in pairs, but it was adopted slowly because it increased the demand for spun thread, which was already in short supply. The

spinning bottleneck was opened by James Hargreaves (d. 1778), who devised a machine known as the jenny. The jenny was a wooden frame containing a number of spindles around which thread was drawn by means of a hand-turned wheel. The first jennies allowed for the spinning of 8 threads at once, and improvements brought the number to over 100. Jennies replaced spinning wheels by the tens of thousands. The jenny was a crucial breakthrough in redressing the balance between spinning and weaving, though it did not solve all problems. Jenny-spun thread was not strong enough to be used as warp, which continued to be wheel spun. But the jenny could spin cotton in unimaginable quantities.

As is often the case with technological change, one innovation followed another. The problem set by improvements in weaving gave rise to solutions for increasing the output of spinners. The need to provide stronger warp threads posed by the introduction of the jenny was ultimately solved by the development of the water frame. It was created in 1769 by Richard Arkwright (1732–92), whose name was also to be associated with the founding of the modern factory system. Arkwright's frame consisted of a series of water-power-driven rollers that stretched the cotton before spinning. These stronger fibers could be spun into threads suitable for warp, and English manufacturers could finally produce an all-cotton fabric. It was not long before another innovator realized that the water frame and the jenny could be combined into a single machine, one that would produce an even finer cotton yarn than that made in India. The mule, so named because it was a cross between a frame and a jenny, was invented by Samuel Crompton (1753–1827), who sold its rights for only £60. It was the decisive innovation in cotton production. By 1811, ten times as many threads were being spun on mules as on water frames and jennies combined.

The original mules were small machines that, like the jennies, could be used for domestic manufactures. But increasingly the mule followed the water frame into purposely built factories, where it became larger and more expensive. The need for large rooms to house the equipment and for a ready source of running water to power it provided an incentive for the creation of factories, but secrecy provided a greater one. The original factories were called "safe-boxes," and whether they were established for the manufacture of silk or cotton, their purpose was to protect trade secrets. Innovators took out patents to prevent their inventions from being copied and fought long lawsuits to prevent their machines from being used. Workers were sworn to secrecy

This hand-colored engraving shows the interior of a German weaver's shop around 1850. Two men are weaving at looms and two women are winding bobbins. The scene is bordered with details of tools such as shuttles and quills.

about the techniques they were taught. Imitators practiced industrial espionage as sophisticated as the age would allow: enticing knowledgeable workers; employing spies; copying inventions. Although the factory was designed to protect secrets, its other benefits were quickly realized. Manufacturers could maintain control over the quality of products through strict supervision of the work force. Moreover, workers in shifts could keep the costly machines in continuous use.

Richard Arkwright constructed the first cotton factories in Britain, all of which were designed to house water frames. The first was established in 1769 at Cromford near Nottingham, which was the center of stocking manufacture. The site was chosen for its isolation, since stockings were an article of fashion in which secrecy was most important. The Cromford mill was a four-story building that ultimately employed over 800 workers. During the next quarter century, Arkwright built over a dozen other mills, most in partnership with wealthy manufacturers. Arkwright's genius lay in industrial management rather than mechanical innovation. As others switched from frames to mules, Arkwright stubbornly stuck to his own invention. When steam power began to replace water, he failed to make the shift. But his methods of constructing and financing factories were undeniably successful. From a modest beginning as a traveling salesman of wigs, Sir Richard Arkwright died in possession of a fortune worth more than £500,000.

The organization of the cotton industry into factories was one of the pivotal transformations in economic life. Domestic spinning and weaving took place in agricultural villages; factory production took place in mill towns. The location of the factory determined movements of population, and from the first quarter of the eighteenth century onward a great shift toward northeast England was under way. Moreover, the character of the work itself changed. The operation of heavy machinery reversed the traditional gender-based tasks. Mule spinning became men's work, while handloom weaving was taken over by women. The mechanization of weaving took longer than that of spinning, both because of difficulties in perfecting a power loom and because of opposition to its introduction by workers known as Luddites, who organized machine-breaking riots in the 1810s. The Luddites attempted to maintain the traditional organization of their industry and the indepen-

The wealth of Britain

Cotton was the first of the new industries that led to British economic domination in the nineteenth century. In producing cotton, new inventions like the spinning jenny and the water frame revolutionized manufacture and the factory system was born. Britain's domination of cotton production impressed contemporaries. In this excerpt, a contemporary tries to explain why Britain took the lead in industrialization.

In comparing the advantages of England for manufactures with those of other countries, we can by no means overlook the excellent commercial position of the country—intermediate between the north and south of Europe; and its insular situation, which, combined with the command of the seas, secures our territory from invasion or annoyance. The German ocean, the Baltic, and the Mediterranean are the regular highways for our ships; and our western ports command an unobstructed passage to the Atlantic, and to every quarter of the world.

A temperate climate, and a hardy race of men, have also greatly contributed to promote the manufacturing industry of England.

The political and moral advantages of this country, as a seat of manufactures, are not less remarkable than its physical advantages. The arts are the daughters of peace and liberty. In no country have these blessings been enjoyed in so high a degree, or for so long a continuance, as in England. Under the reign of just laws, personal liberty and property have been secure; mercantile enterprise has been allowed to reap its reward; capital has accumulated in safety; the workman has "gone forth to his work and to his labour until the evening;" and, thus protected and favoured, the manufacturing prosperity of the country has struck its roots deep, and spread forth its branches to the ends of the earth.

England has also gained by the calamities of other countries, and the intolerance of other governments. At different periods, the Flemish and French protestants, expelled from their native lands, have taken refuge in England, and have repaid the protection given them by practising and teaching branches of industry, in which the English were then less expert than their neighbours.

From Edward Baines, *The History of the Cotton Manufacture in Great Britain* (1835).

---

dence of their labor. For a time, handloom weavers managed to survive by accepting lower and lower piece rates. But their competition was like that of a horse against an automobile. In 1820 there were over 250,000 handloom weavers in Britain; by 1850 the number was less than 50,000. Weaving as well as spinning became factory work.

The transformation of cotton manufacture had a profound effect on the overall growth of the British economy. It increased shipping because the raw material had to be imported, first from the Mediterranean and then from America. American cotton—especially after 1794, when American inventor Eli Whitney (1765–1825) patented his cotton gin—fed a nearly insatiable demand. In 1750 Britain imported less than 5 million pounds of raw cotton; a century later the volume had grown to 588 million pounds. And to each pound of raw cotton, British manufacturers added the value of their technology and their labor. By the mid-nineteenth century, nearly a half million people earned their living from cotton, which alone accounted for over 40 percent of the value of all British exports. Cotton was undeniably the king of manufactured goods.

The Iron Horse

The first stage of the Industrial Revolution in Britain was driven by the production of consumer goods. Pottery, cast-iron tools, clocks, toys, and textiles, especially cottons—all were manufactured in quantities unknown in the early eighteenth century. These products fed a ravenous market at home and abroad. The greatest complaint of industrialists was that they could not get enough raw materials or fuel, nor could they ship their finished products fast enough to keep up with demand. Transportation was becoming a serious stumbling block to continued economic growth. Even with the completion of the canal network that linked the major rivers and improvement in highways and tollways, raw materials and finished goods moved slowly and uncertainly. It was said that it took as long to ship goods from Manchester to Liverpool on the Duke of Bridgewater's canal as it did to sail from New York to Liverpool on the Atlantic Ocean. Furthermore, once the canals had a monopoly on bulk cargo, transportation costs began to rise.

It was the need to ship increasing amounts of coal to foundries and factories that provided the spur for the development of a new form of transportation. Ever since the seventeenth century, coal had been moved from the seam to the pit on rails, first constructed of wood and later of iron. Broad-wheeled carts hitched to horses were as much dragged as rolled, but this still represented the most efficient form of hauling, and these railways ultimately ran from the seam to the dock. By 1800 there was perhaps as much as 300 miles of iron rail in British mines.

In the same year, Watt's patent on the steam engine expired, and inventors began to apply the engine to a variety of mechanical tasks. Richard Trevithick (1771–1833), whose father managed a tin mine in Cornwall, was the first to experiment with a steam-driven carriage. George Stephenson (1781–1848), who is generally recognized as the father of the modern railroad, made two crucial improvements. In mine railways the wheels of the cart were smooth and the rail was grooved. Stephenson reversed this construction to provide better traction and less wear. Perhaps more importantly, Stephenson made the vital improvement in

engine power by increasing the steam pressure in the boiler and exhausting the smoke through a chimney. In 1829 he won a £500 prize with his engine "The Rocket," which pulled a load three times its own weight at a speed of 30 miles per hour and could actually outrun a horse.

In 1830 the first modern railway, the Manchester-to-Liverpool line, was opened. Like the Duke of Bridgewater's canal, it was designed to move coal and bulk goods, but surprisingly its most important function came to be moving people. In its first year, the Manchester-Liverpool line carried over 400,000 passengers, which generated double the revenue derived from freight. The railway was quicker, more comfortable, and ultimately cheaper than the coach. Investors in the Manchester-Liverpool line, who pocketed a comfortable 9.5 percent when government securities were paying 3.5 percent, learned quickly that links between population centers were as important as those between industrial sites. The London-to-Birmingham and London-to-Bristol lines were both designed with passenger traffic in mind.

Railway building was one of the great boom activities of British industrialization. Since it came toward the end of the mechanization of factories, investors and industrialists were psychologically prepared for the benefits of technological innovation. By 1835 Parliament had passed 54 separate acts to establish over 750 miles of railways. Ten years later, over 6000 miles had

In the eighteenth century a number of British inventors patented new machines that transformed the British textile industry and marked the beginning of the Industrial Revolution. Among these inventions was the spinning jenny, invented by James Hargreaves in 1764, and named for his daughter. The jenny, which permitted the spinning of a number of threads at the same time, made possible the automatic production of cotton thread.

Great Britain—Railroads, ca. 1850

been sanctioned and over 2500 miles built; by 1852 over 7500 miles of track were in use. The railways were built on the model of the canals. Private bills passed through Parliament, which allowed a company to raise money through the sale of stock. Most railways were trunk lines, connecting one town to another or joining two longer lines together. They were run by small companies, and few ultimately proved profitable. Only because of the dominant influence of George Stephenson and his son Robert (1803–59) was there an attempt to establish a standard gauge for tracks and engines. Britain was the only country in which the government did not take a leading role in building the railways. Hundreds of millions of pounds were raised privately, and in the end it is calculated that the railroads cost £40,000 a mile to build, more than three times the cost per mile of railroads on the Continent and in the United States.

Nevertheless, the investment paid huge dividends. By the 1850s, the original purpose of the railways was being realized as freight revenues finally surpassed passenger revenues. Coal was the dominant cargo shipped by rail, and the speedy, efficient service continued to drive down prices. The iron and steel industries were modernized on the back of demand for rails, engines,

and cast-iron seats and fittings. In peak periods—and railway building was a boom-and-bust affair—as much as a quarter of the output of the rolling mills went into domestic railroads, and much more into Continental systems. The railways were also a massive consumer of bricks for beddings, sidings, and especially bridges, tunnels, and stations. Finally, the railways were a leading employer of labor, surpassing the textile mills in peak periods. Hundreds of thousands worked in tasks as varied as engineering and ditch digging, for even in this most advanced industry, sophisticated mechanized production went hand in hand with traditional drudgery. Over 60,000 workers were permanently engaged in the industry to run trains, mind stations, and repair track. Countless others were employed in manufacturing engines, carriages, boxcars, and the thousands of components that went into making them.

Most of all, the railroads changed the nature of people's lives. Whole new concepts of time, space, and speed emerged to govern daily activities. As Henry Booth, an early railroad official, observed, "Notions which we have received from our ancestors and verified by our own experience are overthrown in a day. What was slow is now quick; what was distant is now near." Coach travel had ordinarily been limited to those with means, not only because it was expensive, but also because it was time-consuming. Ordinary people could not take off the days necessary to complete relatively short round-trip journeys. When passenger rail service began, there was even a debate over whether provision should be made for third-class passengers, a class unknown on the coaches, where the only choices were riding inside for comfort or outside for savings. Third-class passengers quickly became the staple of railroad service. The cheap excursion was born to provide short holidays or even day trips. The career of Thomas Cook (1808–92), who became the world's first travel agent, began after he took a short excursion. Over 6 million people visited London by train to view the Crystal Palace exhibition in 1851, a number equivalent to one-third of the population of England and Wales. The railways did more than link places; they brought people together and helped develop a sense of national identity by speeding all forms of communication.

entrepreneurs and managers

The Industrial Revolution in Britain was not simply invented. Too much credit is given to a few breakthroughs and too little to the ways in which they were improved

This representation of travel on the Liverpool and Manchester railway illustrates the great difference between first-class (top) and second-class (bottom) travel conditions.

and dispersed. The Industrial Revolution was an age of gadgets when people believed that new was better than old and that there was always room for improvement. "The age is running mad after innovation," the English moralist Dr. Johnson wrote. "All the business of the world is done in a new way; men are hanged in a new way." Societies for the advancement of knowledge sprang up all over Britain. Journals and magazines promoted new ideas and techniques. Competitions were held for the best invention of the year; prizes were awarded for agricultural achievements. Practical rather than pure science was the hallmark of industrial development.

Yet technological innovation was not the same as industrialization. A vital change in economic activity took place in the organization of industry. Putters-out with their circulating capital and hired laborers could never make the economies necessary to increase output and quality while simultaneously lowering costs. This was the achievement of industrialists, producers who owned workplace, machinery, and raw materials and invested fixed capital by plowing back their profits. Industrial enterprises came in all sizes and shapes. A cotton mill could be started with as little as £300 or as much as £10,000. As late as 1840, fewer than 10 percent of the mills employed over 500 workers. Most were family concerns with under 100 employees, and many of them failed. For every story with a happy ending, there was

another with a sad one. When Major Edmund Cartwright (1740–1824) erected a cotton mill, he was offered a Watt steam engine built for a distiller who had gone bankrupt. He acquired his machinery at the auction of another bankrupt. Cartwright's mill, engine, and machinery ended on the auction block less than three years later. There were over 30,000 bankruptcies in the eighteenth century, testimony both to the risks of business and to the willingness of entrepreneurs to take them.

To survive against these odds, successful industrialists had to be both entrepreneur and manager. As entrepreneurs they raised capital, almost always locally from relatives, friends, or members of their church. Quakers were especially active in financing each other's enterprises. The industrial entrepreneur also had to understand the latest methods for building and powering machinery and the most up-to-date techniques for performing the work. One early manufacturer claimed "a practical knowledge of every process from the cotton-bag to the piece of cloth." Finally, entrepreneurs had to know how to market their goods. In these functions, industrial entrepreneurs developed logically from putters-out.

But industrialists also had to be managers. The most difficult task was organization of the workplace. Most gains in productivity were achieved through the special-

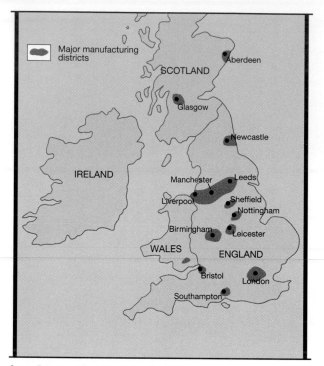

Great Britain—Manufacturing Centers

ization of function. The processes of production were divided and subdivided until workers performed a basic task over and over. The education of the work force was the industrial manager's greatest challenge. Workers had to be taught how to use and maintain their machines and disciplined to apply themselves continuously. At least at the beginning, it was difficult to staff the factories. Many employed children as young as seven from workhouses or orphanages, who, though cheap to pay, were difficult to train and discipline. It was the task of the manager to break old habits of intermittent work, indifference to quality, and petty theft of materials. Families were preferred to individuals, for then parents could instruct and supervise their children. There is no reason to believe that industrial managers were more brutal masters than farmers or that children were treated better in workhouses than in mills. Labor was a business asset, what was sometimes called "living machinery," and its control with carrots and sticks was the chief concern of the industrial manager.

Who were the industrialists who transformed the traditional economy? Because British society was relatively open, they came from every conceivable background: dukes and orphans, merchants and salesmen,

inventors and improvers. Though some went from rags to riches—like Richard Arkwright, who was the thirteenth child of a poor barber—it was extremely difficult for a laborer to acquire the capital necessary to set up a business. Wealthy landowners were prominent in capital-intensive aspects of industries—for example, owning ironworks and mines—but few established factories. Most industrialists came from the middle classes, which, while comprising one-third of the British population, provided as much as two-thirds of the first generation of industrialists. These included lawyers, bankers, merchants, and those already engaged in manufacturing, as well as tradesmen, shopkeepers, and self-employed artisans. The career of every industrialist was different, as a look at two—Josiah Wedgwood and Robert Owen—will show.

Josiah Wedgwood (1730–95) was the thirteenth child of a long-established English potting family. He worked in the potteries from childhood, but a deformed leg made it difficult for him to turn the wheel. Instead he studied the structure of the business. His head teemed with ideas for improving ceramic manufacturing, but it was not until he was 30 that he could set up on his own and introduce his innovations. These encompassed both technique and organization, the entrepreneurial and managerial sides of his business.

Wedgwood developed new mixtures of clays that took brilliant colors in the kiln and new glazes for both useful and ornamental ware. His technical innovations were all the more remarkable in that he had little education in mineral chemistry and made his discoveries by simple trial and error. But there was nothing of either luck or good fortune in Wedgwood's managerial innovations. He was repelled by the disorder of the traditional pottery, with its waste of materials, uneven quality, and slow output. When he began his first works, he divided the making of pottery into distinct tasks and assigned separate workers to them. One group did nothing but throw the pots on the wheel; another painted designs; a third glazed. To achieve this division of function, Wedgwood had to train his own workers almost from childhood. Traditional potters performed every task from molding to glazing and prized the fact that no two pieces were ever alike. Wedgwood wanted each piece to replicate another, and he stalked the works breaking defective wares on his wooden leg. He invested in schools to help train young artists, in canals to transport his products, and in London shops to sell them. Wedgwood was a marketing genius. He named his famed cream-colored pottery Queen's Ware and made special coffee

Jasperware copy of the Portland vase by Josiah Wedgwood. The Portland vase is one of the most famous ancient vases. It was found near Rome in the seventeenth century in a tomb believed to be that of Alexander Severus.

place. He replaced old machinery with new, reduced working hours, and instituted a monitoring system to check theft. To enhance life outside the factory, he established a high-quality company-run store, which plowed its profits into a school for village children.

Owen was struck by the irony that in the mills, machines were better cared for than were humans. He thought that with the same attention to detail that had so improved the quality of commodities he could make even greater improvements in the quality of life. He prohibited children under 10 from mill work and instituted a 10-hour day for child labor. His local school took infants from one year old, freeing women to work and ensuring each child an education. Owen instituted old-age and disability pensions, funded by mandatory contributions from workers' wages. Taverns were closed and workers were fined for drunkenness and sexual offenses. In the factory and the village, Owen established a principle of communal regulation to improve both the work and the character of his employees. New Lanark became the model of the world of the future, and each year thousands made an industrial pilgrimage to visit it.

The wages of progress

Robert Owen ended his life as a social reformer. His efforts to improve the lot of his workers at New Lanark led to experiments to create ideal industrial communities throughout the world. He founded cooperative societies, in which all members shared in the profits of the business, and supported trade unions in which workers could better their lives. His followers planted colonies where goods were held in common and the fruits of labor belonged to the laborers. Owen's agitation for social reform was part of a movement that produced results of lasting consequence. The Factory Act (1833) prohibited factory work by children under nine, provided two hours of daily education, and effectively created a 12-hour day in the mills until the Ten Hours Act (1847). The Mines Act (1842) prohibited women and children from working underground.

Nor was Owen alone in dedicating time and money to the improvement of workers' lives. The rapid growth of unplanned cities exacerbated the plight of those too poor and overworked to help themselves. Conditions of housing and sanitation were appalling even by nineteenth-century standards. The *Report on the Sanitary Condition of the Laboring Population in Britain* (1842), written by Edwin Chadwick (1800–90), so shocked Parliament and the nation that it helped to shift the burden

and tea services for leading aristocratic families. He would then sell replicas by the thousands. In less than 20 years, Wedgwood pottery was prized all over Europe and Wedgwood's potting works were the standard of the industry.

Robert Owen (1771–1858) did not have a family business to develop. The son of a small tradesman, he was apprenticed to a clothier at the age of 10. As a teenager he worked as a shop assistant in Manchester, where he audaciously applied for a job as a manager of a cotton mill. At 19 he was supervising 500 workers and learning the cotton trade. Owen was immediately successful, increasing the output of his workers and introducing new materials to the mill. In 1816 he entered a partnership to purchase the New Lanark mill in Scotland. Owen found conditions in Scotland much worse than those in Manchester. Over 500 workhouse children were employed at New Lanark, where drunkenness and theft were endemic. Owen believed that to improve the quality of work one had to improve the quality of the work-

The sin of wages

Robert Owen was both a successful manufacturer and a leading philanthropist. He believed that economic advance had to take place in step with the improvement of the moral and physical well-being of the workers. He organized schools, company shops, and ultimately utopian communities in an effort to improve the lives of industrial laborers. Owen was one of the first social commentators to argue that industrialism threatened the fabric of family and community life.

The acquisition of wealth, and the desire which it naturally creates for a continued increase, have introduced a fondness for essentially injurious luxuries among a numerous class of individuals who formerly never thought of them, and they have also generated a disposition which strongly impels its possessors to sacrifice the best feelings of human nature to this love of accumulation. To succeed in this career, the industry of the lower orders, from whose labour this wealth is now drawn, has been carried by new competitors striving against those of longer standing, to a point of real oppression, reducing them by successive changes, as the spirit of competition increased and the ease of acquiring wealth diminished, to a state more wretched than can be imagined by those who have not attentively observed the changes as they have gradually occurred. In consequence, they are at present in a situation infinitely more degraded and miserable than they were before the introduction of these manufactories, upon the success of which their bare subsistence now depends. . . .

The inhabitants of every country are trained and formed by its great leading existing circumstances, and the character of the lower orders in Britain is now formed chiefly by circumstances arising from trade, manufactures, and commerce; and the governing principle of trade, manufactures, and commerce is immediate pecuniary gain, to which on the great scale every other is made to give way. All are sedulously trained to buy cheap and to sell dear; and to succeed in this art, the parties must be taught to acquire strong powers of deception; and thus a spirit is generated through every class of traders, destructive of that open, honest sincerity, without which man cannot make others happy, nor enjoy happiness himself.

From Robert Owen, *Observations on the Effect of the Manufacturing System* (1815).

of social reform to government. The Public Health Act (1848) established boards of health and the office of medical examiner, while the Vaccination Act (1853) and the Contagious Diseases Act (1864) attempted to control epidemics. (See "Industry and the Environment," pp. 722–723.)

The movement for social reform began almost as soon as industrialization. The Industrial Revolution initiated profound changes in the organization of British society. Cities sprang up from grain fields almost overnight. The lure of steady work and high wages prompted an exodus from rural Britain and spurred an unremitting boom in population. In the first half of the nineteenth century, the population of England doubled from 9 to 18 million, with growth most rapid in the newly urban north and west. In 1750, about 15 percent of the population lived in urban areas; by 1850, about 60 percent did. Industrial workers married younger and produced more children than their agricultural counterparts. For centuries women had married in their middle twenties, but by 1800, age at first marriage had dropped to 23 for the female population as a whole and to nearly 20 in the industrial areas. This was in part because factory hands did not have to wait until they inherited land or money, and in part because they did not have to serve an apprenticeship. But early marriage and large families were also a bet on the future, a belief that things were better now and would be even better soon, that the new mouths would be fed and the new bodies clothed. This was an investment on the part of ordinary people similar to that made by bankers and entrepreneurs when they risked their capital in new businesses. Was it an investment that paid off?

It is difficult to calculate the benefits of the Industrial Revolution or to weigh them against the costs. What is certain is that there was a vast expansion of wealth as well as a vast expansion of people to share it. Agricultural and industrial change made it possible to support comfortably a population over three times larger than that of the seventeenth century, when it was widely believed that England had reached the limits of expansion. Despite the fact that population doubled between 1801 and 1851, per capita income rose by 75 percent. That means that had the population remained stable, per capita income would have increased by a staggering 350 percent. At the same time, untold millions of pounds had been sunk into canals, roads, railways, factories, mines, and mills.

But the expansion of wealth is not the same as the improvement in the quality of life, for wealth is not equally distributed. An increase in the level of wealth may mean only that the rich are getting richer more quickly than the poor are getting poorer. Similarly, economic growth over a century involved the lives of several generations, each of which experienced different standards of living. One set of parents may have sacrificed for the future of their children; another may have mortgaged it. Moreover, economic activity is cyclical.

Trade depressions, like those induced by the War of 1812 and the American Civil War, which interrupted cotton supplies, could have disastrous short-term effects. The "Great Hunger" of the 1840s was a time of agrarian crisis and industrial slump. The downturn of 1842 threw 60 percent of the factory workers in the town of Bolton out of work at a time when there was neither unemployment insurance nor a welfare system. Finally, quality of life cannot be measured simply in economic terms. People with more money to spend may still be worse off than their ancestors, who may have preferred leisure to wealth or independence to the discipline of the clock.

Thus there are no easy answers to the quality-of-life question. In the first stages of industrialization, it seems clear that only the wealthy benefited economically, though much of their increased wealth was reinvested in expansion. Under the impact of population growth, the Napoleonic wars, and regional harvest failure, real wages seem to have fallen from the levels reached in the 1730s. Industrial workers were not substantially better

Dudley Street, Seven Dials, London, *by Gustave Doré, is a scene of life in the London slums of the early nineteenth century.*

industry and the environment

The Industrial Revolution changed the landscape of Britain. Small villages grew into vast metropolises seemingly overnight. The rates of growth were absolutely staggering: in 1801 there were 75,000 people in Manchester; by 1851 the number had more than quadrupled. This unremitting boom in population did more than strain the resources of local authorities: it broke them apart. It was not that the new industrial cities were unplanned; they were beyond the capacity of planning. Every essential requirement for human survival became scarce and expensive. Shortages of food, water, and basic accommodation were commonplace.

Shantytowns sprang up wherever space would allow, making the flimsily built habitations of construction profiteers seem like palaces. There was loud complaint about these nineteenth-century rip-off artists, but in truth the need for housing was so desperate that people willingly lived anywhere that provided shelter. Houses were built back to back and side by side, with only narrow alleyways to provide sunlight and air. In Edinburgh one could step through the window of one house into the window of the adjoining one. Whole families occupied single rooms where members slept as they worked, in shifts. In Liverpool over 38,000 people were estimated to be living in cellars—windowless underground accommodations that flooded with the rains and the tides.

Most cities lacked both running water and toilet facilities. Districts were provided with either pumps or capped pipes through which private companies ran water for a few hours each day. The water was collected in buckets and brought to the home, where it would stand for the rest of the day and serve indifferently for washing, drinking, and cooking. Outhouse toilets were an extravagant luxury; in one Manchester district 33 outhouses had to accommodate 7095 people. They were a mixed blessing even in the middle-class districts where they were more plentiful, as there was no system of drainage to flush away the waste. It simply accumulated in cesspools, which were emptied manually about every two years. The thing that most impressed visitors as they approached an industrial city was the smoke; what impressed them most when they arrived was the smell.

The quality of life experienced by most of the urban poor who lived in these squalid conditions has been recorded by a number of contemporary observers. Friedrich Engels was a German socialist who was sent to England to learn the cotton trade. He lived in Manchester for two years and spent much of his time exploring the working-class areas of the city. "In this district I found a man, apparently about sixty years old, living in a cow stable," Engels recounted from one of his walking tours in *The Condition of the Working Class in England in* 1844. "He had constructed a sort of chimney for his square pen, which had neither windows, floor, nor ceiling, had obtained a bedstead and lived there, though the rain dripped through his rotten roof. This man was too old and weak for regular work, and supported himself by removing manure with a hand-cart; the dung-heaps lay next door to his palace!" From his own observations Engels concluded that "in such dwellings only a physically degenerate race, robbed of all humanity, degraded, reduced morally and physically to bestiality, could feel comfortable and at home." And as he was quick to point out, his own observations were no different from those of parliamentary commissioners, medical officers, or civic authorities who had seen conditions firsthand.

Among these observers, the most influential by far was Sir Edwin Chadwick, who began his government career as a commissioner for the poor law and ended it as the founder of a national system of public health. Chadwick wrote the report of a parliamentary commission, *The Sanitary Condition of the Laboring Population of Britain* (1842), which caused a sensation among the governing classes. Building on the work of physicians, overseers of the poor, and the most technical scholarship available, Chadwick not only painted the same grim picture of urban life as Engels did, he proposed a comprehensive solution to one of its greatest problems, waste management.

Chadwick was a civil servant, and he believed that problems were solved by government on the basis of conclusions of experts. He had heard doctors argue their theories about the causes of disease, some believing in fluxes that resulted from combinations of foul air, water, and refuse; others believing disease was spread by the diseased, in this case Irish immigrants who settled in the poorest parts of English industrial towns. Although medical research had not yet detected the existence of germs, it was widely held that lack of ventilation, stagnant pools of water, and the accumulation of human and animal waste in proximity to people's dwellings all contributed to the increasing incidence of disease. Chadwick fixed upon this last element as crucial. Not even in middle-class districts was there any effective system for the removal of waste. Chamber pots and primitive toilets were emptied into ditches, which were used to drain rain off into local waterways. The few underground sewers that existed were square containers without outlets that were simply emptied once filled. Chadwick's vision was for a sanitation system, one that would carry waste out of the city quickly and deposit it in outlying fields where it could be used as fertilizer.

Chadwick realized that the key to disposing of waste was a constant supply of running water piped through the system. Traditionally, only heavy rainstorms cleared the waste ditches in most cities, and these were too infrequent to be effective. The river had to be the beginning of the sewerage system as well as its end. River water had to be pumped through an underground construction of sewage pits that were built to facilitate the water's flow. Civil engineers had already demonstrated that pits with rounded rather than angular edges were far more effective, and Chadwick advocated the construction of a system of oval-shaped tunnels, built on an incline beneath the city. Water pumped from one part of the river would rush through the tunnels, which would empty into pipes that would carry the waste to nearby farms.

Chadwick's vision took years to implement. He had all of the zeal of a reformer and none of the tact of a politician. He offended nearly everyone with whom he came into contact, because he believed that his program was the only workable one and because he believed that it must be implemented whatever the price. He was uninterested in who was to pay the enormous costs of laying underground tunnel and building pumping stations and insisted only that the work begin immediately. In the end, he won his point. Sanitation systems became one of the first great public-works projects of the industrial age.

off than agricultural laborers when the high cost of food and rent is considered. But beginning around 1820, there is convincing evidence that the real wages of industrial workers were rising despite the fact that more and more work was semi- and unskilled machine-minding and more of it was being done by women, who were generally paid only two-thirds the wages of men. Although this increase in real wages was still subject to trade cycles, like the Great Hunger of the 1840s, it continued nearly unabated for the rest of the nineteenth century. Thus, in the second half of the Industrial Revolution, both employers and workers saw a bettering of their economic situation. This was one reason why rural workers flocked to the cities and Irish peasants emigrated in the hundreds of thousands to work the lowest paid and least desirable jobs in the factories.

But economic gain had social costs. The first was the decline of the family as a labor unit. In both agricultural and early industrial activity, families labored together. Workers would not move to mill towns without the guarantee of a job for all members of their family, and initially they could drive a hard bargain. The early factories preferred family labor to workhouse conscripts, and it was traditional for children to work beside their parents, cleaning, fetching, or assisting in minding the machines. Children provided an essential part of family income, and youngest children were the agency of care for infirm parents. Paradoxically, it was agitation for improvement in the conditions of child labor that spelled the end of the family work unit. At first young children were barred from the factories and older ones allowed to work only a partial adult shift. Although reformers intended that schooling and leisure be substituted for work, the separation of children from parents in the workplace ultimately made possible the substitution of teenagers for adults, especially as machines replaced skilled human labor. The individual worker now became the unit of labor, and during economic downturns it was adult males with their higher salaries who were laid off first.

The decline of the family as a labor unit was matched by other changes in living conditions when rural dwellers migrated to cities. Many rural habits were unsuited to both factory work and urban living. The tradition of "Saint Monday," for example, was one that was deeply rooted in the pattern of agricultural life. Little effort was expended at the beginning of the work week and progressively more at the end. Sunday leisure was followed by Monday recovery, a slow start to renewed labor. The factory demanded constant application six days a week. Strict rules were enforced to keep workers at their stations and their minds on their jobs. More than efficiency was at stake. Early machines were not only crude, they were dangerous, with no safety features to cover moving parts. Maiming accidents were common in the early factories, and they were the fault of both workers and machines. Similarly, industrial workers entered a world of the cash economy. Most agricultural workers were used to being paid in kind and to barter exchange. Money was an unusual luxury that was associated with binges of food, drink, and frivolities. This made adjustment to the wage packet as difficult as adjustment to the clock. Cash had to be set aside for provisions, rent, and clothing. On the farm, the time of a bountiful harvest was the time to buy durable goods; in the factory, "harvest time" was always the same.

Such adjustments were not easy, and during the course of the nineteenth century a way of life passed forever from England. For some its departure caused profound sorrow; for others it was a matter of rejoicing. A vertically integrated society in which lord of the manor, village worthies, independent farmers, workers, and servants lived together interdependently was replaced by a society of segregated social classes. By the middle decades of the nineteenth century, a class of capitalists and a class of workers had begun to form and had begun to clash. The middle classes abandoned the city centers, building exclusive suburban communities in which to raise their children and insulate their families. Conditions in the cities deteriorated under the pressure of overcrowding, lack of sanitation, and the absence of private investment. The loss of interaction between these different segments of society had profound consequences for the struggle to improve the quality of life for everyone. Leaders of labor saw themselves fighting against profits, greed, and apathy; leaders of capital against drunkenness, sloth, and ignorance. Between these two stereotypes there was little middle ground.

The Industrialization of the Continent

Although Britain took the first steps along the road to an industrial economy, it was not long before other European nations followed. There was intense interest in "the British miracle," as it was dubbed by contemporaries. European ministers, entrepreneurs, even heads of state visited British factories and mines in hope of

exploiting the young

The condition of child laborers was a concern of English legislators and social reformers from the beginning of industrialization. Most of the attention was given to factory workers, and most legislation attempted to regulate the age at which children could begin work, the number of hours they could be made to work, and the provision of schooling and religious education during their leisure. It was not until the mid-1840s that a parliamentary commission was formed to investigate the condition of child labor in the mines. In this extract the testimony of the child is confirmed by the observations of one of the commissioners.

Ellison Jack, 11-years-old girl coal-bearer at Loanhead colliery, Scotland: I have been working below three years on my father's account; he takes me down at two in the morning, and I come up at one and two next afternoon. I go to bed at six at night to be ready for work next morning: the part of the pit I bear in the seams are much on the edge. I have to bear my burthen up four traps, or ladders, before I get to the main road which leads to the pit bottom. My task is four or five tubs: each tub holds 4G cwt. I fill five tubs in twenty journeys.

I have had the strap when I did not do my bidding. Am very glad when my task is wrought, as it sore fatigues. I can read, and was learning the writing; can do a little; not been at school for two years; go to kirk occasionally, over to Lasswade: don't know much about the Bible, so long since read.

R. H. *Franks*, Esq., the sub-commissioner: A brief description of this child's place of work will illustrate her evidence. She has first to descend a nine-ladder pit to the first rest, even to which a shaft is sunk, to draw up the baskets or tubs of coals filled by the bearers; she then takes her creel (a basket formed to the back, not unlike a cockle-shell flattened towards the neck, so as to allow lumps of coal to rest on the back of the neck and shoulders), and pursues her journey to the wall-face, or as it is called here, the room of work. She then lays down her basket, into which the coal is rolled, and it is frequently more than one man can do to lift the burden on her back. The tugs or straps are placed over the forehead, and the body bent in a semicircular form, in order to stiffen the arch.

"Child Labor in the Coal Mines," Testimony to the Parliamentary Investigative Committee (1842).

learning the key industrial secrets that would unlock the prosperity of a new age. The Crystal Palace exhibition of manufacturing and industry held in London in 1851 was the occasion for a Continent-wide celebration of the benefits of technology and a chance for ambitious Europeans to measure themselves against the mighty British. By then many European nations had begun the transformation of their own economies and had entered a period of sustained growth.

There was no single model for the industrialization of the Continental states. Contemporaries continually made comparisons with Britain, but in truth the process of British industrialization was not well suited to any but the coal-rich regions in Belgium and the Rhineland. Nevertheless, all of Europe benefited from the British experience. No one else had to invent the jenny, the mule, or the steam engine. Although the British government banned the export of technology, none of these path-breaking inventions remained a secret for long. Britain had demonstrated a way to make cheap, durable goods in factories, and every other state in Europe was able to skip the long stages of discovery and improvement. Thus, while industrialization began later on the Continent, it could progress more quickly. France and Germany were building a railroad system within years of Britain despite the fact that they had to import most of the technology, raw materials, and engineers.

Britain shaped European industrialization in another way. Its head start made it very difficult for follower nations to compete against British commodities in the world market. This meant that European industrialization would be directed first and foremost to home markets, where tariffs and import quotas could protect fledgling industries. Although European states were willing to import vital British products, they placed high duties on British-made consumer goods and encouraged higher-cost domestic production. Britain's competitive advantage demanded that European governments become involved in the industrialization of their countries, financing capital-intensive industries, backing the railroads, and favoring the establishment of factories.

European industrialization was therefore not the thunderclap it was in Britain. In France it was a slow, accretive development that took advantage of traditional skills and occupations and gradually modernized the marketplace. In Germany industrialization had to overcome the political divisions of the empire, the economic isolation of the petty states, and the wide dispersion of vital resources. Regions rather than states industrialized in the early nineteenth century, and parts of Austria, Italy, and Spain imported machinery and techniques and modernized their traditional crafts. But most of these states and most of the eastern part of Europe remained tied to a traditional agrarian-based economy that provided neither labor for industrial production nor purchasing power for industrial goods.

These areas quickly became sources for raw materials and primary products for their industrial neighbors.

industrialization without revolution

The experience of France in the nineteenth century demonstrates that there was no single path to industrialization. Each state blended together its natural resources, historical experiences, and forms of economic organization in unique combinations. While some mixtures resulted in explosive growth, as in Britain, others made for steady development, as in France.

French industrialization was keyed to domestic rather than export markets and to the application of new technology to a vast array of traditional crafts. The French profited, as did all of the Continental states, from British inventions, but they also benefited from the distinct features of their own economy. France possessed a pool of highly skilled and highly productive labor, a manufacturing tradition oriented toward the creation of high-quality goods, and consumers who valued taste and fashion over cost and function. Thus while the British dominated the new mass market for inexpensive cottons and cast-iron goods, a market with high sales but low profit margins, the French were pro-

The Industrial Revolution on the Continent

*This engraving shows a French steelworks, Manufacture Nationale, in Paris, 1800. At that time this was the only
French steelworks that compared with those in Sheffield, England.*

ducing luxury items whose very scarcity kept both prices and profits high.

Two decisive factors determined the nature of French industrialization: population growth and the French Revolution. From the early eighteenth to the mid-nineteenth centuries, France grew slowly. In 1700, the French population stood at just under 20 million; in 1850 it was just under 36 million, a growth rate of 80 percent. In contrast, Germany grew 135 percent, from 15 to 34 million, and England 300 percent, from 5 to 20 million, during the same period. Nevertheless, France remained the most populous nation in western Europe, second on the Continent only to Russia. There is no simple explanation for France's relatively sluggish population growth. The French had been hit particularly hard by subsistence crises in the seventeenth century, and there is reliable evidence that the rural population consciously attempted to limit family size by methods of birth control as well as by delaying marriages. Moreover, France urbanized slowly at a time when city dwellers were marrying younger and producing larger families. As late as the 1860s, a majority of French workers were farmers. Whatever the cause of this moderate population growth, its consequences were clear. France was not pressured by the force of numbers to abandon its traditional agricultural methods, nor did it face a shortage of traditional supplies of energy. Except during crop failures, French agriculture could produce to meet French needs, and there remained more than enough wood for domestic and industrial use.

The consequences of the French Revolution are less clear. Throughout the eighteenth century, the French economy performed at least as well as the British, and in many areas better. French overseas trade had grown spectacularly until checked by military defeat in the Seven Years' War (1756–63). French agriculture steadily increased output, while French rural manufactures flourished. A strong guild tradition still dominated urban industries, and although it restricted competition and limited growth, it also helped maintain the standards for the production of high-quality goods that made French commodities so highly prized throughout the world. The Revolution disrupted every aspect of economic life. Some of its outcomes were unforeseen and unwelcome. For example, Napoleon's Continental System, which attempted to close European markets to Britain, resulted in a shipping war, which the British won decisively and which eliminated France as a competitor for overseas trade in the mid-nineteenth century. But other outcomes were the result of direct policies, even if their impact could not have been entirely predicted. Urban guilds and corporations were abolished, opening trades to newcomers but destroying the close-knit groups that trained skilled artisans and introduced innovative products. Similarly, the breakup of both feudal and common lands to satisfy the hunger of the peasantry had the effect of maintaining a large rural population for decades.

Despite the efforts of the central government, there had been little change in the techniques used by French farmers over the course of the eighteenth century. French peasants clung tenaciously to traditional rights that gave even the smallest landholder a vital say in community agriculture. Landlords were predominantly absentees, less interested in the organization of their estates than in the dues and taxes that could be extracted from them. Thus the policies of successive revolutionary governments strengthened the hold of small peasants on the land. With the abolition of many feudal dues and with careful family planning, smallholders could survive and pass a meager inheritance on to their children. Even prosperous farmers could not grow into the large-scale proprietors that had enclosed English fields, for little land came on the market, and many parts of France practiced partible inheritance, which, over time, tended to even out the size of holdings. French agriculture continued to be organized in its centuries-old patterns. While it was able to supply the nation's need for food, it could not release large numbers of workers for purely industrial activity.

Thus French industrial growth was constrained on the one hand by the relatively small numbers of workers who could engage in manufacturing and on the other by the fact that a large portion of the population remained subsistence producers, cash-poor and linked only to small rural markets. Throughout the eighteenth century, the French economy continued to be regionally segregated rather than nationally integrated. The size of the state inhibited a highly organized internal trade, and there was little improvement of the infrastructure of transportation. Although some British-style canals were built, it must be remembered that canals in Britain were built to move coal rather than staple goods and France did not have much coal to move. Manufacturing concerns were still predominantly family businesses whose primary markets were regional rather than international. Roads that connected the short distances between producers and consumers were of greater importance to these producers than arterial routes that served the markets of others. Similarly, there was no national capital market until the mid-nineteenth century, and precious few regional ones. French producers were

as thrifty and profit-oriented as any others, but they found it more difficult to raise the large amounts of capital necessary to purchase the most expensive new machinery and build the most up-to-date factories. Ironworks, coal mines, and railroads, the three capital-intensive ventures of industrialization, were financed either by government subsidy or by foreign investment.

All these factors determined the slow, steady pace of French industrialization. Recovery after 1815 came in fits and starts. British inventors, manufacturers, and entrepreneurs were enticed to France to demonstrate new machinery and industrial techniques, but in most places the real engine of growth was skilled workers' steady application of traditional methods. By 1820 only 65 French factories were powered by steam engines, and even water-powered machinery was uncommon. Industrial firms remained small and were frequently a combination of putting-out and factory production. It was not until midcentury that sustained industrial growth became evident. This was largely the result of the construction of railroads on a national plan, financed in large part by the central government. Whereas in Britain the railways took advantage of a national market, in France they created one. They also gave the essential stimulation to the modernization of the iron industry, in which much refining was still done with charcoal rather than coke; of machine making; and of the capital markets. Imported steel and foreign investment were vital ingredients in a process that took several decades to reach fruition.

The disadvantages of being on the trailing edge of economic change were mitigated for a time by conventional practices of protectionism. Except in specialty goods, agricultural produce, and luxury products, French manufactures could not compete with either British or German commodities. Had France maintained its position as a world trader, this comparative disadvantage would have been devastating. But defeat in the wars of commerce had led to a drawing inward of French economic effort. Marseille and Bordeaux, once bustling centers of European trade, became provincial backwaters in the nineteenth century. But the internal market was still strong enough to support industrial growth, and domestic commodities could be protected by prohibitive tariffs, especially against British textiles, iron, and, ironically, coal. Despite the fact that France had to import over 40 percent of its meager requirements of coal, it still insisted upon slapping high import duties on British supplies. This was in part to protect French mine owners, who had never integrated their operations with iron production and therefore had no interest in keeping fuel costs low. Moreover, the slow pace of French industrialization allowed for the skipping of intermediate stages of development. France had hardly entered the canal age when it began to build its railways. Ultimately, industry moved from hand power to steam power in one long step.

While France achieved industrialization without an industrial revolution, it also achieved economic growth within the context of its traditional values. Agriculture may not have modernized, but the ancient village communities escaped the devastation modernization would bring. The orderly progression of generations of farming families characterized rural France until the shattering experiences of the Franco-Prussian War (1870) and the First World War (1914–18). Nor did France experience the mushroom growth of new cities with all of their problems of poverty, squalor, and homelessness. Slow population growth ameliorated the worst of the social diseases of industrialization while traditional rural manufacturing softened the transformation of a way of life. If France did not reap the windfall profits of the Industrial Revolution, neither did it harvest the bitter crop of social, economic, and spiritual impoverishment that was pulled in its train.

industrialization and union

The process of industrialization in Germany was dominated by the historic divisions of the empire of the German peoples. Before 1815 there were over 300 separate jurisdictional units within the empire, and after 1815 there were still more than 30. These included large advanced states like Prussia, Austria, and Saxony as well as small free cities and the personal enclaves of petty nobles who had guessed right during the Napoleonic wars. Political divisions had more than political impact. Each state clung tenaciously to its local laws and customs, which favored its citizens over outsiders. Merchants who lived near the intersection of separate jurisdictions could find themselves liable for several sets of tolls to move their goods and several sets of customs duties for importing and exporting them. These would have to be paid in different currencies at different rates of exchange according to the different regulations of each state. Small wonder that German merchants exhibited an intense localism, preferring to trade with members of their own state and supporting trade barriers against others. Such obstacles had a depressing effect on the economies of all German states but pushed

with greatest weight against the manufacturing regions of Saxony, Silesia, and the Rhineland.

Most of imperial Germany was agricultural land suited to a diversity of uses. The mountainous regions of Bavaria and the Austrian alpine communities practiced animal husbandry; there was a grain belt in Prussia, where the soil was poor but the land plentiful, and one in central Germany in which the soil was fertile and the land densely occupied. The Rhine Valley was one of the richest in all of Europe and was the center of German wine production. The introduction of the potato was the chief innovation of the eighteenth century. While English farmers were turning farms into commercial estates, German peasants were learning how to make do with less land.

Agricultural estates were organized differently in different parts of Germany. In the east, serfdom still prevailed. Peasants were tied to the land and its lord and were responsible for labor service during much of the week. Methods of cultivation were traditional, and neither peasants nor lords had much incentive to adopt new techniques. The vast agricultural domains of the Prussian Junkers, as these landlords were called, were built on the backs of cheap serf labor, and the harvest was destined for the Baltic export trade, where world grain prices rather than local production costs would determine profits. In central Germany, the long process of commuting labor service into rents was nearly completed by the end of the eighteenth century. The peasantry was not yet free, as a series of manorial relationships still tied them to the land, but they were no longer mere serfs. Moreover, western Germany was dominated by free farmers who either owned or leased their lands and who had a purely economic relationship with their landlords. The restriction of peasant mobility in much of Germany posed difficulties for the creation of an industrial work force. As late as 1800, over 80 percent of the German population was engaged in agriculture, a proportion that would drop slowly over the next half century.

Although Germany was well endowed with natural resources and skilled labor in a number of trades, it had not taken part in the expansion of world trade during the seventeenth century, and the once bustling Hanseatic ports had been far outdistanced by the rise of the Atlantic economies. The principal exported manufacture was linen, which was expertly spun and woven in Saxony and the Prussian province of Silesia. The linen industry was organized traditionally, with a mixture of domestic production managed on the putting-out sys-

An engraving of the train from Nuremberg to Fürth. This Bavarian train ran for the first time in 1835. Passengers rode the 7 kilometers between Nuremberg and Fürth in coaches that closely resembled their horse-drawn predecessors.

tem and some factory spinning, especially after the introduction of British mechanical innovations. But even the most advanced factories were still being powered by water, and thus they were located in mountainous regions where rapidly running streams could turn the wheels. In the 1840s there were only 22 steam-driven spinning mills in Germany, several of them established by the Prussian government, which imported British machines and technicians to run them. Neither linens nor traditional German metal crafts could compete on the international markets, but they could find a wider market within Germany if only the problems of political division could be resolved.

These were especially acute for Prussia after the reorganization of European boundaries in 1815 (see Chapter 22). Prussian territory now included the coal- and iron-rich Rhineland provinces, but a number of smaller states separated these areas from Prussia's eastern domain. Each small state exacted its own tolls and customs duties whenever Prussian merchants wanted to move goods from one part of Prussia to the other. Such movement became more common in the nineteenth century as German manufacturing began to grow in step with its rising population. Between 1815

and 1865, the population of Germany grew by 60 percent to over 36 million people. This was an enormous internal market, nearly as large as the population of France, and the Prussians resolved to make it a unified trading zone by creating a series of alliances with smaller states known as the Zollverein (1834). The Zollverein was not a free-trade zone, as was the British empire, but rather a customs union in which member states adopted the liberal Prussian customs regulations. Every state was paid an annual portion of receipts based upon its population, and every state—except Prussia—increased its revenues as a result. The crucial advantage the Prussians received was the ability to move goods and materials from east to west, but Prussia reaped political profits as well. It forced Hanover and Saxony into the Zollverein and kept its powerful rival Austria out. Prussia's economic union soon proved to be the basis for the union of the German states.

The creation of the Zollverein was vital to German industrialization. It permitted the exploitation of natural advantages, like plentiful supplies of coal and iron, and it provided a basis for the building of railroads. Germany was a follower nation in the process of industrialization. It started late and it self-consciously modeled its success on the British experience. British equipment and engineers were brought to Germany to attempt to plant the seeds of an industrial economy. German manufacturers sent their children to England to learn the latest techniques in industrial management. Friedrich Engels (1820–95) worked in a Manchester cotton factory, where he observed the appalling conditions of the industrial labor force and wrote *The Condition of the Working Class in England* (1845). Steam engines were installed in coal mines, if not in factories, and the process of puddling revolutionized ironmaking, though most iron was still smelted with charcoal rather than coke. Although coal was plentiful in Prussia, it was to be found at the eastern and western extremities of Germany. Even with the lowering of tolls and duties, it was still too expensive to move over rudimentary roads and an uncompleted system of canals.

Thus the railroads were the key to tapping the industrial potential of Germany. Here they were a cause rather than a result of industrialization. The agreements hammered out in the creation of the Zollverein made possible the planning necessary to build single lines across the boundaries of numerous states. Initially German railroads were financed privately, with much foreign investment. But ultimately governments saw the practical advantages of rail transport and took an active part in both planning and financing the system. Over a quarter of the track constructed in Prussia before 1870 was owned directly by the government, and most of the rest had been indirectly financed by the government, which purchased land and guaranteed interest on stock issues.

Germany imported most of its engines directly from Britain and thus adopted standard British gauge for its system. As early as 1850 there were over 3500 miles of rail in Germany, with important roads linking the manufacturing districts of Saxony and the coal and iron deposits of the Ruhr. Twenty years later Germany was second only to Britain in the amount of track that had been laid and opened. By then it was no longer simply a

The slavery of Labor

Although born in Germany, Friedrich Engels witnessed industrialization in England firsthand. His father owned a factory in Manchester of which Engels was put in charge. By day he oversaw industrial production, and by night he wandered the city streets overwhelmed by the suffering of the working classes. His analysis of industrialization developed from his own observations. He became first a socialist and then, with Karl Marx, a founder of the Communist party.

Capital is the all-important weapon in the class war. Power lies in the hands of those who own, directly or indirectly, foodstuffs and the means of production. The poor, having no capital, inevitably bear the consequences of defeat in the struggle. Nobody troubles about the poor as they struggle helplessly in the whirlpool of modern industrial life. The working man may be lucky enough to find employment, if by his labour he can enrich some member of the middle classes. But his wages are so low that they hardly keep body and soul together. If he cannot find work, he can steal, unless he is afraid of the police; or he can go hungry and then the police will see to it that he will die of hunger in such a way as not to disturb the equanimity of the middle classes. . . .

The only difference between the old-fashioned slavery and the new is that while the former was openly acknowledged the latter is disguised. The worker *appears* to be free, because he is not bought and sold outright. He is sold piecemeal by the day, the week, or the year. Moreover he is not sold by one owner to another, but he is forced to sell himself in this fashion. He is not the slave of a single individual, but of the whole capitalist class. As far as the worker is concerned, however, there can be no doubt as to his servile status. It is true that the apparent liberty which the worker enjoys does give him some *real* freedom. Even this genuine freedom has the disadvantage that no one is responsible for providing him with food and shelter. His real masters, the middle-class capitalists, can discard him at any moment and leave him to starve, if they have no further use for his services and no further interest in his survival. . . .

From Friedrich Engels, *The Condition of the Working Class in England in 1844* (1845).

follower. German engineers and machinists, trained in Europe's best schools of technology, were turning out engines and rolling stock second to none. And the railroads transported a host of high-quality manufactures, especially durable metal goods that came to carry the most prestigious trademark of the late nineteenth century: "Made in Germany."

The Lands That Time Forgot

Nothing better demonstrates the point that industrialization was a regional rather than a national process than a survey of those states that did not develop industrial economies by the middle of the nineteenth century. These states ranged from the Netherlands, which was still one of the richest areas in Europe, to Spain and Russia, which were the poorest. Also included were Austria-Hungary, the states of the Italian peninsula, and Poland. In all these nations there was some industrial progress. The Bohemian lands of Austria contained a highly developed spinning industry; the Spanish province of Catalonia produced more cotton than did Belgium; and the Basque region was rich in iron and coal. Northern Italy mechanized its textile production, particularly silk spinning, while in the regions around both Moscow and Saint Petersburg, factories were run on serf labor. Nevertheless, the economies of all these states remained nonindustrial and, with the exception of the Netherlands, dominated by subsistence agriculture.

There were many reasons why these states were unable to develop their industrial potential. Some, like Naples and Poland, were simply underendowed with resources; others, like Austria-Hungary and Spain, faced difficulties of transport and communications that could not easily be overcome. Spain's modest resources were located on its northern and eastern edges, while a vast, arid plain dominated the center. To move raw materials and finished products from one end of the country to the other was a daunting task, made more difficult by lack of waterways and the rudimentary condition of Spanish roads. Two-thirds of Austria-Hungary is either mountains or hills, a geographic feature that presented obstacles not even the railroads could easily solve. But there was far more than natural disadvantage behind the failure of these parts of Europe to move in step with the industrializing states. Their social structure, agricultural organization, and commercial policies all hindered the adoption of new methods, machines, and modes of production.

Despite the fact that industrialization created new and largely unmanageable social problems, the follower states were eager for its benefits. All imported the latest products of technology, and the ruling elites in even the most traditional economies lived a material life similar to those in the most advanced. British entrepreneurs and artisans were courted by heads of state and their ministers and were offered riches in exchange for their precious knowledge. British industrialists set up textile factories in Moscow, built spinning machines in Bohemia, and taught Spanish miners how to puddle iron. Railroad pioneer George Stephenson himself surveyed the prospect of creating a passenger rail system in Spain, though he concluded pessimistically, "I have not seen enough people of the right sort to fill a single train." In the later part of the nineteenth century, French, Belgian, and German industrialists served similar roles. There were no traditional economies by choice. Industrialization was seen as a miracle, and the latecomers worshiped avidly at its shrine.

It was work rather than faith that would produce economic salvation. The most common characteristic of the latecomers was a traditional agrarian structure that consumed the lion's share of labor and capital while producing little surplus for any but a small dominant class. In areas as dissimilar as Spain, Italy, and Russia, agriculture was organized in vast estates, which kept the mass of peasants perpetually poor. Sharecropping systems in the west and serfdom in the east differed only in formal organization. Both conditions made it impossible for peasants to accumulate the land necessary to invest in capital improvements or to send their children to towns to engage in industrial occupations. In Hungary, Poland, and Russia it was illegal for people to change occupations, and serfs who engaged in industrial activity paid their lords for the privilege. Although a number of serfs amassed considerable fortunes in organizing domestic or factory spinning, legal constraints restricted the efforts of potential entrepreneurs.

Similarly, the leaders of traditional economies maintained tariff systems that insulated their own producers from competition. Austrian tariffs were not only artificially high, they were accompanied by import quotas to keep all but the smallest fraction of foreign products from Austrian consumers. The Spanish government prohibited the importation of grain, forcing its eastern provinces to pay huge transport costs for domestic grain despite the fact that cheaper Italian grain was readily available. Such policies sapped much-needed capital from industrial investment. There were many reasons for so-called protective tariffs, and it was not only the follower states that imposed them. France and the Zollverein protected domestic industry while Britain was converted to free trade only in the 1840s. But protection was sensible only when it protected rather than isolated. Inefficiently produced goods of inferior quality were the chief results of the protectionist policies of the follower nations. Failure to adopt steam-powered machines made traditionally produced linens and silks so expensive that smuggling occurred on an international scale. Although these goods might find buyers in domestic markets, they could not compete in international trade, and one by one the industries of the follower nations atrophied. Such nations became exporters of raw materials and foodstuffs. The export of Russian linen was replaced by the export of Russian flax. Spain, once the largest exporter of woolen cloth in Europe, now exported mainly wines and fruits. Those economies that remained traditionally organized came to be exploited for their resources by those that had industrialized.

This international situation was not all that different from the dual system that came into effect within the nonindustrialized states. In Austria-Hungary, for example, it was Hungary that was kept from industrializing, first by the continuation of serf-based agriculture, then by the high internal tariffs that favored Austrian over Hungarian manufactures. In Italy the division was between north and south. In Lombardy and Tuscany, machine-based manufacturing took hold alongside

mining and metallurgy; in 1860 northern Italy contained 98 percent of the railways and 87 percent of the roads that existed on the entire peninsula. In Naples and Sicily, half-starved peasants eked out a miserable existence on once-rich soil that was now depleted from overuse. It was estimated that of the 400,000 people living in Naples, over 100,000 were destitute beggars. In Spain, Catalonia modernized while Castile stagnated. Until the loss of its Latin American empire in the first half of the nineteenth century, Spain had a ready market for Catalonian textiles and handicrafts. But since Castile remained the cultural and administrative center of the state, it did little to encourage change, and much government policy was actually counterproductive. The chief problem faced by these dual economies was that neither part could sustain the other. Traditional agriculture could not produce the necessary surplus of either labor or capital to support industry, and industry could not economize sufficiently to make manufactured goods cheap enough for a poor peasantry.

Thus the advantages of being a follower were all missed. Technology could not be borrowed or stages skipped because the ground was not prepared for widespread industrial activity to be cultivated. Even by standing still, followers fell behind. While over the course of the nineteenth century male illiteracy dropped dramatically in the industrialized states—to 30 percent in Britain and France and 10 percent in Prussia—it remained at 75 to 80 percent in Spain and Italy

A Russian peasant tills a field with a primitive horse-drawn wooden plow. Russian fields produced low yields, partly because of the use of such crude farming methods.

and over 90 percent in Russia. There was more than irony in the fact that one of the first railroads built on the Continent was built in Austria but was built to be powered by horses rather than engines. The first railways in Italy linked royal palaces to capital cities. Those in Spain radiated from Madrid and bypassed most cen-

ters of natural resources. In these states, the railroads were built to move the military rather than passengers or goods. They were state-financed, occasionally state-owned, and almost always lost money. They were symbols of the industrial age, but in these states they were symbols without substance.

The industrialization of Europe in the eighteenth century was an epochal event in human history. The constraints on daily life imposed by nature were loosened for the first time. No longer did population growth in one generation mean famine in the next; no longer was it necessary for the great majority of people to toil in the fields to earn their daily bread. Manufacture replaced agriculture as humanity's primary activity, though the change was longer and slower than the burst of industrialization that took place in the first half of the nineteenth century. For the leaders, Britain especially, industrialization brought international eminence. British achievements were envied, British inventors celebrated, Britain's constitutional and social organization lauded. A comparatively small island nation had become the greatest economic power in Europe. Industrialization had profound consequences for economic life, but its effects ran deeper than that. The search for new markets would result in the conquest of continents; the power of productivity unleashed by coal and iron would result in the first great arms race. Both would reach fruition in World War I, the first industrial war. For better or worse, we still live in the industrial era that began in Britain in the middle of the eighteenth century.

mastering the chapter

To review the main points of the chapter, be sure you can explain the significance of each of the following.

Terms/Concepts/Events	People	Places
cottage industry	Thomas Newcomen	Manchester
putting-out system	James Watt	Liverpool
enclosure	Matthew Boulton	Birmingham
fodder crops	Richard Arkwright	Belgium
convertible husbandry	George Stephenson	Rhineland
water frame	Josiah Wedgwood	Ruhr
Factory Act	Robert Owen	
Ten Hours Act		
protectionism		
Zollverein		

suggestions for further reading

general reading

* Carlo Cipolla, ed., *The Fontana Economic History of Europe: The Emergence of Industrial Societies*. 2 vols. (London: Fontana Books, 1973). A country-by-country survey of Continental European industrialization.

* David Landes, *The Unbound Prometheus* (Cambridge: Cambridge University Press, 1969). A vigorously argued study of the impact of technology on British and European society from the eighteenth to the twentieth century.
* Jordan Goodman and Katrina Honeyman, *Gainful Pursuits: The Making of Industrial Europe, 1600–1914* (London: Edward Arnold, 1988). A brief overview of the entire process of industrialization.
* E. L. Jones, *The European Miracle*, 2d ed. (Cambridge: Cambridge University Press, 1987). A comparative study of the acquisition of technology in Europe and Asia and the impact that industrialization had upon the two continents.
* T. S. Ashton, *The Industrial Revolution* (Oxford: Oxford University Press, 1969). A compelling brief account of the traditional view of industrialization.

The Traditional Economy

* E. A. Wrigley, *Continuity, Chance and Change* (Cambridge: Cambridge University Press, 1988). Explores the nature of the traditional economy and the way in which Britain escaped from it.
* L. A. Clarkson, *Proto-Industrialization: The First Phase of Industrialization?* (London: Macmillan, 1985). A study of domestic manufacturing and its connection to the process of industrialization.
* Richard Brown, *Society and Economy in Modern Britain, 1700–1850* (London: Routledge, 1991). A comprehensive survey.
  J. D. Chambers and G. E. Mingay, *The Agricultural Revolution* (London: Batsford, 1966). The classic survey of the changes in British agriculture.
  E. L. Jones, *Agriculture and the Industrial Revolution* (New York: John Wiley & Sons, 1974). A detailed study of the relationship between agricultural innovations and the coming of industrialization in Britain.

The Industrial Revolution in Britain

* Peter Mathias, *The First Industrial Nation*, 2d ed. (London: Methuen, 1983). An up-to-date general survey of British industrialization.
* Phyllis Deane, *The First Industrial Revolution*, 2d ed. (Cambridge: Cambridge University Press, 1979). The best introduction to the technological changes in Britain.
  A. E. Musson, *The Growth of British Industry* (New York: Holmes & Meier, 1978). An in-depth survey of British industrialization that is especially strong on technology.
* John Rule, *The Vital Century: England's Developing Economy, 1714–1815* (London: Longman, 1992). The most up-to-date survey on the British economy.
* N. F. R. Crafts, *British Economic Growth During the Industrial Revolution* (Oxford: Oxford University Press, 1986). A highly quantitative study by a new economic historian arguing the case that economic growth was slow in the early nineteenth century.
  T. S. Ashton, *Iron and Steel in the Industrial Revolution* (Manchester: Manchester University Press, 1963). A lucid account of the transformation of ironmaking, including the story of James Watt.
  Eric Hopkins, *Birmingham: The First Manufacturing Town in the World, 1760–1840* (London: Weidenfeld & Nicolson, 1989). An intimate portrait of one of the greatest of all boom towns.
  Philip Bagwell, *The Transport Revolution from 1770* (London: Batsford, 1974). A thorough survey of the development of canals, highways, and railroads in Britain.
* François Crouzet, *The First Industrialists* (Cambridge: Cambridge University Press, 1985). An analysis of the social background of the first generation of British entrepreneurs.
* Joel Mokyr, *The Lever of Riches: Technological Creativity and Economic Progress* (New York: Oxford University Press, 1992). A compelling argument concerning the role of technology by a leading econometrician.
* Harold Perkin, *The Origins of Modern English Society, 1780–1880* (London: Routledge & Kegan Paul, 1969). An outstanding survey of British social history in the industrial era.

* E. P. Thompson, *The Making of the English Working Class* (New York: Random House, 1966). A brilliant and passionate study of the ways laborers responded to the changes brought about by the industrial economy.

Friedrich Engels, *The Condition of the Working Class in England in 1844* (London: Allen and Unwin, 1952). The classic eyewitness account of the horrors of the industrial city.

The industrialization of the continent

* Tom Kemp, *Industrialization in Nineteenth-Century Europe*, 2d ed. (London: Longman, 1985). Survey of the process of industrialization in the major European states.

* Clive Trebilcock, *The Industrialization of the Continental Powers, 1780–1914* (London: Longman, 1981). A complex study of Germany, France, and Russia.

* Sidney Pollard, *Peaceful Conquest* (Oxford: Oxford University Press, 1981). Argues the regional nature of industrialization throughout western Europe.

Roger Price, *The Economic Transformation of France* (London: Croom Helm, 1975). A study of French society before and during the process of industrialization.

Alain Corbin, *The Lure of the Sea: The Discovery of the Seaside in the Western World, 1750–1840* (Cambridge: Polity Press, 1993). One dimension of European cultural responses to industrialization.

* Richard Sylla and Gianni Toniolo, eds., *Patterns of European Industrialization* (London: Routledge, 1993). A strong collection of essays that presents case studies from both east and west.

W. O. Henderson, *The Rise of German Industrial Power* (Berkeley: University of California Press, 1975). A chronological study of German industrialization that centers on Prussia.

Herbert Kisch, *From Domestic Manufacture to Industrial Revolution: The Case of the Rhineland Textile Districts* (New York: Oxford University Press, 1989). A scholarly study of the slow pace of industrialization in Germany.

* Wolfgang Schivelbusch, *The Railway Journey* (Berkeley: University of California Press, 1986). A social history of the impact of railways, drawn from French and German sources.

*Paperback edition available.

social transformations and political upheavals, 1815-1850

potato politics

Vegetables have histories too. But none has a more interesting history in the West than the humble potato. First introduced to northern Europe from the Andean highlands in South America at the end of the sixteenth century, it rapidly became a staple of peasant diets from Ireland to Russia. The potato's vitamins, minerals, and high carbohydrate content provided a rich source of energy to Europe's rural poor. It was simple to plant, required little or no cultivation, and did well in damp, cool climates. Best of all, it could be grown successfully on the smallest plots of land. One acre could support a peasant family of four for a year. Potato peelings helped sustain the family cow and pig, further supplementing family income.

The French painter Jean-François Millet (1814–75) provides a view of the peasant labor involved in *Planting Potatoes*. Millet, the son of a wealthy peasant family, understood well the importance of the potato crop in the peasant diet. The man and woman in this canvas plant their potatoes as a reverent act, bowing as field laborers might in prayer (laborers actually do pray in Millet's more sentimental work *The Angelus*). The primitive nature of the process is striking: the man uses a short hoe to scrape at what seems to be unyielding soil. The peasants seem part of the nature that surrounds them, patient as the beast that waits in the shade, bent and gnarled and lovely as the tree that arches in the background.

The fleshy root not only guaranteed health, it also affected social relations. Traditionally, peasants had delayed marrying and starting families because of the unavailability of land. The potato changed that behavior. Now the potato allowed peasants with only a little land to marry and have children earlier. Millet's depiction of the man and woman working together in the field resonates with the simple fact that potato cultivation aided in the formation of the couple. Millet's couple are parents whose baby sleeps swaddled in a basket and shaded by the tree. In those peasant homes where family members did putting-out work for local entrepreneurs, potato cultivation drew little labor away from the spinning wheel and loom. It permitted prosperous farmers to devote more land to cash crops, since only a small portion of land was required to feed a family. As the sole item of diet, it provided life-sustaining nutrients and a significant amount of the protein so necessary for heavy labor. The Irish adult male ate an average of 12 to 14 pounds of potatoes a day—a figure that may seem preposterous to us today.

Proverbs warned peasants against putting all their eggs in one basket, but no folk wisdom prepared the Irish, many of whom relied on the potato as a single crop, for the potato disaster that struck them. In 1845 a fungus from America destroyed the new potato crop. Although peasants were certainly accustomed to bad harvests and crop failures, they had no precedent for the years of blight that followed. From 1846 to 1850, famine and the diseases resulting from it—scurvy, dysentery, cholera, and typhus fever—killed over a million people in what became known as the Great Hunger. Another million people emigrated, many to the United States. Total dependence on the potato reaped its grim harvest, devastating all levels of Irish society. Within five years the Irish population was reduced by almost 25 percent.

The Irish potato famine has been called the "last great European *natural* disaster," to distinguish it from the man-made horrors of war and revolution. But it was as much a social disaster as a natural one. Food was the most political issue in the United Kingdom, the political entity created in 1801 consisting of England, Scotland, Ireland, and Wales. Governing one of the world's most prosperous states, British statesmen expected that the free market would solve the problems caused by famine in Ireland once trade barriers were removed in 1847. But the famine had hit the Irish so hard that they simply did not have the means to take advantage of tariff-free grains. Emergency work relief was established and soup kitchens were opened in the spring of 1847, but this meager assistance was withdrawn because the famine coincided with a banking crisis in England. In 1847 the problem was handed over to the Irish Poor Law system imposed on Ireland in

focus Questions

1. What problems did European peace makers confront at the Congress of Vienna and how did they attempt to resolve these problems?
2. How did industrialization change European families?
3. In what ways were liberalism and nationalism compatible with each other; how were they in conflict?
4. What are the connections between various ideologies—for instance, liberalism, romanticism, or socialism—and the revolutions of 1830 and 1848?

1838. The workhouses created by the recent law were not intended to deal with disasters of such proportions. Mass deaths and mass graves were the inevitable result.

As the wealth of European societies expanded in the nineteenth century, so did the number of those who lived on the edge, poised between unemployment and starvation. The Irish Great Hunger was the most striking example of the problem that plagued all Western societies in the first half of the nineteenth century: what to do with the poor.

Poverty was by no means a new social phenomenon, but the scale of impoverishment in both rural and urban areas and the perceived threat that it could disrupt whole societies were. In the case of the Irish famine, the British government was unable to handle an extreme crisis that was different in degree from the economic crises that periodically challenged other European nations. The question of poverty, the social question, lay at the heart of social experience and influenced new ideas about the role of government in solving social problems. It also fueled the firestorm of protest and revolution that swept across Europe after 1830 and, most notably, in 1848. In the context of poverty and the politics of food, Millet's melancholy painting of planting potatoes is not after all a pretty picture.

Europe in 1815

Europe After 1815

In his quest for empire, Napoleon had given Europe a geography lesson. Because no one state had been able to defeat him, Napoleon had made clear the territorial and political interdependence of the European powers. This lesson was not lost on the Great Powers as they sat down to redraw the map of Europe in 1815. The leaders of Russia, Austria, Prussia, and France shared with the British foreign secretary Lord Castlereagh (1769–1822) the vision of Europe as a machine that must be kept in running order. They looked on the whole of Europe as one entity and conceived of peace in terms of a general European security.

The primary goal of the European leaders who met in 1815 was to devise the most stable territorial arrangement possible. The settlement that emerged from their meeting was not simply a reaction to the ideological challenges of the French Revolution, nor was it a restoration of the European state system that had existed before Napoleon. During the negotiations, traditional claims of the right to rule came head to head with new ideas about stabilization. The equilibrium established in 1815 made possible a century-long European peace. Conflicts erupted, to be sure, but they took on the characteristics of the new system that was constructed at Vienna in 1815.

France

The Congress of Vienna

Because of the concern with establishing harmony at the time of Napoleon's defeat, the peace enforced against France was not a punitive one. After Napoleon's abdication in 1814, the victorious powers of Great Britain, Russia, Prussia, and Austria decided that leniency was the best way to support the restored Bourbon monarchy. After 1793, royalist émigrés referred to the young son of the executed Louis XVI as Louis XVII, although the child died in captivity and never reigned. In 1814 the four powers designated the elder of the two surviving brothers of Louis XVI as the appropriate candidate for the restored monarchy. Because of the circumstances of his restoration, the new king, Louis XVIII (1814–15; 1815–24), bore the ignominious image of returning "in the baggage car of the Allies." Every effort was made not to weigh down Louis XVIII with a harsh settlement. The First Peace of Paris, signed by the Allies with France in May 1814, had reestablished the French frontiers at the 1792 boundaries, which included Avignon, Venaissin, parts of Savoy, and German and Flemish territories—none of which had belonged to France in 1789.

After the hundred-day return of Napoleon, the "Usurper," the Second Peace of Paris of November 1815 somewhat less generously declared French frontiers restricted to the boundaries of 1790 and exacted from France an indemnity of 700 million francs. An army of occupation consisting of 150,000 troops was also placed on French soil at French expense but was removed ahead of schedule in 1818. Contrary to the terms of the first treaty, the second treaty also required France to return plundered art treasures to their countries of origin.

Representatives of the victorious Allies agreed to convene in the Austrian capital of Vienna for the purposes of mopping up the mess created in Europe by French rule and restoring order to European monarchies. On the surface, the Congress of Vienna, which began its deliberations in September 1814, seemed to be no more than an excuse for endless partying among Europe's royalty. Glittering balls as costly as battles gave critics the impression that statesmen were waltzing their way through treaty arrangements. The survival of an old system of precedence and etiquette hobbled negotiations. Issues of who should sign a treaty first and who should have the preferred places at the dinner table were the subjects of endless debates and fatal duels. But the image of bewigged men arguing over which criterion should be used to determine who would enter a room first belied the reality of the diplomats' serious negotiations as they sought to fashion a lasting peace by redrawing the map of Europe.

The central actors whose personalities dominated the Congress were Austrian minister of foreign affairs Prince Klemens von Metternich (1812–22), British foreign secretary Viscount Castlereagh, French minister of foreign affairs Charles Maurice de Talleyrand (1814–15), the Russian tsar Alexander I (1801–25), and the Prussian king Frederick William III (1797–1840). In spite of personal eccentricities, animosities, and occasionally outright hostilities among Europe's leaders, all shared a common concern with reestablishing harmony in Europe.

The dominant partnership of Austria and Britain at the Congress of Vienna resulted in treaty arrangements that served to restrain the ambitions of Russia and Prussia. No country was to receive territory without giving up something in return, and no one country was to receive enough territory to make it a present or future threat to the peace of Europe. To contain France, some steps taken prior to the Congress were ratified or expanded. In June 1814, the Low Countries had been set up as a unitary state to serve as a buffer against future French expansion on the Continent and a block to the revival of French sea power. The new Kingdom of the Netherlands, created out of the former Dutch Republic and the Austrian Netherlands, was placed under the rule of William I (1815–40). The Catholic southern provinces were thus uneasily reunited with the Protestant northern provinces, regions that had been separated since the Peace of Westphalia in 1648. Lest there be any doubt about the intended purpose of this new kingdom, Great Britain gave William I of the Netherlands £2 million to fortify his frontier against France. A reestablished monarchy that united the Island kingdom of Sardinia with Piedmont and included Savoy, Nice, and part of Genoa contained France on its southeast border. To the east, Prussia was given control of the left bank of the Rhine. Switzerland was reestablished as an independent confederation of cantons. Finally, Bourbon rule was restored in Spain on France's southwestern border.

Austria's power was firmly established in Italy, either through outright territorial control or influence over in-

United Netherlands

Italy

dependent states. The Papal States were returned to Pope Pius VII (1800–23), along with territories that had been Napoleon's Cisalpine Republic and the Kingdom of Italy. The Republic of Venice was absorbed into the Austrian empire. Lombardy and the Illyrian provinces on the Dalmatian coast were likewise restored to Austria. The Italian duchies of Tuscany, Parma, and Modena were placed under the rule of Habsburg princes.

After the fall of Napoleon, the Allies made no attempt to restore the Holy Roman Empire. Napoleon's Confederation of the Rhine, which organized the majority of German territory under French auspices in 1806, was dissolved. In its place, the German Confederation was created by reorganizing the 300 petty states into 38. The German Confederation was intended as a bulwark against France, not to serve any nationalist or parliamentary function. The 38 states, along with Austria as the thirty-ninth, were represented in a new Federal Diet at Frankfurt, dominated by Austrian influence.

All of these changes were the result of carefully discussed but fairly uncontroversial negotiations. The question of Poland was another matter indeed. Successive partitions by Russia, Austria, and Prussia in 1772, 1793, and 1795 had completely dismembered the land that had been Poland. Napoleon had reconstituted a small portion of Poland as the Grand Duchy of Warsaw. The Congress faced the dilemma of what to do with this Napoleonic creation and with Polish territory in gen-

The German Confederation

In this French cartoon satirizing the Congress of Vienna, left to right, Talleyrand is watching and waiting as Castlereagh balks, Metternich leads the "dancing," the king of Saxony clutches his crown in fear, and Genoa jumps up and down on the sidelines.

Saxony

Poland

eral. Fierce debate over Poland threatened to shatter congressional harmony.

Tsar Alexander I of Russia argued for a large Poland that he intended to be fully under his influence, thus extending Russian-controlled territories to the banks of the Oder. He also envisioned extending Russian dominance farther into central and eastern Europe. He based his claim on the significant contribution the Russian army had made to Napoleon's defeat. But such thinking conflicted with the Austrian minister Metternich's pursuit of equilibrium. Frederick William III of Prussia contended that if a large Poland was to be created, Prussia would expect compensation by absorbing Saxony. Both Great Britain and France distrusted Russian and Prussian territorial aims.

Negotiating for the French, Talleyrand was a man who knew something about survival and taking advantage of opportunities. A bishop under the old regime, a revolutionary who managed to keep his head, an exile in America during the Terror, Napoleon's chief minister, and then the representative of the restored Bourbon monarchy at the Congress, he was a shrewd and experienced diplomat who managed to convince the Allies to accept France, their defeated enemy, as an equal partner in negotiations. In the midst of the crisis over Poland, he persuaded Britain and Austria to sign a secret treaty with France in order to preserve an independent Polish territory. He then deliberately leaked news of the secret agreement of these powers to go to war, if necessary, to block Russian and Prussian aims. Alexander I and Frederick William III immediately backed down. Talleyrand's private opinion of the other four powers was acidic: "Too frightened to fight each other, too stupid to agree."

But under Talleyrand's manipulation, agree they did. In the final arrangement, Prussia retained the Polish territory of Posen and Austria kept the Polish province of Galicia. Krakow, with its population of 95,000, was declared a free city. Finally, a kingdom of Poland, nominally independent but in fact under the tutelage of Russia, emerged from what remained of the Grand Duchy of Warsaw. It was a solution that benefited no one in particular and disregarded Polish wishes.

In addition to receiving Polish territories, Prussia gained two-fifths of the kingdom of Saxony. Prussia also received territory on the left bank of the Rhine, the

Duchy of Westphalia, and Swedish Pomerania. With these acquisitions, Prussia doubled its population to around 11 million people. The Junkers, the landed class of east Prussia, reversed many of the reforms of the Napoleonic period. The new territories that Prussia gained were rich in waterways and resources but geographically fragmented. The dispersal of holdings that was intended to contain Prussian power in central Europe spurred Prussia to find new ways of uniting its markets. In this endeavor, Prussia constituted a future threat to Austrian power over the German Confederation.

In Scandinavia, Russia's conquest of Finland was acknowledged by the members of the Congress, and in return Sweden acquired Norway from Denmark. Unlike Austria, Prussia, and Russia, Great Britain made no claim to territories at the Congress. Having achieved its aim of containing France, its greatest rival for dominance on the seas, Britain returned the French colonies it had seized in war. For the time being, the redrawing of the territorial map of Europe had achieved its pragmatic aim of guaranteeing the peace. It was now left to a system of alliances to preserve that peace.

The Alliance System

Only by joining forces had the European powers been able to defeat Napoleon, and the necessity of a system of alliances was recognized even after the battles were over. Two alliance pacts dominated the post-Napoleonic era: the renewed Quadruple Alliance and the Holy Alliance. The Quadruple Alliance, signed by the victorious powers of Great Britain, Austria, Russia, and Prussia in November 1815, was intended to protect Europe against future French aggression and to preserve the status quo. In 1818 France, having completed its payment of war indemnities, joined the pact, which now became the Quintuple Alliance. The five powers promised to meet periodically over the next 20 years to discuss common problems and to ensure the peace.

The Holy Alliance, very different in tone and intent, was the brainchild of Alexander I and was heavily influenced by his mystical and romantic view of international politics. In this pact, the monarchs of Prussia, Austria, and Russia agreed to renounce war and to protect the Christian religion. The Holy Alliance spoke of

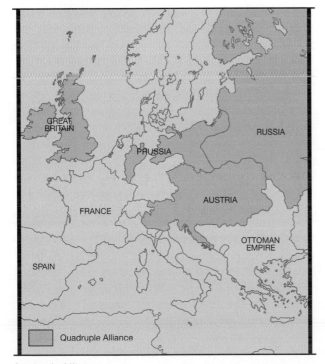

Quadruple Alliance

Holy Alliance

"the bonds of a true and indissoluble brotherhood . . . to protect religion, peace, and justice." Russia was able to give some credibility to the alliance with the sheer size of its army. Career diplomats were aware of its hollowness as a treaty arrangement, but it did indicate the willingness of Europe's three eastern autocracies to intervene in the affairs of other states.

The concept of Europe acting as a whole, through a system of periodic conferences, marked the emergence of a new diplomatic era. Conflict, however, was inherent in the commitment of parliamentary governments to open consultation and the need for secrecy in diplomacy. Dynastic regimes sought to intervene in smaller states to buoy up despots, as was the case in 1822, when European powers met to consider restoring the Bourbon monarchy in Spain. The British acted as a counterbalance to interventionist tendencies, refused to cooperate, and blocked united action by the Alliance. France took military action on its own in 1823, restored King Ferdinand VII, and abolished the Spanish constitution.

Both in the Congress of Vienna and the system of alliances that succeeded it, European nations aimed to establish a balance of power that recognized legitimate rulers and preserved the peace. The upheaval of the French Revolution and the revolutionary and Napoleonic wars had made clear the interdependence of one nation on another as a guarantee of survival. By maintaining an international equilibrium, Europe's statesmen hoped—erroneously, as it turned out—that by keeping the peace abroad, domestic peace would follow.

The Alliance system

May 1814	First Peace of Paris
23 September 1814–9 June 1815	Congress of Vienna
26 September 1815	Formation of the Holy Alliance
20 November 1815	Second Peace of Paris; Formation of the Quadruple Alliance
November 1818	Quadruple Alliance expands to include France in Quintuple Alliance
1823	French restoration of Bourbon Monarchy in Spain

The New European society

The peace that emerged from the Congress of Vienna did not restore the old order, although it did preserve principles of rule that a property-owning elite held dear. The search for stability and a reaction against political changes brought about by French rule characterized national and international affairs after 1815. Social structure and the world of production were undergoing dramatic transformations, and European states had to reckon with the fact that the daily lives of growing numbers of their subjects were transformed between 1815 and 1850. The demands of an international balance of power stood poised against the internal assaults on old social values in new arenas of conflict. Urbanization, industrialization, and economic uncertainties challenged Europeans in new ways in their search for stability.

Urban miseries

In 1800, two of every 100 Europeans lived in a city. By 1850 the number of urban dwellers per hundred had jumped to five and was rising rapidly. In England, the shift was more concentrated than the general European pattern. With one of every two people living in a city, England had become an urban society by midcentury. London was the fastest-growing city in Europe, followed at some distance by Paris and Berlin. The numbers of smaller urban centers were also multiplying.

Massive internal migrations caused most urban growth. People from the same rural areas often lived together in the same urban neighborhoods, and even in the same boardinghouses. Irish emigrants crowded together in the "Little Dublin" section of London. Similarly, districts in other cities were set off by regional accents and native provincial dress. Workers from the same hometowns gravitated to their favorite cafes. These social networks helped make the transition from rural to urban life bearable for the tens of thousands of people who poured into Europe's cities in search of jobs and opportunity. Until midcentury, many migrants returned to their rural homes for the winter when work, especially in the building trades, was scarce in the city. Young migrant women who came to the city to work as servants sent money home to support rural relatives, or worked to save a nest egg—or dowry—with the plan of returning to the village permanently. Before 1850, 20 percent of the workers in London were domestics, and most of them were women.

The Awakening Conscience (1854) *by William Holman Hunt. The painting captures a moment in the relationship of a London man of means and the young woman he has set up in a suburban flat. Such arrangements were common in an era when some women resorted to prostitution to eke out a living.*

Despite the support networks that migrants constructed for themselves, the city was not always a hospitable place. Workers were poorly paid, and women workers were more poorly paid than men. When working women were cut free of the support of home and family, uncounted numbers were forced into part-time prostitution to supplement meager incomes. More and more women resorted to prostitution as a means of surviving in times of unemployment. It is conservatively estimated that in 1850 there were 34,000 prostitutes in Paris and 50,000 in London. The phenomenon of prosti-

tution indicated changing mores about sexuality in the first half of the nineteenth century. The "angel" of middle-class households and the "whore" of the streets were subjects of fascination in fiction and nonfiction. Increased prostitution created a veritable epidemic of venereal diseases, especially syphilis, for which there was no known cure until the twentieth century.

Urban crime also grew astronomically, with thefts accounting for the greatest number of crimes. Social reformers identified poverty and urban crowding as causes of the increase in criminal behavior. In 1829, both Paris and London began to create modern urban police forces to deal with the challenges to law and order. Crime assumed the character of disease in the minds of middle-class reformers. Statisticians and social scientists, themselves a new urban phenomenon, produced massive theses on social hygiene, lower-class immorality, and the unworthiness of the poor. The pathology of the city was widely discussed. Always at the center of the issue was the growing problem of what to do with the poor.

The "social question"

State-sponsored work relief expanded after 1830 for the deserving poor: the old, the sick, and children. Able-bodied workers who were idle were regarded as undeserving and dangerous, regardless of the causes of their unemployment. Performance of work became an indicator of moral worth as urban and rural workers succumbed to downturns in the economic cycle. Those unable to work sought relief from the state as a last resort. What has been called a "revolution in government" took place in the 1830s and 1840s as legislative bodies increased regulation of everything from factories and mines to prisons and schools.

Poverty was not just an urban problem, though it was both more conspicuous and more feared in urban areas. Politicians, social reformers, religious thinkers, and revolutionaries all had different solutions that followed one of two general orientations. There were those who argued, as in the case of the Irish famine, that the government must do nothing to intervene because the problem would correct itself, as Thomas Malthus had predicted 40 years earlier. Malthus argued that the "natural" means of famine and death would keep population from outgrowing available resources and food supplies. The Irish population, one of the poorest in Europe, had indeed doubled between 1781 and 1841, and for Malthusians the Irish famine was the fulfillment of their vision that famine was the only way to correct overpopulation. This first group insisted that poverty was a social necessity; by interfering with it, governments could only make matters worse.

A second group contended that poverty was society's problem, and perhaps society's creation, and not a law of nature. Thus it was the social responsibility of the state to take care of its members. The question of how to treat poverty—or the "social question," as it came to be known among contemporaries—underlay many of the protests and reforms of the two decades before 1850 and fueled the revolutionary movements of 1848. Parliamentary legislation attempted to improve the situation of the poor, especially the working class, during the 1830s and 1840s.

In 1833 British reformers turned their attention to the question of child labor. Against the opposition of those who argued for a free market for labor, Parliament passed the Factory Act of 1833, which prohibited the employment of children under nine years of age and restricted the workweek of children aged nine to thirteen to 48 hours. No child in this age group could work more than 9 hours a day. Teenagers between 13 and 18 years could work no more than 69 hours a week. By modern standards, these "reformed" workloads present a shocking picture of the heavy reliance on child labor. The British Parliament commissioned investigations, compiled in the "Blue Books," that reported the abusive treatment of men, women, and children in factories. Similar studies existed for French and Belgian industry.

British legislation marked an initial step in state intervention in the workplace. Additional legislation over the next three decades further restricted children's and women's labor in factories and concerned itself with improving conditions in the workplace. Fundamentally, the "social question" was the question of what the state's role and responsibility were in caring for its citizens.

smaller families, higher hopes

Industrialization profoundly altered the structure of daily life within the family during the first half of the

---

Recalling a childhood in the factory

In the early 1830s, philanthropists and reformers demanded that the British government do something about the appalling abuses of children laboring in textile factories. In response to public outcry, parliamentary commissions interviewed thousands of women and children workers and compiled a record of horrifying exploitation and abuse.

These investigations resulted in legislation that limited the work hours of children, provided for inspection of work conditions by state agents, and required that young workers receive educational instruction.

Eliza Marshall, who was 18 at the time she gave the following testimony before the commission, recalled her childhood in the factory, beginning at age nine. Crippled by the tasks she performed and beaten frequently by her employer, she endured a grueling life of factory discipline typical of that legion of children who helped Britain maintain its industrial dominance.

I was turned ten when I began to work from five [a.m.] to nine [p.m.]. My sister was nine. There were older than me at Burgess'. Mr. Warburton picked us out, I suppose, because I was sharp at my work, a good hand: so was my sister. I was forced to go to work. I had no father, and my mother could not keep us without working. My mother is dead now. She died about half a year ago, since I was in London. I worked on at Warburton's till better than a year ago. I worked those hours all the time. We sometimes worked from six [a.m.] to seven [p.m.], but it was mostly from five to nine. He has got nearly two rooms full now; when I left him, there were about fifteen hands or so. I went from there to the Infirmary. . . .

It was the work and hours together that hurt me, and always having to stop the flies with my knee. I could stop it with my hand, but I had to hold it with my knee while I pieced it. It was having to crook my knee to stop the spindle that lamed me as much as any thing else.

From Great Britain's *Parliamentary Papers*, 1833, XX, Factory Inquiry Commission, 1st Report.

nineteenth century. Changes affected both middle-class and working-class families, though to varying degrees. With the rise of the state and a growing emphasis on education, the socializing role of the family was gradually transformed. By midcentury, population growth was beginning to slow down throughout Europe as people chose to restrict the size of their families. Europeans of earlier times had delayed marriage, practiced birth control, and employed abortion to limit family size. But the nineteenth century marks the first time in history that the majority of Europeans saw having fewer children as a value and acted on it.

Why decisions about limiting family size were made and how they were implemented are among the most intimate and private of questions; the answers can never really be known. But there is no doubt about the outcome of these decisions: people began having two or three children per family instead of five or six. Economic motivation appears to have been primary. In the nineteenth century, children had little economic value when they were eliminated from the workplace. The hope of a better life for one's progeny required that existing resources be concentrated on fewer children. The

Child labor in the textile factories. The meager wages of children were often necessary for the survival of their families.

middle-class pattern of small families became the dominant one in western Europe in the nineteenth century as middle-class culture became more self-conscious.

Jane Austen (1775–1817), one of Europe's great novelists, created a picture of middle-class life in nineteenth-century England and of women's place in it. In *Pride and Prejudice* (1813) and *Emma* (1815), parents and guardians wait helplessly on the sidelines, hoping their charges will marry well. Young people, freed from the arranged marriages of the previous century, choose mates on the basis of affection and affinity. The couple is a locus for personal fulfillment. Yet the middle-class family exists in a network of value and status. In Austen's novels, families are ranked according to their furniture, carriages, and pianofortes; the numbers of their servants; and the frequency of their trips to London. Austen chronicles the importance of income for marriage and status in a money-oriented society. The family is the primary arena of consumption.

The privacy of family life intensified with the transfer of paid work to a public workplace. Middle-class Europeans, whether French, German, or British, shared with Austen's families a taste for decorated interiors and material comforts in the home. In Germany, the Biedermeier style, named after a popular furniture maker, appeared in 1815 and remained popular until midcentury. Biedermeier stressed coziness, intimacy, and domesticity in the furnishings, clothes, and paintings of the German middle class. To its critics, the style was sentimental and vulgar. During this era, middle-class consumers began collecting on a mass scale. They filled their homes with knickknacks, curios, and mass-produced art. By accumulating these objects, the middle class asserted its right to be arbiter of its own style. At the same time, middle-class collectors aped the great aristocratic connoisseurs of a previous age.

A vast gulf separated working-class families from these middle-class consumers. Factory owner and social critic Friedrich Engels (1820–95) left a bleak but accurate account of working-class life in Manchester in *The Condition of the Working Class in England in 1844*. Working women, unsupervised children, and unemployed husbands figured prominently in his brutal tale of misery and immorality. Western culture redefined family life as the seat of solace, comfort, and consumption, but for the majority of the population that ideal remained out of reach.

Reformers confronted the disparities in family life and placed the blame squarely on women's absence from the home. Women had made industrialization

Cloakroom of the Clifton Assembly Rooms (1817–18) *by Rolinda Sharples is an example of the popular genre scenes that dealt with sentimental romanticized subjects.*

possible as they poured into the British and Continental textile factories and became the primary work force. Employers found women more adept and more dexterous than men in running the intricate new looms. Women worked for cheaper wages and generally were more docile than men in accepting the routinization of the factory. Men were considered more likely to organize, riot, or become rowdy. Women and children worked long hours under dire conditions. The number of women in factories was expanding rapidly in the 1830s and 1840s. The solution to the perceived decline in the working-class family was found in legislation to restrict women from working away from home and return them to care for their husbands and children.

Children were an even cheaper work force than women. Some proponents of child labor argued that the choice was to have children running wild in the streets and unsupervised at home or in the disciplined environment of the factories. The situation at its worst was reflected in one eyewitness account of French silk manufacture. For 18 hours a day, six-year-old girls were harnessed to mechanical wheels to work.

Women's rights, little affected by industrialization, were increasingly disputed in public forums after 1815. In France, the equality of citizens before the law did not extend to women. Women's subservience in marriage was clearly defined: "A husband owes protection to his wife, a wife obedience to her husband." The law preserved a double standard for judging the behavior of women and men. In English law, men could terminate their marriages but their wives had no such access to divorce. Agitation for the right to divorce, converging with notorious public scandals over abused married women, achieved nothing before 1850. Critics blamed the decline in sexual mores on women's refusal to "know their place." By the mid-nineteenth century, women were organizing to demand equal political rights, political representation, assistance in caring for children, and better living conditions. Through their own newspapers, journals, and pamphlets, bourgeois women publicized their political demands for all women. John Stuart Mill, the leading liberal theorist, joined with women reformers in demanding full equality for British women. These movements achieved little

seneca falls resolutions

One of the most influential meetings in furthering the claims of women to full participation in civil life occurred at Seneca Falls, New York, in 1848 where the assembled women declared their rights as individuals equal to men and full members of the body politic. The women present— many of them active in the antislavery and temperance movement—included Elizabeth Cady Stanton (1815–1902) and Susan B. Anthony (1820–1906). In 1840, eight years before Seneca Falls, Stanton and other abolitionists had attended an international antislavery convention in London. The exclusion of the women delegates from the floor of the London convention shocked Stanton and her female colleagues and served as a turning point in their own political consciousness. Their resolutions at Seneca Falls, especially those demanding the right to vote, influenced burgeoning women's movements in Europe and the United States.

Resolved, That such laws as conflict, in any way, with the true and substantial happiness of woman, are contrary to the great precept of nature and of no validity, for this is "superior in obligation to any other."

Resolved, That all laws which prevent woman from occupying such a station in society as her conscience shall dictate, or which place her in a position inferior to that of man, are contrary to the great precept of nature, and therefore of no force or authority.

Resolved, That woman is man's equal—was intended to be so by the Creator, and the highest good of the race demands that she should be recognized as such.

Resolved, That the women of this country ought to be enlightened in regard to the laws under which they live, that they may no longer publish their degradation by declaring themselves satisfied with their present position, nor their ignorance, by asserting that they have all the rights they want.

Resolved, That inasmuch as man, while claiming for himself intellectual superiority, does accord to woman moral superiority, it is pre-eminently his duty to encourage her to speak and teach, as she has an opportunity, in all religious assemblies.

Resolved, That the same amount of virtue, delicacy, and refinement of behavior that is required of woman in the social state, should also be required of man, and the same transgressions should be visited with equal severity on both man and woman.

Resolved, That the objection of indelicacy and impropriety, which is so often brought against woman when she addresses a public audience, comes with a very ill-grace from those who encourage, by their attendance, her appearance on the stage, in the concert, or in feats of the circus.

Resolved, That woman has too long rested satisfied in the circumscribed limits which corrupt customs and a perverted application of the Scriptures have marked out for her, and that it is time she should move in the enlarged sphere which her great Creator has assigned her.

Resolved, That it is the duty of the women of this country to secure to themselves their sacred right to the elective franchise.

Resolved, That the equality of human rights results necessarily from the fact of the identity of the race in capabilities and responsibilities.

Resolved, therefore, That, being invested by the Creator with the same capabilities, and the same consciousness of responsibility for their exercise, it is demonstrably the right and duty of woman, equally with man, to promote every righteous cause by every righteous means; and especially in regard to the great subjects of morals and religion, it is self-evidently her right to participate with her brother in teaching them, both in private and in public, by writing and by speaking, by any instrumentalities proper to be used, and in any assemblies proper to be held; and this being a self-evident truth growing out of the divinely implanted principles of human nature, any custom or authority adverse to it, whether modern or wearing the hoary sanction of antiquity, is to be regarded as a self-evident falsehood, and at war with mankind.

Resolved, That the speedy success of our cause depends upon the zealous and untiring efforts of both men and women, for the overthrow of the monopoly of the pulpit, and for the securing to woman an equal participation with men in the various trades, professions, and commerce.

From Declaration of Sentiments and Resolutions, Seneca Falls Convention of 1848.

in solid reforms before 1850, but they made clear the tensions within the family and within the law.

The growing emphasis on public education added its own special twist to the debate over family life and women's rights. Few agreed with French labor leader Flora Tristan (1801–44) and the utopian reformer Charles Fourier that women had the capacity and the right to receive an equal education with men. Most argued that women should be educated only to fulfill better their natural responsibilities as mothers. Napoleon's dictum "The hand that rocks the cradle rules the nation" became the chief justification for educating girls as mothers.

In 1837, in Great Britain, an 18-year-old became queen. Reigning until her death in 1901, Victoria gave her name to an age and its morals. Girls became queens of Portugal and Spain. They, like the young Victoria, were little more than political figureheads, protecting the survival of dynastic claims and contributing little to the growing debate about women's proper place in society. Although the presence of women on European thrones may have provided inspiration for disenfran-

chised women, it did not affect the broader reality that everywhere women were deprived of the vote and equal protection before the law, that married women could not own property or claim custody of their own children. Victoria, ruler of one of the world's great nations, became the model for domestic bliss. The changing expectations about the emotional rewards of family life, reflected in the publicity of the queen's marriage to Prince Albert of Saxe-Coburg-Gotha in 1840, created a new image of proper womanhood that had little relation to the lives that most women led.

To European societies that had remained stable, if not stagnant, for centuries, the changes in the first half of the nineteenth century were undoubtedly startling and disruptive. More people than ever before lived in cities, and national populations faced the prospect of becoming urban. Industrialization reshaped how people worked, how people lived, and how they consumed. But change did not necessarily mean improvement. Urban congestion brought crime and disease; new factories created the arena for exploitation and misery; and patterns of consumption demonstrated beyond dispute

A family portrait of Queen Victoria, the Prince Consort, and their eldest children, painted by Franz Xavier Winterhalter in 1846. Their first daughter, Victoria, would become the mother of Kaiser Wilhelm II of Germany.

that people were not created equal. New expectations were attached to the family as its size changed and gender roles underwent redefinition. A new European society that challenged existing political ideas and demanded new political formulations was in the process of emerging.

The New Ideologies

Early industrialization had been accomplished without a dramatically new technology. Wood, water, wind, and muscle—animal and human—the sources of energy in the preindustrial period, fueled the early stages of industrialization. Practices began to change slowly as crises in energy supply—deforestation and drought, for example—encouraged the use of coal as a more reliable and eventually more efficient fuel. After 1815, steam-driven mechanical power in production and transportation steadily replaced human and animal power. In deference to what it was replacing, the new mechanical force was measured in units of horsepower. The new technology challenged old values; new definitions of worth emerged from the changing world of work. The fixed, castelike distinctions of the old aristocratic world were under attack or in disarray. Western intellectuals struggled with the changes of the new age as they sought to make sense of the way in which Europeans lived, looked at the world, and defined their place in it.

The political and economic upheavals of the first half of the nineteenth century encouraged a new breed of thinkers to search for ways to explain the transformations of the period. During this period, Europeans witnessed one of the most intellectually fertile periods in the history of the West. The search for understanding during this era gave birth to new ideologies—liberalism, nationalism, romanticism, conservatism, and socialism—that would shape the ideas and institutions of the present day.

Liberalism

The term *liberal* was first used in a narrow political sense to indicate the Spanish party of reform that supported the constitution modeled on the French document of 1791. But the term assumed much broader connotations in the first half of the nineteenth century as its appeal spread among the European middle classes. The

two main tenets of belief that underlay liberalism were the freedom of the individual and the corruptibility of authority. As a political doctrine, liberalism built on Enlightenment rationalism and embraced the right to vote, civil liberties, legal equality, constitutional government, parliamentary sovereignty, and a free-market economy. Liberals firmly believed that less government was better government and that noninterference would produce a harmonious and well-ordered world. They also believed that human beings were basically good and reasonable and needed freedom in which to flourish. The sole end of government should be to promote that freedom.

No single representative thinker embodied all the tenets of liberal thought, but many shared similar ideas and beliefs. Liberal thinkers tried to make sense of the political conflicts of the revolutionary period and the economic disruptions brought on by industrialization. The Great Revolution at the end of the eighteenth century spawned a vast array of liberal thought in France. Republicans, Bonapartists, and constitutional monarchists cooperated as self-styled "liberals" who shared a desire to preserve the gains of the revolution while ensuring orderly rule. Not the least influenced by liberal

This cameo, made by Josiah Wedgwood for the Society for the Abolition of Slavery, shows a chained and manacled slave and bears the inscription "Am I Not a Man and a Brother?" Wedgwood sent a batch of these cameos to Benjamin Franklin for distribution among American abolitionists.

ideas were a variety of political movements in the United States, including those demanding the liberation of slaves and the extension of legal and political rights to women. Abolitionists justified their opposition to slavery on humanitarian Christian grounds and on the liberal principles of freedom and equality. American women who were active in antislavery societies extended their liberal crusade against oppression to their own legal and political status.

By the mid-nineteenth century, liberal thinking constituted a dominant strain in British politics. Jeremy Bentham (1748–1832), trained in British law, fashioned himself into a social philosopher. He founded utilitarianism, a fundamentally liberal doctrine that argued for "the greatest happiness of the greatest number" in such works as *Introduction to the Principles of Morals and Legislation*. Bentham believed that government could achieve positive ends through limited and "scientific" intervention. Only the pursuit of social harmony justified interference with individual liberty. He found the best testing grounds for his theories in prisons, among convicted criminals. By supporting the reform of penal codes and prison regulations in *Rationale of Punishments and Rewards* (1825), he hoped that rewards and punishments could be meted out to convicts in a measurable "geometry" of pain and pleasure. He was sure that behavior could be improved and that prisoners could be rehabilitated and returned as honest citizens to society. (See "The Birth of the Prison," pp. 756–757.)

The Scottish philosopher, economist, and historian James Mill (1773–1836) met Jeremy Bentham in 1808 and dedicated the rest of his life to promulgating Bentham's utilitarian philosophy. James Mill's son John Stuart Mill (1806–73) reacted to his early and intense education in Benthamite ideas by rejecting the tenets of utilitarianism. Forging his own brand of classical liberalism in his treatise *On Liberty* (1859), the younger Mill became the greatest liberal thinker of the age. John Stuart Mill criticized Bentham for ignoring human emotions and for the mass tyranny implicit in his ideas. Mill went beyond existing political analyses by applying economic doctrines to social conditions in *Principles of Political Economy* (1848). With Harriet Taylor (d. 1858), who married him after years of intellectual collaboration, he espoused social reform for the poor and championed the equality of women and the necessity of birth control. By 1848 his writings on liberty and equality were questioning the sacredness of private property. In later life, John Stuart Mill came to believe that a more equitable distribution of wealth was both necessary and possible.

David Ricardo (1772–1823) was a stockbroker prodigy who by the age of 20 had made his fortune. In *Principles of Political Economy and Taxation* (1817), Ricardo outlined his opposition to government intervention in foreign trade and elaborated his "iron law of wages," which contended that wages would stabilize at the subsistence level. Increased wages would cause the working classes to grow, and the resulting competition in the labor market would drive wages down to the level of subsistence. Other liberals, more concerned with social welfare than Ricardo, argued that state intervention was unavoidable but could be limited.

Nationalism

In its most basic sense, nationalism before 1850 was the political doctrine that glorified the people united against the absolutism of kings and the tyranny of foreign oppressors. The success of the French Revolution and the spread of Napoleonic reforms boosted nationalist doctrines, which were most fully articulated on the Continent. In Germany, Johann Gottfried von Herder (1744–1803) rooted national identity in German folk culture. The *Fairy Tales* (1812–14) of the brothers Jacob Ludwig Grimm (1785–1863) and Wilhelm Carl Grimm (1786–1859) had a similar national purpose. The brothers painstakingly captured in print the German oral tradition of peasant folklore. The philosophers Johann Fichte (1762–1814) and Georg Wilhelm Friedrich Hegel (1770–1831) emphasized the importance of the state. Nationalism gave birth to a search for new symbols, just as the tricolor flag replaced the fleur-de-lis and the image of Marianne replaced the monarch as a result of the Great Revolution in France. There was a new concern with history as nationalists sought to revive a common cultural past.

In the period between 1830 and 1850, many nationalists were liberals and many liberals were nationalists. The nationalist yearning for liberation meshed with the liberal political program of overthrowing tyrannical rule. Giuseppe Mazzini (1805–72) represented the new breed of liberal nationalist. A less-than-liberal nationalist was political economist Georg Friedrich List (1789–1846), who formulated a statement of economic nationalism to counter the liberal doctrines of David Ricardo. Arguing that free trade worked only for the wealthy and powerful, List advocated a program of protective tariffs for

young italy (1832)

Giuseppe Mazzini, an Italian patriot and revolutionary, was the principal theorist of national revolution in Europe in the first half of the nineteenth century. He claimed that his strong commitment to equality and democratic principles stemmed from his readings on the French Revolution of 1789 and his study of the Latin classics. As a young man, he resolved to dress always in black as a sign of mourning for his country, disunited and under foreign oppressors. In 1832 he founded the secret society Young Italy. The goal of this revolutionary group was the unification of Italy under a republican form of government through direct popular action.

We have beheld Italy—Italy, the purpose, the soul, the consolation of our thoughts, the country chosen of God and oppressed by men, twice queen of the world and twice fallen through the infamy of foreigners and the guilt of her citizens, yet lovely still though she be dust, unmatched by any other nation whatever fortune has decreed, and Genius returns to seek in this dust the word of eternal life, and the spark that creates the future. . . .

Young Italy: but we chose this term because the one term seems to marshal before the youth of Italy the magnitude of its duties and the solemnity of the mission that circumstances have entrusted to it, so that it will be ready when the hour has struck to arise from its slumber to a new life of action and regeneration. And we chose it because we wanted to show ourselves, writing it, as what we are, to do battle with raised visors, to bear our faith before us, as the knights of medieval times bore their faith on their shields. For while we pity men who do not know the truth, we despise men who, though they know the truth, do not dare to speak it.

developing German industries. He perceived British free trade as merely economic imperialism in disguise. List was one of the few nationalists who did not wholeheartedly embrace liberal economic doctrines. Beyond ideology and political practices, nationalism began to capture the imagination of groups who resented foreign domination. Expanding state bureaucracies did little to tame the centrifugal forces of nationalist feeling and probably exacerbated a desire for independence in eastern and central Europe, especially in the Habsburg-ruled lands.

Romanticism

Unlike liberalism and nationalism, which were fundamentally political ideologies, romanticism designated a variety of literary and artistic movements throughout Europe that spanned the period from the late eighteenth century to the mid-nineteenth century. One could be a nationalist and a romantic or a liberal and a romantic just as easily as one could be a conservative and a romantic. Above all, and in spite of variations, romantics shared similar beliefs and a common view of the world. Among the first romantics were the English poets William Wordsworth (1770–1850) and Samuel Taylor Coleridge (1772–1834), whose collaborative *Lyrical Ballads* (1798) exemplified the iconoclastic romantic idea that poetry was the result of "the spontaneous overflow of powerful feelings" rather than a formal and highly disciplined intellectual exercise. Romantics, in general, rebelled against the confinement of classical forms and refused to accept the supremacy of reason over emotions.

The English gardens designed at the end of the eighteenth century provide one of the best visual examples of the new romanticism. The formal gardens that surrounded the castles and manor houses of Europe's wealthy elite throughout the eighteenth century relied on carefully drawn geometric patterns, minutely trimmed hedges and lawns, and symmetrically arranged flowers planted in rows by size and color to achieve the effect of total mastery of nature. The gardens at the great palace of Versailles are a good example of the formal landscaping chosen by France's kings and emulated by the wealthy everywhere in Europe. The romantic or English garden was, by contrast, a rebellious profusion

the Birth of the prison

There was once a time when modern prisons, what we call penitentiaries, did not exist. Prisons, like modern hospitals and schools, were one of the great achievements of the age of reform in the first half of the nineteenth century. Thanks to the efforts of humanitarians and social reformers, a new rationale for punishment emerged, one that claimed modern prisons were capable of rehabilitating criminals. Reformers argued that the controlled environment of a new prison system would be able to fashion wrongdoers into upstanding citizens through moral instruction, hard work, constant surveillance, and, in some cases, isolation from human contact.

The principles of the new penal arrangement were silence and separation—total or partial, in order to rehabilitate prisoners through supervised activities, including productive work. In French penitentiaries, prisoners were given an occupation and produced goods for the prison system itself—shoes or mattresses, for example—or for sale on the open market. The belief was that through productive labor, prisoners could be taught to be good workers and good citizens. Idle hands were the devil's workshop, so no moment of the prisoner's day was unoccupied or, in theory, unsupervised.

Some of these "new" prisons were built in the shells of ancient military garrisons, seminaries, convents, and retreat houses. Before the beginning of the nineteenth century, prisons existed but they served as waystations, holding areas for those who were about to face their "real" punishments, which could be death, mutilation, forced labor in prison ships, or banishment. After 1820, however, incarceration became a punishment in itself throughout western Europe, with the goal to deprive prisoners of liberty and freedom of movement.

A typical prisoner in the new penitentiaries was a man convicted of theft serving a sentence of from five to seven years. He entered a prison world where every aspect of his life was prescribed and supervised. The experience of the prison was intended to transform the behavior of the prisoner. Prisoners for the first time were required to wear uniforms. In addition to the regimented routine of work, meals, and sleep, the prisoner now also received moral and religious instruction behind bars.

Although populations in the old prisons of the eighteenth century were mixed with women and men, adults and children confined in the same spaces, by contrast, in the nineteenth century convicted women and children were systematically separated from male prisoners and subject to separate rules of confinement. Religious orders and philanthropic groups supervised women and children in prisons and continued to watch them in their lives after prison. Reformers now spoke of the punishment being made to fit the criminal—not the crime.

The most controversial aspect of the new punishment was solitary confinement. Women were usually exempted from these initial isolation experiments, deemed as too "social" or too weak to support total separation. Young boys on the other hand were targeted for the special experimental punishment of solitary isolation, something French observers like historian and political philosopher Alexis de Tocqueville greatly admired on his travels in the United States. In one particularly brutal period of experimentation, beginning in 1838 French prison officials confined boys between the ages of six and sixteen to their cells day and night where they were expected to follow a strict regime of silence, discipline, religious instruction, and constant occupation. Most of these children were court custody cases committed by their fathers because of unruly behavior. The results were dire. There was no accurate way to measure recidivism, and, worse, the children's mortality rates increased sharply. Children in solitary confinement may have been protected from the "moral depravity" of other inmates, but they got sick and died more frequently than their counterparts in free society and than other kinds of prisoners. What began as a humanitarian advance was soon denounced as a form of torture for juvenile offenders.

Why did penitentiaries come into being in the first half of the nineteenth century? The new punishment was considered attractive because, in an age confronted with industrial and political transformations and revolutionary upheavals, it seemed to be a way of controlling criminal disruptions and social unrest. The middle classes, whether in London or Paris, grew increasingly fearful about potential threats to their property and well-being. Industrial workers crowded into substandard urban housing could face long periods of unemployment, when it was feared that desperate men and women would commit crimes to feed themselves and their families. The fear of the poor as dangerous informed many of the prison reforms of the early nineteenth century. Great Britain and France created growing bureaucracies of penal, policing, and judicial institutions to guarantee the safety of honest citizens. At the same time that new prisons opened their doors, policemen started walking their neighborhood beats in European capitals.

Almost from the beginning prisons were deemed a failure. Specialists concluded that prisons did not correct criminals but instead served as schools for crime.

Vincent van Gogh, The Prison Courtyard (1890). *The painting is copied after a wood engraving by Gustave Doré representing Newgate-the Exercise Yard in* London, a Pilgrimage *(1872).*

Statistics—a new scientific practice in itself—proved them right. Recidivism rates rose dramatically, as penal authorities devised new ways—eventually fingerprinting and photography—to follow the activities of released prisoners. It is very likely that what was increasing in this era was not criminality but the ability of the state to track it.

The science of the new punishment evolved directly in relation to political and social changes in the first half of the nineteenth century. The three major spurts of prison reform in France, for example, coincided with the revolutionary upheavals of 1789, 1830, and 1848. Social reformers and legislators turned to the prison system as a crucial mechanism in the regulation of civil society. The new prisons were part of the network of institutions created to maintain an orderly working class in the new democratic age.

of color in which the landscaper rejected the carefully drawn geometric patterns then in vogue and set out instead, deliberately and somewhat paradoxically, to imitate nature. The romantic aesthetic, whether in landscape gardening or in literature, recognized the beauty of untamed nature and the inspiration produced by the release of human emotions.

By rooting artistic vision in spontaneity, romantics endorsed a concept of creativity based on the supremacy of human freedom. The artist was valued in a new way as a genius through whose insight and intuition great art was created. Intuition, as opposed to scientific learning, was endorsed as a valid means of knowing. Building on the work of the eighteenth-century philosopher Immanuel Kant (1724–1804), romanticism embraced subjective knowledge. Inspiration and intuition took the place of reason and science in the romantic pantheon of values.

Germaine de Staël (1766–1817), often hailed as the founder of French romanticism, was an extraordinary woman whose writings influenced French liberal political theory after 1815. Madame de Staël's mother had followed the principles of education spelled out by Jean Jacques Rousseau in Émile (1762), according to which the child was allowed to follow his or her own path of intellectual development. De Staël authored histories, novels, literary criticism, and political tracts that opposed what she judged to be the tyranny of Napoleonic rule. She, like many other romantics, was greatly influenced by the writings of Rousseau, and through him she discovered that "the soul's elevation is born of self-consciousness." The recognition of the subjective meant for de Staël that women's vision was as essential as men's for the flowering of European culture.

"It is within oneself that one must look at what lies outside." Following de Staël's lead, Victor Hugo (1802–85), one of the great French writers of the nineteenth century, identified another essential ingredient in romanticism. The turning "within oneself" so apparent in Hugo's poetry was profoundly influenced by the political events of the French Revolution and its principles of liberty and equality. His greatest novels, including Notre-Dame de Paris (1831) and Les Misérables (1862), offer bold panoramic sweeps of the social universe of Paris across the ages.

Nationalists in the first half of the nineteenth century were often romantics who valued the authenticity of the vernacular and folklore over the language and customs imposed by a foreign ruler. Herder and the brothers Grimm were German examples of the romantic

appreciation of the roots of German culture. While French romantics emphasized the glories of their revolutionary heritage, German romantics stressed the importance of history as the source of one's identity. By searching for the self in a historic past, and especially in the Middle Ages, they glorified their collective cultural identity and national origins. Medievalism in Germany was at the heart of Sturm und Drang (Storm and Stress), a literary movement founded in the 1770s. A founder of the Sturm und Drang movement, Johann Wolfgang von Goethe (1749–1832), hailed as the greatest of modern German writers, inspired generations with his dramatic poem Faust (Part I, 1808; Part II, 1832). In the poem, Goethe recounts the traditional legend of a man who sells his soul to the devil in exchange for greater knowledge. Faust, who achieves mystical salvation in the poem's final scene, symbolizes for Goethe the spiritual crisis plaguing European civilization in the early nineteenth century.

Whether in words or in music or on canvas, romanticism conveyed a new way of understanding the world. The supremacy of the emotions over reason found its way into the works of the great romantic composers of the age. Liberation from the forms that dominated the classical era could be heard in the works of French composer Louis Hector Berlioz (1803–69), who set Faust's damnation to music; Polish virtuoso Frédéric Chopin (1810–49), who created lyric compositions for the piano; and Hungarian concert pianist Franz Liszt (1811–86), who composed symphonic poems and Hungarian rhapsodies.

Artists as different as J. M. W. Turner (1775–1851), the English landscape painter, and Eugène Delacroix (1798–1863), the leader of the French romantic school in painting, shared a commitment to their iconoclastic art. Turner's intense and increasingly abstract vision of an often turbulent natural world and Delacroix's epic historical and political masterpieces shared a rebellious experimentation with color and a rejection of classical conventions and forms. Characteristic of a particular strain within romanticism was the political message of Delacroix's art. In the magnificent painting Liberty Leading the People (1831), for example, Delacroix immortalized the revolutionary events that swept Paris in 1830 in his moving portrayal of valiant revolutionaries of different social classes led into battle by a female Liberty.

In the postrevolutionary years between 1815 and 1850, romanticism claimed to be no more than an aesthetic stance in art, letters, and music, a posture that had no particular political intent. Yet its validation of the individual as opposed to the caste or the estate was the most revolutionary of doctrines, just as its justification of subjective knowledge threatened to erode the authority of classical learning. Artists did not make revolutions, but they supported them. Some stood by on the sidelines; others mounted the barricades; but all romantics, no matter how political or apolitical, helped shape a new way of looking at the world and helped define a new political consciousness.

conservatism

Conservatism was not a rejection of political, economic, or social change. Like liberalism, conservatism represented a dynamic adaptation to a social system in transition. In place of individualism, conservatives stressed the corporate nature of European society; in place of reason and progress, conservatives saw organic growth and tradition. Liberty, argued British statesman Edmund Burke (1729–97) in *Reflections on the Revolution in France* (1790), must emerge out of the gradual development of the old order, and not its destruction. On the Continent, conservatives Louis de Bonald (1754–1840) and Joseph de Maistre (1753–1821) defended the monarchical principle of authority against the onslaught of revolutionary events.

Conservatism took a reactionary turn in the hands of the Austrian statesman Metternich. The Carlsbad decrees of 1819 are a good example of the "Metternich system" of espionage, censorship, and repression in central Europe, which sought to eliminate any constitutional or nationalist sentiments that had arisen during the Napoleonic period. The German Confederation approved decrees against free speech and civil liberties and set up mechanisms to root out "subversive" university students. Students who had taken up arms in the Wars of Liberation (1813–15) against France had done so in hopes of instituting liberal and national reforms. Metternich's system aimed at uprooting these goals. Student fraternities were closed, and police became a regular fixture in the university. Political expression was driven underground for at least a decade. Metternich set out to crush liberalism, constitutionalism, and parliamentarianism in central Europe. His goals, though tolerated, were certainly not shared by more liberal regimes such as Great Britain's.

socialism

Socialists and conservatives shared one point of view: both rejected the world as it was. Socialism, like other ideologies of the first half of the nineteenth century,

Liberty Leading the People (1831) *by Eugène Delacroix captures the spirit of the French romantics, who looked upon revolutionary action as a way to achieve union with the spirit of history.*

grew out of changes in the structure of daily life and the structure of power. There were as many stripes of socialists as there were liberals, nationalists, and conservatives. Socialists as a group shared a concern with "alienation," though they may not all have used the term.

Henri de Saint-Simon (1760–1825) rejected liberal individualism in favor of social organization and, for this reason, has been called the father of French socialism. To Saint-Simon, the accomplishments and potential of industrial development represented the highest stage in history. In a perfect and just society, productive work would be the basis of all prestige and power. The elite of society would be organized according to the hierarchy of its productive members, with industrial leaders at the top. Work was a social duty. The new industrial society that Saint-Simon foresaw would be both efficient and ethical, based on a religion similar to Christianity.

Like Saint-Simon, the French social theorist Pierre-Joseph Proudhon (1809–65) recognized the social value of work. But unlike Saint-Simon, Proudhon refused to accept the dominance of industrial society. A self-educated typesetter of peasant origin, Proudhon gained national prominence with his ideas about a just society, free credit, and equitable exchange. In his famous pamphlet *What Is Property?* (1840), Proudhon answered, "Property is theft." This statement was not, however, an argument for the abolition of private ownership. Proudhon reasoned that industrialization had destroyed workers' rights, which included the right to the profits of their own labor. In attacking "property" in the form of profits amassed from the labor of others, Proudhon was arguing for a socialist concept of limited possession—people had the right to own only what they had earned from their own labor. Proudhon, who did not himself participate in political agitation, held a profoundly anarchistic view of society, hated government, and favored instead small self-ruling communities of producers. Proudhon's ideal world would be one of comfort but not great wealth.

At least one socialist believed in luxury. Charles Fourier (1772–1837), an unsuccessful traveling salesman, devoted himself to the study and improvement of society and formulated one of the most trenchant criticisms of industrial capitalism. In numerous writings between 1808 and his death, this eccentric, solitary man put forth his vision of a utopian world organized into units called phalanxes that took into account the social,

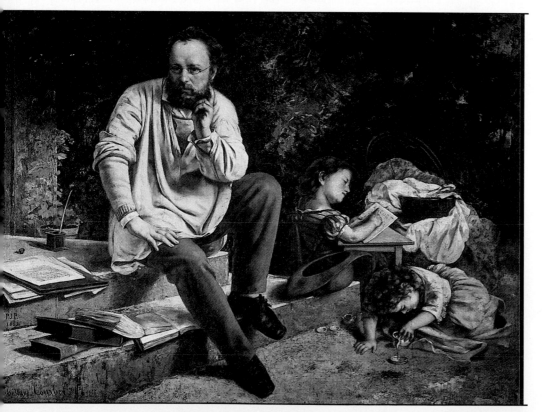

Proudhon and His Children (1865) *by Gustave Courbet. Proudon's literary and political activities often led to trouble with the authorities. He spent a number of years in prison or in exile.*

sexual, and economic needs of their members. With a proper mix of duties, everyone in the phalanx would work only a few hours a day. In Fourier's scheme, work was not naturally abhorrent, but care had to be taken to match temperaments with tasks. Women and men fulfilled themselves and found pleasure and gratification through work. People would be paid according to their contributions in work, capital, and talent. In his vision of a better world, Fourier's phalanxes were always rural and were organized communally, though neither poverty nor property would be eliminated. Education would help alleviate discord, and rich and poor would learn to live together in perfect harmony.

Charles Fourier's work, along with that of Saint-Simon and Proudhon, became part of the tradition of utopian thinking that can be traced back to Thomas More in the sixteenth century. Because he believed in the ability of individuals to shape themselves and their world, Fourier intended his critique of society to be a blueprint for living. Fourier's followers set up communities in his lifetime—40 phalanxes were established in the United States alone—but because of financial problems and petty squabbling, all of them failed.

Women active in demanding their own emancipation were often joined by men who espoused utopian socialist and liberal views. The issue of increased civil liberties for women, tied as it often was to talk of freeing the slaves, was both a moral and political question for social reformers and utopian thinkers, including Fourier, who put the issue of women's freedom at the center of their plans to redesign society. Saint-Simonians argued for woman's social elevation and searched for a female messiah. Other social reformers joined with conservative thinkers in arguing that women must be kept in their place and that their place was in the home. Proudhon, for example, saw women's only choices as working at home as housewives or working in the streets as prostitutes.

Socialists, along with other ideologues in the decades before the middle of the nineteenth century, were aware of how rapidly their world was changing. Many felt that a revolution that would eliminate poverty and the sufferings of the working class was at hand. Followers of Saint-Simon, Fourier, and Proudhon all hoped that their proposals and ideas would change the world and prevent violent upheaval. Not all social critics were so sanguine. In January 1848, two young men, one a philosopher living in exile and the other a businessman working for his father, began a collaboration that would last a lifetime with the publication of a short tract entitled *The Communist Manifesto*. Karl Marx (1818–83) and Friedrich Engels described the dire situation of the European working classes throughout the 1840s. The growing poverty and alienation of the proletariat, the authors promised, would bring to industrialized Europe a class war against the capitalists. Exploited workers must prepare themselves for the moment of revolution by joining with each other across national boundaries: "Workers of the world unite. You have nothing to lose but your chains." In light of subsequent events, the *Manifesto* appears to be a work of great predictive value. But neither Marx nor Engels realized that the hour of revolution was at hand.

Intellectuals and reformers hoped to reshape the world in which they lived with the force of their ideas. Yet the new ideologies were themselves the consequence of the changing role of government and the changing practices of daily life. The technology of industrial production informed people's values and required a new way of looking at the world. Liberals, nationalists, romantics, conservatives, and socialists addressed the challenges of a changing economy in a political universe buffeted by democratic ideas. The new ideologies did not provide easy answers, but they did serve to incite their followers to take up arms in protests and revolutions throughout Europe.

protest and Revolution

Few Europeans alive in 1830 remembered the age of revolution that spanned the period from 1789 to 1799. Yet the legends were kept alive from one generation to the next. Secret political organizations perpetuated Jacobin republicanism. Mutual-aid societies and artisans' associations preserved the rituals of democratic culture. A revolutionary culture seemed to be budding in the student riots in Germany and in the revolutionary waves that swept across southern and central Europe in the early 1820s. Outside Manchester, England, in August 1819 a crowd of 80,000 people gathered in St. Peter's Field to hear speeches for parliamentary reform and universal male suffrage. The cavalry swept down on them in a bloody slaughter that came to be known as the "Peterloo" massacre, a bitter reference to the Waterloo victory four years before.

The fabric of stability began unraveling throughout Europe in the 1820s. The forces of order reacted to protest with repression everywhere in Europe. In the more industrialized countries of England and France, the army was joined by the newly created peacekeeping forces of the police. Yet armed force proved inadequate

A savage satire of the Peterloo Massacre by cartoonist George Cruikshank. One soldier urges the others on by telling them that the more poor people they kill, the fewer taxes they will have to pay for poor relief.

to contain the demands for political participation and the increased political awareness of whole segments of the population. Workers, the middle class, and women's political organizations now demanded, through the vote, the right to govern themselves.

The Revolutions of 1830

Poor harvests in 1829 followed by a harsh winter left people cold, hungry, and bitter. Misery fueled social protest, and political issues of participation and representation commanded a new attention. The convergence of social unrest with long-standing political demands touched off apparently simultaneous revolutions all over Europe. Governmental failure to respond to local grievances sparked the revolutions of 1830. Highly diverse groups of workers, students, lawyers, professionals, and peasants rose up spontaneously to demand a voice in the affairs of government.

In France, the late 1820s were a period of increasing political friction. Charles X (1824–30), the former comte d'Artois, had never resigned himself to the constitutional monarchy accepted by his brother and predecessor, Louis XVIII. When Charles assumed the throne in 1824, he dedicated himself to a true restoration of kingship as it had existed before the revolution. To this end, he realigned the monarchy with the Catholic church and

undertook several unpopular measures, including approval of the death penalty for those found guilty of sacrilege. The king's bourgeois critics, heavily influenced by liberal ideas about political economy and constitutional rights, sought increased political power through their activities in secret organizations and in public elections. The king responded to his critics by relying on his ultraroyalist supporters to run the government. In May 1830, the king dissolved the Chamber of Deputies and ordered new elections. The elections returned a liberal majority unfavorable to the king. Charles X retaliated with what proved to be his last political act, the Four Ordinances, in which he censored the press, changed the electoral law to favor his own candidates, dissolved the newly elected Chamber, and ordered new elections.

Opposition to Charles X might have remained at the level of political wrangling and journalistic protest, if it had not been for the problems plaguing the people of Paris. A severe winter in France had driven up food prices by 75 percent. Most urban dwellers were barely subsisting. The king had erred in hoping that France's recent conquest of Algeria in North Africa would keep the populace quiet. He underestimated the extent of hardship and the political volatility of the population. Throughout the spring of 1830, prices continued to rise and Charles continued to blunder. In a spontaneous uprising in the last days of July 1830, workers took to the streets of Paris. The revolution they initiated spread rapidly to towns and the countryside as people throughout France protested the cost of living, hoarding by grain merchants, tax collection, and wage cuts. In "three glorious days," the restored Bourbon regime was pulled down and Charles X fled to England.

The people fighting in the streets demanded a republic, but they lacked organization and political experience. Liberal bourgeois politicians quickly filled the power vacuum. They presented Charles's cousin Louis-Philippe, formerly the duc d'Orléans, as the savior of France and the new constitutional monarch. This July Monarchy, born of a revolution, put an end to the Bourbon Restoration. Louis-Philippe became "king of the French." The charter that he brought with him was, like its predecessor, based on restricted suffrage, with property ownership a requisite for voting. The voting age was lowered from 30 to 25, and the tax requirement was also lowered. The electorate nearly doubled, from 90,000 to 170,000, but nevertheless voting remained restricted to a small fraction of the population.

Popular disturbances did not always result in revolution. In Britain, rural and town riots erupted over grain prices and distribution, but no revolution followed. German workers broke their machines to protest low wages and loss of control of the workplace, but no prince was displaced. In Switzerland, reformers found strength in the French revolutionary example. Ten Swiss cantons granted liberal constitutions and established universal manhood suffrage, freedom of expression, and legal equality.

In southern Europe, Greece had languished as a subjugated country for centuries. Turkish overlords ruled Greece as part of the Ottoman Empire. The longing for independence smoldered in Greece throughout the 1820s as public pressure to support the Greeks mounted in Europe. Greek insurrections were answered by Turkish retaliations throughout the Ottoman Empire. In 1822 a Turkish fleet captured the island of Chios in the Aegean Sea off the west coast of Turkey and massacred or enslaved the population. The atrocities committed by the Turks against Greeks in Constantinople provoked international reaction in the form of a Philhellenic (literally, "lover of Greece") movement supported by two of Britain's great romantic poets, Lord Byron (1788–1824) and Percy Bysshe Shelley (1792–1822). Byron sailed to the besieged Greek city of Missolonghi in 1824 to help coordinate the military effort, and there

he contracted malaria and died. The sultan of Turkey had been able to call upon his vassal, the pasha of Egypt, to subdue Greece. In response, Great Britain, France, and Russia signed the Treaty of London in 1827, pledging intervention on behalf of Greece. In a joint effort, the three powers defeated the Egyptian fleet. Russia declared war on Turkey the following year, seeking territorial concessions from the Ottoman Empire. Following the Russian victory, Great Britain and France joined Russia in declaring Greek independence.

The concerted action of the three powers in favor of Greek independence was neither an endorsement of liberal ideals nor a support of Greek nationalism. The British, French, and Russians were reasserting their commitment made at the Congress of Vienna to territorial stability. Yet beneath the veneer of their commitment, the Russians intervened, hoping for territorial gains in the Ottoman Empire. The British favored Ottoman stability while distrusting Russian ambitions in the area. The Turks had been unable to maintain stability on their own. Finally, the three powers abandoned their policy of propping up the Ottoman Empire and supported instead the movement for Greek independence. But they did so on their own terms by creating a monarchy in Greece and placing a German-born prince on the new throne.

The overthrow of the Bourbon monarch in France served as a model for revolution in other parts of Europe. Following the French lead, in the midst of the Greek crisis the Belgian provinces revolted against the Netherlands. The Belgians' desire for their own nation struck at the heart of the Vienna settlement. Provoked by a food crisis similar to that in France, Belgian revolutionaries took to the streets in August 1830. As a symbol of their solidarity with the successful French Revolution, they flew the tricolor in defiance of their Dutch rulers. Belgians protested the deterioration of their economic situation and made demands for their own Catholic religion, their own language, and constitutional rights. Bitter fighting on the barricades in Brussels ensued, and the movement for freedom and independence spread to the countryside.

The Great Powers disagreed on what to do. Russia, Austria, and Prussia were all eager to see the revolution crushed. France, having just established the new regime of the July Monarchy, and Great Britain, fearing the involvement of the central and eastern European powers in an area where Britain had traditionally had interests, were reluctant to intervene. A provisional government in Belgium set about the task of writing a constitution. All five great powers recognized Belgian independence, with the proviso that Belgium was to maintain the status of a neutral state.

Russia, Prussia, and Austria were convinced to accept Belgian independence because they were having their own problems in eastern and southern Europe. Revolution erupted to the east, in Warsaw, Poland. Driven by a desire for national independence, Polish army cadets and university students revolted in November 1830, demanding a constitution. Landed aristocrats and gentry helped establish a provisional government but soon split over how radical reforms should be. Polish peasants refused to support either landowning group. Within the year, Russia brought in 180,000 troops to crush the revolution and reassert its rule over Poland. All pretext of constitutional rule ended. Thousands of Poles were executed; others fled to exile in western Europe, including the 5000 who settled in France. Inspired by the poetry of Adam Mickiewicz (1798–1855) and the music of Frédéric Chopin, many of them dedicated themselves to the cause of Polish nationalism and to resurrecting an independent Polish kingdom. The Poles remained a captive people of the Habsburg, Hohenzollern, and Romanov empires until 1918–19.

In February 1831, the Italian states of Modena and Parma rose up to throw off Austrian domination of northern Italy. The revolutionaries were ineffective against Austrian troops. Revolution in the Papal States resulted in French occupation that lasted until 1838 without serious reforms. Nationalist and republican yearnings were driven underground, kept alive there in the Young Italy movement under the leadership of Giuseppe Mazzini.

Although the revolutions of 1830 are called "the forgotten revolutions" of the nineteenth century, they are important for several reasons. First, they made clear to European states how closely tied together were their fates. The events of 1830 were a test of the Great Powers' commitment to stability and a balance of power in Europe. True to the principles of the Vienna settlements of 1815, European leaders preserved the status quo. Revolutions in Poland and Italy were contained by Russia and Austria without interference from the other powers. Where adaptation was necessary, as in Greece and Belgium, the Great Powers were able to compromise on settlements, though the solutions ran counter to previous policies. Heads of state were willing to use the forces of repression to stamp out protest. Although each revolution followed its own pattern of development, all shared origins in domestic crises unsuccessfully addressed by those in power.

The international significance of the revolutions reveals a second important aspect of the events of 1830: the vulnerability of international politics to domestic instability. No state could practice diplomacy in a vacuum. Grain prices and demands for democratic participation had direct impact on the balance of power of European states. The five Great Powers broke down into two ideological camps. On the one hand were the lib-

'Gentlemen,' says Nicholas I, the bear, to the Polish revolutionaries of 1830, 'I know that you wish to address me; but to spare you from delivering a pack of lies, I desire that you hold your tongues.' The Polish rebellion of 1830–31 was brutally suppressed by the Russians. However, this brutality reinforced Polish national sentiment (the Poles rebelled again in 1863) and engaged the sympathy of the West for the Poles—as this English cartoon shows. (2)

This English cartoon of 1832 is titled "The Clemency of the Russian Monster." It shows Nicholas I in the guise of a bear with menacing teeth and claws addressing the Poles after crushing their rebellion against Russian rule.

eral constitutional states of Great Britain and France; on the other stood the autocratic monarchies of Russia, Austria, and Prussia. Yet ideological differences were always less important than the shared desire for internal stability as a prerequisite for international peace.

Finally, the 1830 revolutions exposed a growing awareness of politics at all levels of European society. If policies in 1830 revealed a shared consciousness of events and shared values among ruling elites, the revolutions disclosed a growing awareness among the lower classes of the importance of politics in their daily lives. The cry for "liberty, equality, and fraternity" transcended national borders and the French language. The demands for constitutions, national identity, and civic equality resounded from the Atlantic to the Urals. In a dangerous combination of circumstances, workers and the lower classes throughout Europe were politicized, yet they continued to be excluded from political power.

Reform in Great Britain

The right to vote had been an issue of contention in the revolutions of 1830 in western Europe. Only the Swiss cantons enforced the principle of "one man, one vote." The July Revolution in France had doubled the electorate, but still only a tiny minority of the population (less than 1 percent) enjoyed the vote. Universal male suffrage had been mandated in 1793 during the Great Revolution but not implemented. This exclusion of the mass of the population from participation in electoral politics was no oversight. Those in power believed that the wealthiest property owners were best qualified to govern, in part because they had the greatest stake in politics and society. One also needed to own property to hold office. Because those who served in parliaments received no salary, only the wealthy had the resources and the leisure to represent the electorate. When confronted by his critics, François Guizot (1787–1874), French prime minister and chief spokesman for the July Monarchy, offered this glib advice to an aspiring electorate: "Get rich!"

Landowners ruled Britain too. There the dominance of a wealthy elite was strengthened by the geographic redistribution of population resulting from industrialization. Migration to cities had depleted the population of rural areas. Yet the electoral system did not adjust to these changes: large towns had no parliamentary representation, while dwindling county electorates maintained their parliamentary strength. Areas that continued to enjoy representation greater than that justified by their population were dubbed "rotten" or "pocket" boroughs to indicate a corrupt and antiquated electoral system. In general, urban areas were grossly underrepresented and the wealthy few controlled county seats.

Liberal reformers attempted to rectify the electoral inequalities by reassigning parliamentary seats on the basis of density of population, but vested interests balked at attempted reforms and members of Parliament wrangled bitterly. Popular agitation by the lower classes provoked the fear of civil war, which helped break the parliamentary deadlock. The Great Reform Bill of 1832 proposed a compromise. Although the vast majority of the population still did not have the vote, the new legislation strengthened the industrial and commercial elite in the towns, enfranchised most of the middle class, opened the way to social reforms, and encouraged the formation of political parties.

Years of bad harvests, unemployment, and depression, coupled with growing dissatisfaction with the government's weak efforts to address social problems, put the spur to a new national reform movement in the 1830s. Radical reformers, disillusioned with the 1832 Reform Bill because it strengthened the power of a wealthy capitalist class, argued that democracy was the only answer to the problems plaguing British society. In 1838, a small group of labor leaders, including representatives of the London Working Men's Association, an organization of craft workers, drew up a document known as the People's Charter. The single most important demand of the charter was that all men must have the vote. In addition, Chartists petitioned for a secret ballot, salaries for parliamentary service, elimination of the requirement that one must own property in order to run for office, equal electoral districts, and annual elections. The proposal favored direct democracy, guaranteed by frequent elections that would ensure maximum accountability of officials to their constituents.

Chartist appeal was greatest in periods of economic hardship. A violent mood swept through the movement in 1839. The Irish Chartist leader Feargus O'Connor (1794–1855) and the Irish journalist and orator James Bronterre O'Brien (1805–64) urged an unskilled and poorly organized working class to protest inequities through strikes that on occasion became violent. O'Brien thrilled his working-class listeners by haranguing "the big-bellied, little-brained, numbskull aristocracy." Chartism blossomed as a communal phenomenon in working-class towns and appeared to involve all

THE REFORM BILL.

The *Reform Bill of 1832* is praised by a contemporary cartoonist. "Rotten boroughs" and political corruption are put through a meat grinder by Whig leaders, and a triumphant Britannia emerges.

members of the family: "Every kitchen is now a political meeting house; the little children are members of the unions and the good mother is the political teacher," one Chartist organizer boasted. Chartist babies were christened with the names of Chartist heroes. When Mrs. King of Manchester, England, attempted to register the birth of her son, James Feargus O'Connor King, her choice of names was challenged. The registrar demanded, "Is your husband a Chartist?" Mrs. King replied, "I don't know, but his wife is." Women organized Chartist schools and Sunday schools in radical defiance of local church organizations. Many middle-class observers were sure that the moment for class war and revolutionary upheaval had arrived. The government responded with force to the perceived threat of armed rebellion and imprisoned a number of Chartist leaders.

Throughout the 1840s, bad harvests and economic hardships continued to fan the flames of discontent. National petitions signed by millions were submitted to the House of Commons, which stubbornly resisted the idea of universal manhood suffrage. Strikes and attacks on factories spread throughout England, Scotland, and Wales in 1842. Increased violence served to make the Parliament intransigent and caused the movement to splinter and weaken as moderates formed their own fac-

tions. The final moment for Chartism occurred in April 1848 when 25,000 Chartist workers, inspired by revolutionary events on the Continent, assembled in London to march on the House of Commons. They carried with them a newly signed petition demanding the enactment of the terms of the People's Charter. In response, the government deputized nearly 200,000 "special" constables in the streets. These deputized private citizens were London property owners and skilled workers intent on holding back a revolutionary rabble. Tired, cold, and rain-soaked, the Chartist demonstrators disbanded. No social revolution took place in Great Britain, and the dilemma of democratic representation was deferred.

workers unite

The word *proletariat* entered European languages before the mid-nineteenth century to describe those workers afloat in the labor pool who owned nothing, not even the tools of their labor, and who were becoming "appendages" to the new machines that dominated production. To workers, machines could mean the elimination of jobs or the de-skilling of tasks; almost always machines meant a drop in wages. Mechanization deprived skilled craft workers of control of the workplace. In Great Britain, France, and Germany, groups of textile workers destroyed machines in protest. Workers demanding a fair wage smashed cotton power looms, knitting machines, and wool carding machines. Sometimes the machines were a bargaining point for workers who used violence against them as a last resort. Machine-breakers tyrannized parts of Great Britain from 1811 to 1816 in an attempt to frighten masters. The movement was known as Luddism after its mythical leader, Ned Ludd. Workers damaged and destroyed property for more control over the work process, but such destruction met with severe repression. From the 1820s to the 1850s, sporadic but intense outbursts of machine-breaking occurred in continental Europe. Suffering weavers in Silesia and Bohemia resorted to destroying their looms in 1844.

Craft production continued to deteriorate with the rise in industrial competition. Skilled workers, fearing that they would be pulled down into the new proletariat because of mechanization and the increased scale of production, began organizing in new ways after 1830 by forming associations to assert their control over the workplace and to demand a voice in politics.

In Britain, skilled craft workers built on a tradition of citizenship. They resisted the encroachments of factory production, and some channeled their political fervor into the Chartist movement. Skilled workers in France also built on a cultural heritage of shared language and values to create a consciousness of themselves as an exploited class. Uprisings and strikes in France, favoring the destruction of the monarchy and the creation of a democratic republic, increased dramatically from 1831 to 1834. Many French craft workers grew conscious of themselves as a class and embraced a socialism heavily influenced by their own traditions and contemporary socialist writings. Republican socialism spread throughout France by means of a network of traveling journeymen and tapped into growing economic hardship and political discontent with the July Monarchy. Government repression drove worker organizations underground in the late 1830s, but secret societies proliferated. Increasingly, workers saw the validity of the slogan of the silk workers of Lyon: "Live Working or Die Fighting!"

Women were an important part of the work force in the industrializing societies. Working men were keenly aware of the competition with cheaper female labor in the factories. Women formed a salaried work force in the home too. In order to turn out products cheaply and in large quantities, some manufacturers turned to subcontractors to perform the simpler tasks in the work

Workers known as Luddites, who felt threatened by the mechanization of weaving, organized machine-breaking riots in England. In this illustration English workers and Luddites smash factory looms during the riots of 1811–1816.

process. These new middlemen contracted out work like cutting and sewing to needy women who were often responsible for caring for family members in their homes. This kind of subcontracting, called "sweated labor" because of the exertion and long hours involved in working in one's own home, was always poorly paid.

Cheap female labor paid by the piece allowed employers to profit by keeping overhead costs low and by driving down the wages of skilled workers. Trade unions opposed women's work, both in the home and in the factories. Women's talents, union leaders explained, were more properly devoted to domestic chores. Unions argued that their members should earn a family wage "sufficient to support a wife and children." Unions consistently excluded women workers from their ranks.

French labor leader Flora Tristan, herself a wife and mother, had a very different answer for those who wanted to remove women from the workplace and assign them to their "proper place" in the home. She recognized that working women needed to work in order to support themselves and their families. Tristan told audiences in Europe and Latin America that the emancipation of women from their "slave status" was essential if the working class as a whole was to enjoy a better future. She deplored the economic competition between working men and women and denounced the degradation of women in both the home and the workplace. A working woman earned one-third or less of the average working man's wages, and women's working conditions were often deplorable. In the 1840s, British parliamentary commissions heard the horrifying testimony of one young London dressmaker from the country who was forced to work grueling hours—often 20 hours a day—under unhealthy working conditions that had destroyed her health. She concluded that "no men could endure the work enforced from the dressmakers."

Working women's only hope, according to Tristan, lay in education and unionization. She urged working men and women to join together to lay claim to their natural and inalienable rights. In some cases, working women formed their own organizations, like that of the Parisian seamstresses who joined together to demand improved working conditions. On the whole, however, domestic workers in the home remained isolated from other working women, and many women in factories feared the loss of their jobs if they engaged in political activism. The wages of Europe's working women remained low, often below the level of subsistence. In the absence of a man's income, working women and their children were the poorest of the poor in European society in the middle of the nineteenth century.

For some men and women of the working class, the 1840s were a time of mounting unrest, increased organization, and growing protest. Workers used their unity in associations, unions, and mutual-aid societies to press for full political participation and government action in times of economic distress.

The Revolutions of 1848

Europeans had never experienced a year like 1848. Beginning soon after the ringing in of the New Year, revolutionary fervor swept through nearly every European country. By year's end, regimes had been created and destroyed. France, Italy, the German states, Austria, Hungary, and Bohemia were shaken to their foundations. Switzerland, Denmark, and Romania experienced lesser upheavals. Great Britain had survived reformist agitation, and famine-crippled Ireland had endured a failed insurrection. No one was sure what had happened. Each country's conflict was based on a unique mix of issues, but all were connected in their conscious emulation of a revolutionary tradition.

Hindsight reveals warning signs in the two years before the 1848 cataclysm. Beginning in 1846, a severe famine—the last serious food crisis Europe would experience—racked Europe. Lack of grain drove up prices. An increasing percentage of disposable income was spent on food for survival. Lack of spending power severely damaged markets and forced thousands of industrial workers out of their jobs. The famine hurt everyone—the poor, workers, employers, and investors—as recession paralyzed the economy.

The food crisis took place in a heavily charged political atmosphere. Throughout Europe during the 1840s, the middle and lower classes had intensified their agitation for democracy. Chartists in Great Britain argued for a wider electorate. Bourgeois reformers in France campaigned for universal manhood suffrage. Known as the "banquet" campaign because its leaders attempted to raise money by giving speeches at subscribed dinners, the movement for the vote appeared to be developing a mass following by taking its cause directly to the people. In making demands for political participation, those agitating for suffrage necessarily criticized those in power. Freedom of speech and freedom of assembly were demanded as inalienable rights. The food

The communist Manifesto

The Communist Manifesto is one of the most important documents in world history. Translated into many languages in countless editions, it inspired worker organizations throughout Europe in the second half of the nineteenth century and fired the imagination of Communist leaders in Asia, Latin America, Africa, and Europe well into the twentieth century.

The pamphlet, which in its entirety consists of no more than 12,000 words, was written at the beginning of 1848 by Karl Marx, founder of modern communism, and his collaborator and friend, Friedrich Engels. Their intention was to urge exploited workers throughout Europe to prepare themselves for the coming revolution by uniting across national boundaries. *The Communist Manifesto* is a concise statement of the basic tenets of Marxism. Although mistaken in most of its predictions about the future development of capitalism, it accurately distilled some of the most salient inequities of industrial economies whose remedies, Marx and Engels asserted, could only be found through the revolutionary overthrow of the capitalist system.

Bourgeois and proletarians*

The history of all hitherto existing society is the history of class struggles.

Freeman and slave, patrician and plebeian, lord and serf, guild-master and journeyman, in a word, oppressor and oppressed, stood in constant opposition to one another, carried on an uninterrupted, now hidden, now open fight, a fight that each time ended, either in a revolutionary reconstitution of society at large, or in the common ruin of the contending classes. . . .

The modern bourgeois society that has sprouted from the ruins of feudal society has not done away with class antagonisms. It has but established new classes, new conditions of oppression, new forms of struggle in place of the old ones.

Our epoch, the epoch of the bourgeoisie, possesses, however, this distinctive feature: it has simplified the class antagonisms. Society as a whole is more and more splitting up into two great hostile camps, into two great classes directly facing each other: Bourgeoisie and Proletariat. . . .

The bourgeoisie cannot exist without constantly revolutionizing the instruments of production, and thereby the relations of production, and with them the whole relations of society. Conservation of the old modes of production in unaltered form, was, on the contrary, the first condition of existence for all earlier industrial classes. Constant revolutionizing of production, uninterrupted disturbance of all social conditions, everlasting uncertainty and agitation distinguish the bourgeois epoch from all earlier ones.

All fixed, fast-frozen relations, with their train of ancient and venerable prejudices and opinions are swept away, all new-formed ones become antiquated before they can ossify. All that is solid melts into air, all that is holy is profaned, and man is at last compelled to face with sober senses, his real conditions of life, and his relations with his kind.

The need of a constantly expanding market for its products chases the bourgeoisie over the whole surface of the globe. It must nestle everywhere, settle everywhere, establish connexions everywhere. . . .

The proletariat goes through various stages of development. With its birth begins its struggle with the bourgeoisie. At first the contest is carried on by individual labourers, then by the work-people of a factory, then by the operatives of one trade, in one locality, against the individual bourgeois who directly exploits them. They direct their attacks not against the bourgeois conditions of production, but against the instruments of production themselves; they destroy imported wares that compete with their labour, they smash to pieces machinery, they set factories ablaze, they seek to restore by force the vanished status of the workman of the Middle Ages.

proletarians and communists

In what relation do the Communists stand to the proletarians as a whole?

The Communists do not form a separate part opposed to other working-class parties.

They have no interests separate and apart from those of the proletariat as a whole. . . .

You are horrified at our [Communists'] intending to do away with private property. But in your existing society, private property is already done away with for nine-tenths of the population; its existence for the few is solely due to its non-existence in the hands of those nine-tenths. You reproach us, therefore, with intending to do away with a form of property the necessary condition for whose existence is the non-existence of any property for the immense majority of society. . . .

In short, the Communists everywhere support every revolutionary movement against the existing social and political order of things.

In all these movements they bring to the front, as the leading question in each, the property question, no matter what its degree of development at the time.

Finally, they labour everywhere for the union and agreement of the democratic parties of all countries.

The Communists disdain to conceal their views and aims. They openly declare that their ends can be attained only by the forcible overthrow of all existing social conditions. Let the ruling classes tremble at a Communistic revolution. The proletarians have nothing to lose but their chains. They have a world to win.
WORKING MEN OF ALL COUNTRIES, UNITE!

*By bourgeoisie is meant the class of modern Capitalists, owners of the means of social production and employers of wage labour. By proletariat, the class of modern wage-labourers who, having no means of production of their own, are reduced to selling their labour power in order to live. |Note by Engels to the English edition of 1888.|

crisis and political activism provided the ingredients for an incendiary situation.

In addition to a burgeoning democratic culture, growing demands for national autonomy based on linguistic and cultural claims spread through central, southern, and eastern Europe. The revolts in Poland in 1846, though failures, encouraged similar movements for national liberation among Italians and Germans. Even in the relatively homogeneous nation of France, concerns with national mission and national glory grew among the regime's critics. National unity was primarily a middle-class ideal. Liberal lawyers, teachers, and businessmen from Dublin to Budapest to Prague agitated for separation from foreign rule. Austria, with an

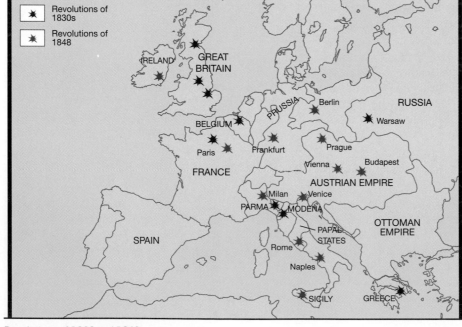

Revolutions of 1830 and 1848

empire formed of numerous ethnic minorities, had the most to lose. Since 1815, Metternich had been ruthless in stamping out nationalist dissent. However, by the 1840s, national claims were assuming a cultural legitimacy that was difficult to dismiss or ignore.

The events in France in the cold February of 1848 ignited the conflagration that swept Europe. Bourgeois reformers had arranged for their largest banquet to date in support of extension of the vote, to take place in Paris on 22 February. City officials became nervous at the prospect of thousands of workers assembling for political purposes and canceled the scheduled banquet. This was the spark that touched off the powder keg. In a spontaneous uprising, Parisians demonstrated against the government's repressive measures. Skilled workers took to the streets, not only in favor of the banned banquet but also with the hope that the government would recognize the importance of labor to the social order. Shots were fired; a demonstrator was killed. The French Revolution of 1848 had begun.

Events moved quickly. The National Guard, a citizen militia of bourgeois Parisians, defected from Louis-Philippe. Many army troops garrisoned in Paris crossed the barricades to join revolutionary workers. The king attempted some reform, but it was too little and too late. Louis-Philippe fled. The Second Republic was proclaimed at the insistence of the revolutionary crowds on the barricades. The Provisional Government, led by the poet Alphonse de Lamartine (1790–1869), included members of both factions of political reformers of the July Monarchy: moderates who sought constitutional reforms and an extension of the suffrage; and radicals who favored universal manhood suffrage and social programs to deal with poverty and work. Only the threat of popular violence held together this uneasy alliance.

The people fighting in the streets had little in common with the bourgeois reformers who assumed power on 24 February. Workers made a social revolution out of a commitment to their "right to work," which would replace the right to property as the organizing principle of the new society. Only one member of the new Provisional Government was a worker, and he was included as a token symbol of the intentions of the new government. He was known as "Albert, the worker," and was not addressed by his surname, Martin. The government acknowledged the demand of the "right to work" and set up two mechanisms to guarantee workers' relief. First, a commission of workers and employers was created to act as a grievance and bargaining board and settle questions of common concern in the workplace.

Headed by the socialist Louis Blanc (1811–82) and known as the Luxembourg Commission, the worker-employer parliament was an important innovation, but accomplished little other than deflecting workers' attention away from the problems of the Provisional Government. The second measure was the creation of "national workshops" to deal with the problems of unemployment in Paris. Although the name was taken from Blanc's plan for worker control of production, the national workshops were no more than an inefficient charity program that paid men minimal wages. The national workshops quickly proved disastrous. Workers from all over France poured into Paris with the hope of finding jobs. However, the workshops had a residency requirement that even Parisians had difficulty meeting. As a result, unemployment skyrocketed. Furthermore, the government was going bankrupt trying to support the program. The need to raise taxes upset peasants in the provinces. National pressure mounted to repudiate the programs of the revolution.

French workers were too weak to dominate the revolution. The government dissolved the workshops and recalled General Louis Cavaignac (1802–57) from service in Algeria to maintain order. In a wave of armed insurrection, Parisian workers rebelled in June. Using provincial troops having no identification with the urban population and employing guerrilla techniques he had mastered in Algeria, Cavaignac put down the uprising. The June fighting was the bloodiest that Paris had ever seen. The Second Republic was placed under the military dictatorship of Cavaignac until December, when presidential elections were scheduled.

The overthrow of the July Monarchy at the end of February set off shock waves of protest in central and eastern Europe. Long-suppressed desires for civil liberties and constitutional reforms erupted in widespread popular disturbances throughout Prussia and the German states. Fearing a war with France and unable to count on Austria or Russia for support, the princes who ruled Baden, Württemberg, Hesse-Darmstadt, Bavaria, Saxony, and Hanover followed the advice of moderate liberals and acceded quickly to revolutionary demands. In Prussia, Kaiser Friedrich Wilhelm IV (1840–61) preferred to use military force to respond to popular demonstrations. Only in mid-March 1848 did the Prussian king yield to the force of the revolutionary crowds building barricades in Berlin by ordering his troops to leave the city and by promising to create a national Prussian assembly. The king was now a prisoner of the revolution.

Meanwhile, the collapse of absolute monarchy in Prussia gave further impetus to a constitutional movement among the liberal leaders of the German states. The governments of all the German states were invited to elect delegates to a national parliament in Frankfurt. The Frankfurt Assembly, which was convened in May 1848, had as its dual charge the framing of a constitution and the unification of Germany. It was composed for the most part of members of the middle class, with civil servants, lawyers, and intellectuals predominating. In spite of the principle of universal manhood suffrage, no members of the working class served among the 800 men elected. To most of the delegates, who had been trained in universities and shared a social and cultural identity, nationalism and constitutionalism were inextricably related.

As straightforward as the desire for a German nation appeared to be, it was complicated by two important facts. First, there were non-German minorities living in German states. What was to be done with the Poles, Czechs, Slovenes, Italians, and Dutch in a newly constituted and autonomous German nation? Second, there were Germans living outside the German states under Habsburg rule in Austria, in Danish Schleswig and Holstein, in Posen (Poznan), in Russian Poland, and in European Russia. How were they to be included within the linguistically and ethnically constituted German nation? No matter how small the circle was drawn, it included non-Germans; no matter how wide, it excluded Germans. After much wrangling over a "small" Germany that excluded Austrian Germans and a "large" Germany that included them, the Frankfurt Assembly opted for the small-Germany solution in March 1849. The crown of the new nation was offered to the unpredictable Friedrich Wilhelm IV of Prussia, head of the largest and most powerful of the German states. Unhappy with his capitulation to the revolutionary crowd in March 1848, the Prussian king refused to accept a "crown from the gutter." He had his own plans to rule over a middle-European bloc, but not at the behest of a liberal parliament. The attempt to create a German nation crumbled with his unwillingness to lead.

Revolution in Austrian-dominated central Europe was concentrated in three places: Vienna, where German-speaking students, workers, and middle-class liberals were agitating for constitutional reform and political participation; Budapest, where the Magyars, the dominant ethnic group in Hungary, led a movement for national autonomy; and Prague, where Czechs were attempting self-rule. By April 1848, Metternich had fallen from power and the Viennese revolutionaries had set up

Club-wielding police break up a radical demonstration in Berlin, the capital of Prussia, in 1848. In March, King Frederick William of Prussia acceded to the demands of liberal reformers. But in November, after uprisings against conservative regimes elsewhere in Europe had been put down, the monarch allowed the Prussian army to regain control of Berlin.

A *satiric cartoon shows Pope Pius IX removing the mask of a liberal "savior" to reveal his true countenance after he failed to support the revolution in Italy.*

1831 by Giuseppe Mazzini. Mazzini, a tireless and idealistic patriot, favored a democratic revolution. In spite of his reputation as a liberal, Pope Pius IX (1846–78) lost control of Rome and was forced to flee the city. Mazzini became head of the Republic of Rome, created in February 1849.

The French government decided to intervene to protect the pope's interests and sent in troops to defeat the

a constituent assembly. In Budapest, the initial steps of the patriot Lajos Kossuth (1802–94) toward establishing a separate Hungarian state seemed equally solid as the Magyars defeated Habsburg troops. Habsburg armies were more successful in Prague, where they crushed the revolution in June 1848.

The Habsburg empire was also under siege in Italy, where the Kingdom of the Two Sicilies, Tuscany, and Piedmont declared new constitutions in March 1848. Championed by Charles Albert of Piedmont, Venice and Lombardy rose up against Austria. Italian middle-class intellectuals and professionals championed the idea of national unification and the expulsion of the hated Austrian overlords. Nationalist sentiments had percolated underground in the Young Italy movement, founded in

protest and revolution

August 1819	Peterloo Massacre
1824	Charles X assumes French throne
1827	Treaty of London to support liberation of Greece
July 1830	Revolution in Paris; creation of July Monarchy under Louis-Philippe
August 1830	Revolution in Belgium
November 1830	Revolution in Poland
1831–1838	Revolutions in Italian states
1831–1834	Labor protests in France
1832	Britain's Great Reform Bill
1838	Drawing up the first People's Charter in Britain
1846	Beginning of food crisis in Europe; revolts in Poland
1846–1848	Europe-wide movements for national liberation
February 1848	Revolution in France; overthrow of the July Monarchy; proclamation of the French Second Republic and creation of Provisional Government
March 1848	Uprisings in some German states; granting of a constitution in Prussia
March 1848– June 1849	Revolutions in Italy
April 1848	Revolutions in Vienna, Budapest, Prague
May 1848	Frankfurt Assembly
June 1848	Second revolution in Paris, severely repressed by army troops under General Cavaignac
December 1848	Presidential elections in France; Louis Napoleon wins

republicans. One of Mazzini's disciples, Giuseppe Garibaldi (1807–82), returned from exile in South America to undertake the defense of Rome. Garibaldi was a capable soldier who had learned the tactics of guerrilla warfare by joining independence struggles in Brazil and Argentina. Although his legion of poorly armed patriots and soldiers of fortune, known from their attire as the Red Shirts, waged a valiant effort to defend the city from April to June 1849, they were no match for the highly trained French army. French troops restored Pius IX as ruler of the Papal States.

Meanwhile, from August 1848 to the following spring, the Habsburg armies fought and finally defeated each of the revolutions. Austrian success can be explained in part because the various Italian groups of Piedmontese, Tuscans, Venetians, Romans, and Neapolitans continued to identify with their local concerns and lacked coordination and central organization. Both Mazzini and Pius IX had failed to provide the focal point of leadership necessary for a successful national movement.

In December 1848, Emperor Ferdinand I (1835–48), whose authority had been weakened irreparably by the overthrow of Metternich, abdicated in favor of his 18-year-old nephew, Franz Josef I (1848–1916). By the fall of 1849, Austria had solved the problems in its own capital and with Italy and Hungary by military dominance. Austria understood that a Germany united under Friedrich Wilhelm IV of Prussia would undermine Austrian dominance in central Europe. In 1850 Austrians threatened the Prussians with war if they did not give up their plans for a unified Germany. In November of that year, Prussian ministers signed an agreement with their Austrian counterparts in the Moravian city of Olmütz. The convention became known as "the humiliation of Olmütz" because Prussia was forced to accept Austrian dominance or go to war. In every case, military force and diplomatic measures prevailed to defeat the national and liberal movements within the German states and the Austrian Empire.

europe in 1850

By 1850 a veneer of calm had spread over central Europe. In Prussia, the peasantry were emancipated from feudal dues, and a constitution, albeit conservative and based on a three-class system, was established. Yet be-

neath the surface, there was the deeper reality of Austrian decline and Prussian challenge. The great Habsburg empire needed to call on outside help from Russia to defeat its enemies within. The imperial giant was again on its feet, but for how long? In international relations, Austria's dominance in the German Confederation had diminished, while Prussia assumed greater political and economic power.

The 1848 revolutions spelled the end to the concert of Europe as it had been defined in the peace settlement of 1815. The European powers were incapable of united action to defend established territorial interests. Perhaps France would have provoked united action if it had attempted to extend its revolution throughout Europe, as in 1792. Instead, pragmatism prevailed. The British failed to support independence for Hungary, for example, because they feared the consequences of Russian ambitions that would be unchecked with a weaker Austria.

The revolutions of 1848 failed in part because of the irreconcilable split between moderate liberals and radical democrats. The participation of the masses had frightened members of the middle classes, who were committed to moderate reforms that did not threaten property. In France, working-class revolutionaries had attempted to replace property with labor. Property triumphed. In the face of more extreme solutions, members of the middle class were willing to accept the increased authority of existing rule as a bulwark against anarchy. In December 1848, Prince Louis Napoleon, nephew of the former emperor, was elected president of the Second Republic by a wide margin. The first truly modern French politician, Louis Napoleon managed to appeal to everyone—workers, bourgeois, royalists, and peasants—by making promises that were vague or unkeepable. Severe repression forced radical protest into hiding. The new Bonaparte bided his time, apparently as an ineffectual ruler, until the moment in 1851 when he seized absolute power.

Similar patterns emerged elsewhere in Europe. In Germany, the bourgeoisie accepted the dominance of the old feudal aristocracy as a guarantee of law and order. Repressive government, businessmen were sure, would restore a strong economy. The attempts in 1848 to create new nations based on ethnic identities were in shambles by 1850.

Nearly everywhere throughout Europe, constitutions had been systematically withdrawn with the recovery of the forces of reaction. With the French and Swiss exceptions, the bid for the extension of the franchise failed. The propertied classes remained in control of political institutions. Radicals willing to use violence to press electoral reforms were arrested, killed, or exiled. The leadership of the revolutionary movements had been decapitated, and there seemed no effective opposition to the rise and consolidation of state power. The 1848 revolutions have been called a turning point at which modern history failed to turn. Contemporaries wondered how so much action could have produced so few lasting results.

The perception that nothing had changed was wrong. The revolutions of 1848 and subsequent events galvanized whole societies to political action. Conservatives and radicals alike turned toward a new realism in politics. Everywhere governments were forced to adapt to new social realities. No longer could the state ignore economic upheavals and social dislocations if it wanted to survive. Revolutionaries also learned the lesson of repression. The state wielded powerful forces of violence against which nationalists, socialists, republicans, and liberals had all been proved helpless. Organizing, campaigning, and lobbying were newly learned political skills, as was outreach across class lines—from bourgeoisie to peasantry—around common political causes. In these ways, 1848 was a turning point in the formation of a modern political culture.

Mastering the chapter

To review the main points of the chapter, be sure you can explain the significance of each of the following.

Terms/Concepts/Events	People	Places
Congress of Vienna	Prince Klemens von Metternich	Kingdom of the Netherlands
liberalism	Viscount Castlereagh	Oder River
utilitarianism	Thomas Malthus	Piedmont-Sardinia
nationalism	Queen Victoria	Lombardy
romanticism	Jeremy Bentham	Papal States
conservatism	Henri de Saint-Simon	German Confederation
socialism	Karl Marx	Posen
The Communist Manifesto	Charles X	Galicia
Chartists	Louis-Philippe	Krakow
Second Republic	Louis Napoleon	

suggestions for further reading

europe after 1815

* Robert Gildea, Barricades and Borders, Europe 1800–1914 (Oxford: Oxford University Press, 1987). A synthetic overview of economic, demographic, political, and international trends in European society.

* Harold Nicolson, *The Congress of Vienna: A Study in Allied Unity,* 1812–1822 (New York: Viking Press, 1965). Dissects the maneuverings of the Allied diplomats and analyzes their cooperation in reconstructing Europe.

* Alan Sked, *The Decline and Fall of the Habsburg Empire,* 1815–1918 (London: Longman, 1989). A revisionist interpretation that demonstrates the strength and viability of Europe's greatest dynasty throughout the nineteenth century.

The New European Society

* Leonore Davidoff and Catherine Hall, *Family Fortunes: Men and Women of the English Middle Class,* 1750–1850 (Chicago: University of Chicago Press, 1991). Through the stories of families during the Industrial Revolution, the authors explain the development of middle-class identity and the role that gender played in the development of property relations, the construction of family life, and the differentiation of the world of the home from the public world of production.

* Gertrude Himmelfarb, *The Idea of Poverty: England in the Early Industrial Age* (New York: Vintage Books, 1983). Traces the concept of poverty in Britain from the mid-eighteenth to the mid-nineteenth century through a discussion of inadequate solutions, changing material conditions of industrialism, and new modes of thought and sensibility.

* Joel Mokyr, *Why Ireland Starved: A Quantitative and Analytical History of the Irish Economy,* 1800–1850 (London: Allen & Unwin, 1983). An analysis of the structural factors that produced poverty in pre-famine Ireland and a thorough examination of the impact of the famine.

  Patricia O'Brien, *The Promise of Punishment: Prisons in Nineteenth-Century France* (Princeton: Princeton University Press, 1982). The author provides an overview of the creation of the penitentiary system in nineteenth-century France and the rise of the new science of punishment, criminology, and the eventual appearance of alternatives to the penitentiary system.

* Redcliffe N. Salaman, *The History and Social Influence of the Potato,* revised impression edited by J. G. Hawkes (Cambridge: Cambridge University Press, 1985). The classic study of the potato. A major portion of the work is devoted to the potato famine.

* Louise A. Tilly and Joan W. Scott, *Women, Work and Family* (New York: Holt, Rinehart and Winston, 1978). An overview of the impact of a wage economy on the family and on women's work.

The New Ideologies

* Jonathan Beecher, *Charles Fourier: The Visionary and His World* (Berkeley: University of California Press, 1986). An intellectual biography that traces the development of Fourier's theoretical perspective and roots it firmly in the social context of nineteenth-century France.

* Craig Calhoun, *The Question of Class Struggle: Social Foundations of Popular Radicalism During the Industrial Revolution* (Chicago: University of Chicago Press, 1982). Presents popular protest of eighteenth- and early nineteenth-century England as the reaction of communities of artisans defending their traditions against encroaching industrialization.

* William H. Sewell, Jr., *Work and Revolution in France: The Language of Labor from the Old Regime to* 1848 (Cambridge: Cambridge University Press, 1980). Traces nineteenth-century working-class socialism to the corporate culture of Old Regime guilds through traditional values, norms, language, and artisan organizations.

  Gareth Stedman Jones, *Languages of Class: Studies in English Working Class History,* 1832–1982 (Cambridge: Cambridge University Press, 1983). A series of essays, on topics such as working-class culture and Chartism, that examine the development of class consciousness.

  Denis Mack Smith, *Mazzini* (New Haven, CT: Yale University Press, 1994). Mazzini is presented as an important force in legitimizing Italian nationalism by associating it with republicanism and the interests of humanity.

* Edward P. Thompson, *The Making of the English Working Class* (New York: Pantheon Books, 1963). Spans the late eighteenth to mid-nineteenth centuries in examining the social, political, and cultural contexts in which workers created their own identity and put forward their own demands.

protest and revolution

* Maurice Agulhon, *The Republican Experiment, 1848–1852* (Cambridge: Cambridge University Press, 1983). Traces the Revolution of 1848 from its roots to its ultimate failure in 1852 through an analysis of the republican ideologies of workers, peasants, and the bourgeoisie.

Clive Church, *Europe in 1830: Revolution and Political Change* (London: Allen & Unwin, 1983). Considers the origins of the 1830 revolutions within a wider European crisis through a comparative analysis of European regions.

Catherine J. Kudlick, *Cholera in Post-Revolutionary Paris: A Cultural History* (Berkeley: University of California Press, 1996). Examines the cultural values of ruling elites and demonstrates the role disease played in shaping political life and class identity in nineteenth-century France.

* Peter N. Stearns, *1848: The Revolutionary Tide in Europe* (New York: Norton, 1974). Surveys the causes, impact, and legacy of the revolutions in France, Germany, the Habsburg Empire, and Italy, which shattered the diplomatic framework established at the Congress of Vienna and served as a transition to a new society.

* Dorothy Thompson, *The Chartists: Popular Politics in the Industrial Revolution* (New York: Pantheon Books, 1984). Thompson demonstrates that Chartism was an extraordinary coalition of women, laborers, artisans, and alehouse keepers whose goals were transforming public life and forging a new political culture.

*Paperback edition available.

state-Building and social change in europe, 1850-1871

The Birth of the German Empire

CHAPTER

23

Secret fancies bubbled in Otto von Bismarck's brain. As he explained in long letters to his wife, he imagined that the Russian king and German princes crowding around him were pregnant women seized by "strange cravings." In the next moment, he imagined himself a midwife assisting at a momentous birth. In spite of his remarkable train of thought, Otto von Bismarck (1815–98) was not a fanciful man. The birth in his daydream was the proclamation of the German Empire on 21 January 1871. The building was the palace of Versailles outside Paris. As the Prussian statesman stood in the great Hall of Mirrors on that fateful day, surrounded by German aristocrats, he could not forget the years of struggle and planning that preceded this event. His tension and anticipation provoked his birthing fantasies.

The newly established Second Reich, successor to the Holy Roman Empire (962–1806), united the German states into a single nation. The unification process had been a precarious pregnancy, with years of foreign wars and a Herculean labor of diplomatic maneuverings. The placid, glossy scene painted by Anton von Werner

(1843–1915) hardly suggests Bismarck's violent emotions on this momentous day. Bismarck saw his task in terms of the female metaphor of birth. Yet this warrior group was the most masculine of gatherings. Look at the painting. The richly marbled and mirrored room, the site of the birth, figures as prominently in the tableau as the uniformed princes and aristocrats who, with sabers, helmets, and standards raised, cheer the new emperor. The massive mirrors reflect more than this soldier society standing before the long windows of the opposite wall; they reflect a humiliation. This is, after all, the great hall built by Louis XIV at Versailles, one of Europe's greatest palaces, designed to reflect and glorify the power of absolutist France. Here the kings of France presided over lavish ceremonies and opulent receptions. Here Napoleon I honored his generals, victorious in conquering central Europe. Here, not long ago, Napoleon III had danced on the parqueted floors with Queen Victoria of Britain. The choice of the Hall of Mirrors as the meeting place for the German princes, who had successfully combined forces to defeat the French Second Empire in only six weeks of war in the fall of 1870, was intended as an assertion of German superiority in Europe.

In less than a decade, German unity had been achieved through military victories over Denmark, Austria, and France. The gilded moldings that commemorate the age of the Sun King are matched by the glitter of golden ribbons, medals, buttons, and cuffs of German uniforms, by the soft glow of burnished Prussian helmets. France is about to be stripped of its territories of Alsace and Lorraine; now the French are to be stripped of their dignity as the Prussian king stands on luxuriant French carpeting to assert his claim. There is an arrogance here in the details on which Werner dwells. The French understood and promised to avenge their humiliation.

Look at the painting again. There on the dais is King Wilhelm I of Prussia, flanked by his son, Crown Prince Friedrich Wilhelm, and his son-in-law, Friedrich I, the Grand Duke of Baden, whose upraised hand signals a cheer for the new emperor. At the foot of the steps, like a loyal retainer, stands the self-described midwife, Otto von Bismarck. Yet there is something amiss here. The new German emperor, the person for whom the event has been orchestrated, stands to one side of the canvas. Bismarck commands its center. If the eyes of most of the cheering princes turn to the emperor, ours are pulled to the chancellor of the new Reich, who is singled out in his pure white uniform. Werner is telling us that this is the statesman's event, for it is he who has crafted a united Germany. Bismarck got what he wanted: a German Empire under the leadership of the Prussian king.

In both hands Bismarck clasps the proclamation of empire, the document wrested out of endless wrangling among the heads of the 38 German states. The kings of Saxony, Bavaria, and Württemberg refused to attend the ceremony. Some who did attend were disgruntled and resentful. Even Bismarck's sovereign was not happy

Focus Questions

1. How did the process of creating nation-states in Germany and Italy differ?
2. What social and political circumstances explain the different reforms undertaken in France, Britain, and Russia?
3. How did industrialization change women's lives, and how did such changes depend on a woman's social class?
4. What are the connections between Darwin's ideas about nature and Marx's ideas about society?
5. What forces inspired the creation of the Paris Commune and what did its fate suggest about the possibility of revolution in the late nineteenth century?

with the document, nor did he like the title assigned to him. He would have preferred to be "emperor of Germany" rather than "German emperor." Before the ceremony, Wilhelm I had refused to speak to Bismarck. Yet the artist reveals none of this in the impassive faces and the sturdy stances of the two men.

Bismarck understood that symbols forge unity. The artist Werner also attends to symbol. Beneath the red-encased document, Bismarck firmly grasps his Prussian military helmet. Military victories had ensured Prussian predominance over a united Germany. To Bismarck's left, in profile facing the emperor, stands Count Helmuth von Moltke (1800–1891), head of the Prussian General Staff and the man responsible for reorganizing the Prussian army with Bismarck's support. Medals for bravery and service to his sovereign adorn Moltke's chest. With one foot forward, Moltke is a man of action, almost caught in mid-stride, a man ready to move into the future.

The unification of Germany was not achieved by democratic means. Bismarck understood the new age. As he explained in a speech to the Prussian Diet, "The great questions of the time are not decided by speeches and majority decisions—that was the error of 1848 and 1849—but by iron and blood." The new Reich was a "state of princes," an empire born of the union of force and military conquest. A century earlier, Voltaire, the French philosopher of the Enlightenment, had his own theory of creation: God gave the English the seas, the French the land, and the Germans the clouds. Fragmented and without a state, Germans could claim a rich, if ethereal, culture of philosophy, music, and literature in the previous century. In 1871, with the proclamation of the German Empire, Germans had put their feet on the ground. The struggle for land and sea, so easily assigned by Voltaire, lay ahead.

Building Nations: The politics of unification

The revolutions of 1848 had occurred in a period of experimentation from below. Radicals enlisting popular support had tried and failed to reshape European states for their own nationalist, liberal, and socialist ends. Governments in Paris, Vienna, Berlin, and a number of lesser states had been swept away. The revolutions had created a power vacuum but no durable solutions. To fill that vacuum, a new breed of politician emerged in the 1850s and 1860s, men who understood the importance of the centralized nation-state and saw the need of reforms from above. They also had an appreciation of the importance of foreign policy successes as a means of furthering domestic programs. Cavour of Italy, Bismarck of Germany, and Louis Napoleon of France shared a new realism about means and ends.

National unification had escaped the grasp of liberals and radicals between 1848 and 1850 with the failure of revolutionary and reform movements. In the 1850s and 1860s, those committed to radical transformations worked from within the existing system. The new realists subordinated liberal nationalism to the needs of conservative state-building. Military force validated what intellectuals and revolutionaries had not been able to legitimate through ideological claims.

The Crimean War

After 1815 Russia, as the greatest military power in Europe, honored its commitment to preserving the status quo by acting as policeman of Europe. It supported Austria against Hungary and Prussia in 1849 and 1850. But Russia sought greater power to the south, in the Balkans. The Bosporus, the narrow strait connecting the Black Sea with the Sea of Marmara, and the strait of the Dardanelles, which connects the Sea of Marmara with the Aegean Sea, were controlled by the Ottoman Empire. Russia hoped to benefit from Ottoman weakness caused by internal conflicts and gain control of these straits, which were the only outlet for the Russian fleet to the warm waters of the Mediterranean, Russia's southern outlet to the world.

At the center of the hope for Ottoman disintegration

lay the "Eastern question," the term used to refer to the disputes over the European territories controlled by the Ottoman Empire. Each of the Great Powers—including Russia, Great Britain, Austria, Prussia, and France—hoped to benefit territorially from the collapse of Ottoman control. In 1853, Great Power rivalry over the "Eastern question" created an international situation that led to war.

In 1853 the Russian government demanded that the Turkish government recognize Russia's right to protect Greek Orthodox believers in the Ottoman Empire. The Russian action was a response to measures taken by the French government during the previous year, which had gained from the Turkish government rights for Roman Catholic religious orders in certain sanctuaries in the Holy Land. In making its claims as protector, Russia demanded that the rights granted Roman Catholic orders also be rescinded. The Turkish government refused Russian demands and the Russians, feeling that their prestige had been damaged, ordered troops to enter the Danubian Principalities held by the Turks. In October 1853, the Turkish government, counting on support from Great Britain and France, declared war on Russia.

Russia easily prevailed over its weaker neighbor to the south. In a four-hour battle, a Russian squadron destroyed the Turkish fleet off the coast of Sinope. Tsar Nicholas I (1825–55) drew up the terms of a settlement with the Ottoman Empire and submitted them to Great Britain and France for review. The two western European powers, fearing Russian aggrandizement at Turkish expense, responded by declaring war on Russia on 28 March 1854, a date that marked a new phase in the Crimean War. Both Great Britain and France, like Russia, had ambitions in the Balkans and the eastern Mediterranean. Great Britain feared Russian expansion as a threat to its trade and holdings in India and had a vested interest in an independent but weak Turkey presiding over the straits. The French hoped that by entering into a partnership with the British to defeat the Russians, they would be able to lay claim to greater power and status in European international politics. The Austrian Empire, frightened by Russia's seizure of the Danubian Principalities of Moldavia and Walachia, remained neutral but threatened to enter the war with Britain and France on the side of Turkey. The Italian kingdom of Piedmont-Sardinia joined the war on the side of the western European powers in January 1855, hoping to make its name militarily and win recognition for its aim to unite Italy into a single nation. Without explicit economic interests, the Great Powers and the

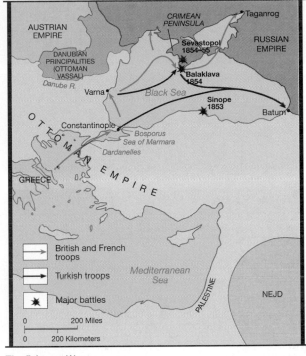

The Crimean War

lesser Italian state of Piedmont-Sardinia were motivated by ambition, prestige, and rivalry in the Balkans.

British and French troops landed in the Crimea, the Russian peninsula extending into the Black Sea, in September 1854, with the intention of capturing Sevastopol, Russia's heavily fortified chief naval base on the Black Sea. In March 1855, Nicholas I died and was succeeded by his son Alexander II (1855–81), who wanted to bring the war to a speedy end. His attempts to negotiate a peace in the spring of 1855 repeatedly failed. In battle, the Russians continued to resist as the allies laid siege to the fortress at Sevastopol, which fell only after 322 days of battle, on 11 September 1855. The defeated Russians abandoned Sevastopol, blew up their forts, and sank their own ships.

Russia, now facing the threat of Austrian entry into the war, agreed to preliminary peace terms. In the Peace of Paris of 1856, Russia relinquished its claim as protector of Christians in Turkey. The British gained the neutralization of the Black Sea. The mouth of the Danube was returned to Turkish control, and an international commission was created to oversee safe navigation on the Danube. The Danubian Principalities were placed under joint guarantee of the powers, and Russia gave

"The charge of the Light Brigade"

Alfred, Lord Tennyson (1809–92) described the bravery of the British Light Brigade in the Crimean War as they charged, hopelessly outnumbered, into the "valley of Death" at the Battle of Balaklava. His poem brought home to the British public both the glory of their troops and the tragedy brought on by a commander's "blunder."

1

Half a league, half a league,
Half a league onward,
All in the valley of Death
　　Rode the six hundred.
"Forward the Light Brigade!
Charge for the guns!" he said.
Into the valley of Death
　　Rode the six hundred.

2

"Forward, the Light Brigade!"
Was there a man dismay'd?
Not tho' the soldier knew
　　Some one had blunder'd.
　　Theirs not to make reply,
　　Theirs not to reason why,
　　Theirs but to do and die.
　　Into the valley of Death
　　　Rode the six hundred.

3

Cannon to right of them,
Cannon to left of them,
Cannon in front of them
　　Volley'd and thunder'd;
Storm'd at with shot and shell,
Boldly they rode and well,
Into the jaws of Death,
Into the mouth of hell
　　Rode the six hundred.

4

Flash'd all their sabres bare,
Flash'd as they turn'd in air

Sabring the gunners there,
Charging an army, while
　　All the world wonder'd.
Plunged in the battery-smoke
Right thro' the line they broke;
Cossack and Russian
Reel'd from the sabre-stroke
　　Shatter'd and sunder'd.
Then they rode back, but not,
　　Not the six hundred.

5

Cannon to right of them,
Cannon to left of them,
Cannon behind them
　　Volley'd and thunder'd;
Storm'd at with shot and shell,
While horse and hero fell,
They that had fought so well
Came thro' the jaws of Death,
Back from the mouth of hell,
All that was left of them,
　　Left of six hundred.

6

When can their glory fade?
O the wild charge they made!
　　All the world wonder'd.
Honor the charge they made!
Honor the Light Brigade,
　　Noble six hundred!

up a small portion of Bessarabia. In 1861 the Principalities were united in the independent nation of Romania.

The Crimean War had the highest casualty rate of any European war between 1815 and 1914. Three-quarters of a million soldiers—Russian, French, British, and Turkish—died. Because no sanitary practices were observed in caring for the wounded, four out of five succumbed to disease, especially typhus and cholera. The English nurse Florence Nightingale (1820–1910) brought medical reforms to the theater of war, introduced sanitation, and organized barracks hospitals, all of which saved the lives of countless British soldiers. (See "A Working Woman," pp. 784–785.) Russians suffered disproportionately, claiming two-thirds of all dead and wounded; 450,000 Russian soldiers died. Of those who died in battle, many died needlessly, under poorly prepared leaders. A typical example occurred during the battle of Balaklava when 600 troops of the British Light Brigade were ordered into battle by incompetent and confused commanders. British soldiers charged down a narrow valley flanked by Russian guns on the heights on both sides and into the teeth of yet another battery at the head of the valley. The battlefield became known as the Valley of Death. When the dust of the fighting had settled, the battlefield lay strewn with the bodies of nearly two-thirds of the soldiers of the Light Brigade. Their horses, slain too, lay beside them.

This was a war no one really won, a war over obscure disagreements in a faraway peninsula in the Black Sea. Nevertheless, it had dramatic and enduring consequences. Russia ceased playing an active role in European affairs and turned toward expansion in central Asia. Its withdrawal opened up the possibility for a move by Prussia in central Europe. The rules of the game had changed. The concert of Europe so carefully crafted by European statesmen in 1815 came to an end with the Crimean War. With the Peace of Paris of 1856, the hope that goals could be achieved by peaceful means also died. Piedmont-Sardinia, an empty-handed victor, realized that only the force of the cannon could achieve the unification of Italy.

Unifying Italy

Italy had not been a single political entity since the end of the Roman Empire in the West in the fifth century. The movement to reunite Italy culturally and politically was known as the Risorgimento (literally, "resurgence") and had its roots in the eighteenth century. Hopes for unification encouraged by reorganization during the Napoleonic era had been repeatedly crushed throughout the first half of the nineteenth century. Revolutionary movements had failed to cast out foreign domination by Austria in 1848.

Both Giuseppe Mazzini's Young Italy movement and Giuseppe Garibaldi's Red Shirts had as their goal in 1848 a united republican Italy achieved through direct popular action. But both movements had failed. It took a politician of aristocratic birth to recognize that Mazzini's and Garibaldi's model of revolutionary action was doomed against the powerful Austrian military machine. Mazzini was a moralist; Garibaldi was a fighter. But Camillo Benso di Cavour (1810–61) was an opportunistic politician and a realist. He knew that only as a unified nation could Italy lay claim to status as a great power in Europe. And he saw that a united Italy could be achieved only through the manipulation of diplomacy and military victory. He understood that international events could be made to serve national ends.

As premier for Piedmont-Sardinia from 1852 to 1859 and again in 1860–61, Cavour was well placed to launch his campaign for Italian unity. The kingdom of Piedmont-Sardinia had made itself a focal point for unification efforts. Piedmont-Sardinia's king, Carlo-Alberto (1831–49), had stood alone among Italian rulers in opposing Austrian domination of the Italian peninsula in 1848 and 1849. Severely defeated by the Austrians, he was forced to abdicate. With his death in exile, Carlo-Alberto became a saint martyred for the cause of unification. He was succeeded by his son Victor Emmanuel II (1849–61), who had the good sense to appoint Cavour as his first minister. From the start, Cavour undertook

Lady Elizabeth Butler, Balaclava *(1876). The painting depicts the Light Brigade coming in after the charge. Troop Sergeant-Major Loy Smith of the 11th Hussars is shown mounted on the left.*

A working woman

Women have always worked, but how society has valued women's work has changed over time. After 1850, women of all income levels, not just the wealthy, were expected to retire from the workplace upon marrying. Woman's proper role was that of wife and mother in the home, caring for her husband and family, watching over her children. Young women worked before they married to help their parents and to save for dowries. There is no doubt that many women continued to work for wages because they had to; they were too poor to live by society's norms. But mid-nineteenth-century European culture reinforced the idea that woman's place was in the separate domestic sphere of private pleasures and unpaid labor. To be a "public" man was a valued trait. The same adjective applied to a woman meant that she was a harlot.

Yet it is this culture that immortalized Florence Nightingale, a woman who valued what she called "my work" above home and family. She was a single woman in an age when more and more women were making the choice to remain unmarried; but it was also an age in which spinster was a term of derision and a sign of failure. Miss Nightingale, as she was known, received the British Empire's Order of Merit for her achievements. Queen Victoria, the most maternal and domestic of queens, hailed her as "an example to our sex." Nightingale was widely regarded as the greatest woman of her age, among the most eminent of Victorians. A highly visible and outspoken reformer, Nightingale deviated from woman's unpaid role as nurturer in the private sphere. How could she be an example to the women of her time?

Florence Nightingale was hailed as a national heroine because of her work during the Crimean War in organizing hospital care at Scutari, a suburb outside Constantinople on the Asiatic side of the Bosporus. In the Crimea, she entered her own field of battle, attacking the mismanagement, corruption, and lack of organization characteristic of medical treatment for British soldiers. She campaigned for better sanitation, hygiene, ventilation, and diet, and in 1855 the death rate plummeted from 42 percent to 2 percent thanks to her efforts. The London *Times* declared, "There is not one of England's proudest and purest daughters who at the moment stands on as high a pinnacle as Florence Nightingale."

It was a pinnacle not easily scaled. Blocked by her family and publicly maligned, Nightingale struggled against prevailing norms to carve out her occupation. She was the daughter of a wealthy gentry family, and from her father she received a man's classical education. Women of her milieu were expected to be educated only in domestic arts. The fashion of the day emphasized woman's confinement to the home: crinolines, corsets, and trains restricted movement and suggested gentility. This was the life of Nightingale's older sister, one that "the Angel of the Crimea" fiercely resisted. Nightingale railed at the inequity of married life: "A man gains everything by marriage: he gains a 'helpmate,' but a woman does not." Her memoirs are filled with what she called her "complaints" against the plight of women.

Nightingale was not a typical working woman. She struck out on her career as a rebel. Because of her wealth, she did not need to work, yet she felt driven to be useful. Her choice of nursing much alarmed her family, who considered the occupation to be on a level with domestic service. For them, nursing was worse, in fact, because nurses worked with the naked bodies of the sick. Thus nurses were either shameless or promiscuous, or both. Nightingale shattered these taboos. She visited nursing establishments throughout Europe, traveling alone—another feat unheard of for women in her day—and studied their methods and techniques. She conceived of her own mission to serve God through caring for others.

As with any exceptional individual, character and capabilities must figure in an explanation of achievements. Nightingale was a woman of drive and discipline who refused to accept the limited choices available to Victorian women. She possessed, in her sovereign's words, "a wonderful, clear and comprehensive head." Yet her unique talents are not enough to explain her success. In many ways, Nightingale was not a rebel, but rather an embodiment of the changing values of her age. In 1860, she established a school to train nurses, just as similar institutions were being created to train young women as teachers. These occupations were extensions of women's roles from the arena of the home into society. In keeping with their domestic roles, women remained nurturers in the classroom and at the sickbed.

These new female professions were also poorly paid. Significantly, Florence Nightingale, honored as she was in her lifetime, received no salary for her contributions to the British state. Her work was supported by donations from the benefactors and administrative protectors she referred to as her "masters." She and other women of her class, including Elizabeth Fry (1780–1845), who was a Quaker minister, prison reformer, banker's wife, and mother of ten, and the English writer and political reformer Harriet Martineau (1802–76), were regarded as philanthropists, women who donated their time and expertise to the public good. Theirs was the moral obligation of the wealthy toward the poor. It also sprang out of the nature of women, contemporary moralists asserted, to mother and to heal. The definition of women's proper role did not need to be dismantled to accommodate these activities. It needed merely to be stretched.

Florence Nightingale spent a good part of the last 45 years of her life in a sickbed suffering from what she called "nervous fever." During this period she wrote incessantly and continued to lobby for her programs, benefiting, one of her biographers claimed, from the freedom to think and write provided by her illness. It may well be true that her invalidism protected her from the claims on her time made by her family and by society. It may also be true that she, like many of her middle-class female contemporaries, experienced debilitation or suffered from hypochondria in direct proportion to the limitations they experienced.

Midcentury Europe had witnessed a series of failed protests on behalf of women against social and political

restrictions. In spite of reform movements, women did not enjoy the franchise or equal property rights. Access to divorce was available only to women wealthy enough to afford it. Yet women did participate in new activities and enter new occupations justified by their role as nurturers. Nightingale herself believed that the right to vote was less important than financial independence for women. New occupations labeled "women's work" were essential to the expansion of industrial society. A healthy and literate population guaranteed a strong citizenry, a strong army, and a strong work force. As helpmeets, women entered a new work sector identified by the adjective service. Women were accepted as clerical workers, performing the "housekeeping" of business firms and bureaucracies.

After midcentury, gender differences, socially defined virtues for men and women, became more set. Individualism, competition, and militarism were the values of the world of men. Familial support, nurturance, and healing were female virtues. These were the separate and unequal worlds created by the factory and the battlefield. The virtues of the private sphere were extended into the public world with the creation of new forms of poorly paid female labor. In this sense, Florence Nightingale was not a rebel. This "Lady with the Lamp," whom fever-ridden soldiers called their mother, was another working woman.

liberal administrative reforms that included tax reform, stabilization of the currency, improvement of the railway system, the creation of a transatlantic steamship system, and the support of private enterprise. With these programs Cavour created for Piedmont-Sardinia the dynamic image of progressive change. He involved Piedmont-Sardinia in the Crimean War, thereby securing its status among the European powers.

Most important, however, was his successful pursuit of an alliance with France against Austria in 1858. Cavour shrewdly secured the French pledge of support, including military aid if necessary, against Austria in the Treaty of Plombières, signed by Napoleon III in 1858. The treaty was quickly followed by an arranged provocation against the Habsburg monarchy. Austria declared war in 1859 and was easily defeated by French forces in the battles of Magenta and Solferino. The peace, signed in November 1859 at Zurich, joined Lombardy to Piedmont-Sardinia. Cavour wielded the electoral weapon of the plebiscite—a method of direct voting that gives to electors the choice of voting for or against an important public question—to unite Tuscany, Parma, and Modena under Piedmont's king.

Cavour's approach was not without its costs. His partnership with a stronger power meant sometimes

The Unification of Italy

following France's lead. French bullying provoked fits of rage and forced Cavour to resign from office temporarily in 1859 over a war ended too early by Napoleon III. The need to solicit French support meant enriching France with territorial gain in the form of Nice and Savoy. However, Piedmont-Sardinia got more than it gave up. In the summer of 1859, revolutionary assemblies in Tuscany, Modena, Parma, and the Romagna, wanting to eject their Austrian rulers, voted in favor of union with the Piedmontese. By April 1860 these four areas of central Italy were under Victor Emmanuel's rule. Piedmont-Sardinia had doubled in size to become the dominant power on the Italian peninsula.

Southern Italians took their lead from events in central Italy and in the spring of 1860 initiated disturbances against the rule of King Francis II (1859–61) of Naples. Uprisings in Sicily inspired Giuseppe Garibaldi to return from his self-imposed exile to organize his own army of Red Shirts, known as the Thousand, with whom he liberated Sicily and crossed to the Italian mainland to expel Francis II from Naples. Garibaldi next turned his attention to the liberation of the Holy City, where a French garrison protected the pope. After his defeat in Rome in 1849, Garibaldi had never lost sight of his mission to free all of Italy from foreign rule, even in the 1850s when he had lived on New York's Staten Island as a candle maker and had become a naturalized citizen of the United States.

As Garibaldi's popularity as a national hero grew, Cavour became alarmed by his competing effort to unite Italy and took secret steps to block the advance of the Red Shirts and their leader. To seize the initiative, Cavour directed the Piedmontese army into the Papal States. After defeating the pope's troops, Cavour's men crossed into the Neapolitan state and scored important victories against forces loyal to the king of Naples. Cavour proceeded to annex southern Italy for Victor Emmanuel, using plebiscites to seal the procedure. At this point, in 1860, Garibaldi yielded his own conquered territories to the Piedmontese ruler, making possible the declaration of a united Italy under Victor Emmanuel II, who reigned as king of Italy from 1861 to 1878.

The new king of Italy was now poised to acquire Venetia, still under Austrian rule, and Rome, still ruled by Pope Pius IX, and he devoted much of his foreign policy in the 1860s to these ends. In 1866, when Austria lost a war with Prussia, Italy struck a deal with the victor and gained control of Venetia. When Prussia prevailed against France in 1870, Victor Emmanuel II took over Rome. The boot of Italy, from top to toe, was now a sin-

Garibaldi's army of liberation sailed from Genoa on May 5, 1860. This lithograph depicts the army's arrival at Marsala in Sicily.

In this British cartoon of 1860, Garibaldi surrenders his power to Victor Emmanuel II, king of Piedmont-Sardinia (soon to be king of a united Italy). The caption reads "Right Leg in the Boot at Last."

gle nation. The pope remained in the Vatican, opposed to an Italy united under King Victor Emmanuel II. The new national government sought to impose centralization with a heavy hand and had little interest in preserving regional differences and regional cultures. Cavour's liberal constitutional principles, combined with moderately conservative stands on social issues, produced alienation, especially in southern Italy, among both the peasantry and the nobility.

Cavour did not live to see the united Italy that he had worked so hard to fashion. He had succeeded where poets and revolutionaries had failed in preparing the ground for unification because he understood that the world had changed dramatically in the first half of the nineteenth century. He appreciated the relationship between national and international events and was able to manipulate it for his own ends. Both Cavour and his counterpart in Germany, Otto von Bismarck, considered themselves realists who shared a recognition of diplomacy as an instrument of domestic policy.

unifying Germany

Seldom in modern history does an individual emerge as a chess master, overseeing international politics and domestic affairs as if the world were a great board game with movable pieces. Otto von Bismarck (1815–98) was aware that he was playing a game of high risks and high stakes. His vision was limited to the pragmatic pursuit of preserving the power of his beloved Prussia. For him the empire was not an end in itself but a means of guaranteeing Prussian strength. In an age of realistic politicians, he emerged as the supreme practitioner of Realpolitik, the ruthless pursuit by any means, including illegal and violent ones, to advance the interests of his country.

Bismarck was a Junker, an aristocratic estate owner from east of the Elbe River, who entered politics in 1847. As a member of the United Diet of Prussia, he made his reputation as a reactionary when he rose to speak in favor of hunting privileges for the nobility: "I am a Junker and I want to enjoy the advantages of it." In the 1850s, he became aware of Prussia's future in the center of Europe: he saw that the old elites must be allied with the national movement in order to survive. The problem was that nationalism was the property of the liberals, who had been defeated in 1848. Bismarck appropriated it. Liberals and Junkers shared an interest in unification, but for different political ends. As a politician, Bismarck learned how to exploit their common ground.

In 1850 Prussia had been forced to accept Austrian dominance in central Europe; the alternative was going to war. Throughout the following decade, however, Prussia systematically undermined Austrian power by wielding the trade agreements of the Zollverein as a tool to exclude Austria from German economic affairs. In 1862, at the moment of a crisis provoked by the new king, Wilhelm I, over military reorganization, Bismarck became minister-president of the Prussian cabinet as well as foreign minister. He overrode the parliamentary body, the Diet, by reorganizing the Prussian army without a formally approved budget. In 1864 he constructed an alliance between Austria and Prussia for the purpose of invading Schleswig, a predominantly German-speaking territory controlled by the king of Denmark, whose population hoped to become part of the German Confederation. Within five days of invasion, Denmark yielded the duchies of Schleswig and Holstein, now to be ruled jointly by Austria and Prussia.

Ascertaining that he had a free hand in central Europe, Bismarck skillfully provoked a crisis between Austria and Prussia over management of the territories. Counting on the neutrality of France and Great Britain, the support of Piedmont-Sardinia, and good relations

The Unification of Germany

with Russia, Bismarck led his country into war with Austria in June 1866. In this Seven Weeks' War—the war took its name from its short duration—Austrian forces proved to be no match for the better-equipped and better-trained Prussian army. Bismarck dictated the terms of the peace, which demonstrated that he had no desire to cripple Austria, only to exclude it from a united Germany in which Prussia would be the dominant force. Austria's exclusion from Germany forced the Austrian government to deal with its own internal problems of imperial organization. In 1867, in response to pressures from the subject nationalities, the Habsburg Empire transformed itself into a dual monarchy of two independent and equal states under one ruler, who would be both the emperor of Austria and the king of Hungary. In spite of the reorganization, the problem of nationalities persisted, and ethnic groups began to agitate for total independence from imperial rule.

Bismarck's biggest obstacle to German unification was laid to rest with Austria's defeat. The south German states, however, continued to resist the idea of Prussian dominance. Prussia's militarism, Protestant religion, and economic strength threatened antimilitarists, Catholics, and the ruling elites of the southern states.

Liberals, democrats, and socialists from the south feared the political consequences of Prussian conservatism. But growing numbers of people in Baden, Württemberg, Bavaria, and the southern parts of Hesse-Darmstadt recognized the necessity of uniting under Prussian leadership.

Many French observers were troubled by the Prussian victory over Austria and were apprehensive over what a united Germany might portend for the future of French dominance in Europe. Napoleon III made clear his opposition to further Prussian growth and attempted unsuccessfully to contain Prussian ambitions through diplomatic maneuverings. Instead, France found itself stranded without important European allies. In the spring of 1870, Bismarck decided to seize the initiative and provoke a crisis with France.

Bismarck recognized that war with France could be the dramatic event needed to forge cooperation and unity among all German states. The issue of succession to the Spanish throne gave him the opportunity he sought. Bismarck skillfully created the impression that the French ambassador had insulted the Prussian king, then leaked news of the incident to the press in both countries. Enraged and inflamed French and Prussian publics both demanded war.

As a direct result of this misunderstanding deliberately manufactured by Bismarck, France declared war on Prussia in July 1870. The southern German princes, as Bismarck hoped, immediately sided with the Prussian king. For years before hostilities broke out, the Prussians had been preparing for war. They had been sending Prussian army officers disguised as landscape painters into France to study the terrain of battle. French troops carried maps of Germany but were ignorant of the geography of their own country, where the battles were waged. Sent into battle against the Germans, French troops roamed around in search of their commanders and each other. The Germans had learned new deployment strategies from studying the use of railroads in the American Civil War of 1861–65. Unlike the Germans, the French had not coordinated deployment with the new technology of the railroad. Although French troops had the latest equipment, they were sent into battle without instructions on how to use it. Finally, the Prussian-led German army was superior, outnumbering French troops 450,000 to 260,000. All these factors combined to spell disaster for the French. Within a matter of weeks, it was clear that France had lost this Franco-Prussian War. The path was now clear for the declaration of the German Empire in January 1871.

The newly established Second Reich, successor to the Holy Roman Empire, united the German states into a single nation. After years of foreign wars and endless

Im Etappenquartier vor Paris, 1871. *This 1894 painting by Anton von Werner shows Prussian troops making themselves at home in a French drawing room on their way to victory in Paris. The Prussians occupied the city for only 48 hours.*

wrangling among the heads of the 38 German states, Bismarck got what he wanted: a German Empire under the leadership of the Prussian king. The Proclamation of Empire was signed on 21 January 1871 in a ceremony in the French palace of Versailles. Bismarck, always the pragmatist, understood clearly that Europe was not the same place that it had been a decade or two earlier. "Anyone who speaks of Europe is wrong—it is nothing but a set of national expressions." This understanding was the key to his success. In unifying Germany, Bismarck built on the constitution of the North German Confederation formed in 1867, which guaranteed Prussian dominance. Bismarck used the bureaucracy as a mainstay of the emperor. The new Reichstag—the national legislative assembly—was to be elected by means of universal male suffrage, a concession to the liberals. Yet the constitution was not a liberal one, since the Reichstag was not sovereign and the chancellor was accountable only to the emperor. Policy was made outside the domain of electoral politics. The federal structure of the constitution, especially with regard to taxation, also kept the central parliament weak. Most liberals supported the constitution, but a minority persisted in a tradition of radical dissent. Critics felt that true constitutional government had been sacrificed to the demands of empire. As one liberal remarked, "Unity without freedom is a unity of slaves." Bismarck spoke in confidence of his aim "to destroy parliamentarianism by parliamentarianism." According to this formula, Bismarck hoped that a weak Reichstag would undermine parliamentary institutions better than any dictatorial ruler.

During the 1860s, another great crisis in state-building had been resolved across the Atlantic. The United States had cemented political unity through the use of force in its Civil War. Just as Bismarck had resolved his crisis through "blood and iron," so did the president of the United States, Abraham Lincoln (1809–65), mobilize the greater human and industrial resources of the North against the agrarian, slave-owning South. Republican democracy triumphed in the United States, while a neo-absolutism emerged in Germany. Yet there is a remarkable similarity between the two events. In both countries, wars eventually resulted in a single national market without internal tariffs. The wars made possible a single financial system through which capital could be raised. In both countries, unified national economies paved the way for the expansion of industrial power.

Nationalism and force

It is commonplace in the Western historical tradition to speak of nations as if they were individuals possessing emotions, making choices, taking actions, having ideas. "Russia turned inward"; "Germany chose its enemies as well as its friends"; "France vowed revenge"; "Great Britain took pride in its achievements." On one level, to attribute volition, feeling, and insight to an abstract entity like a nation is nonsense. But on another level, the personification of nation-states was one of the great achievements of statesmen throughout Europe between 1850 and 1870. The language and symbols they put in place created the nation itself, a new political reality whose forms contain modern political consciousness. The nation-state became an all-knowing being whose rights had to be protected, whose destiny had to be assured. Before the nineteenth century, the person of the king had embodied the nation. With the political upheavals of the midcentury revolutions and the creation of new states, symbols took the place of monarchs to communicate a single undivided entity. A female form, whether it was that of Britannia of Great Britain or Marianne of France, could be used to capture the purity, strength, and vulnerability of the new nationalist concept.

The nation was above all a creation that minimized or denied real differences in dialect and language, regional loyalties, local traditions, and village identities. The crises in state-building in Italy and Germany had been resolved finally by violence. No power was acknowledged to exist above the nation-state. No power could sanction the nation's actions but itself. Force was an acceptable alternative to diplomacy. War was a political act and a political instrument, a continuation of political relations. Violence and nationalism were inextricably linked in the unification of both Italy and Germany in the third quarter of the nineteenth century.

Reforming European society

The revolutions of 1848 had failed to deal with social problems, just as they had failed to realize nationalist aspirations. After the revolutions, government repression silenced radical movements throughout Europe. But repression could not maintain social harmony and promote growth and prosperity. In the third quarter of the nineteenth century, Europe's leaders recognized that reforms were needed to build dynamic and competitive states.

Three different models for social and political reform developed in Europe after 1850. One model is that of France, where the French emperor worked through a highly centralized administrative structure and with a highly valued elite of specialists to achieve social and economic transformation. The French model was a technocratic one that emphasized the importance of specialized knowledge to achieve material progress. Reform in France relied on both autocratic direction and liberal participation.

Great Britain provides another model, in which reform was fostered through liberal parliamentary democracy. In government by "amateurs," with local rather than a highly centralized administration, British legislation alternated between a philosophy of freedom and one of protection. But reforms were always hammered out by parliamentary means with the support of a gradually expanding electorate.

Finally, Russia offers a third model for reform. Like Britain, Russia had avoided revolution at midcentury. Like Britain, it hoped to preserve social peace. Yet the Russian model for reform stands in dramatic contrast to Britain's. Russia was still a semifeudal society in the 1850s. Beginning in the late 1850s, Russia embarked on a radical restructuring of society by autocratic means. Reforms in the three societies had little in common ideologically, but all reflected a commitment to progress and an awareness of the state's role and responsibility in achieving it.

The second Empire in France, 1852–1870

Napoleon III ruled France from the middle of the century until 1870. His apprenticeship for political leadership had been an unusual one. Louis Napoleon (1808–73) was a nephew of the emperor Napoleon I. The child Louis, born at the peak of French glory, was old enough to remember the devastation of his uncle's defeat in 1815. He dedicated his exiled youth to preparing for his family's restoration as rulers of France. With the death of Napoleon's son, the duc de Reichstadt, in 1832, Louis was aware that the mantle of future power and the family destiny fell to him.

In comparing Louis Napoleon with his uncle, Napoleon I, Karl Marx said that history happens the first time as tragedy and the second time as farce. There was much that passed as farcical before Louis Napoleon established France's Second Empire in 1852, as one attempt after another to seize power failed. Yet those who viewed Louis Napoleon as a figure of derision were misled: by 1848 he understood the importance of shaping public opinion to suit his own ends. He wielded the Napoleonic legend to play on the dissatisfaction of millions. He understood that to succeed in an electoral system, he had to promise something to everyone. That is exactly what he did in the fall of 1848 when he spoke of prosperity, order, and the end of poverty, slogans that sent different and incompatible messages to a bourgeoisie who wanted social peace, workers who wanted jobs and social justice, and peasants who wanted land and freedom from taxes. Universal manhood suffrage was for the first time employed in a French national election. Recognizing its legitimating power, Louis Napoleon swept the field, the only candidate supported by all social classes.

In spite of his awareness of his own importance, nobody took Louis Napoleon very seriously, even when as the dark-horse candidate he was elected president of the Second Republic in December 1848. The politicians were sure that he could be managed, so insignificant did he seem. They and the rest of France were literally caught sleeping before dawn on 2 December 1851 when the nephew of the great Napoleon seized power in a coup d'état and became dictator of France. Exactly one year later, he proclaimed himself Emperor Napoleon III and set about the tasks of establishing his dynasty and reclaiming French imperial glory.

Napoleon III's regime has been condemned for its decadence and its spectacle. On the surface, the world of the Second Empire glittered like a fancy-dress ball, with men in sparkling uniforms and women in full-skirted, low-necked gowns waltzing to gay tunes. Courtesans in open carriages, parading through the newly landscaped Bois de Boulogne, became as famous as cabinet members. But to judge the empire on superficial criteria alone would be a mistake. The Second Empire achieved significant successes in a variety of areas. Napoleon III supported economic expansion and industrial development. During his reign, the French economy prospered and flourished. The discovery of gold in California and Australia fueled a demand for French products in international markets and initiated a period of sustained economic growth that lasted beyond Napoleon III's reign into the 1880s. A new private banking system, founded in 1852 by financiers and key political figures, enabled the pooling of investors' resources, small and large, to finance industrial expansion. Stable authoritarian government encouraged increased investment in state public-works programs.

Napoleon III surrounded himself with advisers who saw in prosperity the answer to all social problems. Between 1852 and 1860, the government supported a massive program of railroad construction. Jobs multiplied and investment increased. Agriculture expanded as railroad lines opened new markets. The rich got richer, but the extreme poverty of the first half of the nineteenth century was diminishing. Brutal misery in city and countryside did not disappear, but on the whole, the standard of living increased as wages rose faster than prices.

The best single example of the energy and commitment of the imperial regime was the rebuilding of the French capital. As Sir Edwin Chadwick (1800–1890), Britain's leading public health reformer, put it, Napoleon III found Paris stinking and left it sweet. Before midcentury, Paris was one of the most unsanitary, crime-ridden, and politically volatile capitals in Europe. Within 15 years it had been transformed into a city of lights, wide boulevards and avenues, monumental vistas, parks, and gardens. Napoleon III was the architect of the idea for a new Paris, something his uncle never had the time or resources to accomplish. But the real credit for carrying through these municipal improvements goes to Baron Georges Haussmann (1809–91).

As Prefect of the Seine from 1853 to 1870, Baron Haussmann typified the technocrat in power. He was called "the Attila of the Straight Line" for the ruthless manner in which his protractor cut through city neighborhoods, destroying all that lay in his pencil's path. Poor districts were turned into rubble to make way for the elegant apartment buildings of the Parisian bourgeoisie. The new housing was too expensive for workers, who were pushed out of Paris into the suburbs. The boundaries of the city expanded. As workers from all over France migrated to the capital in search of jobs, the population nearly doubled, increasing by just under one million in the 1850s and 1860s. A poor and volatile population encircled the city of monuments and museums. Paris as the radical capital of France was being physically dismantled and a new, more conservative political entity rose in its place as the middle classes took over the heart of the city. This process was very different from the development of other urban areas like London, where the middle class fled to the suburbs, leaving behind the problems of urban life.

Much has been made of the policing benefits of rebuilding the city of Paris. Wider streets facilitated the movement of troops, which could more easily crush revolutionary disturbances. While the control aspect of urban reconstruction was not lost on Haussmann and Napoleon III, it was not the primary purpose of the vast public-works project that lasted for the whole regime.

View of the Champs-Elysées after the rebuilding of Paris. The renovations were carried out under the direction of Baron Georges Haussmann, who was called "the Attila of the Straight Line" for the ruthless manner in which his pencil cut through city neighborhoods on the map.

Napoleon wanted Paris to be the center of Western culture and the envy of the world. Its wide, straight avenues served as the model for other French cities. The new Paris became an international model copied in Mexico City, Brussels, Madrid, Rome, Stockholm, and Barcelona between 1870 and 1900. American city planners of the City Beautiful movement were also influenced by the "Haussmannization" of Paris. In spite of financial scandals that plagued the reconstruction near the end of the regime, few disputed that Napoleon III had transformed Paris into one of the world's most beautiful cities.

Just as a new Paris would make France the center of culture, Napoleon III intended his blueprint for foreign policy to restore France to its pre-1815 status as the greatest European power. French governments after 1815 had been forced to abandon adventurous foreign policies. By involving France in both the Crimean War and the war for Italian unification, Napoleon III reversed this pattern. The emperor had undertaken both wars with the hope of further increasing French economic and diplomatic prominence on the Continent. Napoleon III supported Piedmont-Sardinia not out of any sense of altruism, in spite of his claim that he was "doing something for Italy." The accession of Nice and Savoy increased French territory—and reversed the settlements of 1815.

The Italian campaign complicated relations with Great Britain, which feared a resurgent French militarism. French construction of the Suez Canal between the Red Sea and the Mediterranean also created tensions with Great Britain, protective of its own dominance in the Mediterranean and the Near East. Nevertheless, the free-trade agreement between the British and the French in 1860—the Chevalier-Cobden Treaty—was a landmark in overseas policy and a commitment to liberal economic policies.

The Second Empire's involvement in Mexico was another matter. It was simply a fiasco. The Mexican government had been chronically unable to pay its foreign debts, and France was Mexico's largest creditor. Napoleon III hoped that by intervening in Mexican affairs he could strengthen ties with Great Britain and Spain, to whom the Mexicans also owed money. The emperor planned to turn Mexico into a satellite empire that would be economically profitable to France. The United States, occupied with civil war, did not interfere in 1861 when Napoleon III sent a military expedition to "pacify" the Mexican countryside. With the backing of Mexican conservatives who opposed Mexican president

Benito Juárez (1806–72), Napoleon III supported the Austrian archduke Maximilian (1832–67) as emperor of Mexico. The reasons for the choice of Maximilian are obscure, although the gesture was probably intended to win favor in the Viennese court. Max, as he was known, was well-meaning but inept. After he was crowned in 1863, the new Mexican emperor struggled to rule in an enlightened manner, but he was stymied from the beginning by the lack of popular support. Napoleon III recalled the 34,000 French troops that, at considerable expense, were keeping Maximilian's troubled regime in place. Abandoned, Maximilian was captured and executed by a firing squad in the summer of 1867. The Mexican disaster revealed the weaknesses of Napoleon III's regime and damaged French prestige in the international arena. Intensely aware of public criticism, the emperor undertook the reorganization of the army and a series of liberal reforms, including increasing parliamentary participation in affairs of state, and granting to trade unions the right of assembly.

The Prussian victory over Austria in the Seven Weeks' War had dramatically changed the situation on the Continent. Pundits in Paris were fond of saying that the Austrian loss really marked the defeat of France. France's position within Europe was threatened, and Napoleon III knew it. In 1870, the humiliatingly rapid defeat of French imperial forces in the Franco-Prussian War brought to an end the experiment in liberal empire.

In 1870 France remained a mixture of old and new. Although industrial production had doubled between 1852 and 1870, France was still an agricultural nation. Foreign trade expanded by 300 percent, growing faster than that of any other nation in Europe. Six times as many miles of railroad track crisscrossed France at the time Napoleon III went into exile as when he came into power. Napoleon III did not create the economic boom from which all of Europe benefited between 1850 and 1880, but he did build on it, using the state to stimulate and enhance prosperity. His policies favored business and initiated a financial revolution of enduring benefits. However, the technocratic model of rule by specialists was not applied to the army in forcing it to modernize. Nor had foreign policy benefited from the careful calculations employed in domestic administration. The empire had become the victim of its own myth of invincibility.

The Victorian Compromise

Contemporaries were aware of two facts of life about Great Britain in 1850: first, that Britain had an enormously productive capitalist economy of sustained growth; and second, that Britain enjoyed apparent social harmony without revolution and without civil war. As revolutions ravaged continental Europe in 1848, the British took pride in a parliamentary system that valued a tradition of freedom. British statesmen were not reluctant to point out to the rest of the world that Great Britain had achieved industrial growth without rending the social fabric.

The political rhetoric of stability and calm was undoubtedly exaggerated. Great Britain at midcentury had its share of serious social problems. British slums rivaled any in Europe. Poverty, disease, and famine ravaged the kingdom. Many feared that British social protests of the 1840s would result in upheavals similar to those in continental Europe. Yet Great Britain avoided a revolution. One explanation for Britain's relative calm lay in the shared political tradition that emphasized liberty as the birthright of English citizens. Building on an established political culture, the British Parliament was able to adapt to the demands of an industrializing society. Adaptation was gradual, but as slow as it seemed, a compromise was achieved among competing social interests. The great compromise of Victorian society was the reconciliation of industrialists' commitment to unimpeded growth with workers' need for the protection of the state. The British political system was democratized slowly after 1832.

The Reform Bill of that year gave increased political power to the industrial and manufacturing bourgeoisie, who joined a landed aristocracy and merchant class. The property qualification meant that only 20 percent of the population was able to vote. The next step toward democracy was not taken for another 35 years. In 1867, under conservative leadership, a second Reform Bill was introduced. Approval of this bill doubled the electorate, giving the vote to a new urban population of shopkeepers, clerks, and workers. In 1884, farm laborers were enfranchised. Women, however, remained disenfranchised; they were not granted the vote until after World War I. Through parliamentary cooperation between Liberals and Conservatives, the male franchise was slowly implemented without a revolution.

The lives and careers of two men, William Ewart Gladstone (1809–98) and Benjamin Disraeli (1804–81), exemplify the particular path the British government followed in maintaining social peace. Rivals and political opponents, both men served as prime ministers and

Eduoard Manet, The Execution of the Emperor Maximilian (1868). *The United States pressured France to withdraw support for the Mexican imperial venture, which led to disaster for Maximilian and the reinstatement of Benito Juarez as president of Mexico.*

both left their mark on the age. From different political perspectives, they contributed to British reform in the second half of the nineteenth century.

William Gladstone was an example of a British statesman with no counterpart elsewhere in Europe: he was a classical liberal who believed in free enterprise and was opposed to state intervention. Good government, according to Gladstone, should remove obstacles to talent, competition, and individual initiative but should interfere as little as possible in economy and society. Surprisingly, this leader of the Liberal party began his long parliamentary career at the other end of the political spectrum, as a Tory. The son of a successful merchant and slave trader, Gladstone enjoyed the benefits of wealth and attended Eton and Oxford, where he studied classics and mathematics. Discouraged by his father from a career in the Church of England, Gladstone used his connections to launch a parliamentary career in 1832. He gradually left behind his conservative opposition to parliamentary reform and his support of protective tariffs. In 1846, as a member of the government, Gladstone broke with Tory principles and voted in favor of free trade. The best government, he affirmed in true liberal fashion, was the one that governed least.

Those who knew Gladstone in these early years were struck not by his brilliance but by his capacity for hard work and assiduous application to the task at hand. He chopped wood for relaxation. In his spare time he wrote

a three-volume study on Homer and the Homeric age. He practiced an overt morality, targeting prostitutes in the hope of convincing them to change their lives. Gladstone was not blind to social problems, but he considered private philanthropy the best way to correct them.

Many of the significant advances of the British liberal state were achieved during Gladstone's first term as prime minister (1868–74). Taking advantage of British prosperity, Gladstone abolished tariffs, cut defense expenditures, lowered taxes, and sponsored sound budgets. He furthered the liberal agenda by disestablishing the Anglican church in Ireland in 1869. The Church had been the source of great resentment to the vast majority of Irish Catholics, who had been forced to pay taxes to support the Protestant state church.

Gladstone reformed the army, in disrepute after its poor performance in the Crimea, so that one could no longer purchase a commission. Training and merit would justify all future advancements. Similarly, Gladstone reformed the civil service system by separating it from political influence and seniority. A merit system and examinations were intended to ensure the most efficient and effective government administration. The secret ballot was introduced to prevent coercion in voting. Finally, the Liberals stressed the importance of education for an informed electorate and passed an education act that aimed to make elementary schooling available to everyone.

William Gladstone rides in an omnibus in this painting titled One of the People *by Alfred Morgan. This mode of transport was thought of as a social leveler because all classes of people could afford the fares.*

These reforms added up to a liberal philosophy of government. Liberal government was, above all, an attack on privilege. It sought to remove restraints on individual freedom and to foster opportunity and talent. Liberal government sought to protect democracy through education. Voting men must be educated men. As one Liberal put it, "We must educate our masters." Liberals governed in the interests of the bourgeoisie and with the belief that what was good for capitalism was good for society. Tariffs, therefore, were kept low or eliminated to promote British commerce. Gladstone believed that all political questions were moral questions and that fairness and justice could solve political problems. In spite of his moral claims, his programs made him enemies among special interests, including farmers and the Church of England, because his policies undermined their security and privileges.

During these years, another political philosophy also left its mark on British government. This was conservatism. Under the flamboyant leadership of Benjamin Disraeli, the Conservative party supported state intervention and regulation on behalf of the weak and disadvantaged. Disraeli sponsored the Factory Act of 1875, which set a maximum of 56 hours for the factory work week. The Public Health Act established a sanitary code. The Artisans Dwelling Act defined minimum housing standards. Probably the most important conservative legislation was the Trade Union Act, which permitted picketing and other peaceful labor tactics.

Disraeli's personal background and training were very different from Gladstone's and made him unique in British parliamentary politics. He was known primarily as a novelist, social critic, and failed financier before he entered the political arena in 1837. His father was a Jewish merchant descended from a family of Spanish refugees in Venice. The senior Disraeli became a British subject in 1801, three years before Benjamin's birth. In embracing English culture, the senior Disraeli had his children baptized in the Anglican church.

The split between Disraeli and Gladstone was clearly apparent in 1846 when they, both Tories, disagreed over the issue of free trade versus tariffs. Disraeli moved on to champion protection and throughout the early 1860s consistently opposed Gladstone's financial system. Unlike the Liberals, Disraeli insisted on the importance of traditional institutions like the monarchy, the House of Lords, and the Church of England. Queen Victoria named him the First Earl of Beaconsfield for his strong foreign policy and social reforms. "Dizzy's" real cleverness and contribution to British politics were in an area

that few contemporaries appreciated at the time. Disraeli's work in organizing a national party machinery facilitated the adaptation of the parliamentary system to mass politics. His methods of campaigning and building a mass base of support were used by successful politicians regardless of political persuasion.

The terms liberal and conservative hold none of the meaning today that they did for men and women in the nineteenth century. Classical liberalism has little in common with its twentieth-century counterpart, which favors an active interventionist state. Disraeli is a far more likely candidate for the twentieth-century liberal label than is Britain's leading nineteenth-century liberal statesman, Gladstone. Disraeli placed value in the ability of the state to correct and protect. Because of his interventionist philosophy, he may be compared with Continental statesmen like Bismarck and Napoleon III.

In spite of Liberal hopes, Great Britain never had a purely laissez-faire economy. As the intersecting careers of Gladstone and Disraeli demonstrate, the British model combined free enterprise with intervention and regulation. The clear issues and the clear choices of the

Political rivals William Gladstone (left) and Benjamin Disraeli (right) prepare to sling mud at each other in a Punch *cartoon.*

two great parties—Liberal and Conservative—dominated parliamentary life after midcentury. In polarizing parliamentary politics, these parties also invigorated it.

Reforming Russia

In 1850 Russia was an unreformed autocracy, a form of government in which the tsar held absolute power. Without a parliament, a constitution, or civil liberties for its subjects, the Russian ruler governed through a bureaucracy and a police force. Economically, Russia was a semifeudal agrarian state with a class of privileged aristocrats supported by serf labor on their estates.

For decades—since the reign of Alexander I (1801–25)—the tsars and their advisers realized that they were out of step with developments in western Europe. An awareness was growing that serfdom was uncivilized and morally wrong. The remnants of feudalism had been swept away in France in the Great Revolution at the end of the eighteenth century. Prussia had abolished hereditary serfdom beginning in 1806. Among the European powers, only Russia remained a serf-holding nation. Russian serfs were tied to the land and owed dues and labor services in return for the lands they held. Peasant protests mounted, attracting public attention to the plight of the serfs. A Russian aristocrat, Baron N. Wrangel (1847–1920), recounted in his memoirs a story from his childhood in the 1850s, when he was about ten years old, that exemplifies the growing social awareness of the problem:

> One day we were sitting quietly on the terrace listening to the reading aloud of *Uncle Tom's Cabin*, a recently translated book that was then in fashion. My sisters could not get over the horrors of slavery and wept at the sad fate of poor Uncle Tom. "I cannot conceive," said one of them, "how such atrocities can be tolerated. Slavery is horrible." "But," said Bunny, in her shrill little voice, "we have slaves too."

In spite of growing moral concern, there were many reasons to resist the abolition of serfdom. Granting freedom to all serfs was a vastly complicated affair. How were serf-holders to be compensated for the loss of labor power? What was to be the freed serf's relationship to the land? Personal freedom would be worthless without a land allotment. Yet landowners opposed loss of land as strongly as loss of their work force. A landless work force would be a serious social threat, if western European experience could be taken as an example.

Hesitation about abolition evaporated with the Russian defeat in the Crimean War. The new tsar,

Alexander II (1855–81), viewed Russia's inability to repel an invasion force on its own soil as proof of its backwardness. Russia had no railroads and was forced to transport military supplies by carts to the Crimea. It took Moscow three months to provision troops, whereas the enemy could do so in three weeks. Alexander II believed in taking matters into his own hands. Russia must be reformed. Abolition of serfdom would permit a well-trained reserve army to exist without fear of rebellion. Liberating the serfs would also create a system of free labor so necessary for industrial development. Alexander interpreted rumblings within his own country as the harbinger of future upheavals similar to those that had rocked France and the Austrian Empire. He explained to the Muscovite nobility, "It is better to abolish serfdom from above than to wait until the serfs begin to liberate themselves from below."

In March 1861 the tsar signed the emancipation edict that liberated the serfs. Serfdom was eliminated in Poland three years later. Alexander II, who came to be known as the "Tsar-Liberator," compromised between landlord and serf by allotting land to freed peasants, while requiring from the former serfs redemption payments that were spread out over a period of 49 years.

Russian Serfs

The Emancipation Proclamation, 1861

Aleksandr Vasilievich Nikitenko, a former serf who had managed through luck and talent to gain an education and a place in the Russian bureaucracy, recorded the joy and excitement he and others felt when Alexander II freed Russia's serfs. Many hoped, and some feared, that the change would revolutionize Russian agriculture and society.

5 March. A great day: the emancipation manifesto! I received a copy around noon. I cannot express my joy at reading this precious act which scarcely has its equal in the thousand-year history of the Russian people. I read it aloud to my wife, my children and a friend of ours in my study, under Alexander II's portrait, as we gazed at it with deep reverence and gratitude. I tried to explain to my ten-year-old son as simply as possible the essence of the manifesto and bid him to keep inscribed in his heart forever the date of March 5 and the name of Alexander II, the Liberator.

I couldn't stay at home. I had to wander about the streets and mingle, so to say, with my regenerated fellow citizens. Announcements from the governor-general were posted at all crossways, and knots of people were gathered around them. One would read while the others listened. I encountered happy, but calm faces everywhere. Here and there people were reading the proclamation aloud, and, as I walked, I continually caught phrases like "decree on liberty," "freedom." One fellow who was reading the announcement and reached the place where it said that manor serfs were obligated to their masters for another two years, exclaimed indignantly "The hell with this paper! Two years? I'll do nothing of the sort." The others remained silent.

I ran into my friend, Galakhov. "Christ has risen!" I said to him. "He has indeed!" he answered, and we expressed our great joy to each other.

Then I went to see Rebinder. He ordered champagne and we drank a toast to Alexander II.

From Aleksandr Nikitenko, *The Diary of a Russian Censor* (1861).

The peasant paid the state in installments; the state reimbursed the landowner in lump sums. To guarantee repayment, the land was not granted directly to individual peasants but to the village commune (*mir*), which was responsible for collecting redemption payments.

Emancipation of the serfs, Alexander's greatest achievement, was a reform of unprecedented scale. It affected 52 million peasants, over 20 million of them enserfed to private landowners. By comparison, Abraham Lincoln's Emancipation Proclamation less than two years later freed four million American slaves. However, beneath the surface of the Russian liberation, peasants soon realized that the repayment schedule increased their burdens and responsibilities. The peasants resented being forced to pay for land they considered rightfully theirs. An old peasant saying reflected this belief: "We are yours"—they acknowledged to the landlords—"but the land is ours." It was not an accident that the mir arrangement prevented mobility; Alexander had no intention of creating a floating proletariat similar to that of western Europe. He wanted his people closely tied to the land, but freed from the servility of feudal obligations.

The abolition of serfdom did not solve the problem of Russian backwardness. Farming methods and farming implements remained primitive. Russian agriculture did not become more productive. Nor did emancipation result in a contented and loyal peasantry. Frustrations festered. A large proportion of peasants received too little land to make their redemption payments. Many peasants in the south received smaller plots of land than they had farmed under serfdom. The commune replaced the landowner in a system of peasant bondage. Redemption payments were finally abolished in 1907, but not before exacerbating social tensions in the countryside.

The real winner in the abolition of serfdom was not the landowners, and certainly not the peasantry, but the state. A bureaucratic hierarchy and a financial infrastructure were expanded. Other reforms in the system of credit and banking contributed significantly to rapid economic growth. With the help of foreign—especially

French—investment, railway construction increased dramatically, from 660 miles of track in 1855 to 14,000 by 1880. Thanks in large part to the new transportation network, Russia became a world grain supplier during this period, with exports increasing threefold. But development was uneven and remained uncoordinated. The coexistence of the old alongside the new, combined with the speed of change, created friction and promised future unrest.

Alexander II, a man conservative by temperament but aware that Russia must move forward, did not stop here. In 1864 he introduced *zemstvos*, local elected assemblies on the provincial and county levels, to govern local affairs. The three classes of landowners, townspeople, and peasants elected representatives who were responsible for implementing educational, health, and other social welfare reforms. Similar statutes governing towns were passed in 1870. In the spirit of modernization, the state also undertook judicial reforms. New provincial courts were opened in 1866. Corporal punishment was to be eliminated. Separate courts for peasants still endured, however, preserving the impression that peasants were a lower class of citizens subject to different jurisdiction.

With the military triumph of Prussia over France in 1870–71, the tsar found the excuse he had been looking for in the 1860s to push through fundamental military reforms. Alexander II had admired the Prussian military model since his childhood. In 1874 he used that model to require that all young men on reaching the age of 20 be eligible for conscription "in defense of the fatherland." Fifteen years of service were specified, but only six were served in active duty. This was a significant reduction from the 25 years of active service that peasant and lower-class conscripts had formerly served. Although length of service was reduced according to educational level, the military reforms were, on the whole, democratizing because they eliminated an important privilege of the wealthy.

In spite of this vast array of "Great Reforms"—emancipating the serfs, creating local parliamentary bodies, reorganizing the judiciary, modernizing the army—Russia was not sufficiently liberalized or democratized to satisfy the critics of autocracy. Between 1860 and 1870, a young generation of intelligentsia, radical intellectuals who benefited from the democratization of education and were influenced by the rhetoric of revolution in the West, assumed a critical stance in protest against the existing order. Although not itself a class, many members of the intelligentsia shared a similar background as the student sons and daughters of petty officials or priests. Young women, who often sought the

Russian peasants at a village meeting. With the abolition of serfdom in 1861, village leaders gained considerable power.

education in Switzerland that was denied to them at home, were especially active in supporting ideas of emancipation.

In 1873 the imperial government considered the Western liberal and socialist ideas of the intelligentsia so threatening that it ordered Russian students studying in Switzerland to return home. Many returning students combined forces with radical intellectuals in Russia and decided to "go to the people." About 2500 educated young men and women traveled from village to village to educate, to help, and, in some cases, to attempt to radicalize the peasants. These populist crusaders sought to learn from what they considered to be the source of all morality and justice, the Russian peasantry. They paid dearly for what proved to be a fruitless commitment to populism in the mass trials and repression of the late 1870s.

Some of the tsarist regime's critics fled into exile to reemerge as revolutionaries in western Europe, where they continued to oppose the tsarist regime and helped shape the tradition of revolution and dissent in Western countries. Other educated men and women who remained in Russia chose violence as the only effective weapon against absolute rule. Terrorists who called themselves "Will of the People" decided on assassination as the best strategy and condemned the tsar to death. In the "emperor hunt" that followed, numerous attempts were made on the tsar's life. Miraculously, Alexander II escaped even the bombing of his own living quarters in the Winter Palace. The tsarist state responded with stricter controls, but repression only fanned the flames of discontent.

In response to attempts on his life and the assassination of public officials intended to cripple the central regime, Alexander II put the brakes on reform in the second half of his reign. The Great Reforms could not be undone, however, and had set in motion sweeping economic and social changes. The state encouraged capitalist growth and witnessed the rise of a professional middle class and the formation of an embryonic factory proletariat. Serfdom was dead forever. Yet reforms had increased expectations for an equally dramatic political transformation that failed to materialize. In the end, the "Will of the People" movement succeeded in its mission. A terrorist bomb killed Alexander II, the "Tsar-Liberator," in St. Petersburg in 1881.

The politics of Leadership

Modern politics emerged in Europe only after 1850. Until that time, traditional political categories had pre-

vailed. When faced with revolutionary upheavals, regimes aimed for stability and permanence. Only after 1850 did a new breed of political leader appear who understood the world of politics and directed it to their own ends. Three statesmen typify the new approach to the public world of power: Camillo di Cavour, Otto von Bismarck, and Louis Napoleon.

In old-regime Europe, power flowed downward from the monarch, who was perched atop a hierarchically organized social system often depicted as a pyramid. The source of royal power was both timeless and historic. As God's appointed agents, the sovereigns of Europe reinforced their right to rule with the continuity of their dynasties. Men of great political acumen ministered to their royal masters and were legitimated by royal power. In the years between 1789 and 1850, this system was challenged as kings were displaced—sometimes restored to power, sometimes executed. In the Austrian Empire, Spain, France, the Low Countries, Italy, and the German states, kingship, even when accepted, no longer went unquestioned. Divine authority was an archaic idea to the growing numbers of those who spoke of democratic principles and rallied to banners that represented new concepts of liberty and equality.

In the first half of the nineteenth century, men and women had learned that those in power could be questioned. The good of the people was the primary justification for government. Power now flowed upward from the citizenry to their appointed and elected representatives. The new power brokers were those who could control and direct the flow, not merely be carried along or swept away by it. These new political men were realists in the same tradition as Machiavelli and reflected the new political culture of the nineteenth century.

Political realists like Cavour, Bismarck, and Louis Napoleon understood the importance of public opinion. Public opinion had been a central fact of political life from the eighteenth century, but as revolutionary events in France demonstrated, public opinion proved unreliable building material for a stable government. The new political leaders appreciated public opinion for what it was—an unreliable guide for policy-making, often a dangerous beast that must be controlled and tamed. But above all, it was a tool for the shaping of consensus, the molding of support. The new political realists also understood the power of the press. Cavour achieved first prominence and then power by founding his own newspaper, Il Risorgimento. Louis Napoleon ran Europe's first modern political campaign, manipulating the printed word to shape his image and tailor his message to different audiences. Bismarck used public opinion and fashioned an image of German power that served his political ends.

The new political men also shared, to varying degrees, a disregard for traditional morality in decision-making. They were often politically amoral, willing to use whatever methods guaranteed success. As Bismarck succinctly put it at the end of his long career in public life, "Politics ruins the character." Machiavelli, too, shared this disregard for traditional morality. The new political men forged their own standards by which they judged the correctness of decisions and policies.

The nation-state was the supreme justification for all actions. Cavour, Bismarck, and Louis Napoleon saw struggle as the central fact of life. Nation-states were inherently competitive, with conflicting objectives. Realpolitik meant that statesmen had to think in terms of military capability, technological dominance, and the acceptable use of force. Without a traditional morality of right and wrong, these leaders recognized that there could be no arbiter outside the interests of the nation-state. From exile in England following his military defeat and his abdication, Napoleon III placed the welfare of France above his failed ambitions. At the former emperor's funeral, his son led a cheer, not for the empire but for France.

Modern European statesmen did not, however, share a common ideological outlook. Cavour leaned toward liberal ideas, while Bismarck was unquestionably conservative and Louis Napoleon held a blend of liberal and conservative views. Yet these leaders willingly enacted similar policies and sponsored similar legislation, not from any shared political commitment, but because of their desire to strengthen and promote their nations. In order to maintain power, they adapted to circumstance; they did not insist on principle. As Bismarck explained it, he always had more than one arrow in his quiver.

Finally, the new political men were risk takers. They acted without the safety net of tradition or political legitimacy under them. Bismarck saw himself on a tightrope, but one he felt prepared to walk. Just as Jeremy Bentham, earlier in the century, had figured the relationship between actions and outcomes in terms of profits and losses, the new statesmen were calculators; they weighed levels of risk appropriate for the ends they sought to achieve. Realpolitik was less the invention of a particular statesman and more a characteristic of the new age of gamesmanship in statecraft.

changing values and the force of new ideas

Like the political world, the material world was changing rapidly after 1850. The world of ideas that explained the place of women and men in this new universe was rapidly changing as well. The railroad journey became the metaphor for the new age. The locomotive hurtling forward signified the strength, power, and progress of materialism. Yet the passenger was strangely dislocated, the landscape between one point and another a blur seen through a carriage window. New points of reference must be found; new roots must be put down. In the period between 1850 and 1870, a materialist system of values emerged as behaviors changed. This was as true for the private world of the home as it was for the public world of high politics.

In any age, changes in material life find their way into literature, philosophy, science, and art. Changes in the environment affect the way people look at the world. In turn, intellectuals can have a profound effect on values and behavior. Truly great thinkers not only reflect their times, they also shape them. The third quarter of the nineteenth century was especially rich in both the creativity and critical stance that shaped modern consciousness. Amid the tumult of new ideas in the period after 1850, two titans stand out. Not artists, but sci-

This cartoon from the London News, 1848, shows newsboys selling election broadsides for Louis Napoleon and his opponent, General Cavaignac. The boys are fighting over the merits of their respective candidates.

entists—one of biology, the other of society—they sought regularity and predictability in the world they observed and measured. The ideas of Charles Darwin and Karl Marx both reflected and changed the world in which they lived.

People alive during the third quarter of the nineteenth century called themselves "modern." They were, indeed, "modern," since in their values and view of the world they were closer to their twentieth-century progeny than they were to their eighteenth-century grandparents.

The politics of Homemaking

At the Great Exhibition of 1851 held in London, the achievements of modern industry were proudly displayed for all the world to see. Engineering marvels and mechanistic wonders dwarfed the thousands of visitors who came to the Crystal Palace to view civilization at its most advanced. In the midst of the machinery of the factory, household items took their place. Modern kitchens with coal-burning stoves were showcased, and the artifacts of the ideal home were carefully displayed. Predictably, mechanical looms, symbols of the new age, were exhibited; but inkstands, artificial flowers, thermostats, and cooking utensils were also enshrined. Visitors did not find strange this juxtaposition of the public world of production with the private world of the home in an exhibition celebrating British superiority.

The world of the home, not immune to changes in society and the economy, was invested with new power and meaning in mid-nineteenth-century Europe. Home was glorified as the locus of shelter and comfort where the harsh outside world could be forgotten. In 1870, an article in a popular Victorian magazine explained that the home functioned as a haven: "Home is emphatically man's place of rest, where his wife is his friend who knows his mind, where he may be himself without fear of offending, and relax the strain that must be kept out of doors: where he may feel himself safe, understood, and at ease."

Throughout Europe, the home served another function, as a symbol of status and achievement. Objects of a proper sort indicated wealth, upward mobility, and taste. In the belief that the more objects that could be displayed the better, the middle-class home of the third quarter of the nineteenth century was usually overdecorated. Drapes hung over doors and windows, pictures and prints covered the walls, and overstuffed furniture filled the rooms. All were intended to convey gentility and comfort.

Industrialization had separated the workplace from the home. Protective legislation before midcentury attempted to ease women out of the work force. Middle-class women were expected to assume primary responsibility for the domestic goals of escape and status. Just as the workplace was man's world, the private world of the home was woman's domain. After 1850, magazines, handbooks, and guidebooks that instructed women on how to fulfill their domestic duties proliferated. The most famous of the instruction manuals in Britain was *Mrs. Beeton's Book of Household Management* (1861). The title is instructive. The business concept of management could now be applied to the home. Mrs. Beeton told her readers, "The functions of the mistress of the house resemble those of the general of an army or the manager

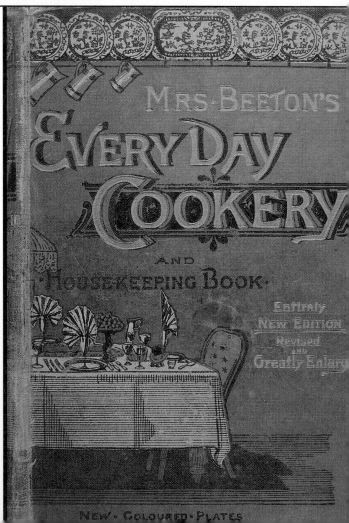

The cover of the 1890 edition of Mrs. Beeton's Everyday Cookery and Housekeeping Book. *Preparing an elaborate table like that shown in the cover illustration was one of women's principal domestic duties, according to Mrs. Beeton.*

of a great business concern." "Home economics" was invented during this period. As the marketplace had its own rules and regulations that could be studied in the "dismal science" of economics, so too, women were told, the domestic sphere could benefit from the application of rational principles of organization.

Women were also well-informed by popular literature on how to get a man and keep him. Manuals cautioned women not to be too clever, since women with opinions were not popular with men. Mrs. Beeton's advice centered on food as the way to a man's heart. A wife's duty, she explained, was above all to provide her husband with a hot meal, prepared well and served punctually. Meals became elaborate occasions of several courses requiring hours of work. Women's magazines bombarded a growing readership with menus and recipes for the careful housewife. Status was communicated not by expensive foods, but by extravagant preparation. Meal-planning was an art, women learned, one whose practice required and assumed the assistance of household servants.

Before this time, women had produced in the home products they could now buy in the marketplace. Purchases of bread, beer, soap, and candles saved housewives hours of labor every week. But with rising expectations about the quality of life in the home, women had more rather than less to do each day. Handbooks prescribed rules on etiquette and proper manners. The rituals of domestic life, from letter-writing to afternoon visits and serving tea, were minutely detailed for middle-class audiences. The woman of the house was instructed in the care and education of her children; in health, cleanliness, and nutrition; and in the management of resources. Thrift, industry, and orderliness, the virtues of the business world, had their own particular meaning in the domestic sphere.

To the Victorian mind, gentility and morality were inextricably interwoven. A woman who failed in her duty to maintain a clean and comfortable home threatened the safety of her family. An 1867 English tract warned:

> The man who goes home on a Saturday only to find his house in disorder, with every article of furniture out of its place, the floor unwashed or sloppy from uncompleted washing, his wife slovenly, his children untidy, his dinner not yet ready, or spoilt in the cooking, is much more likely "to go on a spree" than the man who finds his house in order, the furniture glistening from the recent polishing, the burnished steel fire-irons looking doubly resplendent from the bright glow of the cheerful fire, his well-cooked dinner laid on a snowy cloth, and his wife and children tidy and cheerful.

The ideal was very far from the experiences of most families throughout Europe after the middle of the century. The "science" of homemaking presupposed a cushion of affluence out of reach to the men, women, and children who made up the vast majority of the population. Working-class wives and mothers often had to earn wages if their families were to survive. One Englishwoman, Lucy Luck (1848–1922), began her working career in a silk mill at the age of eight. By law allowed to work only half a day, the child Lucy returned to her foster home at the end of her shift to labor late into the night plaiting straw for baskets. In her reminiscences, she looked back over her life: "I have been at work for forty-seven years, and have never missed one season, although I have a large family of seven surviving children." Lucy, who married at the age of 18, learned that on her own she could not survive without a man's income or without resorting to the "bad life" of crime and prostitution. In the marriage, the couple could not survive without Lucy's wages.

This female aboveground coal-mine worker was photographed in 1864 by Arthur J. Munby. Such women, who sorted the coal, had low status and no prospects.

Like Lucy Luck, many women held jobs outside the home or did piecework to supplement the meager family incomes. In 1866 women constituted a significant percentage of the French labor force, including 45 percent of all textile workers. At the height of the rhetoric about the virtues of domesticity, as many as two married Englishwomen in five worked in the mills in industrial areas like Lancashire. Working women often chose the "sweated labor" that they could perform in their home because it allowed them to care for their children while being paid by the piece. Home workers labored in the needle trades, shoemaking, and furniture making in their cramped living quarters under miserable conditions; and they worked for a third or less of what men earned.

The "haven" of the home was not insulated from the perils of the outside world. Nor was every home a happy one. Venereal diseases rose dramatically in Western nations, belying the image of the devoted couple. By the end of the nineteenth century, 14 to 17 percent of all deaths in France were attributable to sexually transmitted diseases. These diseases were blind to class distinctions. Illegitimacy rates rose in the first half of the nineteenth century and remained high after 1850 among the working classes, defying middle-class standards of propriety. Illegitimate births were highest in urban areas, where household life assumed its own distinctive pattern among working-class families, with couples often choosing free union instead of legal marriage.

Because virtue was defined in terms of woman's roles as wife and mother, working women were regarded as immoral. Social evils were, according to this reasoning, easily attributed to the "unnatural" phenomenon of women leaving the home to work in a man's world. Women continued to work and, in some cases, to organize to demand their rights. Women like Lucy Luck did not and could not accept the prescription that good mothers should not work, since their wages fed their children. The politics of homemaking defined women as mothers and hence legitimated the poor treatment and poor pay of women as workers. Yet the labor of women outside as well as inside the home remained the norm.

Nor did all middle-class women accept approved social roles. Increasing numbers of middle-class women in western Europe protested their circumscribed sphere. Critics argued that designating the home as woman's proper domain stifled individual development. Earlier in the century, Jane Austen, one of Britain's greatest novelists, had to keep a piece of muslin work on her writing table in the family drawing room to cover her papers lest visitors detect evidence of literary activity. In the next generation, Florence Nightingale refused to accept the embroidery and knitting to which she was relegated at home. This period in Western society witnessed both the creation of the cult of domesticity and the stirrings of feminism among middle-class women, whose demand for equal treatment for women was to become more important after 1870. Patterns of behavior changed within the family, and they were not fixed immutably in social practice. Woman's place and woman's role proved to be much-disputed questions in the new politics of homemaking.

The New World of Realism in the Arts

The term *realism* was first used in 1850 to describe the paintings of Gustave Courbet (1819–77), but the spirit of realism characterized a wide array of artistic endeavors. Realism in the arts and literature was a rejection of romantic idealism and subjectivity. Realists responded to the disillusionment with the political failures of midcentury by withdrawing from politics. And they responded directly to the challenges of urban and industrial growth by confronting the alienation of modern existence. In *The Artist's Studio* (1855), Courbet portrayed himself surrounded by the intellectuals and political figures of his day. He may have been painting a landscape, but contemporary political life crowded in; a starving Irish peasant and her child crouch beneath his easel. Of his unrelenting canvases, none more fittingly portrays the harsh realism of bourgeois life than the funeral ceremony depicted in *Burial at Ornans* (1849–50) or better depicts the brutality of workers' lives than *Stone Breakers* (1849).

After midcentury, idealization in romantic literature yielded to novels depicting the objective and unforgiving social world. Through serialization in journals and newspapers, fiction reached out to mass audiences, who got their "facts" about modern life through stories that often cynically portrayed the monotony and boredom of daily existence. In *Hard Times* (1854), set in the imaginary city of Coketown, Charles Dickens (1812–70) creates an allegory that exposes the sterility and soullessness of industrial society through "fact, fact, fact everywhere in the material aspect of the town; fact, fact, fact everywhere in the immaterial."

Gustave Flaubert (1821–80), the great French realist novelist, critiqued the Western intellectual tradition in his unfinished *Dictionary of Accepted Ideas* (1881). In the novel *Bouvard et Pécuchet* (1881), Flaubert satirized modern man's applications of Enlightenment ideas about the environment and progress by showing that they are foolish and often at odds with common sense. The main characters of the novel know everything there is to know about theories and applied sciences, but they know nothing about life. His best-known work, *Madame Bovary* (1856), recounts the story of a young country doctor's wife whose desire to escape from the boredom of her provincial existence leads her into adultery and eventually results in her destruction. Flaubert was put on trial for obscenity and violating public morality with his tale of the unrepentant Emma Bovary. This beautifully crafted novel is marked by an ironic detachment from the hypocrisy of bourgeois life. Mary Ann Evans (1819–80), writing under the pseudonym George Eliot, was also concerned with moral choices and responsibilities in novels like *Middlemarch* (1871–72), a tale of idealism disappointed by the petty realities of provincial English life.

The problem of morality in the realist novel is nowhere more apparent than in the works of the Russian writer Fyodor Dostoyevsky (1821–81). Dostoyevsky's protagonists wrestle with a universe where God no longer exists and where they must shape their own morality. The impoverished student Raskolnikov in *Crime and Punishment* (1866) justifies his brutal murder of an old woman that occurs in the opening pages of the novel. Realist art and literature addressed an educated elite public but did not flinch before the unrelenting poverty and harshness of contemporary life. The morality of the realist vision lay not in condemning the evils of modern life and seeking their political solutions, as an earlier generation of romantics did, but in depicting social evils for what they were, failures of a smug and progressive middle class.

charles Darwin and the New science

Science had a special appeal for a generation of Europeans disillusioned with the political failures of idealism in the revolutions of 1848. This was not an age of great scientific discovery, but rather one of synthesis of previous findings and their technological applications. Science was, above all, to be useful in promoting material progress.

Charles Darwin (1809–82), the preeminent scientist of the age, was a great synthesizer. Darwin began his scientific career as a naturalist with a background in geology. As a young man, he sailed around the world on the *Beagle* (1831–36). He collected specimens and fossils as the ship's naturalist, with his greatest finds in South America, especially the Galapagos Islands. He spent the next 20 years of his life taking notes of his observations of the natural world. In chronically poor health, Darwin produced 500 pages of what he called "one long argument." *On the Origin of Species by Means of Natural Selection* (1859) was a book that changed the world.

Gustave Courbet, Young Ladies from the Village *(1851–52). Here Courbet has painted his sisters walking in a valley near his native Ornans and offering food or money to a young cowherd. The painting, the first in a series about the lives of women, was soundly attacked by critics who objected to the girls' common features and country attire, the lack of unity and traditional perspective and scale. What the critics attacked most strongly are the very attributes that make Courbet a revolutionary figure in the history of art.*

Darwin's argument was a simple one: life forms originated in and perpetuated themselves through struggle. The outcome of this struggle was determined by "natural selection," or what came to be known as "survival of the fittest." Better-adapted individuals survived, while others died out. Competition between species and within species produced a dynamic model of organic evolution. Darwin did not use the word evolution in the original edition, but a positivist belief in an evolutionary process permeated the 1859 text.

Evolutionary theory was not new, nor was materialism a new concept in organic biology. In the 1850s, others were coming forward with similar ideas about natural selection, including most notably A. R. Wallace (1823–1913), who stressed geographic factors in biological evolution. Darwin's work was a product of discoveries in a variety of fields—philosophy, history, and science. He derived his idea of struggle from Malthus's *Essay on Population* and borrowed across disciplines to construct a theory of "the preservation of favored races in the struggle for life" (part of the book's subtitle). The publication of On *the Origin of Species* made Darwin immediately famous. Scientific theory was the stuff of front-page headlines. Like Samuel Smiles, a businessman who published the best-seller *Self-Help* in 1860, Darwin spoke of struggle and discipline, though in nature, not in the marketplace. In the world of biology, Darwin's ideas embodied a new realist belief in progress based on struggle. Force explained the past and would guarantee the future as the fittest survived. These were ideas that a general public applied to a whole range of human endeavors and to theories of social organization.

κarl Marx and the science of society

"Just as Darwin discovered the law of development of organic nature, Marx discovered the law of development of human history." So spoke Friedrich Engels (1820–95), longtime friend of and collaborator with Karl Marx (1818–83), over Marx's grave. Marx would have been pleased with Engels's eulogy: he called himself the Darwin of sociology. Marx footnoted as corroborating evidence Darwin's "epoch-making work on the origin of species" in his own masterwork, *Das Kapital*, the first volume of which appeared in 1867. As the theorist of the socialism that he called "scientific," Marx viewed himself as an evolutionist who demonstrated that history is the dialectical struggle of classes.

Engels first encountered Marx in Paris. It was a meeting of kindred spirits: each had been seeking out the other. Engels had just written *The Condition of the Working Class in England in 1844*. Marx was an iconoclast. The son of a Prussian lawyer who had converted from Judaism to Christianity, Marx had rejected the study of the law and belief in a deity. In exile because of his political writings, Marx was the most brilliant of the German young Hegelians, intellectuals heavily influenced by the ideas of Georg Friedrich Hegel (1770–1831), which held sway over the German intellectual world of the 1830s and 1840s. By the mid-1840s, Marx was in rebellion against Hegel's idealism and was developing his own materially grounded view of society. When Engels and Marx first met, they talked daily for two weeks about their common concern with social injustice and the struggles of the poor. Their momentous encounter was the beginning of a lifelong collaboration.

Engels was a wealthy German businessman whose father owned factories in Manchester, England. When Marx was expelled from France in 1847 at the request of the Prussian government, Engels financed his move to London, where he eventually took up permanent residence in 1849. While Karl Marx studied in the main reading room of the British Museum, Engels paid for the Marx family's expenses, bailed them out in hard times, and even assumed responsibility for Marx's illegitimate son, whose mother was the family maid. Karl Marx, who was to become the foremost critic of the capitalist system, joked self-disparagingly that he could not survive without Engels, since he did not know how to manage money.

The philosophy that evolved in these years of collaboration with Engels was built on a materialist view of society. Human beings were defined not by their souls but by their labor. Labor was a struggle to transform nature by producing commodities useful for survival. Their ability to transform nature by work differentiated men and women from animals. Building on this fundamental concept of labor, Marx and Engels saw society as divided into two camps: those who own property and those who do not. Nineteenth-century capitalist society was divided into two classes: the bourgeoisie, those who owned the means of production as its private property, and the proletariat, the propertyless working class.

This materialist perspective on society was the engine driving Marx's theory of history. For Marx, every social system based on a division into classes carries within it the seeds of its own destruction. Marx and Engels used a biological metaphor to explain this destruction. The growth of a plant from a seed is a dialectical process in which the germ is destroyed by its opposite, the plant. The mature plant produces seed while continuing its form. The different stages of history are determined by different forms of the ownership of production. In a feudal-agrarian society, the aristocracy controlled and exploited the unfree labor of serfs. In a world of commerce and manufacturing, the capitalist bourgeoisie are the new aristocracy exploiting free labor for wages.

Marx was more than an observer: he was a critic of capitalism. His labor theory of value was the wedge he drove into the self-congratulatory rhetoric of the capitalist age. Labor is the source of all value, he argued, and yet the bourgeois employer denies workers the profit of their work by refusing to pay them a decent wage. Instead, he pockets the profits. Workers are separated, or alienated, from the product of their labor. But more profoundly, in a capitalist system all workers are alienated from the creation that makes them human; they are alienated from their labor.

Marx predicted that capitalism would produce more and more goods but would continue to pay workers the lowest wages possible. By driving out smaller producers, the bourgeoisie would increase the size of the proletariat. Yet Marx was optimistic. As workers were slowly pauperized, they would become conscious of their exploitation and would revolt. The force of these ideas mobilized thousands of contemporaries aware of the injustices of capitalism. Few thinkers in the history of the West have left a more lasting legacy than Karl Marx. The legacy has survived the fact that much of Marx's analysis rested on incorrect predictions about the increasing misery of workers and the inflexibility of the capitalist system.

Karl Marx was a synthesizer who combined economics, philosophy, politics, and history in a wide-ranging critique of industrial society. Marxism spread across Europe as workers responded to its message. Marx did not cause the increase in the organization of workers that took place in the 1860s, but his theories did give shape and focus to a growing critique of labor relations in the second half of the nineteenth century. Political parties throughout Europe coalesced around Marxist beliefs and programs. Marxists were beginning to be heard in associations of workers, and in 1864 they helped found the International Working Men's Association in London, an organization of French, German, and Italian workers dedicated to "the end of all class rule." The promise of a common association of workers transcending national boundaries became a compelling idea to those who envisioned the end of capitalism. The importance of the international exchange of ideas and information cannot be underestimated as a means of promoting labor organization in western Europe. In 1871 Marx and his follow-

This illustration by Gustave Doré appeared in The Condition of the Working Class in England in 1844 *by Friedrich Engels. Small and cramped industrial working-class houses with their tiny walled backyards are framed by railway lines.*

ers turned to Paris for proof that the revolution was at hand.

A new Revolution? The siege of paris and the commune

Soundly defeated on 2 September 1870, Napoleon III and his fighting force of 100,000 men became Prussia's prisoners of war. With the emperor's defeat, the Second Empire collapsed. But even with the capture of Napoleon III, the French capital city of Paris refused to capitulate. The dedication of Parisians to the ongoing war with the Prussians was evident from the first. The regime's liberal critics in Paris seized the initiative to proclaim France a republic. If a corrupt and decadent empire could not save the nation, then France's Third Republic could.

In mid-September 1870, two German armies surrounded Paris and began a siege that lasted for over four months. Only carrier pigeons and balloon-transported passengers linked Paris with the rest of France. In the beginning, Parisian heroism, unchallenged by battle, seemed festive and unreal. Bismarck's troops were intent on bringing the city to its knees not by fighting but by cutting off its vital supply lines. By November, food and fuel were dwindling and Parisians

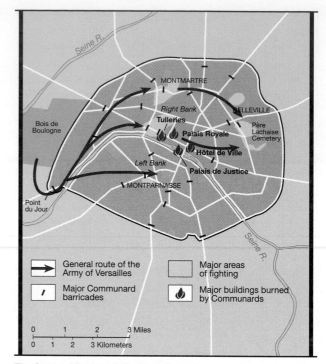

The Siege of Paris and the Paris Commune

Interior of a meat market in Paris during the siege of 1870–71. Food shortages were taking their toll, as the sign advertising dog and cat meat attests.

were facing starvation. Undaunted, they began to eat dogs, cats, and rats. By December, famine threatened to become a reality. Most people had no vegetables and no meat. Rationing was ineffective, and a black market prevailed in which the wealthy could buy whatever was available. Horses disappeared from the streets and the zoo was emptied as antelope, camel, donkey, mule, and elephant became desirable table fare. The Bois de Boulogne, the city's largest park, was leveled for timber to build barricades and for fuel. But the wood was too green and would not burn. The bitter cold of one of the century's most severe winters heightened the horror.

Yet the population was committed to fighting on. Men and women became part of the city's citizen militia, the National Guard, and trained for combat against the Germans. "Siege fever" swept the city. In spite of dire conditions, there were moments of euphoria. Collective delusions, perhaps intensified by empty stomachs, convinced Parisians that they were invincible against the enemy. Citizens joined clubs to discuss pol-

itics and preparedness, and probably to keep warm. Patents on inventions to defeat the Germans proliferated. Most of them were useless and silly, like the musical machine gun that was intended to lure its victims within firing range. The enemy at their gates absorbed the total attention of the urban population. There was no life other than the war.

Apparently with the goal of terrorizing the population, the Germans began a steady bombardment of the city at the beginning of January 1871. The shells fell for three weeks, but Parisian resistance prevailed. However, the rest of France wanted an end to the war. The Germans agreed to an armistice at the end of January 1871 in order that French national elections could be held to elect representatives to the new government. In the elections, French citizens outside Paris repudiated the war and returned an overwhelmingly conservative majority to seek peace.

Thus the siege came to an end. Yet it left deep wounds that still festered. Parisians felt they had

Red women in Paris

Louise Michel, a schoolteacher and a member of the Paris Commune, was one of the many women and men who took up arms to defend the Commune against the forces of the government in Versailles. Men's and women's vigilance committees (Michel attended both) met to ensure that the Commune set up by the people would survive. The Communards believed that the Versailles government would limit their hard-won freedoms by creating a new king of France. When the Versailles government attacked Paris, the Communards fought back.

Learning that the Versailles soldiers were trying to seize the cannon, men and women of Montmartre swarmed up the Butte in a surprise maneuver. Those people who were climbing believed they would die, but they were prepared to pay the price.

The Butte of Montmartre was bathed in the first light of day, through which things were glimpsed as if they were hidden behind a thin veil of water. Gradually the crowd increased. The other districts of Paris, hearing of the events taking place on the Butte of Montmartre, came to our assistance.

The women of Paris covered the cannon with their bodies. When their officers ordered the soldiers to fire, the men refused. The same army that would be used to crush Paris two months later decided now that it did not want to be an accomplice of the reaction. They gave up their attempt to seize the cannon

from the National Guard. They understood that the people were defending the Republic by defending the arms that the royalists and imperialists would have turned on Paris in agreement with the Prussians. When we had won our victory, I looked around and noticed my poor mother, who had followed me to the Butte of Montmartre, believing that I was going to die.

On this day, the eighteenth of March, the people wakened. If they had not, it would have been the triumph of some king; instead it was a triumph of the people. The eighteenth of March could have belonged to the allies of kings, or to foreigners, or to the people. It was the people's.

From Louise Michel, *The Red Virgin: Memoirs of Louise Michel* (1981).

been betrayed by the rest of France. Through four months as a besieged city, they had sacrificed, suffered, and died. Parisians believed that they were defenders of the true republic, the true patriots. Among Parisians, disparities of wealth were more obvious than ever before. Some wealthy citizens had abandoned the city during the siege. The wealthy who stayed ate and kept warm. Poor women who stood in food lines from before dawn every day to provision their families knew that there was food—but not for them.

The war was over, but Paris was not at peace. The new national government, safely installed outside Paris at Versailles, attempted to reestablish normal life. The volatility of the city motivated the government's attempt in March 1871 to disarm the Parisian citizenry by using army troops. In the hilly neighborhood of northern Paris, men, women, and children poured into the streets to protect their cannons and to defend their right to bear arms. In the fighting that followed, the Versailles troops were driven from the city. Paris was in a state of siege once again.

The spontaneity of the March uprising was soon succeeded by organization. Citizens rallied to the idea of the city's self-government and established the Paris Commune, as other French cities followed the capital's lead. Karl Marx hailed this event as the beginning of the revolution that would overthrow the capitalist system and saw in it the beginning of the dictatorship of the proletariat. But what occurred between March and May 1871 was not a proletarian revolution. Rather, it was a continuation of the state of siege that had held Paris through the fall and early winter months. Parisians were still at war. It was not war against a foreign enemy, nor was it a class war. It was a civil war against the rest of France.

The social experiment of self-defense in the Commune lasted for 72 days. Armed women formed their own fighting units, the city council regulated labor relations, and neighborhoods ruled themselves. In May 1871, government troops reentered the city and brutally crushed the Paris Commune. In one "Bloody Week," 25,000 Parisians were massacred and 40,000 others were arrested and tried. Of the 10,000 rebels convicted, 5000 were sent to a penal colony in the southwestern Pacific Ocean. Such reprisals inflamed radicals and workers all over Europe. The myth of the Commune became a rallying cry for revolutionary movements throughout the world and inspired the future leaders of the Russian revolutionary state.

state-building and social change

1853–1856	Crimean War
1859	Austria declares war on Kingdom of Sardinia; France joins forces with Italians
1860	Piedmont-Sardinia annexes duchies in central Italy; France gains Nice and Savoy
3 March 1861	Emancipation of Russian serfs
14 March 1861	Kingdom of Italy proclaimed with Victor Emmanuel II as king
1861–1865	American Civil War
1863	Maximilian crowned emperor of Mexico
1863	Prussians and Austrians at war with Denmark
1866	Seven Weeks' War between Austria and Prussia; Italy acquires Venetia
1867	Emperor Maximilian executed
July 1870	Franco-Prussian War begins
2 September 1870	French Second Empire capitulates with Prussian victory at Sedan
20 September 1870	Italy annexes Rome
18 January 1871	German Empire proclaimed
March–May 1871	Paris Commune

The Commune was important at the time, but not as a revolution. It offered two lessons to men and women at the end of the third quarter of the nineteenth century. First, it demonstrated the power of patriotism. Competing images of the nation were at stake, one Parisian and the other French, but no one could deny the power of national identity to inspire a whole city to suffer and to sacrifice. Second, the Commune made clear the power of the state. No revolutionary movement could succeed without controlling the massive forces of repression at the state's command. The Commune had tried to recapture a local, federal view of the world but failed to take sufficient account of the power of the state that it opposed. In writing of this episode two decades later, Friedrich Engels wondered if revolution would ever again be possible in the West.

Western societies had crossed the threshold into the modern age in the third quarter of the nineteenth century. Strong states from Great Britain to Russia were committed to creating and preserving the conditions of industrial expansion. The machine age, railroads, and metallurgy were spreading industrial development much more widely through western and central Europe than had been possible before 1850. Italians and Prussians, in attempting to join the ranks of nation-states, realized that the road to a strong nation could only be achieved with industrial development and social reforms.

State-building in Western societies went hand in hand with growth in the social responsibilities of government. The national powers that would dominate world politics and economy in the twentieth century all underwent modernizing transitions in the 1860s. These included the United States, France, Great Britain, and Germany. The Austrian Empire, too, undertook programs to modernize its government and economy; and the Russian Empire established social reforms of unparalleled dimensions. New nations came into existence in this period through the limited use of armed force. With the establishment of the German Empire, Otto von Bismarck, the most realistic of politicians, was intent on preserving the peace in Europe by balancing the power of the great European states. Europeans prided themselves on being both modern and realistic in the third quarter of the nineteenth century. Peace was possible if it was armed and vigilant. Reform, not revolution, many were sure, was the key to the future progress of European societies.

mastering the chapter

To review the main points of the chapter, be sure you can explain the significance of each of the following.

Terms/Concepts/Events	People	Places
Crimean War	Florence Nightingale	Crimean Peninsula
Risorgimento	Guiseppe Garibaldi	Bosporus Strait
Realpolitik	Camillo Benso di Cavour	Dardanelles
Junker	Victor Emmanuel II	Sea of Marmara
Seven Weeks' War	Otto von Bismarck	Black Sea
Franco-Prussian War	Louis Napoleon (Napoleon III)	Ottoman Empire
realism	William Gladstone	Danubian Principalities
Marxism	Benjamin Disraeli	Sevastopol
Third Republic	Alexander II	Piedmont-Sardinia
Paris Commune	Charles Darwin	Suez Canal

suggestions for further Reading

Building Nations: The politics of unification

Derek Beales, *The Risorgimento and the Unification of Italy* (London: Allen & Unwin, 1982). Drawing a distinction between unification and national revival, Beales situates the period of unification within the larger process of the cultural and political revival.

* Gordon A. Craig, *Germany, 1866–1945* (New York: Oxford University Press, 1978). This synthetic view of German history provides a thorough examination of German unification. Craig analyzes all aspects of imperial development, with special attention to the institutional framework, its politics, economy, and diplomacy.

James J. Sheehan, *German Liberalism in the Nineteenth Century* (Chicago: University of Chicago Press, 1978). Sheehan explores the problems of transferring Western liberalism to Germany by examining the origins of German liberalism, the revolutions of 1848, and the politics of the Bismarckian state.

Denis Mack Smith, *Cavour* (London: Weidenfeld and Nicolson, 1985). Smith contrasts Cavour and his policies to Garibaldi and Mazzini and considers the challenge of regionalism to the unification process.

Reforming European Society

* David Pinkney, *Napoleon III and the Rebuilding of Paris* (Princeton, NJ: Princeton University Press, 1972). Describes how Paris was transformed into the monumental city that became not only a manifestation of French culture, but also a symbol of European culture as a whole. The planning, financing, and building of Napoleon III's Paris are analyzed, as is the impact of the rebuilding on the city's residents.

* Alain Plessis, *The Rise and Fall of the Second Empire, 1852–1871*, tr. Jonathan Mandelbaum (Cambridge: Cambridge University Press, 1985). Discusses the Second Empire as an important transitional period in French history, when the conflict was between traditional and modern values in political, economic, and social transformations.

* W. H. C. Smith, *Second Empire and Commune: France, 1848–1871* (London: Longman, 1985). Places the reign of Louis Napoleon in its domestic and international context and argues that the Empire was destroyed by external forces.

H. Seton Watson, *The Russian Empire, 1801–1917* (Oxford: Clarendon Press, 1967). This narrative history describes the social and economic background of late imperial Russia, with attention to intellectual trends and political ideologies.

Changing Values and the Force of New Ideas

* Jacques Barzun, *Darwin, Marx, Wagner: Critique of a Heritage* (Garden City, NY: Doubleday Anchor, 1958). A classic study of mid-nineteenth-century intellectual and cultural trends that situates the roots of the modern heritage in the science and art of this period.

Jenni Calder, *The Victorian Home* (London: B. T. Batsford, 1977). A cultural and social history of Victorian domestic life in which the author describes both bourgeois and working-class domestic environments.

* Bonnie G. Smith, *Ladies of the Leisure Class: The Bourgeoises of Northern France in the Nineteenth Century* (Princeton, NJ: Princeton University Press, 1981). Explores the impact of industrialization on the lives of bourgeois women in northern France and demonstrates how the cult of domesticity emerged in a particular community.

Edith Thomas, *The Women Incendiaries*, tr. James and Starr Atkinson (New York: George Braziller, 1966). One of the few studies that examines the prominent role played by women in the Paris Commune, this book considers how instrumental women were in the burning of Paris and also examines contemporary feminist debates.

* Martha Vicinus, *Independent Women: Work and Community for Single Women, 1850–1920* (Chicago: University of Chicago Press, 1985). Chronicles the choices that Victorian women made to live outside the norms of marriage and domesticity in various women's communities, including sisterhoods, nursing communities, colleges, boarding schools, and settlement houses.

*Paperback edition available.

The crisis of european culture, 1871-1914

speeding to the future

"We want to demolish museums and libraries." These are not the words of an anarchist or a terrorist but of a poet. The Italian writer Emilio Marinetti (1876–1944) endeavored—symbolically, at least, through the power of his pen—to destroy the citadels of Western culture at the beginning of the twentieth century. Marinetti was not alone in wanting to pull down all that preserved art and learning in the West. Joined by other artists and writers who called themselves futurists, Marinetti represented a desire to break free of the past. By shocking complacent bourgeois society with their art, futurists hoped to fashion a new and dynamic civilization. Although they were a small group with limited influence, their concerns were shared by a growing number of intellectuals who judged European culture to be in the throes of a serious moral and cultural crisis. Futurist ideas also reflected the growing preoccupation with the future common among European men and women who spurned the value of tradition.

The futurist painter Umberto Boccioni (1882–1916) captures an aspect of the dynamic intensity of this changing world in his *Riot in the Galleria* (1910). Look at the

painting. The setting is a galleria, the equivalent of a modern shopping mall, in front of a respectable *caffé* (an Italian coffee shop), this one frequented by well-dressed men and women, clearly members of the middle class. Here is a modern urban scene, a public space in every way characteristic of the new age of enjoyment and consumption.

There is a story here. In a flurry of light and shadow, a rush of figures moves toward the middle ground of the canvas. At the center of this movement are two women engaged in a brawl that seems to pull the figures of shoppers and strollers toward it. The fact that the brawlers are female is intended to underscore the irrationality of the incident. Yet the brawl itself is not compelling our attention. It is rather the movement of the crowd, like moths to a flame, that Boccioni intends us to see. This is a painting about movement. These objects in motion are little more than vibrations in space, faceless and indistinguishable as individuals. The crowd does not walk or run; it appears instead to be in flight. In his studies for the canvas, Boccioni reduces movement to a series of lines both swirling and directed.

The riot Boccioni depicts here is an irrational event. This is no ordinary rabble: it is a well-dressed mob, as the blurred but sumptuously flowered hats and the occasional yellow straw boaters make clear. Movement is taking place without forethought, fueled by the attraction of violence and the possibility of participating in it. There are those on the periphery who have not joined the frenzy, but we as spectators are confident that they will be swept up in the action as the energy of the brawl sucks everything to its center, like the vortex of a tornado. European society seemed to many contemporaries to be moving into an abyss, a world of tumultuous change but without values.

In the violence of the riot we are shown beauty of movement that surpasses that of an orderly waltz. Boccioni uses the warm glow of the electric lights, symbol of the modern age, to illuminate a "new reality." Golden tones, warm oranges and rosy hues, shadowed in delicate purples, create a mosaic whose beauty in the play of color is strangely at odds with the theme of the two brawling figures who activate the crowd. There is no meaning beyond the movement.

Riot in the Galleria reflects the preoccupation with change in the early twentieth century. Life was moving so fast that European society seemed to have outrun its own heritage by 1900. Technology was transforming Europe with a breakneck speed unmatched in human history. Science undermined the way people thought about themselves by challenging moral and religious values as hollow and meaningless. The natural sciences threw into doubt the existence of a creator. New forms of communication and transportation—the telephone, the wireless telegraph, the bicycle, the automobile, the airplane—were obliterating traditional understandings of time and space. The cinema and the X ray altered visual perception and redefined the ways people saw the world around them. This was a period of intense excitement and vitality in the history of the West, one that traditional values did not always explain.

Like the political revolutionaries of an earlier age, futurist artists issued "manifestos." They sought the liberation of the human spirit from a world that could no longer be understood or controlled. Liberation could only be achieved through immersion in mass society and rapid change. Boccioni's goal was a revolutionary one: "Let's turn everything upside down. . . . Let's split open our figures and place the environment inside them."

Not all contemporary artists went as far in embracing the new age as Marinetti, Boccioni, and the other futurists. Many of Europe's intellectuals understood the attempt to break free of the stranglehold of Western

Focus Questions

1. Why did European economies run through cycles of boom and bust in the late nineteenth century, and how did European governments attempt to regulate the economy?
2. What challenges did liberal ideals and institutions confront in England, Germany, France, and Austria?
3. What social forces brought women and others into the new mass politics of the late nineteenth century?
4. What new ideas were being generated in psychology and the social sciences at the turn of the century, and what impact did this have on the way Europeans thought about gender relations?

tradition. In the arts, French impressionists, including Édouard Manet (1832–83), Claude Monet (1840–1926), Edgar Degas (1834–1917), and Pierre-Auguste Renoir (1841–1919), experimented with capturing the nature of light on canvas. They painted scenes from modern life, including urban subjects, that broke with traditional forms by emphasizing the private, individual lives of the middle class.

The moral dimensions of the cultural crisis affecting the West were grasped early by the German philosophers Arthur Schopenhauer (1788–1860), who made pessimism into a philosophical category, and Friedrich Nietzsche (1844–1900), who argued against all religion and glorified the superman. Georges Sorel (1847–1922) in France reflected on the importance of violence, and his countryman Alfred Jarry (1873–1907) used the stage to show that nonsense and irrationality ruled everywhere.

The futurists went beyond the radical cultural critique of European intellectuals when they proclaimed, "A speeding automobile is more beautiful than *The Victory of Samothrace*." By declaring that modern mechanical invention surpassed the beautiful ancient Greek statue enshrined in the Louvre museum in Paris, Boccioni intended to establish the supremacy of contemporary achievement.

Boccioni has been recognized as one of the great artists of the twentieth century. In his sculpture and painting, he aimed to capture the vitality and excitement of the new age. The desire to destroy all traditional values led Boccioni and the futurists to embrace violence and war as "hygienic." Futurism glorified the masses and rejected traditional elites as sterile. The individual was no longer at the center of the new culture. Change, technology, and, above all, violence were exalted. As the First Futurist Manifesto urged, "Let us leave Wisdom behind. . . . Let us throw ourselves to be devoured by the Unknown." With the figures in his canvas swept up into an irrational mass, Boccioni emphasizes the rush and unpredictability of daily life. Beauty was a speeding car swallowing up the landscape, and it was a crowd sucked into the whirlwind of collective irrationality. Boccioni met his own death in 1916 as a soldier in the war that he welcomed as a purifying event.

The "whirling life of steel, of pride, of fever and of speed" identified by the futurists in their 1910 Manifesto suggested a new universe of continuous upheaval. Futurists were not alone in their confusion over what to keep and what to reject in Western culture or in their inability to break entirely with the past. But they were single-minded in their rebellion against constraints. Before 1914 a new generation of Europeans rushing forward abandoned the lessons of the past for the promise of the future.

European Economy and the Politics of Mass Society

Between 1871 and 1914, the scale of European life was radically altered. Industrial society had promoted largeness as the norm, and growing numbers of people worked under the same roof. Large-scale heavy industries fueled by new energy sources dominated the economic landscape. Great Britain, the leader of the first phase of the industrial revolution of the eighteenth century, slipped in prominence as an industrial power at the end of the nineteenth century, as Germany and the United States devised successful competitive strategies of investment, protection, and control.

The organization of factory production throughout Europe and the proximity of productive centers to distribution networks meant ever greater concentration of populations in urban areas. Like factories, cities were getting bigger at a rapid rate and were proliferating in numbers. Berlin, capital of the new German nation, mushroomed in size in the last quarter of the nineteenth century. In the less industrialized parts of eastern Europe, cities also underwent record growth.

Warsaw, St. Petersburg, and Moscow all expanded by at least 400,000 inhabitants each. Budapest, the city created by uniting the towns of Buda and Pest in 1872, tripled in size between 1867 and 1914 and was typical of the booming growth of provincial cities throughout Europe. With every passing year proportionately fewer people remained on the land. Those who did stay in the agricultural sector were linked to cities and tied into national cultures by new transportation and communications networks.

Changes in the scale of political life paralleled the rise of heavy industry and the increasing urbanization of European populations. Great Britain experienced the transformation in political organization and social structure before other European nations. But after 1870, changes in politics influenced by the scale of the new industrial society spread to every European country. Mass democracy was on the rise and was pushing aside the liberal emphasis on individual rights valued by parliamentary governments everywhere.

In spite of dramatic changes in politics and society, the old order still persisted. Throughout Europe, monarchy remained the dominant form of government, whether in the small German dynasties or the great Habsburg holdings. The progeny of Britain's Queen Victoria married the sons and daughters of Europe's other royal houses, seeming to make Europe's aristocrats one extended family network. But the age of royal influence was in twilight. In 1901, Victoria, Britain's longest-reigning monarch, died; her son and successor Edward VII (1901–11) died ten years later. Their obsequies symbolized the end of an era. New industrial and financial leaders assumed positions of power among Europe's ruling elite. A new style of politics brought new political actors into the public arena at the beginning of the twentieth century.

Women were excluded from national political participation, although the right to vote was gradually being extended to all men in western Europe, regardless of property or social rank. Paradoxically, the extension of the suffrage worked to undermine the significance of parliaments. Political parties developed as interest groups with single issues that were at odds with the liberal policies of the nineteenth century. Demagogues appealing to anti-Semitic, antiliberal, and antilabor voters attracted mass followings. Extraparliamentary groups—lobbies, trade unions, and cartels—grew in influence and power and came to exert pressure on the political process. The politics of mass society made clear the contradictions inherent in democracy. Propaganda, the

Berlin street scene, 1909.

ability to control information, became the avenue to success.

Great Britain, Germany, France, and Austria-Hungary, all with very different political traditions, had to adapt to the new realities of mass politics. The challenges of trade unions in England, socialism in Germany, political scandals in France, and anti-Semitic politics in Austria provide strikingly different vantage points on a common phenomenon: the crisis in European liberalism and the new politics of mass society.

Regulating Boom and Bust

Between 1873 and 1895, an epidemic of slumps battered the economies of European nations. These slumps, characterized by falling prices, downturns in productivity, and declining profits, have been called the

"Great Depression" of the nineteenth century. In reality, the economic downturn of this period was not a great depression like the one that followed the crash of 1929, but instead a period of economic uncertainty and fluctuation. It did not strike European nations simultaneously, nor did it affect all countries with the same degree of severity. But the so-called Great Depression of the late nineteenth century and the boom period of intense economic expansion from 1895 to 1914 did teach industrialists, financiers, and politicians one important lesson: alternative booms and busts in the business cycle were dangerous and had to be regulated.

Too much of a good thing brought on the steady deflation of the last quarter of the nineteenth century. In the world economy, there was an overproduction of agricultural products—a sharp contrast to the famines that had ravaged Europe only 50 years earlier. Overproduction resulted from two new factors in the world economy: technological advances in crop cultivation, and the low cost of shipping and transport, which had opened up European markets to cheap agricultural goods from the United States, Canada, and Argentina. The absolute numbers of those employed in agriculture remained more or less constant, but world output soared. Cheap foreign grains, especially wheat, flooded European markets and drastically drove down agricultural prices. The drop in prices affected purchasing power in other sectors and resulted in long-term deflation and unemployment.

Financiers, politicians, and businessmen dedicated themselves to eliminating the boom-and-bust phenomenon, which they considered dangerous. Why were cyclic downturns considered so dangerous at the end of the nineteenth century when they had not been before? Earlier in the century, manufacturers of textiles could endure "bust" periods of depressed prices and declining profits without great hardship. Small family firms requiring little capital could move in and out of production to meet demand. But by the last quarter of the nineteenth century that situation had changed dramatically. The application of science and technology to industrial production required huge amounts of capital. The two new sources of power after 1880, petroleum and electricity, could only be developed with heavy capital investment. Large mechanized steel plants were costly and out of reach for small family firms of the scale that had industrialized textiles so successfully earlier in the century. Heavy machinery, smelting furnaces, buildings, and transport were all beyond the abilities of the small entrepreneur. In order to raise the capital necessary for the new heavy industry at the end of the nineteenth century, firms had to look outside themselves to the stock market, banks, or the state to find adequate capital resources.

But investors, especially banks, refused to invest without guarantees on their capital. Bankers all over Europe were intent on minimizing risks, and they certainly wanted to avoid the uncertainties of the business cycle. Because investment in heavy industry meant tying up capital for extended periods of time, banks insisted on safeguards against falling prices. The solution they demanded was the elimination of uncertainty through the regulation of markets.

Regulation was achieved through the establishment of cartels, combinations of firms in a given industry united to fix prices and to establish production quotas. Not as extreme as the monopolies that appeared in the United States in the same period and for the same purpose, cartels were agreements among big firms intent on controlling markets and guaranteeing profits. Trusts were another form of collaboration that resulted in the elimination of unprofitable businesses. Firms joined together horizontally within the same industry—for example, all steel producers agreed to fix prices and set quotas. Or they combined vertically by controlling all levels of the production process, from raw materials to the finished product, and all other ancillary products necessary to or resulting from the production process. This type of cartel was exemplified by a single firm that controlled the entire production process and the marketing of a single product, from raw materials and fuel through sales and distribution.

Firms in Great Britain, falling behind in heavy industry, failed to form cartels and for the most part remained in private hands. But heavy industry in Germany, France, and Austria, to varying degrees, sought regulation of markets through cartels. International cartels appeared that regulated markets and prices across national borders within Europe. Firms producing steel, chemicals, coke, and pig iron all minimized the effects of competition through the regulation of prices and output.

Banks, which had been the initial impetus behind the transformation to a regulated economy, in turn formed consortia to meet the need for greater amounts of capital. A consortium—paralleling a cartel—was a partnership among banks, often international in character, in which interest rates and the movement of capital were regulated by mutual agreement. The state, too, played an important role in directing the economy. In capital-poor Russia, the state used indirect taxes on the peasantry to finance industrialization and railway construction at the end of the nineteenth century. Russia industrialized with the sweat of its peasants. Russia also needed to import capital, primarily from France after 1887. The state had to guarantee foreign loans and regulate the economy to pay interest on foreign capital investment. Foreign investors were not willing to leave the export of capital to chance or the vagaries of the business cycle. The state must intervene.

Throughout Europe, nation-states protected domestic industries by erecting tariff barriers that made foreign goods noncompetitive in domestic markets. Only Great Britain among the major powers stood by a policy of free trade. Europe was split into two tiers, the haves and the have-nots—those countries with a solid industrial core and those that had remained unindustrialized. This division had a geographic character, with the north and west of Europe more heavily developed and capitalized and the southern and eastern parts of Europe remaining heavily agricultural. For both the haves and the have-nots, tariff policies were an attractive form of regulation by the state to protect established industries and to nurture those industries struggling for existence.

Economic regulation was not a twentieth-century creation, as critics of the welfare state contend. Intervention and control began in the late nineteenth century, very much under the impetus of bankers, financiers, and industrialists. Capitalists looked on state intervention not as an intrusion but as a welcome corrective to the ups and downs of the business cycle. Regulation did not emerge from any philosophical or ideological assumption about government but came about as a result of the very real need for capital to enable heavy industry to expand and the equally compelling need to protect profits in order to encourage financiers to invest.

challenging Liberal England

Great Britain had avoided revolution and social upheaval in the nineteenth century. It prided itself on the progress achieved by a strong parliamentary tradition. One writer caught the self-congratulatory spirit of the age in an 1885 book on popular government: "We Englishmen pass on the Continent as masters of the art of government." Parliamentary government was based on a homogeneous ruling elite. Aristocrats and businessmen and financial leaders shared a common educational background in England's elitist educational system of the public schools and the universities of Oxford or Cambridge. Schooling produced a common outlook and common attitudes toward parliamentary rule, whether in Conservative or Liberal circles, and guaranteed a certain stability in policies and legislation.

In the 1880s, issues of unemployment, housing, public health, and education challenged the attitudes of Britain's ruling elite and fostered the advent of an inde-

A cartoon from a pamphlet published in Britain by the Tariff Reform League in 1903. The tree represents Britain's free-trade policy. The other nations of the world are harvesting the benefits of the British policy.

pendent working-class politics. Between 1867 and 1885, extension of the suffrage increased the electorate fourfold. Protected by the markets of its empire, the British economy did not experience the roller-coaster effect of recurrent booms and busts after 1873. Nor did Britain experience severe economic crisis between 1890 and 1914, a period of growing labor unrest. But after 1900, wages stagnated, while prices continued to rise. Traditional parliamentary politics had little to offer those workers whose standard of living suffered a real decline. The quality of urban housing deteriorated, as exemplified by the severe overcrowding of London's East End.

Workers responded to their distress by supporting militant trade unions. Trade unions, drawing on a long tradition of working-class associations, were all that stood between workers and the economic dislocation caused by unemployment, sickness, or old age. In addition, new unions of unskilled and semiskilled workers flourished, beginning in the 1880s and 1890s. A Scottish miner, James Keir Hardie (1856–1915), attracted national attention as the spokesman for a new political movement, the Labour party, whose goal was to represent workers in Parliament. In 1892 Hardie was the first independent working man to sit in the House of Commons. Hardie and his party convinced trade unions that it was in their best interests to support Labour candidates instead of Liberals in parliamentary elections after 1900. Unions, as extraparliamentary groups, worked successfully toward achieving a parliamentary voice. By 1906, the new Labour party had 29 seats in Parliament.

Yet Parliament seemed to be failing the poor. So argued a group of intellectuals concerned with social wel-

An election poster of 1895 exhorts voters to send Keir Hardie to Parliament. His positions on labor issues are succinctly stated.

fare who called themselves Fabians. They named themselves after the Roman dictator Fabius, who was noted for his delaying tactics, which enabled him to avoid decisive battle with Hannibal in the Punic Wars. Fabius believed in cutting off the supplies of his enemies and engaging in skirmishes. Following his lead, the Fabians were socialists, not in a Marxist sense of ultimate revolutionary confrontation, but in a gradualist sense of a reformist commitment to social justice. Led by Beatrice Webb (1858–1943) and Sidney Webb (1859–1947), and including in their number playwright and critic George Bernard Shaw (1856–1950), theosophist Annie Besant (1847–1943), and novelist H. G. Wells (1866–1946), the Fabians proved to be successful propagandists who were able to keep issues of social reform in the public eye. They advocated collective ownership of factories and workshops and state direction of production through gradual reform. At the turn of the century, the Fabian Society threw its support and the power of its tracts on social issues behind Labour party candidates. Intellectuals now joined with trade unionists in demanding public housing, better public sanitation, municipal reforms, and improved pay and benefits for working people.

The existence of the new Labour party pressured Conservatives and Liberals to develop more enlightened social policies and programs. After 1906, under threat of losing votes to the Labour party, the Liberal party heeded the pressures for reform. The "new" Liberals supported legislation to strengthen the right of unions to picket peacefully. Led by David Lloyd George (1863–1945), who was chancellor of the exchequer, Liberals sponsored the National Insurance Act of 1911. Modeled after Bismarck's social welfare policies, the act provided compulsory payments to workers for sickness and unemployment benefits. In order to gain approval to pay for this new legislation, Lloyd George recognized that Parliament itself had to be renovated. The Parliament Bill of 1911 reduced the House of Lords, dominated by Conservatives resistant to proposed welfare reforms, from its status as equal partner with the House of Commons. Commons could and now did raise taxes without the consent of the House of Lords to pay for new programs that benefited workers and the poor.

Social legislation did not silence unions and worker organizations. To the contrary, protest increased in the period up to the beginning of World War I in 1914. There was little doubt about the ability of militant trade unions to mobilize workers. In 1910, three of every ten manual workers belonged to a union, and this figure

A union leader addresses striking British coal miners in 1912. Labor unions became increasingly militant after the turn of the century as rising unemployment and declining real wages cut into the gains of the working class.

doubled to 60 percent of the work force between 1910 and 1914. In these years, waves of strikes broke over England. Unions threatened to paralyze the economy. Coal miners, seamen, railroad workers, and dockers protested against stagnant wages and rising prices.

The high incidence of strikes was a consequence of growing distrust of Parliament and distrust, too, of a regulatory state bureaucracy responsible for the social welfare reforms. Workers felt manipulated by a system unresponsive to their needs. Labour's voice grew more strident. The Trade Unions Act of 1913 granted unions legal rights to settle their grievances with management directly. In the summer of 1914, a railway worker boasted, "We are big and powerful enough to fight our own battle without the aid of Parliament or any other agency. There could be no affection between the robber and the robbed." Only the outbreak of war in 1914

ended the possibility of a general strike by miners, railwaymen, and transport workers.

The question of Irish Home Rule also plagued Parliament. In Ulster in northern Ireland, army officers of Protestant Irish background threatened to mutiny. In addition, women agitating for the vote shattered parliamentary complacence. The most advanced industrial nation in the world, with its tradition of peaceful parliamentary rule, had entered the age of mass politics.

political struggles in Germany

During his reign as chancellor of the German Empire (1871–90), Otto von Bismarck formed shrewd alliances that hampered the development of effective parliamentary government. He repeatedly and successfully blocked the emergence of fully democratic participation. In Germany, all males had the right to vote, but the German parliament, the Reichstag, enjoyed only restricted powers in comparison to the British Parliament. Bismarck's objective remained always the successful unification of Germany, and he promoted cooperation with democratic institutions and parties only so long as that goal was enhanced.

Throughout the 1870s, the German chancellor collaborated with the German liberal parties in constructing the legal codes, the monetary and banking system, the judicial apparatus, and the railroad network that pulled the new Germany together. Bismarck backed German liberals in their antipapal campaign, in which the Catholic church was declared the enemy of the German state. He suspected the identification of Catholics with Rome, which the liberals depicted as an authority in competition with the nation-state. The anti-Church campaign, launched in 1872, was dubbed the *Kulturkampf*, the "struggle for civilization," because its supporters contended that it was a battle waged in the interests of humanity.

The legislation of the *Kulturkampf* expelled Jesuits from Germany, removed priests from state service, attacked religious education, and instituted civil marriage. Bishops and priests who followed the instructions of Pope Pius IX (1846–78) not to obey the new laws were arrested and expelled from Germany. Many Germans grew concerned over the social costs of such widespread religious repression, and the Catholic Center party increased its parliamentary representation by rallying Catholics as a voting bloc in the face of state repression. With the succession of a new pontiff, Leo XIII (1878–1903), Bismarck took advantage of the opportunity to negotiate a settlement with the Catholic church, cutting his losses and bringing the *Kulturkampf* to a halt. Bismarck had grown wary of the demands of the National Liberal party for an increasing share of political power.

Bismarck's repressive policies also targeted the Social Democratic party. The Social Democrats were committed to a Marxist critique of capitalism and to international cooperation with other socialist parties. Seeing them as a threat to stability in Germany and in Europe as a whole, he set out to smash them. In 1878, using the opportunity for repression presented by two attempts on the emperor's life, Bismarck outlawed the fledgling Socialist party. The Anti-Socialist Law forbade meetings among Socialists, fund-raising, and distribution of printed matter. The law relied on expanded police powers and was a fundamental attack on civil liberties and freedom of choice within a democratic electoral system. Nevertheless, individual Social Democratic candidates stood for election in this period and quickly learned how to work with middle-class parties in order to achieve electoral successes. By 1890 Social Democrats had captured 20 percent of the electorate and controlled 35 Reichstag seats, in spite of Bismarck's anti-Socialist legislation.

Throughout the 1880s, as his ability to manage Reichstag majorities declined and as Socialist strength steadily mounted, Bismarck grew disenchanted with universal manhood suffrage. Beginning in 1888, the chancellor found himself at odds with the new emperor, Wilhelm II (1888–1918), over his foreign and domestic policies. The young emperor dismissed Bismarck in March 1890 and abandoned the chancellor's anti-Socialist legislation. The Social Democratic party became the largest Marxist party in the world and, by 1914, the largest single party in Germany.

The socialism of the German Social Democrats was modified in the 1890s. Although it had never been violent or insurrectionary, social democracy moved away from a belief in a future revolution and toward a democratic "revisionism" that favored gradual reform through parliamentary participation. Those who continued to maintain a more orthodox Marxist position, such as August Bebel (1840–1913) and Karl Kautsky (1854–1938), believed capitalism would destroy itself, as Karl Marx had predicted, without any violent action by German Social Democrats. Bebel confided to Friedrich Engels in 1885 that he went to bed every night with the confidence that "the last hour of bourgeois society strikes soon."

Revisionism was both practical and democratic. Its leading advocate, Eduard Bernstein (1850–1932), introduced aspects of Fabian state socialism into the German movement. This grass-roots transformation favored evolutionary rather than revolutionary political action. Workers were the primary force behind the shift away from the catastrophe theory of Bebel and Kautsky. Their standard of living had been improving in Germany, and the prospect of the imminent collapse of capitalism seemed slight to workers intent on achieving

The struggle between Bismarck and the pope is symbolized in this cartoon. Bismarck's chessmen include "Germania," the press, and antimonastic legislation. The pope marshals encyclicals, interdicts, and the Syllabus of Errors.

further gains. Union membership grew dramatically among unskilled workers after 1895. Working-class organizations, tolerated earlier by Social Democrats for their future potential, now became centers of power and pressed for practical benefits for their members.

During the period when the Social Democratic movement had been outlawed, Bismarck had employed carrot-and-stick methods to woo the working class away from the Marxists. The stick with which Bismarck beat back the political opposition had been the Anti-Socialist Law. The carrot that he and then Wilhelm II used to win mass support was social welfare legislation, including accident insurance, sick benefits, and old age and disability benefits introduced by the state. But such legislation did not undermine the popularity of socialism, nor did it attract workers away from Marxist political programs, as the mounting electoral returns demonstrated. Social democracy built its rank-and-file union membership by employing sophisticated organizational techniques in order to expand its mass base of support.

The success and popularity of the Social Democratic party cemented a stronger alliance on the Right among Conservatives. Realizing that they could not beat the Left, right-wing groups decided to copy it. Unable to defeat social democracy by force or by state-sponsored welfare policies, Bismarck's successors set out to organize mass support. Agrarian and industrial interests united strongly behind state policies. An aggressive foreign policy was judged as the surest way to win over the masses. Leagues were formed to exploit nationalism and patriotism among the electorate over issues of naval and military expansion and colonial development.

In the end, the Reichstag failed to defy the absolute authority of Emperor Wilhelm II, who was served after 1890 by a string of ineffectual chancellors. Despite its constitutional forms, Germany was ruled by a state authoritarianism in which the bureaucracy, the military, and various interest groups exercised influence over the emperor. A high-risk foreign policy that had a mass appeal was one way to circumvent a parliamentary system incapable of decision-making. Constitutional solutions had been short-circuited in favor of authoritarian rule.

political scandals and mass politics in france

The Third Republic in France had an aura of accidental origins and precarious existence. Founded in 1870 with the defeat of Napoleon III's empire by the Germans, the Third Republic claimed legitimacy by placing itself squarely within the revolutionary democratic tradition. Yet its early days were marked by bloody social conflict and its existence was plagued by ongoing struggles among contenders on the Right and Left who sought to control it.

In spite of surface indications of political conflict, the Third Republic successfully worked toward the creation of a national community based on a common identity for its citizens. Compulsory schooling, one of the great institutional transformations of French government in 1885, socialized French children by implanting in them common values, patriotism, and identification with the nation-state. Old ways, local dialects, superstitious practices, and peasant insularity dropped away or were modified under the persistent pressure of a centralized curriculum of reading, writing, arithmetic, and civics. Compulsory service in the army for the generation of young men of draft age served the same end of communicating national values to a predominantly peasant population.

Technology also accelerated the process of shaping a national citizenry as railroad lines tied people together and the infrastructure of roads made distances shrink. People could now travel back and forth between village and city, town and countryside, with ease and frequency. Common expectations for a better life and upward mobility moved through rural populations that for most of the nineteenth century had not looked beyond the horizon of the village. Young working women were particularly influential in transferring values from urban to rural areas as they moved from villages to towns in search of domestic and industrial jobs and then returned to their villages with new outlooks and new goals for their families.

Information was controlled at the center—Paris—and distributed on a national scale. Villagers in southern France read Parisian newspapers over their morning bowls of coffee and learned—with a previously unimaginable immediacy—about French foreign exploits and parliamentary wrangles. A truly national mass culture emerged in the period between 1880 and 1914. Common symbols like the bust of Marianne appeared in every city hall in France, and a common vocabulary of patriotism spread across the land. French people were not necessarily more political, but they were political in a new way that enabled them to identify their own local interests with national issues.

Two events in particular that occurred in the three decades before World War I indicate the extent of the transformation of French political life. The first, the

Boulanger Affair, involved the attempt of a French general to seize power. The second, the Dreyfus Affair, involved all of French society in the treason conviction of a Jewish army captain.

General Georges Boulanger (1837–91) was a popular and romantic figure who captured the imagination of the French press. As minister of war, Boulanger became a hero to French soldiers when he undertook needed reforms of army life. He won over businessmen by leading troops against strikers. Above all, he cultivated the image of a patriot ready to defend France's honor at any cost. Known as "the Man on Horseback" because of his ability to look dashing in public appearances astride his black horse, Boulanger was a shallow man whose success and national popularity were created by a carefully orchestrated publicity campaign that made him the most popular man in France by 1886.

Boulanger's potential in the political arena attracted the attention of right-wing backers, including monarchists who hoped eventually to restore kingship to France. Supported by big-money interests who favored a strengthened executive and a weaker parliamentary system, Boulanger undertook a nationwide political campaign, hoping to appeal to those unhappy with the Third Republic and promising vague constitutional reforms. General Boulanger's 1889 campaign managers successfully manipulated images that were recognizable to a rural electorate. Religious lithographs carried likenesses of the modern "messiah," the blond-bearded general, in place of Jesus. Campaign workers were recruited at the local level. Boulangists hoped that through universal suffrage an authoritarian government could be established. By 1889 Boulanger was able to amass enough national support to frighten the defend-

General Boulanger's carefully orchestrated publicity campaign included postage stamps bearing the likeness of the messianic general. The stamps shown here were a prototype only; they were never released.

ers of parliamentary institutions. The charismatic general ultimately failed in his bid for power and fled the country because of allegations of treason. But he left in his wake an embryonic mass movement on the Right that operated outside the channels of parliamentary institutions. Boulanger's success was due to a new nationalism that flexed its muscles after 1880. Cultural symbols like the flag and the nation-in-arms moved from the revolutionary tradition of the Left to become part of the appeal of the new right-wing groups that were growing in importance.

A very different type of crisis began to take shape in 1894 with the controversy surrounding the trial of Captain Alfred Dreyfus (1859–1935) that came to be known simply as "the Affair." Dreyfus was an Alsatian Jewish army officer accused of selling military secrets to the Germans. His trial for treason served as a lightning rod for xenophobia—the hatred of foreigners, especially Germans—and anti-Semitism, the hatred of Jews. Dreyfus was stripped of his commission and honors and sentenced to solitary confinement for life on Devil's Island, a convict colony off French Guiana in South America.

Illegal activities and outright falsifications by Dreyfus's superiors in order to secure a conviction came to light in the mass press. The nation was soon divided. Those who supported Dreyfus's innocence, the pro-Dreyfusards, were for the most part on the left of the political spectrum and spoke of the Republic's duty to uphold justice and freedom. The anti-Dreyfusards were associated with the traditional institutions of the Catholic church and the army and considered themselves to be defending the honor of France. Among those who upheld the conviction were right-wing groups, monarchists, and virulent anti-Semites.

Dreyfus was eventually exonerated and granted a full pardon in 1905. On the personal level, the Affair represented the ability of an individual to seek redress against injustice. On the national level, the Affair represented an important transformation in the nature of French political life. Existing parliamentary institutions had been found wanting and unable to cope with the mass politics stirred up by Dreyfus's conviction. New groups entered public life after 1894, coalescing around the question of the guilt or innocence of an individual man. The newspaper press vied with parliament and the courts as a forum for investigation and decision-making. Intellectuals, too, organized. Leagues on the left and on the right took shape; unions, cooperatives, and professional societies all raised their voices. These organizations manipulated propaganda around issues of national defense and republican justice.

Captain Alfred Dreyfus, accused of treason, marches with a "guard of dishonor." After Dreyfus was declared innocent, he became a lieutenant colonel in the French army and was enrolled in the Legion of Honor.

The crises provoked by Boulanger's attempt at power and the Dreyfus Affair demonstrated the major role of the press and the importance of public opinion in exerting pressure on the system of government. The press emerged as a myth-maker in shaping and channeling public opinion. Émile Zola (1840–1902), the great French novelist, spearheaded the pro-Dreyfusard movement with his damning article "I Accuse!" in which he pointed to the military and the judiciary as the "spirits of social evil" for persecuting an innocent man. The article appeared in a leading French newspaper and was influential in securing Dreyfus's eventual exoneration and the discovery of the real culprit, one of Dreyfus's colleagues in the General Staff. The Third Republic had never been in danger of collapsing, but it was transformed. The locus of power in parliament was challenged by pressure groups outside it.

Defeating Liberalism in Austria

In the 1870s, the liberal values of the bourgeoisie dominated the Austro-Hungarian Empire. The Habsburg

"J'Accuse"

The central role of the press during the Dreyfus Affair is nowhere more apparent than in the impact of the novelist Émile Zola's front-page letter to the president of the Third Republic published in Georges Clemenceau's newspaper L'Aurore, on 13 January 1898. "J'Accuse" was an impassioned appeal to the French nation for justice in which Zola pointed to those truly guilty of betraying France in a cascade of ringing accusations. This letter, which was ultimately instrumental in freeing Captain Dreyfus, resulted in Zola's own prosecution for libel.

I accuse Lieutenant-Colonel du Paty de Clam of having been the diabolical artisan of the judicial error, without knowing it, I am willing to believe, and then of having defended his nefarious work for three years throughout the most grotesque and culpable machinations.

I accuse General Mercier of having become an accomplice, out of mental weakness at the least, in one of the greatest iniquities of the century. . . .

I accuse the three handwriting experts, Mssrs. Belhomme, Varinard, and Couard, of having composed deceitful and fraudulent reports, unless a medical examination declares them to be stricken with an impairment of vision or judgment.

I accuse the offices of War of having conducted in the press, particularly in L'Éclair and in L'Echo de Paris, an abominable campaign designed to mislead public opinion and to conceal their wrongdoing.

Finally, I accuse the first Court Martial of having violated the law in convicting a defendant on the basis of a document kept secret, and I accuse the second Court Martial of having covered up that illegality on command by committing in turn the juridical crime of knowingly acquitting a guilty man.

In bringing these accusations, I am not without realizing that I expose myself in the process to Articles 30 and 31 of the press law of July 29, 1881, which punishes offenses of slander. And it is quite willingly that I so expose myself.

As for those whom I accuse, I do not know them, I have never seen them, I have neither rancor nor hatred for them. They are for me no more than entities, spirits of social malfeasance. And the act that I hereby accomplish is but a revolutionary means of hastening the explosion of truth and justice.

I have but one passion, one for seeing the light, in the name of humanity which has so suffered and which is entitled to happiness. My fiery protest is but the cry of my soul. Let me be brought then before a criminal court and let the investigation be conducted in the light of day!

I am waiting.

---

monarchy had adjusted to constitutional government, which was introduced throughout Austria in 1860. Faith in parliamentary government based on a restricted suffrage had established a tenuous foothold. After the setbacks of 1848 and the troublesome decade of the 1860s, when Prussia had trounced Austria and Bismarck had routed the hope of an Austrian-dominated German Empire, the Austrian bourgeoisie counted on a peaceful future with a centralized multinational state dedicated to order and progress.

There is no better symbol of middle-class political and cultural aspirations in this period than the monumental rebuilding of the city of Vienna that took place after 1860. The belt of public and private buildings on the Ringstrasse, or "Ring Street," girding the old central city and separating it from its suburbs was dramatic testimony to bourgeois self-confidence. Grandiose buildings, likened to "cakes on platters," glorified constitutional government, economic vitality, the fine arts, and educational values. Monumental architecture was intended to legitimize bourgeois claims to power and to link Austrian institutions with the great cultural heritage of the West. The buildings were blatant copies of past architectural styles—massive Gothic for the city hall, Renaissance for the university, and early baroque for the theater. Yet this was more than a self-confident statement of Austria's inheritance of a rich cultural tradition. Vienna's ruling class was fortifying itself behind the edifices of Western politics and culture against the onslaught of the new age.

In reality, the Austrian bourgeoisie was weaker than its French or British counterparts. The Austrian ruling class was heavily dependent on the Habsburg emperor and identified itself with the values of the aristocracy. Rapid economic growth had strengthened bourgeois status between 1840 and 1870, but it had also unleashed new social forces that existing institutions were unable to control. Liberal values of constitutional monarchy, centralization, restricted suffrage, and multinational government came up against new and threatening forces of anti-Semitism, socialism, nationalism, and mass politics.

By 1900 liberal politicians were being eliminated as a directing force in national politics. The new politicians who replaced them rejected the liberal-rational values of progress and order and moved into a realm colored by charisma, fantasy, and demagoguery. A new Right wielded mass political strategies that embraced the irrational and the violent.

The new groups laying claim to political power and displacing a weak Austrian bourgeoisie were peasants, workers, urban artisans and shopkeepers, and the colonized Slavic peoples of the empire. Bourgeois politics and laissez-faire economics had offered little or nothing to these varied groups, who were now claiming the right of participation. Mass parties were formed based on radical pan-Germanic feeling; anticapitalism, which appealed to peasants and artisans; hatred of the Jews, shared by students and artisans; and nationalist aspirations that attracted the lower middle classes. In 1895 Karl Lueger (1844–1910) used anti-Semitism in his successful campaign for the office of mayor of Vienna. Lueger's election was the first serious sign of the collapse of Austrian liberalism. Jews were identified with capitalists, and the irrational hatred directed at them unified different groups and helped to sweep Lueger into office.

Austrian poet and playwright Hugo von Hofmannsthal (1874–1929) understood the rejection of bourgeois politics in the age of expanded suffrage: "Politics is magic. He who knows how to summon the forces from the deep, him will they follow." The creation of a scapegoat by means of anti-Semitism and racism became the means of uniting the masses against a common foe and in favor of a common nationalist program. In Austria, antiliberal politics grew stronger in the years before 1914. The great buildings on the Ringstrasse that had attempted to connect Austrian political life with the glories of the European past were mocked as relics of a dead age. Centrifugal forces of pan-Germanism and nationalism were pulling the parliamentary system apart. An urban and capitalist middle class that ruled Austria by virtue of a limited suffrage based on property had lost ground to new groups that were essentially anticapitalist and antiliberal in their outlook and for whom parliamentary deliberations held no promise. The rejection of liberalism was a "revolt against the fathers." A new style of leader had emerged in Vienna at the end of the century, charismatic in style and violent in appeal. The "politics of fantasy" based on a new electorate was fast becoming the nightmare of parliamentary disintegration.

The political experiences of Great Britain, Germany, France, and Austria between 1871 and 1914 make clear the common challenges confronting Western parliamentary systems in a changing era of democratic politics. In spite of variations, each nation experienced its own challenge to liberal parliamentary institutions, and each shaped its own variety of responses to a new international phenomenon—the rise of the masses as a political force.

outsiders in mass politics

By the end of the nineteenth century, the masses were replacing the individual in political culture. A faceless, nameless electorate became the basis of new political strategies and a new political rhetoric. A concept of class identification of workers was devalued in favor of interest-group politics in which lobbies formed around single issues to pressure European governments. But the apparently all-inclusive concept of mass society continued to exclude some groups. Women, ethnic minorities, and Jews were pushed to the margins. Outsiders in mass politics had little in common with one another except for the common experience of repression by the state. But they did not remain quietly on the periphery. Women and ethnic minorities learned to incorporate strategies and techniques of politics and organization that permitted them to challenge the existing political system. Others, including anarchists, rejected both the organizational techniques of mass society and the values of the nation-state. Outsiders, then, were both those intent on being integrated into mass politics and those who sought its destruction.

feminists and politics

Women's emancipation had been a recurrent motif of European political culture throughout the nineteenth century. In the areas of civil liberties, legal equality with men, and economic autonomy, only the most limited reforms had been enacted. The cult of domesticity, important throughout the nineteenth century, assigned women to a separate sphere, that of the home. Glorifying domesticity was a recognition of women's unique contribution to society in the home, but it may itself have been a means of controlling women who protested the separation between public and private space.

European women were paid at most one-third to one-half of what men earned for the same work. In Great Britain, women did not enjoy equal divorce rights until the twentieth century. In France, married women had no control over their own incomes: all their earnings were considered their husbands' private property. From the Atlantic to the Urals, women were excluded from economic and educational opportunities. Serfs had been liberated. Working-class men had gained the right to vote. But the new electoral politics that emerged in the last quarter of the nineteenth century explicitly excluded women.

Growing numbers of women, primarily from the middle classes, began calling themselves "feminist," a term coined in France in the 1830s. The new feminists throughout western Europe differed from earlier generations in their willingness to organize mass movements and to appropriate the techniques of interest-group politics. The first international congress of women's rights, held in Paris in 1878, initiated an era of international cooperation and exchange among women's organizations. Women's groups now positioned themselves for sustained political action.

Feminism as a historic term is worth pondering. Like liberalism, which had pulled down kings and destroyed privilege, feminism aimed at eliminating social inequalities. Like socialism, feminism was a set of principles for action whose purpose was to build a better world. At its base, feminism recognized the equality of the sexes, without denying difference. As John Stuart Mill in Great Britain and Ernest Legouvé (1807–1903), a French dramatist and leading proponent of women's rights, had demonstrated, one need not be female to be a feminist. It was the belief that men and women are equal and should enjoy equal rights that identified the feminist. Most feminists, however, were women, and the leadership of the movement for equal rights was in women's hands. The converse—that most women were feminists—was not true. Contemporary critics often dismissed feminism on the grounds that it represented no more than a tiny minority of women. The same mi-

nority status characterized the trade union movement—which in France, for example, had a smaller membership at the end of the nineteenth century than did feminist organizations.

European feminist organizations did not share a common agenda but instead grouped themselves around a series of related concerns for legal, educational, economic, and political emancipation. Rather than speaking of a single feminism, it is more appropriate to speak of different feminisms. The General German Women's Association agitated for educational opportunities and democratic participation for women. In France, women working for the vote were a minority of the women's organizations. Many French feminists defended a "maternal politics," by which they sought

A young member of the Women's Social and Political Union sells copies of the paper Votes for Women.

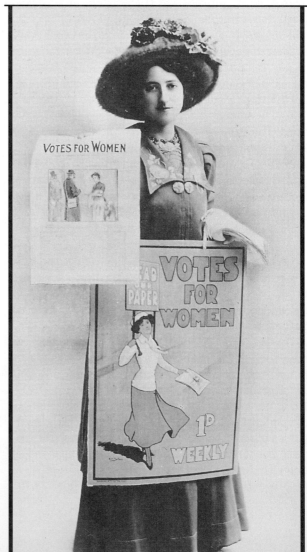

protection for women's responsibilities in the home. Other feminists were involved in abortion reform, birth control issues, and repeal of state control of prostitution. The French League for the Rights of Women stood steadfastly against the vote as an end in itself and worked instead for legal and economic reforms. On the whole, however, feminist organizations were divided into two camps. In the first group were those who agitated for the vote; the second included those who thought that the vote was beside the point and that the central issues were economic, social, and legal reforms of women's status. Constituting the left wing of the second group were socialist women who were dedicated to needs of women of the working class.

The lessons of the new electoral politics were not lost on feminists seeking women's emancipation through the vote. Leaders like Hubertine Auclert (1848–1914) in France and Emmeline Pankhurst (1858–1928) in Great Britain recognized the need for a mass base of support. If women's organizations were to survive as competing interest groups, they needed to form political alliances, control their own newspapers and magazines, and keep their cause before the public eye. Just as cartels, trade unions, and political parties had learned the game of influence and leverage so important for survival in the modern political milieu, so too did feminists rely on organization to achieve their ends. There was a growing willingness by a variety of women's organizations to hold mass demonstrations and rallies and to use violent tactics.

No movement operated more effectively in this regard than the British suffrage movement. In 1903 the Women's Social and Political Union (WSPU) was formed by a group of eminently respectable middle-class and aristocratic British women. At the center of the movement was Emmeline Pankhurst, an attractive middle-aged woman with a frail appearance but a will of iron and a gift for oratory. Emmeline Pankhurst and her two daughters—Christabel (1880–1958), a lawyer by training, and Sylvia (1882–1960), an artist—succeeded in keeping women's suffrage before the British public and brought the plight of British women to international attention. Over the next seven years, the WSPU made considerable progress, attracting a growing number of followers and successfully aligning itself with parliamentary supporters.

Women's demands for political power were the basis of an unheralded revolution in Western culture. In Great Britain, the decade before the Great War of 1914 was a period of profound political education for women seeking the vote. An unprecedented 250,000 women gathered in Hyde Park in 1908 to hear more about female suffrage. Laughed at by men, ridiculed in the press, taunted in public demonstrations, women activists refused to be quiet and to "know their place." If respectable women would never demonstrate for their rights, then the suffragists were willing to cease being respectable. Because they spoke out for voting rights, feminists were demeaned, humiliated, and accused of not being *real* women by their detractors. One of the best examples of the rebellion of women against the limitations of their social roles took place on 18 November 1910, a day that came to be known among feminists as Black Friday. On that day, suffragists marched on Parliament, which had failed to support the vote for women. In a confrontation that lasted six hours, unarmed women battled with police to hold their ground. Rather than returning home as they were ordered, the women relentlessly pushed forward, meeting the blows and the wrath of London's bobbies. Many women were injured and many arrested.

The year 1910 marked the beginning of an era of increased militancy among women, who were derisively called "suffragettes" in the press in order to distinguish them from the nonmilitant suffragists. A basic element in the new militancy was the willingness to use violence to achieve political emancipation. As Emmeline Pankhurst explained it, "The argument of the broken window pane is the most valuable argument in modern politics." Militant women set mailboxes on fire or poured glue and jam over their contents, threw bombs into country houses, and slashed paintings in the National Gallery. All over London the tinkling of thousands of shattered windowpanes ushered in a new age of women's political action. Mrs. Pankhurst was not naive about what her followers were doing: "There is something which governments care for more than human life and that is the security of property, and so it is through property that we shall strike the enemy." Suffragettes set fires in public buildings, churches, and hotels. As frustration grew, some assaulted members of the cabinet. One suffragette, Emily Wilding Davison (1872–1913), probably intent on suicide as an act of protest, was trampled to death when she threw herself under the king's horse on Derby Day at Epsom Downs in 1913. Mrs. Pankhurst and others advocated violence against personal property to highlight the violence done to women by denying them their rights. These tactics seemed to accomplish little before the war, although they certainly kept the issue of female suffrage in the public eye until the outbreak of war in 1914. It was not until 1918 that British women were granted limited suffrage, and not until 1928 that women gained voting rights equal to those of men.

Women suffered for their militancy, for civil disobedience evoked harsh repressive measures from the British government. Previous benevolence toward middle-class female prisoners arrested for attacks on property gave way to a new harshness that included the force-feeding of convicted suffragettes. Using tubes, hoses, and metal jaw clamps, prison guards and doctors poured gruel down the throats of imprisoned women who, as a form of protest, refused to eat. Such repressive measures only increased the solidarity within the women's movement and won the suffragettes international sympathy and support. Stymied, the government passed the Cat and Mouse Act in 1913. Imprisoned women who refused to eat were released, then reincarcerated once they had resumed eating and regained their strength. This "cat-and-mouse" pattern of release and reimprisonment could double or extend indefinitely a three-year sentence served in three-day segments. Many of the more dramatic tactics of the suffragettes, including getting arrested, were not available to working-class activists, who could not put aside their family responsibilities to serve jail sentences.

European women did not easily gain the right to vote. In France and Germany, moderate and left-wing politicians opposed extension of the vote to women because they feared that women would strengthen conservative candidates. Many politicians felt that women were not "ready" for the vote and that they should receive it only as a reward—an unusual concept in democratic societies. Queen Victoria condemned women's agitation for the vote as a "mad, wicked folly." Only after war and revolution was the vote extended to women in the West—in Germany in 1918, in the United States in 1920, and in France at the end of World War II.

Not all activist women saw the right to vote as the solution to women's oppression. Those who agitated for social reforms for poor and working-class women parted ways with the militant suffragettes. Sylvia Pankhurst, for example, left her mother and sister to their political battles in order to work for social reform in London's poverty-stricken East End. Differing from those who focused on woman's right to vote as a primary goal, women socialists were concerned with working-class women's "double oppression" in the home and in the workplace. The largest women's socialist movement existed in Germany, with 175,000 members by 1914. With its own newspaper, it operated independently of the men's socialist movement. German socialist women were opposed to suffrage on the grounds that giving middle-class women the vote did not address social issues.

Socialist women's lot was not an easy one, since union members often denied women's right to work and saw women's employment as a threat to men in the workplace. In Germany, socialist men opposed women industrial workers. Unions supported the concept of separate spheres for men and women and based their demands for a family wage on the need to maintain a separate private domain of the home. Socialist men argued that women's work often resulted in the neglect of

This British suffragette poster, published by the Women's Social and Political Union, graphically depicts the tortuous methods used to force feed women prisoners. A prison guard pulls back the prisoner's head, others hold down her arms and legs, and another ties her foot to the chair. A doctor holds a hose through which he forces gruel into the woman's open mouth.

constance Lytton

Civil disobedience by British women demanding the right to vote often led to their arrest. In protest, incarcerated suffragettes went on hunger strikes to publicize their cause. The British government responded with a brutal policy of force-feeding of prisoners. Constance Lytton, a British aristocrat and suffragette, recounts here the agony of being forcibly fed in prison. Her own health was seriously weakened by the experience.

[The prison's senior medical officer] urged me to take food voluntarily. I told him that was absolutely out of the question, that when our legislators ceased to resist enfranchising women then I should cease to resist taking food in prison. . . . I offered no resistance to being placed in position, but lay down voluntarily on the plank bed. Two of the wardresses took hold of my arms, one held my head and one my feet. One wardress helped to pour the food. The doctor leant on my knees as he stooped over my chest to get at my mouth. I shut my mouth and clenched my teeth. . . . The doctor offered me the choice of a wooden or steel gag; he explained elaborately, as he did on most subsequent occasions, that the steel gag would hurt and the wooden one not, and he urged me not to force him to use the steel gag. But I did not speak nor open my mouth, so that after playing about for a moment or two with the wooden one he finally had recourse to the steel. He seemed annoyed at my resistance and he broke into a temper as he plied my teeth with the steel implement. . . . The pain of it was intense and at last I must have given way for he got the gag between my teeth, when he proceeded to turn it much more than necessary until my jaws were fastened wide apart, far more than they could go naturally. Then he put down my throat a tube which seemed to me much too wide and was something like four feet in length. The irritation of the tube was excessive. I choked the moment it touched my throat until it had got down. Then the food was poured in quickly; it made me sick a few seconds after it was down and the action of the sickness made my body and legs double up, but the wardresses instantly pressed back my head and the doctor leant on my knees. The horror of it was more than I can describe. I was sick over the doctor and wardresses, and it seemed a long time before they took the tube out. As the doctor left he gave me a slap on the cheek, not violently, but, as it were, to express his contemptuous disapproval, and he seemed to take for granted that my distress was assumed. . . . I had been sick over my hair, which, though short, hung on either side of my face, all over the wall near my bed, and my clothes seemed saturated with it, but the wardresses told me they could not get me a change that night as it was too late, the office was shut. I lay quite motionless, it seemed paradise to be without the suffocating tube, without the liquid food going in and out of my body and without the gag between my teeth. Before long I heard the sounds of the forced feeding in the next cell to mine. It was almost more than I could bear, it was Elsie Howey, I was sure. When the ghastly process was over and all quiet, I tapped on the wall and called out at the top of my voice, which wasn't much just then, "No surrender," and there came the answer past any doubt in Elsie's voice. "No surrender."

From Constance Lytton, *Prisons and Prisoners* (1914).

children and could lead to the physical degeneration of the family. Working women, socialist men argued, undermined existing wage scales and aided the exploitation of workers by their willingness to work for lower wages. Class oppression, countered German socialist leader and theorist Clara Zetkin (1857–1933), was the basis of women's oppression. For militants like Zetkin, socialism offered the only means to eliminate sexual inequalities.

The women's movements of the period from 1871 to 1914 differed socially and culturally from nation to nation. Yet there is a sense in which the women's movements constituted an international phenomenon. The rise in the level of women's political consciousness occurred in the most advanced Western countries almost simultaneously and had a predominantly middle-class character. Working-class women, most notably in Germany, united feminism with socialism in search of a better life. In spite of concerted efforts, women remained on the outside of societies that excluded them from political participation, access to education, and social and economic equality.

The Jewish Question and Zionism

The term *anti-Semitism*, meaning hostility to Jews, was first used in 1879 to give a pseudoscientific legitimacy to bigotry and hatred. Persecution was a harsh reality for Jews in eastern Europe at the end of the nineteenth century. In Russia, Jews could not own property and were restricted to living in certain territories. Organized massacres, or *pogroms*, in Kiev, Odessa, and Warsaw followed the assassination of Tsar Alexander II in 1881 and recurred after the failed Russian revolution of 1905. Russian authorities blamed the Jews, seen as perennial outsiders, for the assassination and revolution and the social instability that followed them. Pogroms resulted in the death and displacement of tens of thousands of Russian and eastern European Jews.

Two million eastern European Jews migrated westward between 1868 and 1914 in search of peace and refuge. Seventy thousand settled in Germany. Others continued westward, stopping in the United States. Another kind of Jewish migration took place in the nineteenth century—the movement of Jews from rural to urban areas within nations. In eastern Europe, Jewish migrations coincided with downturns in the economic cycle, and Jews became scapegoats for the high rates of unemployment and high prices that seemed to follow in their wake. Most migrants were peddlers, artisans, or small shopkeepers who were seen as threatening to small businesses. Differing in language, culture, and dress, they were viewed as alien in every way.

In western Europe, Jews considered themselves "assimilated" into their national cultures, identifying with their nationality as much as with their religion. Austrian and German Jews were granted full civil rights in 1867 on the principle that citizens of all religions enjoyed full equality. In France, Jews had been legally emancipated since the end of the eighteenth century. But western and central European politics of the 1890s had a strong dose of anti-Semitism. Demagogues like Georg von Schönerer (1842–1921) of Austria were capable of whipping up a frenzy of riots and violence against Jews. They

Jewish Migration

did not distinguish between assimilated and immigrant Jewish populations in their irrational denunciations.

Western and central European anti-Semitism assumed a new level of virulence at the end of the nineteenth century. Fear of an economic depression united aristocrat and worker alike in blaming a Jewish conspiracy. German anti-Semitism proliferated in the 1880s. "It is like a horrible epidemic," the scholar Theodor Mommsen (1817–1903) observed. "It can neither be explained nor cured."

Fear of the Jews was connected with hatred of capitalism. In France and Germany, Jews controlled powerful banking and commercial firms that became the targets of blame in hard times. Upwardly mobile sons of Jewish immigrants entered the professions of banking, trading, and journalism. They were also growing in numbers as teachers and academics. In the 1880s, more than half of Vienna's physicians (61 percent in 1881) and lawyers (58 percent of barristers in 1888) were Jewish. Their professional success only heightened tensions and condemnations of Jews as an "alien race." Anti-Semitism served as a violent means of mobilizing mass support, especially among those groups who felt threatened by capitalist concentration and large-scale industrialization. For anti-Semitic Europeans, Jews embodied the democratic, liberal, and cosmopolitan tendencies of the culture that they were consciously rejecting in their new political affiliations.

A Jewish leadership emerged in central and western Europe that treated anti-Semitism as a problem that could be solved by political means. For their generation at the end of the nineteenth century, the assimilation of their fathers and mothers was not the answer. Jews needed their own nation, it was argued, since they were a people without a nation. Zionism was the solution to what Jewish intellectuals called "the Jewish problem." Zion, the ancient homeland of Biblical times, would provide a national territory, and a choice, to persecuted Jews. Zionism became a Jewish nationalist movement dedicated to the establishment of a Jewish state. Although Zionism did not develop mass support in western Europe among assimilated Jews, its program for national identity and social reforms appealed to a large following of eastern European Jews in Galicia (Poland), Russia, and the eastern lands of the Habsburg Empire— those directly subjected to the extremes of persecution.

Theodor Herzl (1860–1904), an Austrian Jew born in Budapest, was the founder of Zionism in its political form. As a student in Vienna he had encountered discrimination, but his commitment to Zionism developed as a result of his years as a journalist in Paris. Observing the anti-Semitic attacks in republican France provoked by the scandals surrounding the misappropriation of funds by leading French politicians and businessmen during the construction of the Panama Canal and the divisive conflict over the Dreyfus Affair in the 1890s, Herzl came to appreciate how deeply imbedded anti-Semitism was in European society. He despaired of the ability of corrupt parliamentary governments to solve the problem of anti-Semitism. In *The Jewish State* (1896), Herzl concluded that Jews must have a state of their own. Under his direction, Zionism developed a worldwide organization and its own newspaper with the aim of establishing a Jewish homeland in Palestine.

Jews began emigrating to Palestine. With the financial backing of Jewish donors like the French banker Baron de Rothschild, nearly 90,000 Jews had established settlements there by 1914. Calculated to tap a common Jewish identification with an ancient heritage, the choice of Palestine as a homeland was controversial from the beginning. The problems arising from the choice have persisted through the twentieth century.

The promised land of the Old Testament, Zion is a holy place in Judaism. The Austrian psychoanalyst Sigmund Freud (1856–1939), who described himself as "a Jew from Moravia," was sympathetic to the Zionist cause but critical of the idea of Palestine as a Jewish state. He considered the idea unworkable and one bound to arouse Christian and Islamic opposition. Freud feared that Palestine would arouse the suspicions of the Arab world and challenge "the feelings of the local natives." He would have preferred a "new, historically unencumbered soil."

Some Jewish critics of Zionism felt that a separate Jewish state would prove that Jews were not good citi-

Maurycy Minkowski, After the Pogrom (ca. 1910). Minkowski's works depict Jewish life in Poland before the Russian Revolution. In this painting he has expertly captured the weariness, hopelessness, and fear of the refugees who have interrupted their flight to rest. The sense of isolation and dislocation evoked in the painting may derive from the deaf and mute artist's personal perception of profound separation and detachment.

zens of their respective nation-states and would exacerbate hostilities toward Jews as outsiders. Yet Zionism had much in common with the European liberal tradition because it sought in the creation of a nation-state for Jews the solution to social injustice. Zion, the Jewish nation in the Middle East, was a liberal utopia for the Jewish people. Zionism learned from other mass movements of the period the importance of a broad base of support. By the time of the First Zionist Congress, held in Basel, Switzerland, in 1897, it had become a truly international movement. Herzl was also well aware of the necessity for a charismatic leader and cast himself in the role of messiah for his people.

Zionism did not achieve its goals before World War I, and the Jewish state of Israel was not recognized by the world community until 1948. Before World War I, anti-Semitism and antifeminism were strongly linked in nationalist political programs, which insisted that the place for Jews was on the periphery and the place for women was in the home. Through the Zionist movement, Jews victimized by nationalism planned for their own nation-state as a solution.

workers and minorities on the margins

In 1892 the Parisian trial of a bomb-throwing anarchist named Ravachol attracted great public attention. He and other French anarchists had captured the popular imagination with their threats to destroy bourgeois society by bombing private residences, public buildings, and restaurants. Ravachol's terrorist deeds represented the extreme rejection of participation in electoral politics. The public was frightened—but also fascinated. Ravachol opposed the state and the capitalist economy as the dual enemy that could only be destroyed through individual acts of random physical violence. For his crimes he was condemned to death and publicly executed.

The best-known anarchists of the late nineteenth century were those, like Ravachol, who engaged in terrorist assassinations and bombings. Although not all anarchists were terrorists intent on destruction, all shared a desire for a revolutionary restructuring of society. Most anarchists were loners. They dreamed of the collapse of the capitalist system with its exploitation and inequality and of the emergence of a society based on personal freedom, autonomy, and justice. Anarchists spurned the Marxist willingness to organize and participate in parliamentary politics. They disdained the

tyranny of new organizations and bureaucracies that worked for gradual reforms at the expense of principles of justice.

There was no single anarchist doctrine, but the varieties of anarchism all shared a hope in a future free from constraints. Mikhail Bakunin (1814–76), a member of the Russian nobility, absorbed the works and the message of the French social critic Pierre-Joseph Proudhon. Bakunin became Europe's leading anarchist spokesman. Unlike Proudhon, Bakunin was a man of revolutionary action who espoused the use of violence to achieve individual liberation. All existing institutions must be swept away before ownership of production could be collectivized. Bakunin broke with Marx, whom he considered a "scientific bourgeois socialist" out of touch with the mass of workers.

Bakunin's successor in international anarchist doctrine was also a Russian of aristocratic lineage—Prince

Mikhail Bakunin.

Petr Kropotkin (1842–1921). Kropotkin joined together communism and anarchism, arguing that goods should be communally distributed, "from each according to his ability, to each according to his needs." On the basis of his own empirical observations, Kropotkin argued that competition and dominance were not laws of nature and instead stressed human interdependence.

It is difficult to measure the extent of Bakunin's or Kropotkin's influence, since whatever followers they might have inspired were not overtly or formally organized. Anarchism's greatest appeal was in the less industrialized countries of southern Europe: Spain, Italy, and southern France. In these countries, grass-roots anarchism germinated in working-class communities. In the second half of the nineteenth century, Russia too had developed a strong populist tradition similar to anarchism in its opposition to state tyranny. But anarchism was primarily a western European phenomenon.

Anarchism had special appeal to workers in trades staggering under the blows of industrial capitalism. Calling themselves anarcho-syndicalists, artisans—especially in France—were able to combine local trade union organization with anarchist principles. Alienation from the political process was strong among the French working class, who had recent bitter memories of repression during the Paris Commune in 1871 and who rejected the sterility and corruption of the party politics of the Third Republic. Most of these workers were in skilled trades that suffered from high rates of unemployment and chronically depressed wages.

Unlike union movements in the industrialized countries of Great Britain and Germany, French trade unions remained small, weak, and local, without the resources to undertake sustained action. French unions had gained legal recognition in 1884, eight years after Great Britain but six years before Germany. Workers who combined trade unionism with anarchism shared an apocalyptic vision of social transformation. The contrast between the Labour party in Great Britain and the German Social Democrats on the one hand and the French anarcho-syndicalists on the other highlighted the split between advanced industrial countries and less-developed areas of Europe, where an artisan class was attempting to preserve autonomy and control.

The journalist and social thinker Georges Sorel (1847–1922) captured the philosophy of anarcho-syndicalism in his book *Reflections on Violence* (1908). Sorel described the "myth," or shared belief, in the "general strike," a kind of final judgment day when justice would prevail. Unlike the trade unions of other western European states, anarcho-syndicalist unions were militantly opposed to issues of improved wages and better working conditions. In order to be ready for the collapse of bourgeois society, anarcho-syndicalists must not collaborate with the existing system by accepting benefits and improvements from it. Instead, workers were to hold themselves ready by employing a technique of "direct action" to maintain worker solidarity. "Direct action" was a symbolic gesture that did not advance the revolution but did help workers remain aware of their exploitation. A typical example of "direct action" was the agreement among the militantly revolutionary barbers' union to nick their customers periodically with the razor while shaving them. Acts such as this were meaningless in themselves—except perhaps to those who experienced them—but were intended to raise the level of commitment to a common cause.

The problems of disaffected groups in general intensified before 1914. Anarchists and anarcho-syndicalist workers deplored the centralization and organization of mass society. Yet anarchism posed no serious threat to social stability because of the effectiveness of policing in most European states. As Friedrich Engels observed at the turn of the century, random violence directed against politics and the economy was no match for the repressive forces at the command of the nation-state. The politics of mass society excluded diverse groups—including women, Jews, and ethnic minorities—from participation. Yet the techniques, values, and organization of the world of politics remained available to all these groups. It was the outbreak of war in 1914 that silenced, temporarily at least, the challenge of these outsiders.

shaping the new consciousness

Imagine a world that discovered how to eliminate the difference between night and day. Imagine further a civilization that could obliterate distance or shrink it. Imagine a people who could see for the first time into solid mass, into their own bodies, and send images through space. These are the imaginings of fable and fantasy that can be traced back to prehistory. But what had always been the stuff of magic became reality between 1880 and 1914. The people of the West used science and technology to reshape the world and their understanding of it.

The discoveries of science had ramifications that extended beyond the laboratory, the hospital, and the classroom. Science changed the way people thought and the way they lived. It improved the quality of life by defeating diseases, improving nutrition, and lengthening life span. But scientific knowledge was not without its costs. Scientific discoveries led to new forces of destruction. Scientific ideas challenged moral and religious beliefs. Science was invoked to justify racial and sexual discrimination. Traditional values and religious belief also did combat with the new god of science, with philosophers proclaiming that God was dead. New disciplines claimed to study society scientifically with methods similar to those applied to the study of bacilli and the atom. A traditional world of order and hierarchy gave way to a new reality in which the center was no longer holding and the limits were constantly expanding.

The Authority of science

What may seem commonplace at the end of the twentieth century was no less than spectacular at the end of the nineteenth. Scientific discoveries in the last quarter of the century pushed out the frontiers of knowledge. In physics, James Clerk Maxwell (1831–79) discovered the relationship between electricity and magnetism. Maxwell showed mathematically that an oscillating electric charge produces an electromagnetic field and that such a field radiates outward from its source at a constant speed—the speed of light. His theories led to the discovery of the electromagnetic spectrum, comprising radiation of different wavelengths, including X rays, visible light, and radio waves. This discovery had important practical applications for the development of the electrical industry and led to the invention of radio and television. Within a generation, the names of Edison, Westinghouse, Marconi, Siemens, and Bell entered the public realm.

Discoveries in the physical sciences succeeded one another with great rapidity. The periodic table of chemical elements was formulated in 1869. Radioactivity was discovered in 1896. Two years later, Marie Curie (1867–1934) and her husband Pierre (1859–1906) discovered the elements radium and polonium. At the end of the century, Ernest Rutherford (1871–1937) identified alpha and beta rays in radioactive atoms. Building on the new discoveries, Max Planck (1858–1947), Albert Einstein (1879–1955), and Niels Bohr (1885–1962) dismantled the classical physics of absolute and determined principles and left in its place modern physics

based on relativity and uncertainty. In 1900, Planck propounded a theory that renounced the emphasis in classical physics on energy as a wave phenomenon in favor of a new "quantum theory" of energy as emitted and absorbed in minute, discrete amounts.

The name Einstein has become synonymous with genius in the twentieth century. In 1905 Albert Einstein formulated his special theory of relativity, in which he established the relationship of mass and energy in the famous equation $E = mc^2$. In 1916 he published his general theory of relativity, a mathematical formulation that created a new conception of space and time. Einstein disproved the Newtonian view of gravitation as a force and instead saw it as a curved field in the time-space continuum created by the presence of mass. No one at the time foresaw that the application of Einstein's theory—that a particle of matter could be converted into a great quantity of energy—would unleash the greatest destructive power in history. Einstein, a pacifist, lived to see atomic bombs developed in his lifetime.

Marie Curie was born Manya Sklodowska in Warsaw, Poland. She shared the Nobel Prize in physics in 1903 and was awarded the Nobel Prize in chemistry in 1911.

Although there were no more dramatic discoveries than those in the physical sciences, the biological sciences also witnessed great breakthroughs. Research biologists dedicated themselves to the study of disease-causing microbes and to the chemical bases of physiology. French chemist Louis Pasteur (1822–95) studied microorganisms to find methods of preventing the spread of diseases in humans, animals, and plants. He developed methods of inoculation to provide protection against anthrax in sheep, cholera in chickens, and rabies in animals and humans.

The pace of breakthroughs in biological knowledge and medical treatment was staggering. The malaria parasite was isolated in 1880. The control of diseases such as yellow fever contributed to improvement in the quality of life. Knowledge burst the bounds of disciplines, and new fields developed to accommodate new concerns. Research in human genetics, a field that was only beginning to be understood, was begun in the first decade of the twentieth century. The studies of Austrian botanist Gregor Mendel (1822–84) in the crossbreeding of peas in the 1860s led to the Mendelian laws of inheritance. Scientists at the time ignored Mendel, but after the turn of the century Mendel's discoveries were used to pursue the problem of how hereditary characteristics were transmitted.

Biological discoveries resulted in new state policies. Public health benefited from new methods of prevention and detection of diseases caused by germs. A professor at the University of Berlin, Rudolf Virchow (1821–1902) discovered the relationship between microbes, sewage, and disease that led to the development of modern sewer systems and pure water for urban populations. Biochemistry, bacteriology, and physiology promoted a belief in social progress through state programs. After 1900, health programs to educate the general public spread throughout Europe.

Discoveries that changed the face of the twentieth century proliferated in a variety of fields. This was a time of many firsts. Airplane flights and deep-sea expeditions based on technological applications of new discoveries pushed out boundaries of exploration above the land and below the sea. In 1909, the same year that work began in human genetics, American explorer Robert E. Peary (1856–1920) reached the North Pole. In that year, too, plastic was first manufactured, under the trade name Bakelite. In this period, Irish-born British astronomer Agnes Mary Clerke (1842–1907) did pioneering work in the new field of astrophysics. Ernest Rutherford proposed a new spatial reality in his theory

Robert E. Peary. His claim to the discovery of the North Pole was questioned when Frederick Cook announced that he had reached the pole before Peary. After an investigation, the U.S. Congress upheld Peary's claim.

of the nuclear structure of the atom, which stated that the atom can be divided and that it consists of a nucleus surrounded by electrons revolving in orbits.

The values of an age are often revealed in the accomplishments it chooses to honor. In 1896, Swedish industrialist Alfred Nobel (1833–96), who had invented dynamite and amassed a fortune through the manufacture of explosives, established the Nobel Prizes. To be drawn from a bequest of $9.2 million, the prizes were to recognize achievement internationally in five areas: physics, physiology or medicine, chemistry, literature, and peace. Literary figures, peacemakers, poets, and philosophers had long been recognized as shapers of Western culture. At the end of the nineteenth century, scientists assumed pride of place in their company.

establishing the social sciences

Innovations in the social sciences paralleled the drama of discovery in the biological and physical sciences. The "scientific" study of society purported to apply the same methods of observation and experimentation to human interactions. After 1870, sociology, economics, history, psychology, anthropology, and archaeology took shape at the core of new social scientific endeavors. They, like the "hard" sciences, had benefits to offer Western women and men that improved the quality of life. But just as scientific advances could be applied to destructive ends, so too did the social sciences promote inequities and prejudices in the Western world.

Archaeology uncovered lost civilizations. Heinrich Schliemann (1822–90) discovered Troy. Schliemann, a German businessman, captured the imagination of Europeans when he used his own fortune to open up what he believed to be the ruins of the sites mentioned in Homeric verse. Sir Arthur Evans (1851–1941) began excavations in Crete in 1900 and over the next eight years unearthed the remains of Minoan culture. Both men used scientific procedures to reconstruct ancient cultures. Historians, too, applied new techniques to the study of the past. German historian Leopold von Ranke (1795–1886) eschewed a literary form of historical writing that relied on legend and tradition in favor of objective, "scientific" history based on documentation and other forms of material evidence. Ranke produced influential multivolume histories of Prussia, England, France, and the world.

The social scientific study of economics came to the aid of businessmen. Influenced by the quantum theory of physics, economists posited a new view of the economy that revised the classical models of Adam Smith and David Ricardo. The neoclassical economic theory of Alfred Marshall (1842–1924) and others recognized the centrality of individual choice in the marketplace, while dealing with the problem of overproduction: how can businesses know they have produced enough to maximize profits? Economists concerned with how individuals responded to prices devised a theory of marginal utility, by which producers could calculate costs and project profits in a reliable fashion based on a pattern of consumer response to price changes.

"Scientific" psychology developed in a variety of directions. Wilhelm Wundt (1832–1920) established the first laboratory devoted to psychological research in Leipzig in 1879. From his experiments he concluded that thought is grounded in physical reality. The Russian physiologist Ivan Pavlov (1849–1936) had already received the Nobel Prize for physiology and medicine for his study of the dog's digestive system when he began his famous series of experiments demonstrating the conditioned reflex in dogs. Other psychological models competed for theoretical primacy. With his theory of personality development and the creation of psychoanalysis, the science of the unconscious, Sigmund Freud (1859–1939) greatly influenced the direction of psychology. (See "Sigmund Freud, Explorer of Dreams," pp. 840–841.) Freudian probing of the unconscious was a model greatly at odds with the behavioral perspective of conditioned responses based on Pavlov's work.

The new social science of criminology claimed scientific veracity after 1880. In 1885, Sir Francis Galton (1822–1911), a cousin of Charles Darwin, proved the individuality of fingerprints through scientific study and thereby initiated an important method of identifying criminals. Criminologists joined psychiatrists as expert witnesses in criminal trials for the first time at the end of the nineteenth century. Galton also propagated pseudoscientific ideas about eugenics, the improvement of the human race through selective breeding. Anthropological studies of primitive cultures influenced eugenic assumptions about racial inferiority.

The new specialties of forensic medicine and criminal anthropology came into being at the end of the century. The Criminal Man (1876), written by Italian criminologist Cesare Lombroso (1836–1909), claimed to be a scientific study of the physical attributes of convicted criminals. Through observation and statistical compilation, Lombroso discovered "born criminals," individuals whose physical characteristics proved their deviance. Criminals, he claimed, could be identified by their looks. With statistics Lombroso demonstrated, for example, that left-handed, redheaded people with low foreheads were naturally disposed to a life of crime. Even during his lifetime, Lombroso's ideas were widely disputed, and subsequently they were discredited, but their temporary legitimacy was a good indication of how scientific claims justified prejudicial assumptions. Opposing Lombroso's ideas, the French school of criminology stressed the social determinants of crime, seeing poverty and malnutrition as explanations for the different physical appearance of criminals.

The psychology of crowd behavior originated in the work of the French physician Gustave Le Bon (1841–1931). In Psychology of Crowds (1895), Le Bon argued that the masses were instinctively irrational. Through his "science" he arrived at the political judgment that democracy was a despicable and dangerous form of government. Émile Durkheim (1858–1917) is regarded as the founder of modern sociology. In his famous study of suicide as a social phenomenon, Durkheim pitted sociological theory against psychology and argued that deviance was the result not of psychic disturbances but of environmental factors and hereditary forces.

Heredity became a general explanation for behavior of all sorts. The novels of Émile Zola presented a popular view of biological determinism. Zola's protagonists were doomed by self-destructive characteristics they inherited from their parents. Everything from poverty, drunkenness, and crime to a declining birthrate could be attributed to biologically determined causes. For some theorists, this reasoning teetered on the edge of racism and ideas about "better blood." Intelligence was now measured "scientifically" for the first time with IQ tests developed at the Sorbonne by the psychologist Alfred Binet (1857–1911) in the 1890s. The tests did not acknowledge the importance of cultural factors in the development of intelligence, and they scientifically legitimated a belief in natural elites. Not least of all, science was also invoked in support of a particular system of gender relations, one that itself was undergoing assault and upheaval between 1871 and 1914.

The "new woman" and the new consciousness

New scientific ideas had a formative impact on prevailing views of gender relations and female sexuality. The natural sciences were employed to prove the inferiority of women in the species. In *The Descent of Man* (1871), Charles Darwin, the giant of evolutionary theory, concluded that the mental power of man was higher than that of woman. The female's need for male protection, the father of evolution reasoned, had increased her dependence over time while at the same time increasing the competition of natural selection among men. The result, Darwin argued, was inequality between the sexes. Darwin went on to reject women's emancipation as out of step with biological realities. What Darwin presented was a vicious circle in which women's dependence had made them inferior and their inferiority kept them dependent. These attitudes toward gender and race marked the advent of biological "proofs" to justify social policies. Those of Darwin's disciples who applied biological principles to society came to be known as "social Darwinists," specialists who claimed that "survival of the fittest" was a concept that could be applied to all social interactions between races and the sexes.

Darwin was not the only man of science who had ideas about a woman's proper place. Others made a dubious case for brain size as an index of superiority. The French physiologist Paul Broca (1824–80), a contemporary of Darwin's, countered in 1873 that the skull capacity of the two sexes was very similar and that a case for inferiority could not be based on measurement. But Broca was atypical. Most scientific opinion argued in favor of female frailty and outright inferiority. Social Darwinists adapted evolutionary biology to the debate over inequality between the sexes. They complemented their race theories with evolutionary theories of sexual division: "What was decided among the prehistoric Protozoa cannot be annulled by an Act of Parliament." Sexless prehistoric protozoa held the message for social Darwinists that women should not enjoy the right to vote.

In general, the natural sciences worked to reinforce the idea of women as reproducers whose proper role was nurturing and whose proper domain was the home. The social sciences, in particular sociology, echoed these findings by asserting that the male-dominated household was a proof of social progress.

These "scientific" arguments justified the exclusion of women from educational opportunities and from professions like medicine and law. Biology became destiny as women's attempts at equal education came up against closed doors. Stalwarts broke the prohibitions, but women who gained higher education in these decades were the exception that proved the rule. Those women who were able to get an education were blocked from using it. There was a generalized fear in Western societies that women who attempted to exceed their "natural" abilities would damage their reproductive functions and neglect their nurturing roles. The specter of sickly children and women with nervous disorders was invoked as grounds for opposing demands for coeducation. Women's education was assigned to the church and was intended to meet the needs of the family. The creation of the first separate women's colleges in the late 1860s marked the beginning of the pioneering era of higher education for women.

In this age of scientific justification of female inferiority, the "new woman" emerged. All over Europe the feminist movement had demanded social, economic, and political progress for women. But the "new woman" phenomenon exceeded the bounds of the feminist movement and can be described as a general cultural phenomenon. The search for independence was overwhelmingly a middle-class phenomenon that had a psychological as well as a political significance in the years between 1880 and 1914. Victorian stereotypes of the angel at the hearth were crumbling. The "new woman" was

sigmund freud, explorer of dreams

Sigmund Freud was a disciplined man, precise and punctual in his habits. In many ways, his life was typical of the life of a Viennese bourgeois professional at the end of the nineteenth century. His day was like a railway timetable, scheduled to the minute—whether seeing patients, dining with his family, or taking his daily constitutional. He even calculated his pleasures, counting as his only indulgence the 20 cigars he smoked every day.

The order in Freud's life seemed curiously at odds with his dedication to the study of disorder. He was a man of science, a medical doctor specializing in organic diseases of the nervous system. Early in his career, he began to question physiological explanations for certain nervous disorders and to search for another reason for the disorders of the mind. His exploration took him to Paris in 1885 to study with the leading French neurologist, Jean Martin Charcot (1825–93), whose work on hysteria had won him an international reputation.

Surrounded by hysterics in Charcot's clinic, Freud wondered whether organic physical illnesses could be traced to psychological problems. Freud explored the value of hypnosis as a technique for uncovering the secret workings of the mind. He learned that emotions alone could produce physical symptoms like blindness and paralysis. By hypnotizing patients, Freud caught glimpses of the world of the unconscious as a vast and hidden terrain. He approached this new territory as an explorer.

Freud created a new science of the unconscious, psychoanalysis, when he rejected physiological causes for nervous disorders in favor of psychological ones. He intended psychoanalysis as a theory of personality and a method of treatment or therapy. This was a dramatic break with existing theories of madness and mental disorder. On his seventieth birthday, Freud looked back over his own career and described his achievement: "The poets and philosophers before me discovered the unconscious; what I discovered was the scientific method by which the unconscious can be studied."

The hostile reaction to Freud's break with existing ideas about mental disorders was further aggravated by the importance he attributed to sexuality. Colleagues in Vienna were shocked by the direction that his work was taking. Freud began by hypothesizing that disturbed patients developed neurotic symptoms because of the repression of memories of actual sexual abuse as children. He moved away from this theory of sexual abuse to one in which the subject had *fantasized* about sex as a child and then had repressed the desire. In searching for the root of psychological disorders, Freud argued that sexual conflicts originating in early childhood were the cause of adult neuroses. Repressed sexual desire therefore became the key to understanding human behavior.

Freud's self-described scientific method, which allowed him to probe the unconscious, was free association. Patients were encouraged to talk, or "associate," in a relaxed atmosphere. The couch in the doctor's office has become the enduring symbol of the psychoanalytic method. Patients were particularly encouraged to talk about their dreams. The unconscious, Freud argued, manifests itself in dreams. The role of the psychoanalyst is to examine the content of the dream and interpret it, facilitating recognition and hence a cure in the patient.

Freud's first major work, and probably the most important study of his career, *The Interpretation of Dreams* (1900), heralded the new century. Working with his own dreams and those of his patients, Freud posited that a dream is the fulfillment of a wish. Dreams are not literal in their meaning; their symbols and context must always be interpreted. The experiences of our conscious lives are rearranged in dreams. For Freud, nothing was accidental. Jokes, obsessions, and even slips of the tongue ("Freudian slips") as well as dreams were indicators of unconscious desires. In later life, Freud was supposed to have said, "Sometimes a cigar is just a cigar." But in his dream theory, every object—cigar, banana, flight of stairs, or broken candle—had meaning in the context of the patient's associations. Freud used his own dreams and his relationship with his parents to describe the neurotic personality and the Oedipus complex, so important to his later work on childhood sexuality. Here the child's unresolved desire for the parent of the opposite sex formed the basis for all ego development. In famous case studies such as "Dora," "The Wolf Man," and "The Rat Man," Freud described the symptoms and histories of patients to whom he assigned fictitious names. In subsequent works, Freud went on to detail the uncharted land of the unconscious he discovered in his work on dreams, using designations for the components of personality—the "ego," the "superego," and the "id."

Sigmund Freud gave to Western culture a new vocabulary. His lexicon has survived throughout the twentieth century and has entered common parlance as a way of explaining our daily lives in psychological terms that range from "anal-retentive stage" to "sublimation." He bequeathed to Western men and women a new way of looking at the world. Freud's work sounded the death knell for the nineteenth century's blind faith in reason. For Freud, human beings were driven by subterranean instincts and desires. The horrors of war and destruction in the twentieth century confirmed for Freud his belief in the irrationality of Western civilization.

Freud died in exile in London in 1939, having fled from the Nazi occupation of his beloved Vienna. During his lifetime and ever since, his theories have been refuted, with critics saying that they explain nothing more than the psychic world in which Freud lived—the world of European middle-class men at the beginning of the twentieth century. But there can be no denying that Freud's exploration of the land of dreams in the world of the unconscious was a revolutionary event in the history of Western thought.

a woman characterized by intelligence, strength, and sexual desire—in every way man's equal. The Norwegian playwright Henrik Ibsen (1828–1906) created a fictional embodiment of the phenomenon in Nora, the hero of A Doll's House (1879), who was typical of the restive spirit for independence among wives and mothers confined to suffocating households and relegated to the status of children. Contemporary opinion condemned Nora as immoral for abandoning her home, her husband, and her children.

The "new woman's" pursuit of independence included control over her own body. The term birth control was first used by an American, Margaret Sanger (1879–1966), although the reality itself was not new. Women had always known of and employed contraceptive and abortive techniques to limit family size. What was different in the period before 1914 was the militant public discussion of ways to prevent conception and an awareness of the death and debilitation that resulted from primitive methods. The development of a process of vulcanizing rubber in the mid-nineteenth century had made condoms available to a mass market, but they were little employed. A growing number of women, among whom were medical doctors, decided to take information to the public. A common result was state repression of their activities. Annie Besant, advocating birth control in Great Britain, was charged with corrupting youth by distributing books that dealt with contraception. Aletta Jacobs (1849–1929), the first woman to practice medicine in Holland, opened a contraceptive clinic in 1882. Leagues for distributing contraceptive information were formed elsewhere in Europe. Birth-control advocates aimed to preserve women's health and to give them some control over their reproductive lives.

Discussions of contraception brought into the public arena the premise that women, like men, were sexual beings. This was reinforced by the frank discussions of sexuality in the works of Sigmund Freud. The first English translation of Freud's The Interpretation of Dreams appeared in 1913 with a warning note from the publisher that its sale should be limited to doctors, lawyers, and clerics. Richard von Krafft-Ebing (1840–1902) and Havelock Ellis (1859–1939) also contributed to the public discussion of sex in their works on sexuality and sexual

"Angel" or woman?

Victorian domestic ideals viewed woman as an "Angel in the House" (the title of a poem by Coventry Patmore) who created a paradise of love and nurturance for her husband and children. By the end of the nineteenth century, many women recognized that this description, however rosy, kept women in the home and out of public life. Here Maria Desraismes, a French feminist and republican, rebuts republican and historian Jules Michelet for his popular books that romanticized women and marriage.

Of all woman's enemies, I tell you that the worst are those who insist that woman is an angel. To say that woman is an angel is to impose on her, in a sentimental and admiring fashion, all duties, and to reserve for oneself all rights; it is to imply that her specialty is self-effacement, resignation, and sacrifice; it is to suggest to her that woman's greatest glory, her greatest happiness, is to immolate herself for those she loves; it is to let her understand that she will be generously furnished with every opportunity for exercising her aptitudes. It is to say that she will respond to absolutism by submission, to brutality by meekness, to indifference by tenderness, to inconstancy by fidelity, to egotism by devotion.

In the face of this long enumeration, I decline the honor of being an angel. No one has the right to force me to be both dupe and victim. Self-sacrifice is not a habit, a custom; it is an extra! It is not on the program of one's duties. No power has the right to impose it on me. Of all acts, sacrifice is the freest, and it is precisely because it is free that it is so admirable.

From Maria Desraismes, "La Femme et le droit" public address published in Eve dans l'humanité (1891).

In October 1916 Margaret Sanger opened the first birth-control clinic in the United States in Brooklyn, New York. Police soon raided the clinic, and Sanger was charged with "maintaining a public nuisance." She was convicted and sentenced to 30 days in jail. The New York Court of Appeals upheld the sentence but also ruled that physicians should have broader discretion in prescribing birth control. Later in 1916 Sanger formed the New York Birth Control League to push for even broader discretion. Sanger is shown here leaving the Court of Special Sessions after her arraignment in October 1916.

deviance. By 1900 sexuality and reproduction were openly connected to discussions of women's rights.

The new sciences had worked to change the world. At the same time, those intent on preserving traditional values invoked scientific authority. But as the uncertainty over gender roles at the beginning of the twentieth century makes clear, science was a way of thinking as well as a body of doctrine. Traditional ideas might be scientifically justified, but they would not go unchallenged.

The New Consumption

The great Russian novelist Lev Tolstoy (1828–1910) was an astute observer of the world in which he lived. In 1877 he condemned the materialism that characterized European society: "Money is a new form of slavery, and distinguishable from the old simply by the fact that it is impersonal—that there is no human relation between master and slave." Although he was speaking as a moral philosopher, Tolstoy had put his finger on something that economists were just beginning to understand—the extension of a money economy. Tolstoy was aware of how peasants freed from the land became entangled in a web of financial obligations that constituted a new form of serfdom.

At the end of the nineteenth century, the role of money changed in ways affecting all of Western society. Workers were beginning to share in the benefits of industrial prosperity. This prosperity differed dramatically by geographic region and occupation. But the expansion in the ranks of a salaried working class augured a shift in patterns of behavior. Lagging behind the industrial revolutions but no less important was a revolution in consumption patterns among European populations. The new consumer age is best illustrated by the creation of the big department stores of the last quarter of the nineteenth century. The Bon Marché Department Store in Paris occupied over 52,000 square feet and contained a vast selection of goods. Everything from initialed toilet paper to household furniture was now located under a single roof. The department store was intended to satisfy every need. Advertising and the art of display became industries in themselves, whose goal was to encourage people to buy things they did not need. The promise of the good life, epitomized in the department store and preached by advertising, now seemed accessible to everyone.

Leisure time also became a consumer item in the late nineteenth century. In 1899, the American economist Thorstein Veblen (1857–1929) published a pathbreaking work that was little appreciated at the time. *The Theory of the Leisure Class* argued that leisure was a form of "conspicuous consumption," a term Veblen coined. More than a theory, his work constituted a critique of the values of Western culture. Women and the family were, for Veblen, the primary vehicles for conspicuous consumption. Elegant dress, for example, conveyed status and served as a sign of leisure just as it had done in aristocratic society. Expensive clothing was designed to show that the wearer had no need to earn wages. For this purpose, women were actually "mutilated," in Veblen's term, by the corset that constricted their vitality and rendered them unfit for work. Women immobilized by their clothes and shoes became the ultimate symbols of social status.

The middle and upper classes controlled sufficient disposable income to allow them to spend time in such leisure pursuits as flocking to seaside resorts in Great Britain and on the Continent. However, resort vacations remained out of the financial reach of most working-class people. Instead, in pursuit of leisure-time activities, working-class men congregated in cafes and pubs. Starting in the 1880s, vaudeville and music halls rose in popularity, their low admission price attracting ever larger crowds. There were at least 30 striptease shows in Paris in the 1890s. These activities fostered fear among the middle classes that working-class leisure was degenerate. The newly invented cinema also exercised a growing appeal for European men and women of all ages and classes.

Not least important in the new leisure was the rise of organized sports. The strict organization of work life in mature industrial societies may have made sports an attractive way of organizing leisure. Men—there were few organized sports for women—worked by the clock and now played by the clock as well. Sports also promoted national and regional identification. Beginning in the 1860s, men began playing the games they had learned as boys in English public schools. Rugby, football (soccer), and cricket soon developed national followings. Golf originated in Scotland in this period and spread throughout Europe and to the United States. Spectator sports grew in importance, with audiences of over 100,000 people at British soccer matches at the beginning of the twentieth century. Victorians saw the necessity of recreation and endorsed the renewing, relaxing, and entertaining aspects of organized play.

Scouting also originated at the end of the nineteenth century as another form of organized leisure. Uniformed boys were taught "manly" virtues of self-reliance and teamwork. Team spirit was tied to patriotism. Scouting organizations for girls emphasized domestic virtues and household tasks.

Amateur athletics and track-and-field events grew in popularity, especially after the establishment of an in-

Fashionably dressed customers look over some of the vast array of goods on display in this engraving of the interior of a nineteenth-century department store.

ternational Olympics competition, modeled on the ancient Greek games. The first modern Olympiad was held
in Athens in 1896, and—except for upheavals caused by
war—the Olympic Games have been held at four-year
intervals throughout the twentieth century.

Cycling became a popular competitive sport on the
Continent with the establishment of the Tour de France
at the beginning of the twentieth century. Some saw in
the new pastime of bicycling a threat to the social order.
Women, attracted by the exercise and mobility afforded
by this new means of transportation, altered their costumes in favor of freedom of movement. For eminently
practical reasons, they discarded their corsets and bus-
tles and shortened their skirts. As women gained
greater mobility, some observers saw in the "new
woman" on the bicycle seat the decline of true womanhood and Western values.

*A poster for the World Exhibition held in Paris in 1889 features the star
attraction of the show—the Eiffel Tower. Most of the other exhibition
buildings were subsequently demolished.*

The engineering marvel of the Eiffel Tower, built in 1889 for the World Exposition held
in Paris, became a symbol not only of the French capital but of the values of the new
age. New artifacts of European culture proliferated. Photography, motorcars, bicycles,
motion-picture cameras, and X rays all created sensations when they appeared. London's Inner Circle underground railway was completed in 1884, and other lines soon followed, forming a vast urban subterranean network. In 1898, the miracle of underground
transportation became a reality in Paris with the opening of the Métro, or subway. Yet
some observers saw in this new age upheaval and disruption of traditional liberal values, the collapse of the family, and the disruptions of women and workers who did not
know their place.

The Eiffel Tower was criticized more than it was praised. It was a building, yet it was
not. Its inside and its outside were confused. The admirers of classic architecture
lamented the ugliness of this girdered monument whose main function was to demonstrate structural innovation for its own sake. Critics lamented that science disrupted
people's understanding of the world and their place in it in the same way. The Eiffel
Tower—like the values of the new age (speed, progress, technological innovation, and
mass consumption), critics warned—was hollow and would not endure.

mastering the chapter

To review the main points of the chapter, be sure you can explain the significance of each of the following.

Terms/Concepts/Events	People	Places
cartels	Edward VII	Budapest
Labour party	James Keir Hardie	Ulster
Fabian Society	David Lloyd George	Vienna
National Insurance Act	Captain Alfred Dreyfus	
Trade Unions Act	Emmeline Pankhurst	
Irish Home Rule	Theodor Herzl	
Kulturkampf	Mikhail Bakunin	
feminist	Marie Curie	
pogroms	Albert Einstein	
Zionism	Sigmund Freud	

suggestions for further reading

European Economy and the politics of mass society

Michael Burns, *Rural Society and French Politics: Boulangism and the Dreyfus Affair, 1886–1900* (Princeton, NJ: Princeton University Press, 1984). Examines the impact on rural France of two political watersheds of the Third Republic in order to gauge the importance of national politics in nonurban settings.

* Albert S. Lindemann, *A History of European Socialism* (New Haven, CT: Yale University Press, 1983). Surveys socialist thought in the nineteenth and twentieth centuries and examines the relationships between ideology, institutions, and workers in their historical context.

* Carl E. Schorske, *Fin-de-Siècle Vienna: Politics and Culture* (New York: Alfred A. Knopf, 1980). A series of essays describing the break with nineteenth-century liberal culture in one of Europe's great cities as artists, intellectuals, and politicians responded to the disintegration of the Habsburg Empire.

* Eugen Weber, *Peasants into Frenchmen: The Modernization of Rural France* (Stanford, CA: Stanford University Press, 1976). Views the integration of the French peasantry into national political life through agents of change, including the railroads, schools, and the army. The author contends that a national political culture took the place of traditional beliefs and practices between 1870 and 1914 in France.

* Hans-Ulrich Wehler, *The German Empire, 1871–1918* (Leamington Spa, England: Berg Publishers, 1985). Stresses the institutional continuities of German society and links pre-World War I Germany to the rise of Nazism.

outsiders in mass politics

* Richard J. Evans, *The Feminist Movement in Germany, 1894–1933* (London: Sage Publications, 1976). Considers two conflicting approaches to bourgeois feminism—one radical and the other conservative and authoritarian—and discusses the role of social Darwinism in the women's movement and the place of feminism in political life.

* Steven C. Hause and Anne R. Kenney, *Women's Suffrage and Social Politics in the French Third Republic* (Princeton, NJ: Princeton University Press, 1984). Examines the women's suffrage movement from its origins through its defeat after World War I in the Senate. Aims, tactics, and leadership of the women's movement receive special attention.

* William M. Reddy, *The Rise of Market Culture: The Textile Trade and French Society, 1750–1900* (Cambridge: Cambridge University Press, 1984). A cultural interpretation of the textile trade in the era of industrialization. Reddy examines the creation of market culture and workers' resistance to it through a study of collective action, workers' songs, bourgeois attitudes, and factory organization.

* Richard Stites, *The Women's Liberation Movement in Russia: Feminism, Nihilism, and Bolshevism, 1860–1930* (Princeton, NJ: Princeton University Press, 1978). Situates the Russian women's movement within the contexts of both nineteenth-century European feminism and twentieth-century communist ideology and traces its development from the early feminists through the rise of the Bolsheviks to power. Includes a discussion of the Russian Revolution's impact on the status of women.

shaping the new consciousness

* Stephen Kern, *The Culture of Time and Space, 1880–1918* (Cambridge, MA: Harvard University Press, 1983). Describes how late-nineteenth-century technological advances created new modes of thinking about and experiencing time and space.

* Michael B. Miller, *The Bon Marché: Bourgeois Culture and the Department Store, 1869–1920* (Princeton, NJ: Princeton University Press, 1981). A social and cultural history of the department store as the creation and reflection of bourgeois culture.

  Robert A. Nye, *Crime, Madness, and Politics in Modern France: The Medical Concept of National Decline* (Princeton, NJ: Princeton University Press, 1984). Nye shows how the medical concept of deviance was linked to a general cultural crisis in fin-de-siècle France.

* William M. Reddy, *Money and Liberty in Modern Europe: A Critique of Historical Understanding* (Cambridge: Cambridge University Press, 1987). This essay on the role of money in modern Europe contends that its widespread use in exchange influenced social structure. Arguing that monetary exchange intensified existing social inequities, Reddy examines the expansion of commerce in France, Germany, and England.

* Martin Wiener, *English Culture and the Decline of the Industrial Spirit, 1850–1980* (Cambridge: Cambridge University Press, 1981). A cultural history of growth and decline from Victoria to Thatcher. By drawing on literature, art, architecture, politics, and economics, the author describes the ambiguous attitude of the elite toward industry and argues that English culture was never conducive to sustained industrial growth.

* Rosalind H. Williams, *Dream Worlds: Mass Consumption in Late Nineteenth-Century France* (Berkeley: University of California Press, 1982). A historical overview of attitudes toward consumption and an examination of the creation of the consumer mentality in terms of the consumer revolution and its consequences.

*Paperback edition available.

europe and the world, 1870-1914

the power of words

European conquest of African territories often involved sizable military expeditions and resulted in high death tolls among native populations. But imperial domination also took forms other than those reflected in battles and conquest. Language was an important tool of domination often overlooked in favor of more tangible indicators of control. Imperialist powers were able to extract natural wealth, employ native labor, and administer and control millions of Africans—not with bullets but with the power of words.

For certain kinds of profit, words were not necessary—terror and repression were enough. In the Congo rubber trade, for example, early Belgian adventurers could simply steal from or blackmail whole villages until they were stopped by the force of international opinion. But for other enterprises, like mining, that required organization, technology, and discipline, communication between the colonized and the colonizer was essential. Hierarchies of power and authority had to be established on the basis of orders given and orders understood. A shared language was the only means of moving beyond a state of siege to ongoing economic activity and, ideally, efficiency and profitability.

Europeans did not always choose simply to impose their own languages on colonized populations. Nor did they take the time and trouble to learn the numerous languages and countless dialects of the tribes with whom they came into contact. The politics of language was more complicated than either of these alternatives and varied from region to region.

Particularly instructive is the adoption of Swahili as a *lingua franca*, or common language, in the Congo Free State (later the Belgian Congo, and now Zaire).

Nineteenth-century missionaries had identified Swahili, a Bantu language heavily influenced by Arab traders on the eastern coast of Africa in the seventeenth century, as the easiest language for Europeans to learn. Belgians widely believed that Congolese natives were incapable of learning French, which the Belgians considered to be a superior language. In an area stretching 1300 miles along the Congo River from the west coast of Africa to Stanley Falls, missionaries and explorers encountered at least eight principal languages. Both Catholic priests and various Protestant missionaries, intent on converting natives, recognized the utility of Swahili and set about codifying vocabularies and training manuals for their own missionaries. Priests were sent home if they were not properly trained in Swahili. In the same manner, the Belgian government required basic language instruction in Swahili for administrators before they left Belgium.

Trade with agricultural areas populated by Swahili-speaking natives contributed to the spread of Swahili among African workers moving into newly created urban areas like Elizabethville and into the towns around the Belgian-owned copper mines of the Katanga area of the Congo Free State. Unlike European settlers, Africans showed a willingness to learn new languages quickly. Through the influence of urban migration and the encouragement of Belgian overseers, Swahili became the common tongue of growing numbers of workers and urban dwellers.

While Belgians and other Westerners used Swahili to control native workers, they did not speak the language. This is an important distinction. Many Europeans had access to vocabularies—they used words rather than explained ideas or expressed feelings. In their pidgin Swahili, Europeans knew only how to give orders. Nouns were limited to concrete objects. True signs of language mastery—concern for syntax and grammar—were absent from Belgian training manuals. Verbs were listed only in their imperative forms—including the verb for love, *penda*. Most verbs referred to movements connected with employer-employee relations and domestic and agricultural work. In much the same way that modern-day tourists learn enough of a foreign language to order a meal or ask the location of a restroom, Belgian managers and work bosses often learned how to channel labor and increase output with pidgin-language skills that excluded the possibility of discussion and exchange of ideas. This was also true of the British in east Africa, in the area that is now Tanzania, Uganda, Kenya, and Zanzibar. Natives identified the limited dialect the British spoke as *kisetla* Swahili—the dialect of the settlers.

This situation reinforced stereotypes and prevented communication between Europeans and Africans. Europeans concluded from their limited exchanges that natives were childlike and simple. And what did Africans think of the Europeans? The novelist George Orwell, the

Focus Questions

1. What social, political, and economic forces encouraged the nations of Europe to create overseas empires in the late nineteenth century?
2. How and why did European imperialism differ in Africa and Asia?
3. How did imperial expansion around the globe transform the lives of Europeans at home?
4. What geopolitical factors made the European balance of power so unstable around the turn of the century?

pseudonym of Eric Arthur Blair (1903–50), experienced the reverse of the stereotyping phenomenon in his early career as a British police officer in Burma. Forced against his better judgment to kill an elephant, Orwell concluded, "The imperialist wears a mask and his face grows to fit it." In the mask of authority, Orwell became the violent and destructive imperialist that the natives saw. This was a process without words, in what Orwell described as "the utter silence" experienced by every European in the colonies.

The hierarchy of languages reinforced the silence. The 1908 Charter of the Belgian Congo specified that French was the official language to be used at all state ceremonies. Native Africans, however, had no advanced training in French. Elementary French taught in the mission schools was intended to help the Congolese serve their Belgian masters as servants and low-level clerks. Furthermore, all decrees and regulations were to be published in French and Flemish, but not Swahili. As a result, Africans could not read the laws that governed them. But they could hear the laws translated for them into their regional languages by their own people.

Swahili, promoted by the state as the common language of work, expanded from a few hundred speakers in what is now central Zaire to become the first language of millions, including entire urban populations and a great majority of rural dwellers. Just as the French language was an effective barrier to Congolese participation in public life, Swahili—in its variety of dialects—effectively excluded Europeans from the private lives and popular customs of the Congolese. Within two generations, the Congolese were also able to use Swahili, encouraged as a language of deference and labor, as a bond of common identity and political resistance against their imperial rulers. Such was the power of words that the language imposed by the conqueror became the language of liberation.

The New Imperialism

The concept of empire was certainly not invented by Europeans in the last third of the nineteenth century: European states had controlled empires before 1870. The influence of Great Britain stretched beyond the limits of its formal holdings in India and South Africa. Russia held Siberia and central Asia, and France ruled Algeria and Indochina. Older empires—Spain, for example—had survived from the sixteenth century but as hollow shells. What, then, was new about the "new imperialism" practiced by England, France, and Germany after 1870? In part, the new imperialism was the acquisition of territories on an intense and unprecedented scale. Industrialization created the tools of transportation, communication, and domination that permitted the rapid pace of global empire-building. Above all, what distinguished the new imperialism was the domination by the industrial powers over the nonindustrial world. The United States also participated in the new imperialism, less by territorial acquisition and more by developing an "invisible" empire of trade and influence in the Pacific. The forms of imperialism may have varied from nation to nation, but the basically unequal relationship between an industrial power and an undeveloped territory did not.

Only nation-states commanded the technology and resources necessary for the new scale of imperialist expansion. Rivalry among a few European nation-states—notably Great Britain, France, and Germany—was a common denominator that set the standards by which these nations and other European nation-states gained control of the globe by 1900. Why did the Europeans create vast empires? Were empires built for economic gain, military protection, or national glory? Questions about motives may obscure common features of the new imperialism. Industrial powers sought to take over nonindustrial regions, not in isolated areas but all over the globe. In the attempt they necessarily competed with one another, successfully adapting the resources of industrialism to the needs of conquest.

The Technology of Empire

For Europeans at the end of the nineteenth century, the world had definitely become a smaller place. Steam, iron, and electricity—the great forces of Western industrialization—were responsible for seemingly shrinking the globe. Technology not only allowed Europeans to accomplish tasks and to mass-produce goods efficiently, but it also altered the previous conception of time and space.

Steam, which powered factories, proved equally efficient as an energy source in transportation. Great iron steamships fueled by coal replaced the smaller, slower, wind-powered wooden sailing vessels that had ruled the seas for centuries. Steam-powered vessels transported large cargoes of people and goods more quickly and more reliably than the sailing ships. Iron ships were superior to wood in their durability, lightness, watertightness, cargo space, speed, and fuel economy. For most of the nineteenth century, British trading ships and the British navy dominated the seas, but after 1880 other nations, especially Germany, challenged England by building versatile and efficient iron steamers. In a society in which time was money, steamships were important because, for the first time, ocean-going vessels could meet schedules as precisely and as predictably as railroads could. Just as the imperial Romans had used their network of roads to link far-flung territories to the capital, Europeans used sea-lanes to join their colonies to the home country.

Until 1850, Europeans had ventured no farther on the African continent than its coastal areas. The installation of coal-burning boilers on smaller boats permitted navigation of previously uncharted and unnavigable rivers. Steam power made exploration and migration possible and greatly contributed to knowledge of terrain, natural wealth, and resources. Smaller steam-powered vessels also increased European inland trade with China, Burma, and India.

While technology improved European mobility on water, it also literally moved the land. Harbors were deepened to accommodate the new iron- and then steel-hulled ships. One of the greatest engineering feats of the century was the construction of a hundred-mile-long canal across the Isthmus of Suez in Egypt. The Suez Canal, completed in 1869, joined the Mediterranean and Red seas and created a new, safer trade route to the East. No longer did trading vessels have to make the long voyage around Africa's Cape of Good Hope. The Suez Canal was built by the French under the supervision of Ferdinand de Lesseps (1805–94), a diplomat with no technical or financial background who was able to promote construction because of concessions he received from Said Pasha, the viceroy of Egypt. The canal could accommodate ships of all sizes. Great Britain purchased a controlling interest in the Suez Canal in 1875 to benefit its trade with India.

De Lesseps later oversaw the initial construction of the Panama Canal in the Western Hemisphere. The combination of French mismanagement, bankruptcy,

Elaborate ceremony marked the opening of the Suez Canal to navigation on November 17, 1869. The first convoy of ships to pass through the canal was led by a French ship carrying the Empress Eugénie.

and the high incidence of disease among work crews enabled the United States to acquire rights to the Panama project and complete the canal by 1914. Fifty-one miles long, the Panama Canal connected the world's two largest bodies of water, the Atlantic and Pacific oceans, across the Isthmus of Panama by a waterway containing a series of locks. Now the passage from the Atlantic Ocean to the Pacific Ocean took less than eight hours—much less time than it took using the various overland routes or voyaging around the tip of South America. Both the Suez and Panama canals were built in pursuit of speed. Shorter distances meant quicker travel, which in turn meant higher profits.

Technology also altered time by increasing the speed with which Westerners communicated with other parts of the world. In 1830, for example, it took about two years for a person sending a letter from Great Britain to India to receive a reply. In 1850, steam-powered mail boats shortened the time required for the same round-trip correspondence to about two or three months. But the real revolution in communication came through electricity. Thousands of miles of copper telegraph wire laced countries together; insulated underwater cables linked continents to each other. By the late nineteenth century, a vast telegraph network connected Europe to every area of the world. In 1870 a telegram from London to Bombay arrived in a matter of hours, instead of months, and a response could be received back in London on the same day. Faster communications extended power and control throughout empires. Europeans could communicate immediately with their distant colonies, dispatching troops, orders, and supplies. This communication network eliminated the problem of overextension that had plagued Roman imperial organization in the third century. For the first time, continents discovered by Europeans five centuries earlier were brought into daily contact with the West.

Technological advances in other areas helped foster European imperialism in the nineteenth century. Advances in medicine permitted European men and women to penetrate disease-ridden swamps and jungles. After 1850, European explorers, traders, missionaries, and adventurers carried quinine pills. Quinine, the bitter-tasting derivative of cinchona-tree bark, was discovered to be an effective treatment for malaria. This treatment got its first important test during the French invasion of Algeria in 1830, and it allowed the French to stay healthy enough to conquer that North African country between 1830 and 1847. David Livingstone (1813–73) and Henry M. Stanley (1841–1904) were just two of the

The transatlantic telegraph cable was the first intercontinental communications link of the electric age. This illustration shows the Great Eastern, the largest ship afloat, which finally succeeded in laying the cable in 1866.

many explorers who crossed vast terrains and explored the waterways of Africa, after malaria—the number one killer of European travelers—had been controlled.

Europeans carried the technologies of destruction as well as survival with them into less-developed areas of the world. New types of firearms produced in the second half of the nineteenth century included breech-loading rifles, repeating rifles, and machine guns. The new weapons gave the advantages of both accurate aim and rapid fire. The spears of African warriors and the primitive weaponry of Chinese rebels were no match for sophisticated European arms, which permitted their bearers to lie down while firing and to remain undetected at distances of up to a half mile.

The new technology did not cause the new imperialism. The Western powers used technological advances as a tool for establishing their control of the world. Viewed as a tool, however, the new technology does explain how vast areas of land and millions of people were conquered so rapidly.

Motives for Empire

If technology was not the cause but only a tool, what explains the new imperialism of the late nineteenth century? Were wealthy financiers, searching for high-yielding opportunities for investments, the driving force? Was profit the main motive? Were politicians and heads of state in the game for the prestige and glory that territorial expansion could bring them at home?

There are no easy or simple explanations for the new imperialism. Individuals made their fortunes overseas, and heavy industries like the Krupp firm in Germany prospered with the expansion of state-protected colonies. Yet many colonies were economically worthless. Tunisia and Morocco, acquired for their strategic and political importance, constituted an economic loss for the French, who poured more funds into their administration than they were able to extract. Each imperial power held one or more colonies whose costs outweighed the return. Yet this does not mean that some Europeans were simply irrational in their pursuit of empire or that they were driven by an atavistic desire to recapture the glories of a precapitalist past and willing to incur financial losses in order to do so.

Economics. The test for economic motivation cannot simply be reduced to a balance sheet of debits and credits because, in the end, an account of state revenues and state expenditures provides only a static picture of the business of empire. Even losses cannot be counted as proof against the profit motive in expansion. In modern capitalism, profits, especially great profits, are often predicated on risks. Portugal and Italy, as smaller nations with limited resources, failed as players in the game in which the great industrial powers called the shots. Prestige through the acquisition of empire was one way of keeping alive in the game. Imperialism was influenced by business interests, market considerations, and the pursuit of individual and national fortunes. Not by accident did the great industrial powers control the scramble and dictate the terms of expansion. Nor was it merely fortuitous that Great Britain, the nation that provided the model for European expansion, dedicated itself to the establishment of a profitable worldwide network of trade and investment. Above all, the search for investment opportunities—whether railroads in China or diamond mines in South Africa—lured Europeans into a world system that challenged capitalist ingenuity and imagination. Acquiring territory was only one means of protecting investments. But there were other benefits associated with the acquisition of territory that cannot be reduced to economic terms, and those too must be considered.

Geopolitics. Geopolitics, or the politics of geography, is based on the recognition that certain areas of the world are valuable for political reasons. The term, first used at the end of the nineteenth century, described a process well under way in international relations. Statesmen influenced by geopolitical concerns recognized the strategic value of land. Some territory was considered important because of its proximity to acquired colonies or to territory targeted for takeover. France, for example, occupied thousands of square miles of the Sahara Desert to protect its interests in Algeria.

Other territory was important because of its proximity to sea routes. Egypt had significance for Great Britain not because of its inherent economic potential but because it permitted the British to protect access to lucrative markets in India through the Suez Canal. Beginning in 1875, the British purchased shares in the canal. By 1879 Egypt was under the informal dual rule of France and Great Britain. The British used the deterioration of internal Egyptian politics to justify their occupation of the country in 1882. Protected access to India also accounted for Great Britain's maintenance of Mediterranean outposts, its acquisition of territory on the east coast of Africa, and its occupation of territory in southern Asia.

Leopold II of Belgium, speech to an International conference of geographers, 12 september 1876

Leopold II reigned as king of the Belgians from 1865 until his death in 1909. Although the ruler of a small European country, he had vast territorial aspirations in Africa. As the personal ruler of the Congo Free State, Leopold amassed an immense fortune until abuses of African workers forced him to hand over his authority of what is now Congo to the Belgian government. In addressing geographers, Leopold evinced some of the self-serving goals that made him the architect of the scramble for territory.

The matter which brings us together today is one most deserving the attention of the friends of humanity. For bringing civilization to the only part of the earth which it has not yet reached and lightening the darkness in which whole peoples are plunged, is, I venture to say, a crusade worthy of this century of progress, and I am glad to find how favourable public opinion is to the accomplishment of this task. We are swimming with the tide. Many of those who have closely studied Africa have come to realise that it would be in the interest of the object they are all seeking to achieve for them to meet and consult together with a view to regulating the course to be taken, combining their efforts and drawing on all available resources in a way which would avoid duplication of effort. . . . Among the matters which remain to be discussed, the following may be mentioned:

1. Deciding exactly where to acquire bases for the task in hand . . . on the Zanzibar coast and near the mouth of the Congo, either by means of conventions with chiefs or by purchasing or renting sites from individuals.

2. Deciding on the routes to be successively opened up into the interior, and on the medical, scientific and peace-keeping stations which are to be set up with a view to abolishing slavery, and bringing about good relations between the chiefs by providing them with fair-minded, impartial persons to settle their disputes, and so forth.

3. Setting up—once the task to be done has been clearly defined—a central, international committee with national committees, each to carry out this task in the aspects of it which concern them, to explain the object to the public of all countries, and to appeal to the feeling of charity to which no worthy cause has ever appealed in vain.

These are some of the points which seem worthy of your attention. . . . My wish is to serve the great cause for which you have already done so much, in whatever manner you may suggest to me. It is with this object that I put myself at your disposal, and I extend a cordial welcome to you.

A third geopolitical motive for annexation was the necessity of fueling bases throughout the world. Faster and more reliable than wind-powered vessels, coal-powered ships were nonetheless dependent on guaranteed fueling bases in friendly ports of call. Islands in the South Pacific and the Indian Ocean were acquired primarily to serve as coaling stations for the great steamers carrying manufactured goods to colonial ports and returning with foodstuffs and raw materials. Ports along the southern rim of Asia served the same purpose. The need for protection of colonies, fueling ports, and sea-lanes led to the creation of naval bases like those on the Red Sea at Djibouti by the French, along the South China Sea at Singapore by the British, and in the Pacific Ocean at Honolulu by the Americans.

In turn, the acquisition of territories justified the increase in naval budgets and the size of fleets. Britain still had the world's largest navy, but by the beginning of the twentieth century, the United States and Germany had entered the competition for dominance of sea-lanes. Japan joined the contest by expanding its navy as a vehicle for its own claims to empire in the Pacific.

The politics of geography was land- as well as sea-based. As navies grew to protect sea-lanes, armies expanded to police new lands. Between 1890 and 1914, military expenditures of Western governments grew phenomenally, with war machines doubling in size. In both its impact on domestic budgets and its protection of markets and trading routes, geopolitics had a strong economic component. Governments became consumers of heavy industry; their predictable participation in markets for armaments and military supplies helped control fluctuations in the business cycle and reduce unemployment at home. A side effect of the growing importance of geopolitics was the increased influence of military and naval leaders in foreign and domestic policy-making.

Nationalism. Many European statesmen in the last quarter of the nineteenth century gave stirring speeches about the importance of empire as a means of enhancing national prestige. In his Crystal Palace speech of 1872, Benjamin Disraeli, British prime minister in 1868 and 1874–80, put the challenge boldly to the British:

> I appeal to the sublime instinct of an ancient people. . . . The issue is not a mean one. It is whether you will be content to be a comfortable England, modelled and moulded upon Continental principles and meeting in

due course an inevitable fate, or whether you will be a great country, an imperial country, a country where your sons, when they rise, rise to paramount positions and obtain not merely the esteem of their countrymen but command the respect of the world.

National prestige was not an absolute value but one weighed relatively. Possessing an empire may have meant "keeping up with the Joneses," as it did for smaller countries like Italy. Imperial status was important to a country like Portugal, which was willing to go bankrupt to maintain its territories. But prestige without economic power was the form of imperialism without its substance. Nation-states could, through the acquisition of overseas territories, gain bargaining chips to be played at the international conference table. In this way, smaller nations hoped to be taken seriously in the system of alliances that preserved "the balance of power" in Europe.

Western newspapers deliberately fostered the desire for the advancement of national interests. Newspapers competed for readers, and their circulation often de-

Great Britain originally opposed construction of the Suez Canal but soon recognized its crucial role in the route to India. In this cartoon, The Lion's Share, British Prime Minister Disraeli purchases a controlling interest in the Suez Canal Company from the khedive of Egypt. The British lion in the foreground guards the key to India, the symbol of the canal.

THE LION'S SHARE.

"GARE À QUI LA TOUCHE!"

pended on the passions they aroused. Filled with tales calculated to titillate and entertain, and with advertisements promising miracle cures, newspapers wrested foreign policy from the realm of the specialist and transformed politics into another form of entertainment. The drama and vocabulary of sporting events, whose mass appeal as a leisure activity also dates from this era, were now applied to imperialist politics. Whether it was a rugby match or a territorial conquest, readers backed the "home" team, disdained the opposition, and competed for the thrill of victory. This marked

quite a change for urban dwellers whose grandparents worked the land and did not look beyond the horizon of their home villages. Newspapers forged a national consciousness whereby individuals learned to identify with collective causes they often did not fully comprehend. Some observed what was happening with a critical eye, identifying a deep-seated need in modern men and women for excitement in their otherwise dull and dreary lives.

Information conveyed in newspapers shaped opinion, and opinion, in turn, could influence policy. Lead-

Joseph Chamberlain's speech to the Birmingham Relief Association

Joseph Chamberlain (1836–1914) was an English businessman and statesman and, from 1873 to 1876, the mayor of one of Great Britain's leading industrial cities, Birmingham. He was a national advocate for an expansionist colonial policy as the means of keeping his country strong. On 22 January 1894, with no regard for African people, he spoke before a community group to convince them that British imperialism helped the working class.

Believe me, if in any one of the places [in Africa] to which I have referred any change took place which deprived us of that control and influence of which I have been speaking, the first to suffer would be the working-men of this country. Then, indeed, we should see a distress which would not be temporary, but which would be chronic, and we should find that England was entirely unable to support the enormous population which is now maintained by the aid of her foreign trade. If the working-men of this country understand, as I believe they do—I am one of those who have had good reason through my life to rely upon their intelligence and shrewdness—if they understand their own interests, they will never lend any countenance to the doctrines of those politicians who never lose an opportunity of pouring contempt and abuse upon the brave Englishmen, who, even at this moment, in all parts of the world are carving out new dominions for Britain, and are opening up fresh markets for British commerce, and laying out fresh fields for British labour. [Applause.] If the Little Englanders[i] had their way, not only would they refrain from taking the legitimate opportunities which offer for extending the empire and for securing for us new markets, but I doubt whether they would even take the pains which are necessary to preserve the great

heritage which has come down to us from our ancestors. [Applause.]

When you are told that the British pioneers of civilisation in Africa are filibusters[ii], and when you are asked to call them back, and to leave this great continent to the barbarism and superstition in which it has been steeped for centuries, or to hand over to foreign countries the duty which you are unwilling to undertake, I ask you to consider what would have happened if 100 or 150 years ago your ancestors had taken similar views of their responsibility? Where would be the empire on which now your livelihood depends? We should have been the United Kingdom of Great Britain and Ireland; but those vast dependencies, those hundreds of millions with whom we keep up a mutually beneficial relationship and commerce would have been the subjects of other nations, who would not have been slow to profit by our neglect of our opportunities and obligations. [Applause.]

From Joseph Chamberlain, M.P., *Foreign and Colonial Speeches* (1897).

[i]Britain's anti-imperialists.

[ii]A person engaged in a private military action against a foreign government.

ers had to reckon with this new creation of "public opinion." In a typical instance, French newspaper editors promoted feverish public outcry for conquest of the Congo by pointing out the need to revenge British advances in Egypt. "Colonial fever" in France was so high in the summer of 1882 that French policymakers were pressured to pursue claims in the Congo Basin without adequate assessment or reflection. As a result, the French government evicted Belgians and Portuguese from the northern Congo territory and enforced questionable treaty claims rather than risk public censure for appearing weak and irresolute.

Public opinion was certainly influential, but it also could be manipulated. In Germany, the government often promoted colonial hysteria through the press in order to advance its own political ends. Chancellor Otto von Bismarck used his power over the press to support imperialism and to influence electoral outcomes in 1884. His successors were deft at promoting the "bread and circuses" atmosphere that surrounded colonial expansion in order to direct attention away from social problems at home and to maintain domestic stability.

The printed word was also manipulated in Britain, critics asserted, by business interests during the Boer War (1899–1902) to keep public enthusiasm for the war effort high. J. A. Hobson (1858–1940), a journalist and theorist of imperialism, denounced the "abuse of the press" in his hard-hitting *Psychology of Jingoism* (1901), which appeared while the war was still being waged. Hobson recognized jingoism as the appropriate term for the "inverted patriotism whereby the love of one's own nation is transformed into hatred of another nation, and into the fierce craving to destroy the individual members of that other nation."

Certainly jingoism was not a new phenomenon in 1900, nor was it confined to Britain. Throughout Europe a mass public appeared increasingly willing to support conflict to defend national honor. Xenophobia (hatred of foreigners) melded with nationalism, both nurtured by the mass press, to put new pressures on the determination of foreign policy. Government elites, who formerly had operated behind closed doors far removed from public scrutiny, were now accountable in new ways to faceless masses. Even in autocratic states like Austria-Hungary, the opinion of the masses was a powerful political force that could destroy individual careers and dissolve governments.

Every nation in Europe had its jingoes, those willing to risk war for national glory. Significantly, the term *jingo* was coined in 1878 during a British showdown with the Russians over Turkey. The sentiment that "the Russians shall not have Constantinople" was so strong that the acceptability of war was set to music:

> We don't want to fight,
> But, by Jingo, if we do,
> We've got the men,
> We've got the ships,
> We've got the money too.

This was the most popular music-hall song in Britain that year, and long after the crisis had faded the tune and its lyrics lingered.

To varying degrees, all of these factors—economics, geopolitics, and nationalism—motivated the actions of the three great imperialist powers—Britain, France, and Germany—and their less-powerful European neighbors. The same reasons account for the global aspirations of non-European nations like the United States and Japan. Each of the powers was aware of what the others were doing and tailored its actions accordingly. Imperialism followed a variety of patterns but always had a built-in component of emulation and acceleration. It was both a cause and a proof of a world system of states in which the actions of one nation affected the others.

The European search for Territory and Markets

Most western Europeans who read about the distant regions that their armies and statesmen were bringing under their national flags tended to regard these new territories as no more than entries on a great tally sheet or as colors on a map. The daily press recorded the numbers of square miles gained and the captive populations taken, and for readers that was often the end of the story. Few Europeans looked on imperialism as a relationship of power between two parties and, like all relationships, one influenced by both partners. Fewer still understood or appreciated the distinctive qualities of the conquered peoples.

The areas European imperialism affected varied widely in their political organization. Throughout Africa, states were generally small or even nonexistent, and Europeans considered their governmental institutions too ineffectual to produce the economic changes and growth of trade Europe wanted. Military takeover and direct rule by European officials seemed the only feasible way to establish empire there. In Asia, on the other hand, societies such as China and India were territorially large and possessed efficient institutions of government dominated by established political hierarchies. Although they were more difficult to conquer, their leaders were also more likely to cooperate with the imperial powers because their own interests were often similar to those of the Westerners. For these reasons, European empire builders pursued a variety of models: formal military empires (as in Africa), informal empires (as in China), or formal but indirect rule over hierarchical societies (as in India).

The scramble for Africa: Diplomacy and conflict

In the mid-1860s, a committee of the British Parliament recommended that Britain withdraw from the scattering of small colonies it possessed in West Africa, arguing that they were costly anachronisms in an era of free trade. In 1898 the president of France, when commenting on French policies of the previous 20 years, remarked, "We have behaved like madmen in Africa, having been led astray by irresponsible people called the 'colonialists.'" The "mad" event that had altered the political landscape in Africa was the so-called "scramble for Africa" that is usually considered as extending from around 1875 to around 1912. By its end, virtually all of Africa was under European control.

Africa is a large and complex continent, and the reasons which Europeans pursued specific pieces of African territory were similarly complex. The explanations for the acquisition of a particular colony, therefore, depend largely on the historical context of that particular case. In certain areas, such as the West African desert zones of the Sudan and the Sahara, ambitious French military men sought to advance their careers by carving out grand colonies.

The existence of valuable minerals motivated the scramble for the area now called Zimbabwe, the Zambian-Zairian copper belt, and other areas. Along the West African coast, chronic disputes between traders working in a souring economy seemed to demand European annexation. Some colonies, such as those in what are now Uganda and Malawi, were created to please missionaries already working there. Britain took Egypt and France took Djibouti for strategic reasons. And in Mozambique, Tanzania, Namibia, and Botswana, some Europeans seized areas to keep other Europeans from doing the same.

Yet there were also basic underlying historical factors favoring the scramble as a whole. One was the rapid development in Europe after 1870 of pseudosci-

British General Horatio H. Kitchener (1850–1916) *reviewing the troops. Kitchener, who served in colonial theaters from India to Africa, personified nineteenth-century British imperial expansion.*

entific racist ideas asserting that Europeans were a superior race and that Africans were inferior. The writings of Charles Darwin were critical in gaining broad popular acceptance for the concept of a racial hierarchy governed by natural laws and operating within an evolutionist dynamic. This was not merely because Darwin's *Origin of Species* (1859) and *The Descent of Man* (1871) "scientifically" legitimated the concept of evolution, but also because he himself explicitly suggested its applicability to humanity. His suggestion was quickly taken up by intellectuals such as Herbert Spencer (1820–1903) and subsequently popularized as social Darwinism. According to this notion, the various racial groups not only occupied distinct positions in a staged sequence of "development" over time, with whites the most advanced and blacks the least so, but were also engaged in a natural conflict or struggle with one another. Social Darwinism's strongest message was that the fittest were destined to prevail, an idea especially welcome to racists of the later nineteenth century because it could be used to justify as "natural" the imperial expansion upon which they were then embarked.

A second underlying historical factor was the atmosphere created by an economic downturn in Europe that lasted from 1873 until 1896. This downturn, coupled with Germany's rapid rise to economic power during the second phase of the Industrial Revolution in the 1870s and 1880s, was deeply unsettling to many Europeans.

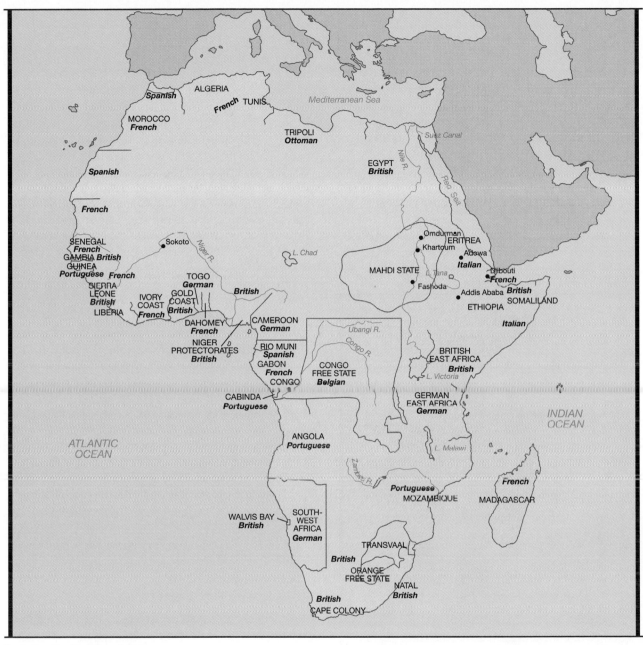

Beginning the Partition of Africa

Protectionist policies springing from new economic anxieties eroded the earlier European faith in free trade. Many Europeans favored acquiring African territory just in case it should turn out to be economically useful. Even Britain, long the major champion of free trade, became ever more protectionist and imperialistic as the century neared its end.

Historians generally agree that the person who provided the catalyst for the scramble was Leopold II, king of Belgium (1835–1909). Sheer greed motivated Leopold. In early 1876 he had read a report about the Congo Basin that claimed it was "mostly a magnificent and healthy country of unspeakable richness" that promised within "30 to 16 months [to] begin to repay any enterprising capitalist." Leopold, an ambitious and frustrated king ruling over a small country, went to work at once to acquire the Congo Basin, an area one-third the size of the United States. Cloaking himself in the mantle of philanthropy and asserting that all he desired was to stamp out the remnants of the East African slave trade, in late 1876 Leopold organized the International African Association. Leopold II's association soon established trading stations on the region's rivers and coerced much valuable ivory from the people.

Leopold skillfully lobbied in Europe for formal recognition of his association's right to rule the Congo Basin. This action provoked objections from France and

A contemporary cartoon characterized King Leopold of the Belgians as a monstrous snake crushing the life out of the black population of the Congo Free State. The territory was under the personal rule of the Belgian king from 1885 to 1908.

IN THE RUBBER COILS.

Portugal, and, after much diplomatic wrangling, an international conference was finally held in Berlin in late 1884 to decide who should rule the Congo. The Berlin Conference was important, not only because it yielded the Congo Basin to Leopold as the Congo Free State, but also because it laid down the ground rules for all other colonial acquisitions in Africa. For international recognition of a claim, "effective occupation" would be required. This meant that no longer would planting a flag in an area be considered adequate for establishing sovereignty; instead, a real presence calculated to produce "economic development" would be needed. If Leopold's actions began the scramble by panicking the European states, the Berlin Conference organized it. However, it is clear in retrospect that the scramble would have occurred even without Leopold II's greedy intervention.

In their disputes over apportioning Africa, the Europeans were remarkably pacific. Although Britain threatened Portugal with war in 1890 in a conflict over the area around Lake Malawi, and although it appeared for a while that Britain and France were headed toward armed conflict in 1898 at Fashoda, in a dispute over the Nile headwaters, peaceful diplomatic settlements that satisfied the imperial powers were always worked out. Deals where states traded territory were common, and peace was maintained. Africa was not worth a war to Europeans. Yet in every instance of expansion in Africa, Europeans were ready to shoot Africans. With Hiram Maxim's invention in 1884 of a machine gun that could fire 11 bullets per second, and with the sale of modern weapons to Africans banned by the Brussels Convention of 1890, the military advantage passed overwhelmingly to the imperialists. As the British poet Hillaire Belloc tellingly observed,

> Whatever happens, we have got
> The Maxim gun, and they have not.

The conquest of "them" became more like hunting than warfare. In 1893, for example, in Zimbabwe, 50 Europeans, using only six machine guns, killed 3000 Ndebele people in under two hours. In 1897, in northern Nigeria, a force of 32 Europeans and 500 African mercenaries defeated the 31,000-man army of the emir of Sokoto. The nature of such warfare is well summed up in a report by Winston Churchill about the battle at Omdurman, in the Sudan, in 1898:

> The [British] infantry fired steadily and stolidly, without hurry or excitement, for the enemy were far away and

the officers careful. Besides the soldiers were interested in the work and took great pains. . . . And all the time out on the plain on the other side bullets were shearing through flesh, smashing and splintering bone: blood spouted from terrible wounds; valiant men were struggling on through a hell of whistling metal, exploding shells, and spurting dust—suffering, despairing, and dying.

After five hours of fighting, the number killed were 20 Britons, 20 Egyptian allies, and over 11,000 Sudanese. Technology had made bravery and courage obsolete for the majority of Africans.

The sole exception to the general rule of easy conquest was Ethiopia. The history of this country illustrates the overriding importance of guns in understanding the essential dynamic of the scramble. In the middle of the nineteenth century, the emperor of Ethiopia possessed little more than a grand title. The empire had broken down into its ethnic and regional components, each of which was fueled by its own "big men," local rulers with little regard for the emperor. Yet the dream of a united empire was alive and pursued by the emperors of the time, Amharic-speaking "big men" with their political base on the fertile plateau that constituted the heartland of the country. In their campaigns to rebuild the empire, they relied increasingly on modern weapons imported from Europe. Their work went forward with some success.

By the early 1870s, however, the emperor realized that his accomplishments in re-creating the Ethiopian empire were endangered by the resistance of the people whom he was then trying to force into his empire and, more ominously, by interference from the outside world, especially Egypt to the north and the Sudan to the west. An expansionary Egypt actually invaded Ethiopian territory, and it was only the Egyptian government's bankruptcy in 1876 that gave the emperor breathing room. The opening of the Suez Canal in 1869 had made the Red Sea and its surroundings attractive not only to Egypt but also to European countries eager to ensure their trade routes to Asia. By the end of the 1870s, when the scramble for Africa was getting seriously under way, Britain, France, and Italy were all contemplating acquiring land in the region. Soon thereafter, Britain occupied Egypt (1882), France took Djibouti (1884), and Italy seized Eritrea (1885).

The Ethiopian emperor, Menelik II (1889–1913), realized that he could exploit rival European interests in the area by playing off one European power against the

others to obtain the weapons he needed for expanding his empire's boundaries. Thus he gave certain concessions to France in return for French weapons. Italy, upset by the growing French influence in Ethiopia, offered weapons as well, and Menelik accepted them. Russia and Britain joined in. More and more modern weapons flowed into Ethiopia during the 1870s and 1880s and into the early 1890s, and Menelik steadily strengthened his military position, both to stop internal unrest and to block encroachment from without. Because each European power feared its rivals' influence in Ethiopia, each sold arms to Menelik, and Ethiopia remained largely unaffected by the scramble going on around it.

In the early 1890s, Menelik's stratagems began to unravel. In 1889 he had signed the Treaty of Wichale with Italy, granting it certain concessions in return for more arms shipments. Italy then claimed that Ethiopia had become an Italian protectorate and moved against Menelik when he objected. By 1896 Italy was ready for a major assault on the Ethiopian army. The Italians were heady with confident racism, believing that their forces could defeat the "primitive" Ethiopians with ease. However, General Oreste Baratieri (1841–1901), the commander of the 18,000-man Italian army in Eritrea, was wisely cautious. He understood that modern weapons functioned the same, whether they were fired by Africans or by Italians. Baratieri knew that Menelik's army of some 100,000 troops had very long supply lines, and his strategy was to wait until Menelik could no longer supply his troops with food. Then, he assumed, the soldiers would simply disappear and the Italians would walk in. But the prime minister of Italy, Francesco Crispi (1819–1901), wanted a quick, glorious victory to enhance his political reputation. Crispi ordered Baratieri to send his army of 18,000 men into battle at once. Hopelessly outnumbered, the Italians lost over 8000 at the decisive battle of Adowa on 1 March 1896. With its army destroyed and its artillery lost to the Ethiopians, Italy had no choice but to sue for peace.

Italy's acceptance of Ethiopia as a sovereign state with greatly expanded imperial boundaries was soon ratified by France and Britain. As a consequence of its victory at Adowa—and attesting to the crucial importance of modern weaponry for survival in late-nineteenth-century Africa—Ethiopia was the only African country aside from the United States' quasi-colony of Liberia not to be occupied in the scramble for Africa. After 1896 Menelik, with his access to modern weapons assured by his country's international recognition, continued his campaign to extend his control forcefully over the Ethiopian empire's subordinate peoples.

Gold, Empire-Building, and the Boer War

Europeans fought white African settlers as well as black Africans during the scramble, as they seized their lands and resources. In South Africa, for example, the British engaged in a long war over access to the world's largest supply of gold with a group of "Afrikaners"—white settlers who had emigrated, mostly from the Netherlands, and settled in South Africa during the eighteenth and early nineteenth centuries.

After the Great Trek (1837–44), in which a large number of Afrikaners had withdrawn from the British-controlled Colony of the Cape of Good Hope (or Cape Colony), the British had grudgingly recognized the independence of the Orange Free State and the Transvaal—the Afrikaner republics in the interior—in a series of formal agreements. The British complacently believed that the Afrikaners, economically weak and geographically isolated, could never challenge British preeminence in the region. Two events of the mid-1880s shattered British complacency. First, in 1884, Germany—Britain's greatest rival—inserted itself into the region by annexing Namibia as a colony as part of its imperial adventures. The British, aware that the Germans and the Afrikaners were as sympathetic to one another as both were hostile to them, worried about the German threat to their regional hegemony and economic prospects.

British fear of the Germans redoubled in 1886 when, in the Witwatersrand area of the Transvaal Republic, huge deposits of gold were discovered. A group of rich British diamond-mine owners moved in quickly to develop the gold mines in the Witwatersrand area, for the gold lay deep in the ground and could be mined only with a large capital investment, which the Afrikaners lacked. The best known of the British investors was Cecil Rhodes (1853–1902), a politician and financier intent upon expanding his wealth through an expansion of British power. Rhodes and his colleagues quickly recognized that Afrikaner governmental policies on agriculture, tariffs, and labor control were major impediments to profitable gold production. Therefore, in 1895, with the connivance of members of the British government, they organized an attempt to overthrow the Afrikaner government. This attempt was led by Dr. L. S. Jameson (1853–1917), Rhodes's lieutenant. It involved the invasion of Transvaal by British South African police and

THE RHODES COLOSSUS
STRIDING FROM CAPE TOWN TO CAIRO.

This cartoon shows Cecil Rhodes astride the continent of Africa like a colossus, fulfilling his dream of a British Africa from the Cape to Cairo.

came to be known as the Jameson Raid. It was faultily executed, however, and to Rhodes's utter humiliation, it failed.

The failure of the Jameson raiders prompted the British government to send a new agent, Alfred Milner (1854–1925), to the area. He was an ardent advocate of expanding the British Empire and of keeping German influence in the region to a minimum. Well aware of the importance of gold to Britain's financial position in the world, Milner was determined to push the Afrikaners into uniting with the British in South Africa, either through diplomacy or war. By 1899 war had become inevitable, and in October it broke out. The British confidently expected to win the war by Christmas, but the Afrikaners did not cooperate. Inept British commanders opposed by skillful Afrikaner guerrilla-warfare leaders guaranteed that the so-called Boer War would drag on and on. (See "African Political Heroes and Resistance to the Scramble," pp. 864–865.)

The British eventually sent 350,000 troops to South Africa, but these forces could not decisively defeat the

65,000 Afrikaner fighting men. Casualties were high, not merely from the fighting, but because typhus epidemics broke out in the concentration camps in which the British interred Afrikaner women and children as they pursued their scorched-earth policies. By the war's end in April 1902, 25,000 Afrikaners, 22,000 British imperial troops, and 12,000 Africans had died. Britain had also been widely criticized for having treated white Afrikaners as if they were black Africans.

In April 1902, the British accepted the conditional surrender of the Afrikaners. The British annexed the Afrikaners to the empire and had the opportunity of making the gold industry efficient. However, they had to promise the Afrikaners that no decisions regarding the political role of the black African majority in a future South Africa would be made before returning political power to the Afrikaners. This crucial concession ensured that segregation would remain the model for race relations in South Africa throughout the twentieth century.

By the time World War I broke out in 1914, the scramble for Africa was over and the map of the continent was colored in imperial inks. France had secured the largest chunk of the continent—some 4 million square miles—but it was mostly desert and tropical forest. Britain had the second-largest empire, but it was richer in minerals and agricultural potential than France's. Germany was the proud possessor of two West African colonies, Togo and Cameroon, as well as Namibia and Tanganyika. Belgium had inherited Leopold II's Congo in 1908. Portugal had finally consolidated its feeble hold on Angola, Mozambique, and Portuguese Guinea. Italy and Spain held unimportant bits

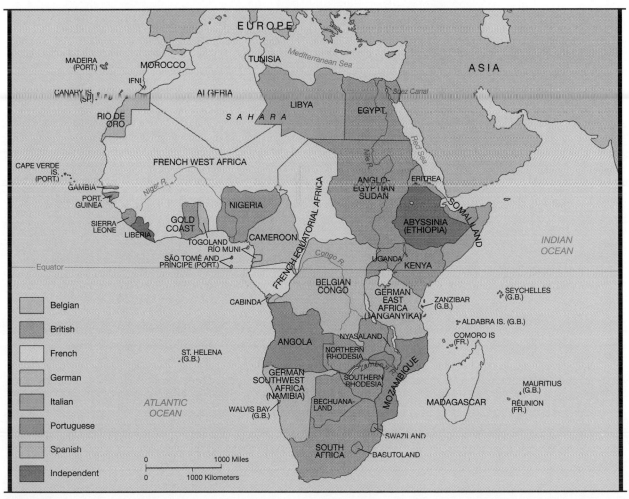

Africa, 1914

african political Heroes and Resistance to the scramble

Often a country's political heroes are its generals and kings, its presidents and states-men—men of power and accomplishment. Paintings and photographs of them empha-size grandeur and majesty, reflecting their larger-than-life importance. Two of the political heroes of contemporary Zimbabwe are very different, however. One is a short, aging woman of about 60 whose name is Nehanda. The other is a short middle-aged man of about 45 called Kagubi. Both appear undistinguished: scruffy, unkempt, and barefoot. Yet both were executed on 27 April 1898 and buried with utmost secrecy. And although they died almost a century ago, their memory is alive in Zimbabwe and stu-dents are taught about them in history books. Why?

In 1889 Cecil Rhodes, the South African financier and politician, convinced that large deposits of gold existed in Zimbabwe, persuaded the British government to support his efforts to seize Zimbabwe and Zambia. He established a private chartered company known as the British South Africa Company (BSAC) and in 1890 invaded the eastern part of Zimbabwe. The people who lived there were Shona people, and conquering them seemed easy because they were politically fragmented into myriad little states with nei-ther strong chiefs nor a military tradition. So easy was the conquest, indeed, that the settlers came to view the Shona with utter contempt.

One of the frequently stated purposes of European imperialism during the scramble for Africa was to carry "civilization" to the "primitive" peoples of Africa—to "bear the White Man's burden" so that the people could improve their lives. For the Shona, how-ever, Rhodes's agents displayed little perceptible civilization and much to be lamented. The Shona soon had a mass of grievances against the BSAC. Some of their land had been taken. They were forced to work for the settlers for little or no pay. They were com-pelled to pay taxes. Europeans took Shona women as concubines. Shona grievances grew steadily. Then, in 1896, their cattle herds were almost wiped out by a new disease, rinderpest, which the Italians who were occupying Eritrea had accidentally imported into Africa in the late 1880s and which was spreading southward. This seemed the last straw.

The Shona got the chance to make their complaints felt. At the end of 1895, most of the BSAC police force had gone over the border into the Transvaal to participate in the Jameson Raid on the Afrikaner state, and in 1896 they were still languishing in jail. With few police around, the Shona reasoned, the time was ripe for revolt against the BSAC. In June, the Shona rose in rebellion, and 100 settlers were slain before the government knew what was occurring.

The BSAC could not believe that the disorganized Shona for whom they had such con-tempt were capable of such an uprising. But despite their lack of chiefs or a military tra-dition, they were. And when the company's officials investigated more closely, they were astounded to discover that the uprising, which came to be known as the *chimurenga*, was being organized and directed by the Shona religious leaders known as mediums. These were people who became possessed by spirits of Shona ancestors and articulated what the ancestors wanted the living to do. These people—obscure and seemingly unthreatening—were able not only to mobilize the attack on the company, but, because of their very lack of notoriety in British eyes, to sustain it by spying on the company, distributing intelligence regarding company troop movements, and relaying messages across Shona country.

The result of the work of the spirit mediums was that the BSAC was unable to conquer the Shona quickly. The effort against the guerrilla war waged by the Shona took over 15 months, almost bankrupting the company. Only in October 1897 did the company track down the leader of the rebellion, Kagubi, and his colleagues, including the important Nehanda. By then, however, the uprising had attracted so much negative publicity in Britain that the company was brought under greater control by the British government. Many of the abuses that had provoked the Shona to rebel were forbidden, and greater regularity in administration was instituted. The Shona had demonstrated to the company that there was a point beyond which the British could not go.

Seven decades later, in the 1970s, the African people again rose up, this time against the white government of Ian Smith, political heir to Cecil Rhodes, and this time successfully. They called their rebellion the "second *chimurenga*." When they finally won, the Africans needed a new group of patriotic heroes from their past about whom to teach in independent Zimbabwe's schools. Two of those chosen were Kagubi and Nehanda, scruffy and unkempt to be sure, but remembered as early patriots and martyrs, the memory of whose work against Rhodes was able to travel across the years and inspire Zimbabweans during the 1970s.

of coastal territory. Only Ethiopia and Liberia were politically independent. Now that the colonial powers had
conquered Africa, they had to face the issue of how their
new colonies could be made to pay off. Now that Africa
had been conquered, Africans had to face the issue of
how they might regain their political independence.

imperialism in asia

The British Parliament proclaimed that on New Year's
Day, 1877, Queen Victoria (1837–1901) would add the ti-

*The Boer War and Queen Victoria. This Dutch caricature is from an
album titled "John Bull in Africa," published in 1900. The war aroused
much criticism among the British liberal opposition.*

tle of Empress of India to her many honors. India, the
great jewel in the imperial crown, was a land Victoria
had never seen. The queen's new title, not universally
popular in Britain and unnoticed by most famine-
stricken Indian peasants, in fact changed nothing about
the way the British ruled India. Yet it was more than
merely a symbolic assertion of dominance over a country long controlled by the British.

India was the starting point of all British expansion,
and it stood at the center of British foreign policy. To
protect its sea routes to India and to secure its Indian
markets, Britain acquired territories and carved out concessions all over the world. Devised by Prime Minister
Benjamin Disraeli to flatter an aging monarch, the
new title of empress was really a calculated warning to
Russia—present on India's northern frontier in
Afghanistan—and to France, busily pursuing its own interests in Egypt.

Formal British rule in India began in 1861 with the
appointment of a viceroy, assisted by legislative and executive councils. Both of these bodies included some
Indian representatives. British rule encountered the
four main divisions of the highly stratified Hindu society. At the top were Brahmans—the learned and priestly
class—followed by warriors and rulers, then by farmers
and merchants, and finally by peasants and laborers.
On the outside of Hindu society were the "untouch-
ables"—a fifth division relegated to performing society's most menial tasks. Rather than disrupt this
divisive caste system, the British found it to their advantage to maintain the status quo.

Britain's relationship with India originated in the
seventeenth century, when the British East India Company—a joint-stock venture free of government control—began limited trading in Indian markets. The need
for regulation and protection firmly established British
rule by the end of the eighteenth century. Conquest of
the Punjab in 1849 brought the last independent areas
of India under British control. Throughout this period,
Britain invested considerable overseas capital in India,
and in turn India absorbed one-fifth of the total of
British exports. The market for Indian cotton, for centuries exported to markets in Asia and Europe, collapsed under British tariffs, and India became a ready
market for cheap Lancashire cotton. The British also exploited India's agricultural products, salt, and opium.

At the end of the eighteenth century, the British were
trading English wool and Indian cotton for Chinese tea
and textiles. But Britain's thirst for Chinese tea grew,
while Chinese demand for English and Indian textiles

slackened. Britain discovered that Indian opium could be used to balance the trade deficit created by tea. British merchants and local Chinese officials, especially in the entry port of Canton, began to expand their profitable involvement in a contraband trade in opium. The British East India Company held a monopoly over opium cultivation in Bengal. Opium exports to China mounted phenomenally: from 200 chests in 1729 to 40,000 chests in 1838. By the 1830s, opium was probably Britain's most important crop in world markets. The British prospered as opium was pumped into China at rates faster than tea was flowing out. Chinese buyers began paying for the drug with silver.

Concerned with the sharp rise in opium addiction, the accompanying social problems, and the massive exporting of silver, the Chinese government reacted. As Chinese officials saw it, they were exchanging their precious metal for British poison. Addicts were threatened with the death penalty. In 1839, the Chinese government destroyed British opium in the port of Canton, touching off the so-called Opium War (1839–42). British expeditionary forces blockaded Chinese ports, besieged Canton, and occupied Shanghai. In protecting the rights of British merchants engaged in illegal trading, Great Britain became the first Western nation to use force to impose its economic interests on China. The Treaty of Nanking (1842) initiated a series of unequal treaties between Europeans and the Chinese and set the pattern for exacting large indemnities.

Between 1842 and 1895, China fought five wars with foreigners and lost all of them. Defeat was expensive, as China had to pay costs to the winners. Before the end of the century, Britain, France, Germany, and Japan had managed to establish major territorial advantages in their "spheres of influence," sometimes through negotiation and sometimes through force. By 1912, over 50 major Chinese ports had been handed over to foreign control as "treaty ports." British spheres included Shanghai, the lower Yangzi, and Hong Kong. France maintained special interests in South China. Germany controlled the Shandong peninsula. Japan laid claim to the northeast.

Spheres of influence grew in importance at the beginning of the twentieth century, when foreign investors poured capital into railway lines, which needed treaty protection from competing companies. Railways necessarily furthered foreign encroachment and opened up new territories to the claims of foreigners. As one Chinese official explained it, the railroads were like scissors that threatened to cut China into many pieces. As a re-

A British gunboat, the Nemesis, *fires on Chinese junks during the Opium War. The* Nemesis *was one of the first ironclad warships ever built.*

sult, China lost control of its trade and was totally unable to protect its infant industries. Foreigners established no formal empires in China, but the treaty ports certainly were evidence of both informal rule and indisputable foreign dominance.

Treaty ports were centers of foreign residence and trade, where rules of extraterritoriality applied. This meant that foreigners were exempt from Chinese law enforcement and that, though present on Chinese territory, they could be judged only by officials of their own countries. Extraterritoriality, a privilege not just for diplomats but one shared by every foreign national, implied both a distrust of Chinese legal procedures and a cultural arrogance about the superiority of Western institutions. These arrangements stirred Chinese resentment and contributed considerably to growing antiforeign sentiment.

In order to preserve extraterritoriality and maintain informal empires, the Western powers appointed civilian representatives known as consuls. Often merchants themselves and in the beginning unpaid in their posts, consuls acted as the chieftains of resident merchant communities, judges in all civil and criminal cases, and spokesmen for the commercial interests of the home country. They clearly embodied the commercial intentions of Western governments. Initially they stood outside the diplomatic corps; later they were consigned to its lower ranks. Consuls acted as brokers for commerce and interpreted the international commercial law being forged. Consulates spread beyond China as Western nations used consuls to protect their own interests elsewhere. In Africa, consuls represented the trading concerns of European governments and were instrumental in the transition to formal rule.

The rise of Western influence in China coincided with and benefited from Chinese domestic problems, including dynastic decline, famine, and successive rebellions. The European powers were willing to prop up the crumbling structure for their own ends, but the Boxer Rebellion of 1900 made clear to the Western powers their limited ability to control social unrest in China. The Boxers—peasants so named by Westerners because of the martial rites practiced by their secret society, the Harmonious Fists—rose up against the foreign and Christian exploitation in north China. At the beginning of the summer of 1900, the Boxers—with the concealed encouragement of the Chinese government—killed Europeans and seized the foreign legations in Beijing. An international expeditionary force of 16,000 well-armed Japanese, Russian, British, American, German, French, Austrian, and Italian troops entered Beijing in August to defend the treaty interests of their respective countries. Led by a German general, the international force followed Kaiser Wilhelm II's urging to remember the Huns: "Show no mercy! Take no prisoners!" Systematic plunder and slaughter followed. Beijing was sacked.

Abandoning earlier discussions of partitioning China, the international powers accepted the need for a central Chinese government—even one that had betrayed their interests—that would police a populace plagued by demographic pressures, famine, discrimination against minorities, excessive taxation, exorbitant land rents, and social and economic dislocations created by foreign trade. During the previous year (1899), the United States had asserted its claims in China in the Open Door policy. This policy, formulated by U.S. Secretary of State John Hay, was as much concerned with preserving Chinese sovereignty as it was with establishing equal economic opportunity for foreign competition in Chinese markets. Europeans and Americans

The claims of the Boxer troops to invulnerability were believed by millions of Chinese. In this Chinese print, the Boxer forces use cannons, bayonets, dynamite, and sabers to drive the Western "barbarians" from the Middle Kingdom.

The New Imperialism in Africa and Asia

1837–1844	Great Trek
1839–1842	Opium War
1869	Suez Canal completed
1884	Berlin Conference held to regulate imperialism in Africa
1886	Gold discovered in the Transvaal Republic
1894–1895	Sino-Japanese War
1896	Battle of Adowa
1899–1902	Boer War
1900	Boxer Rebellion
1904–1905	Russo-Japanese War

Results of a European-Dominated world

Europeans fashioned the world in their own image, but in doing so, Western values and Western institutions underwent profound and unintended transformations. Family values were articulated in an imperialist context, and race emerged as a key factor in culture. The discovery of new lands, new cultures, and new peoples altered the ways in which European women and men regarded themselves and viewed their place in the world. With the rise of new contenders for power—the United States and Japan—and growing criticism about the morality of capitalism, the Western world was not as predictable in 1914 as it had appeared to be in 1870.

A world Economy

Imperialism produced an interdependent world economy, with Europe at its center. Industrial and commercial capitalism linked together the world's continents in a communications and transportation network unimaginable in earlier ages. As a result, foreign trade increased from 3 percent of world output in 1800 to 33 percent by 1913. The greatest growth in trade occurred in the period from 1870 to 1914 as raw materials, manufactured products, capital, and men and women were transported across seas and continents by those seeking profits.

wanted to send bankers to China, not gunboats. A stable central government facilitated their aims. By operating within delineated spheres of influence and using established elites to further their own programs, Westerners protected their financial interests without incurring the costs and responsibilities of direct rule.

European nations pursued imperialist endeavors elsewhere in Asia, acquiring territories on China's frontiers and taking over states that had formerly paid tribute to the Chinese empire. The British acquired Hong Kong (1842), Burma (1886), and Kowloon (1898). The Russians took over the Maritime Provinces in 1858. The French made gains in Indochina (Annam and Tonkin) in 1884, and in 1893 extended control over Laos and Cambodia.

The Sino-Japanese War of 1894–95 revealed Japan's intentions to compete as an imperialist power in Asia. The modernized and westernized Japanese army easily defeated the ill-equipped and poorly led Chinese forces. As a result, Japan gained the island of Taiwan. Pressing its ambitions on the continent, Japan locked horns with Russia over claims to the Liaotung peninsula, Korea, and South Manchuria. Following its victory in the Russo-Japanese War of 1904–05, Japan expanded into all of these areas, annexing Korea outright in 1910. The war sent a strong message to the West about the ease with which the small Asian nation had defeated the Russian giant and contributed to the heightening of anti-imperialist sentiments in China.

Most trading in the age of imperialism still took place among European nations and North America. But entrepreneurs in search of new markets and new resources saw in Africa and Asia opportunities for protected exploitation. Opportunities were not seized but created in nonindustrialized areas of the world as new markets were shaped to meet the needs of Western producers and consumers. European landlords and managers trained Kenyan farmers to put aside their traditional agricultural methods and grow more "useful" crops like coffee, tea, and sugar. The availability of cheaper British textiles of inferior quality drove Indian weavers away from their handlooms. Chinese silk producers changed centuries-old techniques to produce silk thread and cloth that was suited to the machinery and mass-production requirements of the French. Non-European producers undoubtedly derived benefits from this new international trading partnership, but those benefits were often scarce. Trade permitted specialization, but at the choice of the colonizer, not the colonized. World production and consumption were being shaped to suit the needs of the West.

Capital in search of profits flowed out of the wealthier areas of Europe into the nonindustrialized regions of Russia, the Balkans, and the Ottoman Empire, where capital-intensive expenditures (on railways, for instance) promised high returns. Capital investment in overseas territories also increased phenomenally as railroads were built to gain access to primary products. Great Britain maintained its overwhelming dominance in overseas investment, with loans abroad greater than those of its five major competitors—France, Germany, Holland, the United States, and Belgium—combined.

The City of London had become the world's banker, serving as the clearinghouse for foreign investment on a global scale. The adoption of gold as the standard for exchange for most European currencies by 1874 further facilitated the operation of a single interdependent trading and investment system. Britain remained the world's biggest trading nation, with half of its exports going to Asia, Africa, and South America and the other half to Europe and the United States. But Germany was Britain's fastest-growing competitor, with twice as many exports to Europe and expanding overseas trade by 1914. The United States had recently joined the league of the world's great trading nations and was running a strong third in shares of total trade.

Foreign investments often took the form of loans to governments or to enterprises guaranteed by governments. Investors might be willing to take risks, but they also expected protection, no less so than merchants and industrialists trading in overseas territories. Together, trade and investment interests exerted considerable pressure on European states for control through acquisition and concessions. The vast amounts of money involved help explain the expectations of state involvement and the reasons why international compe-

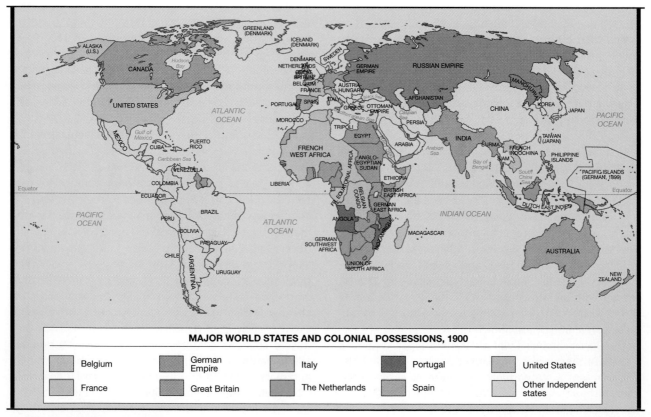

World Colonial Holdings, ca. 1914

A map of the world showing the extent of the British Empire in 1886. The inset in the upper right is a world map showing the extent of the British territories a century earlier.

tition, rivalry, and instability threatened to lead to conflict and war

Race and Culture

The West's ability to kill and conquer as well as to cure was, as one Victorian social observer argued, proof of its cultural superiority. Every colonizing nation had its spokesmen for the "civilizing mission" to educate and to convert African and Asian "heathens." Cultural superiority was only a short step from arguments for racial superiority. Prompted by the U.S. involvement in the Philippines, the British poet Rudyard Kipling (1865–1936) characterized the responsibilities of the advanced West as "the White Man's burden." The smug and arrogant attitude of his poem about the white man's mission revealed a deep-seated and unacknowledged racism toward peoples considered "half-devil and half-child."

Views of cultural superiority received support from evolutionary theories based on the scientific work of Herbert Spencer (1820–1903) and Charles Darwin. In the 1880s, popularizers applied evolutionary ideas about animal and plant life to the development of human society. Just as animals could be hierarchically organized according to observable differences, so too, it was ar-

gued, could the different races of human beings. Race and culture were collapsed into each other. If Westerners were culturally superior, as they claimed, they must be racially superior as well. The "survival of the fittest" came to justify conquest and subjugation as "laws" of human interaction and, by extension, of relations among nations.

Women and Imperialism

Ideas about racial and cultural superiority were not confined to books by pseudoscientists and to discussions among policymakers. Public discussions about marriage, reproduction, motherhood, and child-rearing reflected new concerns about furthering "the imperial race"—the racial identity of white Westerners. Women throughout Western societies were encouraged by reformers, politicians, and doctors to have more children and instructed to take better care of them. "Children are the most valuable of imperial assets," one British doctor instructed his readers. Healthy young men were needed in the colonies, they were told, to defend Western values. State officials paid new attention to infant mortality at the end of the nineteenth century, set up health programs for children, and provided young women with training in home management, nutrition, and child care. These programs were no coincidence in an age of imperialism. Their rhetoric was explicitly imperialist and often racist in urging women to preserve the quality of the white race.

In the poem "White Man's Burden," Kipling advised, "Send forth the best ye breed." All over Europe, newly formed associations and clubs stressed the need for careful mate selection. In Britain, Francis Galton (1822–1911) founded eugenics, the study of genetics for the purpose of improving inherited characteristics of the race. Imperialism, the propagandists proclaimed, depended on mothers—women who would nurture healthy workers, strong soldiers and sailors, and intelligent and capable leaders. High infant mortality and poor health in children were attributed directly to maternal failings and not to environmental factors or poverty. Kaiser Wilhelm II stressed that German women's attention to the "three Ks"—*Kinder, Küche, Kirche* (children, kitchen, church)—would guarantee a race of Germans who would rule the world. British generals and French statesmen publicly applied similar sentiments to their own countries and stressed that the future depended on the devotion of women to their family obligations.

Some European women participated directly in the colonizing experience. As missionaries and nurses, they supported the civilizing mission. As wives of officials and managers, they were expected to embody the gentility and values of Western culture. Most men who traded and served overseas did so unaccompanied by women. But when women were present in any numbers, as they were in India before 1914, they were expected to preserve the exclusivity of Western communities and to maintain class and status differentiations as a proof of cultural superiority.

ecology and imperialism

Ecology—the relationship and adjustment of human groups to their environment—was affected by imperial expansion, which dislocated the societies that it touched. Early explorers had disrupted little as they arrived, observed, and then moved on. The missionaries, merchants, soldiers, and businessmen who came later required that those with whom they came into contact must change their thought and behavior. In some cases, dislocation resulted in material improvements, better medical care, and the introduction of modern technology. For the most part, however, the initial ecological impact of the imperialist was negative. Western men and women carried diseases to people who did not share the Westerners' immunity. Traditional village life was destroyed in rural India, and African tribal societies

A British family in India poses with their domestic staff in front of their bungalow. An 1878 handbook on upper-class life in India recommended 27 servants per family.

disintegrated under the European onslaught. Resistance existed everywhere, but only the Ethiopians, with their defeat of the Italians at Adowa in 1896, managed to have any success in keeping out foreigners.

Education of native populations had as its primary goal the improvement of administration and productivity in the colonies. When foreigners ruled indirectly through existing indigenous hierarchies, they often created corrupt and tyrannical bureaucracies that exploited natives. The indirect rule of the British in India was based on a pragmatic desire to keep British costs low.

When Asian and African laborers started producing for the Western market, they became dependent on its fluctuations. Victimized for centuries by the vagaries of weather, they now had to contend with the instability and cutthroat competition of cash crops in world markets. Individuals migrated from place to place in the countryside and from the countryside to newly formed cities. The fabric of tribal life unraveled. Such migrations necessarily affected family life, with individuals marrying later because they lacked the resources to set up households. The situation paralleled similar disruptions in English society at the beginning of the Industrial Revolution. Women as well as men migrated to find jobs. Many women, cut free of their tribes (as was the case in Nairobi) turned to prostitution—literally for pennies—as a means of survival.

In an extreme example of the colonizers' disdain for the colonized, some European countries used their overseas territories as dumping grounds for hardened and incorrigible convicted criminals. Imitating the earlier example of the British in Australia, the French developed Guiana and New Caledonia as prison colonies in the hope that they could solve their social problems at home by exporting them.

The United States provided another variation on imperial expansion. Its westward drive across the North American continent, beginning at the end of the eighteenth century, established the United States as an imperial power in the Western Hemisphere. By 1848, the relatively young American nation stretched over 3000 miles from one ocean to the other. It had met the opposition and resistance of the Native Americans with armed force, decimated them, and "concentrated" the survivors in assigned territories, and later on reservations.

At the end of the nineteenth century, the United States, possessing both the people and the resources for rapid industrial development, turned to the Caribbean and the Pacific islands in pursuit of markets and investment opportunities. By acquiring stepping stones of islands across the Pacific Ocean in the Hawaiian Islands and Samoa, it secured fueling bases and access to lucrative east Asian ports. And by intervening repeatedly in Central America and building the Panama Canal, the United States had established its hegemony in the Caribbean by 1914. Growing in economic power and hegemonic influence, both Japan and the United States had joined the club of imperial powers and were making serious claims against European expansion.

critiquing capitalism

Not least significant of the consequences of imperialism was the critique of capitalism it produced. Those

French convicts embarking for the penal colony at Guiana, 1903. The penal colony included the notorious Devil's Island, where many prisoners died and from which few managed to escape. If a prisoner was sentenced to a term of less than eight years, he had to spend an equal period of time in Guiana; if his sentence was more than eight years, he had to remain in the colony permanently. After 1885, only criminals with sentences of more than eight years were sent to Devil's Island.

Karl pearson

The following is an excerpt from a lecture titled "National Life from the Standpoint of Science," given by a British professor of mathematics, Karl Pearson (1857–1936), in 1900. Pearson held the first chair in eugenics at the University of London, where he applied statistical methods to the study of heredity and evolution. The term eugenics was introduced by Francis Galton, of whom Pearson was a follower. Pearson was heavily influenced by the pseudoscientific assumptions of social Darwinism and combined prejudices about race and nationalism to justify British imperialism as a proof of "survival of the fittest."

The . . . great function of science in national life . . . is to show us what national life means, and how the nation is a vast organism subject as much to the great forces of evolution as any other gregarious type of life. There is a struggle of race against race and of nation against nation. In the early days of that struggle it was a blind, unconscious struggle of barbaric tribes. At the present day, in the case of the civilized white man, it has become more and more the conscious, carefully directed attempt of the nation to fit itself to a continuously changing environment. The nation has to foresee how and where the struggle will be carried on; the maintenance of national position is becoming more and more a conscious preparation for changing conditions, an insight into the needs of coming environments. . . .

If a nation is to maintain its position in this struggle, it must be fully provided with trained brains in every department of national activity, from the government to the factory, and have, if possible, *a reserve of brain and physique* to fall back upon in times of national crisis. . . .

You will see that my view—and I think it may be called the scientific view of a nation—is that of an organized whole, kept up to a high pitch of internal efficiency by insuring that its numbers are substantially recruited from the better stocks, and kept up to a high pitch of external efficiency by contest, chiefly by way of war with inferior races, and with equal races by the struggle for trade-routes and for the sources of raw material and of food supply. This is the natural history view of mankind, and I do not think you can in its main features subvert it. . . .

Is it not a fact that the daily bread of our millions of workers depends on their having somebody to work for? that if we give up the contest for trade-routes and for free markets and for waste lands, we indirectly give up our food supply? Is it not a fact that our strength depends on these and upon our colonies, and that our colonies have been won by the ejection of inferior races, and are maintained against equal races only by respect for the present power of our empire? . . .

We find that the law of the survival of the fitter is true of mankind, but that the struggle is that of the gregarious animal. A community not knit together by strong social instincts, by sympathy between man and man, and class and class, cannot face the external contest, the competition with other nations, by peace or by war, for the raw material of production and for its food supply. This struggle of tribe with tribe, and nation with nation, may have its mournful side; but we see as a result of it the gradual progress of mankind to higher intellectual and physical efficiency. It is idle to condemn it; we can only see that it exists and recognise what we have gained by it—civilization and social sympathy. But while the statesman has to watch this external struggle, . . . he must be very cautious that the nation is not silently rotting at its core. He must insure that the fertility of the inferior stocks is checked, and that of the superior stocks encouraged; he must regard with suspicion anything that tempts the physically and mentally fitter men and women to remain childless.

From Karl Pearson, *National Life from the Standpoint of Science* (1905).

who condemned capitalism as exploitative and racist saw imperialism as an expression of problems inherent in it. In 1902 J. A. Hobson (1858–1940) published *Imperialism, A Study*, a work that has remained in print ever since. In his book, Hobson argued that underconsumption and surplus capital at home drove Western industrial countries overseas in search of a cure for these economic ills. Rather than solving the problems by raising workers' wages, and thereby increasing their consumption power and creating new opportunities for investment in home markets, manufacturers, entrepreneurs, and industrialists sought higher profits abroad. Hobson considered these business interests "economic parasites," making large fortunes at the expense of national interests.

In the midst of world war, the future leader of the Russian Revolution, Vladimir Ilich Ulyanov (1870–1924)—or to use his revolutionary name, Lenin—added his own critique of capitalism. He did not share Hobson's belief that capitalism was merely malfunctioning in its imperialist endeavors. Instead, Lenin argued in *Imperialism, the Highest Stage of Capitalism* (1916) that capitalism is inherently and inevitably imperialistic. Because he was sure that Western capitalism was in the process of destroying itself, Lenin called World War I the final "imperialist war."

Critics, historians, and economists have since pointed out that these works by Hobson and Lenin are marred by errors and omissions. Yet the works usher in almost a century of debate over the morality and economic feasibility of imperialism. Hobson as a liberal and Lenin as a Marxist highlighted the connections between social problems at home—whether in late Victorian England or in prerevolutionary Russia—and economic exploitation abroad.

Yet if electoral results and the popular press are any indication, Europeans not only accepted but warmly embraced the responsibilities of empire. Criticism of the backwardness of captive peoples prevailed. Victorian social scientist Walter Bagehot (1826–77) told the story of an aged savage who, upon returning to his tribe, informed them that he had "tried civilization for forty years and it was not worth the trouble." No matter how intelligent the judgment of this African might seem with hindsight, the possibility of returning to areas of the world not influenced by the civilization of the West was rapidly disappearing in the years before World War I.

conflict at Home: The European Balance of power

In addition to mounting conflicts in colonized areas, European states were locked in a competition within Europe for dominance and control. The politics of geography combined with rising nationalist movements in southern Europe and the Ottoman Empire to create a mood of increasing confrontation among Europe's great powers. The European balance of power so carefully crafted by Germany's Otto von Bismarck began to disintegrate with his departure from office in 1890. By 1914 a Europe divided into two camps was no longer the sure guarantee of peace that it had been a generation earlier.

The Geopolitics of Europe

The map of Europe had been redrawn in the two decades after 1850. By 1871 Europe consisted of five great powers, known as the Big Five—Britain, France, Germany, Austria-Hungary, and Russia—and a handful of lesser states. The declaration of a German Empire in 1871 and the emergence of Italy, with Rome as its capital, in 1870 unified numerous disparate states. Although not always corresponding to linguistic and cultural differences among Europe's peoples, national boundaries appeared fixed, with no country aspiring to territorial expansion at the expense of its neighbors. But the creation of the two new national units of Germany and Italy had legitimized nationalist aspirations and the militarism necessary to enforce them.

Under the chancellorship of Otto von Bismarck, Germany led the way in forging a new alliance system based on the realistic assessment of power politics within Europe. In 1873 Bismarck joined together the three most conservative powers of the Big Five—Germany, Austria-Hungary, and Russia—into the Three Emperors' League. Consultation over mutual interests and friendly neutrality were the cornerstones of this alliance. Identifying one's enemies and choosing one's friends in this new configuration of power came in large part to depend on geographic weaknesses. The Three Emperors' League was one example of the geographic imperatives driving diplomacy. Bismarck was determined to banish the specter of a two-front war by isolating France on the Continent.

Each of the Great Powers had a vulnerability, a geographic Achilles' heel. Germany's vulnerability lay in its North Sea ports. German shipping along its only coast could easily be bottlenecked by a powerful naval force. Such an event, the Germans knew, could destroy their rapidly growing international trade. What was worse, powerful land forces could "encircle" Germany. As Britain's century-old factories slowly became obsolete under peeling coats of paint, Germany enjoyed the advantages of a latecomer to industrialization—forced to start from scratch by investing in the most advanced machinery and technology. The German Reich was willing to support industrial expansion, scientific and technological training, and social programs for its workers. Yet as Germany surged forward to seize its share of world markets, it was acutely aware that it was hemmed in on the Continent. Germany could not extend its frontiers the way Russia had to the east. German gains in the Franco-Prussian War in Alsace and Lorraine could not be repeated without risking greater enmity. German leaders saw the threat of encirclement as a second geographic weakness. Bismarck's awareness of these geographic facts of life prompted his engineering of the Three Emperors' League in 1873, two years after the founding of the German Empire.

Austria-Hungary was Europe's second largest nation in land and the third largest in population. The same factors that had made it a great European power—its size and its diversity—now threatened to destroy it. The ramshackle empire of Europe, it had no geographical unity. Its vulnerability came from within, from the centrifugal forces of linguistic and cultural diversity. Weakened by nationalities clamoring for independence and self-rule and by an unresponsive political system, Austria-Hungary remained backward agriculturally and unable to respond to the Western industrial challenge. It seemed most likely to collapse from social and political pressures.

Another feature must be added to the picture of Europe in the late nineteenth century. To the southeast lay the Ottoman Empire, a great decaying conglomeration that bridged Europe and Asia. Politically feeble and on the verge of bankruptcy, the Ottoman Empire, with Turkey at its core, comprised a vast array of ethnically, linguistically, and culturally diverse peoples. In the hundred years before 1914, increasing social unrest and nationalist bids for independence had plagued the Ottoman Empire. As was the case with the Habsburgs in Austria-Hungary, the Ottomans maintained power

THE BOILING POINT.

A *Punch* cartoon shows European leaders trying to keep the lid on the simmering kettle of Balkan crises.

with increasing difficulty over these myriad ethnic groups struggling to be free. The Ottoman Empire, called "the sick man of Europe" by contemporaries, found two kinds of relations sitting at its bedside: those who would do anything to ensure its survival, no matter how weak; and those who longed for and sought to hasten its demise. Fortunately for the Ottoman Empire, its enemies were willing to preserve it in its weakened state rather than see one of the other rival European powers benefit from its collapse.

The Ottomans had already seen parts of their holdings lopped off in the nineteenth century. Britain, ever conscious of its interests in India, had acquired Cyprus, Egypt, Aden, and Sudan from the Ottomans. Germany insinuated itself into Turkish internal affairs and financed the Baghdad Railway in the attempt to link the Mediterranean to the Persian Gulf. Russia acquired territories on the banks of the Caspian Sea and had plans to take Constantinople. But it was the volatile Balkan Peninsula that threatened to upset the European power balance. The Balkans appeared to be a territory that begged for dismemberment. Internally, the Slavs sought independence from their Habsburg and Turkish oppressors. External pressures were equally great, with each of the major powers following its own geopolitical agenda.

The Instability of the Alliance system

The system of alliances formed between and among European states was guided by two realities of geopolitics. The first was the recognition of tension between France and Germany. France had lost its dominance on the Continent in 1870–71, when it was easily defeated by Prussia at the head of a nascent German Empire. With its back to the Atlantic, France faced the smaller states of Belgium, Luxembourg, Switzerland, and Italy and the industrially and militarily powerful Germany. It had suffered the humiliation of losing territory to Germany—Alsace and Lorraine in 1871—and was well aware of its continued vulnerability. Geopolitically, France felt trapped and isolated and in need of powerful friends as a counterweight to German power.

The second reality guiding alliances was Russia's preoccupation with maintaining free access to the Mediterranean Sea. Russia, clearly Europe's greatest landed power, was vulnerable because it could be landlocked by frozen or blockaded ports. The ice that crippled its naval and commercial vessels in the Baltic Sea drove Russia east through Asia to secure another ice-blocked port on the Sea of Japan at Vladivostok in 1860 and to seek ice-free Chinese ports. Russia was equally obsessed with protecting its warm-water ports on the Black Sea. Whoever controlled the strait of the Bosporus controlled Russia's grain export trade, on which its economic prosperity depended. All diplomatic arrangements, especially after the turn of the century, took into account these two geopolitical realities.

Ostensibly, Russia had the most to gain from the extension of its frontiers and the creation of pro-Russian satellites. It saw that by championing Pan-Slavic nationalist groups in southeastern Europe, it could greatly strengthen its own position at the expense of the two great declining empires, Ottoman Turkey and Austria-Hungary. Russia hoped to draw the Slavs into its orbit by fostering the creation of independent states in the Balkans. A Serbian revolt began in two Ottoman provinces, Bosnia and Herzegovina, in 1874. International opinion pressured Turkey to initiate reforms. Serbia declared war on Turkey on 30 June 1876; Mon-

tenegro did the same the next day. Britain, supporting the Ottoman Empire because of its trading interests in the Mediterranean, found itself in a delicate position of perhaps condemning an ally when it received news of Turkish atrocities against Christians in Bulgaria. Prime Minister Disraeli insisted that Britain was bound to defend Constantinople because of British interests in the Suez Canal and India. While Britain stood on the sidelines, Russia, with Romania as an ally, declared war against the Ottoman Empire. The war was quickly over, with Russia capturing all of Armenia, forcing the Ottoman sultan, Abdul Hamid II (1842–1918), to sue for peace on 31 January 1878.

Bismarck, a seemingly disinterested party acting as an "honest broker," hosted the peace conference that met at Berlin. The British succeeded in blocking Russia's intentions for a Bulgarian satellite and keeping the Russians from taking Constantinople. Russia abandoned its support of Serbian nationalism, and Austria-Hungary occupied Bosnia and Herzegovina. The peace concluded at the 1878 Congress of Berlin disregarded Serbian claims, thereby promising continuing conflict over the nationalities question.

The Berlin Congress also marked the emergence of a new estrangement among the Great Powers. Russia felt betrayed by Bismarck and abandoned in its alliance with Germany. Bismarck in turn cemented a Dual Alliance between Austria-Hungary and Germany in 1879 that survived until the collapse of the two imperial regimes in 1918. The Three Emperors' League was renewed in 1881, now with stipulations regarding the division of the spoils in case of a war against Turkey.

In 1882 Italy was asked to join the Dual Alliance with Germany and Austria-Hungary, thus converting it into the Triple Alliance, which prevailed until the Great War of 1914. Germany, under Bismarck's tutelage, signed treaties with Italy, Russia, and Austria-Hungary and established friendly terms with Great Britain. A new Balkan crisis in 1885, however, shattered the illusion of stable relations.

Hostilities erupted between Bulgaria and Serbia. Russia threatened to occupy Bulgaria, but Austria stepped in to prevent Russian domination of the Balkans, thus threatening the alliance of the Three Emperors' League. Russia was further angered by German unwillingness to support its interests against Austrian actions in the Balkans. Germany maintained relations with Russia in a new Reinsurance Treaty drawn up in 1887, which stipulated that each power would maintain

The society for national defense, serbia, 1911

The Society for National Defense (*Narodna Odbrana*) was a secret society formed by Serb nationalists. This group sought the liberation of Slavs through propaganda and subversive activities against Austria-Hungary, which had annexed Bosnia-Herzegovina in 1908. The Society for National Defense was a terrorist group, one of whose members was responsible for the assassination of the Austrian Archduke Ferdinand on 28 June 1914. Here the group spells out its program and speaks of a new kind of nationalism, one that is a "holy cause."

The Serbian people has endured during its existence many difficult and bitter days. Among these days is September 24, 1908, when Austria-Hungary illegally annexed Bosnia and Herzegovina. This day can be compared to the worst days of our past. It was especially painful for the Serbian people in that it came at a time when more fortunate peoples had already completed their national unification and had created large states, and when culture and freedom were presumed to be at their peak.

At such a time Austria-Hungary oppressed along with other peoples several million Serbs, whom she penalizes and seeks to alienate from us. They may not openly call themselves Serbs, and may not adorn their homes with the Serbian flag; they may not trade freely, cultivate their soil, erect Serbian schools, openly celebrate the feast of the patron saint [Slava], and may not sing of Kossowo or of Prince Marko and Milosch Obilitsch. Only such a state, only an Austria-Hungary, could carry through such an annexation. . . .

Today everywhere a new concept of nationalism has become prevalent. Nationalism (the feeling of nationality) is no longer a historical or poetical feeling, but the true practical expression of life. Among the French, Germans, and English, and among all other civilized peoples, nationalism has grown into something quite new; in it lies the concept of bread, space, air, commerce, competition in everything. Only among us is it still in the old form; that is, it is the fruit of spiritual suffering rather than of reasonable understanding and national advantage. If we speak of freedom and union, we parade far too much the phrases "breaking our chains" and "freeing the slaves"; we call far too much upon our former Serbian glory and think too little of the fact that the freeing of subjected areas and their union with Serbia are necessary to our citizens, our merchants, and our peasants on the grounds of the most elementary needs of culture and trade, of food and space. If one were to explain to our sharp-eyed people our national task as one closely connected with the needs of everyday life, our people would take up the work in a greater spirit of sacrifice than is today the case. We must tell our people that the freedom of Bosnia is necessary, not just because of their feeling of sympathy with their brothers who suffer there, but also because of commerce and its connection with the sea; national union is necessary because of the stronger development of a common culture. The Italians welcome the conquest of Tripoli not just because of the glory to be won by the success of their arms, but especially because of the advantage they hope to gain by annexing Tripoli. Our people must adopt a more realistic attitude toward politics. We must show them how we would stand culturally and economically if we were united into one state and were in as favorable a position commercially as that of Timok in relation to the Adriatic. . . .

Along with the task of explaining to our people the danger threatening us from Austria, the *Narodna Odbrana* has also the other important tasks of explaining to them, while preserving our holy national memories, this new, healthy, fruitful conception of nationalism, and of convincing them to work for national freedom and unity. . . .

All in all, the *Narodna Odbrana* aims through its work to advance upon the enemy on the day of reckoning with a sound, nationally conscious, and internally reconciled Serbian people, a nation of Sokols, rifle clubs, heroes—in fact, the fear and terror of the enemy—reliant front-rank fighters and executors of Serbia's holy cause.

If this succeeds, all will be well for us; woe to us if we fail.

neutrality should the other find itself at war. Bismarck now walked a fine line, balancing alliances and selectively disclosing the terms of secret treaties to nonsignatory countries with the goal of preserving the peace. He was described by his successor as the only man who could keep five glass balls in the air at the same time.

After Bismarck's resignation in 1890, Germany found itself unable to juggle all the glass balls. Germany allowed the arrangement with Russia to lapse. Russia, in turn, allied itself in 1894 with France. Also allied with Great Britain, France had broken out of the isolation that Bismarck had intended for it two decades earlier. The Triple Entente came into existence following the Anglo-Russian understanding of 1907. Now it was the Triple Entente of Great Britain, France, and Russia against the Triple Alliance of Germany, Austria-Hungary, and Italy.

There was still every confidence that these two camps could balance each other and preserve the peace. But in 1908–09, the unresolved Balkan problem threatened to topple Europe's precarious peace. Against Russia's objections, Austria-Hungary annexed Bosnia and Herzegovina, the provinces it had occupied since 1878. Russia supported Serbia's discontent over Austrian acquisition of these predominantly Slavic territories that Serbia felt should be united with its own lands. Unwilling to risk a European war at this point, Russia was ultimately forced to back down under German pressure. Germany had to contend with its great geopolitical fear—hostile neighbors, France and Russia, on its western and eastern frontiers.

A third Balkan crisis erupted in 1912 when Italy and Turkey fought over the possession of Tripoli in North Africa. The Balkan states took advantage of this opportunity to increase their holdings at Turkey's expense. This action quickly involved Great Power interests once again. A second war broke out in 1913 over Serbian interests in Bulgaria. Russia backed Serbia against Austro-Hungarian support of Bulgaria. The Russians and Austrians prepared for war while the British and Germans urged peaceful resolution. Although hostilities ceased, Serbian resentment toward Austria-Hungary over its frustrated nationalism was greater than ever. Britain, in its backing of Russia, and Germany, in its support of Austria-Hungary, were enmeshed in alliances that could involve them in a military confrontation.

Great Britain did not share Germany's and Russia's fears of strangulation by blockade. And although the

European crises and the balance of power

1871	German Empire created
1873	Three Emperors' League: Germany, Austria-Hungary, and Russia
1874	First Balkan crisis: Serbian revolt in Bosnia and Herzegovina
1875	Russo-Turkish War
1876	Serbia declares war on Turkey; Montenegro declares war on Turkey
1878	Congress of Berlin
1879	Dual Alliance: Germany and Austria-Hungary
1881	Three Emperors' League renewed
1882	Triple Alliance: Germany, Austria-Hungary, and Italy
1885	Second Balkan crisis: Bulgaria versus Serbia
1887	Reinsurance Treaty between Germany and Russia
1894	Russia concludes alliance with France
1907	Triple Entente: Great Britain, France, and Russia
1908	Austria-Hungary annexes Bosnia and Herzegovina
1912	Third Balkan crisis: Italy versus Turkey
1913	War erupts between Serbia and Bulgaria

question of Irish home rule was a nationalities problem for Britain, it paled in comparison with Austria-Hungary's internal challenge. As an island kingdom, however, Great Britain relied on imports for its survival. The first of the European nations to become an urban and industrial power, Britain was forced to do so at the expense of its agricultural sector. It could not feed its own people without importing foodstuffs. Britain's geographic vulnerability was its dependence on access to its empire and the maintenance of open sea-lanes. Britain saw its greatest menace coming from the rise of other sea powers—notably Germany.

From the very beginning of the competition for territories and concessions, no European state could act in Africa or Asia without affecting the interests and actions of its rivals at home. The African scramble made clear how interlocking the system of European states was after 1870. The development of spheres of influence in China underlined the value of world markets and international trade for the survival and expansion of western nations.

A "balance of power" among states guaranteed national security and independence until the end of the nineteenth century. But between 1870 and 1914, industrialization, technology, and accompanying capital formation created vast economic disparities. Conflict and disequilibrium challenged European stability and balance. Ultimately, it was the politics of geography on the European continent, not confrontations in distant colonies, that polarized the European states into two camps. Despite the unresolved conflicts behind all of these crises, European statesmen prided themselves on their ability to settle disputes through reason and negotiation. That was not to be the case with the last and final Balkan crisis that exploded in the summer of 1914.

mastering the chapter

To review the main points of the chapter, be sure you can explain the significance of each of the following.

Terms/Concepts/Events	People	Places
geopolitics	Benjamin Disraeli	Suez Canal
Boer War	Herbert Spencer	Panama Canal
jingoism	Winston Churchill	Singapore
social Darwinism	Menelik II	Fashoda
battle of Adowa	Afrikaners	Ethiopia
the Great Trek	Cecil Rhodes	Cape Colony
Jameson Raid	Alfred Milner	Ottoman Empire
Opium War	Rudyard Kipling	Balkan Peninsula
consuls	Vladimir Ilich Ulyanov (Lenin)	Bosnia
eugenics		Serbia

suggestions for further reading

The New Imperialism

* Michael W. Doyle, *Empires* (Ithaca, NY: Cornell University Press, 1986). Nineteenth-century imperialism is placed in a broad historical context that emphasizes a comparative perspective of the European imperial experience.

* Daniel R. Headrick, *The Tools of Empire: Technology and European Imperialism in the Nineteenth Century* (New York: Oxford University Press, 1981). By focusing on technological innovations in the nineteenth century, the author demonstrates how Europeans were able to establish control over Asia, Africa, and Oceania rapidly and at little cost.

* Daniel R. Headrick, *The Tentacles of Progress: Technology Transfer in the Age of Imperialism, 1850–1940* (New York: Oxford University Press, 1988). Argues that the transfer of technology to Africa and Asia by the Western imperial powers produced colonial underdevelopment.

The European search for Territory and Markets

* Winfried Baumgart, *Imperialism: The Idea and Reality of British and French Colonial Expansion, 1880–1914* (New York: Oxford University Press, 1982). Principally concerned with the motives that led to imperial expansion, the author argues that motives were many and that each action must be studied in its specific social, political, and economic context.

Raymond F. Betts, *The False Dawn: European Imperialism in the Nineteenth Century* (Oxford: Oxford University Press, 1976). Explores the ideology of empire and the process of cultural transmission through colonial institutions.

* Eric Hobsbawm, *The Age of Empire, 1875–1914* (New York: Pantheon, 1987). A wide-ranging interpretive history of the late nineteenth century that spans economic, social, political, and cultural developments.

Thomas Pakenham, *The Scramble for Africa* (New York: Random House, 1991). A narrative history of how Europeans subdivided Africa among themselves.

Ronald Robinson and John Gallagher, with Alice Denny, *Africa and the Victorians: The Official Mind of Imperialism* (London: Macmillan, 1961). A classic, though controversial, analysis of British motivations during the scramble.

G. N. Uzoigwe, *Britain and the Conquest of Africa* (Ann Arbor: University of Michigan Press, 1975). An interpretation of the scramble by an African that disagrees with that of Robinson and Gallagher.

Results of a European-Dominated world

Anna Davin, "Imperialism and Motherhood," *History Workshop* (Spring 1978), no. 5: 9–65. Davin's article links imperialism and economic expansion with the increasing intervention of the state in family life. The author offers an analysis of an ideology that focused on the need to increase population in support of imperial aims and that led to the social construction of motherhood, domesticity, and individualism.

Johannes Fabian, *Language and Colonial Power: The Appropriation of Swahili in the Former Belgian Congo* (Cambridge: Cambridge University Press, 1986). Demonstrates how colonial power was exercised in the Belgian Congo through the study of the growth of Swahili as a lingua franca. The author pays particular attention to the uses of Swahili in industrial and other work situations.

* Anne McClintock, *Imperial Leather: Race, Gender, and Sexuality in the Colonial Contest* (New York: Routledge, 1995). By using novels, diaries, advertisements, and other sources, the author demonstrates the relationship between images of domestic life and an ideology of imperial domination and foregrounds the role of women in the colonial experience.

* Paul B. Rich, *Race and Empire in British Politics* (Cambridge: Cambridge University Press, 1986). An intellectual history of ideas about race in the imperial tradition. Focusing on the years between 1890 and 1970, the author examines the political dimensions of race and race ideology in British society.

Conflict at Home: The European Balance of power

* George F. Kennan, *The Decline of Bismarck's European Order: Franco-Russian Relations, 1875–1890* (Princeton, NJ: Princeton University Press, 1979). A diplomatic history of the origins of the 1894 military alliance between Russia and France, Kennan's book views the alliance as a critical factor in the breakdown of the European balance of power established by Bismarck's diplomacy.

* Alan Sked, *The Decline and Fall of the Habsburg Empire, 1815–1918* (London: Longman, 1989). An overview of the Habsburg Empire's history from Metternich to World War I. The author interprets the various historiographical debates over the collapse of Habsburg rule. Rather than treating the late empire as a case of inevitable decline, the book examines the monarchy as a viable institution within a multinational state.

*Paperback edition available

war and revolution, 1914-1920

selling the great war

Advertising is a powerful influence in modern life. Some feel that it makes us buy goods we do not need. Others insist that advertising is an efficient way of conveying information, on the basis of which people make choices. The leaders of Western nations discovered the power of advertising during the years of World War I, from 1914 to 1918. Advertising did not create the conflict that became known as the Great War. Nor did it produce the enthusiasm that excited millions of Europeans when war was declared in 1914. But when death counts mounted, prices skyrocketed, food supplies dwindled, and the frenzy and fervor for the war flagged, governments came to rely more heavily on the art of persuasion. Survival and victory required the support and coordination of the whole society. For the first time in history, war had to advertise.

By the early decades of the twentieth century, businessmen had learned that it was not enough to develop efficient technologies and to mass-produce everything from hair oil to corsets—they had to sell their goods to the public. People would not buy goods they did not know about and whose merits they did not understand. Modern advertising pioneered sales techniques that convinced people to buy. Now political leaders came to realize that the advertising techniques of the marketplace could be useful. Governments took up the "science" of selling—not products but the idea of war. It was not enough to have a well-trained and well-equipped army to ensure victory. Citizens had to be persuaded to join, to fight, to work, to save, and to believe in the national war effort. Warring nations learned how to organize enthusiasm and how to mobilize the masses in support of what proved to be a long and bloody conflict.

Look at the poster on the facing page. Here is a dramatic appeal to German women to support war work. A stern soldier whose visage and bearing communicate strength and singleness of purpose is backed up by an equally determined young woman. She is in the act of handing him a grenade as she stands with him, her arm on his shoulder, facing the unseen enemy. Grenades hang from his belt and from his left hand, giving us the sense that he is able to enter battle properly armed, thanks to this dedicated woman's efforts. The poster is a good representation of the centrality of women's work to the waging of a new kind of war in the twentieth century. The battlefront had to

TAKE UP THE
SWORD OF JUSTICE

Deutsche Frauen arbeitet im Heimatheer!

Kriegsamtstelle Magdeburg

be backed up by a *home front*—the term used for the first time in the Great War—of working men, women, and even children. The poster communicates the dignity and worth that lay in the concerted partnership of soldiers and civilians to defeat the enemy.

Early war posters stressed justice and national glory. Later, as weariness with the war spread, the need for personal sacrifice became the dominant theme. Look at the sad female figure rising from a sea of suffering and death on the facing page. The woman, both goddess-like and vulnerable, symbolizes Great Britain. She is making a strong visual plea for action, seeking soldiers for her cause. This appeal for volunteers for the armed forces was unique to Great Britain, where conscription was not established until 1916. Yet the image is typical of every nation's reliance on a noble female symbol to emphasize the justice of its cause. The dark suffering and death in the waters lapping at her robes are reflected in her eyes. She evinces a fierce determination as she exhorts, "Take up the sword of justice." In February 1915, Germany declared the waters around the British Isles to be a war zone. All British shipping was subject to attack, as were neutral merchant vessels, which were attacked without warning. In May 1915 the *Lusitania* was sunk, taking with it over 1000 lives, including those of 128 Americans. The poster frames an illuminated horizon where a ship that is probably the *Lusitania* is sinking. We need not read a word to understand the call to arms against the perfidy of an enemy who has killed innocent civilians. The female figure's determined jaw, clenched fist, and outstretched arms communicate the nobility of the cause and the certainty of success.

Focus Questions

1. Why did so many in Europe look forward to war by the summer of 1914, and what had they done to bring it about?
2. How and why did the Great War differ so much from the expectations of both the generals and the majority of Europeans?
3. What is total war, and what made World War I the first such war in history?
4. How was peace at last achieved, and what were the terms of that peace?
5. In what ways did the Great War contribute to revolution in Russia?

Civilians had to be mobilized for two reasons. First, it became evident early in the fighting that the costs of the war in human lives were high. Soldiers at the front had to be constantly replaced by civilian reserves. Second, the costs of the war in food, equipment, and productive materials were so high that civilian populations had to be willing to endure great hardships and to sacrifice their own well-being to produce supplies for soldiers at the front. Advertising was used by nations at war to coordinate civilian and military contributions to a common cause.

The European governments proudly "selling" war to their citizens in 1914 expected quick victories and the triumph of their cause. Instead, what they got was a prolonged global war, costly in human life and material destruction, stretching out over four miserable years. Military technology and timetables called the tune in a defensive war fought from the trenches with sophisticated weapons capable of maiming and killing in new ways. Selling the Great War required selectively communicating information and inspiring belief and a commitment to total victory, no matter how high the cost.

The War Europe Expected

In 1914 Europe stood confidently at the center of the world. Covering only 7 percent of the earth's surface, it dominated the world's trade and was actively exporting both European goods and European culture all over the globe. Proud of the progress and prosperity of urban in-dustrial society, Europeans had harnessed nature to transform their environment. They extended their influence beyond their continent, sure that their achievements marked the pinnacle of civilization.

The values of nineteenth-century liberalism permeated the self-confident worldview of European men and women in 1914. Liberalism assured the middle classes

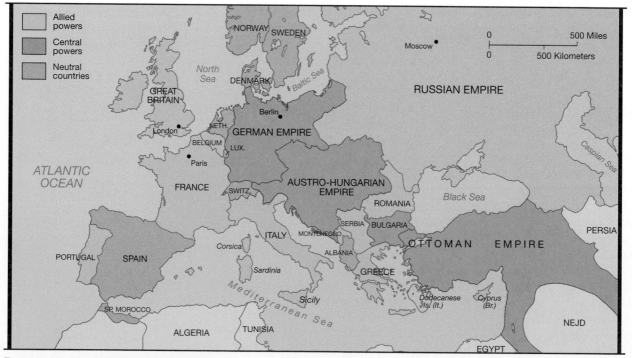

European Alliances on the Eve of World War I

that the world was at peace, governed by rules that could be known. Europeans assumed that they could discover these rules and fashion a better world. Science and industry were their tools for controlling nature and shaping institutions. If life was not yet perfect, it could become so.

Westerners assumed they could discover the rules that governed the world and use them to fashion a better civilization. They took stability and harmony for granted as preconditions for progress. Yet they also recognized the utility of war. In recent times, local confrontations between European states in Africa had been successfully contained in bids for increased territory. While warfare was accepted as an instrument of policy, no one expected or wanted a general war. Liberal values served the goals of limited war, just as they had justified imperial conquest. Statesmen decided there were rules to the game of war that could be employed in the interests of statecraft. Science and technology also served the goals of limited war. Modern weapons, statesmen and generals were sure, would prevent a long war. Superiority in armed force became a priority for European states seeking to protect the peace.

The beginning of the modern arms race resulted in "armed peace" as a defense against war. Leaders nevertheless expected and planned for a war, short and limited, in which the fittest and most advanced nation would win. Planners believed that their rivals could not triumph. War was acceptable because it would be quick and decisive. Previous confrontations among European states had been limited in duration and destruction, as in the case of Prussia and France in 1870, or confined to peripheries, as squabbles among the Great Powers in Africa indicated. The alliance system was expected to defend the peace by defining the conditions of war.

As international tensions mounted, the hot summer days of 1914 were a time of hope and glory. The hope was that war, when it came, would be "over by Christmas." The glory was the promise of ultimate victory in the "crusade for civilization" that each nation's leaders held out to their people. Declarations of war were greeted with songs, flowers, wild enthusiasm, and dancing in the streets. Crowds welcomed the battles to come with the delirium of cheering a favorite team in a sports match. Some embraced war as a test of greatness, a purification of a society that had become lazy and complacent. When war did come in 1914, it was a choice, not an accident. Yet it was a choice that Europeans did not understand, one whose limits they could not control. Their unquestioned pride in reason and progress, which iron-

ically had led them to this war, did not survive the four years of barbaric slaughter that followed.

separating friends from foes

At the end of the nineteenth century, the world appeared to be coming together in a vast international network linked by commerce and finance. A system of alliances based on shared interests also connected states to one another. After 1905, the intricate defensive alliances between and among the European states maintained the balance of power between two blocs of nations and helped prevent one bloc from dominating the other. Yet by creating blocs, alliances identified foes as well as friends. On the eve of the war, France, Great Britain, and Russia stood together in the Triple Entente. Since 1882, Germany, Austria-Hungary, and Italy had joined forces in the Triple Alliance. Other states allied with one or the other of these blocs in pacts of mutual interest and protection. Throughout the world, whether in North Africa, the Balkans, or Asia, the power of some states was intended to balance the power of others. Yet the balance of power did not exist simply to preserve the peace. It existed to preserve a system of independent national societies—nation-states—in a precarious equilibrium. Gains in one area by one bloc had to be offset by compromises in another to maintain the balance. Nations recognized limited conflict as a legitimate means of preserving equilibrium.

The alliance system of blocs reflected the growing impact of public opinion on international relations. Statesmen had the ability to manipulate the newspaper images of allies as good and rivals as evil. But controlling public opinion served to lock policymakers into permanent partnerships and "blank checks" of support for their allies. Western leaders understood that swings in public opinion in periods of crisis could hobble their efforts in the national interest. Permanent military alliances with clearly identified "friends," therefore, took the place of more fluid arrangements.

Although alliances that guaranteed military support did not cause war, they did permit weak nations to act irresponsibly, with the certainty that they would be defended by their more powerful partners. France and Germany were publicly committed to their weaker allies Russia and Austria-Hungary, respectively, in supporting imperialist ambitions in the Balkans from which they themselves derived little direct benefit. Because of treaty commitments, no country expected to face war alone. The interlocking system of defensive alliances

Linguistic Groups in Austria-Hungary

Schlieffen Plan, which he set before his fellow officers in 1905, was a bold and daring one: in the likely event of war with Russia, Germany would launch a devastating offensive against France. Schlieffen reasoned that France was a strong military presence that would come to the aid of its ally, Russia. Russia, lacking a modern transportation system, could not mobilize as rapidly as France.

Russia also had the inestimable advantage of the ability to retreat into its vast interior. If Germany were pulled into a war with Russia, its western frontier would be vulnerable to France, Russia's powerful ally. The Schlieffen Plan recognized that France must first be defeated in the west before Germany could turn its forces to the task of defeating Russia. The Schlieffen Plan thus committed Germany to a war with France, regardless of particular circumstances. Furthermore, the plan, with its strategy of invading the neutral countries of Belgium, Holland, and Luxembourg in order to defeat France in six weeks, ignored the rights of the neutral countries.

Germany was not alone in being driven by military timetables when conflicts arose. Russian military strategists planned full mobilization if war broke out with Austria-Hungary, which was menacing the interests of Russia's ally Serbia. Russia foresaw the likelihood

was structured to match strength against strength—France against Germany, for example—thereby making a prolonged war more likely than would be the case if a weak nation confronted a strong enemy.

Military Timetables

As Europe soon discovered, military timetables restricted the choices of leaders at times of conflict. The crisis of the summer of 1914 revealed the extent to which politicians and statesmen had come to rely on military expertise and strategic considerations in making decisions. Military general staffs assumed increasing importance in state policy-making. War planners became powerful as war was accepted as an alternative to the negotiation of differences. Germany's military preparations are a good example of how war strategy exacerbated crises and prevented peaceful solutions.

Alfred von Schlieffen (1833–1913), the Prussian general and chief of the German General Staff (1891–1905), who developed the war plan, understood little about politics but spent his life studying the strategic challenges of warfare. His war plan was designed to make Germany the greatest power on the Continent. The

The Schlieffen Plan

German War Aims

Theobald von Bethmann-Hollweg (1856–1921) was Chancellor of Germany from 1909 to 1917. Known as a moderate who did not desire war, he nevertheless drew up a statement of "war aims" in September 1914, one month after the outbreak of hostilities. This chilling document, which he intended to implement once Germany was victorious, was no less than a redrawing of the map of Europe with Germany as supreme power. Bethmann-Hollweg's vision of a German-dominated Mitteleuropa was deliberately kept a secret; as he explained to a close colleague, "We are keeping all the cards in our hand hidden from the enemy's eyes."

Bethmann-Hollweg's provisional notes on the Direction of policy on the conclusion of peace, 9 september 1914

[The] general aim of the war [is] security for the German Reich in west and east for all imaginable time. For this purpose France must be so weakened as to make her revival as a great power impossible for all time. Russia must be thrust back as far as possible from Germany's eastern frontier and her domination over the non-Russian vassal peoples broken.

1. *France*. The military to decide whether we should demand cession of Belfort and western slopes of the Vosges, razing of fortresses and cession of coastal strip from Dunkirk to Boulogne.

    The ore-field of Briey, which is necessary for the supply of ore for our industry, to be ceded in any case.

    Further, a war indemnity, to be paid in installments; it must be high enough to prevent France from spending any considerable sums on armaments in the next 15–20 years.

    Furthermore: a commercial treaty which makes France economically dependent on Germany, secures the French market for our exports and makes it possible to exclude British commerce from France. This treaty must secure for us financial and industrial freedom of movement in France in such fashion that German enterprises can no longer receive different treatment from French.

2. *Belgium*. Liège and Verviers to be attached to Prussia, a frontier strip of the province of Luxemburg to Luxemburg.

    Question whether Antwerp, with a corridor to Liège, should also be annexed remains open.

    At any rate Belgium, even if allowed to continue to exist as a state, must be reduced to a vassal state, must allow us to occupy any militarily important posts, must place her coast at our disposal in military respects, must become economically a German province. Given such a solution, which offers the advantages of annexation without its inescapable domestic political disadvantages, French Flanders with Dunkirk, Calais, and Boulogne, where most of the population is Flemish, can without danger be attached to this unaltered Belgium. The competent quarters will have to judge the military value of this position against England.

3. *Luxemburg*. Will become a German federal state and will receive a strip of the present Belgian province of Luxemburg and perhaps the corner of Longwy.

4. We must create a *central European economic association* through common customs treaties, to include France, Belgium, Holland, Denmark, Austria-Hungary, Poland [sic], and perhaps Italy, Sweden and Norway. This association will not have any common constitutional supreme authority and all its members will be formally equal, but in practice will be under German leadership and must stabilise Germany's economic dominance over Mitteleuropa.

5. *The question of colonial acquisitions*, where the first aim is the creation of a continuous Central African colonial empire, will be considered later, as will that of the aims to be realised *vis-à-vis* Russia.

6. A short provisional formula suitable for a possible preliminary peace to be found for a basis for the economic agreements to be concluded with France and Belgium.

7. *Holland*. It will have to be considered by what means and methods Holland can be brought into closer relationship with the German Empire.

    In view of the Dutch character, this closer relationship must leave them free of any feeling of compulsion, must alter nothing in the Dutch way of life, and must also subject them to no new military obligations. Holland, then, must be left independent in externals, but be made internally dependent on us. Possibly one might consider an offensive and defensive alliance, to cover the colonies; in any case a close customs association, perhaps the cession of Antwerp to Holland in return for the right to keep a German garrison in the fortress of Antwerp and at the mouth of the Scheldt.

that Germany would come to the aid of Austria-Hungary. Russia knew, too, that because of its primitive railway network it would be unable to mobilize troops rapidly. In order to compensate for this weakness, Russian leaders planned to mobilize *before* war was declared. German military leaders had no choice in the event of full Russian mobilization but to mobilize their own troops immediately and to urge the declaration of war. There was no chance of containing the conflict once a general mobilization on both sides was underway. Mobilization would mean war.

Like the Schlieffen Plan, the French Plan XVII called for the concentration of troops in a single area, with the intention of decisively defeating the enemy. The French command, not well informed about German strengths and strategies, designated Alsace and Lorraine for the immediate offensive against Germany in the event of war. Plan XVII left Paris exposed to the German drive through Belgium called for in the Schlieffen Plan.

Military leaders throughout Europe argued that if their plans were to succeed, speed was essential. Delays to consider peaceful solutions would cripple military responses. Diplomacy bowed to military strategy. When orders to mobilize went out, armies would be set on the march. Like a row of dominoes falling with the initial push, the two alliance systems would be at war.

assassination at sarajevo

A teenager with a handgun started the First World War. On 28 June 1914, in Sarajevo, the sleepy capital of the Austro-Hungarian province of Bosnia, Gavrilo Princip (1895–1918), a 19-year-old Bosnian Serb, repeatedly pulled the trigger of his Browning revolver, killing the designated heir of the Habsburg throne, Archduke Franz Ferdinand, and his wife, Sophie. Princip belonged to the Young Bosnian Society, a group of students, workers, some peasants, Croats, Muslims, and intellectuals who wanted to free Slavic populations from Habsburg control. Princip was part of a growing movement of South Slavs struggling for national liberation who believed they were being held in colonial servitude by Austria-Hungary.

Struggle over control of the Balkans had been a long-standing issue that had involved all the major European powers for decades. As Austria-Hungary's ally since 1879, Germany was willing to support Vienna's showdown in the Balkans as a way of stopping Russian advances in the area. The alliance with Germany gave Austria-Hungary a sense of security and confidence to pursue its Balkan aims. Germany had its own plans for domination of the Continent and feared that a weakened Austria-Hungary would undermine its own position in central Europe. Independent Balkan states to

Austrian Archduke Franz Ferdinand and his wife, Sophie, leave the Senate House in Sarajevo on 28 June 1914. Five minutes later, Serbian terrorist Gavrilo Princip assassinated the couple.

the south and east were also a threat to Germany's plans. German leaders hoped that an Austro-Serbian war would remain localized and would strengthen their ally, Austria-Hungary. While Austria-Hungary had Germany's support, Serbia was backed by a sympathetic Russia that favored nationalist movements in the Balkans. Russia, in turn, had been encouraged by France, its ally by military pact since 1894, to take a firm stand in its struggle with Austria-Hungary for dominance among Balkan nationalities.

The interim of five weeks between the assassination of Archduke Ferdinand and the outbreak of the war was a period of intense diplomatic activity. The assassination gave Austria-Hungary the excuse it needed to bring a troublesome Serbia into line. Austria-Hungary held Serbia responsible for the shootings. Leaders in Vienna had no evidence at the time to justify their allegations of a Serbian conspiracy, but they saw in this event the perfect pretext for military action. On 23 July 1914, Austria-Hungary issued an ultimatum to the small Balkan nation and secretly decided to declare war regardless of Serbia's response. The demands were so severe that, if met, they would have stripped Serbia of its independence. Austria's aim was to destroy Serbia. In spite of a conciliatory, though not capitulatory, reply from Serbia to the ultimatum, Austria-Hungary declared war on the Balkan nation on 28 July 1914. Russia mobilized two days after the Austro-Hungarian declaration of war against Serbia. Germany mobilized in response to the Russian action and declared war on Russia on 1 August, and on France on 3 August. France had begun mobilizing on 30 July, when its ally, Russia, entered the war.

Great Britain stood briefly outside the fray in the futile attempt to mediate a settlement in the Austro-Serbian conflict. Britain's dependence on its alliance with France as a means of protecting British sea routes in the Mediterranean meant that Great Britain could not remain neutral once France declared war. On 4 August, after Germany had violated Belgian neutrality in its march to France, Great Britain honored its treaty obligations and declared war on Germany. Great Britain entered the war because it judged that a powerful Germany could use ports on the English Channel to invade the British Isles. Italy alone of the major powers remained for the moment outside the conflict. Although allied with Germany and Austria-Hungary, its own aspirations in the Balkans kept it from fighting for the Austrian cause in 1914.

Self-interest, fear, and ambition motivated the Great Powers in different ways in the pursuit of war. The inter-

A World War I British cartoon celebrates the bravery of Belgium in blocking the path of the German bully.

national diplomatic system that had worked so well to prevent war in the preceding decades now enmeshed European states in interlocking alliances and created a chain reaction. The Austro-Serbian war of July 1914 became a Europe-wide war within a month.

The War Europe Got

The expectation of a speedy war of decisive victories and domestic glory drove European leaders and their populations to embrace armed conflict as an acceptable means of mediating grievances in 1914. The peace that had been preserved from the end of the nineteenth century to 1914 was a precarious one indeed, predicated as it was on military timetables that planned for war and alliance systems that guaranteed that local disagreements would become international conflicts. The international mechanisms for keeping the peace led directly to war and guaranteed that once war broke out, it would not remain limited and local.

Early in the war, the best-laid plans of political and military leaders collapsed. In the first place, Europe got a war that was not limited but quickly spread throughout Europe and became global. Switzerland, Spain, the Netherlands, and all of Scandinavia remained neutral, but every other European nation was pulled into the war. In August 1914, Japan cast its lot with the Allies, as the Entente came to be known, and in November the Ottoman Empire joined the Central Powers of Germany and Austria-Hungary. In the following year, Italy joined the war—not on the side of its long-term treaty partners, Germany and Austria-Hungary, but on the side of the Allies, with the expectation of benefiting in the Balkans from Austrian defeat. Bulgaria joined Germany and Austria-Hungary in 1915, seeking territory at Serbia's expense. By the time the United States entered the war in 1917, the war had become a world war.

The second surprise for the European powers was that they did not get a war of movement, nor did they get one of short duration. Within weeks, that pattern had given way to what promised to be a long and costly war of attrition. The war started as German strategists had planned, with German victory in battle after battle. The end seemed near. But in the space of less than a month, the war changed in ways that no one had predicted. Technology was the key to understanding the change and explaining the surprises.

Technology and the Trenches

In the history of nineteenth-century European warfare, armies had relied on mobile cavalry and infantry units, whose greatest asset was speed. Rapid advance had been decisive in the Prussian victory over the French in 1870, which had resulted in the formation of the German Empire. Soldiers of the twentieth century were also trained for a war of movement, high maneuverability, and maximum territorial conquest. But after the first six weeks of battle, soldiers were ordered to do something unimaginable to strategists of European warfare: they were ordered to dig ditches and fight from fixed positions. Soldiers on both sides shoveled out trenches four feet deep, piled up sandbags, mounted their machine guns, and began to fight an unplanned defensive war.

The front lines of Europe's armies in the west wallowed in the 400 miles of trenches that ran from the English Channel to the Swiss frontier. The British and French on one side and the Germans on the other fought each other with machine guns and mortars, backed up by heavy artillery to the rear. Strategists on both sides believed they could break through enemy lines. As a result, the monotony of trench warfare was punctuated periodically by infantry offensives in which immense concentrations of artillery caused great bloodshed. Ten million men were killed in this bizarre and deadly combination of old and new warfare. The glamour of battle that had attracted many young men disappeared quickly in the daily reality of living in mud with rats and constantly facing death. The British poet Wilfred Owen (1893–1918), shortly before his own death in battle, wrote about how the soldier next to him had been shot in the head, soaking Owen in blood: "I shall feel again as soon as I dare, but now I must not."

The invention of new weaponry and heavy equipment had transformed war into an enterprise of increasing complexity. Military and naval staffs expanded to meet the new needs of warfare, but old ways persisted. In their bright blue coats and red trousers, French and Belgian infantrymen made easy targets. Outmoded cavalry units survived despite more efficient mechanization. The railroad made the mobilization, organization, and deployment of mass armies possible. Specialists were needed to control the new war machines that heavy industry had created.

The shovel and the machine gun had indeed transformed war. The machine gun was not new in 1914, but its strategic value had not been fully appreciated before then. The Maxim machine gun had been used by the British in Africa. Strategists regarded the carnage that resulted as a stunning achievement but failed to ask how a weapon of such phenomenal destructive power would work against an enemy armed with machine guns instead of spears. Military strategists drew all the wrong conclusions. They continued to plan an offensive strategy when the weaponry developed for massive destruction had pushed them into fighting a defensive war from the trenches. Both sides resorted to concentration of artillery, increased use of poison gas, and unrestricted submarine warfare in desperate attempts to break the deadlock caused by meeting armed force with force.

"All Quiet on the Western Front"

Eyewitness accounts described the horrors of the new trench warfare. But no one captured the war better than the German novelist Erich Maria Remarque (1898–1970), who drew on his own wartime experiences in *All Quiet on the Western Front*. Published in 1928 and translated subsequently into 25 languages, this powerful portrayal of the transformation of a school boy into a soldier indicts the inhumanity of war and pleads for peace. Stressing the camaraderie of fighting men and sympathy for the plight of the enemy soldier, Remarque also underscored the alienation of a whole generation—the lost generation of young men who could not go home again after the war.

Attack, counter-attack, charge, repulse—these are words, but what things they signify! We have lost a good many men, mostly recruits. Reinforcements have again been sent up to our sector. They are one of the new regiments, composed almost entirely of young fellows just called up. They have had hardly any training, and are sent into the field with only a theoretical knowledge. They do know what a hand-grenade is, it is true, but they have very little idea of cover, and what is most important of all, have no eye for it. A fold in the ground has to be quite eighteen inches high before they can see it.

Although we need reinforcement, the recruits give us almost more trouble than they are worth. They are helpless in this grim fighting area, they fall like flies. Modern trench-warfare demands knowledge and experience; a man must have a feeling for the contours of the ground, an ear for the sound and character of the shells, must be able to decide beforehand where they will drop, how they will burst, and how to shelter from them.

The young recruits of course know none of these things. They get killed simply because they hardly can tell shrapnel from high-explosive, they are mown down because they are listening anxiously to the roar of the big coal-boxes falling in the rear, and miss the light, piping whistle of the low spreading daisy-cutters. They flock together like sheep instead of scattering, and even the wounded are shot down like hares by the airmen.

Their pale turnip faces, their pitiful clenched hands, the fine courage of these poor devils, the desperate charges and attacks made by the poor brave wretches, who are so terrified that they dare not cry out loudly, but with battered chests, with torn bellies, arms and legs only whimper softly for their mothers and cease as soon as one looks at them.

Their sharp, downy, dead faces have the awful expressionlessness of dead children. . . .

I am young, I am twenty years old; yet I know nothing of life but despair, death, fear, and fatuous superficiality cast over an abyss of sorrow. I see how peoples are set against one another, and in silence, unknowingly, foolishly, obediently, innocently slay one another. I see that the keenest brains of the world invent weapons and words to make it yet more refined and enduring. And all men of my age, here and over there, throughout the whole world see these things; all my generation is experiencing these things with me. What would our fathers do if we suddenly stood up and came before them and proffered our account? What do they expect of us if a time ever comes when the war is over? Through the years our business has been killing;—it was our first calling in life. Our knowledge of life is limited to death. What will happen afterwards? And what shall come out of us?

From Erich Maria Remarque, *All Quiet on the Western Front*.

The necessity of total victory drove the Central Powers and the Allies to grisly new inventions. Late in the war, the need to break the deadlock of trench warfare ushered in the airplane and the tank. Neither was decisive in altering the course of the war, though the airplane was useful for reconnaissance and for limited bombing and the tank promised the means of breaking through defensive lines. Chlorine gas was first used in warfare by the Germans in 1915. Mustard gas, which was named for its distinctive smell and which caused severe blistering, was introduced two years later. The Germans were the first to use flame throwers, especially effective against mechanized vehicles with vulnerable fuel tanks. Barbed wire, invented in the U.S. Midwest to contain farm animals, became an essential aspect of trench warfare, as it marked off the no-man's-land between combatants and prevented surprise attacks.

The technology that had been viewed as proof of progress was now channeled toward engineering new instruments of death. Yet technology itself produced a stalemate. New weapons sometimes produced their antidotes. For example, the invention of deadly gas was followed soon after by gas masks. Each side was capable of matching the other's ability to devise new armaments. Deadlocks caused by technological parity forced both sides to resort to desperate concentrations of men and weaponry that resulted not in decisive battles but in ever-escalating casualty rates. By improving their efficiency at killing, the European powers were not finding a way to end the war.

The Battle of the Marne

German forces seized the offensive in the west and invaded neutral Belgium at the beginning of August 1914. The Belgians resisted stubbornly but unsuccessfully. Belgian forts were systematically captured, and the capital of Brussels fell under the German advance on 20 August. After the fall of Belgium, German military might swept into northern France with the intention of defeating the French in six weeks.

In the years preceding the war, the German General Staff, unwilling to concentrate all of its troops in the west, had modified the Schlieffen Plan by committing divisions to its eastern frontier. The absence of the full German fighting force in the west did not appreciably slow the German advance through Belgium. Yet the Germans had underestimated both the cost of holding back the French in Alsace-Lorraine and the difficulty of maneuvering German forces and transporting supplies in an offensive war. Eventually, unexpected Russian advances in the east also siphoned off troops from the west. German forces in the west were so weakened by the offensive that they were unable to swing west of Paris, as planned, and instead chose to enter the French capital from the northeast by crossing the Marne River. This shift exposed the German First Army on its western flank and opened up a gap on its eastern flank.

Despite an initial pattern of retreat and a lack of coordination of forces, Allied French and British troops were ready to take advantage of the vulnerabilities in the German advance. In a series of battles between 6 and 10 September 1914 that came to be known as the First Battle of the Marne, the Allies counterattacked and advanced into the gap. The German army was forced to drop back. In the following months, each army tried to outflank the other in what has been called "the race to the sea." By late fall it was clear that the battles from the Marne north to the border town of Ypres in northwest Belgium near the English Channel had ended an open war of movement on the western front. Soldiers now dug in along a line of battle that

A typical World War I trench. Millions of soldiers lived amid mud, disease, and vermin, awaiting death from enemy shells. After the French army mutiny in 1916, the troops wrung this concession from their commanders: they did not have to charge German machine guns while armed only with rifles.

The British invented the tank, which made its combat debut in 1916. The new weapon terrified the German troops when first used on the western front. The British had developed it in heavy secrecy under the pretext of constructing water tanks; hence the name.

changed little in the long three and a half years until March 1918.

The Allies gained a strategic victory in the First Battle of the Marne by resisting the German advance in the fighting that quickly became known as the "miracle of the Marne." The legend was further enhanced by true stories of French troops being rushed from Paris to the front in taxicabs. Yet the real significance of the Marne lay in the severe miscalculations of military leaders and statesmen on both sides, who had expected a different kind of war. They did not understand the new technology that made a short war unlikely. Nor did they understand the demands that this new kind of warfare would make on civilian populations. Those Parisian taxi drivers foreshadowed how European civilians would be called upon again and again to support the war in the next four years. The Schlieffen Plan was dead. But it was no more a failure than any of the other military timetables of the Great Powers.

"I don't know what is to be done—this isn't war." So spoke Lord Horatio Kitchener (1850–1916), one of the most decorated British generals of his time. He was not alone in his bafflement over the stalemate of trench warfare at the end of 1914. By that time, Germany's greatest fear, a simultaneous war on two fronts, had become a grim reality. The Central Powers were under a state of siege, cut off from the world by the great battlefront in the west and by the Allied blockade at sea. The rules of the game had changed, and the European powers settled in for a long war.

War on the Eastern Front

War on Germany's eastern front was a mobile war, unlike its western counterpart, because there were relatively fewer men and guns in relation to the vast distances. The Russian army was the largest in the world. Yet it was crippled from the outbreak of the war by inadequate supplies and poor leadership. At the end of August 1914, the smaller German army, supported by divisions drawn from the west, delivered a devastating defeat to the Russians in the one great battle on the eastern front. At Tannenberg, the entire Russian Second Army was destroyed, and about 100,000 Russian soldiers were taken prisoner. Faced with this humiliation, General Aleksandr Vasilievich Samsonov (1859–1914), head of the Russian forces, committed suicide on the field of battle.

The German general Paul von Hindenburg (1847–1934), a veteran of the Franco-Prussian war of 1870, had been recalled from retirement to direct the campaign against the Russians because of his intimate knowledge of the area. Assisted by Quartermaster General Erich Ludendorff (1865–1937), Hindenburg followed the stunning victory of Tannenberg two weeks later with another devastating blow to Russian forces at the Masurian Lakes.

The Russians were holding up their end of the bargain in the Allied war effort, but at great cost. They kept the Germans busy and forced them to divert troops to the eastern front, weakening the German effort to knock

By late 1914, the sight of marching soldiers was no longer a novelty in France. These vineyard workers do not even look up as a military column passes.

France out of the war. In the south, the tsar's troops defeated the Austro-Hungarian army at Lemberg in Galicia in September. This Russian victory gave Serbia a temporary reprieve. But by mid-1915, Germany had thrown the Russians back and was keeping Austria-Hungary propped up in the war. By fall, Russia had lost most of Galicia, the Polish lands of the Russian empire, Lithuania, and parts of Latvia and Byelorussia to the advancing enemy. These losses amounted to 15 percent of its territory and 20 percent of its population. The Russian army staggered, with over 1 million soldiers taken as prisoners of war and at least as many killed or wounded.

The Russian army, as one of its own officers described it, was being bled to death. Russian soldiers were poorly led into battle, or not led at all because of the shortage of officers. Munitions shortages meant that soldiers often went into battle without rifles, armed only with the hope of scavenging arms from their fallen comrades. Despite these difficulties, the Russians, under the direction of General Aleksei Brusilov (1853–1926), commander of the Russian armies in the southern part of the eastern front, remarkably managed to throw back the Austro-Hungarian forces in 1916 and almost eliminated Austria as a military power. But this was the last great campaign on the eastern front and Russia's last show of strength in the Great War.

Russia's near-destruction of the Austrian army tremendously benefited Russia's allies. In order to protect its partner, Germany was forced to withdraw 8 divisions from Italy—alleviating the Allied situation in the Tyrol—and 12 divisions from the western front, providing relief for the French at Verdun and the British at the Somme. In addition, Russia sent troops to the aid of a

World War I

new member of the Allied camp, Romania, an act that probably further weakened Brusilov's efforts. In response to Brusilov's challenge, the Germans established control over the Austrian army, assigning military command of the coalition to General Ludendorff.

By the summer of 1917, the tsardom had been overthrown and a provisional government ruled Russia. Tens of thousands of Russian soldiers were walking away from the war. Russia withdrew from the war and in March 1918 signed a separate peace by which Germany gained extensive territorial advantages and important supply bases for carrying on the war in the west. To protect these territories and their resources, the Germans had to maintain an army on the eastern front. No longer fighting in the east, however, Germany could release the bulk of its forces to fight in the west.

war on the western front

Along hundreds of miles of trenches, the French and British tried repeatedly to expel the Germans from Belgium. Long periods of inactivity were punctuated by orgies of heavy bloodletting. The German phrase "All quiet on the western front," used in military communiqués to describe those periods of silence between massive shellings and infantry attacks, reported only the uneasy calm before the next violent storm.

Military leaders on both sides cherished the dream of a decisive offensive, the breakthrough that would win the war. In 1916 the Allies planned a joint strike at the Somme, a river in northern France flowing west into the English Channel, but the Germans struck first at Verdun, a small fortress city in northeast France. By concentrating great numbers of troops, the Germans outnumbered the French five to two. As General Erich von Falkenhayn (1861–1922), chief of the General Staff of the German army from 1914 to 1916, explained it, the German purpose in attacking Verdun was "to bleed the French white by virtue of our superiority in guns."

On the first day of battle, 1 million shells were fired. The battlefield was a living hell as soldiers stumbled across corpse after corpse. Against the German onslaught, French troops were instructed to hold out, though they lacked adequate artillery and reinforcements. General Joseph Joffre (1852–1931), commander in chief of the French army, was unwilling to divert reinforcements to Verdun.

The German troops advanced easily through the first lines of defense. But the French held their position for ten long, horrifying months of continuous mass slaughter from February to December 1916. General Henri Philippe Pétain (1856–1951), a local commander who had been planning an early retirement before the war, bolstered morale by constantly rotating his troops to the point that most of the French army—259 of 330 infantry battalions—saw action at Verdun. Nearly starving and poorly armed, the French stood alone in the bloodiest offensive of the war. Attack strategy backfired on the Germans as their own death tolls mounted.

Pétain and his flamboyant general Robert Georges Nivelle (1856–1924) were both hailed as heroes for fulfilling the instruction to their troops: "They shall not pass." Falkenhayn fared less well and was dismissed from his post. Yet no real winners emerged from the scorched earth of Verdun, where observers could see the nearest thing to a desert created in Europe. Verdun was a disaster. The French suffered over half a million total casualties. German casualties were almost as high. A few square miles of territory had changed hands back and forth. In the end, no military advantage was gained, and almost 700,000 lives had been lost. Legends of the brilliant leadership of Pétain and Nivelle, who both went on to greater positions of authority, and the failed command of Falkenhayn, who retired in disgrace, obscured the real lesson of the battle: an offensive war under these conditions was impossible.

Still, new offensives were devised. The British went ahead with their planned offensive on the Somme in July 1916. For an advance of seven miles, 400,000 British and 200,000 French soldiers were killed or wounded. The American writer F. Scott Fitzgerald (1896–1940), who had served as an army officer in World War I, wrote of the battle of the Somme in his novel Tender Is the Night (1934). One of his characters describes a visit to the Somme Valley after the war: "See that little stream. We could walk to it in two minutes. It took the British a whole month to walk to it—a whole empire walking very slowly, dying in front and pushing forward behind. And another empire walked very slowly backward a few inches a day, leaving the dead like a million bloody rugs." German losses brought the total casualties of this offensive to 1 million men. Despite his experience at Verdun, the French general Robert Nivelle planned his own offensive in the Champagne region in spring 1917, sure that he could succeed where others had failed in "breaking the crust." The Nivelle offensive resulted in 40,000 deaths, and Nivelle was dismissed. The French army was falling apart, with mutiny and insubordination everywhere.

A *painting by François Flameng of Verdun in flames. This city on the Meuse River in northern France has played an important role in resisting enemy invasion since the time of Attila the Hun in the fifth century.*

The British believed they could succeed where the French had failed. Under General Douglas Haig (1861–1928), the commander in chief of British expeditionary forces on the Continent, the British launched an attack in Flanders throughout the summer and fall of 1917. Known as the *Passchendaele offensive* for the village and ridge in whose "porridge of mud" much of the fighting took place, this campaign resulted in the slaughter of almost 400,000 British soldiers for insignificant territorial gain. The Allies and the Germans finally recognized that "going over the top" in offensives was not working and could not work. The war must be won by other means.

war on the periphery

Recognizing the stalemate in the west, the Allies attempted to open up other fronts where the Central Powers might be vulnerable. In the spring of 1915, the Allies were successful in convincing Italy to enter the war on their side by promising that it would receive, at the time of the peace, the South Tyrol, the southern part of Dalmatia, and key Dalmatian islands, which would ensure Italy's dominance over the Adriatic Sea. By thus capitalizing on Italian antagonism toward Austria-Hungary over control of this territory, the Allies gained 875,000 Italian soldiers for their cause. Although these Italian troops were in no way decisive in the fighting that followed, Great Britain, France, and Russia saw the need to build up Allied support in southern Europe in order to reinforce Serbian attempts to keep Austrian troops beyond its borders. The Allies also hoped that by pulling Germans into this southern front, some relief might be provided for British and French soldiers on the western front.

Germany, in turn, was well aware of the need to expand its alliances beyond Austria-Hungary if it was to compete successfully against superior Allied forces. Trapped as they were to the east and west, the Central Powers established control over a broad corridor stretching from the North Sea through central Europe and down through the Ottoman Empire to the Suez Canal so vital to British interests. In the Balkans, where the war had begun, the Serbs were consistently bested by the Austrians. By late 1915, the Serbs had been knocked out of the war in spite of Allied attempts to assist them. Serbia paid a heavy price in the Great War: it lost one-sixth of its population through war, famine, and disease. The promise of booty persuaded Bulgaria to join Germany and Austria-Hungary. Over the next year and a half, the Allies responded by convincing Romania and then Greece to join them.

The theater of war continued to expand. Although the Ottoman Empire had joined the war in late 1914 on the side of the Central Powers, its own internal difficulties attenuated its fighting ability. As a multinational empire consisting of Turks, Arabs, Armenians, Greeks, Kurds, and other ethnic minorities, it was plagued by Turkish misrule and Arab nationalism. Hence the Ottoman Empire was the weakest link in the chain of German alliances. Yet it held a crucial position. The Turks could block shipping of vital supplies to Russia through the Mediterranean and Black seas. Coming to the aid of their Russian ally, a combined British and French fleet attacked Turkish forces at the straits of the Dardanelles in April 1915. In the face of political and military opposition, First Lord of the Admiralty Winston Churchill (1874–1965) supported the idea of opening a new front by sea. Poorly planned and mismanaged, the expedition was a disaster. When the naval effort in the German-mined strait failed, the British foolishly decided to land troops on the Gallipoli Peninsula, which extends from the southern coast of European Turkey. There British soldiers were trapped on the rocky terrain, unable to advance against the Turks and unable to fall back. Gallipoli was the first large-scale attempt at amphibious warfare. The Australian and New Zealand forces (ANZACs) showed great bravery in some of the most brutal fighting of the war. Critics in Britain argued that the only success of the nine-month campaign was the Allied evacuation.

Britain sought to protect its interests in the Suez Canal. Turkish troops menaced the canal effectively enough to terrify the British into maintaining an elaborate system of defense in the area and concentrating large troop reinforcements in Egypt. War with the Ottoman Empire also extended battle into the oil fields of Mesopotamia and Persia. This attempt at a new front was initially a fiasco for the British and Russian forces that threatened Baghdad. The Allies proceeded not only without plans, but also without maps. They literally did not know where they were going. Eventually, British forces recovered and took Baghdad in 1917, while Australian and New Zealand troops captured Jerusalem. The tentacles of war spread out, following the path of Western economic and imperial interests throughout the world.

Most surprising of all was the indecisive nature of the war at sea. The great battleships of the British and German navies avoided confrontation on the high seas. The only major naval battle of the Great War, the Battle of Jutland in the North Sea, took place in early 1916. Each side inflicted damage on the other but, through careful maneuvering, avoided a decisive outcome to the battle. Probably the enormous cost of replacing battle ships deterred both the British and the Germans from risking their fleets in engagements on the high seas. With the demands for munitions and equipment on the two great land fronts of the war, neither side could afford to lose a traditional war at sea. Instead, the British used their seapower as a policing force to blockade German trade and strangle the German economy.

The German navy, much weaker than the British, relied on a new weapon, the submarine, which threatened to become decisive in the war at sea. Submarines were initially used in the first months of the war for recon-

British machine gunners wearing gas masks at the battle of the Somme in 1916.

naissance. Their potential for inflicting heavy losses on commercial shipping became apparent in 1915. Undergoing technological improvements throughout the war, U-boats (*Unterseebooten*), as German submarines were called, torpedoed 6 million tons of Allied shipping in 1917. With cruising ranges as high as 3600 miles, German submarines attacked Allied and neutral shipping as far away as off the shore of the United States and the Arctic supply line to Russia. German insistence on unrestricted use outraged neutral powers, which considered the Germans in violation of international law. The Germans rejected the requirements of warning an enemy ship and boarding it for investigation as too dangerous for submarines, which were no match for battleships above water. The Allies invented depth charges and mines capable of blowing German submarines out of the water. These weapons, combined with the use of the convoy system in the Atlantic Ocean and the Mediterranean Sea, produced a successful blockade and an anti-submarine campaign that put an end to the German advantage.

Adjusting to the unexpected: Total war

The war that Europe got differed from all previous experiences and expectations of armed conflict. Technological advances, equally matched on both sides, introduced a war of attrition, defensive and prolonged. Nineteenth-century wars that lasted six to eight weeks, were confined to one locale, and were determined by a handful of battles marked by low casualties had nothing in common with the long, dirty, lice-infested reality of trench warfare. Warring European nations faced enemies to the west, to the east, and on the periphery, with no end to the slaughter in sight.

The period from 1914 to 1918 marked the first time in history that the productive activities of entire populations were directed toward a single goal: military victory. The Great War became a war of peoples, not just of armies. Wars throughout history have involved non-combatants caught in the crossfire or standing in the wrong place at the wrong time. But this unexpected war of attrition required civilian populations to adjust to a situation in which what went on at the battlefront transformed life on the home front. For this reason, the Great War became known as history's first *total* war.

Adjusting to the unexpected war of 1914, governments intervened to centralize and control every aspect of economic life. Technology and industrial capacity made possible a war of unimaginable destruction. The scale of production and distribution of war-related materials required for victory was unprecedented. To persuade civilians to suffer at home for the sake of the war, leaders pictured the enemy as evil villains who must be defeated at any cost. The sacrifice required for a total war made total victory necessary. And total victory required an economy totally geared to fighting the war.

Mobilizing the Home Front

While soldiers were fighting on the eastern and western fronts, businessmen and politicians at home were creating bureaucracies to control wages and prices, distrib-

Crew on the deck of a German World War I submarine at sea.

War at Home

The total character of World War I meant that it changed life for noncombatants as much as it did for those at the front. Women had to fend for themselves, organizing relief societies, working the fields, and manufacturing weapons and war goods. They often took jobs men had held before. In London, taxi driving had been a male monopoly before the war. Articles from 16 March 1917 in the *Manchester Guardian* show what could happen when both women and men shared jobs. Conflicts could break out when men felt threatened by women's new positions.

Women Taxi-Cab Drivers

The taxi-cab drivers of London threaten to try to bring about a strike, which will include motor-'bus drivers and conductors, if the London County Council does not abandon its intention to license women to drive taxi-cabs. To be successful a strike must in the ultimate event be in defence of a principle that commands a measure of public assent. The only principle for which the men stand in this strike is that even where women are fitted to do men's work they should be debarred from it. It is a principle never tenable in justice, and utterly discredited in the popular mind by the war. If the employment of women as motor-drivers meant a decrease in the general level of skill in the trade, a worsening of conditions, or a lowering of wages a real principle would be involved. Stress of war might make the setting aside of it temporarily necessary, but the point would be at least arguable. In this matter such considerations do not arise. Hundreds of women have taken the place of men as motor-drivers for the army and the Red Cross at home and abroad, thousands more are employed in driving commercial motors. They have proved, if proof were needed, that this work is well within their compass. The woman who can take a man's place fully in the harder sort of tasks involved in work on the railways or in agriculture is an exception, and the employment of women for such work is a war-time necessity that may not to any great extent survive when peace comes. But the woman motor-driver has come to stay, and a strike of taxi-men could be no more than a vain and selfish protest against her arrival.

"Down Cabs" Again

The London taxi-drivers are again threatening trouble—this time because the Home Office refuses to give way on the question of licensing women drivers. Sir George Cave told a deputation of the Licensed Vehicle Workers the other day that there is no intention at present of licensing women as tram and 'bus drivers, but that competent women will certainly be licensed for taxi-driving. The men are holding indignation meetings on Sunday, and threaten to bring all the cab, 'bus, and tram drivers of London out on strike—about 20,000 workers, inclusive of garage men.

ute supplies, establish production quotas, and mobilize human and material resources. Just as governments had conscripted the active male population for military service, the Allies and the Central Powers now mobilized civilians of all ages and both sexes to work for the war.

Women played an essential role in the mobilization of the home front. They had never been isolated from the experiences and hardships of war, but they now found new ways to support the war effort. In cities, women went to work in munitions factories and war-related industries that had previously employed only men. Women filled service jobs, from fire fighting to trolley-car conducting—jobs that were essential to the smooth running of industrial society and that had been left vacant by men. On farms, women literally took up the plow after both men and horses had been requisitioned for the war effort.

By 1918, 650,000 French women were working in war-related industries and in clerical positions in the army, and they had counterparts all over Europe. In Germany, two out of every five munitions workers were women. Women became more prominent in the work force as a whole, as the case of Great Britain makes clear: there the number of women workers jumped from 250,000 at the beginning of the war to 5 million by the war's end

Women also served in the auxiliary units of the armed services, in the clerical and medical corps, in order to free men for fighting at the front. In eastern European nations, women entered combat as soldiers. Although most women were displaced from their wartime jobs with the return of men after the armistice, they were as important to the war effort as the men fighting at the front.

In the first months of the war, the private sector had been left to its own devices, with nearly disastrous results. Shortages, especially of shells, and bottlenecks in production threatened military efforts. Governments were forced to establish controls and to set up state monopolies in order to guarantee the supplies necessary to wage war. In Germany, industrialists Walther Rathenau (1867–1922) and Alfred Hugenberg (1865–1951) worked with the government. By the spring of 1915, they had eliminated the German problem of munitions scarcity. France was in trouble six weeks after the outbreak of the war: it had used up half of its accumulated munitions supplies in the First Battle of the Marne. German occupation of France's northern industrial basin further crippled munitions production. Through government intervention, France improvised and relocated its war industries. The British government got involved in production, too, by establishing in 1915 the first Ministry of Munitions under the direction of David Lloyd George (1863–1945). Distinct from the Ministry of War, the Ministry of Munitions was to coordinate military needs with the armaments industry.

In a war that leaders soon realized would be a long one, food supplies assumed paramount importance. Germany, dependent on food imports to feed its people and isolated from the world market by the Allied block-ade, introduced rationing five months after the outbreak of the war. Other continental nations followed suit. Government agents set quotas for agricultural producers. Armies were fed and supplied at the expense of domestic populations. Great Britain, which enjoyed a more reliable food supply by virtue of its sea power, did not impose food rationing until 1917.

Three factors put food supplies at risk. First, the need for large numbers of soldiers at the front pulled farmers and peasants off the land. The resultant drop in the agricultural work force meant that land was taken out of production and what remained was less efficiently cultivated, so that productivity declined. A second factor was fear of requisitioning and the general uncertainties of war that caused agricultural producers to hoard supplies. What little was available was traded on black markets. Finally, because all European countries depended to some extent on imports of food and fertilizers, enemies successfully targeted trade routes for attack.

silencing dissent

The strains of total war were becoming apparent. Two years of sacrificing, scrimping, and, in some areas, starving began to take their toll among soldiers and civilians on both sides. With the lack of decisive victories, war weariness was spreading. Work stoppages and strikes, which had virtually ceased with the outbreak of war in 1914, began to climb rapidly in 1916. Between 1915 and 1916 in France, the number of strikes by dissatisfied workers increased by 400 percent. Underpaid and tired workers went on strike, staged demonstrations, and protested exploitation. Labor militancy also

E. F. Skinner, For King and Country. The artist's patriotic work celebrates women's contributions in the munitions industry during the war.

intensified in the British Isles and Germany. Women, breadwinners for their families, were often in the forefront of these protests throughout Europe. Social peace between unions and governments was no longer held together by patriotic enthusiasm for war.

Politicians, too, began to rethink their suspension of opposition to government policies as the war dragged on. Dissidents among European socialist parties regained their prewar commitment to peace. Most socialists had enthusiastically supported the declarations of war in 1914. By 1916, the united front that political opponents had presented against the enemy was crumbling under growing demands for peace.

In a total war, unrest at home guaranteed defeat. Governments knew that all opposition to war policies had to be eliminated. In a dramatic extension of the police powers of the state, whether among the Allies or the Central Powers, criticism of the government became treason. Censorship was enforced and propaganda became more virulent. Those who spoke for peace were no better than the enemy. The governments of every warring nation resorted to harsh measures. Parliamentary bodies were stripped of power, civil liberties were suspended, democratic procedures were ignored. The civilian governments of Premier Georges Clemenceau (1841–1929) in France and Prime Minister Lloyd George in Great Britain resorted to rule by emergency police power to repress criticism. Under Generals von Hindenburg and Ludendorff in Germany, military rule became the order of the day. Nowhere was "government as usual" possible in total war.

Every warring nation sought to promote dissension from within the societies of its enemies. Germany provided some aid for the Easter Rebellion in Ireland in 1916 in the hope that the Irish demand for independence that predated the war would deflect British attention and undermine fighting strength and morale. Germany also supported separatist movements among minority nationalities in the Russian empire and was responsible for returning the avowed revolutionary V. I. Lenin under escort to Russia in April 1917. The British engaged in similar tactics. The British foreign secretary Arthur Balfour (1848–1930) worked with Zionist leaders in 1917 in drawing up the Balfour Declaration, which promised to "look with favor" on the creation of a Jewish homeland in Palestine. The British thereby encouraged Zionist hopes among central European Jews, with the intent of creating difficulties for German and Austrian rulers. Similarly, the British encouraged Arabs to rebel against Turks with the same promise of Palestine. Undermining the loyalties of colonized peoples and minorities would be at minimum a nuisance to the enemy. Beyond that, it could erode war efforts from within.

Turning point and victory, 1917–1918

For the Allies, 1917 began with a series of crises. Under the hammering of one costly offensive after another, French morale had collapsed and military discipline was deteriorating. A combined German–Austrian force had eliminated the Allied states of Serbia and Romania. The Italians experienced a military debacle at Caporetto and were effectively out of the war.

The year 1917 was "the blackest year of the war" for the Allies. At the beginning of the year, the peril on the sea had increased with the opening of unrestricted U-boat warfare against Allied and neutral ships. The greatest blow came when Russia, now in the throes of domestic revolution, withdrew. Germany was able to concentrate more of its resources in the west and fight a one-front war. Perhaps more significantly, it was able to utilize the foodstuffs and raw materials of its newly acquired Russian territories to buoy its home front.

Yet in spite of Allied reversals, it was not at all the case that the war was turning in favor of the Central Powers. Both Austria-Hungary and the Ottoman Empire teetered on the verge of collapse, with internal difficulties increasing as the war dragged on. Germany suffered from labor and supply shortages and economic hardship resulting from the blockade and an economy totally dedicated to waging war.

The war had gone from a stalemate to a state of crisis for both sides. Every belligerent state was experiencing war weariness that undermined civilian and military morale. Pressures to end the war increased everywhere. Attrition was not working, attacks were not working. Every country suffered on the home front and battlefront from strikes, food riots, military desertions, and mutinies. Defeatism was everywhere on the rise.

The Allies longed for the entry of the United States into the war. Although the United States was a neutral country, from the beginning of the war it had been an important supplier to the Allies. U.S. trade with the Allies had jumped from $825 million in 1914 to $3.2 billion in 1916. American bankers also made loans and extended credit to the Allies to the amount of $2.2 billion. The United States had made a sizable investment in the Allied war effort, and its economy was prospering.

Beginning with the sinking of the *Lusitania* in 1915, German policy on the high seas had incensed the American public. Increased U-boat activity in 1916 led U.S. President Woodrow Wilson (1856–1924) to issue a severe warning to the Germans to cease submarine warfare. The Germans, however, were driven to desperate measures. The great advantage of submarines was in sneak attacks—a procedure against international rules, which required warning. Germany initiated a new phase of unrestricted submarine warfare on 1 February 1917, when the German ambassador informed the U.S. government that U-boats would sink on sight all ships, including passenger ships—even those neutral and unarmed.

German machinations in Mexico were also revealed on 25 February 1917, with the interception of a telegram from Arthur Zimmermann (1864–1940), the German foreign minister. The telegram communicated Germany's willingness to support Mexico's recovery of "lost territory" in New Mexico, Arizona, and Texas in return for Mexican support of Germany in the event of U.S. entry into the war. U.S. citizens were outraged. On 2 April 1917, Wilson, who had won the presidential election of 1916 on the promise of peace, asked the U.S. Congress for a declaration of war against Germany.

The entry of the United States was the turning point in the war, tipping the scales dramatically in favor of the Allies. The United States contributed its naval power to the large Allied convoys formed to protect shipping against German attacks. In a total war, control and shipment of resources had become crucial issues, and it was in these areas that the U.S. entry gave the Allies indisputable superiority. The United States was also able to send "over there" tens of thousands of conscripts fighting with the American Expeditionary Forces under the leadership of General John "Black Jack" Pershing (1860–1948). They reinforced British and French troops and gave a vital boost to morale.

However, for such a rich nation, the help that the United States was able to give at first was very little. The U.S. government was new to the business of coordinating a war effort, but it displayed great ingenuity in creating a wartime bureaucracy that increased a small military establishment of 210,000 soldiers to 9.5 million young men registered before the beginning of summer 1917. By July 1918, the Americans were sending a phenomenal 300,000 soldiers a month to Europe. By the end of the war, 2 million Americans had traveled to Europe to fight in the war.

The U.S. entry is significant not just because it provided reinforcements, fresh troops, and fresh supplies to the beleaguered Allies. From a broader perspective, it marked a shift in the nature of international politics: Europe was no longer able to handle its own affairs and settle its own differences without outside help.

U.S. troops, though numerous, were not well trained, and they relied on France and Great Britain for their arms and equipment. But the Germans correctly understood that they could not hold out indefinitely against this superior Allied force. Austria-Hungary was effectively out of the war. Germany had no replacements for its fallen soldiers, but it was able to transfer troops from Russia, Romania, and Macedonia to the west. It realized that its only chance of victory lay in swift action. The German high command decided on a bold measure: one great, final offensive that would knock the combined forces of Great Britain, France, and the United States out of the war once and for all by striking at a weak point and smashing through enemy lines. The great surprise was that it almost worked.

Known as the *Ludendorff offensive*, after the general who devised it, the final German push began in March 1918. Secretly amassing tired troops from the eastern front pulled back after the Russian withdrawal, the Germans counted on the element of surprise to enable them to break through a weak sector in the west. On the first day of spring, Ludendorff struck. The larger German force gained initial success against weakened British and French forces. Yet in spite of breaches in its defense, the Allied line held. Allied Supreme Commander General Ferdinand Foch (1851–1929) coordinated the war effort that withstood German offensives throughout the spring and early summer of 1918.

The final drive came in mid-July. More than 1 million German soldiers had already been killed, wounded, or captured in the months between March and July. German prisoners of war gave the French details of Ludendorff's plan. The Germans, now exposed and vulnerable, were placed on the defensive. The German army was rapidly disintegrating. On the other side, tanks, plentiful munitions, and U.S. reinforcements fueled an Allied offensive that began in late September. The German army retreated, destroying property and equipment as it went. With weak political leadership and indecision in Berlin, the Germans held on until early November. The end came finally after four years of war. On 11 November 1918, an armistice signed by representatives of the German and Allied forces took effect.

Thus came to an end a war of slightly more than four years in duration that had consumed the soldiers, material, and productive resources of the European na-

Fighting the Great War

1905	Development of the Schlieffen Plan
28 June 1914	Assassination of Archduke Franz Ferdinand and his wife, Sophie
28 July 1914	Austria-Hungary declares war on Serbia
30 July–4 August 1914	Russia, France, Britain, and Germany declare war in accordance with system of alliances
August 1914	Germany invades Belgium
6–10 September 1914	First Battle of the Marne
1915	Germany introduces chlorine gas
April 1915–January 1916	Gallipoli Campaign
May 1915	Sinking of the *Lusitania*
February–December 1916	Battle at Verdun
1917	First use of mustard gas
2 April 1917	United States enters war
March 1918	Russia withdraws
11 November 1918	Armistice

tions on both sides. Europeans had prided themselves on representing the pinnacle of civilization against the barbarism of other continents. Yet nothing matched the destructiveness of the Great War. Of the 70 million who were mobilized, about one in eight were killed. Battlefields of scorched earth and mud-filled ditches, silent at last, scarred once-fertile countrysides as grim memorials to history's first total war. Home fronts, too, served as battlefields, with those who demanded peace silenced as traitors. In the end, only the entry of the United States into the war on the side of the Allies brought an end to the human misery and staggering bloodletting. The war to end all wars was over; the task of settling the peace now loomed.

Reshaping Europe: After War and Revolution

In the aftermath of war, the task of the victors was to define the terms of a settlement that would guarantee peace and stabilize Europe. Russia was the ghost at the conference table, excluded from the negotiations be-

Allied flags are paraded on Armistice Day in Vincennes, France. The long ordeal was over, but relief and joy soon faded as the bitterness of the peace terms corroded postwar Europe.

cause of its withdrawal from the Allied camp in 1917 and its separate peace with Germany in March 1918. The Bolsheviks were dealing with problems of their own following the revolution, including a great civil war lasting through 1920. Much of what happened in the peace settlements reflected the unspoken concern with the challenge of revolution that the new Soviet Russia represented. A variety of goals marked the peace talks: the idealistic desire to create a better world, the patriotic pursuit of self-defense, a commitment to the self-determination of nations, and the desire to fix blame for the outbreak of the war. In the end, the peace treaties satisfied none of these goals. Meanwhile, Russia's new leaders carefully watched events in the west, looking for opportunities that might permit them to extend their revolution to central Europe.

settling the peace

From January to June 1919, an assembly of nations convened in Paris to draw up the new European peace. Although the primary task of settling the peace fell to the Council of Four—Premier Georges Clemenceau of France, Prime Minister David Lloyd George of Great Britain, Prime Minister Vittorio Emanuele Orlando of Italy, and President Woodrow Wilson of the United States—small states, newly formed states, and non-European states, Japan in particular, joined in the task of forging the peace. The states of Germany, Austria-Hungary, and Soviet Russia were excluded from the negotiating tables where the future of Europe was to be determined.

President Wilson, who captured international attention with his liberal views on the peace, was the central figure of the conference. He was firmly committed to the task of shaping a better world: before the end of the war he had proclaimed the "Fourteen Points" as a guideline to the future peace and as an appeal to the people of Europe to support his policies. Believing that secret diplomacy and the alliance system were responsible for the events leading up to the declaration of war in 1914, he put forward as a basic principle "open covenants of peace, openly arrived at." Other points included the reduction of armaments, freedom of commerce and trade, self-determination of peoples, and a general association of nations to guarantee the peace that became the League of Nations. The Fourteen Points were, above all, an idealistic statement of the principles for a good and lasting peace. Point 14, which stipulated "mutual guarantees of independence and

The representatives of the victorious Allies at Versailles: (left to right) David Lloyd George of Great Britain, Vittorio Orlando of Italy, Georges Clemenceau of France, and Woodrow Wilson of the United States.

territorial integrity" through the establishment of the League of Nations, was endorsed by the peace conference. The League, which the United States refused to join in spite of Wilson's advocacy, was intended to arbitrate all future disputes among states and to keep the peace.

Georges Clemenceau of France represented a different approach to the challenge of the peace, one motivated primarily by a concern for his nation's security. France had suffered the greatest losses of the war in both human lives and property destroyed. In order to prevent a resurgent Germany, Clemenceau supported a variety of measures to cripple it as a military force on the Continent. Germany was disarmed. The territory west of the Rhine River was demilitarized, with occupation by Allied troops to last for a period of 15 years. With Russia unavailable as a partner to contain Germany, France supported the creation of a series of states in eastern Europe carved out of former Russian, Austrian, and German territory. Wilson supported these new states out of a concern for the self-determination of peoples. Clemenceau's main concern was self-defense.

Much time and energy were devoted to redrawing the map of Europe. New states were created out of the lands of three failed empires. To allow self-determination, Finland, Latvia, Estonia, Lithuania, Poland, Czechoslovakia, Austria, Hungary, and Yugoslavia were all granted status as nation-states. However, the rights of ethnic and cultural minorities were violated in some cases because of the impossibility of redrawing the map of Europe strictly according to the principle of self-determination. In spite of good intentions, every new nation had its own national minority, a situation that held the promise of future trouble.

The peace conference produced five separate treaties with each of the defeated nations: Austria, Hungary, Turkey, Bulgaria, and Germany. The treaty signed with Germany on 28 June 1919, known as the Treaty of Versailles because it was signed in the great Bourbon palace, was the first and most important. In that treaty, the Allies imposed blame for the war on Germany and its expansionist aims in the famous War Guilt Clause. If the war was Germany's fault, then Germany must be made to pay. Reparations, once the price of defeat, were now exacted as compensation for damages inflicted by a guilty aggressor.

The principle of punitive reparations was included in the German settlement. By 1920 the German people knew that Germany had to make a down payment of $5 billion against a future bill; had to hand over a signifi-

Europe After World War I

cant proportion of their merchant ships, including all vessels of more than 1600 tons; had to lose all German colonies; and had to deliver coal to neighboring countries. These harsh clauses, more than any other aspect of the peace settlement, came to haunt the Allies in the succeeding decades.

In the end, no nation got what it wanted from the peace settlement. The defeated nations felt that they had been badly abused. The victorious nations were aware of the compromises they had reluctantly accepted. Cooperation among nations was essential if the treaty was to work successfully. It had taken the combined resources, not only of France and the British Empire but also of Russia with its vast population and the United States with its great industrial and financial might, to defeat the power of Germany and the militarily ineffective Austro-Hungarian Empire. A new and stable balance of power depended on the participation of Russia, the United States, and the British Empire. But Russia was excluded from and hostile to the peace settlement, the United States was uncommitted to it, and the British Empire declined to guarantee it. All three Great Powers backed off from their European responsibilities at the end of the war. By 1920 all aspects of the treaty, but especially the reparations clause, had been

A German cartoon, titled "The Mask Falls," depicts German reaction to the terms of the Treaty of Versailles and to the Allies' brand of justice.

questioned and criticized by the very governments that had written and accepted them. The search for a lasting peace had just begun.

Revolution in Russia, 1917–1920

Every country has its prophets. So too did Russia in 1914 when a now-forgotten former government minister advised Tsar Nicholas II (1894–1917) to avoid war or else face a social revolution. Other advisers prevailed: they said that Russia must go to war because it was a Great Power with interests beyond its borders. But within its empire, the process of modernization was widening social divisions. Nicholas preferred to listen to those who promised that a short, successful war would strengthen his monarchy against the domestic forces of change. Little did Nicholas know, when he committed Russia to the path of war instead of revolution, that he had guaranteed a future of war *and* revolu-

tion. He was delivering his nation up to humiliating defeat in global war and a devastating civil war. His own days were numbered, with his fate to be determined at the hands of a Marxist dictatorship.

The Last Tsar. The Romanov dynasty surely needed strengthening. In 1914 Russia was considered backward by the standards of Western industrial society. Russia still recalled a recent feudal past. The serfs had been freed in the 1860s, but the nature of the emancipation exacerbated tensions in the countryside and peasant hunger for land. Russia's limited, rapid industrialization in the 1880s and 1890s was an attempt to catch up with Great Britain, France, and Germany as a world industrial power. But the speed of such change brought with it severe dislocation, especially in the industrial city of Moscow and the capital, St. Petersburg.

Twelve years earlier, in 1905, the workers of St. Petersburg had protested hardships due to cyclical downturns in the economy. On a Sunday in January 1905, the tsar's troops fired on a peaceful mass demonstration in front of the Winter Palace, killing and wounding scores of workers, women, and children, who were appealing to the tsar for relief. The event, which came to be known as Bloody Sunday, set off a revolution that spread to Moscow and the countryside. In October 1905, the regime responded to the disruptions with a series of reforms that legalized political parties and established the Duma, or national parliament. Peasants, oppressed with their own burdens of taxation and endemic poverty, launched mass attacks on big landowners throughout 1905 and 1906. The government met workers' and peasants' demands with a return to repression in 1907. In the half-decade before the Great War, the Russian state stood as an autocracy of parliamentary concessions blended with severe police controls.

What workers had learned in 1905 was the power and the means of independent organization. Factory committees, trade unions, and *soviets*, or workers' councils, proliferated. Despite winning a grant of legal status after 1906, unions gained little in terms of ability to act on behalf of their members. Unrest among factory workers revived on the eve of the Great War, a period of rapid economic growth and renewed trade union activity. Between January and July 1914, Russia experienced 3500 strikes in a six-month period. Although economic strikes were considered legal, strikes deemed political were not. With the outbreak of war, all collective action was banned. Protest stopped, but only momentarily. The tsar certainly weighed the workers' actions in his

This oil painting by N. Vladimirov depicts the shooting of the workers in front of the Winter Palace in St. Petersburg, on a Sunday, 9 January 1905. The day is known in Russian history as Bloody Sunday.

decision to view war as a possible diversion from domestic problems.

Russia was less prepared for war than any of the other belligerents. Undoubtedly it had more soldiers than other countries, but it lacked arms and equipment. Problems of provisioning such a huge fighting force placed great strains on the domestic economy and on the work force. Under government coercion to meet the needs of war, industrial output doubled between 1914 and 1917, while agricultural production plummeted. The tsar, who unwisely insisted on commanding his own troops, left the government in the hands of his wife, the Tsarina Alexandra, a German princess by birth, and her eccentric peasant adviser, Rasputin. Scandal, sexual innuendo, and charges of treason surrounded the royal court. The incompetence of a series of unpopular ministers further eroded confidence in the regime. (See "The Women Who Started the Russian Revolution," pp. 908–909.)

In the end, the war sharpened long-standing divisions within Russian society. Led by exhausted and starving working women, poorly paid and underfed workers toppled the regime in the bitter winter of March 1917. This event was the beginning of a violent process of revolution and civil war. The tsar abdicated, and all public symbols of the tsardom were destroyed. The banner bearing the Romanov two-headed eagle was torn down, and in its place the red flag flew over the Winter Palace.

Dual Power. With the tsar's abdication, two centers of authority replaced autocracy. One was the Provisional Government, appointed by the Duma and made up of progressive liberals led by Prince Georgi Lvov (1861–1925), prime minister of the new government, who also served as minister of the interior. Aleksandr Kerenski (1881–1970), the only socialist in the Provisional Government, served as minister of justice. The members of the new government hoped to establish constitutional and democratic rule. The other center of authority was the soviets—committees or councils elected by workers and soldiers and supported by radical lawyers, journalists, and intellectuals in favor of socialist self-rule. The Petrograd Soviet was the most prominent among the councils. This duality of power was matched by duality in policies and objectives, which guaranteed a short-lived and unstable regime.

The problems facing the new regime soon became apparent as revolution spread to the provinces and the battlefront. Peasants, who made up 80 percent of the Russian population, accepted the revolution and de-

The women who started the Russian Revolution

Women in Russia, like their counterparts all over Europe in 1914, took over new jobs in the workplace as men marched off to war. Four out of every ten Russian workers were women, up from three of ten on the eve of the war. The situation was more dramatic in Petrograd, Russia's capital and principal industrial center, where by 1917 women constituted 55 percent of the labor force. Russian working women faced greater hardships than their sisters in the west. Most women workers in Petrograd held unskilled, poorly paid jobs in the textile industries and worked grueling 12- and 13-hour days. They left work only to stand for hours in long bread lines and then returned home to care for their elderly relatives and often sick children. Infant mortality was alarmingly high, with as many as half of all children dying before the age of three. Factory owners reported that nothing could be done. "The worker mother drudges and knows only need, only worry and grief," one commentator observed. "Her life passes in gloom, without light."

Russia was suffering badly in the war, with over 2 million soldiers killed by the beginning of 1917. News of disasters at the front reached mothers, wives, and sisters at home in spite of the government's efforts to hide the defeats. In the less than three years since the war had begun, prices had increased 400 percent and transport lines for food and coal had broken down. Bread was the main staple of meager diets. Supplies of flour and grain were not reaching towns and cities. People were starving and freezing to death. Young children were now working 11½-hour days in the factories. The situation was dire, and working women knew that something must be done if their families were to survive.

The working women of Petrograd correctly understood that the intolerable state of affairs had come about because the government was unable to control distribution and to ration limited supplies. Carrying a double burden of supporting those at home unable to work and of producing in the factory the armaments essential for the war effort, women workers began demanding that labor organizations take action to alleviate the situation. In the winter of 1916–17, labor leaders advised exhausted and starving workers to be cautious and patient: workers must wait to strike until the time was ripe. Women workers did not agree. On 8 March 1917 (23 February by the Russian calendar), over 7000 women went on strike in acknowledgment of International Women's Day, an event initiated in the United States in 1909 to recognize the rights of working women. These striking women were angry, frustrated, hungry, and tired of watching their families starve while their husbands, brothers, and sons were away at the battlefront. The week before, the city had been placed on severe rationing because Petrograd was down to its last few days' supply of flour. Although the principal concern of the striking women was bread, their protest was more than just a food riot. Women left their posts in the textile mills to demand an end to the war and an end to the reign of Tsar Nicholas II. They were responding not to revolutionary propaganda but to the politics of hunger. Singing songs of protest, they marched through the streets to take their cause to the better-paid and more radical male metalworkers. Women appealed to working men to join the strike. By the end of the day, 100,000 workers had left their jobs to join demonstrations against the government.

The women did not stop there. They took justice into their own hands and looted bakeries and grocery shops in search of food. In the street demonstrations of the next several days, women and men marched by the thousands, attracting growing support from workers throughout the city and the suburbs. Forty demonstrators were killed when government troops fired into a crowd. Still the women were not deterred. Bolshevik leader Leon Trotsky recalled women's bravery in going up to detachments of soldiers: "More boldly than men, they take hold of the rifles and beseech, almost command: 'Put down your bayonets—join us!'" Stories abound of how poor working women persuaded officers and soldiers of the Cossacks—the tsar's privileged fighting force—to lay down their arms. It was rumored that soldiers abandoned the tsar because they would not fire on the crowds of women. A participant in one confrontation reported how women workers stood without flinching as a detachment of Cossacks bore down upon them. Someone in the crowd shouted out that these were the wives and sisters of soldiers at the front. The Cossacks lowered their rifles and turned their horses around. Troops like these, tired of the war, mutinied all over Petrograd. Within four days of the first action taken by women textile operatives, the government had lost the support of Petrograd workers, women and men, and its soldiers, who had joined the demonstrators. The tsar was forced to abdicate. From this point on, the Romanov monarchy and the Russian war effort were doomed.

In those first days of protest, the women of Petrograd took action into their own hands, pouring into the streets to call for bread, peace, and the end of tsardom. They rejected autocracy and war in defense of their communities and their families. The Russian Revolution had begun.

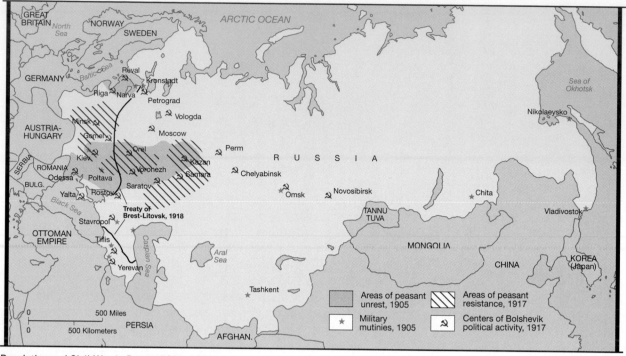

Revolution and Civil War in Russia, 1914–1920

manded land and peace. Without waiting for government directives, peasants began seizing the land. Peasants tried to alleviate some of their suffering by hoarding what little they had. The food crisis of winter persisted throughout the spring and summer as breadlines lengthened and prices rose. Workers in cities gained better working conditions and higher wages. But wage increases were invariably followed by higher prices that robbed workers of their gains. Real wages declined.

In addition to the problems of land and bread, the war itself presented the new government with other insurmountable difficulties. Hundreds of thousands of Russian soldiers at the front deserted the war, having heard news from home of peasant land grabs and rumors of a new offensive planned for July. The Provisional Government, concerned with Russia's territorial integrity and its position in the international system, continued to honor the tsar's commitments to the Allies by participating in the war. By spring 1917, 6 to 8 million Russian soldiers had been killed, wounded, or captured. The Russian army was incapable of fighting.

The Provisional Government tried everything to convince its people to carry on with the war. In the summer of 1917, the Women's Battalion of Death, composed exclusively of female recruits, was enlisted into the army.

Its real purpose, officials admitted, was to "shame the men" into fighting. The all-female unit, like its male counterparts, experienced high losses: 80 percent of the force suffered casualties. The Provisional Government was caught in an impossible situation: it could not withdraw from the war, but neither could it fight. Continued involvement in the lost cause of the war blocked any consideration of social reforms.

While the Provisional Government was trying to deal with the calamities, many members of the intelligentsia—Russia's educated class, who had been exiled by the tsar for their political beliefs—now rushed back from western Europe to take part in the great revolutionary experiment. Theorists of all stripes put their cases before the people. Those who were in favor of gradual reform debated the relative merits of various government policies with those who favored violent revolution. The months between February 1917 and July 1917 were a period of great intellectual ferment. It was the Marxists, or Social Democrats, who had the greatest impact on the direction of the revolution.

The Social Democrats believed that there were objective laws of historical development that could be discovered. Russia's future could be understood only in terms of the present situation in western Europe. Like

Marxists in the West, the Russian Social Democrats split over how best to achieve a socialist state. The more moderate Mensheviks (the term means "minority") wanted to work through parliamentary institutions and were willing to cooperate with the Provisional Government. A smaller faction—despite its name—calling themselves Bolsheviks (meaning "majority") dedicated themselves to preparation for revolutionary upheaval. After April 1917, the Bolsheviks refused to work with the Provisional Government and organized themselves to take control of the Petrograd Soviet.

The leader of the Bolsheviks was Vladimir Ilich Ulyanov (1870–1924), best known by his revolutionary name, Lenin. Forty-seven years old at the time of the revolution, Lenin had spent most of his life in exile or in prison. More a pragmatist than a theoretician, he argued for a disciplined party of professional revolutionaries, a vanguard that would lead the peasants and workers in a socialist revolution against capitalism. In contrast to the Mensheviks, he argued that the time was now ripe for a successful revolution and that it could be achieved through the soviets.

Immediately upon his arrival in Petrograd from Switzerland, Lenin threw down the gauntlet to the Provisional Government. In his April Theses, he promised the Russian people peace, land, and bread. The war must be ended immediately, he argued, because it represented an imperialist struggle that was benefiting capitalists. Russia's duty was to withdraw and wait for a world revolution. This was more than rhetoric on Lenin's part. His years in exile in the west and news of

mutinies and worker protests convinced him that revolution was imminent. His revolutionary policies on land were little more than endorsements of the seizures already taking place all over Russia. Even his promises of bread had little substance. But on the whole, the April Theses constituted a clear critique of the policies of the Provisional Government.

Dissatisfaction with the Provisional Government increased as the war dragged hopelessly on and bread lines lengthened. In the midst of these calamities, a massive popular demonstration erupted in July 1917 against the Provisional Government and in favor of the soviets, which excluded the upper classes from voting. The Provisional Government responded with repressive force reminiscent of the tsardom. The July Days were proof of the growing influence of the Bolsheviks among the Russian people. Although the Bolshevik leadership had withdrawn support for the demonstrations at the last moment, Bolshevik rank-and-file party members strongly endorsed the protest. Indisputably, Bolshevik influence was growing in the soviets despite repression and the persecution of its leaders. Lenin was forced to flee to Finland.

As a result of the July Days, Kerenski, who had been heading the Ministry of Justice, was named prime minister and continued the Provisional Government's moderate policies. In order to protect the government from a coup on the right, Kerenski permitted the arming of the Red Guards, the workers' militia units of the Petrograd Soviet. The traditional chasm between the upper and lower classes was widening as the policies of the

As late as August 1917, the Provisional Government of Aleksandr Kerenski was determined to carry on the war, but the war-weary troops began to quit. In this scene from Galicia, demoralized Russian soldiers throw down their arms and flee after hearing that German cavalry has broken through the lines.

Provisional Government conflicted with the demands of the soviets.

Lenin and the Bolsheviks Seize Power. The second revolution came in November (October according to the Russian calendar). This time it was not a spontaneous street demonstration by thousands of working women that triggered the revolution, but rather the seizure of the Russian capital by the Red Guards of the Petrograd Soviet. The revolution was carefully planned and orchestrated by Lenin and his vanguard of Bolsheviks, who now possessed majorities in the soviets in Moscow and Petrograd and other industrial centers. Returning surreptitiously from Finland, Lenin moved through the streets of Petrograd disguised in a curly wig and head bandages, watching the Red Guards seize centers of communication and public buildings. The military action was directed by Lev Bronstein, better known by his revolutionary name, Leon Trotsky (1879–1940). The Bolshevik chairman of the Petrograd Soviet, Trotsky used the Red Guards to seize political control and arrest the members of the Provisional Government. Kerenski escaped and fled the city.

The takeover was achieved with almost no bloodshed and was immediately endorsed by an All-Russian Congress of Soviets, which consisted of representatives of local soviets from throughout the nation who were in session amid the takeover of the capital. A Bolshevik regime under Lenin now ruled Russia. Tsar Nicholas II and the royal family were executed by the Bolshevik revolutionaries in July 1918.

The Russian Civil War, 1917–1920. Lenin immediately set to work to end the war for Russia. After months of negotiation, Russia signed a separate peace with the Germans in March 1918 in the Treaty of Brest-Litovsk. By every measure, the treaty was a bitter humiliation for the new Soviet regime. The territorial losses sustained were phenomenal. In a vast amputation, Russia was reduced to the size of its Muscovite period: it recognized the independence of the Ukraine, Georgia, and Finland; it relinquished its Polish territories, the Baltic States, and part of Byelorussia to Germany and Austria-Hungary; and it handed over other territories on the Black Sea to Turkey. Lenin felt that he had no choice: he needed to buy time in order to consolidate the revolution at home, and he hoped for a socialist revolution in Germany that would soften the results of the treaty.

The Treaty of Brest-Litovsk was judged a betrayal, not only outside Russia among the Allied powers, but

In this poster from 1922, Lenin points to a utopian future as he proclaims, "Let the ruling class tremble before the Communist revolution." The rising sun in the background symbolizes the dawn of the socialist era.

also inside Russia among some army officers who had sacrificed much for the tsar's war. To these military men, the Bolsheviks were no more than German agents who held the country in their sway. Lacking sufficient organization, unable to coordinate their movements because the Bolsheviks dominated the country's center, and torn apart by different political goals, the White Armies ultimately failed to challenge successfully the Bolshevik hold on the reins of state. But in the three years of civil war between Whites and Reds, the Whites posed a serious threat to Bolshevik policies.

Anti-Bolshevik forces were supplied with materials by the Allies, who intended to keep the eastern front viable. The Allies sent over 100,000 troops and supplies for the purpose of overthrowing the Bolshevik regime by supporting its enemies. Allied support for the White Armies came primarily from the United States, Great Britain, France, and Japan and continued beyond the armistice that ended the Great War in 1918. Although Allied support was not crucial to the outcome of the

proclamation of the "whites," 8 july 1918

In the summer of 1918, opponents of the Bolsheviks organized their own volunteer army with the hope of destroying the communist Red Army and eliminating Bolshevik rule. Dissatisfied military officers, Cossacks who feared the loss of their lands and privileges under a Bolshevik state, moderate republicans, socialist revolutionaries, and detachments of workers, students, and intellectuals rallied together. The only thing they had in common was their enemy. In this proclamation, they paint the Bolsheviks as the enemy of the people.

To the Workers and Peasants:

Citizens! The events of the last few days compel all those who love their country and the Russian people, all true defenders of freedom, to take up arms against the Soviet Government and defeat the usurpers who are disguising their nefarious acts by using the name of the people.

The Soviet of People's Commissars has brought ruin to Russia. . . . Instead of bread and peace it has brought famine and war. The Soviet of People's Commissars has made of mighty Russia a bit of earth dripping with the blood of peaceful citizens doomed to the pangs of hunger. In the name of the people the self-styled commissars have given the most fertile land to the enemies of Russia—the Austrians and Germans. There have been wrested from us the Ukraine, the Baltic and Vistula regions, the Kuban, the Don, and the Caucasus, which fed and supplied us with bread. That bread now goes to Germany. With that bread they are feeding those who, step by step, are conquering us and with the help of the Bolsheviks are placing us in the power of the German Kaiser. With that bread they are feeding the German army, which is slaughtering our people in cities and villages of the Ukraine, on the banks of the Don, in the mountains of the Caucasus, and in the fields of Great Russia.

The Soviet of People's Commissars is a plaything in the hands of the German Ambassador, Count Mirbach.

The Soviet of People's Commissars dictates decrees in the name of the people but Kaiser Wilhelm writes those decrees. Spurning agreement with the best citizens of the country, the Soviet of People's Commissars is not only in complete accord with the German imperialists but is carrying out unhesitatingly all their orders and demands.

By its treacherous policy of executing the orders of Count Mirbach the Soviet of People's Commissars forced the rising of the Czechoslovak army, which was marching to the Western front to fight the Germans. . . .

The Czechoslovaks are true republicans and serve the same sublime cause that we do. They are making war on the usurpers and will not permit the strangling of liberty. The People's Commissars, having long since betrayed the cause of the working class and knowing that the wrath of the people is terrible, now depend upon the bayonets of the Germans and the duped Letts to save their own lives and to keep in power.

The People's Commissars have brought about a terrible fratricidal war, sending detachments of Red Guards and Letts against the peasants to take their grain. The People's Commissars are arresting and shooting workers who do not agree with their policies, are manipulating the elections, and are strangling all civil liberties. . . .

To arms all! Down with the Soviet of People's Commissars! Only by overthrowing it shall we have bread, peace, and freedom! Long live unity and order in Russia! When we put an end to the Soviet power we shall at the same time end civil war and return once more to our former strength and power.

And then the enemies of our country will not be terrifying to us. Down with the hirelings—the People's Commissars and their tools! Long live the coming Constituent Assembly!

Long live the free mighty fatherland!

civil war, it played a significant role in shaping Soviet perceptions of the outside world. For generations of Soviet citizens, anti-Bolshevik assistance has been viewed as an indication that a hostile and predatory capitalist world intended to destroy the fledgling Soviet state for its own ends.

The civil war had another legacy for the future of the Soviet state. To deal with the anarchy caused by the fratricidal struggle, Lenin had to strengthen the government's dictatorial elements at the expense of its democratic ones. The new Soviet state used state police to suppress all opposition. The dictatorship of the proletariat yielded to the dictatorship of the repressive forces.

In the course of the civil war, Lenin was no more successful than Kerenski and the Provisional Government had been in solving the problems of food supplies. Human costs of the civil war were high, with over 800,000 soldiers dead on both sides and 2 million civilian deaths from dysentery and diseases caused by poor nutrition. Industrial production ceased, and people fled towns to return to the countryside. In 1920 it seemed that Russia could drop no lower. Millions had been killed in war or had died from famine. Stripped of territories and sapped of its industrial strength, Russia was a defeated nation. Yet Bolshevik idealism about the success of the proletarian revolution prevailed. No longer sure that a world socialist revolution would come to their aid, Bolshevik leaders set out to build the future.

The Russian Revolution

January–July 1914	Protests and strikes
30 July 1914	Russia enters World War I
March 1917	First Russian Revolution: abdication of Tsar Nicholas II
March 1917	Creation of Provisional Government
April 1917	Bolsheviks take control of Petrograd
July 1917	Massive demonstration against Provisional Government; Lenin is forced to flee Russia
November 1917	Bolsheviks and Red Guards seize political control in what comes to be known as the October Revolution
March 1918	Russia withdraws from World War I and signs Treaty of Brest-Litovsk
July 1918	Tsar Nicholas II and family are executed

By every measure, the Great War was disastrously expensive. Some European nations suffered more than others, but all endured significant losses of life, property, and productive capacity. The cost in human lives was enormous. In western Europe, 8.5 million were dead; total casualties amounted to 37.5 million. France lost 20 percent of its men between the ages of 20 and 44, Germany lost 15 percent, and Great Britain 10 percent. The war also resulted in huge losses in productive capacity. National economies buckled under the weight of foreign debts and resorted to a variety of methods to bail themselves out, including taxes, loans, and currency inflation. The people of Europe continued to pay for the war long after the fighting had ended.

The big winner in the war was the United States, now a creditor nation owed billions of dollars in loans from the Allies and operating in new markets established during the war. The shift was not a temporary move but a structural change. The United States now took its place as a great power in the international system. The world that had existed before 1914 was gone, and what was to replace it was still very much in flux. To the east, Russia was engaged in the vast experiment of building a new society. In the West, the absence of war was not peace.

Mastering the chapter

To review the main points of the chapter, be sure you can explain the significance of each of the following.

Terms/Concepts/Events	People	Places
Schlieffen Plan	Gavrilo Princip	Sarajevo
Easter Rebellion	General Henri-Philippe Pétain	Ypres
Balfour Declaration	Winston Churchill	Tannenberg
Lusitania	David Lloyd George	Verdun
"Fourteen Points"	Nicholas II	the Somme
League of Nations	Aleksandr Kerenski	Passchendaele
Treaty of Versailles	Mensheviks	Dalmatia
reparations	Bolsheviks	Dardanelles
Bloody Sunday	Vladimir Ilich Ulyanov (Lenin)	Gallipoli Peninsula
soviets	Leon Trotsky	Jutland

suggestions for further Reading

The war Europe expected

Marc Ferro, *The Great War, 1914–1918* (London: Routledge & Kegan Paul, 1973). The origins of World War I within a broad social and cultural context. Stressing the importance of an imagined war and patriotism as two factors that precipitated actual conflict, Ferro shows how the gulf between imagination and reality led to domestic conflict and social unrest once war broke out.

* James Joll, *The Origins of the First World War* (New York: Longman, 1984). In an examination of the decisions that brought about war in 1914, importance is placed on the limited options available to decision makers. The July crisis, the international system, the arms race, domestic politics, the international economy, imperial rivalries, and cultural and psychological factors are considered in terms of their contributions to the outbreak of war.

* Keith Robbins, *The First World War* (Oxford: Oxford University Press, 1984). The major cultural, political, military, and social developments between 1914 and 1918. Includes a discussion of the course of the land war and modes of warfare.

The war Europe got

* Frans Coetzee and Marilyn Shevin-Coetzee, eds. *Authority, Identity and the Social History of the Great War* (Providence: Berghahn Books, 1995). Recognizing that 1914 marks the beginning of the twentieth century, contributors examine the variety of national responses involved in waging total war and stress the interrelatedness of the home fronts and the battlefronts in affecting individual lives and identities.

* Gerd Hardach, *The First World War, 1914–1918* (Berkeley: University of California Press, 1977). Describes the changes in the world economy leading up to the war, the war's impact on trade, wartime monetary and fiscal policies, and the war's impact on labor. Each major power is included in an analysis of wartime economic history.

B. E. Schmitt and H. C. Vedeler, *The World in a Crucible, 1914–1919* (New York: Harper & Row, 1984). A broad survey of the military and political history of World War I; the war is viewed here as a period of revolution in both warfare and politics. Includes considerable discussion of the Russian Revolution and a section on the entry of the United States into European affairs.

* Denis Winter, *Death's Men: Soldiers of the Great War* (London: Penguin, 1979). Rather than being an account of military strategy and battlefield tactics, *Death's Men* goes inside the infantrymen's war to convey the experience of war in the trenches.

adjusting to the unexpected: total war

John Williams, *The Homefronts: Britain, France and Germany, 1914–1918* (London: Constable, 1972). A comparative study of the home fronts, their impact on the course of the war, and the war's impact on civilian life.

Reshaping europe: After war and Revolution

* Sheila Fitzpatrick, *The Russian Revolution, 1917–1932* (Oxford: Oxford University Press, 1982). An analysis of the October Revolution of 1917 from the perspective of Stalinist society. The February and October revolutions of 1917, the civil war, and the economic policies of the 1920s are treated as various aspects of a single revolutionary movement.

Tsuyoshi Hasegawa, *The February Revolution: Petrograd, 1917* (Seattle: University of Washington Press, 1981). A thorough examination of the effects of World War I on Russian workers, liberals, and revolutionary parties leads to an interpretation of the February Revolution as the outcome of a conflict between the state and its citizens. Particular attention is given to events leading to the abdication of the tsar, the establishment of the Provisional Government, and the early stages of the Russian Revolution.

Arno J. Mayer, *The Politics and Diplomacy of Peacemaking* (New York: Knopf, 1967). A comprehensive examination of the role of internal political concerns and the foreign policy of the warring nations, as well as a thorough analysis of the struggles between Bolshevism, Wilsonian liberalism, and counterrevolution.

* David Stevenson, *The First World War and International Politics* (Oxford: Oxford University Press, 1988). A study of the global ramifications of World War I, this work traces the development of war aims on both sides, the reasons peace negotiations failed, and why compromise proved elusive.

*Paperback edition available.

The European search for stability, 1920-1939

The screams from Guernica

Rarely does a piece of art scream out. The mural Guernica is different. Listen to the painting shown here. It is a painting whose images convey sounds: the shrieks of terror, fear, suffering, and death. There is a chaos of noise here that seems at odds with the drab grays, black, and white, the monochromatic colorlessness of the artist's palette. But no, the lack of color only heightens the noise and allows us to focus on the sound, the screams that come from the open mouths of human and beast on the canvas. Death and brutality reverberate throughout the painting. The open mouths of the dead baby's mother, the bull standing behind her, the small bird to the right of the bull, and the wounded horse at the center of the canvas emit fear like projectiles—beak and tongues thrusting forth in pointed daggers.

Pablo Picasso (1881–1973) painted this great mural in May and June 1937 for the Spanish Pavilion of the International Exhibition to be held in Paris. He called it *Guernica* in commemoration of the bombing of the small Basque town in Spain by German planes at the end of April 1937. The destruction of Guernica was an event that shocked the world and devastated the Spanish artist, then living in France. Working in collaboration with the insurgent forces of Francisco Franco (1892–1975), German planes dropped bomb after bomb on the ancient city, destroying it in three and a half hours. Their purpose was to cut off the retreat of loyalist government troops and to terrorize civilians through saturation bombing. Picasso demonstrates vividly that noncombatants, represented by the women and child, were no longer just hapless bystanders but were, in fact, the very targets of indiscriminate killing.

Guernica is a huge canvas, measuring over 11 feet high and 25 feet long. It dwarfs spectators who stand before it, enveloping them in a modern-day apocalypse of contorted bodies. We do not look at war directly in the mural but at the terror it creates in this vision of needless slaughter. Picasso deliberately used the traditional religious symbols of the Madonna and Child and the Pietà as models for his terrifying image of maternity. The lips of the baby, who hangs like a rag doll in the arms of its despairing mother on the far left of the canvas, are sealed in the silence of death. The mother finds her counterpoint in the figure of the limping woman in the right foreground, who drags behind her a wounded arm and a swollen knee. Above her a woman, gaping in disbelief and clutching her breasts in anguish, raises a lamp over the scene. On the far right, a fourth woman, trapped in the flames of a burning building, appears to be exploding upward in terrified petition. On the ground under the horse lies a dead man with his head and arm severed from his body, clutching a broken sword and flower whose petals wait to be picked in his right hand. The presentation of his head as a piece of statuary fallen from its pedestal reinforces the bloodless horror of his death. His left palm is crisscrossed with the lines of fate, or perhaps marked with the toil of heavy labor. Suspended over the scene like a huge eye is a naked light bulb, a modern image illuminating the timelessness of the theme of the horror of war.

In one of his rare moments of self-interpretation, Picasso explained to a public eager to grasp the mural's symbolism that the horse whose side is opened by a terrible gash is "the people," victimized by incomprehensible cruelty. The bull is an enigmatic figure symbolizing, Picasso tells us, darkness and brutality. The horned beast appears as a powerful and vulnerable witness to this scene of needless destruction.

Guernica has been hailed as the most significant painting of the twentieth century. His greatness as an artist, Picasso claimed, derived from his ability to understand his time. In the stripped-down, almost cartoonlike figures of *Guernica*, Picasso presents us with a picture of European society that is brutal and horrible. Here is a condemnation of the modern technological war that targets civilian populations; here on this horrifying canvas are portrayed the consequences of totalitarianism and the failure of democracy that characterized the European search for stability between 1920 and 1939. Subsequent events

focus Questions

1. What problems for European stability were created or left unresolved by the armistice ending World War I?
2. What did Stalin's victory over Trotsky mean for economic development in the Soviet Union?
3. What is fascism, and why was it so alluring to Italians, Germans, and other Europeans?
4. How were rearmament, anti-Semitism, and autarky all part of Hitler's vision of *Lebensraum*?
5. Why did Europe's remaining democracies prove to be so frail during the 1930s?

made Germany's actions in the Spanish Civil War seem like a dress rehearsal for atrocities against the population centers of Warsaw, Rotterdam, and London and made this canvas seem a prophecy of horrors to come. Some years later, during the Second World War, a Nazi official challenged Picasso with a photograph of the great mural: "So it was you who did this." The artist answered, "No, you did."

International politics and economic nationalism

The armistice that ended World War I in 1918 did not stop the process of social upheaval and transformations challenging attempts to restore order throughout Europe. In 1918, parts of war-torn Europe faced the possibility of revolution. Russia, where revolution had destroyed tsardom, expectantly watched revolutionary developments in countries from the British Isles to eastern Europe. The Bolshevik leaders of Russia's revolution counted on the capitalist system to destroy itself. That did not happen. By 1921, revolutions had been brutally crushed in Berlin, Munich, and Budapest. The Soviets, meanwhile, had won the civil war against the Whites and survived the intervention of the British, French, Japanese, and Americans. But the new Russian regime

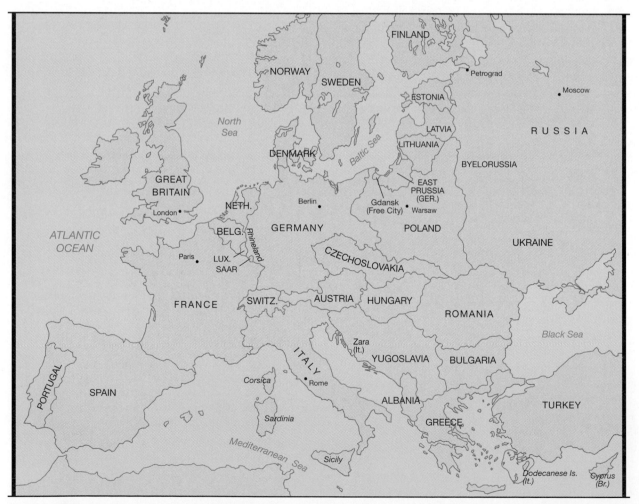

Europe in 1918

was diplomatically isolated and in a state of almost total economic collapse.

In 1917–18, the United States had played a significant and central role in the waging of war and in the pursuit of peace. Under U.S. President Woodrow Wilson, who urged his country to guarantee European security and guide Europe's future, the American nation seemed promising as an active and positive force in international politics. By 1921, however, the United States had retreated to a position, not of isolation, but of selective involvement. With one giant, Russia, devastated and isolated, and the other, the United States, reluctant, Europeans faced an uncertain future.

New Nation-states, New problems

Before World War I, east-central Europe was a region divided among four great empires—the Ottoman, the Habsburg, the Russian, and the German. Under the pressure of defeat, those empires collapsed into their component national parts, and when the dust of the peace treaties had settled, the region had been molded into a dozen sovereign states. The victorious Allies hoped that independent states newly created from fragments of empire would buffer Europe from the spread of communism westward and the expansion of German power eastward.

A swath of new independent states cut through the center of Europe. Finland had acquired its independence from Russia in 1917. Estonia, Latvia, and Lithuania, also formerly under Russian rule, comprised the now independent Baltic states. After more than a century of dismemberment among three empires, Poland became a single nation again. Czechoslovakia was carved out of former Habsburg lands. Austria and Hungary shriveled to small, independent states. Yugoslavia was pieced together from a patchwork of territories. Romania swelled, fed on a diet of settlement concessions. These new nations assured the victorious powers, especially France, that the new political geography of east-central Europe would guarantee the peace.

World War I victor nations hoped that these new states would stabilize European affairs; they could not have been more wrong. They erred in three important ways in their calculations. First, many of the new states were internally unstable precisely because of the principle of national self-determination, the idea that nationalities had the right to rule themselves. Honoring the rights of nationalities was simple in the abstract, but

application of the principle proved complicated and at times impossible. Religious, linguistic, and ethnic diversity abounded in the newly formed nations, and recognizing nationality often meant ignoring the rights of minorities. In Czechoslovakia, for example, the Czechs dominated the Slovaks and the Germans even though the Czechs were fewer in number. Ethnic unrest plagued all of eastern Europe. Minority tensions weakened and destabilized the fragile governments.

Second, the struggle for economic prosperity further destabilized the new governments. East-central Europe was primarily agricultural, and the existence of the great empires had created guaranteed markets. The war disrupted the economy and generated social unrest. The peace settlements only compounded the economic problems of the region. When the Habsburg Empire disintegrated, the Danube River basin ceased to be a cohesive economic unit. New governments were saddled with borders that made little economic sense.

Creating cohesive economic units proved an insurmountable task for newly formed governments and administrations that lacked both resources and experience. Low productivity, unemployment, and overpopulation characterized most of east-central Europe. Attempts to industrialize and to develop new markets confronted many obstacles. Much of the land was farmed on a subsistence basis. What agricultural surplus was created was difficult to sell abroad. East-central Europeans—including Poles, Czechs, Yugoslavs, and Romanians, all tied to France through military and political commitments—were excluded from western European markets and were isolated economically from their treaty allies. Economic ties with Germany endured in ways that perpetuated economic dependence and threatened future survival.

Finally, common borders produced tensions over territories. The peace settlements made no one happy. Poland quarreled with Lithuania, and Czechoslovakia vied with Poland over territorial claims. Poland actually went to war with Russia for six months in 1920 in an effort to reclaim the Ukraine and expand its borders to what they had been more than a century earlier. The Bolsheviks counterattacked and tried to turn the conflict into a revolutionary war in order to spread communism to central Europe. French military advisers came to the aid of the Poles and turned the Russians back. The Treaty of Riga, signed in March 1921, gave Poland much but not all of the territory it claimed.

Hungary, having lost the most territory in World War I, held the distinction of having the greatest number of ter-

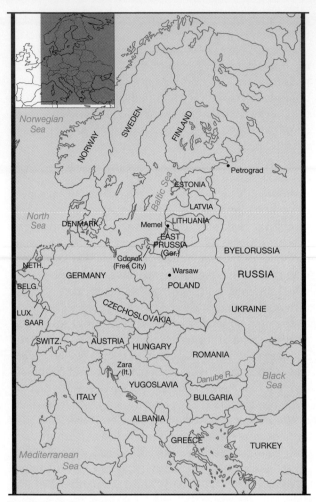

East-Central Europe

Austria, and Albania. The redefined borders of eastern and central Europe produced animosity and the seeds of ongoing conflict. The new states of eastern Europe stood as a picket fence between Germany and Russia, a fence that held little promise of guaranteeing the peace or of making good neighbors.

German Recovery

Germany, the most populous nation in western Europe with 60 million people, emerged strong from defeat. In 1919 the German people endorsed a new liberal and democratic government, the Weimar Republic, so named for the city in which its constitution had been written. The constitution of the new government was unusually progressive, with voting rights for women and extensive civil liberties for German citizens. Because World War I had not been fought in Germany, German transportation networks and industrial plants had escaped serious damage. Its industry was fed by raw materials and energy resources unsurpassed anywhere in Europe outside Russia.

In east-central Europe, Germany had actually benefited from the dismantling of the Habsburg Empire and the removal of Poland and the Baltic states from Rus-

ritorial grievances against its neighbors—Czechoslovakia, Romania, and Yugoslavia. Yugoslavia made claims against Austria. Bulgaria sought territories controlled by Greece and Romania. Ethnicity, strategic considerations, and economic needs motivated claims for territory. Disputes festered, fed by the intense nationalism that prevented the cooperation necessary for survival.

Germany, the Soviet Union, and Italy further complicated the situation with their own territorial claims against their east-central European neighbors. The new German government refused to accept the loss of the "corridor" controlled by Poland that severed East Prussia from the rest of Germany. Nor was Germany resigned to the loss of part of Silesia to Poland. Russia refused to forget its losses to Romania, Poland, Finland, and the Baltic states. Italy, too weak to act on its own, nevertheless dreamed of expansion into Yugoslavia,

Germany

sian control. Replacing its formerly large neighbor to the east were weak states potentially susceptible to Germany's influence. Because the governments of east-central Europe feared communism, they were not likely to ally themselves with the Soviet state. The existence of the small buffer states left open the possibility of German collaboration with Russia, since the two large nations might be able to negotiate their interests in the area.

On its western frontier, Germany's prospects were not so bright. Alsace and Lorraine had been returned to France. From German territory, a demilitarized zone had been created in the Rhineland. The Saar district was under the protection of League of Nations commissioners, and the Saar coal mines were transferred to French ownership until 1935, when a plebiscite returned the region to Germany. Humiliated and betrayed by the geographic consequences of its defeat, Germany looked to recover its status.

Germany's primary foreign policy goal was revision of the treaty settlements of World War I. German politicians and military leaders perceived disarmament, loss of territory, and payment of reparations as serious obstacles in restoring Germany's position as a great power. German statesmen sought liberation of the Rhineland from foreign military occupation; return of the Saar basin; and recovery of the Corridor and Upper Silesia from Poland.

German leaders set economic recovery as the basis of their new foreign policy. In 1922, Germany signed the Treaty of Rapallo with Russia, a peacetime partnership that shocked the western powers. Economics motivated the new Russo-German alliance: German industry needed markets, and the Russians needed loans to reconstruct their economy. Both states wanted to break out of the isolation imposed on them by the victors of World War I. However, Germany quickly learned that markets in Russia were limited and that hopes for recovery depended on financial cooperation with western Europe and the United States. At the end of 1923, Gustav Stresemann (1878–1929) assumed direction of the German Foreign Ministry and began to implement a conciliatory policy toward France and Britain. By displaying peaceful intentions, he hoped to secure American capital for German industry and win the support of the West for the revision of the peace settlement.

Stresemann joined his French and British counterparts, Aristide Briand (1862–1932) and Austen Chamberlain (1863–1937), in fashioning a series of treaties at Locarno, Switzerland, in 1925. In a spirit of cooperation, Germany, France, and Belgium promised never again to go to war against each other and to respect the demilitarized zone that separated them. Britain and Italy "guaranteed" the borders of all three countries and ensured the integrity of the demilitarized zone. The treaties initiated an atmosphere of goodwill, a "spirit of Locarno," that heralded a new age of security and nonaggression.

However, Germany did not renounce its ambitions in eastern Europe. Stresemann expected Germany to recover the territory lost to Poland. He also knew that Germany must rearm and expand to the east. From the early 1920s until 1933, Germany secretly rearmed in violation of Versailles. Undercover, Germany rebuilt its army and trained its soldiers and airmen on Russian territory. In violation of Versailles treaty agreements, Germany planned to be once again a great power with the same rights as other European countries.

france's search for security

Having learned the harsh lessons of 1870–71 and 1914–18, France understood well the threat posed by a united, industrialized, and well-armed Germany. During the years immediately following World War I, France deeply distrusted Germany. France had a smaller population of 40 million people, and lower industrial production than Germany. France had been devastated by the war, and Germany had not. But France did have certain advantages in 1921. It had the best-equipped army in the world. Germany was disarmed. The Rhineland was demilitarized and occupied. But France knew that without the support of Great Britain and the United States, it could not enforce the Treaty of Versailles and keep Germany militarily weak.

The Americans and the British refused to conclude a long-term peacetime alliance with the French. In search of allies on the Continent, therefore, France committed itself to an alliance in the east with Poland and the Little Entente nations of Czechoslovakia, Romania, and Yugoslavia. Treaties with these four states of east-central Europe gave France some security in the event of an attack. But the treaties were also liabilities because France would have to fight to defend east-central Europe.

To keep Germany militarily and economically weak, the French attempted to enforce the Treaty of Versailles fully in 1921–23. They were willing to do so alone if necessary. In 1923 the French army invaded the Ruhr district of Germany and occupied it with the intention of collecting reparations payments. But the Ruhr invasion served only to isolate France further from its wartime al-

Buildings for the future

Buildings tell tales. Archaeologists, trying to understand other civilizations, excavate ancient dwellings in order to reconstruct past lives. Family life, social values, the nature of work, technology, and progress are all embodied in the structures in which people live and work. If future generations had only traces of the buildings of the twentieth century, they would nonetheless hold a key to understanding our civilization and values.

The twentieth-century architecture that we call *modern* was the child born from the union of technology and art in the aftermath of the Great War of 1914–18. In reaction to the horrors of the battlefront, a new generation of architects, many of them ex-soldiers, committed themselves to the creation of buildings as works of art that answered the needs of modern society. Those who followed the lead of the prewar avant-garde disdained imitating past masters. They saw their task as "starting from zero"—that is, striking out in a new direction unencumbered by the cultural baggage of a past that had proven itself to be morally bankrupt. In building for the future, the postwar generation felt that the present must create a new style of its own.

The battle cry for a new architectural style arose from defeated Germany and in particular from a single man, Walter Gropius (1883–1969). In 1919, only a few months after the Treaty of Versailles ended World War I, Gropius, a recent veteran of the front, founded the Bauhaus, a school based on the collaborative efforts of architects, sculptors, artists, and artisans. The untranslatable name Bauhaus (resulting from joining the German words for "building" and "house") soon characterized a new movement in the arts and architecture. As director of the Bauhaus until 1928, Gropius attracted some of Europe's leading artists to the school, including the architects Marcel Breuer (1902–81) and Ludwig Mies van der Rohe (1886–1969). Russian abstract artist Vasili Kandinski (1866–1944) and his Swiss colleague Paul Klee (1879–1940) were also members of the teaching staff at the Bauhaus. Characterized by intense activity, exciting experimentation, and enthusiastic collaboration, the men and women who assembled at the Bauhaus pioneered new designs in everything from kitchen utensils and furniture to lighting fixtures and skyscrapers.

Gropius was a utopian dreamer who saw in buildings and in the humble objects of daily life the means of creating human happiness. Beauty in design was defined by the fit between form and function. Rather than rejecting industrial society, Gropius sought a new way of uniting art with it. Unlike other arts-and-crafts movements, the Bauhaus was willing to make use of the machine to produce for the masses, whether the production involved prefabricated houses or teacups. Gropius knew well that architecture does not move faster than the society it seeks to serve, but he also knew that it must keep pace with the world around it. The school's motto, one that Gropius considered realistic and responsible, proclaimed: "Art and technology—a new unity!"

Pictured here is one of the first Bauhaus models of a skyscraper. Modest by subsequent standards, its 32 stories dwarf the traditional buildings at its base. Steel and glass were expressly used to liberate the structure from supporting walls. With new engineering knowledge about support, loads, stress, and mass, sheer facades of glass opened up inside space to the outside world. Interior walls were eliminated. Gropius admired the new functional factory structures and early skyscrapers in the United States and Canada for their starkness and simplicity and sought to introduce their "majesty" to residential architecture.

The architects of the Bauhaus were in the right place at the right time. Germany needed new buildings, and in the period from 1924 to 1929 the return of economic prosperity allowed them to be built. Under Gropius's direction, working-class apartment blocks with open floor plans, unadorned facades, clean lines, and a stark simplicity spread across the German landscape. Office buildings of reinforced concrete with little to distinguish them from the new residential housing also mushroomed. By the end of the decade, Bauhaus architects had left their mark on German towns and cities. Then, seeking refuge from Hitler (eventually in the United States), Gropius and some of his associates transformed the skylines of America's great cities within a decade. In the second half of the twentieth century, the Bauhaus style of architecture spread throughout the world.

The architects of the Bauhaus changed the appearance of the modern world, and with it the twentieth-century experience. Critics who longed for a traditional architecture of decoration and classical emulation judged the Bauhaus style to be barren and ugly, but its emphasis on design and function prevailed. The skyscrapers of the twentieth century are products of the lessons of war and technology and the idealistic pursuit of a better world that took shape very visibly in the 1920s.

lies. France depended on loans from American banks to balance its budget, and the Americans disapproved of the French use of military might to enforce the treaty.

In 1924–25, France decided to cooperate with the United States and Great Britain rather than continue a policy of enforcing the treaty alone and attempting to keep Germany weak. France withdrew its army from the Ruhr and some troops from the Rhineland. It agreed to lower German reparations payments. In addition, by signing the Locarno treaties, France cooperated with the Anglo-American policy that rejected the use of military force against Germany and promoted German economic recovery.

French anxiety about security continued. Nothing indicated the nature of this anxiety more clearly than the construction, beginning in the late 1920s, of the Maginot Line, a system of defensive fortifications between Germany and France.

Throughout the 1920s, French political leaders tried to engage Great Britain in guaranteeing the security of France and Europe. The British agreed to defend France and Belgium against possible German aggression. They stopped short, however, of promising to defend Poland and Czechoslovakia. After settling this matter at Locarno, Britain largely reverted to its prewar pattern of withdrawing from continental Europe and concentrating its attention on the demands of its global empire.

The United States in Europe

The Treaty of Versailles marked the demise of European autonomy. American intervention had boosted French and British morale during the crucial months of 1917. In providing financial help, ships, troops, and supplies, the United States had rescued the Allied powers. After the war, a balance of power in Europe could not be maintained without outside help. Germany had been defeated, but if it recovered, France and Britain alone would probably not be able to contain it. Security and peace now depended on the presence of the United States to guarantee a stable balance of power in Europe and to defend Western hegemony in the world.

However, the United States was unwilling to assume a new role as political leader of Europe and mediator of European conflict. It refused to sign a joint peace, arranging instead a separate peace with Germany. It also refused to join the League of Nations. Following the war, the League had been devised as an international body of nations committed, according to article 10 of its covenant, to "respect and preserve as against external aggression the territorial integrity and existing political independence" of others. Germany was excluded from membership until 1926, and the USSR (Union of Soviet Socialist Republics) was denied entry until 1934. Otherwise, the League of Nations claimed a global membership. But the absence of U.S. support and the lack of any machinery to enforce its decisions undermined the possibility of the League's long-term effectiveness. Hopes that the international body could serve as a peacekeeper collapsed in 1931 with the League's failure to deal with the crisis of Japanese aggression against Manchuria.

The United States persisted in avoiding political and military obligations in Europe, with the idea of protecting its own freedom and autonomy. Instead, it sought to promote German economic recovery and reasoned that a peaceful and stable Europe would be reestablished without a real balance of power in Europe and without a commitment from the United States.

Many feared that territorial settlements of the peace held the promise of another war. Even efforts at comprehensive international cooperation like the League of Nations did not overcome the problem of competitive nations, nor did the Kellogg-Briand Pact, signed by 23 nations in 1928. Named for U.S. Secretary of State Frank B. Kellogg (1856–1937) and French foreign minister

Western Europe

MARRIED AGAIN

PARIS

FIFTEEN NATIONS

PEACE

KELLOGG TREATIES

DIVORCED 1914

THIS WICKED WORLD

FOREVER - AND EVER AND EVER

IRELAND, *THE COLUMBUS DISPATCH*

"Married Again." This 1928 cartoon shows the wicked world once again pledging eternal fidelity to peace with the signing of the Kellogg-Briand pact. The cynical attitude of the artist was vindicated by the events of the later twentieth century.

Aristide Briand, who devised the plan, the pact renounced war. In the atmosphere of the 1920s, a time of hope and caution, the agreement carried all the weight of an empty gesture.

crisis and collapse in a world economy

In 1918 the belligerent nations—winners and losers alike—had big bills on their hands. Although nations at war had borrowed from their own populations through the sale of war bonds, private citizens could not provide all the money needed to finance four years of war. France borrowed from Great Britain. Both Great Britain and France took loans from the United States. When all else failed, belligerent nations could and did print money not backed by productive wealth. Because more money had claims on the same amount of national wealth, the money in circulation was worth less. When the people who had purchased war bonds were then paid off with depreciated currency, they lost real wealth. Inflation had the same effect as taxation. The people had less wealth and the government had less debt.

The United States, for the first time in history the leading creditor nation in the world, had no intention of wiping the slate clean by forgiving war debts. Nor did it intend to accept repayment in less valuable postwar currencies: loans were tied to gold. Britain, France, and Belgium counted on reparations from Germany to pay their war debts and to rebuild their economies. Reparations were calculated on the basis of the damages Germany had inflicted on the Allies. The postwar Reparations Commission determined that Germany owed the victors 132 billion gold marks ($33 billion), to be paid in annual installments of 2 billion gold marks ($500 million), plus 26 percent of the value of German exports.

For the German people and for German leaders, reparations were an unacceptable punitive levy that mortgaged the prosperity of future generations. Germany, too, wanted to recover from the years of privation of the war. Substantial reparations payments would have transferred real wealth from Germany to the Allies. Transferring wealth would have cut into any increase in the German standard of living in the 1920s, and it would have diminished the investment needed to make the German economy grow.

When French and Belgian troops entered the Ruhr district of Germany in order to exact overdue reparations payments, the German government recommended that German miners, trainmen, and civil servants respond with passive resistance. To pay these idle employees and employers, the German government printed huge amounts of currency. The mark collapsed and world currencies were endangered. With financial disaster looming, the British and Americans decided to intervene. A plan had to be devised that would permit Germany to prosper while funneling payments to France, so dependent on reparations for its own recovery and for its war debt payments to the United States. In 1924 the American banker Charles G. Dawes (1865–1951), along with a group of international financial experts appointed by the Allied governments, devised a solution to the reparations problem. The Dawes Plan aimed to end inflation and restore economic prosperity in Germany by giving Germany a more modest and realistic schedule of payments and by extending a loan from American banks to get payments started.

As important as reparations and war debts are in any understanding of the Western world in the 1920s, they cannot be considered in isolation. Debtor nations, whether Allies paying back loans to the United States or defeated nations paying reparations to the victors, needed to be able to sell their goods in world markets. They saw trade as the principal way to accumulate enough national income to pay back what they owed and to prosper domestically without burying their citizens under a mountain of new taxes.

If trade was to be the stepladder out of the financial hole of indebtedness, open markets and stable currencies were its rungs. The United States recognized that a stable Europe would give it a market for its own agricultural and industrial products and provide a guarantee for recovery of its loans and investments. Yet the proverbial monkey wrench in a smoothly functioning international economy was the trade policy of the United States. Republican political leaders in the United States insisted on high tariffs to protect domestic goods against imports. But high tariffs prevented Europeans from selling in the United States and earning the dollars they needed to repay war debts.

While blocking imports, the United States planned to expand its own exports to world markets, especially to Europe. The problem for American exporters, however, was the instability of European currencies in the first half of the 1920s. All over Europe, governments allowed inflation to rise with the expectation that depreciating currencies would make their goods cheaper in world markets and hence more salable.

Depreciating European currencies on the one hand meant an appreciating dollar on the other. For the "grand design" of U.S. trade expansion, a strong dollar was no virtue. More and more German marks, British

The runaway inflation of the 1920s is dramatized by this photo of a German housewife who is lighting the cooking fire with millions of marks. She declared that it was cheaper to use the worthless currency for kindling than to buy wood with it.

pounds, and French francs had to be spent to purchase American goods. The result was that fewer American exports were sold in European markets. Because two-thirds of Germany's long-term credits came from the United States, Germany's fate was directly linked to the fortunes of American financial centers. Conversely, the soundness of American banks depended on a solvent Germany, which now absorbed 18 percent of U.S. capital exports.

Despite the scaled-down schedule of the Dawes Plan, reparations remained a bitter pill for German leaders and the German public to swallow. In 1929, American bankers devised another plan under the leadership of the American businessman Owen D. Young (1874–1962), chairman of the board of General Electric. Although the Young Plan initially transferred $100 million to Germany, Germans saw the twentieth century stretching before them as year after year of nothing but humiliating reparations payments. To make matters worse, after 1928 American private loans shriveled in Germany as American investors sought the higher yields of a booming stock market at home.

Europe as a whole made rapid progress in manufacturing production during the second half of the decade, and by 1929 it had surpassed its prewar (1913) per capita income. Yet structural weaknesses were present, though they went almost unnoticed. The false security of a new gold standard masked the instability and interdependence of currencies. Low prices prevailed in the agricultural sector, keeping the incomes of a significant segment of the population depressed. But the low rate of long-term capital investment was obscured in the flurry of short-term loans, whose disappearance in 1928 spelled the beginning of the end for European recovery. The protectionist trade policy of the United States conflicted with its insistence on repayment of war debts. Germany's resentment over reparations was in no way alleviated by the Dawes and Young repayment plans. The irresponsibility of American speculation in the stock market pricked the bubble of prosperity. None of these factors operated in isolation to cause the collapse that began in 1929. Taken together, however, they caused a depression of previously unimagined severity in the international economic system.

The Great Depression

In the history of the Western world, the year 1929 has assumed mythic proportions. During one week in October of that year, the stock market in the United States collapsed. This crash set off the Great Depression in an international economic system already plagued with structural problems. It also marked the beginning of a long period of worldwide economic stagnation and depression.

A confluence of factors made Europe and the rest of the world vulnerable to reversals in the American economy. Heavy borrowing and reliance on American investment throughout the 1920s contributed to the inherent instability of European economies. Even Great Britain, itself a creditor, relied on short-term loans; "borrowing short and lending long" proved to be disastrous when loans were recalled. Excessive lending and leniency were fatal mistakes of creditor nations, especially the United States. When in the summer of 1929 American investors turned off the tap of the flow of capital to search for higher profits at home, a precarious situation began to get worse.

A depression is a severe downturn marked by sharp declines in income and production as buying and selling slow down to a crawl. Depressions were not new in the business cycles of modern economies, but what happened in October 1929 was more serious in its extent and duration than any depression before or since. The bottom was not reached until three years after the Great Depression began. In 1932 one in four American workers was without a job. One in three banks had closed its doors. People lost their homes, unable to pay their mortgages; farmers lost their land, unable to earn enough to survive. The great prosperity of the 1920s had vanished overnight.

The plight of the United States rippled through world markets. Americans stopped buying foreign goods. The Smoot-Hawley Tariff Act, passed by the U.S. Congress in 1930, created an impenetrable tariff fortress against agricultural and manufactured imports and hampered foreign producers. The major trading nations of the world, including Great Britain, enacted similar protectionist measures. American investment abroad dried up as the lifelines of American capital to Europe were cut.

European nations tried to staunch the outward flow of capital and gold by restricting the transfer of capital abroad. Large amounts of foreign-owned gold ($6.6 billion from 1931 to 1938) nevertheless were deposited in American banks. In 1931 President Herbert Hoover (1874–1964) supported a moratorium on the payment of reparations and war debts. The moratorium, combined with the pooling of gold in the United States, led to a run on the British pound sterling in 1931 and the collapse of Great Britain as one of the world's great financial centers.

winifred Holtby

Winifred Holtby (1898–1935) was a British novelist, journalist, and social reformer who covered European political events throughout the interwar period. In this selection from her writings she chronicles the differential impact that war and depression had on women's lives. Expectations about woman's proper role, whether of housewife and mother or serving her country in the workplace, were profoundly political and hotly contested.

The effect of the slump upon women's economic position is most obvious, not only in the problems of unemployment among both industrial and professional women, but still more in the bitterness surrounding the question of married women's paid employment, "pin money" office girls, unorganised casual female factory labour, and claims to alimony, maintenance and separation allowances. These are the dilemmas of scarcity. It is here that the shoe pinches when national purchasing power has failed to distribute adequately the products of industry.

During the War, women entered almost every branch of industry and most of the professions. . . . In transport, engineering, chemicals, textiles, tailoring and woodwork, women took the places which, ever since the sorting-out process which followed the first disorganised scramble of the Industrial Revolution, had been reserved to men. They took and they enjoyed them.

Then the men returned, and on demobilisation demanded again the jobs which they had left. The position was not simple.

Some of the men had received promises that their work should be kept for them; but of these, some did not return. Some women surrendered their shovels, lathes and hoes without a grievance. Their work had been "for the duration of the war" and they had no desire to retain it.

But others thought differently. Women, they told themselves, had been excluded from the more highly-skilled and better-paid industrial posts for two or more generations. They had been told that certain processes were beyond their power. It was a lie. During the war they had proved it to be so, by their own skill and efficiency. Why surrender without a word opportunities closed to them by fraud and falsehood? They had as much right to wheel, loom or cash-register as any man. Why then pretend that they were intruders in a world which was as much their own as their brothers'? . . .

After 1928, jobs became not duties which war-time propaganda taught girls that it was patriotic to perform, but privileges to be reserved for potential bread-winners and fathers of families. Women were commanded to go back to the home.

The bitterness began which has lasted ever since—the women keeping jobs and the men resenting it—the men regaining the jobs and the women resenting it. . . .

In Italy, Germany and Ireland a new dream of natural instinctive racial unity was arising, which designed for women a return to their "natural" functions of house-keeping and child-bearing; while in the English-speaking countries a new anti-rational philosophy combined with economic fatalism, militated against the ebullient hopes which an earlier generation had pinned to education, effort, and individual enterprise.

All generalisations are false. In every civilised country are little groups of older women with memories of suffrage struggles, and young women who grew up into the post-war optimism, and whose ideas remain unchanged by the fashions of the hour. It is they who still organise protests against reaction; who in national and international societies defend the political, civil, and economic equality of men and women; who invade new territories of achievement; who look towards a time when there shall be no wrangling over rights and wrongs, man's place and woman's place, but an equal and cooperative partnership, the individual going unfettered to the work for which he is best suited, responsibilities and obligations shared alike.

From Winifred Holtby, *Women in a Changing Civilization* (1934).

international politics

1919	Creation of the League of Nations
1920	War between Poland and Russia
1921	Treaty of Riga
1922	Germany and Russia sign Treaty of Rapallo
1923	French and Belgian troops invade the Ruhr district
1924	Dawes Plan
1925	Locarno Treaties
1928	Kellogg-Briand Pact
1929	Young Plan
October 1929	Collapse of the U.S. stock market; beginning of the Great Depression
1935	Saar region returned to German control
1936	Germany stations troops in the Rhineland in violation of the Versailles Treaty

The gold standard disappeared from the international economy, never to return. So too did reparations payments and war debts when the major nations of Europe met without the United States at a special conference held in Lausanne, Switzerland, in 1932. Something else died at the end of the 1920s: confidence in a self-adjusting economy, an "invisible hand" by which the business cycle would be righted. In 1932–33, the Great Depression, showing no signs of disappearing, reached its nadir and became a global phenomenon. Economic hardship transformed political realities. The Labour cabinet in Great Britain was forced to resign, and a new national government composed of Conservative, Liberal, and Labour leaders was formed to deal with the world economic emergency. Republican government was torn by bitter divisions in France. In the United States, the Republican party, which had been in power since 1920, was defeated in 1932. Franklin D. Roosevelt (1882–1945), a Democrat, was elected president in a landslide victory with a mandate to transform the American economy. German democratic institutions were pulled down in favor of fascist dictatorship.

In the decade following the Great War, peace settlements did not promote a stable international community. Instead, self-determination of peoples created new grounds for national rivalries in eastern Europe, and the lack of any effective means of guaranteeing the peace only exacerbated prewar animosities. The economic interdependence of nation-states through an international system of reparations payments and loans increased the vulnerability of governments to external pressures. With the collapse of the international finance system in 1929, political stability and international cooperation seemed more elusive than ever.

The soviet union's separate path

In the decade following war, revolution, and civil war, the Soviet state committed its people to a program of rapid industrial growth in order to ensure its survival as

This poster for the October 1931 British General Election reflects the National Government's concern over mass unemployment and industrial stagnation. The coalition National Government swamped the opposition Labour Party, taking 556 Parliament seats to Labour's 51.

a great power. The costs of Russia's rapid industrialization were wasted resources, enormous human suffering, and millions of lost lives. Lenin's successor, Joseph Stalin (1879–1953), obliged the Soviet people to achieve in a single generation what it had taken the West a century and a half to accomplish.

The Soviet Regime at the End of the Civil War

Echoing Karl Marx, the Bolshevik leader Lenin declared that the revolution and the civil war had been won in the name of "the dictatorship of the proletariat." The hammer and sickle on the Soviet flag represented the united rule of workers and peasants and were symbolic reminders of the commitment to rule from below. But at the end of the civil war in 1921, the Bolsheviks, not the people, were in charge.

The industrial sector, small as it was, was in total disarray by 1921. Famine and epidemics in 1921–22 killed and weakened more people than the Great War and the civil war combined. The countryside had been plundered to feed the Red and White armies. The combination of empty promises and a declining standard of living left workers and peasants frustrated and discontented. Urban strikes and rural uprisings defied short-term solutions. The proletarian revolutionary heroes of 1917 were rejecting the new Soviet regime. The Bolshe-

vik party now faced the task of restoring a country exhausted by war and revolution, its resources depleted, its economy destroyed.

At the head of the Soviet state was Lenin, the first among equals in the seven-man Politburo. The Central Committee of the Communist party decided "fundamental questions of policy, international and domestic," but in reality the Politburo, the inner circle of the Central Committee, held the reins of power.

Among seven members of the Politburo, three in particular attempted to leave their mark on the direction of Soviet policy: Leon Trotsky, Nikolai Bukharin (1888–1938), and Joseph Stalin. The great drama of Soviet leadership in the 1920s revolved around how the most brilliant (Trotsky) and the most popular (Bukharin) failed at the hands of the most shrewdly political (Stalin).

The two extremes in the debate over the direction of economic development were, on the one hand, a planned economy totally directed from above and, on the other hand, an economy controlled from below. In 1920–21, Leon Trotsky, at that time the people's commissar of war, favored a planned economy based on the militarization of labor. Trade unions opposed such a proposal and argued for a share of control over production. Lenin, however, favored a proletarian democracy and supported unions organized independently of state control.

The controversy was resolved in the short run at the Tenth Party Congress in 1921, when Lenin chose to

Leon Trotsky

Nikolai Bukharin

Joseph Stalin

steer a middle course between trade-union autonomy and militarization by preserving the unions and at the same time insisting on the state's responsibility for economic development. His primary goal was to stabilize Bolshevik rule in its progress toward socialism. He recognized that nothing could be achieved without the peasants. As a result, Lenin found himself embracing a new economic policy that he termed a "temporary retreat" from Communist goals.

The New Economic policy, 1921-1928

In 1921 Lenin ended the forced requisitioning of peasant produce that had been in effect during the civil war. In its place, peasants were to pay a tax in kind, that is, a fixed portion of their yield, to the state. Peasants, in turn, were permitted to reinstate private trade on their own terms. Party leaders accepted this dramatic shift in economic policy because it held the promise of prosperity so necessary for political stability. The actions of Lenin to return the benefits of productivity to the economy, combined with those of the peasants to reestablish markets, created the New Economic Policy (NEP) that emerged in the spring and summer of 1921.

It remained for Nikolai Bukharin to give shape and substance to the economic policy that permitted Russian producers to engage in some capitalist practices. As one of the founding fathers of the Soviet state and the youngest of the top Bolshevik leaders, Bukharin took his place on the Central Committee of the Communist party and on the Politburo as well.

Bukharin set about solving Russia's single greatest problem: how could Russia, crippled by poverty, find enough capital to industrialize? Insisting on the need for long-term economic planning, Bukharin counted on a prosperous and contented peasantry as the mainstay of his policy. Bukharin was also strongly interested in attracting foreign investment to Soviet endeavors as a way of ensuring future productivity.

Bukharin appreciated the importance of landholding to Russian peasants and defended a system of individual farms and private accumulation. Agriculture would operate through a market system, and the peasants would have the right to control their own surpluses. Rural prosperity would generate profits that could be used for gradual industrial development. Bukharin's policy stood in stark contrast to Stalin's later plan to feed industry by starving the agricultural sector.

Collective and large-scale farming had to be deferred indefinitely in order to reconcile the peasantry to the state—a policy profoundly at odds with the programs of the Communist state to pull down the capitalist system and establish socialism. In 1924 the tax in kind was replaced with a tax in cash. With this shift the state now procured grain through commercial agencies and cooperative organizations instead of directly from the peasants. The move toward Western capitalist models seemed more pronounced than ever to critics of the NEP.

Beginning in 1922, Lenin suffered a series of strokes, which virtually removed him from power by March 1923. When he died on 21 January 1924, the Communist leadership split over the ambiguities of the NEP. The backward nature of agriculture did not permit the kind of productivity that the NEP policymakers had anticipated. Cities demanded more food as their populations swelled with the influx of unskilled workers from rural areas. In 1927 peasants held back their grain. The Soviet Union was then experiencing a series of foreign policy setbacks in the West and in China, and Bolshevik leaders spoke of an active anti-Soviet conspiracy by the capitalist powers, led by Great Britain. The Soviet state lowered the price of grain, thereby squeezing the peasantry. The war scare, combined with the drop in food prices, soon led to an economic crisis.

By 1928 the NEP was in trouble. Stalin, general secretary of the Communist party of the Soviet Union, saw his chance. Under his supervision, the state intervened to prevent peasants from disposing of their own grain surpluses. The peasants responded to requisitioning by hoarding their produce and violently rioting. Bukharin and the NEP were in danger. Stalin exploited the internal crisis and external dangers to eliminate his political rivals. Trotsky had been expelled from the Communist party in November 1927 on charges that he had engaged in antiparty activities. Banished from Russia in 1929, he eventually found refuge in Mexico, where he was assassinated in 1940 at Stalin's command.

Bukharin's popularity in the party also threatened Stalin's aspirations. Bukharin was dropped from the Politburo in 1929. Tolerated throughout the early 1930s, he was arrested in 1937, and tried and executed for alleged treasonous activities the following year. The fate that befell Trotsky and Bukharin was typical of what happened to those who stood in the way of Stalin's pursuit of dictatorial control. Stalin was, in a colleague's words, "a gray blur." Beneath his apparently colorless personality, however, was a dangerous man of great political acumen, a ruthless behind-the-scenes politician

This 1931 Russian political poster exhorts workers "Join our kolkhoz [collective farm]." A year later the process of collectivization of Soviet agriculture was nearly complete.

who controlled the machinery of the party for his own ends and was not averse to employing violence in order to achieve them.

Stalin's Rise to Power

Joseph Stalin was born Iosif Vissarionovich Dzhugashvili in 1879. His self-chosen revolutionary name, Stalin, means "steel" in Russian and is as good an indication as any of his opinion of his own personality and will. Stalin, the man who ruled the Soviet Union as a dictator from 1928 until his death in 1953, was not a Russian. He was from Georgia, an area between the Black and Caspian seas, and spoke Russian with an accent. Georgia, with its land occupied and its people subjugated by invading armies for centuries, was annexed to the expanding Russian empire in 1801.

As the youngest of four and the only surviving child of Vissarion and Ekaterina Dzhugashvili, Stalin endured a childhood of brutal misery. Stalin's father was a poor and often unemployed shoemaker who intended that his son be apprenticed in the same trade. Under his mother's protection, young Iosif received an education and entered a seminary against his father's wishes. Iosif's schooling, extraordinary for someone of his poverty-stricken background, gave him the opportunity to learn about revolutionary socialist politics. At the turn of the century, Georgia had a strong Marxist revolutionary movement that opposed Russian exploitation. Iosif dropped out of the seminary in 1899 to engage in underground Marxist activities, and he soon became a follower of Lenin.

Stalin's association with Lenin kept him close to the center of power after the October Revolution of 1917. First as people's commissar for nationalities (1920–23) and then as general secretary of the Central Committee of the Communist party (1922–53), Stalin showed natural talent as a political strategist. His familiarity with non-Russian nationalities was a great asset in his dealings with the ethnic diversity and unrest in the vast Soviet state. Unlike party leaders who had lived in exile in western Europe before the revolution, Stalin had little knowledge of the West.

After Lenin's death in 1924, Stalin shrewdly bolstered his own reputation by orchestrating cult worship of Lenin. In 1929 Stalin used the occasion of his fiftieth birthday to fashion for himself a reputation as the living hero of the Soviet state. Icons, statues, busts, and images of all sorts of both Lenin and Stalin appeared everywhere in public buildings, schoolrooms, and homes. He systematically began eliminating his rivals so that he alone stood unchallenged as Lenin's true successor.

The First Five-Year Plan

The cult of Stalin coincided with the First Five-Year Plan (1929–32), which launched Stalin's program of rapid industrialization. Between 1929 and 1937, the period covered by the first two five-year plans (truncated because of their proclaimed success), Stalin laid the foundation for an urban industrial society in the Soviet Union. By brutally squeezing profits out of the agricultural sector, Stalin managed to increase heavy industrial production between 300 and 600 percent.

Stalin committed the Soviet Union to rapid industrialization as the only way to preserve socialism. The failure of revolutionary movements in western Europe meant that the Soviet Union must preserve "socialism in one country," the slogan of the political philosophy that justified Stalin's economic plans. Stalin made steel the idol of the new age. The Soviet state needed heavy machinery to build the future. An industrial labor force was created virtually overnight as peasant men and women were placed at workbenches and before the vast furnaces of modern metallurgical plants. The number of women in the industrial work force tripled in the decade after 1929. The reliability of official indices varied, but there is little doubt that heavy industrial production soared between 1929 and 1932. The Russian people were constantly reminded that no sacrifice could be too great in producing steel and iron.

When he first began to deal with the grain crisis of 1928, Stalin did not intend collective agriculture to be a solution. But by the end of 1929, the increasingly re-

The Results of the first five-Year plan

Under Joseph Stalin the Soviet Union embarked on rapid industrialization that transformed the peasant-based economy into a leading iron and steel producer. The Five-Year Plan achieved in 4 years what the Western industrialized nations took 150 years to accomplish. The Soviet leader did not tally the cost in human lives or the impact on the quality of life that such brutal economic transformation entailed.

The fundamental task of the Five-Year Plan was to transfer our country, with its backward, and in part medieval, technique, to the lines of new, modern technique.

The fundamental task of the Five-Year Plan was to convert the USSR from an agrarian and weak country, dependent upon the caprices of the capitalist countries, into an industrial and powerful country, fully self-reliant and independent of the caprices of world capitalism.

The fundamental task of the Five-Year Plan was, in converting the USSR into an industrial country, fully to eliminate the capitalist elements, to widen the front of socialist forms of economy, and to create the economic base for the abolition of classes in the USSR, for the construction of socialist society. . . .

The fundamental task of the Five-Year Plan was to transfer small and scattered agriculture to the lines of large-scale collective farming, so as to ensure the economic base for socialism in the rural districts and thus to eliminate the possibility of the restoration of capitalism in the USSR.

Finally, the task of the Five-Year Plan was to create in the country all the necessary technical and economic prerequisites for increasing to the utmost the defensive capacity of the country, to enable it to organize determined resistance to any and every attempt at military intervention from outside, to any and every attempt at military attack from without. . . .

What are the results of the Five-Year Plan in four years in the sphere of *industry*?

Have we achieved victory in this sphere?

Yes, we have. . . .

We did not have an iron and steel industry, the foundation for the industrialization of the country. Now we have this industry.

We did not have a tractor industry. Now we have one.

We did not have an automobile industry. Now we have one.

We did not have a machine-tool industry. Now we have one.

We did not have a big and up-to-date chemical industry. Now we have one.

We did not have a real and big industry for the production of modern agricultural machinery. Now we have one.

We did not have an aircraft industry. Now we have one.

In output of electric power we were last on the list. Now we rank among the first.

In output of oil products and coal we were last on the list. Now we rank among the first.

We had only one coal and metallurgical base—in the Ukraine—which we barely managed to keep going. We have not only succeeded in improving this base, but have created a new coal and metallurgical base—in the East—which is the pride of our country.

We had only one center of the textile industry—in the North of our country. As a result of our efforts we will have in the very near future two new centers of the textile industry—in Central Asia and Western Siberia.

And we have not only created these new great industries, but have created them on a scale and in dimensions that eclipse the scale and dimensions of European industry.

And as a result of all this the capitalist elements have been completely and irrevocably eliminated from industry, and socialist industry has become the sole form of industry in the U.S.S.R.

And as a result of all this our country has been converted from an agrarian into an industrial country; for the proportion of industrial output, as compared with agricultural output, has risen from 48 per cent of the total in the beginning of the Five-Year Plan period (1928) to 70 per cent at the end of the fourth year of the Five-Year Plan period (1932). . . .

The object of the Five-Year Plan in the sphere of agriculture was to unite the scattered and small individual peasant farms, which lacked the opportunity of utilizing tractors and modern agricultural machinery, into large collective farms, equipped with all the modern implements of highly developed agriculture, and to cover unoccupied land with model state farms. . . .

The party has succeeded, in a matter of three years, in organizing more than 200,000 collective farms and about 5,000 state farms specializing mainly in grain growing and livestock raising, and at the same time it has succeeded, in the course of four years, in enlarging the crop area by 21,000,000 hectares.

The party has succeeded in getting more than 60 per cent of the peasant farms, which account for more than 70 per cent of the land cultivated by peasants, to unite into collective farms, which means that we have *fulfilled* the Five-Year Plan *threefold*.

The party has succeeded in creating the possibility of obtaining, not 500,000,000 to 600,000,000 poods* of marketable grain, which was the amount purchased in the period when individual peasant farming predominated, but 1,200,000,000 to 1,400,000,000 poods of grain annually.

The party has succeeded in routing the kulaks as a class, although they have not yet been dealt the final blow; the laboring peasants have been emancipated from kulak bondage and exploitation, and a firm economic basis for the Soviet government, the basis of collective farming, has been established in the countryside.

The party has succeeded in converting the U.S.S.R. from a land of small peasant farming into a land where agriculture is run on the largest scale in the world.

Such, in general terms, are the results of the Five-Year Plan in four years in the sphere of agriculture.

From Joseph Stalin, *Selected Writings* (1942).

*Pood—a unit of weight equivalent to 36.1 lb.

---

pressive measures instituted by the state against the peasants had led both to collectivization and to the deportation of *kulaks*, the derisive term for wealthy peasants that literally means "the tight-fisted ones." Stalin achieved forced collectivization by confiscating land and establishing collective farms run by the state. Within a few months, half of all peasant farms were collectivized. By 1938 private land had been virtually eliminated. The state set prices, controlled distribution, and selected crops with the intention of ensuring a steady food supply and freeing a rural labor force for heavy industry. More as a publicity ploy than a statement of fact, the First Five-Year Plan was declared a success after only three years. It was a success in one important sense: it did lay the foundations of the Soviet planned economy, in which the state bureaucracy made all decisions about production, distribution, and prices.

Collectivization meant misery for the 25 million peasant families who suffered under it. At least 5 million peasants died between 1929 and 1932. Collectivization ripped apart the fabric of village life, destroyed families, and sent homeless peasants into exile. Peasants who resisted collectivization retaliated by destroying their own crops and livestock. Rapid industrial development shattered the lives of millions of people. In attempting to develop an industrial sector overnight, Stalin, like tsars before him, saw that Russia could be carried into the future only on the backs of its peasants.

The comintern, economic Development, and the purges

In addition to promoting its internal economic development, the Soviet Union had to worry about survival in a world political system composed entirely of capitalist countries. After the Bolshevik revolution in 1917, Lenin had fully expected that other socialist revolutions would follow throughout the world, especially in central and western Europe. These revolutions would destroy capitalism and secure Russia's place in a new world order. But as the prospects for world proletarian revolution evaporated, Soviet leaders sought to protect their revolutionary country from what they saw as a hostile capitalist world. They used diplomacy to this end. The end of the Allied intervention in Russia allowed the Bolshevik state to initiate diplomatic relations with the West, beginning with the Treaty of Rapallo signed with Germany in 1921. By 1924 all the major countries of the world—with the exception of the United States—had established diplomatic relations with the Soviet Union. In 1928 the USSR cooperated in the preparation of a world disarmament conference to be held in Geneva and joined western European powers in a commitment to peace. The United States and the Soviet Union exchanged ambassadors for the first time in 1933.

In addition to diplomatic relations, the Soviet state in 1919 encouraged various national Communist parties to form an association for the purpose of promoting and coordinating the coming world revolution. This Communist International, or Comintern, was based in Moscow and included representatives from 37 countries by 1920. As it became clear that a world revolution was not imminent, the Comintern concerned itself with the ideological purity of its member parties. Under Lenin's direction, the Soviet Communist party determined policy for all the member parties.

Bukharin and Stalin shared a view of the Comintern that prevailed from 1924 to 1929: since the collapse of capitalism was not imminent, the Comintern should work to promote the unity of working classes everywhere and should cooperate with existing worker organizations. In 1929, however, Stalin argued that advanced capitalist societies were teetering on the brink of new wars and revolutions. As a result, the Comintern must seek to sever the ties between foreign Communist parties and social democratic parties in order to prepare for the revolutionary struggle. Stalin purged the Comintern of dissenters, and he decreed a policy of noncooperation in Europe from 1929 to 1933. As a result, socialism in Europe was badly split between Communists and democratic socialists.

The Second Five-Year Plan, announced in 1933, succeeded in reducing the Soviet Union's dependence on foreign imports, especially in the areas of heavy industry, machinery, and metal works. The basic physical plant for armaments production was in place by 1937, and resources continued to be shifted away from consumer goods to heavy industrial development. This industrial development, and the collectivization of agriculture, brought growing urbanization. By 1939 one in three Soviet people were living in cities, compared to one in six in 1926. In his commitment to increased pro-

Soviet women were mobilized into the labor force. Here a female tractor driver heads toward the fields.

duction, Stalin introduced into the workplace incentives and differential wage scales at odds with the principles and programs of the original Bolshevik revolution. Stricter discipline was enforced; absenteeism was punished with severe fines or loss of employment. Workers who exceeded their quotas were rewarded and honored.

Amid this rapid industrialization, Stalin inaugurated the Great Purge, actually a series of purges lasting from 1934 to 1938. Those whom Stalin believed to be his opponents—real and imagined; past, present, and future—were labeled *class enemies*. The most prominent of them, including leaders of the Bolshevik revolution who had worked with Stalin during the 1920s, appeared in widely publicized *show trials*. They were intimidated and tortured into making false confessions of crimes against the regime, humiliated by brutal prosecutors, and condemned to death or imprisonment. Stalin wiped out the Bolshevik old guard, Communist party members whose first loyalty was to the international Communist movement rather than to Stalin himself, and all potential opposition within the Communist party. Probably 300,000 people were put to death, among them engineers, managers, technical specialists, and officers of the army and navy. In addition, 7 million people were placed in labor camps. Stalin now had unquestioned control of the Communist party and the country.

The purges dealt a severe blow to the command of the army and resulted in a shortage of qualified industrial personnel, slowing industrial growth. The Great Purge coerced the Soviet people into making great sacrifices in the drive for industrialization. It prevented any possible dissension or opposition within the USSR at a time when the "foreign threat" posed by Nazi Germany was becoming increasingly serious.

The human suffering associated with the dislocation and heavy workloads of rapid, coerced industrialization cannot be measured. Planned growth brought with it a top-heavy and often inefficient bureaucracy, and that bureaucracy ensured that the Soviet Union was the most highly centralized of the European states. The growing threat of foreign war meant an even greater diversion of resources from consumer goods to war industries beginning with the Third Five-Year Plan in 1938.

women and the family in the New soviet state

The building of the new Soviet state exacted particularly high costs from women. Soviet women had been active

The soviet union's separate path

November 1917	Bolsheviks and Red Guard seize power
1919	Creation of the Communist International (Comintern)
1920	Legalization of abortion and divorce
1921	End of the civil war
1921	Introduction of the New Economic Policy
3 April 1922	Stalin becomes secretary general of the Communist party
21 January 1924	Lenin dies
1924–1929	Comintern policy of "Unity of the Working Classes"
1927	Dissatisfied peasants hoard grain
November 1927	Trotsky expelled from Communist party
1928	Stalin introduces grain requisitioning
November 1929	Bukharin expelled from Politburo
1929	Introduction of First Five-Year Plan and the collectivization of agriculture
1929–1933	Comintern policy of noncooperation with Social Democratic parties
1933–1937	Second Five-Year Plan
1934–1938	Great Purge
1936	Abortion declared illegal
1938	Third Five-Year Plan

in the revolution from the beginning. Lenin and the Bolshevik leaders were committed to the liberation of women, who, like workers, were considered to be oppressed under capitalism. Lenin denounced housework as "barbarously unproductive, petty, nerve-wracking, stultifying, and crushing drudgery." In its early days, the Soviet state pledged to protect the rights of mothers without narrowing women's opportunities or restricting women's role to the family.

After the October Revolution of 1917, the Bolsheviks passed a new law establishing equality for women within marriage. In 1920 abortion was legalized. New legislation established the right to divorce and removed the stigma from illegitimacy. Communes, calling themselves "laboratories of revolution," experimented with sexual equality. Russian women were enfranchised in 1917, gaining the right to vote before women in the industrialized countries of western Europe. The Russian revolution went further than any revolution in history toward the legal liberation of women within such a short span of time.

These advances, as utopian as they appeared to admirers in western European countries, did not deal with the problems faced by the majority of Russian women. Bolshevik legislation did little to address the special economic hardships of peasant and factory women. Although paid maternity leaves and nursing breaks were required by law, these guarantees became a source of discrimination against women workers, who were the last hired and first fired by employers trying to limit expenses. Divorce legislation was hardly a blessing for women with children, since men incurred no financial responsibility toward their offspring in terminating a marriage. Even as legislation was being passed in the early days of the new Soviet state, women were losing ground in the struggle for equal rights and independent economic survival.

By the early 1930s, reforms affecting women were in trouble due in large part to a plummeting birthrate. This decline created special worries for Soviet planners, who forecast doom if the trend was not reversed. In 1936, a woman's right to choose to end a first pregnancy was revoked. In the following decade, all abortions were made illegal. Homosexuality was declared a criminal offense. The family was glorified as the mainstay of the socialist order, and the independence of women was challenged as a threat to Soviet productivity. While motherhood was idealized, the Stalinist drive to industrialize could not dispense with full-time women workers.

Women's double burden in the home and workplace became heavier during Stalin's reign. Most Russian women held full-time jobs in the factories or on the farms. They also worked what they called a "second shift" in running a household and taking care of children. In the industrialized nations of western Europe, the growth of a consumer economy lightened women's labor in the home to some extent. In the Soviet Union, procuring the simplest necessities was woman's work that required waiting in long lines for hours. Lack of indoor plumbing meant that women spent time hauling water for their families at the end of a working day. In such ways, rapid industrialization exacted its special price from Soviet women.

In the 1920s and 1930s, the Soviet search for stability and prosperity took the Soviet Union down a path very different from that of the states of western Europe. Rejecting an accommodation with a market economy, Stalin committed the Soviet people to planned rapid industrialization that was accomplished through mass repression and great human suffering. Insulated from world markets and the devastation of the Great Depression, the Soviet Union relied on a massive state bureaucratic system to achieve socialism in one country and to make the Soviet state into an industrial giant.

The promise of fascism

Throughout western Europe, parliamentary institutions, representative government, and electoral politics offered no ready solutions to the problems of economic collapse and the political upheaval on the left and the right. Fascism promised what liberal democratic societies failed to deliver—a way out of the economic and political morass. Fascist rule—dictatorship by a charismatic leader—promised an escape from parliamentary chaos, party wranglings, and the threat of communism. Fascism promised more: by identifying ready enemies—scapegoats for failed economic and national ambitions—fascism promised that it held the answer for those who sought protection and security.

The rise of dictatorships

Dictatorships became the most prevalent form of government in Europe between the world wars. Dictatorships appealed to the middle classes, who feared loss of their property to socialists and loss of their money to the vagaries of international markets. The move toward dictatorship appeared relentless in the period between the wars. In 1920, of the 28 states in Europe, 26 were parliamentary democracies. By the end of 1940, only five democracies remained: the United Kingdom, Ireland, Sweden, Finland, and Switzerland. The rest of Europe was under dictatorial rule. The European dictatorships of the 1930s displayed a variety of forms. On the left, the "dictatorship of the proletariat" in the Soviet Union was in fact a regime driven by the ruthless brutality of Joseph Stalin toward the goal of building socialism. Other dictatorships were on the right. Italy and Germany each constructed fascist dictatorships that regarded Soviet communism as their mortal enemy. The Soviet Union, in turn, saw fascism as a serious threat.

The Law on the Abolition of Legal Abortion, 1936

In his drive to industrialize the Soviet Union as rapidly as possible, Stalin recognized the economic importance of women's roles both as workers and as mothers. At the height of the Second Five-Year Plan, many women's rights were revoked, including the right to an abortion. The "New Woman" of the revolutionary period gave way to the post-1936 woman, depicted by the state as the perfect mother who matched her husband's productivity in the workplace, ran the household, and raised a large family.

When we speak of strengthening the Soviet family, we are speaking precisely of the struggle against the survivals of a bourgeois attitude towards marriage, women and children. So-called "free love" and all disorderly sex life are bourgeois through and through, and have nothing to do with either socialist principles or the ethics and standards of conduct of the Soviet citizen. Socialist doctrine shows this, and it is proved by life itself.

The elite of our country, the best of the Soviet youth, are as a rule also excellent family men who dearly love their children. And vice versa: the man who does not take marriage seriously, and abandons his children to the whims of fate, is usually also a bad worker and a poor member of society.

Fatherhood and motherhood have long been virtues in this country. This can be seen at the first glance, without searching enquiry. Go through the parks and streets of Moscow or of any other town in the Soviet Union on a holiday, and you will see not a few young men walking with pink-cheeked, well-fed babies in their arms. . . .

The toilers of our land have paid with their blood for the right to a life of joy, and a life of joy implies the right to have one's own family and healthy, happy children. Millions of workers beyond the frontiers of our land are still deprived of this joy, for there unemployment, hunger and helpless poverty are rampant. Old maids and elderly bachelors, a rare thing in our country, are frequent in the West, and that is no accident.

We alone have all the conditions under which a working woman can fulfill her duties as a citizen and as a mother responsible for the birth and early upbringing of her children.

A woman without children merits our pity, for she does not know the full joy of life. Our Soviet women, full-blooded citizens of the freest country in the world, have been given the bliss of motherhood. We must safeguard our family and raise and rear healthy Soviet heroes!

War and postwar hardships were the catalysts for the emergence of the new mass movements of fascism in Europe. The Great War had created a political vacuum caused by the crisis in liberal values. In condemning the war and its costs, new fascist leaders, who tended to start their political careers as social reformers and even socialists, proposed a radical reformation of the status quo.

Fascism sounded very like socialism. In the Soviet Union, Bolshevik leaders reassured their people that socialism was the only way of dealing with the weaknesses and inequities of the world capitalist system laid bare in the world war. In their initial condemnations of the capitalist economy and liberal political institutions and values, fascists employed revolutionary language similar to that of the Left while manipulating in radically new ways the political symbols of the Right—the nation, the flag, and the army. Fascism promised to steer a course between the uncertainties and exploitation of a liberal capitalist system and the revolutionary upheaval and expropriation of a socialist system. Fascism was ultranationalist, and the use of force was central to its appeal.

The word *fascism* is derived from the Latin *fasces*, the name for the bundle of rods with ax head carried by the magistrates of the Roman Empire. Fascism was rooted in the mass political movements of the late nineteenth century, which emphasized nationalism, antiliberal values, and a politics of the irrational. The electoral successes of the German variant—National Socialism, or

Nazism—were just beginning in the late 1920s. In the same period, fascist movements were making their appearance in England, Hungary, Spain, and France. But none was more successful and none demanded more attention than the fascist experiment in Italy, which inspired observers throughout Europe to emulate it.

Mussolini's Italy

Italy was a poor nation. Although Italy was one of the victorious Allies in World War I, Italians felt that their country had been betrayed by the peace settlement of 1919 by being denied the territory and status it deserved. A recently created electoral system based on universal manhood suffrage had produced parliamentary chaos and ministerial instability. The lack of coherent political programs only heightened the general disapproval with government that accompanied the peace negotiations. People were beginning to doubt the parliamentary regime's hold on the future. It was under these circumstances that the Fascist party, led by Benito Mussolini (1883–1945), entered politics in 1920 by attacking the large Socialist and Popular (Catholic) parties.

Mussolini had begun his prewar political career as a Socialist. The young Mussolini was arrested numerous times for Socialist political activities and placed under state surveillance. An ardent nationalist, he volunteered for combat in World War I and was promoted to the rank of corporal. Injured in early 1917 by an exploding shell detonated during firing practice, he returned to Milan to continue his work as editor of *Il Populo d'Italia* ("The People of Italy"), the newspaper he founded in 1914 to promote Italian participation in the war.

Mussolini yearned to be the leader of a revolution in Italy comparable to that directed by Lenin in Russia. Although his doctrinal allegiance to socialism was beginning to flag, Mussolini, like Lenin, recognized the power of the printed word to stir political passions. Emphasizing nationalist goals and vague measures of socioeconomic transformation, Mussolini identified a new enemy for Italy—bolshevism. He organized his followers into the Fascist party, a political movement that, by utilizing strict party discipline, quickly developed its own national network.

Many Fascists were former Socialists and war veter-

Gerardo Dottori, Portrait of the Duce (1933). *Dottori was one of a group of Italian Futurist artists whose works reflected their fascination with aircraft, flight, and extraterrestrial fantasy. In 1929 they published a manifesto in which they launched the idea of an art linked to the most exciting aspect of contemporary life. During the 1930s the artists sought to align themselves with Mussolini's Fascist regime.*

ans like Mussolini who were disillusioned with postwar government. They dreamed of Italy as a great world power, as it had been in the days of ancient Rome. Their enemies were not only Communists with their international outlook but also the big businesses, which they felt drained Italy's resources and kept its people poor and powerless. Panicky members of the lower middle classes sought security against the economic uncertainties of inflation and were willing to endorse violence to achieve it. Unions were to be feared because they used strikes to further their demands for higher salaries and better working conditions for their members while other social groups languished. Near civil war erupted as Italian Communists and Fascists clashed violently in street battles in the early 1920s. The Fascists entered the national political arena and succeeded on the local level in overthrowing city governments. In spite of its visibility on the national political scene, however, the Fascist party was still very much a minority party when Mussolini refused to serve as a junior minister in the new government in 1922.

His refusal to serve as representative of a minority party reflected Mussolini's belief that the Fascists must be in charge. On 28 October 1922, the Fascists undertook their famous March on Rome, which followed similar Fascist takeovers in Milan and Bologna. Mussolini's followers now occupied the capital. This event marked the beginning of the end of parliamentary government and the emergence of Fascist dictatorship and institutionalized violence. Rising unemployment and severe inflation contributed to the politically deteriorating situation that helped bring Mussolini to power.

Destruction and violence, not the ballot box, became fascism's most successful tools for securing political power. *Squadristi*—armed bands of Fascist thugs—attacked their political enemies (both Catholic and Socialist), destroyed private property, dismantled the printing presses of adversary groups, and generally terrorized both rural and urban populations. By the end of 1922, Fascists could claim a following of 300,000 members endorsing the new politics of intimidation.

The Fascists achieved their first parliamentary majority by using violent tactics of intimidation to secure votes. One outspoken Socialist critic of Fascist violence, Giacomo Matteotti (1885–1924), was murdered by Mussolini's subordinates. The deed threatened the survival of Mussolini's government as 150 Socialist, Liberal, and Popular party deputies resigned in protest. Mussolini chose this moment to consolidate his position by arresting and silencing his enemies to preserve order. Within two years, Fascists were firmly in control, monopolizing politics, suppressing a free press, creating a secret police force, and transforming social and economic policies. Mussolini destroyed political parties and made Italy into a one-party dictatorship.

In 1925 the Fascist party entered into an agreement with Italian industrialists that gave industry a position of privilege protected by the state in return for its support. Mussolini presented this partnership as the end to class conflict, but in fact it ensured the dominance of capital and the control of labor and professional groups. A corrupt bureaucracy filled with Mussolini's cronies and run on bribes orchestrated the new relationship between big business and the state.

Mussolini, himself an atheist, recognized the importance of the Catholic church in securing his regime. In 1870, when Italy had been unified, the pope had been deprived of his territories in Rome. This event, which became known as the "Roman Question," proved to be the source of ongoing problems for Italian governments. In February 1929, Mussolini settled matters with Pope Pius XI in the Lateran Treaty and the accompanying Concordat, which granted to the pope sovereignty over the territory around St. Peter's Basilica and the Vatican. The treaty also protected the role of the Catholic church in education and guaranteed that Italian marriage laws would conform to Catholic dogma.

By 1929 *Il Duce* (the leader), as Mussolini preferred to be called, was at the height of his popularity and power. Apparent political harmony had been achieved by ruthlessly crushing fascism's opponents. The agreement with the pope, which restored harmony with the Church, was matched by a new sense of order and accomplishment in Italian society and the economy.

Mussolini's plans for Empire

In spite of official claims, Fascist Italy had not done well in riding out the Great Depression. A large rural sector masked the problems of high unemployment by absorbing an urban work force without jobs. Corporatism, a system of economic self-rule by interest groups promoted on paper by Benito Mussolini, was a sham that had little to do with the dominance of the Italian economy by big business. By lending money to Italian businesses on the verge of bankruptcy, the government acquired a controlling interest in key industries, including steel, shipping, heavy machinery, and electricity.

As fascism failed to initiate effective social programs, Mussolini's popularity plummeted. In the hope of boosting his sagging image, *Il Duce* committed Italy to a foreign policy of imperial conquest. Italy had conquered Ottoman-controlled Libya in North Africa in 1911. Now, in the 1930s, Mussolini targeted Ethiopia for his expansionist aims and ordered Italian troops to invade that east African kingdom in October 1935. Using poison gas and aerial bombing, the Italian army defeated the native troops of Ethiopian Emperor Haile Selassie (1892–1975). European democracies, under the pressure of public opinion, cried out against the wanton and unwarranted attack, but Mussolini succeeded in proclaiming Ethiopia an Italian territory.

The invasion of Ethiopia exposed the ineffectiveness of the League of Nations to stop such flagrant violations. Great Britain and France took no action other than to express their disapproval of Italy's conquest. Yet a rift opened up between these two western European nations and Italy. Mussolini had distanced himself from the Nazi state in the first years of the German regime's existence, and he was critical of Hitler's plans for rearmament. Now, in light of disapproval from Britain and France, Mussolini turned to Germany for support. In October 1936, Italy aligned itself with Germany in what Mussolini called the Rome-Berlin Axis. This alliance was little more than a pledge of friendship. However, less than three years later, in May 1939, Germany and Italy agreed to offer support in any offensive or defensive war. The agreement, known as the Pact of Steel, in fact bound Italy militarily to Germany.

Mussolini pursued other imperialist goals within Europe. The small Balkan nation of Albania entered into a series of agreements with Mussolini beginning in the mid-1920s that made it dependent financially and militarily on Italian aid. By 1933 Albanian independence had been undermined by this "friendship" with its stronger neighbor. In order not to be outdone by Hitler, who was at the time dismantling Czechoslovakia, Mussolini invaded and annexed Albania in April 1939, ending the fiction that Albania was an Italian protectorate.

The Beginnings of the Nazi Movement in Germany

Repeated economic, political, and diplomatic crises of the 1920s buffeted Germany's internal stability. Most Germans considered reparations to be an unfair burden, so onerous that payment should be evaded and resisted in every way possible. The German government did not promote inflation in order to avoid paying reparations, but rather to avoid a postwar recession, revive industrial production, and maintain high employment. But the moderate inflation that stimulated the economy spun out of control into destructive hyperinflation.

The Germans blamed the French, with their reparations demands and their invading troops, for the economic plight of Germany. Rampant inflation had negative repercussions for democracy as extremist political groups on both right and left attracted growing numbers of followers by blaming the liberal and democratic Weimar Republic. Because of the horrors of inflation, German governments thereafter were committed to balanced budgets. When the Great Depression hit the German economy in 1929, the fear of a new inflation prevented the government from using deficit spending to bring back prosperity. The Great Depression in turn contributed to the burgeoning appeal of Hitler and the National Socialists. People grew cynical and defiant through suffering and sought security in extraordinary extrademocratic solutions.

The fiscal problems of the Weimar Republic obscure the fact that, in the period after World War I, Germany experienced real economic growth. German industry ad-

Ethiopian soldiers march to meet the invading Italian forces.

vanced, productivity was high, and German workers flexed their union muscles to secure better wages. Weimar committed itself to large expenditures for social welfare programs, including unemployment insurance. By 1930 social welfare was responsible for 40 percent of all public expenditures, compared to 19 percent before the war. All these changes, apparently fostering the well-being of the German people, aggravated the fears of German big businessmen, who resented the trade unions and the perceived trend toward socialism. The lower middle classes also felt cheated and economically threatened by inflation. They were a politically volatile group, susceptible to the antidemocratic appeals of some of Weimar's critics.

Constitutional provisions that allowed for the constant wrangling of a multiparty system divided the Weimar Republic. Political parties formed and destroyed cabinet after cabinet while Germany's real problems remained—the humiliating peace treaty, reparations, and a weak economic structure. As a result, growing numbers of Germans expressed disgust with parliamentary democracy. The Great Depression dealt a staggering blow to the Weimar Republic in 1929 as American loans were withdrawn and German unemployment skyrocketed. By 1930 the antagonisms among the parties were so great that the parliament was no longer effective in ruling Germany. As chancellor from 1930 to 1932, Centrist leader Heinrich Brüning (1885–1970) attempted to break this impasse by overriding the Weimar constitution. This move opened the door to enemies of the republic, and Brüning was forced to resign.

Hitler and the Third Reich

One man in particular knew how to exploit the Weimar Republic's weaknesses for his own political ends. Adolf Hitler was that man. He denounced the betrayal of reparations. He made a special appeal to Germans who saw their savings disappearing, first in inflation and then in the Great Depression. He promised a way out of economic hardship and the reassertion of Germany's claim to status as a world power.

Hitler's Rise to Power

Just as Stalin was born a Georgian and not an ethnic Russian, Adolf Hitler (1889–1945) was born an Austrian

In this satirical painting, The Pillars of Society, George Grosz caricatures the society of the Weimar Republic as composed of corrupt judges, petty bourgeoisie, militarists, and hypocritical pacifists.

outside the German fatherland he came to rule. Hitler, the son of a customs agent who worked on the Austrian side of the border with Germany, came from a middle-class family with social pretensions. Aimlessness and failure marked Hitler's early life. Denied admission to architecture school, he took odd jobs to survive. Hitler welcomed the outbreak of war in 1914, which put an end to his self-described sleepwalking. He volunteered immediately for service in the German army. Wounded and gassed at the front, he was twice awarded the Iron Cross for bravery in action.

Hitler later described what he had learned from war in terms of the solidarity of struggle against a common enemy and the purity of heroism. The army provided him with a sense of security and direction. What he learned from the peace that followed was an equally powerful lesson that determined his commitment to a career in politics. Hitler profoundly believed in the stab-in-the-back legend: Germany had not lost the war, he insisted, it had been defeated from within—or stabbed in the back by Communists, Socialists, liberals, and Jews. The Weimar Republic signed the humiliating Treaty of Versailles and continued to betray the German people by taxing wages to pay reparations. Hitler's highly distorted and false view of the origins of the Republic and its policies was the basis for his demand that the "Weimar System" must be abolished and replaced by a Nazi regime.

For his failed attempt to seize control of the Munich municipal government in 1923, in an event that became known as the Beer Hall Putsch because of the locale in which Hitler attempted to initiate the "national revolution," he served nine months of a five-year sentence in prison. There he began writing the first volume of his autobiography, *Mein Kampf* ("My Struggle"). In this turgid work he condemned the decadence of Western society and singled out for special contempt Jews, Bolsheviks, and middle-class liberals. From his failed attempt to seize power, Hitler learned the important lesson that he could succeed against the German republic only from within, by coming to power legally. By 1928 he had a small party of about 100,000 Nazis. Modifying his anti-capitalist message, Hitler appealed to the discontented small farmers and tailored his nationalist sentiments to a frightened middle class.

Adolf Hitler became chancellor of Germany in January 1933 by legal, constitutional, and democratic means. The Nazi party was supported by farmers, small businessmen, civil servants, and young people. In the elections of 1930 and 1932, the voters made the Nazi party the largest party in the country—although not the majority one. President Paul von Hindenburg (1925–34) invited Hitler to form a government. Hitler claimed that Germany was on the verge of a Communist revolution and persuaded Hindenburg and the Reichstag to consent to a series of emergency laws, which the Nazis used to establish themselves firmly in power. Legislation outlawed freedom of the press and public meetings, and approved of the use of violence against Hitler's political enemies, particularly the Socialists and the Communists. Within two months after Hitler came to office, Germany was a police state and Hitler was a "legal" dictator who could issue his own laws without having to gain the consent of either the Reichstag or the president. After carrying out this "legal revolution" incapacitating representative institutions and ending civil liberties, the Nazis worked to consolidate their position and their power. They abolished all other political parties, established single-party rule, dissolved trade unions, and put their own people into state governments and the bureaucracy.

Many observers at the time considered the new Nazi state to be a monolithic structure, ruled and coordinated from the center. This was not, however, an accurate observation. Hitler actually issued few directives. Policy was set by an often chaotic jockeying for power among rival Nazi factions. Hitler's political alliance with traditional conservative and nationalist politicians, industrialists, and military men helped give the state created by Adolf Hitler a claim to legitimacy based on continuity with the past. Hitler called this state the Third Reich. (The first Reich was the medieval German empire; the second Reich was the German Empire created by Bismarck in 1871.)

The first of the paramilitary groups so important in orchestrating violence to eliminate Hitler's enemies was the SA (Sturmabteilung), or the storm troopers, under Ernst Röhm (1887–1934). Röhm helped Hitler achieve electoral victories by beating up political opponents on the streets and using other thuglike tactics. SA followers, also known as Brownshirts, adopted a military appearance for their terrorist operations. By the beginning of 1934, there were 2.5 million members of the SA, vastly outnumbering the regular army of 100,000 soldiers.

Heinrich Himmler (1900–45) headed an elite force of the Nazi party within the SA called the SS (Schutzstaffel, or protection squad), a group whose members wore black uniforms and menacing skull-and-crossbones insignia on their caps. Himmler seized control of political policing and emerged as Röhm's chief rival. In 1934, with the assistance of the army, Hitler and the SS purged the SA and executed Röhm, thereby making the SS Hitler's exclusive elite corps, entrusted with carrying out his extreme programs and responsible later for the greatest atrocities of the Second World War.

Nazi Goals

Hitler identified three organizing goals for the Nazi state: *Lebensraum* (living space), rearmament, and economic recovery. These goals were the basis of the new foreign policy Hitler forged for Germany, and they served to fuse that foreign policy with the domestic politics of the Third Reich.

Key to Hitler's worldview was the concept of *Lebensraum*, in which he considered the right and the duty of the German master race to be the world's greatest empire, one that would endure for a thousand years. Hitler first stated his ideals about living space in *Mein Kampf*, where he argued that superior nations had the right to expand into the territories of inferior states. Living space meant for him German domination of central and eastern Europe at the expense of Slavic peoples. The Aryan master race would dominate inferior peoples. Colonies were unacceptable because they weakened rather than strengthened national security; Germany must annex territories within continental Europe. Hitler's primary target was what he called "Russia and her vassal border states."

Hitler continued the secret rearmament of Germany begun by his Weimar predecessors in violation of the restrictions of the Treaty of Versailles. He withdrew Germany from the League of Nations and from the World Disarmament Conference, signaling a new direction for German foreign policy. In 1935 he publicly renounced the Treaty of Versailles and announced that Germany was rearming. The following year he openly defied the French and moved German troops into the Rhineland, the demilitarized security zone that separated the armed forces of the two countries. Hitler also reversed the cooperative relationship his nation had established with the Soviet Union in the 1920s. In 1933 the German state was illicitly spending 1 billion Reichsmarks on arms. By 1939 annual expenditures to prepare Germany for war had climbed to 30 billion.

Hitler knew that preparation for war meant more than amassing weapons; it also required full economic recovery. One of Germany's great weaknesses in World War I had been its dependence on imports of raw materials and foodstuffs. To avoid a repetition of this problem, Hitler instituted a program of autarky, or economic self-sufficiency, by which Germany aimed to produce everything that it consumed. He encouraged the efforts of German industry to develop synthetics for petroleum, rubber, metals, and fats.

The state pumped money into the private economy, creating new jobs and achieving full employment after 1936, an accomplishment unmatched by any other European nation. Recovery was built on armaments as well as consumer products. The Nazi state's concentration of economic power in the hands of a few strengthened big businesses. The victims of corporate consolidation were the small firms that could no longer compete with government-sponsored corporations like the chemical giant I. G. Farben.

In 1936 Hitler introduced his Four-Year Plan, dedicated to the goals of full-scale rearmament and economic self-sufficiency. Before the third year of the Four-

Hitler at a Nazi rally. These mass meetings were used by the Nazi mythmakers to enhance Hitler's image as the savior of Germany.

National income of the powers in 1937 and percentage spent on Defense

	National Income (billions of dollars)	Percentage Spent on Defense
United States	68	1.5
British Empire	22	5.7
France	10	9.1
Germany	17	23.5
Italy	6	14.5
USSR	19	26.4
Japan	4	28.2

Year Plan, however, Hitler was aware of the failure to develop synthetic products sufficient to meet Germany's needs. But if Germany could not create substitutes, it could control territories that provided fuel, metals, and foodstuffs. Germany had been importing raw materials from southeastern Europe and wielding increasing economic influence over the Balkan countries. Hitler now realized that economic self-sufficiency could be directly linked to the main goal of the Nazi state: *Lebensraum.*

Thus Hitler was committed to territorial expansion from the time he came to power. He rearmed Germany for that purpose. When economists and generals cautioned him, he refused to listen. Instead, he informed them of his commitment to Lebensraum and of his intention to use aggressive war to acquire it. He removed his critics from their positions of power and replaced them with Nazis loyal to him.

propaganda, Racism, and culture

To reinforce his personal power and to sell his program for the "total state," Hitler created a Ministry of Propaganda under Joseph Goebbels (1897–1945), a former journalist and Nazi party district leader in Berlin. Goebbels was a master of manipulating emotions in mass demonstrations held to whip up enthusiasm for Nazi policies. Flying the flag and wearing the swastika signified identification with the Nazi state. With his magnetic appeal, Hitler inspired and manipulated the devotion of hundreds of thousands of those who heard him speak. Leni Riefenstahl, a young filmmaker working for Hitler, made a documentary of a National Socialist party rally at Nuremberg. In scenes of swooning women

and cheering men, her film, called *Triumph of the Will,* recorded the dramatic force of Hitler's rhetoric and his ability to move the German people. Hitler's public charisma masked a profoundly troubled and incomplete individual capable of irrational rage and sick hatred of his fellow human beings. His warped views of the world were responsible for the greatest outrages ever committed in the name of legitimate power. Yet millions, including admirers in western Europe and the United States, succumbed to his appeal.

Family life, too, was carefully regulated through the propaganda machinery. Loyalty only to the state meant less loyalty to the family. In 1939, 82 percent of all German boys and girls between the ages of 10 and 18 were members of Nazi-controlled organizations. Special youth organizations, including the Hitler Youth, indoc-

Artist Wolfgang Willrich captures the Nazi ideal of domesticity—the small suburban middle-class family.

A propaganda-laden German beer coaster of the Nazi era informs the world that "who buys from the Jews is a traitor."

trinated boys with nationalistic and military values. Organizations for girls were intended to mold them into worthy wives and mothers. Woman's natural function, Hitler argued, was to serve in the home. Education for women beyond the care of home and family was a waste. Adult women had their own organizations to serve the Nazi state. The German Women's Bureau under Gertrud Scholtz-Klink instructed women in their "proper" female duties. In an effort to promote large families, the state paid allowances to couples for getting married, subsidized families according to their size, and gave tax breaks to large families. Abortion and birth control were outlawed, and women who sought such measures risked severe penalties and imprisonment.

By 1937 the need for women workers conflicted with the goals of Nazi propaganda. With the outbreak of war in 1939, women were urged to work, especially in jobs like munitions manufacture formerly held by men. For working women with families the double burden was a heavy one, as women were required to work long shifts—60-hour workweeks were not unusual—for low wages. Many women resisted entering the work force if they had other income or could live on the cash payments they received as the wives of soldiers. At the beginning of 1943, the German people were ordered to make sacrifices for a new era of "total war." Female labor became compulsory, and women were drafted into working for the war.

Propaganda condemned everything foreign, including Mickey Mouse, who was declared an enemy of the state in the 1930s. Purging foreign influences meant purging political opponents, especially members of the Communist party, who were rounded up and sent to concentration camps in Germany. Communism was identified as an international Jewish conspiracy to destroy the German *Volk*, or people. Nazi literature also identified "asocials," those who were considered deviant in any way, including homosexuals, who were likewise to be expelled. Euthanasia was used against the mentally ill and the mentally disabled in the 1930s. Concentration camps were expanded to contain enemies of the state. Later, when concentration camps became sites of extermination and forced labor, gypsies, homosexuals, criminals, and religious offenders had to wear insignia of different colors to indicate the reason for their persecution. The people who received the greatest attention for exclusion from Nazi Germany, and then from Europe, were the Jews.

The first measures against the German Jews—their exclusion from public employment and higher education—began almost immediately in 1933. In 1935 the Nuremberg Laws were enacted to identify Jews, to deprive them of their citizenship, and to forbid marriage and extramarital sexual relations between Jews and non-Jews. On the night of 9 November 1938, synagogues were set afire and books and valuables owned by Jews were confiscated throughout Germany. Jews were beaten, about 91 were killed, and 20,000 to 30,000 were imprisoned in concentration camps. The night came to be called *Kristallnacht*, meaning "night of broken glass," which referred to the Jewish shop windows smashed by the Brownshirts under orders from Goebbels. The government claimed that *Kristallnacht* was an outpouring of the German people's will. An atmosphere of state-sanctioned hate prevailed.

Racism was nothing new in European culture, nor was its particular variant, anti-Semitism—hatred of Jews—the creation of the Third Reich. The link the Nazis cultivated between racism and politics was built on cultural precedents. In the 1890s, in France and Austria and elsewhere in Europe, anti-Semitism was espoused by political and professional groups that formed themselves around issues of militant nationalism, authoritarianism, and mass politics. Hitler was a racist and an anti-Semite, and he placed theories of race at the core of his fascist ideology. "Experts" decided that sterilization was the surest way to protect "German blood." In 1933 one of the early laws of Hitler's new Reich decreed compulsory sterilization of

adolf Hitler on "Racial purity"

The purity of German blood was a recurrent theme in Hitler's speeches and writings from the beginning of his political career. In attacking both liberalism and socialism, Hitler offered racial superiority as the essence of the National Socialist "revolution." This speech, delivered in Berlin on 30 January 1937, lays out his attack on the concept of individual rights and humanity in favor of the *folk community*.

The most important plank in the National Socialist program is to abolish the liberal idea of the individual and the Marxist idea of humanity and to substitute for them the folk community rooted in the soil and held together by the bond of common blood. This sounds simple, but it involves a principle which has great consequences.

For the first time and in the first country our people are being taught to understand that, of all the tasks we have to face, the most noble and the most sacred for all mankind is the concept that each racial species must preserve the purity of blood which God has given to it.

The greatest revolution won by National Socialism is that it has pierced the veil which hid from us the knowledge that all human errors may be attributed to the conditions of the time and hence can be remedied, but there is one error that cannot be set right once it has been made by men—that is, the failure to understand the importance of keeping the blood and the race free from intermingling, and in this way to alter God's gift. It is not for human beings to discuss why Providence created different races. Rather it is important to understand the fact that it will punish those who pay no attention to its work of creation. . . .

I hereby prophesy that, just as knowledge that the earth moves around the sun led to a revolutionary change in the world picture, so will the blood-and-race doctrine of the National Socialist movement bring about a revolutionary change in our knowledge. . . . It will also change the course of history in the future.

This will not lead to difficulties between nations. On the contrary, it will lead to a better understanding between them. But at the same time it will prevent the Jews, under the mask of world citizenship, from thrusting themselves among all nations as an element of domestic chaos. . . .

The National Socialist movement limits its domestic activities to those individuals who belong to one people. It refuses to permit those of a foreign race to have any influence whatever on our political, intellectual, or cultural life. We refuse to give any members of a foreign race a dominant position in our national economic system.

In our folk community, which is based on ties of blood, in the results which National Socialism has obtained by training the public in the idea of this folk-community, lies the deepest reason for the great success of our Revolution.

"undesirables" in order to "eliminate inferior genes." The Nazi state decided who these undesirables were and forced the sterilization of 400,000 men and women.

The Third Reich was a government that delivered on its promises to end unemployment, to improve productivity, to break through the logjam of parliamentary obstacles, and to return Germany to the international arena as a contender for power. Yet Hitler's Nazi state ruled by violence, coercion, and intimidation. With a propaganda machine that glorified the leader and vilified groups singled out as scapegoats for Germany's problems, Hitler undermined democratic institutions and civil liberties in his pursuit of German power.

democracies in crisis

Democracies in the 1930s turned in on themselves in order to survive. In contrast to the Fascist mobilization of society and the Soviet restructuring of the economy, European democracies took small, tentative steps to respond to the challenges of the Great Depression. Democratic leaders lacked creative vision or even clear policy. Both democratic France and Great Britain were less successful than Nazi Germany in responding to the challenges of the Great Depression. France paid a high price for parliamentary stalemate and was still severely depressed on the eve of war in 1938–39. Great Britain maintained a stagnant economy and stable politics under Conservative leadership. Internal dissension ripped Spain apart. Its civil war assumed broader dimensions as the Soviet Union, Italy, and Germany struggled over Spain's future while Europe's democratic nations stood by and accepted defeat.

The failure of the Left in France

France's Third Republic, like most European parliamentary democracies in the 1930s, was characterized by a multiparty system. Genuine political differences often separated one party from another. The tendency toward parliamentary stalemate was aggravated by the Great Depression and by the increasingly extremist politics on both the left and the right in response to developments in the Soviet Union and Germany.

The belief of the French people in a private enterprise economy was shaken by the Great Depression, but no new unifying belief replaced it. Some felt that state planning was the answer; others were sure that state intervention had caused the problem. Distrusting both the New Deal model of the United States and the Nazi response to depression politics, the Third Republic followed a haphazard, wait-and-see policy of insulating the economy, discouraging competition, and protecting favored interests in both industry and agriculture. Stimulating the economy by deficit spending was considered anathema. Devaluation of the franc, which might have helped French exports, was regarded by policymakers as an unpatriotic act. France stood fast as a bastion of liberal belief in the self-adjusting mechanism of the market, and it suffered greatly for it. Party politics worked to reinforce the defensive rather than offensive response to the challenges of depression and a sluggish economy.

In 1936 an electoral mandate for change swept the Left into power. The new premier, Léon Blum (1872–1950), was a Socialist. Lacking the votes to rule with an exclusively Socialist government, Blum formed a coalition of Left and Center parties intent on economic reforms known as the Popular Front. Before Blum's government could take power, a wave of strikes swept France. Although reluctant to intervene in the economy, the Popular Front nevertheless was pushed into some action. It promised wage increases, paid vacations, and collective bargaining to French workers. The reduced workweek of 40 hours caused a drop in productivity, as did the short-lived one-month vacation policy. The government did nothing to prevent the out-

Europe: Types of Government

flow of investment capital from France. Higher wages failed to generate increased consumer demand because employers raised prices to cover their higher operating costs.

German rearmament, now publicly known, forced France into rearmament, which it could ill afford. Blum's government failed in 1937, with France still bogged down in a sluggish and depressed economy. The last peacetime government of the 1930s represented a conservative swing back to laissez-faire policies that put the needs of business above those of workers and brought a measure of revival to the French economy.

The radical Right drew strength from the Left's failures. Right-wing leagues and organizations multiplied, appealing to a frightened middle class. The failure of the Socialists, in turn, drove many sympathizers further to the left to join the Communist party. A divided France could not stand up to the foreign policy challenges of the 1930s posed by Hitler's provocations.

Muddling Through in Great Britain

Great Britain was hard hit by the Great Depression of the 1930s; only Germany and the United States experienced comparable economic devastation. The socialist Labour government of the years 1929 to 1931 under Prime Minister Ramsay MacDonald (1866–1937) was unprepared to deal with the 1929 collapse and lacked the vision and the planning to devise a way out of the morass. It took a coalition of moderate groups from the three parties—Liberal, Conservative, and Labour—to address the issues of high unemployment, a growing government deficit, a banking crisis, and the flight of capital. The National Government (1931–35) was a centrist, nonpartisan coalition whose members included Ramsay MacDonald, retained as prime minister, and Stanley Baldwin (1867–1947), a Conservative with a background in iron and steel manufacturing.

In response to the endemic crisis, the National Government took Britain off the international gold standard and devalued the pound. In order to protect domestic production, tariffs were established. The British economy showed signs of slow recovery, probably due less to these government measures than to a gradual improvement in the business cycle. The government had survived the crisis without resorting to the kinds of creative alternatives devised in the Scandinavian countries where, for example, consumer and producer cooperatives provided widespread economic relief. Moderates and classical liberals in Great Britain persisted in defending the nonintervention of the government in the economy, despite new economic theories such as that of John Maynard Keynes (1883–1946), who urged government spending to stimulate consumer demand as the best way to shorten the duration of the Great Depression.

In 1932 Sir Oswald Mosley (1896–1980) founded the British Union of Fascists (BUF), consisting of goon squads and bodyguards. The BUF was opposed to free-trade liberalism and communism alike. Mosley developed a corporate model for economic and political life in which interest groups rather than an electorate would be represented in a new kind of parliament. He favored, above all, national solutions by relying on imperial development; he rejected the world of international finance as corrupt.

The BUF shared similarities with European Fascist organizations. BUF squads beat up their political opponents and began attacking Jews, especially the eastern European émigrés living in London. The British fascists struck a responsive chord among the poorest working-class people of London's East End; at its peak the group claimed a membership of 20,000. Public alarm over increasingly inflammatory and anti-Semitic rhetoric converged with parliamentary denunciation. Popular support for the group was already beginning to erode when the BUF was outlawed in 1936. By this time, anti-Hitler feeling was spreading in Great Britain.

Mosley's response to harsh economic times had proven to be no match for the steady and reassuring strength of Stanley Baldwin's National Government, which seemed to be in control of an improving economic situation. The traditional party system prevailed not because of its brilliant solutions to difficult economic problems but because of the willingness of moderate parliamentarians to cooperate and adapt, however slowly, to the new need for economic transformation.

The Spanish Republic as Battleground

In 1931 Spain became a democratic republic after centuries of Bourbon monarchy and almost a decade of

Joan Miró, commissioned to design a French stamp to raise funds for the Spanish Republic, created "Aidez L'Espagne," but the stamp was never produced. Because the French people were so deeply divided over the Spanish Civil War, the Popular Front French government was unable to aid the Popular Front in Spain. Miró's stamp design recalls characteristics of his style in the brightly colored distorted forms and twisted shapes, positioned seemingly randomly on the flat background.

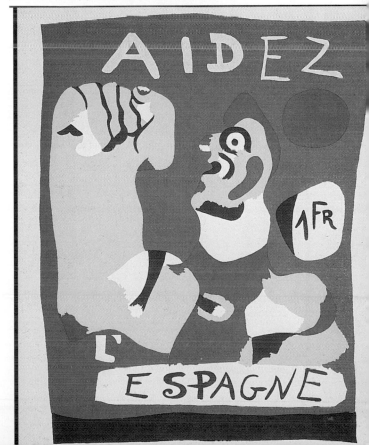

military dictatorship. In 1936 the voters of Spain elected a Popular Front government. The Popular Front in Spain was more radical than its French counterpart. The property of aristocratic landlords was seized; revolutionary workers went on strike; the Catholic church and its clergy were attacked. This social revolution initiated three years of civil war. On one side were the Republicans, the Popular Front defenders of the Spanish Republic and of social revolution in Spain. On the other side were the Nationalists, those who sought to overthrow the Republic—aristocratic landowners, supporters of the monarchy and the Catholic church, and much of the Spanish army.

The Spanish Civil War began in July 1936 with a revolt against the Republic from within the Spanish army. It was led by General Francisco Franco (1892–1975), a tough, shrewd, and stubborn man, a conservative nationalist allied with the Falange, the Fascist party in Spain. The conflict soon became a bloody military stalemate, with the Nationalists led by Franco controlling the more rural and conservative south and west of Spain and the Republicans holding out in the cities of the north and east—Madrid, Valencia, and Barcelona.

Almost from the beginning, the Spanish Civil War was an international event. Mussolini sent ground

The Rise of Fascism and Democracy in Crisis

28 October 1922	Italian Fascists march on Rome
November 1923	Beer Hall Putsch in Munich
1924	Fascists achieve parliamentary majority in Italy
1929	Lateran Treaty between Mussolini and Pope Pius XI
1932	Nazi party is single largest party in German parliament
January 1933	Hitler becomes Chancellor of Germany
30 June 1934	Purge of the SA leaves Hitler and the SS in unassailable position
15 September 1934	Enactment of Nuremberg Laws against Jews and other minorities
March 1935	Hitler publicly rejects Treaty of Versailles and announces German rearmament
3 October 1935	Italy invades Ethiopia
1936	Popular Front government elected in Spain
July 1936	Beginning of Spanish Civil War
October 1936	Rome-Berlin Axis Pact, an Italo German accord
1936–1937	Popular Front government in France
27 April 1937	Bombing of the Spanish town of Guernica
9 November 1938	*Kristallnacht* initiates massive violence against Jews
March 1939	Fascists defeat the Spanish Republic
April 1939	Italy annexes Albania
May 1939	Pact of Steel between Germany and Italy

Spanish capital (Republican stronghold)

★ Nationalist provisional capital

Major battles or bombings

The Spanish Civil War

troops, "volunteers," to fight alongside Franco's forces. Hitler dispatched technical specialists, tanks, and the Condor Legion, an aviation unit, to support the Nationalists. The Germans regarded Spain as a testing ground for new equipment and new methods of warfare, including aerial bombardment. The Soviet Union intervened on the side of the Republic, sending armaments, supplies, and technical and political advisers. Because the people of Britain and France were deeply divided in their attitudes toward the war in Spain, the British government stayed neutral, and the government of France was unable to aid its fellow Popular Front government in Spain. Although Americans volunteered to fight with the Republicans, the American government did not prevent the Texas Oil Company from selling 1.9 million tons of oil to Franco's insurgents, nor did it block the Ford Motor Company, General Motors, and Studebaker from supplying them with trucks.

The Spanish government pleaded, "Men and women of all lands! Come to our aid!" In response, 2800 American volunteers—among them college students, professors, intellectuals, and trade unionists—joined the loyalist army and European volunteers in defense of the Spanish Republic. Britons and antifascist émigrés from Italy and Germany also joined the International Brigades, which were vital in helping the city of Madrid hold out against the Nationalist generals. The Russians withdrew from the war in 1938, disillusioned by the failure of the French, British, and Americans to come to the aid of the Republicans. Madrid fell to the Nationalists in March 1939. The government established by Franco sent 1 million of its enemies to prison or concentration camps.

The fragile postwar stability of the 1920s crumbled under the pressures of economic depression, ongoing national antagonisms, and insecurity in the international arena. Europe after 1932 was plagued by the consequences of economic collapse, Fascist success, and the growing threat of armed conflict. Parliamentary institutions were fighting and losing a tug-of-war with authoritarian movements. A Fascist regime was in place in Italy. Political and electoral defeats eroded democratic and liberal principles in Germany's Weimar Republic. Dictatorships triumphed in Spain and in much of eastern and central Europe. Liberal parliamentary governments were failing to solve the economic and social problems of the postwar years. In the democratic nations of France, Great Britain, and, during the brief period from 1921 to 1936, Spain, parliamentary institutions appeared to be persevering. But even here, polarization and increasing intransigence on both the left and the right threatened the future of democratic politics.

The exclusion of the Soviet Union from Western internationalism in the 1920s both reflected and exacerbated the crisis. The Bolshevik revolution had served as a political catalyst among workers in the West, attracting them to the possibility of radical solutions. That potential radicalization aggravated class antagonisms in the 1930s, when mass politics prevailed and drove political leaders to seek conservative solutions as a means of stabilizing class politics.

Mastering the chapter

To review the main points of the chapter, be sure you can explain the significance of each of the following.

Terms/Concepts/Events	People	Places
Weimar Republic	Lenin	Finland
Politburo	Leon Trotsky	Estonia
New Economic Policy	Nikolai Bukharin	Latvia
Five-Year Plan	Joseph Stalin	Lithuania
Comintern	Benito Mussolini	Baltic states
Great Purge	*Squadristi*	Yugoslavia
Beer Hall Putsch	Adolf Hitler	Romania
Mein Kampf	Joseph Goebbels	Czechoslovakia
Lebensraum	John Maynard Keynes	the Saar
Kristallnacht	General Francisco Franco	Maginot Line

suggestions for further Reading

International politics and economic Nationalism

* Derek H. Aldcroft, *From Versailles to Wall Street*, 1919–1929 (Berkeley: University of California Press, 1977). Traces the recovery of the international economy and the systemic forces of its disintegration in the 1920s, with special attention to such areas as war debts, reparations, the gold standard, the agricultural sector, and patterns of international lending.

Jon Jacobson, *When the Soviet Union Entered World Politics* (Berkeley: University of California Press, 1994). Deals with the revolutionary and diplomatic aspects of early Soviet foreign relations and demonstrates the central importance of foreign relations to Soviet economic development and the struggle for leadership.

Marshall M. Lee and Wolfgang Michalka, *German Foreign Policy, 1917–1933: Continuity or Break?* (Leamington Spa, England: Berg, 1987). A solid and synthetic treatment of Weimar diplomacy that takes into account the historiographical debates over revisionism and expansion.

* Melvyn P. Leffler, *The Elusive Quest: America's Pursuit of European Stability and French Security, 1919–1933* (Chapel Hill: University of North Carolina Press, 1979). Examines the economic and financial imperatives guiding U.S. foreign policy after World War I and identifies a particular Republican party approach labeled *economic diplomacy*. Special attention is paid to European stabilization, French security, and Germany's rehabilitation.

* Joseph Rothschild, *East Central Europe Between the Two World Wars* (Seattle: University of Washington Press, 1983). A balanced survey of interwar developments in Poland, Czechoslovakia, Hungary, Yugoslavia, Romania, Bulgaria, Albania, and the Baltic states highlighting internal weaknesses and external vulnerabilities. A concluding chapter covers cultural contributions.

* Stephen A. Schuker, *The End of French Predominance in Europe: The Financial Crisis of 1924 and the Adoption of the Dawes Plan* (Chapel Hill: University of North Carolina Press, 1976). Locates the decline of France as a great power in the financial crisis of 1924 and the diplomacy of reparations and examines the domestic bases for French powerlessness.

The soviet union's separate path

* Stephen F. Cohen, *Bukharin and the Bolshevik Revolution: A Political Biography*, 1888–1938 (Oxford: Oxford University Press, 1980). This milestone work is a general history of the period, as well as a political and intellectual biography of Bukharin, "the last Bolshevik," who supported an evolutionary road to modernization and socialism and whose policies were an alternative to Stalinism.

* Sheila Fitzpatrick, *The Russian Revolution*, 1917–1932 (Oxford: Oxford University Press, 1985). Arguing from the premise that the revolutionary upheaval did not end with the Bolshevik seizure of power in November 1917, Fitzpatrick interprets the developments of the 1920s and early 1930s, including the NEP and the First Five-Year Plan, as stages in a single revolutionary process.

Sheila Fitzpatrick, *Stalin's Peasants: Resistance and Survival in the Russian Village After Collectivization* (New York: Oxford University Press, 1995). An important study of Soviet peasants during the first decade of collectivization that argues that passive forms of resistance by peasants forced the regime to moderate its policies.

* J. Arch Getty and Roberta Manning, *Stalinist Terror: New Perspectives* (Cambridge: Cambridge University Press, 1994). Leading revisionist scholars of the Stalinist period provide an authoritative reassessment of the regime.

* Robert C. Tucker, *Stalin as Revolutionary, 1879–1929: A Study in History and Personality* (New York: Norton, 1973). Traces Stalin's development from his Georgian childhood to his 50th year, when he established himself as the new hero of the Soviet state. Tucker uses Freudian terms of analysis in considering Stalin's hero-identification with Lenin.

The promise of fascism

* Volker R. Berghahn, *Modern Germany: Society, Economy and Politics in the Twentieth Century* (Cambridge: Cambridge University Press, 1987). Considers the particular challenges of rapid industrialization faced by Germany and how they interacted with social tensions and political conflict.

Eberhard Kolb, *The Weimar Republic*, tr. P. S. Falla (London: Unwin Hyman, 1988). An introduction to the history of Germany's first republic, both as a historic survey and as an examination of the basic problems and trends in research.

* MacGregor Knox, *Mussolini Unleashed, 1939–1941: Politics and Strategy in Fascist Italy's Last War* (Cambridge: Cambridge University Press, 1982). Argues that Mussolini had a consistent foreign policy in the Mediterranean and a genuine program for living space in the Mediterranean and the Middle East. In his bid for power and prestige, Mussolini was willing to risk war and short-term instability at home.

* Adrian Lyttelton, *The Seizure of Power: Fascism in Italy, 1919–1929* (New York: Scribners, 1973). Addresses the question of why fascism first took root in Italy.

Zeev Sternhell with Mario Sznajder and Maia Asheri, *The Birth of Fascist Ideology: From Cultural Rebellion to Political Revolution* (Princeton: Princeton University Press, 1994). Approaches fascism as an ideology rather than a social movement and argues that it was already fully formed before World War I.

Hitler and the Third Reich

* Hilmar Hoffman, *The Triumph of Propaganda: Film and National Socialism, 1933–1945* (Providence: Berghahn Books, 1996). The significance of film to the Nazi propaganda effort is demonstrated through the author's examination of newsreels, documentaries, feature films, and "cultural" films from Hitler's rise to power through the war.

* Ian Kershaw, *The "Hitler Myth": Image and Reality in the Third Reich* (New York: Oxford University Press, 1987). Examines the power of the "Hitler myth" created by the German Propaganda Ministry, the German people, and Hitler. The myth accounted for the stability of the Third Reich throughout the 1930s and in the first years of the war.

* Detlev Peukert, *Inside Nazi Germany: Conformity, Opposition, and Racism in Everyday Life* (New Haven: Yale University Press, 1987). Discusses the informal modes of resistance among the German people.

Democracies in Crisis

M. S. Alexander and H. Graham, *The French and Spanish Popular Fronts: Comparative Perspectives* (Cambridge: Cambridge University Press, 1989). Contributions by specialists on the interwar period.

Herschel B. Chipp, *Picasso's Guernica: History, Transformations, Meanings* (Berkeley: University of California Press, 1988). Documents the creation of Picasso's *Guernica*, rooting it firmly in the context of the Spanish Civil War, and discusses the painting's reception in Spain and abroad.

* John Hiden and Patrick Salmon, *The Baltic Nations and Europe: Estonia, Latvia, and Lithuania in the Twentieth Century* (London and New York: Longman, 1991). Surveys the development of the Baltic states in this century, discussing Baltic independence, the period between the wars, and the states' incorporation into the Soviet Union, as well as renewed efforts toward independence in the Gorbachev era.

* Julian Jackson, *The Popular Front in France: Defending Democracy, 1934–1938* (Cambridge: Cambridge University Press, 1988). The first in-depth study of Leon Blum's government, with a special emphasis on cultural transformation and the legacy of the Popular Front.

Michael Jackson, *Fallen Sparrows: The International Brigades in the Spanish Civil War* (Philadelphia: American Philosophical Society, 1994). A careful description of the members and activities of the International Brigades, which were organized under the direction of the Comintern to save the Spanish Republic.

Maurice Larkin, *France Since the Popular Front: Government and People, 1936–1986* (Oxford: Clarendon Press, 1988). A work of total history that situates French political developments in the history, traditions, social structure, and economy of France. Separates the legend from the legacy of the Popular Front.

*Paperback edition available.

global conflagration: world war II, 1939-1945

building bombs

Scientists in the twentieth century participate in an international community of ideas and discoveries. In the first half of the twentieth century, as is the case now, academic scientists dedicated themselves to basic research—the pursuit of scientific knowledge for its own sake—and published their findings in scholarly scientific journals read only by specialists in their own fields throughout the world. It was not unusual for public-minded critics to accuse scientists and other academicians of living in an ivory tower, producing work without relevance or social value. For that matter, scientists themselves did not dispute the accusation that they gave little thought to the practical and applied scientific outcomes of their research. The transfer of basic research to useful technology was not a primary motivator for the great discoveries in physics and chemistry in the first half of the twentieth century. Einstein's theory of relativity or Heisenberg's uncertainty principle, both meriting the Nobel Prize in physics, seemed to offer little to the average citizen to change the world.

While international in their exchange of information, scientists worked very much within national scientific communities. Because of the demands for interdisciplinary knowledge and highly specialized control, however, scientists began to abandon more individualistic models of doing research in favor of team approaches. In Italy, for example, the creation of a research center at the University of Rome brought together an outstanding and creative research team headed by the physicist Enrico Fermi and dedicated to collaboration on atomic physics. In France, the team led by J. F. Joliot and his wife, Irene Curie Joliot, daughter of Nobel physicists Marie and Pierre Curie, trailblazed new directions in atomic physics with their discovery of artificial radioactivity. In 1932 the team of J. D. Cockcroft and E. T. S. Walton attracted public attention by doing the unimaginable: they split the atom, which hitherto had been considered invisible and indivisible. Few at the time considered that this accomplishment held more than a curiosity value.

The leading national "factories" garnering Nobel Prizes in the sciences were the United States and Germany. Most of the important theoretical breakthroughs in physics were published first in the German language and spread quickly to the research teams of other nations, leading to new perspectives and new insights in pushing back the frontier of scientific knowledge. All of this, while interesting, seemed of little value to people concerned with improving depression economies or keeping the world safe from war.

But politics changed everything. Beginning in 1933, the racial policies directed against the Jews in Germany and Nazi political repression provoked a diaspora of leading chemists and physicists, who fled central Europe for the safer havens of Great Britain and the United States. Enrico Fermi traveled to Stockholm in 1938 to claim his Nobel Prize in physics but did not return home to Italy. Instead, he fled to the United States with his wife, Laura, who was Jewish, because he feared for her safety in Fascist Italy. Two other refugee scientists, Otto Frisch and Rudolf Peierls, left Germany and settled in Great Britain, where, because of their work on uranium-235, they were able to persuade the British government to sponsor the first work on atomic weapons.

And here is where the story of science changed. In 1939 German scientists began to consider the possibility of applying all of the accumulated knowledge about atomic physics to the task of building the ultimate weapon, a new kind of bomb with explosive force unimaginable before the discovery of fission in 1939. The Allies feared that Germany would achieve exactly that goal. Building the ultimate bomb

Building Bombs
The Coming of World War II
    Hitler's Foreign Policy and Appeasement
    Hitler's War, 1939-1941
    Collaboration and Resistance
Racism and Destruction
    Enforcing Nazi Racial Policies
    The Destruction of Europe's Jews
    Who Knew?
Allied Victory
    The Soviet Union's Great Patriotic War
    The United States Enters the War
    Winning the War in Europe
    Japanese War Aims and Assumptions
    Winning the War in the Pacific
    The Fate of Allied Cooperation: 1945

Focus Questions

1. What factors made possible Hitler's diplomatic and military successes between 1933 and 1941?
2. Why did the Nazi regime believe that it needed to destroy the Jews, Gypsies, and other outsiders, and how did it attempt to justify this policy?
3. How did Hitler's invasion of the Soviet Union and the entry of the United States into the war transform the military situation?
4. How did the Allies coordinate their efforts, and what factors strained relations between them?

required a great commitment of resources and highly coordinated management of science, technology, and military needs. We now know that the German scientific community in Germany never really believed that building a massive bomb was possible, nor was it feasible for the Nazi state to dedicate sufficient resources to accomplish the task. German leaders were sure that the war would be over long before such a weapon could be manufactured, and in the meantime, they had more pressing needs for weapons creation and production.

The Allies lacked neither resources nor scientific brainpower to address the task. The U.S. government joined forces with the British in an endeavor known by the code name of the Manhattan Project. By 1945 the budget of the project, entirely underwritten by the U.S. government, was estimated to be equal to that of the entire U.S. auto industry. Refugee scientists from central Europe and their British and American colleagues joined together in a collaboration unique in the annals of scientific culture.

The speed with which the scientists of the Manhattan Project moved from basic to applied research was staggering. Discoveries were made and applied almost instantaneously. Plutonium, an artificial material used in the bomb's explosive chain reaction, had to be manufactured. Detonation of a nuclear core was an especially knotty problem, since the materials comprising the bomb had to be compressed to a critical volume in less than one-millionth of a second. The head of the Manhattan Project, Robert Oppenheimer (1904–67), a physicist who managed the scientific side of the project, spoke of the successive challenges of the production of the atomic bomb as "technically sweet." He explained that the scientists of the Manhattan Project continued to do what they did best—make discoveries, albeit in a highly focused and applied environment. "You go ahead and do it and you argue about what to do about it only after you have had your technical success. This is the way it was with the atomic bomb. I do not think anybody opposed making it; there were some debates about what to do with it after it was made."

The atomic bomb resulting from this new kind of scientific collaboration changed the world. In acknowledging the impact of this product of scientific expertise, it is easy to overlook the culture that itself had changed in order to build bombs. Governments entered laboratories as key players in supporting the research agenda. Scientists, perhaps not for the first time but certainly dramatically, were forced to confront the ethical consequences of their actions in a world where no form of knowledge could be considered innocent.

The coming of world war II

The years between 1933 and 1939 marked a bleak period in international affairs when the British, the French, and the Americans were unwilling or unable to recognize the dire threat to world peace of Hitler and his Nazi state. The leaders of these countries did not comprehend Hitler's single-minded goal to extend German living space eastward as far as western Russia. They failed to understand the seriousness of the Nazi process of consolidation at home. They took no action against Hitler's initial acts of aggression. The war that began in Europe in 1939 eventually became a great global conflict that pitted Germany, Italy, and Japan—the Axis Powers—against the British Empire, the Soviet Union, and the United States—the Grand Alliance.

Even before war broke out in Europe, there was armed conflict in Asia. The rapidly expanding Japanese economy depended on Manchuria for raw materials and on China for markets. Chinese boycotts against Japanese goods and threats to Japanese economic interests in Manchuria led to a Japanese military occupation of Manchuria and the establishment of a Japanese puppet state there in 1931–32. When the powers of the League of Nations, led by Great Britain, refused to recognize this state, Japan withdrew from the League. Fearing that the Chinese government was becoming strong enough to exclude Japanese trade from China, Japanese troops and naval units began an undeclared war in China in 1937. Many important Chinese cities—Peking, Shanghai, Nanking, Canton, and Hankow—fell to Japanese forces. Relentless aerial bombardment of Chinese cities and atrocities committed by Japanese troops against Chinese civilians outraged Europeans and Americans. The governments of the Soviet Union, Great Britain, and the United States, seeking to protect their own ideological, economic, and security interests in China, gave economic, diplomatic, and moral support to the Chinese government of Chiang Kai-shek. Thus the stage was set for major military conflicts in Asia and in Europe.

Hitler's Foreign Policy and Appeasement

For Hitler a war against the Soviet Union for living space was inevitable. It would come, he told some of his close associates, in the years 1943–45. However, he wanted to avoid refighting the war that had led to Germany's defeat in 1914–18. World War I was a war fought on two fronts—in the east and in the west. It was a war in which Germany had to face many enemies at the same time, and a war that lasted until German soldiers, civilians, and resources were exhausted. In the next war, Hitler wanted above all to avoid fighting Great Britain while battling Russia for living space. He convinced himself that the British would remain neutral if Germany agreed not to attack the British Empire. Would they not appreciate his willingness to abolish forever the menace of communism? Were they not Aryans too?

Beginning in 1938, with the non-Nazi conservatives removed from positions of power in Germany, Hitler alone determined foreign policy. He was becoming increasingly impatient, considering time his greatest enemy. He feared that Germany could fail to achieve its destiny as a world power by waiting too long to act. And he became more aggressive and willing to use military force as he set out to remove the obstacles to German domination of central Europe—Austria, Czechoslovakia, and Poland. In March he annexed Austria to the German Reich. Many Austrians wished to be united with Germany; others had no desire to be led by Nazis. Using the threat of invasion, he intimidated the Austrian government into legalizing the Nazi party, which thereby brought pro-Nazis into the Austrian cabinet and Ger-

man troops into the country. Encouraged by his success, Hitler provoked a crisis in Czechoslovakia in the summer of the same year. He demanded "freedom" for the German-speaking people of the Sudetenland area of Czechoslovakia. His main objective, however, was not to protect the Germans of Czechoslovakia but to smash the Czech state, the major obstacle in central Europe to the launching of an attack on living space farther east.

Western statesmen did not understand Hitler's commitment to destroying Czechoslovakia or his willingness to fight a limited war against the Czechs to do so. Hitler did everything possible to isolate Czechoslovakia from its neighbors and its treaty partners. France, an ally of Czechoslovakia, appeared distinctly unwilling to defend it against Germany's menace. Britain, seeking to avoid a war that the government did not think was necessary and for which the British were not prepared, sent Prime Minister Neville Chamberlain (1869–1940) to reason with Hitler. Believing that transferring the Sudetenland, the German-speaking area of Czechoslovakia, to Germany was the only solution—and one that would redress some of the wrongs done to Germany after World War I—Chamberlain convinced France and Czechoslovakia to yield to Hitler's demands.

Chamberlain's actions were the result of British self-interest. British leaders agreed that their country could not afford another war like the Great War of 1914–18. Defense expenditures had been dramatically reduced to devote national resources to improving domestic social services, protecting world trade, and fortifying Britain's global interests. Britain understood well its weakened position in its dominions. In the British hierarchy of priorities, defense of the British Empire ranked first, above defense of Europe; and Britain's commitment to western Europe ranked above the defense of eastern and central Europe.

Hitler's response to being granted everything he requested was to renege and issue new demands. His desire for war could not have been more transparent, nor could his unwillingness to play by the rules of diplomacy have been clearer. One final meeting was held at Munich to avert war. On 29 September 1938, one day before German troops were scheduled to invade Czechoslovakia, Mussolini and the French prime minister, Édouard Daladier (1884–1970), joined Hitler and Chamberlain at Munich to discuss a peaceful resolution to the crisis.

At Munich, Chamberlain and Daladier again yielded to Hitler's demands. The Sudetenland was ceded to Germany, and German troops quickly moved to occupy

A triumphant Hitler enters Austria in 1938. The union of his native country with the German Reich had long been a cherished goal of the Nazi Führer.

the area. The policy of the British and French was dubbed *appeasement* to indicate the willingness to concede to demands in order to preserve peace. Appeasement has become a dirty word in twentieth-century European history, taken to mean weakness and cowardice. Yet Chamberlain was neither weak nor cowardly. His great mistake in negotiating with Hitler was in assuming that Hitler was a reasonable man, who like all reasonable persons wanted to avoid another war.

Chamberlain thought his mediation at Munich had won for Europe a lasting peace—"peace for our time," he reported. The people of Europe received Chamberlain's assessment with a sense of relief and shame—relief over what had been avoided, shame at having deserted Czechoslovakia. In fact, the policy of appeasement further destabilized Europe and accelerated Hitler's plans for European domination. Within months, Hitler cast aside the Munich agreement by annihilating Czechoslovakia. German troops occupied the western, Czech part of the state, including the capital of Prague.

The Slovak eastern part became independent and a German satellite. At the same time, Lithuania was pressured into surrendering Memel to Germany, and Hitler demanded that Germany control Gdansk and the Polish Corridor. No longer could Hitler be ignored or appeased. No longer could his goals be misunderstood.

Hitler's War, 1939-1941

In the tense months that followed the Munich meeting and the occupation of Prague, Hitler readied himself for war in western Europe. To strengthen his position, in May 1939 he formed a military alliance, the Pact of Steel, with Mussolini's Italy. Then Hitler and Stalin, previously self-declared enemies, shocked the West by joining their two nations in a pact of mutual neutrality, the Non-Aggression Pact of 1939. Opportunism lay behind Hitler's willingness to ally with the Communist state that he had denounced throughout the 1930s. A German alliance with the Soviet Union would, Hitler believed, force the British and the French to back down and to remain neutral while Germany conquered Poland—the last obstacle to a drive for expansion eastward—in a short, limited war. Stalin recognized the failure of the western European powers to stand up to Hitler. There was little possibility, he thought, of an alliance against Germany with the virulently anti-Communist Neville Chamberlain. The best Stalin could hope for was that the Germans and the Western powers would fight it out while the Soviet Union waited to enter the war at the most opportune moment. As an added bonus, Germany promised not to interfere if the Soviet Union annexed eastern Poland, Bessarabia, and the Baltic republics of Latvia and Estonia.

Finally recognizing Hitler's intent, the British and the French also signed a pact in the spring of 1939 promising assistance to Poland in the event of aggression. Tensions mounted throughout the summer as Europeans awaited the inevitable German aggression. On 1 September 1939, Germany attacked Poland, which was ill-prepared to defend itself. By the end of the month, in spite of valiant resistance, the vastly outnumbered Poles surrendered. Although the German army needed no assistance, the Russians invaded Poland ten days before its collapse, and Germany and Russia divided the spoils. Almost immediately, Stalin took measures to defend Russia against a possible German attack. The Soviet Union assumed military control in the Baltic states and demanded of Finland territory and military bases from which the city of Leningrad could be defended. When Finland refused, Russia invaded. In the snows of the "Winter War" of 1939–40, the Finns initially fought the Russian army to a standstill, much to the encouragement of the democratic West. The Finns, however, were eventually defeated in March 1940.

Hitler's war, the war for German domination of Europe, had begun. But it had not begun the way he intended. Great Britain and France, true to their alliance with Poland and contrary to Hitler's expectations, declared war on Germany on 3 September 1939, even though they were unable to give any help to Poland. In the six months after the fall of Poland, no military action took place between Germany and the Allies because Hitler postponed offensives in northern and western Europe because of poor weather conditions. This strange interlude, which became known as "the phony war," was a period of suspended reality in which

France and Great Britain waited for Hitler to make his next move. Civilian morale in France deteriorated among a population that still remembered the death and destruction that France had endured in the Great War. An attitude of defeatism germinated and grew before the first French soldier fell in battle.

With the arrival of spring, Germany attacked Denmark and Norway in April 1940. Then, on 10 May 1940, Hitler's armies invaded the Netherlands, Belgium, and Luxembourg. By the third week of May, German mechanized forces were racing through northern France toward the English Channel, cutting off the British and Belgian troops and 120,000 French forces from the rest of the French army. With the rapid defeat of Belgium, these forces were crowded against the Channel and had to be evacuated from the beaches of Dunkirk. France, with a large and well-equipped army, nevertheless re-

A German motorized detachment rides through a bomb-shattered town during the Nazi invasion of Poland in 1939. The invasion saw the first use of the blitzkrieg—lightning war—in which air power and rapid tank movement combined for swift victory.

World War II in Europe

lied on Allied support and was in a desperate situation without it.

In France, the German army fought a new kind of war called a *blitzkrieg*, or "lightning war," so named because of its speed. The British and the French had expected the German army to behave much as it had in World War I, concentrating its striking forces in a swing through coastal Belgium and Holland in order to cap-

ture Paris. French strategists believed that France was safe because of hilly and forested terrain they thought was impassable. They also counted on the protection of the fortress wall known as the Maginot Line that France had built in the period between the wars. The Maginot Line stretched for hundreds of miles but was useless against mobile tank divisions, which outflanked it. With stunning speed, Germany drove its tanks—panzers—

The reaction of this Frenchman watching the Axis powers take over his country was repeated across Europe as defending armies laid down their arms or escaped into exile.

through the French defenses at Sedan in eastern France.

The French could have pinched off the advance of the overextended panzers, but the French army, suffering from severe morale problems, collapsed and was in retreat. On 17 June 1940, only weeks after German soldiers had stepped on French soil, Marshal Henri-Philippe Pétain, the great hero of the Battle of Verdun in World War I, petitioned the Germans for an armistice. Three-fifths of France, including the entire Atlantic seaboard, was occupied by the German army and placed under direct German rule. In the territory that remained unoccupied, Pétain created a collaborationist government that resided at Vichy—a spa city in central France—and worked in partnership with the Germans for the rest of the war. Charles de Gaulle (1890–1970), a brigadier general opposed to the armistice, fled to London, where he set up a Free French government in exile.

French capitulation in June 1940 followed Italian entry into the war on the side of Germany in the same month. The British were now alone in a war against the two Axis Powers as Germany made plans for an invasion of the British Isles from across the English Channel. To prepare the way, the German air force, under Reichsmarshal Hermann Göring (1893–1946), launched a series of air attacks against England—the Battle of

Britain. The German air force first attacked British aircraft, airfields, and munitions centers and then shifted targets to major population centers like London and industrial cities like Coventry. Between 7 September and 2 November 1940, the German air force bombed the city of London every night, inflicting serious damage on the city and killing 15,000 people.

The British resisted these attacks under the leadership of Winston Churchill, who had succeeded Chamberlain as prime minister in 1940. Churchill was a master public speaker who, in a series of radio broadcasts, inspired the people of Britain with the historic greatness of the task confronting them—holding out against Nazism until the forces of the overseas British Empire and the United States could be marshaled to liberate Europe. The British Royal Air Force inflicted serious losses on German aircraft, while British industry was able to maintain steady production of planes, bombs, and armaments. Civilians endured the nightly destruction and air raids in what Churchill termed Britain's "finest hour." Recognizing his lack of success in establishing air superiority over the Channel or in breaking the will of the British people, Hitler abandoned the Battle of Britain and canceled the invasion.

The Division of France, 1940–1944

The London Underground was pressed into service as a bomb shelter during the Battle of Britain.

autonomous Croatian government favorably disposed to the Germans in Zagreb.

German troops then crossed the Yugoslav border into Greece. Moving quickly down the Greek mainland, German soldiers captured the capital of Athens on 27 April 1941. German forces then turned their attention to the Greek island of Crete, where fleeing British soldiers sought refuge. In the first mass paratroop attack in history, Crete was rapidly subdued, forcing the British to evacuate to Egypt. The British were routed and experienced humiliating defeat by the German blitzkrieg.

The Balkans were important to Hitler for a number of reasons. Half of Germany's wheat and livestock came from the countries of southeastern Europe. Romanian and Hungarian oil fields supplied Germany's only non-Russian oil. Greece and Yugoslavia were important suppliers of metal ores, including aluminum, tin, lead, and copper, so necessary for industry and the war effort.

The necessity of protecting resources, especially the oil fields in Romania, also gave the area geopolitical importance for Germany. In launching an attack against the Soviet Union, Hitler was well aware of the strategic significance of controlling the straits linking the Mediterranean and Black seas. The British lifeline to its empire could also be cut by control of the eastern Mediterranean.

collaboration and resistance

No one nation has ever controlled the Balkans, and Hitler understood that he must rule not by occupation but by collaboration. Some Balkan collaborators joined puppet governments out of an ideological commitment to fascism. They were hostile to communism and believed that Hitler's Nazism was far preferable to Stalin's communism. They saw in the German victory the chance to put their beliefs into practice.

Some governments collaborated with the Germans out of national self-interest. Just as the government of Hungary allied with Germany in the hope of winning back territory lost at the end of World War I, Romania allied with Russia. The government of Slovakia was loyal to the Third Reich because Hitler had given it independence from the Czechs. A German puppet state was set up in the Yugoslav province of Croatia. Other collaborators were pragmatists who believed that by taking political office they could negotiate with the German conquerors and soften the effects of the Nazi conquest on their people. Hitler had little affection for local ideological Fascists and sometimes smashed their

It was not in Great Britain but in the Balkans that Hitler was able to engage the British enemy and inflict serious losses. The British had a presence in the Greek Peloponnese, where their air units were deployed to support the valiant resistance of the Greeks against Italian aggression. In his original plans for a limited war, Hitler hoped to establish control over the Balkans by peaceful diplomatic means. But Mussolini's disastrous attempt to achieve military glory by conquering Greece impelled Hitler to make his own plans to attack Greece in Operation Marita. Using Bulgaria as the base of operations, Germany invaded Yugoslavia, whose government had been weakened by a recent military coup. The capital of Belgrade fell in April 1941. Internal ethnic enmity between the Croats and the Serbs led to the mutiny of Croatian soldiers and to the formation of an movements. He preferred to work with local generals and administrators. Pragmatic collaborators often could not or would not negotiate with the German authorities very well. The help they gave in rounding up opponents of Nazi Germany—resistance fighters and Jews—resulted in their punishment after the war.

Resistance against German occupation and collaborationist regimes took many forms. Resisters wrote subversive tracts, distributed them, gathered intelligence information for the Allies, sheltered Jews or other enemies of the Nazis, committed acts of sabotage or assassination or other violent acts, and carried on guerrilla warfare against the German army. Resisters ran the risk of endangering themselves and their families, who, if discovered, would be tortured and killed. Resistance movements developed most strongly after the German attack on the Soviet Union in 1941, when the Communist parties of occupied Europe formed the core of the violent resistance against the Nazi regime. Resistance grew stronger when the Germans began to draft young European men for work on German farms and in German factories. Many preferred to go underground rather than to Germany.

One of the great resistance fighters of the Second World War was Josip Broz (1892–1980), alias Tito. He was a Croatian Communist and a Yugoslav nationalist. Instead of waiting to be liberated by the Allies, his partisans fought against Italian and German troops. Ten or more German divisions that might otherwise have fought elsewhere were tied up combating Tito's forces. He gained the admiration and the support of Churchill, Roosevelt, and Stalin. After liberation, Tito's organization won 90 percent of the vote in the Yugoslav elections, and he became the leader of the country in the postwar era. Resistance entailed enormous risks and required secrecy, moral courage, and great bravery. On the whole, however, the actions of resistance fighters seldom affected military timetables and did little to change the course of the war and Hitler's domination of Europe.

By the middle of 1941, Hitler controlled a vast continental empire that stretched from the Baltic to the

A Yugoslav partisan bayoneting a Nazi soldier.

The white Rose

Resistance to Hitler's rule in Germany was a limited and isolated phenomenon, unable to claim, as the French resistance did, any coordinated leadership or mass following. On 22 February 1943, two students at the University of Munich and their professor were executed for distributing pamphlets that criticized Hitler's regime. The students, Sophie and Hans Scholl, were brother and sister, and along with Professor Kurt Huber they belonged to a small group of students, faculty, scientists, and intellectuals who called their society the White Rose.

Appeal to All Germans!

The war goes on to its certain conclusion. As in the year 1918, the German Government tries to tell us that the U-boat campaign is succeeding, while in the East our armies are retreating without stopping and in the West an Allied invasion is expected momentarily. America has yet to reach the height of its arming for war, and today it is already armed beyond anything like it in the past. With mathematical certainty Hitler is leading the German people to destruction.

Hitler cannot win the war, he can only prolong it. His guilt and that of those who helped him have already gone beyond the point of no return. A just punishment comes nearer and nearer!

What must the German people do? It sees nothing and it hears nothing. Blinded, it staggers on to its destruction. "Victory at any cost!" are the words written on its banners. "I shall fight to the last man," says Hitler—even though the war has already been lost.

Germans! Do you want yourself and your children to suffer the same fate as the Jews? Do you want to be judged the same way your mis-leader will be judged? Shall we forever be the most hated and rejected people in the world? Separate yourself, therefore, from the National Socialist subhumanity! Show by your deeds that you think otherwise!

This is the beginning of a new War of Liberation. The most decent of our people fight on our side! Tear up the cloak of indifference which you have placed around your hearts! *Decide yourself, before it is too late!*

Don't fall for that National Socialist propaganda that has put the fear of Bolshevism in your bones! Do you really think that the salvation of Germany is bound up for better or worse with National Socialism? A criminal conspiracy cannot possibly win a German victory. Abandon *immediately and in time* anything to do with National Socialism! There is going to be a terrible and just verdict for those who have shown themselves to be cowardly and irresolute.

This war was never a national one. What will be its lesson for us?

The imperialist concept of power, no matter from which side it comes, must have its teeth drawn for all time. One-sided Prussian militarism must never again be allowed to win power. Only in noble cooperation with other Europeans can the ground be prepared for a new political structure. Any centralized power, such as that the Prussian state sought to exercise inside Germany and in Europe, must be stifled in its germinal stage. The future Germany can be only a federal state. Only a sound federal state order can give Europe a new life. Workers must be freed by a rational socialism from their condition of abject slavery. The phantom of an autarchic economy must disappear in Europe. Every single person has the right to the good things of the world!

Freedom of speech, freedom of conscience, protection of the individual from despotism of the criminal power-state, these will be the foundation of the new Europe.

Support the Resistance! Distribute these leaflets!

Black Sea and from the Atlantic Ocean to the Russian border. The German army occupied territories and controlled satellites, or Hitler relied on collaborationist governments for support. Having destroyed the democracies of western Europe, with the exception of Great Britain, Hitler's armies absorbed territory and marched across nations at rapid speed with technical and strategic superiority. Military conquest was not the only horror that the seemingly invincible Hitler inflicted on European peoples.

Racism and Destruction

War, as the saying goes, is hell. But the horrors perpetrated in World War II exceeded anything ever experienced in Western civilization. Claims of racial superiority were invoked to justify inhuman atrocities. The Germans and Japanese used spurious arguments of racial superiority to fuel their war efforts in both the European and Asian theaters of battle. In Asia the subjugation of inferior peoples became a rallying cry for conquest. But the Germans and the Japanese were not alone in using racist propaganda. The United States employed racial stereotypes to depict the inferiority of the enemy, and the government interned Japanese-Americans living on the West Coast in camps and seized their property.

Nowhere, however, was the use of racism by the state more virulent than in Germany. German racist ideology distorted pseudoscientific theories for the purpose of separating those they deemed racially superior from the racially inferior. The phrase "the master race" was used to identify those human beings worthy of living; those not worthy were designated "subhuman." Hatred of certain groups fueled both politics and war. Hitler promised the German people a purified Reich of Aryans free of the Jews and the racially and mentally inferior. Slavic peoples—Poles and Russians—were designated as subhumans who could be displaced in the search for *Lebensraum* and German destiny. With the war in eastern Europe, anti-Semitism changed from a policy of persecution and expropriation in the 1930s into a program of systematic extermination beginning in 1941.

Enforcing Nazi Racial Policies

Social policies erected on horrifying biomedical theories discriminated against a variety of social groups in the Third Reich. Gypsies were an example of "outsiders" who were labeled racially and genetically inferior. Gypsy ancestors had migrated to Germany in the fifteenth century, originating in the Punjab region of northern India and converting to the Christian religion in the course of their travels through Persia, Asia Minor, and the Balkans. As German itinerants with their own language, customs, and lifestyle, they were viewed by many other Germans during the Weimar period as a nuisance threatening the morals and hygiene of local communities. Beginning in 1933, police harassment of those

identified as gypsies intensified. In 1936 the Nazi bureaucracy expanded to include the Reich Central Office Against the Gypsy Nuisance, where files on gypsies were assiduously maintained. They were subject to all racialist legislation and could be sterilized because of their "inferiority" without any formal hearing process. In September 1939, even as the war was beginning, high-ranking Nazis planned the removal of 30,000 gypsies to Poland. Over 200,000 German, Russian, Polish, and Balkan gypsies were killed in the course of the war by internment in camps and by systematic extermination. Discrimination against gypsies, however, did not begin with the Nazis, nor did it end with them. Not until 1982 were gypsies officially recognized by the German government as a persecuted group subject to Nazi genocidal policies. In 1989, as East Germans were welcomed in West Germany, gypsies from East Germany were either summarily deported to Yugoslavia or subject to attacks and discrimination in the newly united Germany.

Mixed-race children were also singled out for special opprobrium under Nazi racial policies. Children born of white German mothers and black fathers were a consequence of the presence in the Rhineland of French colonial troops from Senegal, Morocco, and Malaga as part of the French occupation forces during the 1920s and 1930s. The press during both the Weimar Republic and the Nazi regime attacked the children of these unions, probably numbering no more than 500 to 800 individuals, as "Rhineland bastards." In 1937 the Nazis decided to sterilize them without any legal proceedings.

Those suffering from hereditary illnesses were also labeled as a biological threat to the racial purity of the German people. Illegitimate medical tests were devised by state doctors to establish who was feeble-minded and genetically defective. Since the society of the Third Reich was treated as one huge laboratory for the production of the racially fit and the "destruction of worthless life," categories were constructed according to subjective criteria that claimed scientific validation. Medical officials examined children, and those judged to be deformed were separated from their families and transferred to special pediatric clinics where they were either starved to death or injected with lethal drugs. In the summer of 1939, euthanasia programs for adults were organized, and 65,000 to 70,000 Germans were identified for death. Asylums were asked to rank patients according to their race, state of health, and ability to work. These rankings were used to determine candidates for death. In Poland mental patients were simply

Schreibers raffenkundliche Anschauungstafel: Deutsche Raffenköpfe
Bearbeitet von Dr Alfred Eydt

Nordisch   Westisch

Fälisch   Dinarisch

Ostbaltisch   Ostisch

The Nazis attempted to cloak their self-serving racial theories in scientific respectability. A Nazi "race-identification table" displays what were asserted to be the typical heads of different German "races"—a classification that has no basis in anthropology.

shot; in other places they were starved to death. The uncooperative, the sick, and the disabled were purged as racially undesirable.

The umbrella covering hereditary illnesses was broad but not broader than the category covering the "asocial." In this designation, asocial behavior itself came to be interpreted as a hereditary trait. Criminals, beggars, vagrants, and the homeless could be compulsorily sterilized. Alcoholics, prostitutes, and people with sexually transmitted diseases could be labeled asocial and treated accordingly. These forms of behavior were considered to be hereditary and determined by blood.

Homosexuals were likewise treated as "community aliens" by Nazi social policies. The persecution of homosexual men intensified after 1934, when any form of "same-sex immorality" became subject to legal persecution. "Gazing and lustful intention" were left to the definition of the police and the courts. Criminal sentences could involve a term in a concentration camp. But because homosexuality was judged to be a sickness rather than an immutable biological trait, gays did not be-

come the primary object of Nazi extermination policies that began to be enforced against the "biologically inferior." Instead, Nazi treatment of homosexuality might involve castration or indefinite incarceration in a concentration camp.

Gay men in Nazi concentration camps during the war were singled out with the badge of a pink triangle. Although it is not clear how many gay men were actually killed by the Nazis, estimates run as high as 200,000. Gay men rather than lesbian women were singled out by officials of the Third Reich because their behavior was considered a greater threat to the perpetuation of the German race.

The Destruction of Europe's Jews

Although anti-Semitism was an integral part of Hitler's view of the world, he did not think the peoples of Germany and Europe were ready for harsh measures against the Jews. When they came to power in 1933, the Nazis did not have a blueprint for the destruction of Europe's Jews; the anti-Semitic policies of the Third Reich evolved incrementally in the 1930s and 1940s.

After 1938, German civil servants expropriated Jewish property as rightfully belonging to the state. When the war began, Jews were rounded up and herded into urban ghettos in Germany and in the large cities of Poland. For a time the German foreign ministry considered the possibility of deporting the more than 3 million Jews under German control to Madagascar, an island off the southeast coast of Africa. Until 1941, Nazi policies against the Jews were often uncoordinated and unfocused.

The "Final Solution." Confinement in urban ghettos was the beginning of a policy of concentration that ended in annihilation. After having identified Jews, seized their property, and then confined them to ghettos, German authorities began to implement a step-by-step plan for extermination. There appears to have been no single order from Hitler that decreed what became known to German officials as the "Final Solution"—the total extermination of European Jews. But Hitler's recorded remarks make it clear that he knew and approved of what was being done to the Jews. A spirit of

shared purpose permeated the entire administrative system, from the civil service through the judiciary. Administrative agencies competed to interpret the Führer's will. SS guards in the camps and police in the streets embraced Hitler's "mission" of destruction. Those involved in carrying out the plan for extermination understood what was meant by the Final Solution and what their responsibilities were for enforcing it. To ensure that the whole process operated smoothly, a planning conference for the Final Solution was conducted by Reinhard Heydrich (1904–42), leader of the Sicherheitsdienst (SD), or Security Service of the SS, for the benefit of state and party officials at Wannsee, a Berlin suburb, in January 1942.

Mass racial extermination began with the German conquest of Poland, where both Jews and non-Jews were systematically killed. It continued when Hitler's army invaded the Soviet Union in 1941. This campaign, known as Operation Barbarossa, set off the mass execution of eastern Europeans declared to be enemies of the Reich. The tactics of the campaign pointed the way to the Final Solution. To the Nazi leadership, Slavs were subhuman. Russian Jews were, by extension, the lowest of the low, even more despised than German Jews. Nazi propaganda had equated Jews with Communists, and Hitler had used the expression *Judeocommunist* to describe what he considered to be the most dangerous criminal and enemy of the Third Reich, the enemy who must be annihilated at any cost.

The executions were the work of the SS, the elite military arm of the Nazi party. Special mobile murder squads of the SD under Heydrich were organized behind the German lines in Poland and Russia. Members of the army were aware of what the SS squads were doing and participated in some of the extermination measures. In the spring of 1941, Hitler ordered a massive propaganda campaign to be conducted among the armed forces. The army was indoctrinated to believe that the invasion of the Soviet Union was more than a military campaign: it was a "holy war," a crusade that Germany was waging for civilization. SS chief Heinrich Himmler, probably responding to oral orders from Hitler, set about to enforce the Führer's threats with concrete extermination policies. Fearful that the SS would be outstripped by the regular army in the Führer's favor, Himmler exhorted his men to commit the worst atrocities.

Firing squads shot Russian victims en masse, then piled their bodies on top of each other in open graves. Reviewing these procedures for mass killings, Himm-

The Holocaust

Seizing Jews in Warsaw. Nazi soldiers rounded up men, women, and children for "resettlement" in the east.

ler—ever competitive with other Nazi agencies—suggested a more efficient means of extermination that would require less manpower and would enhance the prestige of the SS. As a result, extermination by gas was introduced, using vans whose exhaust fumes were piped into the enclosed cargo areas that served as portable gas chambers. In Poland, Himmler replaced the vans with permanent buildings housing gas chambers using Zyklon B, a gas developed by the chemical firm I. G. Farben for the purpose. The chambers could annihilate thousands at a time.

The Third Reich began erecting its vast network of death in 1941. The first extermination camp was created in Chelmno, Poland, where 150,000 people were killed between 1941 and 1944. The camps practiced systematic extermination for the savage destruction of those groups deemed racially inferior, sexually deviant, or politically dangerous. The terms *genocide, judeocide,* and *holocaust* have been used to describe the mass slaughter of the Jewish people, most of which took place in the five major killing centers in what is now Polish territory—Chelmno, Belzec, Sobibor, Treblinka, and Auschwitz.

Many victims died before ever reaching the camps, transported for days in sealed railroad cars, without food, water, or sanitation facilities. Others died within months as forced laborers for the Reich. People of all ages were starved, beaten, and systematically humiliated. Guards taunted their victims verbally, degraded them physically, and tortured them with false hope. Promised clean clothes and nourishment, camp internees were herded into "showers" that dispensed gas rather than water. Descriptions of life in the camps reveal a systematized brutality and inhumanity on the part of the German, Ukrainian, and Polish guards toward their victims. In all, 11 million people died by the extermination process—6 million Jews and almost as many non-Jews, including children, the aged, homosexuals, Slavic slave laborers, Soviet prisoners of war, Communists, members of the Polish and Soviet leadership, various resistance elements, gypsies, and Jehovah's Witnesses.

"Work Makes You Free." The words ARBEIT MACHT FREI ("Work Makes You Free") were emblazoned over the main gate at Auschwitz, the largest of the concentration camps. It was at Auschwitz that the greatest number of persons died in a single place, including more than 1 million Jews. The healthy and the young were kept barely alive to work. Hard labor, starvation, and disease—especially typhus, tuberculosis, and other diseases that spread rapidly because of the lack of sanitation—claimed many victims.

On entering the camps, the sick and the aged were automatically designated for extermination because of their uselessness as a labor force. Many children were put to work, but some were designated for extermination. Many mothers chose to accompany their children to their deaths to comfort them in their final moments. Pregnant women were considered useless in the forced labor camps and were sent immediately to the "showers." The number of German Jewish women who died in the camps was 50 percent higher than the number of German Jewish men. Starvation diets meant that women stopped menstruating. Because the Nazis worried that women of childbearing age would continue to reproduce, women who showed signs of menstruation were killed immediately. Women who were discovered to have given birth undetected in the camp were killed, as were their infants. Family relations were completely destroyed, as inmates were segregated by sex. It soon became clear that even those allowed to live were only intended to serve the short-term needs of the Nazis.

Resisting Destruction. Could the victims of extermination have effectively resisted? The answer is no. The im-

Felix Nussbaum, Self-Portrait with a Jewish Identity Card (1943). Nussbaum left Germany when the Nazis came to power in 1933. During the Holocaust he went underground, moving from place to place in constant fear of discovery. He painted this work, which captures his deep anxiety, while he was in hiding. Nussbaum and his wife were arrested in 1944, and both perished at Auschwitz.

possibility of any effective resistance was based on two essential characteristics of the process of extermination. First, the entire German state and its bureaucratic apparatus were involved in the policies, laws, and decrees of the 1930s that singled out victims, while most Germans stood silently by. There was no course of appeal and no place to hide. Those who understood early what was happening and who had enough money to buy their way out emigrated to safer places, including Palestine and the United States. But most countries blocked the entry of German and eastern European refugees with immigration quotas. Neither Britain nor the United States was willing to deal with the mass influx of European Jews. Jews in the occupied countries and the Axis nations had virtually no chance to escape. They were trapped in a society where all forces of law and administration worked against them.

A second reason for the impossibility of effective resistance was the step-by-step nature of the process of extermination, which meant that few understood the final outcome until it was too late. Initially, in the 1930s, many German Jews believed that things could get no worse and obeyed the German state as good citizens. Even the policy of removing groups from the ghetto militated against resistance because the hope was that sending 1,000 Jews to "resettlement" would allow 10,000 Jews remaining behind to be saved. The German authorities deliberately controlled information to cultivate this misunderstanding of what was happening.

Isolated instances of resistance in the camps—rioting at Treblinka, for example—only highlight how impossible rebellion was for physically debilitated people in these heavily guarded centers. In the Warsaw ghetto, a resistance movement was organized with a few firearms and some grenades and homemade Molotov cocktails in April 1943. Starvation, overcrowding, and epidemics made Warsaw, the largest of the ghettos, into an extermination camp. As news reached the ghetto that "resettlement" was the death warrant of tens of thousands of Polish Jews, armed rebellion erupted. It did not succeed in blocking the completion of the Final Solution against the Warsaw ghetto the following year, when the SS commandant proclaimed, "The Jewish Quarter of Warsaw is no more!" Polish and Russian Jews account for 70 percent of the total Jewish deaths.

who knew?

It is impossible that killing on such a scale could have been kept secret. Along with those who ordered extermination operations, the guards and camp personnel

manifesto of the jewish resistance in vilna, september 1943

In May 1943, in spite of the valiant resistance of Jewish fighting groups, the Warsaw ghetto was destroyed by the German SS. In August of the same year, inmates revolted in the concentration camp at Treblinka in the face of insurmountable odds. News of the Warsaw ghetto revolt had spread to the camp, where it inspired Jews to rise up and fight against their captors. Few survived the revolt, although considerable damage was done to the gas chambers, the railway station, and the barracks by the armed inmates. The Jews of the ghetto of Vilna (Vilnius) organized active resistance to the Nazis with the rallying cry, "Jews, we have nothing to lose!"

Offer armed resistance! Jews, defend yourselves with arms!

The German and Lithuanian executioners are at the gates of the ghetto. They have come to murder us! Soon they will lead you forth in groups through the ghetto door.

Tens of thousands of us were despatched. But we shall not go! We will not offer our heads to the butcher like sheep.

Jews, defend yourselves with arms!

Do not believe the false promises of the assassins or believe the words of the traitors.

Anyone who passes through the ghetto gate will go to Ponar [death camp]!

And Ponar means death!

Jews, we have nothing to lose. Death will overtake us in any event. And who can still believe in survival when the murderer exterminates us with so much determination? The hand of the executioner will reach each man and woman. Flight and acts of cowardice will not save our lives.

Active resistance alone can save our lives and our honor.

Brothers! It is better to die in battle in the ghetto than to be carried away to Ponar like sheep. And know this: within the walls of the ghetto there are organized Jewish forces who will resist with weapons.

Support the revolt!

Do not take refuge or hide in the bunkers, for then you will fall into the hands of the murderers like rats.

Jewish people, go out into the squares. Anyone who has no weapons should take an ax, and he who has no ax should take a crowbar or a bludgeon!

For our ancestors!

For our murdered children!

Avenge Ponar!

Attack the murderers!

In every street, in every courtyard, in every house within and without the ghetto, attack these dogs!

Jews, we have nothing to lose! We shall save our lives only if we exterminate our assassins.

Long live liberty! Long live armed resistance! Death to the assassins!

Vilna, the Ghetto, September 1, 1943.

---

involved in carrying out the directives were aware of what was happening. Those who brought internees to the camps, returning always with empty railroad cars, knew it too. People who saw their neighbors disappearing believed for a time that they were being resettled in the east. But as news got back to central and western Europe, it was more difficult to sustain belief in this ruse. People who lived near the camps could not ignore the screams and fumes of gas and burning bodies that permeated the environs.

Although never publicly announcing its extermination program, the German government convinced its citizens that the policies of the Nazi state could not be judged by ordinary moral standards. The benefits to the German state were justification enough for the annihilation of 11 million people. Official propaganda successfully convinced millions that the Reich was the supreme good. Admitting the existence of the extermination program carried with it a responsibility on which few acted, perhaps out of fear of reprisals. There were some heroes like Raoul Wallenberg of Sweden, who interceded for Hungarian Jews and provided Jews in the Budapest ghetto with food and protection. The king of Denmark, when informed that the Nazis had ordered Danish Jews to wear the yellow star, stated that he and his family would also wear the yellow star as a "badge of honor." Heroic acts, however, were isolated and rare.

Collaborationist governments and occupied nations often cooperated with Nazi extermination policies. The French government at Vichy introduced and implemented a variety of anti-Jewish measures. All of this was done without German orders and without German pressure. By voluntarily identifying and deporting Jews, the Vichy government sent 75,000 men, women, and children to their deaths.

As the war dragged on for years, internees of the camps hoped and prayed for rescue by the Allies. But such help did not come. The U.S. State Department and the British Foreign Office had early and reliable information on the nature and extent of the atrocities. But they did not act. American Jews were unable to convince President Franklin D. Roosevelt to intercede to prevent

Jewish population loss, 1939-1945

	1939	1945
Austria	60,000	7,000
Belgium	90,000	40,000
Bulgaria	50,000	47,000
Czechoslovakia	315,000	44,000
Denmark	6,500	5,500
France	270,000	200,000
Germany	240,000	80,000
Greece	74,000	12,000
Hungary	400,000	200,000
Italy	50,000	33,000
Luxembourg	3,000	1,000
Netherlands	140,000	20,000
Norway	2,000	1,000
Poland	3,350,000	50,000
Romania	800,000	430,000
USSR	3,020,000	2,500,000
Estonia	4,500	
Latvia	95,000	
Lithuania	145,000	
Yugoslavia	75,000	12,000

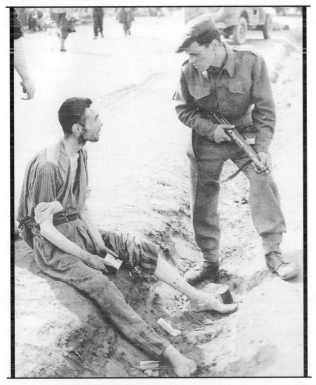

A British soldier listens to the story of an inmate of Bergen-Belsen as the camp is liberated by the Allies.

the slaughter. Appeals to bomb the gas chambers at Auschwitz and the railroad lines leading to them were rejected by the United States on strategic grounds. Those trying to survive in the camps and the ghettos despaired at their abandonment.

The handful of survivors found by Allied soldiers who entered the camps after Germany's defeat presented a haunting picture of humanity. A British colonel who entered the camp at Bergen-Belsen in April 1945 gave a restrained account of what he found:

> As we walked down the main road of the camp, we were cheered by the internees, and for the first time we saw their condition. A great number were little more than living skeletons. There were men and women lying in heaps on both sides of the track. Others were walking slowly and aimlessly about, vacant expressions on their starved faces.

The sight of corpses piled on top of one another lining the roads and the piles of shoes, clothing, underwear, and gold teeth extracted from the dead shocked those who came to liberate the camps. One of the two survivors of Chelmno summed it all up: "No one can understand what happened here."

The Final Solution was a perversion of every value of civilization. The achievements of twentieth-century in-

The atrocity at Lidice

Lidice was a small village in Czechoslovakia. The Nazis decided to raze it to the ground in retaliation for the assassination of Reinhard Heydrich, Nazi head of the Secret Police and the Security Service of the SS. On 10 June 1942, all 173 men of the village were executed by German soldiers, and the women and children were deported to concentration camps. Only 15 of Lidice's 101 children survived the war. So outraged was world opinion by this atrocity that memorials were created everywhere, and many towns and cities changed their name to Lidice as a commemoration. The first extract is from a letter written by a Nazi official by the name of Krumey in charge of the camp at Lodz, Poland, where 38 of Lidice's children had been sent, to his superior, Adolf Eichmann, asking for direction. The second, from a letter addressed to the villagers of Lidice, is from five children in the camp.

In a telegram dated 17 June 1942 I asked the Commander of the Security Police and the Security Service . . . what was to be done with the Czech children. In the meantime, the Race and Resettlement Office has found seven of the children fit to be Germanized. [Note: these seven children were adopted by German families.]

Since I have no word on further disposition of the children and since the children were transferred here without any luggage, I urgently ask you to decide on the further use of the children.

*   *   *

Here it is always cold. We feel homesick for Lidice. We would like to beg you to send us some clothing because we don't own anything beyond what we are wearing, or especially something to eat. . . . Do you know anything about our parents? Send the things as soon as possible because we don't know how long we will remain in this place. Let us know what has become of Lidice. Send something that does not go bad for a long time. We are all here, all the children of the town. We don't know where our parents are. Send also some dresses and shoes. Above all, if you can, at least a bit of bread.

Signed Vera, Marenka, Mila, Anicka, and Valek

dustry, technology, state, and bureaucracy in the West were turned against millions to create, as one German official called it, murder by assembly line. Mass killing was not prompted by military or security concerns. Nor was the elimination of vital labor power consistent with the needs of the Nazi state. The international tribunal for war crimes that met in 1945 in the German city of Nuremberg attempted to mete out justice to the criminals against humanity responsible for the destruction of 11 million Europeans labeled as demons and racial inferiors. History in the end must record, even if it cannot explain, such inhumanity.

Allied victory

The situation at the end of 1941 appeared grim for the British and their dominions and for the Americans who were assisting them with munitions, money, and food. Hitler had achieved control of a vast land empire covering all of continental Europe in the west, north, south, and center. This empire, which Hitler called his "New Order," included territories occupied and directly administered by the German army, satellites, and collaborationist regimes. It was fortified by alliances with Italy, the Soviet Union, and Japan. Hitler commanded the greatest fighting force in the world, one that had knocked France out of the war in a matter of weeks, brought destruction to British cities, and conquered Yugoslavia in 12 days. Much of the world was coming to fear German invincibility.

Then, in June 1941, Hitler's troops invaded the Soviet Union, providing the British with an ally. In December the naval and air forces of Japan attacked American bases in the Pacific, providing the British and the Russians with still another ally. What was a European war became a world war. This was the war Hitler did not want and that Germany could not win—a long, total war to the finish against three powers with inexhaustible resources: the British Empire, the Soviet Union, and the United States.

The soviet union's Great patriotic war

Hitler had always considered the Soviet Union Germany's primary enemy. His hatred of communism was all-encompassing: Bolshevism was an evil invention of the Jewish people and a dangerous ideological threat to the Third Reich. The 1939 Non-Aggression Pact with Stalin was no more than an expedient for him. Hitler rebuked a Swiss diplomat in 1939 for failing to grasp the central fact of his foreign policy:

> Everything I undertake is directed against Russia. If those in the West are too stupid and too blind to understand this, then I should be forced to come to an understanding with the Russians to beat the West, and then, after its defeat, turn with all my concentrated force against the Soviet Union.

That is exactly what happened on 22 June 1941, when German armies marched into Russia. They found the Soviet army larger but totally unprepared for war. In contrast to German soldiers, who had fought in Spain, Poland, and France, Soviet troops had no firsthand battle experience. Nor were they well led. Stalin's purges in the late 1930s had removed 35,000 officers from their posts by dismissal, imprisonment, or execution. Many of the men who replaced them were unseasoned in the responsibilities of leadership.

Russian military leaders were sure they would be ready for a European war against the capitalist nations by 1942, and Stalin refused to believe that Hitler would attack the Soviet Union before then. British agents and Stalin's own spies tried to warn him of German plans for an invasion in the spring of 1941. When the Germans did invade Russian territory, Stalin was so overwhelmed that he fell into a depression and was unable to act for days.

In his first radio address after the attack on 3 July 1941, Stalin identified his nation with the Allied cause: "Our struggle for the freedom of our country will merge with the struggle of the peoples of Europe and America for their independence, for democratic liberties." He accepted offers of support from the United States and Great Britain, the two nations that had worked consistently to exclude the Soviet Union from European power politics since the Bolshevik revolution in 1917. With France defeated and Great Britain crippled, the future of the war depended on the Soviet fighting power and American supplies.

Hitler's invasion of Russia involved 3 million soldiers from Germany and Germany's satellites, the largest invasion force in history. It stretched along an immense battlefront from the Baltic to the Black Sea. Instead of exclusively targeting Moscow, the capital, the German army concentrated first on destroying Soviet armed forces and capturing Leningrad in the north and the oil-rich Caucasus in the south. In the beginning, the German forces advanced rapidly in a blitzkrieg across western Russia, where they were greeted as liberators in the Ukraine. The Germans took 290,000 prisoners of war and massacred tens of thousands of others in their path through the Jewish settlements of western Russia.

Within four months, the German army had advanced to the gates of Moscow, but they concentrated their forces too late. The Red Army rallied to defend Moscow as thousands of civilian women set to work digging trenches and antitank ditches around the city. The Soviet people answered Stalin's call for a scorched-earth policy by burning everything that might be useful to the advancing German troops. German troops had also burned much in their path, depriving themselves of essential supplies for the winter months ahead. The German advance was stopped, and the best ally of the Red Army—the Russian winter—settled in. The first snow fell at the beginning of October. By early November, German troops were beginning to suffer the harsh effects of an early and exceptionally bitter Russian winter.

Hitler promised the German people that "final victory" was at hand. So confident was Hitler of a speedy and decisive victory that he sent his soldiers into Russia wearing only light summer uniforms. Hitler's generals knew better and tried repeatedly to explain military realities to the Führer. General Heinz Guderian (1888–1954), commander of the tank units, reported that his men were suffering frostbite, that tanks could not be started, and that automatic weapons were jamming in the subzero temperatures. Back in Germany, the civilian population received little accurate news of the campaign. They began to suspect the worst when the government sent out a plea for woolen blankets and clothing for the troops.

By early December, the German military situation was desperate. The Soviets, benefiting from intelligence

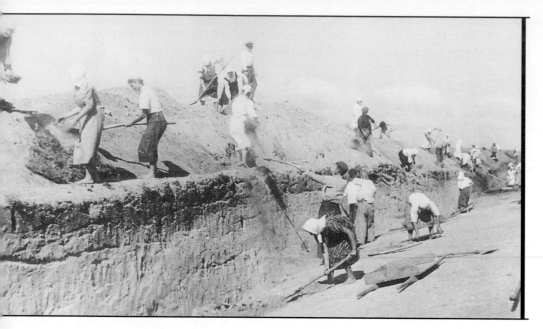

Men and women on a Ukrainian collective farm labor to erect huge antitank traps during the German invasion of the Soviet Union. The steadfast courage of the civilian population contributed greatly to the defeat of Hitler's quest for Lebensraum in the east.

information about German plans and an awareness that Japan was about to declare war on the United States, recalled fresh troops from the Siberian frontier and the border with China and Manchuria and launched a powerful counterattack against the poorly outfitted German army outside Moscow. Under the command of General Gyorgi Zhukov (1896–1974), Russian troops, dressed and trained for winter warfare, pushed the Germans back in retreat across the snow-covered expanses. By February, 200,000 German troops had been killed, 46,000 were missing in action, and 835,000 were casualties of battle and the weather. Thus the campaign cost the German army over 1 million casualties. It probably cost the Soviets twice that number of wounded, missing, captured, and dead soldiers. At the end of the Soviet counterattack in March, the German army and its satellite forces were in a shambles reminiscent of Napoleon's troops, who 130 years earlier had been decimated in the campaign to capture Moscow. An enraged Hitler dismissed his generals for retreating without his permission, and he himself assumed the position of commander in chief of the armed forces.

Hitler was not daunted by the devastating costs of his invasion of Russia. In the summer of 1942, he initiated a second major offensive, this time to take the city of Stalingrad. Constant bombardment gutted the city, and the Soviet army was forced into hand-to-hand combat with the German soldiers. But the German troops, once again inadequately supplied and unprepared for the Russian winter, failed to capture the city. The Battle of Stalingrad was over in the first days of February 1943. Of the original 300,000 members of the German Sixth Army, fewer than 100,000 survived to be taken prisoner by the Soviets. Of those, only 5,000 returned to Germany in 1955, when German prisoners of war were repatriated.

The Soviets succeeded by exploiting two great advantages in their war against Germany: the large Soviet population and their knowledge of Russian weather and terrain. There was a third advantage that Hitler ignored: the Soviet people's determination to sacrifice everything for the war effort. In his successive Five-Year Plans, Stalin had mobilized Soviet society with an appeal to fulfill and surpass production quotas. In the summer of 1941, as Hitler's troops threatened Moscow, he used the same rhetoric to appeal to his Soviet "brothers and sisters" to join him in waging "the Great Patriotic War." The Russian people shared a sense of common purpose, sacrifice, and moral commitment in their loyalty to the nation.

The advancing Germans themselves intensified Soviet patriotism by torturing and killing tens of thousands of peasants who might have willingly cooperated against the Stalinist regime. Millions of Soviet peasants joined the Red Army. Young men of high school age were drafted into the armed forces. Three million women became wage earners for the first time as they replaced men in war industries. Women who remained on the land worked to feed the townspeople and the soldiers. Because the Red Army had requisitioned horses and tractors for combat, grain had to be sown and harvested by hand—and this often meant women's hands. Tens of thousands of Russians left their homes in western Russia to work for relocated Soviet industries in the Urals, the Volga region, Siberia, and Central Asia. More than 20 million Soviet people, soldiers and civilians, men, women, and children, died in the course of World War II. In addition to those killed in battle, millions starved as a direct result of the hardships of war. In 1943 food was so scarce that seed for the next year's crops was eaten. One in every three men born in 1906 died in the war. But Soviet resistance did not flag. The Great Patriotic War had a profound impact on Soviet views of the world and the Soviet Union's place in it. The war left the Soviet people with an enduring fear of invasion. The official falsification of all published maps of the Soviet Union in order to mislead spies and foreign armies was just one indication of the Russian expectation of treachery. (This practice was as recent as 1988.) Today, a visitor to Stalingrad, renamed Volgograd, can still find old tanks in city parks and on streets as reminders of the front line of the Red Army in the Great Patriotic War. Ruins of buildings have been left standing as grim monuments to the need for continued preparedness. The few remaining trees that en-

dured through the war's devastation bear plaques that make their survival a memorial.

The Soviet Union sacrificed 10 percent of its population to the war effort, incurring well over 50 percent of all the deaths and casualties of the war. Few families escaped the death of members in the defense of the nation. Soviet citizens correctly considered that they had given more than any other country to defeat Hitler. For the Soviet people, their suffering in battle made World War II the Soviet Union's war and their sacrifice made possible the Allied victory. But victory still eluded the Allies in western Europe, where now another nation, the United States, had entered the fray.

The united states enters the war

Although a neutral power, the United States began extending aid to the Allies after the fall of France in 1940. Since neither Britain nor the Soviet Union could afford to pay all the costs of defending Europe against Hitler, the U.S. Congress passed the Lend-Lease Act in 1941. This act authorized President Roosevelt to provide armaments to Great Britain and the Soviet Union without payment. America became the "arsenal of democracy." The United States and Britain sent 4,100 airplanes and 138,000 motor vehicles, as well as steel and machinery, to the Soviet Union for the campaign of 1943. In all, America pumped $11 billion worth of equipment into the Soviet war effort between 1941 and 1945. Stalin later told Roosevelt that the USSR would have lost the war

Russian villagers search for loved ones among civilians slain by German troops. Noncombatants were frequent victims of the Nazi policy of enslavement or annihilation.

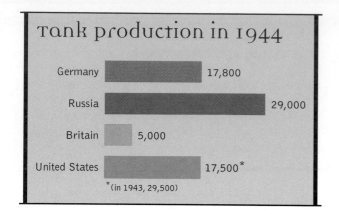

Tank production in 1944

Germany	17,800
Russia	29,000
Britain	5,000
United States	17,500*

*(in 1943, 29,500)

with Germany without the help of the Americans and the British.

President Roosevelt and his advisers considered Germany, not Japan, to be America's primary target for a future war. Japan nevertheless had been threatening American trade interests in Asia and had embroiled the United States in disputes over Japanese imperialist ex-

pansion in the late 1930s. The United States understood Japan to be an aggressive country determined to expand its control over China and southeast Asia, which it opposed initially through economic embargoes. The presence of the Soviet Union pressing eastward across Asia, coupled with the colonial presences in Asia of Great Britain, France, and the United States, severely constrained Japan's capacity to expand its frontiers and ensure its security. The war in western Europe and the German invasion of the Soviet Union in June 1941 meant that the Japanese could concentrate their attention farther south in China, Indochina, and Thailand. Japan's limited reserves of foreign currency and raw materials made it increasingly vulnerable to economic disruptions. Japanese leaders accepted the necessity of grasping oil and raw materials in southeast Asia.

In September 1940, Japan joined forces with the Axis Powers of Germany and Italy in the Tripartite Pact, in which the signatories, promising mutual support against aggression, acknowledged the legitimacy of each other's expansionist efforts in Europe and Asia. Japanese–American relations deteriorated following the

The battleship USS West Virginia in flames at Pearl Harbor. The attack was carried out entirely by carrier-based aircraft—a sign of things to come in naval warfare.

president franklin roosevelt's request for a declaration of war on japan, 8 december 1941

On 7 December 1941, the Japanese naval and air forces attacked the American naval base at Pearl Harbor in Hawaii, killing and wounding 3,457 military personnel and civilians. Most of the U.S. Pacific fleet was moored in Pearl Harbor, and it sustained severe destruction of its naval vessels, battleships, and aircraft. U.S. military and political leaders were taken completely by surprise by the Japanese attack. Roosevelt's declaration of war reflects the outrage over this "infamy."

To the Congress of the United States:

Yesterday, December 7, 1941—a date which will live in infamy—the United States of America was suddenly and deliberately attacked by naval and air forces of the Empire of Japan.

The United States was at peace with that Nation and, at the solicitation of Japan, was still in conversation with its Government and its Emperor looking toward the maintenance of peace in the Pacific. Indeed, one hour after Japanese air squadrons had commenced bombing in Oahu, the Japanese Ambassador to the United States and his colleague delivered to the Secretary of State a formal reply to a recent American message. While this reply stated that it seemed useless to continue the existing diplomatic negotiations, it contained no threat or hint of war or armed attack.

It will be recorded that the distance of Hawaii from Japan makes it obvious that the attack was deliberately planned many days or even weeks ago. During the intervening time the Japanese Government has deliberately sought to deceive the United States by false statements and expressions of hope for continued peace.

The attack yesterday on the Hawaiian Islands has caused severe damage to American naval and military forces. Very many American lives have been lost. In addition American ships have been reported torpedoed on the high seas between San Francisco and Honolulu.

Yesterday the Japanese Government also launched an attack against Malaya.

Last night Japanese forces attacked Hong Kong.

Last night Japanese forces attacked Guam.

Last night Japanese forces attacked the Philippine Islands.

Last night the Japanese attacked Wake Island.

This morning the Japanese attacked Midway Island.

Japan has, therefore, undertaken a surprise offensive extending throughout the Pacific area. The facts of yesterday speak for themselves. The people of the United States have already formed their opinions and well understand the implications to the very life and safety of our Nation.

As Commander-in-Chief of the Army and Navy I have directed that all measures be taken for our defense.

Always will we remember the character of the onslaught against us.

No matter how long it may take us to overcome this premeditated invasion, the American people in their righteous might will win through to absolute victory. . . .

With confidence in our armed forces—with the unbounded determination of our people—we will gain the inevitable triumph—so help us God.

I ask that the Congress declare that since the unprovoked and dastardly attack by Japan on Sunday, December seventh, a state of war has existed between the United States and the Japanese Empire.

Franklin D. Roosevelt

Japan's Declaration of War on the United States and Great Britain, 8 December 1941

Japan's sense of its mission in East Asia is embodied in Emperor Hirohito's declaration of war against the United States and Great Britain on 8 December 1941, the day after Japanese forces attacked the American fleet in Hawaii. Interestingly, the Japanese declaration speaks of "world peace" and "friendship among nations." In spite of marked cultural differences in the form of the two declarations, both the Japanese and the American leaders make clear their country's dependence on the total support of their people to win the war.

We, by grace of heaven, Emperor of Japan, seated on the Throne of the line unbroken for ages eternal, enjoin upon ye. Our loyal and brave subjects.

We hereby declare war on the United States of America and the British Empire. The men and officers of Our Army and Navy shall do their utmost in prosecuting the war, Our public servants of various departments shall perform faithfully and diligently their appointed tasks, and all other subjects of Ours shall pursue their respective duties; the entire nation with a united will shall mobilize their total strength so that nothing will miscarry in the attainment of our war aims.

To insure the stability of East Asia and to contribute to world peace is the far-sighted policy which was formulated by Our Great Illustrious Imperial Grandsire and Our Great Imperial Sire succeeding Him, and which We have constantly to heart. To cultivate friendship among nations and to employ prosperity in common with all nations has always been the guiding principle of Our Empire's foreign policy. It has been truly unavoidable and far from Our wishes that Our Empire has now been brought to cross swords with America and Britain. More than four years have passed since the government of the Chinese Republic, failing to comprehend the true intentions of Our Empire, and recklessly courting trouble, disturbed the peace of east Asia and compelled Our Empire to take up arms. . . .

Patiently have We waited and long have We endured, in the hope that Our Government might retrieve the situation in peace. But our adversaries, showing not the least spirit of conciliation, have unduly delayed a settlement; and in the meantime, they have intensified the economic and military pressure to compel thereby Our Empire to submission. This trend of affairs would, if left unchecked, not only nullify Our Empire's efforts of many years for the sake of the stabilization of east Asia, but also endanger the very existence of Our nation. The situation being such as it is, Our Empire for its existence and self-defence has no other recourse but to appeal to arms and to crush every obstacle in its path.

The hallowed spirits of Our Imperial Ancestors guarding Us from above, We rely upon the loyalty and courage of Our subjects in Our confident expectation that the task bequeathed by Our Forefathers will be carried forward, and that the sources of evil will be speedily eradicated and an enduring peace immutably established in East Asia, preserving thereby the glory of Our Empire.

The 8th day of the 12th month of the 16th year of Showa.

Hirohito

Japanese invasion of southern Indochina in July 1941. The United States insisted that Japan vacate China and Indochina and reestablish the open door for trade in Asia. The United States knew, however, that it was only a matter of time until Japan attacked U.S. interests but was uncertain about where that attack would take place.

On Sunday morning, 7 December 1941, Japan struck at the heart of the American Pacific Fleet stationed at Pearl Harbor, Hawaii. The fleet was literally caught asleep at the switch: 2,300 people were killed, and eight battleships and numerous cruisers and destroyers were sunk or severely damaged. The attack crippled American naval power in the Pacific as the American navy suffered its worst loss in history in a single engagement. The attack on Pearl Harbor led to the United States' immediate declaration of war against Japan. In President

Roosevelt's words, 7 December 1941 was "a date which will live in infamy." In the next three months, Japan captured Hong Kong, Malaya, and the important naval base at Singapore from the British, taking 60,000 prisoners. Like its earlier march into China, the Japanese invasion of southeast Asia moved swiftly to establish control, outstripping the Japanese military's own timetables for advance. In December 1941, the Japanese landed in Thailand and secured immediate agreement for Japanese occupation of strategic spots in the country. They then turned to the Malayan peninsula, decisively defeating the British fleet off Malaya and pushing on the ground toward Singapore, which they conquered in February 1942. They conquered British Borneo in January, drove the Dutch from all of Indonesia but New Guinea, pushed American forces in the Philippines into the Bataan Peninsula, occupied Burma, and inflicted severe defeats on British, Dutch, and American naval power in East Asia. U.S. General Douglas MacArthur (1880–1964) surrendered the Philippines to the Japanese on 2 January 1942 with the promise to return. With the armies of Germany deep in Russian territory, Australia now faced the threat of a Japanese invasion.

Hitler praised the Japanese government for its action against the British Empire and against the United States and its "millionaire and Jewish backers." Germany, with its armies retreating from Moscow, nevertheless declared war against the United States on 11 December 1941. Hitler, in fact, considered that the United States was already at war with Germany because of its policy of supplying the Allies. Within days the United States, a nation with an army smaller than Belgium's, had gone from neutrality to a war in two theaters. Although militarily weak, the United States was an economic giant, commanding a vast industrial capacity and access to resources. America grew even stronger under the stimulus of war, increasing its production by 400 percent in two years. It now devoted itself to the demands of a total war and the unconditional surrender of Germany and then Japan.

winning the war in europe

The Allies did not always share the same strategies or concerns. President Roosevelt and Prime Minister Churchill had already discussed common goals in the summer of 1941 before U.S. entry into the war. The United States embraced the priority of the European war and the postponement of war in the Pacific. Stalin pleaded for the Anglo-Americans to open up a second front against Germany in western Europe to give his troops some relief and save Soviet lives. Anglo-American resources were committed to the Pacific to stop the Japanese advance, and the Americans and the British disagreed as to where a second front in Europe might be opened.

Because of British interests in the Mediterranean, Churchill insisted on a move from North Africa into Sicily and Italy. This strategy was put into effect in 1942. The Italian government withdrew from the war in September, but German troops carried on the fight in Italy. The Anglo-American invasion of Italy did little to alleviate Russian losses, and the Soviet Union absorbed almost the entire force of German military power until 1944. Stalin's distrust of his allies increased. Churchill, Roosevelt, and Stalin met for the first time in late November 1943 at Teheran, Iran. Roosevelt and Churchill made a commitment to Stalin to open a second front in France within six months. Stalin, in turn, promised to attack Japan to aid the United States in the Pacific. The great showdown of the global war was at hand.

On 6 June 1944, Allied troops under the command of American General Dwight D. Eisenhower (1890–1969) came ashore on the beaches of Normandy in the largest amphibious landing in history. In a daring operation identified by the code name Operation Overlord, 2.2 million American, British, and Free French forces, 450,000 vehicles, and 4 million tons of supplies poured into northern France. Allied forces broke through German lines to liberate Paris in late August. The Germans launched a last-ditch counterattack in late December 1944 in Luxembourg and Belgium. This Battle of the Bulge only slowed the Allied advance; in March 1945, American forces crossed the Rhine into Germany. Hitler, meanwhile, refused to surrender and insisted on a fight to the death of the last German soldier. Members of his own High Command had attempted unsuccessfully to assassinate Hitler in July 1944. The final German defeat came in April 1945, when the Russians stormed the German capital of Berlin. Hitler, living in an underground bunker near the Chancellery building, committed suicide on 30 April 1945.

japanese war aims and assumptions

Japan and the United States entered the Pacific War with very different understandings of what was at stake. Initially, the Japanese appealed to southeast Asian leaders as the liberators of Asian peoples from Western colonialism and imperialism. The approach struck a responsive chord as the Japanese established what they called the Greater East Asia Co-Prosperity Sphere. Ba Maw, Burma's leader, said at the Assembly of the Greater East Asiatic Nations held in Tokyo in November 1943, "My Asiatic blood has always called to other Asiatics. . . . This is not the time to think with our minds; this is the time to think with our blood, and it is thinking with the blood that has brought me all the way from Burma to Japan." But the passionate and positive welcome Ba Maw extended to the Japanese liberators did not last long. As he bluntly explained in his memoirs, "The brutality, arrogance, and racial pretensions of the Japanese militarists in Burma remain among the deepest Burmese memories of the war years; for a great many people in southeast Asia these are all they remember of the war."

The Greater East Asia Co-Prosperity Sphere began in 1940 and lasted until the summer of 1945. This reorganization of east and southeast Asia under Japanese

Soldiers raise the hammer-and-sickle flag over the ruins of the Reichstag as Soviet troops occupy Berlin in May 1945. At war's end, the Soviets occupied most of eastern Europe, which gave Stalin an advantage at the Yalta Conference.

hegemony constituted a redefinition of world geography, with Japan at the center. The Japanese fashioned a romanticized vision of the family living in harmony, each member knowing his place and enjoying the complementary division of responsibilities and reciprocities that made family life work smoothly. Behind this pleasant image lurked the reality of a brutal power structure forcing subject peoples to accept massively inferior positions in a world fashioned exclusively for Japanese desires and needs. The Japanese viewed southeast Asia principally as a market for Japanese manufactured goods, a source of raw materials, and a source of profits for Japanese capital invested in mining, rubber, and raw cotton. Plans were made for hydroelectric power and aluminum refining facilities.

Wartime Japanese nakedly displayed their disdain for the people they conquered in southeast Asia. All subject peoples were to bow on meeting a Japanese. At public assemblies a ritual bow in the direction of the Japanese emperor was required, to the dismay of southeast Asians such as Indies Muslims or Philippine Catholics, who regarded Japanese emperor worship as pagan and presumptuous. Japanese holidays, such as the emperor's birthday, were enforced as Co-Prosperity Sphere holidays, and the calendar was reset to the mythical founding of the Japanese state in 660 B.C.

The Japanese were less brazen toward the Chinese in their rhetoric, in part because so much of east Asian civilization had its roots in China. But even if more temperate in their pronouncements, the realities of Japanese aggression in China included one of the worst periods of destruction in modern warfare. When they took over the Nationalist capital of Nanjing in December 1937, 20,000 women were raped, 30,000 soldiers killed, and another 12,000 civilians died in the more than six weeks of wanton terror inflicted by Japanese soldiers.

With regard to Westerners, Japanese propaganda avoided labeling them as inferior. In part this reflected Japan's economic and political emulation of the West since the late nineteenth century. Rather than denigrating Western people, the Japanese chose to elevate themselves as a people descended from divine origins. Stressing their unique mythical history gave the Japanese a strong sense of superiority neither intellectual nor physical, but moral. They believed that virtue was on their side in their mission to stop Western expansion in Asia and to take their "proper place" as the leading people in Asia by tyrannizing the Co-Prosperity Sphere.

Supplies for the Allied forces pour ashore at the beachheads of Normandy during Operation Overlord in 1944. The invasion began the opening of the second front that Stalin had been urging on the Allies since the German armies thrust into Russia in 1941.

To achieve their moral superiority, the Japanese government urged their people to "purify" themselves. Although purification rituals occur in the world's great religions, rarely do governments urge people to cleanse their souls. For the average wartime Japanese citizen, purification meant accepting extreme material poverty and scarcity, rejecting foreign influences, and if called upon, dying for the emperor. The Japanese elevation of patriotism to the level of human sacrifice lay outside Western sensibilities of the time; to expect the spirit to become more purified made little sense to large numbers of Westerners. A bit more comprehensible, perhaps, were Japanese wartime views of Americans as beasts because of the atrocities that American soldiers committed. The grotesque quality of the American soldier's desire for war trophies was captured by a *Life* magazine photograph of a blond young American woman holding a Japanese skull sent to her by her GI sweetheart. What *Life* magazine considered "human interest"

the Japanese found racist. However reasonable this assessment may be, Japanese impressions of Westerners definitely proved fatally false in another matter. The Japanese assumed that individual selfishness and egoism would make Americans and Europeans incapable of mobilizing for a long fight.

winning the war in the pacific

The tide in the Pacific War began to turn when the planned Japanese invasion of Australia was thwarted. Fighting in the jungles of New Guinea, Australian and American troops under the command of General Douglas MacArthur turned back the Japanese army. U.S. Marines did likewise with a bold landing at Guadalcanal and months of bloody fighting in the Solomon Islands. In June 1942, within six months of the attack at Pearl Harbor, American naval forces commanded by Admiral Chester Nimitz (1885–1966) inflicted a defeat on the

World War II in the Pacific, 1941–1945

Japanese navy from which it could not recover. In the battle of Midway, Japan lost 4 aircraft carriers, a heavy cruiser, over 300 airplanes, and 5,000 men. Midway was the Pacific equivalent of the Battle of Stalingrad.

In the summer of 1943, as the Soviet Union launched the offensive that was to defeat Germany, America began to move across the Pacific toward Japan. Nimitz and MacArthur conceived a brilliant plan in which American

land, sea, and air forces fought in a coordinated effort. With a series of amphibious landings, they hopped from island to island. Some Japanese island fortresses, like Tarawa, were taken; others, like Truk, were bypassed and cut off from Japanese home bases. With the conquest of Saipan in November 1944 and Iwo Jima in March 1945, the U.S. Air Force acquired bases from which B-29 bombers could strike at the Japanese home islands. In

"Glittering fragments"

Hara Tamiki (1905–51) was a Japanese poet who was living in Hiroshima when the atomic bomb exploded there on 6 August 1945. His poem "Glittering Fragments" tells about what he saw. A victim of the bomb's radioactivity, he committed suicide in 1951.

Glittering fragments	*All existence, all that could exist*
Ashen embers	*Laid bare in a flash. The rest of the world*
Like a rippling panorama,	*The swelling of a horse's corpse*
Burning red then dulled.	*At the side of an upturned train,*
Strange rhythm of human corpses.	*The smell of smoldering electric wires.*

the summer of 1945, in the greatest air offensive in history, American planes destroyed what remained of the Japanese navy, crippled Japanese industry, and mercilessly firebombed major population centers. The attack ended with the dropping of atomic bombs on the cities of Hiroshima and Nagasaki. (See "The Atomic Wasteland," pp. 986–987.) The Japanese government accepted American terms for peace and surrendered unconditionally on 2 September 1945 on the battleship *Missouri* in Tokyo Bay. Four months after the defeat of Germany, the war in Asia was over.

The Fate of Allied cooperation: 1945

The costs of World War II in terms of death and destruction were the highest in history. Fifty million lives were lost. Most of the dead were Europeans, and most of the Europeans were Russians and Poles. The high incidence of civilian deaths distinguished the Second World War from previous wars—well over 50 percent of the dead were noncombatants. Deliberate military targeting of cities explains this phenomenon only in part. The majority of civilian deaths were the result of starvation, enslavement, massacre, and deliberate extermination.

The psychological devastation of continual violence, deprivation, injury, and rape of survivors cannot be measured. Terrorizing citizens became an established means of warfare in the modern age. Another phenomenon not matched in the First World War emerged in 1945: mass rape. The Soviet officer corps encouraged the advancing Russian army to use sexual violence against German women and girls. The Russians, brutally treated by Hitler's army, returned the savagery in their advance through eastern and central Europe. Collective

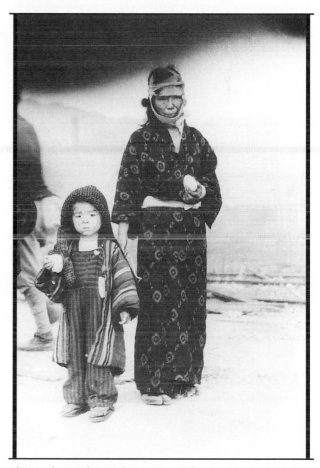

Photographer Yosuke Yamahata was one of three men sent by the Japanese Army to document the effects of the atomic bomb dropped on Nagasaki on 9 August, 1945. The three arrived in Nagasaki just before dawn on August 10, and as the sun rose Yamahata immediately began to take pictures. One of his first was this photo of a young boy and his mother holding riceballs, the only emergency rations available to survivors of the atomic blast.

the atomic wasteland

The sixth of August 1945 was a typical summer day in southwestern Japan. In the city of Hiroshima at 8:15 A.M., people were walking to work, sitting down at office desks, riding buses, weeding gardens, and clearing away breakfast dishes. Suddenly a noiseless flash lit the sky over the city and its environs for miles. A mammoth column of smoke in the shape of a mushroom cloud ballooned up. The United States had dropped history's first atomic bomb.

The explosion had the intensity of a huge blast furnace. In some areas, the brilliant light created by the explosion bleached everything it touched. Near the epicenter of the blast, human bodies were charred to cinders or turned into frightening statues. Flesh melted and bones fused. Buildings were reduced to ashes. Stones bled. The world had never seen a bomb like this. Hiroshima, a city renowned in prewar Japan for its relaxed and agreeable atmosphere, was leveled in an instant by the terrifying force of a single atomic bomb.

There were 78,000 dead in Hiroshima on 6 August. By December the number had reached 140,000 as the sickness caused by radioactive poisoning continued to take its toll. Rescue workers inhaled the dense dust and became contaminated by radioactivity. Surviving victims often lost their hair and eyebrows and experienced nausea, vomiting, diarrhea, and bleeding. Others suffered from internal hemorrhaging, blindness, chronic weakness, and fatigue. Many developed cancers like leukemia, sometimes years later. The bomb scarred and disfigured. Atomic radiation released by the bomb caused unseen damage by attacking the lungs, heart, bone marrow, and internal organs. It poisoned the lymph glands. It worked unobserved to alter genetic structure, deforming unborn babies and those not yet conceived.

Harry Truman, who became president of the United States on 12 April 1945 following the death of Franklin D. Roosevelt, later spoke of his decision to drop the atomic bomb to bring the war to a speedy end. In July 1945, Truman issued an ultimatum to Japan to surrender immediately or face dire consequences. The Japanese ignored the warning. Hiroshima was targeted, according to Truman, to make a point to the Japanese, to demonstrate the unimaginable force of this new American weapon. The city was a military center, a major storage and assembly point that supplied the armed forces. Nagasaki, bombed three days after Hiroshima with an experimental plutonium bomb, was targeted as an industrial center and the place where the torpedoes that had destroyed American ships were manufactured.

It is undoubtedly true that the bombings were responsible for the Japanese surrender a few days later. The atomic bomb did bring the Asian war to an immediate end. But critics of the bombings pointed out that Japan was already close to defeat. Secret U.S. intelligence studies that came to light in the 1980s indicate that American leaders knew that Japan had been weakened by intense American incendiary bombing of its cities. Twenty-six square miles of the working-class and industrial section of Tokyo had been burned at the cost of well over 100,000 lives. Many refugees from other Japanese cities had fled to Hiroshima to live with relatives. The Sea of Japan had been heavily mined, cutting off Japan from its armies on the Asian mainland. Some radical young officers of the Japanese army were preparing to kidnap Emperor Hirohito to keep him from capitulating. The planned American landing on Japan was expected to be costly. U.S. forces had already suffered over 100,000 casualties in the conquest of the Japanese island of Okinawa in April. Truman and his advisers were now prepared to use any means possible to prevent further American casualties. Defenders of the decision have argued that any responsible American leader would have made the same decision to use the atomic bomb. Modern total wars acquire a life of their own, and desperate nations use the science, technology, and weapons available to them.

In the summer of 1945, General Dwight D. Eisenhower, then the victorious Supreme Allied Commander in the European theater of war, was informed by U.S. Secretary of War Henry L. Stimson of what was about to take place in Hiroshima. Eisenhower voiced "grave misgivings" based on his "belief that Japan was already defeated and that the dropping of the bomb was completely unnecessary" to end the war. He was not alone among military men in questioning the use of nuclear force on strategic and moral grounds. Strong opposition to nuclear weapons began to surface among scientists working on the bomb. In opposition to many of their colleagues, they warned that the atomic bomb was an undiscriminating weapon that could not pinpoint supply depots and military targets but would destroy entire civilian populations. The peace movement based on banning nuclear weapons actually began among horrified scientists who were aware, before the rest of the world could know, of the terrible force that they had helped to create.

At the Potsdam Conference in July 1945, Stalin had informed President Truman and Prime Minister Winston Churchill that the Soviet Union was about to invade Manchuria, honoring the promise Stalin had made at Teheran in 1943 to join the war against Japan after Germany was defeated. The Soviet Union would now play a role in determining the future of Asia. Truman told Stalin of the powerful new weapon America had developed. Stalin seemed unimpressed. Secretary of War Stimson was aware that the atomic bomb would be an important weapon to have in the American arsenal when the time came to negotiate a postwar world settlement

Yasuko Yamagata

with the Russians. Truman and his advisers, however, never deviated from their insistence that saving the lives of thousands of American and Japanese soldiers was their only consideration in dropping the bomb.

An American observer called the bombing of Hiroshima "the immersion in death." Survivors repeatedly described Hiroshima after the "flash" as what hell must be like. Photographs of the city record the total destruction of buildings and vegetation. Japanese photographers avoided taking pictures of the devastation the bomb had done to human bodies, believing that what they saw was too horrible to record. Yet the brutality of nuclear war could not be ignored. It has become a central issue of international politics in the second half of the twentieth century. The decision to drop the atomic bomb has had enduring moral and political consequences. On that August morning in 1945, the world had its first terrifying glimpse of the power of total annihilation. In an instant—0.3 second—Hiroshima became an atomic wasteland. The world now lived with the knowledge that it could happen again.

world war II

1937	Japan begins undeclared war on China
March 1938	Germany annexes Austria to the German Reich
29 September 1938	Chamberlain, Daladier, Mussolini, and Hitler meet at Munich conference
May 1939	Pact of Steel: military alliance between Italy and Germany
1939	Non-Aggression Pact between Germany and the Soviet Union
1 September 1939	Germany attacks Poland
3 September 1939	Great Britain and France declare war on Germany
April 1940	Germany attacks Denmark and Norway
May 1940	Germany invades the Netherlands, Belgium, Luxembourg, and then France
June 1940	Italy enters the war on the side of Germany
17 June 1940	French Marshal Pétain petitions Germany for an armistice and creates a collaborationist government at Vichy
September 1940	Japan, Germany, and Italy sign Tripartite Pact
September–November 1940	The Battle of Britain
22 June 1941	Germany invades the Soviet Union
1941	First extermination camp created in Chelmno, Poland
7 December 1941	Japan attacks Pearl Harbor; the following day, the United States declares war on Japan
11 December 1941	Germany declares war on the United States
January 1942	Wannsee Conference, where the Final Solution is planned
September 1942	Italian government withdraws from the war
April 1943	Unsuccessful uprising in the Warsaw ghetto
November 1943	Churchill, Roosevelt, and Stalin meet at Teheran conference
6 June 1944	Allied forces land in northern France—D-Day
February 1945	Churchill, Roosevelt, and Stalin meet at Yalta
March 1945	American forces march into Germany
30 April 1945	Hitler commits suicide
July and August 1945	Churchill, Truman, and Stalin meet at Potsdam
June 1945	Battle of Midway
6 August 1945	United States drops atomic bomb on Hiroshima
2 September 1945	Japan surrenders

rape became a means of direct retaliation. Victorious Japanese soldiers raped Chinese women as part of the spoils of war. Regardless of what country was involved, victorious armies practiced rape against civilian populations as one of the unspoken aspects of conquest.

Material destruction was great. Axis and Allied cities, centers of civilization and culture, were turned into wastelands by aerial bombing. The Germans bombed Rotterdam and Coventry. The British engineered the firebombing of Dresden. Warsaw and Stalingrad were destroyed by the German army. Hiroshima and Na-

gasaki were leveled by the United States. The nations of Europe were weakened after World War I; after World War II, they were crippled. Europe was completely displaced from the position of world dominance it had held for centuries. The United States alone was undamaged and stronger after the war than before, its industrial capacity and production greatly improved by the war.

What would be the future of Europe? The leaders of the United States, Great Britain, and the Soviet Union—the Big Three, as they were called—met three times between 1943 and 1945: first at Teheran; then in February 1945 at Yalta, a Russian Black Sea resort; and finally in July and August 1945 at Potsdam, a suburb of Berlin. They coordinated their attacks on Germany and Japan and discussed their plans for postwar Europe. After Allied victory, the governments of both Germany and Japan would be totally abolished and completely reconstructed. No deals would be made with Hitler or his successors; no peace would be negotiated with the enemy; surrender would be unconditional. Germany would be disarmed and denazified, and its leaders would be tried as war criminals. The armies of the Big Three occupied Germany, each with a separate zone, but the country would be governed as a single economic unit. The Soviet Union, it was agreed, could collect reparations from Germany. With Germany and Japan defeated, a United Nations organization would provide the structure for a lasting peace in the world.

Stalin expected that the Soviet Union would decide the future of the territories of eastern Europe that the Soviet army had liberated from Germany. This area was vital to the security of the war-devastated Soviet Union; Stalin saw it as a protective barrier against another attack from the west. Romania, Bulgaria, Hungary, Czechoslovakia, and Poland, the Big Three decided, would have pro-Soviet governments. Since Soviet troops occupied these countries in 1945, there was little that the Anglo-Americans could do to prevent Russian control unless they wanted to go to war against the USSR. Churchill realistically accepted this. But for Americans who took seriously the proclamations of President Roosevelt that their country had fought to restore freedom and self-determination to peoples oppressed by tyranny, Soviet power in eastern Europe proved to be a bitter disappointment.

Churchill, Roosevelt, and Stalin—the Big Three—at the Yalta Conference. Stalin invoked the Yalta agreements to justify the Soviet Union's control over eastern Europe after the war.

The presence of Soviet armies in eastern Europe guaranteed that communism would prevail there after 1945. In western Europe, the American and British presence fostered the existence of parliamentary democracies. Germany was divided. A similar pattern emerged in Asia. The U.S. forces of occupation in Japan oversaw the introduction of democratic institutions. The USSR controlled Manchuria. Korea was divided. The celebration of victory after a war in which 50 million people died did not last long. Nor did the Anglo-American cooperation with the Soviet Union endure. With the defeat of Germany and Japan, the United States and the Soviet Union were the undisputed giants in world politics. Two ideological systems stood facing each other suspiciously across a divided Europe and a divided Asia.

mastering the chapter

To review the main points of the chapter, be sure you can explain the significance of each of the following.

Terms/Concepts/Events	People	Places
appeasement	Neville Chamberlain	Sudetenland
Non-Aggression Pact	Benito Mussolini	Czechoslovakia
Winter War	Henri-Philippe Pétain	Munich
phony war	Charles de Gaulle	Dunkirk
blitzkrieg	Hermann Göring	Maginot Line
Battle of Britain	Winston Churchill	Vichy
Final Solution	Josip Broz (Tito)	Auschwitz
Wannsee Conference	gypsies	Warsaw ghetto
Zyklon B	Heinrich Himmler	Stalingrad
Operation Overlord	Joseph Stalin	Yalta

suggestions for further reading

the coming of world war II

* Paul Kennedy, *The Realities Behind Diplomacy: Background Influences on British External Policy, 1865–1980* (London: Allen & Unwin, 1981). Essays dealing with the continuity of appeasement in British foreign policy across two centuries.

* Ian Kershaw, *The Nazi Dictatorship* (London: Edward Arnold, 1985). A fine synthesis of key problems of interpretation regarding the Third Reich. Special attention is paid to the interdependence of domestic and foreign policy and the inevitability of war in Hitler's ideology.

* Donald Cameron Watt, *How War Came: The Immediate Origins of the Second World War* (London: Heinemann, 1989). An international historian chronicles the events leading to the outbreak of the war.

racism and destruction

* Renate Bridenthal, Atina Grossmann, and Marion Kaplan, eds., *When Biology Became Destiny: Women in Weimar and Nazi Germany* (New York: Monthly Review Press, 1984). A volume of es-

says pursuing common themes on the relation between sexism and racism in interwar and wartime Germany.

* Raul Hilberg, *The Destruction of the European Jews.* 3 vols. (New York: Holmes and Meier, 1985). An exhaustive study of the annihilation of European Jews beginning with cultural precedents and antecedents. Examines step-by-step developments that led to extermination policies and contains valuable appendixes on statistics and a discussion of sources.

* Charles S. Maier, *The Unmasterable Past: History, Holocaust, and German National Identity* (Cambridge, MA: Harvard University Press, 1988). A thoughtful discussion of the historical debate over the Holocaust and the comparative dimensions of the event. Especially valuable in placing the Holocaust within German history.

* Michael R. Marrus, *The Holocaust in History* (New York: New American Library, 1987). A comprehensive survey of all aspects of the Holocaust, including the policies of the Third Reich, the living conditions in the camps, and the prospects for resistance and opposition.

Allied victory

John Campbell, ed., *The Experience of World War II* (New York: Oxford University Press, 1989). This richly illustrated work provides an overview of the Second World War in both the Asian and European theaters in terms of origins, events, and consequences.

* Akira Iriye, *The Origins of the Second World War in Asia and the Pacific* (London: Longman, 1987). Examines the events of the 1930s leading up to hostilities in the Pacific theaters, with a special focus on Japanese isolation and aggression.

* John Keegan, *The Second World War* (New York: Viking, 1990). Provides a panoramic sweep of "the largest single event in human history," with special attention to warfare in all its forms and the importance of leadership.

Gerhard L. Weinberg, *A World at Arms: A Global History of World War II* (New York: Cambridge University Press, 1994). An overview of the interactions among Germany, the Soviet Union, and Japan, which provides an integrated history of World War II with a helpful bibliographic essay.

*Paperback edition available.

postwar Recovery and crisis: from the cold war to the new europe, 1945-1968

sex, Drugs, and Rock 'n' Roll

CHAPTER

29

"I Wanna Hold Your Hand" seems an unlikely anthem for a generation. Yet this song, performed by the British rock group the Beatles, was known around the world in the early 1960s by an entire generation of the young. Youths screamed and swooned and danced to it. Parents and educators screamed, too, but out of fear that "Beatlemania" signaled the ruination of the younger generation in Western society. Adults worried that young people were being caught up in hedonism, sexual pleasure, and mind-numbing drugs, all because of this loud, cacophonous music.

Young people of the 1950s and 1960s saw the advent of Rock 'n' Roll differently. Rock 'n' Roll emerged as a national phenomenon in the United States in the mid-1950s. It was firmly rooted in the black music of rhythm and blues. White country and western music was also influential in shaping the new sound. Titles like "Rock Around the Clock," "Shake, Rattle, and Roll," "Keep A-Knockin'," and "Blue Suede Shoes" captured the attention of a generation. The experiences of teenagers were at the center of the new rhythms, confronted in the lyrics and amplified with electric guitars. Rock 'n' Roll appealed to the young because it dealt openly with the issues of sex and young love and was aimed at the hypocrisy of the adult white world. Even the sound was revolutionary. It became "the music of the young," something that accentuated their differences from the adult world and their commonalities with one another.

Babies born after World War II, who began entering adolescence at the end of the 1950s, constituted a new audience for mass entertainment. They were also an important international mass market for music: popular recordings began selling in the millions for the first time in history. Music was now an important consumer product. Elvis Presley, a country blues singer from Memphis, Tennessee, emerged as the greatest figure on the Rock 'n' Roll scene in the late 1950s. His overt androgynous sexuality, gyrating hips, and explicit lyrics made him an object of adult fears about losing control of their children. He quickly developed a worldwide following of devoted fans, who hailed him as "the King" and who continue to honor his memory years after his death.

In the 1960s, British groups such as the Beatles from Liverpool entered the international rock scene. Dubbed "the Mop-Tops" because of their long hair, they were condemned for transgressing sex roles in their appearance. Millions of boys copied their idols as hair became a political issue, a symbol of rebellion. Billboards appeared across the United States that proclaimed: "Beautify America—Get a Haircut!" With the new music came a new style of dressing, what adults saw as a uniform of disrespect for traditional values and parental authority. The British group the Rolling Stones were considered more outrageously sexual, vulgar, and lewd than their countrymen the Beatles. Antirock movements cited "specialists" who warned that the new amplified music caused deafness, drug addiction, and excessive sexual activity.

The gap between the generations yawned into a gulf as rock music became political in the mid-1960s. Bob Dylan, an American rock performer, introduced folk music to the genre with songs of social protest like "Blowin' in the Wind" and "Only a Pawn in Their Game." Rock music was denounced as a communist plot, with performers urging their audiences to "Make Love, Not War." Dylan's "Subterranean Homesick Blues" targeted the hypocrisy of his society:

> Ah get born, keep warm
> Short pants, romance, learn to dance
> Get dressed, get blessed
> Try to be a success
> Please her, please him, buy gifts
> Don't steal, don't lift
> Twenty years of schoolin'
> And they put you on the day shift
> Look out kid
> They keep it all hid . . .

Although rock music served as a rallying cry for a generation who opposed war and exploitation, its

Focus Questions

1. What did it mean for postwar European politics that the Continent was divided by an "iron curtain"?
2. What factors encouraged decolonization in the decades after World War II?
3. Why did Western Europe's economy recover so rapidly, and how did this contribute to a gradual process of European economic integration?
4. What is the welfare state, and how did it transform the lives of ordinary Europeans?
5. What were some of the concerns that provoked protests from women, students, and others in the 1960s?

frankness about sexuality did not result in a reformulation of gender roles. Woman's place in rock music was usually as an object of desire. Few of the major rock stars were women. The American singer Janis Joplin was a striking exception. What was known in the rock world as "girl groups"—the Ronettes and the Shangri-Las are two examples—reinforced predominantly male views of sexuality, both by their dress and by the lyrics of their songs. The female body was treated as a commodity itself in the fashions associated with the new youth culture, such as the miniskirt and the bikini. Girls and young women were important consumers of the new music and the values it communicated.

Rock music quickly became an international phenomenon, spreading from the United States and Great Britain to appeal to the young throughout the world. Rock stars were the new self-made millionaires, often from working-class backgrounds, who were able to benefit from advertising and mass-marketing techniques in a new age of consumption. The postwar generation that grew into adulthood in the late 1960s shared a common musical culture. Student protest movements spread throughout Europe and the United States, and in the same period rock music gained acceptance as a legitimate and important musical genre. Through radio, television, and the international distribution of recordings, an international youth culture linked European and American youth together with common symbols and a common language of protest.

Regulating the cold war

With the cessation of the "hot" war that had ripped Europe apart from 1939 to 1945, the armies of the United States and the Soviet Union met on the banks of the Elbe River in 1945. Greeting each other as victors and allies, the occupying armies waited for direction on how to conduct the peace. Europe and Japan had been destroyed, leaving the United States and the Soviet Union as indisputably the two richest and strongest nations in the world. The Soviets understood that they ran a sorry second to American military superiority—the United States was alone in possessing the atomic bomb—and to American wealth, which, measured in GNP, was 400 percent greater than that of the Soviet Union. War had made these two superpowers allies; now the peace promised to make them once again into wary foes. In the three years that followed the war, a new kind of conflict emerged between the two superpower victors, a war deemed "cold" because of its lack of military violence, but a bitter war nonetheless.

The Cold War emerged as ideological opposition between communism and capitalist democracies, dominated by the two superpowers, the Soviet Union and the United States. It affected the entire world. Drawing on

Territorial Gains of the USSR

three decades of distrust between the East and the West, the Cold War was related to the economic and foreign policy goals of both superpowers.

Cold War conflict initially developed because of differing Russian and American notions regarding the economic reconstruction of Europe. The Soviet Union realized that American aid to Europe was not primarily a humanitarian program; it was part of an economic offensive in Europe that would contribute to the dominance of American capital in world markets. The United States recognized that the Soviet Union hoped to achieve its own recovery through outright control of Eastern Europe. Needing the stability of peace, the Soviets saw in Eastern Europe, hostile as the area may have been to forced integration, a necessary buffer against Western competition. The Soviet Union feared U.S. intentions to establish liberal governments and capitalist markets in these states bordering its own frontiers and viewed such attempts as inimical to Soviet interests. For these reasons, Stalin refused to allow free elections in Poland and, by force of occupying armies, annexed neighboring territories that included eastern Finland, the Baltic states, East Prussia, eastern Poland,

Ruthenia, and Bessarabia. With the exception of East Prussia, these annexations were all limited to territories that had once been part of tsarist Russia.

Winston Churchill captured the drama of the new international order in a speech he delivered in Missouri in 1946: "From Stettin in the Baltic to Trieste in the Adriatic an iron curtain has descended across the Continent." The term *iron curtain* described graphically for many the new fate of Europe, rigidly divided between East and West, a pawn in the struggle of the superpowers.

atomic politics

The nuclear arms race began in earnest during World War II, well before the first atomic bomb was dropped in August 1945. The Germans, the Russians, and the British all had teams exploring the destructive possibilities of nuclear fission during the war, but the Americans had the edge in the development of the bomb. Stalin understood the political significance of the weapon and committed the Soviet Union to a breakneck program of development following the war. The result was that the USSR ended the American monopoly and

The first hydrogen bomb test, on November 1, 1952, destroyed an entire island in the Pacific.

The iron curtain

Winston Churchill (1874–1965), prime minister of England during World War II, captured the drama of the postwar international order in a speech he delivered in Missouri in 1946. Churchill had long been suspicious of the political motives of the Soviet Union, though he welcomed Stalin as an ally in defeating Hitler. The term that he coined, *iron curtain,* described graphically the fate of Europe that many feared: a Europe rigidly divided between East and West, no more than a pawn in the struggle of the superpowers.

From Stettin in the Baltic to Trieste in the Adriatic, an iron curtain has descended across the Continent. Behind that line lie all the capitals of the ancient states of Central and Eastern Europe. Warsaw, Berlin, Prague, Vienna, Budapest, Belgrade, Bucharest and Sofia, all these famous cities and the populations around them lie in what I must call the Soviet sphere, and all are subject in one form or another, not only to Soviet influence but to a very high and, in many cases, increasing measure of control from Moscow. Athens alone—Greece with its immortal glories—is free to decide its future at an election under British, American and French observation. The Russian-dominated Polish Government has been encouraged to make enormous and wrongful inroads upon Germany, and mass expulsions of millions of Germans on a scale grievous and undreamed-of are now taking place. The Communist parties, which were very small in all these Eastern States of Europe, have been raised to preeminence and power far beyond their numbers and are seeking everywhere to obtain totalitarian control. Police governments are prevailing in nearly every case, and so far, except in Czechoslovakia, there is no true democracy.

The safety of the world requires a new unity in Europe, from which no nation should be permanently outcast. It is from the quarrels of the strong parent races in Europe that the world wars we have witnessed, or which occurred in former times, have sprung. Twice in our own lifetime we have seen the United States, against their wishes and their traditions, against arguments, the force of which it is impossible not to comprehend, drawn by irresistible forces, into these wars in time to secure the victory of the good cause, but only after frightful slaughter and devastation had occurred. Twice the United States has had to send several millions of its young men across the Atlantic to find the war; but now war can find any nation, wherever it may dwell between dusk and dawn. Surely we should work with conscious purpose for a grand pacification of Europe, within the structure of the United Nations and in accordance with its Charter. That I feel is an open cause of policy of very great importance.

In front of the iron curtain which lies across Europe are other causes for anxiety. In Italy the Communist Party is seriously hampered by having to support the Communist-trained Marshal Tito's claims to former Italian territory at the head of the Adriatic. Nevertheless the future of Italy hangs in the balance. Again one cannot imagine a regenerated Europe without a strong France. All my public life I have worked for a strong France and I never lost faith in her destiny, even in the darkest hours. I will not lose faith now. However, in a great number of countries, far from the Russian frontiers and throughout the world, Communist fifth columns are established and work in complete unity and absolute obedience to the directions they receive from the Communist centre. Except in the British Commonwealth and in the United States where Communism is in its infancy, the Communist parties or fifth columns constitute a growing challenge and peril to Christian civilization. These are somber facts for anyone to have to recite on the morrow of a victory gained by so much splendid comradeship in arms and in the cause of freedom and democracy; but we should be most unwise not to face them squarely while time remains.

tested its first atomic bomb in 1949. Both countries developed the hydrogen bomb almost simultaneously in 1953. Space exploration by satellite was also deemed important in terms of the detection and deployment of bombs, and the Soviets pulled ahead in this area with the launching of the first satellite, Sputnik I, in 1957. Intercontinental ballistic missiles (ICBMs) followed, further accelerating the pace of nuclear armament.

The atomic bomb and thermonuclear weapons contributed greatly to the shape of Cold War politics. The incineration of Hiroshima and Nagasaki sent a clear message to the world about the power of total annihilation available to those who controlled the bombs. The threat of such total destruction made full and direct confrontation with an equally armed enemy impossible. Both the United States and the Soviet Union, the first two members of the "nuclear club," knew that they had the capability of obliterating their enemy, but not before the enemy could respond in retaliation. They also knew that the technology necessary for nuclear arms was available to any industrial power. By 1974 the nuclear club included Great Britain, France, the People's Republic of China, and India. These countries joined the United States and the Soviet Union in spending the billions of dollars necessary every year to expand nuclear arsenals and to develop more sophisticated weaponry and delivery systems.

A new vocabulary transformed popular attitudes and values. *Missile gaps*, *deterrence*, *first strike*, *second strike*, *radioactive fallout*, and *containment* were all terms that heightened popular fears. Citizens in the Soviet Union learned of American weapons stockpiling and American deployment of military forces throughout the world. Americans learned that the Russians had the ability to deliver bombs that could wipe out major U.S. cities. Paranoia on both sides was encouraged by heads of state in their public addresses throughout the 1950s. Traitors were publicly tried while espionage was being sponsored by the state.

The first nuclear test-ban treaty, signed in 1963, banned tests in the atmosphere. Arms limitation and nonproliferation were the subjects of a series of conferences between the United States and the Soviet Union in the late 1960s and pointed the way to limitations eventually agreed on in the next decade. The United Nations, created by the Allies immediately following World War II to take the place of the defunct League of Nations, established international agencies for the purpose of harnessing nuclear power for peaceful uses. On the whole, however, the arms race persisted as a continuing threat in Cold War politics. The race required the dedication of huge national resources to maintain a competitive stance. Conventional forces, too, were expanded to protect Eastern and Western bloc interests. With the aim of containing the USSR, the United States entered into a series of military alliances around the world. In order to provide mutual assistance should any member be attacked, the United States joined with Belgium, Britain, Canada, Denmark, France, Iceland, Italy, the Netherlands, Norway, and Portugal in 1949 to form the North Atlantic Treaty Organization (NATO). Greece and Turkey became members in 1952, West Germany in 1955, and Spain in 1982. The potential military threat of the Soviet Union in Western Europe prompted this peacetime military alliance.

The Southeast Asia Treaty Organization (SEATO) in 1954 and the Baghdad Pact of 1955 (known as the Central Treaty Organization after 1959) followed. The United States strengthened its military presence throughout the period by acquiring 1400 military bases in foreign

Sputnik I on its support stand before launching. The news of the Soviet breakthrough galvanized the Western nations. The United States redoubled its efforts to enter the space age and reorganized school curricula to stress math and science.

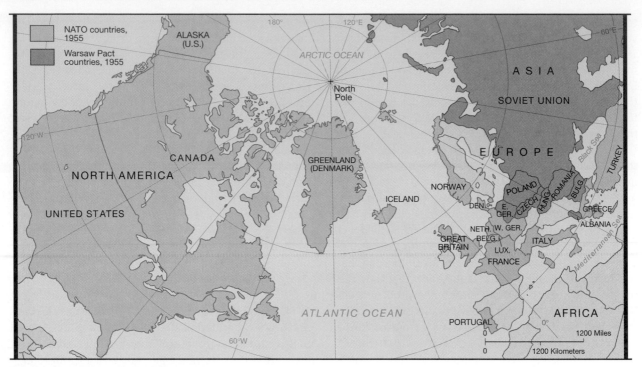

The Cold War: U.S. and Soviet Alliances

countries for its own forces. The Soviet Union countered developments in the West with its own alliances and organizations. In 1949 the USSR established the Council for Mutual Economic Assistance, or Comecon, with bilateral agreements between the Soviet Union and Eastern European states. Comecon was Stalin's response to the U.S. Marshall Plan in Western Europe. Rather than providing aid, however, Comecon benefited the Soviet Union at the expense of its partners, seeking to integrate and control the economies of Eastern Europe for Soviet gain. In 1955, Albania, Bulgaria, Romania, Czechoslovakia, Hungary, Poland, and East Germany—all Comecon members—joined with the Soviet Union to form a defensive alliance organization known as the Warsaw Pact. The USSR intended its Eastern European allies to serve as a strategic buffer zone against the NATO forces.

Atomic politics encouraged *brinksmanship*, a term coined by John Foster Dulles (1888–1959), U.S. secretary of state from 1953 to 1959. Brinksmanship referred to a confrontationist foreign policy that brought the superpowers repeatedly to the edge of armed conflict. It also encouraged a new kind of global politics in which the superpowers vied with each other to find new partners, especially in formerly colonized areas, to join their camps.

decolonization

By the end of the Second World War, European colonial empires had been weakened or destroyed by the ravages of battle, occupation, and neglect. The United States, committed to free and open markets, pushed its advantage at the conclusion of the peace by insisting on the dismantling of its allies' empires as well as those of its enemies. The Soviets, preoccupied with their own recovery, were in no position to assert a global policy at the end of the war.

Nationalist movements had been growing in power in the 1930s, and many nationalist leaders saw the war as a catalyst for independence, especially in Asia. Great Britain knew that it no longer commanded the resources to control India, historically its richest colony, which under the leadership of Mohandas Gandhi (1869–1948) had been agitating for independence since 1920. Given the title of "Mahatma," or "great-souled," by his people, Gandhi advocated passive resistance to achieve independence. He sought by means of civil disobedience, boycotts, and public fasts instead of violence to bring pressure on the colonizers. The British granted self-government to India in 1946 with the proviso that if the bitter conflict between Hindus and Muslims was not settled by mutual agreement, Great Britain would decide on the division of power. As a result, Muslim and Hindu representatives agreed to the division of British India into the independent states of India and Pakistan in 1947. Ceylon (now Sri Lanka) and Burma (now Myanmar) achieved full independence in 1948.

In its march through Asia during the war, Japan had smashed colonial empires. Japan's defeat created a power vacuum that nationalist leaders were eager to fill. Civil wars erupted in China, Burma, Korea, and Indochina. Anticolonial resistance opened the way to Communist insurgence. Indochina declared its independence in 1945 and waged war with France until 1954. South Vietnam was declared a republic, and the United States sponsored a regime that was considered favorable to Western interests. The North Vietnamese state was established under the French-educated leader Ho Chi Minh. The civil war continued, with the North Vietnamese backing the National Liberation Front in the South. After almost two decades of escalating involvement, in 1973 American troops were finally withdrawn from a war they could not win. Cold War politics had enmeshed the United States in Southeast Asia, and Cold War imperatives had kept it there.

The first wave of decolonization after 1945 had been in Asia. A second wave crested and crashed in the late 1950s and early 1960s in Africa, another ready battleground for Cold War dominance. During the Second World War, North Africa had served as a theater of military action, while South Africa was a source of supplies and troops. Wartime experiences and rapid economic development fed existing nationalist aspirations and encouraged the emergence of mass political demands for liberation. A new generation of leaders, many of them educated in European institutions, moved from cooperation with home rule to demands for independence by the early 1960s. British Prime Minister Harold MacMillan (1894–1986) spoke of "the winds of change" in 1960, the year that proved to be a turning point in African politics. Britain and Belgium yielded their colonies. In 1960 Patrice Lumumba (1925–61) became the first prime minister of the Republic of the Congo (present-day Zaire). White European rule continued in

Jubilant Algerians celebrate the granting of independence to their country on 3 July 1962 after a bloody seven-year war. Many Europeans whose families had been settled in Algeria for generations fled during the fighting or left after independence was won.

Rhodesia (now Zimbabwe) and South Africa, despite continued world pressure.

The French, having faced what its officer corps considered a humiliating defeat in Indochina, held on against the winds of change in North Africa. France's problems in Algeria began in earnest in 1954 when Muslims seeking independence and self-rule revolted. Although the Algerian rebels successfully employed ter-

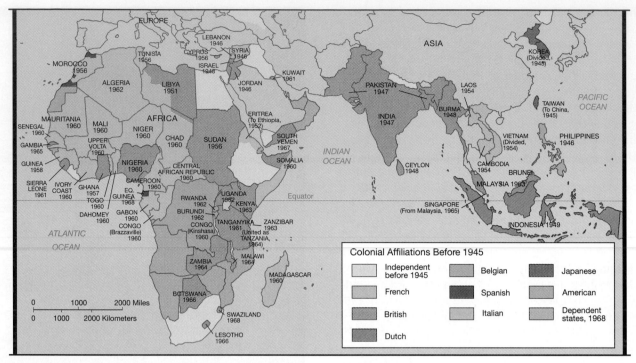

Decolonization

rorist and guerrilla tactics, European settlers and the French army in Algeria refused to accept defeat. The Fourth Republic was on the verge of collapse when General Charles de Gaulle, leader of the Free French resistance in World War II, stepped in to establish the Fifth Republic with a strong executive branch. He ended the war and agreed to Algeria's independence, which was achieved in 1962.

One supporter of the Algerian revolution, Frantz Fanon (1925–61), was working as a French-trained psychiatrist in Algeria when the revolution began. In his writings, especially his book *The Wretched of the Earth* (1961), he argued in favor of national liberation movements and for the necessity of violence. Fanon described the trap of dependence of colonized countries: "We go on sending out raw materials; we go on being Europe's small farmers; we specialize in unfinished products."

Decolonization meant continued dependence for many *third world* countries, as these primarily agricultural countries with weak market infrastructures were now known. *First world* nations were identified as the advanced industrial countries; *second world* countries were those whose lower level of prosperity indicated a transition from agricultural to industrial production. Third

world nations were suppliers of raw materials and food to the countries of the first world. These countries were no longer directly controlled as colonies but continued to be dominated by the Western capitalist powers and Japan, on which they relied for their markets and trade. As Frantz Fanon had described it, these newly independent countries had to continue doing what they had done as colonies: supplying raw materials to their former masters.

African leader Kwame Nkrumah (1909–72) of Ghana denounced this situation of dependence as "neocolonialism" and called for a united Africa as the only means of resistance. Nkrumah argued that "aid" was merely a "revolving credit" plan that returned increased profits to the former colonial masters while extracting wealth from African nations. He led Ghana in a policy of nonalignment in the Cold War. With Jomo Kenyatta (1894–1978) of Kenya, he founded the Pan-African Federation, which promoted African nationalism.

Soviet leader Joseph Stalin limited the Soviet Union's foreign involvement following the Second World War to Communist regimes that shared borders with the USSR in Eastern Europe and Asia. After Stalin's death in 1953, the Soviet Union turned to the third world. Former colonies played an important new role in the Cold War strategies with the accession to power of Nikita Khrushchev (1894–1971) in the mid-1950s. The Soviet Union abandoned its previous caution and assumed a global role in offering "friendship treaties," military advice, trade credits, and general support for attempts at national liberation in Asia, Africa, and Latin America. Cold warriors took advantage of tribalism and regionalism, which mitigated against the establishment of strong central governments. Military rule and fragmentation often resulted. Instability and acute poverty continued to characterize former colonies after emancipation, regardless of which camp the new leaders joined.

The Two Germanys and the World in Two Blocs

In central Europe, Cold War tensions first surfaced over the question of how to treat Germany. The United States and the Soviet Union had very different ideas about the future of their former enemy. In fostering economic reconstruction in Europe, the United States counted on a German economy transfused with American funds that would be self-supporting and stable. To the contrary, the Soviet Union, blaming Germany for its extreme destruction, was explicit in its demands: German resources must be siphoned off for Soviet reconstruction. Stricken as the Soviets were with 20 million dead, millions of homeless refugees in dire poverty, and 1700 cities in ruins, commandeering German labor and stripping Germany of its industrial plant seemed to them only fair.

With Germany's defeat, its territory had been divided into four zones, occupied by American, Soviet, British, and French troops. An Allied Control Commission consisting of representatives of the four powers was to govern Germany as a whole in keeping with the decisions made at Yalta before the end of the war. As Soviet and American antagonisms over Germany's future deepened, however, Allied rule polarized between the East and the West, with the internal politics of each area determined by the ideological conflicts between communism and capitalist free enterprise.

Allied attempts to administer Germany as a whole faltered and failed in 1948 over a question of economic policy. The zones of the Western occupying forces (the United States, Great Britain, and France), now administered as a single unit, issued a uniform and stable currency that the Russians accurately saw as a threat to their own economic policies in Germany. The Soviets blockaded the city of Berlin, which, though behind the frontier of the Russian sector, was being administered in sectors by the four powers and whose western sector promised to become a successful enclave of Western capitalism. With the support of the people of West Berlin, the Allies responded by airlifting food and supplies into West Berlin for almost a year, defending it as an outpost that must be preserved from the advance of communism. The Russians were forced to withdraw the

The Berlin airlift of 1948-49 broke through the Soviet blockade of the city. Called "Operation Vittles," the airlift provided food and fuel for beleaguered West Berliners. Here children wait for the candy American pilots dropped in tiny parachute handkerchiefs. The Soviets ended the blockade in the spring of 1949.

blockade in the spring of 1949. The Berlin blockade hardened the commitment on both sides to two Germanys.

The two new states came into existence in 1949, their founding separated by less than a month. The Federal Republic of Germany, within the American orbit, was established as a democratic parliamentary regime. Free elections brought the Christian Democrat Konrad Adenauer to power as chancellor. The German Democratic Republic was ruled as a single-party state under Walter Ulbricht, who took his direction from the Soviet Union.

The division of Germany became a microcosm of the division of the world into two armed camps. With the support of local Communist parties, Soviet-dominated governments were established in Poland, Hungary, Bulgaria, and Romania in 1947. The following year, Czechoslovakia was pulled into the Soviet orbit. Czechoslovakia serves as a significant marker in the development of Cold War confrontation. The tactics of the Communists in Czechoslovakia taught the West that coalition governments were unacceptable and undoubtedly hardened the resolve of U.S. policymakers in support of two Germanys.

In 1953 the man who had ruled the Soviet Union in his own image for almost three decades died. The death of Joseph Stalin unleashed a struggle for power among the Communist party leadership. It also initiated almost immediately a process of de-Stalinization and the beginnings of a thaw in censorship and repression. A growing urban and professional class expected improvements in the quality of life and greater freedoms after years of war and hardship. In 1956, at the Twentieth Party Congress, Nikita Khrushchev, as head of the Communist party, denounced Stalin as incompetent and cruel. After five years of jockeying for power among Stalin's former lieutenants, Khrushchev emerged victorious and assumed the office of premier in 1958.

De-Stalinization also took place in Eastern Europe. Discontent over collectivization, low wages, and the lack of consumer goods fueled a latent nationalism among Eastern European populations resentful of Soviet control and influence. Violence erupted in 1953 in East Berlin as workers revolted over conditions in the workplace, but it was quickly and effectively suppressed. Demands for reforms and liberalization in Poland also produced riots and changes in Communist party leadership. Wladislaw Gomulka (1905–82), a Communist with a nationalist point of view who had survived Stalin's purges, aimed to take advantage of the power vacuum created by the departure of Stalinist leaders. Gomulka refused to back down in the face of severe Soviet pressure and the threat of a Soviet invasion to keep him from power. Elected as the first secretary of the Communist party in Poland, Gomulka sought to steer his nation on a more liberal course.

Hungarians followed suit with their demands for the withdrawal of Hungary from the Warsaw Pact. On 23 October 1956, inspired by the events in Poland, Hungarians rose up in anger against their old-guard Stalinist rulers. Imre Nagy (1896–1958), a liberal Communist, took control of the government, attempted to introduce democratic reforms, and relaxed economic controls. The Soviets, however, were unwilling to lose control of their sphere of influence in Eastern Bloc nations and to jeopardize their system of defense in the Warsaw Pact. Moscow responded to liberal experimentation in Hungary by sending tanks and troops into Budapest. Brutal repression and purges followed. The Hungarian experience in 1956 made clear that too much change too quickly would not be tolerated by the Soviet rulers. The thaw following Stalin's death had promoted expectations among Eastern Europeans that a new era was dawning. The violent crushing of the Hungarian revolution reminded everyone of the realities of Soviet control and the Soviet Union's defense priorities in Eastern Europe.

East Berlin in the late 1950s and early 1960s posed a particular problem for Communist rule. Unable to com-

The Division of Germany

pete successfully in wages and standard of living with the capitalist western sector of the city, East Berlin saw increasing numbers of its population, especially the educated and professional classes, crossing the line to a more prosperous life. In 1961 the Soviet Union responded to this problem by building a wall that cordoned off the part of the city that it controlled. The Berlin Wall eventually stretched for 103 miles, with heavily policed crossing points, turrets, and troops and tanks facing each other across the divide that came to symbolize the Cold War.

The process of liberalization that had begun after Stalin's death and continued under Khrushchev certainly experienced its setbacks and reversals in the case of Budapest and Berlin. But in 1968 the policy of de-Stalinization reached a critical juncture in Czechoslovakia. Early in 1968, Alexander Dubcek, Czech party secretary and a member of the educated younger generation of technocrats, had supported liberal reforms in Czechoslovakia that included decentralization of planning and economic decision-making, market pricing, and market incentives for higher productivity and innovation. He acted on popular desire for nationalism, the end of censorship, and better working conditions. Above all, he called for democratic reforms in the political process that would restore rule to the people. Dubcek spoke of "socialism with a human face," al-

though, unlike the Hungarians in 1956, he made no move to withdraw his country from the Warsaw Pact or to defy Soviet leadership. Moscow nevertheless feared the erosion of obedience within the Eastern Bloc and the collapse of one-party rule in the Czech state and sent in thousands of tanks and hundreds of thousands of Warsaw Pact troops to Prague and other Czech cities to reestablish control. The Czechs responded with passive resistance in what became known as the Prague Spring uprising. The Soviet invasion made clear that popular nationalism was intolerable in an Eastern Bloc nation.

Alone among Eastern European leaders, Marshal Tito of Yugoslavia resisted Soviet encroachment. As a partisan leader of the Communist resistance during World War II, Tito had heroically battled the Germans. Ruling Yugoslavia as a dictator after 1945, he refused to accede to Soviet directives to collectivize agriculture and to participate in joint economic ventures. For its defiance of Soviet supremacy, in 1948 Yugoslavia was expelled from the Cominform, the Soviet-controlled information agency that replaced the Comintern after 1943.

No part of the globe escaped the tensions generated by the Cold War. Asia was the next arena for the development of Cold War antagonisms. In 1950 the United States and the United Nations intervened when North

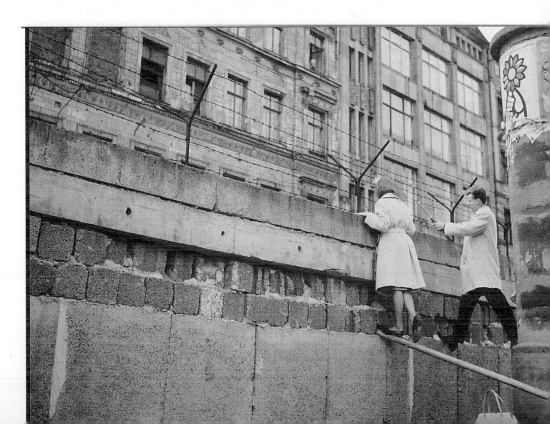

A West Berlin couple has climbed to the top of the Berlin Wall to carry on a conversation with relatives in an East Berlin apartment house.

Soviet tanks rumbled through Prague as troops from the Warsaw Pact countries invaded the Czechoslovakian capital in 1968, bringing an end to Alexander Dubcek's reform movement. Dubcek was rehabilitated in the liberalization of 1989 and elected chairman of the parliament.

Korea attacked South Korea. Korea, formerly controlled by Japan, had been divided following the war as a result of the presence of Russian and American troops. Communist-dominated North Korea refused to accept the artificial boundary between it and Western-dominated South Korea. China, a Communist state following the victory of Mao Zedong (1893–1976) in 1949, intervened in the Korean conflict when American troops advanced on Chinese frontiers in October 1950. After three years of military stalemate, Korea was partitioned on the 38th parallel in 1953. The Soviet Union was not party to the conflict in Korea, but the United States considered China to be in the Soviet camp rather than an independent contender for power.

The Middle East was another theater of confrontation between the superpowers. The United States and the Soviet Union used aid to win support of "client" states. The withdrawal, sometimes under duress, of British and French rule in the Middle East and North Africa and the creation of the state of Israel in 1948 destabilized the area and created the opportunities for new alliances. Egypt and Syria, for example, sought Soviet support against the new Israeli state, which had been formed out of the part of Palestine under British mandate from 1920 and was dependent on U.S. aid.

Oil, an essential resource for rapid industrialization, was the object of Soviet politicking in Iran after the war. Western oil companies, long active in the area, had won oil concessions in Iran in 1946, but such rights eluded the Soviets. In 1951 a nationalist Iranian government sought to evict Westerners by nationalizing the oil fields. The British blockaded Iranian trade in the Persian Gulf, and the newly formed American espionage organization, the Central Intelligence Agency (CIA), subverted the nationalist government and placed in power the shah of Iran, a leader favorable to American interests.

A crisis came in 1956 in Egypt. Egyptian President Gamal Abdel Nasser (1918–70), a nationalist in power by virtue of a military coup d'état in 1952, oversaw the nationalization of the Suez Canal. British and French military forces attacked and were forced to withdraw by pressure from both the Soviet Union and the United States, which cooperated in seeking to avert a disaster. The Middle East, however, remained a Cold War powder keg, with Israeli and Arab nationalist interests and Soviet and American aid running on a collision course. The expansion of the Israeli state at the expense of its Arab neighbors further exacerbated tensions.

The United States was heavily committed as a military presence in Southeast Asia after the French withdrawal from Indochina after the French defeat at Dien Bien Phu in 1954. Arguing the domino theory—that one Southeast Asian country after another would fall like a row of dominoes to Communist takeover—the United States also intervened in Laos and Cambodia. Between 1961 and 1973, the United States committed American troops to a full-scale war—though officially termed only a military action—against Communist guerrilla forces throughout the region.

The United States was also experiencing Cold War problems closer to home. In 1954 the CIA plotted the overthrow of Guatemala's leftist regime to keep Soviet influence out of the Western Hemisphere. In 1958 President Dwight D. Eisenhower sent his vice-president, Richard M. Nixon, on a tour of Latin American countries. Crowds everywhere jeered the American vice-president and hurled stones and eggs at his motorcade in response to U.S. policies. In 1959 a revolution in Cuba, an island nation only 90 miles off the American coast, resulted in the ejection of U.S. interests and the establishment of a Communist regime under the leadership of a young middle-class lawyer, Fidel Castro. In 1962 a direct and frightening confrontation occurred between the United States and the USSR over Soviet missile installations in Cuba. Following the Russian withdrawal from the island, both U.S. President John F. Kennedy and Soviet leader Nikita Khrushchev pursued a policy of *peaceful coexistence*, intent on averting nuclear confrontation. Both sides recognized how close they had come to mutual annihilation in the showdown over Cuba.

Another kind of challenge to Cold War power politics came from within the NATO alliance. General Charles de Gaulle, as president of the French Fifth Republic, rejected the straitjacket of American dominance in Western Europe and asserted his country's independent status by exploding the first French atomic bomb in 1960. Refusing to place the French military under an American general who served as Supreme Allied Commander for NATO, de Gaulle completely withdrew France from participation in NATO in 1966. He forged an independent French foreign policy, taking advantage of the loosening of bloc politics in the mid-1960s.

In May 1965, U.S. Secretary of State Dean Rusk observed, "This has become a very small planet. We have to be concerned with all of it—with all of its land, waters, atmosphere, and with surrounding space." Atomic politics in the Cold War era had helped to shrink the globe by bringing the threat of destruction closer to home. In the mid-1960s, leaders of the two great blocs of East and West began to realize that peaceful coexistence was the only reasonable strategy in the atomic age and that alternatives to the arms race must be found.

Reconstructing Europe

Europe faced peace in 1945 politically disorganized and economically crippled. Allied and Soviet occupation forces carved Germany into zones and its capital, Berlin, into sectors. In the international arena, growing antagonism marked relations between the United States and the Soviet Union, the two nations that controlled the future of Europe.

When the dust from the last bombs settled over Europe's cities, the balance sheets of destruction were tallied. Millions of survivors found themselves homeless, having lost their loved ones, often all of their personal belongings, and the roofs over their heads. Millions returned home from battlefronts and concentration camps to rubble, with wounds beyond healing. There were no jobs; there was nothing to eat. Peacetime rationing dipped below wartime levels. What was not measured in the statistics on physical and human de-

A brother and sister on the way home from school walk down a deserted street in a bombed-out section of Berlin. They carry tin cans for the hot meals they receive in school.

struction, at least immediately, was the psychological devastation that succeeded such loss. There could be no returning to life as normal. For many the war was far gentler than the peace. For these combatants of peacetime, often women and children, digging out and surviving were the greatest battles of all.

The problem: Europe in Ruins

An American military observer reported to his superiors in 1947: "Europe is steadily deteriorating. The political position reflects the economic. One political crisis after another merely denotes the existence of economic distress. Millions of people in the cities are slowly starving." Even the winners were losers as survivors faced a level of human and material destruction unknown in the history of warfare. Economists judged that Europe would need at least 25 years to regain its prewar economic capacity. The worst was also feared: that Europe would never recover as a world economic power.

Large-scale population movements made matters worse. Displaced persons by the millions moved across Europe. The release of prisoners of war and slave workers imprisoned during the Third Reich strained already weak economies. Germans were expelled from territo-

ries that Germany had controlled before the war. Soviet expansionist policies forced others to flee Estonia, Latvia, and Lithuania. Jews who survived the concentration camps resettled outside Europe, primarily in Palestine and the United States.

Industrial production in 1945 was one-third of its level in 1938. Housing shortages existed everywhere. France had lost one-fifth of its housing during the war years; Germany's 50 largest cities had seen two-fifths of their buildings reduced to rubble. Frankfurt, Düsseldorf, Dresden, Warsaw, and Berlin were virtually destroyed. The transportation infrastructure was severely damaged: railways, roads, and bridges were in shambles all over Europe. Communications networks were in disarray. In some cases, industrial plants had not been as adversely affected as urban centers. Yet machinery everywhere had been worn out in wartime production, and replacement parts were nonexistent. German equipment was dismantled and seized by Soviet soldiers to be used in Russia in place of what the Germans had destroyed.

Agriculture, too, suffered severe reversals in wartime economies and was unable to resume prewar production in 1945. In general, European agriculture was producing at 50 percent of its prewar capacity. Livestock had been decimated during the war years—in France,

European Migrations After World War II

for example, 50 percent of all farm animals had been killed—and it was estimated that restoring herds would take decades. Italy suffered greatly, with one-third of its overall assets destroyed. The scarcity of goods converged with ballooning inflation. Black markets with astronomical prices for necessities flourished, while currency rates plummeted. Everywhere the outlook was bleak. Yet in less than a decade, the situation had been reversed. The solution came from outside of Europe.

The solution: The Marshall plan

The Soviet Union implemented an expansion of its territorial boundaries as a way of reversing some of its drastic losses in the war. Above all, it wanted a protective ring of satellite states as security from attack from the west. Stalin also was eager to see the Soviet Union surrounded by "friendly" governments in Eastern Europe to replace the hostile regimes with which the Soviets had had to contend in the period between the wars. Picking up territory from Finland, Poland, and parts of East Prussia and eastern Czechoslovakia; forcibly reincorporating the Baltic states of Estonia, Latvia, and Lithuania; and recovering Bessarabia, the Soviet Union succeeded in acquiring sizable territories. In addition, the Soviet state dedicated itself to economic reconstruction behind a protective buffer of satellite states—Poland, East Germany, Czechoslovakia, Hungary, Romania, and Bulgaria—over which Soviet leaders exercised strong control. Yugoslavia and Albania chose to follow a more independent Communist path. Lacking the capital necessary to finance recovery, the Soviets sought compensation from Eastern and central European territories.

In contrast to the Soviet Union, the United States had incurred relatively light casualties in World War II. Because the fighting had not taken place on the North American continent, U.S. cities, farmlands, and factories were intact. As the chief producer and supplier for the Allied war effort, even before its entry into the conflict, the United States had benefited from the conflict in Europe and actually expanded its economic productivity during the war. In 1945 the United States was producing a full 50 percent of the world's GNP—a staggering fact to a displaced Great Britain, whose former trade networks were permanently destroyed. Furthermore, the United States held two-thirds of the world's gold. A United States bursting with energy and prosperity was a real threat to the Soviet Union viewing the rubble of its destroyed cities and counting the bodies of its dead.

The United States knew that it lacked one important guarantee to secure its growth and its future prosperity: adequate international markets for its goods. After World War I, American officials and businessmen understood that America's productive capacity was outpacing its ability to export goods. In the 1920s, the United States had exported capital to Europe in the form of private loans with the hope that trade would flourish as a result. The decade following the Great Depression of 1929 witnessed the search for a policy to expand U.S. markets. Both Europe and Japan were recognized as potential buyers for American goods, but both areas parried with protectionism to foster their own postdepression recovery.

World War II facilitated the success of an international economic policy consistent with international economic goals identified by U.S. policymakers as early as 1920. In both Europe and Japan, the United States intervened to aid reconstruction and recovery of war-torn nations. These economies, hungry for capital, no longer opposed U.S. intervention or erected trade barriers against American goods. The prospect of a Europe in chaos economically, socially, and politically and on the verge of collapse justified immediate action by the United States.

By the spring of 1947 it was clear to American policymakers that initial postwar attempts to stabilize European economies and promote world recovery were simply not working. The United States had, earlier in the same year, engineered emergency aid to Turkey and Greece, both objects of Soviet aspirations for control. President Truman articulated a doctrine bearing his name: "I believe that it must be the policy of the United States to support free people who are resisting attempted subjugation by armed minorities or by outside pressures." The aid emerged in an atmosphere of opposition between the United States and the Soviet Union over issues of territorial control in Eastern and southern Europe. The Cold War coincided with and reinforced the U.S. need to reconstruct Western Europe.

On 5 June 1947, Secretary of State George C. Marshall (1880–1959) delivered the commencement address at Harvard University. In his speech, Marshall introduced the European Recovery Act, popularly known as the Marshall Plan, through which billions of dollars in aid would be made available to European states, both in the east and in the west, provided that two conditions were met: (1) the recipient states must cooperate with one another in aligning national economic policies and improving the international mone-

The Marshall plan

In the rituals that are part of graduation ceremonies, guest speakers often address the challenges of the future awaiting graduates. Not many of these commencement addresses change the world. The speech given by U.S. Secretary of State George C. Marshall at Harvard University in June 1947 was different. By pledging gifts in aid, the United States helped rebuild war-torn Europe and transform the world's economy.

The truth of the matter is that Europe's requirements for the next three or four years of foreign food and other essential products—principally from America—are so much greater than her present ability to pay that she must have substantial additional help or face economic, social, and political deterioration of a very grave character.

The remedy lies in breaking the vicious circle and restoring the confidence of the European people in the economic future of their own countries and of Europe as a whole. The manufacturer and the farmer throughout wide areas must be able and willing to exchange their products for currencies the continuing value of which is not open to question.

Aside from the demoralizing effect on the world at large and the possibilities of disturbances arising as a result of the desperation of the people concerned, the consequences to the economy of the United States should be apparent to all. It is logical that the United States should do whatever it is able to do to assist in the return of normal economic health in the world, without which there can be no political stability and no assured peace. Our policy is directed not against any country or doctrine but against hunger, poverty, desperation, and chaos. Its purpose should be the revival of a working economy in the world so as to permit the emergence of political and social conditions in which free institutions can exist. Such assistance, I am convinced, must not be on a piecemeal basis as various crises develop. Any assistance that this Government may render in the future should provide a cure rather than a mere palliative. Any government that is willing to assist in the task of recovery will find full cooperation, I am sure, on the part of the United States Government. Any government which maneuvers to block the recovery of other countries cannot expect help from us. Furthermore, governments, political parties, or groups which seek to perpetuate human misery in order to profit therefrom politically or otherwise will encounter the opposition of the United States.

From Department of State Bulletin, 15 June 1947.

tary system, and (2) they must work toward breaking down trade barriers.

Participating countries included Austria, Belgium, Denmark, France, West Germany, Great Britain, Greece, Iceland, Italy, Luxembourg, the Netherlands, Norway, Sweden, Switzerland, and Turkey. Russia and Eastern European countries were also eligible for aid under the original formulation. But Russia opposed the plan from the first, wary of U.S. intentions to extend the influence of Western capitalism. Soviet opposition encouraged members of the U.S. Congress, afraid of a Communist takeover in Europe, to support the plan.

Like the United States, the Soviet Union had its own economic imperatives that dictated its attitudes toward European economic development. Under Stalin's direction, the Soviet Union concentrated all its efforts on re-constructing its devastated economy and, to this end, sought integration with Eastern European states, whose technology and resources were needed for the rebuilding of the Soviet state. U.S. dominance threatened the vital connection with Eastern Europe that the Soviet Union was determinedly solidifying in the postwar years.

The amount of U.S. aid to Europe was massive. Over $23 billion was pumped into Western Europe between 1947 and 1952. By every measure, the Marshall Plan was judged a success in the West. American foreign aid restored Western European trade and production while at the same time controlling inflation. Dean Acheson (1893–1971), Marshall's successor as secretary of state, described the plan in terms of "our duty as human beings" but nevertheless considered it "chiefly as a matter of national self-interest." Soviet critics and Western observers differed dramatically in describing the relationship between self-interest and philanthropy as motives for the plan.

Administering the plan

As significant as the gift of funds to European states undoubtedly was, no less important was the whole administrative apparatus that the American money brought in its wake. In order to expend available monies most effectively and comply with stipulations for cooperation and regulation, the states of Western Europe resorted to intensified planning and limited nationalization. These ideas were not new in the experience of European states: Vichy France, for example, had emphasized the importance of planning and specialization in its corporatist approach to economic development and social-welfare policies. Regulation and state intervention dominated the formulation of economic policy. Special attention was given to workers' welfare through unemployment insurance, retirement benefits, public health, and housing policies. European states recognized the need to provide a safety net for their citizens in order to avoid reexperiencing the disastrous depression and stagnation of the 1930s while attempting to rebuild their shattered economies. These were lessons that had been learned as much from the attempts at recovery before 1939 as from the experiences of running wartime economies.

The economic theory of John Maynard Keynes, applied successfully by neutral Sweden to its economic policies during the war, came into vogue throughout Europe in 1945, and the postwar era saw the triumph of Keynesian economics. Keynes favored macroeconomic policies to increase productivity and argued for an active role for government in "priming the pump" of economic growth. The government should be responsible, according to Keynes, for the control and regulation of the economy, with the goal of ensuring full employment for its people. Governments could and should check inflation and eliminate boom-and-bust cycles, incurring deficits by spending beyond revenues if necessary.

U.S. foreign aid contributed mightily to the extension of central planning and the growth of the welfare state throughout Western Europe. But money alone could not have accomplished the recovery that took place. The chief mechanism for administering Marshall Plan aid was the Office of European Economic Cooperation (OEEC). This master coordinating agency made the requirements for recovery clear. European states had to stabilize their own economies. Cooperation between the public and private sectors was intended to free market forces, modernize production, and raise productivity. Planning mechanisms, including transnational organizations and networks, resulted in the modernization of production and the assimilation of new techniques, new styles of management, and innovative business practices from the United States. This modernization of economies through centrally coordinated planning made Europe once again a major contender in the international economic arena.

The major exception to the establishment of central planning agencies and the nationalization of key industries was West Germany. Deciding against the British and French models of planned growth, the West Germans endorsed a free-market policy that encouraged private enterprise while providing state insurance for all workers. What has been described as "a free enterprise

This poster for the Marshall Plan reads "By the Marshall Plan: Inter-European cooperation for a higher standard of living." Aid given through the Marshall Plan generated a broad industrial revival in Western Europe and created for the United States an enormous reservoir of goodwill.

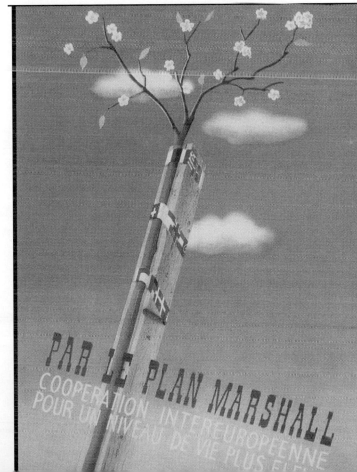

economy with a social conscience" produced the richest economy in Western Europe by the mid-1950s. Some West German industries had been dismantled, but much of West Germany's productive capacity remained intact in the late 1940s. The wealth of great industrialists such as Krupp serving prison sentences as war criminals had not been expropriated, and their commercial empires stood ready to direct the economic revival. The Krupp and I. G. Farben empires were successfully broken up into smaller units. Industries forced to start afresh benefited from the latest technology.

Japanese economic challenges in the postwar era were similar to those of Western Europe. As a defeated and occupied nation in 1945, Japan faced a grim future. U.S. aims for Asia were similar to those for Europe: American policymakers sought to create a multilateral system of world trade and preserve America's sphere of influence against Communist encroachment. The American general Douglas MacArthur was appointed the Supreme Commander for the Allied Powers and the head of occupation forces in Japan. His mission in Japan was to impose rapid economic change from above. The occupation government set out to erect institutions to promote political democratization and to eliminate militaristic institutions, official patronage, and censorship. Planning, both formal and informal, reshaped the economy as U.S. aid flowed into Japan during the late forties and early fifties. These changes in Japan, as in Western Europe, took place alongside growing American fears of communism in the region.

Japan turned its wartime devastation into an advantage by replacing destroyed factories with the latest technology, obtained by license from foreign firms. Through a combination of bureaucracy and patronage devoted to planned growth, Japan's GNP reached prewar levels by 1956. By 1968 Japan had turned defeat into triumph and stood as the third largest industrial nation in the world. Japanese growth paralleled the "economic miracle" of West Germany, with the Japanese economy growing at a rate three times faster than that of the United States between 1954 and 1967.

The abolition of the army and navy was a boon for the Japanese economy, since 16 percent of prewar GNP had been devoted to support of the military. Postwar demilitarization freed Japan of the financial exigencies of the arms race. Funds formerly used for arms now flowed into investment and new technology. Slowed population growth after 1948 and an increased volume of foreign trade contributed to Japanese prosperity. In the 1960s, Japan emerged as an affluent society undergoing a revolution in consumer durables, including televisions, washing machines, refrigerators, and automobiles.

The United States had succeeded in exporting aspects of its own economy abroad. Through management and planning, recipients of American aid surpassed U.S. goals. A multilateral system of world trade emerged out of the ashes of war. The effects of the Great Depression, which the world had been unable to

After the war, Japan concentrated its energies and investments on industrial recovery and technological advances. One result was the high-speed bullet train, which runs between Tokyo and Osaka. Mount Fuji looms in the background.

shake throughout the 1930s, had been laid to rest by global war and its consequences.

western european economic integration

European integration, discussed before and during the war, received added impetus in the postwar period. The Marshall Plan reconciled Western Europe with West Germany through economic cooperation, although that was by no means its original purpose. Realizing that Europe as a region needed the cooperation of its member states if it was to contend in world markets, associations dedicated to integration began to emerge alongside economic planning mechanisms. The Council of Europe dealt with the "discussion of questions of common concern and by agreements and common action in economic, social, cultural, scientific, legal, and administrative matters and in the maintenance and further realization of human rights and fundamental freedoms." Although not itself a supranational institution with its own authority, the Council of Europe urged a federation among European states. Britain alone rejected all attempts to develop structures of loose intergovernmental cooperation.

Belgium, the Netherlands, and Luxembourg were the first European states to establish themselves as an economic unit—Benelux. Internal customs duties among the three states were removed, and a common external tariff barrier was erected. The Schuman Plan joined France and West Germany in economic cooperation by pooling all coal and steel resources, beginning in 1950. The creators of the plan, Jean Monnet (1888–1979) and Robert Schuman (1886–1963) of France, saw it as the first step toward the removal of all economic barriers among European states and as a move toward eventual political integration. In 1951 the Netherlands, Belgium, Luxembourg, France, Italy, and West Germany formed the European Coal and Steel Community (ECSC). While constantly confronting domestic opposition on nationalist grounds, the ECSC succeeded in establishing a "common market" in coal and steel among its member states. In 1957 the same six members created the European Economic Community (EEC) and committed themselves to broadening the integration of markets. This was the beginning of what became known as the Common Market.

The Common Market aimed to establish among its member states a free movement of labor and capital, the elimination of restrictions on trade, common in-

vestment practices, and coordinated social-welfare programs. National agricultural interests were to be protected. Great Britain was initially a vocal opponent of the Common Market and continued to defend its own trading relationship with its Commonwealth countries, eventually founding its own free trade association in 1959. In 1973 Great Britain became a member of the Common Market and joined with other European nations in defining common economic policies. The EEC meanwhile achieved the support of the United States in its transitional period, in which it had 15 years to accomplish its aims.

A train carrying iron ore crosses the France–Luxembourg border, celebrating the joint community in coal and steel that became effective in 1953. The European Coal and Steel Community was the first step in the economic integration of Europe.

European union was a phenomenon of exclusion as much as inclusion. It sharpened antagonisms between the West and the East by its very success. While promoting prosperity, European economic unification favored concentration and the emergence of large corporations. Vast individual fortunes flourished under state sponsorship and the rule of the experts. National parliaments were sometimes eclipsed by new economic decision-making organizations that aimed to make Western Europe into a single free-trade area. The Soviet Union, too, relied on state planning to foster rapid economic growth, but it was central planning emanating from Moscow, based on different assumptions and directed toward different ends.

creating the welfare state

The welfare state, a creation of the post–World War II era throughout Europe, grew out of the social welfare policies of the interwar period and out of the war itself. Welfare programs aimed to protect citizens through the establishment of a decent standard of living available for everyone. The experiences of the Great Depression had done much to foster concern for economic security. In France, the primary concern of the welfare state was the protection of children and the issue of family allowances. In Great Britain, as in Germany, emphasis was placed on unemployment insurance and health care benefits. Everywhere, however, the welfare state developed a related set of social programs and policies whereby the state intervened in the cycles of individual lives to provide economic support for the challenges of birth, sickness, old age, and unemployment. (See "Utopia Lost," pp. 1014–1015.)

Protection of the citizenry took varied forms according to Cold War politics. In the Warsaw Pact countries, the need to industrialize rapidly and to dedicate productive wealth to armament and military protection resulted in a nonexistent consumer economy in which the issues of quality of life and protection took a very different direction. Based on a concept of equal access to a minimum standard of living, welfare states did not treat all its members equally. Women were often disadvantaged in social welfare programs as family needs, men's rights, and the protection of children led to different national configurations.

prosperity and consumption in the west

Despite the different paths toward reconstruction following World War II, every Western European nation experienced dramatic increases in total wealth. Per capita

A traffic jam on the Place de la Concorde in Paris in 1962. Western Europeans learned that prosperity has its price as nineteenth-century cities were thrust into the automobile age.

income was clearly on the rise through the mid-1960s, and there was more disposable wealth than ever before. Prosperity encouraged new patterns of spending based on confidence in the economy. This new consumerism, in turn, was essential to economic growth and future productivity.

The social programs of the welfare state played an important role in promoting postwar consumption. People began to relax about their economic futures, more secure because of the provisions of unemployment insurance, old-age pensions, and health and accident insurance. The state alleviated the necessity of saving for a rainy day by providing protection that had formerly been covered by the savings of workers. In the mid-1950s, all over Western Europe, people began to spend their earnings, knowing that accidents, disasters, and sicknesses would be taken care of by the state.

The main items in the new consumption were consumer durables, above all televisions and automobiles. Refrigerators and washing machines also developed mass markets, as did the increased consumption of liquor and cigarettes. Increased leisure resulted in a boom in vacation travel. In addition to spending their salaries, Western Europeans began to buy on credit, spending money they had not yet earned. This, too, was an innovation in postwar markets. People sought immediate gratification through consumption by means of delayed payment against future earnings.

Welfare programs could be sustained only in an era of prosperity and economic growth, since they depended on taxation of income for their funds. Such taxation did not, however, result in a redistribution of wealth. Wealth remained in the hands of a few and became even more concentrated as a result of phenomenal postwar economic growth. In West Germany, for example, 1.7 percent of the population owned 35 percent of the society's total wealth.

Just as the welfare state did not redistribute wealth, it did not provide equal pay for equal work. In France, women who performed the same jobs as men received less pay. In typesetting, for example, women, who on average set 15,000 keystrokes per hour at the keyboards compared to 10,000 by men, earned 50 percent of men's salaries and held different titles for their jobs. Separate wage scales for women drawn up during the Nazi period remained in effect in West Germany until 1956. The skills associated with occupations performed by women were downgraded, as were their salaries. Women earned two-thirds or less of what men earned throughout West-

ern Europe. Welfare state revenues were a direct result of pay-scale inequities. Lower salaries for women meant higher profits and helped make economic recovery possible.

The Eastern Bloc and Recovery

In the years before his death in 1953, Joseph Stalin succeeded in making the Soviet Union a vital industrial giant second only to the United States. The Soviet economy experienced dramatic recovery after 1945, in spite of the severe damage inflicted on it during the war. The production of steel, coal, and crude oil skyrocketed under state planning. Heavy industry was the top priority of Soviet recovery, in keeping with prewar commitments to rapid modernization. In addition, the postwar Soviet economy assumed the new burdens of the development of a nuclear arsenal and an expensive program for the exploration of space. Stalin maintained the Soviet Union on the footing of a war economy, restricting

Many basic needs are provided for under Britain's cradle-to-grave social welfare system. Here mothers and children line up to receive orange juice. Vitamins and milk are also provided for growing children.

utopia lost

The pig's name is Napoleon. The farmer who drinks too much and loses control of his animals is named Jones. In his "fairy tale" titled *Animal Farm*, George Orwell gives us a deceptively simple but frightening tale of rebellion and tyranny. The barnyard animals of Farmer Jones know they are exploited by their human masters. When they can stand it no longer, they rise up against their oppression. Their revolution succeeds only when one animal, a pig, emerges as the revolutionary leader, the consolidator of revolutionary aims. He is named Napoleon.

The animals' cause is just: they want equality and fair treatment for their labors. They dream of a utopian world, a place free of care and filled with comforts. But in the process of wresting power and consolidating it, their paradise is lost, their utopia distorted. The seven commandments of the animal revolution are rewritten in such a way that all power resides in the dictator pig. All principles are reduced to one commandment: "All animals are equal, but some animals are more equal than others." A desire for a better life has produced a dictatorship that is far worse than the human tyranny the animals overthrew.

George Orwell created a dystopia, a utopia turned inside out, a dream that ends as a nightmare, a paradise lost in a new hell of oppression. In the same tradition as Thomas More's sixteenth-century masterpiece *Utopia*, Orwell's story uses fable to criticize contemporary institutions and events. In his parable of farmyard life, Orwell intended to "fuse political purpose and artistic purpose into one whole" in an assault on totalitarianism. Orwell's novel appeared in 1946. *Animal Farm* is recognizably an indictment of the Russian Revolution, an event that Orwell thought had soured under Stalinist rule and one that had colored the politics of the twentieth century with false hope. It served as a fitting herald to Cold War politics in the West.

Yet *Animal Farm* indicts more than communist rule in one country. It is a fairy tale without a moral, a profoundly cynical appreciation of the advances of civilization in the twentieth century. The civilization that Orwell judged so negatively had made important advances in science, technology, state organization, and a rhetoric of equality and welfare. For the donkeys, horses, and chickens of the farmyard—as for people in his own society—liberal and democratic values shrivel when squared off against the realities of power and force. In the end, the farm grows richer but the animals do not. The dreams of a better life, of the luxuries that electric power could bring, fade. The pigs become the ruling class, controlling information in mysterious files, memoranda, and reports. Neither technology nor government bureaucracy has improved animal life. The animals now work harder to support a greedy and parasitic ruling class.

Most unsettling of all, the animals lack their own history, remembering only what they are told was their past. In the concluding pages of the work, an old donkey by the name of Benjamin, who has lived through the prerevolutionary and revolutionary periods and is now under the yoke of the new tyrant pig, declares that things are little different from the old days: hunger, hardship, and disappointment are the unalterable laws of life. His memory serves as the only historical record. Napoleon now lives in Farmer Jones's house, sleeps in his bed, wears his clothes, and drinks his whiskey. In the greatest perversion of the transfer of power, the pig now walks on his two hind legs, terrifyingly humanized.

Orwell's fusion of politics and art did not stop with *Animal Farm*. In *Nineteen Eighty-Four* (1949), he created an equally horrifying picture of the future, one that does not resort to animal parables but instead portrays a mechanized kind of inhuman tyranny, that of Big Brother, a force that sees all and controls all, down to what people think. Both works were banned in the Soviet Union and in communist Eastern Europe. Many intellectuals of the postwar period shared Orwell's concern for what they saw as the erosion of personal freedom. For Orwell, the liberal traditions of the West were as hollow as the socialist promises of the Soviet world were dangerous. The great principle of equality, the cornerstone of the Western political tradition, served as the instrument of a new oppression. Standing on the edge of the abyss of war, revolution, and human suffering in the twentieth century, Orwell peered into the future and saw ahead only what he was trying to leave behind.

occupational mobility and continuing to rely on forced-labor camps.

The Soviet Union's standard of living remained relatively low in these years when Western Europe was undergoing a consumer revolution. Soviet consumption was necessarily stagnant, since profits were plowed back as investments in future heavy industrial expansion. In the Soviet Union and throughout the Eastern Bloc countries, women's full participation in the labor force was essential for recovery. In spite of their presence in large numbers in highly skilled sectors like medicine, Soviet and Eastern Bloc women remained poorly paid, as did women in the West. Soviet men received higher salaries for the same work on the grounds that they had to support families.

With Stalin's death, new leaders recognized the need for change, especially with regard to the neglected sectors of agricultural production and consumer products. The Soviet population was growing rapidly, from 170 million in 1939 to 234 million in 1967. Khrushchev promised the Russian people lower prices and a shorter workweek, but in 1964, when he fell from power, Russians were paying higher prices for their food than before. With a declining rate of development, the Soviet economy lacked the necessary capital to advance the plans for growth in all sectors. Defense spending nearly doubled in the short period between 1960 and 1968.

The nature of planned Soviet growth exacted heavy costs in the Eastern Bloc countries. Adhering to the Soviet pattern of heavy industrial expansion at the expense of agriculture and consumer goods, East Germany nearly doubled its industrial output by 1955, despite having been stripped of its industrial plants by the Soviet Union before 1948. Czechoslovakia, Bulgaria, Romania, and Yugoslavia all reported significant industrial growth in this period. Yet dislocations caused by collectivization and heavy defense expenditures stirred up social unrest in East Germany, Czechoslovakia, Poland, and Hungary. The Soviet Union responded with some economic concessions but on the whole stressed common industrial and defense pursuits, employing ideological persuasion and military pressure to keep its reluctant partners in line. The slowed growth of the 1960s, the delay in development of consumer durables, and the inadequacy of basic foodstuffs, housing, and clothing were the costs that Eastern Bloc citizens paid for their inefficient and rigid planned economies dedicated to the development of heavy industry. In Eastern Europe and the Soviet Union, poverty was virtually eliminated, however, as the state subsidized housing, health care, and higher education, which were available to all.

family strategies

The pressures on European women and their families in 1945 were often greater than in wartime. Severe scarcity of food, clothes, and housing required careful management. Women who during the war held jobs in industry and munitions plants earned their own money and established their own independence. After the war, in victorious and defeated nations alike, women were moved out of the work force to make room for returning men. Changing social policies affected women's lives in the home and in the workplace and contributed to the politicization of women within the context of the welfare state.

Demography and Birth Control. Prewar concerns with a declining birthrate intensified after World War II. In some European countries, the birthrate climbed in the years immediately following the war, an encouraging sign to observers who saw in this trend an optimistic commitment to the future after the cessation of the horrors of war. The situation was more complicated in France and the United States, where the birthrates began to climb even before the war was over. Nearly everywhere throughout Europe, however, the rise in the birthrate was momentary, with the United States standing alone in experiencing a genuine and sustained "baby boom" until about 1960. In Germany and in Eastern Europe (Poland and Yugoslavia, for example), the costs of the war exacted heavy tolls on families long after the hostilities ended. On average, women everywhere were having fewer children by choice.

Technology had expanded the range of choices in family planning. In the early 1960s, the birth control pill became available on the European and American markets, primarily to middle-class women. Europeans were choosing to have smaller families. The drop in the birthrate had clearly preceded the new technological interventions that included intrauterine devices (IUDs), improved diaphragms, sponges, and more effective spermicidal creams and jellies. The condom, invented a century earlier, was now sold to a mass market. Controversies surrounded the unhealthy side effects of the pill and the dangerous Dalkon shield, an IUD that had not been adequately tested before marketing and that resulted in the death or sterilization of thousands of

Report to the Twentieth party congress

Like Stalin before him, the Soviet leader Nikita Khrushchev perceived that the Soviet Union was locked in a worldwide struggle with the United States and Western capitalist nations. The experiences of the Korean War and the escalation of the nuclear arms race prompted him to proceed with wariness in foreign policy. In his now famous speech before the Twentieth Party Congress in February 1956, Khrushchev, as first secretary of the Communist party, accused the United States, England, and France of imperialism and pleaded for the peaceful coexistence of communism and capitalism, confident that, in the end, communism would win the day.

Soon after the Second World War ended, the influence of reactionary and militarist groups began to be increasingly evident in the policy of the United States of America, Britain, and France. Their desire to enforce their will on other countries by economic and political pressure, threats, and military provocation prevailed. This became known as the "positions of strength" policy. It reflects the aspiration of the most aggressive sections of present-day imperialism to win world supremacy, to suppress the working class and democratic and nation-liberation movements; it reflects their plans for military adventures against the socialist camp.

The international atmosphere was poisoned by war hysteria. The arms race began to assume more and more monstrous dimensions. Many big U.S. military bases designed for use against the USSR and the People's Democracies [East European countries under Soviet control] were built in countries thousands of miles from the borders of the United States. "Cold war" was begun against the socialist camp. International distrust was artificially kindled, and nations set against one another. A bloody war was launched in Korea; the war in Indochina dragged on for years.

. . . The Leninist principle of peaceful coexistence of states with different social systems has always been and remains the general line of our country's foreign policy. . . . To this day the enemies of peace allege that the Soviet Union is out to overthrow capitalism in other countries by "exporting" revolution. It goes without saying that among us Communists there are no supporters of capitalism. But this does not mean that we have interfered or plan to interfere in the internal affairs of countries where capitalism still exists.

When we say that the socialist system will win in the competition between the two systems—the capitalist and the socialist—this by no means signifies that its victory will be achieved through armed interference by the socialist countries in the internal affairs of the capitalist countries. Our certainty of the victory of communism is based on the fact that the socialist mode of production possesses decisive advantages over the capitalist mode of production. Precisely because of this, the ideas of Marxism-Leninism are more and more capturing the minds of the broad masses of the working people in the capitalist countries, just as they have captured the minds of millions of men and women in our country and the People's Democracies. [*Prolonged applause.*] We believe that all working men in the world, once they have become convinced of the advantages communism brings, will sooner or later take the road of struggle for the construction of socialist society.

women. Religious leaders spoke out on the moral issues surrounding sexuality without reproduction. Information about their reproductive lives became more accessible to young women. Illegal abortions continued to be an alternative for women. In France and Italy, birth control information was often withheld from the public. Abortion was probably the primary form of birth control in the Soviet Union in the years following the war.

The Family and Welfare. Concurrent with a low birthrate was a return to family life and family values in the years after the war. Those who had lived through the previous 20 years were haunted by the memories of the Great Depression, severe economic hardships, destructive war, and the loss of loved ones. Women and men throughout Western Europe and the United States embraced family values and a return to normal life, even if they did not opt for large families. Expectations for improved family life placed new demands on welfare state programs. They also placed increased demands on mothers, whose presence in the home was now seen as all-important for the proper development of the child. Handbooks for mothers proliferated, instructing them in the "science" of child-rearing. The best-seller *Baby and Child Care* by Dr. Benjamin Spock was typical of such guides.

European states implemented official programs to encourage women to have more children and to be better mothers. *Pronatalism*, as this policy was known, resulted from an official concern over low birthrates and a decline in family size. It is unlikely that pronatalism was caused by a fear of a decline in the labor force, since the influx of foreign workers, refugees from Eastern Europe, and migrant laborers from poorer southern European nations provided an expanding labor pool. Other considerations about racial dominance and women's proper role seem to have affected the development of policies. In 1945, Lord Beveridge (1879–1960), the architect of the British welfare state, emphasized the importance of women's role "in ensuring the adequate continuance of the British race" and argued that women's place was in the home: "During marriage most women will not be gainfully employed. The small minority of women who undertake paid employment or other gainful employment or other gainful occupations after marriage require special treatment differing from that of single women."

Welfare state programs differed from country to country as the result of a series of different expectations of women as workers and women as mothers. Konrad Adenauer, chancellor of West Germany, spoke of "a will to children" as essential for his country's continued economic growth and prosperity. In Great Britain, the welfare system was built on the ideal of the mother at home with her children. With the emphasis on the need for larger families—four children was considered desirable in England—English society focused on the importance of the role of the mother. Family allowances determined by the number of children were tied to men's participation in the work force; women were defined according to their husbands' status. The state welfare system strengthened the financial dependence of English wives on their husbands.

In Great Britain, anxiety over the low birthrate was also tied to the debate over equal pay for women. Opponents of the measure argued that equal pay would cause women to forgo marriage and motherhood and

should therefore be avoided. There was a consensus about keeping women out of the work force and paying them less in order to achieve that end.

The French system of *sécurité sociale* defined all women, whether married or single, as equal to men; unlike English women, all French women had the same rights of access to welfare programs as men. This may well have reflected the different work history of women in France and the recognition of the importance of women's labor for reconstruction of the economy. As a result, family allowances, pre- and postnatal care, maternity benefits, and child care were provided on the assumption that working mothers were a fact of life. French payments were intended to encourage large families and focused primarily on the needs of children. More and more women entered the paid labor force after 1945, and they were less financially dependent on their husbands than were their British counterparts.

Both forms of welfare state—the British that emphasized women's role as mothers and the French that accepted women's role as workers—were based on different attitudes about the nature of gender difference and equality. Women's political consciousness developed in both societies. The women's liberation movements of the late sixties and early seventies found their roots in the contradictions of differing welfare policies.

The Beginnings of Women's Protest. The 1960s was a period of protest in Western countries as people demonstrated for civil rights and free expression. The movement against U.S. involvement in Vietnam was fueled by the activism of the black civil rights movement. Pacifist and antinuclear groups united to "ban the bomb." Women participated in all of these movements, and by the end of the 1960s had begun to question their own place in organizations that did not acknowledge their claims to equal rights, equal pay, and liberation from the oppression of male society. A new critique began to form within the welfare state that indicated there were cracks in the facade.

One book in particular, written after World War II, captured the imagination of many women who were aware of the contradictions and limitations placed on them by state and society. *The Second Sex* (1949), written by Simone de Beauvoir (1908–86), a leading French intellectual, analyzed women's place in the context of Western culture. By examining the assumptions of political theories, including Marxism, in the light of philosophy, biology, history, and psychoanalysis, de Beauvoir uncovered the myths governing the creation of

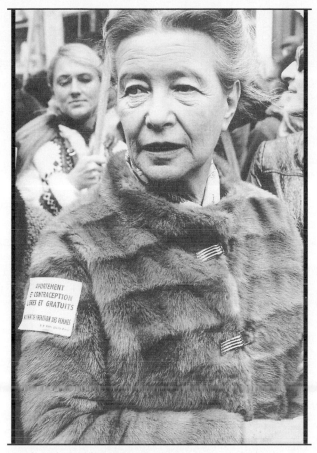

French novelist and feminist Simone de Beauvoir participated in demonstrations for women's issues such as family planning

the female self. By showing how the male is the center of culture and the female is "other," de Beauvoir urged women to be independent and to resist male definitions. *The Second Sex* became the handbook of the women's movement in the 1960s.

A very different work, *The Feminine Mystique*, appeared in 1963. In this work, author Betty Friedan voiced the grievances of a previously politically quiescent group of women. Friedan was an American suburban homemaker and the mother of three children when she wrote about what she saw as the schizophrenic split in her own middle-class world between the reality of women's lives and the idealized image of the perfect homemaker. After World War II, women were expected to find personal fulfillment in the domestic sphere. Instead, Friedan found women suffering from the "sickness with no name" and the "nameless desperation" of a profound crisis in identity.

A new politics centering on women's needs and women's rights slowly took root. The feminist critique did not emerge as a mass movement until the 1970s. Youth culture and dissent among the young further informed growing feminist discontent. But the agenda of protest in the sixties, reinforced by social policies, accepted gender differences as normal and natural.

youth culture and the generation gap

Youth culture was created by outside forces as much as it was self-created. Socialized together in an expanding educational system from primary school through high school, the young came to see themselves as a social force. They were also socialized by marketing efforts that appealed to their particular needs as a group.

The prosperity that characterized the period from the mid-fifties to the mid-sixties throughout the West provided a secure base from which radical dissenters could launch their protests. The young people of the 1960s were the first generation to come of age after World War II. Although they had no memory themselves of the destruction of that war, they were reminded daily of the imminence of nuclear destruction in their own lives. The combination of the security of affluence and the insecurity of Cold War politics created a widening gap between the world of decision-making adults and the idealistic universe of the young. To the criticisms of parents, politicians, and teachers, the new generation responded that no one over 30 could be trusted.

New styles of dress and grooming were a rejection of middle-class culture in Europe and the United States. Anthropologists and sociologists in the 1960s began studying youth as if they were a foreign tribe. The *generation gap* appeared as the subject of hundreds of specialized studies. Adolescent behavior was examined across cultures. Sexual freedom and the use of drugs were subjected to special scrutiny. But, above all, it was the politics of the young that baffled and enraged many observers. When the stable base of economic prosperity began to erode as a result of slowed growth and inflation in the second half of the sixties—first in Western Europe and then in the United States—frustrated expectations and shrinking opportunities for the young served as a further impetus for political action.

The second sex

Simone de Beauvoir, one of France's leading intellectuals, wrote philosophical treatises, essays, and novels that drew on a wide variety of cultural traditions and synthesized philosophy, history, literary criticism, and Freudian psychoanalysis in her studies of the human condition. *The Second Sex*, which first appeared in French in 1949, has subsequently been translated into many languages and has appeared in numerous editions throughout the world. It has served as a call to arms for the feminist movement, provoking debate, controversy, and a questioning of the fundamental gender arrangements of modern society.

A man never begins by presenting himself as an individual of a certain sex; it goes without saying that he is a man. The terms *masculine* and *feminine* are used symmetrically only as a matter of form, as on legal papers. In actuality the relation of the two sexes is not quite like that of two electrical poles, for man represents both the positive and the neutral, as is indicated by the common use of *man* to designate human beings in general; whereas woman represents only the negative, defining by limiting criteria, without reciprocity. In the midst of an abstract discussion it is vexing to hear a man say: "You think thus and so because you are a woman"; but I know that my only defense is to reply: "I think thus and so because it is true," thereby removing my subjective self from the argument. It would be out of the question to reply: "And you think the contrary because you are a man," for it is understood that the fact of being a man is no

peculiarity. A man is in the right in being a man; it is the woman who is in the wrong. It amounts to this: just as for the ancients there was an absolute vertical with reference to which the oblique was defined, so there is an absolute human type, the masculine. Woman has ovaries, a uterus; these peculiarities imprison her in her subjectivity, circumscribe her within the limits of her own nature. It is often said that she thinks with her glands. Man superbly ignores the fact that his anatomy also includes glands, such as the testicles, and that they secrete hormones. He thinks of his body as a direct and normal connection with the world, which he believes he apprehends objectively, whereas he regards the body of woman as a hindrance, a prison, weighed down by everything peculiar to it. "The female is a female by virtue of certain *lack* of qualities," said Aristotle; "we should regard the female nature as afflicted with a natural defective-

sex, drugs, and protest

Increased emphasis on fulfillment through sexual pleasure was one consequence of the technological revolution in birth control devices, and it led to what has been called a revolution in sexual values in Western societies in the 1960s. The sexual revolution drew attention to sexual fulfillment as an end in itself. Women's bodies were displayed more explicitly than ever before in mass advertising in order to sell products from automobiles to soap. Sex magazines, sex shops, and movies were part of an explosion in the marketing of male sexual fantasies in the 1960s.

Sweden experienced the most far-reaching reforms of sexual mores in the 1960s. Sex education became part of every school's curriculum, contraceptive information was widely available, and homosexuality was decriminalized. Technology allowed women and men to separate pleasure from reproduction but did nothing to

alter men's and women's domestic roles. Pleasure was also separated from familial responsibilities, yet the domestic ideal of the woman in the home remained. Some women were beginning to question their exploitation in the sexual revolution. In the early 1970s, this issue became the basis of mass feminist protest.

Just as sexuality was invested with new meaning within the context of protest, so was the use of drugs. Drug use was not new in history: through the ages drugs have been taken as painkillers or pleasure enhancers and used in religious and cultural rituals. Soldiers in nineteenth-century wars in Europe and America returned home addicted to opium and morphine, which they were given when treated for their wounds. In the 1960s American soldiers in Vietnam turned to drugs as an escape from the horrors of war.

Drugs began to pervade Western cultures in apparently harmless ways. At the end of the nineteenth century in the United States, the newly created Coca-Cola ness." And Saint Thomas for his part pronounced woman to be an "imperfect man," an "incidental" being. This is symbolized in Genesis where Eve is depicted as made from what Bossuet called "a supernumerary bone" of Adam.

Now, woman has always been man's dependent, if not his slave; the two sexes have never shared the world in equality. And even today woman is heavily handicapped, though her situation is beginning to change. Almost nowhere is her legal status the same as man's, and frequently it is much to her disadvantage. Even when her rights are legally recognized in the abstract, long-standing custom prevents their full expression in the mores. In the economic sphere men and women can almost be said to make up two castes; other things being equal, the former hold the better jobs, get higher wages, and have more opportunity for success than their new competitors. In industry and politics men have a great many more positions and they monopolize the most important posts. In addition to all this, they enjoy a traditional prestige that the education of children tends in every way to support, for the present enshrines the past—and in the past all history has been made by men. At the present time, when women are beginning to take part in the affairs of the world, it is still a world that belongs to men—they have no doubt of it at all and women have scarcely any. To decline to be the Other, to refuse to be a party to the deal—this would be for women to renounce all the advantages conferred upon them by their alliance with the superior caste. Man-the-sovereign will provide women-the-liege with material protection and will undertake the moral justification of her existence; thus she can evade at once both economic risk and the metaphysical risk of a liberty in which ends and aims must be contrived without assistance. Indeed, along with the ethical urge of each individual to affirm his subjective existence, there is also the temptation to forgo liberty and become a thing. This is an inauspicious road, for he who takes it—passive, lost, ruined—becomes henceforth the creature of another's will, frustrated in his transcendence and deprived of every value. But it is an easy road; on it one avoids the strain involved in undertaking an authentic existence. When man makes of woman the *Other*, he may, then, expect her to manifest deep-seated tendencies toward complicity. Thus, woman may fail to lay claim to the status of subject because she lacks definite resources, because she feels the necessary bond that ties her to man regardless of reciprocity, and because she is often very well pleased with her role as the *Other*.

From Simone de Beauvoir, *The Second Sex* (1949).

was actually made with cocaine, a drug derived from the coca shrub. Another ingredient in the soft drink formula was the kola nut, which contains the stimulant caffeine. In the 1950s and 1960s, chemical technology made possible the manufacture of synthetic drugs. Pharmaceutical industries in Europe and the United States expanded by leaps and bounds with the mass marketing of amphetamines, barbiturates, and tranquilizers. Doctors prescribed these new drugs for a variety of problems from obesity to depression to sleeplessness. People discovered that these drugs had additional mood-altering effects.

Marijuana grew in popularity as a safe "recreational" drug, especially among college and university students in the 1960s. In fact, young people were the primary users of drugs of all sorts, including synthetic drugs like the hallucinogen LSD (lysergic acid diethylamide). Hallucinogens were considered by their proponents to be mind-expanding drugs that permitted the achievement of new levels of consciousness. Drugs used by young people affluent enough to afford them served to widen the gap between the generations still further.

The protests of 1968

Student protest, which began at the University of California at Berkeley in 1964 as the Free Speech movement, by the spring of 1968 had become an international phenomenon that had spread to other American campuses and throughout Europe and Japan. A common denominator of protest, whether in New York, London, or Tokyo, was opposition to the war in Vietnam. Growing numbers of intellectuals and students throughout the world condemned the U.S. presence in Vietnam as an immoral violation of the rights of the Vietnamese people and violent proof of U.S. imperialism.

Student protesters shared other concerns in addition to opposition to the war in southeast Asia. The

The cold war

1947	Marshall Plan starts U.S. aid to European countries
1947	Pro-Soviet governments established in Poland, Hungary, Bulgaria, and Romania
1948	Pro-Soviet government established in Czechoslovakia
1949	European states and United States form North Atlantic Treaty Organization (NATO)
1949	Federal Republic of Germany and German Democratic Republic established
1949	Soviet Union creates Council for Mutual Economic Assistance (Comecon)
1949	Soviet Union tests its first atomic bomb
1950–1953	Korean War, ending with the partition of Korea
1953	United States and Soviet Union develop hydrogen bombs
1955	Formation of Warsaw Pact
1956	Hungarian uprising and subsequent repression by Soviet military forces
1957	The Netherlands, Belgium, Luxembourg, France, Italy, and West Germany form the European Economic Community (EEC), also called the Common Market
1957	Soviet Union launches first satellite, *Sputnik I*
1961	Berlin Wall built
1961–1973	U.S. troops engaged in Vietnam
1962	Cuban missile crisis
1963	Soviet Union and United States sign Nuclear Test-Ban Treaty
1968	Prague Spring uprising in Czechoslovakia, quelled by Soviet Union

the wider society. Student demonstrations met with brutal police repression and violence, and rioting was common.

European students, more than their American counterparts, were also experiencing frustration in the classroom. European universities were unprepared to absorb the huge influx of students in the 1960s. The student–teacher ratio at the University of Rome, for example, was 200 to 1. In Italian universities in general, the majority of over half a million students had no contact with their professors. The University of Paris was similarly overcrowded.

For the most part, student protest was primarily a middle-class phenomenon. In France, for example, only 4 percent of university students came from below the middle class. Higher education had been developed after World War II to serve the increased needs of a technocratic society. Instead of altering the social structure, which politically committed student protesters thought it should do, mass education served as a certifying mechanism for bureaucratic and technical institutions. Many of the occupations that students could look forward to were in dead-end service jobs or in bureaucratic posts.

The Beatles were the icons of the sixties—the era of pacifism, when young people experimented with sexual liberation, the drug culture, and Eastern mysticism.

growing activism on American campuses was aimed at social reform, student self-governance, and a recognition of the responsibilities of the university in the wider community. In West Germany, highly politicized radical activists, a conspicuous minority among the students at the Free University of Berlin, directed protest out into

"subterranean homesick blues"

The gap between the generations yawned into a gulf as rock music became political in the mid-1960s. Bob Dylan, an American rock performer, introduced folk music to the genre with songs of social protest like "Blowin' in the Wind" and "Only a Pawn in Their Game." Rock music was denounced as a communist plot as performers urged their audiences to "Make Love, Not War." Dylan's "Subterranean Homesick Blues" targeted the hypocrisy of his society.

Subterranean Homesick Blues
Bob Dylan

Johnny's in the basement
Mixing up the medicine
I'm on the pavement
Thinking about the government
The man in the trench coat
Badge out, laid off
Says he's got a bad cough
Wants to get it paid off
Look out kid
It's somethin' you did
God knows when
But you're doin' it again
You better duck down the alley way
Lookin' for a new friend
The man in the coon-skin cap
In the big pen
Wants eleven dollar bills
You only got ten

Maggie comes fleet foot
Face full of black soot
Talkin' that the heat put
Plants in the bed but
Look out kid
You're gonna get hit
But users, cheaters
Six-time losers
Hang around the theaters
Girl by the whirlpool
Lookin' for a new fool
Don't follow leaders
Watch the parkin' meters

Ah get born, keep warm
Short pants, romance, learn to dance
Get dressed, get blessed

Try to be a success
The phone's tapped anyway
Maggie says that many say
They must bust in early May
Orders from the D.A.
Look out kid
Don't matter what you did
Walk on your tip toes
Don't try "No Doz"
Better stay away from those
That carry around a fire hose
Keep a clean nose
Watch the plain clothes
You don't need a weather man
To know which way the wind blows

Get sick, get well
Hang around a ink well
Ring bell, hard to tell
If anything is goin' to sell
Try hard, get barred
Get back, write braille
Get jailed, jump bail
Join the army, if you fail
Please her, please him, buy gifts
Don't steal, don't lift
Twenty years of schoolin'
And they put you on the day shift
Look out kid
They keep it all hid
Better jump down a manhole
Light yourself a candle
Don't wear sandals
Try to avoid the scandals
Don't wanna be a bum
You better chew gum
The pump don't work
'Cause the vandals took the handles

Student dissent reflected the changing economy of the late 1960s. Inflation, which earlier in the decade had spurred prosperity, was spiraling out of control in the late sixties. In the advanced industrial countries of Western Europe and later in the United States, the growth of the postwar period was slowing down. Economic opportunity was evaporating and jobs were being eliminated. One survey estimated that only one in three Italian university graduates in 1967 was able to find a job. The dawning awareness of shrinking opportunities in the workplace for students who had attained their degrees and been properly certified further aggravated student frustration and dissent. Anger about the uncertainties of their future mixed with the realization of the boredom of the careers that awaited them upon graduation.

By the late sixties, universities and colleges provided the students a forum for expressing their discontent with advanced industrial societies. In their protests, student activists rejected the values of consumer society. The programs and politics of the student protesters aimed to transform the world in which they lived. Student protesters in France chanted *"Métro, boulot, dodo,"* a slang condemnation of the treadmill-like existence of those who spent their lives in a repetitive cycle of subway riding (*Métro*), mindless work (*boulot*), and sleep (*dodo*). The spirit of protest was expressed in the graffiti and posters that seemed to appear overnight on the walls of Paris:

"Action must not be a reaction—but a creation"

"Power to the Imagination"

"The revolution will be won when the last bureaucrat is strangled in the entrails of the last cop"

"The state is each one of us"

In May 1968, French protest spread beyond the university when workers and managers joined students in paralyzing the French economy and threatening to topple the Fifth Republic. Between 7 and 10 million people went on strike in support of worker and student demands. White-collar employees and technicians joined blue-collar factory workers in the strike. Student demands, based on a thoroughgoing critique of the whole society, proved to be incompatible with the wage and consumption issues of workers. But the unusual, if short-lived, alliance of students and workers shocked those in power and induced reforms.

Students riot in Paris in 1968. The student protests of the late 1960s were sparked by the war in Vietnam and by disillusionment with the present and uncertainty about the future.

The division of the world into two camps framed the recovery of combatant nations dealing with the losses of World War II. The Cold War instilled fear in the populations who lived on both sides of the divide. Yet the Cold War also created the terms for stability following the upheaval of war. It promoted prosperity that preserved the long-term policies of both the United States and the Soviet Union in the twentieth century. The Soviet Union had buffered itself from the West by creating a ring of friendly nations on its borders and had continued its race to industrialize. The belief that the USSR had won the war for the Allies and the sense of betrayal that followed the war determined the outlook of grim distrust shared by postwar Soviet leaders who had survived the years from 1939 to 1945.

The United States, on the other hand, found itself playing the role of rich uncle in bankrolling the European recovery. Its long-term commitment to promoting its own economic interests by helping future trading partners led it also into playing the role of policeman throughout the world. The escalating war in Vietnam made America vulnerable to growing world criticism and to growing domestic discontent.

The gains of economic recovery began to unravel in the mid-1960s. In the West, rising expectations of consumer societies came up against the harsh realities of slowed growth. In the East, frustrated nationalism, the lack of consumer goods, and repressive conditions resulted in low morale, demonstrations, and outright conflict. After Stalin's death, resources were diverted to consumer goods, but there was little measurable improvement in the quality of life.

The nations of Europe and the United States sensed that they stood at a crossroads in 1968. Whether the future inspired confidence or fear remained to be seen. The threat of nuclear annihilation had considerably diminished. The euphoria of students in the West and the Prague Spring in the East seemed to be more an interlude than a turning point. If the rivalry between East and West no longer dominated the international arena, what lay ahead?

Mastering the chapter

To review the main points of the chapter, be sure you can explain the significance of each of the following.

Terms/Concepts/Events	People	Places
Cold War	Mohandas Gandhi	Elbe River
United Nations	Ho Chi Minh	Federal Republic of
NATO	Charles de Gaulle	Germany
Warsaw Pact	Nikita Khrushchev	German Democratic
brinksmanship	Imre NagyRepublic	Republic
de-Stalinization	Alexander Dubcek	Benelux countries
Prague Spring	Marshal Tito	
domino theory	John Maynard Keynes	
Marshall Plan	Jean Monnet	
European Economic Community	Simone de Beauvoir	

suggestions for further Reading

Regulating the cold war

* Franz Ansprenger, *The Dissolution of the Colonial Empires* (London: Routledge, 1989). An analysis of Europe's withdrawal from Asia and Africa following the Second World War, beginning with an examination of post–World War I imperialism.

* Walter Lafeber, *America, Russia, and the Cold War, 1945–1966* (New York: John Wiley and Sons, 1978). A Cold War revisionist interpretation of American foreign policy in the two decades after World War II. Lafeber examines the influence of Soviet and American domestic policies on the two nations' foreign policies.

* William Roger Louis and Roger Owen, eds., *Suez 1956: The Crisis and Its Consequences* (New York: Oxford University Press, 1989). A series of essays resulting from new research into the origins and consequences of the Suez crisis.

  Charles S. Maier, ed., *The Origins of the Cold War and Contemporary Europe* (New York: Franklin Watts, 1978). A series of essays considering the origins of the Cold War and its impact on the political economy of Europe.

* Charles S. Maier, *In Search of Stability: Explorations in Historical Political Economy* (Cambridge: Cambridge University Press, 1987). Covers a wide variety of issues affecting twentieth-century Europe, including the foundation of American international economic policy after World War II and the conditions for stability in Western Europe after 1945.

* Bruce D. Porter, *The USSR in Third World Conflicts: Soviet Arms and Diplomacy in Local Wars, 1945–1980* (Cambridge: Cambridge University Press, 1984). A case study approach to the Soviet Union's changing postwar policies toward the third world that centers on local wars in Africa and the Middle East.

* Tony Smith, ed., *The End of the European Empire: Decolonization After World War II* (Lexington, MA: Heath, 1975). A collection of articles dealing with the rapid decolonization of the overseas holdings of Great Britain, France, the Netherlands, and Belgium and the growing agitation and organization of nationalist movements.

Reconstructing Europe

* Stanley Hoffman and Charles Maier, *The Marshall Plan: A Retrospective* (Boulder, CO: Westview Press, 1984). Based on a commemorative conference held at Harvard University 35 years after George C. Marshall's address there, this collection combines the work of specialists and of actual participants in the plan's implementation.

* Michael J. Hogan, *The Marshall Plan: America, Britain, and the Reconstruction of Western Europe* (Cambridge: Cambridge University Press, 1987). A thoroughly researched argument on the continuity of U.S. economic policy in the twentieth century. Hogan counters the belief that the Marshall Plan was merely a response to the Cold War.

* Derek W. Urwin, *Western Europe Since 1945: A Political History*, 4th ed. (London: Longman, 1989). An updated general survey of postwar politics, with a special focus on the problems of reconstruction and the role of the resistance after 1945.

creating the welfare state

* Simone de Beauvoir, *The Second Sex* (New York: Knopf, 1963). The author, one of France's leading intellectuals in the twentieth century, describes the situation of women's lives in the postwar West by placing them within the context of the history and myths governing Western culture.

* Jane Jenson, "Both Friend and Foe: Women and State Welfare," *Becoming Visible: Women in European History*, ed. Renate Bridenthal, Claudia Koonz, and Susan Stuard (Boston: Houghton Mifflin, 1987). This essay illuminates the mixed blessing of the welfare state for women after 1945 by focusing on the experiences of women in Great Britain and France.

* Walter Laqueur, *Europe Since Hitler: The Rebirth of Europe* (New York: Penguin Books, 1982). Surveys politics, economy, society, and culture in order to explain Europe's postwar resurgence.

  Susan Pederson, *Family, Dependence, and the Origins of the Welfare State: Britain and France, 1914–1945* (Cambridge: Cambridge University Press: 1994). Although this work covers the earlier period, the comparative approach to differing attitudes and policies provides an essential background to understanding family policy in postwar Europe.

* Denise Riley, *War in the Nursery: Theories of the Child and Mother* (London: Virago Press, 1983). Treats social policies of postwar pronatalism within the context of the popularization of developmental and child psychologies in Europe, with special attention to Britain and the United States and an emphasis on the postwar period as a turning point in attitudes toward women and the family.

* Mary Ruggie, *The State and Working Women: A Comparative Study of Britain and Sweden* (Princeton, NJ: Princeton University Press, 1984). A sociological study comparing the economic status of women in two European welfare states.

youth culture and the generation gap

* David Caute, *The Year of the Barricades: A Journey Through 1968* (New York: Harper & Row, 1988). More than its title suggests, this work is an overview of postwar youth culture on three continents. The politics of 1968 is featured, although other topics regarding the counterculture, lifestyles, and cultural ramifications are considered.

  John R. Gillis, *Youth and History: Tradition and Change in European Age Relations, 1770–Present* (New York: Academic Press, 1981). Connects the history of European youth to broad trends in economic and demographic modernization over the last 200 years.

* Margaret Mead, *Culture and Commitment: The New Relationships Between the Generations in the 1970s* (New York: Columbia University Press, 1978). This series of essays, written by one of America's premier anthropologists, explores the origins and consequences of the generation gap, with special attention to Cold War politics, historical conditions, and technological transformations.

*Paperback edition available.

the contemporary west, 1968 to the present

lost in space

The Cold War was waged in many arenas after World War II. None was so novel as the competition for space between the United States and the Union of Soviet Socialist Republics. Committed to space exploration and discovery in spite of the economic demands it placed on its people, the Soviet Union had gained the advantage early over the United States. Soviet leaders proudly reminded the world that they inaugurated the space age in 1957 by launching two Soviet space satellites, *Sputnik* I and *Sputnik* II, thereby establishing the Soviet Union as a world force in science and technology. Adding further to its prestige, Yuri Gagarin, a Soviet citizen, became the first person launched in space in 1961.

The Age of Sputnik set high stakes for the United States, as the other superpower undertaking high-cost space exploration, which included new standards of scientific education for America's children. After 1957, space exploration and achievement became a measure of national prowess and a source of patriotic pride among the citizens of the two nations.

The competition for space was not merely about scientific dominance and prestige. From the very beginning, the exploration of outer space was measured in military terms, both offensive and defensive. The majority of satellites, for example, launched by both sides had military purposes of surveillance, intelligence-gathering, and communications. Manned space missions became a cornerstone of space exploration and appealed to the imaginations of national communities that embraced the conquest of new frontiers in terms similar to justifications of imperial conquest in the nineteenth century.

Space programs in the two nations, always costly, fell on tough times with the winding down of the Cold War and economic hardships and recessions that affected East and West. Missions that laid claim to advancement

During the 313 days that Russian Cosmonaut Sergei Krikalev spent in space, the Soviet Union ceased to exist, and his hometown of Leningrad was renamed St. Petersburg.

of scientific knowledge persisted, and as recently as 1996 the examination of a rock from Mars that indicated the possibility that life existed on that planet billions of years ago fueled political arguments for the ongoing support for the National Aeronautics and Space Agency (NASA).

The Soviets launched one such science-based mission in 1991, apparently routine but with unforeseen consequences. Soviet cosmonaut Sergei Krikalev was sent into space for ten months. His comrade, Aleksandr Volkov, joined him for the last five months of the mission as commander of the Mir space outpost. Both left the earth as Soviet citizens and returned as representatives of a nation that no longer existed, men without a country, wearing uniforms and insignia of a defunct service, and part of a program that had been virtually dismantled. While orbiting the earth, they learned of revolution at home and the collapse of their mother country. They understood the shortages being experienced back home when their own requests for supplies were denied. In place of the requested honey, now no longer available from the former Soviet republic that supplied it, a provisioning ship delivered to them instead horseradish and onions. Strikes on the ground in the former Soviet space center that launched the cosmonauts seemed to pose a threat to their safe return. If the nation that sponsored the mission no longer existed, what country would bring them back? Workers on the ground assured the cosmonauts that they would not be lost in space, even as the wages of ground workers were cut, some lost their jobs, and others went on strike in protest.

When they were brought back to earth, the cosmonauts returned to a vastly altered world. For one thing, communism, an ideology that had inspired followers around the globe, had been defeated in its country of origin, its leaders replaced, and its party disbanded. The official Communist party daily newspaper, *Pravda*, closed its doors. Cosmonaut Krikalev, born in Leningrad, returned as a Russian citizen, not a Soviet one, and his natal city now had a new name, St. Petersburg, to reflect the rejection of its revolutionary past and a return to its czarist roots. The other cosmonaut, Volkov, born in the Ukraine, was now a citizen of a new republic, Ukraine, which enjoyed a troubled relationship with the new Russian state, now in control of what was left of the space program. While it might have looked the same from space, the map of Europe was being redrawn. The space colleagues, formerly both Soviet citizens, were now citizens of rival nations.

Focus Questions

1. How did the ideas of *glasnost* and *perestroika* help bring about the end of the Soviet Union?
2. What social, economic, and political forces contributed to German reunification?
3. How did the collapse of communist regimes in Russia and Eastern Europe promote national and ethnic conflict?
4. How did the treaty signed by the nations of the European Community at Maastricht in 1991 create both hopes and fears of European unity?
5. In what ways have women's lives in Eastern and Western Europe been similar and in what ways have their experiences differed since the 1960s?
6. What is the difference between the European Community and the European Union?
7. How have democracy and nationalism come into conflict since 1968?

The irony of the space program, which had been a centerpiece of the Cold War, was that by the early 1990s it sought to promote international cooperation, as astronauts of different countries were invited to collaborate on teams of mixed national origins. National rivalries on the ground, new borders, and new disputes, however, threatened to undermine cooperation in space as well as on earth. Increased nationalism accompanied the disintegration of empire. These former Soviet citizens touched down to discover that where there once was peace, enmity threatened. They also came home to food riots, shortages, poor working conditions, high unemployment, and an uncertain future for the space program.

The experience of the former Soviet cosmonauts provides a metaphor for what was happening to people throughout central and eastern Europe as well as in the territory of the former Soviet Union. Communism had been toppled, the Cold War was over, and the map of Europe was being redrawn. Millions of Europeans from both East and West struggled to make sense of the new nationalism that motivated breakaway republics, ethnic minorities, and long-standing national communities to express their political aspirations and grievances in new and sometimes violent ways. The alien world was not the one that Krikalev and Volkov explored in outer space but the one they found when they returned to earth.

Toppling communism in the soviet union

The Cold War, while it lasted from the post-1945 period to the late 1980s, had provided a way of ordering the world. It served to divide friend from foe, to create spheres of economic interest, and to promote market relations among blocs of nations. Also, in a seemingly contradictory sense, it was a conflict that promoted stability and peace, no matter how uneasy. Even the Soviet action against Czechoslovakia and other expressions of dissent in eastern Europe in 1968 reminded the world of the power of Communist unity in the Eastern Bloc.

Yet the chinks in the facade of unity were already present by the mid-1960s. The use of military intervention to resolve the Czech crisis opened a new era governed by what came to be known as the Brezhnev Doctrine. Leonid Brezhnev (1906–82), general secretary of the Communist party and head of the Soviet Union from 1966 to 1982, established a policy whereby the Soviet Union claimed the right to interfere in the internal affairs of its allies in order to prevent counterrevolution. Brezhnev was responsible for the decision to intervene in Czechoslovakia, arguing that a socialist state was obliged to take action in another socialist state if the survival of socialism was at stake. The Brezhnev Doctrine influenced developments in eastern Europe throughout the next decade. After 1968, rigidity and stagnation characterized the Soviet, East German, and Czechoslovak governments, as well as rule in other eastern European states.

With repression came protest. At first weak but growing in volume, dissent from within communist countries commanded international attention in the mid-1970s. Criticism of the Soviet Union had been strongly repressed in Eastern Bloc nations. In 1985 the accession to power of Mikhail Gorbachev as general secretary ushered in a new age of openness. A strong critique of domestic and foreign policy aims infused movements for reform throughout the Eastern Bloc, thereby undermining communism and Cold War politics.

soviet Dissent

In response to state repression during the Brezhnev years, dissidence took on a variety of forms. Some dissenters sought an international forum for their cause. Growing numbers of Soviet Jews, for example, petitioned to emigrate to Israel in order to escape anti-Semitism within the Soviet Union and to embrace their own cultural heritage. Some of the 178,000 who were allowed to emigrate found their way to western Europe and the United States, and stories of persecution were published in the world press. In May 1976 a number of Soviet dissidents, including Jewish protesters, commanded interna-

Legend:
- Slavic
- Baltic
- Turkic
- Uralian
- Romance
- Armenian
- Caucasian
- Iranian
- Other languages or sparsely populated areas

Republics

1 Russia S.F.S.R.	9 Armenia
2 Estonia	10 Azerbaijan
3 Latvia	11 Kazakhstan
4 Lithuania	12 Turkmenia
5 Byelorussia	13 Uzbekistan
6 Ukraine	14 Tajikistan
7 Moldavia	15 Kirghizia
8 Georgia	

Republics of the Soviet Union

tional attention by openly declaring themselves united for the purpose of securing human rights in the Soviet Union. The state retaliated by charging organizers with anti-Soviet propaganda and handing out harsh prison sentences or relegating protesters to mental asylums, drawing the criticism of democratic states.

Another vehicle of protest was the self-published, privately circulated manuscripts in either typed or mimeographed form, known as *samizdat*, which became the chief means of dissident communication. For the most part, dissidents were members of a university-trained professional elite. The leading Soviet dissident

The funeral of Andrei Sakharov. The scientist-dissenter was eulogized at a public service held in Lenin Stadium in Moscow.

of this period was Andrei Sakharov (1921–89), internationally renowned as the father of the Soviet hydrogen bomb and a scientist of great eminence. In 1968 he wrote *Thoughts on Progress, Peaceful Coexistence, and Intellectual Freedom*, a work that opposed Communist party rule in favor of a liberal democratic system. For his dissident activities and criticism of the invasion of Afghanistan, Sakharov was sentenced to a life in exile in Gorky in 1980.

Sakharov was not the only figure of stature to engage in protest. The novelist Alexander Solzhenitsyn denounced the abuses of Soviet bureaucracy in *Cancer Ward*, *The Gulag Archipelago*, and *One Day in the Life of Ivan*

Denisovich, works that were highly respected in the West. The historian Roy Medvedev also criticized Stalinism and continued to speak out in favor of peace and democratic principles in the Gorbachev years.

For almost three decades, dissidents waged a lonely battle within the Soviet Union for civil liberties, democratic rights, and the end of the nuclear arms race. In the 1980s it became clear to Soviet watchers in the West that demands for recognition of nationalities were an important part of the dissident movement in the Soviet Union that echoed similar demands throughout eastern Europe. Now cultural, religious, ethnic, and ecological concerns and demands for national autonomy joined

career advancement, communist-style

Interviewed in 1990, Klara Paramova, a Soviet lecturer who taught the English language in Moscow, told of her decision to join the Communist party as a means of upward mobility. Although fluent in English and "the best pupil in the class," she realized that membership in the Party was the only way of getting the job she wanted in higher education. Her disillusionment with the tenets of communism was typical of many Soviet citizens of her generation and younger.

·

I'm thirty-nine and I joined the Party at twenty-four so that means fifteen years as a member in, what is the phrase, good standing—paying my dues, sometimes going to a meeting to elect a delegate to this conference or a representative for that occasion, but not much else. I'm not an active member, I don't take my share of responsibilities. Why? Well, because I am not a good Party member, as I told you. And I'm not a good Party member because I don't believe in Communism, it is as simple as that. Nor do a lot of Party members, does that surprise you? It should not. . . . Joining the Party was for me entirely a calculated way of furthering my career. It had nothing at all to do with ideals. . . .

But . . . I am still a member of the Party and I shall remain one. At its simplest it is because if I was to do something that would draw attention to me, like not continuing my membership and stepping down from it—well, then I think, almost certainly, I would lose my present job as senior lecturer. I got it because of those who were in contention for the vacancy, I was the only one who was in the Party—and from this it is correct to deduce, yes, the members of the appointments committee were nearly all themselves members of the Party. . . .

I am not a Communist, and don't believe in Communism, for the simple reason that I think it takes too rosy a view of human beings and it doesn't work. You could say I am not a Christian either, for almost the same reasons. I know there are good Communists and bad Communists, and not all the bad things done in the name of Communism are the fault of the system of itself. But I think it lacks things, and some of the things it lacks are serious. First I would put self-respect or a feeling of the value of people as individuals. I have never been to the West, but of course at the place where I work I have met a lot of people from the West—and there is something about their manner, their self-assurance, which is unlike that of Russian people. I think this can only be the fault of Communism: it may have done, it has done, many good things, but it has never somehow built up dignity in people. There are many catch-phrases, "the dignity of labour" and such sayings; but there isn't one for the dignity of a person as a person, it's an idea which doesn't even exist.

I think I will not change in my views very much now, not at the age of forty: I think I will remain as I am, a Party member but not a good one because I don't share its beliefs.

forces with protests for civil liberties and economic freedom. The reinstatement of Sakharov, one of the Soviet Union's most visible dissidents, as a national hero just before his death and after years of persecution was one of the best barometers of the social revolution that was transforming Soviet politics in the 1980s. Following the demise of the Soviet Union, Solzhenitsyn returned to his native Russia, a celebrity in the West and still virtually unknown to his countrymen.

Détente: The soviets and the west

The Nuclear Test Ban Treaty of 1963 inaugurated a period of lessening tension between the Eastern and Western blocs. By the early 1970s, both the United States and the Soviet Union recognized the importance of closer relations between the superpowers. The USSR and the United States has achieved nuclear parity. Now, from positions of equality, both sides expressed a willingness to negotiate. The 1970s became the decade of détente, a period of cooperation between the two superpowers. The Strategic Arms Limitation Treaty, known as SALT I, signed in Moscow in 1972, limited defensive antiballistic missile systems.

The refusal of the United States in 1979 to sign SALT II to limit strategic nuclear weapons ushered in the "dangerous decade" of the 1980s, when the possibility of peaceful coexistence seemed crushed. U.S. President Ronald Reagan, during his first term in office, revived traditional Cold War rhetoric and posturing. Nuclear strategists on both sides were once again talking about nuclear war as possible and winnable. Popular concern over the nuclear arms race intensified in the United States, in the Soviet Union, and throughout Europe as the United States pursued the Strategic Defense Initiative (SDI), popularly called "Stars Wars" because of its futuristic, science fiction quality of promised superiority through technology to a single power. At the least, the new system threatened an escalation in nuclear defense spending on both sides in an attempt to end the stabilizing parity between the United States and the Soviet Union.

In spite of grandstanding gestures such as the Star Wars initiative, East–West relations after 1983 were characterized by less confrontation and more attempts at cooperation between the Soviet Union and the United States. The world political system itself appeared to have stabilized, with a diminution of conflict in the three main arenas of superpower competition—the third world, China, and western Europe. By the end of 1989, leaders in the East and West declared that the ideological differences that separated them were more apparent than real. They declared an end to the Cold War and sought a new and permanent détente.

The end of the soviet union

By the mid-1980s, Soviet leaders were weighing the costs of increasing internal dissent and the promise of benefits from improved relations with the West. During the 40 years that followed World War II, a different kind of leader was being forged in the ranks of the Communist party among a generation that favored more open political values and dynamic economic growth. Typical of this new generation of political leaders was Mikhail Gorbachev, who was, above all, a technocrat, someone who could apply specialized technical knowledge to the problems of a stagnant Soviet economy.

As the youngest Soviet leader since Stalin, Gorbachev set in motion in 1985 bold plans for increased openness, which he called *glasnost*, and a program of political and economic restructuring, which he dubbed *perestroika*. Appointing men who shared his vision to key posts, especially in the foreign ministry, Gorbachev extended the olive branch of peace to the West and met with President Ronald Reagan in a superpower summit in Geneva. By 1989, many observers inside and outside the Soviet Union felt that a new age was at hand as the Soviet leader loosened censorship, denounced Stalin, and held the first free elections in the Soviet Union since 1917.

The Soviet Union had undergone dramatic changes after Stalin's death in 1953, and with his death, many Stalinist policies were repudiated. The 1960s witnessed increased prosperity as the population became more urban (180 million people lived in cities by mid-1970) and more literate (the majority of the population remained in school until age 17).

Soviet citizens of the 1960s and 1970s were better fed, better educated, and in better health than their parents and grandparents had been. When people grumbled over food shortages and long lines, the Soviet state reminded them of how far they had come. Yet while economic growth continued throughout the postwar years, the rate of growth was slowing down in the 1970s. Some planners feared that the Soviet Union could never catch up to the United States, Japan, and West Germany. Soviet citizens were increasingly aware of the sacrifices and suffering that economic development had cost them in the twentieth century and of the

perestroika

In describing what he called "New Thinking for Our Country and the World" in his subtitle to his book *Perestroika,* Soviet leader Mikhail Gorbachev offered a cogent explanation of the need for peaceful competition as the means of avoiding a third world war. He justifies perestroika historically by alluding to the history of war and revolution in the West since the nineteenth century.

In developing our philosophy of peace, we have taken a new look at the interdependence of war and revolution. In the past, war often served to detonate revolution. One may recall the Paris Commune which came as an echo of the Franco-Prussian war, or the 1905 Russian Revolution triggered by the Russo-Japanese war. The First World War provoked a real revolutionary storm which culminated in the October Revolution in our country. The Second World War evoked a fresh wave of revolutions in Eastern Europe and Asia, as well as a powerful anti-colonial revolution.

All this served to reinforce the Marxist-Leninist logic that imperialism inevitably generates major armed confrontations, while the latter naturally creates a "critical mass" of social discontent and a revolutionary situation in a number of countries. Hence a forecast which was long adhered to in our country: a third world war, if unleashed by imperialism, would lead to new social upheavals which would finish off the capitalist system for good, and this would spell global peace.

But when the conditions radically changed so that the only result of nuclear war could be universal destruction, we drew a conclusion about the disappearance of the cause-and-effect relationship between war and revolution. The prospects of social progress "coincided" with the prospects of the prevention of nuclear war. At the 27th CPSU [Communist Party of the Soviet Union] Congress we clearly "divorced" the revolution and war themes, excluding from the new edition of the Party Program the following two phrases: "Should the imperialist aggressors nevertheless venture to start a new world war, the peoples will no longer tolerate a system which drags them into devastating wars. They will sweep imperialism away and bury it." This provision admitting, in theory, the possibility of a new world war was removed as not corresponding to the realities of the nuclear era.

Economic, political and ideological competition between capitalist and socialist countries is inevitable. However, it can and must be kept within a framework of peaceful competition which necessarily envisages cooperation. It is up to history to judge the merits of each particular system. It will sort out everything. Let every nation decide which system and which ideology is better. Let this be decided by peaceful competition, let each system prove its ability to meet man's needs and interests. The states and peoples of the Earth are very different, and it is actually good that they are so. This is an incentive for competition. This understanding, of a dialectical unity of opposites, fits into the concept of peaceful coexistence.

From Mikhail Gorbachev, *Perestroika* (1987).

disparities in the standards of living between the capitalist and communist worlds. Due to outmoded technology, declining older industries, pollution, labor imbalances, critical shortages of foodstuffs and certain raw materials, and a significant amount of hidden unemployment in unproductive industries, discontent became more widespread.

Consumer products were either of poor quality or not available. Because of limited provisions, people queued on the average of two hours every day to purchase food and basic supplies. Housing, when it was available, was inadequate, and there were long waiting lists for vacancies. The black market flourished, with high prices on everything from Western blue jeans to Soviet automobiles. People saw corruption in their ruling elite, who drove Western cars, wore Western clothes, had access to material goods not available to the general population, and lived in luxury.

The problem was not salaries. Workers were well paid, with more disposable income than ever before.

But purchasing power far outstripped supplies. The state system of production, which emphasized quantity over quality, resulted in overproduction of some goods and underproduction of others. The state kept prices low in order to control the cost of living, but low prices were a problem because they did not provide sufficient incentive for the production of better-quality goods.

Programs between 1985 and 1988 promised more than they delivered. The promises were part of the problem since they created unmet expectations. Modest increases in output were achieved, but people's demands for food and consumer goods were rising faster than they could be met. The Soviet Union did not increase imports of consumer durables or food to meet the demand, nor did the quality of Soviet goods improve appreciably. Rising wages only gave workers more money that they could not or would not spend on Soviet products. The black market was a symbol both of the economic failures of the state and of the growing consumerism of Soviet citizens. Rather than purchase poor-quality goods, Soviets chose to purchase foreign products at vastly inflated prices.

Although his economic reforms broke sharply with the centralized economy established by Stalin in the 1930s, Gorbachev candidly warned that he would not implement a consumption revolution in the near future. Many critics, including fellow communist Boris Yeltsin, felt that Gorbachev did not go far or fast enough with his economic reforms. In place of a controlled economy, Gorbachev offered a limited open market free of state controls for manufacturing enterprises organized on a cooperative basis and for light industry. He loosened restrictions on foreign trade, encouraged the development of the private sector, and decentralized economic decision-making for agriculture and the service sector.

Price increases and the importation of foreign goods, the two essential measures necessary for progress in the Soviet consumer economy, had been resisted by Gorbachev's predecessors as politically explosive. The state kept prices down in order to maintain the low cost of living. In contrast to the ingrained conservatism of his predecessors, Gorbachev represented experimentation, innovation, vitality, and a willingness to question old ways. For him, economic and political reforms had to be accomplished in concert; the economy, in other words, could only be restructured by "a democratization of our society at all levels."

Gorbachev's foreign policy also served his economic goals. Military participation in decision-making declined as state expenditures on defense were cut. Moscow had always borne larger military costs than Washington. Gorbachev recognized that Cold War defense spending must decline if the Soviet Union was to prosper: consumer durables had to take the place of weapons on the production lines. But here the transformation was bound to be slow. To this end, Gorbachev met with American President Ronald Reagan and agreed to systematic arms reduction and greater cooperation. In 1988, Soviet troops began the withdrawal from Afghanistan and completed the process by the fol-

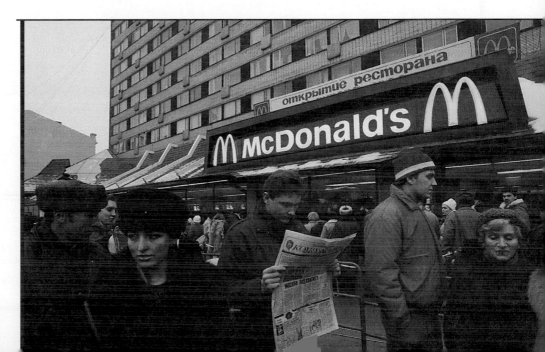

The Big Mac comes to Moscow. McDonald's opened its first Soviet fast-food outlet in 1990, just a few blocks from the Kremlin. Muscovites stood in long lines for milkshakes, fries, and the "Bolshoi Mak."

lowing year. Also in 1989, in a stunning reversal of the Brezhnev doctrine, the Soviet state refused to intervene in the upheavals that were sweeping eastern Europe.

Tensions became increasingly apparent internally over how Communist party rule and centralization could be coordinated with the demands for freedom and autonomy that Gorbachev's own reforms fostered. To gain credibility and backing, Gorbachev supported the formation of new parliamentary bodies, including a 2250-member Congress of People's Deputies in 1988. The new Congress soon became the forum for attacks on the Communist party and the KGB. In March 1989, in the first free elections held in the Soviet Union since 1917, Communist party officials suffered further reversals. Early in 1990, Gorbachev ended the Party's constitutional monopoly of power; the Party now no longer played a leading role in Soviet political life.

New political parties proliferated, some defending the old order but many demanding a total break with the past and with Communist ideology and programs. Among Gorbachev's harshest critics was his former ally and supporter, the former Moscow Party leader Boris N. Yeltsin, who began in 1987 to criticize Gorbachev's caution in implementing reforms. Later, as the popularly elected president of the Russian republic in 1990, Yeltsin called for a true democracy and decisive economic action.

Aware of his precarious political position, Gorbachev appeared to retrench by increasing control over the media and by attempting to consolidate his base of power. (See "Television and Revolutions," pp. 1038–1039.) In spite of these attempts, many felt that the regime was becoming authoritarian. Gorbachev was clearly walking a fine line in attempting to maintain stability, yet he was making no one happy— neither Communist party hardliners nor Western-oriented supporters of capitalism.

The shocking end to the Gorbachev experiment came in August 1991. A quasi-military council of Communist hard-liners seized power in order to restore Communist rule and reverse democratic reforms. Gorbachev was taken prisoner in his vacation home in the Crimea. Soviet citizens from the Baltic republics to Siberia protested the takeover, and tens of thousands of Muscovites poured into the streets to defy the tanks and troops of the rebel government. Three people were killed outside Russia's parliament building, which had become a rallying point for the protesters. The timing of the coup was probably determined by the fact that Gorbachev was scheduled to sign a new union treaty with nine of the republics the day following his house

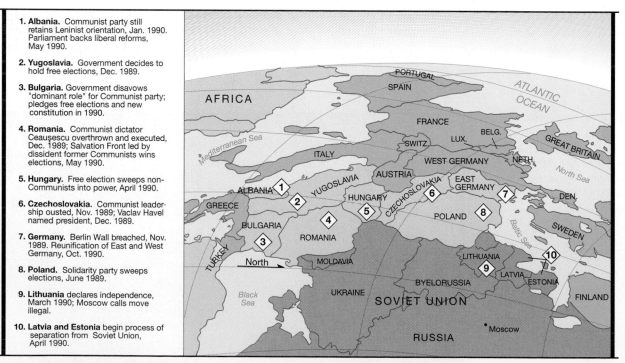

1. **Albania.** Communist party still retains Leninist orientation, Jan. 1990. Parliament backs liberal reforms, May 1990.

2. **Yugoslavia.** Government decides to hold free elections, Dec. 1989.

3. **Bulgaria.** Government disavows "dominant role" for Communist party; pledges free elections and new constitution in 1990.

4. **Romania.** Communist dictator Ceauşescu overthrown and executed, Dec. 1989; Salvation Front led by dissident former Communists wins elections, May 1990.

5. **Hungary.** Free election sweeps non-Communists into power, April 1990.

6. **Czechoslovakia.** Communist leadership ousted, Nov. 1989; Vaclav Havel named president, Dec. 1989.

7. **Germany.** Berlin Wall breached, Nov. 1989. Reunification of East and West Germany, Oct. 1990.

8. **Poland.** Solidarity party sweeps elections, June 1989.

9. **Lithuania** declares independence, March 1990; Moscow calls move illegal.

10. **Latvia and Estonia** begin process of separation from Soviet Union, April 1990.

Events in Eastern Europe, 1989–1990

arrest, which would have effectively broken up the Soviet empire.

Boris Yeltsin became a hero overnight, publicly defying the plotters, rallying popular support behind him, and helping convince Soviet army troops to disobey orders to attack the White House, as the parliament building in Moscow is called. After only two days, the coup d'état failed; Gorbachev returned to Moscow and banned the Communist party. Although Gorbachev retained his title of Soviet president, his prestige had been seriously damaged by the coup and by the challenge of Yeltsin's new dominance as a popular hero. In the national elections for the Congress of People's Deputies that followed, Boris Yeltsin, who had been dismissed as the head of the Moscow party in 1987, garnered 89 percent of the popular vote. As Yeltsin's star was on the rise, the Soviet Union was now in full collapse.

Russia and the New Republics

Following the events of August 1991, Russia embarked on a drive toward westernization in playing catch-up with capitalist nations. Liberal reformers pressed for privatization of industry and the lifting of price controls. The long lines in front of stores disappeared but inflation galloped to new heights, wiping out savings and pensions overnight. The black market, always in the shadows even in the most repressed of times, emerged boldly as a corrupt "mafia" became the new business leaders of Russia. New markets relied on dollars, and neither banks nor police had the power to stem illegal activities. A visitor to St. Petersburg (the former Leningrad) could ride in taxis whose meters registered the fare in dollars and could eat in restaurants in sections reserved for dollar-paying customers where the service and the food were better—all violations of government policy and law, although dealing in dollars was outlawed. The combined crises of inflation and rule by a gangster elite weakened the barely emergent market economy and undermined the Russian ruble, whose value crashed in October 1994. Recent figures indicate that, while a new wealthy class was emerging, as many as 30 percent of the population were indigent and lived below the poverty line. In 1996, the average monthly salary amounted to about $140 in its U.S. currency equivalent.

The economy was not the only problem facing the new Russian state. A crucial element in understanding the end of the Soviet Union was the nationalities problem—the claim to self-determination made by Soviet minorities. The Soviet Union listed 102 separate nationalities in its 1979 census. Twenty-two of those nationalities had populations of 1 million or more people. This very diversity contributed to the disintegration of the Soviet Union from within. As Gorbachev supported the demands for self-determination in eastern Europe, he faced similar claims to autonomy in a growing number of Soviet republics. The nationalities problem proved to be even more challenging to Gorbachev's regime than the free-market economy. In fact, the demands for more freedom in the marketplace went hand in hand with demands for greater cultural self-expression and political autonomy among minority nationalities.

The three major areas of nationalist conflict—Central Asia, Armenia, and the Baltic states—had been voicing grievances against the Soviet state since the

Economic problems, including high prices and shortages of food and goods, plague post–Soviet Union Russia. Here a woman tries to exchange a used sweater for fish at a flea market in Moscow.

television and revolutions

Television became the principal means of communicating current events to mass populations in the second half of the twentieth century. It was one of the chief consumer durables purchased by the newly prosperous populations of Europe and the United States beginning in the 1950s. Many intellectuals in the West feared that television, because of its uninspired programming, would dull the sensibilities of the masses and serve as a kind of opiate to cloud political judgment. Yet the role of television in politics was more complex, as events after 1968 made clear.

As East Germans in large numbers began buying televisions in the 1960s and 1970s, they faced a dilemma. Should they heed the prohibition of the East German government against watching West German television programs, whose signals were easily accessible to them, or should they disobey the law and take advantage of the varied entertainment that West German television afforded? East German leaders feared that the "corrupt" and "decadent" images of West Germany might attract their citizens. The East German head of state, Walter Ulbricht, warned ominously in 1961 that "the enemy of the people stands on the roof." He was talking about television antennas. However, the East German ban was impossible to enforce. Millions of East German viewers tuned in daily to West German programs and were able to compare the different standards of living in the two German nations and to learn of their own deprivation. The irony of awareness was that as East Germans achieved a higher standard of living and were able to buy more televisions, they became more and more discontented over their relatively low standard of living. Television contributed to rising expectations and the exodus of East Germans to the West.

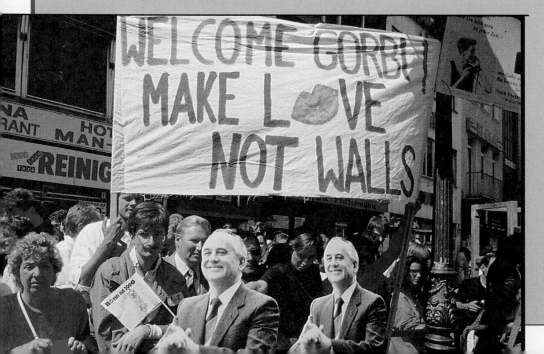

Soviet leader Mikhail Gorbachev enjoys a "photo op" during his visit to Bonn, Germany, in 1989.

Television played a central role in the Romanian revolution of 1989, spreading information and encouraging coordinated action throughout the country. One of the first acts of the Bucharest revolutionaries was to seize the headquarters of the state television station in order to transmit their own view of the conflict. When Nicolae and Elena Ceausescu were executed, the event was videotaped for broadcast to the Romanian nation and the world. In a still heavily rural society undergoing modernization, television provided the essential link between city and countryside. Television promoted concerted action. Romanians in Timosoara, a small city near the Hungarian border, and Bucharest, the nation's capital, simultaneously espoused the same revolutionary program and adopted the same symbols, as similarly doctored national flags made clear. The new regime governed by means of the television screen.

Politicians on both the left and the right used television for political ends. The political utility of television was exploited in France, where 60 percent of the population owned TV sets in 1968. Charles de Gaulle, president of the Fifth Republic, used the medium to appeal directly to the French people against the student-worker revolt that began in Paris in May 1968. Television was decisive in maintaining de Gaulle in power and mobilizing conservatives against the activists.

No one in the late twentieth century was better at grasping the power of the televised image than the Soviet leader Mikhail Gorbachev, who from the very beginning used the small screen to appeal directly to the Soviet people. He carefully cultivated his own image and used television to build a personal power base outside of the Communist party. Gorbachev was so successful in creating his own televised publicity that he became a popular figure within the Western capitalist world as well as within Soviet bloc countries. Crowds everywhere greeted him with the affectionate nickname "Gorby"; he was as easily recognizable in the streets of New York and Paris as in the streets of Moscow. Even the new revolutionaries in eastern Europe, who were intent on breaking their bonds with the Soviet state and who espoused democracy and capitalism, saw in Gorbachev the guarantee of their aspirations. Romanians chanted his name in public squares as they set about pulling down the Communist regime that ruled them.

Above all, television contributed to the revolution in expectations in Communist countries in the last quarter of the twentieth century. The contrast between the quality of life in the East and the West became inescapable for many educated eastern European and Soviet men and women who had access to travel and to television. Modern video technology did not cause revolutions, but it did convey information and provide political platforms. Television also publicized revolutions and, in some cases, sold dreams.

1920s. The protests of the 1980s differed from earlier outcries because claims were now being advanced by a new and educated urban elite, formed after World War II. Moscow relied on these groups of university-educated and upwardly mobile professionals to further its economic reforms. These groups now became the driving force behind demands for nationalist reforms. Gorbachev's challenge was to harness their protests for autonomy without undermining the Communist party's authority, and to make the Party the vehicle for these new social groups and their local needs. Because of the Party's inability to accommodate these new political ends, Gorbachev ultimately failed.

Ethic minorities, especially in the Soviet Baltic republics of Latvia, Lithuania, and Estonia, threatened the dominance of Party rule in favor of immediate self-determination. Endorsing diversity of opinion, individual rights, and freedom as the bases of good government, Gorbachev now had to deal with vocal nationalities who took him at his word. Large-scale riots erupted in Lithuania over demands for nationalist rights. In 1988 Estonians demanded the right of veto over any law passed in Moscow. The Russian minority in Estonia protested attacks and prejudicial treatment in the Estonian republic. In the same year, outright violence erupted in Azerbaijan as tens of thousands of Armenians took to the streets to demand the return of the Armenian enclave of Nagorno-Karabakh, incorporated into Azerbaijan in 1921. In the Azerbaijan capital of Baku, the center of Russia's oil-producing region, demonstrators demanded greater autonomy for their republic and the accountability of their deputies in Moscow. Violence between Azerbaijanis and Armenians resulted in 32 deaths and the displacement of tens of thousands. The state upheaval climaxed in December 1988, when an earthquake in Armenia killed 25,000 people. Soviet troops were placed in the area, ostensibly to deal with the aftermath of the natural disaster.

In 1986 university students in the central Asian republic of Kazakhstan incited two days of demonstrations and rioting over the removal of a corrupt local leader who was replaced with a Russian Party official. The Soviet government's attempts to clean up politics in the area betrayed a clumsy disregard for ethnic issues and seemed at odds with Gorbachev's commitment to decentralization. Crimean Tatars, who had been exiled in Islamic fundamentalist Kazakhstan since World War II, agitated for a return home.

One by one, all 15 of the Soviet republics proclaimed their independence, following the lead of the breakaway Baltic republics of Estonia, Lithuania, and Latvia. Having failed to agree on a new plan for union, Gorbachev and the leaders of ten republics transferred authority to an emergency State Council in September 1991 until a plan could be devised. By the end of the year, the Soviet Union was faced with serious food shortages and was bankrupt, unable to pay its employees and dependent on the financial backing provided by Yeltsin as head of the Russian state. Rejecting all Soviet authority, Russia, Belarus, and Ukraine joined together in December 1991 to form the Commonwealth of Independent States (CIS). Eight other republics followed their lead. The Soviet Union thereby came to its end on 21 December 1991 with the resignation of Mikhail Gorbachev, who had become a man without a state to rule. Russian President Yeltsin moved into Gorbachev's Soviet presidential offices at the Kremlin.

Many issues remained unresolved. The new political organization did not address the endemic problems of economic hardship, and left unanswered the questions of who would control the former Soviet Union's vast military machine, including its nuclear arsenal, and how trade networks and a stable monetary policy would be determined. Just as there were millions of Russians living beyond the borders of the Russian state with the rise of independent republics, there continued to be ethnic minorities within Russia who sought independence. Russia, on a smaller scale than its Soviet predecessor, was a federation of different ethnic minorities and a Russian majority population with no clear policy for autonomy or self-rule.

In the elections of December 1993 a post-Soviet constitution was approved. Ominously, ultranationalists and their demagogic leader, Vladimir Zhirinovsky, became a troubling presence in Russian politics as they combined forces with communists and other groups to receive almost 50 percent of the votes cast. Yeltsin's grasp of the reigns of power slipped as he faced challenges both from inside and outside the government. In the vacuum of power that resulted from the collapse of Soviet rule, regions operated autonomously and local rule was often supreme. After easily winning the national election in the summer of 1996, Yeltsin began his second term in failing health, hidden from public view, and under a heavy cloud of doubt about his ability to rule.

yeltsin and the chechen challenge

In the midst of this crisis of rule, in December 1994, Russia committed itself and 30,000 Russian troops to a war with another of its ethnic minorities, the secessionist Chechens. Russia began a 20-month war with rebel forces in Chechnya, a territory of plains and peaks in the Caucasus, which had also posed a problem for the former Russian Empire. In the nineteenth century, Muslims of the area waged a series of what they called "holy wars" to fend off the Russian invaders, but to no avail.

Following in the footsteps of their forebears and in a long tradition of resistance, secessionist Chechens challenged Russian rule that appeared insensitive to local needs. After almost two years of battle, Russian officials estimated that the death toll stood at 80,000, with some 240,000 wounded. The war was denounced in the international arena because of Russian attacks against the civilian population. Reportedly, 60 percent of schools, kindergartens, and nurseries were partly or fully destroyed. An estimated 80 percent of the war dead were civilian. Russian warplanes bombed rebel-occupied villages, and thousands of refugees fled their homes in search of shelter. By the summer of 1996, Russia appeared to have lost the war, despite the fact that it possessed the largest army in Europe deployed against an enemy estimated to be about 4000. Russian estimates were undoubtedly low, but the disparity in forces was nonetheless real.

Yeltsin promised to end the war, which proved so unpopular among Russians, in his 1996 reelection campaign. Yet critics of the truce negotiations that took place in August 1996 felt that he had attracted votes in bad faith. Yeltsin appeared to be reverting to his hawkish ways, with renewed bombing. Chechen forces responded by regaining control of Grozny, the region's capital city, in August 1996. A Chechen rebel leader also claimed responsibility for two terrorist bombings in Moscow during this period. Russian troops began a systematic withdrawal from Chechen cities following the fall of Grozny. Both sides agreed to a truce, similar to a half dozen such efforts in the preceding two years. The development of a peace plan that would acknowledge Chechen autonomy within the Russian state was acceptable to the rebels, who saw the advantage of regrouping their forces and the need for a break in the hostilities. The agreement proposed in the summer of 1996 called for a referendum in Chechnya in the year 2001 for the purpose of determining the future of the republic. But attempts at implementation of a peace plan demonstrated the fissures in Russian leadership as the national security adviser, Aleksandr Lebed, appeared to act without the full support of the Russian president. Yeltsin continued to remain out of public view, giving rise to speculation about his ability to rule. Kremlin officials expressed dismay that the move from Chechen autonomy threatened "Russian territorial integrity."

What had begun as a period of openness, restructuring, and commitment to democratic values had turned by the late 1990s into conflict, instability, and political uncertainty. Just as the ethnic question had ultimately pulled down the Soviet Union, it posed the single greatest threat to the stability of Russia, at least as powerful as economic hardship in threatening the future of the new Russian state. And economic hardship was great. Tied for most of the twentieth century to the control of a state-run economy, Russia appeared to lack the re-

Gathered in Electoral Headquarters, members of the Electoral Commission and the media monitor the late returns in the 1996 Russian presidential election that resulted in Boris Yeltsin's reelection.

Chechen women and Russian soldiers' mothers united in a peace march to try to bring an end to the war in Chechnya. Russian troops halted the women, who were on their way to the village of Samashki in western Chechnya, the site of an alleged massacre by Russian soldiers.

sources—infrastructural, financial, and human—to join the top ranks of productive nations.

Redrawing the Map of Europe

The year 1989 marked a watershed in the history of European politics. The beginnings of transformation were first evident in the Soviet Union. But no less dramatic transformations in central and eastern Europe among Warsaw Pact allies rivaled the democratization of Soviet political life in 1989. The democratic tide appeared irreversible as symbols of freedom and democratic cooperation proliferated throughout the region. One million people joined hands in a widely publicized event to form a 370-mile-long human chain that stretched across the Soviet Baltic republics of Estonia, Latvia, and Lithuania in protest against Soviet annexation in 1940. Other bodies defied borders, as in September 1989, when East Germans began a mass exodus into West Germany, voting with their feet for economic prosperity

and democracy. Poland and Hungary opted for democratic regimes, and Bulgarians ended the 35-year reign of the dictator Todor Zhivkov and endorsed parliamentary government. Tens of thousands of Czech demonstrators in the capital city of Prague typified the peaceful "velvet revolution" of the democratic movement that swept through eastern and central Europe as they poured into the streets to sing songs about freedom and cheer their new heroes, dissidents persecuted and jailed under the former communist regime, one of whom became president of the newly formed Czech Republic.

But by far the most dramatic symbol of communism's fall came late in 1989. In November, bulldozers moved against the Berlin Wall, the tangible symbol of Cold War politics that had cut Berlin in two since 1961. As this tangible barrier came down, people spoke of the birth of a new democratic age of free markets and free expression. Yet freedom was not the only force unleashed with the collapse of communism. Ugly battles based on longstanding grievances erupted. Groups intent on autonomy and independence vied with each other over territories and borders. Nowhere was violence more pronounced than in Bosnia, where a bloody

The crumbling of the eastern bloc

1972	East and West Germany normalize relations with the Basic Treaty
1980	Polish non-Communist labor union Solidarity established under the leadership of Lech Walesa
1985	Mikhail Gorbachev assumes leadership of the Soviet Communist party, introducing glasnost (increased openness) and perestroika (political and economic restructuring)
1989	Free elections in Poland lead to the ouster of the Communist regime
September 1989	Hungary opens its borders to the West
November 1989	German Democratic Republic lifts travel restrictions between East and West Germany
1990	Boris Yeltsin elected president of the Russian Republic
1990	Gorbachev ends the Communist party's monopoly of power
1990	Lech Walesa elected president of Poland
October 1990	Federal Republic of Germany and German Democratic Republic reunited
December 1991	Eleven former Soviet republics form Commonwealth of Independent States (CIS); Mikhail Gorbachev resigns and the Soviet Union is dissolved

war dragged on for years in the former Yugoslavia, and where the term *ethnic cleansing* laid bare the barbarity and genocide that were still very much a part of the Europe of the late twentieth century.

The unification of germany

The German Democratic Republic (East Germany) and the German Federal Republic (West Germany), divided by the victorious Allies following World War II, continued to develop after 1968 as two separate countries with different social, economic, and political institutions. On the surface, these differences seemed insurmountable. The Berlin Wall, erected by the East German government in 1961, bifurcated the former German capital and served its intended purpose of keeping East Germans confined behind it. East Germany's chief problem in the 1950s was the exodus of skilled workers and professionals in search of a better life in the West. The flow of emigration throughout the 1950s turned into a torrent in the first eight months of 1961, when the number of refugees fleeing from East to West Germany reached 160,000 people. The Berlin Wall was, more than anything else, erected to keep skilled and professional workers in East Germany. German leaders in the West continued to voice their long-term commitment to reunification, while East German leaders insisted on the independence and autonomy of their state.

From the 1960s through the 1980s East Germany underwent a series of economic transformations. By 1969 East Germany's economy was the strongest among Eastern Bloc nations, with the highest per capita output. But the oil crises of the 1970s undermined its prosperity by driving up the costs of production, so dependent on foreign fuel, and thereby driving up consumer prices. Trade deficits soared and consumer industries faltered.

In West Germany, meanwhile, politics took a new direction in 1969. Under the chancellorship of Social Democrat Willy Brandt, the new government promised to make the welfare state more responsive to social needs, to involve labor more directly in economic decision-making, and to attend to feminist demands regarding abortion, divorce, and pornography. Brandt captured international acclaim with his bold foreign policy of *Ostpolitik*, the establishment of cooperative politics with the East, for which he was awarded the Nobel Peace Prize in 1971. *Ostpolitik* was a clear break with superpower hegemony, as Brandt, in his own version of détente, seized the initiative without waiting for directions from the United States. At home, however, he was not always regarded as a hero, as his domestic policies underwent reversals and the fabric of the social–liberal coalition began to fray. The 1973 oil crisis brought about rising unemployment and a decline in consumer demand. Shrinking tax revenues and a high rate of inflation further limited Brandt's options.

Brandt resigned over an espionage scandal affecting one of his aides in 1974 and was succeeded by Social Democrat Helmut Schmidt, who continued Brandt's policies of rapprochement with the East. In 1981, Erich

"Nothing Lasts Forever" reads the sign hanging from the battered bust of Communist dictator Joseph Stalin being carried through the streets of Prague by Czech demonstrators celebrating the end of the Communist regime in their country.

Honecker, head of the East German state, met with Schmidt, head of the West German state, to discuss common concerns. Bonn and East Berlin were engaging in their own détente that, in retrospect, could be seen as securing the foundation for the subsequent unification. Helmut Kohl, a Christian Democrat who became chancellor in 1982, stressed the importance of individual enterprise and competition and ran a winning campaign with the slogan "Less State, More Market."

The two Germanies had been linked economically, if not politically, throughout most of the postwar period. When West Germany entered the European Community in 1957, it insisted that in matters related to trade the two Germanies were to be treated as one country. As a result, East Germany benefited from its free trade relationship with West Germany. This advantage provided an important part of East Germany's prosperity since the 1960s. West Germany, in turn, achieved much of its prosperity through export-led growth, and it found markets in East Germany.

In the 1980s West Germany stood as an economic giant, second in foreign trade only to the United States and far ahead of Japan. East Germany also established itself as an important trading nation—15th in the world in 1975. Nevertheless, citizens in East Germany were lured by the greater prosperity of the West. Applications for authorized immigration to West Germany increased in the 1980s, and in 1984 East Germany allowed 30,000 citizens to emigrate to the West. Throughout the late 1980s the emigration rate remained high, with an average exodus of 20,000 a year. With Hungary's refusal to continue to block the passage of East Germans into West Germany, the floodgates were opened: 57,000 East Germans migrated via Hungary within a matter of weeks. In the face of angry demonstrations, Honecker was forced to resign. The new government opened the Berlin Wall on 9 November 1989, ending all restrictions on travel between East and West. An East Germany with open borders could no longer survive as its citizens poured into the promised land of the West in record numbers. The West German government intervened to assist East Germany in shoring up its badly faltering economy; the West German deutsche mark was substituted for the East German currency. Monetary union

"There Are No Better-fed Refugees"

East Germany built the strongest economy in the Soviet bloc, but its standard of living lagged far behind that of West Germany

	Federal Republic of Germany (West)	German Democratic Republic (East)
Population	61 million	17 million
Life Expectancy	For men, 71.2 years; for women, 78.1 years	For men, 69.5 years; for women, 75.4 years
Gross National Product	$1.12 trillion	$207.2 billion
Public Spending on Education	9.4% of all government expenditures	5.5% of all government expenditures
New Books Published	50,903 volumes	5636 volumes

Source: Statistical Yearbook, Unesco, 1988; Demographic Yearbook, United Nations; CIA World Factbook, 1988.

prefigured political unification. In October 1990 Germany became a single, united nation once again.

Germans represent the largest nationality in Europe west of Russia. Other Europeans feared the prospect of a united Germany, although publicly European leaders endorsed the principle of the self-determination of peoples. In addition, western Europeans were troubled by the impact a united Germany might have on plans for European unification in the European Union. Not least of all, Germans themselves feared reunification. Former East Germans were wary about marginalization and second-class citizenship, while West Germans worried that their poor cousins from the east would act as a brake on West Germany's sustained economic expansion. Nevertheless, Germany committed itself to a course of action that promised to make of the German nation a unified people whose economy would continue to dominate European and world markets.

Eastern Europe: Nationalism and Ethnicity

The Soviet example of restructuring and Gorbachev's calls for reforms and openness gave the lead to eastern Europe. In 1988 Gorbachev, speaking before the United Nations, assured the West that he would not prevent eastern European satellites from going their own way:

Reunified Germany, October 1990

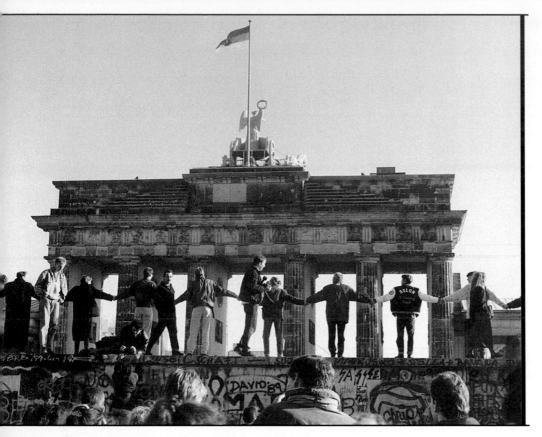

In a scene that symbolizes the end of the Cold War, people dance atop the Berlin Wall in November 1989. Soon pieces of the demolished wall were being sold as souvenirs.

"Freedom of choice is a universal principle," the Soviet head of state declared. Poland's first free elections in 40 years were part of a vast mosaic of protest from which a pattern began to emerge in the spring of 1989.

Poland, the most populous nation in eastern Europe, had played an important role in the Soviet bloc because of its strategic location as a corridor for supplies to the Soviet Union's 380,000 troops in East Germany. Yet its economy was never robust, and it had a 20-year history of worker protest and resistance. When economic hardship was aggravated in December 1970 by major price increases for food, workers spontaneously went on strike, with demonstrations beginning in the shipyards of Gdansk, the Baltic seaport in northern Poland, and spreading to other cities. The Polish government responded by sending the militia to teargas the workers, some of whom were killed in the melee.

More protests followed before prices were rolled back and the Soviet Union provided economic aid. Throughout the 1970s, the Polish government, based on one-party rule, drew loans from abroad for investment in technology and industrial expansion. The government increased its foreign indebtedness rather than raise prices at home. In 1976, however, price increases were again decreed. A new wave of spontaneous strikes erupted, forcing the government to rescind the increases.

Poland's indebtedness to the West rose from $2.5 billion in 1973 to $17 billion in 1980. Poland was sinking into the mire of ever higher interest payments that absorbed the country's export earnings. At the beginning of July 1980, the government was forced yet again to raise food prices. Shipyard workers in Gdansk were ready, solidly organized in a new noncommunist labor union called Solidarity under the leadership of a politically astute electrician named Lech Walesa. The union staged a sit-down strike that paralyzed the shipyards. Union committees coordinated their activities from one factory to the next and succeeded in shutting down the entire economy. The government agreed to a series of union-backed reforms known as the Gdansk Accords, which, among other measures, increased civil liberties and acknowledged Solidarity's right to exist.

Within a year, Solidarity had an astounding 8 million members out of a population of 35 million. The Catholic church lent important support to those who opposed Communist rule. Dissident intellectuals also cast their lot with the organized workers in demanding reforms. General Wojciech Jaruzelski became prime minister in February 1981, but the situation of shortages did not change appreciably. Jaruzelski attempted to curb the union's demands for democratic government and participation in management by harsh measures: he declared martial law on 13 December 1981. Jaruzelski was trying to save the Polish Communist party by using the Polish military to crack down on the dissidents. The Soviet response was to do nothing. Soviet leaders knew that the size of the Polish protest would require a massive retaliation, which they were unwilling to undertake—especially since to do so would fly in the face of Western opinion that supported the Solidarity movement. In addition, the Soviet Union had other problems in this period: in 1979 it began a war in Afghanistan to secure Communist rule. Moscow feared that the Islamic fundamentalism at its border threatened to stir up the rapidly growing Muslim populations in six Soviet republics—Azerbaijan, Kazakhstan, Uzbekistan, Tadzhikistan, Turkmenistan, and Kirgizia. Poland, as a result, was left to Polish rule.

Martial law in Poland produced military repression. Solidarity was outlawed and Walesa was jailed. The West did not lose sight of him: in 1983 the union leader was awarded the Nobel Peace Prize for his efforts. After years of negotiations and intermittent strikes, Solidarity was legalized once again in 1989. The economy was in dire straits, and Jaruzelski knew that he needed Solidarity's cooperation: he agreed to open elections. At the polls, Solidarity candidates soundly defeated the Communist party. Poland was the first country anywhere to turn a Communist regime out of office peacefully. Yet Poland did not pull out of the Warsaw Pact. As Lech Walesa explained it in 1989 on West German television, "Poland cannot forget where it is situated. You know we are in the Warsaw Pact. That cannot be changed." Poland needed above all its own perestroika, its own restructuring of its economy and administration.

The great challenge before the Solidarity government, as for the Communist regime that preceded it, was economic recovery. Inflation drove food prices up at the rate of 50 percent a month. The Polish government committed itself to freeing the zloty from state control and making it a convertible currency, one that could be bought and sold for other currencies on the international currency market, so that Polish goods could compete in world markets. Poland faced the task of earning enough foreign trade credits to alleviate its indebtedness and to justify foreign investment. In the mid-1990s, Poland continued its pursuit of a free market economy by attracting Western companies and corporations to open subsidiaries and to do business within its borders, as inflation slowed to a still high 20 to 30 percent. A prosperous management class began emerging.

Poland sought economic recovery through aggressive pursuit of foreign investment. Daewoo Motor Company of Korea invested more than $1 billion to refurbish two automotive assembly plants in Poland. By the year 2000 it is estimated that the two plants will manufacture nearly 100,000 vehicles, half of them for export.

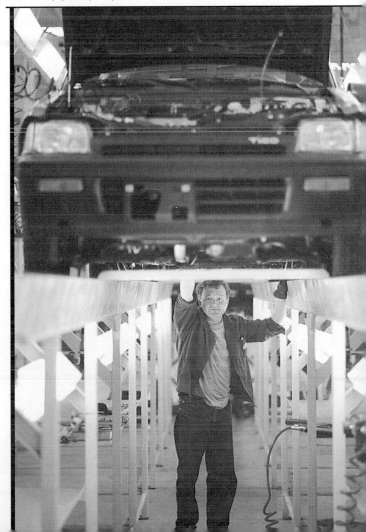

In the same period as the Polish free elections, Hungary dismantled the barbed-wire fences on its Austrian border; all of its borders to the West were opened in September 1989. People wanted freedom of movement and freedom of expression. Everywhere East Europeans demanded democratic institutions modeled on those of Western nations. "People power" swept away Communist leaders and ousted the Communist party, many believed for good. The leader of the New Socialist party in Hungary, Imre Pozsgay, declared: "Communism does not work. We must start again at zero." Unlike other eastern European countries, Hungary had begun experimenting cautiously with free markets and private control as early as the 1970s. As a result, Hungary was best positioned to engage in serious trade with western Europe and made the most prosperous adjustment to democratic autonomy.

Czechoslovakia's revolution began with angry university students. Singing Czech versions of protest songs like "We Shall Overcome," student protesters were reminiscent of the student activists of 1968. They tried to give flowers to police, who responded by bludgeoning the protesters. This spark touched off a mass movement that within days drove out the Czech Communist party. Idealism and growing public sympathy were on the side of the protesters. The dissident playwright Vaclav Havel, released from jail just before the demonstrations began, emerged as the leader of the democratic opposi-

tion and was elected president of the new government. He became a powerful spokesperson for democratic institutions and oversaw a relatively peaceful separation of the Czech Republic from Slovakia.

All of these countries underwent what were considered "velvet revolutions," characterized by a lack of violence and an apparently smooth passage to a new order. The year 1989 did not end, however, without bloody upheaval. Romania under communist dictator Nicolae Ceaucescu appeared to be successfully pursuing a peaceful path. It had evaded its military responsibilities in the Warsaw Pact; it alone of the member states had refused to participate in the Czechoslovak intervention of 1968. Yet Romania was a state that could not tolerate internal protest. In December 1989, Ceaucescu ordered his troops to fire on demonstrators. Thousands of men, women, and children were killed and buried unceremoniously in mass graves. The slaughter set off a revolution in which Ceaucescu and his wife and co-ruler, Elena, were captured, tried, and executed by a firing squad. They were charged with genocide—the slaughter of 64,000 people—and the mismanagement of the economy. In the days that followed, Romanians spoke in the international media of their newly won freedom, as videotaped images of the slain leaders were broadcast to the world. (See "Television and Revolutions.") But the events of 1989 made it clear that Ceaucescu was far from an enlightened leader; instead he ruled in the

Czech students wearing headbands proclaiming "democracy" hold a solidarity march in support of the ill-fated Chinese pro-democracy movement, which was crushed when the tanks of the Communist government rolled into Tiananmen Square in Beijing.

most totalitarian fashion, with repressive policies and a cadre of thugs who enforced them.

War in Bosnia

The most enduring and bloody of the ethnic crises came in Yugoslavia, where in 1991 festering differences erupted in civil war between Serbs and Croats, as Serbian nationalists overran multiethnic Bosnia and Herzegovina in a bid for territorial aggrandizement of Serbia. Yugoslavia was a federation of six people's republics, with Serbia, Croatia, and Bosnia and Herzegovina the three largest in descending order. With the collapse of Yugoslavia, Serbs became an aggrieved minority in Croatia and Bosnia. Serbia and Croatia were more than long-standing rivals. They were enemies with a history of hostility that had been masked by their federated status in the Yugoslav state.

The question of national independence in the Balkans had caused war before in the twentieth century. A Serbian nationalist intent on independence for Serbia from Austria-Hungary assassinated an Austrian archduke in 1914, sparking the outbreak of World War I. The nation of Yugoslavia had been created in 1918 by consolidating different ethnic groups as part of the peace that settled the war. The divide between the Serbs and Croats was partly identified with religious differences— the Croats were historically Catholic, the Serbs Orthodox—but for the most part, their enmity was based on the competing claims over the South Slavic lands, Bosnia and Herzegovina, that were part of the former Ottoman and Austro-Hungarian empires.

Various historic milestones have been commemorated on both sides as part of their litany of grievances against each other. In 1928, for example, a Croatian nationalist was assassinated in the Serbian city of Belgrade, capital of Yugoslavia. The Croats blamed the Serbs for the death. In World War II, Croatians sympathized with the Nazi occupiers and committed atrocities against the Serbs. The legacy of these and similar events was the creation of an unauthorized history of ethnic independence distinct from that of the official Yugoslav history that stressed the independence of the Yugoslav state within the Soviet bloc, apparently prosperous and united under the World War II communist hero and Croatian leader, Marshal Tito.

Conflicting territorial claims of the Serbs and Croatians were considerably exacerbated by two facts. First, a large number of Serbs lived in Croatia, and, of course, Croatians were present in the Serbian-claimed lands of Bosnia. Under Tito's rule, ethnic differences were held in check. After 1991, land claims were considerably complicated by the mixed population of Bosnia and Herzegovina. Second, another group, neither Catholic nor Orthodox but Muslim, amounting to 9 percent of the population of the former Yugoslavia and a majority of the Bosnian population, got caught in the crossfire of the war between Serbs and Croats and became a target for massacre and atrocities by the Serbs.

Under Serbian President Slobodan Milosevic, Serbs launched an offensive for a "Greater Serbia." With both Serbs and Croats in pursuit of maximum territorial control, war was almost a foregone conclusion. But what could not be foreseen was its brutality. In 1992, the Serbian army evicted 750,000 Muslim civilians from their homes. Serb forces also continued to bomb civilians in the Bosnian capital of Sarajevo. It later came to light that in 1992 Serb leaders had authorized a policy of *ethnic cleansing*, the term used to connote the genocide and atrocities—including concentration camps, rape, and starvation—used against Muslims. In 1995 the Serb military was also responsible for the mass killings of Muslims from Srebenica. Such barbarity contributed heavily to forging a strong sense of national identity among Bosnian Muslims, who controlled the Bosnian army and the presidency.

Beginning in 1992, Muslims from other parts of the world, including Afghanistan, Iran, Turkey, Pakistan, and Arab countries such as Egypt, volunteered to fight alongside the soldiers of the Bosnian army as Muslim holy warriors or *moujahedeen* against the Serb nationalists. Used as shock troops by Bosnia commanders, they quickly earned a reputation as fierce fighters, who inspired religious fervor among the Bosnian army.

In the course of the war, with over a quarter of a million lives lost and 2 million people displaced, the Bosnia conflict was recognized as the bloodiest ground war in Europe in 50 years. The Bosnian Serb political leader and the Bosnian Serb military commander were indicted as war criminals for "crimes against humanity," although they were allowed to remain at large. More than 150,000 Serbs living in Croatia also became refugees as the Croat government ousted them from their homes in the summer of 1995. The United Nations placed forces in Bosnia on a peace-keeping mission, which allowed it to take neither side in the war. NATO intervened against the Serbian attempt to overrun Bosnia after the outbreak of hostilities, and in September 1995 NATO stepped up the bombing of Bosnian Serb military installations and Serbian-held positions

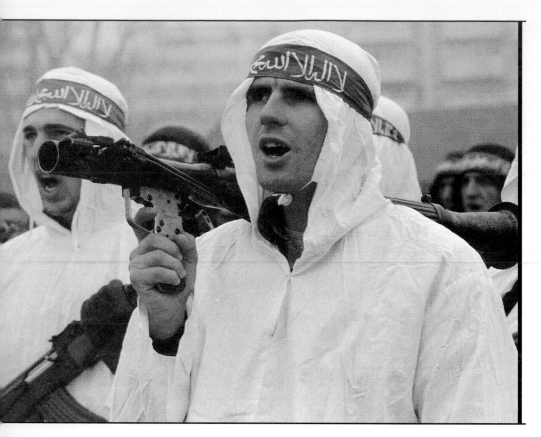

Bosnian soldiers in 1996 show the solidarity of their cause with the Muslim "holy war" by wearing headbands with Muslim phrases and chanting their readiness to die in Allah's name in pursuit of Bosnian independence.

in Bosnia with the policy of avoiding civilian targets. European leaders looked to the United States for intervention, but two U.S. presidents, George Bush and Bill Clinton, sought to avoid involvement in Bosnia.

The Dayton Peace Accord brokered by the United States brought Muslim, Croat, and Serb leaders together to Ohio in November and December 1995. The aim of the accord was to create a unified country in Bosnia while recognizing ethnic interests. As part of the commitment to the accord, the Clinton Administration sent 20,000 U.S. troops to join the 60,000 NATO troops already present to help enforce the peace.

The West hoped that free elections would provide the answer. In Bosnia and Herzegovina, 2.9 million people were eligible to vote in the elections of September 1996. The concept of a shared three-person presidency, with the one gaining the most votes carrying the title of President, as spelled vaguely in the Dayton Peace Accord, offered little hope, in the judgment of some Western diplomats, of a stable and enduring peace. Despite the accord, Serbs, who controlled 49 percent of Bosnia at the time of the election, continued to speak of their

own desire for an independent state in Bosnia and of their refusal to return homes to their former Muslim occupants. Bosnia remained a partitioned country, with Croats, Serbs, and Muslims still struggling for separate rule.

Other eastern European states were also riddled with ethnic troubles—including Czechs and Slovaks in Czechoslovakia, the Hungarians and Romanians over the border region of Transylvania, and the Bulgarians and Turks in Bulgaria—but none of these disputes involved the bloodshed of the Balkan crisis.

The iceberg of communism had melted. As dictators were replaced by democrats, some observers wondered if counterrevolution was waiting in the wings, should the new capitalist experiments fail. Proto-fascist and anti-Semitic groups became more vocal in the early 1990s amid the economic chaos. One potentially unifying force was the marketplace. Democratic institutions seemed least stable in those countries whose economies were least developed. In the former Yugoslavia, for example, little had changed for the better since the fall of the communist regime. The new Serbia remained a tightly controlled state economy. A good indication of the state of affairs was the criticism by one Serbian official of the Chinese economy as being "too market-oriented." Privatization was unconstitutional in Serbia as late as 1996. Former communist officials continued to run things, as before, as feudal fiefdoms for the profit of a few. Bosnia had no economy at all, and foreign investors, so necessary for economic recovery and trade, avoided putting funds in a country lacking financial institutions and a market orientation.

Russia itself suffered from a similar problem of economic readjustment and restructuring. Even where political reforms had been accomplished, economic reforms lagged behind or were nonexistent. Western Europe and the United States realized the devastation industrialization had wrought in their own countries after a century and a half of development, and were taking steps to control pollution and to clean up the air and the environment. Yet in eastern Europe, ecological concerns were a luxury as industries struggled uncontrolled to establish footholds in competitive markets. In spite of emergence of a new world order of democratic states, many Europeans, both in the East and in the West, saw an uncertain future of misery and repression fueled as long as virulent nationalism remained unchecked.

The west in the global community

Western European nations had met the challenges of wartime devastation with miraculous economic recoveries in the 1950s and 1960s. A key component in achieving growth was not only the U.S. capital that helped fuel recovery, but also the availability to Western European economies of a floating labor pool of workers from southern Europe and from former colonies in Asia and Africa. The phenomenal growth and prosperity of western Europe came up against a new set of harsh realities in the 1970s with skyrocketing oil prices, inflation, and recession. The permanent presence of foreign workers, many of them unemployed or erratically employed during the economic downturns of the 1970s and 1980s, came to be seen as a problem by welfare-state leaders and politicians of the New Right. Europe's new working class became the brunt of racist antagonism.

With the goal of reviving the economy, in the 1980s, the 12 member states of the European Economic Com-

munity devoted themselves to making western Europe competitive as a bloc in world markets. They hoped that by uniting they could serve as a counterweight to American economic hegemony in the West. At the same time that Russian satellites in eastern Europe were breaking free of Soviet control and attempting to strike out on their own, the nations of western Europe were negotiating a new unity based on a single market and centralized policy-making.

Europe, both East and West, seemed on the verge of a new renaissance, united economically, committed to democratic institutions, and looking forward to the twenty-first century as a global power in its own right. Yet social and economic problems persisted, the costs of the welfare state rose, terrorism tyrannized democratic societies, and a new nationalism vied with cooperation across borders. The rosy vision of the West in a global community that many foresaw in 1990, and that prompted U.S. President George Bush to dub the age a "new world order," seemed to have a cloudy future as West faced the new century.

european union and the American superpower

In 1957 the founders of the European Economic Community, Robert Schuman and Jean Monnet, envisioned the idea of a United States of Europe. Both men perceived that Europe's only hope of competing in a new world system was through unity. The European Community (EC) had been created in 1967 by merging the three transnational European bodies—the European Coal and Steel Community, the European Economic Community, and the European Atomic Energy Community. It operated with its own commission, parliament, and council of ministers, though it had little real power over the operations of member states. In 1974 a European Council was created within the European Community, made up of heads of government who met three times a year. Almost since its inception, the European Community has been committed to European integration.

The oil crisis of the 1970s encouraged isolationism among the members of the EC and eroded foreign markets, causing growing dependence on national suppliers and thereby undercutting the goals of the Common Market. In 1973, the international politics of oil prices provoked an economic crisis followed by a recession. The Organization of Petroleum Exporting Countries (OPEC) raised prices and cut back production. Western

European countries depended heavily on imported oil, which they used to fuel their prosperity through the early 1970s. As the crisis abated, competition and efficiency reemerged as priorities within the EC. Europeans were well aware that the United States and Japan had surged ahead after the 1973 crisis. They also recognized that the Common Market had been successful in promoting European growth and integration since 1958. They now realized that integration was the only defense against the permanent loss of markets and dwindling profits. In unity there was strength, as the aggregate economic indicators for 1987 made clear.

In 1985 the EC negotiated the Single European Act, which by 1987 had been ratified by the parliamentary bodies of all the member nations. Final steps were initiated to establish a fully integrated market by 31 December 1992. The 12 members of the EC intended to eliminate internal barriers and to create a huge open market among the member states with common external tariff policies. In addition, the elimination of internal frontier controls with a single-format passport was intended to make travel easier and to avoid shipping delays at frontiers, thereby lowering costs. An international labor market based on standardized requirements for certification and interchangeable job qualifications would result. The easier movement of capital to areas where profitability was greatest was encouraged. All aspects of trade and communication, down to electrical plugs and sockets, had to be standardized. The goal behind the planning was to make the EC think and act as a single country. Supporters compared it to the 50 individual American states participating in one nation.

In 1989 there were 320 million European citizens of the 12 countries of the EC: the original Common Market six of France, West Germany, Belgium, the Netherlands, Luxembourg, and Italy were joined by Britain, Denmark, and Ireland in 1973, Greece in 1981, and Portugal and Spain in 1986. Plans for European economic integration moved dramatically forward in October 1991 when the 12-nation European Community and the 7 nations of the European Free Trade Association (EFTA) joined forces to form a new common market to be known as the European Economic Area. The EFTA countries that joined forces with the EC include Austria, Finland, Iceland, Liechtenstein, Norway, Sweden, and Switzerland. Several of the EFTA nations announced plans to join the EC as well. The European Economic Area constituted the world's largest trading bloc, stretching from the Arctic Circle to the Mediterranean and consisting of about 380 million consumers. The nations of the EFTA

agreed to abide by the EC's plans for economic integration and adopted the vast array of laws and regulations that governed the EC.

Meeting in Maastricht, the Netherlands, in December 1991, the heads of the 12 EC countries ratified the Treaty on the European Union. They agreed that a common currency, the *euro*, would replace the national currencies of eligible nations as early as 1997 and no later than 1999. A single central banking system, known as the European Monetary Institute, would begin operations on 1 January 1994 for the purpose of guiding member nations in reducing inflation rates and budget deficits. Economic union would be reinforced by political union, with member states sharing a common European defense system and common social policies regulating immigration and labor practices. In this sense, the new European Union (EC) was intended as something more than the EC, which had been primarily an economic entity. Prior to the Maastricht Treaty, President François Mitterrand of France had endorsed the goals of the 1992 integration: "One currency, one culture, one social area, one environment." Many worried, however, that the long histories, traditions, and national identifications of the individual member states would stand in the way of a fully integrated and politically united Europe.

Britain was the most reluctant of the member states at the prospect of European integration. British negotiators strongly resisted plans for monetary union because of fear of losing national sovereignty rights. Nonetheless, Prime Minister Margaret Thatcher and her successor, John Major, solidly committed Great Britain to the EU. As Thatcher explained it: "Our destiny is in Europe." In addition to resisting monetary union, British public opinion polls reflected cynicism over the 1991 Maastricht negotiations and a social policy affecting working hours, minimum wages, and conditions of employment throughout Europe.

Some planners were wary about the prospect of including all of eastern Europe, whose troubled economies, they feared, would dilute the economic strength of the EU. Others predicted a fully integrated Europe, including the Eastern European nations, by the year 2014. The more optimistic predictions recognized the potential of an available labor pool and the possibility of new markets in the former Soviet bloc. Three of the new regimes—Poland, Czechoslovakia, and Hungary—were admitted with the status of associate members.

The plan for a single European market affected more than just economics. Education, too, faced standardiza-

Citizens of France attend a rally in support of the treaty on European economic and political union, which came out of the Maastricht Conference. French voters approved the treaty by a narrow margin.

tion of curricula and requirements for degrees. There were proposals for a common European history textbook that, in place of national perspectives, would emphasize the values of a single political entity in its discussion of battles, wars, social change, and culture.

Export-producing nations, including Japan and the United States, expressed concerns over "Fortress Europe," that is, Europe as a global trading bloc with a common external tariff policy that would exclude them. A united Europe, with the world's largest volume of trade and the highest productivity, would constitute a formidable presence in the world arena. With the thawing of the Cold War and the bloc politics of East versus West no longer dominating the international system, the move might easily place Europe at the center of world politics.

Originally intended to offset American dominance in European markets, in the 1990s the EU offered the opportunity of a closer economic relationship with the United States. The EU has been the largest customer for American products. In addition, Ford, IBM, Digital, Boeing, Unisys, Otis, General Electric, Pratt & Whitney, McDonnell Douglas, and Pacific Telesis are just a few of the American companies entering into partnerships and joint ventures with EU firms. The possibility of the

emergence of a truly global marketplace seemed, paradoxically, more likely with the creation of the EU and other regional associations throughout the world. By fostering economic competition as well as cooperation, the EU offered a counterbalance to the void filled by the end of the Cold War and the promise of peace based on productivity and trade.

A New Working Class: Foreign Workers

Foreign workers played an important role in the industrial expansion of western Europe beginning in the 1950s. Western European nations needed cheap, unskilled laborers. Great Britain, France, and West Germany were the chief labor-importing countries; their economic growth in the fifties and sixties had been made possible by readily available pools of cheap foreign labor. The chief labor-exporting countries included Portugal, Turkey, Algeria, Italy, and Spain, whose sluggish economic performance spurred workers to seek employment opportunities beyond national borders. Great Britain imported workers from the West Indies, Ireland, India, Pakistan, Africa, and southern Europe. Migrant employment was by definition poorly paid, unskilled or semiskilled manual work. Italian workers in

West Germany, for example, commonly worked factory night shifts that German workers refused. France employed a large number of foreign laborers in agriculture, public works, commerce, and engineering. Foreign male workers found employment on construction sites all over western Europe. Foreign women worked in domestic service, personal care, and factories.

Commonly, married men migrated without their families, with the goal of earning cash to send home to those left behind. Switzerland actually discouraged family migration with restrictions on income and housing. Nevertheless, prosperous and underpopulated Switzerland had Europe's highest percentage of foreign workers—16 percent of the total Swiss population in 1975. The prohibition against permanent settlement, however, hampered assimilation among this sizable percentage of foreign workers.

Most immigrants who came looking for jobs carried with them the "myth of return," the belief that they would someday go back home. For the most part, however, foreign workers stayed in the host country. Irish workers were alone in following the pattern of return to the home country.

The lot of foreign workers was difficult and sometimes dangerous. Onerous and demanding labor was common. Foreign workers were often herded together in crowded living quarters, socially marginalized, and identified with the degrading work they performed. Street cleaning and refuse collection in France were jobs typically performed by black Africans. Foreign workers were frequently denied the rights of citizenship and subjected to the vagaries of legislation. In economic downturns they were the first to be laid off. Yet the obligations of foreign workers to send money back home to aged parents, spouses, children, and siblings persisted. Children who resided in the host country with their foreign-worker parents suffered from severe identity problems, experiencing discrimination in schools in the countries in which they were born and with which they identified. A rising incidence of violence among second-generation Algerian adolescents in France, for example, indicated tensions and a new kind of rebellion among migrant populations in the 1970s and 1980s. Third and fourth generations of foreign workers born on West German soil were refused the rights of citizenship and denied the possibility of naturalization.

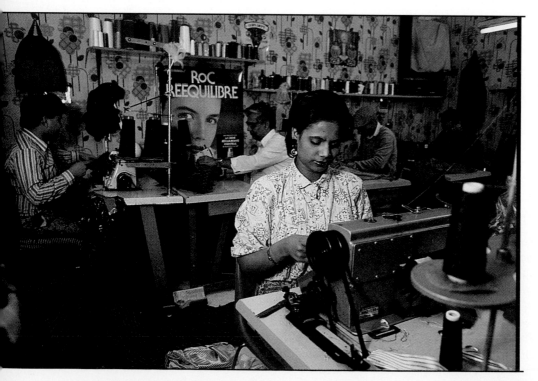

Indian immigrants in France sewing in a sweatshop. Immigrant workers in European countries took low-paying, menial jobs. They faced resentment from xenophobic native Europeans.

Women endured special problems within the foreign work force. Between 1964 and 1974, the majority of Portuguese immigrants to France came with families, but there were few social services to support them on their arrival. Dependable child care was either too expensive or unavailable to female workers with children. Increasing numbers of single women began migrating to western Europe independently of their households. Like men, they worked in order to send money back home. Often housed in dormitories provided by their employers, Spanish and Portuguese women factory workers in Germany and France were isolated from the communities of their compatriots.

Opposition to the presence of foreign workers was often expressed in an ultranationalist rhetoric and usually flared up in periods of economic reversals. Right-wing politicians sometimes complained that foreign workers deprived native workers of jobs. This argument seemed baseless, since many of the jobs filled by migrants were spurned by native workers as too menial, too poorly paid, or too physically demanding. Opposition to foreign workers nonetheless became virulent. In 1986 in France, the xenophobic National Front campaigned on a platform of "France for the French" and captured 10 percent of the vote in national elections. Racism was out in the open in western countries that had depended on a foreign labor force for their prosperity. Arab and black African workers in France resorted to work stoppages to protest police discrimination and identity controls that they likened to the yellow Stars of David that Jews had been required to wear in Nazi Germany. In 1996, the French government chartered planes to return undocumented Africans to Africa. Riots in Great Britain in 1980 and 1981, particularly in the London ghetto of Brixton, were motivated by racial discrimination against blacks, severe cuts in social welfare spending, and deteriorating working conditions.

Before 1973, most countries in western Europe, including Great Britain, had actively encouraged foreign labor. After that date, restrictions became the order of the day. It is no coincidence that restrictions on foreign labor followed the 1973 oil crisis. Western governments enforced new conservative policies throughout the 1970s and 1980s aimed at keeping out third world refugees. Exceptions were made for political refugees from eastern Europe. Racial considerations lay beneath the surface of discussions about political asylum. In 1989 the British government sent back to Vietnam the "boat people" who had escaped to Hong Kong in search of a better life. Britain earned the condemnation of other Western governments and humanitarian groups for its refusal to provide a haven for Asian refugees, many of whom were children.

On the whole, restrictions failed to achieve what they set out to do—remove foreign workers from western countries by repatriation. Foreign workers in West Germany learned to get around the restrictions and sent for their families to join them. British laws also had the effect of converting temporary migration by single men into permanent family migration, actually increasing the total annual rate of immigration. In 1974 the French government halted immigration altogether. The state withdrew subsidies from businesses employing large numbers of foreign workers and instituted police identity checks two years later. In 1977 foreign workers were offered cash incentives to encourage them to return to their home countries, but to little avail. Governments refused to acknowledge the reality of the plight of foreign workers.

By the end of the 1970s, there were 10 million foreign workers settled in Europe. Their presence heightened racism and overt antagonism from a resurgent extreme Right. In the late 1980s, when movements for democratic freedom and human rights were being endorsed in eastern Europe, the problem of permanent resident "aliens" was without a solution in western Europe. Yet the need for cheap labor made the preservation of such a labor pool likely. After 1990, economic analysts began assessing the potential of eastern European workers to fill that need.

women's changing lives

During the last quarter of the twentieth century, the lives of Western women reflected dramatic social changes. Women were more educated than ever before. Access to institutions of higher learning and professional schools had allowed women to participate in the work force in the areas of education, law, medicine, and business throughout the world, whether in France, the United States, or the Soviet Union. Women had been active in calling for the liberation of oppressed groups in the 1960s. These activities served to heighten women's collective awareness of the disparities between their own situations and those of men in Western societies: women worked at home without pay; in the workplace, women received less pay than men for the same work.

In this period of increased educational and work opportunities, an international women's movement

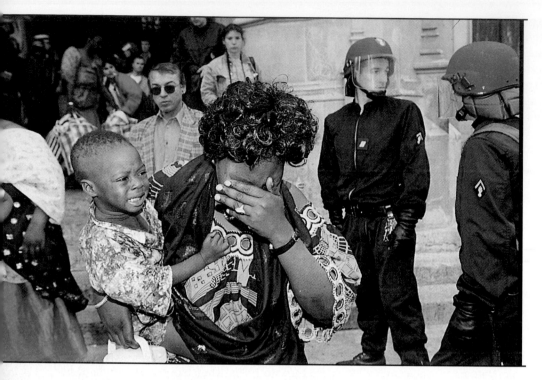

A weeping African woman and her child leave St. Bernard Church in Paris after riot police stormed the church to disperse the 300 African immigrants who had gathered there to protest French treatment of immigrants.

emerged. International conferences about issues related to women were media events in the 1970s. In 1975 the United Nations Conference on the Decade for Women was convened in Mexico City. Women activists felt that something more was needed than this conference, which was accused of seeking only to integrate women into existing social structures dominated by men. On 8 March 1976—International Women's Day—the International Tribunal of Crimes Against Women was convened in Brussels.

Modeling the conference on tribunals like the Nuremberg Commission, which dealt with Nazi atrocities in World War II, the feminists who convened in Brussels concentrated on crimes against women for the purpose of promoting greater political awareness and action. Fertility and sexuality were at the center of the new politics of the women's movement, justified in the slogan "The personal is political." Rape and abortion were problems of international concern. "Sisterhood is powerful!" gave way to a new organizing slogan, "International sisterhood is *more* powerful!"

In Italy, political action by women yielded a new law in 1970 that allowed divorce under very restricted circumstances. Italian feminists used the legal system as a

public forum. In France, the sale of contraceptives was legalized in 1968. French feminists, like their Italian counterparts, worked through the courts to make abortion legal: they achieved their goal in 1975. Important in the victory were two manifestos: one signed in 1971 by 343 French women, many of them prominent, who acknowledged having had an abortion; the other signed in 1975 by 345 French doctors who acknowledged having performed abortions. Widespread opposition from religious and conservative groups did not reverse the legal gains.

The feminist movement also created a new feminist scholarship that sought to incorporate women's experiences and perspectives into the disciplines of the humanities and the social sciences. Women's studies courses, which emphasized the history of women and their contributions to civilization, became part of university and college curricula throughout Europe and the United States. Reformers also attempted to transform language, which, they argued, had served as a tool of oppression.

In addition to promoting political action throughout Europe, issues of domestic violence, incest, and heterosexuality entered the political arena. In 1970 Western feminism was discovering that "socialism was not enough," and that women had to address problems of discrimination in terms of gender as much as class. As two French feminists explained it in 1974: "If we maintain that our sex unites us across all class differences because we are oppressed as women, regardless of class, race, and age, then even those men who serve the revolution start to react violently and brutally against us. Since we conceive of ourselves as an oppressed sex, we naturally resist those who oppress us." This was a declaration of war between the sexes. In its most radical form, lesbian separatism meant a total rejection of men as enemies. Separatists provoked a rift in the women's movement.

Feminists continued to be politically active in the 1970s and 1980s in the peace movement, in antinuclear protests, and in ecological groups concerned with protecting the environment. As Petra Kelly, the West German leader of the Green party, an ecological and pacifist coalition, described it: "Women all over the world are rising up, infusing the antinuclear, peace, and alternative movements with a vitality and creativity never seen before."

The women's movement recognized that women in socialist and capitalist countries alike shared similar problems. Increasingly, well-educated Soviet women demanded reforms, and the beginnings of a women's protest literature in the 1970s indicated an awakening concern for women's issues. Soviet women enjoyed more representation in parliamentary bodies than women in the West. More than half of the 2.3 million deputies to the local Soviets in the 1980s were women. One-third of the 1500 members of the Supreme Soviet were women. Gorbachev appointed a woman as one of the 12 Central Committee secretaries—the most politically influential people in the country. In spite of greater participation, however, women enjoyed little real authority in the higher echelons of political life, and most Soviet women rejected feminism as a political movement.

The same pattern held true for women in the work force. Over 85 percent of Soviet women worked, compared to about 60 percent of women in the West. Although 70 percent of doctors and 73 percent of teachers were women, women held few positions of authority. Both their pay and their status were lower than men's, as the example of primary school teaching reveals: 80 percent of primary school teachers were women, but two out of three head teachers were men.

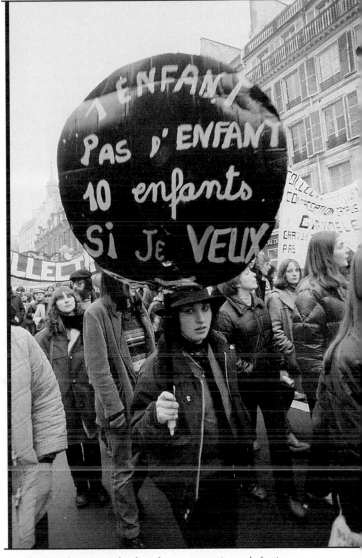

French women demonstrate for the right to contraception and abortion. The sign says, "A baby, no baby, ten babies if I wish."

Unlike western European women, many Soviet women—two out of three on average, according to censuses in the 1970s—performed heavy manual labor. Older women, for example, still chopped ice from Soviet streets. This practice had begun 40 years earlier because of the heavy losses of men in World War II—15 million had died in the war. In her doctoral dissertation on the sociology of the rural village of Stavropol, Raisa Gorbachev, wife of the Soviet leader, argued that while men were trained to run machines and tractors, women were expected more and more to perform the heavy physical labor associated with farm work.

Birthrates fell in the Soviet Union as in Western countries; women were bearing fewer children. Technology had made controlled fertility possible in safer, more dependable ways, but most birth control devices remained unavailable to Soviet women, and what was available was often unreliable. Abortion continued to be a common form of birth control in the Soviet Union, with two abortions for every live birth. Women were also choosing to have their children later, often because of work and financial considerations, with a growing percentage delaying childbearing until their thirties. Women complained of lack of quality in maternity hospital care. As one young mother explained, "The only experience worse than an abortion is having a baby in a Soviet hospital."

In the late 1980s, Soviet President Mikhail Gorbachev made direct appeals for women's support by promising preschool nurseries and kindergartens for every child. Gorbachev also committed himself to supporting increased sick leave for mothers of sick children, paid maternity leave for a period of 18 months, increased child-care allowances, and shorter workdays for women who worked at home. In support of women's voice in the workplace, women's councils were to be revived.

Women's work experience in the East and the West varied in degree, but a startlingly similar pattern of home and work life prevailed in the late twentieth century. Neither state institutions nor the law met the needs of women.

The Threat of Terrorism

Terrorism persisted as a force of political violence in the second half of the twentieth century. So serious had the threat become, as the end of the century approached, that U.S. President Bill Clinton in 1996 called it "the enemy of our generation." Understanding that America was a target because of its "unique position in the world," he continued, "Fascism and Communism may be dead or discredited but the forces of destruction live on." Terrorism was, however, a global phenomenon that erupted without warning in London or Rome or Athens. In 1995 Paris was paralyzed by a series of bombings in its center, and Tokyo subway riders experienced nerve gas attacks.

The history of contemporary terrorism began after World War II. The creation of the state of Israel in part of the land of Palestine in 1948 led to conflict between the Israelis and the Palestinian Arabs, who refused to accept the new Jewish state. Israel's Arab neighbors went to war to support the Palestinians but were defeated by Israel in late 1948. Hundreds of thousands of Palestinians became refugees in neighboring Arab states, and Palestinian guerrillas decided that the best way to attack Israel and its protectors was with a global strategy of terrorist violence. The first Palestinian hijacking took place in the summer of 1968. Ejected from

Draped in her country's flag, a Moroccan delegate to the women's conference held in Beijing, China, in 1995, shouts for women's rights in her homeland.

Jordan, Palestinian guerrillas set up their headquarters in Syria and Lebanon in order to continue their terrorist activities.

By the late 1970s, terrorism had become a tool of European revolutionaries, and its use had intensified with political killings in western Europe. A small group of left-wing radicals known as the Red Army Faction executed key industrial, financial, and judicial leaders in West Germany. The Red Army Faction was also responsible for a number of bombings, including that of the West German embassy in Stockholm. In Italy, a small group known as the Red Brigades, which claimed to represent the masses, was responsible for violent incidents, including the "kneecapping"—that is, crippling people by shooting them in the knees—of leading Italian businessmen and the kidnapping and murder of the former Italian prime minister Aldo Moro. In 1981 the Red Brigades targeted the United States for their terrorist reprisals when they abducted an American general, James Dozier.

Terrorism was heir to an anarchist tradition in Western society. Anarchism in nineteenth-century Europe fought against the rise of the state and in favor of an older way of life that existed before central control and industrialization. Anarchism was also a tool of oppressed nationalist minorities. The assassination of the Archduke Ferdinand in 1914 was the single most consequential act of an anarchist nationalist—it started World War I. Although modern-day terrorists did not agree on a unified political program, they were alike in their desperation, as evidenced by graffiti scrawled on the wall of a French university in the late 1970s: "Hope betrayed arrays itself in bombs." Terrorists lacked access to channels of peaceful change and shared a utopian vision of a better world that could be achieved only by the use of violence for political ends. Groups as disparate as the Provisional Wing of the Irish Republican Army (IRA), the West German Baader-Meinhof gang, and the Palestine Liberation Organization (PLO) shared these common features.

Another influence figured prominently in terrorism of the late twentieth century: Islamic fundamentalism. Muslim militants intent on waging a "holy war" for the oppressed could be found throughout the world in areas as different as Algeria, Bosnia and Herzegovina, France, and the Philippines. Muslim radicals in these and other countries shared a truly global commitment and were often heavily influenced by their formative volunteer experiences in the Afghan war of the 1980s. Conceiving of their mission as a holy one, they were able to form a series of loose connections with like-minded Muslims from other countries for the purposes of recruitment, training, and deployment of dedicated fighters. A taxi driver from Egypt, for example, who fought in the Afghan war was convicted for the bombing of New York's World Trade Center. A conspiracy led by the convicted Egyptian cleric Omar Abdel Rahman plotted to bomb the United Nations building, FBI headquarters in lower Manhattan, and the Lincoln and Holland tunnels linking Manhattan with New Jersey. The French blamed Afghan-trained Algerian Muslims for the 1994 Christmas Eve hijacking of an Air France airbus in which three passengers were killed in the initial shoot-out in Algiers.

In some cases, peace-loving Muslims were demonized because of fundamentalists' actions. Following the 1995 bombing of the federal building in Oklahoma City, Arabs and Muslims across the country were singled out for reprisals and intimidation until it was discovered that the Oklahoma City bombing was the act of domestic terrorists protesting U.S. government policies. The Oklahoma City attack, which terrorized the nation, fit the mold of a violent act against innocent civilians whose purpose was to undermine the power of the government.

An ancient Chinese proverb captures terrorism's strategic rationale: "Kill one, frighten ten thousand." Terrorism meant politically motivated violence performed by groups claiming to represent some greater political or religious cause. Victims were targeted by terrorists not because they themselves merited punishment, but as a means of attracting international attention to the terrorists' cause. Victims—whether American tourists or German capitalists—were considered pawns in a battle against a greater oppression. In the bombing of Pan Am Flight 103 over Lockerbie, Scotland, in 1988, no group came forward to claim credit. Terrorist experts explained that the menace of silence and uncertainty worked to strengthen the impact of the terrorist act and reinforce the perception that the government was not only unable to protect its citizens, it was also unable to identify the force that destroyed them.

Western Europe served as an important arena for terrorist acts. In order to succeed—that is, to terrify—terrorism had to be publicized: terrorists relied on media exposure and claimed responsibility for their acts after they had been successfully completed. In September 1972, members of the Palestinian Black September movement kidnapped 11 Israeli athletes at the Olympic Games in Munich. An estimated 500 million people

Blast-shattered building in Dhahran, Saudi Arabia, June 1996, where at least 19 died and over 200 were injured when a gasoline tanker was detonated at the military base housing U.S. soldiers.

watched in horror as all 11 were slaughtered during an American sports broadcast. In a dramatic televised shootout, five of the terrorists also died. Later in the decade, OPEC oil ministers were held hostage in Vienna.

A recurrent pattern of terrorism prevailed throughout the 1980s, highlighted by international media coverage. In 1981 a Turkish fascist attempted to kill the pope. In 1983 a Lebanese Shiite guerrilla blew up the American garrison in Beirut, taking hundreds of American lives along with his own. In October 1985, the cruise ship *Achille Lauro* was hijacked by a Palestinian ultranationalist group. One aged American Jewish passenger, confined to a wheelchair, was killed in a senseless act. In 1985 Palestinian terrorists bombed the airports in Vienna and Rome.

The Provisional Wing of the IRA justified its bombing of Christmas crowds in London with the need to unite Northern Ireland with the independent Irish Republic. Like the Provisional Wing of the IRA and the PLO, many terrorists saw themselves as representing nationalist liberation movements: "One man's freedom fighter is another man's terrorist." Resistance fighters in World War II had used bombs and assassinations as their means of fighting a more powerful enemy. Seeing themselves engaged in wars of liberation, revolution, and re-

A hooded Arab terrorist stands on a balcony during the attack on the Israeli Olympic team headquarters at the Munich Olympics in 1972.

The Return of Fascism?

In the following two excerpts from the *New York Times* (2 December 1992), neo-Nazi attacks in Germany by gangs of skinheads gave rise to renewed fears about the resurgence of racism in Europe. Attacks on foreigners—gypsies, Cambodians, Turks, and other ethnic groups—are not unique to Germany in the last decade of the twentieth century. With renewed emphasis on nationalism, extremist groups have designated enemies based on racist terms throughout central, eastern, and western Europe.

Music of Hate Raises the Volume in Germany

Were it not for the lyrics, it might be just another teen-age rock show. But this is a concert in Zwickau, in eastern Germany, by Störkraft, a Düsseldorf-based skinhead band whose name means "destructive force." They are performing hits like their 1990 song "Kraft für Deutschland," or "Strength for Germany," and the lead singer, Jörg Petrisch, howls the words:

> We fight shaved, our fists are hard as steel,
> Our heart beats true for our Fatherland.
> Whatever may happen, we will never leave you,
> We will stand true for our Germany,
> Because we are the strength for Germany,
> That makes Germany clean.
> Germany awake!

"Germany awake!" is a slogan the Nazis used during their rise to power in the early 1930's. When the concert ends, the audience of about 1,000 young people begins chanting "Sieg Heil." Some give the stiff-armed Fascist salute. Several young men unfurl a black-white-and-red Third Reich battle flag emblazoned with the swastika.

Two Germans Admit Arson Attack That Killed Three Turkish Nationals

BERLIN, Dec. 1 (AP)—German officials said today that two men arrested in connection with the firebombing that killed a Turkish grandmother and two girls had confessed to their part in the attack, the country's worst case of neo-Nazi violence.

The two right-wing radicals have been charged with murder, attempted murder and arson after confessing to the attack on November 23 in the northern town of Mölln, Alexander von Stahl, the chief federal prosecutor, said.

Moving to counter a wave of violence by right-wing groups, officials have banned a neo-Nazi political party and expanded federal antiterrorist operations over the last week.

Justice Minister Sabine Leutheusser-Schnarrenberger said in Bonn today that dozens of neo-Nazi and skinhead hate-music bands would be investigated under the new ban. Critics say that the bands' racist lyrics, set to a derivative of punk and metal music, may have inspired some attacks.

Rightists have made nearly 1,800 attacks that have killed 16 people in Germany this year.

Officials are worried that the violence is hurting Germany's image abroad and could harm the export-dependent economy, leading to boycotts of German products or declining foreign investment.

In a statement issued in Cologne today, the Federation of German Industries said the world must know that "Germany is not an anti-foreigner country."

In the Mölln firebombing case, Lars Christiansen, 19 years old, and Michael Peters, 25, confessed to carrying out two bombings on houses where Turks lived, Mr. von Stahl said.

After each attack, the prosecutor said, Mr. Peters called the police from a telephone booth to claim responsibility, closing each call by shouting "Heil Hitler!"

sistance, terrorists argued that they used the only weapons at their disposal against the great imperialist powers. Plastic explosives in suitcases, nearly impossible to detect by available technology in the 1980s, became the weapon of choice. If all was fair in war—and World War II demonstrated that both sides had bombed innocent civilian victims in pursuit of victory—then, terrorists countered, they were fighting the war with the only weapons and in the only arena at their disposal.

Terrorism was not a single movement but a wide variety of groups and organizations on both the left and the right. Some organizations were Marxist, as was the

Popular Front for the Liberation of Palestine (PFLP); some were nationalist, as was the PLO and the IRA. Some were Islamic fundamentalists intent on waging a holy war. All defined the enemy as an imperialist and a colonizer. Western capitalist nations, especially the United States and Israel, were common targets of terrorist attacks. Terrorists all shared a utopian vision of the world based on the commonly held belief that the destruction of the existing order was the only way of bringing about a more equitable system. The Japanese Red Army, in support of the PFLP, massacred 24 passengers at Lod Airport in Israel in 1972.

By 1990, terrorism challenged the tranquility of Western capitalist nations in effective ways. One reason for terrorism's success was the vulnerability of advanced industrial societies to random terror. Modern terrorists were able to evade police detection. Surveillance had not prevented terrorists from striking at airplanes and cruise ships. In December 1988 hundreds of people died when a Pan American flight was bombed over Lockerbie, Scotland, probably in retaliation for the accidental downing of an Iranian passenger airliner by the U.S. Navy in the Persian Gulf. Yet terrorism accomplished little to bring about political change or solutions to problems like the question of a Palestinian homeland in the Middle East.

Western European governments often refused to bargain with terrorists. Yet at times, European nations have been willing to negotiate for the release of kidnapped citizens. They have also been willing to use violence themselves against terrorists. Israel led the way in creating antiterror squads. In 1976 Israeli commandos succeeded in freeing captives in Entebbe in Uganda.

The following year, specially trained West German troops freed Lufthansa passengers and crew held hostage at Mogadishu in Somalia, on the east coast of Africa. The Arab kidnappers had hoped to bargain for the release of the imprisoned leaders of the Red Army Faction; the West German government refused. In 1986 the United States bombed Libya, long recognized as a training ground for international terrorist recruits, in retaliation for the bombing of a discotheque frequented by American service personnel in West Germany. Israel bombed refugee camps to retaliate against Palestinian nationalists. The goal of this "counter-terrorism" was the undermining of support for terrorists among their own people, which made it very similar in tactics and ends to the terrorism it was opposing.

The advanced industrial states of western Europe and the United States were vulnerable to an invisible terrorist enemy who could terrorize populations and incapacitate the smooth functioning of the modern industrial state. More serious threats to stability and demands for some kind of armed response came from the ethnic unrest in central and eastern Europe. Nationalist feelings and war were intensifying within eastern Europe at the very moment that integration appeared to accelerate in the west. Demands for autonomy lay behind the revolutionary events in Poland, the Baltic Soviet states, Hungary, Bulgaria, and Romania. Talk of ethnic purity ominously echoed the despicable racial policies of Nazi Germany. Meanwhile, in western Europe, planners spoke of a European Union in which national differences would be muted for the common good.

In describing all the changes that accompanied the collapse of communism, then U.S. President George Bush spoke of the emergence of a new world order. The Western world was undoubtedly a different place in the last quarter of the twentieth century from all that had gone before. But was the world really so transformed that one could speak of its being ordered in a different way? Problems that plagued Western states in the modern era persisted. The triumph of the nation-state in the nineteenth century had always carried the seeds of violence and destruction, as two world wars and countless local conflicts had proven. Democracy, likewise viewed as the best hope for a new world order, struggled in new settings that lacked the institutions, the culture, and the experience of democratic values. Elected elites from Russia to Romania used positions of power for aggrandizement, both political and economic. As the benefits of the welfare state in the West dwindled with slowed economic growth, the gap between the rich and the poor widened. This widening gulf characterized the new capitalist economies of the former Soviet bloc as well as those of the West. In the United States, the richest 1 per-

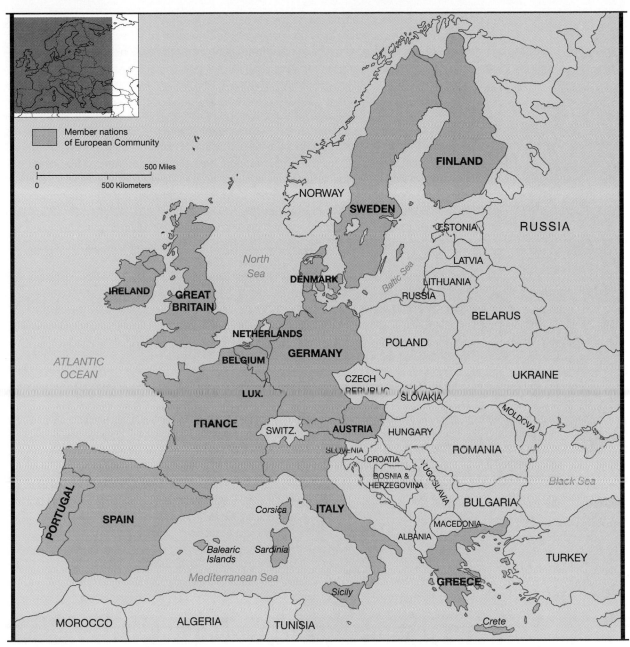

Europe, 1997

cent of households controlled about 40 percent of the nation's wealth. In Germany, high wage-earning families earned about $2\frac{1}{2}$ times as much as low wage workers.

At the end of the twentieth century, Western women and men faced the birth of a new century and a new millennium in the year 2001. Some did so apprehensively, just as inhabitants of Europe in medieval Europe at the end of the tenth century did, and perhaps with some of the same superstition about what the future held. Investing a date with such meaning is not new in the history of Western societies. At the end of the nineteenth century, Europeans defined a new sensibility of progress and advancement at the fin-de-siecle, aware that they were on the threshold of a new age. And they were right. But with that new age of the twentieth century, Europeans ushered in the bloodiest and most violent period in history.

What of those who foresee the beginning of the third millennium? Technology certainly plays a central role in forecasts, positive and apocalyptic. But it is the commitment to human cooperation that holds the key. Jacques Delors, president of the EC's Executive Commission, stated simply: "I don't want to live in a Europe that is like it was in 1914." Commentators warned of new nationalist conflicts on the horizon. Social change threatened to wither without producing fruit as governments cut free of the security of old ways grappled with new political challenges and economic chaos. Yet there was hope, too, as leaders of democratic and former communist states that had once been enemies spoke of a common European destiny based on security, freedom, and democratic principles. And citizens of Western democracies, women and men, grappled with the demands that equality, justice, and freedom make on free societies.

Mastering the chapter

To review the main points of the chapter, be sure you can explain the significance of each of the following:

Terms/Concepts/Events	People	Places
Cold War	Leonid Brezhnev	Baltic republics
Nuclear Test Ban Treaty	Mikhail Gorbachev	Armenia
détente	Boris Yeltsin	Nagorno-Karabakh
SALT	Vladimir Zhirinovsky	Belarus
Congress of People's Deputies	Aleksandr Lebed	Ukraine
ethnic cleansing	Erich Honecker	Commonwealth of
Berlin Wall	Lech Walesa	Independent States
Ostpolitik	Vaclav Havel	Chechnya
Solidarity	Nicolae Ceaucescu	Bosnia
OPEC	Slobodan Milosevic	Yugoslavia
		Sarajevo

suggestions for further reading

Toppling communism in the soviet union

Archie Brown, *The Gorbachev Factor* (New York: Oxford University Press, 1996). Traces the career and examines in detail Gorbachev's attempts to convert the Soviet Union into a social democratic variant of socialism.

* Patrick Cockburn, *Getting Russia Wrong: The End of Kremlinology* (London: Verso, 1989). A Moscow correspondent takes the measure of the politics of the Gorbachev era while attempting to correct Western misconceptions about the Soviet Union.

* Stephen F. Cohen, *Rethinking the Soviet Experience: Politics and History Since 1917* (New York: Oxford University Press, 1985). Offers a revisionist analysis of the historiographical debates in Soviet studies, with the intention of casting light on contemporary Soviet politics.

Geoffrey Hosking, *The Awakening of the Soviet Union* (Cambridge, MA: Harvard University Press, 1990). Published in the midst of the dramatic changes taking place in the Soviet Union, this study emphasizes the social bases of reform and the challenges to Soviet leadership.

Walter Laqueur, *The Dream That Failed: Reflections on the Soviet Union* (New York: Oxford University Press, 1994). This work recognizes the tenuous hold of capitalism in Russia and the possibility of a Communist party return.

Martin Malia, *The Soviet Tragedy: A History of Socialism in Russia, 1917–1991.* (New York: Maxwell Macmillan International, 1994). A reevaluation of the failure of communism by a leading Russian historian.

* Brian McNair, *Images of the Enemy: Reporting the New Cold War* (London: Routledge, 1988). Focuses on the importance of television in conveying the East–West debate to a mass audience in the 1980s. McNair demonstrates that the Soviets learned in the 1980s to manage communication techniques to their own advantage.

* Adam B. Ulam, *Dangerous Relations: The Soviet Union in World Politics, 1970–1982* (New York: Oxford University Press, 1983). Discusses the making of détente and the relationship between internal developments in the Soviet Union and their impact on foreign policy.

Redrawing the Map of Europe

Timothy Garton Ash, *In Europe's Name: Germany and the Divided Continent* (London: Jonathan Cape, 1993). An original and complex thesis that looks at German reunification from its origins in the 1970s.

Michael Ignatieff, *Blood and Belonging: Journeys into the New Nationalism* (Toronto: Viking Press, 1993). A companion to a BBC television series, the volume provides a sophisticated exploration of expressions of nationalism throughout Europe.

David Owen, *Balkan Odyssey* (New York: Harcourt Brace, 1996). Working with much unpublished documentation, Lord Owen defends his original plan for bringing a compromise peace to the former Yugoslavia and offers important insights into the nature of the conflict.

* Joseph Rothschild, *Return to Diversity: A Political History of East Central Europe* (New York: Oxford University Press, 1989). A historical and analytical survey of Poland, Czechoslovakia, Hungary, Yugoslavia, Romania, Bulgaria, and Albania that appeared just before the great changes that swept through eastern Europe in 1989. Rothschild highlights the tensions between nationalist aspirations and Communist rule.

* Teresa Rakowska-Harmstone and Andrew Gyorgy, eds., *Communism in Eastern Europe* (Manchester, England: Manchester University Press, 1984). Provides a comprehensive, country-by-country approach, with consideration of nationalism and shared regional problems.

Laura Silber and Allan Little, *Yugoslavia: Death of a Nation* (New York: TV Books/Penguin USA, 1995). An indictment of Serbian leadership that examines European responsibility in the unfolding of events.

Henry Ashby Turner, Jr., *The Two Germanies Since 1945* (New Haven, CT: Yale University Press, 1987). A political history of the postwar division of Germany until 1987 that bridges a period the author contends was one of increasing involvement and underlying mutual interests between the two nations.

The West in the Global Community

* J. Bowyer Bell, *Transnational Terror* (Washington, DC: American Enterprise Institute, 1975). Presents a compelling argument about the social revolutionary origins of terror and its threat to Western democracies.

* Richard Clutterbuck, *Guerrillas and Terrorists* (London: Faber and Faber, 1977). Clutterbuck considers terrorism as a kind of war rooted in historical experience and global in nature. His purpose is to consider protection against terrorists by examining the roles of the media, the police, and the public.

* Michael Emerson et al., *The Economics of 1992: The E.C. Commission's Assessment of the Economic Effects of Completing the Internal Market* (Oxford: Oxford University Press, 1988). A work replete with em-

pirical data that give a comprehensive assessment of the potential impact of establishing a single internal market in the European Economic Community.

Paul Michael Lutzer, ed., *Europe After Maastricht: American and European Perspectives* (Providence, RI: Berghahn Books, 1994). A collection of essays by an international team of experts who address the relationship between the United States and Europe in the era of the European Union.

Wolfgang Mommsen and Gerhard Hirschfeld, eds., *Social Protest, Violence and Terror in Nineteenth- and Twentieth-Century Europe* (London: Macmillan, 1982). Places terrorism within a historical context in Europe over the last century and a half in a series of articles that take a national case-history approach.

Richard E. Rubinstein, *Alchemists of Revolution: Terrorism in the Modern World* (New York: Basic Books, 1987). Examines the local root causes of terrorism in historical perspective and argues that terrorism is the social and moral crisis of a disaffected intelligentsia.

*Paperback edition available.

credits

document credits

chapter 1

p. 16, "The Code of Hammurabi," and p. 21, "A Homesick Egyptian": From James B. Pritchard, *The Ancient Near East: An Anthology of Texts and Pictures*. Copyright © 1958 by Princeton University Press. Reprinted by permission of Princeton University Press.

p. 29, "The Kingdom of Israel": Excerpts from 1 Samuel 8:9-10. Scripture quotations are from the Revised Standard Version of the Bible. Copyright 1946, 1952, 1971 by the Division of Christian Education of the National Council of Churches in Christ in the USA. Used by permission.

chapter 2

p. 43, "Hector and Andromache": From *The Iliad of Homer*, translated by Richmond Lattimore. Copyright 1951 by the University of Chicago. Reprinted by permission of the University of Chicago Press.

p. 55, "All Things Change": Excerpts from Heraclitus in John Burnet, *Early Greek Philosophy*.

p. 59, "Two Faces of Tyranny": Excerpts from Herodotus translated by A. D. Godley; excerpts from Aristotle's *Athenian Constitution*, translated by H. Rackham.

chapter 3

p. 73, "The Two Faces of Athenian Democracy": Excerpts from Thucydides's *History of the Peloponnesian War*, translated by Rex Warner.

p. 82, "Socrates the Gadfly": From Plato's *Apology*, translated by F. J. Church.

p. 91, "Greeks and Barbarians": From Herodotus, *The Histories*, Book III, translated by A. D. Godley.

p. 94, "Alexander Calls a Halt": From Arrian's *Campaigns of Alexander*, translated by Aubrey de Selincourt.

chapter 4

p. 116, "The Twelve Tables": From *Roman Civilization*, Volume I, by Naphtali Lewis and Meyer Reinhold. Copyright © 1990 by Columbia University Press, New York. Reprinted with the permission of the publisher.

p. 122, "Polybius Describes the Sack of New Carthage": From Polybius's *Rise of the Roman Empire*, translated by Ian Scot-Kilvert.

p. 131, "Cato's Slaves": From Plutarch's *Lives of the Noble Grecians and Romans*, translated by John Dryden and revised by Arthur Hugh Clough.

chapter 5

p. 139, "The Reforms of Tiberius Gracchus": From *Roman Civilization*, Volume I, by Naphtali Lewis and Meyer Reinhold. Copyright © 1990 by Columbia University Press, New York. Reprinted with the permission of the publisher.

p. 142, "Cicero on Justice and Reason": From Cicero's *De Re Publica de Legibus*.

p. 159, "Peter Announces the Good News": Excerpts from Acts 3:17-26. Scripture quotations are from the Revised Standard Version of the Bible. Copyright 1946, 1952, 1971 by the Division of Christian Education of the National Council of Churches in Christ in the USA. Used by permission.

chapter 6

p. 175, "Tacitus on the Germans": From Tacitus's *Germany*.

p. 182, "Religious Toleration and Persecution": Excerpts from *Roman Civilization*, Volume II, by Naphtali Lewis and Meyer Reinhold. Copyright 1951 by Columbia University Press, New York. Used with the permission of the publisher. Excerpt from the Theodosian Code translated by Clyde Pharr.

p. 188, "Love in the Two Cities": From Saint Augustine, *The City of God* (Garden City, NY: Image Books, 1958), pp. 321-322.

chapter 7

p. 202, "The Justinian Code": From Justinian's *Digest of Roman Law*, translated by C. F. Kolbert. Copyright © C. F. Kolbert, 1979. Reproduced by permission of Penguin Books Ltd.

p. 213, "The Qur'an": From the Qur'an, sura 2.

p. 223, "An Arab's View of Western Medicine": From *Arab Historians of the Crusades*, selected and translated from the Arabic sources by Francesco Gabrielli, translated from the Italian by E. J. Costello (Berkeley: University of California Press, 1969), pp. 76-77.

chapter 8

p. 239, "Two Missionaries": From Bede, *A History of the English Church and People*, translated by Leo Sherley-Price, revised by R. E. Latham. Copyright © Leo Sherley-Price, 1955, 1968. Reproduced by permission of Penguin Books Ltd.

p. 241, "From Slave to Queen": From *Sainted Women of the Dark Ages* by Jo Ann McNamara and John E. Halborg. Copyright © 1992 Duke University Press. Reprinted with permission of the publisher.

p. 250, "Charlemagne and the Arts": From Einhard's *Life of Charlemagne*.

chapter 9

p. 275, "Visions Like a Flame": From *Hildegard of Bingen: Mystical Writings*. Edited by Fiona Bowie and Oliver Davies, with new translations by Robert Carver. Copyright © 1990 by Bowie, Davies, and Carver. Reprinted by permission of The Crossroad Publishing Company.

p. 284, "Word from the Fair": From *Medieval Trade in the Mediterranean World*, edited by Robert S. Lopez and Irving W. Raymond. Copyright © 1990 by Columbia University Press. Reprinted with permission of the publisher.

p. 289, "Saint Francis of Assisi on Humility and Poverty": From *The Rule of St. Francis of Assisi*, in E. F. Henderson, ed., *Select Historical Documents*.

p. 301, "The Great Charter": Excerpt from Magna Carta, in Stephenson and Marcham, eds., *A Selection of Documents from A.D. 600 to the Interregnum*.

chapter 10

p. 320, "The Black Death in Florence": From Boccaccio's *Decameron*.

p. 325, "A Letter to Babbo": From *Babylon on the Rhone: A Translation of Letters by Dante, Petrarch, and Catherine of Siena on the Avignon Papacy* by Robert Coogan. Copyright © 1983 Robert Coogan. Reprinted by permission of José Porrue Turanzas, S.A.

p. 328, "A Woman Before the Inquisition": From "Jacques Fournier, Inquisition Records," in *Readings in Medieval History*, edited by Patrick J. Geary. Copyright © 1989 by Broadview Press Ltd. Reprinted by permission.

chapter 11

p. 345, "On the Family": From Leon Battista Alberti, "On the Family," in *The Family in Renaissance Florence* by Renee Watkins. Reprinted by permission of Renee Watkins.

p. 354, "The Renaissance Man": From Giorgio Vasari, "Life of Leonardo da Vinci," in *Lives of the Most Eminent Painters, Sculptors, and Architects*, translated by Gaston DuC. De Vere (London: Warner, 1912-14).

p. 358, "The Lion and the Fox": From *The Prince* by Niccolò Machiavelli, translated and edited by Robert M. Adams (New York: Norton, 1977).

p. 365, "The Siege of Constantinople": From Kritovoulos, *The History of Mehmed the Conquerer*, pp. 324-325.

chapter 12

p. 377, "A Momentous Discovery": From Christopher Columbus, *Letter from the First Voyage* (1493), in *Letters of Christopher Columbus*, trans. R. H. Major (London: Hakluyt Society, 1947).

p. 381, "The Halls of Montezuma": From Bernal Diaz, *The True History of the Conquest of New Spain*, in *The Bernal Diaz Chronicles*, translated and edited by Albert Idell, pp. 169-171.

p. 394, "Last Words": From Anne Boleyn, scaffold speech.

p. 396, "The Kingdom of France": From Claude de Seyssel, *The Monarchy of France*, translated by J. H. Hexter and edited by Donald R. Kelley. Copyright © 1981 by Yale University Press. All rights reserved. Reprinted by permission.

chapter 13

p. 414, "A Dutch Wit": From Desiderius Erasmus, *In Praise of Folly* (London: Reeves & Turner, 1876).

p. 418, "Luther on Marriage": From Martin Luther, *On Good Works*, translated and edited by William Hazlitt (London: George Bell and Sons, 1895).

p. 425, "The Eternal Decree": From John Calvin, *Institutes of the Christian Religion*, in *John Calvin, Selections from His Writings*, edited and with an introduction by John Dillenberger.

p. 435, "Heavenly Vision": From *The Life of St. Teresa of Ávila* (1611), translated by David Lewis.

chapter 14

p. 453, "Catholics and Huguenots": From the Edict of Nantes, translated by James Harvey Robinson, in *Readings in European History*. Volume II: *From the Opening of the Protestant Revolt to the Present Day* (Boston: Ginn & Company, 1906).

pp. 458-459, "Cannibals": From Montaigne, "Of Cannibals." Reprinted from *The Complete Essays of Montaigne*, translated by Donald M. Frame, with the permission of the publishers, Stanford University Press. Copyright © 1958 by the Board of Trustees of the Leland Stanford Junior University.

p. 468, "War Is Hell": From Hans Jacob Cristoph Von Grimmelshausen, *The Adventurous Simplicissimus*, translated by A. T. S. Goodrick (1912).

p. 472, "Fire and Sword": From *The Destruction of Magdeburg*.

chapter 15

p. 482, "Living by One's Wits": From *The Life of Lazarillo des Tormes*, translated and edited by Louis How, with an introduction by Charles Philip Wagner (New York: Mitchell Kennerly; 1917).

p. 499, "The Peasants' Revolt": From the Twelve Articles of the Peasants of Swabia, in *Readings in European History*. Volume II: *From the Opening of the Protestant Revolt to the Present Day*, edited by James Harvey Robinson (Boston: Ginn & Company, 1906).

p. 503, "A Feminine Perspective": From Arcangela Tarabotti, *Innocence Undone*, translated by Brendan Dooley. Reprinted by permission of Brendan Dooley.

p. 507, "The Devil's Due": From "Medieval Witchcraft," in *Translations and Reprints from the Original Sources of European History*, Volume III. Reprinted by permission of The University of Pennsylvania Press.

chapter 16

p. 520, "A Glimpse of a King": From *Memoirs of the Duke of Saint-Simon*, translated by Bayle St. John (London: Swan Sonnonschein & Co., 1900).

p. 535, "A Short, Sharp Shock": From an eyewitness account of the execution of Charles I.

p. 541, "Fathers Know Best": From Sir Robert Filmer, *Patriarcha*.

p. 544, "A Close Shave": From "De Missy's Life of Peter" in *Readings in European History*. Volume II: *From the Opening of the Protestant Revolt to the Present Day*, edited by James Harvey Robinson (Boston: Ginn & Company, 1906).

chapter 17

p. 556, "Stargazing": From Copernicus, *On the Revolutions of Heavenly Spheres* (1543), in *Movement of the Earth* by Thomas S. Kuhn.

p. 558, "The Telescope": From Galileo, *The Starry Messenger*, in *Discoveries and Opinions of Galileo* by Galileo Galilei. Copyright © 1957 by Stillman Drake. Used by permission of Doubleday, a division of Bantam Doubleday Dell Publishing Group, Inc.

p. 577, "Eastern Traders": From *The Low Countries in Early Modern Times: A Documentary History* by Herbert H. Rowen, p. 353. Copyright © 1972 by Herbert H. Rowen. Reprinted by permission of HarperCollins Publishers, Inc.

p. 578, "Defining Commerce": From Adam Smith, *The Wealth of Nations*, edited by James E. Thorold Rogers. Volume I, 2d ed. (Oxford: Clarendon Press, 1880).

chapter 18

p. 602, "Childhood Traumas": From *The Memoirs of Catherine the Great*, edited by Dominque Maroger.

p. 607, "A King's-Eye View": From Frederick the Great, *An Essay on Forms of Government*, translated by T. Holcroft.

p. 609, "Military Discipline": Excerpt from Marshal de Saxe, *Memoirs on the Art of War* (1757), in *War, Diplomacy, and Imperialism, 1618-1763*, edited by Geoffrey Symcox. Copyright © Geoffrey Symcox. Reprinted by permission of the author.

p. 619, "Unalienable Rights": From the Declaration of Independence.

chapter 19

p. 628, "The All-Knowing": From Denis Diderot, *Encyclopedia* (1751-1752).

p. 629, "The Human Condition": From *Voltaire's Philosophical Dictionary*, Volume One, by Peter Gay. Copyright © 1962 by Basic Books, Inc. Reprinted by permission of Basic Books, a division of HarperCollins Publishers, Inc.

p. 631, "Of the People": From Baron de Montesquieu, "Of the Republican Government...," in *The Spirit of the Laws* by Montesquieu, translated by Thomas Nugent, 1900.

p. 632, "The Good of All": From Jean-Jacques Rousseau, *The Social Contract*, translated by Rose M. Harrington, 1906.

chapter 20

p. 671, "What Is the Third Estate?": *A Documentary Survey of the French Revolution* by John Hall Stewart. Copyright © 1951. Reprinted with permission of Prentice-Hall, Inc., Upper Saddle River, NJ.

p. 677, "Declaration of the Rights of Man and Citizen": From *Readings in European History*, Volume II: *From the Opening of the Protestant Revolt to the Present Day*, edited by James Harvey Robinson (Boston: Ginn & Company, 1906).

pp. 684-685, "Declaration of the Rights of Woman and Citizen": From Olympe de Gouges, *Declaration of the Rights of Woman and Female Citizen*, in *Women in Revolutionary Paris, 1789-1795*, translated by Darline Gay Levy, Harriet Branson Applewhite, and Mary Durham Johnson (Urbana: University of Illinois Press, 1979).

chapter 21

p. 714, "The Wealth of Britain": From Edward Baines, *The History of the Cotton Manufactures in Great Britain* (1835).

p. 720, "The Sin of Wages": From Robert Owen, *Observations on the Effect of the Manufacturing System* (1815).

p. 725, "Exploiting the Young": From "Child Labor in the Coal Mines," Testimony to the Parliamentary Investigative Committee (1842).

p. 731, "The Slavery of Labor": From Friedrich Engels, *The Condition of the Working Class in England in 1844*, translated by Florence Kelley Wischnewetsky (London: Allen and Unwin, 1892).

chapter 22

p. 748, "Recalling a Childhood in the Factory": From testimony by Eliza Marshall, *Parliamentary Papers* (Great Britain, 1833), XX, Factory Inquiry Commission.

p. 751, "Seneca Falls Resolutions": From Declaration of Sentiments and Resolution, Seneca Falls (New York) Convention of 1848.

p. 755, "Young Italy (1832)": From Giuseppe Mazzini, *Young Italy* in *Metternich's Europe*, edited and translated by Mack Walker, 1968.

pp. 769-770, "The Communist Manifesto": From Karl Marx and Friedrich Engels, *Manifesto of the Communist Party* (1848).

chapter 23

p. 782, "The Charge of the Light Brigade," by Alfred Lord Tennyson.

p. 798, "The Emancipation Proclamation, 1861": Reprinted by permission from *Diary of a Russian Censor: Aleksandr Nikitenko*, abridged edition translated by Helen Saltz Jacobson (Amherst: The University of Massachusetts Press, 1975). Copyright © 1975 by The University of Massachusetts Press.

p. 809, "Red Women in Paris": Used by permission of the University of Alabama Press from *The Red Virgin: Memoirs of Louise Michel*,

chapter 30

p. 1032, "Career Advancement, Communist-Style": From *Russian Voices* by Tony Parker, 1991. Published by Jonathan Cape, Ltd., London, and Henry Holt & Co., Inc. Reprinted by permission.

p. 1034, "Perestroika": From *Perestroika* by Mikhail Gorbachev. Copyright © 1987 by Mikhail Gorbachev. Reprinted by permission of HarperCollins Publishers, Inc.

p. 1061, "The Return of Fascism?": From "Two Germans Admit Arson Attack That Killed Three Turkish Nationals," as appeared in *The New York Times*, December 2, 1992. Reprinted by permission of the Associated Press. From "Music of Hate Raises the Volume in Germany" by Ferdinand Protzman in *The New York Times*, December 2, 1992. Copyright © 1992 by The New York Times Company. Reprinted by permission.

photo credits

Unless otherwise acknowledged, all photographs are the property of Addison Wesley Educational Publishers, Inc. Page abbreviations are as follows: (T) top, (C) center, (B) bottom, (L) left, (R) right.

Prints appearing on the following pages were hand-colored for Addison Wesley Educational Publishers, Inc. by Cheryl Kucharzak: 375, 411, 416, 429, 432, 450, 453, 463, 464, 465, 467, 497, 508, 511, 525, 540, 545, 572, 599, 611, 612, 632, 633, 647, 663, 667, 701, 707, 721, 764, 787(B), 796, 801, 808, 819, 821, 822, 852, 855, 860, 862, 866, 889, 906, 927.

chapter 1

2 European Space Agency 5 The Cleveland Museum of Natural History 6 Kazuyoshi Nomachi/Pacific Press Service 7 Kathleen M. Kenyon/Jericho Excavations 10(T) Copyright British Museum 10(B) Copyright British Museum 11 © bpk, Berlin 12 Copyright British Museum 13 Hirmer Fotoarchiv, Munich 15 Scala/Art Resource, NY 17 Hirmer Fotoarchiv, Munich 20 Copyright British Museum 22 The Metropolitan Museum of Art, Rogers Fund, 1931 (31.3.157) 23 Hirmer Fotoarchiv, Munich 25 Erich Lessing/Art Resource, NY 26 Bridgeman/Art Resource, NY 27 Lee Boltin 30 Courtesy of The Oriental Institute of The University of Chicago 31 Erich Lessing/Art Resource, NY 33 Erich Lessing/Art Resource, NY

chapter 2

36 William Francis Warden Fund. Courtesy, Museum of Fine Arts, Boston 40(T) The Metropolitan Museum of Art, Rogers Fund, 1947 (47.100.1) 40(B) Scala/Art Resource, NY 41 Hirmer Fotoarchiv, Munich 42(L) Ronald Sheridan/Ancient Art & Architecture Collection 42(R) Hirmer Fotoarchiv, Munich 44 Copyright British Museum 45 Copyright British Museum 47 Scala/Art Resource, NY 48 Bibliothèque Nationale, Paris 50 Scala/Art Resource, NY 51 © bpk, Berlin, Antikenmuseum 53 Alexander Tsiaras/Stock Boston 55 Scala/Art Resource, NY 56 Hirmer Fotoarchiv, Munich 57 Hirmer Fotoarchiv, Munich 58 Giraudon/Art Resource, NY 63 Lee Boltin

chapter 3

68 Scala/Art Resource, NY 69 Scala/Art Resource, NY 70 © 1989 Raymond V. Schoder, S. J., Loyola University of Chicago 72 American Museum of Classical Studies at Athens: Agora Excavations 74 © bpk, Berlin, Antikenmuseum 76(L) The Metropolitan Museum of Art, Fletcher Fund, 1931 (31.11.10) 76(R) Staatliche Antikensammlungen und Glyptothek, Munich 78 Michael Holford 81 Copyright British Museum 84 The Metropolitan Musuem of Art, Rogers Fund, 1952 (52.11.4) 85 Super Stock 88 Alinari/Art Resource, NY 90 Alinari/Art Resource, NY 92 Copyright British Museum 98(L) Giraudon/Art Resource, NY 98(R) The Metropolitan Museum of Art, Bequest of Walter C. Baker, 1971 (1972.118.95)

chapter 4

104 Istituto Geographico De Agostini, Milan. Photo: A. De Gregorio 106 Hirmer Fotoarchiv, Munich 108 Arxiu Mas 110 Hirmer Fotoarchiv, Munich 111 Scala/Art Resource, NY 113 Hirmer Fotoarchiv, Munich 115 Bibliothèque Nationale, Paris 118 Alinari/Art Resource, NY 121 Museo Nazionale, Naples 124 Giraudon/Art Resource, NY 126 Giraudon/Art Resource, NY 127 Alinari/Art Resource, NY 128 The Metropolitan Museum of Art 129 Scala/Art Resource, NY 130 Scala/Art Resource, NY

chapter 5

134 Worcester Art Museum 136 Copyright British Museum 137 Romische-Germanisches Zentralmuseum Mainz 138 The Metropolitan Museum of Art, Rogers Fund, 1903 (03.14.13) 141 Scala/Art Resource, NY 144 Roger-Viollet 145 Alinari/Art Resource, NY 146 Alinari/Art Resource, NY 148 Erich Lessing/Art Resource, NY 149 Scala/Art Resource, NY 150 Alinari/Art Resource, NY 151 Staatliche Skulpturensammlung, Dresden 153 Nimatallah/Art Resource, NY 156 Ronald Sheridan/Ancient Art & Architecture Collection 157 Alinari/Art Resource, NY 158 Catacomb of Priscilla 165 Copyright British Museum 166 Alinari/Art Resource, NY

chapter 6

170 Copyright British Museum 174(T) Bibliothèque Nationale, Paris 174(B) Alinari/Art Resource, NY 177 Alinari/Art Resource, NY 178 Erich Lessing/Art Resource, NY 180 Bibliothèque Nationale, Paris 181 André Held 183 Scala/Art Resource, NY 185 Ronald Sheridan/Ancient Art & Architecture Collection 187 Scala/Art Resource, NY 191 © Photo R.M.N. 192 Copyright British Museum 194 Germanisches Nationalmuseum, Nuremberg 195 Hirmer Fotoarchiv, Munich

chapter 7

198 SuperStock 199 SuperStock 200 Scala/Art Resource, NY 204 Erich Lessing/Art Resource, NY 205(L) Copyright British

Bettmann **531** © Photo R. M. N. **534** Parker Gallery, London **536** By permission of the Earl of Rosebery, on loan to the Scottish National Portrait Gallery **543** Mondadori Photo Archives **547** Scala/Art Resource, NY **548(L)** Mansell Collection **548(R)** Scala/Art Resource, NY

chapter 17

552 Photograph © Mauritshuis, The Hague **555** The British Library **557** Courtesy of The Newberry Library, Chicago **561** Biblioteca Nazionale Centrale, Florence **563** National Library of Medicine **564** Reproduced by courtesy of the Trustees, The National Gallery, London **565** Erich Lessing/Art Resource, NY **566** Städelsches Kunstinstitut, Frankfurt am Main. Photo: Blauel/Gnamm-Artothek **569** The Metropolitan Museum of Art, Gift of Mrs. Albert Blum, 1920 (20.79) **572** Bibliothèque Nationale, Paris **573** Rijksmuseum Foundation, Amsterdam **574** Städelsches Kunstinstitut, Frankfurt am Main. Photo: Ursula Edelmann **576** Rijksmuseum Foundation, Amsterdam **579** National Maritime Museum, London **582** Reproduced by courtesy of the Trustees, The National Gallery, London **583** Copyright British Museum **584** A. F. Kersting **585** National Portrait Gallery, London

chapter 18

590 © bpk, Berlin, Nationalgalerie **594** Rijksmuseum Foundation, Amsterdam **596** Sonia Halliday Photographs **598** Central Naval Museum, St. Petersburg **599** Slavonic Division, The New York Public Library, Astor, Lenox and Tilden Foundations **605** Kunstsammlungen zu Weimar **608** © bpk, Berlin, Kunstbibliothek **610** Kunsthistorisches Museum, Vienna **615** Bridgeman/Art Resource, NY **618** Library of Congress

chapter 19

624 Samuel H. Kress Collection, © Board of Trustees, National Gallery of Art, Washington **626** Copyright British Museum **627** Bulloz **630** Scottish National Portrait Gallery **633** Brown Brothers **635** Erich Lessing/Art Resource, NY **637** Mary Evans Picture Library **638** The Metropolitan Museum of Art, Rogers Fund, 1932 (32.12) **639** Private Collection **640** © bpk, Berlin, Gemäldegalerie **642** Palace of Versailles, France/Bridgeman Art Library, London/SuperStock **644** Scala/Art Resource, NY **645** The Metropolitan Museum of Art, Bequest of William K. Vanderbilt, 1920 (20.155.8) **652** Germanisches Nationalmuseum, Nuremberg **654** Copyright British Museum **655** Mary Evans Picture Library

chapter 20

660 Giraudon/Art Resource, NY **661** Giraudon/Art Resource, NY **665** Bulloz **672** Bulloz **673** Musée Carnavalet, Paris **674** Bulloz **675** Mansell Collection **678** Library of Congress **680(T)** Bibliothèque Nationale, Paris **680(B)** Giraudon/Art Resource, NY **682** Giraudon/Art Resource, NY **688** Francisco José de Goya y Lucientes, Spanish, 1746-1828, *Neither Do These (Ni Por Esas)*, etching, 1863, 16 x 21cm, Gift of J. C. Cebrian, 1920.1316, photograph © 1994, The Art Institute of Chicago. All Rights Reserved. **689** Giraudon/Art Resource, NY **691** Musée des Beaux-Arts, Rouen

chapter 21

696 Claude Monet, French, 1840-1926, *Arrival of the Normandy Train, Gare Saint-Lazare*, oil on canvas, 1877, 59.6 x 80.2 cm, Mr. and Mrs. Martin A. Ryerson Collection, 1933.1158, photograph © 1994, The Art Institute of Chicago. All Rights Reserved. **702** British Library, London/Bridgeman Art Library, London/SuperStock **704** Reproduced from the original in Bedfordshire Record Office **707** The British Library **709** Yale Center for British Art, Paul Mellon Collection **710** The Granger Collection, New York **711** The Granger Collection, New York **713** Museum of American Textile History **715** The Granger Collection, New York **717** Mansell Collection **719** Victoria & Albert Museum, London/Art Resource, NY **721** Mansell Collection **722** John R. Freeman/Fotomas Index, London **727** Bulloz **730** Ullstein Bilderdienst **733** Courtesy of the Print and Picture Department, Free Library of Philadelphia

chapter 22

738 Gift of Quincy Adams Shaw through Quincy A. Shaw, Jr. and Mrs. Marian Shaw Haughton. Courtesy, Museum of Fine Arts, Boston **745** Bibliothèque Nationale, Paris **747** Tate Gallery, London/Art Resource, NY **749** The British Library **750** Bridgeman/Art Resource, NY **752** Royal Collection; © Her Majesty Queen Elizabeth II **753** Trustees of the Wedgwood Museum, Barlaston, Staffordshire **757** Scala/Art Resource, NY **759** Giraudon/Art Resource, NY **760** Giraudon/Art Resource, NY **762** Copyright British Museum **767** The Granger Collection, New York **772** © bpk, Berlin **773** Copyright British Museum

chapter 23

778 © bpk, Berlin, Bismarck-Museum **783** *Balaclava*, 1876 by Lady E. Southerden Thompson Butler. Manchester City Art Galleries/Bridgeman/Art Resource, NY **785** Weidenfeld Archives **787(T)** Collection Bertarelli, Milan. Photo: Saporetti **789** © bpk, Berlin, Nationalgalerie **792** Roger-Viollet **794** Erich Lessing/Art Resource, NY **795** Bridgeman/Art Resource, NY **799** By courtesy of the Board of Trustees of the Victoria & Albert Museum **802** Mary Evans Picture Library **803** The Master and Fellows, Trinity College, Cambridge **805** The Metropolitan Museum of Art, Gift of Harry Payne Bingham, 1940 (40.175)

chapter 24

814 Bridgeman/Art Resource, NY **817** Märkisches Museum **820** Hulton Getty **824** © Photothèque des Musées de la Ville de Paris. Photo: Remi Briant **825** Bibliothèque Nationale, Paris **828** Museum of London **830** Mary Evans Picture Library **833** Jewish Museum/Art Resource, NY **834** Corbis-Bettmann **836** AP/Wide World **837** U. S. Information Agency/National Archives **841** Corbis-Bettmann **843** Sophia Smith Collection, Smith College **844** The Granger Collection, New York **845** © Photothèque des Musées de la Ville de Paris. Photo: L. Degraces

chapter 25

848 Corbis-Bettmann **851** Mary Evans Picture Library **858** René Dazy, Paris **865** National Archives of Zimbabwe **867** National Maritime Museum, London **868** Copyright British Mu-

index